C. L. French

President of the Society, 1983 - 1984

THE SOCIETY OF NAVAL ARCHITECTS AND MARINE ENGINEERS

TRANSACTIONS

Volume 90

1982

Published in 1983 by

The Society of Naval Architects and Marine Engineers
One World Trade Center, Suite 1369, New York, N. Y. 10048

Printed by the Mack Printing Company, Easton, Pa.

ISSN 0081-1661   ISBN 0-9603048-4-3

Contents

Officers and Council—1982

President: John J. Nachtsheim

Secretary and Executive Director: Robert G. Mende   Treasurer: Robert Axelrod

Past Presidents

Phillip Eisenberg	L. V. Honsinger	John R. Newell
Matthew G. Forrest	Ralph K. James	Lester Rosenblatt
James J. Henry	Albert G. Mumma	Daniel D. Strohmeier
Donald A. Holden		Robert T. Young

Honorary Vice Presidents

Harry Benford	James F. Goodrich	Douglas C. MacMillan
Richard B. Couch	A. Dudley Haff	Richards T. Miller
Hollinshead de Luce	George H. Hodges	Jack A. Obermeyer
E. Scott Dillon	John R. Kane	Harry W. Pierce
J. Harvey Evans	Edward V. Lewis	Harold F. Robinson
James M. Farrin	John A. Livingston	William A. Sheehan
John T. Gilbride	Richard Lowery	Nathan Sonenshein

Vice Presidents

1982	1983	1984
Thomas M. Buermann	Keith P. Farrell	Donald P. Courtsal (APS)
Arthur J. Haskell	J. Randolph Paulling, Jr.	Ronald K. Kiss (T&R)
Monroe D. Macpherson	Robert Taggart	Alan C. McClure
Robert I. Price	George A. Uberti	Perry W. Nelson

Elected Members

Representing Members and Associate Members

1982	1983	1984
Roy L. Harrington	Jose Femenia, Jr.	William M. Benkert
William N. Johnston	Harry A. Jackson	Chester L. Long
James A. Lisnyk	T. Francis Ogilvie	J. Randolph Paulling, Jr.
P. Takis Veliotis	Edward Renshaw	Ellsworth L. Peterson

Representing Affiliates

David H. Klinges	Edwin M. Hood	J. Radcliff Maumenee

1982 Executive Committee

John J. Nachtsheim, President

Robert Axelrod	Donald A. Holden	William F. Rea, III
Clarence R. Bryan	L. V. Honsinger	Donald E. Ridley
Everett A. Catlin	Ralph K. James	Lester Rosenblatt
Donald P. Courtsal	Ronald K. Kiss	Bruce C. Skinner
Phillip Eisenberg	John A. Livingston	Daniel D. Strohmeier
Matthew G. Forrest	Monroe D. Macpherson	George A. Uberti
C. L. French	Robert G. Mende	Kenneth E. Wilson, Jr.
James J. Henry	Albert G. Mumma	Robert T. Young
	John R. Newell	

NOTE: Dates at heads of columns listing vice presidents and council members indicate years in which term expires.

Chairmen of Standing Committees

Advisory Public Service	Donald P. Courtsal
Applications	Arnold M. Stein
Awards	Kenneth E. Wilson, Jr.
Budget and Endowments	William C. Freeman
Education	William E. Zimmie
Fellows	Richard B. Couch
Finance and Audit	John A. Livingston
Journal of Ship Research	Ralph D. Cooper
Marine Technology	Perry W. Nelson
Member Insurance	Robert Axelrod
Membership	William H. Hunley
Nominating	George A. Uberti
Papers	Jack A. Obermeyer
Pension	Douglas C. MacMillan
Publications	Roy L. Harrington
Scholarships	Robert E. Stark
Sections	Monroe D. Macpherson
T & R Advance Planning	William O. Gray
T & R Finance and Administration	John T. Gilbride
T & R Steering	Ronald K. Kiss

Chairmen of Sections

September 1, 1982 to August 31, 1983

Arctic Section	Malcolm I. Comyn
Canadian Maritime Section	Pieter Nieuwburg
Chesapeake Section	J. Richard Gauthey
Eastern Canadian Section	Alexander N. Elliott
Great Lakes/Great Rivers Section	Thomas J. Stewart
Gulf Section	Ronald J. McAlear
Hampton Roads Section	Roy L. Harrington
Hawaii Section	Thomas A. Marnane
Los Angeles Metropolitan Section	George F. Henning
New England Section	Lee F. Mount
New York Metropolitan Section	John C. Daidola
Northern California Section	James C. Stokesberry
Pacific Northwest Section	John T. Mitchell
Philadelphia Section	Dean S. Champlin
San Diego Section	Kurt Schmidt
Southeast Section	Lee W. Dana
Texas Section	William A. Horn

Past Presidents

1893–1903	Clement A. Griscom*		1947–1948	Edward L. Cochrane*
1904–1909	Francis T. Bowles*		1949–1950	J. B. Woodward, Jr.*
1910–1912	Stevenson Taylor*		1951–1952	J. H. King*
1913–1915	R. M. Thompson*		1953–1954	William E. Blewett, Jr.*
1916–1918	Stevenson Taylor*		1955–1956	Earle W. Mills*
1919–1921	Washington L. Capps*		1957–1958	Walter L. Green*
1922–1924	Walter M. McFarland*		1959–1960	Albert G. Mumma
1925–1927	David W. Taylor*		1961–1962	John R. Newell
1928–1930	Homer L. Ferguson*		1963–1964	Ralph K. James
1931–1933	J. Howland Gardner*		1965–1966	Matthew G. Forrest
1934–1936	George H. Rock*		1967–1968	Donald A. Holden
1937–1938	Joseph W. Powell*		1969–1970	James J. Henry
1939–1940	H. Gerrish Smith*		1971–1972	Daniel D. Strohmeier
1941–1942	Emory S. Land*		1973–1974	Phillip Eisenberg
1943–1944	John F. Metten*		1975–1976	L. V. Honsinger
1945–1946	William S. Newell*		1977–1978	Robert T. Young
			1979–1980	Lester Rosenblatt

Past Secretary-Treasurers

1893–1895	Washington L. Capps*		1904–1911	William J. Baxter*
1896–1900	Francis T. Bowles*		1912–1931	Daniel H. Cox*
1901–1903	Washington L. Capps*		1932–1938	H. Gerrish Smith*

1939–1946   J. H. King*

Past Treasurers

1947–1948	J. H. King*		1957–1963	David P. Brown*
1949–1951	O. B. Whitaker*		1964–1970	Clifford C. Knerr*
1951–1956	Walter L. Green*		1971–1975	Ralph C. Christensen

Past Secretaries

1947–1964   Wilbur N. Landers*
1964–1969   Marvin H. Gluntz

Honorary Members

Egil Abrahamsen	Jens T. Holm	Manley St. Denis
Harry Benford	L. V. Honsinger	Henry A. Schade
Evers Burtner	Jerome C. Hunsaker	Karl E. Schoenherr
Hollinshead de Luce	Ralph K. James	Blakely Smith
E. Scott Dillon	Edward V. Lewis	Olin J. Stephens, II
Hans Edstrand	John A. Livingston	Daniel D. Strohmeier
Phillip Eisenberg	Albert G. Mumma	Frederick H. Todd
J. Harvey Evans	John R. Newell	Jan D. van Manen
Matthew G. Forrest	Lester Rosenblatt	Edgerton B. Williams
James J. Henry	Viscount Runciman	E. Alvey Wright
Donald A. Holden		Robert T. Young

* deceased

Honorary Members (cont'd)
Deceased Honorary Members

Sir Amos Ayre
Louis A. Baier
William A. Baker
James L. Bates
William Binley
William E. Blewett, Jr.
Roger E. M. Brard
Richard L. Burke
Vannevar Bush
Washington L. Capps
Edward L. Cochrane
Karl T. Compton
John P. Comstock
Homer L. Ferguson
Morris Douw Ferris
Sir E. Julian Foley
J. Howland Gardner
William Francis Gibbs

Walter L. Green
Charles J. Hawkes
John W. Hendry
Eads Johnson
William M. Kennedy
J. H. King
Emory S. Land
Wilbur N. Landers
A. M. Main, Sr.
Frank M. Lewis
Walter M. McFarland
Andrew I. McKee
John F. Metten
C. W. Middleton
Earle W. Mills
William S. Newell
John F. Nichols
John C. Niedermair

W. Selkirk Owen
Joseph W. Powell
John D. Reilly, Sr.
Samuel M. Robinson
George H. Rock
Harold E. Saunders
Herbert L. Seward
James H. Sharp
H. Gerrish Smith
C. Richard Soderberg
Edwin L. Stewart
John W. Stewart
Viscount Stonehaven
David W. Taylor
Edmund V. Telfer
Viscount Weir
Charles D. Wheelock
John B. Woodward, Jr.

Permanent Members

Harold F. Robinson

Successors to Deceased

Academy of Arts and
  Sciences, Boston
Donald T. Burkhardt

Daniel T. Cox
James A. Pennypacker

Webb Institute of
  Naval Architecture

Deceased Permanent Members

Francis T. Bowles
John E. Burkhardt
Washington L. Capps
Daniel H. Cox
John J. Demey
Clayton M. DuBosque
Francis L. DuBosque
Morris Douw Ferris
Andrew Fletcher (Sr.)

Andrew Fletcher (Jr.)
Frederick D. Herbert
James O. Heyworth
J. H. King
Frank E. Kirby
Robert C. Lee
Joseph H. Linnard
Emmet J. McCormack
John F. Metten

C. W. Middleton
Albert V. Moore
William S. Newell
Antonio C. Pessano
Joseph W. Powell
H. Gerrish Smith
Stevenson Taylor
Stevenson Pierce Taylor
Robert M. Thompson

Staff

Robert G. Mende, Secretary and Executive Director

Linda B. Bass . . . . Publications Coordinator
William F. Greulich . . . . Assistant for Operations
Trevor Lewis-Jones . . . . Manager—Publications and Technical Programs
Carolyn L. Marus . . . . Administrative Assistant
Virginia C. Nagle . . . . Assistant Manager—Administration
Carl H. Turner . . . . Accountant

4

1982 Spring Meeting

The word is "aloha" in Hawaii and the aloha spirit prevailed as the most noteworthy aspect of the 1982 Spring Meeting/STAR Symposium in Honolulu, April 19–23. The relaxed, at-home aloha feeling allowed active participation in all technical sessions without the oft-felt "hurry-up" of many conventions.

Some 350 participants enjoyed Hawaii's mild weather as mainland winter hurled a last snowball. Major-General Robert W. Sennewald, USA, standing in for Admiral Robert J. Long, USN, Commander-in-Chief Pacific, opened the sessions with a presentation of the Pacific area in relation to other United States' areas of concern. He discussed focus, commitments and problems. From that point on, the stage was set for lively discussion on all the technical papers.

Although some of the mainland visitors didn't realize it, the light sprinkle on the open-air President's Reception Tuesday night was a blessing in true Hawaiian fashion. Wednesday night's dinner cruise was a sell-out, and over 200 members and guests attended Thursday night's luau, where several SNAME folk, including Society President John J. Nachtsheim, learned to hula!

Aside from the technical sessions, the awards presented by President Nachtsheim at the President's Luncheon on Wednesday were the focus of SNAME business. The William M. Kennedy Award for "outstanding service and contribution in the development of systems and planning, as applied to shipbuilding and ship repair," was presented to Daniel M. Mack-Forlist.

Mr. Lyssimachos Vassilopoulos accepted the 1981 Spring Meeting Paper Award for the paper, "The Performance of the Controllable Pitch Propellers on the U.S. Coast Guard Polar Class Icebreakers," which he coauthored with CDR Donald G. Langrock, USCG, and Dr. Wolfgang Wuhrer.

Honorary Membership Certificates were presented to E. Scott Dillon, Hans Edstrand, and Jens T. Holm (in absentia). Certificates of Appreciation were presented to Hugh W. Kaiser, chairman of the Steering Committee for the 1982 Spring Meeting/STAR Symposium and to Manley St. Denis, chairman of the Hawaii Section.

The theme of Mr. Nachtsheim's address at the President's Luncheon was what the Society can *do* to influence and strengthen our important national marine capabilities. Areas of growth and progress as well as those requiring more attention were pointed out by Mr. Nachtsheim, who concluded by saying, "all of us can be proud of the continued progress being made in our Society."

The full text of President Nachtsheim's luncheon address appears below.

For those members fortunate enough to be able to extend their stay, the Hawaiian islands provided a delightful setting for a spring vacation. And all mainland participants carried home with them some of that aloha spirit (for a while, at least).

The titles of the 1982 Spring Meeting papers and the authors follow:

Tuesday, April 20

1. "Pacific Ocean Power," Long
2. "On the Design and Sailing Performance of the Polynesian Voyaging Canoe HOKULE'A," Choy/St. Denis/Rhodes
3. "Space Shuttle Booster Retrieval Platform for the United States Air Force," Daidola/Graham/Bister/Hultberg
4. "Planning Ocean Resource Development in Hawaii," Keith
5. "Ocean Engineering Challenges in Deep-Sea Mining," Halkyard

Wednesday, April 21

6. "Ship Design Trends in the Pacific: The Changes of the 70's Projected into the 80's," Hunley
7. "Experimental Evaluation of a Destroyer-Type Hull Optimized for Seakeeping," Bales/Day, Jr.
8. "Hydrodynamic Loads on the Hull Surface of a Seagoing Vessel," Kim
9. "Amphibious Assault Landing Crafts JEFF A and JEFF B: Seakeeping Full-Scale Trials," Davis/Turner/Peters/McGuigan
10. "Technical and Economic Implications of the Marine Transport of Alaskan Coal and Coal Products," Roseman/Howritz/Barr/Kirshenbaum

Thursday, April 22

11. "Fleet Maintenance in the Pacific," Wyatt, III
12. "Naval Commercial Maintenance Developments for the 1980's," Ruditzky
13. "Pearl Harbor Naval Shipyard," Marnane
14. "Containership Operator's Program of Bottom Maintenance for Reducing Fuel Consumption," Gronwall/Zink
15. "Application of Vibration Analysis to Determine the Condition of Ship Machinery," Lundgaard

Friday, April 23

16. "Renewable Energy Resources for the Pacific Islands," Shupe
17. "The Effect of Ocean Thermal Energy Technology on the Laws and Regulations of the Sea," Craven
18. "Mini-OTEC: A Hardware Perspective," Steinbach
19. "Hawaiian Water Cable Demonstration Program," Bell/Chapman
20. "At-Sea Testing of an OTEC Cold Water Pipe," McHale/Jones

President John J. Nachtsheim's Remarks at 1982 Spring Meeting/STAR Symposium

April 21, 1982

Ladies and Gentlemen: On behalf of all the members of the Society and its staff, let me thank the members of the Hawaii Section for your efforts in hosting this meeting. This is my first visit to Hawaii and I really wonder why all those members who have been here before have not started a concerted effort to hold all our Spring Meetings here. It is just a magnificent site for a meeting and every element of the entire program has been carried out in a wonderful way.

To you, Hugh Kaiser, the general chairman, and to all the members of the Steering Committee as well as the members of the Technical Program Committee and its very able chairman, Alvey Wright; and Manley St. Denis, chairman of the Hawaii Section and all of your members, we offer our heartfelt thanks. Won't all of you, chairmen, members of the committees, and all members of the local Section please rise and let us express our genuine appreciation for your efforts.

Now I have a 10-minute talk and a 20-minute talk. Since we have no technical meetings, only free time, this afternoon, I'm sure you'd all prefer the 10-minute version. The trouble is there's no difference between the two. I just lose my place a lot more in the 20-minute version.

Speaking of losing one's place, time has truly flown since I was honored by all of you by being selected to serve as president of this great Society. It is truly an honor and I can assure you, there is no greater sense of professional achievement and pleasure. Let me thank all of you again for the high honor you have accorded me in this respect.

As all of you know, I served in the Navy for three years, I worked for the Navy for 21 years, and I worked for the Maritime Administration for 11 years. Having had a foot in both the Navy and merchant marine camps, I don't feel it necessary for me to use the presidency of the Society as a platform to speak for a strong U.S. Navy and for a strong U.S. merchant marine. With my deep and lasting involvement in both, I would be concerned that, to do so, would appear self-serving, in fact. I feel my concern for a strong U.S. Navy and a strong U.S. merchant marine is a given; it's understood.

Rather, what I am more concerned with, in my opportunities to speak for the Society as a whole, is to point out what the Society can *do*, not say, to influence and strengthen our important national marine interests. For example, the Society's continuing Technical and Research Program is strongly supportive of our naval and commercial marine capabilities. The publications, the papers, the technical meetings, the opportunity to bring highly capable people together in common technical pursuits, have all provided a continued high level of technological support. To further enhance this capability, the Society has just added a seventh committee to augment the present six T&R committees. This new committee will deal with the subject of ship design and will be chaired by Dr. Bob Johnson. Various elements of this very important subject have been covered in other T&R areas in the past but some aspects have not. It's believed this new Society initiative will be of help to both the Navy and merchant marine.

Another recent initiative is the addition of an Education and Training Panel to our Ship Production Committee. While we have been concerned with education in the Society in the past, its thrust has been in connection with academic subjects, not ship production. This is an important addition, to bring the field of ship production to a higher level of professional interest.

Another important addition in this area has been the creation of a Design/Production Panel to the Ship Production Committee. Through this group's activities, a much closer integration of ship design, planning and production will be possible in keeping with rapidly changing, increased productivity, ship construction techniques.

Another new initiative will be seen at this fall's Annual Meeting. At that time we will include exhibits as part of the technical program. There are great advantages, truly educational benefits, from the opportunity to see, touch and otherwise kick-the-tires for new equipments, materials, and technologies as well as have the opportunity to meet and discuss these with a very important professional sector of our industry who otherwise don't normally participate in our Annual Meetings.

Symposia in selected special subjects such as propellers, habitability and structures have been extremely successful professional activities in the past. We will continue in this vein. Plans are underway for a Computer Aided Design/Computer Aided Construction Symposium in June, a Ship Energy Conservation Symposium this fall, a Planing Boat Symposium to be initiated by the Southeast Section shortly and, in joint sponsorship with the Navy, a Pan-American Naval Engineering meeting, involving most of our South and Central American colleagues to be convened a little over a year from now.

While our membership grew by 2½ percent the past year, we have a serious lacking in our membership. This relates to the very low number of professional military members. The engineering and management positions held by many Navy and Coast Guard officers provide a wealth of valuable professional experience. The opportunity to interchange this rich experience with our current membership is thereby limited and results in a two-way, losing proposition to both our members and those who are not members. A new initiative to overcome this deficiency is now underway. Just last week we received the personal, full support and encouragement of both Vice Admiral Fowler, Commander of the Naval Sea Systems Command and Admiral Gracey, the newly designated Commandant of the U.S. Coast Guard in this initiative.

As I've said on a number of occasions, we can be proud of the current Society efforts but I am still convinced we are not doing enough. In the past I've spoken of three particular areas where I feel we must do more. I won't repeat the reasons I think we're doing too little in these areas but I will repeat where I think we should be doing more.

These include, first, providing a service to the maritime research community on information and data dealing with ongoing research. A great void has been created by the government's withdrawal from providing this service through the Maritime Research Information Service. We must, in my opinion, step up and do this for this very important segment of our membership. We have not done anything as yet. Second, the Society should take positive steps to encourage greater private-sector maritime research and development efforts. Through the Advanced Planning Committee, now chaired by Bill Gray, we will begin to look at this very important issue. Third, the Society should be more of a spokesman for advanced marine technology. We have spoken out to a limited degree in the past but we have not as yet reached the position where our opinion is sought on difficult, highly technical issues, which bear on important national maritime issues. Technology is difficult to understand and what's not understood is usually ignored. It is our job to make the subject of technology and the benefits of technology better understood. Through the Advisory Public Service Committee, chaired by Don Courtsal, we are seeking ways to be more effective in this area.

Progress sometimes comes quickly, sometimes it is painfully slow. Sometimes it doesn't even happen. Yet, let me repeat that I think all of us can be proud of the continued progress being made in our Society. Each of you individually, your spouses, and your families who also support the Society's activities, can feel this pride. However, I still feel we have the obligation to do more.

With your continued support of our present Society activities, your acceptance of the continuing need to reassess, to change, to adapt to new conditions; and your continued insistence on high professional standards for all Society activities, we will continue to grow in strength and stature. We will in that way benefit our membership, our merchant marine, our Coast Guard, our Navy, and our nation.

Thank you.

90th Annual Meeting

The First International Maritime Exposition was held November 17–19, 1982 at the New York Hilton Hotel in conjunction with the Society's 90th Annual Meeting. Some people on the Society's committees and staff were apprehensive that the Exposition would detract from the technical program. Such was not the case. Probably what was the most successful maritime exposition in New York since 1946 did not cut down the attendance of the papers by one whit; in fact, several of the technical sessions had well over 200 listeners, reinforcing the idea that the Exposition would bolster the Annual Meeting attendance.

Thus, the 90th Annual Meeting of our Society was a landmark meeting, the first of a series of expanded conventions (with an educational exhibition) that could go on to greater things over the next 90 years.

Likewise, the social functions didn't suffer either. The President's Luncheon was filled to capacity. And the Annual Banquet was obviously a sell-out with every table on the balcony occupied (right up to above the dais area). The total registration was 1310, not counting those who registered for the Exposition only. This totals approximately one-tenth of the entire membership. As before, as might be expected, the largest portion of registrants were members of the New York Metropolitan Section.

Besides the Exposition and the Technical Sessions on Thursday and Friday, there were meetings of the T&R Steering Committee and of some of the T&R Panels, taking place at the hotel and other conference rooms in the area.

The ribbon-cutting ceremony outside the Rhinelander Gallery, which was admirably performed by Society President John Nachtsheim with members of the Exposition Committee looking on, lasted only a few minutes and was an elevator ride away from the beginning of the Council meeting held at noon on Wednesday, November 17, in the hotel's West Penthouse.

After luncheon, about 70 members of Council sat at the cleared tables and listened to and discussed approximately 20 reports by the Secretary and Executive Director of the Society, the Treasurer, the Chairmen of the Standing Committees, the Vice President–Technical and Research, the Vice President–Advisory Public Service, and other special committees. These reports are intended to give the Council, the ultimate governing body of the Society, a clear picture of all that is occurring within the Society.

Robert G. Mende gave his Secretary and Executive Director's Report after the introductions. This is roughly a review of all the activity of his office for the past fiscal year (September 1, 1981–August 31, 1982), and can be found, along with the Treasurer's Report, word-for-word, beginning on page 8. Thus, it is available to every member. Touching on membership, Mr. Mende said the potential membership at the end of the calendar year would be 13 201 if all applications are approved. And the Treasurer reported total assets of about $3.4 million (page 12), both attesting to the continued growth of the Society.

It is also at this meeting of the Council that the new members of Council are named, the result of the voting of the entire membership. The Canvassing Committee presented the tallies to the Council which accepted them as follows:

Elected to represent Members and Associate Members for a term of three years (to December 31, 1985) were Ralph J. Bradford, Edward J. Campbell, William N. Johnston and Henry S. Marcus. Elected to Council for a two-year term to fill the unexpired term of Ellsworth Peterson was Roger L. Potash. And J. Gordon German was elected to Council for a term of one year to fill T. Francis Ogilvie's unexpired term. David H.

Klinges was elected to represent Affiliate Members on the Council for a term of three years (to December 31, 1985).

The Council accepted unanimously the report of the Nominating Committee which put forward the name of Clarence L. French to be President of the Society for the two-year period from January 1, 1983 to December 31, 1984. This nomination was to be carried into the Annual Business Meeting the next day for seconding and membership vote.

Others also were nominated for election by the Council. Recommended to be Vice Presidents for a three-year term were Richard Broad, Jean E. Buhler, David A. O'Neil and Ellsworth L. Peterson. Recommendations for Honorary Vice Presidents (for life) were Arthur J. Haskell and Monroe D. Macpherson; Honorary Members (for life) were John J. Nachtsheim, Cedric Ridgely-Nevitt and William A. Sheehan. The Nominating Committee also put forward the names of three members to serve for a three-year term on the Executive Committee. They were William M. Benkert, Jack A. Obermeyer and T. Francis Ogilvie. Roy L. Harrington was named to the Executive Committee to fill the unexpired term of Clarence L. French.

Finally, the Nominating Committee renominated the Society's two administrative officers for a term of one year. These were Robert G. Mende, Secretary and Executive Director and Robert Axelrod, Treasurer. The nomination of an Assistant Treasurer for a one-year term also was made for Donald M. Birney.

The Fellows Committee presented eleven names to the Council with its recommendations that they be made Fellows. These nominations were accepted without reservation:

Donald L. Blount
John P. Breslin
Richard H. Broad
Lawrence R. Glosten
Harry A. Jackson
Ronald K. Kiss
Philip Mandel
T. Arthur McLaren
Walter H. Michel
Frank L. Pavlik
Robert Taggart

Excellent breakfasts were again provided for the key people of the Annual Meeting. Jack A. Obermeyer, chairman of the Papers Committee again did a masterful job in organizing the authors and session presiding officers, clearing up last minute details as to the discussions and getting the group pictures taken. He was ably assisted by Linda Bass, Publications Coordinator of the Staff.

Monroe Macpherson, chairman of the Sections Committee, presided at the Sections Breakfast and William H. Hunley, at the Membership Breakfast.

The President's Luncheon on Thursday was preceded by a General Reception in the East Ballroom Foyer and after a half-hour, all sat down in the Grand Ballroom for the repast. Seated on the dais were the award recipients of the Cochrane, Linnard and Student Paper prizes, the presenters, Society President John J. Nachtsheim, all seven of the technical committee chairmen of the SNAME T&R Program, and the Secretary and Executive Director and others. Special tables on the floor were set up for the spouses of the principals on the dais, a table for staff members and a table for representatives of the press presided at by Trevor Lewis-Jones.

Over coffee and the famous Hilton cheesecake, the ceremonies began with the presenting of the Golden Award 50-year Membership Certificates *in absentia* by John Nachtsheim to

Philip N. Israel, Robert H. Macy, Bertram B. Naschke, Henry A. Schade and Morris Weitzner. Details of these and the rest of the awards begin on page 13. The presentations were followed by the President's Annual Address, which appears in full beginning on page 17.

The annual Business Session took place at 4:00 P.M. in the Trianon Ballroom. After a quorum was established, the members heard placed in nomination the name of Clarence L. (Larry) French for President of the Society to hold office from January 1, 1983 to December 31, 1984. Mr. French is President and Chief Operating Officer of National Steel and Shipbuilding Company, San Diego, Calif. and is the first westerner in history to be elected President of the Society, although he was born in New Haven, Conn. and graduated from Tufts University in Mass. Mr. French's name was placed in nomination by George Uberti, the chairman of the Nominating Committee, who is also with NASSCO. Seconding Mr. French's nomination were past presidents, Phillip Eisenberg, Lester Rosenblatt, L. V. Honsinger and Mr. Nachtsheim. The vote for election was unanimous.

At the end of the program, Walter Schmid, chairman of the 1983 Spring Meeting/STAR Symposium Steering Committee, described the Chesapeake Section's planning for the meeting which has as its theme, "Maritime Technology for a Changing World." He said that the Technical Committee under Marvin Pitkin has done an excellent job in getting together a fascinating technical program which will include key leaders of the maritime scene in Washington. Likewise, an excellent social program has been planned, including a reception and a boat trip on the Potomac. The hotel is to be the L'Enfant Plaza located only a few steps from the Smithsonian Institution on one side and excellent waterfront restaurants on the other. It is interesting to note that this is the same hotel in which the first STAR Symposium was held in August 1975. This will be the eighth STAR Symposium, the acronym "STAR" standing for "Ship Technology and Research."

Ronald K. Kiss then stood up to say that this will not be the only meeting of interest to members in the Washington area in 1983. He invited all the members to return to Washington, September 11–18, 1983 for the Eighth Pan American Congress on Naval Engineering (IPEN) which is to be co-sponsored by the Pan American Institute of Naval Engineering, the U.S. Navy and the Society. This will be the first such congress ever held in the United States and the locale will be the new Hyatt Regency Hotel in Crystal City, Virginia. Members will be advised by mail of registration information as the year progresses.

The 14 papers comprising the technical program were presented on Thursday and Friday in the Mercury and Trianon Ballrooms. Selection of papers for the Annual Meeting is carried out by the Papers Committee, chaired by Capt. Jack Obermeyer, USN (Ret.). These papers together with discussions and authors' closures appear in full in this volume, beginning on page 41.

The presiding and assistant presiding officers for each paper were, respectively:

No. 1, A. Dudley Haff and Richard W. Thorpe, Jr. No. 2, William M. Hannan and James A. Lisnyk. No. 3, Thomas M. Buermann and Jacques B. Hadler. No. 4, Richard B. Couch and Perry W. Nelson. No. 5, Jack A. Obermeyer and Andrew A. Szypula. No. 6, Harry Benford and Spencer Reitz. No. 7, Donald P. Courtsal and Chester L. Long. No. 8, William O. Gray and Keith P. Farrell. No. 9, Nathan Sonenshein and J. Richard Gauthey. No. 10, Robert Taggart and William E. Zimmie. No. 11, William C. Freeman and Edward N. Dunlay. No. 12, Stanley G. Stiansen and James A. Lisnyk. No. 13, George A. Uberti and James F. Dunne. No. 14, T. Francis Ogilvie and Eric W. Linsner.

On Friday evening, 1778 people sat down to the Society's 90th Annual Banquet in the Grand Ballroom of the Hotel. This number fills the Grand Ballroom almost to capacity. Officiating at this black-tie affair was Society President John J. Nachtsheim. After the huge three-tier dais was seated, the Banquet opened with the traditional rendition of the Canadian and the United States National anthems, a toast to the Queen of England and to President Reagan.

Following dinner, the presentation of the Society's prestigious Davidson, Land and Taylor Medals took place, as described on pages 13–15. The medals were awarded to, respectively, Dr. John P. Breslin, VADM Robert I. Price, USCG (Ret.), and Prof. Jacques B. Hadler.

Following the presentation of the three medals, President Nachtsheim introduced the speaker for the evening, John M. Rau. Mr. Rau is national president of the Navy League and spoke in that capacity. A resident of Orange, Calif., Mr. Rau has been active in the Navy League for many years and, as its president, has travelled to the four corners of the earth visiting Navy, Coast Guard and Marine Corps and merchant marine ships and facilities. His speech appears in this volume on pages 19–22.

The Dinner Dance always provides a festive close to the Annual Meeting and for the Ninetieth Meeting on Saturday, it was possibly the largest (1090 dinners served) that the Society has ever had. Five hundred couples danced to the music of a fine orchestra, enjoyed the entertainment provided and witnessed the Ceremony of the Roses, whereby bouquets of roses were presented to the President's wife, Ruth Nachtsheim and the newly elected President's wife, Jean French.

Report of the Secretary and Executive Director

TO THE COUNCIL OF THE SOCIETY OF NAVAL ARCHITECTS AND MARINE ENGINEERS, November 17, 1982

I am pleased to submit the following report for the fiscal year ending August 31, 1982, a year in which the Society continued to make progress in all of its programs and activities.

Membership

The Society's membership shows a net increase of 249 in the past fiscal year, whereas, at this time a year ago, I reported a net increase of 348 members. If the applications submitted today are approved, and when the remaining new members elected by the Executive Committee in September 1982 are entered on the rolls, the potential membership will be 13 201. Clearly, the Membership Committee, under the chairmanship of Mr. William H. Hunley, has done a commendable job.

A comparison of the membership of the Society as of August 31, 1981 and August 31, 1982 is as follows:

	1981	1982
Members	5459	5587
Affiliates	378	389
Associate Members (over 30 years of age)	3235	3296
Associate Members (under 30 years of age)	2322	2453
Student Members	818	752
Honorary Members	13	13
Honorary Members/Fellow	18	19
Fellows	41	44
Permanent Members and Successors	5	4
Special Members	43	39
Reciprocal Members	112	97
	12 444	12 693

Applications

The Applications Committee, chaired by Mr. Arnold M. Stein, recommended for approval 1399 applications. Of these, 1313 were for new membership and 86 for transfer in grade. The Committee has continued to see that the qualifications of each applicant meet the Society's high standards for membership.

Necrology

It is my sad duty to report that the following members died during the fiscal year:

Raymond F. Ackerman, Sr.	Robert H. Jones
Robert F. Allan	Sergio Jurman
L. Stanley Baier	George P. Kenney
William A. Baker	James P. Klima
Nathan K. Bales	Harry E. Knif
Adolph Bednar	Claus B. Kuehl
William C. Brayton	Adrian J. LaRouche
Hugh J. Brown	Clarence W. Levingston
J. Gordon Calvin	Theodore J. Lund
Carl D. Colonna, Jr.	Walter L. Martignoni
James J. Convy	J. Davis Minster
Leslie Coward	Johan H. Mohr
Myron F. Dallen, III	John A. Murtha
Carlos H. Danao	Andrew Neilson
Gerard J. DeCourville	John C. Niedermair
Samuel T. Demro	Nelson Ogden
Clayton Dubosque	D'Arcy E. Phillips
Edward Freeman	Jacob Y. Pyo
Walter B. Gallagher	Charles P. Reddall
Rodolfo A. Garcia	William C. Reynolds
Tobia H. Gordon	Henry W. Runyon
David H. Green	Theodore C. Schoening
Carl E. Habermann	Irving W. Smith
Preston H. Hadley, Jr.	Umberto Spadette
Philip Handler	Alexander P. Stewart
Richard V. Hatfield	Theodore A. Taylor
J. Grant Hebble	Girard T. Tranchin
Henry A. Hoffmann	Leendert van der Tas
Henry M. Horn	Nils A. Wirstrom
Harry F. Huf	

Sections

Under the general direction of Mr. Monroe D. Macpherson, Chairman, Sections Committee, our 17 local Sections have completed another successful year. They held 111 meetings at which some 118 papers were presented. In addition, active programs were held at the seven Student Sections.

The vitality demonstrated by our regular Sections plus the Student Sections serves to support my belief that the continued growth and strength of the Society are directly affected by the ideas and motivations which develop at the local level. To this end it is of paramount importance that the Sections continue to elect officers dedicated to advancing the goals and objectives of the Society.

Finances

We have ended this fiscal year with a substantial operating fund balance. Complete details of the Society's financial operation, a proposed budget for fiscal year 1983 and a four-year projection are contained in the Report of the Budget and Endowments Committee.

A statement of the Society's assets, liabilities and fund balances will be presented by the Treasurer, Mr. Robert Axelrod.

The auditor's fully detailed financial report is available for inspection at Society headquarters.

The performance of the Society's investments has been assiduously monitored by the Finance and Audit Committee under the chairmanship of Mr. John A. Livingston.

Research

The Society's Technical and Research Program continued to make progress during the year. Initially this was under the direction of Captain Richards T. Miller, USN (Ret.), who completed his term as vice president–Technical and Research on December 31, 1981. He was succeeded in this office by Mr. Ronald K. Kiss, who also serves as chairman of the Technical and Research Steering Committee. This organizational change was brought about through Bylaw amendments approved on November 19, 1981. Also, Mr. William O. Gray was appointed chairman of the Technical and Research Advance Planning Committee to fill the unexpired term of Captain Steven N. Anastasion, USN (Ret.).

During the year, several research projects were initiated having to do principally with ship resistance, structure strength, and propeller theory. In addition, the following bulletins were published:

1-39 "The Status of Commercial Seakeeping Research"
1-40 "Ship Control Bibliography"
2-27 "Application of Probabilistic Design Methods to Wave Loads Prediction for Ship Structure Analysis"
3-32 "Furnace Performance Criteria for Gas, Oil and Coal Fired Boilers"
3-33 "Guide for the Disposal of Shipboard Wastes"
3-34 "A Guide for a Coal-Fired Boiler System"
3-35 "Utilization of Coal as a Marine Fuel"
4-17 "Guide to Sources of Data on the Costs of Construction and Operation of Merchant Ships"

The Technical and Research Finance and Administration Committee under the chairmanship of Mr. John T. Gilbride has continued to direct the fund-raising activity. A booklet entitled *The Society's Role in Maritime Research* was distributed internally and also mailed to about 550 leaders of the maritime industry. This effort resulted in total contributions of $59 406, an increase of about 17 percent over the preceding two years.

The Technical and Research Advance Planning Committee has accelerated its activity and is developing significant new directions for the future of the Society's research programs. The ad hoc Committee on Marine Energy, chaired by Mr. David A. O'Neil, continues work on its final report. The ad hoc Committee on Ship Design completed its work which has resulted in formation of the Society's seventh technical committee, that is, the Ship Design Committee, which is chaired by Dr. Robert S. Johnson. Two technical committee chairmanships changed hands, namely, the Ships' Machinery Committee where Mr. Chester L. Long succeeded Mr. Robert P. Giblon and the Marine Systems Committee where Mr. Edward M. MacCutcheon succeeded Captain William M. Nicholson, USN (Ret.).

Two co-sponsored symposia were very well received. These were the Extreme Loads Symposium, held in Arlington, Virginia in October 1981 and co-sponsored with the interagency Ship Structure Committee and the Fishing Industry Energy Conservation Conference held in Seattle, Washington also in October 1981 and co-sponsored by the National Marine Fisheries Service of NOAA. Planning continued with the cooperation of the New York Metropolitan Section for a Symposium on Ship Costs and Energy to be held in New York City.

The *1982 Technical and Research Organization and Procedures Manual* was published and new Committee stationery prepared for general use.

The Society's Technical and Research program continues as one of its more outstanding activities with about 1340 individuals serving on a total of 74 committees, panels and task groups which met about 105 times during the year.

Publications

The Publications Committee, chaired by Mr. Roy L. Harrington, continues to monitor closely the Society's publication policies, thereby maintaining the high standards which are one of SNAME's hallmarks.

Our two quarterly journals, *Journal of Ship Research* and *Marine Technology*, continue in their usefulness to those in the maritime professions. The editorial committees, under the direction of Mr. Ralph D. Cooper and Captain Perry W. Nelson, USN (Ret.), respectively, have maintained the high level of manuscript selectivity which has been responsible for the fine reputation enjoyed by these journals.

The Papers Committee, under the chairmanship of Captain Jack A. Obermeyer, USN (Ret.), has planned an interesting program of fourteen papers for our 90th Annual Meeting. Volume 89–1981 TRANSACTIONS was published and available to those members requesting it in June of this year.

The Control Committee for the new edition of *Principles of Naval Architecture* was confronted with additional delays which has postponed the anticipated publication date to late 1984.

Hydrodynamics in Ship Design, Volume III, published in 1965, went into its second printing.

Also published and made available to members during the year were a booklet entitled *Your Career in the Maritime Industry*, a 1982 *Publications Catalog*, *Proceedings* of the 1982 STAR Symposium, the 1982 edition of the *Biennial Directory and Information Book*, a booklet of discussions and closures for the 1981 STAR Symposium, the *Proceedings* of the Extreme Loads Response Symposium and the *Proceedings* of the Fishing Industry Energy Conservation Conference.

An ad hoc committee charged with investigating the feasibility of a new publication on small powered craft determined that this should be initiated through a series of T&R Bulletins under the overall direction of Panel H-12 (Planing Boats).

Annual Meeting

The 89th Annual Meeting was held November 19–21, 1981 in New York City. The 1291 registrants participated in eight technical sessions, at which 14 papers were presented. Included in the several social activities was the Annual Banquet attended by 1693 members and guests.

Spring Meetings

The 1982 Spring Meeting/STAR Symposium hosted by the Hawaii Section with the theme "Pacific Ocean Power '82" was a technical, social and financial success due principally to the excellent work of the Steering Committee under the chairmanship of Mr. Hugh W. Kaiser and the Technical Program Committee under the chairmanship of Rear Admiral E. Alvey Wright, USN (Ret.).

The 1983 Spring Meeting/STAR Symposium will be hosted by the Chesapeake Section and have as its theme, "Maritime Technology for a Changing World." This will take place April 5–8, 1983 in Washington, D.C.

The 1984 Spring Meeting/STAR Symposium will be hosted by the Los Angeles Metropolitan Section and will take place April 11–14, 1984 in Los Angeles, California.

Future Spring Meetings are scheduled with the Hampton Roads Section in 1985, the Pacific Northwest Section in 1986, the Philadelphia Section in 1987, the Great Lakes/Great Rivers Section in 1988 and the Gulf Section in 1989.

Joint Meetings

During the year the Society participated as a co-sponsor in the Oceans '81 Conference, Offshore Technology Conference, Extreme Loads Symposium, Fishing Industry Energy Conservation Conference and the Fourth International Conference on Computer Applications in the Automation of Shipyard Operation (ICCAS '82).

Appointments

Society representatives to other organizations and other appointments:

Accreditation Board for Engineering and Technology
Board of Directors . . . . Mr. William E. Zimmie
Board of Directors-Alternate . . VADM C. R. Bryan, USN (Ret.)

Engineering Accreditation
Commission . . . . Dr. Laskar Wechsler
Technology Accreditation
Commission . . . . Prof. Clifford F. Anderson
Visitors . . . . Prof. Clifford F. Anderson
Mr. Robert E. Apple
Prof. Amelio M. D'Arcangelo
Mr. Alexander Delli Paoli
Prof. Ira Dyer
Prof. J. Harvey Evans
Prof. Jose Femenia, Jr.
Mr. Jerome L. Goldman
Mr. Raymond Kaufman
Mr. Keatinge Keays
Mr. Ronald K. Kiss
Mr. Edward M. MacCutcheon
Mr. Alan C. McClure
RADM Lauren S. McCready, USMS (Ret.)
Mr. Owen H. Oakley
Dr. J. Randolph Paulling, Jr.
Dr. William R. Porter
Prof. Lawrence W. Ward
Dr. Laskar Wechsler
Dr. Roderick M. White

Advisory Public Service Liaison Representatives
Office of Management and
Budget . . . . Mr. James A. Higgins
National Committee on
Oceans and Atmosphere . . . CAPT Steven N. Anastasion, USN (Ret.)
National Academy of Sciences . RADM Randolph W. King, USN (Ret.)
Office of Technology
Assessment . . . . Mr. Edward M. MacCutcheon

American National Standards Committee
—*Gas Turbine Standards*
  B133 . . . . Dr. Dean A. Rains
Council of Engineering and Scientific Society
  Executives . . . . Ms. Linda B. Bass
Mr. William F. Greulich
Mr. Trevor Lewis-Jones
Mr. Robert G. Mende

Marine Engineering Council
  Underwriters Laboratories Mr. Robert G. Mende

NSPE Liaison Society
   Executive Directors . . . . . . .Mr. Robert G. Mende
Offshore Technology Confer-
ence
   Executive Committee . . . . .Mr. William duBarry
                                Thomas
   1981/82 Program Committees
   . . . . .Mr. Roderick J. Allan
Pan American Institute of
   Naval Engineering . . . . . . .Mr. John J. Nachtsheim
Ship Structure Subcommittee Mr. Norman O. Hammer
Sperry Board of Award . . . . . .Mr. John L. Horton
                                  VADM Robert I. Price,
                                  USCG (Ret.)
U.S. National Committee on
   Theoretical and Applied Me-
   chanics . . . . .Mr. Ralph D. Cooper

Scholarships

Eight Graduate Scholarship recipients have just started their academic year. They bring the number of Graduate Scholarships awarded since 1933 to a total of 162. Completing their scholarship awards in June were: Stephen R. Breit, Joseph Miorelli, Thomas M. Herder, Douglas G. Dommermuth and Stephen J. Harding. Starting their advanced studies this fall are: Jon J. LaBerge, Michael L. Gerardi, Matthew D. Blake, David G. St. Amand, Christopher Wiernicki, David P. Keenan, Douglas B. Colbourne and David H. Milligan.

The Undergraduate Scholarship Program, inaugurated in 1957, has made 357 awards to date. In addition, annual contributions have been given to Webb Institute of Naval Architecture for the past 27 years. Students receiving undergraduate scholarship assistance are attending Massachusetts Institute of Technology, The University of Michigan, State University of New York Maritime College and Florida Atlantic University. In addition, several students at the University of California at Berkeley are receiving Society-sponsored Grants-in-Aid.

Since inception, the total dollar support provided by these two scholarship programs and for the annual contribution to Webb comes to about $1 010 600 of which $144 000 had been in the form of grants from the National Sea Grant Program, NOAA, U.S. Department of Commerce. Unfortunately, the support from NOAA was discontinued in 1981.

The Scholarships Committee, chaired by Captain Robert E. Stark, USN (Ret.), has continued to give the selection process the dedicated care that has characterized the various Scholarships Committees' work through the years.

Awards

The David W. Taylor Medal. The 42nd award of the Taylor Medal was made at the 89th Annual Banquet on November 20, 1981 to Erwin C. Rohde "for notable achievement in marine engineering." The presentation was made by Mr. John J. Nachtsheim, President and Fellow of the Society.

The Vice Admiral "Jerry" Land Medal. The 30th award of the Land Medal was made at the 89th Annual Banquet to Ellsworth L. Peterson "for outstanding accomplishment in the marine field." The presentation was made by Rear Admiral L. V. Honsinger, USN (Ret.), Past President and Honorary Member of the Society.

The Blakely Smith Medal. The second award of the Smith Medal was made at the 89th Annual Banquet to Ben C. Gerwick, Jr. "for outstanding accomplishment in ocean engineering." The presentation was made by Mr. Blakely Smith, Honorary Member of the Society.

The Captain Joseph H. Linnard Prize. The award of the Linnard Prize for the best paper contributed to the proceedings of the Society and published in Volume 88–1980 TRANSACTIONS was awarded to Helge Johannessen and Knut T. Skarr for their paper "Guidelines for the Prevention of Excessive Ship Vibration." The presentation of the certificates of award was made at the President's Luncheon on Thursday, November 19, 1981 by Captain Jack A. Obermeyer, USN (Ret.), Honorary Vice President and chairman of the Papers Committee.

The Vice Admiral E. L. Cochrane Award. This award for the best paper presented at a Section meeting during the 1980/1981 Program Year was presented to Roy L. Harrington for his paper "Rudder Torque Prediction" given before the Hampton Roads Section on January 28, 1981. The presentation was made at the President's Luncheon by Captain Perry W. Nelson, USN (Ret.), chairman of the Marine Technology Committee.

The Spring Meeting Paper Award. The award for the best paper delivered at the 1981 Spring Meeting/STAR Symposium in Ottawa, Canada was presented to Lyssimachos Vassilopoulos and, in absentia, to Donald G. Langrock and Wolfgang Wuhrer for their paper "The Performance of the Controllable Pitch Propellers on the U.S. Coast Guard Polar Class Icebreakers." The presentation was made at the 1982 Spring Meeting in Honolulu, Hawaii by Mr. John J. Nachtsheim, President and Fellow of the Society.

The William M. Kennedy Award. The first Kennedy Award "for outstanding service and contribution in the development of systems and planning applying to shipbuilding and ship repair" was presented to Louis D. Chirillo at the 1981 Spring Meeting in Ottawa, Canada. The second Kennedy Award was presented to Daniel M. Mack-Forlist at the 1982 Spring Meeting in Honolulu, Hawaii. Both awards were presented by Mr. John J. Nachtsheim, President and Fellow of the Society.

STUDENT PAPER AWARDS

The Graduate Paper Honor Prize was awarded to Ygal Shapir and Gregory J. White for their paper "An Analysis of the Ultimate Strength of Deck Structures Under Inplane Loads" presented at the Northern California Section on April 9, 1981.

The Graduate Paper Award was awarded to Rodney D. Peltzer for his paper "The Effect of Upstream Shear and Surface Roughness on the Vortex Shedding Patterns and Pressure Distributions Around a Circular Cylinder in Transitional Re Flows" presented to the Chesapeake Section on May 20, 1980.

The Undergraduate Paper Honor Prize was awarded to Michael R. Ales and Joseph L. McGettigan for their paper "An Experimental Analysis of the Effects of Pitch Gyradius on Ship Motions in Head Seas" presented to the Chesapeake Section on April 14, 1981.

The Undergraduate Paper Award was awarded to K. Scott Hunziker for his paper "The Hood Canal Bridge: Dynamic Loading from Wind and Waves" presented at the Pacific Northwest Section on March 14, 1981.

Presentation of the Student Paper Awards was made at the President's Luncheon on November 19, 1981 by Rear Admiral Kenneth E. Wilson, Jr., USN (Ret.), chairman of the Awards Committee.

CERTIFICATES OF APPRECIATION

Certificates of Appreciation "for outstanding leadership and service to the Society as its President" were presented to Phillip

Eisenberg, L. V. Honsinger, Albert G. Mumma, Lester Rosenblatt, and Robert T. Young and, in absentia, to Matthew G. Forrest, James J. Henry, Donald A. Holden, Ralph K. James, John R. Newell, and Daniel D. Strohmeier.

Also presented were Certificates of Appreciation to Howard B. Little "for outstanding services to the Society as Accountant and Auditor 1937–1981" and to Andrew A. Szypula "for outstanding leadership and service to the Society as Chairman of several Propellers Symposia."

Presentation of the Certificates of Appreciation was made at the President's Luncheon on November 19, 1981 by Mr. John J. Nachtsheim, President and Fellow of the Society.

GOLDEN MEMBERSHIP CERTIFICATES

Golden Award Membership Certificates representing 50 years of Society membership were presented to James C. Clarke and G. Gilbert Wyland and, in absentia, to John Beattie Muir, James A. Pennypacker, Maurice L. Sellers, Ivar D. Soelberg, Leopold E. Starr, and John L. Stevens, Jr. The presentations were made at the President's Luncheon by Mr. John J. Nachtsheim, President and Fellow of the Society.

Georg P. Weinblum Memorial Lecture

The fourth Weinblum Memorial Lecture was given by Dr. Louis Landweber, professor and research engineer at The University of Iowa and Davidson Medalist.

Headquarters Staff

The staff suffered a great loss through the death, on January 7, 1982, of Mr. Walter B. Gallagher, manager, Administration. This, plus some extended absences for reasons of illness and a vacancy in the position of Technical Coordinator, created another difficult year for the Society's small staff. However, this lends added significance to my commendation to the Council of all the members of the staff for their spirit of cooperation and dedication to serving our members. I feel that the Society has made good progress in all areas during the past year and will maintain a pattern of growth in the future. My continuing confidence is based upon the dedication of this Council, the Executive Committee, the Sections and our many hard-working committees.

I also would like to record a personal expression of appreciation to our president, our officers, committee chairmen and numerous other members whose help and cooperation this past year have been so valuable to me.

Respectfully submitted,

ROBERT G. MENDE, *Secretary and Executive Director*

Report of the Treasurer

TO THE COUNCIL OF THE SOCIETY OF NAVAL ARCHITECTS AND MARINE ENGINEERS November 17, 1982

As Treasurer of the Society, I submit a Comparative Statement of Assets, Liabilities and Fund Balances as at August 31, 1982, and August 31, 1981, indicated below, as well as a Comparative Cash Flow covering the fiscal year September 1 through August 31 for 1981 and 1982.

	As at August 31 ($000 omitted)	
ASSETS	1982	1981
Current		
Cash in bank and on hand (Note 1)	$ 716	$ 375
Other Current Assets (Note 2)	131	186
Total Current Assets	$ 847	$ 561
Investments at cost (Note 3)	2547	2501
Total Assets	$3394	$3062
CURRENT LIABILITIES/FUND BALANCES		
Advanced Dues and Receipts	$ 2	$ 3
Special Accounts T&R	79	52
Other Current Liabilities	200	33
Total Current Liabilities	$ 281	$ 88
FUND BALANCES		
Operating	$1109	$ 998
Endowment	1356	1338
Kennedy	629	619
Davidson	4	4
Land	6	6
Linnard	1	1
Weinblum Memorial	8	8
Total Fund Balances	$3113	$2974
Total Liabilities and Fund Balances	$3394	$3062

Note (1)—Includes Savings Accounts—$8 (1982)—$8 (1981) Dreyfus Liquid Assets—$606 (1982)—$329 (1981)
Note (2)—Includes $91 OTC second payment received September 1981 for August 1981—For 1982 second OTC payment received during August 1982
Note (3)—Market Value—$2822 (1982)—$3098 (1981)

CASH FLOW

	As at August 31 ($000) omitted	
	1982	1981
Cash in banks and on hand 9/1	$ 716	$ 424
RECEIPTS		
Dues and Entrance Fees	519	534
Publication Sales	285	354
Contributions	121	151
Investment Income	281	245
Functions & Meetings	315	300
Total Receipts	$1521	$1584
Total Cash Available	$2237	$2008
Less:		
DISBURSEMENTS		
Fringe Benefits & payroll taxes	$ 104	90
Salaries, fees & prof. services	409	361
Facility expense	98	89
Cost of publications	305	424
Supplies & services	93	73
Headquarters & Section expense	78	80
Research	89	47
Awards & scholarships	82	78
Investment purchase	68	226
Functions & meetings	195	165
	$1521	$1633
Cash in bank and on hand	$ 716	$375

Respectfully submitted,

ROBERT AXELROD, Treasurer

Awards and Citations

Certificates of Appreciation

Hugh W. Kaiser, chairman of the Steering Committee for the 1982 Spring Meeting/STAR Symposium, and Manley St. Denis, chairman of the Hawaii Section, received Certificates of Appreciation from Society President John J. Nachtsheim. The presentations were made at the President's Luncheon on Wednesday, April 21, 1982, during the 1982 Spring Meeting/STAR Symposium in Honolulu.

At the President's Luncheon during the 90th Annual Meeting on Thursday, November 18, Mr. Nachtsheim presented a Certificate of Appreciation to Richard H. Roberts for his outstanding service as Steering Committee chairman for the 1976 and 1980 New England Sailing Yacht Symposia.

Fifty-Year Golden Award Membership Certificates

During the President's Luncheon on November 18, Mr. Nachtsheim presented Fifty-Year Golden Award Membership Certificates *in absentia* to Philip N. Israel, Robert H. Macy, Bertram B. Naschke, Henry A. Schade, and Morris Weitzner.

Student Paper Awards

Kenneth E. Wilson, Awards Committee chairman, presented the following Student Paper Awards at the President's Luncheon on November 18:

—the Graduate Paper Honor Prize ($300 plus citation) given *in absentia* to CDR Edward A. Chazal, Jr., USCG, for his paper, "Maritime Opportunities for the New England Utility Coal Trade," delivered at the New England Section on January 20, 1982;

—the Undergraduate Paper Honor Prize ($300 plus citation) to Brian D. Emch, Christopher D. Johnson and Lautaro A. Montgomery for their paper, "Coal Fired Commercial Vessels—A Practical Alternative," delivered at the New England Section on October 22, 1981;

—the Graduate Paper Award ($150 plus citation) given *in absentia* to Anil K. Thayamballi for his paper, "Fatigue Reliability of the Ship Hull Girder," delivered at the Northern California Section on April 15, 1982;

—the Undergraduate Paper Award ($150 plus citation) to William Kenneth Stewart for his paper, "A System for Dynamic Stress Analysis of a Launch and Recovery Crane at Sea with Some Preliminary Results," delivered at the Southeast Section on March 20, 1982.

Cochrane Award

The Vice Admiral E. L. Cochrane Award for 1982, given for the best paper presented before a Section of the Society, went to Robert D. Tagg for his paper, "Damage Survivability of Cargo Ships," delivered at the Northern California Section on March 11, 1982. The award was presented at the President's Luncheon by Perry W. Nelson, chairman of the Marine Technology Committee. Mr. Tagg's paper appears in this volume on page 26.

Spring Meeting Paper Award

The Spring Meeting Paper Award for the 1981 Spring Meeting/STAR Symposium was presented by John J. Nachtsheim on April 21, 1982, to Lyssimachos Vassilopoulos for the Spring Meeting Paper, "The Performance of the Controllable Pitch Propellers on the U.S. Coast Guard Polar Class Icebreakers," which was co-authored with CDR Donald G. Langrock, USCG, and Dr. Wolfgang Wuhrer. The presentation was made during the President's Luncheon at the Spring Meeting/STAR Symposium in Honolulu.

Linnard Prize

The Captain Joseph H. Linnard Prize for 1982, given for the best paper contributed to the proceedings of the Society during the Annual Meeting of the previous year, was presented to William H. Garzke, Jr. and George D. Kerr for their paper, "Major Factors in Frigate Design." Jack A. Obermeyer, chairman of the Papers Committee, made the presentation during the President's Luncheon on November 18.

William M. Kennedy Award

Daniel M. Mack-Forlist, a consulting engineer from Dobbs Ferry, New York, was the second recipient of the William M. Kennedy Award, which was presented by Mr. Nachtsheim at the President's Luncheon during the 1982 Spring Meeting/STAR Symposium in Honolulu. This Society award was established in 1980 and is given annually for outstanding service and contribution in the development of systems and planning as applied to shipbuilding and ship repair. It consists of a suitably framed certificate and $1000.

Davidson Medal

The Davidson Medal was awarded to Dr. John P. Breslin, professor and head of the Department of Ocean Engineering at Stevens Institute of Technology, and former director of the Davidson Laboratory. Dr. Breslin is best known for directing and conducting research on propeller-induced laboratory forces on ship hulls and propeller shafts. Professor Louis Landweber of the University of Iowa presented the Davidson Medal to Dr. Breslin at the 90th Annual Banquet. The following citation accompanied the presentation:

DAVIDSON CITATION

John Breslin is a very unassuming person. When he first came to the Taylor Model Basin, during World War II, as an ensign and was assigned to my group, performing work related to mine sweeping, he spoke mostly about people that he admired, like Demo Young, a classmate of his, or Frank Lewis, his professor, and later he spoke about his MS advisor at the University of Maryland, the famous Alex Weinstein. It was very easy for him to admire others. But our attention tonight is to express our admiration of him. So, we will reverse the stories that he told us.

After the War, John elected to stay at the Taylor Model Basin as a civilian, working under Phil Eisenberg. There, he worked on some very important problems in hydrodynamics, such as the stability of laminous flows and methods of measuring turbulence in water. But then after some years of research, John decided it was time for a change. After all, the purpose of research in ship hydrodynamics is to design safer and more economical ships. Unfortunately, the research information sinks down very slowly to design officers. Well John decided to accelerate the process. He accepted a position with Gibbs & Cox. He told me a story about Mr. Gibbs sending him, in a taxi, to a dry dock to look at the bow of a ship which had suffered damage from cavitation. John looked at this ship and returned to the office and tried to explain to Mr. Gibbs how, by making certain changes in the shape of the bow, he could have prevented this cavitation. Subsequently, John and I were on the Flow Study Panel of the Society and were directed by the Panel to write a bulletin on cavitation, on "How to Predict Cavitation Inception on Two Dimensional Forms Approximately Representing Bow Shapes." John decided afterwards that perhaps he should return to research and enter academia. He joined the staff of the Experimental Towing Tank, which is now called the Davidson Laboratory, acquired a Ph.D. and then, after Ken Davidson's untimely death, he was selected to become his successor.

On several occasions, I have written letters of recommendation, on his behalf, and when I accepted to present this medal to John, I looked through my old files and I found that 17 years ago I had written some letters of recommendation for him. I have selected some excerpts from the letters that I wrote. I find that the comments that I made at that time are still appropriate and not only that, even more so, to some extent.

Let me quote from a letter that I wrote recommending him for a fellowship, a senior fellowship at the National Science Foundation, "To a great extent, the status and prosperity of the Laboratory, of the Davidson Laboratory, depends upon his ability as an original thinker. This is because there are many laboratories competing for the limited funds available for research in ship hydrodynamics." That's a point that I would like to emphasize . . . not so much with respect to John's ability but for the inadequacy of research support in ship hydrodynamics.

Another quote: "Dr. Breslin's relationships with others are eased by his modest and friendly nature which make him readily available to students and colleagues for the discussion of ideas, the resolving of differences and the evaluation of criticisms. My impression is that the high morale and the productivity of his staff can be attributed to a great extent to his relationship with them."

And, lastly, concerning his personal contributions, I wrote at that time, "Dr. Breslin is one of the most productive researchers in ship hydrodynamics who combines physical insight with the ability to express and solve his problems mathematically."

When I first knew him, he had only the basic undergraduate training in naval architecture. It has been interesting to me to observe how the level of his contributions has risen as he has studied and matured. Even now, after undertaking the duties of a laboratory director, he produces papers on a sophisticated, mathematical level on the principal problems of his field.

That was 17 years ago. His paper presented at this meeting is a good example of the level of his current work. John has not stopped producing. His work is becoming even stronger. More power to you, John.

It's very appropriate, John, that you, who carried on so well the work that Ken Davidson had begun, should be awarded the Davidson Medal and it is my great privilege to present it to you now.

Land Medal

The Vice Admiral "Jerry" Land Medal for 1982 was presented to VADM Robert I. Price, USCG (Ret.) for outstanding accomplishment in the marine field by Land Medalist John T. Gilbride at the 90th Annual Banquet, accompanied by the following citation:

LAND CITATION

It is a particular privilege for me to present this very cherished award to one of our colleagues who has contributed so outstandingly to advancement in the marine field. I remember the awe and deserved admiration which all of us in the shipbuilding industry had during the prewar, the World War II and the post-war years for Admiral Land. Few realize that after a long and distinguished career in the U.S. Navy Construction Corps, a career capped by service as chief of the Bureau of Construction and Repair, he retired to become a member and then chairman of President Roosevelt's Maritime Commission. There, he became the driving force during the war years behind the tremendous U.S. Merchant Fleet shipbuilding effort. He rightfully could be called "the major architect of the historical bridge of ships which contributed to the winning of World War II." I can assure you he would be enthusiastic over the choice of Admiral Bob Price, this year's recipient of the "Jerry Land Award," for truly Bob Price is Jerry Land's type of professional. And Jerry Land, and I remember it well, had the habit of saying, "my candidate tonight has these attributes." And I can tell you, Bob Price has all the attributes that Jerry Land cherished.

Admiral Price's contributions to our profession have been too extensive to enumerate tonight but I will touch on a few.

His accomplishments derive from his service career as a Coast Guard officer, after graduation from the Coast Guard Academy and from his professional technical career following his 1953 graduation from M.I.T. with a master of science degree. First, his service career has included such traditional Coast Guard plums as Commanding Officer of a Patrol and Rescue Vessel, Captain of the Port of Philadelphia, Commanding Officer of the Coast Guard Base, Gloucester City, New Jersey, and Commander of the 11th Coast Guard District, Long Beach, California. In this command, which most of us would consider primarily a management position, he conducted a series of technical debates with some badly misinformed State of California Air Quality Administrators in an attempt, unfortunately and unsuccessfully, to make a case for an oil terminal. Finally, he was named Commander, Atlantic Area and 3rd Coast Guard District, Governors Island, New York.

Wearing his professional technical hat, his first assignment was technical secretary to the U.S. Delegation to the International Safety of Life at Sea Conference in London in 1959 and 1960 and continued with such billets as chief of the Hull Branch in the Merchant Marine Technical Division at the Coast Guard Headquarters and later, assistant chief of that same division; Chief of Planning and Special Projects Staff in the Office of Merchant Marine Safety and Chief of the Office of Marine Environment and Systems, Coast Guard Headquarters.

It can truly be stated that national regulations and international conventions in the area of fire protection, ship stability, subdivision, life-saving appliances, safety of navigation, hazardous materials and pollution prevention reflect the results of his sound application, of engineering principles, and his firmness of purpose. Without a doubt, his extraordinary leadership qualities and technical competence through the application of basic and advanced naval architectural and marine engineering principles have resulted in significant contributions to increase ship safety and ultimately safer ships in the United States and throughout the world.

Furthermore, throughout his career he has written and published more than 40 papers or comments on papers in a variety of maritime publications including our Society's Section papers, TRANSACTIONS and *Marine Technology*, and many other naval, Governmental and association publications.

His attention to his favorite theme, "Safety at Sea" has earned him recognition as a leading authority in that area.

And, after all of this, it seems improbable but he is now starting a new career with our good friend, Jim Henry, and judging by his past accomplishments will no doubt scale new heights and continue his outstanding contributions to our industry and to our Society.

Bob, it gives me great pleasure to present to you the prestigious "Jerry" Land Medal.

Taylor Medal

The 1982 David W. Taylor Medal for "notable achievement

in naval architecture" was awarded to Professor Jacques B. Hadler, Director of Research at Webb Institute of Naval Architecture. President and Taylor Medalist John J. Nachtsheim presented the medal to Professor Hadler at the 90th Annual Banquet with the following citation:

TAYLOR CITATION

It's now my great pleasure to present the David W. Taylor Medal to Jack Hadler.

Jack Hadler directs research at the Webb Institute Center for maritime studies, following a long and distinguished career as a naval officer and as naval architect at the David Taylor Model Basin.

I had the pleasure to meet Jack when I was a trainee in the Bureau of Ships and was assigned out to the Model Basin in 1948. He was so much brighter than I thought I could ever be. I tried to impress him with the fact that I had gone to Webb Institute. He told me that wasn't going to make a lot of difference here, you had to produce. Then I told him I had a friend who wanted to get into Webb Institute but he only had an IQ of 77 and he said there was no way that anybody is going to become a student at Webb Institute with an IQ of 77. He could teach . . . but no way could he be a student.

You know, John Breslin chewed me out one time when I received the Taylor Medal for not mentioning my heritage of Webb but you made up for it tonight, John.

It's my great pleasure, Jack, to present to you, the David W. Taylor Medal and add your name to a very distinguished list of recipients, all of whom I think, but one, have IQ's greater than 77.

Business Session

The Business Session on Thursday, November 18, 1982, following Paper No. 5 and presided over by President Nachtsheim, included on its agenda the election of a new president, an amendment to the Bylaws, a report on elections by the Secretary and Executive Director, and a presentation by Walter Schmid, chairman of the Steering Committee for the 1983 Spring Meeting/STAR Symposium. This meeting will take place April 5–8, 1983 in Washington, D.C. There was also a presentation for the Eighth Congress of the Pan American Institute of Naval Engineering to be held in Washington, D.C., September 12–17, 1983. This presentation was made by Ron Kiss, a member of the steering committee for the Congress.

Election of New President

Mr. George A. Uberti, chairman of the Nominating Committee: "It is my privilege to place in nomination for President of the Society the name of one of our members who's a strong supporter of this society and a leading spokesman for the shipbuilding industry. Before I tell you more about this candidate, it might be a good idea if we were to review the process by which a president is selected for nomination since we do this exercise every two years.

"Now you may not know this, but the process is a rational one.

"I didn't say "pause for laughter," but nevertheless there are no kingmakers and there is no smoke-filled back room. The Society Bylaws place this responsibility on a Nominating Committee, and I think you should know what the provisions of the Bylaws are that make this happen. I'll read you a very brief excerpt.

"The Nominating Committee shall be elected by the Executive Committee and shall consist of at least 12 members and shall include members from at least five different Sections. The membership of the Nominating Committee shall represent the broad interests of the Society. The president shall not be a member of the Nominating Committee, and membership on the committee shall be for a term of two years coinciding with the office of the president.

"The key thoughts here are geographic dispersion and diversity of professional interests. And I'm sure that you will discern that these requirements are satisfied by the composition of the 1981–82 Nominating Committee. I'll read these names off to you so you can have a feeling as to who did what we are doing today. These names are in alphabetical order.

"Nick Bachko—for many years a ship operator, now a consultant. He's in New York.

"Mike Benkert—many years a Coast Guard officer. He is now president of the American Merchant Marine Institute representing ship operators, and this is in Washington.

"Russ Bryan—again many years—a vice admiral (retired), naval career. He is now in academia, Webb Institute of Naval Architecture, and he said he's the warden of that school earlier today.

"Al Cox—who is in ship design, J. J. Henry Company, New York.

"Art Haskell—who is a ship operator. He is in San Francisco, California.

"Jack Heyrman—a builder/operator, in Vancouver, Canada.

"Jim Lisanby—active duty, U.S. Navy. He is a deputy commander of ship design, NAVSEA, in Washington.

"Syd Mathews—also in Canada, in Ontario, on the National Research Council of Canada.

"Alan McClure—who is in design, consulting, and offshore; McClure Associates in Texas.

"Ellsworth Peterson—Peterson Builders Inc., Sturgeon Bay, Wisconsin.

"George Plude—who is a Great Lakes design agent in Cleveland, Ohio; Marine Consultants and Designers.

"Captain Bruce Skinner—Coast Guard (active duty) who is in marine and ocean engineering in the Department of Engineering, the Coast Guard Academy.

"Stan Stiansen—VP of American Bureau of Shipping, the classification society, and he is in New York.

"Myself—George Uberti. I'm in shipbuilding in San Diego.

"And Ken Wilson—again many years active-duty Navy but now retired, who is a ship operator, in tanker operations for Exxon.

"If you were to count the cities and the places where these folks come from, we do have the Sections very adequately represented.

"Now of equal importance is the policy stated in the Bylaws that the office seeks the individual. To this end all Sections of the Society are invited to send in names of members to be considered for the office of president as well as for other offices. These names are considered by the Nominating Committee along with other names that the committee members themselves propose. After eligibility is verified and qualifications are reviewed and we do debate, a candidate is selected by ballot.

"Now these are the two key things that many don't know: Every member of the Society has an opportunity to have his voice heard in the process. Every member is contacted through the sections to send in nominations. And finally, the selection of a candidate is performed by a committee representing all Society members. So what we do has wide support of all 14 000 members of our Society.

"Now let's get back to our candidate. The Nominating Committee was unanimous in its selection of the president and chief operating officer of a major U.S. shipyard as the nominee for president of this Society. Our candidate rose to the presidency of his company through successive positions as director of engineering, vice president of engineering, and executive vice president and general manager of this shipyard. He's also a member of the Executive Committee of our Society; and he's been a long supporter of the Society, often encouraging his employees to be active in its affairs locally and nationally.

"Our candidate is a leading spokesman for the shipbuilding industry and has testified frequently on behalf of the industry. He was the first chairman of the Shipbuilders Council of America and presently of the board of directors and on the Executive Committee of the Shipbuilders Council. Our candidate is a member of the American Bureau of Shipping and a member of its Technical Committee. He's also a member of the board of trustees of Webb Institute of Naval Architecture.

"Our candidate is a graduate of Tufts University, a registered professional engineer in the state of California, and a member of several other technical societies. Having a sound engineering background, he maintains a strong practical management approach as he guides his company through these uncertain times. He has brought a good measure of success to his business enterprise, and your Nominating Committee feels that this individual will provide the guidance and leadership necessary for continued success of this great Society.

"Ladies and gentlemen, it gives me great pleasure to offer your committee's nomination as president of this Society for a two-year term beginning January 1, 1983. And this is Mr. C. L. (Larry) French."

President Nachtsheim: "We have a number of past presidents who have indicated they would like to second this nomination. Phil Eisenberg, would you come forward please."

Mr. Phillip Eisenberg: "Thank you. I've remarked in the past that this Society is the only one that I know of in which the membership covers the whole spectrum of the industry—the research, the engineering, the design, the shipbuilding. In the past the presidents generally have represented these various disciplines and generally their jokes have been just as diverse.

"I want to remark that the candidate that's been placed before us is particularly appropriate it seems to me since his background covers several of the disciplines that are represented in this Society. And I do consider it really quite an honor and indeed a pleasure to second the nomination of Larry French as President of The Society of Naval Architects and Marine Engineers."

President Nachtsheim: "Bob Young, would you come forward please."

Mr. Robert T. Young: "Fellow members, it's my great pleasure indeed to second the nomination of Larry French. He's a man who has devoted his whole career to our industry; and like a lot of us, he entered it you might say through the back door. He started in the steel industry and from there switched into one of the major purchasers of the steel industry itself—I mean shipbuilding. I feel absolutely sure that Larry will carry on the great traditions of this Society. He has devoted many, many years of his time to the Society.

"It's with great pleasure that I second his nomination."

President Nachtsheim: "Mike Honsinger, would you come up please."

RADM L. V. Honsinger: "Mr. President, fellow members, I'm delighted to stand here and speak for Larry French. I am impressed by his strong engineering background. This is a professional Society. I'm impressed by the fact that he is the first one in many years who comes from the waterfront, currently being president of a shipyard. It's been a long time since we've had a shipyard man as the president.

"I'm impressed by his executive ability there in the shipyard and also in the Shipbuilding Council—first chairman. I'm impressed by the fact that those of us who thought the Eastern Establishment had to establish the presidency of this Society now find we don't have to have him wholly from the East Coast where he was born and brought up, but we can look a few thousand miles away and expect the kind of service that the Society has had from the Eastern Establishment presidents.

"I am delighted and honored to be able to stand up here and second the nomination of Larry French to be leader for the next two years of this great Society."

President Nachtsheim: "And now it's my pleasure to introduce our immediate past president. Lester?"

Mr. Lester Rosenblatt: "Thank you, John. Anyone with a head of hair like Larry French's can't be all good.*

"It gives me great pleasure to second the nomination of Larry for the position of President of our Society.

"I have known Larry since he first joined National Steel and Shipbuilding Company on the LST program in the 1960's and have followed his steady rise through the ranks from project engineer, to chief materials engineer, to director of engineering, to executive vice president and finally to president.

"I think he's held his present position at NASSCO longer than any other there, and as a Morrison-Knudsen stockholder, I'm glad he's finally found a spot where he can last more than a couple of years!

"Two serious thoughts: I'm glad Larry is from the West Coast. When I became President of this Society, the charge was that all previous Presidents came from the East Coast, between Bath, Maine and Newport News, Virginia. I carefully explained that my own company's practice was worldwide with a geographic center nearer Colorado than the East. But, Larry *is* from good old California.

"Finally, there are those among us who see these immediate times as leading toward the greatest military peril to our nation due to lack of U.S. merchant ships and U.S. merchant shipyards. This vision is, in my view, either not seen or foolishly ignored by our national leaders. Larry has become an articulate spokesman for our industry. Perhaps he can be effective for our nation.

"It is a great honor and sincere privilege to second the nomination of Larry French to the presidency of this venerable but sprightly Society."

President Nachtsheim: "Recognizing the sense of the group, I call for a motion to close the nominations."

A member: "So moved."

President Nachtsheim: "All in favor."

Members: "Aye."

President Nachtsheim: "I now ask for a vote for the presidency. All in favor of Larry French as our next president raise your hands . . . I think we have a simple majority."

(The motion was seconded, it was put to a vote and carried.)

President Nachtsheim: "Larry, would you be good enough to come up and make a few remarks. We're hoping you'll accept."

President-elect C. L. French: "I really wasn't prepared to come up here. John said tomorrow night I might be asked to say a couple of words.

* [L. ROSENBLATT'S NOTE: "Mr. French has a very full head of handsome, wavy, steel-grey hair. I'm quite bald."]

"I'm deeply appreciative of the honor; and I think that to be recognized by your peers is certainly going to be for me a very moving experience. I pledge that I will do my best to follow in the footsteps of the fellows you've seen up here today. They've done a magnificent job, and I hope I can do as well.

"I have to say the two guys just prior to me had better joke writers than I'll ever have. So I'm afraid the speeches I make are not going to be as humorous as the ones you've heard for the past four years. But other than that, I hope to be able to do the job the fellows who have been here before have set the example for.

"Thank you very, very much."

Amendment Approved

The amendment pertained to the Executive Committee quorum. The Executive Committee had a problem in achieving a quorum mainly because the members of the Executive Committee included, in their method of constituting a quorum, all past presidents. With eleven past presidents, however, as their presidency extended from the immediate past, their attendance at Executive Committee meetings became less and less frequent, causing some difficulty in making a quorum.

The change continues all past presidents of the Society as members of the Executive Committee for life, but they will not be counted in the membership of a quorum, in the making up of a quorum. The amended quorum will always be the same number. The quorum as previously defined was 13 members, three of whom had to be elected members. Under the amendment, the quorum will be eight members, three of whom will be elected members, making it significantly easier for the Executive Committee to conduct its activities.

The wording of Section C(2)(3) of the Bylaws, Quorum, has therefore been changed from a simple majority to include all past presidents, to exclude them in the counting of the quorum.

Election of Officers

Robert G. Mende, Secretary and Executive Director, made the following report on the election of officers.

Elected by the Council:

Honorary Members for life: John J. Nachtsheim, Cedric Ridgely-Nevitt, and William A. Sheehan.

Fellows: John P. Breslin, Ronald K. Kiss, Philip Mandel, Walter H. Michel, Frank L. Pavlik, Robert Taggart, Donald L. Blount, Harry A. Jackson, Lawrence R. Gloston, T. Arthur McLaren, and Richard Broad.

Honorary Vice Presidents for life: Arthur J. Haskell, and Monroe D. MacPherson.

Vice Presidents for a term of three years (to December 31, 1985): Richard Broad, Jean E. Buhler, David A. O'Neil, and Ellsworth L. Peterson.

To serve on the Executive Committee for a term of three years (to December 31, 1985): William M. Benkert, Jack A. Obermeyer, and T. Francis Ogilvie.

Member of the Executive Committee for a term of one year (to December 31, 1983): Roy L. Harrington.

Administrative officers for a term of one year (to December 31, 1983): Secretary and Executive Director, Robert G. Mende; Treasurer, Robert Axelrod; and Assistant Treasurer, Donald M. Birney.

Elected to Council by ballot of the membership

Representing Members and Associate Members for a term of three years (to December 31, 1985): Ralph J. Bradford, Edward J. Campbell, William N. Johnston, and Henry S. Marcus.

Representing Members and Associate Members for a term of two years (to December 31, 1984): Roger L. Potash.

Representing Members and Associate Members for a term of one year (to December 31, 1983): J. Gordon German.

Representing Affiliates for a term of three years (to December 31, 1985): David H. Klinges.

1983 Executive Committee

C. L. French, president; Robert Axelrod, treasurer; William M. Benkert (1985); Clarence R. Bryan (1984); Donald P. Courtsal, vice president–Advisory Public Service (1984); Phillip Eisenberg, past president; Matthew G. Forrest, past president; Roy L. Harrington (1983); James J. Henry, past president; Donald A. Holden, past president; L. V. Honsinger, past president; Ralph K. James, past president; Ronald K. Kiss (1983) and vice president–Technical and Research (1984); John A. Livingston, chairman, Finance and Audit Committee; Robert G. Mende, secretary and executive director; Albert G. Mumma, past president; John J. Nachtsheim, past president; John R. Newell, past president; Jack A. Obermeyer (1985); T. Frances Ogilvie (1985); Donald E. Ridley, chairman, Sections Committee; Lester Rosenblatt, past president; Bruce C. Skinner (1984); Daniel D. Strohmeier, past president; George A. Uberti (1984); Kenneth E. Wilson, Jr. (1983); Robert T. Young, past president.

President John J. Nachtsheim's Annual Address

November 18, 1982

(Amenities to guests) . . . This is the occasion for the President's Address. Someone told me, why don't you give the same address you did last year, 9504 Boyer Place, Silver Spring. That hasn't changed.

But, really, after two years of the very high honor to serve as the President of this Society, I have been able to see firsthand how many things we do and how well we do them. This is truly a great, great organization.

The Society continues to grow professionally, financially and in its membership. The technical committees and the panels and our local Sections develop and carry out excellent programs, ever-growing in technical competence and interest. Those committees that are other than technical committees and the staff continue to show increased vigor and continued achievement. Financially, I said we made a 10 percent profit this year, and Trevor corrected me. Because we're a nonprofit organization, our income exceeded our outgo by 10 percent . . . and we had another 2 percent increase in membership.

The first International Maritime Exposition which we are sponsoring in conjunction with this, our 90th Meeting, is a resounding success and a fine, truly fine, addition to our program. It adds a tremendously valuable educational dimension and it brings together several segments of our Society in a much closer relationship than ever before.

A great number of the businesses—many of those with which our Society deals—are in tough times but they continue to support this Society and its activities and I think we should thank all of them for that.

Now, in comparison, the Navy projects an expanded 600-ship program by 1990. It's healthy and strong and is gaining continued support everywhere. This program is not, of itself, sufficient to maintain a shipbuilding and supplier base of the size and diversity that we know today but it is the core of a shipbuilding and supplier system capability that is essential to shipbuilding and maintaining shipbuilding in this country.

Many suppliers, however, do not now see a sufficient market to justify staying in business to supply the necessary equipment for the Naval Ship Construction Program alone and this creates an anomaly, I think. Much of the equipment and materials specified by the Navy is done in what is called Mil Specs, Military Specifications. Much of that equipment doesn't even require what we think of as a Mil Spec for its procurement. Many of those materials and much of that equipment have no military requirement; they are just necessary equipments to go aboard a ship in a marine environment. The Military Specification System was used, however, to specify those equipments because the Navy had to use something to invoke the requirements that they wanted met and there was no commercial equivalent . . . there was no commercial mechanism to establish an alternative way of producing a specification which they could use. The Naval Sea Systems Command is responsible, technically, for 9000 Military Specifications and 2500 standard drawings. They have publicly admitted that 35 percent of those standards are out of date and many of them need significant work to bring them into a state of what you might call readiness . . . at the very time they are accelerating a shipbuilding program! I think that here lies a great opportunity for this Society to render significant assistance. One of the Society's activities which has received very little notice is the Standards Program. You've noticed out in the reception area there is a booth and many of the exhibitors are now showing a little sign that says they support the National Ship Building Standards Program. That is a part of what we are involved with and it is an effective alternative.

The Society has been involved with the development and implementation of what are now called—and this is what they are as against Military Specifications—National Consensus Standards, since 1977. This has been done via a program together with the American Society of Testing and Materials, ASTM. They have established, in order to accommodate the needs of the marine industry at that time, an ASTM Committee, called F25 on Ship Building Standards. At the present time, they've had in process over 100 such standards where none exist today. The Navy representation and participation in that program has been extensive. The Navy has recognized that that would be useful to them and, in fact, Vice Admiral Faller, Commander of the Naval Sea Systems Command, just this month issued a decision paper reiterating the continued Navy support and participation in the ASTM Program. The Maritime Administrator, Harold Shear, in a later dated June 23 to all Ship Building Presidents, strongly endorsed the program spelled out in the ASTM Ship Building Program, and the long-range objectives of that Program. I think I even mentioned this at our meeting last year, when Admiral Hayes asked the Society's help in standards since the Coast Guard had to reduce its regulatory capabilities.

Now, do you see the same significance that I do in these two points? First, the Navy has outdated specs vital to an expanded Ship Building Program, many of which don't even need to be Mil Specs, and those standards will be an obstruction to a pro-

ductive capability for the shipbuilder. Second, the Society has the capability and the expertise as well as the support of the Navy, the Coast Guard and the Maritime Administration to do the technical backup work in developing industry consensus standards. An ideal mechanism that is working through the ASTM F25 Ship Building Committee is available to bring them into being. Now I have personally looked at the Navy's priority list for these specifications, those that have to be updated, and I can confirm that many hundreds don't need to be Mil Specs. We in the Society could take the technical data contained in those specifications, update and quickly process them through the ASTM Panel SP6 Committee System, thereby producing an instant update of a very important series of specifications. The result would be updated consensus industry standards that meet Navy needs and satisfy the needs of the Coast Guard and the Maritime Administration. The cost of the equipment thereby purchased under those specifications as compared with a Military Specification would be considerably less. And, the specification would be current and its currency would be guaranteed because under the ASTM system currency has to be evaluated each and every five years. Thousands of Mil Specs are involved. The Navy Accelerated Program for Ship Building is NOW. From these two conditions, I see a tremendous opportunity for the Society to render great national service, but, on a very urgent time frame if it's to be effective. I see the need to recognize this opportunity and volunteer basically the entire T&R Committee and Panel system. The expertise that they possess toward this effort, not just Panel SP6 and ASTM Committee F25 alone . . . that much talent that's represented by our T&R Program is needed to do this job quickly. And if it's not done quickly, it will not have very much of an impact on the Accelerated Ship Building Program.

I have appealed to the T&R Steering Committee to answer this call, to reorder their priorities in the coming year, to help the Navy meet its serious obligation, to assist in lowering the cost of shipbuilding, and in so doing to retain many vital suppliers of marine equipment who otherwise might not continue to meet the Navy's equipment needs. I'm asking all members of the T&R Steering Committee and its panels to join the Navy for a short hitch. I ask all of the members of this Society to support this challenging effort.

Ron Kiss, the chairman of the T&R Steering Committee, assures me, as a result of a discussion that was held on this subject yesterday morning at their meeting, that they will indeed tackle this problem at the soonest.

We have a real opportunity—or is it an obligation?—to do more. I'm sure we will.

On another subject, we are seeking greater participation by both Navy and the U.S. Coast Guard officers in our Society activities and membership. We have received great support from Admiral Faller, the Commander of the Naval Sea Systems Command, and Admiral Gracey, the Commandant of the Coast Guard, in this effort. We have concluded the initial steps of a drive to attract more than 2000 of these officers to membership in the Society. I want to assure you that this is not for the purpose of increasing our numbers; rather, it is aimed at increasing a quality of our membership. Most of these officers hold key positions in interesting jobs. They're involved in shipbuilding, naval engineering, ship operations, ship maintenance, ship repair and managerial jobs of great significance. Their absence from our membership denies us that experience. Likewise, they deny themselves experience to be gained by active participation with our 14,000 highly competent and experienced members. The first signs of that effort have proven, I think, very encouraging and I'm hopeful that we will have great progress in this coming year and I'm sure the Society as a result will be technically richer.

You may recall that last year I asked the question, "Are we, The Society of Naval Architects and Marine Engineers, doing enough?" And after I spoke a little bit, I said, in answer to that question, "Today, more than ever, the Society has the opportunity, the challenge, maybe even the obligation to do more." Now in recognition of the very important national need in this standards area to support the Navy, which I've just described, I am confident the Society will indeed do more.

In conclusion, I would like to thank you all for the opportunity you have so generously afforded me to serve as your President for the past two years. I'm grateful for the support of all of the members of the Society and to the loyal staff and I want to acknowledge the importance of the support of all the members of their employers who, in less-than-ideal economic times, have been so generous and supportive of the Society's activities and its membership. And, finally, I want to thank the families, the wives and the children of the members whose support also makes what we do possible. Without all three, the members, their employers and their families, this Society would not be the great Society it is. Please believe me when I say all of that support is genuinely appreciated. I've seen, from this sort of position that you provided, how much it means. I really loved the job. I love all of you. Thank you and God Bless you.

Remarks by John M. Rau

President, the Navy League of the United States

Delivered at the Annual Banquet, November 19, 1982

Introduction by John J. Nachtsheim, President:

Our speaker, John M. Rau, is the president of a company he formed himself, David Industries, and he is the national president of the Navy League of the United States. He has been a truly outspoken proponent of United States sea power and his definition of sea power does not include only the Navy. He includes Navy, Coast Guard, Marine Corp and the Merchant Marine in that definition.

Mr. Rau is a resident of Orange, California. And I might mention to you, John—your name is John, you can't be all bad—that our recently elected president, Larry French, is also from California and he will work with you, I'm sure, for the next two years.

Mr. Rau holds degrees in engineering and business from M.I.T. He served in the U.S. Navy during World War II and again during the Korean War. He has been active in the Navy League for over 21 years and has held many offices; he is now, of course, its president. He has traveled on behalf of the Navy League over 200 000 miles a year. Last year alone, he was in London three times. His luggage was there once. He has sailed with carrier battle groups in the Indian Ocean. He's spent two weeks on winter maneuvers with the Marines in northern Norway. He has been on interdiction and icebreaking missions with the Coast Guard. He has deployed in all three oceans as well as the Mediterranean and Caribbean Seas. A true leader. A proponent of U.S. sea power. Someone who tells it like it is. It's my pleasure and high honor to introduce Mr. John M. Rau.

Mr. Rau's remarks:

Thank you very much, John. And thank you ladies and gentlemen.

I'm well aware that the mind can absorb only what the posterior can endure so I will attempt to recognize that fact. I almost think we ought to have a seventh-inning stretch right now. Would you all like to get up for about twenty seconds and stand. Up until the gong rings.

Okay, Bob, want to hit the gong. Well, everybody is going to . . . okay. (Sounding of the bell.)

I know how that feels.

I want you to know that sitting here, listening to your president—your outgoing president, he keeps reminding me—is that nobody in his right mind will come up to the podium and follow Groucho Marx, so you can be sure that I am not going to start telling you any stories.

I do want to tell you one thing about your president which could possibly have led to his impeachment were he not already supplanted. Some time ago he asked for an appointment and took me and our executive director, Bob Scarborough, to lunch at a rather expensive restaurant in Washington and I probably imagine that your Society paid for it, and I want you to understand that that was truly, in the words of this Administration, waste, fraud and abuse, because I would have taken him for lunch for the privilege of addressing such a fine group of people about the concepts of sea power. So, you really wasted your money, John.

I feel a certain kinship as an electrical engineer, and not a naval architect, with your first president, Clement A. Griscom, who was told "there were only two requirements for office either one of which would qualify him to know all about the subject of shipbuilding and marine engineering or nothing at all." And we are advised that he took the job on the basis of this second criterion.

That is not entirely true in my case because while at Tech I did room for a while with a naval architect and that was an experience.

I have concluded from that experience that yours is an art composed primarily of memorizing empirical, abstruse empirical formulae, because I used to drill him for exams for the marine engineering professor named Bilgey Bertner—Evans Bertner, I think—who some of you obviously know; I see a laugh in the audience. Anyway, that was my first experience with your fine professsion.

I find having had the benefit through the courtesy of Bob Price of reviewing an address that was given by your then president, Don Holden, about your Society to the Newcomen Society back in 1968, that there are some interesting parallels with the Navy League. This is your 90th year; this is our 80th year. We support the same goals. We shared a national President. Robert M. Thompson was president of your Society in 1912 and moved on over to the Navy League in 1915 and was a major supporter of the League. We have also had, as things have changed for better and worse in this country and in the world, a similar ebb in flow of our organization of our membership. We have had ups and downs in the industry, together. We have had our dollar problems and our frustrations.

Let me borrow, as I set the stage for some of my further remarks, let me borrow from some of President's Holden's remarks in his account of the Society to establish some historical perspective. Someone once said that, in the spirit, things are ever changing yet everlastingly the same.

"In 1893," he related, "the opening remarks at our first meeting"—speaking of your Society—"were in reference to lack of enough shipbuilding orders to maintain our skills in international competition and the abandonment of ship opening in foreign trades." How little things have changed.

In 1894, a paper was presented to the meeting also citing the apathy of the great bulk of the American public toward the merchant marine . . . an apathy that we in the Navy League are still today trying to dissipate.

In 1898, however, it was still said that the proportion of imports and exports in American bottoms was too small to mention. And I think 4 percent is still too small to mention.

Furthermore, in a paper given in the year 1900, the question was asked, "Can the American shipbuilder, under present conditions, compete with Britain and Germany in the production of commercial steamships." Today, we would substitute Japan, Taiwan, Korea and still have the same question.

President Holden also commented that in 1906 the Secretary of State, after returning from a study trip abroad, observed that the disadvantages of our shipowners were created by our own Government's actions. First by raising standards of wages and living by protective tariffs and, second, by foreign governments paying subsidies to their ships for the promotion of their own trade. For the American shipowners it is not a contest of intelligence, skill, industry and thrift against similar qualities in its competitors; it is a contest against his competitor's government and his own Government.

During 1907, our maritime industry was further frustrated by the transfer of two large ships to foreign registry because of high operating costs. This left only five United States ships in operation to the coasts of Europe.

All before 1910, and 75 years later we can still say much the same things.

We can also recognize that only in wartimes, twice in this century, have we seen those sad things changed around.

Again from Mr. Holden: more destroyers were produced in a year and a half—this is during World War I—than were built in the previous 25 years. We all know how that has happened in merchant ships, in naval ships and everything.

Let's turn now from those recitals from history, sad history, which do set the stage for some of the things I want to discuss with you tonight, to an area that perhaps I do have some competence in and certainly some firsthand knowledge and that's the status of U.S. sea power in the world today. Your President has told you that I've traveled over 300 000 miles visiting the fleets, marines, coastguardsmen, shipyards, etc.

We have a three-ocean problem in this country and we have a one-and-a-quarter-ocean Navy. I would hardly characterize in any language fit for this group the status of our merchant marine and our shipbuilding base. It's so far down as to be a disaster. And what about our principal competitor? Well I'll tell you what Admiral Shepp Shapiro, the Director of Naval Intelligence, said in testimony before the Senate Armed Services Committee. The evidence is most persuasive that not withstanding the severe economic problems they face now and in the coming years, the Soviet leadership has elected to make a major capital investment in building and maintaining a Navy and merchant marine that can project Soviet influence throughout the world. This maritime power represents a direct and growing challenge to the economic, political and strategic interests of the United States and our allies. There must be recognition of the very problems we face in this country and a different decision to be made. There can be little doubt that

despite severe and growing economic problems with the Warsaw Pact, Fleet Admiral Gorshov (phonetic) continues to receive substantial support for the balanced fleet he seeks to create. And in a civilian economy starved for capital investment and faced with other growing domestic economic dilemmas, the Kremlin has lavished funds on warship building yards coupled with huge operating expenses to keep these underused facilities opened. That's what we're up against. Well, one of the reasons, I submit to you, that they have had that success, is that Admiral Gorshov has been there over a quarter of a century and during that time we have had seven C&O's, eight Secretaries of the Navy, countless Chairmen of the House and Senate Armed Services Committee, and they have had a consistency of purpose far beyond ours. Part of the problem we have in our system.

Well now, what have I observed as I have been around the world and in the Indian Ocean and the Med and maneuvering with the Marines in North Norway, etc? Let me give you a little feel for some of the things that are happening out there, because in a few minutes I'm going to lay something on you.

In the Indian Ocean it is hot. We keep a carrier battle group out there all the time. We give our sailors two cans of beer for every 60 days at sea. Nobody has made a six-pack cruise yet but the *Eisenhower* had a 154 days straight without touching port. It's in the high 90's in atmosphere; it's in the high 90's in humidity and the water is 90 plus degrees and that's right down to the keel and that means cooling systems don't work, means air conditioning doesn't work. The sand off the Sahara hangs in the air. You're cleaning antenna insulators every week or two instead of every six months. F14 pilots are on the deck ready to launch in the cats. Canopy is open; their arms are hanging outside the cockpit and do you know why that is? That's because the air conditioning is of course not on and they want the sweat to run down and drip outside the airplane and not into the electrical and electronic equipment in the cockpit. That's tough duty. Sailors are working 12 and 16 hours a day, 7 days a week. You want to work on the electronic bay of an airplane on a hanger deck; you've got to push it around so it isn't partly under the overhead where water is dripping down, becoming condensation, because you don't want water in that electronics again.

I was in Antartica, on board a 27-year-old icebreaker. We keep saying we're going to take it out of service and we put it back in without a yard overhaul. Down in the engine room, you've got six of those ten Fairbanks Morse diesels running; you're in great shape, because the parts have lead times as long as 600 days because Fairbanks Morse doesn't make them anymore and down in that engine room there's a young lady, greasy and dirty, tearing down one of those engines and she gets a shower every five days. And I got down there with a First Class, and I'm an old First Class Petty Officer myself, so I really know what's happening down there. The guy says "Sir, I want to show you what is the most important thing I got in this ship." And he says, "See there, see there, see there, see there . . ." and he's pointing with his flashlight at the hose clamps that he's got around the pipes on that ship because they're all leaking. That's the sort of thing they're coping with.

We send our Marines to North Norway on maneuvers, up above the Arctic Circle, and I was there last winter with a pack and a rifle and, in the tent, the ranking officer was a corporal. Those kids are there because they have to show the Russians that we have the means and the will to reinforce the Norwegians if they come around from the Cola Peninsula, where the largest single concentration of Russian force exists. And those marines are ready, but let me tell you, you can't carry on your back an awful lot of ammunition. And the rates of fire, the weapons that we are now giving our infantry platoons, are pretty high. And if they really had to do that job with only 67 amphib ships

Remarks by John M. Rau

and over 40 of them hitting block obsolescence, and with no real sealift capacity or capability, I don't know how long we can stay and that's true of the Rapid Deployment Force; it's true of a marine amphibious unit, or a MAB or a MAF, or the Army, wherever we put it.

When I was in the amphibs and landed on some of those islands, 600 or 700 amphib ships were nothing and we've got 67.

I was in the Med with those same groups and with others, and it was the same marines that came back to the States for about two months, and now they're back over there in Lebanon. We've got a carrier battle group there; we've got an amphib squadron; we've got that MAL landed. But in all of these incidences, whether it's the Indian Ocean or the Med or the Caribbean or Lebanon—all around—we're right at the very limit of what we can do. We've stretched our people. We're taking it out of the hides of our people and their families. And that's something else you ought to know. We've got a family Navy now and Marine Corps and Coast Guard. When I was in the Navy, a seaman made 54 bucks a month, he couldn't afford to get married, he knew he couldn't afford to get married, and he didn't get married. Today, a seaman gets about $650 a month, he can't afford to get married but he thinks he can afford to get married and he does get married. So we've got 19-year-old sailors out there with wives, with kids. We've got to rotate them. We've got long deployments. Got all these problems. They have second jobs. When they deploy at sea, they lose that second income. Let me tell you a little something about family life in the military service and particularly for our sea services because they are the ones that are facing the family separations, the economic impact, as well as the emotional impact, the lack of both financial and emotional support of both partners of the marriage. I was, a year ago, at Lamour Naval Air Station in central California for Navy Day, toured around, was taken to the Family Service Center or room where the families would come in—where, as they come onto the base, they are told what kind of resources are available and things like that—and there was a big rack, had a lot of pamphlets in that rack, and I took off the top of that rack this pamphlet. . . . This was the pamphlet that was at the top of that rack, this is what was highest priority for those families to read: "How to Apply For and Use Food Stamps." Does that make you proud? Does that make us feel good? I think not.

Now I hope I have your attention, and I think I do. So, what, in my judgment, is the fundamental problem? Why have I burdened you with this account, laid a guilt trip on you? Well I think that it's very simple; there are not enough ships. There are not enough ships just as in all the years before except those two wartime intervals. And why don't we have enough ships? Well, there are a lot of reasons. But I submit to you that basically in our society today we don't have enough ships because they cost too much to build, they cost too much to operate, they cost too much to man, they cost too much to maintain and they cost too much to repair and overhaul. Now we can blame all of that on Government regulations, on politics, on taxes, on the unions, on the environmental movement, on coastal commissions, on foreign subsidies, etc., etc., etc. But I won't accept that and I don't think you should and I'll tell you why. I believe that since the coming of the industrial maturity of this nation we have always had those kinds of problems or similar problems in many competitive situations, and we have solved those problems, and we have solved them—and I say this as a technologist myself—we have solved them through superior technology, of design, of tooling, of manufacture. We don't work cheaper in this country, we work smarter. We think smarter. We innovate. We lead. We've done that in aircraft, in automobiles, in radio and television and telephones, in plumbing, in computers and on and on and on. But I'm not satisfied that

we have done it but rarely in ships or in house construction, but the thing is, in a house, you've got to buy it where you're going to live, you can't buy houses offshore.

So, the challenge is yours. You are the ones to lead the way to technical revolution in this industry . . . this industry which is so basic to our economic health and so vital to our national defense. You, individually, as a profession, as a society, have to foster a quantum jump, no small measures. Crises and catastrophe are at hand. I read in your history that in the 1960's this Society had a magnificent budget of $80 000 for research and development. It's a slightly mixed crowd or I'd characterize that the way it deserves.

You have to provide the leadership, the ideas, the rallying point, the radical breaks with the past, for new legislative initiatives—yes, that is required—for new unanimity in the industry, and we all know that has been the rock on which our maritime industry in the broad sense has foundered shipbuilders, shipowners, shipyards, repair yards, unions, shippers, all the other elements of the industry, including the Navy and the Administration and all the other people, always coming together but never reaching critical mass and falling apart. And above all, to lead the way in searching for technological breakthroughs that can stock this cost too much, that litany, that I just articulated.

And we and you may well have to lead a renaissance in the United States Navy because, and I'm quoting President Holden once again, it was stated in 1896 and it's true today, "even at this early point in our history, it is obvious that most of our progress in naval architecture and marine engineering was in connection with advances made in naval ship construction."

Your president said I was free to speak. I've got a couple of good friends to my right and left and I'm going to step on their toes, just like I'm pounding you on the top of your heads, because this is serious. I have been out in those fleets and I see what we're doing to our people to make up for the lack of these technological breakthroughs which are your responsibility. As I go out on these ships, let me tell you they look awful familiar. There's a hell of a lot of gear there that's just like it was in World War II and those ships are a third my age. They're younger than I was when I was a kid joining the Navy, the first time. The crews are too large and that's a compound exponential problem because every time you put 50 or 100 sailors on board a ship to work that ship you've got to have yeomen and storekeepers and mess cooks and laundrymen and all the other compartment cleaners, etc., and there's a growth factor in ship crews just like there is in an aircraft, weight. So there's also an exponential payoff if you can pull people off.

Now, in the old days, of course, it didn't matter because you had to have enough crew to fight the ship. The USS *New Jersey* is going to be commissioned pretty soon; it went out in World War II with well over 3000 people. It's going to go to sea now with probably under 1500. The 20 millimeters are gone, the 40 millimeters are gone, the quad mounts are all gone, there's all kinds of stuff that's gone. The gunnery division is weighed down; therefore, the crew can be smaller. Habitability can be better. The ship is more economical to operate but I'll bet you there's still too many people on board. And it's still too costly to build the ships as we build them today in our Navy. Switchboxes, this big around; brass covers, big toggle things; heavy armored cable coming in, just the same as 40 years ago. Surely there's a way to meet all of the explosion-proofing, the reliability, the ability to withstand shock and salt water and everything else, that's smaller and lighter and cheaper. There's got to be a better way to dog a hatch than we have been doing it for 50 years.

We have made some improvements, some radical improvements. I don't want to let you think that I don't know that you all have done some things: Trident submarines, the new form of manufacture. End loading of the modules; manufacturing these giant steel rings to tight tolerances now on a mass-production basis. Big improvement. Be a hell of a lot easier if we'd build four or five a year instead of one because then we could really get some economies out of those plants. That's a political problem. I've been on some Coast Guard cutters—lots of stainless steel and formica, you can tell, these are Bay class. Four people can stand watch: an officer, one person in the engine room and two on the bridge. I've been icebreaking on the *Polar* class as well as that 27-year-old icebreaker and that's got what's called the white bow, and it's really a miracle. With half the horsepower you can just crunch right through that 8-foot-thick ice, steady. And on the other ship, with twice the horsepower, it's back and ram, it's herringbone and everything. Yeah, there have been improvements. You can probably name a lot of them, but not enough. They cost too much, to build, to man, to operate, to maintain, to repair, to overhaul.

So, ladies and gentlemen, in my judgment, the sea services need your help. It's up to you to make a major breakthrough in this problem. You're the cream of the technological brains in this industry, and I hope I haven't beaten you so hard on the head that I've dulled your brains because we need you and because I'm going to ask one more thing from you, besides opening your minds to wild, new, different, innovative, challenging, radical steps, one out of a hundred of which will work but when it does it will give us what we need. Because finally I'd like to go back to the people problem and talk to you just as another audience that I want to carry a message to from the sea services. Because in addition to doing that innovation technically I want to ask you to do one more thing. I know many of you do these things, but let's support those people, be active politically, individually if not as a society, to meet some of these problems that I've tried to articulate very briefly for you. Let's keep up the pressure on the supply side of shipbuilding even though they cost too much, because we have 15 years of erosion of our capital, of our seagoing capital, to make up for, and that's

not going to be done in one year or two years or even in one Administration; it's going to take a long time, and you and I know that the American public isn't very patient. I'd like to ask you to help us in our mission of educating the citizens of our country about the importance of sea power, of foreign trade, of American bottoms, of freedom of the seas of ship lanes that we defend, the power projection of flexible mobile sea power, conventional power, so that we are not left only with the choice of surrender or nuclear conflict. You might even join the Navy League. Work on pay for our families, sea service families. And, finally, at the same time you're worrying about the hardware and thinking about new ways, see what you can do to put something in psychic dollars in the paychecks of our sea service people. When you see them, give them a smile, give them a hello. If you're in a bus station, railroad station, airport, on the street, you see a sailor or a marine or a soldier or an airman or airwoman, a Coast Guard lady, who looks a little lost, ask them if you can help them. See if you can help them out in your community, they need guidance for lawyers and doctors and where to live and real estate agents and bankers. Help their families when their menfolks or others are deployed. Help them when the ships are in your yard because that's a traumatic experience for the crew and for the families as well as for you and the ship. Do what you can. And let me give you one last thing. When you see a little clipping in your newspaper and it says, Seaman Jones was commended by his commanding officer for outstanding performance; Corporal Smith received the meritorious promotion, etc., tear that out of the newspaper and clip it to your stationery and write on it "Thanks" or "Great" or "You're doing a real job for us," or "We appreciate it," or "We know what you're doing," or anything like that and sign it and, because you're somebody important in the community, they'll know and I promise you when that hits a ship it will go around it like wildfire. Four or five thousand people on a carrier will know if you did something like that. If you'll try to put some of those psychic dollars in our people's paychecks, they'll be very grateful and so will I.

Thank you very much for having me.

Remarks by John M. Rau

Section Officers

September 1, 1982 to August 31, 1983

Arctic Section (org. Nov. 18, 1981)

Chairman: Malcolm I. Comyn
Vice Chairman: James F. Owler
Treasurer: Deborah R. Dumka
Secretary: Willem H. Jolles

Canadian Maritime Section (org. Jan. 23, 1962)

Chairman: Pieter Nieuwburg
Vice Chairman: Iain P. MacInnes
Secretary-Treasurer: Donald P. Adamson

Chesapeake Section (org. Aug. 23, 1945)

Chairman: J. Richard Gauthey
Vice Chairman: Alexander C. Landsburg
Secretary-Treasurer: Amos Baki

Eastern Canadian Section (org. Sept. 25, 1952)

Chairman: Alexander N. Elliott
Vice Chairman: Ian F. Glen
Secretary-Treasurer: Richard M. Bertrand

Great Lakes/Great Rivers Section (org. Sept. 12, 1946)

Chairman: Thomas J. Stewart
Vice Chairmen: Great Lakes: John O. Greenwood
Great Rivers: Ira J. Singleton, Jr.
Secretary-Treasurer: Wayne E. Bratton

Gulf Section (org. May 25, 1949)

Chairman: Ronald J. McAlear
Vice Chairmen: East Area: Thomas E. Page, Jr.
Central Area: David H. Whitten
Secretary-Treasurer: Henry Fray, Jr.

Hampton Roads Section (org. June 5, 1957)

Chairman: Roy L. Harrington
Vice Chairman: Robert L. Kelly
Secretary-Treasurer: Samuel A. Tatum

Hawaii Section (org. Jan. 26, 1955)

Chairman: Thomas A. Marnane
Vice Chairman: Edwin L. Parker
Secretary-Treasurer: William G. Speed

Los Angeles Metropolitan Section (org. Apr. 29, 1948)

Chairman: George F. Henning
Vice Chairman: Maxwell C. Cheung
Secretary-Treasurer: Gary W. Cash

New England Section (org. June 12, 1944)

Chairman: Lee F. Mount
Vice Chairman: Russell W. Brown
Secretary-Treasurer: John J. Bryan

New York Metropolitan Section (org. Nov. 11, 1942)

Chairman: John C. Daidola
Vice Chairman: Joseph D. Connors
Secretary-Treasurer: William H. Garzke, Jr.

Northern California Section (org. June 12, 1944)

Chairman: James C. Stokesberry
Vice Chairman: Peter A. Fisher
Secretary-Treasurer: Allan T. Maris

Pacific Northwest Section (org. Sept. 12, 1946)

Chairman: John T. Mitchell
Vice Chairmen:
British Columbia Area: Gordon Fenwick
Columbia River Area: J. Cameron McKernan
Puget Sound Area: Edward W. H. Clendenning
Secretary-Treasurer: George A. Lundgren

Philadelphia Section (org. Nov. 12, 1941)

Chairman: Dean S. Champlin
Vice Chairman: Charles W. Lofft
Secretary-Treasurer: Keith W. Lawrence

San Diego Section (org. Jan. 24, 1967)

Chairman: Kurt Schmidt
Vice Chairman: Stephen M. Donley
Secretary-Treasurer: Kenneth R. Cooley

Southeast Section (org. Apr. 5, 1965)

Chairman: Lee W. Dana
Vice Chairman: South: Jean E. Buhler
North: Norman N. DeJong
West: Chester F. Swenson
Secretary-Treasurer: William L. Lane

Texas Section (org. Sept. 1, 1979)

Chairman: William A. Horn
Vice Chairman: G. Curtis Gibby
Secretary-Treasurer: Charles E. Purcell

Papers Presented at Meetings of Sections

from January 1982 to December 1982

Arctic Section

Jan. 22: "Esso Resources and Arctec Canada—Ice Test Basin Presentations"

Feb. 10: "Model Testing of Offshore Structures," R. Edwards

March 17: "Collisions and Grounding. Practical Analysis Methods," J. Pondret, M. Huther, and W. Wood; "Selection of Steel Qualities for Welded Elements," J. Charleux and O. Mogensen

April 14: "The Garoupa Sub-Sea Production System," J. DeJong

May 15: "The IHI Developed IP System, Pulp Plant," I. H.

I.; "Barge Mounted Plants for the Arctic—Little Cornwallis Island (Film)," B. Case; "The Arctic Pilot Project LNG Plant on a Barge," G. Pottinger, and J. Owler; "Ship-Ice Interaction Models. Designer's Approach," V. Laskow; "Ice Impact Loads on Ships," C. Daily and I. Glen; "Ultimate Safe Conditions for Ship's Operation in Ice," A. Tunik

June 16: "Manned Submersible for Arctic Engineering Research," L. LeSchack

Sept. 22: "Azimuthing Units as Main Propulsion for Arctic and Semi-submersible Use," D. Longdale

Oct. 20: "Island Construction in the Beaufort Sea and Its Constraint on the Equipment," J. Brakel

Nov. 24: "Thyssen-Waas Forebody for Icebreaking. Result of Spring 1981, 1982 Full Scale Trials with the Modified Max Waldeck," A. Freitas

Dec. 15: "History of Icebreaking," D. Miller

Canadian Maritime Section

Feb. 9: "The Salvaging of the MV *Kurdistan*," McAllister Towing

April 13: "Concept Design of Type 1100 Navigation Aids Vessel," R. Armour

Nov. 13: "Equipment and Services Used in Offshore Operations," J. Warner

Chesapeake Section

Feb. 4: "Expanding Navy's Shipbuilding Program" (Panel Discussion—George Sawyer, Keynote speaker)

March 10: "Russian Strength Standards for Commercial Ships," Y. Raskin, E. Suhir, and A. Tunik

April 6: "Foreign and Domestic Material Specifications for Ships Components—A Comparison," J. Early and H. Hime

May 25: "Collision Resistance of Ship Structures," W. Wood and D. Edinberg; Student Papers: "The Monoform Ship Concept: Design Principles and Preliminary Performance Characteristics," H. VanHemmen, and "A Parametric Analysis of a COGAS Power System," K. Thorne and J. Volkoff

Sept. 23: "Designing a Naval Frigate—with the Aid of Hindsight," R. Toman, A. Dallas, and G. Garbe

Oct. 30: "An Assessment of the Merit of Using Small Models to Predict Effect of Hull Form Changes on Resistance," S. Fisher; "The Use of Small Models in the Ship Design Process," H. Fireman, J. Hough, J. Hoyt, III, and A. Lones

Dec. 9: "Preliminary Design Study of a Sail-Assisted Oceanographic Research Ship," J. Walter, T. Hooper, and C. Foltis

Eastern Canadian Section

Jan. 19: "Submarine Terminals," B. F. Ackerman and W. H. German

Feb. 16: "DDH Structural and Corrosive Problems," D. Hussey

March 23: "Background of the Future," R. G. A. Lawrence

April 13: "Planing Hull Hydrodynamics," H. Meneian

Oct. 19: "Recent Marine Casualties" (oral), J. Hornsby

Nov. 9: "The Role of Naval Architects in Marine Casualties Investigations" (oral), P. M. Troop

Great Lakes and Great Rivers Section

Jan. 28: "Mathematical Performance Models for River Tows," W. Toutant; "River Towboat Hull and Propulsion," B. Christopoulos and R. Latorre; "Onboard Blending and Engine Performance on Medium Speed Propulsion Engine," S. Kobayashi; "The ACBL Blended Fuel Development Program," R. P. Spock

May 13: "Operational Economics of ITB Rail Ferry Systems on Lake Michigan," R. J. Rotundo; "Strength of Vessels for River, Great Lakes and Coastal Service," F. Kandel, E. Fuhir, and Y. Raskin

Oct. 7: "Marine Diesel Engines for Future Fuels," D. Paro and E. Waryas; "A Knights Move—Machinery Standards in the Global Arena," F. Narbut and D. Ridley; "Deflections of Great Lakes Ore Carrier Hull Structure by Finite Element Analysis," J. Woodward, M. Kaldjian, and W. Reid

Gulf Section

Jan. 21: "Electrical Cables For Ships—Past, Present, Future," Dieter Popoff

April 16: "Justification & Implementation of a 23,000 Ton Floating Dry Dock," O. H. Gatlin; "Structural Design of River Tank Barges," Dan W. Billingsley; "The Use of Externally Swaged Fittings On Marine Piping System," Roger D. Christianson

July 15: "The Construction and Operation of the EAGLE I Split Hull Hopper Dredge," Edward Geoff Webster

Sept. 24: "New Developments in Water Lubricated Propeller Shaft Bearings," George (Sandy) Thomson; "Effect on Environment on Shipping Operations at Offshore Marine Terminals," Roderick A. Barr, Eugene R. Miller, Jr., and Ron Gress; "Sail Assisted Mobilization of Offshore Jack-up Rigs," Jim B. Davis

Oct. 21: "Naval Architecture and Marine Engineering at the University of New Orleans," Frederick Munchmeyer

Hampton Roads Section

Jan. 20: "Some Elementary Criteria for Assessing Surface Force Excitation," Michael B. Wilson

Oct. 6: "Operating Experience of the General Electric LM 2500 Gas Turbines in Navy Ships," R. E. Reed, F. B. Lash, and D. E. Tempesco

Dec. 12: "Modern Shipboard Corrosion Control Technology," W. B. LaGrande and F. H. Porter

Hawaii Section

Feb. 10: "Pre-Stressed Concrete Honeycomb Design for Mounting Structure," A. Yee

June 9: "A Design for an 80 ft SWATH Crew Boat," L. James Wilkie

Oct. 16: "Operating Considerations for an Ocean-Going Cruise Ship" (Discussion), Paul Mead

Dec. 1: "AO-177 Propeller/Hull Form Integration: Know the Limits of the Model," Dave Stone

Los Angeles Metropolitan Section

Jan. 21: "Historical and Recent Developments in Deep Submersible Research Vehicle (DSRV) Technology," Don Walsh

Feb. 11: "Improving Steam Turbine Availability Through Technology Transfer," Ralph J. Ortolano

March 11: "Offshore Anchoring," Quan Y. Choo

April 8: "Tanker Weight Estimates 1930–1980," Roger P. Johnson

May 13: "Velocity and Stroke Meter for Racing Shells," Dan Teninty

Sept. 9: "CIDS—A Mobile Concrete Island Drilling System for Arctic Offshore Operations," Sherman B. Wetmore and Harold D. Ramsden

Oct. 8–10: "Offshore Storage and Treatment of Crude Oil Aboard a Modified Oil Tanker," Joe Godfrey and Walter B. Devine; "Dome and LNG," Arthur G. Berndt; "Transportation of LNG from the Arctic by Commercial Submarine," L. Jacobson, K. Lawrence, K. Hall, T. Canning, and E. Gardner

Nov. 11: "The *Queen Mary* and the Spruce Goose," John Gregory

New England Section

Jan. 21: "Maritime Opportunities for the New England Coal Trade," Edward A. Chazal, Jr.

Feb. 10: "Standard Waste Heat Recovery Systems," P. Schneider

March 10: "Sailing Yacht Capsizing," Karl K. Kirkman

May 20: "New N/C Blade Machining Facility," Donald E. Ridley

Oct. 21: "Problems in Oil Lubricated Outboard Shafting Bearings," F. Everett Reed and Frank Archibald

Dec. 2: "Marine Tank Gauging Applications," Albert D. Ehrenfried

New York Metropolitan Section

Jan. 13: "The Research Vessel *Westward*, Where Future Oceanographers Learn Under Sail," Corwith Cramer, Jr.

Feb. 18: "Loading Instruments—The Why, How and When," Peter Ebbutt

March 24: "A New Approach to Vessel Routing and Performance Analysis," George L. Petrie, Kenneth J. Bongort, and Walter M. Maclean

April 15: "Recent Developments in the Carriage of Bulk Cargoes," S. Fraser Sammis

May 20: "Staten Island Ferries for the 1980's," Carl Berkowitz, Leonard Piekarsky, Allen Chin, Eli Shaprut, and Walter Schiels

Sept. 9: "An Overview of the Navy's Fleet Oiler Class from the Operator's Perspective," Alan Reid, Donald Stein, and Timothy Sumner

Oct. 27: "An Overview of Marine Hull Insurance," Raymond M. Hicks

Dec. 13: "Systems Design for Future Fuels—Steam and Diesel," M. Winkler and T. Pakula

Northern California Section

Feb. 11: "Waste Heat Recovery for Diesel Propulsion Plants: An Economic Evaluation," L. R. Greif

March 11: "Damage Survivability of Cargo Ships," Robert D. Tagg

April 15: "Fatigue Reliability of the Ship Hull Girder," Anil Thayamballi

May 13: "The Liberty Ship SS *Jeremiah O'Brien*," D. J. Seymour and T. T. Patterson

Sept. 9: "Boiler Flu Gas Analysis and Automatic Combustion Air Trim Control by the Measurement of Carbon Monoxide, Unburned Hydrocarbons, and Opacity," James J. Sweeney

Nov. 11: "Current Experience in Model Scale Simulation of Vertically Tethered Platforms," Jeff Dillingham, Rod Edwards, and John McDowall

Dec. 6: "Graphic Presentation of Marine Salvage," Alex Rynecki and Robert Umbdenstock

Pacific Northwest Section

Jan. 22: "Coal Fired Marine Boilers," Steve Sabo

Feb. 27: "Shipbuilding is a Science," Louis D. Chirillo; "Determination of Ship Resistance for a Tugboat Using Model Studies in a Circulating Water Channel," Miles A. Webb

April 10: "Fuel Conservation for High Output Diesel Engines Through Electronic Combustion Analysis" Konrad J. Hambrick

May 15: "Development of Ship Repair Facilities," David J. Alsop; "Marine Power Conversion Instrumentation for Ship Propulsive Efficiency Analysis," Hendrick W. Haynes

June 3: "Machinery Condition Analysis," Bertel Lundgaard

Oct. 23: "The Seattle Harbor Craft; a Case Study of the Design Process," Paul A. Gow and Edward C. Hagemann;

"Impulse Response Techniques for Floating Bridges and Breakwaters Subject to Short-Crested Seas," Bruce L. Hutchison

Philadelphia Section

Jan. 22: "Dustpan Dredging—A Unique Concept," James P. Butler and Richard C. Lockwood

Feb. 25: "Repowering for Coal Fired Ships," John Burns and Raub W. Smith

March 18: "Productivity Navy Style," James W. Tweeddale

April 16: "Advanced Oil Recovery Vessel ZRV, Design, Construction and Operation," S. H. Cowen and R. Browning

Oct. 21: "Low Pressure Steam Catapult," George DiBiase

Dec. 10: "Marine Epoxy Resin Chocks," J. M. Wilson

San Diego Section

Jan. 20: "The Pipelay Ship *Apache*," Stan Uyeda

Feb. 17: "Model Testing in Multi-Directional Seas," Jeff Dillingham

March 24: "Design and Construction of the Cable Ship T-ARC 7," George Uberti

May 14–16: "The Role of Politics and International Law in Sea-Bed Mining," Pam Sematones; "Recent Operational Experiences of the Navy's Deep Submergence Forces," Stan Newton

Sept. 15: "The Role of the American Bureau of Shipping," John McCoy

Dec. 1: "Self-Help Program—Habitability," Mackie Burcham

Southeast Section

Feb. 19: "A Preliminary Report on a Numerical Method for Finding Bridge Deck Loadings for Catamarans Under 30 M. (100 ft.) in a Seaway," B. Justin Chippendale; "Computer-Aided Method for Determining Stability Curves of Multi-Chine Hulls in a Small Computer," David Breault

March 20: "Advantages of Kevlar 49 Aramid in Marine Composite Structures," C. K. Deeakyne and H. W. James; "A System for Dynamic Stress Analysis of a Launch and Recovery Crane at Sea—With Some Preliminary Results," Ken Stewart; "U.S.C.G. Plan Review for New Vessel Construction," D. H. Whitten; "Coal Powering of Ships," Michael S. Triantafyllou

Dec. 4: "A Family of Practical Design Programs for the Small Craft Designer Using the TI-59 Programmable Calculator with Printer," Chet Swenson; "A Proposed Microcomputer-Aided Design and Analysis Software Library for the Small Craft Specialist," John W. Shortall III; "A Correlated Hull Design System," J. Richard Cavanagh

Texas Section

Feb. 12: "Vemar Heavy Lift System (Short Stroke 1200)," Jon H. Matthews; "Barge Motion Predictions," Alan C. McClure; "Semi-Submersible Ship for Personnel Transport," Roy D. Gaul; "A Classification Society's Experience With IMCO Requirements for Crude Oil Washing and Gas Systems," Sudheer Chand, Eugene B. Dumbleton, and John W. Reiter

March 15: "Factors in the Selection of Dry-Docking Systems for Shipyards," J. Richard Salzer

May 14: "Offshore Industry and Golden Triangle," R. Novotny; "Amphibious Vehicle for Offshore Drilling," Penn Johnson; "The Offshore Supply Vessel," L. Patton; "Slo-Rol Motion Supervision for Drilling Vessels," Cam Shaar; "The Continental Shelf Land Act of 1978," Ron Rabago

Oct. 26: "Deep Water Development—A Challenge to the Marine Community," Andrew F. Hunter

SNAME *Transactions*, Vol. 90, 1982, pp. 26–40

Damage Survivability of Cargo Ships

Robert D. Tagg,[1] Associate Member

The traditional "one compartment" standard for evaluating the damage stability of cargo ships has several inherent deficiencies. Damage survivability criteria based on probabilistic procedures, as currently employed in the passenger ship regulations, represent a superior method for evaluating the relative safety of ships exposed to collision damage. A review of the applicable national and international regulations is presented along with the historical background of their development. The principles of probabilistic analysis are discussed, and a procedure is developed to determine a ship's survivability index. An analysis of four sample ships is presented to illustrate inconsistencies in the current criteria, and to demonstrate the effectiveness of alternative forms of subdivision on survivability. It is recommended that the proposed criteria, essentially a modified version of the 1973 IMCO Passenger Regulations, be applied to cargo ships.

Introduction

CURRENT regulations regarding the damage survivability of cargo ships, if any such regulations are applicable at all, are generally based on a "one compartment" standard. The philosophy behind a one-compartment standard is to make ships safer by requiring sufficient transverse compartmentation to keep the ship floating upright after breaching any one main compartment. This one-compartment standard assumes that a high enough portion of damages will fall between the transverse bulkheads to insure a reasonable level of safety for the ship.

In the real world the location and extent of damage has no respect for transverse bulkheads. This means that the portion of damages that falls between transverse bulkheads is dependent upon the specific bulkhead spacing for each ship. Therefore, ships of different bulkhead spacing, while meeting the same one-compartment damage standard, can have differing levels of true safety. In fact, it has been demonstrated that for ships designed to meet the minimum stability of a one-compartment standard, smaller transverse bulkhead spacing may actually reduce the overall safety [1, 2].[2]

In general, one-compartment standards are applied using a fixed damage extent in the longitudinal, transverse, and vertical directions. Lesser extents resulting in less severe flooding or heeling are not considered. The result of these fixed damage assumptions are that the potentially beneficial effects of longitudinal subdivision (both vertical and horizontal) are minimized or not considered at all.

Compliance with any damage survivability standard, one-compartment or otherwise, has its price. This price tag can be in the form of construction costs for additional transverse bulkheads or watertight doors; or it can be in the form of additional fuel consumption due to increased ballast requirements. This price tag may also show up as lost revenue from the reduction in cargo-carrying capacity to meet the damage stability standards. Compliance with an arbitrary damage survivability standard that does not reflect true safety will impose unequal economic penalties to some ship designs.

Damage survivability criteria based on probabilistic analysis procedures, as first proposed by Wendel in 1960 [3], proposed for cargo ships in 1971 [4], and incorporated into the 1973 Intergovernmental Maritime Consultative Organization (IMCO) Passenger Ship Regulations, represent a superior method for evaluating the relative safety of ships exposed to damage. While somewhat more complicated and extensive from the naval architect's viewpoint, criteria based on probabilistic principles are much less arbitrary and can be applied uniformly to ships of all types. The resulting yardstick for ship safety is in the form of a survivability index, which is proportional to the likelihood that a ship will survive collision damage. A required survivability index may be set at a desired level of safety in consideration of the likelihood of damage occurring and its potential consequences in terms of loss of life and property, or environmental impact.

Historical[3]

Regulation of ship subdivision and damage survivability dates back at least to 1854 with the British Marine Shipping Act, which required transverse bulkheads at the peaks and engine room. In the years following, the International Conferences on the Safety of Life at Sea (SOLAS) have been one of the primary initiators of international safety regulations, including subdivision standards.

The 1914 SOLAS conference, convened largely in response to the loss of the *Titanic*, established subdivision and lifesaving standards for passenger ships. The conference was never officially adopted by the participating countries because of World War I. The 1929 SOLAS conference proposed a "Factor of Subdivision" and "Criterion of Service" regulations for passenger ships which in effect established a minimum bulkhead spacing based on the ship length and the number of passengers. These regulations considered sinking or floodable length only, and contained no requirement for flooded stability.

In 1936, following the *Mohawk* and *Morro Castle* losses in the early 1930's, the United States adopted SOLAS 29; and in 1937 a U.S. Senate Report established more stringent criteria

[1] Herbert Engineering Corporation, San Francisco, California.

[2] Numbers in brackets designate References at end of paper.

Presented at the March 11, 1982 meeting of the Northern California Section of THE SOCIETY OF NAVAL ARCHITECTS AND MARINE ENGINEERS.

Author Tagg received the 1982 Vice Admiral E. L. Cochrane Award for this paper, chosen as the best paper presented before a Section of the Society.

[3] For additional information, see references [1, 2, 5, 6].

based on the SOLAS "Factor of Subdivision" format. This Senate Report also first established the one-compartment standard for U.S. cargo ships. The 1948 SOLAS convention proposed mostly minor modifications to SOLAS 29, but did include the important addition of flooded stability criteria to the regulations.

During the early 1950's it was becoming increasingly recognized that combined fuel and ballast double-bottom tanks, often required to be ballasted following burnout to meet damage stability requirements, were becoming an operational problem. When these tanks were used to the designer's instructions, they were causing oil pollution of harbors along with fuel contamination and tank cleaning problems. If these tanks were not used as designed, as was generally the case, the ships could often not meet damage stability criteria. In 1954 a 32-nation conference convened on the Prevention of Pollution of the Sea by Oil. This convention banned oil discharge within 50 miles of land and called for the installation of oily-ballast receiving facilities at all ports.

Following the *Andrea Doria* loss in 1956, IMCO was established, and shortly thereafter the SOLAS 60 Conference was convened. In recognition of the many inherent deficiencies in the SOLAS 48 regulations, a number of delegations proposed new approaches and substantial changes to the passenger ship rules. However, agreement could not be reached and the basic approach of SOLAS 48 was left unchanged. The conference did add regulations requiring that, in general, water ballast should not be carried in fuel tanks. This SOLAS 60 Conference also made General Recommendations No. 6 and No. 8 for further study on the standards for watertight subdivision of passenger and cargo ships. In 1961, acknowledging the recommendations of SOLAS 60, IMCO established the Subcommittee on Subdivision and Stability. Among other issues the work of the committee was to consider the deficiencies in SOLAS 60, new trends in ship design, and the possible range of damage lengths.

The International Conference on Load Lines (ICLL) in 1966, sponsored by IMCO, proposed a one-compartment standard for tankships and also for other reduced-freeboard (B-60 percent) cargo ships. Dry-cargo ships with minimum freeboard (B-100 percent) were required to meet a two-compartment standard, exclusive of the engine room. All damage requirements applied to the summer load line (SLL) draft only. Cargo ships with conventional freeboards were required only to have forepeak, aft peak, and engine room watertight bulkheads in addition to those normally required by the classification society.

During the mid-1960's several technical changes in tankship design and operation were affecting their safety. Prior to the mid-1960's tankers had a high degree of safety in the loaded condition due to the high watertight integrity of their main decks, adequate compartmentation, and the low permeability of the loaded cargo spaces. Following the closing of the Suez Canal in 1967, the trend toward larger tankers gained momentum rapidly. Along with this increase in overall size, the increase in tank sizes, the incorporation of segregated wing ballast tanks, and an increase in multiple-port operations with partial loadings, all tended to reduce tanker safety. With these factors in mind, and in the wake of the *Torrey Canyon* disaster, the U.S. Coast Guard imposed a two-compartment standard for liquid bulk carriers in 1971.

In 1971, culminating many years of research, the IMCO Subcommittee on Subdivision and Stability submitted new passenger ship rules based on probability of damage principles. These rules were adopted in 1973 as an alternative to the provisions of SOLAS 60.

In 1973 the International Conference on Marine Pollution (MARPOL 73) established a two-compartment standard for most tankships along with regulations regarding tank size limitations, and segregated ballast requirements. While this conference is not officially validated internationally, it is incorporated in the U.S. Port and Tanker Safety Act of 1978 and in the regulations of several other countries.

The IMCO Chemical and Gas Codes of 1975 essentially apply the MARPOL 73 criteria to these types of ships. Minor modifications include the addition of minor damage and the protective location of some types of cargo.

SOLAS 74 consists of the SOLAS 60 regulations plus a number of adopted amendments made during the 1966-to-1974 period. No substantial changes were made to the subdivision and stability standards.

The IMCO Protocol of 1978 relating to SOLAS 74 provides additional requirements for crude oil washing and the protective location of segregated ballast spaces for tankers. No substantial changes were made to the MARPOL 73 damage stability standards.

Current damage stability requirements

International regulations generally define the highest level on which agreement was possible at the time they were proposed. They are often not the best level achievable within the state of the art. The following is a brief summary of some of the major points of the current damage stability regulations. See Table 1 for a comparison of the technical features of the various criteria.

SOLAS 74 [7]. Passenger and cargo ship standards from these regulations are based on a "Factor of Subdivision" and a "Criterion of Service" formulas. The rules establish a maximum compartment length based on floodable length and a "Criterion of Service" which is dependent on ship length and the number of passengers. Cargo ships of conventional size and crew are essentially required to have forepeak, aft peak and engine room bulkheads, and double bottoms only.

ICLL 66 [8]. This international standard basically requires a one-compartment standard for tankships and other reduced freeboard (B-60 percent) cargo ships at the SLL draft only. Dry-cargo ships with minimum freeboard (B-100 percent) are required to meet a two-compartment standard exclusive of the engine room, also at the SLL draft only. Conventional Type (B) dry-cargo ships are not required to meet any survivability standard.

MarAd (1965) [9]. These criteria apply to all major vessels built under U.S. Government subsidy or mortgage insurance programs. The regulations consist of a traditional one-compartment standard, basically incorporating the same damage extents, flooded permeabilities, and allowable damage effects as SOLAS 60, applied to all operating drafts.

MARPOL 73 [10,11]. This international conference established regulations for new oil tankers (extended to other product's carriers with the IMCO Chemical and IMCO Gas Codes). Damage extents are based on the statistical averages for side and bottom damage data compiled by the IMCO Subcommittee on Subdivision and Stability for the 1973 passenger regulations. It provides basically for a two-compartment standard with the damage extents applied to all conceivable locations over the ship's length as follows:

• Tankers more than 225 m[4] in length—anywhere in the ship's length.

• Tankers between 150 and 225 m in length—anywhere in the ship's length excluding the engine room. The engine room is to be treated as a single flooded compartment.

• Tankers less than 150 m—anywhere between transverse bulkheads (one-compartment standard).

---

[4] m = meter = 3.28 ft.

Table 1 Comparison of technical features criteria

DAMAGE EXTENT			SOLAS 74	ICLL 66	MARAD	MARPOL 73	IMCO Passenger 73
			1, 2 or 3 compts. Passenger ships only	1-compt.A or B-60% 2-compt. B-100% At SLL only	one-compartment All operating drafts	two-compartment New tankers only All loaded drafts	multiple compartment probabilistic
SIDE	Longitudinal		10' + .031, max 35'	as above	10' + .03L	$1/3L^{2/3}$, max 14.5m	up to .24L, max 48m
	Transverse		B/5	B/5	B/5	B/5, max 11.5m	up to .80B
	Vertical		baseline upwards	D	keel to margin line	baseline upwards	baseline upwards
	Minor/Local		---	---	any lesser extent	---	one-compartment
BOTTOM	Trans	Fwd .3L	---	---	---	$1/3L^{2/3}$, max 14.5m	---
		Aft .7L	---	---	---	L/10, max 5m	---
	Longl	Fwd .3L	---	---	---	B/6, max 10m	---
		Aft .7L	---	---	---	5m	---
	Vertical		---	---	---	B/15, max 6m	---
PERMEABILITIES							
Accommodations			.95	.95	.95	.95	.95
Cargo, Stores			.60	.95	.60	.60	.60 - .95 (based on draft)
Machinery			.85	.85	.85	.85	.85
Liquid or Void			.95 or 0	.95 or 0	.95 or 0	.95 or 0	.95 or 0
DAMAGE EFFECTS							
Max. Heel			7° or 15°	17°/15°	15°	30°/25°	12°
Sinkage Limit			Margin Line	Progressive Flooding	Margin Line	Progressive Flooding	Bulkhead Deck
GM			2" upright	positive	positive	---	function of freeboard
GZ			---	20° range, max .1 m	---	20° range, max .1m	---
Minor/ Intermediate			---	---	---	---	20° heel
Equalization Time			15 minutes	---	"practical"	---	10 minutes

All loaded and partially loaded conditions are to be considered exclusive of the ballast conditions. Larger angles of static heel are permitted (up to 25 deg) provided that the ship has sufficient residual stability beyond the static angle. Neither "margin line" nor bulkhead deck is considered to limit sinkage, and heel is limited to 25 deg or immersion of progressive flooding points.

IMCO Passenger Regulations 73 [12,1,13]. These regulations are currently the most thorough and comprehensive rules on subdivision and damage survivability. The regulations are based on damage extents and locations determined in the statistical analysis of actual collisions. The required "Subdivision Index" is, like SOLAS, based on the length of the ship and the number of passengers and crew aboard. The attained Subdivision Index is the sum of the probabilities from survivable damages involving single, double, or any higher number of adjacent compartments within the damage extents. Account is also taken for the probability of transverse penetration when applied to combined transversely and longitudinally subdivided ships. The use of floodable length calculations has been eliminated. The "margin line" is not used, and flooding is allowed to the "relevant bulkhead deck." A one-compartment standard is also imposed to prevent the vulnerability "that even a very small damage, flooding even only one compartment, might result in the loss of the ship" [1]. The assumed damage is based on the probability of location along the length of the ship, the probability of the damage length, and the probability of the damage penetration. The criteria assume no probability of vertical location or extent, and are instead conservatively simplified to assume the most unfavorable extent of vertical damage. Flooded stability criteria are based on damage GM (metacentric height) and effective freeboard.

Probabilistic analysis of damage survivability

As discussed in [1], there are basically three main probabilities that apply to damage survivability:
- probability that the ship will encounter damage,
- probability of damage location and extent, and
- probability of ship surviving the damage.

Evaluation of each of these probabilities would constitute a fully probabilistic evaluation for a specific ship on a specific trade.

Probability that ship will encounter damage. Based on the compilation of statistics on the world shipping fleet, it has been shown that the general risk of serious collisions (that is, penetration of the hull below the waterline) to ships is about four or five a year per 1000 ships [14–16]. The risk of damage is not the same for all ships but is dependent upon many factors. Route densities are a major component of the probability of encountering damage, and reasonable assumptions of collision likelihood can be based on traffic densities alone [17]. Since high traffic densities are generally encountered in harbor or harbor approaches, the amount of time spent in these high-density areas affects this probability. Collisions, therefore, are more likely for ships on shorter routes where a higher percentage of the voyage time is spent in congested areas [18].

The probability of being involved in a collision can also be influenced by ship characteristics such as, speed, size and maneuverability [18]. Tankers over 150 000 dwt have a significantly lower casualty and collision rate than for other sizes of tankers [14]. The competance of the crew or pilot as well as the effectiveness and reliability of navigation instrumentation are also factors in this probability. Reduction in the likelihood of collision damage has also been achieved through traffic separation and monitoring schemes [17, 18], and through the institution of the Ice Patrol following the loss of the *Titanic*.

Probability of damage location and extent. This probability is based on the following factors:
- characteristics of the striking object (that is, shape, speed, mass, etc.),
- damage location, and
- resulting damage extent.

The probable effects of these three factors can be estimated from statistical surveys of past collision damage, as was done in references [3] and [13] and in work by the IMCO Subcommittee on Subdivision and Stability leading up to the 1973 Passenger Rules.

This overall probability, and specifically the resulting damage extent, can be affected by the ship type as well. The collision protection or resistance of ships is provided mainly by the horizontal deck structure in way of the collision [19]. Therefore, ships with multiple decks or tween decks provide more collision resistance, while tankers or bulkers are more prone to larger damage due to the lack of tween decks to absorb the collision energy [1]. Where the potential risk of breaching a compartment is unusually high (for example, nuclear vessel or hazardous material transportation), additional collision resistance is sometimes provided by the installation of horizontal stringers, or even honeycomb or nested tube structures which offer high energy absorption.

Probability of ship surviving damage. This probability is primarily based on the following factors:
- the intact condition of the ship,
- the extent of flooding, and
- the criteria for determining whether the ship survives, or does not survive.

The intact condition is the probable condition of the ship at the time of the collision in terms of draft, trim, intact stability, and the permeability of the flooded spaces. There is, in theory, a separate probability distribution for each of these factors.

The extent of flooding is determined by the specific damage incurred and the arrangement of the ship's internal watertight subdivisions.

The probability of the ship surviving damage is based on the specific flooded condition and the probability of survival in a seaway. The criteria for determining the survival of the ship consist of insuring that the ship does not sink or capsize.

The ship must retain intact buoyancy greater than its weight in order for it not to sink, and any opening through which progressive flooding might eventually sink the ship must not be immersed below the flooded waterplane.

Capsizing itself will not directly result in the loss of the ship, assuming all openings for potential progressive flooding are closed watertight. This requirement for flooded stability is basically to ensure a condition in which the ship may be abandoned or later reboarded for salvage. Remaining upright in a seaway is also based on the dynamic effects on the ship. Survival is dependent on wind and sea states as well as other dynamic factors, such as entrapped water on the deck.

In regard to sea states at the time of collisions, the conditions are generally reported to be less severe than statistical averages would indicate. This is again the result of the greater probability of collisions occurring in harbor or harbor approach areas,

or during fog, where low sea states are more prevalent.

At this time the determination of the applicable probabilities for all of these components of the overall survival probability is not possible. Any realistic criteria to calculate the survival probability of ships must make certain assumptions and simplifications, leading to an index of survivability which, while it may not represent the actual probability of survival, will be proportional to the true safety.

The probabilistic determination of this survivability was first proposed in depth in 1960 [3]. Probabilistic procedures proposed to date have dealt with the probability of damage location and extent, and the probability of survival of that damage. Probabilistic procedures have not considered the probability of the ship encountering damage, but rather, acknowledging that the risk does exist, determine the probability that the ship will survive the damage.

Proposed damage survivability criteria

The following is a description of proposed criteria for calculating a probabilistic survivability index. These criteria are basically similar in principle to the 73 IMCO Passenger Regulations. The resulting survivability index represents the probability that a given ship will survive damages based on a statistical review of past damages. The index does not include any probability of the ship encountering damage or the probability of variance of the resulting hull damage due to the internal structure and collision resistance of a specific ship. These factors, collision likelihood and collision resistance, should be considered along with the consequences of the potential damage (in terms of loss of life, loss of investment in the ship and cargo, and environmental damage) to determine the appropriate required index of survivability for a specific ship.

These proposed survivability criteria differ from criteria previously proposed for cargo ships [4] in that the longitudinal and vertical probabilistic extents are considered in addition to the probable damage location and transverse extent.

Damage location and extent. Damage is assumed to occur anywhere along the length of the ship regardless of internal subdivision and structure. Figure 1 shows an assumed density distribution of the longitudinal location of damage. This distribution was developed from the histograms of damage surveys presented in [13] and is the same as that used to formulate the 73 IMCO Passenger Regulations. It can be seen that collisions are more likely in the forward half of the ship, and are generally decreasing in likelihood toward the stern.

The longitudinal and transverse extents of damage, shown in Figs. 2 and 3, are also based on the histograms presented in [13], and were used to formulate the 73 IMCO Passenger Regulations. The assumed damage length varies from zero up to 24 percent of the ship's length (maximum 48 m for ships longer than 200 m). For most ships this maximum damage, while statistically rather likely, would damage three or more watertight compartments. The assumed transverse penetration varies from zero to 80 percent of the ship's beam at the load waterline (measured at the longitudinal center of the damage).

The statistics analyzed for the 73 Passenger Ship Regulations in general show that, up to certain limits, average damage lengths as a percent of ship length and average damage penetration as a percent of ship beam are fairly constant. This is assumed to be due to the trend that ships are likely to collide with others of similar size, rules of the road notwithstanding.

Vertical location and extent of damage were not considered in the 73 Passenger Rules, and only the most unfavorable extent of vertical damage was assumed. The reasoning for this simplification was that " . . . the error made by neglecting the favorable extent of horizontal subdivision is not great . . . . " [13].

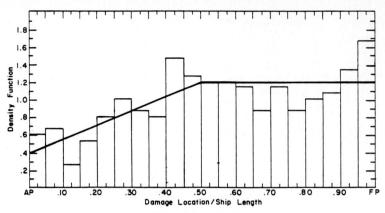

Fig. 1 Density distribution—longitudinal location of damage [13]

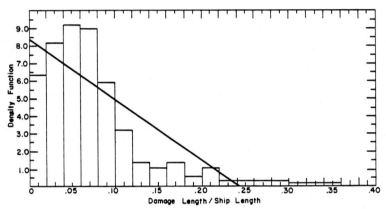

Fig. 2 Density distribution—damage length [13]

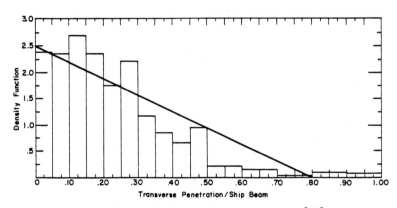

Fig. 3 Density distribution—damage penetration [13]

This, however, is not the case for some current ship designs, especially roll-on/roll-off ships (RO/RO's) or containerships with horizontal subdivision. Data pertaining to the vertical location and extent should be reanalyzed to determine their probabilistic distributions. While such an analysis is beyond the scope of this paper, a typical vertical extent of damage is presumed, Fig. 4, to point out trends in the resulting damage survivability. The center of the proposed extent of vertical damage is located at the load waterline. The vertical extent varies linearly from zero, with the mean damage extending from baseline to the height of a standard fo'c'sle deck on a similar-size ship [20].

Intact condition of ship. Damage stability calculations

should be evaluated for all possible groupings of watertight compartments resulting from the damage extents over a range of intact drafts. In general, no trim or heel is to be assumed, but it may be appropriate at some drafts to evaluate a specific trimmed condition (that is, normal ballast condition at the actual trimmed waterline).

Permeabilities should generally conform to the established practice (that is, 0.60 for cargo or stores, 0.85 for machinery spaces, and 0.95 for liquid or empty compartments. These permeabilities, however, should be modified to suit the specific characteristics of actual cargo. Full-load cases should utilize full cargo hold permeabilities. Ballast conditions should utilize empty hold permeabilities. Intermediate drafts should be evaluated at the worst conceivable permeability, or, alternatively, a probability distribution of permeability may be developed. The surface permeability is assumed to be the same as the volumetric permeability.

In some circumstances it may be necessary to impose operating restrictions on the ship to meet the required criteria, (for example, alternate ballast wing tanks to be filled at ballast drafts for tankers). If such restrictions call for tanks to be filled, damage calculations should assume that the tank completely empties upon damage, and then fills to the flooded equilibrium waterline with seawater.

Criteria for ship survival. To insure survival after damage, sufficient intact GM should be available to
• prevent immersion of progressive flooding openings below the static waterline,
• limit static heel to 25 deg,
• provide a dynamic range of positive righting levers (GZ) to 20 deg beyond the static heel angle, to both port and starboard, with a maximum value of at least 0.1 m, and
• maintain positive upright damaged GM for cases of symmetrical flooding.

Progressive flooding points include vents, overflows, and weathertight doors and hatches, except those in way of already breached compartments. Watertight doors, manholes, and small watertight hatch covers are assumed closed and are not to be considered as points of progressive flooding. Practical arrangements should be made to limit progressive flooding in piping and air ducts within the extent of flooding [24].

Cross-flooding should not be employed as a means to reduce the heel to within the 25-deg static angle. Cross-flooding, if installed between ballast wing or void tanks, can of course be used to reduce heel to some lesser angle after the initial flooding.

The foregoing criteria for determining survival are essentially the same as MARPOL '73, and are believed to represent reasonable criteria for cargo ships. More stringent survival standards are justifiably imposed upon passenger ships due to the potential for large-scale evacuation of untrained passengers into lifeboats. The righting energy requirements are essentially equivalent to those of [2], which are considered adequate based on model tests of damaged ships in a seaway [1].

Determination of Survivability Index (SI). Based on the assumed damage distributions, a probability of damage can be calculated for each compartment and grouping of compartments that fall within the damage extents (see Appendix 2). For each appropriate draft, damage calculations are to be made to determine the required intact GM to meet the survival criteria for all possible groups of damaged compartments. The Survivability Index can then be determined for any given available GM by summing the probabilities of all cases in which the available GM exceeds the required GM to meet the survival criteria (see Appendix 3).

Evaluation of sample ships

On Figs. 5 through 8 indicate the results of damage stability calculations based on various criteria. The results are presented in the standard required "GM versus mean draft" format in which the results of an entire damage investigation can be presented on one graph. In each case the solid lines represent the required GM based on existing regulations. It should be noted that not all of the existing regulations apply to each of these designs. (In fact, the containership and the RO/RO are not governed by any international regulations.) The family of curves, shown in dotted lines, is the resulting survivability index curves based on the proposed criteria. The survivability indexes, while not identical, are essentially comparable to results that would be obtained using the 73 Passenger Regulations, with

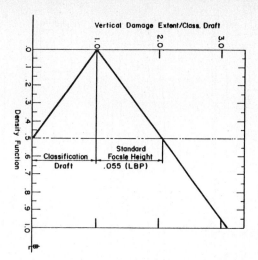

Fig. 4 Density distribution—vertical damage extent

the exception of the 25-deg heel, the vertical extent of damage, and the cargo space permeability.

The Survivability Index, while indicating the relative level of safety, should closely approximate the actual survivability of ships involved in collisions. For the sample ships, SI's of 0.50 to 0.60 are typical at their normal operating GM's. Actual collision statistics indicate, however, that real survival rates after serious collisions are in the order of 0.85 for all cargo ships [16]. The discrepancy between calculated and actual survival rates is due to the increased survivability of striking ships, and to conservative assumptions in the survivability criteria (for example, capsize is considered nonsurvivable but may in fact not result in the total loss of the ship) or conservative assumptions regarding the intact condition, permeability, or GM.

In the absence of an established safety level for cargo ships based on probabilistic survivability, a modified formula for Required Subdivision Index from the 73 Passenger Regulations is proposed:

$$\text{Required SI} = 1 - \frac{1000}{4\,LBP + 1500}, \quad LBP \text{ in meters}$$

This essentially is formula(I) from reference [12] modified to exclude the portion of the index required for additional passenger safety. The resulting Survivability Indexes from this formula seem reasonable based on the proposed survival criteria and are also indicated in Figs. 5–8.

Tanker. The sample tanker shown in Fig. 5 is a fairly typical 80 000-dwt AFRA Large Range 1 tanker. Alternate wing tanks are for segregated saltwater ballast and are carried empty in the loaded condition. These empty ballast wing tanks can have an adverse effect on the one-compartment damage effects due to the large nonsymmetrical flooding. However, when damage involves a main transverse bulkhead (two compartments), the alternate ballast wings can improve survivability since the flooding of the ballast wing will be compensated for by the outflow from the damaged cargo tank. This improved survivability is based on the stipulation that the cargo wings are filled at the loaded draft. Operational restrictions regarding minimum cargo required to be carried in the alternate cargo wings will usually be necessary to arrive at reasonable survivability levels or to meet MARPOL 73 requirements for this type of design.

For this specific tanker sample, both the MARPOL and MarAd criteria are governed by breaching of the forward ballast wing tank. The difference in the resulting required GM curves are due to the difference between the margin line (MarAd) and the tank vents (MARPOL).

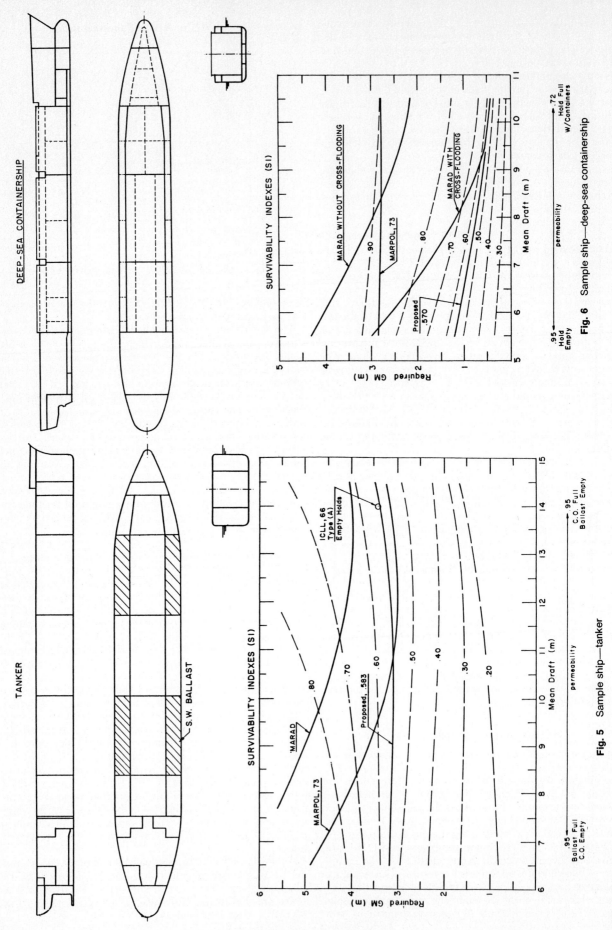

TANKER

DEEP-SEA CONTAINERSHIP

S.W. BALLAST

SURVIVABILITY INDEXES (SI)

MARAD WITHOUT CROSS-FLOODING

MARPOL, 73

.90

.80

MARAD WITH CROSS-FLOODING

.70

.60

.50

.40

.30

Proposed .570

Required GM (m)

Mean Draft (m)

.95 Hold Empty   .72 Hold Full W/Containers

permeability

Fig. 6   Sample ship—deep-sea containership

SURVIVABILITY INDEXES (SI)

ICLL, 66 Type (A) Empty Holds

MARAD

MARPOL, 73

.80

.70

Proposed, .583

.60

.50

.40

.30

.20

Required GM (m)

Mean Draft (m)

.95 Ballast Full C.O. Empty   .95 C.O. Full Ballast Empty

permeability

Fig. 5   Sample ship—tanker

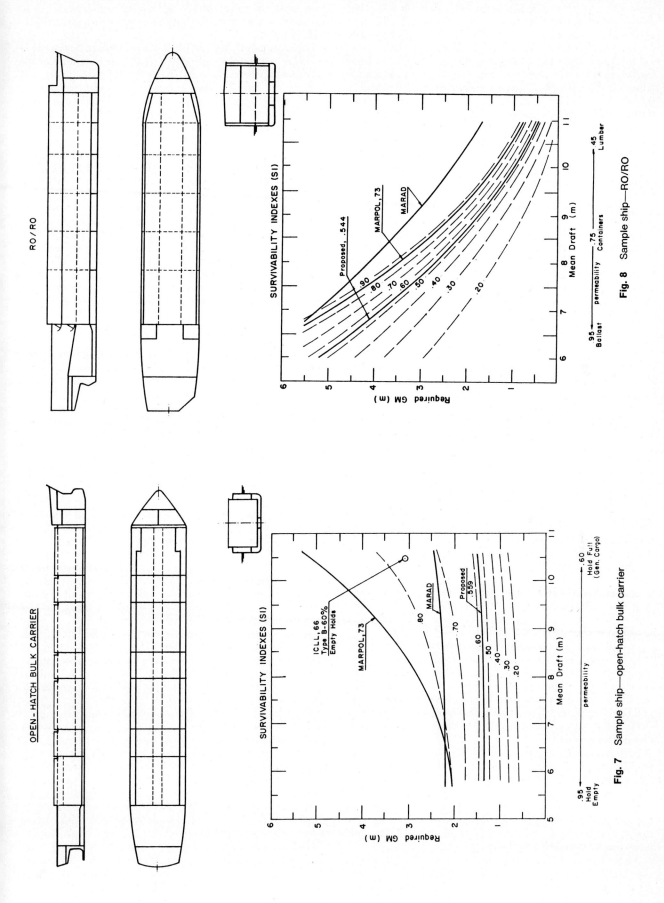

RO/RO

OPEN-HATCH BULK CARRIER

Fig. 8   Sample ship—RO/RO

Fig. 7   Sample ship—open-hatch bulk carrier

In general, based on damage considerations, the longitudinal bulkheads should be as far inboard as possible while still being able to survive the resulting nonsymmetrical flooding. Because of their low freeboard, these types of ships will usually be unable to survive damage beyond this longitudinal bulkhead.

Containership. The sample ship shown in Fig. 6 is a high-freeboard, fine hull ($C_B = 0.63$) containership with full double bottom and wing tanks. The hatchways are the full width of the hold for cellular loading and the holds are as long as practical to minimize the number of transverse bulkheads.

Due mainly to the large wing tanks, the required GM's to meet the existing MarAd or MARPOL '73 standards are quite high. U.S. designs of this type are often required to utilize cross-flooding of the wing tanks to comply with the MarAd criteria for 15-deg angle. While not fully recognized in the traditional 1- or 2-compartment standards, the addition of wing tanks generally improves the survivability of these ships.

It must also be noted that transverse subdivision of the wing tanks, while usually not considered in any existing criteria, has a large influence on survivability. For this sample containership, subdivision of the wing tanks at midhold contributes over 0.10 to the Survivability Index when not considering cross-flooding. For this type of ship the damage results indicate that subdivision of the wing tanks may be more beneficial to survivability than would further subdivision of the cargo holds.

This specific design also receives some improvement in survivability from the upper wing passageways since in approximately 15 percent of the damage cases this compartment is not breached. Additional improvement in survivability could be gained by the use of watertight doors subdividing the passageway at the main transverse bulkheads.

Open-hatch bulk carrier. The sample ship shown in Fig. 7 is a minimum-freeboard (B-60 percent), full-form ($C_B = 0.76$) bulk carrier of about 36 000 dwt with 100 percent open hatches. Incorporated in the design are full wings and double bottoms to provide rectangular cargo holds. The ship is designed to carry full cargoes of lumber in the holds and as deckload, and other forest products, and the ship may also carry heavy ore in the short holds.

In general, the effects of the wing tanks are similar to those for the containership except that the effects of the nonsymmetrical flooding are increased due to the reduced freeboard. The ship has little chance of meeting any two-compartment flooding at the loaded draft due to the nonsymmetrical moment and the reduced freeboard.

Roll-on/roll-off ship. The sample RO/RO ship shown in Fig. 8 is a high-deadweight (42 500 dwt), full-form ($C_B = 0.83$) RO/RO designed for a full load of lumber. The main cargo hold has no transverse subdivision between the forward deep tank bulkhead and the engine room bulkhead. The design incorporates a deep double bottom and fairly narrow (1.37 m) wing tanks. The main deck, at 18.4 m above baseline, is a main horizontal watertight boundary. There is also a line of watertight doors above the forward engine room bulkhead. Vents and overflows from all tanks are terminated above the shelter deck, so the ship, in effect, has 15.75 m of freeboard above the classification draft.

In the typical damaged conditions the entire forward cargo hold floods and buoyancy is provided by the forward and aft "air pockets," the double bottom and the wing tanks. In this condition the ship is essentially "waterlogged" and small changes in GM greatly affect the heel caused by the relatively minor nonsymmetrical flooding in the narrow wing tanks. For damage at full load, the survival effects are predominately governed by the 25-deg heel requirement.

Approximately 26 percent of the damage cases do not breach the main deck and the upper hold will remain intact. Virtually all of these cases will be survivable at normal operating GM's.

The worst condition of damage would involve the watertight doors and bulkhead at the forward engine room boundary. In this case the ship could not survive unless the upper hold remained intact.

The aforementioned sample is not believed to be typical of RO/RO's currently in operation. With the exception of the most recent generation of RO/RO's [24, 25], damage survivability has not generally been a consideration due to the absence of international regulations and the unadaptability of the basic RO/RO design to transverse subdivision. It is not surprising, therefore, that statistically RO/RO's are considerable less likely to survive a major collision [7].

Since main transverse subdivision is not applicable to the RO/RO design, and large watertight doors in the cargo hold should be considered as a last resort, other types of subdivision must be employed. Improvements in RO/RO survivability can be provided by utilizing wing tanks, which can offer considerable protection from minor damage, horizontal subdivision at the upper deck levels, or watertight doors in the upper hold only. Decks located near the waterline will likely be damaged in the event of a collision and, therefore, need not be made watertight. It may, in fact, be beneficial for decks near the waterline to allow rapid down-flooding to the lower deck to gain stability and reduce the multiple-deck free-surface effects.

Methods of subdivision

Various combinations of transverse, vertical longitudinal, and horizontal longitudinal subdivision are used in almost all ships. The cargo handling and stowing methods used in modern cargo ships often dictate the adaptability to specific subdivision schemes. Within the constraints imposed by the cargo handling and stowing requirements, the designer must use any or all methods of subdivision available to insure adequate survivability of the ship. Some of these methods of subdivision and their relative effectiveness are given in the following.

Main transverse bulkheads. Transverse bulkheads are the traditional method used for watertight subdivision. Considering sinkage or floodable length criteria only, the closer the transverse spacing generally, the safer the ship. In consideration of damage stability, nearly the opposite is true. While it is usually true that closer transverse bulkhead spacing will result in greater safety for a given GM, in practice this closer spacing is used to reduce the required GM or freeboard based on some standard criteria. In effect, the designer may be raising the family of Survivability Indexes by providing closer subdivision and giving back those gains by reducing the GM and moving down to a lower survivability percent.

Double bottoms. It is believed that the standard rule double bottom significantly reduces the risk of loss from bottom and grounding damage. Since statistically the upwards penetration of bottom damages averages about $B/15$, for most ships about half of the bottom damages will be confined to the double bottom.

When considering side collisions, double bottoms may or may not be beneficial. If sinking is the predominate damage effect, double bottoms will usually be of benefit due to the reduced flooded volume. (This is true even if the damage extends below the tanktop, since double bottoms are usually transversely divided.) If damage stability or heel angle is the predominate damage effect, double bottoms usually have negligible or adverse effects depending upon whether the added stability gained from flooding the low volume is negated by the increase in nonsymmetrical flooding.

Wing tanks. For many ships, wing tanks significantly reduce the risk of loss from minor side damage [23]. Wing tanks are also usually necessary to reduce the hypothetical outflow from liquid bulk ships. For low-freeboard ships, wing tanks may or may not be beneficial to survivability depending upon whether or not the additional nonsymmetrical flooding can be compensated for by the reduced flooded volume of the center holds. For ships with ample freeboard the net effect of wing tanks will usually be beneficial.

It should be noted that if the allowable damage effects require heel to be limited to relatively smaller angles (for example, 12 or 15 deg), the beneficial effects of wing tanks would be minimized or eliminated. Smaller required heel angles often lead to designs employing cross-connected wing tanks. Cross-connected wing tanks will nearly always improve survivability on paper; however, considering the practical problems in their operation, they should be considered only as a very last resort for cargo ships.

Horizontal subdivision. In general, horizontal subdivision can be beneficial to survivability if the compartment is high enough above the waterline not to be damaged in a significant portion of the potential damages. For ships with high freeboard, horizontal subdivision (that is, upper wing tanks or passageways, or watertight shelterdecks) is believed to significantly improve survivability.

Conclusion

The overall survivability of cargo ships from damage can be determined from the probable likelihood of damage occurrence, the probable location and extent of the damage, and the probability of surviving such damage. These probabilities encompass three main technical areas which affect the overall survivability:

- damage avoidance
- damage resistance
- damage survivability

All three of these areas must be pursued to improve the overall survivability of ships at sea. This paper mainly addresses the area of damage survivability.

The traditional means for insuring an adequate level of survivability of cargo ships are based on a "one compartment" damage standard. This standard has evolved from criteria which primarily considered transverse compartmentation and floodable length only. The one-compartment standard may provide an arbitrary level of safety due to its deficiencies in considering various bulkhead spacings and nonstandard compartmentations. These inconsistencies in the current criteria, as well as the absence of subdivision requirements for some ships, can impose unequal economic penalties upon modern ship designs.

Damage survivability criteria based on probabilistic procedures represent a superior method for evaluating the relative safety of ships exposed to collision damage. These procedures are applicable to any type of ship and permit the use of nonconventional subdivision to meet specific design requirements. The required survivability for a specific ship or type of ship may then be established at a desired safety level.

It is recommended that the probabilistic damage survivability criteria, as proposed by this paper, be applied in the design and evaluation of cargo ships.

The proposed criteria are essentially the same as the 1973 IMCO Passenger Regulations except for the relaxation of the allowable heel angle to 25 deg, a modified treatment of cargo space permeabilities, and incorporating a vertical extent of damage. Required Survivability Indexes should be established based on the likelihood of damage and the potential consequences of the loss in terms of life, ship, cargo, and marine pollution. In the absence of an established safety level, the 73 Passenger Regulation formula for the Required Subdivision Index, modified to include the ship length only and to exclude the number of passengers, is proposed as a reasonable standard for cargo ships based on the relaxed survival criteria.

Possible areas for subsequent investigation include:

- determination of the distribution of vertical location and extent,
- effects of internal ship structure on damage extents,
- probabilistic treatment of permeabilities, trims, and drafts,
- economic evaluation of alternative methods of subdivision, and
- determination of reasonable safety levels based on collision likelihood of damage and consequences of loss.

References

1 Robertson, Nickum, Price, Middleton, "The New International Regulations on Subdivision and Stability of Passenger Ships," TRANS. SNAME, Vol. 82, 1974.

2 Comstock, Robertson, "Survival of Collision Damage Versus the 1960 Convention on Safety of Life at Sea," TRANS. SNAME, Vol. 69, 1961.

3 Wendel, K., "Die Wahrscheinlich des Uberstenens von Verletzungen" (The Probability of Survival from Damages), Schiffstechnik, Vol. 36, April 1960.

4 Herbert, Liu, "Special Ships for Forest Products Transportation," Joint Meeting, SNAME, California Sections, Oct. 2, 1971.

5 Robertson, J. B., Jr., "Subdivision and Stability in Damaged Condition," Principles of Naval Architecture, SNAME, 1967.

6 Kime, Johnson, Price, "Damage Stability Requirements for Tankship, Chemical Ships, and Gas Ships," Marine Technology, Vol. 13, No. 2, April 1976.

7 "International Conference on Safety of Life at Sea, 1974," IMCO Publication.

8 "International Conference on Load Lines, 1966," IMCO Publication.

9 U.S. Department of Commerce, Maritime Administration, Design Letter No. 3, April 28, 1965 (retyped December 1976).

10 "International Conference on Marine Pollution, 1973," IMCO Publication.

11 "Port and Tanker Safety Act of 1978," Department of Transportation, U.S. Coast Guard.

12 IMCO Resolution A.265 (VIII), "Regulations on Subdivision and Stability of Passenger Ships as Equivalent to Part B of Chapter II of the International Convention for the Safety of Life at Sea, 1960."

13 IMCO MSC/Circular 153, "Regulations on Subdivision and Damage Stability of Passenger Ships as Equivalent to Part B of Chapter II of the International Convention for the Safety of Life at Sea, Explanatory Notes to the Regulations."

14 "Analysis of Serious Casualties to Sea-Going Tankers, 1968–1980," IMCO Publication.

15 "Tanker Casualties Report (1968–1977)," IMCO Publication No. 78.16.

16 Jansson, B., "Safety of Ro/Ro Vessels—Ro/Ro Vessel's Casualty Statistics," DNV (Det norske Veritas) Paper No. 81/021, Presented at the 5th International Conference & Exhibition on Marine Transport Using Roll-on/Roll-off Methods.

17 Macduff, T., "The Probability of Vessel Collisions," Ocean Industry, Sept. 1974.

18 Heller, Pegram, "Probabilistic Assessment of Collisions Involving Seagoing Ships," IEEE Transactions on Reliability, Oct. 1979.

19 Jones, N., "On the Collision Protection of Ships," Nuclear Engineering and Design, Vol. 38, 1976.

20 Saunders, H. E., Hydrodynamics in Ship Design, SNAME 1957.

21 IMCO LL/Circular 23, "Recommendations for Uniform Application and Interpretation of Regulation 27 of the Convention," May 1968.

22 VanHees, "Cargo Ship or Passenger Ship?," Schiff und Hafen, Vol. 3, 1977.

23 "Survival Capabilities of Cargo Ships," Norwegian Maritime Directorate, Oslo, Sept. 1978.

24 Ando, Miura, Namba, "The Third-Generation Deep-Sea RO/RO," Marine Technology, Vol. 17, No. 3, July 1980.

25 Michel, K., "The Skaugran Class 42 400-DWT RO/RO's," Marine Technology, Vol. 18, No. 4, Oct. 1981.

26 "Protocol at 1978 Relating to the International Convention for the Prevention of Pollution from Ships, 1973," IMCO Publication.

Appendix 1

Proposed criteria for damaged survivability of cargo vessels

A. Damage location and extent

1. The damage extents and locations should be applied to all locations along the entire length of the ship according to the density distributions from Figs. 1 through 4.
2. All possible combinations of flooded compartments are to be determined along with the corresponding probability of occurrence based on these density distributions (see Appendix 2).

B. Intact condition of ship

1. Calculations to be made for all possible combinations of flooded compartments, as determined in A.2 preceding, over the range of operating drafts.
2. In general, no trim or heel assumed except to evaluate a specific operating condition (that is, ballast draft).
3. Permeabilities:
   a. Hold spaces normally occupied by containers, break-bulk cargo or stores: 60%
   May be modified to suit specific characteristics of actual cargo or to suit draft variations.
   b. Open hold spaces around containers (occupied by open container cell structure, etc.), behind sparring, or at ends of holds: 95%
   c. Appropriated for cargo or stores but not necessarily occupied at the intact draft under consideration, or spaces intended for vehicles or other cargo having a similar high proportion of floodable volume: 95%
   d. Accommodations or passages for passengers and crew: 95%
   e. Machinery: 85%
   f. Void or liquid compartments: 95%
   Fluid contents of tanks specified as filled or partially filled shall be considered to be first emptied and subsequently replaced with seawater to the static flooded waterline.
   g. In general, full load drafts should use full hold permeabilities; ballast conditions should use empty hold permeabilities; and intermediate drafts should use the worst conceivable permeability. Alternatively, a probability distribution at permeability can be developed for any draft.
   h. Surface permeability assumed equal to volumetric permeability.

C. Criteria for ship survival

1. The ship shall have sufficient intact metacentric height (*GM*), so that in the final flooded equilibrium position the ship will:
   a. Prevent immersion of progressive flooding openings. (Progressive flooding openings include vents, overflows, hatches, and weathertight doors, except those in way of already breached compartments. Watertight doors, manholes, and small watertight covers need not be considered.)
   b. Limit static heel to 25 deg.
   c. Provide a dynamic range of positive righting levers (*GZ*) to 20 deg beyond the static heel angle, to both port and starboard, with a maximum value of at least 0.10 m.
   d. Maintain positive upright damaged *GM* for cases of symmetrical flooding.
2. Practical arrangements should be made to limit progressive flooding in piping and air ducts within the extent of flooding.
3. Cross-flooding should not be considered as a means to reduce heel to within the 25-deg static heel requirement.

D. Determination of Survivability Index (SI)

1. The Survivability Index is determined for a specific draft and intact condition for any available *GM* by summing the probabilities of occurrence (from A.2) for all cases in which the available *GM* exceeds the required *GM* to meet criteria for survival.

Appendix 2

Determination of compartment groupings and probabilities

Rather than developing specific formulas for probability to apply to the designer's choice of damaged compartments, a more straightforward method is to apply the damage distributions directly to the specific ship design.

Since the damage survivability calculations will undoubtedly be carried out by computer, a complete numerical description of the hull and all compartments must be made. Once this description has been made it is a relatively easy task for the computer to calculate the compartment groupings and probabilities for every possible damage extent and location. Since damage, according to the proposed criteria, comprises four factors (longitudinal location, longitudinal extent, transverse extent, and vertical extent), the computer program must apply every permutation of these four factors to the ship. The damaged compartments for each permutation are determined along with the probability of the permutation. The probabilities are then summed for each unique combination of compartments.

Definitions of variables

L = longitudinal location of damage
Linc = increment for L
Lprob = probability of longitudinal location
X = longitudinal extent of damage
$X1$ = forward longitudinal boundary
$X2$ = aft longitudinal boundary
Xinc = increment of X
Xprob = probability of longitudinal extent
$Y1$ = upper boundary of damage
$Y2$ = lower boundary of damage
Yinc = increment for Y
Yprob = probability of vertical extent
Z = transverse extent of damage
Zinc = increment for Z
Zprob = probability of transverse extent
Lbp = ship's *LBP*, maximum 200 m
Beam = ship's beam
Sdraft = ship's Summer Load Line draft
No = compartment number
Cn = Maximum number of comp'ts
Tprob = total probability of a given damage extent

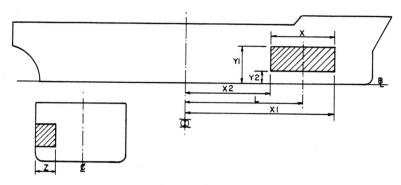

Appendix 2—*continued*

PROGRAM FLOWCHART

```
┌─────────────────────────────────────────────────────────┐
│ FOR L = Lbp/2 - Linc/2 TO -Lbp /2+ Linc/2 STEP - Linc    │
└─────────────────────────────────────────────────────────┘
        ┌──────────────────────────────────────────────────┐
        │ FOR X = Xinc/2 TO .24 * Lbp - Xinc/2 STEP Xinc    │
        │              X1 = L + X/2                         │
        │              X2 = L - X/2                         │
        └──────────────────────────────────────────────────┘
      ┌────────────────────────────────────────────────────┐
      │ FOR Z = Zinc/2 TO .80 * Beam - Zinc/2 STEP Zinc     │
      └────────────────────────────────────────────────────┘
        ┌──────────────────────────────────────────────────┐
        │ FOR Y = Yinc/2 TO 1 - Yinc/2 STEP Yinc            │
        │         Y1 = Sdraft + .11 * Lbp * Y               │
        │         Y2 = Sdraft - 2 * Sdraft * Y              │
        └──────────────────────────────────────────────────┘
              ┌──────────────────────────┐
              │ FOR No = 1 TO Cn          │
              └──────────────────────────┘
```

IS COMPARTMENT WITHIN DAMAGE BOUNDARIES ?

YES → Save Compartment Number

NO

ALL COMPARTMENTS CHECKED ?

NO

YES

CALCULATE PROBABILITIES

IF L >= 0 THEN Lprob = 1.2 * Linc/Lbp
IF L < 0 THEN Lprob = Linc/Lbp * (1.2 + 1.6 * L/Lbp)
Xprob = Xinc/Lbp * (25/3 - 25/3/.24 * X/L)
Zprob = Zinc/Beam * (2.5 - 3.125 * Z/Beam)
Yprob = Yinc
Tprob = Lprob * Xprob * Zprob * Yprob

IS THIS COMBINATION UNIQUE OR EXISTING ?

UNIQUE → NEW CASE

EXISTING

Save compartment groupings and sum probabilities for this case

NEXT Y

NEXT Z

NEXT X

NEXT L

Program flowchart—Appendix 2

Damage Survivability of Cargo Ships

Appendix 3

Sample calculation of Survivability Index (SI)

Tanker

SAMPLE CALCULATION OF SURVIVABILITY INDEX (SI)

TANKER

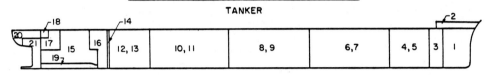

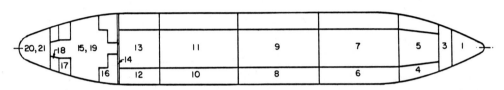

CASE	DAMAGED COMPARTMENTS	DAMAGE PROBABILITY	SURVIVAL CRITERIA		APPLIED PROBABILITY (@ 4.0 m GM)
			GOVERNING	REQ.GM	
1	1,2	.03250	.10 m GZ	.05	.03250
2	1,2,3	.02725	.10 m GZ	.08	.02725
3	1,2,3,4	.01998	20° Range	.47	.01998
4	1,2,3,4,5	.02569	Prog. Flooding	99.	–
5	2,3,	.00558	.10 m GZ	.10	.00558
6	3,4	.00510	20° Range	1.49	.00510
7	3,4,5	.00656	20° Range	2.11	.00656
8	2,3,4	.00419	20° Range	1.55	.00419
9	2,3,4,5	.00539	20° Range	2.34	.00539
10	1,2,3,4,6	.00252	Prog. Flooding	99.	–
11	1,2,3,4,5,6,7	.00323	Prog. Flooding	99.	–
12	4	.01794	20° Range	1.30	.01794
13	4,5	.02306	Prog. Flooding	1.73	.02306
14	2,3,4,6	.00207	Prog. Flooding	99.	–
15	2,3,4,5,6,7	.00267	Prog. Flooding	99.	–
16	3,4,6	.00193	Prog. Flooding	99.	–
17	3,4,5,6,7	.00248	Prog. Flooding	99.	–
18	4,6	.02877	Prog. Flooding	1.50	.02877
19	4,5,6,7	.03698	Prog. Flooding	99.	–
20	6	.05819	Prog. Flooding	3.40	.05819
21	6,7	.07481	Prog. Flooding	99.	–
22	4,6,8	.00007	Prog. Flooding	2.98	.00007
23	4,5,6,7,8,9	.00009	Prog. Flooding	99.	–
24	6,8	.03569	Prog. Flooding	1.75	.03569
25	6,7,8,9	.04589	Prog. Flooding	99.	–
26	8	.05778	Prog. Flooding	2.00	.05778
27	8,9	.07429	Prog. Flooding	4.20	–
28	6,8,10	.00004	Prog. Flooding	6.44	–
29	6,7,8,9,10,11	.00005	Prog. Flooding	99.	–

SAMPLE CALCULATION OF SURVIVABILITY INDEX (SI)

TANKER

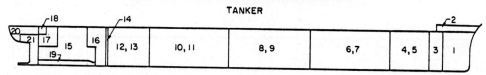

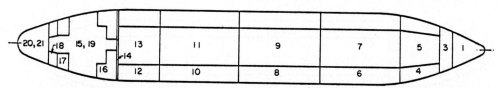

CASE	DAMAGED COMPARTMENTS	DAMAGE PROBABILITY	SURVIVAL CRITERIA		APPLIED PROBABILITY (@ 4.0 m GM)
			GOVERNING	REQ. GM	
30	8,10	.03465	Prog. Flooding	1.58	.03465
31	8,9,10,11	.04455	Prog. Flooding	99.	−
32	10	.04770	Prog. Flooding	2.79	.04770
33	10,11	.06133	Prog. Flooding	3.50	.06133
34	10,12	.02195	Prog. Flooding	1.75	.02195
35	10,11,12,13	.02822	Prog. Flooding	99.	−
36	8,10,12	.00003	Prog. Flooding	3.09	.00003
37	8,9,10,11,12,13	.00004	Prog. Flooding	99.	−
38	10,12,14	.00038	Prog. Flooding	2.90	.00038
39	10,11,12,13,14	.00049	Prog. Flooding	99.	−
40	10,12,14,16	.00197	Prog. Flooding	3.45	.00197
41	10,11,12,13,14,16	.00253	Prog. Flooding	99.	−
42	12	.01114	20° Range	1.33	.01114
43	12,13	.01432	20° Range	1.57	.01432
44	10,12,14,15,16	.00177	Prog. Flooding	99.	−
45	10,11,12,13,14,15,19	.00227	Prog. Flooding	99.	−
46	12,14,16	.00474	20° Range	1.66	.00474
47	12,13,14,16	.00610	20° Range	1.99	.00610
48	12,14	.00082	20° Range	1.37	.00082
49	12,13,14	.00106	20° Range	1.63	.00106
50	12,14,15,16	.00980	Prog. Flooding	4.38	−
51	12,13,14,15,16,19	.01259	Prog. Flooding	99.	−
52	16	.00220	20° Range	.42	.00220
53	15,16	.00669	20° Range	.84	.00669
54	15,16,19	.00861	20° Range	.84	.00816
55	14,15,16	.00103	Prog. Flooding	99.	−
56	14,15,16,19	.00133	Prog. Flooding	99.	−
57	12,14,15,16,17	.00128	Prog. Flooding	99.	−
58	12,13,14,15,16,17,19	.00164	Prog. Flooding	99.	−
59	15	.00498	.10 m GZ	.14	.00498
60	15,19	.00640	20° Range	.12	.00640

SAMPLE CALCULATION OF SURVIVABILITY INDEX (SI)

TANKER

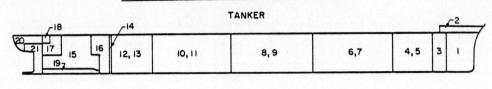

CASE	DAMAGED COMPARTMENTS	DAMAGE PROBABILITY	SURVIVAL CRITERIA GOVERNING	REQ.GM	APPLIED PROBABILITY (@ 4.0 m GM)
61	12,14,15,16,17,18	.00041	Prog. Flooding	99.	–
62	12,13,14,15,16,17,18,19	.00052	Prog. Flooding	99.	–
63	15,16,17	.00150	Prog. Flooding	99.	–
64	15,16,17,19	.00193	Prog. Flooding	99.	–
65	12,14,15,16,17,18,20,21	.00016	Prog. Flooding	99.	–
66	12,13,14,15,16,17,18,19,20,21	.00021	Prog. Flooding	99.	–
67	15,16,17,18	.00063	Prog. Flooding	99.	–
68	15,16,17,18,19	.00081	Prog. Flooding	99.	–
69	14,15,16,17,18,20,21	.00016	Prog. Flooding	99.	–
70	14,15,16,17,18,19,20,21	.00020	Prog. Flooding	99.	–
71	15,17	.00466	20° Range	.54	.00466
72	15,17,19	.00599	20° Range	.53	.00599
73	15,16,17,18,20,21	.00107	Prog. Flooding	99.	–
74	15,16,17,18,19,20,21	.00138	Prog. Flooding	99.	–
75	15,17,18	.00326	20° Range	.60	.00326
76	15,17,18,19	.00419	20° Range	.60	.00419
77	15,17,18,20,21	.01105	20° Range	.84	.01105
78	15,17,18,19,20,21	.01421	20° Range	.88	.01421
79	20,21	.00427	.10 m GZ	.11	.00427
Total		1.00000	SI (at 4.0 m GM)		= .61030

Note: A required GM of 99. indicates that the progressive flooding openings
are immersed at 0° heel. Therefore the condition is non-survivable at
any GM.

SNAME Transactions, Vol. 90, 1982, pp. 41–54

Modal Perturbation Methods for Marine Structures

Robert E. Sandström,[1] Associate Member and **William J. Anderson**,[2] Visitor

Perturbation methods in vibration analysis of structures have been used since Lord Rayleigh's time. Current developments, however, have led to matrix forms of perturbation which allow intricate frequency and mode shape changes. Furthermore, one can synthesize a new structure to meet frequency and mode goals by using inverse perturbation analysis, or can perform system failure identification to locate damaged members. The methods discussed herein require specification of small changes from a baseline case, which is either a nonacceptable design (in the case of synthesis), or is an undamaged structure (in the case of failure identification). This paper presents the theory, methodology, and several illustrative engineering examples.

Background

TECHNIQUES for determining the vibratory characteristics (natural frequencies and mode shapes) of a structure are well established. The structure is defined and then vibratory characteristics are computed or measured. Information obtained is used to determine whether or not the structure will experience a vibratory problem. If a vibration problem exists, one can either minimize the excitation forces, or perform structural redesign. Typically, the redesign process relies on engineering intuition to identify the most promising parts of the structure to change. Subsequently, reanalysis is used to measure the effect of structural changes on the natural frequencies and mode shapes. This process (later called the forward solution) can be quite expensive when one considers computer time and man-hour effort. Furthermore, the redesign is often only marginally adequate with no guarantees that the structural modifications represent the least structural change. An alternative approach is a direct redesign of the desired structure (later called the inverse solution), where one specifies desired natural frequency and mode shape changes and computes the least structural changes directly.

The modal perturbation method presented in this paper offers an efficient approximate solution of the redesign problem. The solution gives usable results when structural changes and modal changes are small. The perturbation methods presented herein will enable a designer to identify those parts of the structure which have the greatest influence on a specified frequency or mode shape goal and to estimate how much each structural component should be modified to reach this goal.

The use of the inverse perturbation method for structural redesign was previously investigated by Stetson [1–3][3] for the redesign of a turbine blade. The goal of that investigation was to adjust the thickness distribution of a turbine blade so that it

would meet specified vibratory characteristics. The NAS-TRAN finite-element program was used.

The current work alters Stetson's solution procedure for the inverse perturbation equations. His solution procedure involves substantial computational effort [1, 3] and has the disadvantage of being mathematically more abstract; consequently, it is less obvious to the user. The solution procedure presented herein is computationally much easier. In fact our scheme is so simple to use that the application of perturbation methods to small problems is now possible with hand calculations. Larger problems can be easily solved using a computer to assist in the required matrix operations, as will be demonstrated later. A second benefit of our solution procedure is that it provides a direct indication as to which structural changes would be the most effective in controlling modal changes. For engineers, it is particularly appealing to use methods, such as those presented herein, that expose the physical characteristics of the structural system.

In the following section, the mathematical formulation of the first-order perturbation method as proposed by Stetson [4, 5] is described. New solution procedures for these equations are then developed, followed by example problems which demonstrate the potential of the new solution procedure as an effective engineering tool. In this, their first paper presented before the Society, the authors feel that it would be more appropriate to give a clear description of modal perturbation methods with only minimal emphasis on related design methodology issues.

Theory

Mathematical development

Vibration studies typically involve an eigenvalue analysis of a structural system defined by

$$[m]_{n \times n} \{\ddot{\psi}\}_{n \times 1} + [k]_{n \times n} \{\psi\}_{n \times 1} = \{0\}$$

which produces the eigenvectors

$$[\phi] = [\{\psi_1\}, \{\psi_2\}, \ldots, \{\psi_n\}]$$

and the natural frequencies

---

[1] Adjunct assistant professor, Department of Naval Architecture and Marine Engineering, The University of Michigan, Ann Arbor, Mich.; now research engineer, Exxon Production Research Co., Houston.

[2] Professor, Department of Aerospace Engineering, The University of Michigan, Ann Arbor, Michigan.

[3] Numbers in brackets designate References at end of paper.

Presented at the Annual Meeting, New York, N. Y., November 17–20, 1982, of THE SOCIETY OF NAVAL ARCHITECTS AND MARINE ENGINEERS.

$$[\ulcorner \omega^2 \lrcorner] = \begin{bmatrix} \omega_1^2 & & & & 0 \\ & \omega_2^2 & & & \\ & & \cdot & & \\ & & & \cdot & \\ 0 & & & & \omega_n^2 \end{bmatrix}$$

Suppose we introduce *small* changes in the system.

New mass $\qquad [m'] = [m] + [\Delta m]$
New stiffness $\qquad [k'] = [k] + [\Delta k]$
New frequencies $\qquad \ulcorner \omega'^2 \lrcorner = \ulcorner \omega^2 \lrcorner + \ulcorner \Delta \omega^2 \lrcorner$
New eigenvectors $\qquad [\phi'] = [\phi] + [\Delta \phi] = [\phi]([I] + [C])T$

where $C_{ii} = 0$ and C_{ij} are small.

The expression describing the new mode shapes $[\phi']$ is a bit puzzling at first glance; however, the logic behind this expression can be seen by expanding $[\phi']$:

$$[\phi'] = [\{\psi'_1\}, \{\psi'_2\}, \ldots, \{\psi'_n\}]$$

$$= [\{\psi_1\}, \{\psi_2\}, \ldots, \{\psi_n\}] \begin{bmatrix} 1 & C_{21} \ldots & C_{n1} \\ C_{12} & 1 & \\ \vdots & & \vdots \\ C_{1n} & \ldots & 1 \end{bmatrix}$$

where

$$\{\psi'_1\} = \{\psi_1\} + C_{12}\{\psi_2\} + \ldots + C_{ln}\{\psi_n\}$$
$$\{\psi'_2\} = C_{21}\{\psi_1\} + \{\psi_2\} + \ldots + C_{2n}\{\psi_n\}$$
$$\vdots$$
$$\{\psi'_n\} = C_{n1}\{\psi_1\} + C_{n2}\{\psi_2\} + \ldots + \{\psi_n\}$$

The new eigenvectors are simply expressed in terms of the original eigenvectors, where the C_{ij} terms relate the participation of the jth mode to changes in the ith mode.

In the development it will be convenient to express the equations of motion in uncoupled form using the calculated natural frequencies and eigenvectors. The uncoupled equations for the baseline structure are given by

$$[\ulcorner K \lrcorner] = [\ulcorner M \lrcorner][\ulcorner \omega^2 \lrcorner]$$

where

Generalized stiffness $\ulcorner K \lrcorner = [\phi]^T[k][\phi]$
Generalized mass $\ulcorner M \lrcorner = [\phi]^T[m][\phi]$

The perturbed quantities representing the modified structure must also satisfy the equations of motion. Hence

$$[\ulcorner K' \lrcorner] = [\ulcorner M' \lrcorner][\ulcorner \omega'^2 \lrcorner]$$

where

$$\ulcorner K' \lrcorner = [\phi']^T[k'][\phi']$$
$$\ulcorner M' \lrcorner = [\phi']^T[m'][\phi']$$

In this procedure we will consider only small perturbations which are of order Δ. Consequently, terms involving order Δ^2 and higher will be neglected. After a bit of manipulation and neglecting terms of Δ^2 and higher, we obtain the general form of the first-order perturbation equations:

$$[\phi]^T[\Delta k][\phi] - [\phi]^T[\Delta m][\phi][\omega^2] = [\Delta] \qquad (1)$$

where changes to the ith mode are given by

$$\Delta_{ji} \equiv \begin{cases} M_i \Delta \omega_i^2 & j = i \\ M_j C_{ij}(\omega_i^2 - \omega_j^2) & j \neq i \end{cases}$$

This is essentially the same result derived by Stetson [1, 2, 4, 5]. The left-hand side of equation (1) involves only structural changes while the right-hand side involves only frequency and mode shape changes.

The perturbation equations, (1), can be used in a forward or an inverse procedure. One could solve directly for the changes in natural frequencies and mode shapes as a result of specifying small changes in the mass and stiffness of the structural system (the forward solution). One could also determine the changes to the stiffness and mass in order to satisfy specified small

---

Nomenclature

C_{ij} = participation of jth mode to changes in ith mode
$[I]$ = identity matrix
$[K]$ = generalized stiffness of baseline structure
$[K']$ = generalized stiffness of modified structure
$[M]$ = generalized mass of baseline structure
$[M']$ = generalized mass of modified structures
P_e^k = perturbation influence term associated with stiffness changes of element e and physical mode shape constraints
P_e^m = perturbation influence term associated with mass changes of element e and physical mode shape constraints
$[\ ]^T, \{\ \}^T$ = denotes transpose of a matrix and vector, respectively
$[T_i]$ = transformation matrix taking nonphysical modal constraints to physical modal constraints
e = eth structural element
i = index associated with ith modal constraint

j = index associated with jth participation of jth mode in mode i constraints
$[k]$ = stiffness matrix of the baseline structure
$[k']$ = stiffness matrix of the modified structure
$[k_e]$ = stiffness matrix of element e
$[\Delta k]$ = small change to stiffness matrix
l = number of structural changes
$[m]$ = mass matrix of baseline structure
$[m']$ = mass matrix of modified structure
$[m_e]$ = mass matrix of element e
$[\Delta m]$ = small change to stiffness mass
n = number of degrees of freedom of structural model
n' = number of nonphysical modal constraints
p_e^k = perturbation influence term associated with stiffness changes of element e and nonphysical mode shape changes
p_e^m = perturbation influence term associated with mass changes of element e and nonphysical mode shape constraints

r = number of physical modal constraints
$[\Gamma_i]$ = transformation matrix related to $[T_i]$
$\{\Delta\}$ = nonphysical modal constraints
Δ = prefix denoting small changes
$\{\alpha\}$ = structural change vector
α_e^k = fractional stiffness change of element e
α_e^m = fractional mass changes of element e
$[\delta]$ = physical modal constraints
$[\lambda_i]$ = matrix related to $[T_i]$
$[\phi]$ = matrix of mode shape vectors of baseline structure
$[\phi']$ = matrix of mode shape vectors of modified structure
$[\Delta\phi]$ = matrix of mode shape vector changes relative to baseline structure
$\{\psi_i\}$ = ith mode shape vector of $[\phi]$
ω_i = ith baseline structure natural frequency
ω'_i = ith modified structure natural frequency
$\Delta\omega_i$ = small change to ith baseline structure natural frequency

Model Perturbation Methods for Marine Structures

changes in the natural frequencies and mode shapes (the inverse solution).

To facilitate the anticipated solution procedures, one expresses the first-order perturbation equations (1) in an alternate form. We note that each Δ_{ji} term is equal to

$$\Delta_{ji} = \{\psi_j\}^T[\Delta k]\{\psi_i\} - \omega_i^2\{\psi_j\}^T[\Delta m]\{\psi_i\} \qquad (2)$$

The perturbation equations in this form exhibit some interesting characteristics. First, the structural changes $[\Delta k]$ and $[\Delta m]$ are separated from the modal changes $\Delta\omega_i^2$ and C_{ij}. Furthermore, equations corresponding to $j = i$ relate the structural changes to changes of the ith natural frequency without involving the mode shape changes. Similarly, equations corresponding to $j \neq i$ relate the structural changes to mode shape changes through C_{ij} without involving the natural frequency changes. This characteristic is attractive since the formulation allows us to uncouple the equations simply in terms of $[\Delta k]$, $[\Delta m]$, $[\Delta\omega^2]$, and $[C]$.

Interpretation of $[\Delta k]$ and $[\Delta m]$

To deal effectively with the inverse solution, one must give the structural changes $[\Delta k]$ and $[\Delta m]$ a practical interpretation. This can be accomplished by decomposing the system changes into l element changes. For the stiffness changes, one obtains

$$[\Delta k]_{\text{SYSTEM}} = \sum_{e=1}^{l} [\Delta k_e]$$

Furthermore, each element change can be expressed as a fractional change from the original stiffness

$$[\Delta k_e] = [k_e]\alpha_e^k$$

where α_e^k represents the fractional change in the stiffness of element e. We now write

$$[\Delta k]_{\text{SYSTEM}} = \sum_{e=1}^{l} [k_e]\alpha_e^k \qquad (3)$$

and similarly for the masses

$$[\Delta m]_{\text{SYSTEM}} = \sum_{e=1}^{l} [m_e]\alpha_e^m \qquad (4)$$

where the superscript k refers to stiffness changes whereas superscript m refers to mass changes.

The system structural changes can therefore be expressed in terms of elemental structural changes. In the implementation of this procedure at an industrial level it will be necessary to define element changes in a more realistic sense. For example, a general three-dimensional beam element contains several stiffness effects

$$[k_{\text{BEAM}}] = [k_{\text{AXIAL}}] + [k_{\text{BENDING}}] + [k_{\text{TORSIONAL}}]$$

Axial effects are controlled by cross-sectional area changes, bending effects by moment of inertia changes, and torsional effects by torsional stiffness changes. Furthermore, changes in elemental mass are directly related to cross-sectional area changes. With this in mind, we could express beam element changes as

$$[\Delta k_{\text{BEAM}}] - \omega^2[\Delta m_{\text{BEAM}}] = [k_{\text{AXIAL}} - \omega^2 m_{\text{BEAM}}]\alpha_{\text{BEAM}}^{\text{AREA}}$$
$$+ [k_{\text{BENDING}}]\alpha_{\text{BEAM}}^I + [k_{\text{TORSION}}]\alpha_{\text{BEAM}}^I$$

Returning to the perturbation equations, one can now use equations (3) and (4) to relate changes in the mode shapes and natural frequencies to changes in the stiffness and mass of each element of the system

$$\Delta_{ji} = \{p^k\}^T\{\alpha^k\} + \{p^m\}^T\{\alpha^m\}$$

where the p^k and p^m are perturbation influence terms

$$p_e^k = \{\psi_j\}^T[k_e]\{\psi_i\}, \qquad p_e^m = -\omega_i^2\{\psi_j\}^T[m_e]\{\psi_i\}$$

Specification of modal constraints

The inverse solution requires that we specify modal changes, $\{\Delta\}$. Natural frequency changes Δ_{ii} are specified directly, while mode shape changes, Δ_{ji}, are not so easy as given by (1). When a mode shape change is required, one normally thinks in terms of physical changes, $\{\Delta\psi_i\}$, rather than mode participation, C_{ij}. Also, the C_{ij} terms may not be easy to compute. Recall

$$\{\Delta\psi_i\} = C_{i1}\{\psi_1\} + C_{i2}\{\psi_2\} + \ldots + C_{i,i-1}\{\psi_{i-1}\}$$
$$+ C_{i,i+1}\{\psi_{i+1}\} + \ldots + C_{in}\{\psi_n\}$$

Computing the C_{ij} terms is a new problem in itself! Furthermore, the solution for C_{ij} may not always be unique; hence, the accuracy of the total method is quite dependent on a proper solution for the C_{ij} terms.

To diffuse the disadvantages of the C_{ij} terms and to bring the problem into a more physical space, an important modification to the perturbation equations is introduced. Isolating our attention to changes associated with the ith mode, the Δ_{ji}'s can be transformed into physical modal constraints, δ_i, using the following mapping matrix

$$\{\delta_i\} \equiv \left\{\frac{\Delta\omega_i^2}{\Delta\psi_i}\right\} \quad \text{(a partitioned matrix)}$$

$$\begin{bmatrix} 1 & 0 \\ 0 & \Gamma_i \end{bmatrix}\{\Delta_{ji}\} \qquad (6)$$

$$\equiv [T_i]\{\Delta_{ji}\}$$

where

$$[\Gamma_i] = [\{\psi_1\},\ldots\{\psi_{i-1}\},\{\psi_{i+1}\}\ldots\{\psi_n\}][\lambda_i] \qquad (7)$$

$$\{\Delta_{ji}\} = \begin{Bmatrix} M_i\Delta\omega_i^2 \\ M_1(\omega_i^2 - \omega_1^2)C_{i1} \\ \vdots \\ M_{i-1}(\omega_i^2 - \omega_{i-1}^2)C_{i,i-1} \\ M_{i+1}(\omega_i^2 - \omega_{i+1}^2)C_{i,i+1} \\ \vdots \\ M_n(\omega_i^2 - \omega_n^2)C_{in} \end{Bmatrix} \qquad (8)$$

and

$$[\lambda_i] = \begin{bmatrix} \frac{1}{M_1(\omega_i^2 - \omega_1^2)} & & & & \\ & \ddots & & & 0 \\ & & \frac{1}{M_{i-1}(\omega_i^2 - \omega_{i-1}^2)} & & \\ & & & \frac{1}{M_{i+1}(\omega_i^2 - \omega_{i+1}^2)} & \\ 0 & & & & \ddots \\ & & & & & \frac{1}{M_n(\omega_i^2 - \omega_n^2)} \end{bmatrix} \qquad (9)$$

This transformation may appear to be somewhat mysterious at first glance; however, when expanded it should become obvious that this is only the definition of $\Delta\psi_i$.

The modified perturbation equations for the ith mode now take on the following form:

$$\{\delta_i\}_{r\times1} = [T_i]_{r\times n'}[p^k]_{n'\times l}\{\alpha^k\}_{l\times1} + [T_i]_{r\times n'}[p^m]_{n'\times l}\{\alpha^m\}_{l\times1}$$

or $\qquad (10)$

$$\{\delta_i\}_{r\times1} = [P^k]_{r\times l}\{\alpha^k\}_{l\times1} + [P^m]_{r\times l}\{\alpha^m\}_{l\times1}$$

where r equals the number of modal constraints in terms of $\Delta\omega_i^2$ and $\Delta\psi_i$, and n' equals the number of modal constraints in terms of $\Delta\omega_i^2$ and C_{ij}. Finally, r and n' must be less than or equal to n.

Interpretation of the P-terms.

The perturbation influence terms P^k and P^m provide important information for vibration design. They indicate which structural elements will be the most effective in controlling modal changes defined by the δ_i terms. Large values for P suggest that small structural changes would be required to meet the design specification. Small values for P, on the other hand, suggest that large structural changes would be required. Obviously, small structural changes produce the least alteration to the structural system and also allow solutions of higher accuracy since the method is linear. The perturbation influence terms can be used to identify structural elements which have no effect on the modal changes. These elements would be characterized by P-values close to zero.

Solution concepts for perturbation equations

The solution of these perturbation equations falls into three categories. They include:

1. Overconstrained case $r > 2l$
2. Unique case $r = 2l$
3. Underconstrained case $r < 2l$

The unique solution simply involves inverting the perturbation matrix, provided it is not singular. The remaining cases can be solved using a quadratic programming algorithm [6]. For the overconstrained case the error in modal constraints is minimized. For the underconstrained case, the least structural change as defined by $\{\alpha\}^T\{\alpha\}$, which satisfies all the modal constraints exactly, is obtained.

In a more general setting the perturbation equations could be used to form constraint equations. These could take the form of equality constraints, as suggested by the development of the perturbation equations, or as inequality constraints. Inequality constraints have the advantage of expanding the set of permissible structural changes by softening the constraints, and increasing the chances of finding the "best" least structural change. For example, specifying two frequency changes with equality constraints might be too restrictive. Specifying upper or lower limits or both to those frequency constraints may produce more acceptable structural changes. The linear programming technique would be recommended when inequality constraints are imposed.

Additional constraints can also be imposed on this system of equations. From a practical standpoint, it may be required that certain elements grow or change at the same rate. This constraint is imposed by modifying the perturbation equations in the following manner. Suppose, for example, that four elements will be involved in a change to satisfy one modal constraint. The perturbation equations can be written as follows:

$$\delta_1 = P_1^k\alpha_1^k + P_2^k\alpha_2^k + P_3^k\alpha_3^k + P_4^k\alpha_4^k \\ + P_1^m\alpha_1^m + P_2^m\alpha_2^m + P_3^m\alpha_3^m + P_4^m\alpha_4^m \quad (11)$$

If we require that Elements 2 and 3 grow together as "linked" design variables:

$$\alpha_2^k = \alpha_3^k$$
$$\alpha_2^m = \alpha_3^m$$

then this equation can be written as

$$\delta_1 = P_1^k\alpha_1^k + (P_2^k + P_3^k)\alpha_2^k + P_4^k\alpha_4^k \\ + P_1^m\alpha_1^m + (P_2^m + P_3^m)\alpha_2^m + P_4^m\alpha_4^m$$

Computationally, this involves adding together the columns

associated with the "linked" elements in each of the matrices $[P^k]$ and $[P^m]$.

Another constraint which could be imposed on the system involves specifying the magnitude of some structural changes while the remaining element changes satisfy the conditions of least structural change. This type of constraint is useful when positive control of the structural changes on a particular element is required. Suppose that the solution from the previous example suggests that a 15 percent reduction in stiffness for Element 4 is required ($\alpha_4^k = -0.15$). Furthermore, suppose that we can only tolerate a 10 percent reduction. We then fix the value of $\alpha_4^k = -0.10$ and modify the perturbation equations as follows:

$$\delta_1 + 0.1(P_4^k) = P_1^k\alpha_1^k + (P_2^k + P_3^k)\alpha_2^k + P_1^m\alpha_1^m \\ + (P_2^m + P_3^m)\alpha_2^m + P_4^m\alpha_4^m$$

A least-change solution can then be used to find the remaining structural changes α_1^k, α_2^k, α_1^m, α_2^m, and α_4^m. It should be noted that limits on permissible structural changes can be imposed through inequality constraints when linear programming is used.

Methodology

To use the perturbation analysis one must first obtain the vibratory characteristics of a baseline structure (Fig. 1). All subsequent modifications using the perturbation analysis are relative to the baseline case. The inverse solution (Fig. 2) uses the baseline stiffness, mass, natural frequency, and mode shape data as input. The user then specifies new natural frequencies and modes shapes and the perturbation analysis subsequently estimates the required structural changes.

In cases where large changes are required, reanalysis can be used to update the baseline model so that small improvements can be used in an incremental approach as indicated in Fig. 3. This theory produces useable results when the changes are small. A direct nonlinear inverse analysis which permits larger changes has been formulated; the solution algorithm is presently under development.

A word of warning is in order here. The method as developed in this paper does not include any check on the stress levels within the structure. Users should be advised to check the modified structure to insure that the stresses are within acceptable levels. It is important that one problem not be traded for another.

Applications

Some applications of perturbation analysis include:

1. Structural redesign to meet specified frequency and mode shape characteristics.
2. Correlation of finite-element models with measured results.
3. Failure analysis.

All of these applications are essentially *redesign* problems. In each application one specifies mode shape and natural frequency changes and utilizes perturbation analysis to determine required structural modifications. *Correlation of finite-element models with measured results* is equivalent to modal redesign where the specified modal goals are the measured results. *Failure analysis* is closely related to model correlation. The finite-element model is first redesigned to agree with data measured from an existing and presumably sound structure. Since structures which experience failure will often show signs of decreasing natural frequency and changing amplitude of vibration, perturbation analysis can be used to indicate which parts of the structure are most likely to be losing stiffness.

Two-element cantilever beam

The cantilever beam model in Fig. 4 can be used to illustrate the working details and the accuracy of the perturbation equations, (10). Data for the baseline model are given in Table 1. Only lateral vibration in the xz-plane is allowed.

The format of this example will be to first analyze the baseline model and three modified designs "close to" the baseline case. The analysis of these four designs is exact; the results form a data base. Subsequent inverse perturbation solutions will be posed in which one attempts to project from the baseline design to each of the modified designs. The "projection" will be done with the *a priori* knowledge of how the modified structures should behave (from the data base). This allows us to evaluate the accuracy of the inverse perturbation method in an environment where known physical changes are the goal.

The baseline model vibration modes are summarized in Table 2. The structural modifications to the baseline cantilever model are:

Modification 1: 10 percent reduction in I_1
Modification 2: 10 percent reduction in I_2
Modification 3: 10 percent reduction in I_1 and I_2

Exact results for these modified structures are given in Table 3.

Formation of perturbation equations—Now let us use inverse perturbation equations, (10), to attempt to reach the same modifications as in the data base. One can propose a set of perturbation equations involving mode shape changes in tip displacements (Node 3 translation) and in natural frequencies. Furthermore, suppose that only changes in the bending stiffness of each beam (I_1, I_2) will be used to accomplish this change. The perturbation equations corresponding to this problem are a set of four equations in two unknowns:

$$\begin{Bmatrix} \Delta\omega_1^2 \\ \Delta\psi_{1,\text{TIP}} \\ \Delta\omega_2^2 \\ \Delta\psi_{2,\text{TIP}} \end{Bmatrix} = \begin{bmatrix} 9.730 & 0.559 \\ 0.0235 & -0.0235 \\ 195.4 & 130.3 \\ -0.0486 & 0.04876 \end{bmatrix} \begin{Bmatrix} \alpha_{\text{BEAM 1}} \\ \alpha_{\text{BEAM 2}} \end{Bmatrix} \quad (12)$$

where

$\Delta\omega_1^2$ = natural frequency change squared ($\text{rad}^2/\text{sec}^2$) of Mode 1

$\Delta\psi_{1,\text{TIP}}$ = Mode 1 shape change corresponding to translation at Node 3

$\alpha_{\text{BEAM 1}}$ = fractional moment of inertia change to Beam 1

The P_{11} perturbation term is computed from

$$P_{11} = \{\psi_1\}^T[k_{\text{BEAM 1}}]\{\psi_1\} = 9.730$$

where

$$\{\psi_1\} = \begin{Bmatrix} 0.0 \\ 0.0 \\ 0.6144 \\ 2.1327 \end{Bmatrix}$$

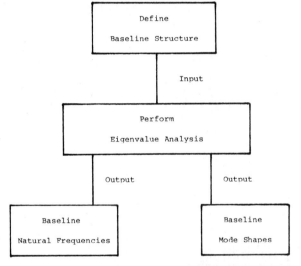

Fig. 1   Forward solution of baseline structure

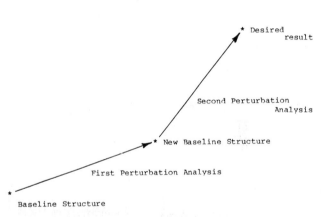

Fig. 3   Incremental solution using small changes

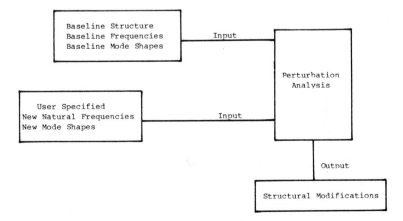

Fig. 2   Inverse solution producing the modified structure

Model Perturbation Methods for Marine Structures

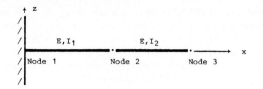

Fig. 4 Cantilever beam model

Table 1   Nondimensional beam model details

Nodal Coordinates			Lumped Masses	Beam Properties
Node	x	z	$\dots$	$E = 1.0$
1	0.0	0.0	$\dots$	$I_1 = 1.0$
2	0.5	0.0	Node $2 = 0.50$	$I_2 = 1.6$
3	1.0	0.0	Node $3 = 0.25$	$A = 1.0$

Table 2   Baseline model vibration modes

Mode 1 $\omega_1 = 3.208$ rad/sec

$$\{\psi_1\} = \begin{Bmatrix} 0.0 \\ 0.0 \\ 0.6144 \\ 2.1327 \\ 1.8014 \\ 2.4947 \end{Bmatrix}$$

0.0	Node 1 translation
0.0	Node 1 rotation
0.6144	Node 2 translation
2.1327	Node 2 rotation
1.8014	Node 3 translation
2.4947	Node 3 rotation

Mode 2 $\omega_2 = 18.047$ rad/sec

$$\{\psi_2\} = \begin{Bmatrix} 0.0 \\ 0.0 \\ -1.2738 \\ 0.6005 \\ 0.8689 \\ 6.1279 \end{Bmatrix}$$

0.0	Node 1 translation
0.0	Node 1 rotation
-1.2738	Node 2 translation
0.6005	Node 2 rotation
0.8689	Node 3 translation
6.1279	Node 3 rotation

$$[k_{\text{BEAM 1}}] = \frac{EI_1}{l^3} \begin{bmatrix} 12 & & & \\ 6l & 4l^2 & \text{SYM} & \\ -12 & -6l & 12 & \\ 6l & 2l^2 & -6l & 4l^2 \end{bmatrix}$$

The P_{21} term has been computed from

$$P_{21} = [\Gamma_1][p_1{}^k] = +0.0235$$

where

$$\Gamma_1 = \frac{\psi_{2,\text{TIP}}}{\omega_1^2 - \omega_2^2} = \frac{0.8689}{3.208^2 - 18.047^2} = -2.75 \times 10^{-3}$$

$$p_1^k = \{\psi_2\}^T [k_{\text{BEAM 1}}]\{\psi_1\} = -8.537$$

$$\{\psi_2\} = \begin{Bmatrix} 0.0 \\ 0.0 \\ -1.2738 \\ 0.6005 \end{Bmatrix}$$

$$\{\psi_1\} = \text{as before}$$

Solution—In general, one could prescribe all four vibratory properties [left-hand side (LHS)] to determine the two α_e [right-hand side (RHS)]. This overdetermined problem would require a least-square error solution or other generalized inverse ideas. For the present, let us simplify the inverse perturbation even further by specifying only changes to the first natural frequency and the tip translation of Mode 1. The perturbation equations are then well posed:

$$\begin{Bmatrix} \Delta\omega_1^2 \\ \Delta\psi_{1,\text{TIP}} \end{Bmatrix} = \begin{bmatrix} 9.730 & 0.559 \\ 0.0235 & -0.0235 \end{bmatrix} \begin{Bmatrix} \alpha_{\text{BEAM 1}} \\ \alpha_{\text{BEAM 2}} \end{Bmatrix} \qquad (13)$$

A solution of equation (13) by specifying the LHS and solving for the RHS can be done to project from the baseline structure to each of the modified structures of Table 3. The results of the inverse calculations are given in Table 4. One finds that for these cases, with changes of I_e on the order of 10 percent, the α_e are typically within 1 percent of the desired change, with the exception of α_2 for Modification 2, where 9 percent error is found. The predicted values of I_e using the α_e's exhibit errors less than 1 percent for all cases in this example.

These results indicate that for small structural changes the perturbation equations provides a simple but useable rela-

tionship between modal characteristics and structural changes. Furthermore, this example and tabulated results can be used as a self-teaching tool to assist potential users to learn the perturbation method presented in this paper.

Mode shape renormalization by energy criterion—In presenting results for mode shapes, a question of normalization of the vectors arises. If one consistently normalizes to a unit generalized mass in the baseline and modified structure, then the scale of the motion may be nonintuitive. For instance, Fig. 5 shows Mode 1 for the baseline and first modification. The first modification involves softening the root bending stiffness of the beam, and one would expect larger tip displacements, especially in some sort of constant input energy environment. There is no mathematical problem here; Fig. 5 is perfectly correct. If, however, one renormalizes a mode of the modified structure as in Fig. 6, the less-stiff modified structure has a larger amplitude. This may appeal to design engineers who have a more intuitive approach. The details of this renormalization follow.

The mode shapes used up to this point in this analysis have been normalized so that the *generalized mass equals unity*. Consequently, the generalized stiffness equals the natural frequency squared. If these mode shapes are used to compute the total strain energy in the system, then the strain energy will equal one-half the natural frequency squared:

$$\text{Baseline strain energy} = \tfrac{1}{2}\,\omega_i^2 = \tfrac{1}{2}\,\{\psi_i\}^T [k_{\text{SYSTEM}}]\{\psi_i\}$$

The frequencies of the modified structure may have changed. Consequently if one uses a modified mode normalized by a unit modal mass, then strain energy

$$\text{Modified strain energy} = \tfrac{1}{2}\,\bar{\omega}_i^2$$

in the modified mode has changed.

In contrast to the foregoing, if one expects the *strain energy of the system to remain constant* with respect to structural changes, then renormalization of the new mode shape such that

$$\text{Modified state energy} = \frac{1}{2}\,\bar{\omega}_i^2 \left(\frac{\omega_i^2}{\bar{\omega}_i^2}\right)$$

$$= \frac{1}{2}\,\omega_i^2 = \text{Baseline strain energy}$$

Model Perturbation Methods for Marine Structures

Table 3 Data base for evaluating accuracy of inverse perturbation

	Baseline	Modified Structure		
		Variation 1 $0.9I_{\text{BEAM 1}}$	Variation 2 $0.9I_{\text{BEAM 2}}$	Variation 3 $0.9I_{\text{BEAM 1}} + 0.9I_{\text{BEAM 2}}$
ω_1 (rad/sec)	3.208	3.051	3.198	3.043
$\Delta\omega_1^2$	...	−0.9827	−0.0641	−1.0314
% Frequency change	...	−4.89%	−0.31%	−5.14%
ω_2 (rad/sec)	18.047	17.477	17.661	17.121
$\Delta\omega_2^2$	...	−20.25	−13.78	−32.57
% Frequency change	...	−3.16%	−2.14%	−5.13%
$\psi_1{}^a$				
Node 2	0.6144	0.6178	0.6106	06144
Node 3	1.8014	1.7990	1.8040	1.8014
$\psi_2{}^a$				
Node 2	−1.2738	−1.2721	−1.2756	−1.2738
Node 3	0.8689	0.8738	0.8635	0.8689

^{a} Only vertical translation components are shown above.

Table 4 Structural changes computed from equation (13)

	Original	Modification 1 $0.9I_1$	Modification 2 $0.9I_2$	Modification 3 $0.9I_1 + 0.9I_2$
$\Delta\omega_1^2$	0.0	−0.9827	−0.0641	−1.0314
$\Delta\psi_{1,\text{TIP}}$	0.0	−0.0024	+0.0026	0.0
$\alpha_{\text{BEAM 1}}$	0.0	−0.1009	−0.0003	−0.1002
$\alpha_{\text{BEAM 2}}$	0.0	−0.0009	−0.1087	−0.1002
I_1 exact	1.0	0.90	1.00	0.90
I_1 predicted	...	0.90	1.00	0.90
I_2 exact	1.6	1.60	1.44	1.44
I_2 predicted	...	1.60	1.43	1.44

requires that the new mode shape be interpreted after multiplying by $\omega_i/\overline{\omega}_i$. This renormalization (Fig. 6) gives the appearance that reducing the bending stiffness of Beam 1 does in fact result in greater tip displacements as expected.

This concept of renormalization is useful when one wants to relate a measured or intuitive mode shape change to the mode shape specified in the analysis:

$$\Delta\psi_{i,\text{specified}} = \frac{\overline{\omega}_i}{\omega_i}\,\psi_{i,\text{observed}} - \psi_{i,\text{baseline}}$$

$$\Delta\psi_{i,\text{observed}} = \frac{\omega_i}{\overline{\omega}_i}\,\overline{\psi}_{i,\text{specified}} - \psi_{i,\text{baseline}}$$

where the baseline and specified modes have been normalized by unit generalized mass and the observed modes have been normalized by the constant strain energy concept referred to earlier.

Offshore light tower

A 442-element computer model of an offshore light tower, provided by the American Bureau of Shipping (ABS), was used to evaluate the utility of the perturbation equations (10) in the analysis of large complex structures. The perturbation equations when applied to simple structures provide usable results as evidenced by the last example and previous work [5, 7]; however, they have not been previously tested on large structural models.

Two basic studies were performed using the ABS offshore light tower. First, *model correlation* was attempted. The goal was to adjust the model so that the finite-element model produced natural frequencies which were in agreement with full-scale tower measurements. The second study examined the use of the perturbation equations for the *identification of a structural failure*.

Model correlation—Model correlation of this tower was attempted earlier in a study performed by ABS [8]. The ABS study considered several modeling parameters such as soil properties, marine growth, and ineffectiveness of concrete. Changes in these parameters were related to changes in the stiffness and mass of the structure. In the ABS study each parameter considered was varied and its effect on the tower model natural frequencies was measured. A set of "best" changes was selected for model correlation. The recomputed natural frequencies are given in Table 10.

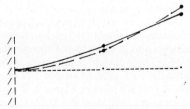

Fig. 5 Mode 1 for baseline and modified model normalized by unit generalized mass

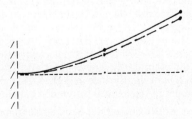

Fig. 6 Renormalization of Mode 1 by energy criterion

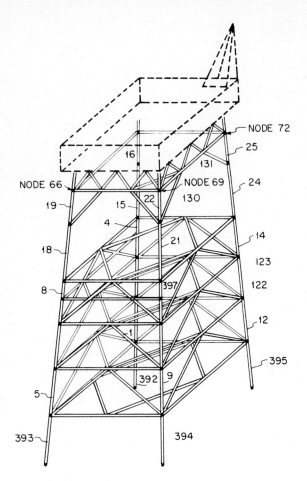

Fig. 7 Offshore light tower—computer model

Table 5 Perturbation influence normalized by frequency squared for Mode 1

Beam No.	Area	$I_2 + I_3$	Total
1	0.230	0.772	1.003
4	−0.118	1.276	1.158
5	−0.099	0.633	0.534
8	−0.121	0.957	0.836
9	0.195	0.960	1.155
12	−0.200	1.152	0.952
14	−0.431	2.325	1.894
15	−0.431	4.800	4.369
16	−0.723	1.988	1.265
18	−0.530	3.640	3.110
19	−0.592	1.514	0.922
21	−0.565	6.015	5.450
22	−0.874	2.494	1.620
24	−0.916	7.104	6.188
25	−1.011	2.960	1.948
122	1.009	0.007	1.016
123	1.001	0.008	1.009
130	1.000	0.133	1.133
131	0.968	0.145	1.113
392	7.709	3.957	11.666
393	1.013	3.274	4.287
394	7.722	4.851	12.573
395	1.016	5.755	6.771
397	−0.141	1.626	1.485
Sum	15.110	58.346	73.456

In the present study the perturbation equation (10) was developed from the baseline model supplied by ABS. Modal constraints used included only changes to the first three natural frequencies of the baseline model, since these frequencies were the only frequencies measured from the full-scale tower reported in reference [8]. Structural changes included in this analysis consisted of element stiffness and mass changes; changes to discrete lumped masses were not used.

The perturbation equations were used first to identify those parts of the structure which influenced the natural frequencies of each mode. Figure 7 illustrates those elements which exhibit a 1 percent or greater influence on the first three modes. The percent influence on the natural frequency of each mode of each member indicated is given in Tables 5, 6, and 7, respectively. For example, Element 394 has a 12.573 percent influence on $\Delta\omega_1^2$. This element, 394, also has the greatest effect on changing the natural frequency of Mode 1.

Many elements share the same geometric properties; consequently, for the correlation study it was decided that elements with the same geometry would be required to change together. For example, Element 394 uses Beam ID (beam geometry description) number 56. A review of the model description data set shows that four elements are described by Beam ID 56; they include elements 392–395 and represent a total influence of 35.3 percent on the natural frequency of Mode 1. Table 8 lists all of the Beam ID's of significance and gives their percent influence on changes to the natural frequencies of each mode.

Using the perturbation influence on terms from Table 8 and the specified frequency changes, one computes the "least

structural change" for each of the beam ID's. The results are given in Table 9. These structural changes were incorporated into the baseline model and the natural frequencies from the modified model were computed. Refer to Table 10 for a summary of computed results.

Several observations can be made on the results given in Table 9. First, assuming that the structural modifications made represent permissible changes, one could conclude that the perturbation equations, (11), do produce usable results at a (substantially) reduced cost. Furthermore, those elements which have been identified as the most influential with regard to natural frequency changes appear to be quite consistent with the ABS study (Elements 392–395) and agree with intuitively conceived expectations.

The fact that the ABS study does not produce results with the same accuracy as results of this study is not to the discredit of work performed by ABS, but rather serves as an important reminder that the permissibility of the structural change should be incorporated into the analysis. Perhaps if the perturbation method had been available and utilized in the ABS work, then their results could be improved.

Identification of a structural failure—Let us consider the use of the perturbation equations for the identification of a structural failure using the ABS-supplied light tower model. First the baseline model was used to represent the sound structure prior to experiencing a structural failure. Then a known defect in the structure is planted: the stiffness of one of the lower support members, Element 394, was degraded by 10 percent. Reducing the stiffness of this element was used to represent a structural failure of the baseline model. Next, the natural frequencies and mode shapes of the degraded structure were computed. These natural frequencies and mode shapes from the degraded structure were used to determine the actual effect of reducing the stiffness of Element 394 and to permit the collection of admissible modal data for use in the failure analysis. The frequencies for the sound baseline model and the degraded model are given in Table 11.

Model Perturbation Methods for Marine Structures

Table 6 Perturbation influence normalized by frequency squared for Mode 2

Beam No.	Area	$I_2 + I_3$	Total
1	−0.163	0.937	0.774
4	−0.163	1.505	1.342
5	0.221	0.863	1.084
8	−0.133	1.394	1.261
9	−0.150	0.869	0.719
12	0.215	0.888	1.102
14	−0.308	1.776	1.468
15	−0.767	5.594	4.827
16	−0.847	2.329	1.482
18	−0.501	5.302	4.801
19	−0.802	2.192	1.390
21	−0.713	5.098	4.385
22	−0.786	2.119	1.333
24	−0.516	5.418	4.902
25	−0.824	2.262	1.438
122	0.104	0.002	0.106
123	0.106	0.002	0.108
130	−0.049	0.054	0.005
131	−0.056	0.067	0.010
392	1.016	4.740	5.756
393	7.947	4.402	12.349
394	1.013	4.412	5.424
395	7.935	4.521	12.456
397	−0.155	1.348	1.193
Sum	11.622	58.093	69.715

Table 7 Perturbation influence normalized by frequency squared for Mode 3

Beam No.	Area	$I_2 + I_3$	Total
1	−0.404	1.419	1.015
4	−0.218	1.630	1.412
5	−0.529	1.776	1.248
8	−0.288	1.911	1.624
9	−0.349	1.251	0.902
12	−0.243	0.896	0.653
14	−0.284	1.436	1.152
15	−1.145	6.258	5.113
16	−1.203	2.553	1.350
18	−1.442	7.446	6.004
19	−1.502	3.039	1.537
21	−0.998	5.662	4.664
22	−1.054	2.309	1.256
24	−0.710	4.471	3.761
25	−0.756	1.830	1.075
122	0.361	0.004	0.365
123	0.377	0.004	0.381
130	0.228	0.147	0.375
131	0.290	0.127	0.417
392	0.219	6.377	6.596
393	0.008	8.038	8.046
394	0.227	5.592	5.819
395	0.010	3.939	3.949
397	−0.185	1.474	1.289
Sum	−9.589	69.589	60.000

Table 8 Percent influence on natural frequency

Structural Changes		Influence on Natural Frequency $\Delta\omega_i^2/\omega_i^2 \times 100$		
Beam ID	geometry parameter	Mode 1	Mode 2	Mode 3
1	area	1.476	1.364	2.765
1	moment of inertia	1.379	1.356	2.293
10	area	3.650	3.605	4.261
10	moment of inertia	0.049	0.005	0.069
11	area	−7.569	−7.718	−11.394
11	moment of inertia	30.537	30.334	33.607
56	area	17.459	17.91	0.463
56	moment of inertia	17.838	18.074	23.946
57	area	−1.609	−1.673	−5.085
57	moment of inertia	10.661	10.587	12.948
Sum		92.227	92.676	96.831

From Table 11 it is evident that Mode 1 exhibits the largest downward shift. It is also interesting to note that a frequency change of less than 1 percent may indicate that substantial structural degradation, 10 percent in this case, has occurred. This raises several questions from a feasibility standpoint. How accurately can such a small frequency change be detected? What percent reduction in stiffness will represent a threat to the structural integrity of the tower? Needless to say these are areas which require further study. Effort in this study is restricted to evaluating the ability of the perturbation equations to perform their task, that is, identification of a structural failure from measured modal changes.

Suppose modal changes measured in the x,z-plane, parallel to the water surface, are monitored at three positions. Nodes 66, 69, and 72 shown in Fig. 7 are the positions monitored in this pseudo case study. Mode changes for Mode 1 are presented in Table 12.

The perturbation influence terms were computed for each of the mode shape changes given in Table 12. Beam Elements 392, 393, 394, and 395 seemed to show the greatest influence on these mode shape changes, while the beams near the water surface exhibited secondary importance. Perturbation equations were formed for those beams exhibiting primary importance, Beams 392–395. Modal constraints included the $\Delta\psi_1$'s given in Table 12 as well as the frequency change, $\Delta\omega_1^2$, for Mode 1. The resulting perturbation equation is

$$\{\delta\} = [P]\{\alpha\}$$

Table 9 Structural change results

Beam ID	Geometry Parameter	% Change
1	area	2.8 increase
1	inertia	2.9 increase
10	area	8.7 increase
10	inertia	0.1 increase
11	area	16.9 decrease
11	inertia	74.1 increase
56	area	53.8 increase
56	inertia	41.4 increase
57	area	2.1 decrease
57	inertia	25.2 increase

Table 10 Comparison of recomputed natural frequencies

Mode	Baseline f_n	Baseline % Error	ABS f_n	ABS % Error	Present Analysis f_n	Present Analysis % Error	Measured f_n
1	0.931	−16.9	0.998	−10.9	1.069	−4.6	1.12
2	0.937	−16.3	1.004	−10.4	1.077	−3.4	1.12
3	1.230	−15.8	1.362	−6.7	1.387	−5.0	1.46
Relative Cost	$1.00		$22.20		$2.20		

NOTE: f_n given in hertz.

Table 11 Natural frequency changes due to degradation of Element 394

Mode	Sound Structure	Degraded Structure	Frequency Reduction
1	0.9306 Hz	0.9246 Hz	−0.64%
2	0.9367	0.9344	−0.25%
3	1.230	1.237	−0.24%

$$\begin{Bmatrix} -1.28675 \\ 0.001727 \\ -0.000961 \\ 0.001726 \\ -0.000963 \\ 0.001732 \\ -0.000963 \end{Bmatrix} =$$

$$\begin{bmatrix} 11.666 & 4.287 & 12.573 & 6.771 \\ -0.040484 & 0.035110 & -0.025300 & 0.030470 \\ 0.018714 & -0.019501 & 0.012652 & -0.013193 \\ -0.040477 & 0.035100 & -0.025310 & 0.030450 \\ 0.018994 & -0.015989 & 0.011743 & -0.014421 \\ -0.040180 & 0.038620 & -0.026220 & 0.02922 \\ 0.18894 & -0.015989 & 0.01732 & -0.014421 \end{bmatrix} \begin{Bmatrix} \alpha_{392} \\ \alpha_{393} \\ \alpha_{394} \\ \alpha_{395} \end{Bmatrix}$$

These equations can now be solved to determine the structural changes responsible for this modal change. The solution procedure, however, must be chosen with great care. A generalized inverse-type solution will select α's which produce a minimum error in the δ terms. Blindly applying this method produces the following structural changes:

Element Number	Stiffness Change
392	244 percent increase
393	47 percent decrease
394	295 percent decrease
395	140 percent increase

These results signal the need to place certain bounds on the results. First, an element can never lose more than 100 percent of its stiffness, therefore, stiffness changes should be constrained to be less than 100 percent. Second, it is difficult to imagine that a structure in service gains stiffness. Hence, another constraint is imposed which requires that the stiffness be allowed only to decrease.

To solve a problem with such inequality constraints as well as with equality constraints (the perturbation equations), one uses a mathematical programming technique. If one develops a cost function which is linear, then linear programming can be used and this was done. The following structural changes were determined:

Table 12 Measured Mode Shape 1 changes due to degradation of Element 394

Node	Direction	Sound Structure Displacements	Observed Change, %	$\Delta\psi$ Used in Analysis
66	x	0.0054507	32.5	0.001727
66	z	0.013529	−6.5	−0.000961
69	x	0.0054562	32.5	0.001726
69	z	0.016851	−5.1	−0.000963
72	x	0.008790	20.5	0.001732
72	z	0.016850	−5.1	−0.000963

Element Number	Stiffness Change
392	0 percent
393	0 percent
394	9.16 percent decrease
395	1.97 percent decrease

These results are not only believable, they are surprisingly accurate. Recall, the failure data were generated by reducing the stiffness of Element 394 by 10 percent.

While it is tempting to wave the flag of success, the use of this method should be approached with caution. This example has demonstrated that the perturbation equations can be used to help identify the location and magnitude of a structural failure by monitoring the modal changes of a structure. This example has also shown that blind application of equation solvers may not produce meaningful results. Furthermore, it was not until very late in the project that a workable relationship between mode shape changes and structural changes was found; hence, more test cases involving failure analysis should be performed. It should be added, however, that the numerical experiment just described represents the first and only attempt at failure analysis on this light tower and it was highly successful. Although the authors do not claim that this method will find all structural failures, they are confident that the method can be used to identify many "probable" failure locations.

Perturbation techniques could be used in concert with acoustic emission techniques for structural monitoring. The acoustic emission would process rapid structural changes while the perturbation techniques would analyze the slow or "quiet" structural changes.

Further reading relevant to failure identification can be found in references [10–15].

Conclusions

1. The perturbation equations presented in this paper do provide a meaningful and useable relationship between modal changes and structural changes.

2. Structural redesign for small frequency changes is obtainable with the help of the perturbation equations at a substantially reduced cost.

Model Perturbation Methods for Marine Structures

3. Structural redesign for small mode shape changes has been demonstrated directly through the cantilever beam example and indirectly through the pseudo failure analysis of an offshore light tower.

4. Perturbation equations can be used to assist in the identification of probable structural failures by monitoring modal changes.

We feel that this method is of significant value to engineers. Consequently, the authors have included this method in their structural courses. The method is now being taught at the senior and graduate level and the student reaction has been most favorable. For years they have been learning how to detect vibration problems and now they are learning how to fix them.

Work on the inverse perturbation method is continuing. We are presently developing an improved formulation which includes the accuracy of the nonlinear terms and retains the efficiency of the first-order solution given in this paper. Furthermore, we are developing computer codes to perform perturbation analysis. Algorithms associated with the SAP programs and NASTRAN's DMAP facility are being programmed. We anticipate that "sailor-proof" algorithms will be available to the industry within the next two to five years.

Acknowledgment

Support for the development of the perturbation methods described herein has been provided by the Ship Structure Committee under their University Research Grant and Scholarship Program and by the National Science Foundation under Grant MEA 8019642.

The Ambrose Light Tower data provided by the American Bureau of Shipping, the support provided by the University of Michigan, and the typing of this manuscript by Mrs. Paula Bousley are also very much appreciated.

References

1 Stetson, K. A., Harrison, I. R., and Cassenti, B. N., "Redesign of Structural Vibration Modes by Finite Element Inverse Perturbation," United Technologies Research Center Final Report R78-992945, Feb. 1978.

2 Stetson, K. A., Harrison, I. R., and Palma, G. E., "Redesigning Structural Vibration Modes by Inverse Perturbation Subject to Minimal Change Theory," *Computer Methods in Applied Mechanics and Engineering*, 1978, pp. 151–175.

3 Stetson, K. A. and Harrison, I. R., "Redesign of Structural Vibration Modes by Finite Element Inverse Perturbation," American Society of Mechanical Engineers Gas Turbine Conference and Products Show, New Orleans, Paper No. 80-GT-167, March 1980.

4 Stetson, K. A., "Perturbation Method of Structural Design Relevant to Holographic Vibration Analysis," *AIAA Journal*, Vol. 13, No. 4, April 1975, pp. 457–459.

5 Stetson, K. A. and Palma, G. E., "Inversion of First Order Perturbation Theory and Its Application to Structural Design," *AIAA Journal*, Vol. 14, No. 4, April 1976.

6 Noble, B., *Applied Linear Algebra*, Prentice-Hall, Englewood Cliffs, N.J., 1969, pp. 142–146.

7 Sandström, R. E., "Inverse Perturbation Methods for Vibration Analysis," *Proceedings*, NATO Advanced Study Institute on Optimization of Distributed Parameter Structural System, University of Iowa, May 20–June 4, 1980.

8 Wojnarowski, M. E., Stiansen, S. G., and Reddy, N. E., "Structural Integrity Evaluation of a Fixed Platform Using Vibration Criteria," Paper No. OTC 2909, Ninth Annual Offshore Technology Conference, Houston, May 1977.

9 Bathe, K. J. and Wilson, E. L., *Numerical Methods in Finite Element Analysis*, Prentice-Hall, Englewood Cliffs, N.J., 1976.

10 Coward, L. and Savage, R. J., "SHRIMP—a companion paper to VIBRATIONS—SOME OTHER ASPECTS," SNAME, Pacific Northwest Section, Oct. 14, 1978.

11 Dobbs, M. W., Blakely, K. D., and Gundy, W. E., "System Identification of Large Scale Structures," Society of Automotive Engineers Technical Paper Series (811050), Aerospace Congress and Exposition, Anaheim, Calif., Oct. 5–8, 1981.

12 Vandiver, J. K., "Detection of Structural Failure on Fixed Platforms by Measurement of Dynamic Response," Paper No. OTC 2267, Seventh Annual Offshore Technology Conference, Houston, May 1975.

13 Mittleman, J. and Wyman D. B., "Underwater Inspections: Credibility and Technology," Paper No. OTC 4030, Thirteenth Annual Offshore Technology Conference, Houston, May 1981.

14 Lepert, P., Chay, M., Heas, J., and Narzul, P., "Vibro-Detection Applied to Offshore Platforms," Paper No. OTC 3918, Twelfth Annual Offshore Technology Conference, Houston, May 1980.

15 Rubin, S., "Damage Detection in Offshore Structures by Vibration Measurements," U.S. Geological Survey Open-File Report 81-704.

Discussion

W. Page Glennie, Member

[The views expressed herein are the opinions of the discusser and not necessarily those of the Department of Defense or the Department of the Navy.]

I would like to commend the authors for their excellent work in developing this design tool, which I was first introduced to while attending courses taught by the authors at the University of Michigan. I have applied their technique to solve simple problems similar to the two-element beam example illustrated in the paper.

This technique is a very valuable tool for vibration analysis to help both the design engineer and fleet support engineer. It permits the calculation of a participation factor for each structural member, thereby determining which member will have the greatest change upon the natural frequencies or mode shapes versus the required weight increase. In the past, the critical member has been estimated using engineering judgment. The method incorporates both forward and inverse perturbation techniques, enabling the engineer to determine the changes caused or required by mass, stiffness, natural frequency, or mode shape changes.

The power of the technique lies in the linear formulation providing for the use of available optimization methods and in the uncoupling of the natural frequencies and mode shapes. The natural frequency perturbation is straightforward; however, the mode shape perturbation is complicated by the selection of the mode participation terms.

The Navy will realize the most utility from the method in the area of mast design and modification. Vibration problems can be determined prior to construction or modification and solved by the most effective means, thereby minimizing topside weight. Due to the numerous antenna changes and mast rearrangements during a naval vessel's service life, the technique should be very valuable to the Navy.

The authors have developed, for the Ship Structure Committee, a computer program of the method which performs forward or inverse perturbation as well as optimization. The program has recently been installed in the NAVSEA VAX computer; however, it has not been verified or used to date.

This method is a major advance in the area of vibration analysis—of as much importance as the finite-element techniques.

Peter M. Palermo, Member

[The views expressed herein are the opinions of the discusser and not necessarily those of the Department of Defense or the Department of the Navy.]

Weight reduction is the goal in any ship design, but reduction of high weight is essential for stability purposes. Therefore, mast structures are closely scrutinized for vibratory characteristics at all stages of the design. Even though every possible precaution is taken in the design stage, vibration problems have been encountered during a ship's first sea trial. The resulting back-fix can be of sufficient weight high up in the ship as to cause serious concern for service life stability characteristics and therefore require more periodic inclinings or removal of other items. Individual cases such as this, though undesirable and expensive, can be coped with. However, warship requirements are such that changing threats and technology advances usually mean not only newer but more mast-mounted sensors being installed during the 25 or more years of service life of the ship.

Relocation of antenna and addition of other sensors can change the vibration characteristics of the ship. In addition, advances in other ship systems and/or structural modifications can alter the vibration frequencies of the hull girder. In the past, these "facts of life" problems associated with capability improvements caused many a designer's hair to turn gray. But more importantly it is safe to say that they resulted in brute-force back-fits that did the job but were less than optimum. Therefore the ship and/or other ship characteristics were penalized.

The authors offer a ray of hope for the solution of these real-life problems. Tools exist for initial design considerations, but this discusser wants better tools for back-fit design problems. The authors are offering such a tool. Final opinion must await actual evaluation, and verification.

Bruce L. Hutchison, Member

The authors have presented an interesting paper that should increase the effectiveness with which the profession can analyze and design structures subject to vibration constraints.

While the theory presented should work well for the numerous problems of marine structures vibrating in air, and in many instances for those deeply submerged, it may not be capable of addressing structures vibrating at or near the free surface. This is because, as is well known, the gravity wave systems generated by the vibrating structure result in frequency-dependent hydrodynamic coefficients for added mass and damping. In the presence of frequency-dependent coefficients the equations of motion in the time domain must be expressed in terms of convolution integrals.

I observe that the authors have made use of standard finite-element structural programs. Unfortunately most standard finite-element structural programs are not designed to handle frequency-dependent coefficients or convolution integrals.

More serious for the application of the current methods, the eigenvalues and eigenvectors exist, in a sense, but they cannot be obtained through the usual methods. Also, the eigenvectors do not form an orthogonal basis in the usual sense for use in renormalizing the equation system. These difficulties may, I suspect, restrict the immediate usefulness of this approach to those marine vibration problems that do not involve frequency-dependent coefficients.

A most useful application if it were possible would be the inverse regression problem to correlate with field data and thereby obtain improved analytical models including improved estimates of the hydrodynamic coefficients.

I would like the authors to comment on the possibilities for extending their work to include vibration problems involving frequency-dependent coefficients.

Schelte Hylarides,[4] Visitor

I would like to compliment the authors on this work, which I expect will prove to be a milestone in the development of theoretical tools to handle the dynamics of complex structures. I hope that their "sailor-proof" algorithms will soon be available.

Before getting it sailor-proof, I think that some more clarification of the underlying approximations is needed. One such approximation is that, for the new eigenvectors, $[\phi']$ the following relationship is used with the old eigenvectors:

$$[\phi'] = [\phi]([I] + [C])^T$$
$$= [\phi][C^*]^T$$

where $C^*_{ii} = 1$ and $C^*_{ij} = C_{ij}$ as mentioned by the authors. My main difficulty lies in the fact that the diagonal terms of this C^*-matrix equal one. Theoretically this is not true, as is explained in the following.

The original construction has its normal modes along the n-axes of the principal coordinate system. The modified structure is still in this n-dimensional space, but its principal coordinate system differs from the first set of axes. This new set, however, originates from the original one by a shift of the origin and a rotation around the new origin. Now the shift does not alter the mode patterns along each axis, but the rotation does. From this latter follows that essentially the new mode "i" can contain only a portion of the original mode "i." Therefore, of the C^*-matrix the diagonal terms are essentially different from one. They will in fact be less than one.

For small structural changes, however, this rotation of the principal co-ordinate system is done over a small angle. Therefore one may expect that the diagonal terms of the C^*-matrix differ a little from one. A good approximation is then obtained by putting these diagonal terms equal to one.

Because this approximation is one of the most essential assumptions in the theory, one may expect that the authors should have proven the validity of it. In my opinion this proof should have been included in the paper and I hope that they will be able to include it in their closure to the discussions.

Donald Liu, Member

The forward procedure, which is used to measure the effect of structural changes on the natural frequencies and mode shapes, has been known for some time, and the use of it is rather straightforward. The inverse procedure, however, is much more difficult and the approach proposed by the authors illustrates that the perturbation equations, when properly used, can be both computationally economical and accurate in transforming the desired frequency and modal changes into structural changes.

It should be noted, however, that since the changes (or perturbation) in the perturbation equations are confined to being small, as indicated by the authors, their applications to model correlation and failure identification may not always be possible. Structural modeling by the finite-element method often involves approximations, idealization and assumptions which may very well contribute to discrepancies between frequency measurements of the real structure and predictions of the structural model. Furthermore, for a complex structure with a high degree of redundancy, such as the offshore light tower presented in the paper, failure in a secondary member may not result in any significant or even noticeable change in

[4] Maritime Research Institute (MARIN), Wageningen, The Netherlands.

frequencies, particularly in the lower modes. Even if a small frequency change, say one tenth of a percent, can be detected, failure identification is still a formidable task when taking into account all members in the structure. The failure can be in any secondary member or any combination of such members.

In the example application of the light tower, the authors use only the four major supporting members (Elements 392–395) in the perturbation equations, which, as indicated by the authors, may yield undesirable and sometimes unreasonable results and therefore some inequality constraints are to be placed on the solution. It would be beneficial if the authors could elaborate more on how they eventually arrived at the prespecified structural changes in this case. Imagine the situation when considering all 422 members together.

For the inverse perturbation method to be accurate in failure detection, the structural failure has to be of considerable magnitude, which would require a modal perturbation method that would be applicable to large structural changes. As the authors indicate, they are developing an approach in this direction. Finally, for a tall structure, the geometric nonlinear effects may be important, which would not be reflected in the linear elastic perturbation equations presented in this paper. Further study in this area is needed.

H. Matthies,[5] Visitor

Perturbation methods make it possible for the important question of design rather than just analysis of a given system to be addressed. As the authors demonstrate, the method may also be used for parameter identification, which is another important topic.

A word of caution has to be added though. The procedure as it is formulated in the paper fails on structures with equal eigenvalues, that is, when there are several eigenvectors with identical natural frequencies. Expressed mathematically, the eigenvectors are then only uniquely determined with othogonal invariance of the eigenspace. It is obvious that the matrix $[\lambda_i]$ in equation (9) will not exist in this case.

Marine structures often exhibit spatial symmetries which automatically result in multiple eigenvalues, so this case is of practical relevance. It should not be hard to extend the procedure to this case, however, as this problem was encountered and solved some time ago (see reference [16], p. 296) (additional reference follows this discussion). This extension would permit treatment of the very interesting symmetry-breaking perturbations in such spatially symmetric structures.

Additional reference

16 Courant, R. and Hilbert, D., *Methoden den mathematischen Physik I*; 3rd ed., Springer-Verlag, Berlin, 1968.

F. Everett Reed, Member

My first comment is that I will have to do a lot of studying of the basic references before I understand the theory well enough to apply it effectively.

My second comment is that I can see how the procedures that are developed can be very helpful for the three types of problems mentioned by the authors, namely,

1. structural redesign to change natural frequencies and mode shapes,
2. correlation of calculations with measurements, and
3. failure analysis.

Let us consider its application to typical problems that might arise in ship hull vibration:

(a) A ship during her trial run is found to vibrate badly. During the design process the problem of vibration was treated in a superficial manner and so there are no analyses to guide

[5] Germanischer Lloyd, Hamburg.

the engineer who is called upon to correct the trouble.

For this case the time and cost required to develop a finite-element model and apply the analysis could well be prohibitive.

(b) A ship has a problem with longitudinal vibration of the shafting. The problem had been studied in the design stage, and the recommendation has been made that careful attention be given to the rigidity of the thrust bearing foundation. The foundation is rigid. A finite-element study had been made of the machinery space with the objective of avoiding response to propeller excitation at the stern. This study showed a mode of vibration in which the vibration pattern had a node between the forward and after bulkheads. Although the frequency of this mode was close to the blade frequency, it was expected that there would be low coupling with the vertical excitation from the propeller. The perturbation process would not have pointed out the obvious, after it happened, coupling of the bottom with longitudinal motion of the shaft.

(c) As a ship approaches full speed, the vibration level throughout the ship seems to be high with no apparent peaks with frequency. The perturbation study would not indicate that the trouble comes from high excitation by the propeller.

(d) In the vibration analysis of a ship the predictions indicate that there will be a large vibration on the bridge at just less than full power. In this case, assume that a good finite-element model of the structure has been developed. The perturbation analysis could be valuable in finding which elements should be changed to give an acceptable level of predicted vibration.

What are the alternatives? At the present time the search for a fix would involve reviewing the mode shape for the vibration in question to find out regions where the potential energy of deformation is particularly large. The possibilities of modifying the structure in this region would be considered and a new calculation made. I would expect that the perturbation program, as presently developed, would not give information on the effects upon vibration of adding additional structure.

My final comment relating to ship vibration is that most troubles with ship vibration occur because inadequate effort has been made to minimize them in the design stage. Shipbuilders are very cost conscious when it comes to studies for minimizing hull vibration. There are aversions to making the thorough analysis that requires a development of a good finite-element model of a ship. The additional cost of perturbation analyses might be difficult to find. The most inhibiting factor in developing good procedures for predicting vibrations is that there are very few measurements taken on ships that have been carefully analyzed.

Authors' Closure

Mr. Glennie and Mr. Palermo: The authors appreciate the favorable comments from Mr. Glennie and Mr. Palermo and agree that the method should be useful for redesign of masts. Our goal has been to make the method applicable to "real" engineering design of structures composed of beam, plate and truss members. It is most satisfying to learn that the U.S. Navy is in the process of implementing modal perturbation procedures for mast design as a result of our work.

Mr. Hutchison: The method at present does not apply to systems with frequency-dependent coefficients. The authors are not certain this extension is possible, although desirable, because of our dependence upon classical modes and frequencies as our building blocks. We will keep this extension in mind, however, in future research.

Dr. Hylarides has commented on the normalization of the perturbed eigenvectors, as seen in the diagonal terms of the C_{ij} matrix. It is true that our perturbed eigenvectors differ from unity by a small amount for small modal and structural changes. The magnitude of the perturbed eigenvector is arbitrarily normalized, and the fact that the vector differs slightly from unity does not present a problem within the context of small changes. For large modal changes, as studied in work following this paper, vector length is considered.

Dr. Liu has correctly pointed out a problem area when the linear perturbation method is used for failure identification, where the failure is in a minor member. The effect of the failure might not influence the measured modes and frequencies. Fortunately, the probability of finding a failure location is higher for more important members. It is likely that a failing member which seriously degrades the strength of the structure will measurably affect some of the vibration modes and should also have substantial perturbation influence coefficients. As a result, the shortcoming of the method is somewhat compensated for in terms of low need.

Dr. Liu has also identified a limitation of the method in the "large change" region. For the case when a structural member has failed completely, the linear method will not predict the correct magnitude of the failure; however, it should identify the member as a suspicious candidate. We believe the method is accurate for structural changes in mass and stiffness from 0 to 15 percent. It can also be used in an approximate sense, or with several incremental redesigns of up to 30 percent change. Current research, involving more complicated equation solvers, is allowing large changes in the redesign problem at increased computational cost. Improved procedures for the large-change problem are currently under study at the University of Michigan.

The light tower example did involve consideration of all 422 members as implied in the paper. Perturbation influence terms were computed for all members; however, only those elements exhibiting primary importance, Beams 392, 393, 394, and 395, were used to form the inverse perturbation equations for this problem.

Dr. Matthies has correctly pointed out a limitation of the method, as currently formulated. The method in its current form will not allow perturbations to a structure with repeated eigenvalues. Fortunately, many problems encountered in practice process *some* degree of asymmetry; hence repeated eigenvalues do not usually appear. Dr. Matthies points out that the procedure can be extended to cover symmetric structures with repeated eigenvalues, and it is out intention to do so in future versions of the algorithm.

Mr. Reed: The authors would like to thank Mr. Reed for posing some practical problems which can be used to emphasize proper uses of the perturbation methods.

It is important to remember that the perturbation method is an engineering tool for structural redesign. The user must first identify the required modal changes and then the method can be used to predict the structural changes (in the inverse solution). The method does not identify the vibration problem; this responsibility belongs to the designer.

One must also keep in mind the fact that structural redesign is not the only cure for a vibration problem. Minimizing excitation is an option that cannot be ignored.

One of the objections commonly expressed is the need to generate complex models before the perturbation method can be used; however, this is not necessarily true. The method can be applied to simplified models, the results from which can be used to identify regions within the structure where redesign would be most effective as well as some indication of the stiffness and mass change required within each region.

The authors would like to thank the Society for giving them the opportunity to present a paper on such a technically important topic: modal perturbation methods. The effort expended by the discussers of this paper is also greatly appreciated. Their comments have helped to emphasize strengths and weaknesses of the perturbation methods presented herein.

We are pleased by the interest shown in the marine community in modal perturbation methods. The fact that the U.S. Navy is now installing perturbation programs on their computing systems for mast redesign is the kind of response we find most encouraging.

Improvements to the methods presented in this paper are under development. We hope that we can continue to work with the marine community in an effort to derive maximum benefits from the modal perturbation methods.

SNAME *Transactions*, Vol. 90, 1982, pp. 55–83

Preliminary Design Estimation of Hull Girder Response to Slamming

J. Harvey Evans,[1] Honorary Member/Fellow

In an era of high-speed ships and tight schedules, it is important that hull girder whipping stresses be reckoned with. Studies with a proven lumped-mass-model computer program emphasize the importance of the slam center location and the distributions of ship and added masses. The distribution of bending stiffness (*EI*) is of less importance but has special significance for hull bending moments at about the ship's quarter-lengths. Variations in the magnitudes of slam impact loading, ship mass, added mass and hull girder stiffness are shown to conform to the nondimensional relationships of dynamic load factor theory between bending moments and the ratio of slam duration to hull vibration period. Finally, a semi-empirical expression is presented which may be useful for estimating whipping bending moments amidships in the early stages of preliminary design.

Introduction

IN 1978, a paper was presented before this Society on the subject of hull girder stiffness [1].[2] It attempted to catalog the undesired results of too little or too much stiffness and isolated the girder response to slamming and springing as those aspects most necessary to be taken into account in the preliminary stages of design. Thereafter, the paper was confined to an investigation of slamming response based upon results using a proven lumped-mass-model computer study [2] with four different types of ship: a Mariner cargo vessel, a 330.74-m (1085 ft) tanker, a 243.84-m (800 ft) bulk carrier and a Great Lakes ore carrier (Appendix 1). It was concluded that a ship's hull girder, when struck by a half-sine pulse representing a slam, responds in a manner which is essentially predictable by means of dynamic load factor (DLF) theory. Furthermore, uniform proportional changes in the *EI* product from end to end of the girder cross section do not destroy conformity of the response to the ship's own particular nondimensional DLF curve, all other load characteristics remaining constant. It remains, then, to establish the means of defining the DLF signature for any particular ship and its specific loading from which whipping bending moments may be determined and from them the whipping stresses.

Before going further, better definition will be given to the terms and the procedures used.

Dynamic load factors

As discussed in [3, 4, 5] and in detail in Appendix 2, the differential equation of motion for the vibratory response of a mass and spring system, having a single degree of freedom, and acted upon by a force varying with time, may be expressed as

$$m \ddot{x} + c \dot{x} + k x = P(t) \tag{1}$$

where

  m = vibrating mass
  c = a damping coefficient
  k = spring constant
  $P(t)$ = forcing function variable with time

Having chosen a half-sine impulse as that most suitable to represent a slam, then

$$P(t) = P_1 \sin\Omega t$$

while the force is applied, that is, when $0 \le \Omega t \le \pi$, that is

$$0 \le t \le \frac{\pi}{\Omega} \text{ or } 0 \le t \le t_1$$

$$\text{and } P(t) = 0$$

after it is removed, that is, when

$$t > \frac{\pi}{\Omega} \text{ or } t > t_1$$

where

  P_1 = maximum value of forcing function impulse
  Ω = circular frequency of loading (that is, $\Omega = \pi/t_i$)
  t_1 = impulse duration

If x_0 is the static deflection which would be produced by the peak load P_1, then

$$x_0 = \frac{P_1}{k} = \frac{P_1}{m \left(\dfrac{2\pi}{T}\right)^2} = \frac{P_1 T^2}{4\pi^2 m} \tag{7}$$

where T is the natural period of vibration of the system and m is the vibrating mass.

Now if $x(t)$ is the instantaneous dynamic displacement, its nondimensional form may ultimately be expressed as

$$\frac{x(t)}{x_0} = \frac{2}{\dfrac{4t_1}{T} - \dfrac{T}{t_1}} \left\{ \frac{2t_1}{T} \sin\frac{\pi t}{t_1} - \sin\frac{2\pi t}{T} \right\} \tag{2e}$$

$$\text{for } 0 \le t \le t_1$$

[1] Emeritus professor of naval architecture, Massachusetts Institute of Technology, Cambridge, Massachusetts.
[2] Numbers in brackets designate References at end of paper.
Presented at the Annual Meeting, New York, N. Y., November 17–20, 1982, of THE SOCIETY OF NAVAL ARCHITECTS AND MARINE ENGINEERS.

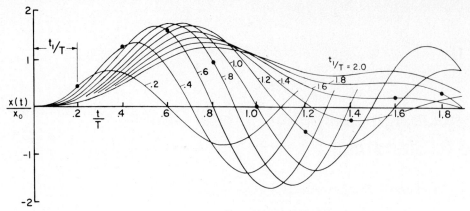

Fig. 1 Response of a system of one degree of freedom to a half-sine pulse of duration t_1

and

$$\frac{x(t)}{x_0} = \frac{-2}{\frac{4t_1}{T} - \frac{T}{t_1}} \left\{ \sin\frac{2\pi t}{T} + \sin\frac{2\pi}{T}(t - t_1) \right\} \quad (2f)$$

$$\text{for } t > t_1$$

Figure 1, taken from St. Denis [4], shows the variation of these nondimensional displacements as a function of time for several values of t_1/T.

For many purposes of structural analysis, it is the maximum values which are of interest. By the usual means, these maxima are found to be, when $t_1/T \leq 0.50$:

$$\left[\frac{x(t)}{x_0}\right]_{max} = \frac{-2}{\frac{4t_1}{T} - \frac{T}{t_1}} \left\{ \sin\pi\left(\frac{1}{2} + \frac{t_1}{T}\right) \right.$$

$$\left. + \sin\pi\left(\frac{1}{2} - \frac{t_1}{T}\right) \right\} \quad (2h)$$

and, when $t_1/T > 0.50$:

$$\left[\frac{x(t)}{x_0}\right]_{max} = \frac{2}{\frac{4t_1}{T} - \frac{T}{t_1}} \left\{ \frac{2t_1}{T} \sin\pi\left[\frac{2\left(\frac{t_1}{T}\right)^2}{1 + \frac{2t_1}{T}}\right] \right.$$

$$\left. - \sin\pi\left[\frac{\frac{4t_1}{T}}{1 + \frac{2t_1}{T}}\right] \right\} \quad (2g)$$

Figure 2 is a graphical representation of these nondimensional maxima, which are the quantities usually given the name of "dynamic load factors." They are, in words, ratios of the maximum dynamic displacement to that displacement produced by the same peak load when applied statically.

For comparison, DLF curves for other than the half-sine pulse shape have been added to Fig. 2. They were taken from Frankland [3]. It is noteworthy that those pulses having an instantaneous time rise (such as the blast and rectangular impulses) ultimately converge upon a value of two, whereas elongating the duration of the three with a gradual time rise causes a peaking of the DLF curves and, ultimately, convergence on a value of one. The DLF curve for the blast pulse when given a gradual rise time, and defined in terms of[3] t_0 rather than t_1, is strikingly similar to that for the first pulse shown in Fig. 2, but with smaller secondary humps, after $t_1/T = 1$.

Because of the direct one-to-one relationship between a structural loading and the bending moment (as well as, and in addition to, the deflection response), it follows that stresses too should be subject to the same magnification factors between the dynamic and static cases as are the deflections themselves.

Dynamic load factors and the hull girder

The limitations of dynamic load factor theory, as reviewed in Appendix 2, made it appropriate to examine its suitability for application to a structure such as a ship's hull girder. For example, even structures much less complex depart in principle from the concept of simple systems having but one degree of freedom. Frankland [3] points out that even an ideally simple system does not conform when the impulse is of extremely short duration. He also notes that when a system has many degrees of freedom the DLF may vary with the point at which the impulse is applied and the DLF for bending may not be the

---

[3] The time t_0 is to the peak value of the pulse, P_1.

Nomenclature

C_{AM} = added-mass coefficient
C_B = block coefficient
C_{BS} = buoyancy spring coefficient
C_{EI} = bending stiffness coefficient
C_{WP} = waterplane coefficient
E = modulus of elasticity, psi
I = moment of inertia, in.$^2 \times$ ft^2
L = length of ship
l = distance from impact center to effective fulcrum point; that is, effective

moment arm, ft
M_s = slam or whipping bending moment, ton·ft
$M_s(\text{⊗})$ = slam or whipping bending moment amidships, tons
m = vibrating mass
P_1 = maximum value of forcing function impulse; that is peak value of impulsive loading, tons
p = distance from impact center to the

forward perpendicular, ft
T = natural first mode period of vibration, sec
t = time, sec
t_1 = impulse or slam duration, sec
t_0 = time to peak load, P_1, sec
x_0 = static deflection produced by peak load, P_1
$x(t)$ = instantaneous dynamic displacement

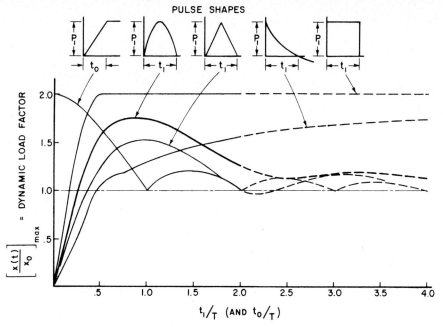

Fig. 2 Dynamic load factors

same for shear. Nevertheless, in certain time domains, the fundamental mode of vibration may be sufficiently uncoupled from higher modes and be so predominant that it would be legitimate, by means of the DLF, to replace the dynamic load with an equivalent static load and continue with the procedures of estimation and analysis thus simplified, which that conversion implies.

Studies with ships

Limited though such an elementary structural model is, an examination of four ships for which sufficient computed data were available from the Kline-Clough program with lumped masses indicated that the hull girder structural response conformed extremely well with the character of the nondimensional dynamic load factor curves [1]. With all other factors unchanged, the plotted points for five slam durations for each of five variations of hull bending stiffness lay on a well-defined curve having a form strongly reminiscent of a theoretical DLF curve for the half-sine shape of a slam pulse assumed. Figure 3 is a sample, that is, for one ship, while Fig. 4 shows those for the four ships together.[4] The impulse magnitude in all cases was 100 ton·sec.

On the evidence of Fig. 4, there is a distinct order and a measured separation relating these DLF curves which suggest

[4] It will be found that the curve for the tanker differs from that shown for the same vessel in Figs. 22 and 25 of [1]. In searching for an explanation for the strangeness of the tanker curve as plotted originally, a careful review of [6] and the graphical data inherited from that study indicated incorrect labeling of the slam durations on the graphical output. Correspondingly, incorrect values of the peak loads were also used originally. Of course, the fundamental conclusion regarding the usefulness of the DLF curves is unimpaired.

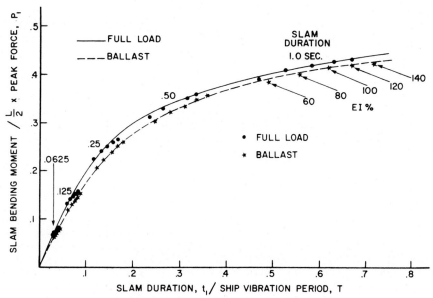

Fig. 3 Nondimensional whipping moments—bulk carrier *Fotini-L*, as built

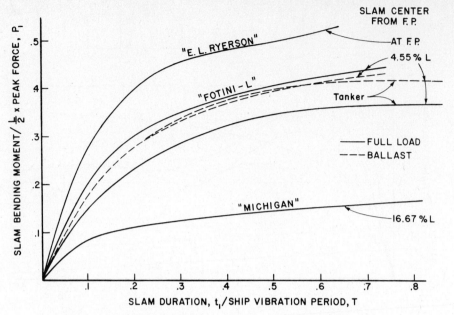

Fig. 4 Nondimensional whipping moments—four diverse ships, as built

that the location of the impact center is an important factor in the arrangement of the resulting nondimensional bending moments (DLF curves).

Vibratory response factors

From vibration theory and a review of the input parameters for the Kline-Clough computer program, a list of factors relevant to vibratory response would include the following:

1. slam center location
2. ship mass magnitude
3. added-mass magnitude
4. "buoyancy spring" stiffness
5. ship mass distribution
6. added mass distribution
7. bending stiffness (EI) magnitude
8. bending stiffness (EI) distribution
9. shear stiffness distribution
10. bottom stiffness at impact point
11. damping

Damping was mentioned in earlier discussions and eliminated from further consideration because its effects are minimal during the very first vibratory cycles when whipping, a transient response, is greatest.

Nor is bottom stiffness a significant consideration. It had been included in earlier work [2, 6, 7] in attempts to discriminate between slams centered at a stiff transverse bulkhead, or midway between two of them, but very little effect could be found. As the response was minutely greater with the softer bottom condition, it was adopted throughout the series of calculations considered here.

Shear stiffness is a very minor component of the total girder stiffness and has been taken as the same fixed fraction of the bending stiffness with all four ships so nothing can be attributed to that as an influence except as related to the bending stiffness itself.

Changes in bending stiffness were covered previously [1]. For each computer run the ship's actual EI-values were multiplied at all stations by the factor for the particular stiffness then under investigation. The alignment of those data points along a very narrow band is typified by Fig. 3 for the bulk carrier *Fotini-L*.

The remaining items of the preceding list (1 through 6 and 8) were therefore selected for study using the *Fotini-L* characteristics as a base of departure but were not limited to them. In fact, the range of variation extended to unrealistic values of each parameter in order to cover all ship cases likely to be encountered. One of these parameters at a time was systematically varied and three locations of the slam center were used with each: at 4.55, 13.64, and 22.73 percent of the ship's length between perpendiculars. Four combinations of slam duration and peak force for the 100-ton·sec impulse were used, in all cases, in order to delineate adequately the DLF response curves.

Slam center location

Figure 5 is for the *Fotini-L* as built and the slam applied at the three evenly spaced locations at the bow. Having adopted a constant slam impulse and, what is more, a constant (but different) peak force at each slam duration, it is noteworthy that at the longer durations the bending moments produced are very closely related linearly to the shifting position of the slam center.

As shown in [1], the largest whipping bending moments are to be found in association with small dynamic load factors. If such very-short-duration impulses (0.0625 sec) have a significant probability of occurrence, conditions at the origin, particularly the slope, would be of special interest and should be given considerable attention ultimately in trying to formulate a sound and adequate means of estimating whipping response. The disposition of the DLF curves at the origin is evidently not so linearly related to the slam center location as it is for the longer durations. In fact, if the maximum bending moment anywhere within the midship 40 percent of length is used rather than the bending moment exactly amidships, the lowest DLF curve, near the origin, tends to rise up and override the middle curve. In other words, the bending moments at some point within the midship 40 percent, with short duration slams applied well aft of the forward perpendicular (FP), may be larger than those produced within the 40 percent L amidships by slams applied farther forward.

The accumulated midship-bending-moment-versus-time output reveals that the higher-order vibratory modes are

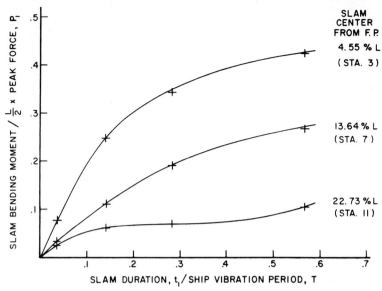

Fig. 5 Nondimensional whipping moments—bulk carrier *Fotini-L* (as built), slam locations varied

prevalent throughout the slam duration range when the slam center approaches the nodal point of the fundamental mode, whereas their presence is seen only at the short slam durations when the slam center is closer to the ship's forward perpendicular. Only the fundamental mode is much in evidence with long durations centered remote from the nodal point. The irregularity of the response, due to the varying intensity and shifting combinations of the higher orders, is reflected to some degree in the DLF curves for a slam center at 22.73 percent *L*. Additional data points would probably show it to be even more irregular, but bending moment and stress magnitudes are obviously smaller and of less consequences with DLF curves for slam locations so far aft.

Ship mass magnitude

Without changing the longitudinal distribution, the full-load displacement lumped masses of the ship were doubled to pro-

duce Fig. 6. The same DLF curves for the *Fotini-L*, as built (Fig. 5), are superimposed and show almost no measurable differences although the data points defining the two sets are displaced as a reflection of the change in ship's vibration period and attendant altered response.

Added-mass magnitude

When the added mass was doubled in similar fashion, and without any other parameter being changed, the results shown in Fig. 7 were produced. Again the DLF curves defined were not significantly different from the originals.

"Buoyancy spring" stiffness

The "buoyancy spring" stiffness is a measure of the added buoyancy for a unit increase of displacement from point to point so it is directly related to the fullness of the waterplane,

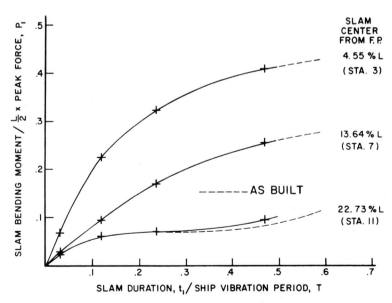

Fig. 6 Nondimensional whipping moments—bulk carrier *Fotini-L*, ship masses doubled

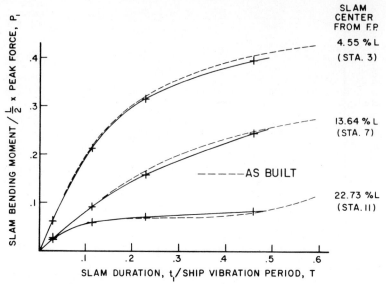

Fig. 7 Nondimensional whipping moments—bulk carrier *Fotini-L*, added masses doubled

or to the "tons per inch," on a segmented basis. Once the ship's breadth is taken into account it is the *shape* of the waterplane which next matters most.

Normalized waterplane distributions for the four ships of this study are given in Fig. 8. The *Fotini-L* happens to typify the fullest waterline likely to be found in oceangoing vessels, having a "buoyancy spring coefficient," C_{BS} (or waterplane coefficient, C_{WP}), of 0.88. The *Michigan* is at the other extreme and with slight modification, as given in Fig. 9, its waterplane was adopted for the fine distribution. In that case $C_{BS} = 0.69$. No matter how unlikely the combination, this waterplane was also used, with all other characteristics being true to the *Fotini-L*. Earlier results and reason indicated very little sensitivity of bending movement response with change of buoyancy spring coefficient, so only the two extremes were included in this study. Figure 10 presents the results, which confirm the opinion that variations of waterplane area distribution are of very little consequence.

Ship mass distribution

The distribution of the ship's displacement and of its added mass obviously play an important part in the whipping bending moment response regardless of the displacement remaining constant. "Weight curves" for the *Fotini-L* in full load and ballast conditions are shown on Fig. 11 with the unit weight amidships in the full-load condition having been taken as unity for convenience. Figure 12 presents the two as if the displacement was the same in both cases and only the fore and aft distribution differed. (The approximated lumped-mass distributions of the full-load condition of Fig. 12 may be compared with the original of Fig. 11.)

The other three ships (for which the data were readily available) are treated in similar fashion in Figs. 13 through 15.

The point of the exercise was to establish a systematic family of mass distributions to cover in very general terms the range likely to be found in actuality. The minor perturbations are of no consequence and cannot all be known and precisely delineated at the preliminary design stage in any case.

Three symmetrical distributions of equal area are given in Fig. 16. The loaded *Fotini-L* is closest to the "sag" case. One after another of these were used together with other charac-

teristics of the *Fotini-L* as built. The three slam centers were used with each. Figure 17 gives the results. It hardly needs to be said that the quantitative differences are significant. It will be found that the "sag" distribution produces results almost identical to those for the *Fotini-L* in full-load condition despite the local irregularities exhibited by Fig. 11 compared with Fig. 16 and the double-ended symmetry imposed by Fig. 16.

Added-mass distribution

Smooth versions of the added-mass distributions for the three seagoing ships can be seen in Fig. 18. From these, a uniform spread of the three forms was developed. They are nonsymmetrical and conform to normal ship practice for overall coefficients of 0.80, 0.65 and 0.50. They are given on Fig. 19. The tanker provided the model for the fullest form and the *Michigan* is closely approximated by the finest. Figure 20 makes it clear that for all slam locations, estimates of added-mass distribution may strongly influence the situation of the DLF curves as would be supposed. This is more so at the full end of the C_{AM} range.

Bending stiffness distribution

From ship to ship, no uniformity at all should be expected with the local irregularities of bending stiffness (EI). This is the case partly because of the differences in hull form and differing extents of effective material. Frequently, for example, partially effective superstructures are involved and these seldom have any relationship to the structural demands of longitudinal strength.

In addition to the distributions for the four ships of this study (Fig. 21), EI distributions for six others were found in the literature, including a pair of naval types. In order to afford a reasonable degree of discrimination, two families of two distributions were used. Both a fine-ended and a blunt-ended family included the same overall full- and fine-form coefficients, namely, $C_{EI} = 0.85$ and 0.65 (Fig. 22).

For the sake of clarity, findings for the sharp-ended pair are in Fig. 23 while those for the blunt-ended pair are in Fig. 24.

Insofar as bending moments amidships are concerned, even large changes of bending stiffness at the girder ends (within the

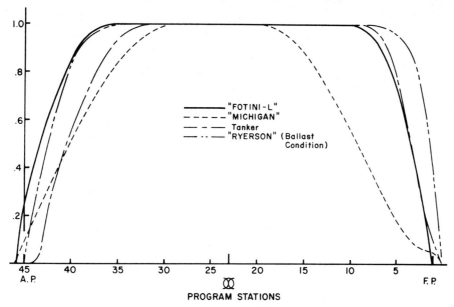

Fig. 8 Buoyancy spring distributions, actual ships

realm of shape reality) appear to make significant changes in bending response only with slams applied near the forward perpendicular. Even so, with long slams, the absolute change of bending moment magnitude with EI coefficient is small; namely, 1000 ton·ft (3037 kN·m) and no more than 6000 ton·ft (18 222 kN·m) even for very short slams.

Between the blunt and sharp families it is probably fair to designate the differences amidships as "inconsequential" throughout, and hereafter to deal with only one or the other shape type and not both.

Including the entire midship length of 40 percent L fails to produce any markedly different whipping bending moments between full and fine, sharp and blunt forms. Nor are there any significantly greater than those amidships except for the very shortest slam durations applied well aft at 22.73 percent L from the FP. Table 1 shows how rapid is the decay with increasing slam duration, in the excess of the greatest midbody

bending moments over those maxima exactly amidships, for such a slam center location. Slams farther forward reduced the excess to inconsequential values.

Beyond the midship length of 40 percent L the situation is

Table 1 Excess midbody bending moments, tons·ft

Sharp-Form EI's	Slam Duration	
C_{EI}	0.0625 sec	0.25 sec
0.85	12725	2176
0.65	10354	2376
Blunt-Form EI's	Slam Duration	
C_{EI}	0.0625 sec	0.25 sec
0.85	15120	1944
0.65	8621	1976

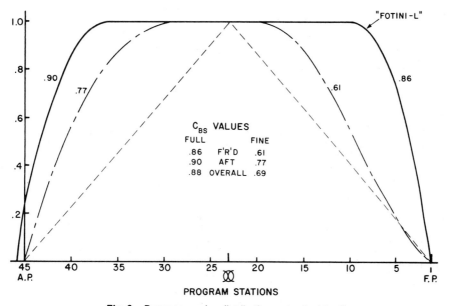

Fig. 9 Buoyancy spring distributions, standard family

Preliminary Design Estimation of Hull Girder Response to Slamming

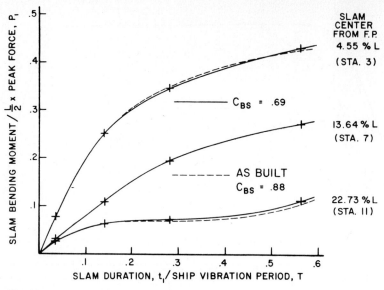

Fig. 10 Nondimensional whipping moments—bulk carrier *Fotini-L*, buoyancy spring distribution modified

equally unique when slams are far from the FP. Bending moments in the ends may then be much larger than amidships, especially with short, sharp impulses. Although midship bending moments are smallest when the slam is applied at the location farthest aft, the bending moments in the end sections are so augmented that they may be perhaps two to three times the worst midship value for the same slam duration and location. They usually occur at 15 to 20 percent L from both perpendiculars, where the section moduli may be greatly reduced.

On the basis of bending moments only, no clear preference can be expressed for either the sharp or blunt forms as best representing the more critical EI distribution for design purposes, but the full C_{EI} coefficients evidently produce the greatest differences between midship and end-section values.

Figure 25 is a composite of the three bending distribution envelopes for the sharp, full-form EI subjected to a 0.25-sec

slam at 4.55 percent, 13.64 percent and 22.73 percent L from the FP. It typifies those for the sharp, fine and both blunt EI shapes as well. The hump at each end of the 22.73 percent slam center curve becomes more exaggerated and the bending moment distribution more irregular throughout, with short sharper slams and the increased importance of higher-order vibratory modes.

Proceeding to the matter of stresses, it is readily apparent that while the fine EI distributions (of both sharp and blunt families) produce the larger midship bending moments for far-forward impulses,[5] the bending stresses with the fine EI distributions could make an unsatisfactory situation remote from amidships even more so. This follows from the fact that the section modulus at each hull cross section, I/c, must closely follow the change of moment of inertia, I, from point to point. In fine forms, then, whipping stresses in the end zones might possibly

---

[5] They being the ones of greatest interest (Figs. 23 and 24).

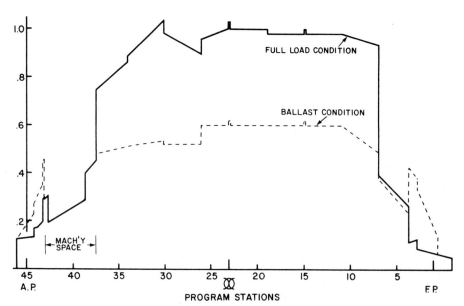

Fig. 11 Displacement mass distributions from weight curves—bulk carrier *Fotini-L*

Preliminary Design Estimation of Hull Girder Response to Slamming

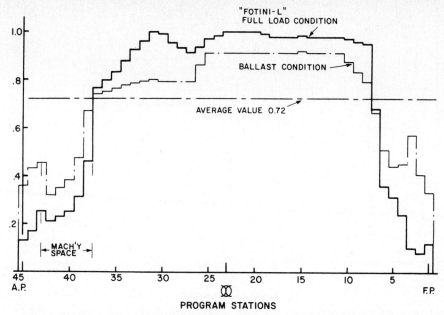

Fig. 12 Lumped-mass distributions with constant area (actual ships)—bulk carrier *Fotini-L*

exceed those expected and provided for amidships. It might also be borne in mind that if even shorter slam durations are possible, the accentuation of bending moments in the ends for Station 11 (22.73 percent *L* from the FP) slams would become greater than shown in Fig. 25, so that stresses there would be further enhanced, even though the moments be quite nominal amidships.

Summation

All computed results from the lumped-mass models stood up to the tests of logic. All data points of each individual computer run related well to all others of the run. The displacement of one plotted curve from another in the same family of variants was always justifiable. And as an example, the fact that neither a uniform change of ship mass, nor of added mass, had any effect in displacing a plotted curve is confirmation of the truly nondimensional nature of the DLF curves produced. Also positive are the strikingly similar characteristics of the curves for the four different ships relative to those of the base ship, *Fotini-L*, when it was given the properties of each of the other three in turn.

Because of the entirely general nature of the studies carried out and the wholly unexceptional character of the findings, it seems justifiable to summarize the broad conclusions as follows and presume them suitable for general application.

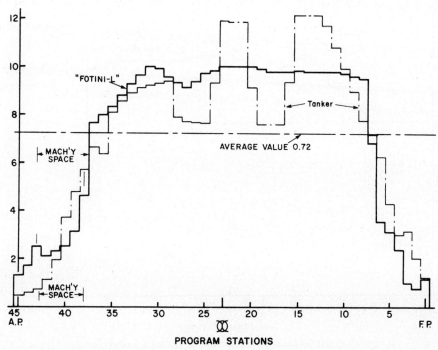

Fig. 13 Lumped-mass distributions with constant area (actual ships, loaded condition)—tanker

Preliminary Design Estimation of Hull Girder Response to Slamming

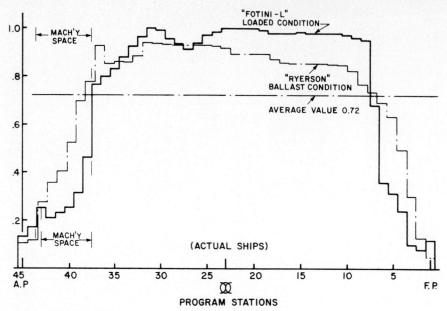

Fig. 14 Lumped-mass distributions with constant area (actual ships)—Great Lakes ore carrier
E. L. Ryerson

1.   Given the dynamic load factor[6] curve for a particular vessel in a particular load condition and struck by a particular impulse at a particular location, modifying the ship masses, the added masses or the *EI* product by a constant factor throughout the ship's length results in the new performance points not deporting significantly from the established DLF curve.

2.   Extreme variations of the buoyancy spring (waterplane area) distribution exert no significant influence in tending to displace the given DLF curve.

---

[6] Perhaps more properly designated a dynamic *response* factor in view of its derivation here.

3.   Those factors which do have a marked influence on the displacement (but not the general shape) of the DLF curve are:

    —slam center location
    —ship mass distribution
    —added mass distribution

and, to a lesser extent,

    —bending stiffness (*EI*) distribution

4.   At least when independently varied, the largest whipping bending moments amidships are generated when the slam center is farthest forward, when the masses are concentrated

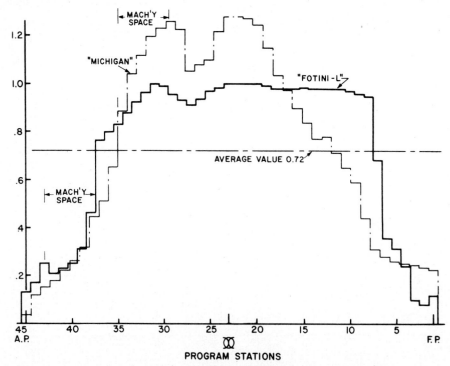

Fig. 15 Lumped-mass distributions with constant area (actual ships, loaded condition)—general cargo carrier *Michigan*

Preliminary Design Estimation of Hull Girder Response to Slamming

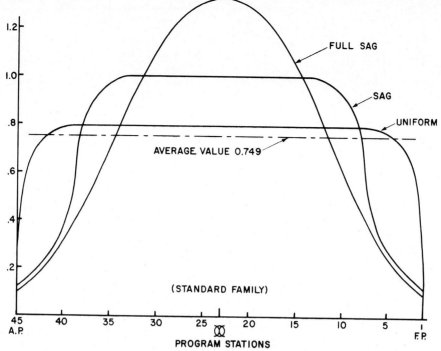

Fig. 16 Displacement mass distributions with constant area (constant displacement)

amidships, and when the bow and stern lines (end values of added mass) are fine rather than full.

Preferences for either full or fine forms for optimum bending stiffness are not clearly visible and the effects of change are less striking. Fine forms produced larger bending moments amidships, at least with slams far forward. However, differences were not substantial except for short slams. With other slam centers, inconsequential differences favored one, then the other, form.

Formulation of an estimation procedure for slam bending moments

To make these findings useful in preliminary design esti-

mation, it is necessary to be able to reproduce the nondimensional load factor relationship peculiar to the ship and to its particular loading at the time in question.

For the longest slam durations, the nondimensional bending moments relate linearly with the point of slam application, regardless of the mass distribution. As the peak forces remain constant for a particular slam duration, the effective moment arms with the long slam durations are also linearly related to the point of application. This suggests one possible approach for estimating the moments, namely, using a moment arm concept.

From output for the *Fotini-L* as built and loaded (as shown in Fig. 5), Fig. 26 illustrates the point made in the preceding. It also indicates that with short slam durations the prevalence

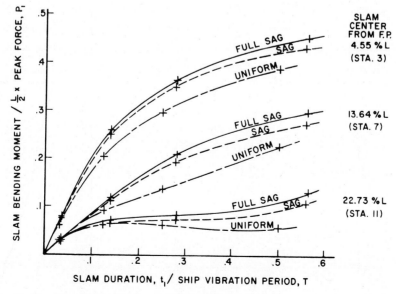

Fig. 17 Nondimensional whipping moments—bulk carrier *Fotini-L*, ship mass distributions modified

Preliminary Design Estimation of Hull Girder Response to Slamming

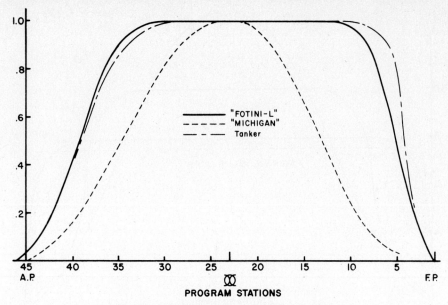

Fig. 18 Added mass distributions, actual ships

of ever-changing higher-order vibratory modes, which are made very evident with one form of the computer output, will make generalized predictions for small values of t_1/T quite uncertain (see Appendix 3). As would be expected, there is also ample evidence that with long slam durations the fulcrum point is a roving one, shifting with t_1/T and the slam center; for when $t_1/T = 0.57$, for example, and $p = 0$, $l = 25$ percent L, but when $l = 0$, $p = 29$ percent L.[7] But its range of movement may not be large enough to be very detrimental for early estimations.

Again with reference to the data supporting Fig. 5, the variation of moment arm with t_1/T for all three slam centers is well matched by the expression

$$l(\%L) = 7.8\,(100\,t_1/T)^{0.3} \qquad (10)$$

so long as t_1/T is greater than about 0.2. By intent, the fit is

[7] p is the distance from the slam center to the FP and l is the distance from the slam center to the effective fulcrum point.

best for $p/L = 0.0455$, with which the bending moments are largest.

Allowing for the slam center location, this becomes

$$l(\%L) = 7.8(100\,t_1/T)^{0.3}\left(1 - \frac{100\,p}{27L}\right) \qquad (10a)$$

Substituting a more refined expression for the denominator coefficient of 27 seems unwarranted at this time.

The smooth distributions of mass adopted for the parametric study are shown in Fig. 16. As with the other variables, they are presumed to cover, in general form, the full range of ship distributions. All have the same area, that is, displacement. In this preliminary investigation no attempt was made to identify the individual types except by name. Figure 17 shows the sensitivity of the *Fotini-L* bending moments to the effects of these mass distribution changes. To include them in the reckoning, a coefficient ⓙ has been introduced so that (10a) becomes

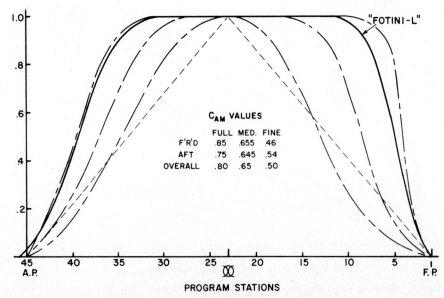

Fig. 19 Added mass distributions, standard family

Preliminary Design Estimation of Hull Girder Response to Slamming

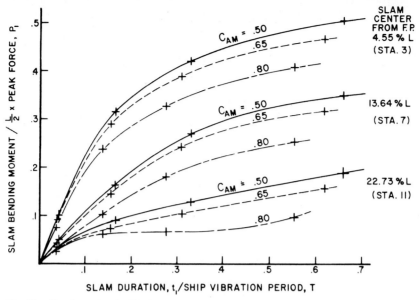

Fig. 20 Nondimensional whipping moments—bulk carrier *Fotini-L*, added-mass distributions modified

$$l(\%L) = 7.8\,(100\,t_1/T)^{0.3}\left(1 - \frac{100\,p}{27L}\right)\!\mathbb{J} \qquad (10b)$$

where

$\mathbb{J} = 1.08$ for "full sag"

$\;\;\; = 1.00$ for "sag"

$\;\;\; = 0.90$ for "uniform"

Rather than adopt such gross gradations as these, a fullness coefficient might have been assigned to each distribution as with the added-mass factor discussed in the following paragraphs. However, the interpolation which this might have implied is hardly consistent with the roughness of the method or the irregularity of the mass distributions as exemplified by the likes of Figs. 11 through 15.

The range of added-mass distributions investigated was also intended to include the full range of ship cases likely to be found. The evidence suggested that these should not be symmetrical about amidships. By defining these in terms of fullness relative to midship values and devising a family of systematic variations (Fig. 19), a fullness coefficient, C_{AM}, can be used and interpolations performed as necessary.

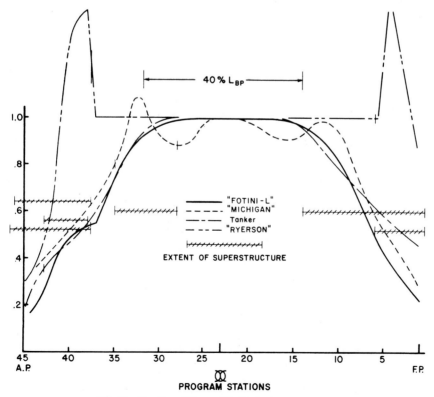

Fig. 21 Bending stiffness (*EI*) distributions, actual ships

Preliminary Design Estimation of Hull Girder Response to Slamming

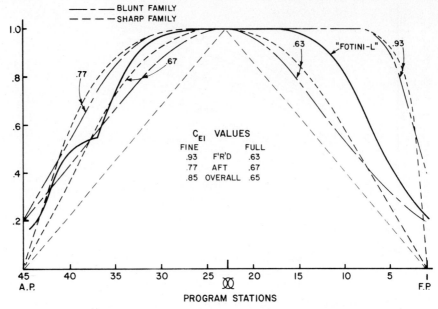

C_{EI} VALUES

	FINE		FULL
	.93	F'R'D	.63
	.77	AFT	.67
	.85	OVERALL	.65

PROGRAM STATIONS

Fig. 22 Bending stiffness (EI) distributions, standard family

As with the ship mass distributions, it has been shown that scale effects, as expressed in terms of the midship value, can be taken care of adequately in the ship's vibration period,[8]T (and the ship's length, L). This can be seen by relating the curves and plotted points of Fig. 6 versus Fig. 5 and Fig. 7 versus Fig. 5 when in the latter figure the masses were doubled.

Taking into account both the *Fotini-L* parametric study and the three other ships, an added-mass modifier was formulated expanding the expression for the virtual moment arm to

$$l(\%L) = 7.8(100\,t_1/T)^{0.3}$$
$$\times \left(1 - \frac{100\,p}{27L}\right) \textcircled{J}(1.45 - 0.60C_{AM}) \quad (10c)$$

Obviously, the virtual moment arms, l, decrease as mass dis-

-----
[8] Which must be independently estimated [1].

tributions and added-mass distributions spread toward the ship's extremities.

The best means of estimating values of C_{AM} for the present would seem to be by means of the block coefficient C_B. It is hardly adequate to do so on the basis of four ships only, but temporarily the expression

$$C_{AM} = 0.88\,C_B + 0.03 \quad (11)$$

might be used.

Finally, then, the slam bending moment amidships, $M_{s(\text{00})}$, is estimated to be

$$M_{s(\text{00})} = P_1\left\{7.8\,(100\,t_1/T)^{0.3} \right.$$
$$\left. \times \left(1 - \frac{100\,p}{27L}\right)\textcircled{J}(1.45 - 0.60C_{AM})\right\}\frac{L}{100} \quad (12)$$

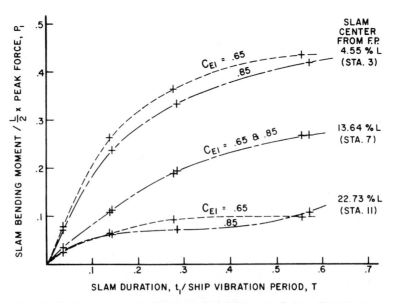

Fig. 23 Nondimensional whipping moments—bulk carrier *Fotini-L*, *EI* distributions modified, sharp ends

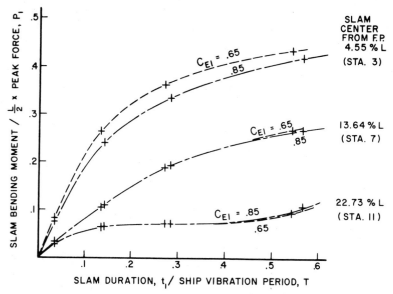

Fig. 24 Nondimensional whipping moments—bulk carrier *Fotini-L, EI* distributions modified, blunt ends

so long as $0.20 \leq t_1/T \leq 0.60$ and, in a nondimensional form:

$$\frac{2M_s(\text{⊗})}{P_1 L} = P_1 l(\% L) \times \frac{L}{100} \times \frac{2}{P_1 L} = l(\% L)/50. \quad (13)$$

In Appendix 3 it is argued that this expression (with the *half*-length as an ingredient) is quantitatively in keeping with the DLF values for a simple one-degree-of-freedom system (Fig. 2), in spite of maxima differing by a factor of about 3.

Evaluation

Figure 27, for the *Fotini-L* with different slam centers, is Fig. 5 with curves from equation (13) added for comparison. Figure 28 provides the same comparison for the four ship cases of Fig. 4. Of the eight data-point curves,[9] only the lowest on Fig. 27 (with small bending moments) has a unique curvature different from the others and whose character is not well served by (13). An expression such as (10c), but with the exponent continually decreasing with increasing t_1/T, would provide

[9] *Fotini-L* loaded, with a 4.55 percent L slam center, appears in both figures.

a better fit even into the region of $t_1/T < 0.2$. But the added complexity cannot be justified on rational grounds. That is, however, the region of largest bending moments for a given impulse, and so it may be a region of great interest if such extremely short slam durations are deemed to be reasonable possibilities.

In delineating the data-point curves for the four ships, only with the *Ryerson* was it necessary to depart significantly from the midship points to include *all* points within the 40 percent L amidships (Fig. 23 of [1]). Expression (10c) is confined to midship values precisely and, thus limited, it suits the *Ryerson* very well.

The distinction between *Fotini-L* loaded and in ballast is too subtle to be dealt with by (13) and only one calculated curve has been drawn (for $Ĵ = 1.00$). However, the difference in mass distribution (shown in Fig. 12) favors a smaller $Ĵ$-value in ballast as better agreement with the data-point curves would require.

The coarse progression of mass distributions of Fig. 16 cannot be expected to deal precisely with the quite irregular distribution of the tanker in loaded condition as shown in Fig. 13. The "sag" form used to produce the result shown in Fig. 28 ($Ĵ$

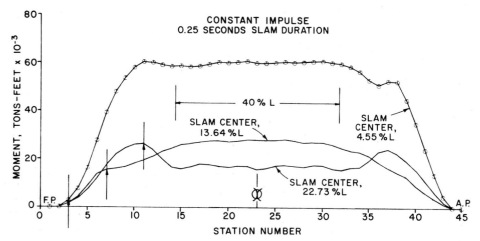

Fig. 25 Whipping bending moment envelopes—bulk carrier *Fotini-L* with slam location variations

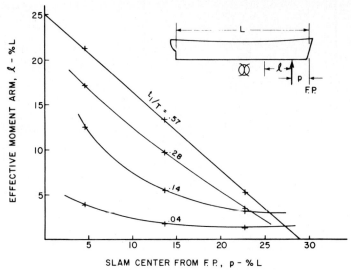

Fig. 26   Effective slam moment arms

= 1.00) has at least *over*estimated the response.   Perhaps it could be argued that the "uniform" distribution ($\textcircled{J}$ = 0.90) is more suitable.

The mass distribution for the tanker in ballast is not known, but the one calculated curve is a reasonable match for the "ballast" data-point curve.

Whereas in the other seven cases it was reasonably good, agreement between calculated and data-point curves for the *Michigan* is unsatisfactory.   Of the four ships studied, the *Michigan* was unique in its fine hull form (Appendix 1).   The other three were uniformly full forms.   The single-variable parametric investigation based upon *Fotini-L* may therefore be insufficient for the fine forms in not accounting for the synergistic effect of more than one parameter being varied at a time.   For example, is it adequate, as in the case of the *Michigan*, simply to sum the individual effects of a "full sag" mass distribution, a very fine added-mass distribution and a slam center well aft of the FP as developed from such a very full base ship as the *Fotini-L*?   The question seems worthy of somewhat more study with a fine hull model.   As they stand, equations (12) and (13) overestimate the whipping moments for the *Michigan*.

Recommendations

It seems reasonable to maintain that (12) provides the basis for a rough but adequate means, suitable for preliminary design, of estimating a vessel's bending moment response amidships to an impulsive loading.   For the present it should be limited to ships of full hull form in the range $0.2 \leq t_1/T \leq 0.6$.[10]   The particular importance of dynamic shock loadings in contributing to buckling failures has been documented by McCallum [8].   Such loadings are also acknowledged to be possible instigations of brittle fracture.

Apart from the specific method proposed, the study emphasizes that in estimating bending moment response:

1.   The important factors are impulse magnitude, impulse center location, mass distribution, added-mass distribution and, to a lesser extent, the bending stiffness distribution in that it will affect other points than amidships within the 40 percent L midship span.

---

[10] From the evidence of Fig. 2 and the tanker of Fig. 4, it would appear that maximum values of the DLF for the constant half-sine impulse shape will appear at t_1/T of about one, so that larger values of t_1/T would be of much less interest.

2.   A reliable means of estimating slam impulse magnitude, suitable for preliminary design, should be sought.

3.   Following from Step 2, estimating procedures for slam duration and for locating the slam center should be investigated so that the worst of a reasonable range of combinations can be found for each design case.

4.   A parametric study stemming from a fine hull form model should be conducted (beginning with verification and extension of the *Michigan* output) to extend the usefulness of, and probably refine, equation (12).

5.   The possibility of extending the method (or devising another) should be explored for the region $t_1/T < 0.2$.   If such short-duration slams are realistic, the resultant transient bending moments may be the ones most critical for structural design.

6.   To moderate the effects of slamming, "V" rather than "U" cross sections forward should be adopted because, for a given impulse, reducing the peak load, P_1, is more beneficial than reducing the slam duration, t_1.   Excessive bow flare should be avoided as it aggravates the problem by locating the slam center far forward.

7.   More study is needed of the phase relationships and associated magnitudes between bending moments due to slamming and wave bending.   The allowance of an additional 60 percent to the wave bending moment, given by Aertssen [10] and discussed by Lewis and Zubaly [11], is obviously tentative and very preliminary.

Acknowledgments

Over a number of years the American Bureau of Shipping has taken an interest in this work and has supported it completely.   It has been a most happy experience to work under such benign auspices, which, it is hoped, will show in the care taken with the planning and analysis, and the value of the results.

Also, thanks are most gratefully extended to the following: to Mr. Roger Kline for his painstaking assembly of program input data and careful review of the raw results, to Professor J. G. deOliveira for reformulating the dynamic load factor derivation to suit the specific conditions of interest here, to Mrs. Muriel Bernier Morey for the knowing and artistic development of the figures and to Miss Cheryl Gibson for the typing of the text which, regrettably, only the printer and the Papers Committee will have seen and be able to appreciate.

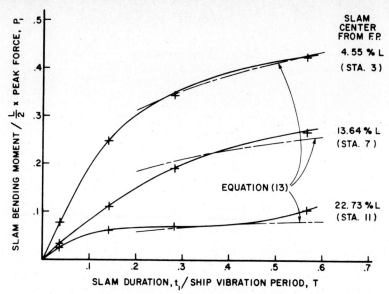

Fig. 27 Nondimensional whipping moments—comparison of computer model with formula, bulk carrier *Fotini-L* (as built)

References

1 Evans, J. Harvey and Kline, Roger G., "Effect of Hull Girder Stiffness Variations on Ship Structural Performance," TRANS. SNAME, Vol. 86, 1978, p. 101.

2 Kline, Roger G. and Clough, R. W., "The Dynamic Response of Ships' Hulls as Influenced by Proportions, Arrangement, Loading and Structural Stiffness," *Proceedings*, SNAME Spring Meeting, Montreal, 1967, p. 4-1.

3 Frankland, J. M., "Effects of Impact on Simple Elastic Structures," David Taylor Model Basin Report 481, April 1942; also, *Proceedings*, Society for Experimental Stress Analysis, Vol. 6, No. 2, 1948, p. 7.

4 Denis, M. St., "Dynamic Strength," *Journal of the Society of Naval Engineers*, Nov. 1948, p. 505.

5 Norris, C. H., Hansen, R. J., Holley, M. J., Jr., Biggs, J. M., Namyet, S., and Minami, J. K., *Structural Design for Dynamic Loads*, McGraw-Hill, New York, 1959.

6 Kline, Roger G. and Daidola, J. C., "Ship Vibration Prediction Methods and Evaluation of Influence of Hull Stiffness Variation on Vibratory Response," Ship Structure Committee Report SSC-249, 1975.

7 Patel, R. K., "Analysis of Ship Hull Girder Response to Slamming," unpublished Master's degree thesis, MIT, Cambridge, Mass., Jan. 1978.

8 McCallum, J., "The Strength of Fast Cargo Ships", *Trans.* RINA, 1975, p. 1.

9 Report of Committee II.3, "Transient Dynamic Loadings and Response," 7th International Ship Structure Committee Symposium, Paris, 1979, p. II. 3–12.

10 Aertssen, G., "Longitudinal Strength of Ships," *International Shipbuilding Progress*, Vol. 17, No. 193, 1970, p. 269.

11 Lewis, E. V. and Zubaly, R. B., "Dynamic Loadings Due to Waves and Ship Motions," SNAME-Ship Structure Committee Symposium, Washington, 1975, p. M-1.

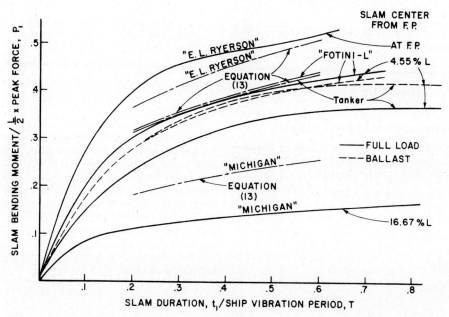

Fig. 28 Nondimensional whipping moments—comparison of computer models with formula, four diverse ships

Preliminary Design Estimation of Hull Girder Response to Slamming

Ship characteristics

Ship Type	Fotini-L Bulk Carrier	Tanker	Ed. L. Ryerson Great Lakes Ore Carrier	Michigan General Cargo Carrier
Length overall, L_{0A}, m	261.56	351.44	222.51	176.48
(ft)	(858.13)	(1153.0)	(730.0)	(579.0)
Length between perpendiculars, L, m	243.84	330.74	217.02	165.81
(ft)	(800.0)	(1085.08)	(712.0)	(544.0)
Breadth, B, m	32.31	51.82	22.86	24.99
(ft)	(106.0)	(170.0)	(75.0)	(82.0)
Depth, D, m	18.30	25.60	11.89	13.87
(ft)	(60.04)	(84.0)	(39.0)	(45.4)
Draft, full load, H, m	13.58	19.20	8.08	8.23
(ft)	(44.54)	(63.0)	(26.5)	(27.0)
Displacement, full load, Δ, t	92 100	290,881	34,681	18 390
(tons)	(90 650)	(286,300)	(34,135)	(18 100)
Draft, ballast, H_B, m	9.12	8.99	5.18	...
(ft)	(25.92)	(29.5)	(17.0)	...
Displacement, ballast, Δ_B, t	59 974	128 016	21 470	...
(ft)	(59 030)	(126 000)	(21 132)	...
Shp	...	32 000	9 000	24 000
@ rpm	...	80	150	...
Speed, knots	...	15.7	14.55	23
L/B	7.55	6.38	9.49	6.63
L/D	13.32	12.92	18.26	11.96
B/H	2.38	2.70	2.83	3.04
B/D	1.77	2.02	1.92	1.80
C_B	0.84	0.86	0.84	0.53
C_B (design)	0.84	0.89	0.86	0.53
Section modulus, deck, Z_d, cm$^2 \times$ m	311 131	772 304	85 723	84 280
(in.$^2 \times$ ft)	(158 256)	(392 830)	(43 603)	(42 869)
Section modulus, bottom, Z_b, cm$^2 \times$ m	346 236	771 641	101 041	103 701
(in.$^2 \times$ ft)	(176 112)	(392 493)	(51 394)	(52 747)
Distance from neutral axis to deck, c_d, m	9.63	12.80	6.43	7.65
(ft)	(31.6)	(41.98)	(21.1)	(25.1)
Distance from neutral axis to bottom, c_b, m	8.66	12.81	5.46	6.22
(ft)	(28.4)	(42.02)	(17.9)	(20.4)
C_b/D	0.473	0.500	0.459	0.448
Moment of inertia, I, cm$^2 \times$ m^2	2 998 964	9 887 223	551 568	645 065
(in.$^2 \times$ ft^2)	(5 002 272)	(16 491 888)	(920 016)	(1 075 968)

Appendix 2

Review of dynamic load factor theory

The general equation of motion for the vibratory response of a mass with a single degree of freedom, under a forcing function varying with time, may be expressed as

$$m\ddot{x} + c\dot{x} + kx = P(t) \tag{1}$$

where

c = damping coefficient
k = spring constant
m = vibrating mass

This may be written as

$$\ddot{x} + \frac{c}{m}\dot{x} + \frac{k}{m}x = \frac{P(t)}{m} \tag{1a}$$

or

$$\ddot{x} + 2\beta\dot{x} + \omega^2 x = \frac{P(t)}{m} \tag{1b}$$

After the first few cycles of vibration under a short-term impulse, and during the ensuing free vibration, the system's motions decay over a number of cycles during which damping plays an important part in describing the response. However, maximum displacements and stresses must occur during the first one or two cycles. Thus, while damping is a vital ingredient in the solution for all characteristics of long-term or steady-state response, under the impulsive loading of interest here (that is, slamming) this is not the case. Therefore the second term of (1a) and (1b) may be neglected.

A half-sine wave is most nearly representative of the slam impulse in its elementary form,[11] so

$$P(t) = P_1 \sin\Omega t$$

---

[11] In recent investigations a very short "spike" superimposed at the origin has also been noted.

when

$$0 \leq \Omega t \leq \pi \text{ or } 0 \leq t \leq \frac{\pi}{\Omega}$$

and

$$P(t) = 0$$

when

$$\pi < \Omega t \text{ or } t > \frac{\pi}{\Omega}$$

where

P_1 = maximum value of sinusoidal forcing function
Ω = circular frequency of loading whose duration is t_1
(that is, $t_1 = \pi/\Omega$)
T = natural period of vibration of system

The homogeneous solution of (1b) (omitting the second term) gives the free part of the motion, namely

$$x(t) = C_1 \sin\omega t + C_2 \cos\omega t \qquad (2)$$

where ω has been taken as $\sqrt{k/m}$ and is also, in fact, $2\pi/T$.

The particular solution, for the forced part of the vibration must have the form $A \sin\Omega t$, where A is not a function of time (for $0 \leq t \leq \pi/\Omega$), so

$$x_p = A \sin\Omega t$$

$$\dot{x}_p = A\Omega \cos\Omega t$$

$$\ddot{x}_p = - A\Omega^2 \sin\Omega t$$

Therefore (1b) becomes

$$\ddot{x}_p + \omega^2 x_p = -A\Omega^2 \sin\Omega t + A\omega^2 \sin\Omega t$$

$$= \frac{P_1}{m} \sin\Omega t$$

$$= A(\omega^2 - \Omega^2) = \frac{P_1}{m} \qquad (1c)$$

or

$$A = \frac{P_1}{m(\omega^2 - \Omega^2)} \qquad (3)$$

The solution

$$x_p = \frac{P_1}{m(\omega^2 - \Omega^2)} \sin\Omega t$$

then represents a vibration with the same frequency and period as the half-sine load.

Thus the total solution is given by the sum of the homogeneous and particular solutions, namely

$$x(t) = C_1 \sin\omega t + C_2 \cos\omega t + \frac{P_1}{m(\omega^2 - \Omega^2)} \sin\Omega t \qquad (2a)$$

which is valid for $0 \leq t \leq \pi/\Omega$

To determine the constants C_1 and C_2, assume the system is initially at rest so that $x(t = 0) = \dot{x}(t = 0) = 0$. Then

$$x(t = 0) = C_1 \sin\omega 0 + C_2 \cos\omega 0 + \frac{P_1}{m(\omega^2 - \Omega^2)} \sin\Omega 0 = 0$$

so

$$C_2 = 0$$

also

$$\dot{x}(t = 0) = C_1 \omega \cos\omega 0 - 0 + \frac{P_1\Omega}{m(\omega^2 - \Omega^2)} \cos\Omega 0 = 0$$

so

$$C_1 = - \frac{P_1\Omega}{m\omega(\omega^2 - \Omega^2)}$$

Thus

$$x(t) = - \frac{P_1\Omega}{m\omega(\omega^2 - \Omega^2)} \sin\omega t + \frac{P_1}{m(\omega^2 - \Omega^2)} \sin\Omega t$$

$$= \frac{P_1}{m(\omega^2 - \Omega^2)} \left[\sin\Omega t - \frac{\Omega}{\omega} \sin\omega t \right]$$

$$= \frac{\dfrac{P_1}{m\omega^2}}{1 - \left(\dfrac{\Omega}{\omega}\right)^2} \left[\sin\Omega t - \frac{\Omega}{\omega} \sin\omega t \right]$$

$$= \overline{X} \left[\sin\Omega t - \frac{\Omega}{\omega} \sin\omega t \right] \qquad \text{so long as } 0 \leq t \leq \frac{\pi}{\Omega} \quad (2b)$$

where

$$\frac{\dfrac{P_1}{m\omega^2}}{1 - \left(\dfrac{\Omega}{\omega}\right)^2} = \overline{X}$$

For $t \geq \pi/\Omega$ the forcing function becomes zero, so the solution reverts again to the form of (2), namely

$$x(t) = C_1 \sin\omega t + C_2 \cos\omega t$$

and in order to determine displacements at times $t > \pi/\Omega$, the initial displacement for the start of free vibration (that is, $t = \pi/(\Omega)$) must be found.

At $t = \pi/\Omega$ the displacement is given by

$$x\left(t = \frac{\pi}{\Omega}\right) = \frac{\dfrac{P_1}{m\omega^2}}{1 - \left(\dfrac{\Omega}{\omega}\right)^2} \left[0 - \frac{\Omega}{\omega} \sin\omega \frac{\pi}{\Omega} \right]$$

Then

$$x\left(t = \frac{\pi}{\Omega}\right) = - \overline{X} \frac{\Omega}{\omega} \sin\left(\frac{\omega\pi}{\Omega}\right)$$

and the velocity becomes

$$\dot{x}(t) = \overline{X}\left(\Omega \cos\Omega t - \Omega \cos\omega t\right)$$

and

$$\dot{x}\left(t = \frac{\pi}{\Omega}\right) = \overline{X}\left[\Omega \cos\pi - \Omega \cos\left(\frac{\omega\pi}{\Omega}\right)\right]$$

$$= - \overline{X}\Omega \left[1 + \cos\left(\frac{\omega\pi}{\Omega}\right)\right]$$

From (2), then

$$x\left(t = \frac{\pi}{\Omega}\right) = C_1 \sin\left(\frac{\omega\pi}{\Omega}\right) + C_2 \cos\left(\frac{\omega\pi}{\Omega}\right)$$

$$= - \overline{X} \frac{\Omega}{\omega} \sin\left(\frac{\omega\pi}{\Omega}\right)$$

and

$$\dot{x}\left(t = \frac{\pi}{\Omega}\right) = C_1 \omega \cos\left(\frac{\omega\pi}{\Omega}\right) - C_2 \omega \sin\left(\frac{\omega\pi}{\Omega}\right)$$

$$= - \overline{X}\Omega \left[1 + \cos\left(\frac{\omega\pi}{\Omega}\right)\right]$$

After multiplying the expression for $x(t = \pi/\Omega)$ by $\sin(\omega\pi/\Omega)$ and the expression for $\dot{x}(t = \pi/\Omega)$ by $\cos(\omega\pi/\Omega)$, these become

$$C_1 \sin^2\left(\frac{\omega\pi}{\Omega}\right) + C_2 \cos\left(\frac{\omega\pi}{\Omega}\right)\sin\left(\frac{\omega\pi}{\omega}\right) = -\,\overline{X}\left(\frac{\Omega}{\omega}\right)\sin^2\left(\frac{\omega\pi}{\Omega}\right)$$

and

$$C_1 \cos^2\left(\frac{\omega\pi}{\Omega}\right) - C_2 \cos\left(\frac{\omega\pi}{\Omega}\right)\sin\left(\frac{\omega\pi}{\Omega}\right)$$
$$= -\,\overline{X}\left(\frac{\Omega}{\omega}\right)\left[\cos\left(\frac{\omega\pi}{\Omega}\right) + \cos^2\left(\frac{\omega\pi}{\Omega}\right)\right]$$

Adding these two expressions produces the result

$$C_1 = -\,\overline{X}\left(\frac{\Omega}{\omega}\right)\left[1 + \cos\left(\frac{\omega\pi}{\Omega}\right)\right]$$

from which, by substitution, it follows that

$$C_2 = \overline{X}\left(\frac{\Omega}{\omega}\right)\sin\left(\frac{\omega\pi}{\Omega}\right)$$

so finally, where $t \geq \pi/\Omega$:

$$x(t) = -\,\overline{X}\left(\frac{\Omega}{\omega}\right)\left[1 + \cos\left(\frac{\omega\pi}{\Omega}\right)\right]\sin\omega t + \overline{X}\left(\frac{\Omega}{\omega}\right)\sin\left(\frac{\omega\pi}{\Omega}\right)\cos\omega t$$

or

$$x(t) = \overline{X}\left(\frac{\Omega}{\omega}\right)\left\{-\left[1 + \cos\left(\frac{\omega\pi}{\Omega}\right)\right]\sin\omega t + \sin\left(\frac{\omega\pi}{\Omega}\right)\cos\omega t\right\}$$
$$= \overline{X}\left(\frac{\Omega}{\omega}\right)\left\{-\sin\omega t - \sin\omega t\,\cos\left(\frac{\omega\pi}{\Omega}\right) + \cos\omega t\,\sin\left(\frac{\omega\pi}{\Omega}\right)\right\}$$
$$= \overline{X}\left(\frac{\Omega}{\omega}\right)\left\{-\sin\omega t - \sin\left[\omega\left(t - \frac{\pi}{\Omega}\right)\right]\right\} \qquad (2c)$$

Recalling that

$$\Omega = \frac{\pi}{t_1}$$

where t_1 is the impulse duration, then

$$\Omega t = \frac{\pi t}{t_1} \qquad (4)$$

Since $T = 2\pi/\Omega$, then

$$\frac{\omega\pi}{\Omega} = \frac{\dfrac{2\pi}{T}\,\pi}{\pi/t_1} = \frac{2\pi t_1}{T}$$

and

$$\omega t = \frac{2\pi t}{T} \qquad (5)$$

From (4) and (5)

$$\frac{\Omega}{\omega} = \frac{T}{2t_1} \qquad (6)$$

Using this notation

$$\overline{X} = \frac{\dfrac{P_1}{m\omega^2}}{1 - \left(\dfrac{\Omega}{\omega}\right)^2} = \frac{\dfrac{P_1}{m}\left(\dfrac{T}{2\pi}\right)^2}{1 - \left(\dfrac{T}{2t_1}\right)^2}$$

so $(2b)$, for $0 \leq t \leq \pi/\Omega$, becomes

$$x(t) = \frac{P_1}{m}\frac{\left(\dfrac{T}{2\pi}\right)^2}{1 - \left(\dfrac{T}{2t_1}\right)^2}\left[\sin\left(\frac{\pi t}{t_1}\right) - \frac{T}{2t_1}\sin\left(\frac{2\pi t}{T}\right)\right]$$

$$= \frac{P_1}{m}\frac{\left(\dfrac{T}{2\pi}\right)^2}{1 - \left(\dfrac{T}{2t_1}\right)^2}\frac{T}{2t_1}\left[\frac{2t_1}{T}\sin\left(\frac{\pi t}{t_1}\right) - \sin\left(\frac{2\pi t}{T}\right)\right]$$

$$= \frac{P_1}{m}\frac{\dfrac{T^2}{4\pi^2}}{\dfrac{2t_1}{T} - \dfrac{T}{2t_1}}\left[\frac{2t_1}{T}\sin\left(\frac{\pi t}{t_1}\right) - \sin\left(\frac{2\pi t}{T}\right)\right]$$

$$= \frac{P_1 T^2}{2\pi^2 m}\frac{1}{\dfrac{4t_1}{T} - \dfrac{T}{t_1}}\left[\frac{2t_1}{T}\sin\left(\frac{\pi t}{t_1}\right) - \sin\left(\frac{2\pi t}{T}\right)\right] \qquad (2d)$$

If x_0 is the static deflection which would be produced by the peak load P_1, then

$$x_0 = \frac{P_1}{k} = \frac{P_1}{m\omega^2} = \frac{P_1}{m\left(\dfrac{2\pi}{T}\right)^2} = \frac{P_1 T^2}{4\pi^2 m} \qquad (7)$$

and, from the definition of $\overline{X}$ and (6):

$$\overline{X} = \frac{x_0}{1 - \left(\dfrac{\Omega}{\omega}\right)^2} = \frac{x_0}{1 - \left(\dfrac{T}{2t_1}\right)^2}$$

Therefore, in nondimensional form $(2d)$ becomes

$$\frac{x(t)}{x_0} = \frac{2}{\dfrac{4t_1}{T} - \dfrac{T}{t_1}}\left[\frac{2t_1}{T}\sin\left(\frac{\pi t}{t_1}\right) - \sin\left(\frac{2\pi t}{T}\right)\right] \qquad (2e)$$

For the case when $t > \pi/\Omega$, the nondimensional form of $(2c)$ may be written

$$\frac{x(t)}{x_0} = \frac{1}{1 - \left(\dfrac{\Omega}{\omega}\right)^2}\left(\frac{\Omega}{\omega}\right)\left\{-\sin\omega t - \sin\left[\omega\left(t - \frac{\pi}{\Omega}\right)\right]\right\}$$

$$= \frac{-1}{1 - \left(\dfrac{T}{2t_1}\right)^2}\left(\frac{T}{2t_1}\right)\left\{\sin\left(\frac{2\pi t}{T}\right) + \sin\left[\frac{2\pi}{T}(t - t_1)\right]\right\}$$

$$= \frac{-2}{\dfrac{4t_1}{T} - \dfrac{T}{t_1}}\left\{\sin\left(\frac{2\pi t}{T}\right) + \sin\left[\frac{2\pi}{T}(t - t_1)\right]\right\} \qquad (2f)$$

Expressions $(2e)$ and $(2f)$ are, then, *instantaneous* values of the ratio of dynamic displacement (or stress) to that displacement (or stress) produced by the same peak load when applied statically, for the forced and free portions of vibration, respectively. For a particular value of t_1/T, maximum and minimum values may be found in the usual way, by differentiating and equating to zero. Then, when $0 \leq t \leq t_1$

$$\frac{\dot{x}(t)}{x_0} = \frac{2}{\dfrac{4t_1}{T} - \dfrac{T}{t_1}}\left[\frac{2\pi}{T}\cos\frac{\pi t}{t_1} - \frac{2\pi}{T}\cos\frac{2\pi t}{T}\right]$$
$$= 0 \qquad (8)$$

which is the case when

$$\cos\frac{\pi t}{t_1} = \cos\frac{2\pi t}{T}$$

that is, $t_1 = T/2$, or when

$$\cos\frac{\pi t}{t_1} = \cos\left(2\pi - \frac{2\pi t}{T}\right)$$

that is

$$\frac{t}{T} = \frac{2}{2 + \dfrac{T}{t_1}}$$

The maximum occurs during the pulse if

$$\frac{t}{T}\left(= \frac{2}{2 + \dfrac{T}{t_1}}\right) < \frac{t_1}{T}; \quad \text{that is, so long as } \frac{t_1}{T} > 0.50$$

For the free vibration, when $t \geq t_1$:

$$\frac{\dot{x}(t)}{x_0} = \frac{-2}{\dfrac{4t_1}{T} - \dfrac{T}{t_1}}\left[\frac{2\pi}{T}\cos\frac{2\pi t}{T} + \frac{2\pi}{T}\cos\frac{2\pi}{T}(t - t_1)\right]$$

$$= 0 \qquad (9)$$

Such an expression holds true if

$$\cos\frac{2\pi t}{T} = -\cos\frac{2\pi}{T}(t - t_1)$$

or

$$\frac{t}{T} = \frac{1}{4}\left(1 + \frac{2t_1}{T}\right)$$

So the maximum occurs after the pulse if

$$\frac{t}{T}\left(= \frac{1}{4}\left[1 + \frac{2t_1}{T}\right]\right) > \frac{t_1}{T}; \quad \text{that is so long as } \frac{t_1}{T} < 0.50$$

Thus, in conclusion, when $t_1/T > 0.50$, the maximum occurs when

$$\frac{t}{T} = \frac{2}{2 + \dfrac{T}{t_1}}$$

implying that $t < t_1$, and when $t_1/T < 0.50$, the maximum occurs when

$$\frac{t}{T} = \frac{1}{4}\left(1 + \frac{2t_1}{T}\right)$$

implying that $t > t_1$.

Therefore, the maximum magnitude when $t_1/T > 0.50$ is

$$\left[\frac{x(t)}{x_0}\right]_{\max} = \frac{2}{\dfrac{4t_1}{T} - \dfrac{T}{t_1}}\left[\frac{2t_1}{T}\sin\pi\left(\frac{t_1}{T}\cdot\frac{2}{2 + \dfrac{T}{t_1}}\right)\right.$$

$$\left. - \sin 2\pi\left(\frac{2}{2 + \dfrac{T}{t_1}}\right)\right]$$

$$= \frac{2}{\dfrac{4t_1}{T} - \dfrac{T}{t_1}}\left[\frac{2t_1}{T}\sin\pi\left(\frac{2\left(\dfrac{t_1}{T}\right)^2}{1 + \dfrac{2t_1}{T}}\right) - \sin\pi\left(\frac{\dfrac{4t_1}{T}}{1 + \dfrac{2t_1}{T}}\right)\right] \quad (2g)$$

and, when $t_1/T < 0.50$, the maximum magnitude is

$$\left[\frac{x(t)}{x_0}\right]_{\max} = \frac{-2}{\dfrac{4t_1}{T} - \dfrac{T}{t_1}}\left\{\sin\left(2\pi\left(\frac{1 + \dfrac{2t_1}{T}}{4}\right)\right) + \right.$$

$$\left. + \sin\left[2\pi\left(\frac{1 + \dfrac{2t_1}{T}}{4} - \frac{t_1}{T}\right)\right]\right\}$$

$$= \frac{-2}{\dfrac{4t_1}{T} - \dfrac{T}{t_1}}\left\{\sin\pi\left(\frac{1}{2} + \frac{t_1}{T}\right) + \sin\pi\left(\frac{1}{2} - \frac{t_1}{T}\right)\right\} \quad (2h)$$

Appendix 3

Nondimensional bending moments for the Fotini-L, Ryerson, Michigan, and a tanker

It may be of interest to discuss the legitimacy of using the moment-arm approach and of using simply the half-length of the ship as the standard on which to base the nondimensional bending moments, that is, the dynamic load factors.

It can be seen in Fig. 4 that with a slam center at the FP, as with the *Ryerson*, the response factors have about one-third the magnitude of the theoretical DLF curve for the simple one-degree-of-freedom system of Fig. 2. If the infinite complexities of the ship and its loading were to be dominated by those common to the elementary one-degree-of-freedom model, this 3:1 relationship might suggest a slam moment arm taken to a point $L/6$ from the FP, reinforcing the suspicion that a nodal point other than the half-length is a more rational fulcrum point. That nature is not so obliging is immediately apparent in the case of the *Michigan*. Here the slam was applied exactly at $L/6$ and bending moments were generated nevertheless. The obvious conclusion is that, even if all else were analogous between ship and simple model, the fact that differing combinations of vibratory modes are excited with differing slam locations means that no single nodal point exists which is common to all individual modes, let alone when several modes coexist simultaneously.

Nevertheless, Fig. 4 for the four different ships, and all the corresponding response curves for different slam locations with the *Fotini-L* (Fig. 5) in its many reincarnations (Figs. 5–7, 10, 17, 20, 23, 24), exhibit a quite linear relationship between bending moment and the slam center location. This, even though the virtual fulcrum point may be translating as the predominance of first-order response gives way to more complex combinations as t_1/T decreases, and with the gradually increasing importance of each higher-order mode in its turn.

At one time, among the several possibilities tested, the bending moments amidships were related to the peak force, P_1, multiplied by the distance of the slam center from amidships (that is, $L/2 - p$), rather than by the half-length, $L/2$. Of course, that did not cause the nondimensional bending moment curves of Figs. 4 or 5, say, to coincide. It also destroyed the linearity of moment arm with slam center location, p (for the largest values of t_1/T), which is a feature of Fig. 26.

Figure 29 has samples of instantaneous bending moment distributions when the moment is maximum amidships, and instantaneous shearing force distributions when the shearing force is maximum at the forward quarter point. The curves are typical of all at the larger values of t_1/T wherein first-mode bending and deflection prevail. The maximum bending moment and the maximum shearing force described do not necessarily occur simultaneously, but the classical relationship between bending force and shearing force clearly obtains.

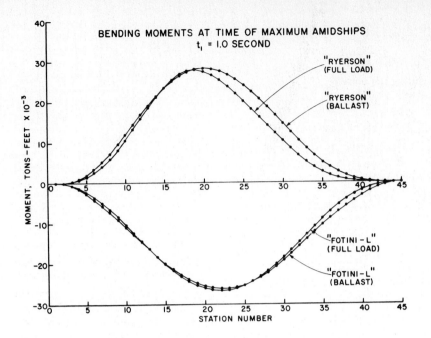

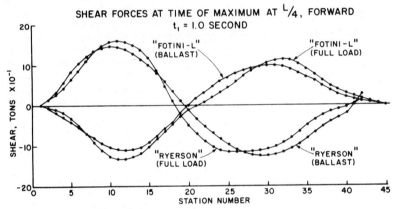

Fig. 29 Dynamic bending moments and shear forces

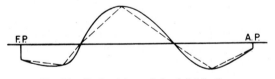

Fig. 30 Derived dynamic load distribution

Another differentiation produces a loading curve such as in Fig. 30 which, along with the shearing force curve, shows little or no evidence of force concentrated at the slam center, only a continuous smooth distribution. This is consistent with Frankland's admonition [3] that a concentration of load in space or time would produce increased contributions from the higher modes. This fundamental-mode bending moment and its static counterpart have been taken as the dimensional reference, $P_1L/2$, in the sense that their deflected forms are not unlike that of a double cantilever and the bending moments diminish steadily from a maximum amidships.

As to the 3:1 ratio between the dimensionless bending moments and the DLF values for the elementary system . . . curiosity might tempt toward further enquiry, but there could be no merit in it. Quantitatively there can be no connection between two such dissimilar systems as the simple one and the full ship.

Discussion

C. Guedes Soares, Member

The author has provided us with an interesting parametric study of the response of ship hulls to impact loads in the forward region. The work is most useful in identifying the parameters to which the response is most sensitive and the ones that do not deserve much effort with the accuracy of their representation.

My discussion raises two minor points and then concentrates on the important question of the definition of a "design slam."

Equation (13) has been derived by fitting the dynamic load curves in their flat region, that is, for ratios of t_1/T larger than 0.2. It is believed that the duration of a slam can be considered to be somewhat insensitive to the type and/or size of the ships.

However, the same does not happen with T and, in fact, the first-mode natural period of vibration of the ships considered in the paper shows a variation of about 3 to 1. This means that the useful range of t_1/T will vary somewhat with the ship, and it is believed that the case of the tanker can be in a different range than the other ships, that is, $t_1/T < 0.2$. In this case a line steeper than equation (13) results for tankers.

It is conceded, however, that in face of the large uncertainties related to the definition of the design slam, it may be questionable if such a distinction is justified.

The second point has to do with the longitudinal distribution of the slam-induced bending moments. The author has pointed out that the bending moments are relatively constant for about 70 percent of the length of the ships. However, the rules of most classification societies require a full section modulus for only 40 percent of the length, allowing tapering toward the ends. Therefore, an important consequence of this fact is that the two zones of $0.15L$ adjacent to the middlebody may be critical with respect to slam-inducing bending moments. The situation may be even more critical for the after part since some classification societies already require an increased section modulus toward the bow for ships liable to slamming.

The rules assume that the maximum wave-induced bending moment will be originated by a wave of length equal to the ship and, if this assumption is correct, the wave-induced bending moments would be quite reduced outside the middlebody zone. Recent results [12] (additional references follow some discussions) have shown that the stillwater bending moments may have significant values outside this length of $0.4L$ and therefore the combined bending moments may be such as to suggest a reevaluation of the length of the middlebody.

Finally, I would like to point out some difficulties in defining one slam for design purposes and ask the author his views on this problem. This is in fact a necessary step before the method presented in the paper can be applied since equation (12) presupposes a knowledge of the intensity, duration and location of the slam.

The prediction of the occurrence of a slam is at present based on the use of strip theories of ship motions, which were developed for linear motions. The occurrence of a slam is, however, the result of a largely nonlinear motion. An engineering approach can be devised for this problem by using strip theory in conjunction with hydrodynamic coefficients varying as a function of instantaneous draft, as done for example in [13].

The slam force, which is just a particular case of these nonlinear forces, can be determined for a section as

$$F = \frac{d}{dt}[M_a W_r] + N\dot{w}_r + \rho gS$$

$$= M_a\ddot{W}_r + \frac{dM_a}{dz}\dot{w}_r^2 + N\dot{w}_r + \rho gS$$

where M_a is the two-dimensional sectional added mass, N is the damping coefficient, S is the instantaneous sectional area, and $\dot{w}_r$ is the relative vertical velocity of the section.

This term is very much the same as the term that describes the nonlinear forces associated with large motions, so it is difficult and somewhat artificial to separate the "nonlinear force" from the "slam force."

The initiation of a slam is easily defined as the moment that a section reenters the water. In this respect it is thought that the concept of threshold velocity is an artificial one which may be more related to the slams that can be perceived on the bridge than to the real physical phenomenon.

On the other hand, the ending of the slam is again artificial and different authors have used different definitions. Should one consider it finished when the section has a draft of 10 percent of the stillwater draft? Or 20 percent? Or 100 percent? Agreeing to a sort of hierarchy of force terms such as the linear

ones accounted for by strip theory, the nonlinear ones due to large motions, and the slam forces due to emergence of the bow, the result is that the latter must be confined to small drafts.

Some of these difficulties have been avoided in the past by defining a slam force as proportional to $\dot{w}_r^2$ and obtaining an empirical K-factor from experiments. This was possible because the most important term in the foregoing expression is in fact the one proportional to $\dot{w}_r^2$ and therefore the contribution of the other terms could be represented in the multiplicative K-factor.

In either case it seems that the resulting slam durations are somewhat smaller than considered by the author. My own, as yet unpublished, calculations resulted in slam forces that resemble very much the ones in Fig. 1 of reference [14]. The durations are such as to lead one to expect most of the slams to be in the range of $t_1/T < 0.3 \sim 0.4$.

Other observation from the calculations is that sometimes the slam propagates forward and sometimes backward. Therefore, the simplification made by the author of considering the slam force applied at one point during the whole slam duration may be somewhat unrealistic, and may influence the higher modes that are excited.

In any event, due to the many possible types of cases that can occur, it is believed that meaningful design values can only be obtained with the help of probabilistic formulations and of statistical measures that define average or extreme conditions.

In conclusion, I believe that the definition of a slam duration and magnitude as well as its point of application is still an open question. As the author has concluded that these parameters had a large influence on the slamming dynamic load factor, it seems that we are not yet able to produce meaningful preliminary design estimates of slam bending moments. However, the work presented in this paper is undoubtedly one step in that direction and I would like to congratulate the author for it.

Additional references

12   Guedes Soares, C. and Moan, T., "Statistical Analysis of Still-Water Bending Moments and Shear Forces in Tankers, Ore and Bulk Carriers," *Norwegian Maritime Research*, Vol. 10, No. 3, Sept. 1982.

13   Juncher Jensen, J. and Terndrup Pedersen, P., "Wave-Induced Bending Moments in Ships—A Quadratic Theory," *Trans.* RINA, Vol. 120, 1978, pp. 151–165.

14   Belik, O., Bishop, R. E. D., and Price, W. G., "On the Slamming Response of Ships to Regular Head Waves," *Trans.* RINA, Vol. 122, 1980, pp. 325–337.

Wm. A. Cleary, Jr., Member

[The views expressed herein are the opinions of the discusser and not necessarily those of the Department of Transportation or the U.S. Coast Guard.]

Professor Evans's paper takes us a step nearer to an actual design criterion for dynamic loading. However, as stated in the Introduction, it is only proposed for determination of "whipping stresses." Since these stresses and the "whipping bending moments" which produce them are high-impact short-cycle transient activities, they must remain differentiated from the relatively continuous short- and long-cycle vibratory stress phenomenon (springing and seaway systems).

Yet the fact that they are different resultants of seaway system force generation does not mean that they are separately endured by the hull girder. The long-standing discussion about the proper method of combining springing and wave stresses (or bending moments) is temporarily on hold because both the Coast Guard and the American Bureau of Shipping are satisfied that the current minimum required section modulus (and moment of inertia) is adequate for moderately strong Great Lakes seaway conditions. However, there is not yet any positive evidence that the section modulus has enough conservatism for the maximum Great Lakes storm seaway. Nor do we wish to find out by endangering people and ships in a deliberate full-scale test as long as the more intelligent *option* of using the many ports of refuge in the Great Lakes remains available to the Great Lakes bulk carrier master. This matters to ocean-going ships because

(a) they do not always have the option of a port of refuge,

(b) seaway actions and reactions are much more severe,

(c) the question of how these dynamic hull loadings interact with one another is still unknown and very important. (Note: Recommendation No. 7 by Professor Evans.)

It is interesting that damping by the hull girder is considered "minimal." Similar conclusions have been drawn in the Great Lakes hull girder stress work accomplished over the past 15 years in *Ryerson*, *Cort*, *Beeghly*, and others. The general conclusion thus far on structural damping seems to be that a hull girder is going to respond to any exterior force and, in certain situations, may respond strongly since the *structural* portion of overall damping is quite low. By apparently proving this low damping, we naval architects have made ourselves even more vulnerable to criticism from the public and the courts than we already were. There is no alternative but to press on with research and find some real answers.

MarAd's research funding has been curtailed, the Coast Guard's R&D Commercial Vessel Safety program currently has virtually no research funding, and the Ship Structures Committee is on a tight budget too. Government funding is therefore not the complete answer for the foreseeable future.

An answer could be found in industry if a group of ships on similar trade routes but having both fine and full forms were similarly instrumented and the results reduced (as nearly as possible) to a nondimensional approach such as that proposed in Professor Evans's paper.

J. R. Cheshire, Member

Lloyd's Register have always been involved in matters concerning slamming, and they are fully aware of the damage to ship structure which this hydrodynamic phenomenon can incur. This has been clearly demonstrated by my predecessor in Lloyd's Register, John McCallum, whose paper concerned with bow flare slamming to the Royal Institution of Naval Architects in 1975 is referred to in the present paper. This particular form of slamming, which became of major importance in respect to fast, large-flare, low-block cargo ships, was identified after a series of case histories was investigated in the mid-seventies. Since then, Lloyd's Register has not only been concerned with improving its knowledge of this particular slamming problem, but has carried out several major studies in respect to bottom slamming.

In brief, the studies consisted of assessing which ships were involved by an examination of the Society's technical records data base, determination of 'theoretical' impact pressures, and matching such applied pressures to the structural capability of stiffened panels. This was done for damaged and undamaged ships to establish the necessary strength criteria to prevent local collapse.

During the course of the studies, it was evident that

(a) short, fine ships had a higher incidence of local damage than longer, fuller ships, which underlines the importance of high relative vertical motion and effects of nonlinearities;

(b) there was no evidence of hull girder damage amidships due to bottom forward slamming;

(c) bottom damage, when it did occur, extended over a considerable distance, suggesting either a variable center of pressure or, more likely, overall high-pressure areas; and

(d) theoretical pressures were very dependent on forward draft, assumed speed and sea state, stressing the importance of ship condition and handling.

Coming to the author's paper, it would be fair to say that the main feature has been to create a mathematical model which can enable the ship's dynamic behavior to be investigated. With this, it has been possible to demonstrate how such parameters as mass distribution, hull stiffness, hydrodynamic added mass, and force-time impulse and its "effective" application at various points along the ship's length influence the characteristic dynamic behavior. Of course, the mathematical model is not reality, and one must always be aware of its shortcomings and treat the results and conclusions accordingly.

While the author is obviously fully aware of this, I feel that it is a matter which should not be lost sight of when recording investigations of response to slamming.

Equation (12) enables a designer to obtain the additional *BM* resulting from a "worst design" slam provided, as indicated by the author in his conclusions, that P_1 is known. The value of P_1, however, must be a force which is feasible when operating under service conditions.

Slamming is a hydrodynamic phenomenon resulting from the contact of the hull with the water, and the resultant pressures are dependent on hull shape, relative velocity of impact, wave shape, pitch angle and air entrapment. The slam is a result of the integrated effect of these pressures of the ship's forebody form, and while we may wish to think of a fixed point as the source of the impact, this is only a simple approach to a complex situation in space and time. This may account for the type of damage I referred to earlier.

F. Everett Reed, Member

The evaluation of the response of a ship hull to slamming is an interesting and important subject, and Professor Evans has made a good contribution. Early in the paper the author lists the factors influencing vibratory response. I suggest that another factor relating to the duration of the slam be added. This might be nondimensionalized by dividing it by the period of the ship fundamental frequency in vertical bending. For example, if the duration of slam is 0.0625 sec and the fundamental frequency of vertical bending is 1.0 Hz, the period of the slam is $1/16$ that of the hull so that even to represent the total energy in the slam, not considering how it is distributed, a computer program suitable for a frequency 16 times the fundamental would be required. To get a clear picture of sharp slams requires a very fine modeling of the ship.

When a short-duration slam is imposed on a ship, it generates bending and shear traveling waves which pass through the ship. These waves gradually degenerate to bending of the ship in its normal modes. The existence of these waves was noted in Fig. 7 of the paper by Dow et al. "Evaluation of Ultimate Hull Strength," presented at the 1981 Extreme Loads Response Symposium, in the little pip which leads all the vibration. (The aforementioned figure is reproduced for this discussion as Fig. 31.) This pip progresses along the length, with time, and broadens out as it proceeds. Although it does not appear to be large, it is of short duration and steep. The shear stress associated with this might be much higher. As this wave proceeds along the ship, it tends to broaden as the speed of the shear wave is different than that of the bending wave and the high-frequency components are damped. When it hits a structural or mass discontinuity, it is partially reflected and the sum of the reflection and the original wave is larger than the free wave. The bending developed by Professor Evans is, I believe, equivalent to the residue after the traveling wave has passed through the ship and the higher harmonics have been damped. I believe that the damping of the ship structure is important in

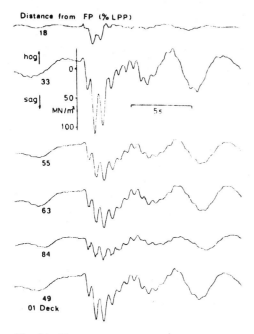

SHIP 'A' LONGITUDINAL DECK STRESS
22 Knots Head Seas

Distance from FP (% LPP)

Fig. 31 Measured slam-induced whipping stresses

the travel of this wave, because it rapidly attenuates the higher harmonics, the steep wave front.

Because of the short distance that this wave proceeds during a sharp slam, a very fine representation of the structure in the region of the slam is required to correctly model its behavior. However, for understanding how the wave progresses, a model that represents the ship as a continuous structure having mass elastic (bending and shear) and damping properties can be useful. Such a model has been developed by Littleton Research and Engineering Corp. for evaluating steady-state excitation. It would require some development to deal with the transient response of a slam.

Additional reference

15   Reed, F. E., "Development of a Criterion for Evaluating the Acceptability of Hull Excitation Forces," MarAd P.O. 3101-0093-2269, April 1981.

C. Daley, Member

The problem addressed has application to the study of ship/ice impact where the load pulse may well be similar in many respects to a slam pulse. In a paper presented before the Arctic Section of the Society [16] a similar approach was taken to predict the general response to ice impact. In that paper the assumption of a sine pulse shape was also made, with the assumption of $t/T = 0.75$ so that the DLF was 1.77. Two ice-breaking ships were examined for the purposes of calculating the effective moment arm for the ice load. In that case the effective moment arm was found to be $0.36L$, after all dynamic and mass factors were accounted for, so that the midbody stress could be expressed as

$$\sigma = \frac{0.36PL}{S}$$

where P is the amplitude of the ice load, L the ship length at the waterline, and S the section modulus.

On the second page of the paper, Professor Evans states that "stresses too should be subject to the same magnification factors" while on the next page: "it would be legitimate, by means of

the DLF, to replace the dynamic load with an equivalent static load and continue with the procedures. . . . " The question to Professor Evans relates to the use of Fig. 26 in the paper. With an effective moment arm of 25 percent of L for a load at the FP, does that mean that dynamic stresses could be calculated for the slam pulse?

$$\sigma = \frac{0.25\,PL}{S}$$

What would this change to if t/T were raised to 0.75 where the DLF curve peaks?

Additional reference

16   Glen, I. F. and Daley, C., "Ice Impact Loads on Ships," Presented at the Spring Meeting, Arctic Section, SNAME, Calgary, Sask., 1982.

Y. Raskin, Member

Professor Evans has presented a most interesting, design-oriented paper. Investigation of the bending moments induced by slamming is of interest to ABS.

The calculation of bending moment due to slamming is complicated as it requires the joint solution of both ship motion and ship bending. For the approximate determination of hull girder response to slamming, the problem could be separated into two independent parts: calculation of hydrodynamic loads and subsequent calculation of ship's hull girder response under the action of these known loads. To calculate the hydrodynamic loads it is necessary, first of all, to compute the ship motion for a family of ships. The approximate solution for the relative vertical displacement of the ships' bow sections can then be found. Using these displacements the hydrodynamic forces can be calculated based on existing theoretical procedures and results of experiments. The slam bending moment can then be determined using the calculated forces.

The bending moment due to slamming depends upon ship motion parameters which in turn depend upon ship's length, block coefficient, speed, weight distribution, and wave conditions. These parameters influence the slamming bending moment in a complex manner. For example, the influence of added-mass distributions on the slam bending moment is more complicated than indicated by the influence of the added-mass coefficient [C_{AM} of equation (12)]. This is because the hydrodynamic loads depend upon the added-mass distribution along the ship and also upon time. This can be seen in the bottom and flare slamming bending moments which depend in different manners upon the ship's draft and fullness of bow. For instance, the loads due to bottom slamming increase with decreasing draft and increasing fullness of bow. On the other hand, the loads due to bow flare impact increase with increasing draft and with decreasing fullness of bow.

Professor Evans's paper is dedicated to the solution of one part of the general problem described in the foregoing—calculation of slam bending moment under the action of presumed loads. This comparative investigation indicates that there is a substantial difference between the nondimensional bending moments for the ships of Fig. 4 and the simple one-degree-of-freedom theoretical dynamic load factor of Fig. 2. We should note that this comparison does not fully reflect the possibility of using the theoretical dynamic load factor of Fig. 2 for calculating the slam bending moment for the ships. To investigate this possibility it is desirable to determine the non-dimensional quasi-static slam bending moment for a value of large slam duration and then determine the dynamic load factor for the ships. This resultant dynamic load factor can be close to the theoretical one of a simple one-degree-of-freedom system. The high-frequency modes of vibration mainly influence the initial maximum peak of the bottom slam bending moment. The subsequent amplitudes of bottom slam bending moment, which can coincide with the maximum sagging wave-induced bending moment, depend mainly upon the first-mode natural frequency of vibration.

A half-sine shape of the slam pulse was assumed for the investigation described in this paper. The shape of the slam pulse has a very small influence in bottom slamming. However, for bow flare slamming it is necessary to describe more precisely the changing of hydrodynamic load with time. This is because the time of increasing load is determined by the time of the submergence of the ship's cross section under consideration. In this case the maximum dynamic bending moment can occur almost simultaneously with the maximum wave-induced sagging moment.

With regard to the influence of ship mass distribution on slam bending moment we would like to note that the ship mass distribution also influences the first-mode period of vibration. Was this taken into account when the influence of ship mass distributions was introduced?

The location of slam center depends upon the ship and ship motion parameters and it is difficult to say where this location is. Sometimes the slam center is assumed for the most severe conditions. For example, the maximum extent of slamming force may be assumed to be about 20 to 30 percent of ship's length aft of the FP. Another possibility, which we believe is more correct, is to calculate the hydrodynamic forces as a function of space and time using seekeeping calculations and results of tests. The ship's hull can then be calculated as a free-free nonuniform beam under the action of these distributed forces. This was done for example by Ochi and Motter some years ago and by ABS in a research project.

Joao G. de Oliveira, Member

Professor Evans's contributions to the field of ship structural design have always been outstanding and this one is, as expected, no exception. This discusser would just like to offer a few minor comments in the hope that they might help to amplify some of the important points raised in the paper.

This paper deals with the hull girder response to slamming from a global point of view, when the hull girder is treated as a beam bending in the vertical plane due to bottom impact. The author indicates that the bottom stiffness at the impact point is not a significant consideration, as far as the hull girder's vibratory response is concerned. However, it should be noted that when the hull girder is subjected to severe transient loads, the local response can be critical, in the sense that local damage due to impact can seriously affect the ship's safety. This is not necessarily only the case of bottom impact, but can be even more critical in side shell impact, since the side shell is in general a much weaker structure than the bottom. A potentially dangerous type of side impact can be caused by breaking waves, and at least in one case this type of environmental condition has been thought to have been the main cause of extensive damage on a large tanker. One of the difficulties in treating such a problem concerns the lack of data on pulse magnitudes and durations, and this echoes Recommendations 2 and 3 offered by the author.

It appears that the method developed in this paper is not directly applicable to the case of side impact, in which the horizontal modes of vibration are primarily excited, for the simple reason that the port/starboard symmetry no longer exists. However, large hull girder bending moments can conceivably occur in such cases, and it might be useful to extend this method to cover such problems.

This study shows that under certain circumstances the higher modes of vibration can have an important role on the hull response to slamming. Shear stiffness affects the higher modes, and it might not be advisable to consider it as a fixed fraction of the hull's bending stiffness. In this respect it might be worthwhile to include a shear stiffness related parameter, such as the L/D ratio, in the design formula (12).

Simple design formulas such as the ones presented in this paper can be of great value to the profession. They identify the main parameters which are relevant for a particular type of phenomenon, and they enable the designer to make the best choices at a preliminary stage, and while the main parameters can still be changed.

Naresh M. Maniar, Member

The design community owes Professor Evans a word of gratitude for his attempts to develop an engineering solution after laborious analysis to what may be considered one of the more elusive hull girder loads and associated response, that is, slamming and vibration. The substance of the paper does well to extend the past research work to isolate the significant design parameters with respect to slamming, and assess their sensitivity. It also provides an additional building block for the eventual development of a rational procedure for the design of the main hull girder. By rational procedure is meant the capability to estimate separately each component of the primary load and then superimpose it correctly in accordance with its respective phase relationship to deduce the total primary load.

It is desirable to test the proposed semi-empirical expression for estimating the whipping bending moments amidships. It seems that the only way to do it is by applying the expression to ship designs for which full-scale or model test records have been obtained for the total bending moments, and the whipping bending moment components have been isolated. If the semi-empirical expression can be widely validated, it would be very helpful to determine in the early stages of the design whether the slamming-induced bending moment will be within acceptable levels.

An example of what I am suggesting is to use the results of the Ship Structure Committee Report 287 where the full-scale hull girder stress data were analyzed for three ships and the vibration bending moment components were separated; the ships were the containership SL-7, the bulk carrier *Fotini L* and the tanker *Universe Ireland*. I might mention that, in case of the SL-7, the vibration stress was as high as 10 to 15 kpsi on occasion. In case of the other two ships, the stress in question was quite small. In applying the semi-empirical expression to the SL-7, we may find out what combinations of the three unknown, namely, peak pressure, lever arm and pulse duration, result in bending moments which correlate with the full-scale measurements.

Lastly, it is possible that the expression will be helpful in tracing damage in secondary structure which may have been caused by excessive primary loads due to a large whipping moment component. Of course, this assumes that the main hull girder is not damaged.

Christopher T. Loeser, Member

[The views expressed herein are the opinions of the discusser and not necessarily those of the Department of Defense or the Department of the Navy.]

Professor Evans has presented a very interesting paper developing an approach introduced in his earlier work concerning the nature of the ship response to a slam impulse. He has examined the sensitivity of the ship's response to the variation of a number of parameters and found that the characteristics of the load, including the duration and the location of the impulse, are significant. The design equation resulting from the parametric analysis includes both pulse duration and location, but no guidance is provided for selection design values for these parameters. As the author states, the nature of the slam impulsive load is not well understood. I have two examples to illustrate values of these parameters for particular cases.

Recent model tests using a SWATH (small waterplane area, twin hull) ship model, performed for the Navy at Stevens Institute of Technology, were made to examine slam pressures. A typical pulse duration on a panel gage measuring 4 ft² (0.37 m²) full scale was about 0.067 sec full scale. Although the author examines a range of slam pulse durations of 0.0626 to 1.0 sec in the parametric study, the design equation was developed for a range of slam durations roughly 0.3 sec and longer, significantly greater than the pulse duration measured on the SWATH model. Although the slam pulse characteristics of monohulls are undoubtedly different from those of a SWATH, this is an indication that slam pulses of very short duration are possible.

The approach developed by Ochi and Motter [17] for estimating slamming characteristics provides a statistical look at slam location. They presented results of calculations for the Mariner which indicated that most slam activity occurred between 10 and 15 percent of the ship's length from the bow. The author has covered this range in the parametric analysis and in the design equation.

Further research is needed in all areas of slamming, including pulse duration, magnitude and location. Although some investigators have focused on the nature of the slamming load, most studies and measurements have concerned the structural response. The author has shown that the nature of the load is an important factor in slamming response and it is evident that an improved understanding of slamming will aid in the development of structural design approaches. A method for the selection of the design slam impulse load, perhaps based on Ochi and Motter, could be developed which will give pulse magnitude, duration and location based on an accepted set of operational limits, for example, a limiting number of slams per hour, and a limiting vertical velocity. This could be coupled with structural design approaches, such as those presented by the author.

Additional reference

17 Ochi, M. K. and Motter, L. E., "A Method to Estimate Slamming Characteristics for Ship Design," *Marine Technology*, Vol. 8, No. 2, April 1971.

Walter M. Maclean, Member

[The views expressed herein are the opinions of the discusser and not necessarily those of the Department of Transportation or the Maritime Administration.]

I knew Professor Evans could only retire to do more interesting and comprehensive work. This paper is an excellent example of his thoroughness. Those of us interested in slamming can only be pleased by the treatment given. Although I can only agree with the work and thoughts presented, there are several aspects which should receive more attention.

Of first concern is the magnitude of loads to be considered. This has been elusive throughout the history of slamming investigations. Well-documented, full-scale data need to be obtained for correlation with model and theoretical studies. The statistics of response must also be established. Shipboard monitoring instrumentation is needed for this work.

Secondly, the location of load needs to be related to the magnitude and time history of load application. The loads of longer duration discussed in the paper generally are associated with bow flare slamming near the FP, exciting all modes of primary response (at least the first half dozen, the higher modes damp quickly). Loads of shorter duration, $t_1/T \leq 0.2$, can be expected on the forward bottom surfaces farther aft. The finer the hull form, the farther aft the location of slam load. The shorter the duration, the higher the local pressures. The total

force and/or impulse effective on the hull girder is likely to be much less as well.

To my knowledge bow flare slamming is of consequence not only to the hull girder but to the local bow flare structure while the bottom slam is of primary concern to the bottom secondary and tertiary structure. Although hull girder failures have occurred due to forward bottom slamming, these have affected the structure in the vicinity of the forward quarter point as in Yamamoto's work; midship $0.4L$ structure seems affected only to a second-order extent.

Surveys of bottom structure subjected to heavy slamming show the relatively local extent of loadings even though there may be evidence of numerous such high loadings. Bow flare structure may have large sections set in in a single event, often claimed to have occurred by encounters with "rogue" waves.

There is today, I believe, open recognition that ship structures have been refined to such an extent that ship masters can, without being aware of and therefore without appreciating the full significance of their action, drive their large, powerful vessels to their own destruction. Ships with bows torn away, hatch covers and bow flare structures stove-in, and total losses result too frequently. Yamamoto challenged the recent ISSC attendees with "What are you going to do about it?" No one gave an answer.

Aside from the definition of load, location and time history, a careful look should be taken at hull structure forward. The transition from forward bottom to midship structure is not adequately related to hull form, power and seakeeping characteristics of a ship. The use of half girders to reduce plate span/thickness ratio and transmit loads to the primary structure requires more thoughtful consideration. The buckling of local bottom structure internals and the fracturing of weldments over many years is still being inadequately addressed, and no proven guidance is even in a formative state either for design or fabrication of the bow structure of commercial ships. Damaged structures are generally repaired to the original condition rather than to an upgraded condition.

Author's Closure

I am extremely pleased with the interest this paper seems to have been somewhat responsible for and for the very thoughtful discussions which have been presented. Evidently the subject is believed to be of importance and that, by itself, is rather complimentary in that it tends to confirm the rightness of the subject chosen for study. Some may have expected a miracle to be brought forth. I can only claim to have provided a crude instrument but not *all* the input data needed. So the slam load still awaits definition although the form in which it may be most useful is suggested.

Mr. Guedes Soares raises several interesting points which I will refer to in order.

First, I have great doubt that "the duration of a slam can be considered to be somewhat insensitive to the type and/or size of the ships" because both a ship's pitching period and its heaving period must be related to its mass and distribution. Furthermore, whether the bow sections are U-shaped or V-shaped must affect slam duration too. The opinion, stated by Mr. Guedes Soares, that values of t_1/T will generally fall in the range between 0.3 and 0.4 is not only interesting but so small it must be supposed that an increase of the ship's period, T, say, will be accompanied by some increase in the slam duration, t_1, also (and vice versa) to accomplish this concentration. The opinion that tankers fall in the t_1/T range of less than 0.2 seems no more to nullify this point than to confirm it as tanker and bulk carrier mass distributions are very uniform longitudinally and so produce larger vibration periods than most other classes.

At this stage the only help to be offered for delineating DLF curves below t_1/T values below 0.2 is that ultimately all must go through the origin! This obvious fact may be helpful if it is not overlooked.

Both in this paper and its predecessor the point was made that slam response bending moments some distance beyond the 40 percent length may be greater than those amidships, a point confirmed by Mr. Guedes Soares. Although Fig. 25, for example, shows this to be true for one slam location, in that particular case even greater bending moments would occur at the points in question if far-forward slams were a possibility. However, Fig. 25 is but one ship, one mass distribution and one slam duration. Given the significant mass of data already compiled for the four subject vessels, more complete study should and could easily be made to help predict when hull end bending stresses are likely to be most critical and sufficient to warrant special attention.

I regret that I can offer no help in defining the most likely or most extreme slam, whether as to magnitude, duration or center of application. Much more data, greater understanding and statistical studies will be necessary to answer those questions. A principal virtue of such a study as this is to expose what information is most badly needed and the form which will make it most immediately useful. Even more obviously, it hopes to make clear which are the most important design variables and their relative magnitudes. From this study too it is possible to estimate with considerable confidence the change of midship bending moment with a given change of hull girder bending stiffness, all other factors being unchanged (See Fig. 3). That fact should have been emphasized more in the paper. The effect of greater or less hull flexibility in all its manifestations was, in fact, the reason for this study in the first place.

It was not intended to imply, because the formula given was limited to t_1/T values greater than 0.2, that no smaller values are possible or likely. Of course smaller values might be anticipated.

The distinction between slamming response and springing response is well made by Mr. Cleary. Originally Roger Kline and I had hoped to shed a little light on the springing problem too, at least to the point of ferreting out the major control factors and offering some help with preliminary design estimations. However, that work has had to be suspended. Damping in the springing problem, no matter how large or small its influence is found to be, is surely more important than in slamming response where it is the earliest of response cycles which are important.

Mr. Cheshire's report of some generalized findings at Lloyd's is most interesting and I find it hard not to be drawn into discussing his discussion. However, to stay on course I must deal only with his second conclusion, that "there was no evidence of hull girder damage amidships due to bottom forward slamming" in the ships studied. Nor was midship damage from slamming the reason for this study. However, I was curious about several things influenced by hull girder stiffness and among them was the question of how much the stiffness might be reduced before such damage *was* felt. Mention has already been made of some of the other insights gained—as, for example, clear of the midship rule length. Mr. Daley's discussion is a reminder that there are other dynamic loadings forward than slamming, icebreaking being one, and these too may be handled. Also, I would maintain that it is usually even nicer to know, when true, that *no* problem exists rather than that it does exist.

Probably one is always aware of most of the discrepancies between full-scale reality and such investigations as this. One artificiality I do *not* have qualms about is the use of the "point"

load because it is applied, in all cases, so far from the cross section of concern, amidships, and because the computer model is so finely articulated.

There is, of course, the other side and in *favor* of laboratory research. Controlled scale experiments and verified calculative procedures can be stretched beyond normal current practice to establish "end points" or to discover what might lie ahead in time.

Mr. Reed and I evidently have an initial misunderstanding. The nondimensional form of slam duration which he advocates as "another" is, in fact, the very one used throughout the paper on most of the figures; it is, namely, t_1/T.

There were several forms of graphical output for every computer run on which this paper was based. One was a plot of midship bending moment versus time. Samples were shown in Figs. 7 and 8 of the 1978 paper. From such as these it is very clear that several higher-order vibration modes are generated and superimposed, especially with short slam durations. As no damping has been included, over several first-order cycles the phase shifts will insure that an arithmetic total bending moment of the several maxima will almost certainly be achieved. I really have no fear at all then that the envelope bending moment diagrams relied upon here represent any but the most realistically severe occurrences, or at least encompass them.

I am delighted to learn of Mr. Daley's parallel experience with ice impact and I am very interested to read the paper by himself and Mr. Glen.

I have converted the formula for the estimated bending moment as given in the paper [equations (12) or (13)] to Mr. Daley's expression for stress. If the added-mass distribution during icebreaking is not greatly different than for slamming, the two cases should be comparable as far as this simple formula is concerned. The limits of suitability of equations (10c), (12) and (13) are: t_1/T between 0.20 and 0.60, p between 0 and 22.73 percent, J between 0.90 and 1.08, and C_{AM} between 0.50 and 0.80. Within these limits the maximum effective lever for $t_1/T = 0.20$ is 23.8 percent L and for $t_1/T = 0.60$ it is 33 percent L. These are for the impulse being applied at the FP, so $p = 0$. Extrapolation to $t_1/ = 0.75$ produces an effective lever of 35.4 percent L for an impulse at the FP. Thus it seems reasonable to expect that

$$\sigma = \frac{0.36PL}{S}$$

at $t_1/T = 0.75$ although I myself have no data to support values at quite such large slam durations.

Apparently I confused Mr. Daley by using the term "magnification factors" in one place and "DLF" in another. I meant one and the same thing in both cases.

I have gone carefully over Mr. Raskin's exposition principally to detect any areas of disagreement or question and there are only two points which need to be made.

As indicated earlier, I hope it is not implied anywhere in the paper that slam loadings are being assumed in any way except in the very general terms of their growth and decay with time. The load magnitude, duration and center of application are left as open questions. Only a *means* of using that information is suggested and that for *first-order* estimations. There should be no misunderstanding regarding how elusive still is the goal of defining such a slam design load for all shapes, types and sizes of vessel. Even the nature of slamming is not wholly agreed upon. Perhaps the bow may not have to emerge. An introductory pressure spike is introduced by some investigators. If forefoot impact with the surface is required, some maintain it occurs linearly fore and aft while others claim the sharpest slams occur when the surface contact is convergent from points both forward and aft of the slam center.

On strictly theoretical grounds Mr. Raskin is far too optimistic about the DLF curves for ships (each with its infinite number of degrees of freedom) ever matching the elemental DLF curve for a system with only one degree of freedom. Appendix 3 elaborates upon this point. The important thing is that, speaking graphically, the calculated ordinates for nondimensional bending moments inevitably defined a line (for example, Fig. 2). That a similarity exists is reassuring but hardly more than that and no doubt indicates a strong predominance of the first-order vibration mode over much of the t_1/T range. I will say that in discussing our 1978 paper, Mr. McCallum said "The consistency with which the points corresponding to different slam durations and different hull stiffnesses fit the characteristic curves for each ship indicates a very promising basis for a potentially simple and practical method for estimating slam-induced bending moments at an early design stage," and he called this "the most important feature of the paper." I am inclined to agree with that assessment.

As damping has had so little time to act during the first few whipping response cycles, it appears justifiable to add the envelope, or maximum, slam bending moments discussed here to whatever wave bending moment it is in phase with. Also, the first-mode period of vibration used throughout *was* that for the particular ship in question and its particular load distribution at the time.

I would like to thank Prof. de Oliveira for his kind remarks and also for his assistance in rounding out the theory supporting the fundamental DLF sine curve which is contained in Appendix 2. With further work the design-use formulation given in the paper *should* be refined and its application to transverse vibration may indeed prove feasible.

Perhaps it should be reaffirmed by me that local bottom stiffness is very definitely of importance with regard to local damage, machinery and equipment foundations and the like. It is only of little importance here because it has little effect in moderating or intensifying the transmission of an impact to the hull girder.

I echo Mr. Maniar's plea for full-scale verification of the formulation. At the same time the whipping stress response is measured, the slamming impulse should be defined also, of course, both in space and time. Such information is probably the most badly needed of all and, no doubt, will not be easy or inexpensive to obtain. I am grateful for his suggestions and I am most interested in the stress magnitude he quotes.

Mr. Loeser's principal comment again calls for improved understanding of the slamming force, reinforcing Mr. Maniar's comment and confirming my own feelings. May it soon come to pass.

Dr. Maclean is something of an expert on the subject of slamming so I welcome his confirmation that our greatest need now is for much better physical and statistical descriptions of the slamming force, how it relates to the ship, the sea state, the hull form and for the full range of its occurrence in space and time.

I hope there is no misunderstanding the fact that the DLF approach seems valid also for very short slam durations. It is only the formula given to delineate the DLF curves ahead of time that has been limited to t_1/T values greater than 0.2.

Graphical output for this study has shown the ability to detect the higher orders of vibration and does so most consistently with short slams applied well aft of the FP. Conversely, long slams applied at or near the FP are seen to induce pure first-order responses almost exclusively. At present I have no explanation for this being in disagreement with Dr. Maclean's statement.

I must now reiterate my thanks to the numerous discussors for their various insights and additional information. It is my hope that a useful tool has been provided and that our greatest areas of ignorance and need relative to slamming are now more clearly seen.

SNAME *Transactions*, Vol. 90, 1982, pp. 85–109

Cavitation-Induced Excitation Forces on the Hull

Erling Huse,[1] Member, and **Wang Guoqiang,**[2] Visitor

The paper describes a practical procedure to determine the hull surface excitation force induced by propeller cavitation. The procedure is based on combining pressure fluctuations at a few positions on the hull, experimentally determined by traditional model testing, with a theoretical calculation of the total excitation force. The idea is that the pressure fluctuations measured at a few positions are used to calculate an "equivalent singularity distribution" to represent the propeller. From this singularity distribution the total excitation force is calculated. The procedure includes the possibility of calculating the "generalized force" for each vibratory mode of the hull, provided the vibratory modes are known. The possibility of including the effect of finite propagation velocity of the pressure waves in water is also discussed. As part of the total procedure, theoretical methods are developed for calculating the solid boundary factor of the hull as well as the influence of the free surface upon propeller-induced pressure amplitudes. Experimental investigations are described which verify these theoretical methods. Furthermore, the paper presents practical information on the magnitude of such solid boundary and free-surface effects. Such information may be of practical value in correcting for such effects when doing propeller-induced pressure measurements in cavitation tunnels in general.

Introduction

DURING the past 20 years much attention has been paid to the subject of propeller-induced hull vibrations. The excitation forces are of two types. First, there are the so-called shaft forces, which are the forces acting on the propeller due to its operation in a non-homogeneous wake field. Secondly, there are the so-called surface forces, which are excitation forces due to the pressures induced by the propeller on the hull surface. There are today several methods available for theoretical as well as experimental prediction of shaft forces. The main problem in predicting shaft forces is the limited accuracy of the input data, that is, the wake field itself. A survey of these problems is given in references [1, 2].[3]

Regarding the surface forces the situation today is such that we have satisfactory methods for calculating the pressures induced by a noncavitating propeller. The first theories for prediction of such forces were published about 20 years ago. Several later investigations have shown, however, that the main source of surface force excitation for merchant vessels is not the noncavitating propeller, but the cavities on the propeller blades [1–5].

The free space pressure field induced by cavities of known geometry can be easily calculated from hydrodynamic theory [1]. (By free space pressure field is meant the pressure field induced by propeller and cavities, provided the propeller is operating in the relevant wake distribution, but without the hull and free surface affecting the pressure field.) In order to obtain the excitation pressures on the hull itself, one also has to include the solid boundary effect of the hull and the effect of the free water surface. The basic principles of a theory for calculating solid boundary and free-surface effects are well known [6–8]. The preceding references primarily aim at calculating the total excitation force and only for noncavitating propellers. However, no information has been published showing how solid boundary and free-surface effects influence the pressure distribution over hulls of arbitrary geometry. One of the objectives of the present paper is to provide numerical calculations as well as experimental data for the distribution of solid boundary and free-surface effects over the afterbody.

As mentioned earlier, one can easily calculate the free space pressure field induced by cavities of known geometry as a function of time. However, for practical applications this is not very interesting as long as our methods for predicting the cavity geometry itself are not very reliable. Considerable effort has been spent in recent years in developing methods for theoretical calculations of cavity geometry from known propeller geometry, load conditions and wake distribution. In spite of all this effort there are still many physical processes in connection with the generation and volume variation of cavities that we are not able to describe and calculate theoretically to a reasonable degree of accuracy. Thus, model testing is still considered the most accurate way of predicting cavitation-induced pressures on the hull. This is normally done by pressure transducers so that one obtains the pressure fluctuations at a few positions on the afterbody only. Evaluation of propeller design regarding excitation forces is often based on these pressure amplitudes alone. This philosophy is satisfactory when local vibration problems such as fatigue cracking of welds and hull plating just above the propeller are concerned. However, when overall vibrations of afterbody and superstructure are concerned, a physically more correct basis for the evaluation is the integrated pressures, that is, the total excitation force on the hull. Such integration based on experimental measurements of pressures at a few positions is, however, not very ef-

---

[1] Professor, Norwegian Hydrodynamic Laboratories, Trondheim, Norway.

[2] Visiting scientist, Norwegian Hydrodynamic Laboratories, Trondheim, Norway; on leave from Shanghai Jiao Tong University, Shanghai, Peoples Republic of China.

[3] Numbers in brackets designate References at end of paper.

Presented at the Annual Meeting, New York, N. Y., November 17–20, 1982, of THE SOCIETY OF NAVAL ARCHITECTS AND MARINE ENGINEERS.

fective. The main reason is that at large distances from the propeller the pressure amplitudes become very small and difficult to measure to a satisfactory accuracy. Furthermore, for the integration of the pressures to obtain the total force it is necessary also to have the phase angles of the pressure fluctuations at each position on the hull, phase angles that are even more difficult to measure accurately. As a third reason it should be mentioned that wall effects in cavitation tunnels can become significant when measuring hull pressures at large distances from the propeller [9]. Even if the pressures at large distances from the propeller are small, they may still contribute significantly to the total excitation force due to the large integration area. The situation is therefore not satisfactory regarding practical procedures for predicting the total surface excitation force on a ship at the design stage.

The second objective of the present paper is to describe a possible procedure to improve upon this situation. The basic idea behind this procedure has been published in [10]. The procedure consists in combining experimentally determined pressure fluctuations at a few positions on the hull by traditional model testing, with a theoretical calculation of the total excitation force. The idea is that the pressure fluctuations measured at a few positions are used to calculate an "equivalent singularity distribution" to represent the propeller. From this singularity distribution the total excitation force is calculated. The procedure includes the possibility of calculating the "generalized force" for each vibratory mode of the hull, provided the vibratory modes are known. The possibility of in-

cluding the effect of finite propagation velocity of the pressure waves in water is also discussed.

Theoretical considerations

Outline of new procedure

The complete procedure for predicting the surface excitation force includes the following steps:
- *Step I:* Model tests are carried out in a cavitation tank or tunnel, including measurements of pressure fluctuations on the afterbody at a certain number of transducer positions. The measurements are done in the cavitating as well as the noncavitating condition. The pressure signals are Fourier-analyzed to determine the amplitude and phase angles of the various harmonics at each transducer position.
- *Step II:* The solid boundary and free-surface effects upon the distribution of pressure amplitudes on the hull are calculated theoretically. The results of this calculation are presented in the form of factors S_b, S_f and S_{tot}. Here, S_{tot} is the combined solid boundary and free-surface factor defined as the ratio between the resulting pressure amplitude on the hull surface and the corresponding free space pressure amplitude. As suggested in [11], S_{tot} can be expressed as a product

$$S_{tot} = S_b \cdot S_f$$

where S_b is the solid boundary factor which represents the image effect of the hull upon the pressures. S_f is a further

---

Nomenclature

A = wetted area of hull

c = tip clearance measured vertically to section above propeller

C_{xo}, C_{yo}, C_{zo} = coordinates of propeller center

E = energy absorbed per unit time by ship from pressure field of propeller

F_z = instantaneous force in vertical direction

F_{zk} = "generalized excitation force" amplitude

f_w = weighting function

G = number of transducers

g = acceleration of gravity

n = propeller rate of revolutions

n_z = vertical component of unit vector normal to hull surface

$\vec{n}$ = outward unit vector normal to the surface

p_c = blade frequency pressure amplitude due to cavitation alone

p_f = free space pressure field generated by pulsating source

p_{fk} = amplitude of kth harmonic of p_f

p_{mk} = pressure amplitude of kth harmonic due to cavitation alone

p_{nc} = blade frequency pressure amplitude measured in cavitation tunnel at such high cavitation numbers that there is no cavitation on the propeller

p_{wc} = blade frequency pressure amplitude measured in cavitation tunnel with cavitation number correctly modeled

Q_k = strength of the kth harmonic of pulsating source representing cavities of propeller

Q_{ko} = amplitude of kth harmonic of pulsating source strength

R = distance from field point (ξ, η, ζ) to source point

R_i = distance from field point (ξ, η, ζ) to source point of image distribution

R_b = radial distance from shaft center to center of rotating balls

R_p = radius of propeller

R_s = distance from shaft center to pulsating source

R_T = distance between transducer position and pulsating source

S_b = solid boundary factor

S_f = free-surface factor

S_{tot} = combined solid boundary and free-surface factor ($= S_b \cdot S_f$)

t = time

$T_1 \, T_2 \, T_3 \, T_4$ = transducers

$\vec{u}$ = onset flow at each control point

$\vec{u}_k$ = amplitude of kth harmonic of $\vec{u}$

v_k = amplitude of kth harmonic of vibratory velocity of hull surface

$x \, y \, z$ = coordinates of pulsating source

Z = number of propeller blades

α = section angle of V-shaped plate arrangement

α_s = defined in Fig. 4

Δs_j = area of panel number j

$\xi \, \eta \, \zeta$ = coordinates of the field point

σ_j = source density on panel number j

σ_k = complex amplitude of source distribution over surface of hull

Φ = velocity potential of onset flow and source distribution on double hull

Φ_D = potential of the flow arising from propeller/hull interaction

Φ_{Dk} = complex amplitude of kth harmonic of potential Φ_D

Φ_j = potential at field point due to σ_j

Φ_p = propeller potential

Φ_{pk} = complex amplitude of kth harmonic of Φ_p

$\Phi_k = \Phi_{pk} + \Phi_{Dk}$

Φ_{pi} = potential due to image of propeller

Φ_s = steady disturbance flow about bare hull in presence of free surface

ϕ_c = blade frequency pressure phase angle due to cavitation alone

ϕ_k = phase angle of source strength

ϕ_{mk} = phase angle of p_{mk}

ϕ_{nc} = phase angle of p_{nc}

ϕ_{pk} = phase angle of p_{fk}

ϕ_{vk} = phase angle of v_k

ϕ_{wc} = phase angle of p_{wc}

$\omega = 2\pi n$

　　　　Cavitation-Induced Excitation Forces on the Hull

correction due to the effect of the presence of the free water surface upon the pressures.

• *Step III:* From the measured pressure fluctuations at the transducers, and the calculated solid boundary and free-surface effect, one determines an "equivalent singularity distribution" which is representative for the propeller and cavitation as far as generation of free space pressure field is concerned. This system of equivalent singularities will in principle consist of sources, sinks and possibly vortices or other types of hydrodynamic singularities.

• *Step IV:* The free space pressure field generated by the "equivalent singularity system" is calculated at a large number of positions covering the whole area of the hull over which pressures are to be integrated. These pressures are multiplied by the solid boundary and free-surface factor S_{tot} to obtain the distribution of pressure amplitudes and phase angles over the hull. These pressures are finally integrated to obtain total excitation force. In connection with this integration one may take into account the effect of finite propagation velocity of the pressure waves in water and one may also take into account the vibratory modes of the hull to obtain the "generalized excitation force" for each mode of vibration.

In the subsequent sections we discuss in more detail how each of these steps should be carried out.

Cavitation tests

There are various types of test facilities and test procedures in use for evaluating the cavitation performance of propellers and for measuring propeller-induced pressures. The procedure for obtaining the total excitation force discussed in this paper can be combined with the application of any such test facility or test procedure. The only requirements are that the pressures are being measured at a certain number of positions on the hull model. Furthermore, these pressures must be Fourier-analyzed to produce amplitude and phase angles. As discussed later in this paper, we shall restrict ourselves primarily to the pressures and excitation forces induced by volume variation of the cavities. This means that it is very important in connection with the cavitation tests that the wake distribution of the ship be correctly modeled during the cavitation tests (see reference [5]).

Calculation of solid boundary and free-surface effects

The problem of solid boundary and free-surface effects is solved by traditional potential theory. The concept of a double hull is applied; that is, above the free surface one introduces an "image hull" as shown in Fig. 1. This image hull and the real submerged part of the hull are symmetric with respect to the water surface (see, for example, [8]). The flow around this double hull and the pressure distribution over it are solved for an onset flow of the following characteristics:

1. The onset flow vector is of arbitrary direction over the various parts of the hull.

2. The onset flow is a periodic function of time so that it can be expressed in terms of Fourier components.

The boundary condition of no flow through the solid surface is satisfied by applying a continuous source distribution over the hull and its image. This source distribution will thus be a function of position on the hull, and of time. At the free surface the following boundary condition has to be satisfied:

$$\frac{\partial^2 \Phi}{\partial t^2} - g \cdot \frac{\partial \Phi}{\partial z} = 0 \text{ at } z = 0$$

where

Φ = velocity potential of onset flow and source distribution on double hull

t = time

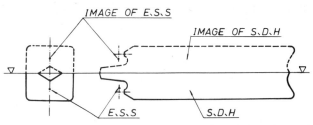

Fig. 1 Singularity distribution used for calculating solid boundary and free surface effect: E.S.S. = "equivalent singularity system"; S.D.H. = source distribution representing solid hull surface

g = acceleration of gravity

z = vertical coordinate, positive downward, $z = 0$ at level of still water free surface

The free-surface boundary condition stated in the preceding equation contains two terms. In the frequency range of interest here one can apply the "high-frequency approximation," which means neglecting the second term in the equation. The simplified free-surface boundary condition will then become

$$\frac{\partial^2 \Phi}{\partial t^2} = 0$$

The validity of this approximation for typical ship geometries and for frequencies from typical blade frequencies and up has been checked. One finds that the second term in the equation will typically be of the order of one thousandth of the first term. The simplified boundary condition is satisfied if the singularity system is such that the potential is always zero at $z = 0$. This is achieved by choosing the source distribution strength on the image part of the hull to be of opposite sign compared with the source distribution on the submerged part of the hull. Furthermore, we have to introduce a negative image of the singularity system describing the propeller.

If we choose the sign of the image source distribution and image propeller to be the same as the sign of the submerged part of the hull and the propeller, then we do not satisfy the condition of zero potential at the free surface. Instead we satisfy the condition of zero flow normal to the surface $z = 0$. The latter case is also an interesting and relevant situation regarding cavitation—induced hull pressures. It corresponds to fitting a solid horizontal plate at the level of the free surface. This is exactly the test setup applied at several cavitation laboratories around.

Since the onset flow is a periodic function of time with a fundamental frequency equal to the blade frequency of the propeller, it can be expressed in the form of a Fourier series, specifying the sine and cosine component of each harmonic. This fact is made use of in the numerical calculation of the source distribution over the hull surface. As shown in the Appendix we can treat the sine and cosine components of the onset flow in the same way as a stationary inflow and use a conventional "Hess and Smith method" [12] to calculate the source distribution over the hull.

The numerical procedure for calculating the solid boundary and free surface effects developed at the Norwegian Hydrodynamic Laboratories (NHL) thus consists in dividing the hull surface into a suitable number of panels. The sine and cosine components of the relevant onset flow are determined at the center point of each panel. Each panel is ascribed a certain source distribution. This source distribution is determined by solving the system of linear equations generated by requiring the boundary condition to be satisfied for each panel. Having calculated the source strength of each element, we calculate the potential at each element numerically by a procedure commonly used in seakeeping applications; see, for instance, [13]. The complete procedure for calculating solid boundary and free-surface effects developed at NHL is described in more detail in the Appendix.

Determination of equivalent singularity distribution to represent the propeller

A cavitating propeller can be represented by a system of singularities, for example, as follows:

1. A source/sink distribution along the mean line of the blade profile to represent the effect of blade thickness.
2. A vortex system to represent the mean and fluctuating lift on the propeller blades.
3. A source/sink distribution to represent the motion of the cavities, a source distribution which will come in addition to the source distribution representing the blade thickness.
4. A system of sources of pulsating strength to represent the volume variation of the cavities.

The pressure signal is measured at a certain number of altogether G transducer positions on the hull. The signal at each position is Fourier-analyzed to produce the amplitudes and phase angles of a certain number of harmonics. For each harmonic the experimental information can be presented in the form of G amplitudes and G phase angles, altogether 2G quantities describing the pressure fluctuations on the hull. This means that we can construct a singularity system to represent the propeller, a singularity system described by altogether 2G unknown coefficients. By setting up the connection between singularity distribution on the propeller and measured pressures, one can thus produce altogether 2G equations and solve for the 2G unknown coefficients describing the singularity system. This procedure can be repeated for each harmonic component in the pressure signal to be investigated. The complexity of the system of singularities that one can choose to represent the propeller is thus theoretically limited only by the number of pressure transducers in the afterbody.

Let us then consider what is a suitable system of singularities for practical applications. First of all, as mentioned in the Introduction, one has today reliable methods for theoretical calculation of the free space pressure field induced by the noncavitating propeller. In fact, those methods are also based on determining a singularity system to represent the propeller. The difference is that for the noncavitating propeller the singularity system and thus the free space pressure field can be calculated directly from basic theory. By combining this pressure field with the solid boundary and free-surface calculation described in the previous section, one can obtain the pressure fluctuations induced by the noncavitating propeller at any position of the hull. Furthermore, these pressures can be integrated to obtain the total excitation force induced by the noncavitating propeller. This means that there is no need for including the effect of the noncavitating propeller in our new procedure for determining equivalent singularity system and excitation forces by a combination of experiments and theoretical calculations. In the subsequent sections we shall therefore limit ourselves to the contribution of the cavities on the propeller.

When choosing the singularity system to represent the cavities on the propeller, one should consider the following two cases. The first case is when the cavitation occurs as a flare-up of cavities over a limited part of the circumference at the top of the propeller disk. If the cavitation occurs over a sufficiently short part of the circumference, for example, well below 90 deg of the circumference, it would be reasonable to model the cavities by

1. a stationary pulsating source at the top of the propeller

disk to account for the volume variation of the cavities, and
2. a stationary dipole of pulsating strength at the same position to account for the motion of the cavity.

The second case to be considered is when the wake distribution is so homogeneous that cavitation on the propeller blade occurs more or less constant during the whole revolution of the propeller. In that case it would be reasonable to model the cavities by

3. a dipole of constant strength positioned at the blade tip and rotating with the blades to account for the motion of the cavities on the blades, and
4. a source of constant strength, positioned at the blade tip and rotating with the propeller blades, to account for a possible tip vortex cavity.

A discussion of the principles for mathematical modeling of the cavities can be found in [4]. For intermediate cases where there is a significant flare-up of cavities at the top of the propeller disk, and also a certain cavitation during the rest of the revolution of the propeller blades, one may consider applying a singularity system which consists of all four contributions mentioned in the foregoing. For each contribution it is now possible to develop an analytical expression which gives the relationship between strength, phase, position, etc. of the various singularities and their corresponding free space pressure field, so that the equations can be solved and the constants describing the singularity system can be determined.

In our further calculations in this paper we shall restrict ourselves to the first case mentioned in the preceding, that is, the case where the main cavitation occurs as a flare-up of cavities at the top of the propeller disk. In order to illustrate the relative importance of cavity volume variation compared with cavity motion, let us consider the following two hypothetical examples: The first example is that of a six-bladed propeller with cavities at the outer parts of the blades, the cavities being constant in time and rotating with the propeller. The second example is meant to illustrate a flare-up of cavitation at the top position of the propeller disk each time a blade passes through this wake peak. The flare-up is assumed to be such that the volume varies between zero and a maximum equal to the volume of each of the stationary cavities in example 1. Furthermore, the frequency of pulsation in Example 2 is equal to the blade frequency in Example 1. Figure 2 illustrates the two situations. Figure 3 shows the resulting nondimensional blade frequency amplitude calculated at a position on the afterbody vertically above the propeller. Results are shown in Fig. 3 as a function of the tip clearance. From this diagram we draw the conclusion that the single pulsating cavity produces a much larger pressure amplitude than the rotating six cavities. The ratio between the pressure amplitudes is 4 at a tip clearance of 10 percent of the diameter and 24 at a tip clearance of 40 percent of the diameter. At more distant positions on the afterbody the ratio becomes even larger.

It can also be mentioned that when looking at the excitation force on the afterbody in the two examples the difference will be even more pronounced. This is due to the fact that the single pulsating cavity produces a pressure field of equal phase all over the afterbody. The six rotating cavities, however, will produce a pressure field where the phase angle of the pressure fluctuation is different at different positions along each section. Thus, in the latter case there will be a canceling effect due to the difference in phase angles when integrating the pressures to obtain the total excitation force.

From the preceding considerations, and in order to simplify the procedure as much as possible, the numerical calculations on the four ships described later in this paper were done by applying only a pulsating source (Item 1) to represent the cavity. The validity of the approximation is discussed later in the sec-

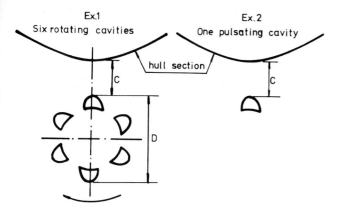

Fig. 2 Examples for illustrating the relative importance of cavity volume variation compared to cavity motion

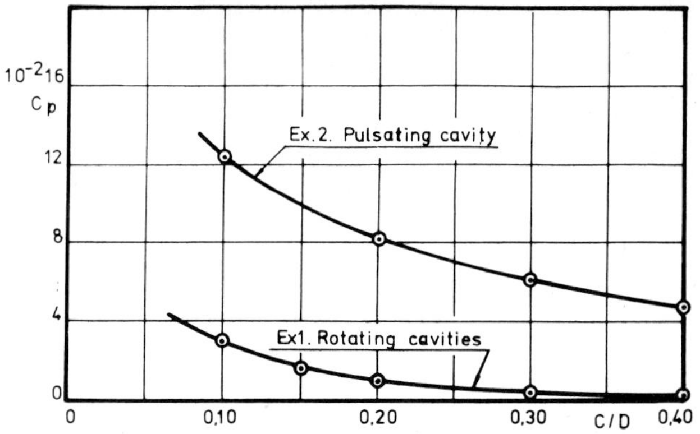

Fig. 3 Resulting blade frequency amplitude calculated at a position on the afterbody vertically above the propeller

tion "Verification of equivalent singularity calculation."

Figure 4 shows the coordinate system. The singularity system which now consists of a pulsating source, is located at (x,y,z). According to the standard cavitation testing technique at NHL, four pressure transducers are fitted in the afterbody. They are denoted by T_1 through T_4 as shown in Fig. 4, and their coordinates are ξ_1, η_1, ζ_1 through ξ_4, η_4, ζ_4, respectively.

The strength of the kth harmonic of the pulsating source representing the cavities of the propeller may be expressed as

$$Q_k(x,y,z;t) = Q_{ko}(x,y,z) \cos(kZ\omega t + \phi_k)$$

where

Q_{ko} = amplitude of kth harmonic of source strength
$\omega = 2\pi n$
n = propeller rate of revolutions
Z = number of propeller blades
t = time
ϕ_k = phase angle of source strength

The potential arising from the singularity system then has the following form:

$$\Phi_k = \frac{Q_{ko}}{R_T} \cos(kZ\omega t + \phi_k)$$

where

Φ_k = potential due to kth harmonic of pulsating source
R_T = distance between field point and source point

$$R_T = [(\xi - c_{xo})^2 + (\eta - R_s \cdot \sin\alpha_s)^2 + (\zeta - c_{zo} + R_s \cos\alpha_s)^2]^{1/2}$$

and

c_{xo}, c_{yo}, c_{zo} = coordinates of propeller center
α_s = as shown in Fig. 4
R_s = as shown in fig. 4

The position in space of the source is determined by R_s and α_s (Fig. 4). For practical applications we shall here assume that R_s is known: for instance, 0.95 times the propeller radius. (This distance can of course be chosen otherwise if the cavitation observations should indicate so.) For practical applications of the procedure, α_s is determined from observations during the cavitation test.

The free space pressure field generated by the pulsating source can be calculated from Bernoulli's equation. In the

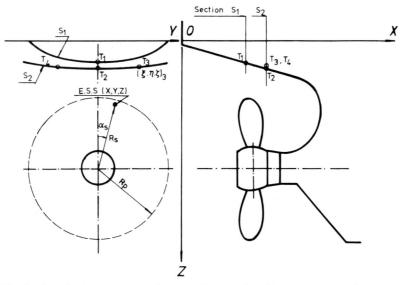

Fig. 4 Coordinate system, transducer positions, and position of equivalent singularity system (E.S.S.)

Cavitation-Induced Excitation Forces on the Hull

Fig. 5 Example of hull vibratory mode

high-frequency range of propeller-induced pressures, we may neglect the velocity dependent term in Bernoulli's equation. Furthermore, all constant terms are of no interest so that the pressure becomes

$$p_f(\xi,\eta,\zeta;t) = -\rho \frac{\partial \Phi_k}{\partial t} = \rho \frac{Q_{ko}kZ}{R_T} \frac{\omega}{} \cdot \sin(kZ\omega t + \phi_k) \quad (1)$$

During the cavitation tests one measures the amplitudes and phase angles of various harmonic components of propeller-induced pressure at each transducer on the hull. The standard cavitation test procedure at NHL includes pressure measurements at altogether four transducer positions as indicated in Fig. 4. Tests are carried out for cavitating as well as noncavitating conditions. The pressure measured in the noncavitating condition is subtracted from the pressure measured in the cavitating condition. This difference then represents the pressure due to the cavities alone. The subtraction is done vectorially, taking phase angle as well as amplitude into account for each harmonic component. The corresponding free space pressure field can be expressed as

$$p_f(\xi,\eta,\zeta;t) = \frac{p_{mk}}{S_{tot}} \cdot \sin(kZ\omega t + \phi_{mk}) \quad (2)$$

where

p_{mk} = pressure amplitude of kth harmonic due to cavitation alone

ϕ_{mk} = phase angle of p_{mk}

S_{tot} = solid boundary and free-surface factor theoretically calculated at the pressure transducer position and at conditions (with or without free surface) relevant to the cavitation test facility in question.

The relationship between the pressure due to propeller cavities and the pulsating source strength is obtained by combining (1) and (2):

$$Q_{ko} = \frac{p_{mk} \cdot R_T}{S_{tot} \cdot kZ\omega\rho} \quad (3)$$

For the numerical calculations for the four ships described later, the source strength Q_{ko} was determined for each transducer and the average value was applied as input in the final calculation of total excitation force.

Our experience from calculating the solid boundary factor (without the presence of a free surface) is that for most afterbody forms it will be very close to 2.0 for normal transducer positions. When determining Q_{ko} from equation (3) we therefore put S_{tot} equal to 2.0. Only when the section angle α (see Fig. 7) is more than about 20 degs, S_{tot} should be calculated for the afterbody in question.

If the present procedure for predicting total excitation force is to be applied in connection with other types of cavitation facilities, for instance, free surface tanks or tunnels where the free surface is substituted by a solid plate, an S_{tot}-value relevant to each facility should be calculated and used for determining the equivalent singularity. When calculating the final pressure

distribution and excitation force on the full scale ship, one will of course use the S_{tot}-values calculated for the ship at correct draft, taking the water level rise due to stern wave, squat, etc. into account.

Calculation of excitation force

Having now determined the equivalent singularity system to represent the propeller, it is easy to obtain the excitation force. For instance, the instantaneous force in vertical direction will be given by:

$$F_z(t) = \int_A p_f(\xi,\eta,\zeta;t) \cdot n_z \cdot S_{tot} \, dA \quad (4)$$

where

$p_f(\xi,\eta,\zeta;t)$ = free space pressure induced by equivalent singularity (pulsating source) representing the propeller cavitation

n_z = vertical component of unit vector normal to hull surface

S_{tot} = solid boundary and free-surface factor, now calculated for conditions relevant to the full-scale ship and for the onset flow field induced by the actual "equivalent singularity system"

A = wetted area of hull

The "generalized excitation force" amplitude can be expressed as:

$$F_{zk} = \int_A p_{fk}(\xi,\eta,\zeta) \cdot n_z \cdot S_{tot} \cdot f_w(\xi,\eta,\zeta) \, dA \quad (5)$$

where $p_{fk}(\xi,\eta,\zeta)$ is the amplitude of the kth harmonic of $p_f(\xi,\eta,\zeta;t)$.

Here $f_w(\xi,\eta,\zeta)$ is a weighting function introduced to make it possible to calculate a "generalized excitation force" relevant to various vibration modes of the hull. For instance, by choosing f_w equal to unity all over the hull, one obtains the total vertical excitation force on the hull. However, no ship vibrates vertically as a stiff body. Figure 5 indicates a more relevant type of vibration. Higher modes than shown in Fig. 5 may well be the most important in the context of propeller excited vibrations. The physical quantity which most accurately describes the excitation from the propeller is the energy absorbed by the ship from the pressure field of the propeller. The energy absorbed per unit time can be expressed as

$$E = \frac{1}{\tau} \int_0^\tau \int_A p_{fk} \cdot \sin(kZ\omega t + \phi_{pk}) \cdot n_z \cdot S_{tot}$$
$$\cdot v_k \sin(kZ\omega t + \phi_{vk}) dA dt \quad (6)$$

where

v_k, ϕ_{vk} = amplitude and phase angle of kth harmonic of vibratory velocity of hull surface.

ϕ_{pk} = phase angle of p_{fk}

Considering a resonant vibratory mode of a ship excited by the pressure field, ϕ_{vk} will be either equal to ϕ_{pk} or 180 deg out of phase. Performing the time integration of (6), we thus obtain

$$E = \frac{1}{2} \int_A p_{fk} \cdot n_z \cdot S_{tot} \cdot f_w \cdot dA$$

where

$f_w = v_k$ at positions where phase angles are equal
$f_w = -v_k$ at positions of opposite phase.

Thus we see that a formula as shown in (5) is a relevant expression for the generalized excitation force for a specific vibratory mode. What one has to do is insert a weighting function equal to the amplitude curve of the vibration as shown in Fig. 5.

The ideal way of analyzing the ship vibration problem would be to apply finite-element structural analysis of the ship with the distributed pressures as excitation force at each element. Such complete analysis is at present not normally carried out for every ship at the design stage. Until such complete analysis becomes standard the application of the weighting function as introduced in the foregoing may be a useful tool when evaluating the propeller design. For making full use of the "generalized excitation force," however, one needs systematic information of typical vibratory modes and structural damping for various types of ships.

The theory outlined herein can be extended to include the effect of the compressibility and thus the finite propagation velocity of the pressure waves. More specifically, this would have to be done when formulating the boundary condition of no flow through the surface at the control points of each element as described in the Appendix. When reformulating the boundary condition, one would take into account the finite propagation velocity, or correspondingly the phase shift, of the velocities induced by the equivalent singularity system as well as by all the other elements. The usefulness of such a theory might still be limited, however, because of limited knowledge of the real compressibility of the water. It is well known that the pressure wave propagation velocity in pure water is about 1500 m/s (4920 fps). It is also known that even small amounts of free air bubbles in the water will reduce the propagation velocity significantly. What we do not know much about today is the real air content in the top layer of the sea surrounding the propeller. In the subsequent numerical calculations in this paper we have neglected compressibility and assumed infinite propagation velocity. It should be noted that the formula (5) is valid only when the pressure occurs at equal phase all over the hull (opposite phase over part of the hull taken care of by negative value of f_w). To account for a possible phase shift due to the compressibility, or due to a more sophisticated equivalent singularity system than applied here, an additional factor taking care of such phase shift has to be introduced in equation (5).

Numerical methods, computer programs

A computer program subroutine has been produced according to the theory outlined in the Appendix. The subroutine accepts arbitrary onset flows as input. The onset flow is specified in terms of x, y, and z components of the velocity at each control point.

The hull is subdivided into a certain number of elements, so-called panels. On each of the panels a constant source distribution is assumed. Together with the onset flow these sources will give contributions to the total flow field. The number of unknown source strengths is equal to the number of panels. By defining a control point on each panel where the boundary condition is required to be fulfilled, one obtains a system of equations with the same number of equations as the number of unknown source strengths. In the present version of the computer program the centroid of each panel is used as the control point and not the "null point" as defined in reference [12]. The hull geometry is specified by giving the rectangular coordinates of the vertices of these panels.

The coordinate system is as given in Fig. 4 where the x-axis is positive forward, the y-axis points to starboard, and the z-axis vertically downward. Since the hull is symmetrical with respect to the centerplane and is reflected in the free surface, only the panels of the first quarter part of the double hull are necessary as input data. The region in way of the propeller is much

more finely subdivided than the remainder of the hull.

The program provides a possibility to determine the equivalent singularity system representing the cavity volume variation of the propeller in terms of the measured pressure amplitudes and phase angles in the cavitation tunnel as explained in a previous section.

The computer program was designed with the following two requirements in mind:

• An ordinary "Hess and Smith type" of program was to be applied with minimum modifications.

• The program should be able to handle any type of pulsating onset flow with arbitrary phase distribution over the hull. (When using the onset flow of a pulsating source, this requirement is not strictly necessary. It was introduced in order to facilitate possible future extension of the program in the direction of more complex equivalent singularity systems or inclusion of compressibility effects.)

In order to fulfill these requirements the onset flow at each control point is split into a sine and cosine component as follows:

$$\vec{u}(\xi,\eta,\zeta;t) = \sum_{k=0}^{\infty} \vec{u}_k(\xi,\eta,\zeta) \sin(kZ\omega t + \phi_k)$$

$$= \sum_{k=0}^{\infty} (\vec{u}_k \cdot \cos\phi_k \cdot \sin(kZ\omega t) + \vec{u}_k \cdot \sin\phi_k \cdot \cos(kZ\omega t))$$

where $\vec{u}_k \cdot \cos\phi_k$ and $\vec{u}_k \cdot \sin\phi_k$ are called sine and cosine components, respectively. Having split the onset flow like this, the "Hess and Smith method" can be applied to each component separately as if it represented a stationary onset flow field. The consequence is that we now have to solve two sets of linear equations in order to obtain the sine and cosine components of the source distribution corresponding to the sine and cosine components of the onset flow, respectively.

The program is next employed to find the values of the velocity potential at the control point of each panel due to the equivalent singularity system representing the propeller cavitation, the hull singularity system, and their images.

Upon solving for the velocity potential all other quantities of interest, for instance, pressure distribution on the hull and so on, can be determined.

The maximum number of panels that may be used to approximate a body surface is 800 for the computer for which this method has been programmed—UNIVAC 1100.

If the number of iterations during solving the set of linear equations exceeds 20, it is assumed that the routine will not converge. The usual number is between three and seven (at least up to 120 panels). Geometric quantities such as panel area, direction vector, diagonal and center of gravity are exact. However, the source strength will typically have an error in its fourth or fifth significant digit. If desired, the accuracy can be improved by changing a parameter in the program input.

The total machine time is about 13 minutes for 140 panels in the first quarter part. The total number of statements in the whole program is about 1300. The program is written in FORTRAN V.

Experimental verification

Experiments on solid boundary and free-surface effects

At the Norwegian Hydrodynamic Laboratories a series of experimental investigations on solid boundary and free surface effects has been carried out. The objective of this experimental work has been:

• to provide general information on solid boundary and free-surface effects upon propeller-induced pressures, and

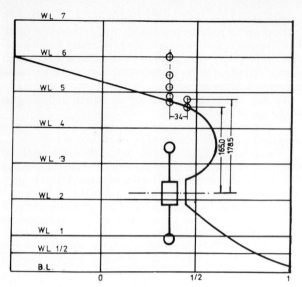

Fig. 6 Aft end of paraffin wax hull model

as well as free-surface effects. The V-shaped plate arrangement was tested at various angles α as well as various degrees of submergence. The flat plate was tested at various distances between rotating balls and the plate, but only at such large submergence that the free surface did not affect the results.

The reason for testing the flat plate was to determine the free space pressure field as a function of distance from the rotating balls. In the case of an infinite flat plate the solid boundary factor is equal to 2.0, so that in order to obtain the free space pressure field one only has to divide the measured pressure amplitudes on the flat plate by this value. Having thus determined the free space pressure field around the rotating balls, one obtains the combined solid boundary and free-surface factor in the case of the afterbody and the V-shaped plate arrangement by dividing the pressure amplitudes measured on these bodies by the free space pressure amplitude. Since the measurements were made at various distances from the free surface, it is possible to analyze the measurements in such a way that the solid boundary and free-surface effect can be separated in the results.

A complete description of the experimental results can be found in [11]. For the V-shaped plate arrangement, tests were done at various angles of rise α (see Fig. 7) and at various drafts. The experimental results can be summarized in the following two formulas:

$$S_b = 2.00 + 0.0019\alpha - 0.00024\alpha^2$$

$$S_f = 9.341 \left(\frac{\zeta}{C_{zo}}\right) - 30.143 \left(\frac{\zeta}{C_{zo}}\right)^2$$

$$+ 33.19 \left(\frac{\zeta}{C_{zo}}\right)^3, 0 < \frac{\zeta}{C_{zo}} < 0.35$$

$$S_f = 1.0, \frac{\zeta}{C_{zo}} > 0.35$$

where

- to verify the theoretical methods for calculating such effects as described in the previous paragraphs.

The experiments have been described in detail in reference [11]. During the experiments the pressure fluctuation is generated by two spherical balls fitted to a rod as indicated in Fig. 6. When rotating around the shaft centerline these balls will generate a pressure field that rotates with the balls and that will be felt as a pressure fluctuation on a hull or other solid body fitted above the balls. The experiments consisted in measuring the pressure fluctuations by means of pressure transducers fitted in bodies above the rotating balls. Three types of bodies were tested:

- a paraffin wax hull model as shown in Fig. 6,
- a "two-dimensional" plate arrangement forming a V-shaped section of adjustable angle α as shown in Fig. 7, and
- an "infinite" flat plate as shown in Fig. 8.

All tests were carried out at zero forward speed in the towing tank of depth 6 m (19.6 ft) and width 10.5 m (34.4 ft). The transducer positions are shown in the Figs. 6–8. For the hull model, pressure measurements were made at various drafts of the model in order to obtain information about solid boundary

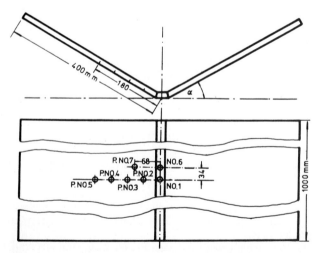

Fig. 7 A "two-dimensional" plate arrangement forming a V-shaped section of adjustable angle α

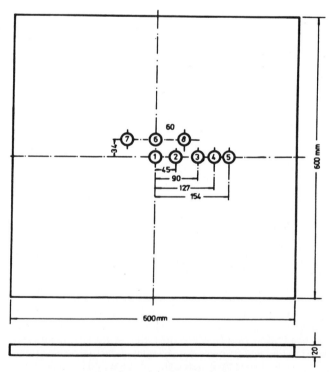

Fig. 8 An "infinite" flat plate

Cavitation-Induced Excitation Forces on the Hull

α = angle of section rise, deg

ζ = distance from waterline to field point measured vertically

C_{zo} = submergence of propeller shaft center

The preceding formulas refer to a constant tip clearance ratio

$$\frac{C}{2R_b} = 0.439$$

where C and R_b are defined as shown in Fig. 9.

Figure 9 shows the values of S_{tot} along the section for one specific angle of rise and submergence. Experimental results are shown as well as theoretical values obtained by using the onset flow due to two rotating sources and two rotating dipoles (each ball represented by a source and a dipole, respectively).

The reason for choosing sources and dipoles is as follows. In the hypothetical case of an ideal fluid a rotating dipole would be an exact representation of each ball. Wake effects generated by the viscous flow around the balls would tend to give a pressure field more like the one generated by a rotating source. The real case should be expected to be most accurately described by a combination of the two. This means that the experimental results should be expected to be somewhere between the two extremes of a pure dipole field and a pure source field, respectively.

Figure 10 shows the free-surface factor S_f as a function of the field point submergence ratio ζ/C_{zo} for the V-shaped plate arrangement. The experimental values of S_f have been explicitly separated from the measured S_{tot} as explained in [11]. The theoretical values shown in Fig. 10 have been obtained correspondingly by the theory outlined in the section "Calculation of solid boundary and free-surface effects."

Figures 9 and 10 both indicate that the source gives a more correct representation of each ball than the dipole. The overall conclusion seems to be that the theory predicts the solid boundary effect and the free-surface effect to an accuracy which is within the limits of experimental error, at least better than 10 percent.

Verification of equivalent singularity calculation

A direct experimental verification of the total excitation force as predicted by the principles presented in this paper is very difficult. However, in the previous paragraph the experimental verification covers the main parts of the theory that go into the calculation of total excitation force. The only main item left for verification is the choice and calculation of equivalent singularity system. A possible way of doing such a verification would be to compare the equivalent singularity system (in our case the strength of the pulsating source Q_{ko}) obtained when using different pressure transducers in the afterbody as the basis for calculating Q_{ko}. Table 1 gives such a comparison for all the transducers and for all four ships for which total excitation force has been calculated and presented in the next section. If all transducers for each ship in question give approximately identical values of Q_{ko}, this can be taken as an indication that the single pulsating source is a valid approximation for the pressure field and thus the equivalent singularity system.

Furthermore, the phase angle ϕ in Table 1 should be identical for all pressure transducers in order to conclude that the single pulsating source is a valid approximation (neglecting compressibility effects).

From Table 1 we see that for Ship A all four transducers give the same value of Q_{ko} to within about 4 percent. For Ships B and C the maximum deviation of any transducer from the average is about 14 percent. For Ship D the maximum deviation

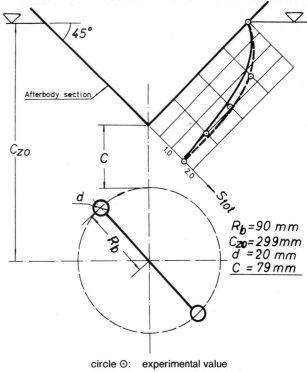

circle ⊙: experimental value
solid line —: theory, rotating dipoles
dotted line - - -: theory, rotating sources

Fig. 9 Comparison between experimental and theoretical values of S_{tot}

from the average is about 30 percent. The relatively large spread in the case of Ship D can be a consequence of the relatively small pressure amplitudes measured in the cavitation tunnel and correspondingly large spread of the experimental results. The phase angle ϕ_c is approximately the same for all four transducers of each ship, indicating again that the single pulsating source is a reasonably valid approximation of the

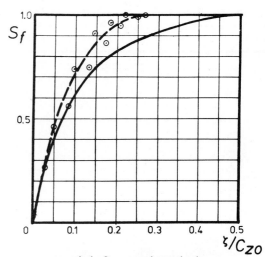

circle ⊙: experimental value
solid line —: theory, rotating dipoles
dotted line - - -: theory, rotating sources

Fig. 10 Comparison between experimental and theoretical values of S_f

Table 1 Experimental blade frequency pressures and corresponding source strength

Ship No.	T No.	ξ_T (m)	η_T (m)	ζ_T (m)	p_{nc} (N/m²)	ϕ_{nc} (deg)	p_{wc} (N/m²)	ϕ_{wc} (deg)	p_c (N/m²)	ϕ_c (deg)	Q_{ko} (m³/s)
	1	11.47	1.20	1.53	1370	285	6540	336	5770	103	0.248
	2	11.17	0.00	1.88	2140	177	7600	249	7230	185	0.241
A	3	12.14	0.00	2.02	3190	153	6390	238	6890	185	0.248
	4	12.14	1.80	1.44	430	217	5010	272	4770	174	0.253
	average	...	...	...	...	...	...	...	...	...	0.248
	1	8.74	0.30	3.15	920	186	8230	95	8460	101	0.406
	2	9.37	0.30	3.30	1110	201	7870	94	8260	87	0.393
B	3	9.37	1.83	2.95	539	144	7040	81	6810	77	0.405
	4	9.37	−1.83	2.95	823	182	4210	89	5020	91	0.337
	average	...	...	...	...	...	...	...	...	...	0.385
	1	6.29	1.26	0.79	2700	324	8280	308	5590	298	0.150
	2	6.29	0.00	0.83	4900	60	8680	350	8380	317	0.172
C	3	5.66	0.00	0.79	3230	24	9630	336	7850	318	0.142
	4	6.29	−1.26	0.79	2640	139	1380	310	4010	316	0.133
	average	...	...	...	...	...	...	...	...	...	0.149
	1	12.95	−0.85	1.45	951	33	3730	128	3930	308	0.270
	2	15.00	0.85	1.80	588	42	2340	130	2390	306	0.229
D	3	15.00	−2.05	1.70	813	343	1370	125	2070	311	0.333
	4	17.00	0.05	3.52	510	4	1110	114	1370	316	0.174
	average	...	...	...	...	...	...	...	...	...	0.252

NOTE: ξ_T, η_T, ζ_T = coordinates of transducers.
1 m³ = 35.31 ft³.
1 m = 3.28 ft.
1 N/m² = 1.45·10⁻⁴ psi.

pressure field. The conclusion to be drawn from Table 1 is that at least for these four ships the single pulsating source describes the pressure field to a general accuracy of better than 20 percent.

Numerical results

Extensive calculations have been performed for altogether four different ships, denoted A, B, C and D. The main specifications of the ships and their propellers are given in Table 2. For these ships, cavitation tests have been performed and pressures measured at four different transducer positions in the afterbody. The results of these measurements were used as input data for calculating the equivalent singularity system consisting of a pulsating source. Table 1 gives the transducer positions (ξ,η,ζ) on the various ships. p_{nc} and ϕ_{nc} are blade frequency pressure amplitude and phase angle, respectively, measured in the cavitation tunnel at such high cavitation numbers that there was no cavitation on the propeller. p_{wc} and ϕ_{wc} are the corresponding quantities measured with the cavitation number correctly modeled. p_c and ϕ_c are the corresponding values due to cavitation alone, obtained by subtracting p_{nc} from p_{wc}, taking phase angles into account. The average value of Q_{ko} for each ship was used as input for the force calculation. Solid boundary and free-surface effects were calculated as described in the previous sections. The distribution of pressure amplitudes and phase angles over the hull were

calculated and the vertical force integrated to obtain the total excitation force. In this integration the weighting function was kept equal to 1.0 all over the hull.

The position of the pulsating source has been chosen to be at the 0.95 radius of the propeller and at angular position $\alpha_s = 7.5$ deg. These quantities are input data in the computer program and should be chosen according to observations of the cavitation pattern during the tests. However, when the tests of the four ships here were originally carried out, no such observations aiming at calculation of total excitation force were done. Therefore, the foregoing choice of pulsating source position is to some extent arbitrary.

Figure 11 shows the resulting solid boundary and free-surface factor S_{tot} as a function of position along the section above the propeller for each of the four ships.

Figure 12 shows the distribution of the solid boundary and free-surface effect at various stations of Ship A. The longitudinal positions of the various sections are shown in the same figure.

In order to investigate the possible effect of propeller position or propeller clearance upon the solid boundary and free-surface effects, an additional set of calculations was performed. The V-shaped section used during the experiments was chosen as the basis for these calculations. An equivalent singularity system consisting of just one single pulsating source was chosen. The distribution of combined solid boundary and free-surface factor was calculated along the section for various distances c

Table 2 Specification of main data of ships

Ship	Type of Vessel	$\dfrac{L_{pp}}{B}$	$\dfrac{B}{T_{AP}}$	C_B	∇ (1000 m³)	Propeller D (m)	Z	N (rpm)	C/D
A	RO/RO	6.5	3.6	0.61	29	6.0	5	133	0.25
B	container	7.0	2.9	0.55	38	6.1	5	139	0.39
C	RO/RO	6.2	3.7	0.54	6	4.2	4	190	0.21
D	RO/RO	6.5	3.6	0.60	37	6.7	5	114	0.32

1 m³ = 35.31 ft³
1 m = 3.28 ft

between the position of the pulsating source and the bottom corner of the section. Figure 13 shows the result of this calculation. As can be seen from this figure, there is a significant influence of tip clearance upon the combined solid boundary and free-surface factor.

Many cavitation laboratories carry out their experiments with the free surface replaced by a horizontal solid plate during the measurements. In order to investigate the effect of this solid plate compared with a real free surface, calculations were carried out for the V-shaped plate arrangement as shown in Fig. 14. The upper diagram in this figure is the same result as has been shown in Fig. 11 for a real free surface. The calculations were repeated but now with the modification that the negative image system was replaced by a positive image system in order to fulfill a boundary condition of no flow at right angles to the water plane. This will then mathematically model the situation of the free surface being substituted by a solid plate. The result is shown in the lower diagram in Fig. 14. Comparing the two we see that the combined solid boundary and free-surface effect tends to zero as we approach the free surface for a real free surface, while it increases as we move upward along the section in the case of a solid flat plate.

Table 3 gives the single amplitude of the excitation force calculated for the various ships in vertical direction. The table also gives the maximum pressure amplitude measured during the cavitation tests for each ship. Looking at the vertical excitation force amplitude, which is considered to be more important than the horizontal force, we find that the ship with the minimum pressure amplitude does not have the minimum excitation force. This is of course due to the size and geometry of the hull.

Discussion

As mentioned in a previous section the accuracy of the theory for calculating solid boundary and free-surface effects seems to be of the order of 10 percent or better. The accuracy of the equivalent singularity system determined as described in the previous section seems to be of the order of 10 to 20 percent. The overall accuracy of the total excitation force defined by choosing the weighting function equal to 1.0 and by neglecting compressibility effects is expected to be better than 30 percent.

An important question is now, How relevant in this excitation force that we have calculated, and how can we make use of this information for practical applications? Ideally, the best way of applying this theory would be in combination with finite-element analysis of the ship structure, using the distributed pressures as input to such analysis. Another and more direct way of using the results would be to consider the excitation force as a relevant quantity for evaluating the propeller design. For that application we need a criterion on which to do our evaluation of the excitation force. For many years several model tanks have evaluated propeller designs on a basis of maximum pressure amplitude measured on the hull, comparing the amplitude with limits or criteria that have been obtained from empirical data. The total excitation force can be applied in the same way, provided one has a sufficient number of cases to develop a criterion from. This would ideally require information about total excitation force and vibratory level for a large number of ships. Development of such a criterion is beyond the scope of the present paper. In this paper a basic method has been described. Furthermore, we have calculated the excitation force for a total of four ships. As indicated in Table 3, two of the ships, B and C, have experienced certain vibration problems in service. For Ships A and D no such problems have been reported. Table 3 gives the impression that a critical level of the total excitation force for Ships A, B

and D, that is, ships of a length of about 200 m (656 ft), would be of the order of 50-tonnes single-amplitude blade frequency. Ship C in Table 3 is a much smaller vessel, only 117 m (384 ft) long and has only about half the excitation force. The excitation force amplitude alone is of course not a relevant basis of a criterion valid for all ships. More relevant parameters could be the ratio between excitation force amplitude and mean thrust, or the ratio between excitation force amplitude and ship displacement, or other possible parameters. Reference [2] gives a survey of such criteria as suggested by various model tanks. It should be noted that the excitation force on which the criteria of reference [2] are based is estimated by different methods. When predicting the total force by the method described in this paper, Table 3 indicates as a first approximate criterion that the total blade frequency single-amplitude excitation force in vertical direction should not exceed about 30 percent of the mean thrust. Ideally, the structural stiffness of the ship should also be taken into account. In any case, in order to develop a reasonably reliable criterion for acceptable excitation force, one needs a lot more cases than the four ships dealt with in this paper.

The theory and numerical procedure presented herein still suffer from certain shortcomings. First of all, as mentioned in the Introduction, only the contribution to excitation force originating from cavity volume variation is taken into account. It is believed that for ships suffering from vibration problems this is in most cases a main source of excitation compared to, for example, the contribution from the noncavitating propeller. However, this has still to be proved. If it should turn out in future studies that the noncavitating propeller and cavity motion are also important, then those effects can easily be included in the theory.

Phase shifts of the pressure signal due to compressibility of the water are not taken into account. This will also be a subject of future studies. Finally, more information about typical vibratory modes of ships is necessary in order to make full use of the "weighting function" concept introduced in this paper.

Conclusions

A theory has been described for calculating the effect of solid boundary and free surface upon propeller-induced pressure fluctuations on the hull. Numerical calculations have been carried out to produce information on such solid boundary and free-surface factors for different ships. Experimental investigations have been carried out that seem to confirm the theoretical calculations of solid boundary and free-surface effects quite well.

The paper also presents a method for obtaining the distribution of propeller-induced pressures over the whole hull, as well as the total excitation force obtained by integrating such pressures. The method is based on a combination of experimental measurements and theoretical calculations. Propeller-induced pressures are measured at a few positions on the afterbody during ordinary cavitation tests. From these measurements one calculates an "equivalent singularity distribution" to represent the propeller. From this equivalent singularity system one obtains the pressure distribution all over the hull by theoretical calculations according to traditional potential-flow theory. The theory as described in the paper is restricted to the effect of the volume variation of the cavities. However, contributions from cavity motion as well as from the noncavitating propeller can easily be taken into account according to well-established theoretical methods. As examples of the application of the new method the total excitation force has been calculated and presented in the paper for a total of four different ships.

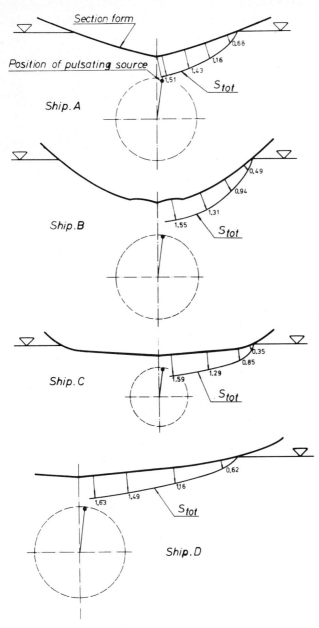

Fig. 11 S_{tot} along section above propeller for all four ships

The main conclusions to be drawn from the investigations are as follows:

• The present theory predicts, within an error of less than 10 percent, the effects of solid boundary and free surface. For the ships used as examples in this paper, and for which cavitation and volume variation of the cavities are a significant source of excitation, it seems that an equivalent singularity system consisting of a single pulsating source describes the pressure field generated by the propeller to an accuracy of the order of 10 to 20 percent. The accuracy of the total excitation force, neglecting compressibility effect and vibratory modes of the hull, is expected to be better than 30 percent.

• As a first approximation of a criterion based on this work, it seems that the total blade frequency single-amplitude excitation force in the vertical direction should not exceed about 30 percent of the mean propeller thrust.

• The free space pressure field due to cavity volume variation decays proportionally to the inverse of the distance from

the propeller. The free surface produces the effect that the real pressure amplitudes on the hull will decay much more rapidly than this with increasing distance. For the hull sections a few propeller diameters ahead of the propeller, the free-surface effect will be very significant even under the bottom of the ship.

• A pulsating source type of pressure field will be subject to a larger influence from the free surface than would the pressure fields of rotating sources or dipoles.

• The lack of free surface in a cavitation tunnel will have a certain effect upon the measured pressure amplitudes. This can be corrected for according to the theory developed in this paper. Such correction is particularly important when the cavitation tests are carried out with the free surface replaced by a solid horizontal plate.

• As recommendations for future work it is suggested that the total excitation force be calculated for a large number of ships in order to form, it is hoped, a more reliable basis of a criterion for acceptable excitation force amplitudes. Furthermore, compressibility effects upon the velocity of propagation of the pressure waves, and thus upon phase shift of pressure signal, over the hull should be investigated. The final objective of future development should be to combine the foregoing theory for calculating pressure distributions over the hull with finite-element methods for structural analysis of the hull. Only in this way can an entirely rational way of evaluating the vibration level while the ship is still at the design stage be achieved.

References

1 15th International Towing Tank Conference, Propeller Committee Report, The Hague, 1978.

2 16th International Towing Tank Conference, Propeller Committee Report, Leningrad, 1981.

3 Huse, E., "The Magnitude and Distribution of Propeller-Induced Surface Forces on a Single-Screw Ship Model," Norwegian Ship Model Experiment Tank, Publication No. 100. Trondheim, Dec. 1968.

4 Huse, E., "Pressure Fluctuations on the Hull Induced by Cavitating Propellers," Norwegian Ship Model Experiment Tank, Publication No. 111, Trondheim, March 1972.

5 Huse, E., "Cavitation Induced Hull Pressures, Some Recent Developments of Model Testing Techniques," *Proceedings*, Symposium on High Powered Propulsion of Large Ships, Wageningen, The Netherlands, Dec. 1974.

6 Breslin, J. P. and Eng, K., "A Method for Computing Propeller-Induced Vibratory Forces on Ships," *Proceedings*, First Conference on Ship Vibration, Stevens Institute of Technology, Hoboken, N.J., 1965.

7 Cox, B. D., Vorus, W. S., Breslin, J. P., and Rood, E. P., "Recent Theoretical and Experimental Developments in the Prediction of Propeller-Induced Vibratory Forces on Nearby Boundaries," *Proceedings*, Twelfth Symposium on Naval Hydrodynamics, Office of Naval Research, Washington D.C., June 1978.

8 Breslin, J. P., "Propeller-Induced Hull Forces," *Schiffstechnik*, Vol. 26, 1979.

9 Huse, E., "Effect of Tunnel Walls upon Propeller-Induced Pressures in Cavitation Tunnels," *Proceedings*, Institution of Mechanical Engineers Cavitation Conference, Edinburgh, 1974.

10 Huse, E., "Propeller-Induced Excitation Forces and Vibrations, Cavitation Noise and Erosion," *Proceedings*, International Symposium on Advances in Marine Technology, Vol. 1, Trondheim, 1979.

11 Guoqiang, Wang, "The Influence of Solid Boundaries and Free Surface on Propeller-Induced Pressure Fluctuations," *Norwegian Maritime Research*, No. 2, Vol. 9, 1981.

12 Hess, J. L. and Smith, A. M. O., "Calculation of Non-Lifting Potential Flow about Arbitrary Three-Dimensional Bodies," Douglas Aircraft Division Report No. E.S. 40622, Long Beach, Calif., March 1962.

13 Garrison, C. J., "Hydrodynamic Loading of Large Offshore Structures: Three-Dimensional Source Distribution Methods," in *Numerical Methods in Offshore Engineering*, O. C. Zienkiewcz, R. W. Lewis, and K. G. Stagg, Eds., Wiley, New York, 1979.

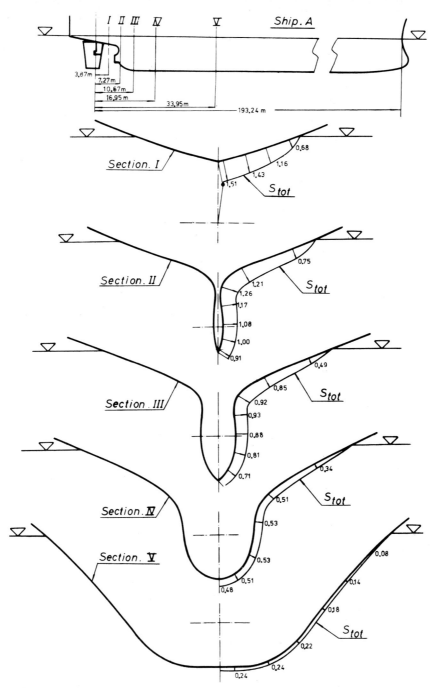

Fig. 12 S_{tot} for Ship A at different sections

14 Newman, J. N., *Marine Hydrodynamics*, MIT Press, Cambridge, Mass. 1977.

15 Faltinsen, O. M. and Michelsen, F. C., "Motion of Large Structures in Waves at Zero Froude Number," *Proceedings*, Symposium on the Dynamics of Marine Vehicles and Structures in Waves, Paper No. 11, The Institution of Mechanical Engineers, 1974.

Appendix

Theoretical calculation of hull pressure, solid boundary, and free-surface effects

Basic potential theory

Let us consider a ship moving at constant speed U through otherwise undisturbed water. We seek to determine the periodic forces exerted on the ship hull surface arising from the unsteady propeller velocity and pressure fields. The fluid is considered to be incompressible and inviscid. Under these circumstances a fluid velocity potential exists which can be expressed in terms of steady and unsteady components as

$$\Phi(\xi,\eta,\zeta;t) = Ux + \Phi_s(\xi,\eta,\zeta) + \Phi_p(\xi,\eta,\zeta;t) + \Phi_D(\xi,\eta,\zeta;t)$$

where

$\Phi_s(\xi,\eta,\zeta)$ = steady disturbance flow about bare hull in presence of free surface

$\Phi_p(\xi,\eta,\zeta;t)$ = propeller potential

$\Phi_D(\xi,\eta,\zeta;t)$ = potential of flow arising from propeller-hull

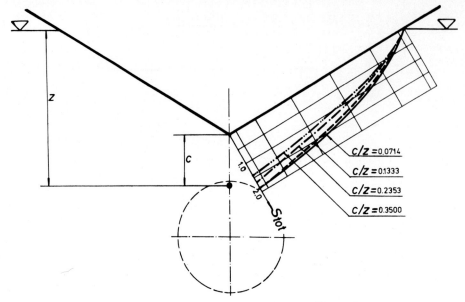

Fig. 13 Effect of singularity position on S_{tot}

interaction, often termed scattering or diffraction potential

Within the framework of linear theory, Φ_s does not contribute to propeller-induced pressure fluctuations, and can therefore be omitted here.

The propeller potential is periodic in time and, by virtue of the symmetry of identical, equally spaced blades, its fluctuating part may be expressed as a Fourier series with harmonics of blade passage frequency as

$$\Phi_p(\xi,\eta,\zeta;t) = \sum_{k=1}^{\infty} \Phi_{pk}(\xi,\eta,\zeta)\cdot e^{ikZ\omega t}$$

with Φ_{pk} being the complex amplitude of the kth harmonic. (In this and all subsequent expressions involving $e^{ikZ\omega t}$ the real part is understood to be taken.) Similarly, the diffraction potential will be of the form

$$\Phi_D(\xi,\eta,\zeta;t) = \sum_{k=1}^{\infty} \Phi_{Dk}(\xi,\eta,\zeta)\cdot e^{ikZ\omega t}$$

We now consider the boundary-value problem for the potential $\Phi = \Phi_p + \Phi_D$. Within the fluid domain the potential must satisfy Laplace's equation

$$\nabla^2\Phi(\xi,\eta,\zeta;t) = 0$$

At large depth and distances upstream of the hull and propeller the disturbance must vanish

$$\nabla\Phi \to 0 \qquad x \to \infty$$
$$\nabla\Phi \to 0 \qquad z \to \infty$$

The boundary condition on the hull surface denoted by S requires that the fluid velocity must be tangent to the surface or

$$\vec{n}\cdot\nabla\Phi_k(\xi,\eta,\zeta) = 0 \text{ on } S \qquad (7)$$

where

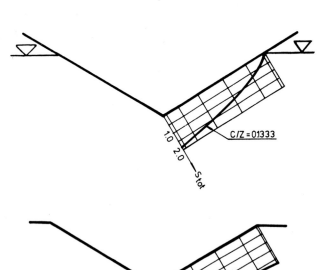

Fig. 14 S_{tot} for V-shaped plate arrangement in case of free surface (*above*) and free surface replaced by solid plate (*below*)

Table 3   Measured pressure and calculated total force

| Ship | Maximum Pressure (N/m²) | Vertical Excitation Force Amplitude | | General Level of Ship Excitation |
		Absolute Value (kN)	In Percent of Propeller Thrust	
A	7230	300	30	acceptable
B	8460	587	38	higher than acceptable
C	8480	237	49	higher than acceptable
D	3920[a]	504	34	acceptable

[a] The transducer was not situated at the position where the maximum pressure appeared.

1 N/m² = 1.45 · 10⁻⁴ psi.
1 kN = 0.1 ton f.

Cavitation-Induced Excitation Forces on the Hull

$$\Phi_k = \Phi_{pk} + \Phi_{Dk}$$

n = outward unit vector normal to surface

On the free surface the pressure has to be constant (atmospheric). The general boundary condition that has to be fulfilled on the free surface is (see, for instance, reference [14])

$$\frac{\partial^2 \Phi}{\partial t^2} - g \frac{\partial \Phi}{\partial z} = 0$$

As explained in the main body of the paper this reduces to

$$\frac{\partial^2 \Phi}{\partial t^2} = 0$$

which can be fulfilled by requiring

$$\Phi_k(\xi,\eta,\zeta) = 0 \text{ on } \zeta = 0$$

A solution for the potential Φ_k which satisfies the foregoing boundary conditions is constructed by choosing a source distribution $\sigma_k(x,y,z)e^{ikZ\omega t}$ over the surface of the hull. Furthermore, one has to introduce an image system of singularities symmetric with respect to the undisturbed free surface and of opposite sign.
The total potential will thus be

$$\Phi_k(\xi,\eta,\zeta) = -\frac{1}{4\pi} \int\!\!\int_S \sigma_k(x,y,z)$$
$$\cdot \left(\frac{1}{R} - \frac{1}{R_i}\right) dS + \Phi_{pk} + \Phi_{pi} \quad (8)$$

where

R = distance from field point (ξ,η,ζ) to source point (x,y,z)

R_i = distance from field point (ξ,η,ζ) to source point of image distribution

S = surface of hull

Φ_{pk} = potential due to singularity system representing propeller

Φ_{pi} = potential due to image of propeller

It should be noted that the x,y,z coordinate system refers to each panel with the x-y plane coinciding with the plane of the panel. Thus, x, y, z in the Appendix are not the same as in the main body of the paper.
With the potential given by equation (8) the boundary condition (7) can be written

$$\frac{\partial}{\partial n}(\Phi_{pk} + \Phi_{pi}) = -\left\{\frac{\sigma_k}{2} - \frac{1}{4\pi}\int\!\!\int_S \sigma_k \frac{\partial}{\partial n}\left(\frac{1}{R} - \frac{1}{R_i}\right) dS\right\}$$

This is the equation that has to be solved numerically in order to determine the source distribution over the hull surface.

Numerical calculation of source distribution over the hull

There are well-established methods available for solving the problem of stationary potential flow around bodies of arbitrary geometry (see, for instance, the "Hess and Smith method" given in [12]). However, in our case we have a periodic pulsating flow and not a stationary one. This means that each harmonic component of the onset flow as well as the source distribution over the hull can be described by its complex amplitude. By splitting this complex amplitude in its real and imaginary component, and by applying the Hess and Smith procedure independently to the real and imaginary parts, we arrive at a complex source density for each panel of the hull. Splitting the complex amplitudes in real and imaginary parts is of course identical to decomposing into sine and cosine components.
The original Hess and Smith procedure of [12] is for uniform

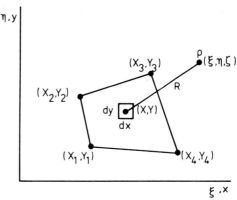

Fig. 15 Plane quadrilateral source element

onset flow only. In order to cope with the present problem it had to be extended to deal with onset flow of arbitrary direction at each control point on the hull.

Numerical calculation of potential and pressure distribution over the hull

When the source densities σ_j have been found, the normalized potential Φ_j may be obtained from

$$\Phi_j = \sigma_j \int\!\!\int_{\Delta s_j} \frac{1}{R(\xi_i,\eta_i,\zeta_i;x,y,z)} ds$$

where

σ_j = source density on panel number j

Φ_j = potential at field point (ξ_i,η_i,ζ_i) due to σ_j

Δs_j = area of panel number j

ξ_i,η_i,ζ_i = field point

x,y,z = source point on panel

The integrand in this integral is not gradually varying when the point i is near the panel over which the integration is to be carried out and is, in fact, singular as $R \to 0$. Therefore, when point i is very near the jth panel or when $i = j$ the integration is carried out as follows.
The integral written in terms of local coordinates ξ,η,ζ and x,y, where the ξ,x and η,y axes lie in the plane of the panel as indicated in Fig. 15, is

$$\int\!\!\int_{\Delta s} \frac{ds}{R} = \int\!\!\int_{\Delta s} \frac{dx\, dy}{[(\xi - x)^2 + (\eta - y)^2 + \zeta^2]^{1/2}}$$

Following a procedure similar to the one used by Hess and Smith for the velocity components [12], Faltinsen and Michelsen [15] have correspondingly obtained for the velocity potential:

$$\int\!\!\int_{\Delta s} \frac{1}{R} dS = -\int_{x_1}^{x_2} dx \log$$
$$\{\eta - y_{12} + \sqrt{(\eta - y_{12})^2 + (\xi - x)^2 + \zeta^2}\}$$
$$- \int_{x_2}^{x_3} dx \log \{\eta - y_{23} + \sqrt{(\eta - y_{23})^2 + (\xi - x)^2 + \zeta^2}\}$$
$$- \int_{x_3}^{x_4} dx \log \{\eta - y_{34} + \sqrt{(\eta - y_{34})^2 + (\xi - x)^2 + \zeta^2}\}$$
$$- \int_{x_4}^{x_1} dx \log \{\eta - y_{41} + \sqrt{(\eta - y_{41})^2 + (\xi - x)^2 + \zeta^2}\}$$

$$(9)$$

where

$$y_{ij} = y_i + \frac{y_j - y_i}{x_j - x_i}(x - x_i)$$

The integrals in the equation (9) may be directly evaluated through numerical integration in most cases. However, the integrand of the first integral is singular when $\zeta = 0$, $x = \xi$, and $\eta - y_{12} < 0$ and in this case the first integral may be replaced by

$$\int_{x_1}^{x_2} dx \, \log((\xi - x)^2 + \zeta^2) - \int_{x_1}^{x_2} dx \, \log\{-(\eta - y_{12}) + \sqrt{(\eta - y_{12})^2 + (\xi - x)^2 + \zeta^2}\}$$

The first term of this alternative form can easily be integrated analytically. The second term, which has no singularity, can be integrated numerically. The difficulties with the integrands of the other integrals are handled in a similar manner.

For panels at large distances from the field point we use the approximation

$$\phi_j = \frac{\sigma_j}{R} \Delta s_j$$

If the distance is less than $2\sqrt{\Delta s_j}$, the exact formula of equation (9) is used [13].

Discussion

Carl-Anders Johnsson,[4] Visitor

First I want to compliment the authors for having accomplished a very elegant procedure for calculating the solid boundary factor.

In its original appearance this concept is, at first hand, of interest to those working out procedures for theoretical calculations of the pressure fluctuations from a propeller (noncavitating or cavitating). However, when the importance of the free surface on the amplitudes of these fluctuations was recognized, this concept became of interest also for those who prefer to determine the pressure fluctuations by measurements in cavitation tunnels, the setup normally not including a free surface. If a complete ship model is placed in front of the propeller the factor S_b is included in the result. Accordingly, our main interest is in the factor S_f. It is therefore a pity that in the present paper separate values of S_f are given for only one configuration; see Fig. 14. Particularly in Fig. 12 I would like to have seen separate curves for S_f, one reason being to find out if the very low values of S_{tot} shown for Section V, far away from the propeller, are due mainly to the influence of the free surface or not.

To try to clarify these matters empirically, two investigations were recently made at SSPA:

(a) The available model/full-scale material was reexamined, emphasizing the aspects of the free-surface effect. The main result of this study was a two-parametric correction factor, the two parameters being the immersion of the transducer and the Froude number.

(b) Well-controlled measurements of pressure fluctuations (and vibration) were carried out on a fisheries research ship and corresponding model tests were performed in the SSPA large cavitation tunnel.

Some results of these measurements, which might be of interest in this context, are shown in Fig. 16, the positions of the transducers being shown in Fig. 17. The values of the empirical correction for the free-surface effect referred to in the foregoing are also included in Fig. 16.

The results of Fig. 16 indicate that there seems to be an influence of the free surface for the transducers close to the water surface, that the empirical correction improves the model/full-scale comparison.

The results of the correlation study referred to in the preceding indicate that the shape of the stern wave is very important for the factor S_f. This result is of significance also when S_f is calculated in the way outlined in the paper.

The results of Fig. 16 illustrate the difficulties of investigating these matters experimentally. When the distance between the propeller and the measuring point increases, the disturbing influence of the vibration of the plating very soon becomes predominant and, also when great efforts are expended to make

[4] Swedish Maritime Research Centre SSPA, Göteborg, Sweden.

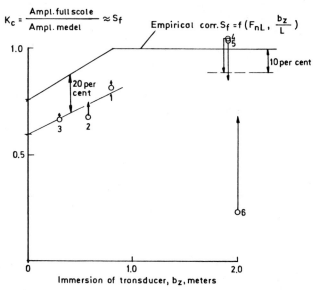

O Uncorrected model and full scale values.

↑ Magnitude of correction of full scale values due to hull vibration (correction based on exciter tests).

Note. Figures denote number of transducer.

$$K_c = \frac{\text{Ampl. full scale}}{\text{Ampl. model}} \approx S_f$$

Empirical corr. $S_f = f\left(F_{nL}, \dfrac{b_z}{L}\right)$

Fig. 16 Comparison between amplitudes of pressure fluctuations in full scale and cavitation tunnel: MS *Argos;* blade frequency; ship speed = 13.6 knots

an accurate correction for this effect, the uncertainty of the measured pressure amplitudes becomes too large. This might explain my keen interest in theoretical calculations of S_f for the cases shown in the present paper, as well as for the fisheries research ship.

F. Everett Reed, Member

This is a valuable paper on a subject of great importance to the prediction of propeller excited hull vibration. I particularly appreciated the values for S that the authors developed. If their calculation methods make it easy to distinguish between S_b and S_f in forming S_{tot}, this would be interesting.

There is another way to determine the values of S_b for surfaces that are wedge-shaped, cylindrical, or conical using Green's functions [16] (additional references follow some discussions). I have been unable to find the time to develop the process, but since it results in an equation for surface pressure, it might be a less expensive, although surely less general, way

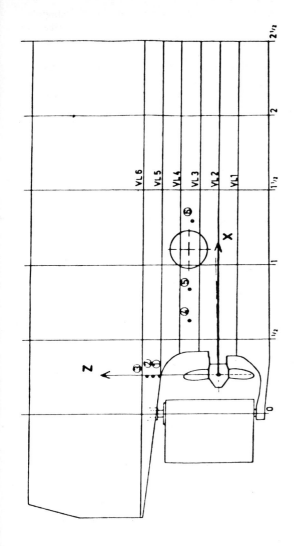

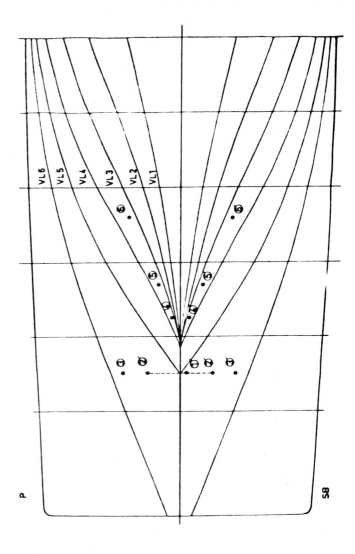

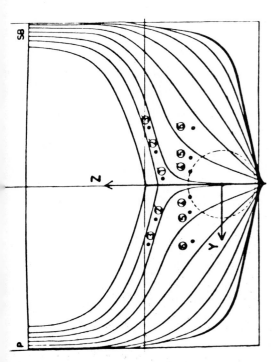

Length of ship
(10 stations), L_{PP} = 54.60 m
Total length = 61.25 m
Propeller diameter, D = 2.5 m

Fig. 17 MS *Argos*: positions of pressure transducers

Cavitation-Induced Excitation Forces on the Hull

of determining S_b than the Smith-Hess procedure.

With regard to the development of the hull pressure data for use in hull response programs, it has been the practice of Littleton Research to use its program for determining hull pressure (assuming $S_{tot} = 2.0$) to calculate the harmonic force and moment inputs at several NASTRAN grid points in the vicinity of the propeller. These excitations then are a direct input to the NASTRAN calculation for hull response (even to the point of being punched on cards).

Additional reference

16   Vildiz, M. and Mawardi, O. K., "On the Diffraction of Multiple Fields by a Semi-infinite Rigid Wedge," *Journal of the Acoustical Society of America*, Vol. 32, No. 12, Dec. 1961, p. 1685.

J. van der Kooij,[5] Visitor

The authors have presented very valuable information about solid boundary effects and free-surface effects. Also, their procedure to determine the pressure distribution over a large part of the ship hull is interesting.

I wonder, however, whether such an extensive pressure distribution is useful, particularly in the design stage of a ship. I fully agree with the authors that the pressure fluctuations at a few positions on the hull above the propeller are not enough to judge the vibration excitation level; see, for example, reference [17] appended to this discussion. It is much better indeed to consider the forces obtained by integration of the pressures over a certain area. The question is how large that area should be, and how the integration should be performed.

The authors state that the pressure fluctuations at large distances from the propeller, although being very small, may contribute significantly to the total excitation force due to the large integration area. However, this total excitation force is not a correct measure for the vibration excitation level either, because of the cancellation effect of the hull vibration modes. Sometimes the authors seem to agree with this view—for example, when they are talking about weighting functions and generalized forces—but finally they stick to the total excitation force, and they even propose to develop criteria for allowable values of this force. I think we should not go that way.

The pressure distribution over a large area is valuable when it can be used as input for finite-element calculations to determine the hull response. Such calculations, however, are not frequently performed, because they require detailed knowledge of the ship structure, which is available only at a late stage of the design of the ship when desired changes are almost impossible.

Nothing is gained in this respect when generalized forces are considered, because the determination and the effect of all relevant generalized forces require a detailed finite-element calculation as well. Possibly, the generalized forces belonging to the first few vibration modes may be derived from what the authors call "systematic information of typical vibratory modes and structural damping for various types of ships." It seems impossible, however, to obtain in this way the generalized forces related to the higher-order modes, which play a dominant role at the excitation frequencies of interest.

For the higher-order vibration modes, the mode-weighted pressures tend to cancel each other over a large part of the hull so that integration over a restricted area in the vicinity of the propeller already yields representative values of the generalized forces. At MARIN we usually consider an integration area with sides equal to 1.5 to 2 times the propeller diameter; see reference [17]. The pressure distribution over such a restricted area can be measured accurately in our depressurized towing tank. The

pressures are integrated over the area considered, and criteria have been developed to judge the resulting forces; see reference [2] of the paper. We have good experience with this method.

Additional reference

17   van der Kooij, J., "Experimental Determination of Propeller-Induced Hydrodynamic Hull Forces in the NSMB Depressurized Towing Tank," *Proceedings*, Symposium on Propeller Induced Ship Vibration, London, Dec. 1979.

Tetsuji Hoshino,[6] Visitor

The authors are to be congratulated for developing a new method of predicting the total surface force by a combination of experimental measurements and theoretical calculations. The results of their calculations of the total excitation force seem to be reasonable.

The authors introduced the equivalent singularity (that is, the strength of pulsating source Q_{ko}) in order to calculate the pressure fluctuation at any point based on the measured pressure fluctuations. It can be well understood why they have attempted this approach rather than the original method based on cavity behavior. But in this discusser's opinion, we should make a further effort to link the pressure fluctuation and the cavity behavior, since the cavity is the only source from which we can learn much more about the complicated phenomenon of unsteady cavitation.

In the following is briefly described the method developed by the discusser to interrelate the pressure fluctuation with the cavity volume observed on a propeller blade [18]. This observed cavity is expressed by a spherical pulsating bubble located on the 0.9 radius of the propeller blade. Then the pressure fluctuations induced by the spherical pulsating bubble are approximately expressed as

$$\Delta P(t) = \frac{\rho}{4\pi} \frac{1}{R_c} \frac{d^2 V_c(t)}{dt^2} \tag{10}$$

where

$V_c(t)$ = volume of pulsating bubble
R_c = distance between field point and center of pulsating bubble

For example, the measured cavity volume is shown in Fig. 18 accompanying this discussion and the results of pressure fluctuation calculations in comparison with measured ones are shown in Fig. 19.

From equation (10) the cavity volume is expressed as

$$V_c(t) = \frac{4\pi R_c}{\rho} \iint \Delta P(t) dt^2 \tag{11}$$

If the pressure fluctuation induced by the pulsating cavity is expressed as

$$\Delta P(t) = \sum_{k=0}^{\infty} \Delta P_k \cos(kz\omega t - \phi_k) \tag{12}$$

where

ΔP_k = amplitude of kth harmonics of pressure fluctuation
ϕ_k = phase angle
k = order of harmonics of blade frequency
z = number of blades
ω = angular velocity
t = time

we get the volume variation of the pulsating cavity as

---

[5] Maritime Research Institute Netherlands (MARIN), Wageningen, The Netherlands.

[6] Nagasaki Experimental Tank, Mitsubishi Heavy Industries, Ltd., Nagasaki, Japan.

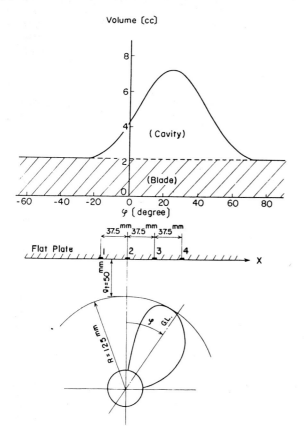

Fig. 18 Volume variation of cavity and positions of pressure pickups

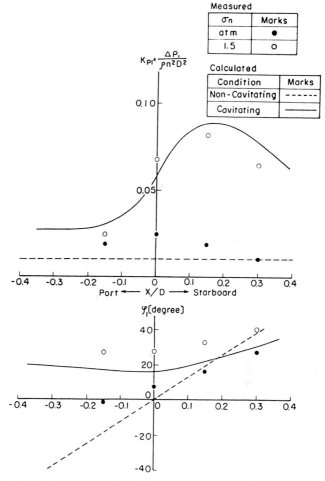

Fig. 19 Comparison of amplitude and phase angle of first harmonic component of pressure fluctuation

$$V_c(t) = \frac{4\pi R_c}{\rho} \sum_{k=0}^{\infty} \frac{\Delta P_k}{(kz\omega)^2} \cos(kz\omega t - \phi_k) \quad (13)$$

Thus, we can verify the theory by comparing the calculated cavity volume with the measured one.

Additional reference

18 Hoshino, T., "Pressure Fluctuation Induced by a Spherical Bubble Moving with Varying Radius," *Transactions*, West-Japan Society of Naval Architects, No. 58, Aug. 1979.

J. P. Breslin, Member

This interesting paper presents a pragmatic procedure for the determination of propeller-induced vibratory vertical forces on ship hulls. The authors advocate the concept of representing the propeller by lumped singularities and deal in detail with the use of an effective, nonrotating pulsating source to represent the contribution of intermittent blade cavitation to pressures induced on the hull. They argue that this effective source strength can be found by measuring the amplitude and phase of the pressures at selected positions on the afterbody in a water tunnel. To verify the assumption that this simple representation is sufficiently valid, they show that determinations of effective source strength and phase are reasonably close when employing the difference in pressure with and without cavitation measured at four locations and on four hulls. The results summarized in their Table 1 are impressive.

Kerwin [19] has shown analogous results for the theoretical potential at a point directly over a propeller, employing a stationary pulsating source having the same cavity volume velocity harmonic as that deduced from a complete calculation of the intermittent cavitation on a 5-bladed propeller. His effective

source was located at $x = 0$, $r/r_0 = 0.9$ and $\theta = 0$ and the potential evaluated at $r/r_0 = 1.4$.

A tacit assumption in the authors' procedure is that the contribution from blade loading and thickness is the same with and without cavitation. This cannot be exactly true, but, as the cavitation-induced pressures predominate, the error is not significant.

As the actual cavitation is distributed chordwise and radially and persists over a sizable angular transit of each blade, it is necessary to determine why the concept of "a center of cavitation" is so effective in capturing the major contribution at hull points which are close to the propeller. Is the effective singularity really only a pulsating point source fixed at $r/r_0 = 0.95$ in the neighborhood of 12 o'clock in the plane of the propeller as "seen" by points in the near field?

The instantaneous velocity potential of a blade-sited cavity as shown in Fig. 20 (of this discussion) can be expressed as

$$\phi_c = -\frac{1}{4\pi} \int_{r_c(\theta)}^{r_0} ds \int_{\alpha(s,\theta)}^{\beta(s,\theta)}$$

$$\times \frac{s\,d\theta' \left[\frac{\partial}{\partial t} - \frac{V}{s} \frac{\partial}{\partial \theta'} \right] \eta(s,\theta';\theta)}{[x^2 + r^2 + s^2 - 2rs\cos(\gamma - \theta - \theta')]^{1/2}} \quad (14)$$

where dependence on the blade angular position θ is embedded in the radial penetration of the cavity $r_c(\theta)$; in the chordwise

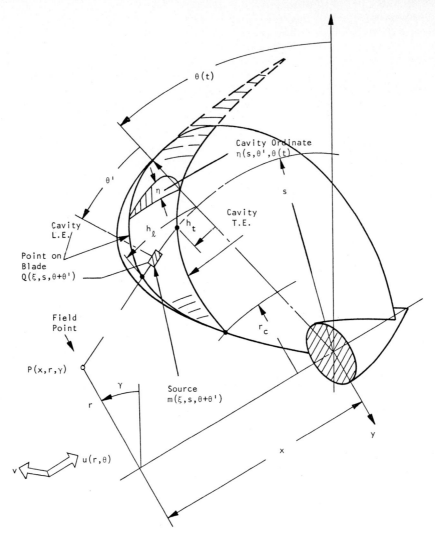

Fig. 20 Schematic of intermittently cavitating propeller blade

limits α, β; in the cavity ordinate η, and in the Decartes distance given by the *denominator*; x, r, γ are the coordinates of any field point; s, θ' are dummy radial and angular coordinates of any point within the cavity; V is the convection velocity $V = [(\omega s)^2 + \overline{U}^2]^{1/2}$.

Expansion of Decartes' distance in a complex Fourier series yields

$$\phi_c = -\frac{1}{4\pi^2} \sum_{-\infty}^{\infty} \int_{r_c}^{r_0} ds \int_{\alpha}^{\beta}$$

$$\times \frac{sd\theta' \left(\dfrac{\partial}{\partial t} - \dfrac{V}{s}\dfrac{\partial}{\partial \theta'}\right) \eta}{\sqrt{rs}} A_m e^{-im\theta'} \cdot e^{im(\gamma-\theta)} \quad (15)$$

where

$$A_m = \frac{Q(Z)}{|m| - \frac{1}{2}} \quad (16)$$

the associated Legendre function of half integer order and

$$Z = \frac{x^2 + r^2 + s^2}{2rs} \quad (17)$$

We may now place the blade angular dependence of the s- and θ'-integrals in evidence by defining

$$C_\lambda^m = \frac{\epsilon_\lambda}{2\pi} \int_{-\pi}^{\pi} d\theta'' e^{-i\lambda\theta''} \int_{r_c(\theta'')}^{r_0}$$

$$\times ds \int_{\alpha(\theta'')}^{\beta(\theta'')} sd\theta' \left(\frac{\omega\partial}{\partial\theta''} - \frac{V}{s}\frac{\partial}{\partial\theta'}\right) \eta e^{im\theta'} A_m e^{im\gamma} \quad (18)$$

so that ϕ_c takes the compact form

$$\phi_c = -\frac{1}{4\pi^2} \sum_{m=-\infty}^{\infty} \sum_{\lambda=-\infty}^{\infty} C_\lambda^m e^{i(\lambda-m)\theta} \quad (19)$$

For an n-bladed propeller, only the terms yielding multiples of blade frequency contribute. Hence $\lambda - m$ is constrained to the values

$$\lambda - m = qn; \quad q = 0, \pm 1, \pm 2 \ldots \quad (20)$$

or

$$m = \lambda - qn$$

Hence, the total cavity potential for an n-bladed propeller is

$$(\phi_c)_{\text{tot}} = -\frac{n}{4\pi^2} \sum_{q=-\infty}^{\infty} \sum_{\lambda=-\infty}^{\infty} C^{\lambda-qn} e^{iqn\theta} \quad (21)$$

Now approximations are made:
• *Approximation* 1—The weighting factor $e^{i(\lambda-qn)\theta'}$ in (18)

when (20) is used as required in (21) may be taken to be unity when the chordwise extent of the cavity, $\beta - \alpha$, is small and the product qn is not large. Then the θ'-integral can be manipulated to produce an operation on the cavity sectional area $S(s,\theta'')$.

After an integration by parts, we have

$$(\phi_c)_{\text{tot}} \sim \frac{in\omega}{4\pi^3} \sum_{q=-\infty}^{\infty} \sum_{\lambda=-\infty}^{\infty} \lambda$$

$$\times e^{i(\lambda-qn)\gamma} \int_{\theta_i}^{\theta_c} d\theta'' e^{-i\lambda\theta''}$$

$$\times \int_{r_c(\theta'')}^{r_0} ds\, S(s,\theta'')\, \frac{A(Z)}{\lambda - qn}\, e^{iqn\theta} \quad (22)$$

The λ-sum can be converted through the use of a substitution $\nu = \lambda - qn$ to a form in which the ν-sums can be accomplished to yield

$$(\phi_c)_{\text{tot}} \simeq -\frac{n\omega}{4\pi^2} \sum_{q=-\infty}^{\infty} \int_{\theta_i}^{\theta_c}$$

$$\times d\theta'' e^{-iqn\theta''} \left\{ \int_{r_c(\theta'')}^{r_0} ds\, S(s,\theta'') \frac{\partial}{\partial\gamma} \right.$$

$$\times \frac{1}{\sqrt{x^2 + r^2 + s^2 - 2rs\cos(\gamma - \theta'')}} + iqn \int_{r_c(\theta'')}^{r_0}$$

$$\times \left. \frac{ds\, S(s,\theta'')}{\sqrt{x^2 + r^2 + s^2 - 2rs\cos(\gamma - \theta'')}} \right\} e^{iqn\theta} \quad (23)$$

where θ_i and θ_c are the key blade position angles at which cavitation inception and collapse take place, respectively. We now require additional assumptions to simplify further.

• *Approximation 2*—The radial extent of the cavity is limited such that the quantities in the radicals can be evaluated at some effective radius $s = \bar{s}$. Thus, the radial integral will yield the cavity volume.

• *Approximation 3*—The angular range in which cavitation ensures is small; that is, $\theta_c - \theta_i$ is small so that the variation of the radicals with θ'' in equation (23) is small.

Then the θ''-integrals produce the qnth harmonic of the cavity volume and we are left with

$$(\phi_0)_{\text{tot}} \simeq -\frac{n\omega}{4\pi} \sum_{q=-\infty}^{\infty} \forall_{qn} e^{iqn\omega t}$$

$$\times \left\{ \frac{qn}{\sqrt{x^2 + r^2 + \bar{s}^2 - 2r\bar{s}\cos\gamma}} \right.$$

$$\left. - \frac{r\bar{s}\sin\gamma}{[x^2 + r^2 + \bar{s}^2 - 2r\bar{s}\cos\gamma]^{3/2}} \right\}$$

(using $\theta = \omega t$).

For any fixed harmonic order, q, the potential is the sum of that for a point source at $x = 0$, $r = \bar{s}$, and $\gamma = 0$ of strength equal to $\omega qn^2 \forall_{qn}$ and pulsating at frequency qn plus the potential of a tangential dipole at the same location of moment $\omega n\bar{s}\forall_{qn}$ and pulsating at the same frequency.

In the vertical longitudinal plane through the propeller, $\gamma \equiv 0$ and, hence, only the source term contributes. However, at athwartship locations, the ratio of the dipole to the source term for $x = 0$ is nearly

$$\frac{r\bar{s}\sin\gamma}{qn(r - \bar{s})^2}$$

For $r = 1.5r_0$, $\bar{s} = 0.95r_0$, $q = 1$, $n = 5$, and $\gamma = \pm 30$ deg, this ratio is ± 0.47. Thus, in lateral regions in the vicinity of the propeller, the dipole contribution is the order of that from the source. Clearly, as x becomes large, the dipole effect decays as $1/x^3$ and the source as $1/x$ in the absence of the water surface.

In the presence of the free surface, the source potential ultimately decays as $1/x^3$ and the dipole as $1/x^5$.

It would be interesting to use the effective source plus dipole representation to see if less variation in their strengths could be secured as compared with the source-alone procedure of the authors.

I agree that corrections must be applied to pressure measurements made on models in water tunnels in which the water surface is replaced by what appears to be a rigid wood cover. I have elaborated on this in our paper, which follows on page 111 of this volume.

The authors' attention is invited to our method of solving the Neumann boundary-value problem on the hull in which the propeller-induced potential is annulled by that of the hull as represented by normal dipoles evaluated on the inner side of the hull boundary. The computational effort is reduced by about two thirds.

Drs. Huse and Guoqiang are to be highly commended for their innovative engineering approach to the prediction of hull forces.

Additional reference

19 Kerwin, J. E., "Flow Field Computations for Non-Cavitating and Cavitating Propellers," Fourteenth Symposium on Naval Hydrodynamics, The University of Michigan, Ann Arbor, 23–27 Aug. 1982.

Paul Kaplan, Member

There are many features of interest in this excellent paper, and my comments are directed toward the basic model for representing a cavitating propeller as well as the nature of the results for the various boundary factors due to the hull and the free surface.

The authors believe that a noncavitating propeller has an adequate theoretical model allowing calculation of the pressure field, while a cavitating propeller does not have such a development presently available. While the model is not claimed to be perfect, we believe that our theory in reference [20] (following this discussion) provides a good approximation of the singularity system that represents a cavitating propeller. In addition to a rotating and pulsating source distribution for the cavity region, the propeller pressure field also has a contribution due to dipoles associated with the loading. Our results in reference [20] as well as in reference [21] show that the loading contribution has an important influence in the near field, and that the loading for a cavitated propeller is different from that for a noncavitated propeller. Since the authors do not even consider the possible influence of such loading dipoles in their paper (they ascribe all loading effects to be present only for the noncavitated propeller), there is the possibility of an error in the determination of the source singularity strength when considering measurements in the near field. As the measurement point is taken farther away from the propeller, this dipole effect falls off fast and has a negligible influence.

The procedure used in the paper to determine the effects of the hull boundary and the free surface involves a three-dimensional analysis, which is generally complicated and uses a large amount of computer time. The approach used in reference [21] is two-dimensional, with only limited computation required due to the analytical solution of an integral equation, conformal mapping, etc. Some of our theoretical results are of interest since they are similar in some respects to those in the present paper, but also serve to illustrate certain differences.

One ship section considered in reference [21] is a wedge, as shown in Fig. 21 accompanying this discussion. The pressure distribution ratio (relative to cavitated propeller free space pressure) is equivalent to the factor S_{tot} in the paper, and our results in Figs. 22 and 23 show the effect of loading and the

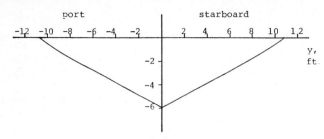

Fig. 21 Section shape of AO-177 at Station 19.5

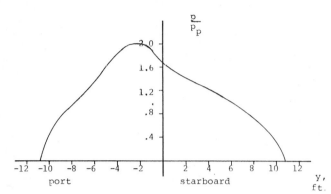

Fig. 22 Variation of pressure relative to local propeller free space pressure along ship section corresponding to AO-177 Station 19.5 flow field due to AO-177 propeller in wake with fins, $x = 5$-ft location

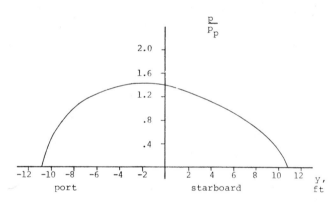

Fig. 23 Variation of pressure relative to local propeller free space pressure along ship section corresponding to AO-177 Station 19.5 flow field due to AO-177 propeller in ship wake, $x = -6$-ft location

influence of the particular onset wake (and resulting free space pressure) as well as the spatial position of the section relative to the propeller. Since we show such behavior, I would like to know if the authors also exhibit variability in the factors as a function of longitudinal location, especially for the free-surface effect. The results shown in Fig. 12 of the paper imply that some difference is present, but is that due only to the hull effect? I can understand the dependence of S_f on vertical distance as shown in Fig. 10 of the paper, but how do the authors account for forward locations that lie below the propeller cavity, as in Fig. 12.

In addition to finding the boundary factors by the method in reference [21], we also show how to determine the total force as well as the generalized excitation force by use of modal weighting functions. There are so many similarities, and yet certain differences, in the results of these two methods, that I

look forward to the response of the authors to my questions and comments.

A final note: There is an error in the conversion of metric to English units in Tables 1 and 3. The correct values should be 1000 N/m^2 = 0.145 psi, or an error of 10^6, which magnifies the problem of propeller excitation forces well beyond their present disturbing effect.[7]

Additional references

20 Kaplan, P., Bentson, J., and Breslin, J. P., "Theoretical Analysis of Propeller Radiated Pressures and Blade Forces Due to Cavitation," *Proceedings* Symposium on Propeller-Induced Ship Vibration, Royal Institution of Naval Architects, London, Dec. 1979.

21 Kaplan, P., Bentson, J., and Benatar, M., "Analytical Prediction of Pressures and Forces on a Ship Hull Due to Cavitating Propellers," paper presented at the Fourteenth Symposium on Naval Hydrodynamics, The University of Michigan, Ann Arbor, Aug. 1982.

D. Catley,[8] Visitor

The authors are to be congratulated on a clear exposition of their procedure for the calculation of hull surface forces. The philosophy is quite similar to the approach developed recently at BSRA [22, 23, 24] in that pulsating free space pressures arising from the propeller are modified by suitable solid boundary factors (SBF) to give the calculated surface forces. It is on the choice of SBF to which the discussion is now directed and important distinctions are drawn compared with the approach suggested in the paper.

The SBF should be mode shape dependent, but those of the paper depend only on the hull geometry and relative position of the excitation source. We at BSRA have found significant variation of SBF with mode shape for a given surface element of the mathematical model; see our Fig. 24 for an example which illustrates the modeling of a products tanker. In the paper this interaction is not considered when calculating the generalized excitations. Furthermore the mode dependence of the SBF implies that correlation with rigid, scale-model results as discussed in the paper will only be, at best, approximate.

The discusser considers that it is more efficient to solve directly for the perturbation potential rather than to solve indirectly for the source strengths as suggested in the paper. In the BSRA scheme, a matrix of influence coefficients is inverted once only and applied via the Chertock relations [25] to obtain the solid, boundary factors for each mode shape in turn. Some 5 min cpu time is required for 10 modes on an ICL 1900 series machine compared with the 13 min quoted for the analysis by the authors using a faster, Univac 1100 machine.

Incidentally, the BSRA model for vertical vibrations of the hull is of a symmetric half of the wetted surface of the hull rather than the double-body model used by the authors. The local free space pressures and their associated phases are then multiplied by the SBF obtained using the aforementioned symmetry to give the required asymmetric pressure loading for each mode. These generalized pressures are then summed vectorially to give the modal forces. Figure 25 shows the longitudinal distribution of the modal force per unit length for the products tanker. As described in reference [23], these modal forces have been used to calculate the vibration response due to propeller blade rate forces and agreement with full-scale measured data is encouraging.

Additional references

22 Catley, D., "Applications of a Surface Singularity Technique to Ship Hydroelastics," IMA Conference on Numerical Methods in Fluid Dynamics, Reading, U.K., March 1982.

---

[7] This error has since been corrected in the TRANSACTIONS.

[8] British Ship Research Association (BSRA), Tyne and Wear, U.K.

Cavitation-Induced Excitation Forces on the Hull

MODE 1 FREQUENCY 50.9 c/min

0.98	0.95	0.91	0.85	0.80	0.77	0.71	0.64	0.53	0.39	VY
1.28	1.57	1.68	1.60	2.08	1.85	1.74	1.68	1.35	0.87	
			2.42	1.91	1.67	1.76	1.71	1.66	1.07	
				1.70	0.99	1.14	1.24	1.38	1.06	
				1.31	0.77	0.58	0.75	1.02	0.97	
					0.37	0.24	0.42	0.71	0.84	SBF
					0.27	0.14	0.29	0.57	0.79	
					0.22	0.17	0.33	0.57	0.85	
					0.26	0.33	0.45	0.71	0.93	
					0.27	0.55	0.78	1.04	1.25	
bottom elements					0.73		1.12		1.33	

MODE 7 FREQUENCY 384 c/min

0.68	0.63	0.57	0.45	0.34	0.26	0.13	$\overline{0}$.05	$\overline{0}$.22	$\overline{0}$.31	VY
1.21	1.46	1.54	1.44	1.78	1.56	1.30	2.19	1.30	0.81	
			2.06	1.64	1.43	1.36	2.09	1.58	0.98	
				1.36	0.85	0.90	1.46	1.31	0.98	
				1.02	0.63	0.45	0.88	0.97	0.89	
					0.19	0.16	0.51	0.68	0.78	SBF
					0.10	0.08	0.35	0.55	0.74	
					0.08	0.15	0.38	0.56	0.80	
					0.19	0.36	0.47	0.70	0.88	
					0.28	0.74	0.68	1.03	1.19	
bottom elements					2.32		1.11		1.27	

MODE 8 FREQUENCY 452 c/min

0.91	0.84	0.75	0.56	0.40	0.27	0.07	$\overline{0}$.18	$\overline{0}$.40	$\overline{0}$.40	VY
1.20	1.45	1.51	1.41	1.70	1.46	0.71	1.78	1.28	0.83	
			1.98	1.58	1.35	0.85	1.75	1.57	1.00	
				1.27	0.81	0.61	1.25	1.30	1.00	
				0.94	0.58	0.29	0.76	0.96	0.91	
					0.12	0.06	0.43	0.67	0.80	SBF
					0.04	0.01	0.30	0.55	0.75	
					0.02	0.11	0.34	0.55	0.81	
					0.16	0.40	0.45	0.70	0.89	
					0.28	0.91	0.75	1.02	1.21	
bottom elements					0.43		1.11		1.28	

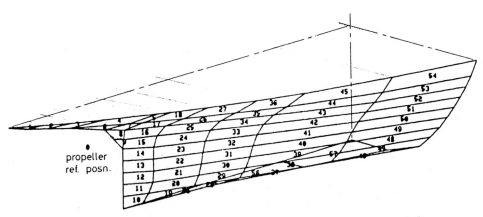

Fig. 24 Calculated solid boundary factors for 25 000-dwt products tanker (loaded)

propeller
ref. posn.

Cavitation-Induced Excitation Forces on the Hull

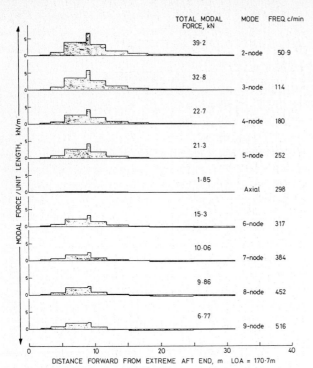

TOTAL MODAL FORCE, kN	MODE	FREQ c/min
39·2	2-node	50·9
32·8	3-node	114
22·7	4-node	180
21·3	5-node	252
1·85	Axial	298
15·3	6-node	317
10·06	7-node	384
9·86	8-node	452
6·77	9-node	516

DISTANCE FORWARD FROM EXTREME AFT END, m   LOA = 170·7m

Fig. 25 Propeller blade order modal forces at 119 rpm for 25 000-dwt products tanker

23   Ward, G., "The Application of Current Vibration Technology to Routine Ship Design Work," RINA Spring Meeting, 1982.

24   Odabasi, A. Y. et al., "An Integrated Method for the Determination of Vibration Excitation from a Cavitating Propeller," paper presented at Euromech 146 "Flows of Liquid Past Bodies with Developed Cavities" Villard de Lans, Sept. 1981.

25   Ogilvie, T. F., "The Chertock Formulae for Computing Unsteady Fluid Dynamic Forces on a Body," *Zeitschrift fuer Angewandte Mathematik und Mechanik*, Vol. 53, 1973, pp. 573–582.

R. Verbeek,[9] Visitor

The authors have presented a very useful paper on the subject of propeller-induced forces on a ship hull. The results of the solid boundary and free-surface effects on propeller-induced pressures on the hull are especially of value for propeller design purposes.

It is clear from the presented results that the use of a correction factor 2 for the free space pressures leads to an overestimation of the propeller-induced pressures and has to be corrected for free-surface effects. For the calculation of the correction factors the authors used a pulsating source at $0.95R$ and an angular position of 6.5 deg. It is not clear from the results if the calculated correction factors are equal for the port and starboard sides of the section considered; especially for larger values of the angular position, one could suspect that differences could arise. Did the authors make such calculations?

During the design of propellers, long calculation runs for correction factors should be avoided, but they should only be performed after finalizing the design. From Fig. 13 in the paper the influence of clearance on the correction factors is evident. In the calculation of propeller-induced pressures the propeller is represented by many sources, each having a different clearance. This is a very time-consuming procedure. Could the authors give a suggestion which overall correction factor value could be used in order to get useful results?

[9] Lips Propeller Works, Drunen, The Netherlands.

Authors' Closure

The authors would first like to thank all the discussers for their kind interest in our paper.

Mr. Johnsson comments on the calculated result that the combined solid boundary and free-surface factor becomes very small at large distances from the propeller. This phenomenon is definitely due to the free-surface effect and not the solid boundary effect. The physical explanation of this phenomenon is that at large distances from the propeller the relative difference in the distances from the field point to the propeller and the distance from the field point to the negative image of the propeller becomes small. Thus, at large distances the total pressure field including the free-surface effect will become more like a dipole-type pressure field with its characteristic rapid decay with increasing distance from the propeller.

Mr. Johnsson describes empirical solid boundary and free-surface factors applied at SSPA. In our opinion it will be difficult to obtain by empirical methods correction factors that are generally applicable for practical applications. We think that it will be more convenient and accurate to calculate the corrections theoretically. After all, as explained in our paper, the calculations can be done in a relatively simple and straightforward manner and at acceptable computer cost. Since it is all a matter of potential theory, we also expect the calculations to be quite accurate.

Dr. Reed asks if the free-surface and solid boundary factors can be calculated separately. Our methods and computer program can be applied to calculate the solid boundary factor separately only in the case when the free surface is substituted by a solid boundary. This is achieved by using a positive image of propeller and hull. By doing the calculation with negative images one obtains the combined free-surface and solid boundary effect. This is the closest we can get to evaluating solid boundary and free-surface effects separately.

We agree with Dr. Reed that the solid boundary effect could be calculated in certain cases by a simple application of Green's functions. However, our procedure developed from a Hess and Smith type of program is certainly more generally applicable.

Mr. van der Kooij comments that pressure distribution over a large area is valuable when used as input for structural finite-element response calculations. As already stated in our paper, we fully agree in this view. His next point is the choice of integration area when using the force as a basis for propeller evaluation. Our method gives the pressure distribution over the whole hull and thus we are completely free to choose whatever integration area we like. We do not agree that choosing an integration area with sides 1.5 to 2.0 times the propeller diameter, as suggested by Mr. van der Kooij, is quite satisfactory. First of all his choice seems quite arbitrary. Secondly, why should the integration area be proportional to the propeller disk area? The relationship between disk area and area of the hull subjected to significant excitation will depend on several parameters such as tip clearance, size of ship relative to the propeller, and afterbody shape. As a conclusion we consider it more natural to use complete hull surface. A basically more correct procedure is to calculate the generalized force associated with each vibratory mode in question by applying the weighting function as suggested in our paper. However, we agree with Mr. van der Kooij that this procedure is not so attractive from a practical point of view because one seldom has sufficient information on the vibratory modes.

Dr. Hoshino draws attention to the possibility of determining cavity volume and volume variation from the generated pressure field. We certainly agree that this is a convenient way of verifying certain types of theoretical calculations of cavity volume.

Dr. Breslin shows by mathematical development that the singularity system should not be just a pulsating source. It should also include a system of dipoles. In fact, when developing our method, we started out by using sources and dipoles of more general distributions as singularity systems in our calculations. However, this did not seem to give more correct or consistent results for practical applications. We checked the consistency of various singularity systems by using the results from three pressure transducers to determine the singularity system and then checked with the measurements on the fourth transducer how well the singularity system worked. Our conclusions was in the cases we tested that the more sophisticated singularity systems did not improve the accuracy significantly, and the simple pulsating source was therefore chosen for the calculations presented in our paper.

Parts of *Dr. Kaplan*'s comments are along the same lines as those of Dr. Breslin. They both draw attention to the tacit assumption made in our paper that the contribution from blade loading and thickness is the same with and without cavitation. We agree that this assumption may lead to considerable error in certain cases where the ship is operated at such conditions that the cavitation has a significant influence on fluctuating blade loading. Although we have no proof for it, we feel that the resulting errors in our procedure will not be very significant, at least not for ordinary merchant vessels. The argument is that they are not normally operated at such extreme cavitating conditions. Naval vessels under certain types of operations might, however, be different in this respect. We agree that this possible error should be kept in mind when applying our procedure for different types of ships.

The calculations presented by Dr. Kaplan shows a certain nonsymmetry about the centerplane of the ship. This is due to the fact that a significant dipole contribution is included in his propeller singularity system. Our calculations are based on only a pulsating source situated very close to the centerplane and will therefore show a more symmetrical behavior of the solid boundary and free-surface effects.

As mentioned before, we consider that the changes of S_{tot} with longitudinal location are due mainly to the free surface-effect and are not so much a consequence of the hull shape.

Finally, we would like to thank Dr. Kaplan for making us aware of the printing error in the conversion factors. We expect that this will be corrected in the TRANSACTIONS.

Mr. Catley shows calculations carried out at BSRA and claims that the solid boundary factor should be mode shape dependent. We believe that the difference is a matter of definition of the term solid boundary factor. In our setup the solid boundary factor is by definition referring to the rigid hull. The effect of the mode shape is in our calculation taken care of by the weighting function that we have introduced.

We have no problem accepting that the computer programs referred to by Mr. Catley are more efficient with respect to computer time than the programs we have developed. In our program development we have optimized with respect to programming effort rather than with respect to computer time efficiency. That is the reason why we used an existing Hess and Smith type program, and by relatively small modifications converted to a program suitable for the new purpose. If our program had been developed as a completely new program, it could certainly have been written to do the calculations more efficiently than is the case now.

Mr. Verbeek also comments on the possible nonsymmetry between port and starboard sides. As mentioned in the foregoing, when using a pulsating source close to the centerplane as a propeller singularity system, the solid boundary and free-surface effects will be correspondingly symmetric. The behavior in the dipole type of pressure field is shown by the figures presented by Dr. Kaplan. The numerical calculations that we have shown in the paper are based on a single pulsating source and not sources distributed along the propeller radius. As indicated by Table 1 of our paper, we consider this singularity system to be acceptable for most practical purposes. Distributing the source along the radius as indicated by Mr. Verbeek should therefore not normally be necessary. In cases where the extent of cavitation in the radial direction is very large (for example, of the same order of magnitude as tip clearance), one would have to use a more sophisticated singularity system to get correct results. At present we can hardly see how this effect could be taken into account by introducing an overall correction factor.

SNAME *Transactions*, Vol. 90, 1982, pp. 111–151

Theoretical and Experimental Propeller-Induced Hull Pressures Arising from Intermittent Blade Cavitation, Loading, and Thickness

J. P. Breslin,[1] Member, **R. J. Van Houten,**[2] Associate Member, **J. E. Kerwin,**[3] Associate Member, and **C-A. Johnsson,**[4] Visitor

This paper is a report of progress of recent theoretical and experimental research efforts at Stevens Institute of Technology (SIT), Massachusetts Institute of Technology (MIT) and the Swedish Maritime Research Centre (SSPA) directed at the prediction of vibratory pressures, forces and moments induced by intermittently cavitating propellers (ICP). The central purpose here is to provide theoretical predictions resulting from a coupling of a propeller-hull program (developed at Davidson Laboratory, SIT) with the output of the ICP program (evolved at MIT) and to compare these results with recent model hull pressure and cavity outline measurements made at SSPA. The physical effects attending rapid growth and collapse of large cavities are qualitatively treated to provide a basis for the more detailed development of unsteady blade cavitation which follows. The mathematical foundation for representation of a hull in the joint presence of an ICP and the water surface is outlined showing that the problem can be solved employing a double hull and a single propeller. The basic assumptions and the procedures developed to solve, for the first time, the three-dimensional, unsteady, mixed boundary-value problem presented by an ICP are given in part in the body of the paper with much mathematical detail relegated to several appendices. A description of the SSPA large cavitation tunnel is followed by a delineation of the characteristics of a model of a RO/RO ship, its propeller, wake and operating conditions. SSPA test results are provided and the correlations with theoretical results exhibited. Tentative conclusions are extracted from this experience and suggestions are advanced for the direction of future work required to enhance the practical applicability of theory and experiment.

Introduction

THIS PAPER is essentially a progress report of recent theoretical and experimental research efforts at Stevens Institute of Technology (SIT), Massachusetts Institute of Technology (MIT), and the Swedish Maritime Research Centre (SSPA) (Göteborg) directed to the prediction of vibratory pressures, forces and moments induced on ship hulls by intermittently cavitating propellers. The significance of this class of cavitation phenomenon to generation of ship vibration needs no elaboration. It has been with us for more than two decades with the advent of increased propeller loadings attending the growth in the size of bulk carriers and express cargo liners. Prior to this evolution, ship vibration arising from the shaft and hull forces induced by noncavitating propellers was long identified as an outstanding problem in ship design and considerable theoretical and experimental studies have been devoted to reveal the roles of the various parameters involved. The appearance of transient cavitation with its generally order-of-magnitude increase in the induced forces at blade frequency (*bf*), and the drastically large forces at twice and thrice *bf*, at which heretofore there were virtually no propeller effects, has riveted our attention and demands that means be developed to predict and mitigate these excitations.

Our response to this challenge is to develop a rational procedure for prediction of hull pressures and forces so that reliable comparisons of competing stern configurations can be made. A sound, proven theoretical method also provides a secure foundation for the analysis of vibration data, whence criteria for acceptable excitation levels can be deduced with confidence.

Here we deal with the coupling of the MIT unsteady propeller cavitation program to drive the SIT propeller-hull program. To ascertain the legitimacy of this marriage, the procedure is applied to a hull-propeller configuration examined experimentally in the large SSPA cavitation tunnel at Göteborg. In the process of this comparison, it is found necessary to consider the probable effects of test boundary conditions.

We present sequentially, physical interpretations of the field effects attending intermittent cavitation (IC) under different conditions; the "creation" of a hull in the presence of its propeller (and the character of the required input from the propeller); a delineation of the procedures for generating the solution of the hitherto unattempted unsteady, three-dimensional

[1] Professor and head, Department of Ocean Engineering, Stevens Institute of Technology, Hoboken, New Jersey.
[2] Associate professor of ocean engineering, Massachusetts Institute of Technology, Cambridge, Massachusetts.
[3] Professor of ocean engineering, Massachusetts Institute of Technology, Cambridge, Massachusetts.
[4] Senior research scientist, Swedish Maritime Research Centre, Göteborg, Sweden.

Presented at the Annual Meeting, New York, N. Y., November 17–20, 1982, of THE SOCIETY OF NAVAL ARCHITECTS AND MARINE ENGINEERS.

(*text continued on page 114*)

Sections 1, 2, 4, and Appendices 1, 2, 3

a = aft extent of ship waterplane at design draft

a' = acceleration ratio; see equation (108) in Appendix 2

a_{qn} = Fourier coefficient of $\cos qn\theta$ at order qn

$A(s,t)$ = cavity cross-sectional area at radius s and time t

b_{qn} = Fourier coefficient of $\sin qn\theta$ at order qn

$c(t)$ = function of time alone arising from integration of fluid motion equation

C_λ^m = Complex Fourier amplitude; see equation (33)

D = propeller diameter

D_e = unbounded domain exterior to surface S

D_i = interior domain bounded by S

f = forward extent of ship waterplane at design draft; also, camber ordinate of blade section

$f_1(y), f_2(y)$ = arbitrary functions of y; see equation (107)

F^+ = representation of cavity surface; $F_{x'}^+, F_{y'}^+, F_r^+$, partial derivatives of F^+

F^- = functional representation of lower or pressure face of blade

g = acceleration due to gravity

h = helical arc length along blade surface measured from center of blade; also used to designate depth of propeller axis below water surface; see equation (48)

$h_l[s, \theta(t)]$ = helical arc length to leading edge of cavity at radius s and angular position of blade $\theta(t)$

$h_t[s, \theta(t)]$ = helical arc length to trailing edge of cavity

J = propeller advance ratio U/ND; U-ship speed, N = revolutions per second (rps), D = diameter

k = blade summing parameter; see equation (35); $-k(\xi)$ designates keel or maximum depth of hull along centerplane including aperture; $\vec{k}$ or $\mathbf{k}$ denotes unit vector in z-direction

K_p = pressure amplitude coefficient defined by SSPA as $(2\sqrt{2}\,p_{rms})/(\rho D^2 n^2)$

K_T = thrust coefficient $T/(\rho n^2 D^4)$; T = propeller thrust

m = source density, cubic units per unit time per unit of area; also used to designate harmonic order number in Fourier expansion of R^{-1}; see equation (29)

m_0 = source density representing blade thickness

$M(t)$ = time-dependent strength of a point source

$\dot{M}(t)$ = time derivative of $M(t)$

n = number of blades; also used as rps in definition of dimensionless pressure amplitude and force coefficients

$n_{x'}, n_{y'}, n_r$ = components of unit normal to cavity surface

p' = pitch of blade at radius r divided by 2π

p = pressure in fluid at any field point at any time

p_a = ambient total pressure

p_c = pressure induced by changing spherical vapor cavity

p_e = net excitation pressure; see equation (13)

p_i = propeller pitch at radius r

p_l = field pressure due to blade loading

p_0 = static pressure at propeller shaft center

p_v = vapor pressure

p_{rms} = root-mean-square of pressure measured at SSPA

q = indicator of order of harmonic $q = 1$ corresponds to blade frequency

$Q(z)\,|m|-\!{}^{1}\!/_2$ = associated Legendre function of second kind of half-integer order; $|m|$ is absolute values of order number m

r = radial coordinate measured outward from propeller axis

$r_c(t)$ = instantaneous lower radial penetration of leading edge of cavity

r_0 = propeller radius

R = radius of a spherical surface; also, distance between a dummy point in a distribution to a field point

R_e = indicates "real part of"

R_i = distance from an image point in free surface to propeller or hull element

s = arc length along any ship section; s' = vertical derivative of section arc length

s = dummy radial variable

S = surface area in general; also, sum of series defined by equation (35)

S_g = sum of a geometric series

$S_c(t)$ = region of blade covered by sheet cavitation at any time t

S_i = surface area of image of hull above plane of water surface

t = time, sec

U = freestream speed directed along negative x

$\overline{U}(r)$ = circumferential mean axial velocity in plane of propeller at any radius r

$v(R, t)$ = radial velocity in a spherically symmetric flow

V = resultant relative velocity at any blade section

V_c = cavity volume on a single blade

$(V_c)_{qn}$ = qnth harmonic of volume of cavity on a single blade

V^+ = fluid velocity on upper or cavity side of blade $V_{x'}^+$, $V_{y'}^+$, V_r^+ components of v in indicated directions

w = arc length along any ship waterplane; w' = axial derivative along waterline

x = axial coordinate measured from center of propeller positive forward

Z = given by $e^{i2\pi(\lambda-m)/n}$; see equation (35)

Z = argument of associated Legendre function of second kind; see equation (30)

Greek letters

$\alpha[s, \theta(t)]$ = angle subtended by trailing edge of cavity at a blade section

$\beta[s, \theta(t)]$ = angle subtended by leading edge of cavity section on a blade

γ = angular coordinate measured from positive z-axis in clockwise direction looking forward in direction of positive x

$\Gamma(N)$ = gamma function with argument N

∇ = vector differential operation $\vec{i}\,\partial/\partial\xi + \vec{j}\,\partial/\partial n + \vec{k}\,\partial/\partial\zeta$

∇ = vector operation; see equation (111) in Appendix 3

∇ = vector operation; see equation (111) in Appendix 3

ϵ_λ = a coefficient; $\epsilon_0 = 1$, $\epsilon_\lambda = 2$, $\lambda \neq 0$

ϵ = phase angle defined by equation (44); angle of key blade when pressure is a positive maximum is given by ϵ/qn

$\zeta(x, y, t)$ = deflection of water surface with respect to horizontal plane $z = 0$

$\eta(s, \theta', t)$ = cavity ordinate at any section $r = s$ and chordwise location θ' at any time t; also, dummy athwartship variable

$\dot{\eta}$ = time derivative of η

η_0 = propeller efficiency

θ' = dummy angular variable measured from blade reference line to any dummy point on blade

θ'' = dummy angular variable of integration; see equation (38)

$\theta(t)$ = angular position of reference line attached to key blade measured clockwise looking forward

μ = dipole strength density on hull in presence of free surface

$\tilde{\mu}_{qn}$ = complex amplitude of qnth harmonic of dipole density $\mu(w, s, t)$

ν = dipole density of double hull

ξ = dummy x-wise variable; also, dummy vertical variable

ρ = mass density of water

$\sigma_{0.7R}$ = cavitation number at 0.7 radius defined by SSPA as $(P_0 - P_v)/[\rho/2(V_{0.7}^2)]$

σ_{VA} = cavitation number based on speed of advance

σ_n = cavitation number based on (revolutions)^2

τ = blade semithickness function; $\tau_{x'}, \tau_r$ = partial derivatives of τ

ϕ = velocity potential of a single blade due to cavitation and loading; see equation (20); also, velocity potential of a propeller in a boundless fluid

ϕ_c = potential of cavity on a blade

ϕ_h = potential of ship hull

ϕ_p = velocity potential of a propeller in presence of free surface

ϕ_{qn} = velocity potential at frequency order qn, $q = 0, 1, 2$; n = number of blades

ϕ_s = velocity potential of a point source

ϕ_d = velocity potential of an exterior driving flow producing cavitation

$\phi(x,y,z)$ = complex amplitude of general potential $\phi(x,y,z,t)$

ω = propeller angular velocity, positive for right-handed propeller

Abbreviations

IC = intermittent cavitation

ICP = intermittently cavitating propeller

WS = water surface

MIT = Massachusetts Institute of Technology

SIT = Stevens Institute of Technology

SSPA = Statens Skeppsprovingsanstalt

Section 3 and Appendices 4–8

a_{pq} = coefficient matrix, defined in eq. (157) of Appendix 8

c = blade section chord length

d_{ij} = defined in equation (129) of Appendix 4

D = propeller diameter

e_{ij} = defined in equation (154) of Appendix 7

f_0 = maximum blade section camber at a given radius

F = defined in equation (142) of Appendix 6

F_r = propeller Froude number based on propeller rotational speed, $F_r = n^2 D/g$

h = cavity thickness function

H_{ijnm} = induced velocity at (i,j)th control point due to (n,m)th unit strength cavity source

I = total number of knowns, $I = N + 1 + N_Q$

i,j = chordwise and spanwise indices of control point, respectively

J_A = advance coefficient, $J_A = V_A/nD$

K = number of blades

K_{ijnm} = induced velocity at (i,j)th control point due to (n,m)th unit strength vortex

K_T = mean thrust coefficient, $K_T = T/\rho n^2 D^4$

l = cavity length

M = number of chordwise panels over radius

n = propeller rotational speed, rps

$\mathbf{n}$ = vector normal to blade camber surface

N = number of spanwise vortices within a chordwise strip

N_Q = number of cavitating elements at each radial interval

N_w = number of discrete time steps since beginning of motion

n,m = chordwise and spanwise indices of singularity, respectively

p = pressure

P_v = vapor pressure

P_∞ = pressure at depth of the shaft center at upstream infinity

P = propeller pitch

q = strength of continuous sources per unit area

Q_{nm} = strength of (n,m)th concentrated line source per unit length

r = radial coordinate

r_H = hub radius

R = propeller radius

R_e = Reynolds number

R_n = defined in equation (140) of Appendix 6

s = fraction of chord from leading edge

t_0 = maximum blade section thickness at a given radius

T = thrust

u,v,w = perturbation velocities in the (ξ,ω,ζ) directions

U_r = helical inflow velocity, defined in equation (133) of Appendix 5

v = resultant velocity

$\overline{V}_A(r,\theta_0)$ = inflow velocity at coordinate (r,θ_0) in propeller plane

w_g = gust velocity normal to camber surface

x_m = rake

x,y,z = cartesian coordinate system fixed on propeller: x positive downstream, y positive radially outward, and z being determined to complete the right-hand system

x_0,y_0,z_0 = cartesian coordinate system fixed on ship: x_0 identical to x, positive downstream, y_0 measured positive upward from shaft center, and z_0 positive when pointing port

Γ_{nm} = strength of (n,m)th discrete vortex element

ϵ = angle of spanwise vortex line relative to η coordinate

θ_0 = angular coordinate of key blade relative to y_0 coordinate fixed on ship

θ_m = skew angle

ξ,η,ζ = coordinate system defined on camber surface: ξ intersection of camber surface and a cylindrical surface concentric with x-axis, positive when pointing downstream, ζ normal to camber surface, positive when pointing upstream, and η being determined to complete the right-hand system on camber surface

σ_n = cavitation number based on propeller rotational speed, $\sigma = (p_\infty - p_v)/\frac{1}{2}\rho n^2 D^2$

ϕ_{ijnm} = velocity potential at (i,j) control point due to (n,m)th unit strength source element

ϕ = perturbation velocity potential

$\Box$ = closed vortex; see equation (130) of Appendix 4

$\Box_w$ = shed vortex quadrilateral; see equation (130) of Appendix 4

problem posed by the IC propeller and the resulting field potential; a description of the SSPA cavitation tunnel with a synopsis of its more than a decade of service; and a summary of a specific SSPA model test and a comparison of the theoretical estimates with cavitating model pressure measurements. Finally, tentative assessments are given and recommendations for possible improvements in theory and measurements are proffered.

1. Basic aspects of the pressure field generated by unsteady cavitation

The growth and recession of large transient vapor cavities on ship propeller blades as they transit the region of low inflow in the wake abaft the hull is a complicated phenomenon. As a prelude to the detailed developments which follow, it is thought to be helpful to portray an elementary time-varying cavity-generated flow to motivate and provide insight to the mathematical representations employed later.

To demonstrate the physics of a cavity-generated flow, we may consider a spherically symmetric, irrotational, incompressible, radial flow emanating from a single point (taken as the origin of coordinates) in a boundless fluid. Then, if $v(R,t)$ is the radial velocity at any radius R and time t, the total volume rate of flow threading through the surface of a sphere of radius R and center at the origin is $4\pi R^2 v$. This volume rate is (from continuity of material) equivalent to the rate of input at the origin, say, $M(t)$ cubic units/unit time. Hence

$$v(R,t) = \frac{M(t)}{4\pi R^2} \tag{1}$$

which can be written as

$$v(R,t) = \frac{\partial}{\partial R}\left(-\frac{M(t)}{4\pi R}\right)$$

As the flow is irrotational, the quantity in the parentheses defines the velocity potential function of a time-dependent point source

$$\phi = -\frac{M(t)}{4\pi R} \tag{2}$$

and

$$v(R,t) = \frac{\partial \phi}{\partial R} \tag{3}$$

To secure the relationship between velocity and pressure, a differential mass of the fluid is examined as an element of a spherical shell. Neglecting gravitational forces, the application of Newton's second law of motion, namely,

(Mass) (acceleration)

= Net force acting on elementary mass yields

$$\rho \frac{dv}{dt} = \frac{\partial p}{\partial R} \tag{4}$$

when the substantive derivative is

$$\frac{dv[r,(t),t]}{dt} = \frac{\partial v}{\partial t} + \frac{\partial R}{\partial t}\frac{\partial v}{\partial R} = \frac{\partial v}{\partial t} + \frac{v\partial v}{\partial R} = \frac{\partial v}{\partial t} + \frac{1}{2}\frac{\partial v^2}{\partial R} \tag{5}$$

In general, for irrotational motions, the velocities can be expressed as the derivatives of a potential function, that is $v = \partial\Phi/\partial R$, and hence (4) with (5) becomes

$$\frac{\partial}{\partial R}\left[\frac{\partial \Phi}{\partial t} + \frac{1}{2}\left(\frac{\partial \Phi}{\partial R}\right)^2 + \frac{p}{\rho}\right] = 0 \tag{6}$$

Integrating and making use of the requirement that Φ vanish at infinity, we obtain

$$\frac{\partial \Phi}{\partial t} + \frac{1}{2}\left(\frac{\partial \Phi}{\partial R}\right)^2 = \frac{p_a - p(R,t)}{\rho} \tag{7}$$

where p_a is the ambient total pressure at large R. For a cavity driven or developed by the action of a flow having a potential ϕ', we take the total potential to be

$$\Phi = \phi + \phi' \tag{8}$$

The kinematic condition on the surface $R = r$ is

$$\frac{\partial \Phi}{\partial R} = \frac{\partial r}{\partial t} = \dot{r} \tag{9}$$

or

$$\frac{M}{4\pi r^2} + \frac{\partial \phi'}{\partial R} = \dot{r} \qquad \text{on } R = r(t) \tag{10}$$

We assume that the driving potential provides only a weak distortion to the spherical surface $R = r(t)$ and can be neglected in (10) to give

$$M \simeq 4\pi r^2 \dot{r} \tag{11}$$

and, hence (2) becomes

$$\phi \simeq -\frac{r^2 \dot{r}}{R} \tag{12}$$

The use of (12) in (8) and thence to (7) produces

$$-\left(\frac{2r\dot{r}^2 + r^2\ddot{r}}{R}\right) + \dot{\phi}' + \frac{1}{2}\frac{r^4\dot{r}^2}{R^4} = \frac{p_a - p(R,t)}{\rho} \tag{13}$$

where $\dot{\phi} = \dot{\phi}'(R,t)$.

When evaluating (13) on the cavity surface $R = r$, we may take $\dot{\phi}'$ as $\dot{\phi}(0,t)$ since the bubble radius is very small compared with the spatial scale of the driving potential ϕ' (which may be considered to be that arising from the changing blade loading during transit of the wake peak). The pressure on the cavity surface is taken to be the vapor pressure (ignoring surface tension) so $p(r,t) = p_v$, a constant, and then (13) on $R = r$ yields the relation

$$-(2\dot{r}^2 + r\ddot{r}) + \frac{\dot{r}^2}{2} = \frac{p_a - p_v}{\rho} - \dot{\phi}'(0,t)\left(r\ddot{r} + \frac{3}{2}\dot{r}^2\right)$$

$$= \frac{\rho\dot{\phi}'(0,t) - p_a + p_v}{\rho}$$

or

$$\frac{1}{2r^2\dot{r}}\frac{d}{dt}(r^3\dot{r}^2) = \frac{p_v - (p_d + p_a)}{\rho} = \frac{P}{\rho} \tag{14}$$

where $p_d = -\rho\dot{\phi}(0,t)$ = the driving pressure.

In order for the cavity to expand, the right side of (14) must be positive. This occurs when the driving pressure p_d becomes more negative than the ambient pressure (composed of the atmospheric pressure plus the static pressure of the fluid at the depth of the cavity).

Integrating (14) under the assumption that P does not vary significantly in the very short time for the cavity to grow yields

$$r^3\dot{r}^2 \simeq \frac{2P}{3\rho}\int_0^t \frac{d}{d\tau}r^3\,d\tau$$

whence

$$\dot{r} = \left(\frac{2P(0)}{3\rho}\left\{1 - \left[\frac{r(0)}{r(t)}\right]^3\right\}\right)^{1/2} \tag{15}$$

After the initial period, then, $r(0)/r(t) \ll 1$ and we see that the rate of growth approaches a constant, namely, $[2P(0)/3\rho]^{1/2}$. Then the first-order pressure increment at any field radius R due to the expanding cavity is

$$\Delta p_c = -\rho \frac{\partial \phi}{\partial t} = \rho \frac{(2r\dot{r}^2 + r^2\ddot{r})}{R} \tag{16}$$

and for $\dot{r} \simeq$ a constant, $\ddot{r} \simeq 0$, then

$$\Delta p_c \sim \frac{2\rho}{R}\left[\frac{2}{3}\frac{P(0)}{\rho}\right]^{3/2} t \tag{17}$$

or

$$\Delta p_c \sim \frac{2\rho}{R}\left[\frac{2}{3\rho}(p_v - (p_d + p_a))\right]^{3/2} t \tag{18}$$

Thus, at a distance from an expanding spherical cavity, the pressure signature is proportional to the $3/2$-power of the net pressure causing vaporization, that is, the amount that p_d is more negative than the cavitation inhibiting pressure $p_a - p_v$.

Returning to (11), we see that the source strength $M(t)$ can be written

$$M(t) = 4\pi r^2 \dot{r} = \frac{4}{3}\pi\frac{d}{dt}r^3$$

or $M(t) = \dot{V}$ where V is the cavity volume and the dot denotes the time derivative. Then the potential of a spherical cavity is

$$\phi = -\frac{\dot{V}}{4\pi R}$$

and the incremental pressure is

$$\Delta p_c = -\rho\frac{\partial \phi}{\partial t} = \frac{\rho\ddot{V}}{4\pi R} \tag{19}$$

a pressure source whose strength is proportional to the acceleration of the cavity volume.

On propeller blades, cavities are clearly far from spherical, being stretched out into sheets because of the high tangential velocity of the blade. Consequently, such cavities are modeled by area distribution of sources (and sinks). Nevertheless, a formula quite analogous to (19) is found for the pressure at relatively large distances from the propeller.

It is important to note that, when cavitation occurs near the water surface, the effect of the presence of that surface is to reduce the pressures at field points. As the motion is rapid, gravity is negligible in the near field and the pressure change due to cavitation would be given by

$$\Delta p_c = \frac{\rho}{4\pi}\ddot{V}\left(\frac{1}{R} - \frac{1}{R_1}\right)$$

$$R = \sqrt{x^2 + y^2 + z^2} \qquad R_i = \sqrt{x^2 + y^2 + (2h - z)^2}$$

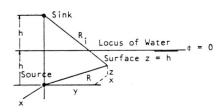

Clearly, along the locus $z = h$, $\Delta p_c = 0$. Now if we ask how the pressure varies as $x \gg h$ for $y = 0$, say, then expanding each radical by the binomial theorem:

$$\Delta p_c \sim \left\{\frac{1}{x}\left(1 - \frac{1}{2}\left(\frac{z}{x}\right)^2 + \dots\right) - \frac{1}{x}\left(1 - \frac{1}{2}\left(\frac{2h - z}{x}\right)^2 + \dots\right)\right\}$$

or

$$\Delta p_c \sim \frac{2h(h - z)}{x^3}$$

This decay with distance is to be contrasted with that from the source in the absence of the free surface, namely, as $1/x$. Thus, the signature at distance from unsteady cavitation can be rapidly quenched when the free surface is present.

It is hoped that the foregoing rather lengthy development provides an explanation as to how intermittent cavitation (IC) can produce large field pressures even though the pressure on the expanding (or contracting cavity surface) is only the vapor pressure of water at the ambient temperature.

Another question is posed by the experimentally observed pressures (from IC propellers) which have frequently been found to have components at twice and thrice blade frequency that are comparable to those at blade frequency. This has never been the case for noncavitating propellers. We may now attempt to answer this question by considering a representation of unsteady cavitation on propeller blades.

The velocity potential generated by a single IC blade (in the absence of boundaries other than the blades) can be expressed by

$$\phi = \frac{1}{4\pi}\iint_{S_c(t)}\frac{m}{R}dS + \frac{1}{4\pi\rho U}$$
$$\times \int_x^\infty p_l\left(\xi,r,\gamma;t - \frac{x - \xi}{U}\right)d\xi - \frac{1}{2\pi}\iint_S\frac{V\tau'}{R}dS \tag{20}$$

where the first term is a source distribution of density m over the instantaneous area of the blade, $S_c(\theta(t))$, on which the cavitation extends. The second term is the contribution from the pressure field generated by the distribution of the jump in pressure (or loading) across the blade elements. The third term is the potential induced by the blade thickness τ.

We shall focus only on the source or cavity term which is designated as ϕ_c. More explicitly

$$\phi_c(x,r,\gamma;\theta(t)) = -\frac{1}{4\pi}\int_{r_c}^{r_0}\int_{h_t}^{h_l}$$
$$\times \frac{m(s,h,t)\,dh\,ds}{[(x - \xi)^2 + r^2 + s^2 - 2rs\cos(\gamma - \theta - \theta')]^{1/2}} \tag{21}$$

Here, as may be observed in Fig. 1, $r_c = r_c(\theta(t))$ is the instantaneous lowest radial extent of the cavity at any blade angular position $\theta(t)$; r_0 is the blade radius; $h_t = h_t(s,\theta(t))$ is the cavity trailing edge along the helix arc; $h_l = h_l(s,\theta(t))$ is the leading-edge location; s is the dummy radius along the surface (a ruled surface); and the denominator is the straight-line distance between any field point x,r,γ and any dummy point $\xi,s,\theta + \theta'$.

From the helical geometry, we have $h = \sqrt{p'^2 + s^2}\theta'$ with $p' = p_i/2\pi$, p_i the pitch at radius s, and the connection between the dummy x-variable and dummy angular variable θ' is $\xi = p_i\theta'/2\pi = p'\theta'$. [We have not allowed for blade skew for simplicity; to do so, simply replace θ by $\theta - \sigma(s)$ where σ is the skew angle.] Employing these helicoidal-cylindrical coordinate relationships places (21) in the form

$$\phi_c(s,r,\gamma;\theta(t)) = -\frac{1}{4\pi}\int_{r_c}^{r_0}\int_\alpha^\beta$$
$$\times \frac{m(s\sqrt{p'^2 + s^2}\theta',t)\sqrt{p'^2 + s^2}d\theta'ds}{[(x - p' - \theta')^2 + r^2 + s^2 - 2rs\cos(\gamma - \theta - \theta')]^{1/2}} \tag{22}$$

Although (22) is precise, it is cumbersome. For our purposes here, since we seek to interpret effects at some distance, we place the sources on the plane $x = 0$ by noting that $\sqrt{p'^2 + s^2} \simeq s$ (in the outer reaches of the blade) and consider only those $x \gg p'\theta'$ (an easy condition since the fore-aft extent of the blade is small). Thus, (22) is approximated by

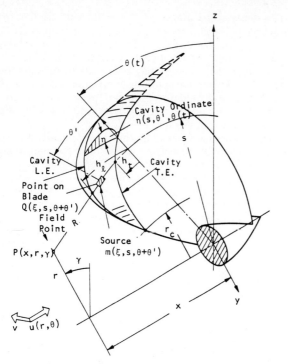

Fig. 1 Schematic of instantaneous intermittent cavitation on a single blade

$$\phi_c = -\frac{1}{4\pi} \int_{s=r_c}^{r_0} \int_{\alpha}^{\beta}$$

$$\times \frac{m(s,\theta's,t)\,sd\theta'ds}{[x^2 + r^2 + s^2 - 2rs\cos(\gamma - \theta - \theta')]^{1/2}} \quad (23)$$

with $\alpha = \alpha(s,\theta(t))$ and $\beta = \beta(s,\theta(t))$ being the angles subtended by the trailing and leading edges of the cavity. Now it is known that the source density m is given by the *jump* in the normal derivative to the source sheet. It is also known that the cavity ordinate η is connected to this jump in the normal velocity by

$$\frac{\partial \eta(s,\theta';t)}{\partial t} - \frac{V}{s}\frac{\partial \eta(s,\theta';t)}{\partial \theta'} = m \quad (24)$$

as shown in Appendix 1. Here V is the resultant relative velocity at radius s, that is, $V = [\overline{U} + (\omega s)^2]^{1/2}$, $\overline{U}$ being the mean axial velocity and ω the angular velocity of the blade. Then (23) becomes [with (24) and integration by parts]:

$$\phi_c = -\frac{1}{4\pi}\Bigg[\frac{\partial}{\partial t}\int_{r_c}^{r_0}$$

$$\times \frac{A(s,t)ds}{[x^2 + r^2 + s^2 - 2rs\cos(\gamma - \theta - \beta)]^{1/2}}$$

$$-\frac{\partial}{\partial t}\int_{r_c}^{r_0}\int_{\alpha}^{\beta}\int_{\alpha}^{\theta'}\eta s d\theta''\frac{\partial}{\partial \theta'}\left(\frac{1}{R}\right)d\theta'ds$$

$$+\int_{r_c}^{r_0}\int_{\alpha}^{\beta}(\omega s - V)\,\eta\frac{\partial}{\partial \theta'}\left(\frac{1}{R}\right)d\theta'ds\Bigg] \quad (25)$$

where $A(s,t)$ is the cavity cross-sectional area at s and t. The first term can be recognized as the time derivative of the potential of a line source along the cavity leading edge whose lineal density is A. The remaining terms are chordwise-directed dipoles, the first of which has a dipole density of the partial cavity area $\int_{\alpha}^{\theta'}\eta s d\theta''$ and the last having a density of $(\omega s - V)\eta$.

Thus, an educated seal (with a degree from SIT or MIT!) could say, when swimming along with a strange ship having only a single-bladed IC propeller—"Aha! At large distances, I see a point source whose strength is the time derivative of the cavity volume—and, behold!, this transforms to a time-varying line source as I move closer and then, when very close, there, is in addition, a distributed mess of chordwise dipoles!" Thus, for $x^2 + r^2 = R_0^2 \gg r_0$

$$\phi_c \rightarrow -\frac{1}{4\pi}\frac{\partial}{\partial t}\frac{\int_{r_c}^{r_0} A(s,t)ds}{R_0} = -\frac{\dot{V}_c}{4\pi R_0} \quad (26)$$

because the integrands of the dipole terms are varying as

$$\frac{\partial}{\partial \theta'}\frac{1}{R} = \frac{rs\sin(\gamma - \theta - \theta')}{[x^2 + r^2 + s^2 - 2rs\cos(\gamma - \theta - \theta')]^{3/2}}$$

$$\rightarrow \frac{rs\sin(\gamma - \theta - \theta')}{R_0^3} \quad (27)$$

and, hence, they fade out much faster than the line source.

We must now remove the restrictions to a single blade and, for the sake of demonstration, consider only the first term of (25). To exhibit the harmonic dependence of the spatial propagation function $1/R$, we use the identity

$$\frac{1}{R} = \frac{1}{[x^2 + r^2 + s^2 - 2rs\cos(\gamma - \theta - \theta')]^{1/2}} \quad (28)$$

$$= \frac{1}{\pi\sqrt{rs}}\sum_{m=-\infty}^{\infty}Q_{|m|-1/2}(Z)e^{im(\gamma-\theta-\theta')}$$

$$= \frac{1}{\pi\sqrt{rs}}\sum_{m=0}^{\infty}\epsilon_m\,Q(Z)_{|m|-1/2}\cos m(\gamma - \theta - \theta'); \quad (29)[5]$$

$$\epsilon_0 = 1, \quad \epsilon_m = 2, \quad m > 0$$

$$Z = \frac{x^2 + r^2 + s^2}{2rs} \quad (30)$$

where $Q_{|m|-1/2}$ is the associated Legendre function of the second kind, of half-integer order. Thus the harmonic components of $1/R$ are individually secured.

Then, at sufficient distances where the first term of (25) dominates, (25) can be written

$$\phi_c \simeq -\frac{1}{4\pi^2}\frac{\partial}{\partial t}\sum_{-\infty}^{\infty}\int_{r_c(t)}^{r_0}\frac{A(s,t)}{\sqrt{rs}}$$

$$\times Q_{|m|-1/2}(Z)\,e^{-im\beta(s,t)}ds\,e^{im(\gamma-\theta)} \quad (31)$$

Now we see that there is harmonic or cyclic variation imbedded in the limit $r_c(t)$, in $A(s,t)$ and $\beta(s,t)$. This cavity-generated harmonic contribution can be placed in evidence by writing

$$\int_{r_c(\theta)}^{r_0}\frac{A}{\sqrt{rs}}Q_{|m|-1/2}e^{im\beta}ds = \sum_{\lambda=-\infty}^{\infty}C_\lambda^m(x,r)e^{i\lambda\theta(t)} \quad (32)$$

where, in the usual procedure, the "cavitation amplitude" functions are calculated from

$$C_\lambda^m(x,r) = \frac{\epsilon_\lambda}{2\pi}\int_0^{2\pi}$$

$$\times \int_{r_c(\theta'')}^{r_0} A\,Q_{|m|-1/2}e^{im\beta(\theta'')}\,ds\,e^{-i\lambda\theta''}d\theta''$$

$$\epsilon_0 = 1, \epsilon_\lambda = 2, \lambda \neq 0 \quad (33)$$

where the superscript m denotes the parametric dependence on the "propagation" order number. Use of (32) in (31) gives

---

[5] The function $1/R$ can be regarded as the propagator of disturbances emanating from $x = 0$, $r = s$, $\gamma = \theta - \theta$ to field points at all frequencies of orders m.

$$\phi_c = -\frac{1}{4\pi^2}\frac{\partial}{\partial t}\sum_{m=-\infty}^{\infty}\sum_{\lambda=-\infty}^{\infty}C_\lambda^m(x,r)e^{im\gamma}\cdot e^{i(\lambda-m)\theta(t)} \quad (34)$$

a Fourier equivalent representation whose sum must yield $\phi_c = 0$ for the blade outside of the cavitating interval $\phi_i \le \theta < \theta_c$, θ_i, the blade angle at which inception occurs, and θ_c, the angle of cavity collapse. Now the potential for each blade is amenable to the same kind of representation with the blade angle indexed appropriately. To achieve the total potential for an n-bladed propeller, we may replace θ by $\theta + (2\pi k/n)$ and sum over k from $k = 0$ (the key blade) to $k = n - 1$ (to the one following the key blade). Thus, one is confronted with the sum

$$S = \sum_{k=0}^{n-1}e^{i(\lambda-m)(\theta+2\pi k/n)} = e^{i(\lambda-m)\theta}\sum_{k=0}^{n-1}e^{i2\pi(\lambda-m)k/n} \quad (35)$$

The k-sum can be recognized as a geometric series by writing

$$Z = e^{i2\pi(\lambda-m)/n}$$

and thus

$$S_g = \sum_{k=0}^{n-1}Z^k = \frac{1-Z^k}{1-Z} = \frac{1-e^{i2\pi(\lambda-m)}}{1-e^{i2\pi(\lambda-m)/n}}$$

$$= 0 \text{ (as } e^{i2\pi(\lambda-m)} \equiv 1, \lambda - m \text{ integers)}$$

for $\lambda - m \ne \pm qn$ where $q = 0,1,2,\dots$, but for $\lambda - m = \pm qn$, we see that $S_g = 0/0$, that is, indeterminate. To resolve this, put $\lambda - m = \pm qn$ in (35) and we achieve

$$S = e^{iqn\theta}\sum_{n=0}^{n-1}e^{i2\pi qnk/n} = ne^{iqn\theta} \quad (36a)$$

and

$$S = ne^{-iqn\theta} \text{ for } -qn \quad (36b)$$

Thus, we have for the sum of all possibilities the two sets, that is

$$\begin{array}{ll} \text{for} \quad \lambda - m = qn & \text{for} \quad \lambda - m = -qn \\ m = \lambda - qn & m = \lambda + qn \end{array} \quad (36c)$$

So, upon eliminating the m-series for both conditions, and considering each λ-term

$$(\phi_c)_{qn,\lambda} = -\frac{n}{4\pi^2}\frac{\partial}{\partial t}(C_\lambda^{\lambda-qn}e^{i(\lambda-qn)\gamma}$$
$$\cdot e^{iqn\theta} + C_\lambda^{\lambda+qn}e^{i(\lambda+qn)\gamma}e^{-iqn\theta}) \quad (37)$$

Out of this menagerie of terms, the only ones which can be simply interpreted in terms of a gross property of the cavity are those for which $\lambda = qn$ and $\lambda = -qn$, that is, for $m = 0$, as we can see from (36c); for $\lambda = qn$:

$$C_{qn}^0 = \frac{1}{\pi}\int_0^{2\pi}\int_{r_c(\theta'')}^{r_0}\frac{A(s,\theta'')}{\sqrt{rs}}Q_{-1/2}(Z)ds\, e^{iqn\theta''}d\theta'' \quad (38)$$

This involves the slowest spatial decay and, from (37), we see that there is no dependence on the angular coordinate γ and, hence, this term is sourcelike.

We are still faced with a radial integration. As seen in Fig. 2, the quantity

$$\frac{1}{\pi\sqrt{rs}}Q_{-1/2}(Z) \cong \frac{1}{\sqrt{x^2+r^2+s^2}}$$

for the space outside of the torus defined by $Z = 3/2$. Then, outside of the spherical volume defined by $x^2 + r^2 = (2)^2$, the foregoing radical can be taken to be independent of s to first order. Thus, for such distances:

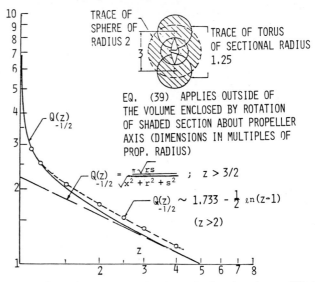

Fig. 2 Comparison of associated Legendre function of second kind with asymptotic approximation and definition of region in which cavitation appears to be due to a single source located at the center of the propeller

$$C_{qn}^0 = \int_0^{2\pi}\int_{r_c(\theta'')}^{r_0}\frac{A(s,\theta'')ds\, e^{-q\theta''}d\theta''}{\sqrt{x^2+r^2}} \quad (39)$$

and the radial integral is simply the cavity volume V_c; the θ''-integral is $\pi\cdot(V_c)_{qn}$, the qnth harmonic of the cavity volume on a single blade. Then, as C_{-qn}^0 is the complex conjugate of C_{qn}^0, (37) is seen to yield twice the real part of the first term or

$$(\phi_c)_{qn,qn} = \frac{-2nR_e}{4\pi}\frac{\partial}{\partial t}\{(V_c)_{qn}\, e^{iqn\theta}\}\frac{1}{\sqrt{x^2+r^2}} \quad (40)$$

and as

$$\frac{\partial}{\partial t} = \frac{\partial}{\partial t}\frac{\partial}{\partial\theta} = \frac{\omega\partial}{\partial\theta}$$

this contribution to the qnth harmonic of the cavity-generated potential is

$$(\phi_c)_{qn} = -\frac{n}{2\pi}R_e(iqn\,\omega(V_c)_{qn}e^{iqn\theta})\cdot\frac{1}{\sqrt{x^2+r^2}} \quad (41)$$

As the dominant linearized pressure is

$$(p_c)_{qn} = -\frac{\rho\partial}{\partial t}(\phi_c)_{qn}$$

we secure

$$(p_c)_{qn} = \frac{\rho n}{2\pi}R_e((qn)^2\omega^2(V_c)_{qn}e^{iqn\theta})\cdot\frac{1}{\sqrt{x^2+r^2}} \quad (42)$$

Now, as $(V_c)_{qn}$ is the complex Fourier coefficient, it is given by

$$(V_c)_{qn} = \frac{(a_{qn}-ib_{qn})}{2} \quad (43)$$

and

$$R_e(V_c)_{qn}e^{iqn\theta} = a_{qn}\cos qn\theta + b_{qn}\sin qn\theta$$

so that (42) reduces to a form, more familiar to engineers, given by

$$(p_c)_{qn}^0 = \frac{\rho n}{4\pi} \frac{(qn\omega)^2(a_{qn}\cos\theta qn + b_{qn}\sin qn\theta)}{\sqrt{x^2 + r^2}}$$

or

$$= \frac{\rho n}{4\pi} \frac{(qn\omega)^2\sqrt{a_{qn}^2 + b_{qn}^2}}{\sqrt{x^2 + r^2}} \cos(qn\theta - \epsilon) \qquad (44)$$

where

$$\epsilon = \tan^{-1}\left(\frac{b_{qn}}{a_{qn}}\right)$$

Thus, if the modulus of the qnth harmonic of the cavity volume does not decrease faster than $1/q^2$, the higher harmonics of the pressure can be larger than the first order ($q = 1$). This is then the answer (at long last) to the question posed earlier.

In contrast to the simplicity of (44), the terms provided by $\lambda = 0$ (hence $m = -qn$ and $+qn$) are again complex conjugates as seen from (37) and (33):

$$(\phi_c)_{qn,0} = -\frac{2n}{4\pi^2}\frac{\partial}{\partial t} R_e C_0^{-qn} e^{-iqn\gamma} e^{iqn\theta} \qquad (45)$$

where, from (33):

$$C_0^{-qn} = \frac{1}{2\pi} \int_0^{2\pi} \int_{r_c}^{r_0} \frac{A}{\sqrt{rs}} Q_{qn-1/2} e^{-iqn\beta(\theta'')} ds\, d\theta''$$

Upon use of the first term in the asymptotic expansion of the associated Legendre function

$$\frac{1}{\pi\sqrt{rs}} Q_{qn-1/2}(Z)$$

$$\rightarrow \frac{\Gamma^2(qn + \frac{1}{2})}{\sqrt{2\pi}(2qn)!} \frac{(2rs)^{qn}}{(x^2 + r^2)^{qn+1/2}} ; x^2 + r^2 \gg s^2$$

Then

$$C_0^{-qn} = \frac{2^{qn}\,\Gamma^2(qn + \frac{1}{2})r^{qn}}{2\sqrt{2}\,(2qn)!}$$

$$\times \int_0^{2\pi} \int^{r_0} \frac{A(s,\theta'')s^{qn}e^{-iqn\beta(\theta'')}ds\,d\theta''}{(x^2 + r^2)^{qn + 1/2}} \qquad (46)$$

This shows that the cavity area in the vicinity of the blade tip is heavily weighted (because of the factor s^{qn}) and all that can be done to simplify is to say that the modulus is less than (but of the order of) $\pi(V_c)_0$, $(V_c)_0$ being the zero harmonic or mean cavity volume. Thus

$$\left|(\phi_c)_{qn,0}\right| \simeq \frac{n}{2\sqrt{2\pi}} \frac{(qn\omega)\Gamma^2(qn + \frac{1}{2})}{(qn)!}$$

$$\times (V_c)_0 \left\{\frac{r^{qn}}{(x^2 + r^2)^{qn+1/2}}\right\} \qquad (47)$$

Now, although this contribution vanishes very rapidly with increasing $x^2 + r^2$, the coefficient is large. The ratio of the coefficients of this contribution to that from $(\phi_c)_{qn,qn}$ is [for $q = 1$ and $n = 5$ (blades)] $32.3(V_c)_0/(V_c)_s$. As the mean cavity volume is likely to be larger than the 5th harmonic of that volume, *we see that this term can dominate the near field, whereas the contribution involving the qnth harmonic of the cavity volume will dominate at distance.* Moreover, because of the absence of dependence on the angular coordinate γ, the $(V_c)_{qn}$ contribution to the hull force will be greater than that from $(V_c)_0$ which is attended by $e^{iqn\gamma}$ and, hence, upon integration, will be largely self-annulling.

It is interesting to note that completely analogous behavior for the contributions from mean blade loading and thickness in the absence of cavitation were observed in 1959 in reference [1].[6]

---

[6] Numbers in brackets designate References at end of paper.

This result could have been extracted immediately from (25) by taking $R = \sqrt{x^2 + r^2}$ without all the preceding detail. However, we would have had no measure of the region in which the space point must lie for the validity of the approximation, nor would we see the multiplicity of terms which can contribute in the near field. All other terms can be interpreted as weighted integrals of the cavity area and ordinates, the weighting function being multipoles of various orders. As in the case of the spherically expanding cavity volume, the magnitude of $|V_{qn}|$ and the other cavity dimensions involved depends upon the orchestrated interaction between the loading Δp (and the blade thickness) and the cavity sources which evolve from the simultaneous satisfaction of the kinematic condition on the wetted portions of the blades and the spatial constancy of pressure on the cavitating region in the presence of all other blades. The solution of this problem, involving as it does simultaneous integral equations, is addressed in the Section 3.

Finally, it is to be noted that this double Fourier expansion procedure could be applied to the last two "dipole" integrals in (26) to secure analogous structures involving weighted integrals of the partial cavity areas and the cavity ordinates. As this would not add further insight and would burden the reader with more unpalatable mathematics, we will omit additional elaboration and turn to the description of a procedure for generating a hull in the presence of a propeller and a free surface.

2. Representation of the hull in the presence of a propeller and water surface

It has been demonstrated in the foregoing that a propeller operating in a temporally uniform but spatially varying hull wake produces, through the concerted action of all the blades, a potential flow and pressure field composed of many components, all of which are at frequencies $qn\omega$. As these frequencies are large compared with those which can give rise to wave generation on the free water surface, the appropriate linearized boundary condition imposed by the presence of the water surface is that the total velocity potential in the undisturbed locus of that surface must be zero. A proof of this is presented, for sake of completeness, in Appendix 2.

Thus, if $\phi(x,y,h + z,t)$ is the potential of a propeller at depth h below the plane $z = 0$ in an infinite fluid with the origin of coordinates above the center of the propeller (x forward, y to port and z vertically upward), then the potential of the propeller in the presence of the water surface (WS) at $z = 0$ is

$$\phi_p(x,y,z,t) = \phi(x,y,h + z,t) - \phi(x,y,h - z,t) \qquad (48)$$

since, at $z = 0$ (the plane of the undisturbed water surface), we have $\phi_p(x,y,0,t) \equiv 0$ for all x,y,t. Thus, (48) is constructed to satisfy the high-frequency boundary condition. The second term (with sign) in (48) is referred to as the negative image of the propeller in the WS.

If we wished to insert a ship hull into this flow field, we (at Davidson Laboratory) first employed a surface distribution of sources plus their negative images over the wetted hull. The determination of the source strength-densities is effected by solving an integral equation generated from the requirement that the normal velocity imposed by the propeller and its negative image must be balanced or annulled at each and every hull element by the normal velocity induced by the concerted action of all the hull sources. This process was found to require excessive computer effort since three components of the propeller-induced velocity must be dot-produced with the normal vector. This effort is reduced by two-thirds by solving this exterior Neumann problem by exploiting the interior Dirichlet problem through the use of normal dipoles whose concerted potential evaluated on the interior side of the hull surface is required to annul the propeller potential (one function) at each and every element. A proof of this equivalent procedure is given in Appendix 3.

The potential of the hull, ϕ_h, as represented by a distribution of normal dipoles and their negative free surface images on the wetted hull surface, is expressed by

$$\phi_h(x,y,z,t) = -\frac{1}{4\pi} \int_{\xi=-a}^{f} \int_{\zeta=-k(\xi)}^{0}$$
$$\times \mu(\xi,\zeta)\, \vec{n} \cdot \vec{\nabla} \left(\frac{1}{R} - \frac{1}{R_i} \right) w's'd\zeta d\xi \quad (49)$$

where a is the aft extent of waterplane, f is forward extent, $k(\xi)$ the depth of the hull along the centerplane; μ the as-yet unknown normal dipole density, $\vec{n}$ is the normal vector to the hull,

$$\vec{\nabla} = \vec{i}\frac{\partial}{\partial \xi} + \vec{j}\frac{\partial}{\partial \eta} + \vec{k}\frac{\partial}{\partial \zeta},$$

the vector differential operator; w and s the waterline and sectional arc lengths, respectively, $w' = dw/d\xi$, $s' = ds/d\zeta$

$$\frac{1}{R} = \frac{1}{[(x-\xi)^2 + (y-\eta)^2 + (z-\zeta)^2]^{1/2}} = \frac{1}{R(x,y,z;\xi,\eta,\zeta)} \quad (50)$$

and

$$\frac{1}{R_i} = \frac{1}{[(x-\xi)^2 + (y+\eta)^2 + (z+\zeta)^2]^{1/2}}$$
$$= \frac{1}{R_i(x,y,z;\xi,\eta,\zeta)} \quad (51)$$

It is clear that $\phi_h(x,y,0,t) \equiv 0$ ($R_i = R$ on $z = 0$). On the inner side of the hull, satisfaction of the condition $\phi_h = -\phi_p$ requires that μ be such that

$$\frac{\mu(x,z)}{2} - \frac{1}{4\pi} \int_{-a}^{f} \int_{-k}^{0} \mu(\xi,\zeta)\, \vec{n} \cdot \vec{\nabla} \left(\frac{1}{R} - \frac{1}{R_i} \right) w's'd\zeta d\xi$$
$$= -\phi_{pfs}(x,z) = -(\phi(x,h+z) - \phi(x,h-z)) \quad (52)$$

where $-\infty < z \leq 0$ and y has been replaced by

$$y = \pm b(x,z); + \text{ for starboard}; - \text{ for port side} \quad (53)$$

the equation defining the hull half-breadths at each x,z.

This integral equation is not of the form available from the previous work of Hess and Smith [2], who developed an inversion procedure for the same kind of Fredholm equation, but having a kernel $\vec{n} \cdot \vec{\nabla}(R^{-1})$. However, it will now be shown that the problem posed by (52) can indeed be solved by converting to an equation having the Hess-Smith kernel.

The solution of (52) can be obtained in terms of dipole strengths ν required to solve the problem posed by the *double* hull in the presence of a *single* propeller as depicted schematically in the following sketch:

k=k(ξ)

The integral equation for this problem is

$$\frac{\nu}{2}(x,z) - \frac{1}{4\pi} \int_{-a}^{f} \int_{-k}^{k} \nu(\xi,\zeta)\, \vec{n} \cdot \vec{\nabla}$$
$$\times \left\{ \frac{1}{[(x-\xi)^2 + (y-\eta)^2 + (z-\zeta)^2]^{1/2}} \right\} s'w'd\zeta d\xi$$
$$= -\phi(x,y,h+z) \quad (54)$$

To achieve a right-hand side identical to that in (52), replace z by $-z$ throughout and subtract the result from (54) to secure

$$\frac{\nu(x,z) - \nu(x,-z)}{2} - \frac{1}{4\pi} \int_{-a}^{f} \int_{-k}^{k} \nu(\xi,\zeta)\, \vec{n} \cdot \vec{\nabla}$$
$$\times \left\{ \frac{1}{R} - \frac{1}{R_i} \right\} s'w'd\zeta d\xi = -[\phi(h+z) - \phi(h-z)] \quad (55)$$

where $1/R$ and $1/R_i$ are defined by (50) and (51)

Now write the ζ-integral in symbolic form

$$\int_{-k}^{k} F(\zeta)d\zeta = \int_{-k}^{0} F(\zeta)d\zeta + \int_{0}^{k} F(\zeta)d\zeta$$

and, in the last, replace ζ by $-\zeta$ and reverse the limits. Then

$$\int_{-k}^{k} F(\zeta)d\zeta = \int_{-k}^{0} (F(\zeta) + F(-\zeta))d\zeta$$

As both $\vec{n}(\xi,\eta,\zeta)$ and $\vec{\nabla}(\xi,\eta,\zeta)$ are odd functions of ζ, the dot product is even and, as $[R^{-1}(-\zeta) - R_i^{-1}(-\zeta)] = -[R^{-1}(\zeta) - R_i^{-1}(\zeta)]$, then (55) becomes

$$\frac{\nu(x,z) - \nu(x,-z)}{2}$$
$$- \frac{1}{4\pi} \int_{-a}^{f} \int_{-k}^{0} (\nu(\xi,\zeta) - \nu(\xi,-\zeta)) \left(\frac{1}{R} - \frac{1}{R_i} \right) w's'd\xi d\xi$$
$$= -[\phi(h+z) - \phi(h-z)] \quad (56)$$

Comparison of (56) and (52) shows that

$$\sigma(x,z) = \nu(x,z) - \nu(x,-z) \quad (57)$$

Thus, the dipole strength required for the solution of the wetted hull in the presence of the propeller and its high-frequency image in the free surface is obtained by solving the double hull in the presence of only the propeller and the results used as indicated by (57).

If a rigid surface condition is imposed on the locus of the WS (the zero-frequency condition as defined in Appendix 2), then the analogous result is

$$\sigma_{rs} = \nu(x,z) + \nu(x,-z) \quad (58)$$

Equation (57) implies that tests of noncavitating and cavitating propeller-hull configurations can be carried out using a double model well submerged in an open-to-atmosphere towing tank. Of course, for cavitation to ensue, sufficient speed must be provided to match the ship cavitation number. The speed required will be somewhat less than ship speed.

It is important to note that, as shown in Appendix 3, the dipole density ν gives, in our case, the sum of the double-hull potential ϕ_h and the propeller potential, that is

$$\nu(x,z,t) = -\{\phi_h(x,z,t) + \phi(x,z,t)\}$$
$$\text{[see equation (122), Appendix 3]} \quad (59)^{7}$$

and, for the hull in the joint presence of the free surface and the propeller (with its negative image), we have

$$\mu(x,z,t) = -\{\phi_h(x,z,t) - \phi_h(x,-z,t)\}$$
$$+ \{\phi_p(x,z,t) - \phi_p(x,-z,t)\} \quad (60)$$

---

[7] The factor $1/4\pi$ does not appear here because it is included in equation (49) and suppressed in the definition (112).

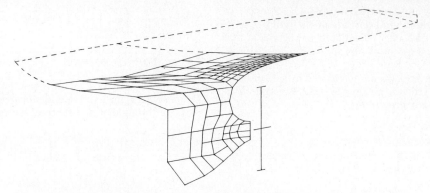

Fig. 3 Panel isometric representation of SSPA 2148-A hull in vicinity of propeller; only port side shown (dotted lines indicate extent of hull to load waterline and to transom)

To secure the numerical inversion of (54), the hull is divided into quadrilateral elements as shown in Fig. 3 and the coordinates of their corners are supplied to the modified Hess-Smith program. The *right-hand* side is the single propeller potential evaluated at the hull panels. This potential includes the contributions from intermittent cavitation, blade loading variations and blade thickness. The methods applied at MIT to secure this required input propeller potential are elaborated in the following section.

Selection of panel size is dictated by the behavior of the propeller potential in the longitudinal and athwartship directions with respect to the propeller. Forward of the propeller, all the various terms attenuate monotonically with longitudinal distance x. The strongest loading and cavity harmonics yield spatial signatures which decay very "rapidly" as $x^{-(2qn+1)}$ and x^{-2qn}, respectively, whereas the component generated by blade-rate loading on the blade falls off as x^{-2} and that from the blade frequency harmonic of the cavity volume decays as x^{-1}. Thus, beyond one diameter the panel lengths can be increased substantially.

Downstream of the propeller, however, the potentials have similarly attenuating components *plus* nondecaying constituents arising from the helically distributed vortex wake. The nonvanishing parts vary with axial distance as $\exp(\pm iqn\,\omega x/U)$. When, for example, $q = 1$ and $n = 4$, these spatial oscillations pass through a complete cycle for an x variation given by

$$\Delta x = \frac{\pi U}{2\omega} = \frac{J}{2}$$

where J is the advance ratio and x is in fraction of propeller radius. As J is the order of 0.6, then $\Delta x = 0.3$ and to have four panels in each of these intervals yields a panel length of $0.075r_0$.

It is envisoned that the net effect of these "rapid" x-wise undulations will produce small contributions to forces from residuals arising from the changes in hull sections with x.

The athwartship variations of the propeller potentials are, in general, decaying, but with oscillations varying as $\exp(\lambda - qn)\gamma$ and $\exp[-(\lambda + qn)\gamma]$ where the space angle γ is given by $-\tan^{-1}(y/z)$, y being athwartship distance and z the vertical distance of any hull point from the propeller axis. The value $y = y_1$ at which $\cos(\lambda + qn)\gamma$ first changes sign for $\lambda = 4$, $q = 1$ and $n = 4$ is $|\tilde{y}_1| = 0.20z_1$. As z_1 is of the order of $3/2\,r_0$, the buttock at which $\cos8\gamma$ changes sign is $y_1 = 0.3r_0$. To secure a minimum panel distribution over the domain wherein this onset potential changes sign, one may choose two panels of width $0.15r_0$. As we move out a frame line, the amplitude of the potential decreases and the panel width can be increased. For the strong local contribution arising from mean propeller loading given by specifying $\lambda = 0$ and, say, $qn = 4$ (for blade

rate contribution of a four-bladed propeller), we note that the complete cycle of

$$\genfrac{}{}{0pt}{}{\sin}{\cos}\left\{4\tan^{-1}\frac{y}{z}\right\}$$

is achieved only for $y \rightarrow \pm\infty$. It is also to be noted that, for the contributions arising from the blade rate harmonics of the cavity and the blade rate harmonics of the blade loading given by $\lambda = \pm qn$, there are no variations with space angle γ so that the panels are beset with monotonically descending onsets which would permit the use of relatively large panels.

As in all finite-element methods, a compromise has to be struck between the estimated requirements for accuracy and the computing capacity and expense. Here we have used 512 panels over the double hull with a distribution of panel size which is thought to be adequate.

3. Numerical solution of intermittently cavitating propeller problem

There are several computer-effected solutions for noncavitating propellers based on unsteady lifting-surface theory which are of such demonstrated accuracy as to be used for practical design purposes. Such is not the case for the ICP. In the past, Johnsson and Søntvedt [3] and Noordzij [4] have employed the steady, partially cavitating two-dimensional section theory of Guerst [5] in a parametric sense with the variations of local angle of attack being looked after via lifting-line theory. More recently, Kaplan et al [6] improved upon Noordzij by employing the equivalent unsteady angle of incidence as provided by the Davidson Laboratory unsteady propeller program developed by Tsakonas et al [7]. Comparison with measured cavity outlines and hull pressures predicted by the methods of references [3] and [4] have been fairly good, but they have not been adopted as reliable predictors.

Evaluation of the method of reference [6], when compared with several measured model and ship hull pressures as carried out by Lloyds Register of Shipping [6], have shown remarkable agreement. To obtain hull forces, Vorus et al [8] have applied the reciprocity procedure, which relies entirely on an arbitrary estimate of cavity thickness. Lately, Stern and Vorus [9] are advancing a nonlinear theory in which the cavity cross section is constrained to be a semi-ellipse. However, none of the cited formulations have addressed the complete, three-dimensional, unsteady mixed-boundary condition problem posed by an IC blade in the presence of all other blades.

Numerical solutions of various cavity flows at MIT using discrete singularity elements have been effected by Golden [10], Jiang [11] and van Houten [12]. In the last reference, numerical solutions of the unsteady, partially cavitating high-aspect-ratio hydrofoil are given which show significant time-varying, cross-sectional cavity areas. This is in apparent contradiction to the analytical finding of Peters et al [13], which demonstrates that the second derivative of cavity area varies inversely as the square of aspect ratio. However, this contradiction does not bear upon the current three-dimensional procedure developed at MIT by Kerwin and Lee and which is outlined next. Although this work was detailed by Lee [14] at the 13th Symposium on Naval Hydrodynamics in Tokyo in October 1980, the paper is not generally available and, hence, we find it necessary to provide herein the basis of the procedure in sufficient detail to yield a coherent account.

Formulation of the problem

Fundamental assumptions—The propeller blades are considered to be a set of symmetrically arranged thin blades of arbitrary form, rotating with a constant angular velocity about a common axis in an unbounded, incompressible fluid. The presence of extraneous boundaries such as the propeller hub, the rudder, and the ship hull is neglected, except that the last is recognized as a body generating the nonuniform flow field.

The blades are assumed to operate at a small angle of attack, and the spatial variation of the ship wake is assumed small accordingly. The blade boundary layer and shed vortex wake thickness are assumed to be thin so that the fluid rotation due to the propeller is confined in a thin layer.

It is assumed that the formation and decay of the cavity occurs instantaneously, depending only upon whether the pressure as determined from potential flow drops below or exceeds the vapor pressure, which is assumed to be constant. The thickness of the cavity is also assumed to be small so that linearization in thickness is possible. It is assumed that the cavity starts at the leading edge of the blade, and that only the suction side of the blade is cavitating.

The cavitation number, σ_n, is defined, based on the propeller rotational speed, as

$$\sigma_n = (p_\infty - p_v)/\tfrac{1}{2}\rho n^2 D^2 \qquad (61)$$

where p_∞ is the pressure at shaft center, p_v the vapor pressure, ρ the density of the water, n the number of revolutions per second, and D the diameter of the propeller. The Froude number, F_r, is also defined based on the propeller rotational speed as

$$F_r = n^2 D/g \qquad (62)$$

where g is the gravitational acceleration. The inverse of the Froude number serves as a direct measurement of the hydrostatic pressure (or local cavitation number) variation from the shaft center to the top of the propeller plane. The cavitating flow field will be uniquely characterized by the preceding two nondimensional parameters.

The propeller is considered to be operating in a known effective inflow field representing the wake field of the ship. The components of the wake field are customarily specified only in the plane of the propeller, and it is assumed that their variation over the axial extent of the propeller can be ignored.

Boundary-value problem—Let us consider a propeller operating in an unbounded, incompressible fluid. The propeller may be in either a noncavitating or cavitating condition. The principle of conservation of mass in the governing equation in the fluid region encompassing the blades, the shed wake, and the cavity is

$$\nabla \cdot \mathbf{V} = 0, \text{ throughout the fluid} \qquad (63)$$

where $\mathbf{V}$ is the total fluid velocity. The problem is uniquely

defined by imposing the boundary conditions as follows:

1. Quiescence condition at infinity: At infinity upstream, the perturbation velocity due to the presence of the propeller and cavity should vanish.

2. Tangency condition on the wetted surface: The kinematic boundary condition on the wetted portion of the blade surface is the impermeability to the fluid, and is best described in a blade-fixed coordinate system rotating with the propeller

$$\mathbf{n} \cdot \mathbf{V} = 0, \text{ on the wetted surface} \qquad (64)$$

where $\mathbf{n}$ is the vector normal to the camber surface, defined positive when pointing upstream.

3. Kutta condition at the trailing edge: The flow should leave the trailing edge in a tangential direction.

4. Kelvin's theorem for the conservation of circulation.

5. Kinematic and dynamic conditions in the wake: The velocity jump must be purely tangential to shed vortex wake sheet, and the pressure must be continuous across this vortex wake sheet.

The preceding five boundary conditions are sufficient to define the fully wetted, subcavitating unsteady propeller problem. For the cavitating propeller, additional conditions are necessary due to the presence of the cavity. The interface of the cavity and the surrounding fluid is termed the cavity surface, $F(\mathbf{x},t) = 0$.

6. Kinematic condition on the cavity surface: Since the interface is moving with the fluid particles, the substantial derivative of the quantity $F(\mathbf{x},t)$ must vanish:

$$DF/Dt = 0, \text{ on the cavity surface} \qquad (65)$$

7. Cavity closure condition: It is assumed that the cavity thickness is zero along the edges of the cavity surface, that is

$$h(\mathbf{x},t) = 0, \text{ along the cavity perimeter} \qquad (66)$$

8. Dynamic condition on the cavity surface: The pressure on the cavity surface is considered to be the same as the prescribed vapor pressure inside the cavity, p_v, that is

$$p = p_v, \text{ on the cavity surface} \qquad (67)$$

Under the smallness assumptions made in the earlier section, the propeller blades, cavity, and loading can be represented by the distribution of sources and vortices lying on the mean camber surface of each blade and shed wake. This representation is shown in Fig. 4.

Source distributions are employed to provide jumps of the normal velocity at the camber surface. There are two distinct sets of source sheets; the first is to represent the thickness of the blades, and the second is to represent the cavity thickness. We will assume at the outset, however, that the source distribution for the blade thickness is independent of time, and that its spatial distribution may be derived from a stripwise application of thin-wing theory at each radius. The source strength for the cavity thickness will be determined by solving the boundary-value problem. It should also be noted that the extent of the cavity is not known in advance and *must* be determined as a part of the solution.

Vortex distributions are employed to represent the jumps of the tangential velocity both at the camber surface and in the trailing wake sheet. The vortex strength is a vector lying in the surface and may be resolved into components along two arbitrarily assigned directions on the surface. The vortex distribution on the blade will be resolved into "spanwise" and "chordwise" components while the corresponding components in the wake will be termed "shed" vorticity and "trailing" vorticity. The vortex strength will also be determined as a part of the solution to the boundary-value problem.

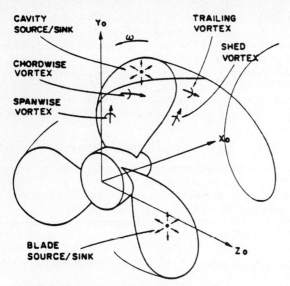

Fig. 4 Pictorial of propeller to illustrate basic singularities

When the method of singularity distribution is employed, the principle of conservation of mass is satisfied in the fluid region away from the singular sheet. The quiescence condition at upstream infinity is also satisfied by the nature of the singularity, since the induced velocity is, at most, inversely proportional to the distance from the singular point. The application of the remaining boundary conditions will lead to coupled integral equations. An approach to the solution of the integral equation is to discretize the continuous distribution of singularities into discrete singularities of unknown strengths, and to form a set of simultaneous equations for the determination of these strengths by satisfying the boundary conditions on selected collocation points or control points.

Mathematical modeling of propeller-cavity system

Blade geometry—The singularities representing the flow disturbance due to propeller loading, thickness and cavitation are distributed on the exact camber surface of the blades. This surface is uniquely defined by the radial distribution of pitch, rake, skew, chord length and maximum camber, and by the chordwise form of the camber function at each radius. For convenience, the latter may be left unspecified, in which case an NACA $a = 0.8$ camber function is presumed to apply at each radius. Formulas for constructing the blade surface geometry from these quantities may be found in [15].

Geometry of the trailing wake—The trailing and shed vortices illustrated in Fig. 4 are placed on surfaces which approximate the slipstream contraction and vortex roll-up observed in practice. A transition wake region is defined as the region from the trailing edge to a "roll-up" point a specified angular distance along the tip vortex. This angular distance is generally taken to be 90 deg. The radial coordinate of the roll-up point is also specified, permitting the introduction of slipstream contraction.

Downstream of the roll-up point, the trailing vortex wake consists of a concentrated helical tip vortex from each blade, and a concentrated hub vortex along the rotational axis. The strength of the ultimate wake is derived from the time-average propeller loading.

Shed vorticity due to unsteady blade loading is convected down the transition wake region only up to the roll-up point, at which point it is ignored. To prevent an abrupt change in the wake representation at the roll-up point, the strength of the shed vorticity is artificially decayed, so that its value goes smoothly to zero.

Details of this wake model, and of its sensitivity with respect to computed propeller performance, may be found in [15].

Discretization of singularity distribution—The continuous distribution of vortices and sources is replaced by a lattice of concentrated straight line-elements of constant strength for the purpose of digital computation.

The discretization scheme in the chordwise direction should, in principle, be determined so as to satisfy the Kutta condition. For the steady two-dimensional noncavitating flow, James [16] showed that the Kutta condition can be satisfied implicitly by suitable arrangements of vortices and control points. For the two-dimensional cavitating hydrofoil, Van Houten [12] used a unique spacing, which gives good agreement with Guerst's [5] steady solution. A similar arrangement is used for the chordwise discretization of the propeller blade, together with uniform spacing in the radial direction.

The *radial* interval from the hub, r_H, to the tip, R, is divided into M equal intervals with the end points of the discrete spanwise vortices located at radii

$$\rho_m = r_H + \frac{(R-r_H)(4m-3)}{4M+2} \qquad m = 1, 2 \ldots M+1 \quad (68)$$

The chord from the leading to the trailing edge at radius ρ_m is divided into N intervals, with the boundaries of each element defined as

$$\tilde{s}_n = 1 - \cos(n\pi/2N), \quad n = 0, 1.2, \ldots N \quad (69)$$

where $\tilde{s}_0$ denotes the leading edge.

Equations (68) and (69) are sufficient to define the vertices of $M \times N$ four-sided elements on the camber surface. The spanwise vortices are placed on the quarter chord of each element with their ends at points

$$s_n^\Gamma = \tilde{s}_{n-1} + \delta\tilde{s}_n/4, \quad n = 1, 2, \ldots N \quad (70)$$

where

$$\delta\tilde{s}_n = \tilde{s}_n - \tilde{s}_{n-1} \quad (71)$$

The line sources are placed on the midchord of the chord segments defined by s_n^Γ. Thus, the nondimensional chordwise coordinates of the line sources are

$$s_n^Q = (s_n^\Gamma + s_{n+1}^\Gamma)/2, \quad n = 1, 2, \ldots, N-1 \quad (72)$$
$$s_N^Q = (s_N^\Gamma + 1.0)/2$$

The control points for the tangency boundary condition are placed on the midspan of the line segment connecting the two points (s_i^Q, ρ_m) and (s_i^Q, ρ_{m+1}). The normal vector is calculated as a cross-product of the vectors tangent to the spanwise and chordwise curves passing through the tangency boundary control points. It should be noted that the control points for the tangency boundary condition lie in the center of the quadrilateral elements formed by the vortex lattice.

The control points for the dynamic boundary condition on the cavity surface are placed on the midspan of the spanwise vortex lines defined by equation (70). Jiang [11] found that the positions of the line sources and control points for the dynamic boundary condition nearest the leading edge should be interchanged to simulate the proper singular behavior of the source strength at the leading edge; that is, there must not be a dynamic boundary condition control point ahead of the leading line source. The vortex arrangement and control points for the tangency boundary condition are illustrated in Fig. 5.

In order to facilitate compution of the convection of the discretized shed vorticity in unsteady flow the transition wake angular spacing, $\delta\theta$, and the time increment, δt, are related by

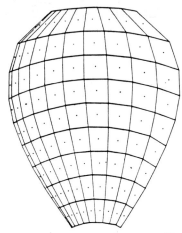

Fig. 5 Illustration of discrete vortex elements and tangency control points on key blade

Fig. 6 Illustration of discrete singularity elements on key blade and other blades

$$\delta\theta = \omega\delta t \tag{73}$$

In this way, if the influence of the tangential induced velocity on convection speed is ignored, the strength of the nth shed vortex at the current time step will be equal to the $(n-1)$st shed vortex at the preceding time step.

In order to extend equation (70) beyond the trailing edge, equation (71) is modified as

$$\delta\tilde{s}_n = \rho\delta\theta \text{ for } n > N \tag{74}$$

where the angular increment, $\delta\theta$, is defined in equation (73). The application of equations (70) and (71), extended to allow $n > N$, and equation (72) will determine the position of the singularities and control points in the wake. For a given blade geometry, the discretized system is uniquely determined by the two parameters M and N. In the present work, $\delta\theta$ is set to 6 deg for all computations.

Representation of other blades and wake—While the discrete singularity arrangement used to represent the key blade and its wake can be reproduced exactly on each of the other blades, such an approach would obviously be inefficient. Due to the relatively large distance between the control points on the key blade and the singularities on the other blades, a coarse spacing may be used on the latter with no significant change in results. In addition, induced velocities need not be computed at all control points, but only at a sufficient number to enable the value at the remaining control points to be obtained by interpolation.

As described in the following, the strengths of the singularities on the other blades are known in terms of the corresponding values on the key blades at a previous time step.

Figure 6 shows a projected view of all five blades of a propeller illustrating this reduction in the number of elements on the other blades.

Methods of solution

Calculation of induced velocities—Once the propeller-cavity-wake systems are discretized, the induced velocities at any point in space by these line source or vortex elements can be very easily computed; see, for example, Kerwin and Lee [15].

From the law of Biot-Savart, the induced velocity at any point x due to a vortex element of strength Γ situated on the curve C may be expressed as

$$\mathbf{v}^\Gamma(\mathbf{x}) = \frac{\Gamma}{4\pi} \int_{C(\xi)} \frac{d\xi \times \mathbf{D}}{|\mathbf{D}|^3} \tag{75}$$

where $\mathbf{D}$ is a vector extending from each point ξ on the vortex curve C to the field point $\mathbf{x}$.

For sources, the induced velocity at any point $\mathbf{x}$ due to a source element of strength Q may be expressed in a similar manner:

$$\mathbf{v}^Q(\mathbf{x}) = -\frac{Q}{4\pi} \int_{c(\xi)} \nabla\left(\frac{1}{D}\right) d\xi \tag{76}$$

Applying equations (75) and (76), the induced velocities at the control point $\mathbf{x}_{ij}$ due to a set of discrete vortices or sources may now be expressed as

$$\mathbf{v}_{ij} = \sum_{n,m} \mathbf{K}_{ijnm} \Gamma_{nm} \tag{77}$$

$$\mathbf{v}_{ij}^Q = \sum_{n,m} \mathbf{H}_{ijnm} Q_{nm}$$

where

$$\mathbf{K}_{ijnm} = \frac{1}{4\pi} \int_{C(\xi_{nm})} \frac{d\xi \times D}{|\mathbf{D}|^3}$$

$$\mathbf{H}_{ijnm} = \frac{-1}{4\pi} \int_{C(\xi_{nm})} \nabla\left(\frac{1}{D}\right) d\xi$$

$$\mathbf{D} = \mathbf{x}_{ij} - \xi_{nm}$$

The equations for boundary conditions, stated earlier, can be formulated in terms of strengths of vortices and sources by applying equation (77) to the control points for kinematic and dynamic boundary conditions. The derivation of these equations is, in principle, straightforward and is given in detail in Appendices 4 through 7. Then, in Appendix 8 we obtain a set of simultaneous equations arising from the boundary conditions. These equations, which would otherwise be coupled integral equations with continuous distributions of sources and vortices, are simple in structure and can be solved in various ways.

Stepwise solution in time domain—The discretized boundary-value problem is established in Appendix 8, where the unknown variables are the strengths of the vortices and sources on the key blade and a pressure inside the cavity.

The stepwise solution method is employed for the solution of the boundary-value problem in the time domain, in which the results from the key blade are used to update the strengths of singularities on the remaining blades, while trailing and shed vortices are being convected downstream to account for propeller advance.

The solution process for the cavitating propeller is significantly more expensive than for the fully wetted propeller. Therefore, the initial start-up procedure is carried out for the fully wetted propeller only. Then the solution for the cavitating propeller is started from the solution to the associated unsteady wetted flow problem, by introducing the cavity source terms. Since the cavity closure condition equation contains the cavity shape of the previous time step on the right-hand side, a bad approximation for it may slow the convergence. It is recommended, therefore, to "turn on" the process for the cavity solution just before the key blade enters the high-wake region, at which the blade will start cavitating. The process may be considered to have converged when two successive propeller revolutions produce results which are identical to within the desired accuracy.

Iterations for cavity extent—To determine the cavity extent and source distribution, two spatial iteration processes are employed in addition to the updating procedure illustrated in the preceding section.

Unknown cavity length and source distribution will always be confined to one chordwise (or streamwise) strip by assuming that the cavity extent and source and vortex distributions on the other streamwise strips be known either by an initial approximation or by the most recent solutions on those strips. The iteration starting from the hub strip (or from the tip strip) to the tip strip (or to the hub strip) and then back to the other end of the propeller blade is found to be very efficient, showing a very fast and stable convergence character. For most cases tested, two or three radial (outward or inward) iterations were sufficient to get the converged values.

To determine the cavity length and source strength for a particular strip, we begin by guessing the cavity length (again from the adjacent strip or from the previous iteration) corresponding to the discretized element boundaries. Pressure (or the cavitation number) corresponding to the assumed cavity length will be determined in (157) of Appendix 8. If the computed cavity pressure is lower than the vapor pressure, a longer cavity length will be tried until the computed pressure becomes higher than vapor pressure. If the initial computed pressure is higher than vapor pressure, a shorter cavity length is used until the computed pressure becomes too low.

A linear interpolation formula can be used to determine the cavity length corresponding to the vapor pressure using the results of the two final trials. The strength of the cavity sources, as well as that of the vortices on that strip, can also be interpolated in a similar manner as is done to get the cavity length, since the dynamic boundary condition [equation (153)] on the cavity surface is linear. It is assumed that linear interpolation is appropriate for the present computer program.

Although we can solve the simultaneous equations (157) directly, an alternative approach can be deduced by closely examining the elements of the coefficient matrix, a_{pq}. As is the case in the fully wetted problem, the coefficients of the vortex strength in the tangency condition equation (155) are invariant in time for given chordwise panel and, hence, this portion can be inverted once in the beginning and used to solve the simultaneous equations (157). This procedure, called the partitioning method in algebra, is found to be particularly useful for the solution of simultaneous equations with a large invertible submatrix.

Determination of blade forces—The force and moment acting on the propeller blade can be obtained by integrating the pressure jump over the blade camber surface

$$\mathbf{F} = \int \Delta p \, \mathbf{n} \, dA$$
$$\mathbf{M} = \int \Delta p \, (\mathbf{r} \times \mathbf{n}) \, dA \quad (78)$$

where Δp is the pressure jump across the camber surface, $\mathbf{n}$ the normal vector on the camber surface defined positive when pointing upstream, and $\mathbf{r}$ the position vector from the origin to the point of integration.

Determination of the propeller potential at any field point

The velocity potential generated by the blade pressure loading elements is calculated from the potential of a point dipole whose normal is perpendicular to the plane formed by the diagonals of the quadrilateral element. The strength of the dipole is equal to the product of the circulation Γ (attached to the element) multiplied by the area of the element. The total velocity potential due to loading induced at any fixed point in space is secured by summing over all the elements. For elements on the blade, it is found that the use of a point dipole is accurate at distances of four or more element lengths. To secure the contribution from the portion of the helical vortex wake shed by each blade beyond the point where it is taken to be composed of rolled-up tip and hub vortices, the dipole substitution scheme had to be altered. The potential of such an array is given by a uniform distribution of dipoles whose strength density is equal to the circulation around the tip or hub vortex, and whose normals lie along the normal to the helicoidal surface joining the rolled-up tip vortex and the hub vortex. Dividing this surface into four equal radial segments was found to give requisite accuracy.

The velocity potentials generated by the blade thickness and cavity ordinate distribution are obtained by replacing each line source element by a point source whose strength is the line source strength multiplied by the length of the element. The total effect at any field point is the sum of all such point source potentials.

These sums are obtained for a single blade (in the presence of all other blades) for 60 time steps per revolution and are then harmonically analyzed to yield the harmonic components at once, twice and thrice blade frequency. The calculations are made for each hull panel as required by the Davidson Laboratory propeller-hull program. This completes the description of the theory and procedures employed for evaluation and we now turn to the experimental results obtained at SSPA.

4. Description of SSPA facility, experimental program and test results

SSPA large cavitation tunnel (Tunnel No. 2)

SSPA cavitation tunnel No. 2 has been in operation since 1970. It is fitted with two test sections: one circular high-speed test section and one rectangular low-speed test section, the latter being used mainly for tests with combinations of propellers and ship models.

The main data of the test sections are given in Table 1 and a sketch showing the tunnel with the low-speed test section in place is given in Fig. 7. In Table 1 data are also given for the low-speed section when fitted with an insert used for testing high-speed propellers in behind condition (insert marked in Fig. 7).

The tunnel is powered by a 1000-hp (746 kW) dc electric motor, the speed control being carried out by a thyristor unit. The blades of the pump are adjustable at standstill and it has been found important to have different pitch settings for the two test sections in order to ensure a good flow distribution.

The low-speed test section is covered by a recess in which the ship model is placed. The model is the one used for self-propulsion tests in the towing tank and is made of paraffin wax, wood or fiberglass. The vertical portion of the model is adjusted in such a way that the waterline, corresponding to the level of the free water surface in the towing tank, is flush with the top of the test section. Individually cut wooden plates are fitted to simulate the free water surface and the test section and the recess are completely filled with water.

For driving the model propellers, a dc electric motor was originally placed in a watertight cylinder inside the model. Recently ac motors were introduced for this purpose, having the advantages of being cheap, light and of small diameter.

A strain-gage dynamometer for measuring thrust and torque is placed in the shaft, close to the propeller.

The total weight of the upper part to be shifted is about 30 tons [27 tonnes (t)]. By using two traversing cranes with a lifting capacity of 20 tons (18 t) each and by using hydraulic jackets to separate the connecting flanges, the shift is accomplished very smoothly in a total time of about five hours.

The insert in the low-speed section, indicated in Fig. 7 and Table 1, is a recent addition to the tunnel. When the tunnel was built the size of the main circuit was limited, for economical reasons. The low-speed test section, however, has to be of a certain size to ensure that no serious blockage effects occur. As a compromise between these two conflicting test conditions, a somewhat unfavorable area ratio between the test section and the downstream corner was chosen, causing cavitation in that corner to be the limiting factor for the minimum cavitation number, rather than the water speed in the test section.

As an operating range covering ship speeds of up to about 30 knots was obtained, such a compromise could be accepted. Lately it has also become evident that for high-speed ships there is a demand for investigations into propellers in the behind condition. Accordingly an insert was manufactured extending the range of operation to cavitation numbers corresponding to ship speeds of about 45 knots; see Fig. 7.

The design principles of the tunnel are outlined in [17] where reference is given to earlier research work done in the low-speed test section. Some results obtained with high-speed propellers in behind condition, using the insert, are given in [18].

Measurements of pressure fluctuations and measuring techniques—For measuring of the pressure fluctuations in the stern, induced by the propeller, transducers were placed in four different positions in the present case (see Fig. 8).

As high-frequency excitation was regarded important in the present case, hydrophones (Bruel and Kjaer Type 8103) were used for two of the measuring points (Points 1 and 3). These hydrophones have a flat response curve (within ±2 db) within the frequency range 0 to 140 kHz. The diameter is 9.5 mm (0.38 in.).

For the two other points, strain-gage transducers [Statham PM 397 ± 15 (103 kPa), membrane diameter 6.35 mm (0.254 in.)] were used, together with amplifiers having an upper limitation of about 5 kHz.

The signals from the transducers were recorded on a Honeywell 5600 C type recorder (maximum 14 channels). Signals from the Bruel and Kjaer transducers were recorded on FM wide-band channels 0 to 40 kHz at a tape speed of 60 in./sec (1.5 m/sec) and signals from the Statham transducers recorded on ordinary FM channels (0 to 20 kHz). To obtain as stable as possible signals in the low-frequency range for Transducers 1 and 3, recordings were also made from these transducers using a filter, eliminating frequencies below 0.5 × blade frequency and above 5.5 × blade frequency.

When running the tests the propellers were painted with paint having small roughness in order to stabilize the cavitation patterns on the blades.

Analysis of signals—The normal way of analyzing the registrations by the transducers in the cavitation tunnel is described in [17, 22]. Briefly, it can be summarized as follows:

Table 1 Main data for test sections of cavitation tunnel No. 2

	High Speed	Low-Speed Section Original	Low-Speed Section With Insert
Length, m	2.5	9.6	9.6
Area $B \times H$, m²	diam = 1 m	2.6 × 1.5	2.6 × 1.15
Maximum speed m/sec	23	6.9	8.8
Minimum cavitation number	0.06[a]	1.45[b]	0.50[b]

[a] Empty tunnel; in propeller tests cavitation on right-angle gear dynamometer sets $\sigma = 0.15$ as the lower limit.
[b] At propeller shaft in a position 0.2 m below roof.

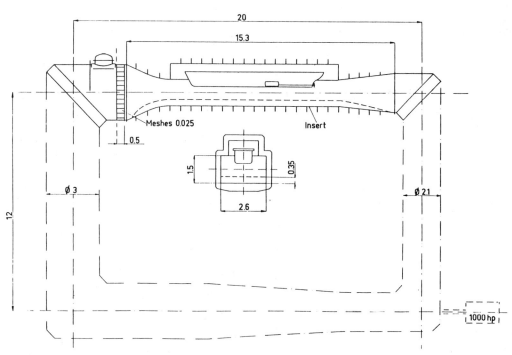

Fig. 7   The SSPA large cavitation tunnel with low-speed test section in place (dimensions in meters)

Theoretical and Experimental Propeller-Induced Hull Pressures

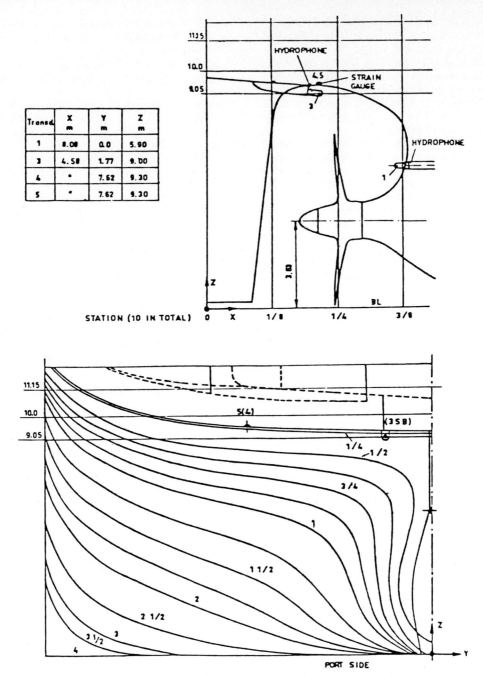

Transd.	X m	Y m	Z m
1	8.08	0.0	5.90
3	4.58	1.77	9.00
4	"	7.62	9.30
5	"	7.62	9.30

Fig. 8   RO/RO ship model: stern shape and transducer positions

The signals are recorded on magnetic tape. For final analysis, the analog tape is converted to digital form and the amplitudes and phase angles of the different harmonics are calculated for each blade separately.   The amplitudes for each harmonic are stored in accordance with their magnitude and the following information is printed for each harmonic (for each separate blade and mean values for all blades):

Maximum, minimum and mean value
Mean value of 0 to 5 percent largest amplitudes
Mean value of 5 to 15 percent largest amplitudes
Mean value of 15 to 35 per cent largest amplitudes
Mean value of 35 to 55 per cent largest amplitudes
Mean value of 55 to 85 per cent largest amplitudes
Standard deviation
Corresponding phase angles

In Fig. 9, analysis results from the cavitation tunnel and the corresponding full-scale results, obtained for the first four harmonics, are compared for a particular project [22].

It is evident from Fig. 9, and from the complete signals shown in reference [22], that the signals obtained at full scale are more stable than those registered in the model case.   It is also evident that the higher harmonics are systematically smaller on the model scale than at full scale, the main reason for this difference being strong phase modulations in the model case; see [22]. This modulation is most likely caused by laminar separation on the blades of the model propeller and temporal variations in the wake behind the ship model.

In most cases, the main purpose of the measurements is to predict the relevant excitation at full scale as accurately as possible.   If the mean values of the amplitudes of the different

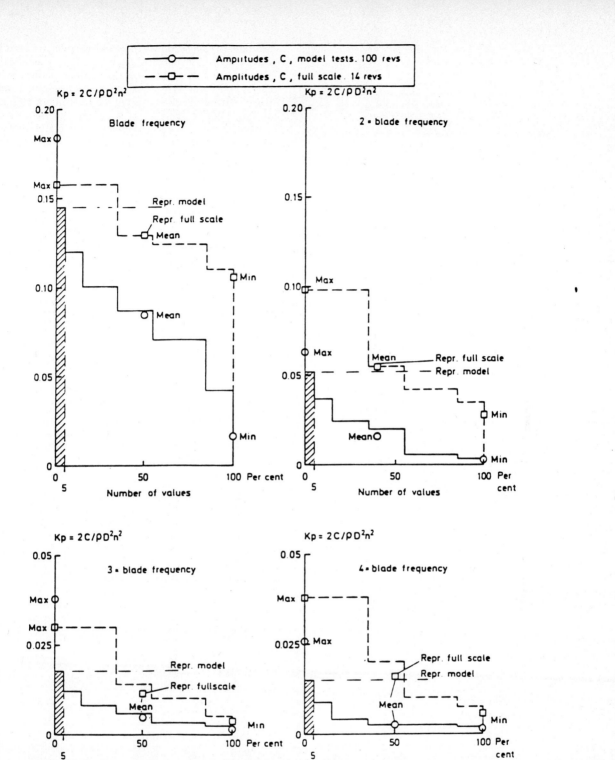

Fig. 9 SSPA analysis of measurements of pressure fluctuations; comparison of model and full-scale normalized amplitudes

harmonics over a large number of revolutions are regarded as representative of the excitation level in the full-scale case, it is evident from Fig. 9 that the corresponding mean values from the model tests will give values which are too low. It has been decided, therefore, to base the predictions on the mean value of the 5 percent largest amplitudes as they give reasonably good agreement with full scale for all harmonics compared. This applies to the case shown in Fig. 9 as well as to other similar comparisons between tests in the large tunnel at SSPA and corresponding full-scale results.

Presentation of results—An example of the measurements of pressure fluctuations of blade frequency and twice the blade frequency is given in Fig. 10, the diagram showing the amplitudes coefficient

$$K_p = \frac{2\sqrt{2}\,P_{\text{rms}}}{\rho D^2 n^2} \qquad (79)$$

on the basis of the cavitation number

$$\sigma_{0.7R} = P_0 - P_v / \frac{\rho}{2}\,V_{0.7}^2 \qquad (80)$$

Theoretical and Experimental Propeller-Induced Hull Pressures

127

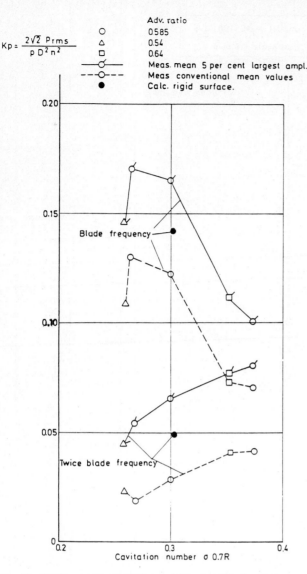

$$K_p = \frac{2\sqrt{2}\ P_{rms}}{\rho\,D^2\,n^2}$$

	Adv. ratio
○	0.585
△	0.54
□	0.64

—○— Meas. mean 5 per cent largest ampl.
--○-- Meas. conventional mean values
● Calc. rigid surface.

0.20

0.15

Blade frequency

0.10

0.05

Twice blade frequency

0
0.2   0.3   0.4
Cavitation number σ 0.7R

Fig. 10 SSPA propeller P-1841: normalized amplitudes of pressure fluctuations—Transducer 3 (centerline, above propeller)

where

P_{rms} = root-mean-square values of pressure fluctuations
D = propeller diameter
n = propeller speed
ρ = density of water
P_0 = static pressure at propeller shaft center
P_v = vapor pressure

$$V_{0.7R} = V_A \sqrt{1 + \left\{\frac{0.7\pi}{J}\right\}^2}$$

= inflow velocity, blade section 0.7R

Results obtained at different advance ratios J are shown in Fig. 10.

Propeller model—The propeller model is one of a systematic series of five model propellers used for studying the influence of different design parameters on efficiency, cavitation erosion and vibration excitation properties, the results of which will be published in reference [19]. The propeller selected for this investigation is characterized by moderate skewback and a slight unloading of the blade tip region. The general charac-

teristics are conveyed by the drawings shown in Figs. 11(*a*) and 11(*b*) and the distribution of pitch, chords, camber and thickness are given in Table 2. Design calculations made at SSPA were carried out using lifting-surface theory using the loading and wake distribution of an existing roll-on/roll-off (RO/RO) ship as shown in Fig. 12.

Ship model—A glass fiber model of a RO/RO ship was employed having a scale ratio of 1:27.2. The principal dimensions of the ship are:

Length	210.0 m (689 ft)
Breadth	31.16 m (102.2 ft)
Scantling draft	10.8 m (fore & aft) (35.42 ft)
Corresponding disp.	50 330 m³ (1 763 867 ft³)
Normal draft	9.05 m (fore & aft) (29.68 ft)
Corresponding disp.	40 400 m³ (1 415 860 ft³)

The ship stern is shown in Fig. 8.

The propeller was designed for the 9.05-m draft at the following operating conditions:

Ship speed	22.0 knots
Propeller speed	126 rpm
Full-scale mean eff. wake coefficient	0.290
Thrust	159 080 kp
Height of waterline above propeller at zero speed	5.42 m (17.77 ft)

The following parameters are determined from the preceding:

Advance ratio	$J = 0.580$
Thrust coef.	$K_T = 0.182$
Loading coef.	$K_T/J^2 = 0.5410$
Cavitation numbers	$\sigma_{VA} = 4.64$
	$\sigma_n = 1.56$
	$\sigma_{0.7R} = 0.302$

When mounting the model in the tunnel, the draft aft was adjusted to level with the stern wave at a draft of 11.15 m (36.57 ft) full-scale. [Measurements conducted later in the towing tank showed that the height of the stern wave was overestimated by about 0.5 m (1.64 ft).] The cavitation numbers cited in the foregoing were, however, used as the increase of static pressure does not fully correspond to the height of the stern wave.

Test results—Open-water tests for determining the propeller characteristics were conducted in the towing tank and the corresponding characteristics in the "behind" condition at at-

Table 2 Characteristics of SSPA propeller model P-1841

	Pitch	Section Lengths		Camber	Thickness
	P/D	CF/D	CA/D	F_{MAX}/C	S/D
0.191	0.987	0.128	0.121	0.0	0.0488
0.25	0.958	0.139	0.134	0.0290	0.0444
0.3	0.935	0.146	0.144	0.0269	0.0408
0.4	0.900	0.157	0.163	0.0211	0.0341
0.5	0.886	0.160	0.182	0.0164	0.0278
0.6	0.883	0.154	0.200	0.0144	0.0221
0.7	0.882	0.138	0.218	0.0131	0.0168
0.8	0.882	0.105	0.232	0.0135	0.0120
0.9	0.857	0.048	0.236	0.0153	0.0078
0.95	0.830	0.0003	0.226	0.0178	0.0058
1.0	0.788	−0.136	0.136	. . .	0.0040

Dimensions of Prototype Propeller	
Diameter	6.6 m
No. of blades	5
Blade area ratio	0.80
Hub ratio	0.191
Blade section mean line	NACA, a = 0.80
Blade thickness	NACA 16

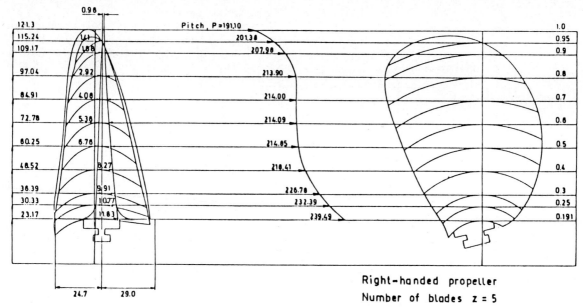

Fig. 11(a) SSPA propeller model P-1841: blade form and pitch distribution

Right-handed propeller
Number of blades z = 5
Diameter D = 242.6
Pitch ratio at 0.7 R $P_{0.7}/D = 0.848$
Blade area ratio $A_D/A_0 = 0.80$

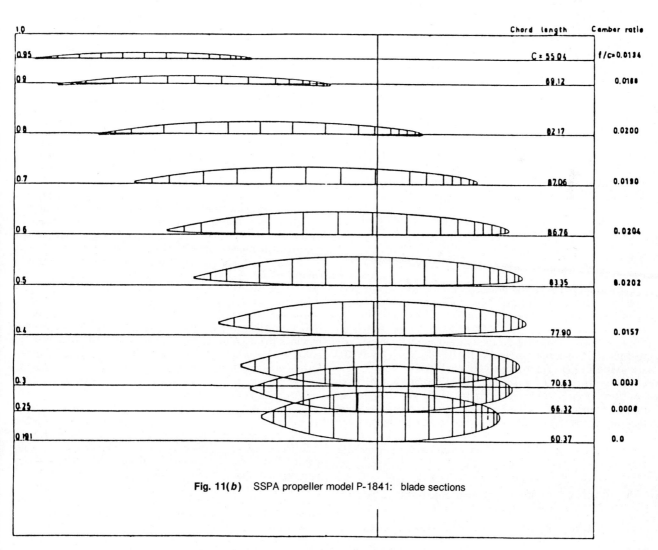

Fig. 11(b) SSPA propeller model P-1841: blade sections

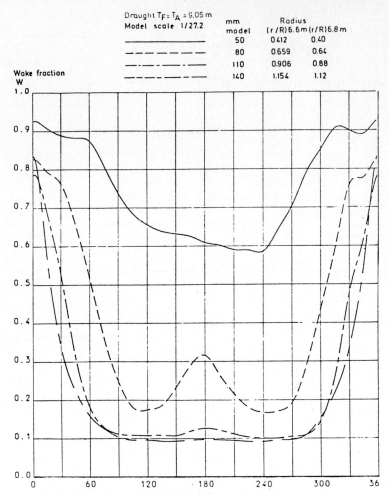

Draught $T_F = T_A = 9.05$ m
Model scale 1/27.2

	mm model	Radius $(r/R)6.6$ m	$(r/R)6.8$ m
———————	50	0.412	0.40
— — — —	80	0.659	0.64
—·—·—·—	110	0.906	0.88
– – – –	140	1.154	1.12

Fig. 12 RO/RO ship model wake distribution measured in towing tank with Prandtl tubes

mospheric conditions in the cavitation tunnel. At the design advance ratio, the following comparisons between calculated and measured thrust coefficients and efficiency were secured:

	OPEN WATER	BEHIND CONDITION		
Thrust coef.	0.181	0.185	0.187	(thrust identity)
Efficiencies	0.613	0.600	0.608	

Cavitation patterns and pressure amplitudes—Cavitation tests in the tunnel were carried out at different combinations of advance ratio and cavitation number. Cavitation patterns were TV-filmed, from which the patterns can be sketched. Pressure fluctuations at blade and twice-blade frequencies are registered. Cavitation patterns at $J = 0.588$ and $\sigma_{0.7R} = 0.301$ are shown in Fig. 13 for propeller model 1841.

In Fig. 10, amplitudes of the pressure fluctuations, measured by Transducer 3, are given as curves of K_p versus $\sigma_{0.7R}$ for propeller model 1841. These results confirm earlier experience that there is very little influence of advance ratio on the pressure magnitude variation when plotted in this way. Table 3 compares amplitudes obtained at three transducers with theoretical results.

5. Evaluation of theory and comparison with SSPA measurements

The MIT program for intermittently cavitating propellers,

designated as PUF-3, was initially applied to SSPA propeller P1842 using the nominal model wake. Cavity outlines were found to correlate poorly with SSPA observations. A second calculation was made using an effective wake derived from the nominal wake in the manner described in the following. Again the cavity geometry did not comport with measurements and, in the vicinity of cavity collapse, the results showed negative cavity ordinates. Examination of SSPA cavity outlines showed that, in the collapsing phase, the leading edge of the cavity retreats from the leading edge of the blade. As PUF-3 is designed to accommodate only cavities which extend from the locus of the leading edges of the blades, it was necessary to secure data in which this aspect of cavity behavior obtained throughout the episode. Fortunately, SSPA Model P-1841 performed in this fashion and the geometry of that design, as given in Table 2, was employed as input to PUF-3 together with an effective wake, deduced as described in the following.

The nominal axial wake, as defined at four radii from SSPA measurements, shown in Fig. 12, is interpolated by spline cubics to give the wake at 10 radii as displayed in Fig. 14 (curve at $r/R = 0.191$ not shown). The harmonics of this nominal wake are provided in Table 4. This nominal wake, however, is not an appropriate wake to use as input to PUF-3. It is well known that an operating propeller causes incoming vortex lines to move relative to each other, rather than merely to convect at advance velocity. This relative motion changes the corresponding wake velocities. In PUF-3, however, this nonlinear effect is not ac-

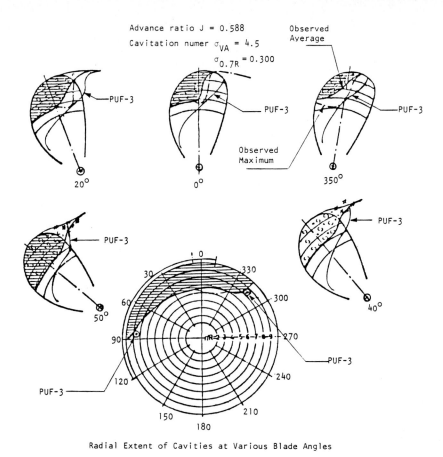

Radial Extent of Cavities at Various Blade Angles

Fig. 13 Measured and computer cavity outlines on SSPA propeller model P-1841 operating aft of RO/RO hull

counted for, so that the distortion of the nominal wake by the propeller must be estimated, and the resulting "effective wake" used as input to PUF-3. Unfortunately, there is no rigorous method available for the prediction of effective wakes in the general, nonaxisymmetric case. For the present work, the method of Huang and Groves [21], which predicts effective wakes in the axisymmetric case, is used as the basis for an approximate scheme, described in the following:

(*a*) The method of Huang and Groves is used to modify the circumferential mean (zeroth harmonic) velocity field. Al-

though this method assumes that the wake is axisymmetric, a recent experimental investigation indicates that it can be used to predict changes in the circumferential mean velocity field in a typical "V"-wake, such as the one considered here. The method predicts not only the (circumferential mean) effective wake velocities, but also the amount of contraction of the stream tubes which occurs forward of the propeller disk.

(*b*) The modification of the circumferential gradients in the nominal wake is based on the assumption that they are due to radial vortex lines which are convected with the axisym-

Table 3 Comparison of measured and computed dimensionless pressure coefficient double amplitudes for two conditions on locus of water surface

$$C_p = \frac{2|p|}{\rho n^2 d^2}$$

Gage	Measured	Calculated Amplitudes		Ratio Meas'd./Calc'd.		Ratio Calc. Free Surface
		Free Surface	Rigid Surface	Free	Rigid	Calc. Rigid Surface
		Blade Frequency				
3 ₵	0.165	0.123	0.141	1.34	1.17	0.87
4 St'bd.	0.105	0.039	0.066	2.69	1.59	0.59
5 Port	0.069	0.031	0.055	2.23	1.25	0.56
		Twice Blade Frequency				
3 ₵	0.065	0.042	0.048	1.52	1.33	0.87
4 St'bd.	0.024	0.015	0.024	1.60	1.00	0.63
5 Port	0.016	0.010	0.018	1.60	0.89	0.56

NOTE: Calculated blade angles for maximum positive pressures for Gages 3, 4, 5, are 15.5, 16.5, and 13.6 deg, respectively, at blade frequency and 1.8, 2.5, and 1.7 deg at twice blade frequency. This indicates the dominance of the source behavior of the cavity. Positive blade angle is counterclockwise from 12 o'clock looking forward.

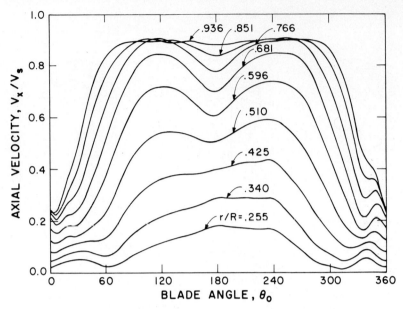

Fig. 14 Computer-interpolated nominal wake of RO/RO ship model

metric wake assumed in (*a*). These radial vortex lines are assumed to remain radial, and to remain at the same azimuthal position as the wake is contracted. As the axisymmetric stream surfaces contract, the radial vortex lines contract and move to smaller radii; see Fig. 16.

(*c*) As the vortex lines are reduced in length, the vorticity equation dictates that the vorticity decreases proportionally, as do the circumferential velocity gradients:

$$\frac{\omega_{r_{eff}}}{\omega_{r_{nom}}} = \frac{\dfrac{1}{r_{eff}}\dfrac{\partial V_{a_{eff}}}{\partial \theta}}{\dfrac{1}{r_{nom}}\dfrac{\partial V_{a_{nom}}}{\partial \theta}} = \frac{\Delta r_{eff}}{\Delta r_{nom}} \qquad (81)$$

where r_{eff}, r_{nom}, Δr_{eff}, and Δr_{nom} are indicated in Fig. 16. Thus, all wake harmonics at a given radius (except circumferential mean) are multiplied by a constant factor, given by

$$\frac{A_{n_{eff}}(r_{eff})}{A_{n_{nom}}(r_{nom})} = \frac{B_{n_{eff}}(r_{eff})}{B_{n_{nom}}(r_{nom})} = \frac{r_{eff}\Delta r_{eff}}{r_{nom}\Delta r_{nom}} \qquad n = 1, 2 \ldots \tag{82}$$

where A_n and B_n are the cosine and sine coefficients at a particular radius of the effective or nominal wake, as indicated by subscript.

This procedure produces the curves of effective wake shown in Fig. 15, and the cosine and sine coefficients of their harmonic series in blade angle are given in Table 5.

It was again noted that employment of the *nominal* wake yielded cavity outlines much larger than those observed on Model P-1841 in the SSPA tunnel. Use of the *effective* wake gave outlines labeled PUF-3 in Fig. 13. Although it is seen there that the prediction of cavity extent is greater than observed *in the mean* by SSPA, the discrepancy in the velocity of the cavity volume is not nearly as great since Fig. 17 shows

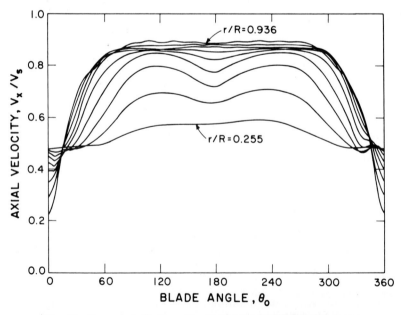

Fig. 15 Computed effective wake distribution for RO/RO ship model

Theoretical and Experimental Propeller-Induced Hull Pressures

Table 4   Nominal wake harmonics

Axial Wake Harmonics

r/R	A_0	A_1	A_2	A_3	A_4	A_5	A_6	A_7
0.191	0.049	−0.046	0.014	0.008	−0.002	−0.007	−0.002	−0.003
0.300	0.126	−0.102	0.015	0.018	−0.000	−0.011	−0.004	−0.005
0.400	0.231	−0.162	−0.009	0.028	0.003	−0.008	−0.004	−0.004
0.500	0.370	−0.224	−0.065	0.037	0.010	0.002	−0.003	−0.001
0.600	0.516	−0.270	−0.132	0.035	0.015	0.015	−0.001	0.004
0.700	0.637	−0.283	−0.174	0.011	0.009	0.020	0.003	0.008
0.800	0.715	−0.261	−0.180	−0.034	−0.010	0.013	0.005	0.008
0.900	0.760	−0.228	−0.166	−0.076	−0.031	−0.000	0.004	0.005
0.950	0.774	−0.214	−0.159	−0.089	−0.039	−0.008	0.000	0.001
1.000	0.784	−0.205	−0.152	−0.095	−0.045	−0.015	−0.005	−0.003

r/R		B_1	B_2	B_3	B_4	B_5	B_6	B_7
0.191	...	−0.006	0.009	−0.001	−0.003	−0.000	−0.002	−0.002
0.300	...	−0.012	0.014	−0.001	−0.004	−0.000	−0.003	−0.004
0.400	...	−0.017	0.015	−0.001	−0.002	−0.000	−0.004	−0.005
0.500	...	−0.021	0.008	0.000	0.004	−0.001	−0.003	−0.005
0.600	...	−0.022	−0.003	0.000	0.009	−0.001	−0.002	−0.005
0.700	...	−0.021	−0.011	−0.002	0.009	−0.002	−0.002	−0.005
0.800	...	−0.017	−0.014	−0.005	0.002	−0.004	−0.004	−0.005
0.900	...	−0.011	−0.011	−0.008	−0.005	−0.004	−0.005	−0.006
0.950	...	−0.009	−0.009	−0.007	−0.007	−0.004	−0.005	−0.005
1.000	...	−0.006	−0.007	−0.006	−0.006	−0.003	−0.004	−0.004

Tangential Wake Harmonics

r/R	A_0	A_1	A_2	A_3	A_4	A_5	A_6	A_7
0.191	0.000	0.000	0.000	0.000	0.000	0.000	0.000	0.000
0.300	−0.003	0.001	0.001	0.001	0.001	0.000	0.000	0.000
0.400	−0.005	0.002	0.002	0.002	0.002	0.001	0.000	0.000
0.500	−0.007	0.004	0.004	0.003	0.003	0.001	0.001	0.000
0.600	−0.010	0.005	0.005	0.004	0.003	0.001	0.001	0.001
0.700	−0.012	0.006	0.006	0.005	0.004	0.002	0.001	0.001
0.800	−0.009	0.004	0.003	0.003	0.003	0.001	0.001	0.001
0.900	−0.001	0.001	−0.001	−0.001	−0.001	−0.000	0.000	0.000
0.950	−0.000	0.000	−0.002	−0.002	−0.001	−0.001	0.000	0.000
1.000	−0.000	0.000	−0.002	−0.002	−0.001	−0.001	0.000	0.000

r/R		B_1	B_2	B_3	B_4	B_5	B_6	B_7
0.191	...	0.000	0.000	0.000	0.000	0.000	0.000	0.000
0.300	...	−0.024	−0.004	0.001	0.001	0.000	0.000	0.000
0.400	...	−0.046	−0.007	0.002	0.003	0.001	0.000	0.000
0.500	...	−0.068	−0.011	0.003	0.004	0.001	0.000	0.000
0.600	...	−0.090	−0.014	0.004	0.005	0.002	0.000	0.000
0.700	...	−0.112	−0.018	0.005	0.006	0.002	0.000	0.001
0.800	...	−0.123	−0.026	0.000	0.004	0.001	0.000	0.000
0.900	...	−0.128	−0.036	−0.008	−0.001	−0.000	0.000	−0.000
0.950	...	−0.129	−0.038	−0.009	−0.002	−0.001	0.000	−0.001
1.000	...	−0.129	−0.038	−0.009	−0.002	−0.001	0.000	−0.001

Radial Wake Harmonics

r/R	A_1	B_1
0.191	0.000	0.000
0.300	0.023	0.006
0.400	0.044	0.012
0.500	0.065	0.017
0.600	0.086	0.023
0.700	0.107	0.029
0.800	0.118	0.032
0.900	0.123	0.033
0.950	0.124	0.033
1.000	0.124	0.033

that the predicted cavities are quite thin in those areas of the blade where no cavitation was observed by SSPA.

The angular extent of cavitation at $r/R = 0.85$, as predicted by PUF-3, is also superimposed on Fig. 13 (bottom, center) and agrees very well near inception and collapse. It is to be noted that inception and collapse are defined by extrapolation in Fig. 18 by cutting off the region of nearly constant short cavity length. The latter has no significance since PUF-3 presently has no means of determining cavity details within the first chordwise elements.

The course of calculated cavity volume with blade position angle is illustrated in Fig. 19, showing that the maximum cavity volume lags the minimum of the wake (at zero degrees) by 30 deg. Harmonics of the time rate of change of cavity volume are listed in Table 6. We note that the amplitude of the cavity volume velocity at blade frequency (5th harmonic) is 0.01303, and that at twice blade frequency is 0.00328 (10th harmonic). As the pressure at distance is approximately proportional to the qNth harmonic of the cavity acceleration, the ratio of the pressure at twice blade frequency to that at blade frequency may be expected to be in the ratio of $2(0.00328)/0.01303 = 0.503$. We conclude that the pressures at twice blade frequency will be less than those at blade frequency. This is found to be the case upon examination of the pressure amplitudes as measured at SSPA and as calculated at DL.

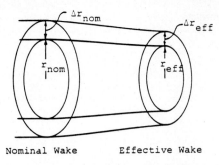

Nominal Wake   Effective Wake

Fig. 16 Contraction of axisymmetric effective wake

To calculate the pressures on the hull, the harmonics of the flow potential, as obtained from the PUF-3 field point output code, are used as input to the DL Propeller-Hull Program as described in Section 2.

The calculated pressure amplitudes and phases are compared with SSPA determinations in Table 3. Computed results are provided for two conditions imposed on the locus of the undisturbed water surface, one being the high-frequency boundary condition (zero potential), the other for the rigid surface condition (zero vertical derivative of the potential) as described in Section 2.

Concentrating on the 5th and 6th columns of Table 3, we see that the comparison with measurement is generally very good when the theoretical value is computed for the rigid-wall condition on the free surface. Consistently, the values of the amplitudes with the free-surface condition are smaller, as they should be. It is noteworthy that the calculated amplitudes under the two surface conditions are not markedly different for Gage 3, which is very close to the propeller. This is highly consistent because the hull pressures at that point are dominated by the cavity on the propeller itself, whereas the contributions from the positive and negative images of the propeller are both weak, being distant from this gage. Consistently, the pressure with the rigid surface condition applied is somewhat higher (15 percent) than that with the free surface. In contrast, the rel-

ative effect of these surface conditions is marked for Gages 4 and 5, which are distant from the propeller. They are consistently different in the right sense.

The character of this correlation strongly suggests that the replacement of the free surface in the SSPA facility by a rigid surrounding wood cover between the model and the top steelwork of the tunnel results in scaled hull pressure observations which are in excess of what would be secured on the ship for the same effective position of the water surface in way of the propeller. This is not to say that SSPA measurements will necessarily disagree with comparable measurements made on the prototype. Indeed, SSPA has demonstrated many successful correlations with ship measurements at sea. In such correlations, many facets of the phenomenon are operative, such as the dynamics of the cavity which are dependent on the time history of the angle of attack at the blade sections resulting from the wake harmonics, which themselves are subject to variable scale effects from one type of hull to another.

However, in direct comparison of theory and experiment under controlled model test conditions, it is the opinion of the senior author that the rigid boundary condition imposed by the test procedure at SSPA, as well as in other cavitation tunnels, can give rise to a bias, and apparently does so, if the free water surface is close to the pressure transducers.

This situation has been recognized at SSPA for some time, as the main interest of the customers has gradually shifted from large tankers of large draft to ferries, RO/RO ships and containerships of more limited draft. Particularly for the latter types of ships, the free-surface effect comes into the picture, as the correlation model/full scale has normally been based on full-scale measurements in connection with the acceptance trials, which are usually carried out in ballast condition. In many cases (as the one referred to in the present report) this means that the pressure transducers of primary interest for predicting the vibration levels are above the water surface at zero speed. Results of correlation studies on commercially tested projects indicate, however, that the free-surface effect can be mastered, and approximate corrections have been es-

Table 5 Effective wake harmonics

Axial Wake Harmonics								
r/R	A_0	A_1	A_2	A_3	A_4	A_5	A_6	A_7
0.191	0.495	−0.003	0.001	0.000	−0.000	−0.000	−0.000	−0.000
0.300	0.575	−0.088	−0.028	0.014	0.004	0.001	−0.001	−0.000
0.400	0.660	−0.141	−0.078	0.014	0.007	0.009	0.000	0.003
0.500	0.722	−0.161	−0.107	−0.009	−0.001	0.010	0.003	0.005
0.600	0.759	−0.156	−0.113	−0.043	−0.017	0.003	0.003	−0.004
0.700	0.779	−0.151	−0.112	−0.066	−0.030	−0.008	−0.001	−0.000
0.800	0.789	−0.154	−0.113	−0.074	−0.040	−0.020	−0.011	−0.008
0.900	0.794	−0.166	−0.120	−0.075	−0.048	−0.032	−0.025	−0.018
0.950	0.796	−0.173	−0.124	−0.074	−0.052	−0.038	−0.031	−0.023
1.000	0.797	−0.177	−0.127	−0.074	−0.055	−0.044	−0.037	−0.027

r/R		B_1	B_2	B_3	B_4	B_5	B_6	B_7
0.191	. . .	0.000	−0.001	0.000	0.000	0.000	0.000	0.000
0.300	. . .	0.008	−0.003	−0.000	−0.002	0.000	0.001	0.002
0.400	. . .	0.011	0.004	0.000	−0.005	0.001	0.001	0.002
0.500	. . .	0.011	0.008	0.002	−0.003	0.002	0.002	0.003
0.600	. . .	0.009	0.008	0.005	0.002	0.003	0.003	0.004
0.700	. . .	0.006	0.006	0.005	0.005	0.002	0.003	0.003
0.800	. . .	0.003	0.002	0.002	0.003	0.001	0.002	0.002
0.900	. . .	0.001	−0.000	−0.001	0.000	0.001	0.002	0.001
0.950	. . .	0.001	−0.000	−0.002	−0.001	0.002	0.003	0.002
1.000	. . .	0.002	0.000	−0.002	−0.001	0.003	0.004	0.003

NOTE: Nominal values assumed for tangential and radial wake harmonics.

tablished based on statistical analysis of a large correlation material. An extensive study on a fishing research ship will give further material. This study would benefit from calculations of the kind presented in the preceding, as preliminary results indicate a more even distribution of the free-surface effect over the stern than that demonstrated in Table 3 of the present paper. It is, of course, recognized that [as in the old saying "One swallow does not make a summer"—John Heywood, *Proverbs* (1546)], a single set of correlations showing relatively better results with rigid over free-surface conditions cannot be taken as conclusive.

It is interesting to note that multiplication of each computed result for the rigid condition by a factor of about 0.6 in the cases of the distant gages 4 and 5 (at both frequencies) would yield the computed answer found for the imposed free-surface condition. This correction factor is of the same order as may be found from an elementary analysis in which the cavity is modeled by a pulsating point source with appropriate images in the waterplane and a simplified hull surface. (Such a simple model is possible only when the field point is not close to the propeller.) The behavior of the computed results is therefore qualitatively consistent with physically based expectations.

6. Summary and suggested direction for future work

The foregoing theoretical developments provide procedures for calculating pressures and forces induced by noncavitating and intermittently cavitating propellers operating in the wakes of hulls of quite arbitrary forms. Correlation with measurements made on a model of a RO/RO ship at SSPA at three lo-cations at blade and twice-blade frequencies shows remarkably close agreement for conditions deemed appropriate to the test configuration used in the SSPA cavitation tunnel.

Application at MIT of a program for generating the flow patterns developed on intermittently cavitating propellers has revealed that, to secure realistic cavity geometry variations, it is necessary to convert the measured model nominal wake to an effective wake which is then used as input. It was also noted that, as expected, the PUF-3 program can be applied only to cases in which the leading edges of the cavities remain attached to the leading edges of the blades throughout the episode.

It is urged that work on the following tasks be supported in the immediate future:

1. Correlations with measurements of model hull pressures available at NSMB and SSPA for cases to which the programs are considered applicable.

2. Definitive experiments to further the development of the MIT procedure for prediction of effective wake.

3. Extension of the PUF-3 program to accommodate blade cavities which recede from the blade leading edge during the contracting or collapse phase.

4. Application of the coupled MIT-DL programs to eval-uate the comparative attributes of alternative hull designs while they are being evolved by shipyards or design agents.

Acknowledgments

Support of the development and coupling of the MIT and SIT programs by the U.S. Maritime Administration through the efforts of Mr. R. Falls, program manager, is gratefully ac-knowledged. The cooperation with SSPA and release of their

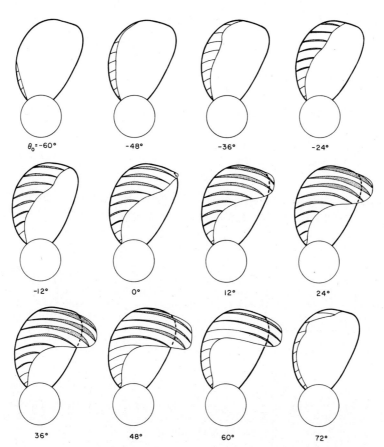

Fig. 17 Computed PUF-3 cavity outlines and thickness distributions for SSPA propeller model P-1841 on RO/RO ship model based on computed effective wake

Theoretical and Experimental Propeller-Induced Hull Pressures

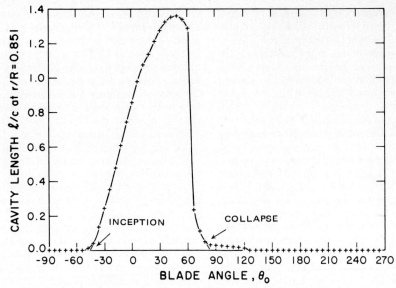

Fig. 18 Calculated variation of cavity length with blade rotation angle at 0.851 radius for SSPA propeller P-1841 on RO/RO ship model

data have been made possible by Dr. H. Edstrand, former director general, SSPA. Mr. D. Greeley, formerly graduate student, MIT, Mr. J. Teeters, formerly assistant research engineer, DL, and Mr. P. F. Wang, graduate student, SIT, are thanked for development of computer codes and conduct of the calculations. The authors also wish to acknowledge the major contribution of Dr. Chang-Sup Lee to the development of the PUF-3 program at MIT and to portions of the text adapted from [14]. Misses J. Jones and M. Palazzo, DL, are commended for their painstaking typing of the manuscript.

References

1   Breslin, J. P. and Tsakonas, S., "Marine Propeller Pressure Field Due to Loading and Thickness Effects," TRANS. SNAME, Vol. 67, 1959, pp. 386–422.
2   Hess, J. and Smith, A. M. O., "Calculation of Non-Lifting Potential Flow About Arbitrary Three-Dimensional Bodies," Douglas Aircraft Report No. E.S. 40622, 15 March 1962.
3   Johnsson, C-A. and Søntvedt, T., "Propeller Excitation and Response of 230,000 TDW Tankers," Ninth Symposium on Naval Hydrodynamics, R. Brard and A. Castera, Eds., Office of Naval Research No. ACR203, Vol. 1, 1972, pp. 581–669.
4   Noordzij, L., "Pressure Field Induced by a Cavitating Propeller," *International Shipbuilding Progress*, Vol. 6, No. 260, 1976, pp. 93–105.
5   Guerst, J. A., "Linearized Theory for Partially Cavitated Hydrofoils," *International Shipbuilding Progress*, Vol. 6, No. 60, 1959, pp. 369–384.
6   Kaplan, P., Bentson, J., and Breslin, J. P., "Theoretical Analysis of Propeller Radiated Pressures and Blade Forces Due to Cavitation," RINA Symposium on Propeller-Induced Ship Vibration, London, Dec. 1979.
7   Tsakonas, S., Jacobs, W. R., and Ali, M. R., "Documentation of a Computer Program for Pressures, Forces and Moments on Ship Propellers in Hull Wakes," Davidson Laboratory Report SIT-DL-

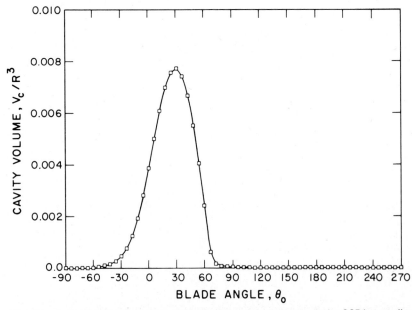

Fig. 19 Calculated cavity volume variation with blade rotation angle for SSPA propeller P-1841 in effective wake of RO/RO ship model

Theoretical and Experimental Propeller-Induced Hull Pressures

76-9-1863, Stevens Institute of Technology, Hoboken, N.J., Jan. 1976.

8   Vorus, W. S., Breslin, J. P., and Tein, Y. S., "Calculation and Comparison of Propeller Unsteady Pressure Forces on Ships," Ship Vibration Symposium '78, Washington, D.C., Oct. 1978.

9   Stern, F. and Vorus, W. S., "A Non-Linear Method for Predicting Unsteady Sheet Cavitation on Marine Propellers," submitted to *Journal of Ship Research*.

10   Golden, D. W., "A Numerical Method for Two-Dimensional, Cavitating, Lifting Flow," MIT, Department of Ocean Engineering, Cambridge, Mass., 1975.

11   Jiang, C. W., "Experimental and Theoretical Investigation of Unsteady Supercavitating Hydrofoils of Finite Span," Ph.D. Thesis, MIT, Department of Ocean Engineering, Cambridge, Mass., 1977.

12   Van Houten, R. J., "The Numerical Prediction of Unsteady Sheet Cavitation on High Aspect Ratio Hydrofoils," 14th Symposium on Naval Hydrodynamics, Ann Arbor, Mich., Aug. 1982.

13   Peters, A. S., Goodman, T. R., and Breslin, J. P., "A Partially Cavitating Hydrofoil in a Gust," Davidson Laboratory Report SIT-DL-80-9-2118, Stevens Institute of Technology, Hoboken, N.J., 1980.

14   Lee, Chang-Sup, "Prediction of the Transient Cavitation on Marine Propellers by Numerical Lifting Surface Theory," 13th Symposium on Naval Hydrodynamics, Tokyo, Oct. 1980.

15   Kerwin, J. E. and Lee, C. S., "Prediction of Steady and Unsteady Marine Propeller Performance by Numerical Lifting-Surface Theory," TRANS. SNAME, Vol. 86, 1978.

16   James, R. M., "On the Remarkable Accuracy of the Vortex Lattice Method," *Computer Methods in Applied Mechanics and Engineering*, Vol. 1, 1972.

17   Johnsson, C-A., "Some Experiences from Vibration Excitation Tests in the SSPA Large Cavitation Tunnel," RINA Symposium on Propeller-Induced Ship Vibration, London, Dec. 1979.

18   Rutgersson, O., "Cavitation on High-Speed Propellers in Oblique Flow—Influence on Propeller Design and Interaction with Ship Hull," 13th Symposium on Naval Hydrodynamics, Tokyo, Oct. 1980.

19   Johnsson, C-A., "Propeller Parameter Studies" in *Noise Sources in Ships: 1. Propellers*, A. C. Nilsson and N. P. Tyvand, Eds., Nordforsk, Miljovardsserien, Stockholm, 1981.

20   Kellogg, O. D., *Foundation of Potential Theory*, F. Ungar Publishing Company, New York, 1929, pp. 160–172.

21   Huang, T. T. and Groves, N. C., "Effective Wake: Theory and Experiment," 13th Symposium on Naval Hydrodynamics, Tokyo, 1980; also presented as DTNSRDC Report No. 81/003.

22   Johnsson, C-A., Rutgersson, O., Olsson, S., and Bjorheden, O., "Vibration Excitation Forces from a Cavitating Propeller. Model and Full-Scale Tests on a High-Speed Container Ship," 11th Symposium on Naval Hydrodynamics, London, April 1976.

Appendix 1

Source-density cavity ordinate relation

The kinematic condition imposed on the cavity-surface motion is that its velocity along its normal must be equal to the component of fluid velocity along that same normal. In symbols defined in Fig. 20, this condition imposes

$$\dot{\eta} = \frac{\partial \eta}{\partial t} = \vec{n} \cdot \vec{V}^+ = n_{x'} V_{x'}^+ + n_{y'} V_{y'}^+ + n_r V_r^+ \quad (83)$$

the radial component being out of (or perpendicular to) the plane of the sketch. The (+) superscript indicates that the fluid velocity is evaluated on the upper or cavity surface.

Now, if $F^+(x',y',r,t) = 0$ is the equation of the cavity surface in terms of the indicated local coordinates, then we know from the calculus of surfaces that the components of the unit normal to that surface are given by

$$n_{x'} = \frac{F_{w'}^+}{|n|}; n_{y'} = \frac{F_{x'}^+}{|n|}; n_r = \frac{F_r^+}{|n|} \quad (84)$$

where

Table 6   Harmonic amplitudes of cavity volume velocity for SSPA Propeller P-1841 in effective wake of RO/RO ship model (PUF-3 output)

Shaft Harmonic Number	Cavity Volume Velocity Harmonics			
	Nondimensionalized on $N*R**3$			
	$A(N)$	$B(N)$	Amp (N)	Phase (N)
0	0.00000	0.00000	0.00000	0.000
1	0.00590	−0.01274	0.01404	155.142
2	0.01752	−0.01438	0.02267	129.373
3	0.02356	−0.00449	0.02399	100.787
4	0.01817	0.00741	0.01962	67.808
5	0.00602	0.01156	0.01303	27.522
6	−0.00332	0.00649	0.00729	332.939
7	−0.00442	−0.00106	0.00455	256.510
8	−0.00002	−0.00410	0.00410	180.224
9	0.00342	−0.00154	0.00375	114.245
10	0.00242	0.00222	0.00328	47.530
11	−0.00102	0.00277	0.00295	339.867
12	−0.00263	0.00015	0.00264	273.262
13	−0.00104	−0.00219	0.00242	205.428
14	0.00153	−0.00171	0.00229	138.159
15	0.00206	0.00067	0.00217	72.000

$$|n| = \sqrt{F_x^{+2} + F_y^{+2} + F_r^{+2}}$$

subscripts on F^+ indicating partial derivatives. From Fig. 20, it is seen that the explicit composition of F^+ is

$$F^+(x',y',r,t) = y' - (f + \tau + \eta(x',r,t)) = 0 \quad (85)$$

and, hence

$$F_{x'}^+ = -(f_{x'} + \tau_{x'} + \eta_{x'}); F_{y'}^+$$
$$= 1; F_r^+ = -(f_r + \tau_r + \eta_r) \quad (86)$$

As the section and cavity are thin, all partial derivatives are very small compared with unity and this yields $|n| \simeq 1$. The boundary condition (83) then reduces to

$$\frac{\partial \eta}{\partial t} = -(f_{x'} + \tau_{x'} + \eta_{x'}) V_{x'}^+$$
$$+ (1) V_{y'}^+ - (f_r + \tau_r + \eta_r) V_r^+ \quad (87)$$

where the subscripts on V^+ indicate the component.

The equation of the lower surface of the section in way of the cavity is

$$F^-(x',y',r) = y' - (f - \tau) = 0 \quad (88)$$

The boundary condition corresponding to (87) on the lower surface is

$$0 = -(f_{x'} - \tau_{x'}) V_{x'}^- + (1) V_{y'}^- - (f_r - \tau_r)V_r^- \quad (89)$$

As f_r, τ_r and η_r are very small, and the radial component velocities, V_r, are also small, we may readily neglect the last terms in (87) and (89). As (87) and (89) hold over the same range of x' (in way of the cavity), we may subtract (89) from (87) to secure

$$\frac{\partial \eta}{\partial t} + \eta_{x'}V^+ = -f_x'(V_{x'}^+ - V_{x'}^-)$$
$$- \tau_{x'}(V_{x'}^+ + V_{x'}^-) + V_{y'}^+ - V_{y'}^- \quad (90)$$

Now, from Fig. 20

$$V_{x'}^+ = \left(-r\omega - U_w + \frac{1}{r}\frac{\partial}{\partial\gamma}\phi^{\pm}\right)\cos\theta_p$$
$$+ \left(-\overline{U} + \frac{\partial\phi^{\pm}}{\partial x}\right)\sin\theta_p \quad (91)$$

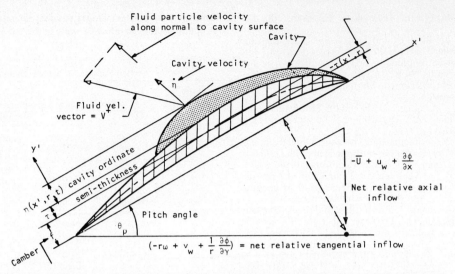

Fig. 20 Schematic of blade section at radius r displaying relative velocities: u_w, v_w hull axial and tangential wake; $\partial\phi/\partial x$, $(1/r)(\partial\phi/\partial\gamma)$, axial and tangential inductions from loading, thickness and cavity

Then

$$V_{x'}^+ - V_{x'}^- = \frac{1}{r}\frac{\partial}{\partial\gamma}(\phi^+ - \phi^-)\cos\theta_p$$
$$+ \frac{\partial}{\partial x}(\phi^+ - \phi^-)\sin\theta_p \quad (92)$$

and as $f'_x(V_{x'}^+ - V_{x'}^{-1})$ is seen to involve products of only second-order terms, no first-order contribution is secured. In contrast

$$\tau_{x'}(V_{x'}^+ + V_{x'}^-) \simeq 2\tau_x\{-r\omega\cos\theta p - \overline{U}\sin\theta p\}$$
$$= -2\sqrt{\overline{U}^2 + (r\omega)^2}\,\tau_{x'} \quad (93)$$

again neglecting products of $\tau_{x'}$ and perturbations.

The jump in the y'-component $V_{y'}^+ - V_{y'}^-$ can arise only from the source distributions m_0 modeling the thickness and the cavity, $m(x',r,t)$. As may be seen in Kellogg [20], the jump in normal velocity across a source sheet is equal to the source density, in this case $m_0 + m$. Consequently, (90) reduces to

$$\frac{\partial\eta}{\partial t} - (r\omega\cos\theta_p + \overline{U}\sin\theta_p)\frac{\partial\eta}{\theta x'}$$
$$= 2\tau_x\sqrt{\overline{U}^2 + (r\omega)^2} + m_0 + m$$

As we know from thin section theory that $m_0 = -2\tau_x V$, then we obtain finally

$$\frac{\partial\eta}{\partial t} - V\frac{\partial\eta}{\partial x'} = m \quad (94)$$

The chordwise variable $x' \simeq s\theta'$; hence we have in dummy variables

$$\left(\frac{\partial}{\partial t} - \frac{V}{s}\frac{\partial}{\partial\theta'}\right)\eta(s,\theta',t) = m \quad (95)$$

Appendix 2

Boundary conditions imposed by water surface at high and low frequencies

The relation between pressure p, velocity potential ϕ, and

vertical location in the fluid z, in the presence of gravity and a uniform stream, $-U$, is

$$\frac{p}{\rho} + \frac{1}{2}\left[\left(-U + \frac{\partial\phi}{\partial x}\right)^2 + \left(\frac{\partial\phi}{\partial y}\right)^2 + \left(\frac{\partial\phi}{\phi z}\right)^2\right]$$
$$+ \frac{\partial\phi}{\partial t} + gz = \frac{p_{at}}{\rho} + \frac{1}{2}U^2 \quad (96)$$

where p_{at} is the atmospheric pressure and the reference datum is $z = 0$, the undisturbed level of the water surface. When on the free surface

$$z = \zeta(x,y,t) \quad (97)$$

or

$$F(x,y,z,t) = z - \zeta(x,y,t) = 0 \quad (98)$$

the pressure $p = p_{at}$ and, upon neglecting the squares of the perturbation terms, (96) yields the physical condition on ζ, namely

$$\zeta = \frac{1}{g}\left(U\frac{\partial\phi}{\partial x} - \frac{\partial\phi}{\partial t}\right) = \frac{1}{g}\left(U\frac{\partial}{\partial x} - \frac{\partial}{\partial t}\right)\phi \quad (99)$$

The kinematic condition that the velocity of the free surface along its local normal must be equal to the component of the fluid velocity along that normal imposes that

$$\frac{d}{dt}F(x,y,z,t) = \frac{\partial F}{\partial t} + \frac{\partial x}{\partial t}\frac{\partial F}{\partial x} + \frac{\partial y}{\partial t}\frac{\partial F}{\partial y} + \frac{\partial z}{\partial t}\frac{\partial F}{\partial z} = 0$$
$$(100)$$

The particle velocities are

$$\frac{\partial x}{\partial t} = -U + \frac{\partial\phi}{\partial x} \simeq -U; \frac{\partial y}{\partial t} = \frac{\partial\phi}{\partial y}, \frac{\partial z}{\partial t} = \frac{\partial\phi}{\partial z}$$

Then, using (98) in (99):

$$-\frac{\partial\zeta}{\partial t} - U\left(\frac{-\partial\zeta}{\partial x}\right) + \frac{\partial\phi}{\partial y}\left(\frac{\partial\zeta}{\partial y}\right) + \frac{\partial\phi}{\phi z} = 0$$

and, as the third term is of second order, one obtains

$$\left(\frac{\partial}{\partial t} - \frac{U\partial}{\partial x}\right)\zeta = \frac{\partial\phi}{\partial z} \quad (101)$$

ζ may be eliminated between the physical (99) and the kinematic (101) conditions to yield the combined requirement on ϕ imposed by the presence of the free surface in the form

$$\left(\frac{\partial}{\partial t} - \frac{U\partial}{\partial x}\right)^2 \phi + \frac{g\partial\phi}{\partial z} = 0 \qquad (102)$$

Here we are interested in potentials in which the time-dependence can be split off, that is

$$\phi = \tilde{\phi}(x,y,z)e^{iqn\omega t} \qquad (103)$$

Then (102) becomes

$$\left(iqn\omega - \frac{U\partial}{\partial x}\right)^2 \tilde{\phi} + \frac{g\partial\tilde{\phi}}{\partial z} = 0 \qquad (104)$$

where $\tilde{\phi}$ and its derivative are to be evaluated on $z = 0$, assuming ζ to be small everywhere. If we now replace $\tilde{\phi}$ by $\omega r_0^2 \tilde{\phi}$, x by $r_0 x$, and z by $r_0 z$ (r_0 the propeller radius, ω the angular velocity) and extract $iqn\omega r_0$ from the first term, there results the dimensionless equation

$$\left(1 + i\frac{J}{\pi qn}\frac{\partial}{\partial x}\right)^2 \tilde{\phi} - \frac{g}{r_0(qn\omega)^2}\frac{\partial\tilde{\phi}}{\partial z} = 0 \qquad (105)$$

where $J = U/ND$, the advance ratio (N, revolutions per second; D, propeller diameter). Now, for $r_0(qn\omega)^2$ sufficiently large so that the acceleration ratio

$$\frac{g}{r_0(qn\omega)^2} \ll 1 \qquad (106)$$

then

$$\left(1 + i\frac{J}{\pi qn}\frac{\partial}{\partial x}\right)^2 \tilde{\phi} \to 0$$

Taking zero as the right side, this equation admits of the possible solution

$$\tilde{\phi} = f_1(y)e^{i\pi qnx/J} + f_2(y)xe^{i\pi qnx/J} \qquad (107)$$

where f_1 and f_2 are to be determined to meet available conditions. *But this solution is inadmissible* since $\tilde{\phi}$ must approach zero as $x \to \infty$. Hence, f_1 and f_2 must be taken as identically zero. Hence

$$\tilde{\phi}(x,y,0,t) \to 0 \qquad (108)$$

provided the acceleration ratio

$$a' = \frac{g}{r_0(qn\omega)^2} \ll 1$$

The value of a' [for $r_0 = 12$ ft, $g = 32.2$ ft/sec, $q = 1$ (blade frequency), $n = 5$ (blades) and $\omega = 2\pi(3/2)$ (90 rpm)] is $a' = 0.0012$. Thus, for applications of interest, we see that the approximation that $a' \ll 1$ is well accommodated.

In contrast, when gravity dominates, that is, $a' \gg 1$, then (105) may be recast to read

$$\frac{\partial\phi}{\partial z} - \frac{r_0(qn\omega)^2}{g}\left(1 + i\frac{J}{\pi qn}\frac{\partial}{\partial x}\right)^2 \tilde{\phi} = 0$$

and, as the second term approaches zero, one is left with the condition:

$$\frac{\partial\phi}{\partial z} \simeq 0$$

or the surface $z = 0$ acts like a nonporous, rigid cover.

Appendix 3

Replacement of the exterior Neumann problem by an interior Dirichlet problem

The problem posed by the generation (or creation) of a double hull in the presence of a single propeller requires a hull potential ϕ_h which meets the *Neumann condition*

$$\frac{\partial\phi_h}{\partial n} = -\frac{\partial\phi}{\partial n}; \text{ on } S = S_h + S_i \qquad (109)$$

where ϕ is the potential of the propeller, n the outward normal from S, S_h the hull surface, and S_i is the image or reflected hull; thus S is the double hull. The difficulty with solving the hull generation problem to meet (109) directly is that the right side of (109) is composed of three terms:

$$\frac{\partial\phi}{\partial n} = n_x\frac{\partial\phi}{\partial x} + n_y\frac{\partial\phi}{\partial y} + n_z\frac{\partial\phi}{\partial z}$$

and this calculation is highly consumptive of computer effort. Fortunately, the same Neumann condition can be met by solving the interior Dirichlet problem requiring within the interior of S that $\phi_h = -\phi$ (a single scalar function).

Let S denote a bounded, simple, smooth, closed surface. Let D_i denote the bounded interior domain of S, and let D_e indicate the unbounded exterior of S. Define $\mathbf{n}$ as the unit normal to S directed from D_i to D_e. Designate

$$\begin{aligned} R_s &= [(x - \xi)^2 + (y - \eta)^2 + (z - \zeta)^2]^{1/2} \\ R &= [(X - \xi)^2 + (Y - \eta)^2 + (Z - \zeta)^2]^{1/2} \end{aligned} \qquad (110)$$

where $Q(\xi,\eta,\zeta)$ and $P(x,y,z)$ are points on S and $T(X,Y,Z)$ is a point in either D_i or D_e. Let

$$\mathbf{\nabla} = \mathbf{i}\frac{\partial}{\partial\xi} + \mathbf{j}\frac{\partial}{\partial\eta} + \mathbf{k}\frac{\partial}{\partial\zeta} \qquad (111)$$

$$\mathbf{\nabla} = \mathbf{i}\frac{\partial}{\partial X} + \mathbf{j}\frac{\partial}{\partial Y} + \mathbf{k}\frac{\partial}{\partial Z}$$

in which $\mathbf{i},\mathbf{j},\mathbf{k}$ are unit vectors defining the orthogonal coordinate system.

Consider the surface integral of normal dipoles

$$\phi_h(T) = -\int \nu(Q)\,\mathbf{n}\cdot\mathbf{\nabla}\left(\frac{1}{R}\right)dS \qquad (112)$$

which satisfies

$$\mathbf{\nabla}\cdot\mathbf{\nabla}\,\phi_h(T) = 0$$

for T in either D_i or D_e. The potential (112) is discontinuous at S (as shown, for example, in Kellogg [20]). If

$$\phi_h^+(P) = \lim_{T\to P}\phi_h(T) \quad T \text{ in } D_e \qquad (113)$$

and

$$\phi_h^-(P) = \lim_{T\to P}\phi_h(T) \quad T \text{ in } D_i \qquad (114)$$

Then

$$\phi_h^+(P) = -2\pi\nu(P) - \int_S \nu(Q)\,\mathbf{n}\cdot\mathbf{\nabla}\left(\frac{1}{R_s}\right)dS \qquad (115a)$$

$$\phi_h^-(P) = 2\pi\nu(P) - \int_S \nu(Q)\,\mathbf{n}\cdot\mathbf{\nabla}\left(\frac{1}{R_s}\right)dS \qquad (115b)$$

where

$$\nu(P) = -\frac{1}{4\pi}(\phi_h^+(P) - \phi_h^-(P)) \qquad (115c)$$

On the other hand, it is shown (Kellogg) that, if $\nu(Q)$ is continuous of S and *if either of the limits*

$$\lim_{T \to P} \mathbf{n} \cdot \nabla \phi_h = \left(\frac{\partial \phi_h}{\partial n}\right)_e \quad T \text{ in } D_e \quad (116)$$

or

$$\lim_{T \to P} \mathbf{n} \cdot \nabla \phi_h = \left(\frac{\partial \phi_h}{\partial n}\right)_i \quad T \text{ in } D_i \quad (116) \text{ (Cont'd)}$$

exists, then the other does and

$$\left(\frac{\partial \phi_h}{\partial n}\right)_e = \left(\frac{\partial \phi_h}{\partial n}\right)_i = \left(\frac{\partial \phi_h}{\partial n}\right)_P \quad (117)$$

that is, the normal derivative or velocity is continuous through the dipoled surface. Now suppose that

$$\phi_h(T) = -\int_S \nu(Q) \mathbf{n} \cdot \nabla \left(\frac{1}{R}\right) dS \quad T \text{ in } D_c \quad (118)$$

is to be such that

$$\left(\frac{\partial \phi_h}{\partial n}\right)_e = -\left(\frac{\partial \phi}{\partial n}\right) = \left(\frac{\partial \phi}{\partial n}\right)_i \quad (119)$$

where, in our case, ϕ is the potential of the propeller which is, of course, a regular harmonic function *in the domain containing the double hull surface S and its interior.*

In accordance with the cited properties of surface dipole distributions cited in the foregoing, this Neumann condition (119) can be satisfied if we demand that the dipole density $\nu(Q)$ be such that

$$\phi_h(T) = -\phi(T) = -\int_S \nu(Q) \mathbf{n} \cdot \nabla \left(\frac{1}{R}\right) dS \quad (120)$$

for all points T in D_i. This insures the satisfaction of

$$\left(\frac{\partial \phi_h}{\partial n}\right)_i = -\left(\frac{\partial \phi}{\partial n}\right)_i$$

and we see that the exterior Neumann problem is thus reduced to an interior Dirichlet problem for, as $T \to P$ (on interior of S). We see from (115b) that ν must satisfy

$$-\phi(P) = 2\pi \nu(P) - \int_S \nu(Q) \mathbf{n} \cdot \nabla \left(\frac{1}{R_s}\right) dS \quad (121)$$

a Fredholm integral equation of the second kind of the form identical to that for which procedures are available for its numerical inversion.

Since $\phi_h^-(P) = -\phi(P)$, then, from the jump relation (115c), we obtain

$$\nu(P) = -\frac{1}{4\pi} \left(\phi_h^+(P) + \phi(P)\right) \quad (122)$$

Hence, once ν is found on the hull, the total pressure on the hull can be calculated from

$$\frac{p}{\rho} = -\left(\frac{\partial}{\partial t} + \frac{U\partial}{\partial x}\right)(\phi_h^+ + \phi) = 4\pi \left(\frac{\partial}{\partial t} + \frac{U\partial}{\partial x}\right) \nu(w,s,t)$$

where w is arc length along a waterline and s is arc length along a section or frame line. If the half-breadths of the ship are expressed as $b = b(x,z)$, then the pressure at frequency qn can be deduced from

$$\frac{p_{qn}}{\rho} = 4\pi(-iqn\omega\tilde{\nu}_{qn}(w,s)) + n_x - U \left(\frac{\partial \hat{\nu}}{\partial w'}\right)_{qn} e^{iqn\theta}$$

where n_x is the x-component of the unit normal or the direction cosine (n,x). As ν_{qn}, the complex amplitude is known only numerically, the evaluation of the second term requires numerical differentiation. Alternatively, $\tilde{\nu}_{qn}$ can be inserted into (120) and the quadrature presented by $\partial \phi_h / \partial x$ on S evaluated by converting the integral to a sum.

Appendix 4

Tangency condition on wetted surface (from [14])

The kinematic boundary condition on the wetted parts of the blade surface is that the resultant normal velocity in the body-fixed surface coordinate system should vanish; see equation (64) of text. The total fluid velocity may be written as a summation of the individual contributions as follows:

$$0 = \mathbf{n} \cdot \mathbf{V} = n \cdot (\mathbf{V}^\Gamma + \mathbf{V}^Q + \mathbf{V}^I + \mathbf{V}^B + \mathbf{V}^O)$$

$$\text{on the camber surface} \quad (123)$$

The superscripts Γ and Q denote the velocities induced by the vortices and cavity sources lying on the key blade and its wake, the superscript O denotes the velocity induced by the singularities lying on the other blades and wakes, the superscript B denotes the velocity induced by the sources representing blade thickness, and the superscript I denotes inflow velocity, including the ship wake and propeller rotational velocity. Applying equation (77), the induced velocity can be written as a summation of the contributions of each discrete singularity element representing the propeller and its wake and, hence, equation (123) may be rewritten for the (i,j)th control point

$$0 = \sum_{m=1}^{M} \sum_{n=1}^{N} K_{ijnm}^s \Gamma_{nm}^s + \sum_{n=1}^{Nw} K_{ijnm}^w \Gamma_{nm}^w \Big]$$

$$+ \sum_{m-1}^{M+1} \left[\sum_{n=1}^{N} K_{ijnm}^c \Gamma_{nm}^c + \sum_{n=1}^{N_w-1} K_{ijnm}^t \Gamma_{nm}^t \right]$$

$$+ \sum_{m=1}^{M} \sum_{n=1}^{N_Q} H_{ijnm} Q_{nm}$$

$$+ \mathbf{n}_{ij} \cdot [\mathbf{V}_{ij}^I + \mathbf{V}_{ij}^B + \mathbf{V}_{ij}^O] \quad (124)$$

where Γ_{nm} is the strength of discrete vortex element located at the nth chordwise and mth spanwise element, and the superscripts s,c,w and t stand for spanwise, chordwise, shed wake, and trailing vortices, respectively. The symbol Q_{nm} denotes the strength of line source element per unit length located at the (n,m)th element, and N_Q denotes the number of cavitating elements at each radial interval, which will be determined as a part of a solution to the boundary-value problem. The strength of the chordwise vortices is expressed by satisfying the principle of vortex conservation at each vortex lattice intersection. Thus, for the (n,m)th intersection

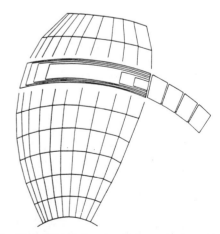

Fig. 21 Illustration of closed vorticies on blade and in wake

$$\Gamma^c_{nm} = \Gamma^s_{n,m-1} - \Gamma^s_{nm} + \Gamma^c_{n-1,m} = \sum_{l=1}^{n} \{\Gamma^s_{l,m-1} - \Gamma^s_{l,m}\} \tag{125}$$

Kelvin's theorem is applied to each chordwise panel of the blade and wake to determine the strength of the first shed vortex, the chordwise panel being the area between two adjacent chordwise vortex lines and their associated trailing vortices. The total circulation around the blade section and its shed wake must be zero; thus

$$\Gamma^w_{lm} = -\left\{\sum_{n=1}^{N}\Gamma^s_{nm} + \sum_{n=2}^{N_w}\Gamma^w_{nm}\right\} \tag{126}$$

Substituting equations (125) and (126) into (124), and rearranging the summations for the shed vortices, one obtains

$$\sum_{m=1}^{M}\left\{\sum_{n=1}^{N}\left[K^s_{ijnm} + \sum_{l=n}^{N}(K^c_{ijl(m+1)} - K^c_{ijlm})\right.\right.$$
$$\left.- K^w_{ijlm}\right]\Gamma^s_{nm} + \sum_{n=2}^{N_w}[K^w_{ij(n-1)m} + K^t_{ij(n-1)(m+1)}$$
$$\left.- K^t_{ij(n-1)m} - K^w_{ijnm}]T^{(t-n+1)}_m\right\}$$
$$+ \sum_{m=1}^{M}\sum_{n=1}^{N_Q}H_{ijnm}Q_{nm} = d_{ij} \tag{127}$$

where $T^{(t)}_m$ is the total circulation around the mth blade section at time t

$$T^{(t)}_m = \left\{\sum_{n=1}^{N}\Gamma^s_{nm}\right\}^{(t)} \tag{128}$$

where t is the time index for the present time step, and d_{ij} the following combination of known quantities:

$$d_{ij} = -\mathbf{n}_{ij}\cdot\{\mathbf{V}^I_{ij} + \mathbf{V}^B_{ij} + \mathbf{V}^O_{ij}\} \tag{129}$$

Focusing on one chordwise panel, it can be seen that the coefficient of Γ^s_{nm} represents the induced velocity by a closed vortex, which is composed of the (n,m)th spanwise vortex on the blade, the first shed vortex in the wake, and two chordwise vortices connecting the ends of the spanwise vortex and first shed vortex as shown schematically in Fig. 21. The coefficient of $T_m(t-n+1)$ represents the velocity induced by shed vortex quadrilaterals at time $(t-n+1)$. It should be noticed that Kelvin's conservation-of-vorticity theorem is satisfied automatically by the closed-vortex structures. It seems natural to introduce another notation for closed vortices and, hence, equation (127) can be rewritten

$$\sum_{n=1}^{M}\sum_{n=1}^{N}{}^wK^\square_{ijnm}\Gamma_{nm} + \sum_{m=1}^{M}\sum_{n=1}^{N_Q}{}^wH_{ijnm}Q_{nm}$$
$$= d_{ij} - \sum_{m=1}^{M}\sum_{n=2}^{N_w}{}^wK^{\square w}_{ijnm}T^{(t-n+1)}_m \tag{130}$$

where the left superscript w is introduced to distinguish the normal component of induced velocites from the tangential component that will be defined later.

Appendix 5

Kinematic condition on cavity surface (from [14])

In order to derive the equation for the kinematic boundary condition (65) on the cavity surface, we will define a system of curvilinear coordinates (ξ, η, ζ) which is useful in dealing with quantities on or near the camber surface. We define that the ξ-coordinate be the intersection of the camber surface and a cylindrical surface concentric with the x-axis and positive when pointing downstream. The ζ-coordinate is defined to be normal to the camber surface and positive when pointing upstream. The η-coordinate is defined on the camber surface to complete the orthogonality of the coordinate system; therefore, it is positive when pointing toward the tip of the blade of a right-handed propeller.

Since the singularities will be distributed on the camber surface, $\zeta = 0$, this coordinate system is particularly convenient to represent the local singularity effects; the tangential velocity jump due to vorticity is in the ξ-η plane, and the normal velocity jump due to the source is in the ζ-direction.

Let us define the ζ-coordinate of the cavity surface by $g(\xi, \eta, t)$. The exact kinematic boundary condition can be derived by requiring that the substantial derivative of the quantity $F(\xi, \eta, \zeta, t) = \zeta - g(\xi, \eta, t)$ vanish on the cavity surface, that is

$$DF/Dt = (\partial/\partial t + \mathbf{V}\cdot\nabla)(\zeta - g) = 0 \tag{131}$$

After differentiating, we obtain the exact equation for the kinematic boundary condition

$$U_3 + w = \partial g/\partial t + (U_1 + u)\partial g/\partial\xi + (U_2 + v)\,\partial g/\partial\eta,$$
$$\text{on } \zeta = g(\xi, \eta, t) \tag{132}$$

where (U_1, U_2, U_3) and (u, v, w) are the inflow and induced velocities, respectively, in the (ξ, η, ζ)-directions.

We define the helical inflow velocity, U_r, as

$$U_r = \sqrt{\overline{V}^2_A(r) + (\omega r)^2} \tag{133}$$

where $\overline{V}_A(r)$ is the longitudinal inflow velocity averaged over one propeller revolution and ω is the radian rotational velocity of the propeller. Under these assumptions, the geometric quantities such as angle of attack of the section, camber ratio, and thickness ratio are small. Chordwise fluctuations in the incoming flow will be assumed to be small compared with U_r, and spanwise velocities will be neglected. Gusts or perturbations normal to the camber surface will be taken into account. Hence, we may write

$$U = U_r, U_2 = 0, U_3 = w_g \tag{134}$$

where w_g denotes the gust. The perturbation velocities are assumed to be small accordingly and, hence, higher-order terms in equation (132) can be neglected to result in a linearized kinematic boundary condition equation

$$w_g + w = \partial g/\partial t + U_r\partial g/\partial\xi, \quad \text{on } \zeta = 0 \tag{135}$$

The assumption of small thickness allows the boundary condition to be applied on the camber surface, $\zeta = 0$, consistent with the linearization.

Let us define the cavity thickness, $h(\xi, \eta, t)$, in terms of the cavity surface and the camber surface, $f(\xi, \eta)$:

$$h(\xi, \eta, t) = g(\xi, \eta, t) - f(\xi, \eta) \tag{136}$$

If we apply equation (135) to the upper and lower surface of the cavity, and if we introduce the source density $q(\xi, \eta, t)$ as the velocity jump across the cavity thickness, then, for the cavity thickness, the following relation is secured:

$$q(\xi, \eta, t) = \partial h/\partial t + U_r\partial h/\partial\xi \quad \text{on } \zeta = 0 \tag{137}$$

Appendix 6

Cavity closure condition (from [14])

The closure condition (66) for the cavity states that the cavity

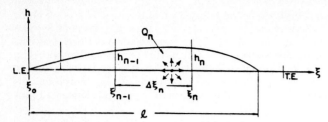

Fig. 22 Illustration of cavity thickness form

thickness be zero along the leading and trailing edges of the cavity, and also along the inner (hub) and outer (tip) boundaries of the cavity. This condition can be stated in the discretized space by

$$h_0 = 0, \ h_L = 0 \qquad (138)$$

where the subscripts 0 and L are indices for the leading and trailing edges of cavity, respectively.

In order to derive an expression for the cavity closure condition, it is first necessary to recast equation (137) into a discretized form, that is, for the (n,j)th element, omitting the radial index j for simplicity, unless otherwise required for clarity:

$$q_n = \frac{\bar{h}_n - \bar{h}_n{}^{(t-1)}}{\Delta t} + U_r \frac{h_n - h_{n-1}}{\Delta \xi_n}$$

$$\bar{h}_n = \frac{h_n + h_{n-1}}{2} \qquad (139)$$

where h_n is the cavity thickness at the panel boundary as shown in Fig. 22, $\Delta \xi_n$ is the chord length of the element, and the superscript $(t-1)$ denotes the previous time step. The quantities at the present time will be described without the superscript.

To simplify the manipulation, we introduce notations

$$\begin{aligned} R_n &= \Delta \xi_n / 2 U_r \Delta t \\ Q_n &= q_n \Delta \xi_n \cos\epsilon \end{aligned} \qquad (140)$$

where Q_n is the strength of line source element, consistent with the definition used in the main text, and ϵ is the tilted angle of line source relative to the η-coordinate. Equation (139) is now rearranged to result in the recurrence formula for the cavity thickness

$$h_n = \frac{1 - R_n}{1 + R_n} h_{n-1} + \frac{1}{1 + R_n} \frac{Q_n}{U_r} \sec\epsilon$$
$$+ \frac{F R_n}{1 + R_n} (h_n + h_{n-1})^{(t-1)} \qquad (141)$$

where a factor F is introduced to account for the relative position of the cavity trailing end at the previous time step with respect to the spanwise boundaries of the element. This factor is defined as follows (referring to Fig. 23):

$$F = \begin{cases} \dfrac{l^{(t-1)} - \xi_{n-1}}{\Delta \xi_n} & , & \text{for} & (a) \\ 0 & , & \text{for} & (b) \\ 1 & , & \text{for} & (c) \end{cases} \qquad (142)$$

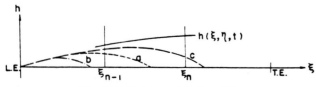

Fig. 23 Sketch for definition of F

where $l^{(t-1)}$ is the cavity length at the previous time step.

Recursive use of the thickness formula (141), together with the closure condition relations (138), after tedious algebraic work, will result in a numerical closure condition equation in discretized form:

$$\sum_{n=1}^{L-1} \left(\prod_{k=n+1}^{L} \frac{1 - R_k}{1 + R_k} \right) \cdot \frac{1}{1 + R_n} \cdot \frac{Q_n}{U_r} \sec\epsilon + \frac{1}{1 + R_L} \cdot \frac{Q_L}{U_r} \sec\epsilon$$

$$= \begin{cases} -\displaystyle\sum_{n=1}^{L-1} \left(\prod_{k=n+1}^{L} \frac{1 - R_k}{1 + R_k} \right) \cdot \frac{R_n}{1 + R_n} (h_n + h_{n-1})^{(t-1)} \\ \qquad - F \cdot \dfrac{R_L}{1 + R_L} \cdot h_{L-1}{}^{(t-1)} \ \dots\dots \ \text{for } L^{(t-1)} = L \\ \qquad \text{where } F = \dfrac{l^{(t-1)} - l_{L-1}}{\Delta \xi_L}, \\[2ex] -\displaystyle\sum_{n=1}^{L^{(t-1)}} \left(\prod_{k=n+1}^{L} \frac{1 - R_k}{1 + R_k} \right) \cdot \frac{F \cdot R_n}{1 + R_n} (h_n + h_{n-1})^{(t-1)} \\ \qquad\qquad \dots\dots \ \text{for } L^{(t-1)} < L \\ \qquad \text{where } F = \begin{cases} 1 & \text{for } n < L^{(t-1)} \\ \dfrac{l^{(t-1)} - l_{L^{(t-1)}} - 1}{\Delta \xi_{L^{(t-1)}}} & \text{for } n = L^{(t-1)} \end{cases} \\[3ex] -\displaystyle\sum_{n=1}^{L-1} \left(\prod_{k=n+1}^{L} \frac{1 - R_k}{1 + R_k} \right) \cdot \frac{R_n}{1 + R_n} (h_n + h_{n-1})^{(t-1)} \\ \qquad - \dfrac{R_L}{1 + R_L} (h_L + h_{L-1})^{(t-1)} \ \dots\dots \ \text{for } L^{(t-1)} > L \end{cases} \qquad (143)$$

where $L^{(t-1)}$ is the number of the cavitating elements at the previous time step along the chordwise strip of interest.

To facilitate further manipulation, it may be found convenient to rewrite equation (143) in the form

$$\sum_{n=1}^{L} \lambda_n Q_n = \lambda_R \qquad (144)$$

where λ_R is the abbreviated notation of the right-hand side of equation (143) and

$$\lambda_n = \begin{cases} \left(\displaystyle\prod_{k=n+1}^{L} \frac{1 - R_k}{1 + R_k} \right) \frac{1}{1 + R_n} \cdot \frac{\sec\epsilon}{U_r} & \text{for } n \le L - 1 \\[2ex] \dfrac{1}{1 + R_L} \cdot \dfrac{\sec\epsilon}{U_r} & \text{for } n = L \end{cases} \qquad (145)$$

It should be noted that this closure condition is applied to each chordwise strip.

Appendix 7

Dynamic condition on cavity surface (from [14])

The linearized form of Bernoulli's equation, applicable to each chordwise strip, can be written as

$$p - p_\infty = \rho \frac{\partial \phi}{\partial t} - \rho u U_r - \rho g y_0 \qquad (146)$$

where ϕ is the perturbation potential, y_0 is the vertical coordinate fixed on ship measured positive upward from the shaft center, and p_∞ is the pressure at infinity upstream at the depth of the shaft center.

We will use a backward difference formula for the time rate of change of the velocity, that is

$$\frac{\partial \phi}{\partial t} = \frac{1}{\Delta t} (\phi - \phi^{(t-1)}) \qquad (147)$$

Equation (146) may then be written in a form

$$= \frac{\rho}{\Delta t}\phi - \rho u U_r - (p - p_\infty) = -\frac{\rho}{\Delta t}\phi^{(t-1)} + \rho g y_0 \quad (148)$$

The streamwise component of induced velocity, u, in the left-hand side of equation (148) is expressed as linear functions of the strengths of vortices and sources, in a manner similar to what was done for the normal component in equation (124). Therefore, the expression for the streamwise component of induced velocity at the (i,j)th control point is written as

$$u_{ij} = \sum_{n,m} {}^u K_{ijm}^{\square} \Gamma_{nm}^s + \sum_{n,m} {}^u H_{ijnm} Q_{nm} + u_{ij}{}^O \quad (149)$$

where the coefficients of Γ_{nm}^s and Q_{nm} are defined as in equation (130) with the left superscript, u, denoting the streamwise component of induced velocity, and $u_{ij}{}^O$ is the streamwise component of induced velocity due to singularities other than those on the key blade.

The potential at the (i,j)th control point along the suction side of the blade may be written as

$$\phi_{ij} = \phi_{ij}^\Gamma + \phi_{ij}^Q + \phi_{ij}^O \quad (150)$$

where $\phi^\Gamma{}_{ij}$ is the odd part of the velocity potential across the camber surface, which is approximated by

$$\phi_{ij}^\Gamma = \frac{1}{2}\sum_{n=1}^i \Gamma_{nj}^s \quad (151)$$

ϕ_{ij}^Q is the cavity-induced potential and may be written as

$$\phi_{ij}^Q = \sum_{n,m} \phi_{ijnm} Q_{nm} \quad (152)$$

where ϕ_{ijnm} is the potential due to a unit source element; ϕ_{ij}^O is the potential due to the cavity sources on the other blades and is computed much the same way as ϕ_{ij}^Q.

Substitution of equations (149) through (152) into (148) leads to the following result for the (i,j)th control point

$$-\frac{\rho}{\Delta t}\left\{\frac{1}{2}\sum_{n=1}^i \Gamma_{nj}^s + \sum_{m=1}^M \sum_{n=1}^{N_Q} \phi_{ijnm} Q_{nm}\right\}$$
$$- \rho U_r \left\{\sum_{m=1}^M \sum_{n=1}^N {}^u K_{ijnm}^\square \Gamma_{nm}^s\right.$$
$$\left.+ \sum_{m=1}^M \sum_{n=1}^{N_Q} {}^u H_{ijnm} Q_{nm}\right\}$$
$$- (p - p_\infty) = e_{ij} \quad (153)$$

The right-hand side containing all the known terms will be defined as

$$e_{ij} = -\frac{\rho}{\Delta t}\left(\phi_{ij}^{\Gamma(t-1)} + \phi_{ij}^{Q(t-1)}\right) + \frac{\rho}{\Delta t}\left(\phi_{ij}^O - \phi_{ij}^{O(t-1)}\right)$$
$$+ \rho g y_0 + \rho u_{ij}^O U_r \quad (154)$$

Formation of the simultaneous equations (from [14])

Equations (130), (144) and (153), derived from the boundary conditions, must be solved simultaneously with a suitable choice of control points. However, equation (153), the dynamic boundary condition on the cavity, should be applied only to the cavitating region, whose extent is not known á priori. Hence, iterative techniques must be used to determine the cavity extent. Since we assumed that the cavity starts at the leading edge, the task is now to determine the spanwise and chordwise extent of the cavity. The iterative procedures to find the cavity extent are very long and time-consuming. It is found to be efficient to consider the unknowns in one chordwise strip at a time. The procedure reduces the size of the matrix. The cavity length is determined for the chordwise strip being considered. Then spanwise strip-by-strip iteration becomes necessary to update the interactions of the adjacent strips. These two steps were described in detail in Section 3.

Let us assume that we are solving the problems for the jth chordwise strip with assumed N_Q cavitating elements, and that the values on the other strips are known from previous calculations. Then equation (130) may be rewritten for the jth strip

$$\sum_{n=1}^N {}^w K_{ijnj}^\square \Gamma_{nj}^s + \sum_{n=1}^{N_Q} {}^w H_{ijnj} Q_{nj} = d_{ij}, \quad \text{for } i = 1, \dots, N \quad (155)$$

where d_{ij} is the combination of known contributions, especially including the influence from adjacent strips. Equation (153) may also be rewritten, for the jth strip, with a slight rearrangement

$$-\frac{\rho}{2\Delta t}\sum_{n=1}^i \Gamma_{nj}^s - \rho U_r \sum_{n=1}^N {}^u K_{ijnj}^\square \Gamma_{nj}^s - (p - p_\infty)$$
$$- \sum_{n=1}^{N_Q}\left(\frac{\rho}{\Delta t}\phi_{ijnj} + \rho U_r {}^u H_{ijnj}\right) Q_{nj} = \tilde{e}_{ij}$$
$$\text{for } i = 1, 2, \dots, N_Q \quad (156)$$

where $\tilde{e}_{ij}$ is again defined for convenience as in d_{ij}. Equations (155), (144) and (156) are sufficient to determine $I = N + 1 + N_Q$ unknowns, which are composed of N unknown strengths of vortices, N_Q unknown strengths of sources, and a pressure inside the cavity. A set of simultaneous equations may take the familiar form

$$\sum_{q=1}^I a_{pq} x_q = b_p, \quad \text{for } p = 1, 2, \dots, I \quad (157)$$

where a_{pq} is the coefficient matrix obtained by suitably arranging coefficients of Γ_{nj}^s, $(p - p_\infty)$, and Q_{nj} from equations (155), (144) and (156), x_q is the qth unknown of a vector

$$\mathbf{x} = \{\Gamma_{1j}^s, \Gamma_{2j}^s, \dots, \Gamma_{Nj}^s (p - p_\infty), Q_{1j}, Q_{2j}, \dots, Q_{N_Qj}\}^T \quad (158)$$

and b_p is the pth element of a vector composed of the right-hand sides of equations (155), (144) and (156), respectively. The solution to this matrix equation is straightforward, at least conceptually!

(Discussion follows overleaf)

Discussion

Paul Kaplan, Member

This paper is interesting and informative, as we would expect from this group of well-known authors. The main task that they have set out to accomplish is quite difficult, namely, to establish a three-dimensional calculation method for an unsteady cavitating propeller in the presence of a ship hull, and the fact that they have managed to achieve some correlation of theory with experiment is certainly commendable. However, there are certain features of the theoretical approach which do raise some questions.

Whenever a comparison is made with a pressure measurement on a hull, there are two different elements that contribute to the calculated value; that is, the free space pressure (and appropriate image contributions) as well as the interaction due to the presence of the hull in the propeller flow field. Each of these elements has to be correctly modeled in order to obtain a correct predicted hull pressure value, although it is also possible that both are in error yet result in a correct overall answer due to compensating effects. A natural question arises as to the necessity of using the effective wake as the inflow velocity field in order to obtain good cavity region outlines with the PUF-3 program, when conventional propeller theories use only the nominal wake. Is there any other basis to demonstrate that this method of using an effective wake inflow velocity would improve the correlation of other predicted propeller results for noncavitated propellers by the MIT theory, or is the agreement on cavity extent on the blades the only reason? A consistent approach should manifest itself throughout the entire range of utility of any theory.

The method of solution of the hull boundary-value problem by replacing it by an equivalent interior Dirichlet problem is an ingenious method that allows solutions for either of the two free-surface boundary conditions being considered (zero pressure or the rigid-wall condition). As far as what free-surface boundary condition is appropriate for the SSPA tunnel, I agree with the point of view expressed in the paper that the rigid-wall condition is more suitable. A description of a two-dimensional method of solution for this same type of problem is given in reference [23] (additional references follow some discussions), with the discussion of that paper also considering the question of the appropriate free-surface boundary conditions for test facilities such as that at SSPA although no numerical illustrations or comparison with experiments are given there.

All of the procedures described in the paper represent the present methods for determining three-dimensional solutions for the pressure on a ship hull due to an IC propeller. While the correlation presented is only limited to a single ship case, the authors should be encouraged to continue their work and apply it to other possible cases in order to provide further validations of their methods. At the same time, consideration should also be given to the use of other procedures, such as the method of reference [6] combined with [23] herewith which is computationally simpler since some aspects involve two-dimensional methods. Since the basic objective is to be able to predict the hull pressures due to IC propellers in an early design stage, there may be a number of available methods that can be applied for that purpose which should be considered by our profession.

Additional references

23 Kaplan, P., Bentson, J., and Benatar, M., "Analytical Prediction of Pressures and Forces on a Ship Hull Due to Cavitating Propellers," paper presented at the Fourteenth Symposium on Naval Hydrodynamics, The University of Michigan, Ann Arbor, Aug. 1982.

Torben Munk,[8] Visitor

This excellent paper has been read with great interest at the Danish Ship Research Laboratory (SL). In particular, the description of the very complicated theory behind the calculation method and the demonstration of the criterion for obtaining pressure amplitudes at the higher harmonics, which are greater than the first-order pressure, is found most admirable. It would be interesting to know if this latter has been verified by calculation for actual propeller wake combinations.

The description of the model test results and the comparison with the calculated results are remarkably open and therefore show clearly the very complicated nature of these matters. In the comparison of the model test results with the full-scale results, the results shown in Fig. 9 are specially surprising. It is seen that both the full-scale and the model test results show rather a lot of scatter, which is not in agreement with the experience at SL. In several cases we have found very stable full-scale results when the measurements were performed in calm weather. The presence of waves may, however, cause some variations in the results. We agree that the model-scale results may contain rather a lot of scatter but, according to our experience, this may to some extent be remedied by a careful control of the content of free gas nuclei in the tunnel water. Small differences of the blade geometry may also cause variations of the pressures, but this phenomenon may be avoided if the recording of the signals is limited to the time intervals when a specific blade passes the cavitation zone.

Another surprising point is the disagreement between the model-scale results and the full-scale results, which is also seen in Fig. 9. In our opinion this may be due to the fact that the steel plates of a ship will reflect the incoming signals nearly totally, while this is not the case for a glass fiber reinforced polyester ship model according to tests carried out at SL. It is possible to show that the theoretical factor, with which signals received on a model should be multiplied before making a comparison with signals received on a ship hull, is about 1.65. We wonder if this is taken into account in the results in Fig. 9. If not, it will certainly improve the correlation considerably, at least for the three lowest orders of the blade frequency. Regarding the higher orders, it is mentioned that phase modulation in model scale may reduce the pressure amplitudes. At the same time it should be mentioned that resonance of the steel structure in the ship may increase the pressure impulses at the higher orders in full scale. This can be shown if accelerometers are mounted on the ship hull alongside the pressure transducers.

The SSPA practice of using only the highest 5 percent of the results is, in our opinion, also causing some confusion in the interpretation of Table 3. It is not mentioned whether the calculated results are compared with mean values of the tests, or with the 5 percent values described earlier, or whether the possibly reduced reflection at the model is taken into account. A clarification of this may perhaps lead to an explanation of the fact that the extent of cavitation is larger in the calculations than in the tests, while the opposite is the case for the pressure impulses.

We agree fully with the suggestions for future work, but would like to include further investigation into the dynamics of the cavitation bubble itself.

Finally, we would like to express our appreciation of the important work carried out by the authors and to thank them for an open, thorough and interesting paper.

[8] Danish Ship Research Laboratory, Lyngby, Denmark.

Michael Wilson, Member

[The views expressed herein are the opinions of the discusser and not necessarily those of the Department of Defense or the Department of the Navy.]

There is a great deal of interesting and important work represented in this landmark paper. We are indebted to the authors for their sophisticated assault on this problem, joining two main analytical tools available from separate research efforts, and combining the predictions with results from careful water tunnel experiments.

My remark centers on a point about the comparative results for periodic pressure pulse amplitudes shown in Table 3. Displayed there are results for two different assumptions of the waterline boundary condition: rigid and free surface (or pressure-relief). The calculations with the rigid plane assumption here certainly seem to produce pressure pulse results that are closer to the tunnel-measured values than with the pressure-relief assumption. However, the discrepancies evident in these comparisons may be due to a physical effect involving the actual water tunnel upper boundary, not necessarily only the effect of differences in the analytical boundary conditions on the accuracy of the calculation method. Specifically, the structural response of the wood plate cover will be characterized by neither a free surface nor a rigid plane. The compliance of the plate and its mounting will enter the problem. The net hydrodynamic boundary condition will involve the vibration impedance of the fluid loaded plating system, which means that at least the density, elastic modulus, and plate thickness could influence the magnitudes of the pressure pulses. Unfortunately I cannot provide even a guess about the magnitude of this plate compliance effect, or whether it is even significant enough to show up in either analytical result or experiments. However, it may be noted that this type of physical influence could be important to the phase angles as well as the pressure amplitudes.

Is it known why the calculation scheme had trouble with the other propeller, P1842? Was it a skewed propeller? Is this symptomatic of a limitation on the generality of the entire scheme?

In his discussion of the Huse/Guoqiang paper earlier in this volume, Dr. Johnsson has noted that a correction scheme for pressure pulse amplitudes obtained in water tunnel experiments is under development that depends on the submergence depth of the pressure transducer and on the Froude number. Can this empirical correction approach be reconciled with the results of the present calculation method, especially with respect to Froude number or speed effect?

H. Tanibayashi,[9] Visitor

The authors are to be commended for their comprehensive study to develop a rational procedure for prediction of hull pressures arising from propeller cavitation, loading and thickness. The discusser fully agrees with the authors in that only an orthodox approach to the problem will give us a key for radical improvement in predicting propeller excitation, which takes growing importance nowadays.

Now having understood that the objective of this paper is essentially a progress report of theoretical and experimental research efforts of internationally colloborating institutions, the discusser would like to ask the authors' opinion from the viewpoint of practical application of the present achievements.

1. There have been proposed several methods for predicting propeller-induced fluctuating pressures. Almost all of them claim that "his" method of prediction, though not purely

theoretical but usually including some empirical factor or correction (that is, not purely theoretical), yields good correlation with the experimental measurements. Figure 24 accompanying this discussion shows plots of theoretical versus experimental fluctuating pressures obtained from some of the papers presenting the method, where O shows full-scale data and ● shows model data (see references [24–26] following this discussion and [3] and [6] of text). Figure 25 shows the same type of plot from Table 3 of the present paper. Comparing both figures, it is difficult to find a clear difference in the degree of agreement between theory and experiment. The discusser would like to ask the authors in this context how the present method compares with those proposed previously.

2. Looking at Fig. 9, which illustrates comparison of model and full-scale normalized pressure fluctuations, it is found that the difference between model and full scale is considerably larger than the mean values. If the 5 percent large amplitudes represent the model values, how should we consider the correlation between the computed and the model cavity behaviors as shown in Fig. 13?

Additional references

24 Tanibayashi, H., "The Propeller-Induced Vibratory Forces—State of the Art," Symposium on Ship Vibration and Noise, Society of Naval Architects of Japan, 1980 (in Japanese).
25 Fitzsimmons, P. A., "Cavitation Induced Hull Pressure: A Comparison of Analytical Results, Ship and Model Measurements," Symposium on Propeller Induced Ship Vibration, RINA, 1979.
26 Chiba, N., Sasajima, T., and Hoshino, T., "Prediction of Propeller-Induced Fluctuating Pressures and Correlation with Full Scale Data," 13th Symposium on Naval Hydrodynamics, ONR, 1980.

W.-H. Isay,[10] Visitor

The authors give an impressive and complete theoretical approach to predict the propeller-induced vibratory pressure amplitudes on ship hulls. This is an old and persistent problem of great practical importance. The reason for the permanent research activities in this field is the fact that nobody at present is able to give purely theoretically a correct prediction of the pressure amplitudes induced on a hull by a cavitating propeller. Therefore further theoretical and experimental research work is needed to solve the problem.

Naturally, also, the scientific staff at the Institute of Shipbuilding (Hamburg University) and at the Hamburg Model Basin (HSVA) are concerned with this problem. A paper concerning quite the same problems as treated by the German authors was presented at the annual meeting of the German Society of Naval Architects in Berlin in November 1982 [27]. In this paper the calculation of the pressure distribution is made by combining propeller design methods and hydrofoil theory developed by Chao [28]. To get the unsteady cavitation pattern we apply an extended version of a singularity method for partially and fully cavitating hydrofoils [29–32].

Comparing the SNAME paper and reference [27] herewith, it can be stated that the theory of the present authors has the advantage of being fully three dimensional and can be applied to every wake geometry and blade form. A propeller calculation using two-dimensional hydrofoil theory with correction factors [27] remains, however, an approximation.

Nevertheless, the foundation of a method to calculate the cavitation pattern of propeller blades is an accurate knowledge of the pressure distribution in the noncavitating state. Did the authors compare the results of their theory with experimental data published during the past four years, for example, in Japan [33–35]? We also were concerned with this question and we found out that the cavity geometry and extent on a propeller blade depend strongly on the pressure distribution. I have some

---

[9] Nagasaki Experimental Tank, Mitsubishi Heavy Industries, Ltd., Nagasaki, Japan.

[10] Institute of Shipbuilding, University of Hamburg, Germany.

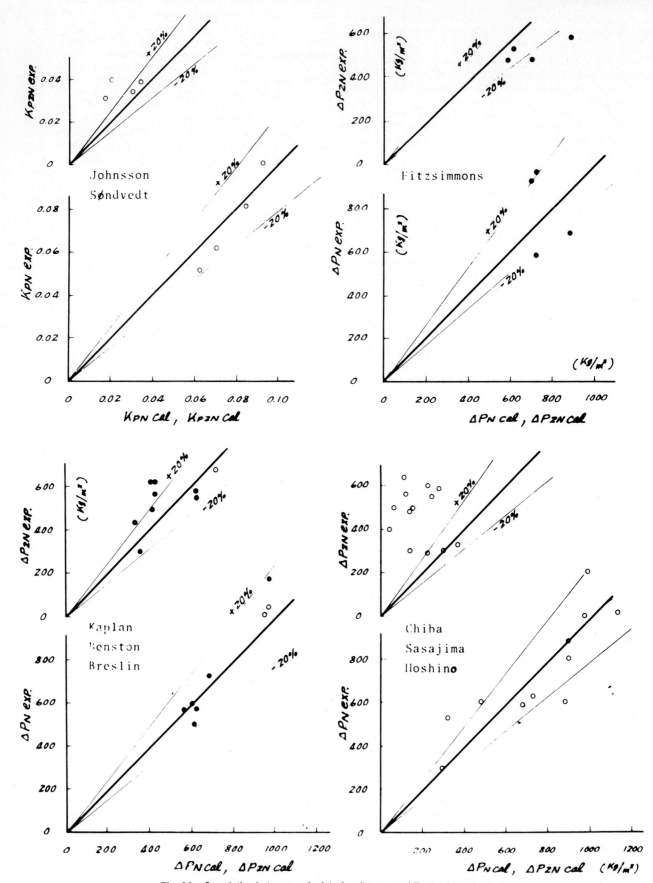

Fig. 24 Correlation between calculated and measured fluctuating pressures

Theoretical and Experimental Propeller-Induced Hull Pressures

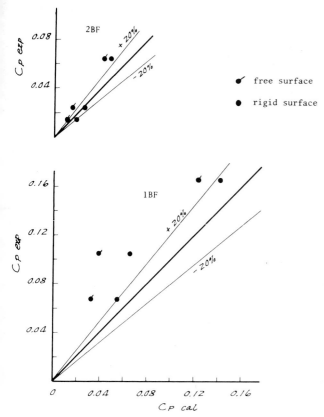

Fig. 25 Correlation between calculated and measured fluctuating pressures

doubt that it is sufficient to consider only the result calculated by assuming potential flow. In a ship's wake, certainly turbulence and boundary-layer effects will play an important role.

The three-dimensional finite-element method applied by the authors to calculate the cavity geometry certainly has advantages in comparison with classical propeller-lifting-surface methods, because this theory applied to cavitating propellers leads to a very complicated system of coupled integral equations for the additional (due to the influence of cavitation) vortex and source distributions. Looking at the authors' numerical calculations, the question arises whether they can give some example as to how strong the results depend on the number of elements used for the mathematical modeling and on the geometrical position of these elements. This question would also be of interest in connection with Prof. Van Houten's results [36] for the cavitation pattern of unsteady loaded hydrofoils. I have some doubt that the influence of the aspect ratio is calculated correctly, because it is physically unrealistic, according to hydrofoil theory, for the differences between the cavity values for length and volume obtained for $AR = 1$ and $AR = 10$ to be of the same order as between $AR = 10$ and $AR = 100$ [36].

Looking at the authors theory to calculate the unsteady hull pressure amplitudes, I must say that this theory has reached a rather high level, because their method is able to treat exactly the complicated mixed boundary-value problem, that is, the rigid-wall condition on the hull and the free water surface condition for high Froude number outside the hull.

Additional references

27 Alwardt, P., Chao, K. Y., Isay, W. H., and Westphal, N., "Berechnung der Druckverteilung, der Kavitationserscheinungen sowie der induzierten Druckschwankungen an der Außenhaut für Propeller im Nachstrom," *Jahrb. d. Schiffbautechn. Ges.*, Bd. 76, 1982.

28 Chao, K. Y., "Entwicklung eines praktikablen EDV-Programms zur Berechnung von Druckschwankungen an der Schiffsaußenhaut infolge kavitierender Propeller im Nachstrom und einige Berechnungsergebnisse, HSVA-Bericht Nr. 1525, 1982.

29 Isay, W. H., *Kavitation, Schiffahrtsverlag "Hansa,"* C. Schroedter & Co. Hamburg, 1981.

30 Alwardt, P. and Isay, W. H., "Zur Behandlung der Teilkavitation an Flügeln mit Methoden der Profiltheorie," Bericht-Nr. 399, Inst. f. Schiffbau, Univ. Hamburg, 1980; *Z. angew. Math. Mech.*, No. 62, 1982.

31 Gasau, H., "Zur Behandlung der stationären Teil- und Superkavitation an Tragflügelprofilen, Ber. Nr. 416, Inst. f. Schiffbau, Universität Hamburg, 1982.

32 Alwardt, P., "Beitrag zur Berechnung von instationären Kavitationserscheinungen am Tragflügel und Schiffspropeller; Ber. Inst. f. Schiffbau, Univ. Hamburg, 1983.

33 Hoshino, T., "A Method to Predict Fluctuating Pressures Induced by a Cavitating Propeller, "Mitsubishi Technical Bulletin No. 150, 1982.

34 Takahshi, M., and Oku, M., "The Cavitation Characteristics of MAU-Type Propeller," *Naval Architecture and Ocean Engineering*, Vol. 17, 1979.

35 Takei, Y., Koyama, K., and Kurobe, Y., "Measurement of Pressures on a Blade of a Propeller Model," Paper No. 55, Ship Research Inst. Tokyo, 1979.

36 Van Houten, R. J., "The Numerical Prediction of Unsteady Sheet Cavitation on High Aspect Ratio Hydrofoils, *Proceedings*, 14th Symposium on Naval Hydrodynamics, Ann Arbor, 1982.

R. Verbeek,[11] Visitor

One of the main problems in the prediction of propeller-induced pressures lies in the calculation of the cavities. The cavity calculation in turn is strongly affected by the wake field used in the calculation process. Errors in the measured wake field affect the predicted cavities and thus the predicted pressure pulses.

We observed that for a certain case variations of wake field velocities caused far more than proportional variations in pressure pulses, especially when the errors in the wake field are located in the region where cavitation on the propeller occurs. Therefore, not only a reliable model for the effective wake must be developed, but also the measurement of the nominal wake field should be as accurate as possible, especially in those regions where cavitation on the propeller occurs. In their calculations the authors used the method of Huang and Groves for the prediction of the effective wake. Has the effect of wake field on the resulting pressure pulses been investigated by the application of different effective wake field prediction methods?

For design purposes a quick, reliable method as used by Noordzij and Kaplan is preferable.

Considering the good results achieved, this method can, certainly in the first stages of the propeller design, be used as a predictor of the resulting pressure fluctuations. In Fig. 26 herewith a comparison is shown between measured pressure pulses in several towing tanks and calculated pressure pulses using this method and a computer program used by Lips [37].

After finalization of the design, more sophisticated methods such as the one presented herein can be used.

Could the authors give some indication of the amount of computer time needed for an analysis such as the one presented in the paper?

Additional reference

37 Verbeek, R., Wiegant, W., and van Oirschot, P., "Prediction of Hull Pressure Fluctuations for Propeller Design Purposes," *Schiff und Hafen*, Oct. 1982.

[11] Lips Propeller Works, Drunen, The Netherlands.

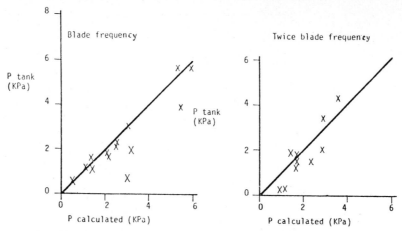

Fig. 26 Comparison of calculations with tank results (five different ships)

Fred Stern, Member

I believe that the amount of cavitation predicted in the example calculation may be excessive. Fig. 19 of the paper shows a maximum cavity volume of $\sim$0.3 m³ (10 ft³), which means a 0.15-m-thick (6 in.) cavity covering one third of the blade. Unfortunately, experimental data for the cavity thickness or volume variation are not available for comparison. Would the authors comment on some of the difficulties in obtaining these data and when they will become routinely available? Would the authors comment on the influence of the amplitude of the harmonics of the cavity volume (or volume velocity) on the amplitude of the predicted hull surface pressures (as is well known, this relationship is linear in the "free-space/factor of 2" method)? Using the "free-space/factor of 2" method and the fifth harmonic of the cavity volume velocity from Table 6 a value of $K_p = 0.22$ is obtained for comparison with the blade frequency result ($K_p = 0.141$) shown in Fig. 10. Would the authors comment on whether it is free-surface pressure relief effects or hull reflection factors of <2 (or both) which cause this reduction in K_p? Lastly, in an earlier paper, Dr. Breslin has shown hull reflection factors >2 for regions of the hull of concave curvature shielded from the free surface. Was this effect also found in the present study?

Additional reference

38 Breslin, J., "Propeller-Induced Hull Pressures and Forces," *Proceedings*, 3rd International Conference on Numerical Ship Hydrodynamics, Paris, 1981.

Erling Huse, Member

The authors are to be congratulated on a very interesting and well-written paper. Especially they should be commended on their very stringent mathematical formulations.

The paper represents another brave attempt at calculating cavity geometry as well as pressure fluctuations induced on the afterbody by the cavitating propeller. Like several other recent publications, this one also ends up with a fairly satisfactory correlation between theoretical calculation and experiments. This correlation was not achieved at the first attempt, however, but only after some correction of the wake input data. Other recent publications have also obtained good correlation but without correcting the wake. In my opinion we still have a long way to go until we can predict cavity geometry theoretically at a reasonable level of accuracy. There are still a lot of physical phenomena involved in the cavitation process that we do not account for in a proper way in our theoretical predictions. First of all there is, as shown in the paper, a question of

effective wake or the interaction between wake distribution and propeller in operating condition. Secondly, the scale effect of the wake distribution still represents a considerable unknown source of error. Thirdly, the paper assumes that the cavitating flow field will be uniquely characterized by the cavitation number and the Froude number. I would like to add that the Reynolds number can also be very important to the cavitation phenomena and this is an effect that is not taken into account at all in the paper. In conclusion I would suggest that one make certain reservations as to the general validity of the apparent correlation achieved in this case.

My second comment is on the statement on page 134 that "... it is the opinion of the senior author that the rigid boundary condition imposed by the test procedure at the SSPA as well as in other cavitation tunnels can give rise to bias, and apparently does so, if the free water surface is closed to the pressure transducers." I would like to ask what is the opinion of the other three authors on this matter. Personally I certainly agree with the senior author.

My last comment is on the statement on page 135 that a simple pulsating point source can be a representative model only when the field point is not close to the propeller. I would very much like to see a quantification of what the authors mean by "not close to." In cases of serious vibrations, which often mean very pronounced volume variation of cavities in the upper part of the propeller disk, the single pulsating source is in my opinion not only a simple but also a quite valid representation of the main features of the cavitation-induced surface force.

Authors' Closure

The authors would like to thank the discussers for the interest they have shown in our paper and for their thoughtful comments on it.

Mr. Munk's first remark is that the scatter (or time variations) of the model and full-scale amplitudes in the example given in the paper is larger than he is used to. Particularly in the full-scale case there is no reason to believe that results of Swedish measurements should behave differently than the corresponding Danish results. Thus a good guess would be that the main reason for the different behavior is that the signals from the transducers are analyzed in different ways in the two laboratories.

The diagrams in Fig. 27 with this closure illustrate how large the influence of the analysis method can be. These diagrams apply to model tests in the SSPA cavitation tunnel. The diagrams show the results of pressure fluctuation measurements

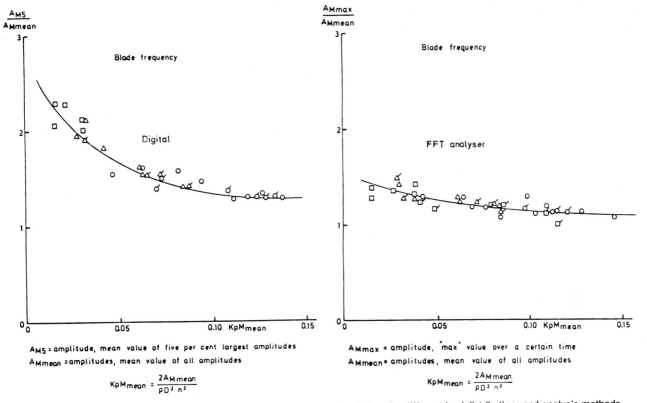

Fig. 27 Amplitudes of pressure fluctuations. Magnitude of temporal variations for different load distributions and analysis methods

from a series of propellers for which the radial load distribution and skew were varied over a large range. (The two propellers mentioned in our paper are included in this series.) The degree of unloading of the blade tips and/or skew is represented on the horizontal axis by the pressure amplitude coefficient Kp_{mean}. The vertical axis represents the ratio of the maximum or nearly maximum amplitude over the mean amplitude. The left diagram applies to the digital method discussed in the paper. In the right diagram results obtained from a modern FFT-analyzer are given. The diagrams show that the propellers with unloaded tips or large skew have larger temporal variations. The temporal variations determined by the digital analysis are much larger than those obtained with the FFT-analyzer. The reason for this is that the so-called maximum or peak values obtained on an FFT-analyzer have in fact gone through an averaging process and are therefore not true maximum values. As we believe that Mr. Munk's laboratory is using FFT-analyzers, we think this answers his first remark.

The second remark by Mr. Munk is about model/full-scale correlation of pressure fluctuation amplitudes. How this problem is handled by SSPA is discussed in some detail in the paper. We will add only that the idea of using what could be called "nearly maximum values" is supported by comparisons between photographs of cavitation patterns in model and full scale. They indicate that the fairly steady cavitation extension observed in full scale agrees with the maximum extension observed in the tunnel rather than the average.

We do not agree with Mr. Munk's idea of applying a correction factor of 1.65 on the model results instead, for two reasons. The first reason is that the theoretical basis for this factor is a simple formula for transmission through a wall, which only applies to high frequencies, as one underlying assumption is that the wall is thick relative to the wavelength. Furthermore, the experimental verification of this factor has only been made at high frequencies. The second reason is that, for the propellers for which the difference between maximum and mean amplitudes is rather small, that is, those with loaded blade tips, SSPA obtains good correlation with full scale with both analysis methods. One example of this is the one referred to in Mr. Johnsson's discussion of Dr. Huse's paper.

Mr. Munk's suggestion that accelerometers be fitted to the hull in full scale was also addressed in Mr. Johnsson's discussion of Dr. Huse's paper. In order to obtain useful information from such accelerometers, one must establish a transfer function between acceleration and pressure, including the phase relation, for instance, by making exciter tests. This is not a trivial task, especially for a large ship, but it can be done.

In response to Dr. Kaplan's assertions that conventional propeller theories use only nominal wakes rather than effective wakes, the authors would like to point out that, when properly applied, all theories should use an effective wake. The mean value of the effective wake is generally obtained from self-propulsion tests, using thrust or torque identity. For the design of a wake-adapted propeller or the analysis of propellers in steady or unsteady flow, the effective wake is commonly approximated by simply scaling the nominal wake field so that its mean value agrees with the mean effective wake obtained in the self-propulsion test. Properly, however, one would have to either calculate or measure the effective wake field as a function of spatial position. Since such measurements are difficult to make behind a self-propelled model, a calculation procedure has great utility. Although there are theories, such as that of Huang and Groves, for making such a calculation in the case of an axisymmetric wake, no rigorous theory exists for the case of nonaxisymmetric wakes. A number of ad hoc methods, such as that used in the present paper, have been used to treat the nonaxisymmetric case.

In noncavitating flow, the errors involved in using the simple scaling approach are not too severe due to the linearity of the problem. In other words, a 20 percent error in estimating the wake gradients will cause a 20 percent error in the unsteady forces. The nonlinearity of the cavitation process, however, can yield cavity volumes which are in error by factors of two or more. For this reason, questions of effective wake estimation are particularly critical when trying to predict cavitating flows.

In response to Mr. Verbeek, no sensitivity analysis was conducted on the effect of wake field variations in the computed pressure amplitudes. However, the authors generally find that reasonable effective wake estimates reduce the cavity volume by approximately a factor of two as compared with results using a scaled nominal wake.

The computer time necessary for making the calculations reported in this paper is as follows:

Program	CPU Time	Machine
PUF-3	15 min	IBM 370/168
FPP	5 min	IBM 370/168
Hull diffraction	20 min	Cyber 170/173

Dr. Tanibayashi, Dr. Kaplan, and Mr. Verbeek all raise the question as to the relative merits of the method presented in this paper compared with the various semi-empirical and ad hoc methods presented elsewhere for the computation of cavitation-induced hull forces. The authors believe that although most of these methods have been shown to yield good agreement with some experimental data, care must be taken when applying them to configurations different from those for which they were developed. The method presented here contains fewer approximations than any other formulation proposed to date so that its applicability should be more general. The computer time needed is not excessive, and the procedure can easily be integrated into a computerized design method.

Dr. Tanibayashi also questions whether some of the differences shown in Fig. 9 between full scale and model scale pressure fluctuations can be attributed to differences in the wake field. This is certainly possible, but it is difficult to say for sure, since no full scale wake data are available. No attempts were made to estimate the full-scale wake for the present work, since the comparison with experimental data was made at model scale.

The authors agree with Dr. Huse that our ability to predict effective wake fields must be improved, as must our knowledge of wake scale effects. The authors believe, however, that the Reynolds number is not of primary importance in predicting the cavitation performance of a full-scale propeller, particularly if the extent of cavitation is fairly large. It is more important at model scale and near inception. This is one reason why a reliable computer prediction can be superior to model testing in predicting full-scale performance.

In response to Dr. Huse's question about the different authors' opinions on the possible existence of a bias in cavitation tunnels due to the rigid boundary conditions, Mr. Johnsson would refer him to pages 134 and 135 in the paper, where it is indicated how SSPA has tried to follow up this problem. All model tests have their limitations. It is therefore absolutely essential that model/full-scale comparisons be carried out in as many cases

as possible and above all that they be ambitiously analyzed. By doing so, unexpected discrepancies or a bias can hopefully be mastered relatively soon.

Rather than try to answer Dr. Huse's question as to how far one must be from a propeller in order to model it as an oscillating point source, the authors would refer Dr. Huse to the paper presented by Professor Kerwin at the Fourteenth Symposium on Naval Hydrodynamics, entitled "Flow Field Computations for Non-Cavitating and Cavitating Propellers." Subsequent calculations made at Davidson Laboratory for the case of the RO/RO ship and the Navy oiler AO-177 have shown that the oscillating point source model as advanced by Dr. Huse produces hull pressures well in excess of both the measured and calculated values (by the procedure of this paper).

In response to Dr. Stern, the authors feel that the cavity volumes predicted are not excessive, and in fact are probably too small, since the predicted hull pressures are too small. Far from the propeller, the hull surface pressure predicted by the present method should be approximately linear with respect to the blade rate cavity volume acceleration. This is not necessarily the case at a position as close as transducer No. 3, data from which are shown in Fig. 10.

As an answer to Mr. Stern's question about the possibilities of measuring the cavity thickness, we refer to the following different methods tried by different research groups:

Stereophotography was tried both in cavitation tunnel tests [39] and at full scale [40] (additional references follow this closure), the latter application being rather successful. In the model tests it was found that the accuracy was not good enough.

In Japan the simple way of putting pins on the blades was tried with some success, [41,42], although the flow was somewhat disturbed. A comparison of observations using this method with measurements using the laser scattering technique showed good agreement [42]. The last method, although very elaborate, seems the most promising one.

The authors agree with Dr. Isay that a comparison with experimental blade pressure data would be useful in verifying the results of fully wetted lifting-surface theory, but feel that the current state of the art in making these measurements is unsatisfactory for comparison purposes. The problems include calibration errors, flow disturbance by the gages, and scale effects.

Dr. Isay points out the limitations of potential-flow theory in predicting the performance of a propeller operating in a ship's boundary layer. This limitation can be minimized by estimating the steady effective wake field which exists at the propeller plane. This is obviously a simplified model of the actual flow situation, where time-varying wake vorticity is continuously modified by the propeller's presence, but the authors believe it can yield useful results.

As to the effect of varying element number, Dr. Isay is referred to reference [15], which presented the lifting-surface method used for noncavitating propellers. It showed the effect of varying element number, both spanwise and chordwise. The effect of varying element number in the case of a two-dimensional cavitating foil was shown in reference [12]. Systematic variations in element number in the case of the cavitating propeller have not been performed. On the basis of the work cited in the preceding, however, the authors believe the discretization used in the present paper is sufficient for most cases.

In response to Dr. Wilson, the authors agree that the wood plate surrounding the model hull in the cavitation tunnel is not truly a rigid surface. However, it may approximate a rigid surface in the case of source-like loading if there exists no pressure relief in the recessed area above the plate. In any case, it does not seem to be worthwhile to incorporate the dynamic characteristics of the plate in the calculation procedure, since similar characteristics for the hull surface itself are not included, and the plate is present only when comparing the calculated results with those from experiments.

For experimental purposes, the influence of the plate must, of course, be considered. The approach taken by SSPA is to develop a correction factor as a function of transducer depth and Froude number. This correction factor is found by analyzing available model and full-scale results, and includes the effect of pressure relief at the free surface, as well as the fact that the free surface is nonplanar.

Although the former effect is correctly handled in the present calculation scheme, the latter is not. In order to include the influence of the steady wave pattern, the free surface would have to be paneled as well as the hull itself. The pressure relief boundary condition would then be explicitly imposed at the free-surface control points. This extension of the theory would be a worthwhile subject of future research.

Dr. Wilson also asks why the calculation procedure had difficulty with Propeller P1842. During the collapse phase the cavity on that propeller pulled back from the leading edge of the blade. Although P1842 is highly skewed, this behavior is not necessarily correlated with high skew. In one series of experiments conducted at MIT it was found that for a given wake and propeller, the collapse occurred toward the leading edge at higher cavitation numbers, and toward the trailing edge at lower cavitation numbers. The inability of PUF-3 to deal with the latter collapse mode is certainly a limitation of the theory—one which hopefully will be relaxed as the result of further research.

Additional references

39 Øfsti, O., "Measurement of the Extent and Thickness of Cavitation by Photogrammetry," *Proceedings*, 14th International Towing Tank Conference, Ottawa, Vol. 2, 1975, p. 281.

40 Holden, K. and Søntvedt, T., "On Stability and Volume of Marine Propeller Cavitation and Corresponding Spectral Distribution in Hull Pressure Fields," Symposium on High Powered Propulsion of Large Ships, Publ. No. 490, NSMB, Wageningen, The Netherlands 1974.

41 Hoshino, T., "A Method to Predict Fluctuating Pressures Induced by a Cavitating Propeller," Mitsubishi Technical Bulletin No. 150, May 1982.

42 Ukon, Y. et al., "Pressure Fluctuations Induced by Cavity Volume on Highly Skewed Propellers for a Ro-Ro Ship," Report of Ship Research Institute, Vol. 19, No. 3, May 1982 (in Japanese).

SNAME *Transactions*, Vol. 90, 1982, pp. 153–194

Large-Diameter Propellers of Reduced Weight

Jacques B. Hadler,[1] Fellow, **Richard P. Neilson,**[2] Member, **Alan L. Rowen,**[3] Associate Member, **Robert D. Sedat,**[4] Associate Member, **Frederick Seibold,**[5] Member, and **Robert B. Zubaly,**[6] Member

This paper describes the design, manufacture, performance and fuel economy of large, slow-turning lightweight marine propellers. The concepts studied include cast hollow blades, fabricated hollow blades, hollow hubs, tip-attached tandem propellers and fiber-reinforced plastic (FRP) propellers. When applied to a 120 000-dwt tanker with a 27.5-ft-diameter propeller, the best solution for weight reduction is a cast hollow bladed propeller with hollow hub, which reduces weight by 48.8 percent while losing only 0.5 percent efficiency. The same design concept was applied to propellers of increased diameter and reduced rpm. It is shown that a 30.2-ft-diameter lightweight propeller in compliance with the U.S. Coast Guard regulations can achieve annual savings of about $250 000. If the Coast Guard regulations on propeller immerson were relaxed, a 42.5-ft-diameter, 30.8-rpm propeller with 17 percent tip emergence could be used. The ship would then require 23 percent less power, consume 19 percent less fuel and save one million dollars annually.

Introduction

THE EVER-RISING price of fuel oiil has made owners and operators of ships increasingly aware of the need to improve the fuel economy of their propulsion system. Much research is now underway on various components of the propulsion system to improve the fuel economy of ships. One of the major components is the propeller. In the past, propeller size has been limited by several technical and operational factors:

- the ability to manufacture them by conventional means,
- the size of the propeller aperture,
- draft restrictions in channels or harbors, and
- inability of stern tube bearing to support heavy weight of large propeller.

The last restriction not only affects the fuel economy of vessels operating today but effectively limits the maximum horsepower of high-speed single screw ships in the design stage. Recent studies [1, 2][7] have recommended that research be undertaken to identify means of manufacturing large-diameter propellers of reduced weight to further improve the fuel economy of ships. In this paper the design, manufacture and performance of large, lightweight propellers for tankers are addressed. Most of the ideas advanced here are also applicable to other ship types.

The many possible approaches for reducing the weight of marine propellers may be classified into one or more of the following categories:

- new or modified fabrication techniques,
- modification of blade design to better utilize the strength properties of the material, and
- use of a lighter weight material of equal strength.

Of these, the last would require extensive development time to verify that the new material can stand up to the rigors of the marine environment and withstand over 10^9 cycles of load variation throughout its lifetime. For near future applications, techniques should be devised for reducing the weight of propellers made of conventional materials.

An analysis of the weight distribution of conventional marine propellers show that approximately two thirds of the weight is contained in the blades and one third in the hub. Thus, while the blades offer the greatest potential for possible weight reduction, it is also desirable to reduce the weight of the hub. Significant weight reduction can be achieved by hollowing the propeller blades and hub while maintaining acceptable stress levels throughout. This paper describes various design schemes and manufacturing techniques for making substantial reductions in weight of large-diameter, slow-turning propeller blades and hubs.

The following sections of the paper describe various propeller lightening schemes and the prototype tanker chosen for comparative evaluations. Then design methodologies are developed and applied to the most promising lightweight propeller concepts, and a comparison is made of their weight savings and performance characteristics. An economic analysis is then made of the base tanker operating with large-diameter propellers of various sizes. A detailed investigation is made of a propeller 54 percent larger than the base design, operating with blade tips emerged in the ballast condition to achieve maximum economic benefits. Finally, the major conclusions of the paper are summarized and recommendations are made for future research.

---

[1] Director of research, Webb Institute of Naval Architecture, Glen Cove, New York.

[2] Professor of naval architecture, Webb Institute of Naval Architecture, Glen Cove, New York.

[3] Professor of marine engineering, Webb Institute of Naval Architecture, Glen Cove, New York.

[4] Research associate, Webb Institute of Naval Architecture, Glen Cove, New York.

[5] Program manager, Maritime Administration, Office of Maritime Technology, Washington, D.C.

[6] Research associate, Webb Institute of Naval Architecture, Glen Cove, New York.

[7] Numbers in brackets designate References at end of paper.

Presented at the Annual Meeting, New York, N.Y., November 17–20, 1982, of THE SOCIETY OF NAVAL ARCHITECTS AND MARINE ENGINEERS.

Preliminary evaluation of lightweight propeller alternatives

At the outset of the study, five alternatives for lightweight propeller blades were considered, namely:

1. Cast hollow blades with separately cast tips.
2. Hollow blades integrally cast with hub segments.
3. Hollow blades partly fabricated.
4. Tip-attached tandem propeller.
5. Lightweight advanced materials.

Also, four methods of reducing hub weight were considered:

1. Saddled hollow hub.
2. Major coring with keyway insert.
3. Major coring with keyless insert.
4. Major coring with flanged connection.

Since there are many possible approaches to reducing propeller weight, it was necessary to reduce the number to a few for detailed investigation. To do this, each suggested blade lightening alternative was subjectively evaluated, using an evaluation system which considered a series of eight factors and assigned ratings ranging from 1 to 5 to each factor, with 5 being the best rating possible.

The factors graded were:

1. Ease of manufacture.
2. Potential weight saving.
3. Degree to which each alternative could be adapted to innovative blade shapes.
4. Ease with which shipyard personnel could handle the propeller.
5. Ease with which a damaged propeller could be repaired.
6. Expected propulsive efficiency achievable by the alternative as compared with a solid propeller of the same diameter and rpm.
7. Probable acceptability of the concept by the industry.
8. Need for additional technological development to implement the alternative.

In every category, the rating for a conventional propeller was assigned first so that the others could be rated in comparison to it. The hub evaluation system considered only four factors (Nos. 1, 2, 4 and 7 from the foregoing list) and assigned ratings ranging from 1 to 3 to each factor with 3 being the highest. Each candidate alternative is described briefly next, followed by the results of the merit evaluation. Then the most promising concepts are identified for detailed study.

Blade lightening alternatives

1. Cast hollow blades with separately cast tips—This is a means of creating a hollow blade by casting the blade tips separately from the hub and blade roots. The hub and blade stubs would be cast out to approximately the 0.5 radius and the remainder of the blade cast separately, both castings containing a cavity. The tips could then be welded to the roots.

2. Hollow blades integrally cast with hub segments—This actually combines the concept of decreasing the weight of the blade and the weight of the hub. It involves casting each blade integrally with a section of hub, the hollow being created in the blade during the casting process by making a mold that joins the blade cavity to the hub cavity. The sections of the hub could then be joined at each end by a shrink-fit forged ring or a bolted ring.

3. Hollow blades partly fabricated—This alternative would involve the use of steel in the manufacture of the propeller. The hub and blade tips would be cast steel and the remainder of the blades would consist of fabricated sections, built of webs and diaphragms and covered with steel plates much like a rudder. These three components would then be welded together to form the propeller. The entire propeller would then be covered with a material to protect it from galvanic action. Copper-nickel or nickel-chromium alloys, in a sheathed, clad or flame-spray coated form are potential candidates for this covering. Urethane coatings may also be promising.

4. Tip-attached tandem propeller—This hydrodynamic concept essentially consists of connecting the tips of the blades of a tandem propeller. Since the blades are no longer cantilevered but form an arch, the loads at the root are much reduced and therefore the thickness can be reduced there. This will result in a weight saving and there is evidence that a gain in propulsive efficiency can be achieved over a conventional propeller of the same size.

5. Lightweight advanced materials—This involves manufacturing propellers from lightweight materials not normally used in the marine industry but developed to some extent by the aircraft industry. These might include fiber-reinforced plastics (see later section) or titanium, for example.

Hub lightening alternatives

1. Saddled hollow hub—A significant coring of material achieved from the inside diameter with the hub keyed to the shaft.

2. Major coring with keyway insert—Removal of large amounts of material from the inside diameter of the hub with a steel keyway insert to provide resistance to the torque.

3. Major coring with keyless insert—Removal of large amounts of material from the inside diameter of the hub with a sleeve attached to the inside diameter of the hub to allow keyless mounting of the propeller on the shaft.

4. Major coring with flanged connection—Removal of large amounts of material from the inside diameter of the hub, utilizing a flange to make the connection between the propeller and the shaft. This connection would be similar to what is common practice for controllable-pitch propellers.

Comparative evaluations of the alternative concepts began with a subjective evaluation of the conventional propeller or hub. Then each candidate design was carried out to the extent that difficulties in construction sequences, matching, joining, coating, structural analysis, blade finishing, hydrodynamic analysis, and repair and maintenance procedures could be compared with their counterparts in the conventional designs. The resulting evaluations are shown in Tables 1 and 2. Individual ratings were then added, and the totals were used for comparing the alternatives.

As a result of the ratings, four alternatives for blades and one for hubs were chosen for further analysis. They are:

- Cast hollow blades with separately cast tips.
- Hollow blades partly fabricated.
- Tip-attached tandem propeller.
- Lightweight advanced materials.
- Hollow hub with major coring and flanged connection.

It is apparent that any of the blade lightening alternatives could be combined with the hollow hub to achieve maximum weight reduction.

Since the numerical ratings were assigned before any of the concepts were designed in detail, small differences in the total ratings were not considered significant. As a result of the detailed designs and weight estimates described later, a clearly best alternative emerged.

Base ship and propeller description

In order to compare the relative merits of each lightweight propeller alternative, a base ship was needed. Since large tankers seem to offer the best opportunity for the use of large-diameter propellers, a 120 000-dwt tanker designed and built by Bethlehem Steel in 1971 was chosen. This vessel was chosen because of its large draft in the full-load condition and because

Table 1 Technical evaluation of lightweight propeller alternatives

Alt. No.	Description	Ease of Manu.	Weight Savings	Dimen. Free	Ease of Handling	Ease of Repair	Prop. Eff.	Level of Acc.	Level of Dev.	Total
	conventional propeller	5	1	1	3	3	3	5	5	26
1	hollow blade: separate tips	3	3	4	3	3	3	3	3	25
2	hollow blade: segmented hub	1	4	2	3	2	3	1	2	18
3	hollow blade: partly fabricated	1	4	5	3	4	2	2	2	23
4	tip attached tandem	3	3	1	3	2	5	3	4	24
5	lightweight advanced materials	2	5	3	3	2	3	2	1	21

Table 2 Technical evaluation of hub lightening alternatives

Alt.	Description	Ease of Manu.	Weight Savings	Ease of Handling	Level of Acc.	Total
	conventional hub	2	1	1	3	7
1	saddled hollow hub	2	2	1	3	8
2	major coring, keyway insert	1	2	1	2	6
3	major coring, keyless insert	1	2	2	2	7
4	major coring, flanged connection	3	3	3	2	14

Table 3 Characteristics of base ship and propeller, 120 000-dwt tanker

LBP, ft-in.	850-0
Beam (mld), ft-in.	138-0
Depth (mld), ft-in.	68-0
Design draft (DWL), ft-in.	51-9
Displacement at DWL, tons	143 098
Shp	26 000 geared steam turbine
Rpm	85
C_B	0.825
Prop. diameter, ft-in.	27-6
P/D	0.795
BAR	0.588
No. of blades	5
Prop. weight (original), lb	122 800
(redesigned), lb	79 100
Material (original)	manganese bronze, ABS Type 2
(redesigned)	manganese bronze, ABS Type 4

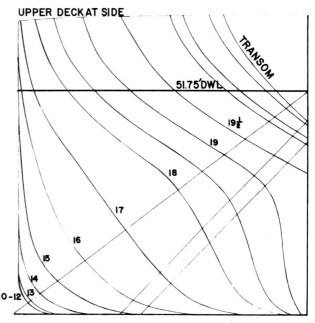

Fig. 1 Stern body plan of 120 000-dwt tanker

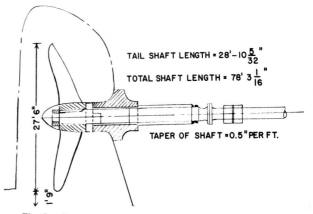

Fig. 2 Arrangement of propeller, stern tube and shafting of 120 000-dwt tanker

all data needed for this study, including the details of the propeller design, were available. The principal characteristics of the vessel and propeller are given in Table 3, the vessel's form is shown in the body plan of Fig. 1, and a centerline profile through the shafting, stern tube and propeller aperture is shown in Fig. 2.

The propeller designed for this ship was one of the largest in the United States at that time (1971) and there was concern about its weight and the impact upon the stern tube bearing. Wake analysis and hull and shaft vibration analysis dictated a 27.5 ft-diameter, 5-bladed propeller with 29.1 in. of rake and 16.5 deg of skew at the tip. This propeller has met all design expectations in service; thus, it serves as a good design around which to develop the lighter-weight propellers.

In choosing a ship for the study, it was also important to have adequate model test data and a method for predicting the effect of changes in both propeller diameter and loading upon the power performance. Model self-propulsion tests had been conducted at both full load and ballast load conditions of the base ship covering the speed range from 13 to 17 knots. It was found that the Netherlands Ship Model Basin (NSMB) regres-

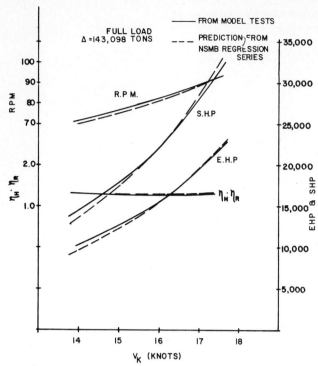

Fig. 3 Predicted power performance of 120 000-dwt tanker

sion equations [3] compared well with the self-propulsion tests. These, in combination with the regression equations for the NSMB propeller series [4], provided a suitable technique for predicting the effects of changes in hull or propeller proportions upon resistance and propulsion factors. The predicted values of shp, rpm, and hull efficiency times relative rotative efficiency ($\eta_H \eta_R$) are shown in Fig. 3 along with the measurements from the model tests. The agreement is quite good, particularly at the design full-load speed of 16 knots, which lends credence to predictions made later in this paper for larger-diameter propellers.

The propeller installed on the ship was made of American Bureau of Shipping (ABS) Type 2 material and was designed more than ten years ago, but it was decided for this study to redesign the propeller using ABS Type 4, a higher-strength and lighter material. Since the original propeller has given good performance in service, no change was made in its hydrodynamic characteristics, but a more uniform radial distribution of stress was obtained, and hub length was minimized. The result of these changes was a redesigned propeller which weighed 79 100 lb, or 35.6 percent less than the original 122 800-lb propeller. Reducing the section thickness also resulted in an increase in propeller efficiency of 0.7 percent, which gave a 1.2 percent reduction in power consumption.

This redesigned propeller of high-strength material established the baseline propeller updated to 1982 technology, to which the candidate lightweight propellers were compared. References in subsequent sections of this paper to the "solid propeller" refer to this redesigned propeller.

Design methodology of lightweight propellers

In developing the various hollow-blade concepts, it was first necessary to establish a design methodology which would retain all of the desirable characteristics of the solid propeller while minimizing weight with minimum loss in propeller efficiency.

As a consequence of the good performance achieved with the original propeller, it was decided to maintain as many of its hydrodynamic characteristics as possible in the various lightened-propeller concepts. A computer routine was developed for the design of hollow-blade propellers which maintained the following characteristics of the solid propeller:

- blade area ratio,
- chord-length and thickness-chord ratios at 0.9 radius,
- radial load distribution, and
- skew.

It was thus expected that both the cavitation and propeller-induced vibration characteristics would remain unchanged.

In order to minimize the weight with minimum loss of efficiency and without jeopardizing strength, the following criteria were incorporated into the design approach:

- The maximum stress at each section should be the same as that of the solid propeller.
- The thickness-chord ratio should not exceed 0.20 for any section
- The ratio of the section thickness to the space between the blades measured on a reference cylinder at any radius should not exceed 1.0.

Maintaining adequate blade strength

The most critical element of the redesign was the development of the hollow sections, particularly those at the root, so that the design stresses were the same as those of the solid propeller and so that it still met all the other criteria established earlier.

This was achieved through the following relationship: The stress in a symmetrical propeller blade section is

$$\sigma = \frac{M_{x_0}\frac{t}{2}}{I_{x_0}} \tag{1}$$

where

M_{x_0} = bending moment about nose-tail line
t = maximum section thickness
I_{x_0} = moment of inertia of section

The equal-stress criterion requires that

$$\left(\frac{t}{I_{x_0}}\right)_{\text{hollow}} = \left(\frac{t}{I_{x_0}}\right)_{\text{solid}} \tag{2}$$

The exact calculation of the moment of inertia, I_{x_0}, for hollow symmetric NACA 66 Mod section with uniform wall thickness is discussed in Appendix 1. The results may be approximated by the following equation:

$$I_{x_0} = t^3 l \left[a + b\left(\frac{2t_w}{t}\right) + c\left(\frac{2t_w}{t}\right)^2 + d\left(\frac{2t_w}{t}\right)^3\right] \tag{3}$$

where

t = maximum section thickness
l = chord length
t_w = wall thickness

where quantities:

$a = 0.43788 \times 10^{-4}$ $b = 0.14423$
$c = 0.17420$ $d = 0.07447$

Substituting equation (3) into (2) and recognizing that $2t_w/t$ for the solid section = 1.0

$$\left(\frac{2t_w}{t_H}\right)^3 + \frac{c}{d}\left(\frac{2t_w}{t_H}\right)^2 + \frac{b}{d}\left(\frac{2t_w}{t_H}\right) + \frac{a}{d} = \left(\frac{a+b+c+d}{d}\right)\frac{l_S t_S^2}{l_H t_H^2} \tag{4}$$

where subscript H refers to the hollow section and subscript S to the solid section.

Equation (4) permits determination of any one of the three quantities t_H, l_H, or t_w if the other two are assumed. Thus, in the root sections, the limitations on chord length and chord thickness imposed by the foregoing restrictions result in increased wall thickness to meet the strength requirements. Blade outline and blade area were determined by the equations developed by Schoenherr [5].

After designing the hollow blades using the preceding procedure, the frequency of the first cantilever mode of vibration of the hollow blade was calculated as described in Appendix 1. The hollow-bladed 27.5-ft-diameter propeller was found to have a natural frequency in water of 17.4 cps, more than twice that of the solid propeller, and well above any likely blade frequency excitation. Thus, no blade vibration problem is expected for a hollow propeller in fully submerged operation.

Blade thickness effects

In order to determine the effect of greater blade thickness in the root sections upon propeller performance, a search was made of cascade data in the aeronautical and turbomachinery literature. A comprehensive set of two-dimensional cascade experiments was found [6], using NACA 65 sections tested over a wide range of lift coefficients and with blade section thicknesses and spacings similar to ship propellers. Section drag was measured, from which the additional two-dimensional section drag associated with blade interference was determined. This was developed into the following equation:

$$\frac{C_D}{C_{Do}} = 12.378 \left(\frac{t_c}{s}\right)^3 - 24.482 \left(\frac{t_c}{s}\right)^2 + 14.598 \left(\frac{t_c}{s}\right) + 0.0547\,\phi$$

$$+ 0.0612 \left(\frac{t_c}{s}\right)^2 \phi - 0.001284 \left(\frac{t_c}{s}\right)\phi^2 - 1.424 \quad (5)$$

where

C_D = blade section drag coefficient in cascade
C_{Do} = blade section drag coefficient in open, or in isolation
t_c = circumferential blade "thickness" measured through blade section centroid in circumferential direction
s = blade spacing measured in circumferential direction
ϕ = face pitch angle of blade section

The developments leading to this equation are discussed in Appendix 2.

The approach taken in calculating propeller efficiency was to assume that the efficiency of the solid propeller was known either from open-water model tests or from lifting-line or lifting-surface calculations. The hollow blade sections differ from the solid sections in chord length, chord-thickness ratio, and the interference between blades. Therefore, each of these components was determined for each section of both the solid-bladed and the hollow-bladed propellers. At each section of each propeller, the frictional and the form drag were calculated using the following equations derived by Hoerner [7]:

$$D = C_D \frac{\rho}{2} c U^2 \quad (6)$$

and

$$C_D = 2C_f[1 + 2t/c + 60(t/c)^4] \quad (7)$$

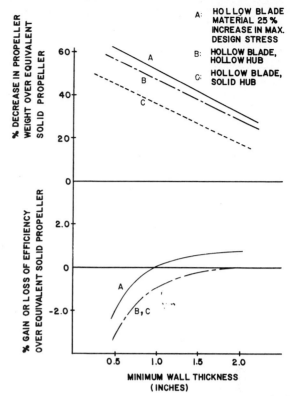

Fig. 4 Effects of hollow blade wall thickness on 5-bladed, 27.5-ft-diameter propeller

where

D = section drag, pounds per unit of radius
t = thickness, in.
c = chord length, in.
$C_f = 0.075/(\log_{10} Re - 2)^2$ (8)
Re = Reynold's number, cU/ν
ρ = mass density
ν = kinematic viscosity
U = section inflow velocity

Then the increased drag due to the interference of the blades with each other was calculated from equation (5) for each blade section. These changes in drag were resolved into changes in thrust and torque and the results summed over the whole blade. Thus, it was possible to determine the change in K_T and K_Q of the hollow propeller from the values measured on the solid propeller. In this way, small changes in efficiency could be determined more precisely than would be possible with model experiments.

All of the foregoing developments were incorporated into a propeller design routine, including calculations of the weight and WR^2 of the solid as well as the hollow-bladed propellers. In this routine, it was possible to vary the blade outline (root chord lengths) as well as the wall thickness of the hollow-bladed propellers. Parametric studies were conducted on nominal wall thickness varying from $\frac{1}{2}$ to 3 in. These results are presented in Fig. 4, which shows the reduction in blade weight over the solid propeller and the loss in propeller efficiency. From these studies, a design wall thickness of $1\frac{1}{4}$ in. was chosen. This provided substantial blade weight reductions, only a small penalty in propeller efficiency, and a wall thickness that was easily cast or fabricated and welded.

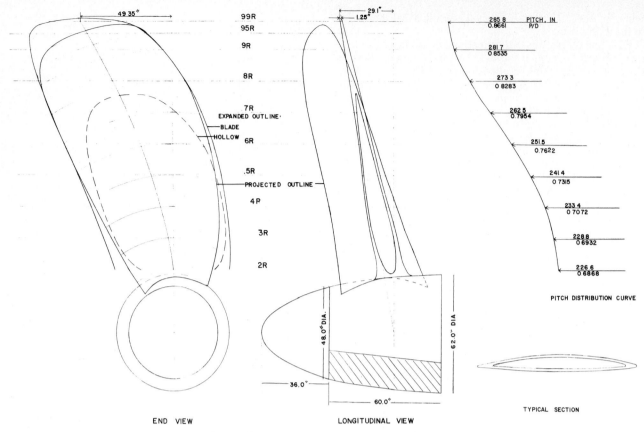

Fig. 5 Cast hollow-blade propeller concept No. 1

Lightweight propeller concepts

Cast propellers

Since the preliminary evaluations indicated that a cast hollow blade utilizing conventional propeller materials was the most promising candidate, two different cast-blade concepts were developed. Concept No. 1, made of nickel-aluminum bronze (ABS Type 4), has five separately cast blade tips which extend from the 0.5 radius to the tip. The portion out to the 0.7 radius is hollow with wall thickness of $1\frac{1}{4}$ in. The hub and the five blades out to the 0.5 radius are one integral casting. Each blade is hollow with full section thickness at about the 0.4 radius. Each blade tip is welded to the blade root prior to finishing the surface. A plan of the propeller is shown in Fig. 5. With conventional hub, this propeller weighs 63 200 lb (a 20.1 percent reduction from the solid propeller) with only a $\frac{1}{2}$ percent decrease in efficiency.

Concept No. 2 is identical in both interior and exterior shape of the blades but the propeller is cast as a unit, omitting part of the face of each blade. Faceplates are cast separately and welded into place after the core is removed from the hollow of the blade. Details are shown in Fig. 6. The weight and efficiency of this propeller are approximately the same as the preceding propeller.

Of the two concepts, the first one has the best potential for casting in very large diameters using existing facilities in the United States. Since the blade tips are cast separately, the reduced diameter of the center casting permits existing molding facilities to be used and keeps the "pour" within the limits of current foundry capabilities. The only equipment that would have to be enlarged would be the pitchometer measuring equipment and the pit for dynamic balancing.

Fabricated propellers

The possibility of fabricating propeller blades of webs, diaphragms and cover plates has always been an intriguing alternative to casting the blades. It appears most practical in this approach to cast the hub and the root section stubs of each blade as well as the tips of the blades, which for reasons of cavitation performance have to be quite thin. The fabricated portion is then limited to the region between the 0.3 and 0.65 radii. As methods of fabrication were being conceived, two different approaches evolved which are identified here as fabricated Concepts No. 1 and No. 2. Concept No. 1 consists of a built-up section of each blade made up of webs, diaphragms, and plates which closely approximates the blade shape of the cast propeller while maintaining straight lines along the blade sections in order to simplify construction. This version is shown in Figs. 7(a) and 7(b), and can be described as follows:

1. The build-up section of the blade extends from the 0.3 radius to 0.65 radius.
2. Both the back and the face consist of nine individual plates (total of 18) which extend as shown in the plate layout sketch [Fig. 7(a)].
3. Castings are used to create the approximate shapes desired at the leading and trailing edges. The extent of these castings are defined by a minimum throat dimension of 4 in., which assures noninterference of the heat-affected zones from the face and back plate welds.
4. The "mid-chord plates" for both the face and back are parallel to the noise-tail line in order to simplify construction.
5. The other six plates, back and face, have knuckles in order to align them with the midchord plates to facilitate the welding of these plates to the midchord plates and to simplify

their attachment to the vertical backing bar [see Fig. 7(b)].

6. Horizontal webs are provided at the 0.3, 0.475, and 0.65 radii.

7. Order of construction:
   (a) Weld vertical backing bars to vertical webs, creating T-sections which vary in depth along the propeller radius.
   (b) Connect back plates to these T-sections.
   (c) Connect horizontal webs to back plates and vertical webs.
   (d) Attach faceplates over T-sections and horizontal webs. At the 0.475 radius, this will require the use of slot welds.
   (e) Weld leading-edge and trailing-edge castings to the assembly.
   (f) Weld the root and tip castings to the assembly.

The fabrication of the blade results in discontinuities in the section shape; thus it is necessary to machine or grind the surface to the shape similar to the procedure used for cast propeller blades. Therefore, the fabricated part should be the same material as the hub and blade tip, probably nickel-aluminum bronze.

Although the design wall thickness of this propeller is the same as that of the cast hollow-bladed propellers, the webs and diaphragms increase the weight somewhat. It is estimated that this propeller with conventional hub would weigh approximately 68 300 lb, a reduction in total propeller weight of about 13.7 percent. The loss in propeller efficiency is 0.5 percent, as for the cast propellers.

Fabricated Concept No. 2 was intended to utilize developable surfaces to create a simplified blade shape. In this version, the part of the blade from the 0.3 to the 0.7 radii is replaced with plates which are bent to the desired shape and welded to leading and trailing edge castings; see Figs. 8(a) and 8(b). Three web frames are used to give the desired shape of the face and back plates, which are attached by plug welds. After each fabricated section is completed, it is welded to the hub and tip castings. The result is to significantly reduce the number of pieces and welding and finishing man-hours over fabricated Concept No. 1.

Fabricated Concept No. 2 could be made of nickel-aluminum bronze castings for the hub and blade tips, with the fabricated section of either the same material or steel clad with copper-nickel alloy. Alternatively, it could be made of a cast steel hub flame-spray coated with a nickel-chromium alloy, tip castings of Inconel, the fabricated section made of steel clad with Inconel, the leading- and trailing-edge castings of Inconel. Urethane coating could also be used. This latter alternative would substantially reduce the cost of materials.

This propeller when made of nickel-aluminum bronze has a weight estimated at 67 200 lb, a 15 percent reduction from the solid propellers.

The requirement that the surface shape of fabricated Concept No. 2 should be quite simple for ease of manufacturing causes a significant change in pitch distribution as shown in Fig. 8(a). Although it was expected that this would reduce the efficiency somewhat, the lifting-line calculations showed a major reduction of 6 percent in propeller efficiency, a value much too large to be acceptable in today's economic environment. As a consequence, no further effort has been devoted to investigating this concept. It is possible that with further study and a slight increase in fabrication complexity, a developable surface might be evolved which better suits the hydrodynamic requirements.

Hub with major coring and flanged connection

As indicated previously, the hub of a conventional propeller makes up approximately one third of its total weight, enough

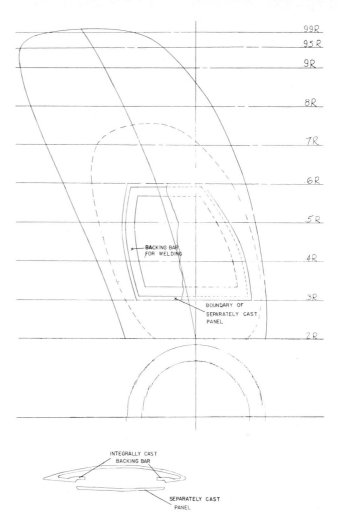

Fig. 6 Cast hollow-blade propeller concept No. 2

to justify a study of means for reducing hub weight. The preliminary studies clearly indicated that to save much weight, a different concept than the usual attachment of the propeller on a tapered section of the tailshaft would be required. Experience with controllable-pitch propellers suggested the possibility of substituting a flange on the tailshaft to which the propeller could be bolted, thus reducing the hub weight and also eliminating the whole tapered section of the tailshaft. The flange on the tailshaft requires that it be withdrawn outboard, using a removable-flange coupling, a muff-coupling, or a split stern tube bearing, for example [8, 9]. The flanged hollow hub was so attractive that all effort on hub weight reduction was devoted to developing the design technology for this type of hub.

The primary effort was devoted to determining
1. hub wall thickness required to carry thrust and torque loads on the blades,
2. attachment of the tailshaft flange, and
3. development of a weight algorithm to be incorporated into the design routine so that minimum total propeller weight rather than minimum blade weight could be achieved.

To determine the required wall thickness of a hollow hub, a stress analysis of a cylindrical shell loaded at its surface by the propeller blade forces and moments was made. The method used was that of Bijlaard [10] in which the loads and deformations of the cylinder are represented by double Fourier series.

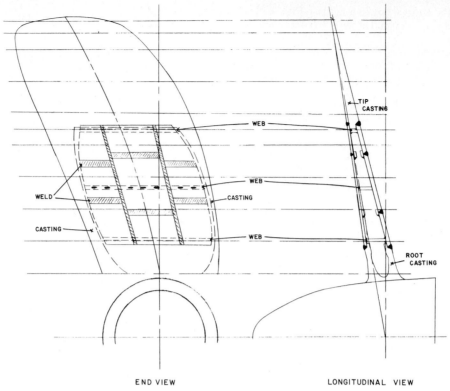

END VIEW   LONGITUDINAL VIEW

Fig. 7(a)   Fabricated hollow-blade propeller concept No. 1

These series are then inserted into the three simultaneous partial differential equations of thin-shell theory [11], which can be reduced to an eighth-order differential equation for the radial displacement of the shell at any point. The solution of that equation leads to expressions for the bending moments and membrane forces, and hence for the stresses in the hub. The method of solution is described in Appendix 3.

The hub was assumed loaded at each propeller blade with a centrifugal force and two blade-root moments, which were determined from the blade bending moments computed at the blade root and resolved into the longitudinal and circumferential directions.

These three loads, each described by double Fourier series, were superimposed for each blade, and the resulting membrane forces and bending moments were calculated in the hub wall at any point ("around the clock"). A second superposition was then required to account for the forces and moments caused by the other blades.

Parametric studies of the hub stresses were made, covering a range of applied forces and moments, blade root areas, hub radii and hub thicknesses. Held constant were hub length (60 in.), Poisson's ratio (0.36 for manganese bronze), and number of blades (five). The parametric studies showed that the maximum stress occurs in the hub at a point near the edge of the blade-root area. A second general finding was that the externally applied longitudinal moment had a negligibly small influence on the stresses.

Plotted results of the parametric studies were used to derive an empirically fitted simplified stress equation

$$\sigma = k_1 \frac{P}{t^2} + k_2 \frac{M}{ct^2} \qquad (9)$$

where

σ = maximum hub stress, psi
P = centrifugal force per blade, lb

M = circumferential blade-root moment, in.-lb
c = half-thickness of blade root, in. ($2c$ = blade root thickness)
t = hub wall thickness, in.

k_1 and k_2 are coefficients determined by regression analysis as follows:

$$k_1 = -0.0036\,c^2 + 0.0283\,c + 0.00075\,ca$$
$$+ 0.005\,a - 0.175 \qquad (10)$$

$$k_2 = 0.00169\,ca - 0.0088\,a + 0.170 \qquad (11)$$

and a is the radius of the hub in inches.

These equations were tested against the computed stresses and were found to give values within ±5 percent of the computed results.

Substituting for σ the allowable stress of the hub material (σ_a), the foregoing equation can be solved for t, the minimum permitted hub thickness. Finally, the thickness was increased for the following uncertainties:

• nonuniform distribution of P and M
• uncertain end fixity of hub
• stress concentrations in blade root

These three effects gave rise to a doubling of the required thickness, as documented in Appendix 3. The design hub thickness at the midlength of the hub is then

$$t_m = 2.0 \sqrt{\frac{1}{\sigma_a}\left(k_1 P + \frac{k_2 M}{c}\right)} \qquad (12)$$

At the coupling with the tailshaft, the required thickness was shown to be 20 percent greater than that at midlength.

The required dimensions of other parts of the hollow hub were determined from the ABS Rules [12] and from several papers describing common practice in shaft and hub design [13, 14].

Finally, a weight algorithm for calculating the weight of a

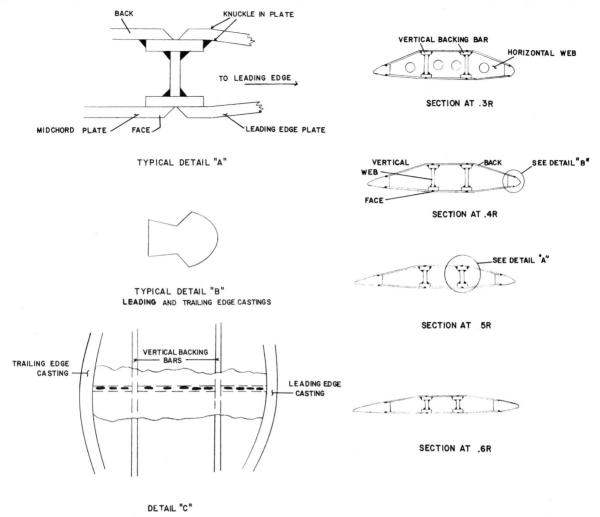

Fig. 7(b) Fabricated hollow-blade propeller concept No. 1

hollow hub designed as described in the foregoing was derived. Assuming a tailshaft of ABS Grade 2 steel, 16 bolts of high-strength steel (ultimate strength 102 000 psi) connecting the hub to the tailshaft, and a hub of ABS Type 4 bronze (allowable stress 7500 psi), the weight of a hollow hub for the example ship is 12 380 lb compared to 34 030 lb for the standard solid hub keyed to a tapered tailshaft. This weight reduction includes the reduced weight of the removed tapered tailshaft section and the added weights of the flange, bolts, and flange cover on the new tailshaft configuration.

As a consequence of the hub study, a hub for the cast hollow-bladed propeller was developed (Fig. 9). This results in a total propeller weight for the cast propeller with hollow blades and hollow hub of 53 200 lb, a 32.7 percent reduction in weight from the solid propeller. If the change in weight of the tailshaft is taken into account, that is, the taper removed and a flange added, the effective weight of the propeller becomes 40 500 lb, a reduction of 48.8 percent from that of the solid propeller. It is thus clear that it is possible to achieve substantial weight reductions by using cast hollow propellers and hubs without requiring significant changes in fabrication techniques except for some increase in coring complexity during casting.

Tip-attached tandem propeller

It was decided to investigate the feasibility of the tip-attached tandem propeller since it held prospects of increasing propeller efficiency as well as reducing weight by virtue of the arch formed by the attachment of the tips of the blades of the forward propeller to the tips of the blades of the after propeller (Fig. 10).

The experimental evidence indicating a gain in propeller efficiency is contained in two different sets of experiments. In reference [15], Sun et al have shown that tandem propellers under heavily loaded conditions are somewhat more efficient than a single propeller. Gonzalez et al [16] show that suppressing the tip vortex by a fence can improve propeller efficiency. The tip-attached tandem propeller takes advantage of both of these features. There are also indications from the lifting-line and lifting-surface work being done by Pien that significant gains in propeller efficiency could be achieved through tip-attached tandem propellers. Hence, it was decided to utilize Pien's lifting-line theory to make the design.

To investigate the structural properties, a simplified finite-element model of a loaded arch was developed. In this model, the loads on the blades were assumed to be distributed equally between the forward and aft propellers, and the radial load distribution was assumed to be similar to that on the single propellers. With this load distribution, a structural analysis was made to determine how the blade might be shaped to satisfy both the hydrodynamic and structural requirements. The loading distribution and the resultant bending moments are shown in Fig. 11. For comparison, the bending moments for

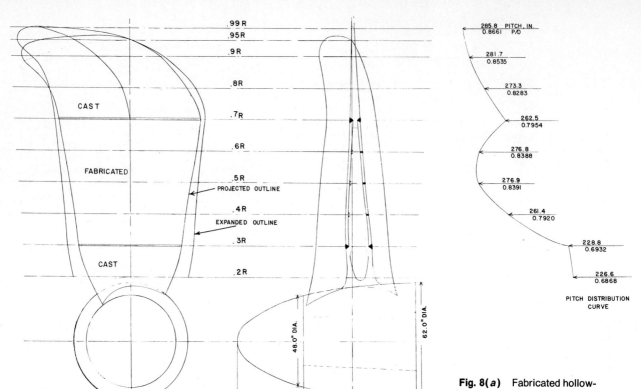

Fig. 8(a) Fabricated hollow-blade propeller concept No. 2

PITCH DISTRIBUTION CURVE

END VIEW

LONGITUDINAL VIEW

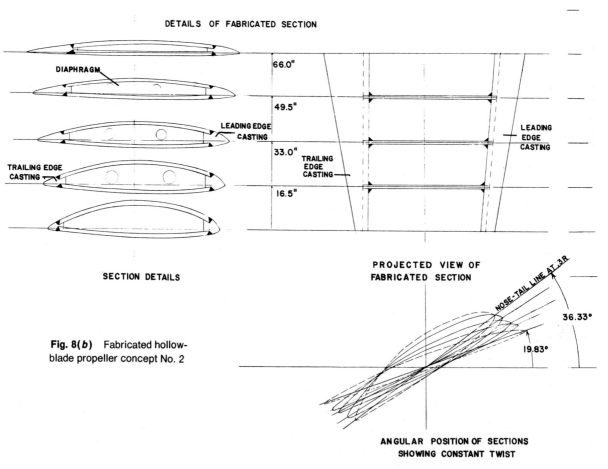

DETAILS OF FABRICATED SECTION

SECTION DETAILS

Fig. 8(b) Fabricated hollow-blade propeller concept No. 2

PROJECTED VIEW OF FABRICATED SECTION

ANGULAR POSITION OF SECTIONS SHOWING CONSTANT TWIST

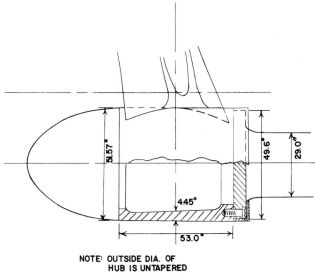

NOTE: OUTSIDE DIA. OF
HUB IS UNTAPERED

Fig. 9   Hollow hub

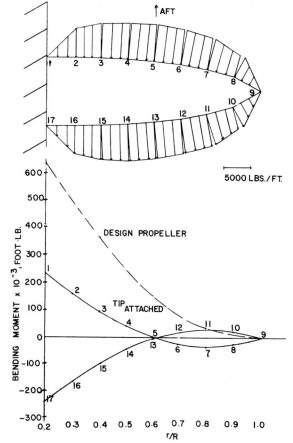

5000 LBS./FT.

Fig. 11   Load and bending moment distribution on tip-attached tandem
propeller

the single propellers are also shown.   As would be expected, the bending moments in the root section (0.2 to 0.6 radius) are substantially reduced and they actually reverse in the tip region (0.7 to 1.0 radius).   Unfortunately, the magnitude of the bending moments at the tip is actually greater than for the single propeller.   This indicates that the blade area can be very substantially reduced in the root region but has to be increased in the tip region to accommodate the structural requirements. The blade shape is somewhat similar to that of a Kaplan rotor. Cavitation criteria at the 0.8 and 0.9 sections require that certain thickness-chord ratios not be exceeded, which further increases the area in this region.   The net effect is an increase in blade area for the set of tandem propellers over that required for the single propeller.

With this information on blade shapes, a number of lifting-line studies were made in which variations in the angular spacing of the blades between the two propellers were investigated.   The best efficiency was achieved with an angular spacing in which the aft propeller leads the forward by 27.8 deg. The spacing between the propellers' centerplanes was 21 percent of the propeller diameter, or 5.78 ft.   Hence, the tip of the forward propeller was raked aft 2.89 ft and skewed forward 13.9 deg whereas the aft propeller was raked forward 2.89 ft and skewed aft 13.9 deg.

Calculations were made for two different blade area ratios, one which matched the single propeller (BAR = 0.56) and one in which the same cavitation criteria are maintained at the 0.8 and 0.9 radius as for the single propeller (BAR = 0.840).   These showed gains in propeller efficiency over the single propeller

Fig. 10   Tip-attached tandem propeller blade

of 8.3 and 3.0 percent, respectively.   Since the cavitation performance of the tip-attached propeller is expected to be somewhat different from that of conventional propellers, it is expected that the blade area required for comparable performance would be between the two values studied.   Therefore, it is concluded that tip-attached propellers can be expected to increase efficiency by between 3 and 8 percent over a comparable single propeller.

Weight estimates were made of the tandem propeller with the larger blade area ratio and with a hollow hub in order to minimize the total weight.   The total estimated weight of the propeller was 81 000 lb or about 3.2 percent heavier than the conventional solid-bladed propeller.   The elimination of the tailshaft weight associated with the solid-bladed propeller would reduce the weight to 68 900 lb, or 12.9 percent less than the solid propeller.

In summary, it appears that there are significant gains to be made in propeller efficiency with the tip-attached tandem propeller, but that there will probably be little if any reduction in propeller blade weight.   Only by using a hollow hub can weight reduction be achieved.   It is also apparent that much more experimental work in both open water and in variable-pressure water tunnels will be required to refine the concept in order to delineate the best blade outline, minimize the blade area, determine the best load distribution between the two propellers, and determine the best angular relationship between the forward and after propeller blades.   Refinements also have to be made in the finite-element structural model to more accurately determine maximum blade bending moments and stresses.

Lightweight advanced materials

A preliminary investigation of the feasibility of constructing a large-diameter ship's propeller from fiber-reinforced plastics (FRP) showed that there should be no insurmountable problems although extensive development effort will be required before practical application is possible. The principal difficulties with FRP construction are flexibility, water absorption and loss of strength due to fatigue, but it appears that all can be controlled by the proper combination of materials and design. While additional research is needed, particularly on the interaction between water absorption and fatigue strengths, it appears that the exotic fibers and resins have properties which are adequate, and that even a comparatively inexpensive glass/polyester matrix may be sufficient for propellers of conventional configuration.

A survey of the physical properties of various plastics and fibers [17, 18] showed that epoxy resin materials have ultimate strengths substantially greater than that of manganese bronze, while polyester glass matrices are comparable or slightly weaker than bronze. With respect to stiffness, however, only a graphite/epoxy combination has a Young's modulus greater than conventional bronze. Therefore blade deflections will be larger for FRP propellers than for bronze propellers.

Calculations described in Appendix 4 were made to compare the deflection of a propeller blade made of nickel-aluminum bronze with that of a comparable blade made of FRP using a polyester matrix of mat, cloth and woven roving (S-glass). The blade was assumed wedge shaped and similar to the blades on the 27.5-ft-diameter solid propeller of the base tanker. The bronze blade was uniformly loaded and sized such that the maximum stress was 8000 psi at the root. The FRP blade was also wedge shaped with the same thickness-chord ratio (0.165) at the root, representing the likely FRP propeller design. A maximum stress of 4000 psi was used for the design assuming the same loading as for the metal blade. These requirements led to blade thickness of 12.44 in. at the root for the FRP blade compared with 9.87 in. for the bronze blade. The corresponding blade-root chords were 6.3 and 5.0 ft, respectively.

Blade tip deflection was then calculated for both materials, with the result that the FRP blade deflects 0.305 ft, which is 2.4 times that of the bronze blade (0.129 ft). It is expected that deflections of this magnitude would present no significant problem, particularly if these deflections and consequent changes of pitch are allowed for in the design stage. That is, a propeller may be designed so that it assumes the designed pitch distribution in its deformed state. It appears possible, therefore, to fabricate an efficient FRP propeller without resorting to the more exotic (and expensive) resins and fibers.

There remains, however, the question of durability in service, particularly as it pertains to fatigue. Fatigue properties of FRP materials are highly dependent upon the care exercised in lay-up of the material and on the extent of water penetration into the material (see Appendix 4).

The stress reversals on a marine propeller blade are due to the variation in the inflow velocity to the blade as it makes each revolution, and their magnitude is influenced by the stern design. Typically a tanker's propeller experiences load variations of about ±25 percent during each revolution [19], thus the amplitude of the resultant stress variation will be about one quarter of the design stress. Calculations (Appendix 4) for the example FRP propeller show that it must have a fatigue stress limit of at least 2140 psi over the life of the propeller. For a tanker operating at 85 rpm over a life span of about 20 years, the propeller blade can be expected to experience 7×10^8 cycles. All of the fiberglass fatigue data except Dixon's [20] show that a stress reversal amplitude of 2140 psi can easily be withstood with some margin for the uncertain effect of saltwater

submergence for the full 20 years. No comparable data were found for epoxy resins. The fatigue resistance of Kevlar is particularly notable; despite a somewhat lower initial yield point than glass, its long-term resistance to fatigue is markedly superior and will permit designing to higher stress levels.

Dixon's data [20] show the deleterious effect of water penetration on both the static and fatigue strengths of fiber-reinforced polyester. These data were taken from cut samples where unfinished ends were directly exposed to water. They are, thus, perhaps overly pessimistic but do indicate the need for preventing water penetration.

One possible means of protecting the FRP using polyurethane has been suggested by chemists of the Upjohn Chemical Company. A structural skeleton of FRP would be inserted in a slightly oversized mold which would then be filled by a poured mixture of polyurethane and catalyst. This would provide a complete barrier against water penetration, a tough erosion-resistant coating,[8] and could include organo-tin compounds for antifouling.

In order to facilitate replacement of a damaged or failed blade, it is suggested that each blade be molded separately, each with a segment of the hub, and held together by interlocking keys bolted to end plates at each end of the hub. This substantially reduces the size of the required molds, and spare blades could be carried aboard ship.

Although much needs to be learned about FRP materials before they can be routinely used for ship propellers, they seem to be promising for future development. A possible first step might be to use FRP propellers as spares, thus reducing the cost and weight of providing spare propellers aboard ships.

Summary of comparative studies

The results of the concepts developed in the preceding are summarized in Table 4. The table shows the estimated final weight and the percentage decrease (or increase) of the weight in relation to the comparable solid propeller. Also tabulated is the estimated propeller efficiency of each concept compared with that of the solid propeller as a percent gain (or loss) in propeller efficiency. From this table and the preceding discussions, it is clear that the cast hollow blade propeller with the hollow hub offers the greatest potential for weight reduction with only a small loss in propeller efficiency. This concept also requires little technological change in current methods of propeller fabrication. Therefore it was selected as the model for an economic case study in which several propellers of increased diameter and reduced rpm were designed for the candidate ship so that potential reductions in operating costs could be predicted.

Since large propeller diameter involves reduced rpm, a detailed study was made of the effects of propeller weight and rpm upon the performance of stern tube bearings and seals.

Effect of propeller weight and rpm on stern tube bearings

The study involved calculations to predict the minimum shaft rpm required to sustain an oil film in the stern tube bearing, that is, the rpm below which the journal would come into metal-to-metal contact with the bushing. By calculating this threshold rpm for the example tanker fitted alternatively with solid and lightweight propellers, the bearing performance could be compared. Similar comparisons were then made assuming that the two types of propellers were designed for reduced design rpm operation in order to determine the extent to which

---

[8] Little data are available on the erosion resistance of FRP but it is suspected that conventional gel coats may be susceptible to cavitation and other damage.

Table 4   Summary of various propellers investigated

All 27.5 ft Diameter—5 Blades

No.	Prop. Type	Hub	Material	Prop. Wt., 1000 lb	% Change in Wt. from Prop. 3	Prop. Eff. at Design	% Change in Eff. From Prop. 3
1	original solid installed on base tanker	solid—long hub	ABS Type 2	122.8	55.2	0.563	−1.2
2	revised solid	solid—long hub	ABS Type 4	83.8	5.9	0.570	0
3	revised solid "baseline propeller"	solid—minimum length hub	ABS Type 4	79.1	0	0.570	0
4	hollow cast	solid	ABS Type 4	63.2	−20.1	0.567	−0.5
5	hollow cast	hollow	ABS Type 4	53.2	−32.7	0.567	−0.5
5a	hollow cast	hollow hub plus reduction in tail shaft wt.	ABS Type 4	40.5	−48.8	0.567	−0.5
6	fabricated No. 1	solid	ABS Type 4	68.3	−13.7	0.567	−0.5
7	fabricated No. 2	solid	ABS Type 4	67.2	−15.0	0.536	−0.6
8	tip attached	hollow	ABS Type 4	81.6	3.2	about 0.599	+5.0

the design rpm could be reduced by using lightweight propellers while still preventing metal-to-metal contact in the bearings at very low ship speeds.

The calculation procedure, briefly described here, is detailed in Appendix 5. Four design rpm cases were studied: 85 rpm as in the original design of the example ship, then 66, 44 and 33 rpm. For each rpm case, solid and hollow propellers were designed to suit the reduced rpm and the corresponding reduced shp and thrust, and increased propeller diameters. Then the propeller weights were calculated for each of the eight cases. For each case, the following elements were calculated or assumed as explained in Appendix 5:

1. required shaft diameter
2. stern tube bearing reactions
3. bearing length-to-diameter ratio
4. bearing clearance ratio
5. shaft alignment
6. shaft bowing

A worst-case alignment is caused by hull deflections which differ from those when the shaft was originally aligned for the full-power condition. In a special case assuming a self-aligning bearing, misalignment was set at zero. Bowing of the shaft is caused by the overhung propeller weight, and is dependent on propeller weight and location, thrust and thrust eccentricity, shaft diameter and length.

An iterative calculation procedure was performed, starting with initial estimates of the minimum rpm for hydrodynamic lubrication (rpm$_{min}$) and the attitude angle at midlength (ψ, see Appendix 5). Calculated values of misalignment and bowing, at the assumed attitude angle, were added to yield a required oil film thickness at midlength (h_r) which would enable the shaft to just clear the bushing at the after edge of the bearing. The h_r value was used to enter a Sommerfeld chart to obtain a calculated rpm$_{min}$. The calculations were repeated, using calculated rpm$_{min}$ and ψ-values until convergence was obtained.

The results of these calculations are shown in Fig. 12, in which the bearing performance for solid and hollow propellers at each design rpm are compared. The minimum rpm for the base ship (solid propeller at 85-rpm design) compares favorably with values in the literature for similar situations. Therefore, the ratio rpm$_{min}$/rpm$_{design}$ ≈ 0.13 was adopted as an acceptable performance criterion for bearings in all cases. The rpm ratio can be assumed to be representative of the ship speed ratio at minimum and design operating conditions, respectively. As the curves indicate, solid propellers designed for 66 and 44 rpm at full ship speed require increasingly higher minimum ship

speeds to maintain bearing lubrication than are currently achieved in practice, and at 33 rpm design and solid propeller arrangement cannot achieve hydrodynamic lubrication even at design speed. The situation is improved in all cases by using lightweight hollow propellers, which at all of the tested design rpm-values will perform satisfactorily within acceptable minimum speed limitations. The effect of the lightweight propellers is to reduce bearing load and shaft bowing, and therefore to improve bearing load distribution.

Additional studies were made of the solid propeller at 33 design rpm to confirm that increasing bearing length would not improve the situation, and as suspected, this proved to be the case—none of the lengthened bearings tried could achieve hydrodynamic lubrication at design speed. Finally, the use of short self-aligning bearings was assumed for the same 33-rpm solid-propeller case. Misalignment is then zero, but bowing is still present. With self-aligning bearings, the situation does improve but not as much as with lightweight propellers; see Fig. 12.

Other points in regard to improving bearing performance which arose during the study, and are further discussed in Appendix 5 are:

1. Hydrostatically lubricated bearings for very-low-rpm applications may be helpful if long periods at sea buoys or in channels are anticipated.
2. Reinforced phenolic resin bushings, which retain some oil within the material and which deform elastically to a greater

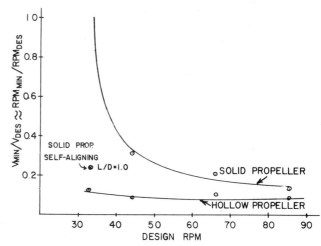

Fig. 12   Stern tube bearing performance with large slow-turning propellers

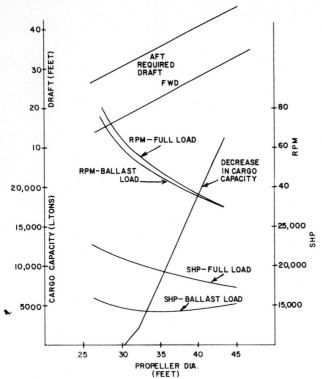

Fig. 13 Effects of increasing propeller diameter on ship performance—compliance with IMCO Rules

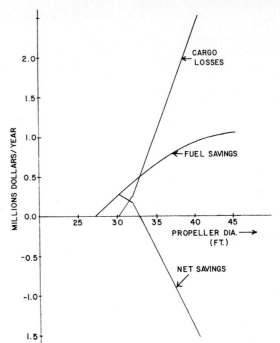

Fig. 14 Economic effects of increasing propeller diameter—compliance with USCG and IMCO

extent than white metal, can reduce the harmful effects of low-rpm operation. With modest design rpm reductions, this could offer a low-risk approach to the problem.

3. Stern seal failures are likely to be reduced with low-rpm operation, since rubbing speeds are reduced, and seal failure incidence increases with rubbing speed.

Economic analysis of large-diameter propellers

The development of a technique for manufacturing very-large-diameter propellers with acceptable weight characteristics makes it possible to determine the impact of a large-diameter propeller upon ship performance and to determine the economic gains that can be achieved. For this case study, the base ship was used assuming that the stern would be redesigned to accommodate the larger-diameter propeller. Studies were made of propellers ranging in size from the 27.5 ft of the original design to 42.5 ft. This study was limited to determining the economic gains only in operating costs.

Impact of U.S. Coast Guard regulations

United States Coast Guard regulations for tankers require that they observe the Intergovernmental Maritime Consultative Organization (IMCO) Rules regarding propeller submergence. These rules require that the draft aft must be sufficient to cover the propeller at all times. The ballast capacity of the base ship as designed is insufficient to meet these requirements with the existing 27.5-ft-diameter propeller; therefore additional segregated ballast had to be allocated. To do this, existing tanks were chosen to be converted for segregated ballast, assuming that cargo tanks would not be subdivided. When the tanks best suited for conversion to satisfy these requirements with the 27.5-ft propeller were determined, the resulting ballast condition was actually sufficient to submerge a propeller of 30.2 ft in diameter. Larger propellers could be used and still be in

compliance with the regulations only if the base ship's cargo capacity were progressively reduced so that segregated ballast capacity could be increased. The specific Coast Guard regulations referred to here are described in Appendix 6.

It was assumed that the ship would make 16 knots in service as the original ship was powered to achieve 17 knots on trial at full load. For the purposes of this study, it was assumed that this speed would be maintained in both full-load and ballast conditions. Power requirements were determined for each propeller size for the operating speed of 16 knots using the NSMB regression equations for hull resistance and propulsion factors as previously cited. The results of these calculations are presented in Fig. 13, which shows that the shp for full load decreases with diameter whereas shp for ballast load goes through a minimum due to the IMCO requirements for propeller submergence.

For the economic analysis, a trade route scenario was developed between Aruba and Rotterdam. From this scenario and the operating profile, the number of round trips per year was determined for the 16-knots operating speed. Annual fuel costs savings (based on $23.50/bbl) and annual cargo revenue losses (based on $10/ton/round trip) were then calculated. These are related to the base case 27.5-ft-diameter propeller and the results shown in Fig. 14. It can be seen that cargo revenue losses rapidly outweigh the fuel cost savings associated with the larger-diameter propellers. Thus, despite the potential for substantial fuel savings, regulatory limitations impose unacceptable losses in cargo revenue and dictate an optimum propeller diameter of about 30.2 ft. Use of a propeller of this size would generate an annual saving of a little over a quarter million dollars. The assumptions and calculations associated with this analysis are in Appendix 7. This appendix includes a sensitivity study showing the effect of changes in fuel costs, cargo revenue, and operating speed upon the net annual savings and upon the optimum propeller diameter. It showed that these changes have little effect upon the optimum propeller diameter, but the net annual savings are most sensitive to fuel prices, and to a lesser degree to ship operating speed.

Large-Diameter Propellers of Reduced Weight

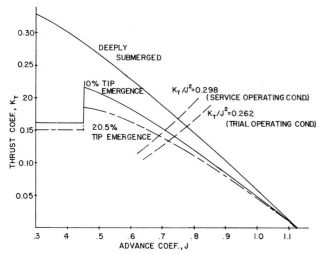

Fig. 15 Open-water performance of partially submerged 42.5-ft propeller for base tanker

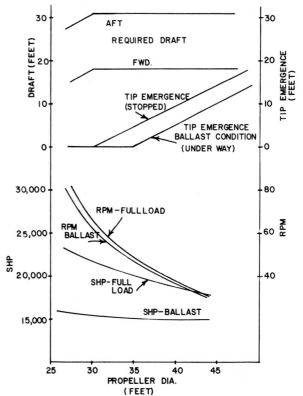

Fig. 16 Effects of increasing propeller diameter on ship performance—rules relaxed, blade tips emerged

The fuel savings curve in Fig. 14 clearly shows the economic advantage of large-diameter propellers if cargo revenue losses could be eliminated. This suggests that if the Coast Guard implementation of the IMCO Rules on draft limitation could be modified without jeopardizing safe operation, fuel economy of tankers similar to this case study would be improved substantially. The present rules require that a tanker have sufficient segregated ballast capacity to submerge the propeller at all times even when stopped. Most tankers, when underway in the ballast condition, experience a wave rise at the stern, which in a ship of this size at 16 knots would be in the order of 4 ft. It is also known that if a small amount of the propeller tips should emerge when underway there is no deleterious effect upon performance. Thus, it was desired to predict performance of a large-diameter propeller with a small percentage of the tips emerged in the ballast condition.

Propellers with blade tips emerged

It was noted that in the past, tankers and other ships frequently operated in the ballast condition with the propeller tips emerged. Thus, there is field evidence of successful operating experience with propeller tips partially exposed.

Discussions with representatives of the Coast Guard revealed that on a case-by-case basis, relief from U.S. regulations can be granted provided equivalent vessel safety can be assured. This is termed achieving an "equivalence" to the regulations. In this case, it would seem an equivalence could be obtained if the following characteristics of a conventional fully immersed propeller are achieved by the tip-emerged propeller:
1. equivalent thrust
2. equivalent vibration characteristics
3. equivalent fuel efficiency
4. equivalent stopping conditions

Within the limits of this project, a number of the foregoing equivalences were studied, namely, 1, 3 and 4 to see if the performance of a large-diameter propeller with tips emerged would compromise any of them. The extensive study by Shiba on air drawing of propellers [21] provided the necessary data. He conducted systematic open-water tests on a series of models of merchant ship propellers with various tip emergences. This provided the basic information, along with the previous resistance information, to determine the effect of tip emergence upon the performance factors just cited. A study of 37.5- and 42.5-ft propellers with 6 and 17 percent tip emergence, respectively (this assumes a 4-ft wave rise at the propeller), in the

ballast condition at 16 knots showed that there is no danger of propeller ventilation. This is shown in Fig. 15, in which the propeller open-water curves are given for deeply submerged and for 10 and 20 percent tip emergences of the 42.5-ft-diameter propeller. Included are the K_T/J^2 curves for the ship in both the service and trial conditions. Their intersections with the propeller open-water curves define the ship operating points. Since the intersections are well clear of the region for air drawing, it is clear that this propeller is a long way from ventilating even when there is substantial propeller emergence.

The performance predictions for 16 knots full load and ballast for the various diameter propellers are presented in Fig. 16. In this instance, the shp for both full load and ballast condition continues to decrease with increasing propeller diameter. The calculations also show that the required increase in rpm for the tip-emerged propellers to develop the required thrust is quite small (about 1.7 rpm). Thus, this presents no problem in propeller or machinery design.

Starting and stopping predictions

The more critical condition is producing the requisite thrust during the stopping or starting maneuver when more of the propeller tip is out of the water and the momentary loading on the propeller is quite large. A transient calculation was made using a quasi-steady approach similar to that developed by Miniovich [22].

Since the open-water experiments conducted by Shiba were performed with propellers operating in the ahead condition only, the transient studies had to be limited to the accelerating conditions, but it is believed that the trends shown for acceleration will be the same as for deceleration. The calculations determined the time needed to accelerate the ship from 0 to 10

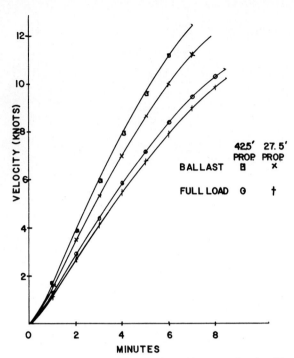

Fig. 17 Starting acceleration of tanker with conventional and large tip-emerged propellers

Table 5 Characteristics of large slow-turning propeller

Diameter	42.5 ft
Number of blades	5
BAR	0.382
BTF	0.0324
Skew at tip	8 deg from reference line
Rake	29.1 in. at tip
Hub length	60 in.
Hub diameter	89.8 in.
Design conditions:	
speed	16.0 knots
rpm	30.8
shp	17 780
Material	ABS Type 4
Blade weight	120 000 lb
Propeller weight	185 500 lb
WR^2 (in air)	15.5×10^6 lb-ft^2
Strength requirements	ABS

knots utilizing but not exceeding the maximum power that would be available for each size propeller; see Fig. 17.

In undertaking such calculations, it is necessary to recognize when air drawing occurs. Since both Froude scaling and surface tension (Weber number) must then be considered, these were taken into account in the calculations, using the data from the Shiba experiments.

The study in the full-load condition showed that there is a tendency to reduce the time to accelerate to a given speed when the propeller diameter is increased. The magnitude of the reduction is small. In the case of the 42.5-ft-diameter propeller compared with the 27.5-ft propeller, there was a 2 percent decrease in the time to accelerate from stop to 10 knots. It would be expected that a similar trend would occur in stopping. No air drawing would occur on either propeller due to the large head of water.

In the ballast condition, the calculations were made assuming no wave rise at the stern as the ship came up to speed; thus, the calculated acceleration is possibly slightly less than would be achieved in actuality. The calculations showed that some loss in thrust does occur at the lower speeds for both the 27.5- and 42.5-ft propellers when operating near full power (low advance ratio, J) due to a small amount of air drawing. They also showed that this condition prevails for only a few minutes until the ship is making sufficient headway to get out of the air-drawing regime. The net effect is that the 42.5-ft propeller actually accelerates somewhat more rapidly than the 27.5-ft propeller. In this instance, the decrease in time to accelerate to 10 knots was more significant, 13 percent. From this analysis, it appears that the safety aspects (stopping and collision avoidance) of the tankers in both the full-load and ballast condition will be slightly better with the larger-diameter propeller, even with tip emergence.

Design of large, slow-turning propeller

As a consequence of the results from the preceding study, it was decided to develop the propeller design for the 42.5-ft

propeller in more detail to show the potential which exists for large slow-turning propellers with acceptable weight characteristics. The approach used was similar to that previously described for the development of the 27.5-ft propellers. An adequate conventional solid propeller was first designed and then a cast hollow-bladed design was developed from the conventional propeller. In developing the conventional propeller design, most of the criteria used in the 27.5-ft propeller design were maintained, namely:

1. ABS Type 4 material
2. Same cavitation criteria
3. Five blades
4. 8-deg skew at the tip
5. 29.1 in. of rake at the tip

Since the diameter was established as 42.5 ft, optimization studies were done to determine the rpm for minimum power. The rpm was found to be 30.8 with shp of 17 800 for a ship speed of 16 knots. This was the design point. Cavitation studies showed that a BAR of about 0.38 should be adequate. A radial wake distribution similar to that of the original ship was assumed, in the absence of model test results, for determining the radial pitch distribution. The characteristics of the propeller which evolved are given in Table 5.

The hollow-bladed propeller was developed from the propeller of Table 5. The hollow blade sections were designed to have the same strength characteristics as the solid propellers. Studies were made with various shell thicknesses, and it was found that a wall thickness of 1.25 in. offered the best compromise between weight reduction and loss in propeller efficiency as was true for the 27.5-ft propeller. A hollow hub was developed based upon the work in Appendix 3. This resulted in a substantial reduction in hub diameter from 89.8 in. for the solid to 63.2 in. for the hollow, due to the sizing of the flange on the tailshaft. The hollow hub weight was reduced by 44 000 lb or 67 percent. The reduction in blade weight was also about 44 000 lb, thus a 47.4 percent reduction in total weight. The WR^2 in air was also significantly reduced about 41 percent. A profile drawing of the resulting propeller is shown in Fig. 18. Its characteristics are the same as those in Table 5, except for the weights and hub diameter. The low operating rpm of 30.8 means that the weight of the solid propeller would be unacceptable from the point of view of hydrodynamic lubrication of the stern tube bearing (see Appendix 5); thus it is necessary to use the reduced-weight propellers.

Operating costs of the base ship fitted with this propeller were calculated using the same operating profile and unit cost assumptions as described previously, with the result that the 42.5-ft-diameter propeller with tip emergence would save about one million dollars in operating costs annually.

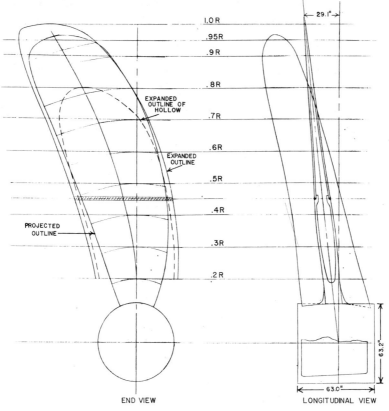

EXPANDED
OUTLINE OF
HOLLOW

EXPANDED
OUTLINE

PROJECTED
OUTLINE

1.0 R
.95R
.9 R
.8R
.7R
.6R
.5R
.4R
.3R
.2 R

29.1"

63.2"

63.0"

END VIEW

LONGITUDINAL VIEW

Fig. 18 Large slow-turning hollow-blade propeller

Advantages of the large slow-turning propeller

The use of a 42.5-ft-diameter propeller would result in the following gains:

1. A 23 percent reduction in installed horsepower.
2. An increase in the full-load propulsive coefficient from 0.675 to 0.815.
3. An increase in ballast condition propulsive coefficient from 0.750 to 0.792.
4. A 19 percent reduction in fuel consumption based on the scenario previously discussed.
5. A 13 percent reduction in time to accelerate (or decelerate) from 0 to 10 knots when in ballast.
6. There appears to be no significant difference in machinery, hull and propeller capital costs for a large-diameter slow-turning propeller versus the conventional propeller and power plant (Appendix 7).

Some "costs," both known and unknown, have been incurred in achieving these gains. The most critical of these is the necessity to establish "equivalence" of performance of the large-diameter propeller when its tips are exposed in the ballast condition. To do this, the magnitude of the propeller blade unsteady forces as the propeller blade tip emerges from and reenters the water must be determined. The effect upon the propeller blade fatigue stresses must be known as well as the unsteady bearing forces which are transmitted to the ship hull. The unsteady hydrodynamic forces upon the hull from the propeller would probably be reduced because much of the stern counter area is out of the water.

The more minor costs are those associated with handling a larger diameter propeller, larger propeller shaft sizes, a higher-aspect-ratio rudder, the maintenance of a third reduction gear and the removal for maintenance of a tailshaft with coupling flanges on both ends.

The "bottom line" appears, for the tankers under study, to be a fuel saving of approximately one million dollars per year without incurring any additional capital costs.

Conclusions

The conclusions derived from this work will be treated in a number of sections to conform to the work as it developed.

Reducing propeller weight

1. The most promising approach to reducing propeller blade weight using current materials and manufacturing facilities is to cast hollow blades. The tips from the 0.5 radius outward are cast separately and welded to the part of the blades cast integral with the hub.
2. The hollow blade designed to have the same maximum stresses as the parent solid propeller will have increased blade thickness resulting in some reduction in propeller efficiency. Parametric studies of effect of wall thickness of hollow blades on blade weight and propeller efficiency show that a wall thickness of about $1\frac{1}{4}$ in. combines substantial blade weight reduction (40 to 50 percent) with small efficiency penalty (less than $\frac{1}{2}$ percent).
3. Substantial weight reduction (over 60 percent) of the propeller hub can be achieved by using a hollow hub with a flanged connection to the tailshaft, thus eliminating the weight of the tapered tailshaft section as well as that of the solid hub.
4. Of all the combinations studied, the combination offering the greatest potential for weight reduction (about 50 percent) with only a small loss in propeller efficiency (0.5 percent) is the cast hollow blades combined with hollow hub and flanged tailshaft connection.

5. The study on first cantilever mode of blade vibration showed that hollow blades raised the resonant frequency substantially (over 100 percent), thus reducing the likelihood on large-diameter propellers of blade fatigue failure due to stresses arising from this mode of vibration.

6. Although the tip-attached tandem propeller did not show any likely weight saving, the study revealed that there may be a substantial gain in propeller efficiency, somewhere between 3 and 8 percent, from this form of propeller.

Tanker case study—propeller blades immersed

1. When operating in harbors at maneuvering speeds, ships having design shaft speeds as low as 30 rpm can achieve satisfactory stern tube bearing lubrication if they have propellers with hollow blades and hollow hubs. If they have solid propellers, proper low-speed lubrication is difficult to achieve in this case with propellers designed for less than 80 rpm and appears impossible for those designed for less than 45 rpm.

2. Adherence to the U.S. Coast Guard regulations requiring propeller blade immersion for tankers in ballast, and requiring segregated ballast tanks, will limit the propeller diameter of the example ship to 30.2 ft if cargo capacity is not reduced. A propeller of this diameter can achieve an annual fuel saving of over one quarter million dollars compared with that of the 27.5-ft propeller currently installed for the operating scenario assumed in the study.

3. For propeller diameters so large that additional ballast tankage is required to immerse the tips, the cargo revenue losses outweigh fuel cost savings due to the Coast Guard regulations cited in the foregoing and preclude taking advantage of the further gains in fuel savings. It appears that review or waiver of this rule may be desirable if further gains in fuel saving are to be achieved with large-diameter slow-turning propellers.

Tanker case study—propeller blade tips emerged

1. The 42.5-ft-diameter propeller at 30.8 rpm with blade tips emerged does not draw air or ventilate and shows a slightly higher rpm at maximum power in the ballast as compared to the full load condition. This should pose no problem in propeller or machinery design.

2. The large, tip-emerged propeller showed shorter acceleration times compared to the 27.5 ft conventional propeller. Thus, it is expected that the larger-diameter propeller is safer in respect to stopping and collision avoidance.

3. No shaft bearing force or hydrodynamic vibration studies were conducted on the large-diameter propeller in ballast condition.

4. The capital costs of the hull, machinery and propeller for a large, slow-turning propeller installation as compared to those for a 27.5 ft, 85-rpm propeller appear to be about the same. A propeller of this diameter can achieve an annual fuel saving of about one million dollars compared with the 27.5-ft propeller currently installed for the operating scenario assumed in the study.

Recommendations for further research

This work has spawned a number of ideas which need further development. These are outlined briefly in the following paragraphs.

1. The study showed the major weight reduction which can be achieved by using a hollow hub attached to a flange on the tailshaft in lieu of fitting the hub on a shaft taper. Thin-shell theory and simplified blade-root geometry were used to determine the minimum hub wall thickness required. These calculations showed that a hub could be much thinner than is normally employed in propeller design. It would be well to further check these calculations with a finite-element model

subjected to steady and vibratory loads caused by propeller blade unsteady loading.

2. The thrust of this investigation was directed toward the reduction of propeller weight with minimum departure from current technology. This has largely been achieved in the hollow cast blade with separately cast tips utilizing well-established propeller materials. It is clear from preliminary studies (Appendix 4) that reinforced plastics (FRP) may prove to have great potential for further weight savings with minimal effect on propeller performance. Much work needs to be done to determine the fatigue properties of these materials when submerged in salt water indefinitely. It is also necessary to determine the effect of the elastic characteristics of these materials on propeller performance.

3. A surprising result from this study was that while the tip-attached tandem propeller does not significantly reduce propeller weight, it should achieve a significant increase in propeller efficiency. The evidence for this is computational and based on simplified models. Research should be done on two aspects of tip-attached tandem propellers: model tests to confirm their hydrodynamic performance, and finite-element studies to check their strength. If the predicted advantages are confirmed, actual ship installations should be tried.

4. The IMCO regulation on submergence of the propeller in the ballast condition, which are implemented by the Coast Guard for ships operating in U.S. waters, should be critically reviewed. The regulations require that the propeller be underwater when stopped. Most tankers when underway in ballast experience a rise in the waterline at the stern due to the pressure distribution around the hull. This rise can be as much as four or five feet on large tankers. It is suggested, at the least, that these rules should take this into account. The technical evaluations performed in this study with the large-diameter propeller seem to show that safety of operation is not reduced even when the propeller tips are emerged.

5. If the potential gains of the large-diameter propeller with tips sometimes emerged are to be commercially exploited, it is necessary to investigate the propeller-induced vibration and the action of such propellers in the transient condition.

(a) Two aspects of the propeller induced vibration should be examined: the magnitude of the forces induced by the propeller upon the hull and the magnitude of the unsteady loads upon the propeller blade due to the exposure of the tip of the blade. Modification of analytic techniques available today can provide some guidance on the possible magnitude of these forces, but ultimately model or full-scale experiments will be required to verify the analytic prediction.

(b) The action of a propeller with tip emerged can be effectively studied by model propeller experiments in a model basin. An extensive program of model testing both in open water and behind the hull can contribute significantly to our understanding of air drawing while building a body of design data.

Acknowledgments

The authors express their thanks to the U.S. Maritime Administration, which sponsored this research, and to the Bethlehem Steel Corporation for providing details of the base tanker and propeller. Dr. P.C. Pien of the David W. Taylor Naval Ship Research and Development Center (DTNSRDC) contributed to the study of tip-attached tandem propellers, and Mr. V. Atkins of the Doran Propeller Company made many helpful suggestions and comments. Ms. E. Palumbo of the Webb research staff did the computer analyses and drafting work, assisted by Mr. M. Rabinowitz. Typing and report preparation were done by Ms. K. Albanese and Ms. G. Sujecki.

References

1 Chang, Pin Yu et al., "Limitations on the Maximum Power of Single-Screw Ships," TRANS. SNAME, Vol. 87, 1979.

2 Kadoi, Hiroyuki, "Reduction of Power of Ships Resulting from Improved Propulsive Efficiency (Power Saving by Means of Large, Slow-Turning Propeller)," *Bulletin of the Marine Engineering Society of Japan*, Vol. 8, No. 4, Dec. 1980.

3 Holtrop, J. and Mennen, G. G. J., "A Statistical Power Prediction Method," *International Shipbuilding Progress* Vol. 25, No. 290, Oct. 1978.

4 Oosterveld, M. W. C. and Van Oossanen, P., "Further Computer-Analyzed Data of the Wageningen B-Screw Series," *International Shipbuilding Progress*, Vol. 22, No. 251, July 1975.

5 Schoenherr, Karl E., "Formulation of Propeller Blade Strength," TRANS. SNAME, Vol. 71, 1963.

6 Emery, J. C. et al, "Systematic Two-Dimensional Cascade Tests of NACA 65-Series Compressor Blades at Low Speeds," NACA Report 1368, 1959.

7 Hoerner, S. F., *Fluid-Dynamic Drag*, 1965.

8 *Marine Engineering*, H. L. Seward, Ed., Vol. 1, SNAME, 1942.

9 Eames, C. F. W. and Sinclair, L., "Methods of Attaching a Marine Propeller to the Tailshaft," *Trans.* IME, (TM), Vol. 92, London, 1980.

10 Bijlaard, P. P., "Stresses from Local Loadings in Cylindrical Pressure Vessels," *Trans.* ASME, 1954.

11 Timoshenko, S. and Woinkowsky-Krieger, S., *Theory of Plates and Shells*, McGraw-Hill, New York, 1981.

12 *Rules for Building and Classing Vessels 1981*, American Bureau of Shipping, New York, 1981.

13 Fielding, S. A., "Design Improvements and Standardization of Propulsion Shafting and Bearings," *Marine Technology*, Vol. 3, No. 2, April 1966.

14 Rothamel, R., "Mechanical Design of Propellers and Tailshafts," SNAME Gulf Section, Mobile, Alabama, Sept. 1979.

15 Qin, Sun, Yun-de, Gu, and Shu-zhen, Zheng, "On the Open Water Series Test of Model Tandem Propellers and Its Design Method with Charts," *Trans.* Chinese Society of Naval Architects and Marine Engineers, No. 66, July 1979.

16 Gonzalez, R. Ruiz-Rornells et al, "Fuel Savings from a New Type of Propeller," *Marine Propulsion International*, Dec. 1981/Jan. 1982.

17 Beadmore, R. et al, "Fiber Reinforced Composites: Engineered Structural Materials," *Science Magazine*, Vol. 208, No. 4446, May 23, 1980.

18 Sonneborn, Ralph H. et al, *Fiberglass Reinforced Plastics*, 1st ed., Reinhold, New York, 1954.

19 Hadler, J. B. and Palumbo, E., "Study of Unsteady Propeller Blade Bending Moments," American Bureau of Shipping, Dec. 1981.

20 Dixon, "Design of HMS *Wilton*," RINA Symposium on GRP Ship Construction, Oct. 1972.

21 Shiba, H., "Air Drawing of Marine Propellers," *Journal of the Society of Naval Architects of Japan*.

22 Miniovich, I. Y., "Investigation of Hydrodynamic Characteristics of Screw Propellers under Conditions of Reversing and Calculation Methods for Backing of Ships," Bureau of Ships Translation No. 697, dated 1960.

23 Conn, J. F. C., "Marine Propeller Blade Vibration," *Trans.* NECIES, Vol. 57, Jan. 10, 1939.

24 Baker, G. S., "Vibration Patterns of Propeller Blades," *Trans.* NECIES, Vol. 57, 1940.

25 Burrill, L. C. and Robson, W., "Virtual Mass and Moment of Inertia of Propellers," *Trans.* NECIES, Vol. 78, March 23, 1962.

26 Tse, F. S., Morse, I. E., and Hinkle, R. T., *Mechanical Vibrations Theory and Applications*, 2nd ed., Allyn and Bacon, Inc., 1978.

27 Schlicting, *Boundary Layer Theory*, 6th ed., McGraw-Hill, New York, 1968.

28 Robinson, A. and Laurmann, J. A., *Wing Theory*, Cambridge University Press, 1956.

29 Wislicenus, G. F., "A Study of the Theory of Axial-Flow Pumps," *Trans.* ASME, Vol. 67, 1945.

30 Schlicting, H., "Application of Boundary-Layer Theory in Turbomachinery," *Journal of Basic Engineering, Trans.* ASME, Vol. 81, 1959.

31 Schlicting, H. and Das, A., "Recent Research on Cascade-Flow Problems," *Journal of Basic Engineering, Trans.* ASME, Vol. 88, 1966.

32 Mellor, G. L., "An Analysis of Axial Compressor Cascade Aerodynamics," *Journal of Basic Engineering, Trans.* ASME, Vol. 81, 1959.

33 Mani, R., "A Method of Calculating Quasi Two-Dimensional Flows Through Cascades," Report No. E-79.10, Engineering Division, California Institute of Technology, July 1967.

34 Wilson, M. B. and Acosta, A. J., "A Note on the Influence of Axial Velocity Ratio on Potential Flow Cascade Performance," Report No. E-79.11, Engineering and Applied Science Division, California Institute of Technology, Jan. 1969.

35 Erwin, J. R., Savage, M., and Emery, J. C., "Two-Dimensional Low-Speed Cascade Investigation of NACA Compressor Blade Sections Having a Systematic Variation in Mean-Line Loading," NACA Technical Note 3817, Nov. 1956.

36 Gearhart, W. S. and Ross, J. R., "Two-Dimensional Cascade Tests of a Compressor Blade Designed by the Mean Streamline Method," Pennsylvania State University Ordanance Research Laboratory Technical Memorandum TM 71-32, 1971.

37 Abbott, I. H. and von Doenhoff, A. E., "*Theory of Wing Sections*, Dover Publications, New York, 1959.

38 Bijlaard, P. P., "Stresses from Radial Loads in Cylindrical Pressure Vessels," *Welding Research Supplement, Welding Journal*, Dec. 1954.

39 Bijlaard, P. P., "Stresses from Radial Loads and External Moments in Cylindrical Pressure Vessels," *Welding Research Supplement, Welding Journal*, December 1955.

40 Cameron, A., *Basic Lubrication Theory*, Longman Group Ltd., London, 1971.

41 Trumpler, P. R., *Design of Film Bearings*, MacMillan Co., New York, 1966.

42 Larsen, O. C., "Some Considerations of Shaft Alignment of Marine Shaftings," Norwegian Maritime Research, 1976; (substantially repeated, but with discussion) *Trans.* IME, 1979.

43 Hill, A. and Martin, F. A., "Some Considerations in the Design of Stern Tube Bearings and Seals," *Trans.* IME, 1979.

44 Telephone conversation with D. O. Carson, Waukesha Bearings Corp., Waukesha, Wis., June 29, 1981.

45 Gardner, W. W., "Design and Test Data on the Sternlign Bearing," Waukesha Bearing Corp., Waukesha, Wis., 1972.

46 Crambie, G., "Stern Bearings-In Service Measurements of Tailshaft Attitude, Bearing Clearance and Other Parameters," *Trans.* IME, 1977.

47 Hyakutake, J. et al, "Measurements of Relative Displacement Between Stern Tube Bearing and Shaft of 210,000 DWT Tanker," *Japan Shipbuilding and Marine Engineering*, 1973.

48 "Design and Operation of Stern Tube Bearings: An Assessment of the State of the Art," Mechanical Technology Inc., Report No. MA-RD-920-78010, Latham, N.Y., Sept. 1977.

49 Volcy, G. C. and Ville, R., "Actual Shaft Behavior on Oil Film Thickness Taking Account of Propeller Forces and Moments," *Trans.* IME, 1979.

50 Emerson, A., Sinclair, L., and Milne, P. A., "The Propulsion of a Million Ton Tanker," *Trans.* IME, 1971.

51 "Sternlign Tailshaft Bearings," Waukesha Brochure W-6A.

52 McIlvean, W., "Stern Tube Seals and Plastic Bearings—A Ship Owner's Development and Experiences," *Trans.* IME, 1976.

53 Saunders-Davies, D. L. and Cunningham, G. L., "Operating VLCC—What Have We Learned?" with discussion by Volcy, *Trans.* IME, 1975.

54 "Bearing and Seal Materials for Stern Tube Applications—Assessment of the State of the Art," Mechanical Technology Inc., Report No. MA-RD-920-77090, Latham, N.Y., June 1977.

55 Rose, A., "Hydrostatic Stern Gear," *Trans.* NECIES, 1974.

56 Hill, A., "Modern Bearing Design and Practice," *Trans.* IME, 1976.

57 Koons, H. O., "Stern Bearings and Seal Failures," *Trans.* IME, 1971.

58 "Large Roller Stern Bearing in Service," *Shipbuilding and Marine Engineering International*, Dec. 1974.

59 Crambie, G. and Clay, G. F., "An Improved Stern Bearing System—Design Features of and Operating Experience with Turnbull Split Stern Bearings," *Trans.* IME, 1972.

60 "A Statistical and Economic Evaluation of Stern Tube Bearing and Seal Failures," Mechanical Technology Inc., Report No. MA-RD-940-77091, Latham, N.Y., July 1977.

61 Attwood, J. D. et al, "How to Save Fuel on Steam Tankers," *Marine Engineers Review*, Feb. 1980.

62 Rein, H., "A Case Study of the Effect of Reduced Ship Speed and Off Design Operation of the Power Plant on the Net Earning Rate of a Steam Turbine Powered VLCC," *Trans.* IME, 1977.

63   Brembo, J. C., "Energy Conservation in Turbine Powered Ships," Norwegian Maritime Research, 1979.

64   Stott, C. W. and Casey, J. P., "An Updated Analysis of Fuel Consumption: Steam and Diesel," *Marine Technology*, Vol. 17, No. 4, Oct.1980.

65   Larsen, G. W., "VAP Turbine Plant and Its Economy," *Trans.* IME (Series C), 1978.

66   Femenia, J. F., "Efficient Low-Power Operation of Steam Turbine Marine Power Plants," Maritime Administration, 1975.

67   Larsen, G. A., "New Techno-Economic Scenarios and Optimum Steam Cycles," Stal-Laval, New York, 1975.

68   Spears, H. C. K., "Steam Propulsion for Modern Ships," *Trans.* IME (Series C), 1978.

69   Stott, C. W., "Modern Steam or Diesel Propulsion? Some Corporative Technical Economics," General Electric Co., New York, 1977.

70   "Power Plants for the 70's," T&R Bulletin No. 3-26, SNAME, 1974.

71   *Marine Design Manual for Fiberglass Reinforced Plastics*, Gibbs & Cox, Inc., Sponsored by Owens-Corning Fiberglass Corporation, McGraw-Hill New York, 1960.

72   Neal, *Properties and Usage of Kevlar 49*, Dupont Chemical Company, 1979.

Appendix 1

Natural frequency and moment of inertia of hollow propeller blade

It is desired to determine whether the natural frequency of a large propeller blade may become so low that resonance with the blade exciting frequency will occur. As a first approximation, the blade may be treated as a nonuniform cantilever beam, fully fixed at the hub. Torsional vibration and possible coupling effects are ignored. The effect of blade twist is quite complicated, but as a first approximation the blade may be assumed to vibrate normal to the nose-tail chord at each r/R. Thus, the blade is imagined to be untwisted and the moments of inertia are calculated about a neutral axis assumed parallel to the nose-tail chord at each r/R. Damping (structural and hydrodynamic) is ignored, but the added hydrodynamic mass is included. Thus, the problem can be modeled as a nonuniform cantilever beam fixed at one end and free at the other.

Approximations using simplified blade geometries

The literature contains several empirical methods for estimating the lateral natural frequency of a propeller blade. Conn [23] suggests two simplified models for a propeller blade, shown in Fig. 19. These models have natural frequencies of flexural vibration parallel to blade breadths as follows:

Model No. 1

$$f = 0.845 \frac{a}{l^2} \sqrt{\frac{gE}{3\rho}} \qquad (13)$$

Model No. 2

$$f = 0.29 \frac{t}{l^2} \sqrt{\frac{gE}{\rho}} \qquad (14)$$

where

a, t, l = defined in figure
E = Young's modulus
ρ = density,

Conn's method has been applied to the solid blade of the 27.5-ft-diameter five-bladed propeller of the example ship. At 85 rpm the exciting frequency of this propeller is 7.1 cps. Conn's approximations give natural frequencies of the wedge (Model 1) and parabolic (Model 2) blades (parallel to blade breadth) as follows:

Model No. 1: $f = 16.3$ cps

Model No. 2: $f = 19.4$ cps

Baker [24] develops a slightly more complex model based on an NACA 66 section shape at all radii, and an assumed parabolic blade outline. His formula for f_n in air is

$$\text{Frequency (cps)} = 0.305 \frac{t_r}{l^2} \left(\frac{b_r}{b_m} \times \frac{t_m}{t_r} \right)^{1/2} \sqrt{\frac{gE}{\rho}} \qquad (15)$$

where b_r and t_r are breadth and maximum thickness at root, respectively, and b_m and t_m are mean breadth and mean maximum thickness, respectively, of the blades. All dimensions are in inches.

Baker's approximation for the example ship solid propeller yields a natural frequency of 17.4 cps in air.

Another empirical approach suggested by Burrill [25] includes the influence of added hydrodynamic mass. He shows that the natural frequency in water is lower than that for the corresponding blade in air.

Calculated natural frequency using actual blade geometry

Various computational methods have been devised for calculating the natural frequency of beams of arbitrarily varying cross section. The Rayleigh-Ritz method [26] was selected for this study because of its computational simplicity. The method can also accommodate the effect of added mass and the geometry of hollow blades.

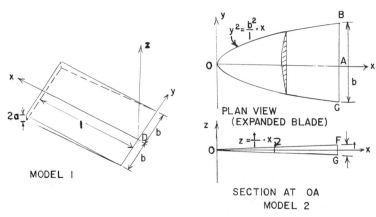

Fig. 19   Simplified propeller blade models

	Solid Blade				Hollow Blade			
(1) $x = r/R$	(2) Area (ft^2)	(3) I_0 (ft^4)	(4) Structural Mass (slugs/ft)	(5) Total Mass (slugs/ft)	(6) Area (ft^2)	(7) I_0 (ft^4)	(8)(9) Structural Mass (slugs/ft)	Total Mass (slugs/ft)
0.2	3.98	0.2360	58.32	106.68	2.65	0.2165	38.92	80.93
0.3	3.76	0.1653	55.08	113.40	1.40	0.2010	20.60	71.24
0.4	3.42	0.1083	50.16	117.48	1.20	0.1521	17.53	76.09
0.5	3.00	0.0662	44.04	118.56	1.30	0.0942	19.02	84.29
0.6	2.51	0.0366	36.84	115.68	1.37	0.0530	20.14	89.89
0.7	1.97	0.0177	28.92	107.88	1.44	0.0230	21.26	92.87
0.8	1.41	0.0069	20.64	93.36	1.58	0.0109	23.12	91.38
0.9	0.83	0.0018	12.12	67.68	0.94	0.0027	13.80	69.37
1.0	0.20	0.0003	3.00	22.00	0.34	0.0008	5.00	32.00

NOTES:
Total mass = structural mass + added mass.
Added mass assumed equal to mass of water displaced by circular cylinder whose diameter = c, the local nose-tail chord.
$\rho = 0.273$ lb/in.^{3} for ABS Type 4 bronze.
$E = 14.5 \times 10^6$ psi for ABS Type 4 bronze.

To use this method, the blade cross-sectional area, moment of inertia, structural mass and hydrodynamic added mass must be calculated for each radius. For the example solid propeller blade with NACA 65 section, of Type 4 ABS bronze, these properties are given in Table 6.

For initial design estimates, the moments of inertia of the hollow blade sections were approximated using the formula for a solid symmetric NACA 66 section, $I = 0.0424\ t^3 c$. If the neutral axis of a solid section with the same outer offsets is assumed coincident with that of the hollow cavity, the moments of inertia of these two figures can be subtracted to give the moment of inertia of the outer shell.

A more rigorous calculation was performed for the vibration analysis. The nose-tail chord was divided into 10 segments and each element of the shell area was approximated by a quadrilateral shape.

A simple computer program was written to calculate the mass and moment of inertia of the hollow blade by summing these segments at each r/R. The results are given in Table 6.

The Rayleigh-Ritz method may be applied as follows for a nonuniform cantilever beam:

1. Assume a mode shape of the form $y(x) = a_1 x^2 + a_2 x^3$. Note that $y(0) = y'(0) = 0$, the usual fixed-end boundary conditions, but the usual free-end condition that $y''(L) = 0$ is not satisfied.

2. Define:

$$U_{max} = \frac{1}{2} \int_0^L EI(x) \left|\frac{d^2 y}{dx^2}\right|^2 dx \qquad (16)$$

$$T^*_{max} = \frac{1}{2} \int_0^L m(x)y(x)^2 dx \qquad (17)$$

3. Let $I(x)$ and $m(x)$ be represented by known cubic polynomials

$$I(x) = C_1 x^3 + C_2 x^2 + C_3 x + C_4 \qquad (18)$$

$$m(x) = b_1 x^3 + b_2 x^2 + b_3 x + b_4 \qquad (19)$$

Thus, analytical expressions for the integrals in Step 2 may be derived in terms of the unknown coefficients a_1 and a_2.

4. Define:

$$\frac{\delta U_{max}}{\delta a_1} = K_{11}a_1 + K_{12}a_2 \qquad (20)$$

$$\frac{\delta U_{max}}{\delta a_2} = K_{21}a_1 + K_{22}a_2 \qquad (21)$$

$$\frac{\delta T^*_{max}}{\delta a_1} = m_{11}a_1 + m_{12}a_2 \qquad (22)$$

$$\frac{\delta T^*_{max}}{\delta a_2} = m_{21}a_1 + m_{22}a_2 \qquad (23)$$

Then the K's and m's may be determined as follows:

$$K_{11} = 4E \left[\frac{C_1}{4} (L_2 - L_1)^4 + \frac{C_2}{3} (L_2 - L_1)^3 \right.$$
$$\left. + \frac{C_3}{2} (L_2 - L_1)^2 + C_4(L_2 - L_1) \right] \qquad (24)$$

$$K_{21} = K_{12} = 12E \left[\frac{C_1}{5} (L_2 - L_1)^5 + \frac{C_2}{4} (L_2 - L_1)^4 \right.$$
$$\left. + \frac{C_3}{3} (L_2 - L_1)^3 + \frac{C_4}{2} (L_2 - L_1)^2 \right] \qquad (25)$$

$$K_{22} = 36E \left[\frac{C_1}{6} (L_2 - L_1)^6 + \frac{C_2}{5} (L_2 - L_1)^5 \right.$$
$$\left. + \frac{C_3}{4} (L_2 - L_1)^4 + \frac{C_4}{3} (L_2 - L_1)^3 \right] \qquad (26)$$

$$m_{11} = \frac{b_1(L_2 - L_1)^8}{8} + \frac{b_2(L_2 - L_1)^7}{7} + \frac{b_3(L_2 - L_1)^6}{6}$$
$$+ \frac{b_4(L_2 - L_1)^5}{5} \qquad (27)$$

$$m_{21} = m_{12} = \frac{b_1(L_2 - L_1)^9}{9} + \frac{b_2(L_2 - L_1)^8}{8} + \frac{b_3(L_2 - L_1)^7}{7}$$
$$+ \frac{b_4(L_2 - L_1)^6}{6} \qquad (28)$$

$$m_{22} = \frac{b_1(L_2 - L_1)^{10}}{10} + \frac{b_2(L_2 - L_1)^9}{9} + \frac{b_3(L_2 - L_1)^8}{8}$$
$$+ \frac{b_4(L_2 - L_1)^7}{7} \qquad (29)$$

where L_1 and L_2 are the limits of integration.

5. It can be shown that minimization of Rayleigh's quotient is mathematically equivalent to solution of the matrix equation

$$\begin{vmatrix} K_{11} - \omega^2 m_{11} & K_{12} - \omega^2 m_{12} \\ K_{21} - \omega^2 m_{21} & K_{22} - \omega^2 m_{22} \end{vmatrix} = 0 \qquad (30)$$

Thus, ω^2 may be determined solely from the length of the beam and the coefficients from Step 3.

In order to use the Rayleigh-Ritz method, the data already given for $I(x)$ and $m(x)$ in Table 6 were approximated by the following polynomials:

$$I_{\text{solid prop}} \text{ (ft}^4) = -0.0001281\, x^3 + 0.004792\, x^2 \\ - 0.05865\, x + 0.236 \quad (31)$$

$$I_{\text{hollow prop}} \text{ (ft}^4) = 0.007309\, x^3 - 0.010193\, x^2 \\ + 0.0037682\, x + 0.217 \quad (32)$$

$$m_{\text{structural solid prop}} \text{ (slugs/ft)} = 0.01321\, x^3 - 0.43636\, x^2 \\ - 1.9181\, x + 58.32 \quad (33)$$

$$m_{\text{total solid prop}} \text{ (slugs/ft)} = 0.16329\, x^3 + 0.93117\, x^2 \\ + 1.81745\, x + 106.68 \quad (34)$$

$$m_{\text{total hollow prop}} \text{ (slugs/ft)} = -0.31153\, x^3 + 4.07246\, x^2 \\ - 11.5561\, x + 81.0 \quad (35)$$

No coefficients are given for the structural mass of the hollow propeller because the curve could not be accurately fit by a cubic polynomial. The fit for total mass of the hollow propeller was not very good, but is considered adequate to approximate the natural frequency.

Using the Rayleigh-Ritz method, the lowest natural frequencies are determined as follows:

	FREQUENCY, cps
Solid propeller in air	17.9
Solid propeller in water	8.0
Hollow propeller in water	17.4

Thus, it is concluded that the Rayleigh-Ritz method correlates well with Conn's and Baker's approximations for the solid propeller in air, and gives reasonable results for the solid propeller in water.

The hollow 27.5-ft-diameter propeller in water is found to have a natural frequency more than twice that of the solid propeller and well above the calculated exciting frequency of 7.1 cps. Thus, no resonant vibration problem is expected for the 27.5-ft hollow propeller.

Appendix 2

Cascade effects on propeller blade drag

The efficiency of a lifting device such as a screw propeller blade is measured by its lift/drag ratio, commonly expressed in terms of the lift and drag coefficients:

$$C_L = \text{Lift coefficient} = \frac{L}{\frac{1}{2}\rho A V^2} \quad (36)$$

$$C_D = \text{Drag coefficient} = \frac{D}{\frac{1}{2}\rho A V^2} \quad (37)$$

Thus

$$\frac{L}{D} = \frac{C_L}{C_D} = \text{Lift/drag ratio}$$

where

L = lift force on blade section, perpendicular to incident flow direction

D = drag force on blade section, parallel to incident flow direction

ρ = mass density of fluid

A = sectional area of blade section

V = velocity of incident flow

Since the efficiency of a blade section depends partly on the section (or profile) drag, it follows that any condition which alters the profile drag will influence the blade's efficiency.

One such condition arises when several identical blades at the same angle of attack to the incident flow are brought into proximity with one another. In this configuration, known as a cascade, the mutual interference of the flow by the blades on each other causes an augment of their drag forces.

Although cascade effects have been known to exist for more than 40 years [27, 28, 29], they have not generally been considered important in ship screw propeller design because the spacing of blades is usually very large compared with blade thickness, so that the blades have negligible influence on each other so far as drag is concerned. If relative blade spacing decreases, however, cascade effects may have to be investigated. This would be the case for propellers with larger numbers of blades, small hubs (thus, reducing blade spacing at the blade roots), or thicker blades (as in hollow or built-up blade designs) than have been common in past propeller design practice.

Two-dimensional cascade

Cascade effects have been of concern to those involved in the design of turbomachinery such as aircraft turbines and compressors. Theoretical treatments by Schlicting [27, 30, 31], Mellor [32], and others [33, 34] and experimental work by various investigators for the National Advisory Council on Aeronautics (NACA) [6, 35, 36] contain thorough analyses and measurements of the flow of fluids through two-dimensional cascades, which are simplified models of turbine or compressor blades. Schlicting [30] shows that in two-dimensional incompressible, viscous flow through a cascade, the flow is uniform in front of the cascade and at a large distance behind the cascade, but in the wake of the blades nonhomogeneous flow is caused by the influence of viscosity in the boundary layers of the blades.

The main purpose of the cascade in turbomachinery is to deflect the flow through a "turning angle" (inflow angle minus outflow angle), giving an increased circumferential velocity component. In a viscous fluid, the boundary layers on the blades cause an energy loss, measured by the loss in total head of the flow through the cascade, or alternatively, measured by the lift and drag coefficients.

Cascade tunnel experiments

An extensive series of tests on a two-dimensional cascade of NACA 65-series compressor blades was reported in reference [6]. In the tests, systematic variations of blade camber, blade angle, angle of attack, and blade spacing were made, and plots were provided of turning angle, lift coefficient, drag coefficient, and lift-drag ratio. The tests described in [6] were used as the principal source of data for this study because of the broad range of parameters covered, and because the NACA 65-series blade form is similar to typical ship propeller blade forms.

Drag forces and drag coefficients

In order to assess the increase in drag caused by propeller blades in cascade, the drag forces measured in cascade tests [6] must be compared with those on the same airfoil sections measured in isolation, or "open" [37]. The drag penalty is then expressed as the ratio of drag in cascade to drag is open. Both forces are expressed as drag coefficients. Thus

$$C_D = \frac{\text{Cascade drag}}{\frac{\rho}{2} W_1^2 bc} = \text{Drag coefficient in cascade} \quad (38)$$

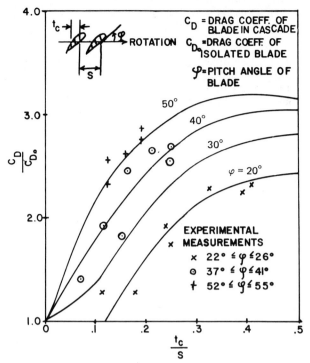

Fig. 20 Effect of cascading on propeller drag coefficient

$$Solidity = \frac{t_c}{s} \qquad (41)$$

where t_c is the blade "thickness" measured through the blade section centroid in the circumferential direction, and s is the blade spacing in the circumferential direction [same as s in equation (40)].

The transformation from σ to t_c/s is as follows:

$$t = t_c \sin\phi \qquad (42)$$

where t is the maximum blade thickness measured perpendicular to nose-tail line and ϕ is the pitch angle

$$\frac{t_c}{s} = \frac{c}{s}\frac{t_c}{c} = \frac{\sigma}{\sin\phi}\left(\frac{t}{c}\right) \qquad (43)$$

Test results and cascade effect equation

Cascade tests on NACA 65-series compressor blades [6, 35] tested at a range of inlet angles and solidities were analyzed to determine cascade drag coefficients as described in the foregoing. The resulting C_D/C_{DO}-values are plotted against t_c/s in Fig. 20. A polynomial regression fit to the plotted results gives the curves shown in the figure for various pitch angles. The equation of these curves is

$$\left.\begin{array}{c} \dfrac{C_D}{C_{DO}} = -1.42 + 14.6\left(\dfrac{t_c}{s}\right) - 24.5\left(\dfrac{t_c}{s}\right)^2 \\[2mm] + 12.4\left(\dfrac{t_c}{s}\right)^3 + 0.0547\,\phi \\[2mm] - 0.00128\left(\dfrac{t_c}{s}\right)\phi^2 + 0.0615\left(\dfrac{t_c}{s}\right)^2\phi \\[2mm] \text{for } \dfrac{t_c}{s} \geq 0.10 \end{array}\right\} \qquad (44)$$

For $\dfrac{t_c}{s} < 0.10$, the recommended equation is

$$\frac{C_D}{C_{DO}} = \frac{10\,t_c}{s}\left[\left(\frac{C_D}{C_{DO}}\right)_{0.1} - 1.0\right] + 1.0 \text{ or } \frac{C_D}{C_{DO}} = 1.0$$

whichever is greater, where

$$\left(\frac{C_D}{C_{DO}}\right)_{0.1} \text{ means } \frac{C_D}{C_{DO}} \text{ at } \frac{t_c}{s} = 0.10$$

$$C_{DO} = \frac{\text{Open foil drag}}{\frac{\rho}{2}V_R^2\,bc} = \text{Drag coefficient in open} \qquad (39)$$

$$\frac{C_D}{C_{DO}} = \text{Cascade effect drag ratio}$$

where

b = blade span
c = blade chord
W_1 = inflow velocity to cascade
V_R = resultant inflow velocity to open foil

Calculating the ratio requires a transformation of the cascade drag coefficient as measured in the tests, because in the cascade tests the drag force was measured parallel to the vector mean velocity of inflow and outflow, whereas in open airfoil tests the drag is measured parallel to the inflow velocity vector, V_R.

The quantities needed to calculate C_D are given in the cascade test plots. They are inflow angle, turning angle, angle of attack, section lift coefficient and section drag coefficient.

For the open-foil coefficient, plotted tests results are given in [37], or alternatively the Hoerner equation [7], fitted to the data in [37], can be used.

Cascade solidity

Solidity is an expression of the relative size of the gap or spacing of the foils or blades in cascade, and, therefore, it has a major influence on the extent of flow restriction and interference among the blades. In the two-dimensional cascade literature, the solidity (or solidity ratio) is usually given as:

$$\sigma = \frac{c}{s} = \frac{\text{Blade chord}}{\text{Blade gap or spacing}} \qquad (40)$$

but it was found that the test results gave more predictable trends if they were crossplotted against a modified solidity defined as follows:

Appendix 3

Stress analysis and design of a hollow propeller hub

Rational design of a hollow hub requires the calculation of the stresses in the hollow hub when it is subjected to the forces imposed on it from the propeller blades during normal operation. As the hollow hub is basically a circular cylinder, the literature on the stress analysis of cylindrical shells was searched for analytical methods to determine the hub stresses.

Classical treatises on the three-dimensional theory of elasticity applied to shell structures include analyses of cylindrical thin-walled shells [11] subject to axisymmetric loads. The analytical solution of the axisymmetrically loaded shell is not easily modified to calculate the stresses caused by local forces and moments applied to the shell, as for example by the centrifugal forces and blade-root bending moments of propeller blades. This type of loading was investigated by Bijlaard [10, 38, 39] by representing the loads on the cylinder and the displacement of the cylindrical shell by double Fourier series.

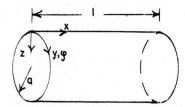

Fig. 21 Hollow hub coordinate system

$$w = \sum\sum w_{mn} \cos m\phi \sin\frac{\lambda}{a}x \qquad (49)$$

$$Z = \sum\sum Z_{mn} \cos m\phi \sin\frac{\lambda}{a}x \qquad (50)$$

where

$$\lambda = \frac{n\pi a}{l} \qquad (51)$$

These series are inserted into the three simultaneous partial differential equations of thin-shell theory [11], which can be reduced to an eighth-order differential equation for the radial displacement of the shell at any point in terms of the applied loads. The solution of that equation leads to double Fourier

Solving (45) with w and Z given by (49) and (50) yields

$$w_{mn} = \Phi mn Zmn \frac{l^4}{2D} \qquad (52)$$

where Φ_{mn} depends only on the geometry of the cylinder and on Poisson's ratio, as follows:

$$\Phi_{mn} = \frac{2(m^2\alpha^2 + n^2\pi^2)^2}{(m^2\alpha^2 + n^2\pi^2)^4 + 12(1-\nu^2)n^4\pi^4\alpha^4\gamma^2 - m^2\alpha^4[2m^4\alpha^4 + (6+\nu-\nu^2)n^4\pi^4 + (7+\nu)m^2\alpha^2n^2\pi^2]} \qquad (53)$$

series expressions for the axial and circumferential displacements and for the bending moments and membrane forces.

Calculation procedure

Bijlaard's method was used to calculate the bending moments and membrane forces in a hollow propeller hub subjected to the propeller blade centrifugal forces and longitudinal and circumferential blade-root moments. The three solutions were then combined by superposition to calculate the resulting membrane forces and bending moments in the hub. Finally, the stresses on the outside and inside surfaces of the hollow hub were calculated, and maximum values of the stresses were determined as a function of hub thickness. The coordinate system is shown in Fig. 21.

The equation for axial deflection w, derived from the three equations of thin-shell theory [11], and omitting terms containing $(t/a)^4$ since t/a is small (<0.1), is

$$\nabla^8 w + \frac{12(1-\nu^2)}{a^2t^2}\frac{\partial^4 w}{\partial x^4} + \frac{1}{a^2}\left[\frac{2\partial^6 w}{a^6\partial\phi^6}\right.$$
$$+ (6+\nu-\nu^2)\frac{\partial^6 w}{a^2\partial x^4\partial\phi^2} + (7+\nu)\frac{\partial^6 w}{a^4\partial x^2\partial\phi^4}\right]$$
$$- \frac{1}{D}\nabla^4 Z = 0 \quad (45)$$

where

a	= radius of cylinder (hub)
l	= length of hub
u,v,w	= displacements (deformations) of hub in the x, y or ϕ, and z directions, respectively
ν	= Poisson's ratio
Z	= radial loading per unit surface, psi (Z takes different forms for the three types of loads induced by the propeller blades)

D = flexural rigidity of shell wall

$$D = \frac{Et^3}{12(1-\nu^2)} \qquad (46)$$

E = modulus of elasticity, psi

$$\nabla^4 Z = \left(\frac{\partial^2 Z}{\partial x^2} + \frac{\partial^2 Z}{a^2\partial\phi^2}\right)^2 \qquad (47)$$

$$\nabla^8 w = \nabla^4\nabla^4 w \qquad (48)$$

This equation is solved by writing the axial deflection w and the external load Z in double Fourier series as follows:

$$\alpha = \frac{l}{a} \qquad (54)$$

$$\gamma = \frac{a}{t} \qquad (55)$$

From the axial deflection, w, the membrane forces and bending moments in the shell wall are derived in references [10] and [11] as follows:

$$N_x = -6\pi^2(1-\nu^2)\alpha^6\gamma^2 a\sum\sum\Phi_{mn}Z_{mn}$$
$$\times \frac{m^2n^2}{(m^2\alpha^2 + n^2\pi^2)^2}\cos m\phi\sin\frac{\lambda}{a}x \quad (56)$$

$$N_\phi = 6\pi^4(1-\nu^2)\alpha^4\gamma^2 a\sum\sum\Phi_{mn}Z_{mn}$$
$$\times \frac{n^4}{(m^2\alpha^2 + n^2\pi^2)}\cos m\phi\sin\frac{\lambda}{a}x \quad (57)$$

$$M_x = \frac{1}{2}\alpha^2 l^2\sum\sum\Phi_{mn}Z_{mn}$$
$$\times \left[\left(\frac{n^2\pi^2}{\alpha^2}\right) + \nu(m^2-1)\right]\cos m\phi\sin\frac{\lambda}{a}x \quad (58)$$

$$M_\phi = \frac{1}{2}\alpha^2 l^2\sum\sum\Phi_{mn}Z_{mn}$$
$$\times \left[m^2 - 1 + \left(\frac{\nu n^2\pi^2}{\alpha^2}\right)\right]\cos m\phi\sin\frac{\lambda}{a}x \quad (59)$$

where

N_x	= longitudinal membrane force in shell wall, per unit width (circumference) of wall, lb/in.
N_ϕ	= circumferential membrane force in shell wall, per unit width (longitudinal) of wall, lb/in.
M_x	= longitudinal bending moment in shell wall, per unit width (circumference) of wall, in-lb/in.
M_ϕ	= circumferential bending moment in shell wall, per unit width (longitudinal) of wall, in-lb/in.

The stresses arising from these forces and moments are

$$\sigma_x = \frac{N_x}{t} \pm \frac{6M_x}{t^2} \text{ (longitudinal)} \qquad (60)$$

$$\sigma_\phi = \frac{N_\phi}{t} \pm \frac{6M_\phi}{t^2} \text{ (circumferential)} \qquad (61)$$

in which the sums and differences of the two terms represent stresses at the inside and outside surfaces of the cylinder, respectively. Designating the stresses at the inside surface [+ signs in equations (60) and (61)] as σ_{xi} and $\sigma_{\phi i}$, and those at the outside surface (− signs) as σ_{x0} and $\sigma_{\phi 0}$, the resultant stresses on each surface are

$$\sigma_i = \sqrt{\sigma_{xi}^2 + \sigma_{\phi i}^2} \text{ (inside surface)} \tag{62}$$

$$\sigma_0 = \sqrt{\sigma_{x0}^2 + \sigma_{\phi 0}^2} \text{ (outside surface)} \tag{63}$$

Load factors

It remains to describe the specific form to be used for the load factors, Z_{mn} in equation (50) and in the force and moment equations. Three load factors were defined, representing the centrifugal force and the longitudinal and circumferential blade-root moments, respectively.

All three applied forces are treated as if they were distributed uniformly over a rectangular area representing the blade-root intersection with the hub. The rectangle is oriented with sides of length $2C_1$ in the circumferential and $2C_2$ in the longitudinal directions. The actual blade-root area and the longitudinal dimensions of the blade-root attachment are retained in the simplified model.

1. Centrifugal force—A centrifugal force per blade of P pounds is directed radially outward. It is modeled as a load (p) per unit surface, uniformly distributed within the rectangle, where

$$p = \frac{-P}{4C_1C_2} \tag{64}$$

where

P = centrifugal force per blade, lb
C_1 = half-length of loading surface in circumferential direction, in.
C_2 = half-length of loading surface in longitudinal direction, in.
p = uniformly distributed load, lb/in.²

This distributed radial load is developed in [10] into two periodic functions represented by Fourier series, defining load factors as follows:

$$\left.\begin{array}{l} Z_{mn} = (-1)^{\frac{n-1}{2}} \dfrac{4\beta_1}{\pi^2} \dfrac{p}{n} \sin\dfrac{n\pi}{\alpha}\beta_2 \text{ when } \begin{cases} m = 0 \\ n = 1,3,5 \ldots \end{cases} \\[4mm] Z_{mn} = (-1)^{\frac{n-1}{2}} \dfrac{8}{\pi^2} \dfrac{p}{mn} \sin m\beta_1 \sin\dfrac{n\pi}{\alpha}\beta_2 \\[4mm] \qquad\qquad\qquad \text{ when } \begin{cases} m = 1,2,3 \ldots \\ n = 1,3,5 \ldots \end{cases} \end{array}\right\} \tag{65}$$

where

$$\beta_1 = \frac{C_1}{a} \tag{66}$$

$$\beta_2 = \frac{C_2}{a} \tag{67}$$

For even values of n, $Z_{mn} = 0$.

2. Longitudinal blade-root moment—The external blade-root moment per blade in the longitudinal direction, denoted by M_{OL}, is modeled as distributed radial loads which are proportional to their lengthwise distances from the hub midpoint. The maximum value of the distributed load per square inch, p_{OL}, is determined by:

$$p_{OL} = \frac{3M_{OL}}{4C_1C_2^2} \tag{68}$$

This loading is represented by load factors:

$$\left.\begin{array}{l} Z_{mn} = \dfrac{2\alpha'\beta_1}{\pi^3\beta_2} p_0 \dfrac{(-1)^n}{n^2}\left(\sin\dfrac{n\pi}{\alpha'}\beta_2 - \dfrac{n\pi}{\alpha'}\beta_2\cos\dfrac{n\pi}{\alpha'}\beta_2\right) \\[4mm] \qquad\qquad \text{when } \begin{cases} m = 0 \\ n = 1,3,5 .. \end{cases} \\[6mm] Z_{mn} = \dfrac{4\alpha'}{\pi^3\beta_2} p_0 \dfrac{(-1)^n}{mn^2}\left(\sin\dfrac{n\pi}{\alpha'}\beta_2 - \dfrac{n\pi}{\alpha'}\beta_2\cos\dfrac{n\pi}{\alpha'}\beta_2\right)\sin m\beta_1 \\[4mm] \qquad\qquad \text{when } \begin{cases} m = 1,2,3 \ldots \\ n = 1,3,5 \ldots \end{cases} \end{array}\right\} \tag{69}$$

$$\alpha' = \frac{\alpha}{2} = \frac{l'}{a} \tag{70}$$

$$l' = \frac{l}{2} \tag{71}$$

Since the longitudinal period of this load is l, rather than $2l$ as in the case of the centrifugal load, the calculation described in equations (49) through (59) will apply if, in those equations, a, l, and λ are replaced by a', l', and λ', where

$$\lambda' = 2\lambda = \frac{n\pi a}{l'} = \frac{2n\pi a}{l} \tag{72}$$

3. Circumferential blade-root moment—When distributed over the loading area, the circumferential blade-root moment, $M_{0\phi}$, is modeled as radial loads proportional to their circumferential distance from the centerline of the loading area, and invariant with x. This gives, for the maximum unit value of the distributed load

$$p_{0\phi} = \frac{3M_{0\phi}}{4C_1^2C_2} \tag{73}$$

The load factors for the circumferential blade-root moment are given by:

$$\begin{array}{l} Z_{mn} = (-1)^{\frac{n-1}{2}} \dfrac{8}{\pi^2\beta_1} \dfrac{p_0}{m^2n} \\[4mm] \qquad \times (\sin m\beta_1 - m\beta_1\cos m\beta_1)\sin\dfrac{n\pi}{\alpha}\beta_2 \\[4mm] \qquad\qquad \text{when } \begin{cases} m = 1,2,3 \ldots \\ n = 1,3,5 \ldots \end{cases} \end{array} \tag{74}$$

and the double Fourier series summations must for this load be rewritten by changing $\cos m\phi$ to $\sin m\phi$ in equations (49), (50), and (56) through (59).

Superposition of loads

Each of the load factors described in the preceding is for a single load of each type, with the loaded area centered at hub midlength and at "top dead center."

The calculation for a propeller having Z blades (for example, the five-bladed propeller investigated in this report) requires two types of superposition of loads, as follows:

1. The effects of the three types of loads on one blade are superimposed to determine the total membrane forces and bending moments in the hub wall at any point. Thus equations (56) through (59) are each executed three times, using the three sets of load factors given by equations (65), (69), and (74). The total longitudinal membrane force at any point (x,ϕ) in the hub caused by *one blade* is then

$$N_{xT1}(x,\phi) = N_{xCF}(x,\phi) + N_{xLM}(x,\phi) + N_{xCM}(x,\phi) \tag{75}$$

where subscripts

$T1$ = total, Blade No. 1
CF = centrifugal force
LM = longitudinal moment
CM = centrifugal moment

Similar summations are used to determine the total values of N_ϕ, M_x, and M_ϕ for Blade No. 1.

2. The effects of multiple blades at constant circumferential spacing are then superimposed. This is done by incrementing the circumferential loading point by $2\pi/Z$ radians and repeating the calculation described in (75) Z times.

$$N_{xT}(x,\phi) = \sum_{n=1}^{Z} N_{xTn}(x,\phi) \qquad (76)$$

in which N_{xT1} is given by (75) and

$$N_{xTn}(x,\phi) = N_{xT1}\left(x,\phi - \frac{2\pi(n-1)}{Z}\right) \qquad (77)$$

On a five-bladed propeller, for example, the total longitudinal membrane force at any point (x,ϕ) can be determined by adding five values of $N_{xT1}(x,\phi)$ as described by

$$Z = 5, \text{ hence } \frac{2\pi}{Z} = 1.257 \text{ radians} = 72 \text{ deg}$$

The membrane force at $\phi = 0$ (the centroid of Blade Root No. 1), for example, consists of five terms, namely:

$$N_{XT1}, N_{XT2}, N_{XT3}, N_{XT4}, N_{XT5}$$

caused by Blades 1 through 5, respectively, at $\phi = 0$. Since the blades are equally spaced at 72 deg, the contribution of Blade 2 to the force at the centroid of Blade 1 is the same as the force caused by Blade 1 at a point 72 deg "behind" (counterclockwise) Blade 1. Thus

$$N_{XT2}(x,0) = N_{XT1}(x, -72°)$$
$$N_{XT3}(x,0) = N_{XT1}(x, -144°)$$

and so on, as given in (77). This superposition of five terms is repeated for each membrane force and bending moment, and any hub location (x,ϕ).

In summary, the total longitudinal membrane force at any point (x,ϕ) in the hub of a five-bladed propeller is the sum of 15 forces caused by three loads on each of the five blades, each of which is determined from equation (56). The same summations are required for the other forces and moments given by (57), (58), and (59).

End support adjustment

The foregoing analysis applies to a cylinder simply supported at both ends, in which case the longitudinal moments and membrane forces in the shell are zero at the ends. A propeller hub is more appropriately represented at a cylinder built in at the forward end where it is bolted to the flanged tailshaft, and unsupported at the after (fairwater) end. A correction to the calculated stresses was made to account for the change in end support. The effect of this change of end fixity was estimated by analogy to straight single-span beams.

A beam of length L simply supported at both ends and subjected to a concentrated load $-P$ and a concentrated moment M_0 at midspan has a maximum bending moment of

$$M_{max} = -\frac{PL}{4} - \frac{M_0}{2} \qquad (78)$$

just to the left of midspan. If the same beam with the same loading is free at the left end and fixed at the right end (cantiliver), the maximum bending moment is

$$M_{max} = M_0 + \frac{PL}{2} \qquad (79)$$

at the fixed end. Thus, the cantilever beam has a maximum longitudinal bending moment which is twice that of the simply supported one.

The cylinder analyzed by Bijlaard is analogous in end fixity and (simplified) loading to the foregoing simply supported beam, while the propeller hub is analogous to the cantilever beam. A correction was therefore made to the longitudinal stress formula, equation [60], as follows:

$$\sigma_x = \frac{N_x}{t} \pm \frac{6M_x}{t^2} \qquad (60)$$

[repeated]

was changed to

$$\sigma_x = \frac{N_x}{t} \pm \frac{12M_x}{t^2} \qquad (80)$$

which is equivalent to doubling the longitudinal bending moment. The equation is then not valid for any point x. It requires that the stress be calculated for $x = L/2$ at which M_x is maximum for the simply supported cylinder, but the stress defined by (80) is assumed to apply at the fixed end.

Stress calculation results

Parametric studies of the hub stress calculations just described were made, varying the following parameters:
- Applied centrifugal force, longitudinal and circumferential moments.
- Hub thickness.
- Circumferential location of stress.
- Dimensions of loaded area.
- Radius of hub.

Held constant in all studies were the following:
Hub length = 60 in.
Poisson's ratio = 0.36 (manganese bronze)
Longitudinal locations of stress calculations = hub midlength and hub coupling
Number of blades = 5

Early runs revealed several general findings, namely:

1. The externally applied longitudinal moment has a negligibly small influence on hub stresses.

2. For a given loading condition and hub thickness, the circumferential location of the maximum stress is near the longitudinal edge of the loaded area, and within that area. Figure 22 shows the circumferential variation of the resultant hub stresses on the outside hub surface [equation (63)] for a typical loading of five-bladed propeller. A series of such calculations with different loads, hub radii, and blade-root dimensions showed that the mean angle defining the point of maximum stress is 60 percent of the angle of the blade-root edge.

Derivation of simplified stress equation

Based on these preliminary findings, routine calculations of the maximum hub stresses were made for a range of the variables listed earlier.

The principal parameters governing maximum hub stress at the critical point and the ranges of values studied in the calculations, are:

Radius of hub, in.	$20 \leq a \leq 40$
Thickness of hub, in.	$2 \leq t \leq 14$
Centrifugal force per blade, lb	$0 \leq P \leq 300\,000$
Circumferential moment per blade in.-lb	$0 \leq M \leq 2\,000\,000$
Blade root thickness, in.	$10.3 \leq 2c_1 \leq 23.0$
Circumferential location of stress	$\delta = 0.6\,\beta_1$

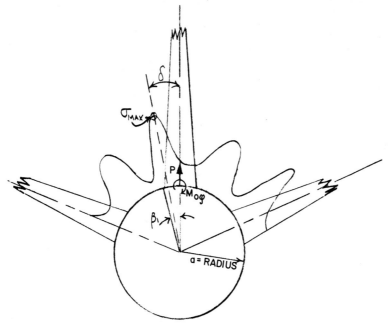

Fig. 22 Circumferential location of maximum hub stress

As stated earlier, the longitudinal moment was eliminated as a principal parameter, and therefore the blade-root length ($2c_2$) has little influence on stress.

Simplified maximum stress equations were then derived, based on four observations from Bijlaard's results:

1. Membrane forces N_x and N_ϕ due to external force P vary as P/a.

2. Bending moments M_x and M_ϕ due to external force P vary as P.

3. Membrane forces N_x and N_ϕ due to external circumferential moment M vary as M/ac_1.

4. Bending moments M_x and M_ϕ due to external circumferential moment M vary as M/c_1.

These relationships were combined with stress equations like (60) and (61) which show how the stresses vary with thickness t as well as with the membrane forces and bending moments. Taken together, these observations suggest a stress equation of the type

$$\sigma = k_2 \frac{P}{t^2} + k_4 \frac{M}{C_1 t^2} \qquad (81)$$

where k_2 and k_4 depend on a and c_1. A regression analysis of k_2 and k_4 against a and c_1 yielded the following equations:

$$k_2 = -0.0036\,c_1{}^2 + 0.0283\,c_1 + 0.00075\,c_1 a \\ + 0.005\,a - 0.175 \qquad (82)$$

$$k_4 = 0.00169\,c_1 a - 0.0088\,a + 0.170 \qquad (83)$$

The resulting simplified equation was tested against the computed stresses and found to give values within ±5 percent of the computed results.

Hollow hub thickness

Equations (81), (82), and (83) were verified for estimating the maximum stress at the outside surface of the hub at midlength, assuming simple support at the ends. For use as a design equation to determine the required hub thickness, equation (81) is solved for t, using an allowable stress for σ:

$$t_{min} = \sqrt{\frac{1}{\sigma_a}\left(k_2 P + \frac{k_4 M}{C_1}\right)} \qquad (84)$$

where

t_{min} = minimum midlength thickness, in.
σ_a = allowable stress of hub material, psi

Finally, design thicknesses at the coupling, midlength, and fairwater ends were calculated by making adjustments for the following uncertainties:

1. P and M are not uniformly distributed over the loaded area, but may have peak values up to 27 percent higher than uniformly distributed loads, as would be the case for elliptical load distribution.

2. End constraints are of uncertain fixity. An increase of 10 percent of thickness is added as a safety factor.

3. Stress concentrations have not been addressed. Assume stresses at concentrations are doubled, hence thickness multiplied by $\sqrt{2}$.

In the absence of a more elaborate stress analysis (a finite-element analysis, for example), it is therefore recommended that for design purposes the midlength thickness calculated in equation (84) be increased by a factor of

$$1.27 \times 1.10 \times 1.414 = 1.98 \text{ (say 2.0)}$$

Thus, the design thickness at midlength is:

$$t_m = 2.0 \sqrt{\frac{1}{\sigma a}\left(k_2 P + \frac{k_4 M}{C_1}\right)} \qquad (85)$$

A procedure like that described by equations (81) through (85) was applied to the stress at the coupling. This showed that the thickness required at the coupling was about 1.2 times that at midlength. For ease of construction, a straight hub wall taper is assumed. Thus, the thicknesses at coupling, midlength, and fairwater are:

$$\left.\begin{array}{l} t \text{ coupling} = 1.2\,t_m \\[4pt] t \text{ midlength} = t_m \\[4pt] t \text{ fairwater} = 0.8\,t_m \end{array}\right\} \qquad (86)$$

Hollow hub details

Dimensions of features of the hollow hub other than the

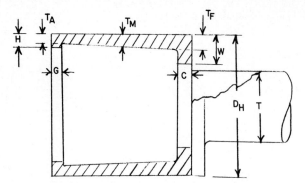

Fig. 23 Nomenclature of hollow hub details

thickness were determined from references [8], [12], [13] and [14].

The characteristics to be chosen are illustrated in Fig. 23. Dimensions of the tailshaft and its flanged coupling and bolts are determined first, since they govern some of the hub dimensions.

The tailshaft diameter is

$$T = 1.236\,d \quad \text{Ref [12]} \tag{87}$$

where

T = tailshaft diameter, in.
d = lineshaft diameter, in.

$$d = C \sqrt[3]{\frac{H}{R}} \quad \text{Ref [12]} \tag{88}$$

$C = 3.504$ for ocean and coastwise operation
H = shp at rated speed
R = rpm at rated speed

Assuming the flanged coupling between tailshaft and hub is equivalent to a lineshaft flanged coupling, the minimum bolt diameter is

$$d_b = 0.65 \sqrt{\frac{D^3(U + 23180)}{NBU_b}} \quad \text{Ref [12]} \tag{89}$$

where

d_b = bolt diameter, in.
D = shaft diameter, in. (= T in preceding)
N = number of bolts
B = bolt circle diameter, in.
U = minimum tensile strength of shaft, psi
U_b = minimum tensile strength of bolts, psi

The bolt material must be steel with at least 16 percent elongation. High-strength steel may be used so long as $U \leq U_b \leq 1.7\,U$ but $U_b \leq 145\,000$ psi. The typical bolt circle diameter [8] is 1.5 times the shaft diameter and the number of bolts required depends on the shaft diameter, according to [13].

The tailshaft flange diameter is then determined from the diameters of the bolt circle and the bolts, by an empirical formula derived by Fielding [13]:

$$F = B + 1.66\,d_b \tag{90}$$

where F is the flange diameter in inches.

The flange diameter should be checked to assure that there is at least one inch of flange material outside of the bolts all around, and thus F must be two inches greater than the diameter of a circle to the outside of the bolt holes. That is

$$\text{Minimum } F = B + d_b + 2.0 \tag{91}$$

The governing equation for the flange diameter is the greater of equations (90) and (91).

A minimum hub diameter can then be determined. It must exceed the flange diameter by 2 in. to permit a flange bolt cover to be fitted and sealed:

$$D_H = F + 2.0 \tag{92}$$

where D_H is the minimum hub diameter in inches.

The internal flange at the forward end of the hub is sized to accommodate the coupling bolts so that they are centered on the face of the flange. Its width is therefore twice the distance from the bolt circle to the outside hub diameter:

$$W = 2\left(\frac{D_H}{2} - \frac{B}{2}\right) = D_H - B \tag{93}$$

where W is the width of forward hub flange in inches.

The thickness of the flange is assumed to be equal to that required for the tailshaft flange, which is

$$C = 0.2\,T \text{ or } C = d_b \quad \text{Ref [12]} \tag{94}$$

whichever is greater. C is the flange thickness in inches.

Lastly, the width and thickness of an internal flange at the after end of the hub must be chosen to accommodate a bolted fairwater. No rules govern these dimensions. An examination of typical propeller hub drawings shows that adequate dimensions of this flange are

$$H = 5.5 \text{ in.}$$
$$G = 3.0 \text{ in.}$$

where H is the width of aft flange and G the thickness of aft flange in inches.

Appendix 4

Feasibility of fiber-reinforced plastic propellers

Properties of FRP

Some of the physical properties of various types of plastics and reinforcing fibers which might serve as possible propeller materials are given in Table 7 [17, 18]. For anisotropic materials, the values are given for the principal fiber direction, as it is assumed that these would be properly oriented in a good design. Included in the table for comparison are some of the corresponding properties of manganese bronze, ABS Type 2, and nickel-aluminum bronze, ABS Type 4. In comparing the physical properties of laminate with homogeneous metals, it should be recognized that for metals most design stresses and safety factors are based upon the yield point, whereas for laminate they are based upon the ultimate strength. This arises from the characteristic difference in the stress-strain curves of the different-type materials. Most metals show an extended ductile range between yield and ultimate stress whereas the FRP materials do not have this characteristic. The table for the polyester resins show that the ultimate flexure stresses are slightly higher than the tensile. A propeller blade receives much larger flexural loading than tensile from the centrifugal forces particularly on a material with as low density as FRP; thus, the flexural stresses should be used in making comparisons with the propeller bronzes.

FRP propeller blade deflection

The calculations which follow compare the deflection of a propeller blade made of nickel-aluminum bronze with that of a comparable blade made of FRP using a polyester matrix of

Property	Propeller Bronzes		Polyester (Ref. [18])				Epoxy (Ref. [17])				
	ABS Type 2	ABS Type 4	Chopped Strand	Woven Roving	Parallel Roving[c]	Fabric S-Glass[b]	Graphite I	Graphite II	S-Glass	E-Glass	Kevlar
Specific gravity	8.4	7.59	1.5 to 1.6	1.7 to 1.9	1.7 to 1.9	1.7 to 1.9	1.75	1.85	2.63	2.63	1.45
Glass content (% by wt.)	...	...	35 to 45	55 to 75	50 to 70	62 to 67	65	65	65	65	65
Tension (psi $\times 10^{-3}$)	65 (25)[a]	85 (35)[a]	15 to 23	35 to 60	80 to 130	78 to 86	200	159	241	159	180
Flexure (psi $\times 10^{-3}$)	...	...	25 to 38	40 to 55	100 to 200	85 to 100	...	...	...	...	...
Compression (psi $\times 10^{-3}$)	(25)[a]	(35)[a]	18 to 26	...	50 to 75	40 to 50	...	...	...	...	...
Tensile modulus (psi $\times 10^{-6}$)	15.0	15.5	0.8 to 1.8	2.0 to 3.5	...	4.0 to 5.0	18.0	26.1	7.0	5.1	9.0
Flexural modulus (psi $\times 10^{-6}$)	...	...	1.0 to 2.0	2.5 to 4.0	5.0 to 7.0	4.5 to 5.5	...	...	...	...	...
Shear (psi $\times 10^{-3}$)	42	47	12 to 17	...	...	19 to 34	...	...	...	...	...

[a] Numbers in ( ) are yield strengths for propeller metals.
[b] Tested parallel to warp.
[c] Tested in direction of glass.

mat, cloth and woven roving (S-glass). The blade for these calculations is assumed wedge shaped and is similar to the blades on the 27.5-ft-diameter solid propeller of the base tanker. The bronze blade is uniformly loaded and sized such that the maximum stress is 8000 psi at the root. The FRP blade is also wedge shaped and the same thickness-chord ratio (0.165) is maintained at the root, representing the likely FRP propeller design. A maximum stress of 4000 psi was used for the design assuming the same loading as for the metal blade. This value was assumed as representing a reasonable compromise for the uncertainties which exist in FRP technology for both manufacturing and fatigue life in the saltwater environment.

The required thickness at the blade root (that is, at the 0.2 radius) is calculated from

$$\sigma_{des} = \frac{6M}{ct^2} \qquad (95)$$

where

σ_{des} = design stress, psi
M = blade root bending moment, ft-lb
c = blade chord, ft
t = blade root thickness, in.

For the two blades, the foregoing quantities are:

M = 650 000 ft-lb (from original design data)
c = 5.0 ft (for bronze propeller; for FRP maintain same t/c)
σ_{des} = 8000 psi (bronze)
    = 4000 psi (FRP)

and the required thicknesses and chord length at the root are:

MATERIAL	THICKNESS	CHORD (ft)
Nickel-aluminum bronze	9.87 in.	5.0
FRP	12.44 in.	6.3

Each has a linear taper to zero thickness at the blade tip. The required blade section moments of inertia at various radii are:

$$I_x = \frac{M_x t_x}{\sigma} \qquad (96)$$

and the angular deflections are given by

$$\theta_x = \int_0^x \frac{M_x}{EI_x} dx \qquad (97)$$

where $x = 0$ represents the blade root (0.2 R).

The tip deflection can be calculated:

$$\delta_{tip} = \int_0^{11.0} \theta_x dx \qquad (98)$$

where $x = 11.0$ ft is the blade tip (1.0 R), since $R = 13.75$ ft and $x = R (r/R - 0.2)$.

Table 8 summarizes the foregoing calculations for both propeller blades. Integrating the θ-values gives the tip deflection as follows:

$$\delta_{Tip} = 0.129 \text{ ft for the bronze blade}$$

$$\delta_{Tip} = 0.305 \text{ ft for the FRP blade}$$

As seen from Table 8, the greater moment of inertia of the FRP blade partially offsets the six-fold difference in stiffness, but the tip deflection of the FRP blade is still 2.4 times that of the bronze. It is expected that deflections of this magnitude would present no significant problem, particularly if these deflections and consequent changes of pitch are allowed for in the design stage.

Flexural fatigue strength

Figure 24 shows typical data on stress amplitude versus cycles to failure for ABS Type 2 and 4 bronzes and possible FRP ma-

Table 8   Propeller blade deflection calculations

r/R	x (ft)	M (ft-lb)	Manganese-Bronze Blade $E = 15 \times 10^6$			S-Glass/Polyester Blade $E = 2.5 \times 10^6$ psi		
			t (ft)	I (ft⁴)	θ (radians)	t (ft)	I (ft⁴)	θ (radians)
0.2	0	650 000	0.820	0.230	0	1.040	0.591	0
0.4	2.75	374 000	0.615	0.097	0.0042	0.780	0.249	0.0098
0.6	5.50	159 000	0.410	0.029	0.0100	0.522	0.075	0.0234
0.8	8.25	30 500	0.205	0.004	0.0183	0.263	0.0096	0.0433
1.0	11.0	0	0	0	0.0305	0	0	0.0735

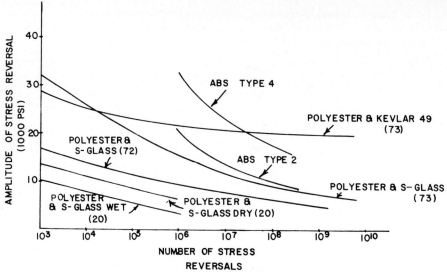

Fig. 24 Fatigue strength of FRP composites

terials. The data on the FRP materials are not as well developed and are highly dependent upon the care exercised in lay-up. The stress reversals on a tanker propeller blade are typically about ±25 percent during each revolution [19], or about one quarter of the design stress. If we assume a design stress of about 4000 psi, this will result in an amplitude of stress variation of about 1000 psi, which is superposed upon the steady stress. Since a material which is preloaded and subjected to stress reversals will fail sooner than if the mean stress were zero, the stress level from the usual zero mean fatigue tests must be modified as follows:

$$S_{max} = S_e \left(\frac{3}{2 - r} \right) \qquad (99)$$

where

S_{max} = endurance limit for a given number of cycles of stress with a steady load
S_e = endurance limit for a given number of cycles of stress, pure alternating stress
r = ratio of minimum to maximum stress during a cycle

For example, at a mean stress of 4000 psi with a variation of ±25 percent:

$$r = \frac{3000}{5000} = 0.6$$

Thus,

$$S_{max} = 1000 \left(\frac{3}{2 - 0.6} \right) = 2140 \text{ psi}$$

Thus, the FRP material must have a fatigue stress limit of at least 2140 psi over the life of the propeller.

Appendix 5

Effect of large, low-rpm propellers on stern tube bearings and seals

Classic analysis of bearing behavior

This material can be found in textbooks on lubrication theory. References [40] and [41] are two excellent examples.

The difference in bearing inner diameter and shaft (or journal) outer diameter is the bearing clearance, C_D, equal to twice the radial clearance, C_R. The clearance ratio is then C_D/D or C_R/R. In a bearing which is running with journal and bushing centerlines parallel, the distance between the centerlines is the eccentricity ratio, ϵ. A line through these centers will be at the attitude angle, ψ, from the vertical at the bottom. It can be proven that this relates to ϵ as follows:

$$\psi = \tan^{-1} \frac{\pi}{4} \cdot \frac{1 - \epsilon^2}{\epsilon} \qquad (100)$$

The least oil film at this section occurs at this angle, so that

$$h_{min} = C_R(1 - \epsilon) \qquad (101)$$

The load on a bearing is conveniently characterized by dividing the bearing by the plan area, to yield the unit load or nominal bearing pressure, P:

$$P = \frac{W}{L \times D} = \frac{W}{(L/D) D^2} \qquad (102)$$

where

P = unit load, psi
W = bearing reaction, lb
L = bearing length, in.
D = bearing or shaft diameter, in.

The Sommerfeld number

The Sommerfeld number is a nondimensional group usually used, along with the length-to-diameter ratio (L/D), to characterize bearing behavior:

$$S = \frac{\mu \times N}{P(C_D/D)^2} \qquad (103)$$

where

P = bearing unit load, psi
μ = oil viscosity, in reyns (lb-sec/in.²)
N = shaft speed, revolutions per second
C_D/D = clearance ratio

For a perfectly aligned bearing of particular L/D ratio and what is best visualized as oil groove location, the Sommerfeld number can be related to the eccentricity ratio by analytic and empirical means, usually in the form of charts, with those of Reference [41] used here.

Nonaligned bearings

When the bearing is not aligned, Sommerfeld charts provide

a relationship which is approached at midlength of the bearing. This provides a mechanism for approximating the limiting conditions of operation for a stern tube bearing. A distinction was made between the misalignment of the shaft within the bearing due mostly to hull deflection from the initial alignment conditions, and bowing of the shaft due mostly to overhung weight of the propeller, nut and tailshaft. Both are affected by thrust eccentricity.

When the thrust center is below the center of the propeller, a moment which compounds the weight of the propeller is created. This moment will increase the bowing of the shaft and also increase the slope of the shaft. The thrust center is usually below the propeller center for tankers in ballast and will rise at deeper drafts. The thrust center may rise above the propeller center, countering the weight of the propeller [42, 43], but this situation did not obtain in the case under study.

Misalignment of the shaft within the bearing will be present at all conditions other than the static condition under which the shafting was initially aligned. For large tankers, Larsen [42] explains that in ballast, a hogging deflection in way of the cargo tanks changing to a sagging deflection of the engine room double bottom may obtain, while a fully loaded ship may have a sagging deflection in way of the cargo tanks changing into a hogging deflection of the engine room double bottom. Thus a worst-case misalignment might occur in the ballast condition at full power, when hull deflection tilts and stern tube forward while a thrust eccentricity below the propeller center combined with a high thrust at full power act to tilt the shaft aft.

For this study a worst cast misalignment was assumed at full power, with a value of $\alpha = 2 \times 10^{-4}$ radians, and allowed to decrease in linear relation to the thrust, since it was found that the center of thrust eccentricity varied little with power level in each case. Since full-power thrust was maintained constant in all cases, the same worst case misalignment was used at full power in each rpm case. Thus, the effect of misalignment of the shaft in the bearing between the edge of the bearing and the section at midlength can be calculated as follows:

$$\Delta h = \alpha \frac{L}{2} \frac{\text{Thrust at rpm}}{\text{Thrust at MCR}} \qquad (104)$$

where

Δh = effect of misalignment, in.
α = worst-case alignment, radians
MCR = maximum continuous rating (at design rpm)

If the bearing were provided with a self-aligning bushing then within the range of capability of the bearing, there would be no misalignment, only bowing.

Bowing of the shaft is caused by the overhung propeller weight, to the effect of which must be added the moment due to eccentric thrust when this acts below the propeller center. From a faired alignment curve for a specific case, the effects of bowing can be calculated as the distance between the alignment curve at the bearing after end, and the tangent to the alignment curve at bearing midlength. This distance, in inches, is called δ.

The shaft will deviate from the tangent in relation to the overhung weight of propeller, shaft and nut, thrust, and shaft stiffness, as follows:

$$\delta = \frac{Wb \pm Ta}{D^4} \times \left(\frac{L}{D}\right)^{5/3} \qquad (105)$$

where

W = overhung weight of propeller, shaft and nut
b = distance from propeller center of gravity to the line of action of bearing resistance
T = thrust

a = thrust eccentricity in vertical plane, positive when below propeller center
D = shaft diameter
L = bearing length

Bowing of the shaft will be present even if the bearing is perfectly aligned or is self-aligning.

Estimates of bearing performance for a specific ship

The material in the foregoing paragraphs was used to develop a procedure for comparing the performance of the stern tube bearing for the specific ship when fitted with solid and hollow propellers, over the whole range of rpm. While other indices of performance could have been selected, such as least oil film thickness at operating rpm, or transition rpm, it was decided that a criterion of lowest rpm for a given minimum oil film thickness was most direct. By selecting this minimum oil film thickness at zero (or, alternatively, at a low value similar to machining tolerances of the journal and bushing), the calculated rpm is then the rpm at or below which the journal would come into metal-to-metal contact with the bushing, provided the bushing was inelastic and in rigid supports. In actual fact considerations of elasticity would reduce the minimum rpm, while considerations of surface finish would raise it. Somewhere in this region, however, metal-to-metal contact, partial seizure and stick-slip operation begin to occur.

Procedure for bearing performance case study

The procedure involves a certain amount of trial-and-error iteration which encourages the use of a computer. The steps are as follows:

1. Shaft diameters were determined from ABS Rules with a 3 percent margin added.

2. Bearing reactions and bowing geometry were obtained for the base ship from a shaft alignment program.

3. Bearing length-to-diameter ratio was at first selected in general accord with Lloyds Rules for white metal-lined, oil-lubricated bushings (Table 9). In Table 10 this restriction was lifted to explore the effects of higher L/D ratios and to simulate self-aligning bearings where higher unit loads have been accepted [44, 45].

4. Bearing clearance ratio was taken as 0.00175, a value within the range of experience [43, 44, 46, 47, 48]. Decreased bearing clearances will result in slightly thicker oil films [41, 43] but will not alter the trend.

5. Worst-case misalignment was calculated as described in the preceding, allowing it to decrease in proportion to thrust and bearing length.

6. Bowing was determined from the shaft alignment curve as described earlier for the base case, static shaft. The effect of thrust was incorporated assuming a constant eccentricity of 10 percent of the propeller radius, and this was thereafter used across the board as it was found to change only slightly from case to case.

7. Oil viscosity was taken as that of SAE 30 oil at about 100°F. Heavier oil would increase the film thickness but would also increase power losses in the bearing.

With this material defined, the trial-and-error procedure to find minimum RPM was as follows:

- An initial estimate of rpm$_{\text{min}}$ was made and used to determine a corresponding level of thrust.
- An initial estimate of the attitude angle (ψ) at midlength was also made.
- The estimated thrust was used to calculate trial values of the effect of misalignment and of bowing using the two relations of equations (104) and (105).
- The sum of the bowing and misalignment (Δh_b), transposed circumferentially around the bushing to the plane of the

	Solid	Hollow	Solid	Hollow	Solid	Hollow	Solid	Hollow
Rpm @ MCR	85.	85.	66.	66.	44.	44.	33.	33.
Shp @ MCR	26000.	26000.	23000.	23000.	21500.	21500.	20000.	20000.
Thrust @ MCR (lb)	437496.	437496.	434182.	434182.	431458.	431458.	426112.	426112.
Prop. weight in air (lb)	97102	74915	129000	74200	165000	86000	229000	105000
Tailshaft dia. (in.)	30.79	30.79	32.16	32.16	35.99	35.99	38.67	38.67
Est. stern tube brg. reaction (lb)	140353	120701	173541	127004	220411	150439	288564	178735
Selected L/D ratio	1.5	1.5	1.5	1.5	1.5	1.5	1.7	1.5
Unit load (psi)	99.	85.	112.	82.	113.	77.	115.	80.
Clearance ratio	0.00175	0.00175	0.00175	0.00175	0.00175	0.00175	0.00175	0.00175
Radial clearance (in. $\times 10^{-3}$)	26.9	26.9	28.1	28.1	31.5	31.5	33.8	33.8
Worst-case misalignment (radians $\times 10^{-4}$)	2.0	2.0	2.0	2.0	2.0	2.0	2.0	2.0
Minimum oil film thickness (in. $\times 10^{-3}$)	0.0	0.0	0.0	0.0	0.0	0.0	0.0	0.0
At minimum rpm:								
Shaft bowing (in. $\times 10^{-3}$)	1.3	1.0	1.5	0.9	1.3	0.6	2.2	0.6
Effect of misalignment (in. $\times 10^{-3}$)	0.1	0.0	0.2	0.0	0.5	0.0	6.5	0.1
Delta Hb (in. $\times 10^{-3}$)	1.4	1.1	1.7	0.9	1.8	0.7	8.7	0.6
Delta Hpsi (in. $\times 10^{-3}$)	1.2	0.9	1.5	0.8	1.5	0.6	6.7	0.6
Req'd. oil film thickness (in. $\times 10^{-3}$)	1.2	0.9	1.5	0.8	1.5	0.6	6.7	0.6
Eccentricity ratio @ mid brg. length	0.955	0.966	0.948	0.971	0.953	0.981	0.802	0.983
Attitude angle at mid brg. length (deg)	13.	12.	14.	12.	14.	9.	21.	9.
Sommerfeld number	0.009	0.007	0.011	0.006	0.010	0.004	0.043	0.003
Minimum rpm	11.	7.	14.	7.	13.	4.	above 33.	4.

attitude angle (Δh_ψ), and then added to the least-permissible oil film (in this case, zero) yielded a required oil film thickness (h_r). Achieving h_r at midlength, at ψ, would enable the shaft to just clear the bushing at the edge (if as mentioned, the bushing is smooth, inelastic, and rigidly supported).

• This value of h_r was used to enter a Sommerfeld chart (incorporated in the program as a subroutine) to obtain a Sommerfeld number, which yielded a calculated rpm$_{min}$.

• The calculated ψ and rpm$_{min}$ were then used in a reiterative routine until convergence obtained.

Results of bearing performance case study

Table 9 compares the bearing performance for solid and hollow propellers in each rpm case. Table 10 is an analysis of several possibilities for the lowest rpm case. It is less valid to interpret the results in absolute terms than it is to compare the results from case to case because of the assumptions that had to be made (especially the assumption of "worst-case mis-

alignment"). Nevertheless, the value of minimum rpm for the base ship conforms to values appearing in the literature for similar situations [42, 47, 49, 50].

In the 66- and 44-rpm solid-propeller cases, the absolute value of the minimum rpm does not change much, but as a percentage of the MCR rpm in each case, which is a parameter roughly representative of ship speed, the minimum value can be seen to rise significantly. The situation is, in all cases, improved by the lighter weight hollow propellers. The effect is not only to reduce the bearing load but also to improve the load distribution by reducing shaft bowing.

At 33 rpm, the indication for the solid propeller is that hydrodynamic lubrication is not achieved even at the MCR rpm, given the constraints and assumptions, while for the hollow propeller at this speed a situation hardly different from the conventional case is created. An examination of the data for the 33-rpm solid-propeller case shows the problem to be about evenly split between misalignment and bowing. In Table 10,

	$L/D = 1.7$	$L/D = 2.0$	$L/D = 2.5$	Self-Aligning Bearings	
Rpm @ MCR	33.	33.	33.	33.	33.
Shp @ MCR	20000.	20000.	20000.	20000.	20000.
Thrust @ MCR (lb)	426112.	426112.	426112.	426112.	426112.
Prop. weight in air (lb)	229000.	229000.	229000.	229000.	229000.
Tailshaft dia. (in.)	38.67	38.67	38.67	38.67	38.67
Est. stern tube brg. reaction (lb)	288564.	288564.	288564.	288564.	288564.
Selected L/D ratio	1.7	2.0	2.5	1.7	1.0
Unit load (psi)	115.	96.	77.	115.	193.
Clearance ratio	0.00175	0.00175	0.00175	0.00175	0.00175
Radial clearance (in. $\times 10^{-3}$)	33.8	33.8	33.8	33.8	33.8
Worst-case misalignment (radians $\times 10^{-4}$)	2.0	2.0	2.0	0.0	0.0
Minimum oil film thickness (in. $\times 10^{-3}$)	0.0	0.0	0.0	0.0	0.0
At minimum rpm:					
Shaft bowing (in. $\times 10^{-3}$)	2.2	3.0	4.3	1.6	0.6
Effect of misalignment (in. $\times 10^{-3}$)	6.5	7.7	9.7	0.0	0.0
Delta Hb (in. $\times 10^{-3}$)	8.7	10.7	13.9	1.6	0.6
Delta Hpsi (in. $\times 10^{-3}$)	6.7	7.7	9.8	1.4	0.6
Req'd. oil film thickness (in. $\times 10^{-3}$)	6.7	7.7	9.8	1.4	0.6
Eccentricity ratio @ mid brg. length	0.802	0.772	0.711	0.960	0.983
Attitude angle at mid brg. length (deg)	21.	25.	27.	13.	8.
Sommerfeld number	0.043	0.046	0.052	0.008	0.004
Minimum rpm	above 33.	above 33.	above 33.	11.	8.

the first three columns demonstrate that increased bearing length and commensurate reductions in unit load only serve to aggravate the situation.

The last two columns of Table 10 assume the journal to be perfectly aligned in the bushing, a situation that can be achieved if a self-aligning bearing is used. What a self-aligning bearing cannot do is eliminate the effects of bowing, although if the bearing can be made shorter, the situation improves, even though unit load rises. These columns indicate that the self-aligning bearing offers possibilities worthy of further study; for example, it is possible to "preload" a tilting pad bearing permitting the use of lower-than-normal radial clearance [51].

Reinforced phenolic resin bushing

This material has been considerable service in stern tube bushings of large tankers since 1973. It is reported to be tolerant of low-rpm operation by virtue of a certain amount of oil retention within the surface and will deform elastically to better match tailshaft attitude. Except for the difference in material and the use of slightly greater bearing clearances it does not require significant departure from the current practice in stern tube design. This coupled with the experience to date make it a low-risk approach with the added advantage of working satisfactorily with water lubrication should the stern seal fail [42, 52, 53, 54].

Hydrostatic stern tube bearing

Hydrostatic bearings have been used in large, slow, heavily loaded bearings in steel mills and have been proposed for stern tubes [48, 55]. The concept appears aboard ship only to the extent that "jacking oil" systems have been fitted in a few cases to allow sustained operation at very low rpm [56]. Power required for the oil pumps will rise rapidly with slight changes in shaft alignment [48] and it is probably this requirement which has limited their further application.

Self-aligning bearings

Self-aligning bearings of the tilting-pad type have seen limited but successful application as stern tube bearings for smaller shafts [48, 57]. The following factors are usually cited in their favor:

1. Misalignment within the normal range is eliminated.
2. Bowing is reduced as higher unit loads are permitted (to 300 psi, reference [45]) and, therefore, L/D ratios of unity are considered normal.
3. The bearing can be "preloaded" to permit the use of lower than normal clearances (51).

The effects of Factors 1 and 2 were demonstrated for the case study, with results discussed earlier. Because of their compact nature, these bearings can be arranged for inboard withdrawal afloat, an added advantage [45].

Spherically seated roller bearings have been used on smaller shafts [48, 57] and in 1973 one was installed on a very large crude carrier (VLCC). Successful operation was reported a year later [58]. No other installations on large ships are known. Roller bearings provide hydrodynamic lubrication at low rpm but the disadvantages usually mentioned are their susceptibility to vibration-induced fretting, and sensitivity to corrosion by even trace quantities of seawater in the lubricating oil [48, 50, 59].

Stern seals

Stern seal failure, leading to bearing failure, is a more likely occurrence than bearing failure alone. The likelihood of seal failure appears to increase with diameter and rubbing speed. The causes of failure are usually related to the temperature rise and increased opportunity for abrasion in larger shafts moving at high peripheral speeds, or to the loading on the seal due to the static head of seawater and the balancing head of oil, or to the difference between them; and to lateral and axial vibration [1, 43, 54, 57, 60].

Seal diameter is not a cause of seal failure except as it relates to rubbing speed, but it is one index used to correlate data on performance and failure. Seal diameter will be larger than shaft diameter by some 10 to 15 percent in the case of lip seals, or by 50 to 60 percent in the case of face seals. Calculations show that at the levels of power and rpm under consideration, rubbing speeds of under 3 m/sec can be anticipated, lower than the range of about 3.5 to 6.0 m/sec common to the largest tankers and containerships, and much below the 7 to 8 m/sec limits of current experience [1, 43].

The problems relating to static head and unbalanced pressures across seals have largely been resolved by proper design of the lubricating oil system [43, 57], enabling variation of pressure with draft. Shaft vibration can cause seals to fail in fatigue, or can cause fluctuations of pressure within the seal compartments leading to loss of oil and water contamination [43]. To whatever extent shaft movements are made more severe for the cases under consideration, these problems become more likely to occur. The problem of seal failure due to fatigue cracking is coupled with seal temperature [50, 54, 57] and is certain to be alleviated by the relatively low rubbing speeds of the installation under study.

While not a solution to the potential problem of seal failure, the use of a phenolic resin bushing would certainly reduce the consequences of such a failure since the material can run with seawater lubrication until repairs can be made [52, 53, 54].

Conclusions

It may be useful to define ranges of design rpm, or MCR rpm, as follows:

Above 75	. . . .	state of the art
40 to 75	. . . .	moderately reduced
Below 40	. . . .	severely reduced

At the MCR rpm the ship will make its best speed, and at reduced ship speeds the required rpm will be closely proportional to ship speed.

1. It appears that even at the most severely reduced values of MCR rpm, conventional stern tube bearings can be provided for lightweight propellers which would have adequate oil film thicknesses even at low ship speeds. This does not appear to be the case with solid propellers, where in the range of even moderately reduced MCR rpm the bearing would no longer be hydrodynamically lubricated at higher ship speeds than those at which this transition occurs today. It further appears that a solid propeller designed for operation in the severely reduced range cannot be fitted with a conventional stern tube bearing.

2. Self-aligning bearings may have possibilities for application to solid propellers in the severely reduced range, but would not appear to offer a better solution than the lightweight propeller.

3. The provision of a hydrostatic system for very-low-rpm operation may be attractive if long periods at sea buoys or in channels are anticipated.

4. The use of phenolic resin bushings in otherwise conventional stern tube bearings would appear advantageous in reducing the effects of operation at low RPM, and of reducing the consequences of a seal failure.

5. At modest power levels, seal diameters are unlikely to exceed the present range of experience when coupled with the low rpm. This yields rubbing speeds on the order of a third to a half of those of some seals in service today. This could lead to a conclusion that seals for low-rpm propellers are likely to be more reliable than those for higher-rpm propellers, even though shaft diameter increases.

Table 11   Cargo losses due to increased ballast requirements for various propeller diameters

Propeller Diameter (ft)	Draft Aft (ft)	Draft Fwd (ft)	Decrease in Cargo Capacity (l. tons)[a]
27.5	28.49	15.73	0
32.5	33.49	20.73	2,700
37.5	38.49	25.73	13,600
42.5	43.49	30.73	24,400

[a] Assumes cargo is crude oil at 47.5° API (8.1051 bbl/l. ton).

Appendix 6

Effect of Coast Guard regulations

Section 33 of the Code of Federal Regulations (CFR) Part 157 contains the pollution prevention requirements for oil tankers in order to implement the regulations of the 1978 MARPOL Protocol for segregated ballast tanks (SBT), clean ballast tanks (CBT) and crude oil washing (COW). The regulations are now applicable to any new tanker in the size range of the base ship and will apply to all tankers of this size in the near future. Of these requirements, the one of most concern to this study is that for segregated ballast tanks. Basically, these regulations state that in the minimum-ballast case (that is, the only weight items included are the vessel's light weight and the ballast contained in segregated tanks) the vessel must meet three conditions:

1.
$$d_m = 2.0 + 0.02\,L$$

where d_m is the mean draft in meters and $L = 0.96 \times LWL$ in meters.

2. The propeller tip must be immersed.

3. Conditions 1 and 2 preceding must be achieved with a trim by the stern not in excess of $0.015\,L$.

For the base ship, this results in the following requirements:

$$d_m = 23.58 \text{ ft}$$
Draft at plane of propeller = 29.25 ft
(propeller tip is 1.75 ft above baseline)
Maximum allowable trim = 12.765 ft

Again for the base ship, with the existing tankage arrangement and sufficient tanks dedicated to ballast to immerse the existing propeller, which is consistent with that provided for a typical modern vessel, the following conditions can be achieved:

Mean draft = d_m = 24.50 ft
Trim = 12.65 ft
Draft at propeller = 30.99 ft
Draft at after perpendicular = 31.23 ft

This condition satisfies the regulations and essentially takes full advantage of the maximum allowable trim. If the propeller shaftline were lowered so that the tip were 9 in. above the baseline, the configurations could accommodate a propeller 30.24 ft in diameter and meet the provisions of 33 CFR 157 without any additional ballast. However, if a larger-diameter propeller is to be installed, then additional ballast must be made available in order to keep the propeller tip submerged. Since the stated condition is essentially at the maximum trim, any further increase in draft must be the result of parallel sinkage. However, the stated condition does not take full advantage of the capacity of the fore peak tank. In fact, there remains volume for 2600 long tons of salt water in this tank. Therefore, if the assumption is made that the required additional saltwater ballast could be located in a longitudinal position such that parallel sinkage occurs, and that this increased ballast tankage results in no increase in light ship weight and all increased ballast volume results in decreased cargo volume, the result is the values contained in Table 11. The gist of these calculations is shown graphically in Fig. 13.

With any reasonable freight rate obtainable for crude oil, the savings in fuel oil from decreased displacement does not balance out the loss in revenue resulting from carrying less cargo. Therefore, the maximum-diameter propeller which can be installed on the base ship without invading the cargo block for ballast and yet meeting the requirements of 33 CFR 157 would be the optimum economically.

Appendix 7

Economic analysis

The economic study has been conducted in two parts. The first is concerned with the net annual savings that can be achieved by using larger, slower-turning propellers. This part is concerned only with the annual operating costs of the tanker and does not consider any capital costs associated with building a ship with a larger-diameter slower-turning propeller. The objective is to determine the best propeller diameter to utilize when living within the constraints of the IMCO Rules on propeller immersion and segregated ballast (see Appendix 6).

The second part is concerned with the capital construction costs of a larger, slower-turning propeller installation as compared with the 27.5-ft propeller installed in the ship. The as-

Table 12   Operating assumptions for economic studies

Propeller Diameters Studied (ft)	Decreased Cargo[a] Using Cargo Tanks to Hold Ballast Required for Tip Immersion in Ballast (long tons)	MCR shp Selected so Vessel Attains 16 Knots Full Load at 80% of MCR shp (HP, English)	Propulsion SHP's					
			Full load			Ballast		
			12	16	20 knots	12	16	20 knots
27.5	0	26 000	9297	22 252	46 331	9781	15 582	24 693
32.5	2 694	23 000	9100	19 837	45 000	8898	14 151	22 364
37.5	13 608	21 500	8753	17 380	42 790	9052	14 246	22 258
42.5	24 376	20 000	8320	15 499	40 019	9347	14 677	22 933

Data held constant:
trade route (Aruba/Rotterdam): 10 000 miles/round trip
days idle/round trip (loading + unloading): 6
other days idle/yr (drydocking and repair): 5

Data varied for sensitivity studies:
(base-case values given).
Speed: 16-kt full load and ballast
fuel cost: $23.50/bbl
cargo revenue (one way): $10/ton

[a] No change in trim from design condition assumed.

sumed propeller is approximately 42.5 ft in diameter and operates at about 30.8 rpm. This represents an extreme upper limit on possible propeller size.

Operating costs and savings

In order to determine the economic advantages of a large-diameter slow-turning propeller, it was necessary to establish an operating scenario. For the purposes of this study, the trade route and operating practices as described in Table 12 was the scenario assumed. In accordance with the IMCO Rules outlined in Appendix 6, as propeller diameter increases, increasing amounts of cargo tankage must be converted to segregated ballast, reducing the revenue potential of the vessel. The IMCO Rules also establish the ballast draft condition for each propeller diameter. The same full-load condition was assumed for all propeller diameters. The technique described in the main report was used to determine the shp for each of the load conditions. The shp values are tabulated in Table 12 for three different ship speeds along the with MCR shp required for each propeller diameter. The analysis was made assuming that the ship operated in full load and ballast condition at 16 knots.

With these data, the number of round trips per year was calculated. The fuel rates used are those given in Fig. 25 which were synthesized from data in references [61] through [70]. Total fuel consumption was determined for both full load and ballast conditions and, in turn, total fuel costs per year were determined. The cost of the cargo revenue losses (relative to the 27.5-ft propeller) were deducted from the annual fuel savings for each case. The further assumption was made that the large slow-turning propeller would not incur any significant additional maintenance costs.

For the cost and revenue calculations, a fuel cost of $23.50/bbl and a cargo revenue of $10.00/ton was assumed based on world scale rates at the time (October 1981). The results are presented in Fig. 13 as a function of propeller di-

ameter. The optimum propeller diameter is 30.2 ft, beyond which compliance with IMCO Rules causes a loss in cargo revenue. The revenue losses rapidly exceed the savings in fuel consumption as the propeller diameter is further increased. The fuel savings with an increase in diameter up to this point indicates the desirability of trying to avoid the loss in cargo revenue, hence the need to examine the justification for the IMCO Rules on ballast draft limitations.

Since this analysis is very dependent upon the assumed cost of fuel and cargo revenue, a sensitivity study was conducted to determine the importance of these two variables, along with the effect of ship operating speed. The results are presented in Fig. 26, which shows the sensitivity of optimum propeller diameter and net annual savings to these variables. These studies show that the optimum propeller diameter is relatively insensitive to moderate changes in fuel costs, cargo revenue or operating speed. Not surprisingly, the net annual savings is quite sensitive to both fuel costs and ship operating speed, and less sensitive to cargo revenue.

Machinery and hull fabrication costs

This part of the economic analysis is an attempt to estimate the changes in machinery and hull costs in making and installing a 42.5-ft, 30.8-rpm propeller versus a 27.5-ft, 85-rpm propeller. Because the development of detail plans was beyond the scope of this project, these costs must be considered approximate.

Comparative costs of the major machinery components including the hollow-bladed propeller are contained in Table 13.

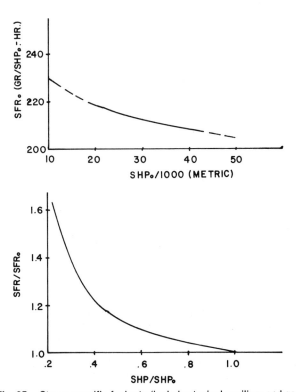

Fig. 25 Steam specific fuel rate (includes typical auxiliary and generator loads)

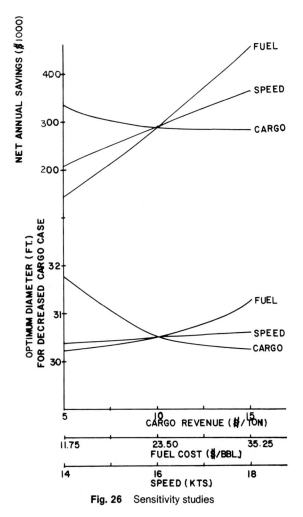

Fig. 26 Sensitivity studies

Table 13 Comparative machinery costs (1981 dollars)

Item	Base Prop	Large Prop	See Notes
1. Propeller:			
Diameter (ft)	27.5	42.5	
rpm	85	31	
shp	26 000	20 000	
2. Basic steam plant cost	$16 125 000	$14 140 000	*a*
3. Tanker machinery increment	$2 420 000	$2 420 000	*b*
4. Gear adjustments			
(*a*) Reduced cost of 1st/2nd red.	. . .	$−240 000	*c*
(*b*) Added cost for 3rd red.		$1 520 000	*d*
5. Shafting system including spare stern tube and bearing	$530 000	$1 040 000	*e*
6. Propeller adjustment	. . .	$200 000	
Total	$19 075 000	$19 080 000	

NOTES:

a Obtained from work in progress for SNAME Panel M15-1.

b 15% of base plant cost allowed for tanker system.

c Propeller shaft speed of 31 rpm was obtained using Curtis Wright/MarAd planetary reduction gear with a 4.59 speed reduction as the final reduction gear. Input to this planetary gear set was obtained from the output of a conventionally configured 1st/2nd reduction gear set. Because the output from the gear set is increased to 140 rpm in lieu of the 85 rpm required for the base plant, this savings results.

d Estimated cost of Curtis Wright/MarAd epicyclic (4.59:1) reduction gear.

e Based on a shipyard estimate for a conventional oil-lubricated solid-steel propeller shafting system.

As noted there, most of these costs were derived from data obtained from machinery manufacturers or were estimated from costs for other installations, adjusted for the change in component size. The net results indicates that there should be no significant difference in machinery costs between the two plants.

A more subjective approach had to be taken to assess the changes in the hull needed to accommodate the large-diameter propeller. An examination of the machinery space indicated that there was adequate room to accommodate the additional stage of reduction gearing; thus no change was required in major dimensions. The rise in propeller position removes the need for shaft inclination. The enlargement of the propeller aperture would reduce some of the steel and welding required in the stern area. On the other hand, the rudder would have to have a higher aspect ratio, thus increasing the size of the rudder bearing foundations and reducing the size of the steering gear room which is quite large on the original ship. In the absence of costing out detail plans, it would appear that the extra costs associated with the rudder and steering gear installation would be compensated by the savings in propeller shaft installation and stern hull structure fabrication.

In summary, it appears that there are no easily identifiable differences in capital costs between the two configurations and that the economic effect of the large-diameter, slow-turning propeller is confined to the gain in fuel savings.

Metric Conversion Table

Original experimental data herein were measured in U.S. customary units. Following is a list of standard factors for conversion to metric (SI) values:

$$1 \text{ ft} = 0.3048 \text{ m}$$
$$1 \text{ in.} = 25.4 \text{ mm}$$
$$1 \text{ mile} = 1.60 \text{ km}$$
$$1 \text{ nautical mile} = 1.852 \text{ km}$$
$$1 \text{ dwt} = 1.016 \text{ metric tonnes}$$
$$1 \text{ psi} = 6.894 \text{ kPa}$$
$$1 \text{ shp} = 0.7457 \text{ kW}$$
$$1 \text{ slug} = 14.59 \text{ kg}$$

Discussion

Richard Tweedie, Member

[The views expressed herein are the opinions of the discusser and not necessarily those of the Department of Transportation or the U. S. Coast Guard.]

The potential fuel savings of large-diameter, slow-turning propellers appear to be quite dramatic.

One of the primary design constraints of these propellers is the International Maritime Organization (IMO, formerly known as IMCO) standards for tankers which require sufficient segregated ballast tank (SBT) capacity to submerge the vessel's propeller. The authors correctly point out that the Coast Guard may consider an "equivalence" that is as effective as the measure required by the standard. One addition stipulation specified in Regulation 3 of the MARPOL Convention is that operational procedures may not be substituted for design or construction features.

First, a little background. In order for the SBT concept to work, a tank vessel must be designed to have sufficient ballast capacity to provide safe and seaworthy performance under most weather and sea conditions without needing to put ballast water in cargo tanks. The SBT capacity standards which accomplish this were developed after extensive studies involving vessel logs, model tests, and surveys of tank vessel masters. The cumulative data indicated the need/desirability of having the propeller tips immersed during the ballast voyage.

While the authors looked at four areas they felt should be considered in an "equivalency" determination of the SBT standards, the Coast Guard is obliged, under the Convention, to ensure that all effects touching on vessel safety or pollution prevention be considered. This would include indirect as well as direct effects.

The impact of large-diameter propellers on stopping distance

Large-Diameter Propellers of Reduced Weight

was explored by the authors. However, the Coast Guard would have to be concerned with all maneuvering characteristics of the vessel. For instance, did the authors consider the possible effects of the vessel's turning diameter? It seems that the reduction in velocity of water flowing past the rudder coupled with a larger percentage of the rudder being out of the water during the ballast voyage could have a negative impact on maneuverability.

From the pollution prevention side there are several indirect effects that would have to be considered. For instance, under the present standards a master would put ballast in a cargo tank only under severe weather conditions—the only time there would be an impetus to do so. However, there might be considerable motivation to do so if, while operating on a ballast voyage, a vessel could achieve greater fuel efficiency by ballasting some cargo tanks to immerse a greater portion of a large-diameter propeller.

The point I am making is that all aspects of the redesigned vessel that touch on safety or pollution prevention would have to be fully developed before an "equivalency" to the IMO SBT capacity standards could be considered.

L. Hawdon, Member

This is an interesting paper covering a wide field of propulsion-related subjects, many of which are perhaps worthy of a paper in their own right, but it is understood that in the general context of the title it was necessary to try to deal with each in this one paper. Comments have therefore been related principally to the propeller design and economic aspects.

As a member of a leading propeller design and manufacturing organization, I would hasten to assure the authors that we, along with other manufacturers, are constantly striving to keep the weight of propellers to a minimum, consistent of course with all the other important features which must be taken into account in the design and manufacture of efficient, inexpensive and reliable marine propellers.

The first comment relates to the list of factors given on the second page which were graded as part of the propeller lightening alternatives. Two other very important factors should have been added: (a) cost of manufacture, and (b) time of manufacture.

Referring to Tables 1 and 2, it would be interesting to have some comments on the reasoning behind the allocation of the ratings to each factor. Some of the ratings are puzzling, notably the following:

(a) Why is "Dimen. Free" allocated only 1 for a conventional propeller? Manufacturers worldwide are casting propellers to most unusual shapes with no insurmountable manufacturing problems.

(b) Following the above, why is Alt 1 given a rating of 5? The sketches in Fig. 7 suggest that there is considerable restriction with regard to blade section shape. The section profiles shown would be unacceptable.

(c) The hollow blade with separate tips is given a rating 3 under ease of manufacture. Have the authors considered the problems involved in casting a hollow blade to give a wall thickness of $1\frac{1}{4}$ in., or the welding problems involved in fitting the outer parts of the blades, or closing plates, bearing in mind that stress-relieving will be necessary and that the propeller will still have to be finished to within ISO dimensional tolerances?

(d) Why is Alternative 4, the tip-attached tandem propeller, given a weight saving grading of 3, when it is heavier than the conventional propeller?

(e) Ease of repair should be given 4 or 5 for conventional propellers and certainly no more than 2 for hollow-bladed propellers.

(f) Why is the conventional hub given only a rating of 2 for ease of manufacture? Every propeller manufacturer currently produces propellers having conventional hubs with no problem, and this rating should surely be 5.

(g) The flange-mounted hub is graded 3 for ease of manufacture. The hub shown in Fig. 9 could not in practice be cast to the dimensions shown, and would require to be machined out of substantial casting allowances. The boss wall thicknesses should in any case be considerably greater, and for guidance the authors are referred to Fig. 5 in their reference [9].

(h) It is not understood why ease of handling is given a rating of 1 for the conventional hub since no problems have been experienced to date with propellers of all sizes and all types of boss fittings.

(i) Since conventional hubs have been accepted by shipbuilders, owners and ship repairers worldwide, it is puzzling to see that level of acceptability is given a rating of only 3.

The authors' comments of the preceding would be welcomed because presumably on the basis of their evaluations—many of which seem to be of doubtful validity—it was decided to proceed with their long and detailed investigation.

On the question of cast lightweight and fabricated propellers, it would be interesting to know how much advice the authors took from propeller manufacturers or elsewhere to assess the practical feasibility, the cost, and the manufacturing time using these methods. Some ten years ago the practicability of hollow and fabricated propellers was investigated in the United Kingdom. While considerable weight savings could be achieved, these were more than offset by the very large increase in man-hours of work involved, and the uncertainties of the structure when subjected to corrosion fatigue.

It would seem from their comments that the authors may have felt restricted by the propeller casting facilities in the United States. It should be noted that in the United Kingdom facilities for casting conventional propellers with a finished weight of up to 120 tonnes have been available for many years.

The idea of the tip-attached tandem propeller is very interesting but Fig. 10 does not clearly show this proposal. Would it therefore be possible for the authors to enlarge their data on this type of propeller and give some more detailed drawings so that the advantages and manufacturing possibilities may be assessed?

It is agreed that the IMO rules on draft limitation do seriously restrict propeller design and the choice of optimum shaft rpm, and overall fuel economy. Representations have already been made to IMO on this subject but have been met with a negative response without clear justification of the reason for the rule. It is agreed that these regulations should be critically reviewed.

F. Everett Reed, Member

This is an interesting paper. Its effect will be to further decrease the rpm of propellers, which will have strong influences not only on propeller and hull design but also on propulsion plants. Geared units would appear to be a necessity even with diesel power plants.

In studying the lateral vibration of shafting on many ships, Littleton Research has been impressed with how difficult it is to develop rigidity in the stern bearing. The bearing is not only flexible in translation but also in rotation about axes perpendicular to the shaft rotation axis. Because of this conformity, even bending, of the stern bearing, length in the bearing is useful in reducing the loads and the difficulties in alignment are less than might otherwise be expected. It did not appear that this flexibility of the bearing was considered in evaluating the propeller weight limitations imposed by the stern bearing.

It is also noted that No. 30 oil was expected to be used for all bearings. Since the friction of a bearing is determined by the product of viscosity and velocity, it is entirely reasonable, and the common practice, to utilize higher viscosity lubricants for slow-turning journals. In fact, the Sommerfeld number which is used for evaluating the bearing contains the product $\mu \times N$.

V. K. Atkins, Member

The authors are to be commended for a pioneering paper on a heretofore generally neglected subject. They have imaginatively considered the myriad ways of constructing large-diameter propellers of reduced weight and provided a subjective discipline evaluating practical alternatives. From that ranking, several configurations were selected, the literature comprehensively reviewed, and a design methodology developed.

The concepts chosen seem producible with existing materials and facilities. In production they will cost more than the displaced conventional bronze propeller, and the authors' estimate of $200 000 (1982 dollars) more than base is reasonable. During detailed design, careful consideration should be given to facilitating nondestructive testing of all welded connections in metal propellers. Likewise, state-of-the-art failure indication devices should be incorporated in lightweight advanced-material designs.

Repairs should be readily accomplished with present equipment and facilities. Detailed techniques will require adjustment for hollow regions and more stringent reinspection of connections. I estimate lightweight metal propeller repairs to cost about 170 percent of base. The most difficult problems will occur when an accident causes cavities to collapse.

Costs to repair lightweight advanced-material propellers are more speculative. However, other experience indicates that major repairs are possible at reasonable cost.

R. Verbeek,[9] Visitor

The authors have presented a very comprehensive paper covering various consequences of the introduction of large-diameter propellers. The idea to save fuel by application of large-diameter, slow-running propellers has already been adopted and realized by various ship operators. Our company has supplied various large-diameter propellers with diameters up to 10.5 m for this purpose. These propellers were all solid monobloc castings and did not cause any problems in the foundry.

Application of hollow blades with a wall thickness of about 3 cm as mentioned in the paper will cause severe molding and casting problems and a big research effort is needed to overcome these difficulties. Lips has already started a long-term investigation program in order to establish and control the metal flow and solidification of cast material within the mold.

Reduction of hub scantlings is another attractive alternative to reduce the weight of a marine propeller. Of course case has to be taken that the stresses in the propeller blades and the hub remain within allowable limits. Detailed studies with advanced numerical techniques are therefore necessary. This can be illustrated by a study in which a five-bladed propeller was represented by an axial slice containing a hub sector with two attached blade root regions at maximum blade thickness. The expected stress distribution has a predominant plane strain behavior, which justifies this two-dimensional approach. Figure 27 accompanying this discussion shows the finite-element mesh. Figures 28 and 29 present contours of calculated equivalent stresses in the hub due to only the shrinkage fit of the hub on the shaft and due to the superposition of blade bending on the shrinkage fit. From these diagrams it can be

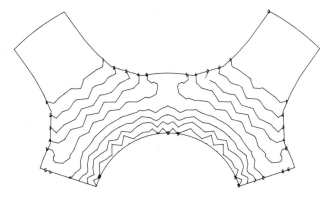

Fig. 27

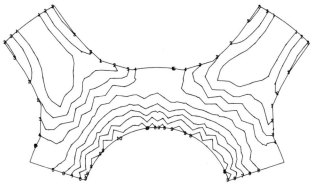

Fig. 28

Fig. 29

easily concluded that the stresses in the hub surface are almost independent of blade loading and consequently not subject to fatigue damage.

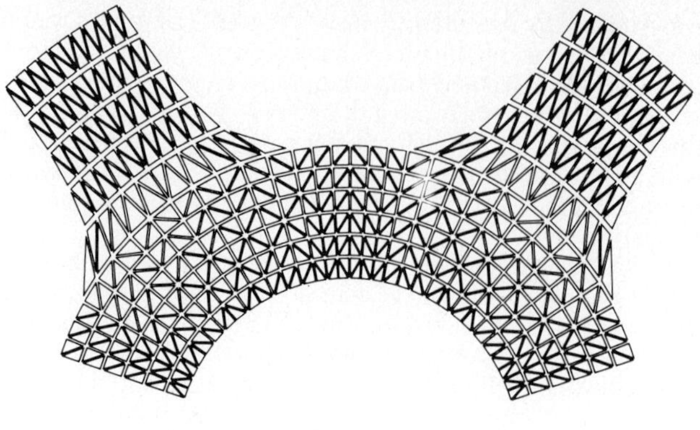

In the paper the repairability of the hollow-bladed propeller was hardly mentioned. In case of an accidental impact on the blade, the danger of plate buckling exists which will complicate repair. Can the authors comment on this aspect?

Another aspect concerns the strength of the propeller blades. In order to reduce vibration problems, skew is often applied to lower the propeller-induced pressures on the hull. The application of skew has the consequence that the location of the maximum stresses in the blade sections moves from maximum thickness toward the trailing edge, and commonly appears between $0.4R$ and $0.6R$. The stress level also increases.

To what extent the calculations for the stress levels in hollow blades used by the authors remain valid for skewed propellers

---

[9] Lips Propeller Works, Drunen, The Netherlands.

Large-Diameter Propellers of Reduced Weight

is questionable, and again finite-element techniques must provide the solution, as the applied basic beam theory probably is even less applicable than for solid skewed propellers.

To conclude, the ideas presented in the paper are very interesting but should be investigated further—especially the aspects of repairability, strength and production of hollow-bladed propellers.

Peter M. Kimon, Member

The authors have presented a methodical analysis of very-low-rpm large-diameter propellers and have made a strong argument for reducing propeller weight to take advantage of the low rpm. They recommend a hollow hub with a flanged connection to the tailshaft, and cast hollow blades, as the best approach to reduce the weight and achieve the benefits of low rpm.

These schemes appear to be attractive, and are worthy of further study prior to implementation. In this connection, I would suggest an approach which sets priorities of modifications in order of least cost to most benefit, with additional consideration of lowest-risk items first. For example, consider first the "baseline propeller" which the authors indicate as being 36 percent lighter than the original installed propeller. Also, lower shp requirements associated with future high fuel costs would suggest that cavitation requirements can be satisfied with smaller blade area ratios and therefore lighter conventional propellers. Smaller number of blades should be another consideration, which in addition to reducing weight would also improve efficiency. Next, before the consideration to go to hollow blades, I would consider the authors' suggestion of a hollow hub with flanged tailshaft. A number of these suggestions are currently under implementation, with one 15 500-bhp ore carrier under construction with a 45 rpm 11-m propeller.

While directionally I agree with the authors, I doubt that their "bottom line" conclusion of being able to save one million dollars per year is realistic. Newbuildings are likely to have diesel engines as main propulsion or advanced steam power plants. In either case basic fuel consumption will be substantially lower than the values used in the paper. Moreover, in today's environment it is likely that tankers, for example, would operate at one quarter to three quarters of their continuous service power rating a large portion of the time. Consequently the annual savings, most likely, will be much less than one million dollars.

Finally, while we at Exxon International are familiar with the NSMB Holtrop Program, we have some doubts regarding its ability when extrapolating hull efficiency down to 33 rpm. Some model test work would be appropriate to substantiate the gains of these very-low-rpm propellers.

Otto Scherer,[10] Visitor

The fact that, on many large ships, the propeller is limited to less than an optimum diameter because of weight is a graphic example of the fundamental scaling law—weight increases as the cube of the scale while the bearing area increases only as the square. I first became aware of the resulting significant efficiency penalty through our work on high-powered ships, reported in reference [1] of the paper, and have remained interested in finding methods to reduce propeller weight. I therefore read this excellent paper with much interest and wish to commend the authors for their thorough and convincing presentation of the feasibility for achieving significant efficiency improvements on large ships through large-diameter propellers of reduced weight.

I would like to comment briefly on the 42.5-ft-diameter

[10] Hydronautics, Inc., Laurel, Maryland.

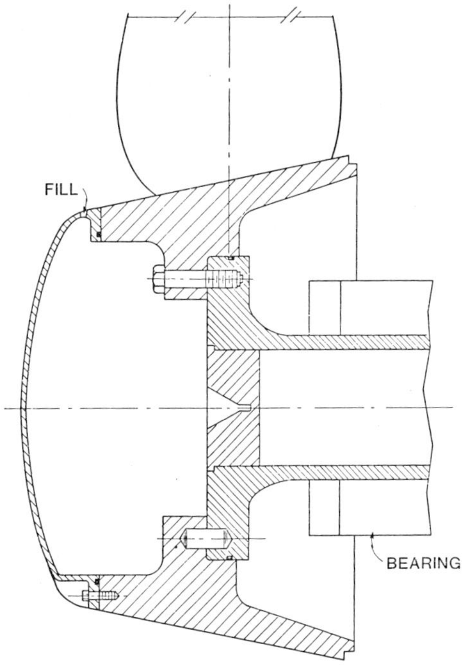

Fig. 30 Lightweight hub, 0.3 hub-diameter ratio

hollow-bladed propeller design. In particular, I am surprised at the very small hub diameter for two reasons:

First, it seems inconsistent with the torque requirements for this design. Taking into account the 23 percent reduction in power associated with the improved efficiency of the large propeller, the torque is still over twice that of the 27.5-ft design, yet the hub is only 1.2 in. larger in diameter. In addition, the solid version of the 42.5-ft propeller has a 17.6 percent hub ratio, which I would judge to be about normal, yet the hollow version has only a 12.4 percent hub. Could you comment on how this hub diameter was selected?

Secondly, and more important, the limited studies we have done indicate that a lighter propeller results from using a larger hub diameter. That is, a minimum combined hub and blade weight occurs with a hollow hub of 25 to 35 percent of the propeller diameter. In fact, if the hollow hub is not flooded, a further significant weight reduction will occur from the buoyancy of a large hub when the propeller is immersed. For conventional-stern, single-screw ships, these large hubs appear to result in a negligible loss of efficiency.

Figure 30 herewith shows a 30 percent diameter, hollow, flange-mounted hub we designed for a smaller ship. Note that the flange is set into the hub. This provides a stiffening ring under the blades to take the blade root bending loads as well as permitting the stern bearing to be closer to the propeller, which reduces the shaft bending moment due to the overhung load.

Edward V. Lewis, Member

This interesting paper suggests that the large slow-turning propeller may be an idea whose time has finally come, especially for large, low-speed ships. Two reasons for this may be that, first, the high price of fuel oil is forcing greater attention to propulsive efficiency, and second the research reported here has demonstrated that practical solutions to the engineering problems are now available. The paper presents and analyzes many novel and interesting ideas in a very thorough fashion.

Although mention is made that "large tankers seem to offer the best opportunity for the use of large-diameter propellers," the dimensional relationships that account for this are not explained. In going to ever larger and larger bulk carriers the conditions for geometrical similarity include, of course, $V \propto \sqrt{L}$ and propeller $D \propto L$. But the vital rpm condition is $N \propto 1/\sqrt{L}$. Hence, as noted in an earlier paper, [73] (additional reference follows this discussion), "The increase in size of bulk carriers . . . poses serious problems of declining propulsive efficiency. It is not generally realized that for a 900-ft tanker to match the propulsive efficiency of a geometrically similar ship of 450-ft length it would require a single propeller of 44-ft diameter instead of 22 ft, operating at 64 rpm instead of 90. . . ." One idea "would be to develop techniques of building larger propellers, along with gear designs which can economically furnish larger shaft speed reductions." It is gratifying that work on how to build larger propellers has finally been undertaken, as reported in this paper.

The proceeding quotation also suggests the importance of the parallel problem—reducing propeller rpm—since simply increasing diameter without optimizing rpm is not worthwhile. The paper merely suggests that a third reduction gear is required (and gives cost estimates in Appendix 7). This may involve some marine engineering problems that deserve a little more attention. This is particularly true of diesel power plants, where higher-than-optimum rpm's are often accepted and therefore even bigger fuel savings from large propellers and low rpm may be attainable. Economic studies are needed, as in this paper, to determine optimum overall economy with different diesel engines and various degrees of speed reduction.

No doubt the authors have considered the fact that smaller, faster ships than the example selected for study may not show the same advantages of larger propellers. Perhaps their investigation should be expanded to show the range of ship size, speed and power plant type for which larger propellers would be advantageous. This suggestion is not a criticism of an excellent paper but a recognition of the fact that any good piece of research usually suggests a worthwhile sequel.

Additional reference

73   Lewis, E. V., "Research Toward More Efficient Transportation by Sea," TRANS. SNAME, Vol. 69, 1961.

David O. Carlson, Member

The purpose of this discussion is to comment upon several of the authors' observations and conclusions concerning stern tube bearings.

While it does not explicitly so state, this paper may give the reader the impression that to operate a marine propulsion shafting system below a calculated minimum rpm invites bearing failure. I don't believe that this is the authors' intention, and such an interpretation would be erroneous and a considerable disservice to the thousands of babbitted, oil-lubricated stern tube bearing installations in operation throughout the world. For a considerable part of their service life, vessels having oil-lubricated bearings operate on turning gear or in the maneuvering mode without bearing damage. Records maintained by this discusser's company document numerous vessels having large-diameter [greater than 22 in. (560 mm)] shafts that have operated for periods of more than 10 years during which time bearing weardown did not exceed 0.015 in. (0.4 mm). I am certain that most shipowners and operators can verify this history of satisfactory service.

These facts do not invalidate the authors' analysis, but merely point out that additional parameters exist which promote successful bearing operation. While it may not exist to the degree found in reinforced phenolic resin or other types of plastic bushings, a babbitt does possess conformability such that a misaligned shaft can "bed" into the bearing, thus reducing edge

loading and distributing the effective shaft load over a larger area. The compatibility of a babbitt bearing surface and a steel shaft journal in conjunction with the lubricity of the stern tube oil have undoubtedly also contributed to the successful history of these components.

The authors outline a procedure for calculating the "minimum" rpm. It is stated that the results from the calculations made for the various configurations, using this procedure, are less valid in absolute terms than on a comparative basis, and the discusser is in agreement with this. The calculation procedure for misaligned shafts (Appendix 5) works with a midlength film thickness and then uses a plot of film thickness versus Sommerfeld number to determine the Sommerfeld number, from which the corresponding rpm is calculated. This implies that the operating conditions at midlength hold true (as an average) for the full bearing length in the misaligned condition. Numerical calculation procedures for misaligned journal bearings (references [74] and [75] herewith) show significant oil film pressure peaks axially biased toward the point of closest approach of the shaft and bearing. These high-pressure areas tend to modify the film conditions as obtained by the midlength averaging procedure. The location of these high pressures axially away from the bearing midpoint (generally toward the propeller) results in positive film thicknesses under some conditions in which the authors' procedure would indicate zero film thickness.

Moving the center of the reaction load aft also increases the natural frequency of the shafting system which, generally, increases the system's resistance to shaft whirl.

The latter serendipitous result can also be obtained by reducing the bearing length; and, as the authors indicate, a shorter bearing may also produce a lower minimum rpm. The classification societies have traditionally been reluctant to reduce bearing L/D ratios below 2:1. Thus, this paper verifies that there are additional technical advantages as well as economic reasons for permitting shorter stern tube bearings.

The authors temper their recommendations concerning the use of hydrostatic lift bearings with the note that slight changes in shaft misalignment will rapidly increase the power required by the lift pump. The obvious solution is to equip self-aligning bearings with hydrostatic lift capability; the technology for such a combination is readily available since this design has been in use for many years.

The discusser does agree with the authors' conclusion that the use of large-diameter, slow-speed propellers will require changes in the conventional stern tube bearing. The incorporation of a self-aligning stern tube bearing will eliminate shaft misalignment from the list of parameters that faces the designer of a vessel employing this propulsion system. And, as has previously been shown [76], a self-aligning tilting pad journal bearing will provide a lower "minimum" rpm than an equivalent aligned sleeve bearing.

Additional references

74   Asanabe, S., Akahoshi, M., and Matsunbu, T., "Theoretical and Experimental Investigation on Stern-tube Bearing Lubrication," *Mitsubishi Heavy Industries Technical Review*, Nagasaki Technical Institute, Nagasaki, Japan, Oct. 1972.

75   "Analysis and Design of Advanced Stern-Tube Bearing Systems," Mechanical Technology Inc., Report No. MA-RD-920-79009, Latham, N.Y., Nov. 1978.

76   Gardner, W. W., "Journal Bearing Operation at Low Sommerfeld Numbers," *Trans.* ASLE, Vol. 19, No. 3, 1976, pp. 187–194.

Al Herrington,[11] Visitor

I would like to compliment the authors on the volume and

---

[11] Waukesha Bearings Corp. (WBC), Waukesha, Wisconsin.

the quality of the work spent in this effort. Our Mr. Jerome Gruber (vice president), who is an honorary lifetime member of SNAME, stated that he believed it to be the "paper of the decade."

My first point is to bring to your attention (with reference to the "Self-aligning bearings" subsection of Appendix 5) that 300 psi is considered by WBC as a reasonable design load for self-aligning bearings; 150 psi is more reflective of the current thinking of most classification societies worldwide. We have run tests well beyond 300 psi.

My second and last point deals with the fact that WBC has a 4000-vessel experience factor worldwide—all running on oil-lubricated stern tube bearings. The mode of power varies from turbines to slow-speed diesels running at all speeds from 1/6 rpm turning gear to nominal operating levels of approximately 100 rpm. We selected weardown records from 50 vessels at random from our records in Waukesha. These vessels ran anywhere from 5 to 15 years of service with weardown records indicating dimensional changes of from 0.000 to 0.034 maximum. These records were available for examination in our booth during the Exposition hours at the Annual Meeting.

Authors' Closure

We wish to thank all of the discussers for the points which they have raised. They add substantially to the value of the material in the paper.

In response to CDR Tweedie's comments, we would first like to say that we are familiar with all aspects of Regulation 3 of the MARPOL Convention and with the spirit in which this regulation was conceived. Secondly, we agree that all aspects of vessel safety and pollution prevention should be investigated prior to the granting of an equivalence for the actual installation of a large diameter propeller. The areas touched upon in the paper were illustrative in nature and not intended to imply that a more complete investigation would be unnecessary. However, in connection with the question CDR Tweedie raises regarding maneuverability, we would like to say that while it might be true that a reduction in water velocity flowing past the rudder would occur, there is no reason to believe that "a larger percentage of the rudder" would be out of the water. We are not proposing to reduce the amount of ballast carried from that required for a vessel with a "conventional" diameter propeller, but to not add to the ballast requirements for a vessel with a greatly increased propeller diameter. Thus, the draft at the after perpendicular for the two propeller diameters would be the same, so that the amount of rudder immersed in the ballast condition would be identical.

Mr. Hawdon raised a large number of questions based on his long experience in propeller design and manufacturing. Many of his questions center upon the preliminary evaluation that we made at the beginning of the project to determine what configurations would warrant further study. These were subjective judgments made by a team composed of a propeller manufacturer, propeller designer, general naval architect and propeller hydrodynamicist. No great significance should be given to the values assigned to each of the factors. This same team, after completion of this project, would undoubtedly give different values to many of these items. As a matter of fact, some of the ideas that were favorite candidates of the team members in the preliminary analysis did not fare well in the detailed study—the basic objective of the project.

The idea of hollow-bladed and fabricated propellers is not new. They have been rejected in the past due to cost because there was no need to reduce weight. This study showed that there would be such a need if very low rpm's were to be

achieved with very-large-diameter propellers. The choice of fabrication method was decided from ease of manufacturing and was in no way guided by manufacturing facilities in the United States or any other country.

Since the tip-attached tandem propellers fell by the wayside, no drawings were developed to assist in evaluating the manufacturing process; thus, there are no detail drawings available to further clarify this concept.

In reference to the IMO rules, we hope a project such as this, which helps quantify the economic liabilities of the rule, will result in possible modifications without violating the intended spirit of the rules. Rules are not written in stone but should be modified as knowledge grows.

We appreciate the additional information that Mr. Atkins provided regarding the manufacturing and repair of hollow-bladed propellers. The advice and support of Mr. Atkins throughout this project was essential to ensure that the concepts were feasible to manufacture.

Mr. Verbeek emphasizes the need for research and development in casting processes to ensure proper solidification of thin-walled hollow propeller blades, and we agree. Once the desirability of adopting hollow blades has been established as we have done here, implementation will require careful attention to all details of the fabrication process.

We recognize that casting hollow blades will require more effort in molding and casting. We are glad to learn that Lips has initiated some of the research effort that will be required to overcome some of the difficulties.

The repair of damaged hollow blades was not part of this study; hence, we cannot offer any opinion on this other than referring to the comments of Mr. Atkins.

The technique of design developed in this project would not be applicable to cases in which the maximum stresses did not occur at the point of maximum thickness such as in highly skewed propellers. A different technique would then have to be developed for sizing the sections. In all circumstances, it would be desirable to make a finite-element study before manufacturing.

From his finite-element studies of stresses in the hub at the blade roots, Mr. Verbeek concludes that hub surface stresses are nearly independent of blade loading for a shrink-fit of hub to tailshaft. What we have suggested for further research is that similar studies should be done on hollow hubs in which there are no stresses from a shrink-fit. Hub stresses may, in that case, be more influenced by unsteady blade loads.

We agree with Mr. Kimon that the most cost-effective approaches from this study should be selected in reducing propeller weight. Careful design of the propeller to minimize material requirements is undoubtedly the most cost-effective approach followed by the design of a hollow hub such as suggested by the paper or by Mr. Scherer. In minimizing blade weight, care has to be taken to insure that neither strength nor fatigue nor cavitation characteristics are jeopardized. Minimizing blade area can result in excessive surface roughness from general cavitation erosion, thus reducing the propeller hydrodynamic performance.

Mr. Kimon questioned the use of the Holtrop data for such a large-diameter propeller and suggested model tests. We would agree that model tests would be a required adjunct for a full-scale installation; however, the Holtrop equations are probably adequate for preliminary design and feasibility studies such as this. The propeller diameter (42.5 ft) to draft (57.0 ft) ratio is about 0.75. The "super" tankers of yesteryear frequently had propeller diameter-to-draft ratios which exceeded that value. Undoubtedly, the data from such models are contained in the data base used in developing these equations.

Mr. Scherer asks how hub diameter was selected. The hub

diameter for our 42.5-ft-diameter propeller was deliberately minimized by sizing the tailshaft to ABS requirements, then adding a flange of sufficient size to accommodate the bolts and studs needed to couple it to the hub. The hub weight was thus minimized. We did not make a parametric study of hub diameters to assess the tradeoff of hub weight against blade weight such as that suggested by Mr. Scherer. That would be a next logical step. Whether the same optimum percent hub would emerge with hollow blades as with the solid blades in Mr. Scherer's comments could only be answered after such a study. His design which puts the flange inside the hub is intriguing, and it is an alternative which should be stress-analyzed along with our design as we have recommended in our suggestions for future research.

In regard to comments by Mr. Reed and Mr. Carlson, we certainly agree that additional parameters exist which would promote successful bearing operation even at very low rpm. Accounting for the flexibility of the bearing and its housing, and the resulting improvement in surface conformity, would reduce bearing load and lower the minimum rpm appearing in the tables. (As Mr. Carlson points out, extremes might be reached in this regard with the phenolic resin bushings and with self-aligning bearings.) In all cases, however, the situation would improve for both solid and hollow propellers. The use of a higher-viscosity lubricant as suggested by Mr. Reed would have a similarly beneficial effect, as would the incorporation of an allowance for the uneven pressure distribution mentioned by Mr. Carlson. It is not that these factors were not taken into account, but rather that they are victims of simplifications made in developing the procedure in an effort to establish trends. In fact, other items which were averaged or taken as constant, such as the initial orientation of the stern tube and shaft, for example, might have had an even greater effect on the absolute values of minimum rpm, but, we think, not on the general trend.

Refinements to the procedure and additional parametric studies would be interesting routes for further development. We thank Mr. Reed and Mr. Carlson for their comments and their support.

The compliments offered by Mr. Herrington and Mr. Gruber are most generous and rewarding, and we accept them with thanks. Mr. Herrington's explanation of load limits for self-aligning bearings is well taken. The cases evaluated in Table 10 were loaded to 115 and 193 psi (L/D of 1.7 and 1.0, respectively) with the generally satisfactory results shown. If a load limit of 300 psi or higher were acceptable, then the results would approach those obtained with the lightweight propeller. The effect here is that while the self-aligning bearing eliminates the problem of shaft alignment, it cannot entirely eliminate the effect of shaft bowing. The shorter the bearing, however, (and the higher the resulting load), the lower the effect of bowing. Mr. Herrington's company must be complimented on their excellent performance record, also mentioned by Mr. Carlson.

Professor Lewis has offered his usual insightful comments on our paper. As he so succinctly explains, the increases in size of any carrier results in larger propellers turning at lower speeds if geometric similarity is to be maintained. We chose the tanker for this project because of their obvious rapid growth in size over the past 20 years without a corresponding growth in propeller size. The principles demonstrated in this study are equally applicable to any other large carrier.

Professor Lewis's suggestion that the study should be extended to include the diesel engine working at very low rpm is appropriate as it is the most likely propulsion system in today's economic environment.

We thank the discussers for their valuable comments, and the Society for the opportunity to present the results of our study to the membership.

SNAME *Transactions*, Vol. 90, 1982, pp. 195–228

Maneuvering Performance of Ships in Critical Channels[1]

Haruzo Eda,[2] Life Member, **Frederick Seibold,**[3] Member, and **Frank W. DeBord,**[4] Associate Member

Results of experimental and computer-aided studies are presented relative to a two-phase research program in which the maneuvering characteristics of Great Lakes ships in critical channels are examined. The Phase I study identified specific problem situations in terms of channels, vessel types, and design variables. Subsequently, in the Phase II study, maneuvering characteristics of two Great Lakes bulk carriers (that is, the 1000-ft and 730-ft ships) are evaluated in captive model tests, full-scale trials, and digital simulations under ice-free and ice-covered water conditions (deep and shallow). Results indicate that the ice and shallow waters have significant stabilizing effects on inherent course stability and reduce turning performance to a great extent. Therefore, shiphandling in ice-covered channels is a critical problem as is clearly shown in full-scale trials and digital simulations. Recommendations are included to improve ship-handling performance in critical channels in terms of ship-waterway-systems design.

Introduction

WITH the expansion of ship size, traffic level, and operational season on the Great Lakes, ship maneuvering is becoming increasingly important in the restricted channels of connecting waterways. This is illustrated by the fact that industry personnel identified maneuvering in critical channels as a high-priority research item [1–3].[5] Both industry and governmental regulatory personnel are concerned with the ability of existing channels to accommodate future marine transportation.

Accordingly, a two-phase program has been carried out to study the maneuvering characteristics of Great Lakes ships in critical channels. The purpose of this study is to examine and to improve the capability of ships and channels of the Great Lakes and St. Lawrence Seaway systems under ice-free and ice-covered conditions through experimental and computer-aided analyses.

The first phase of the program was to identify the most important design and operating problems involving Great Lakes ship maneuvering in both ice-free and ice-covered channels. In order to define these problems and thereby facilitate development of the Phase II Study Plan, waterways, ship types, design parameters and operating variables were ranked according to their estimated importance in ship maneuvering. Specific problems were then defined by combining the highest-ranked ships, waterways, design parameters and operating variables as follows:

1. The most critical ship type is the 1000 × 105-ft Great

Lakes bulk carrier, which is currently the largest size ship capable of navigating the connecting waterways. The 730 × 75-ft bulk carrier is also considered to be of importance.

2. Results of the survey identified the Neebish Island Channel in the St. Mary's River as the highest-priority waterway.

On the basis of these results, the Phase II study was carried out to determine the adequacy of channel size, ship size, and ship maneuvering response, as follows:

1. Captive model tests of two ships (that is, the 1000- and 730-ft ships) were carried out under ice-free and ice-covered conditions to obtain hydrodynamic data needed for the development of the mathematical simulation model.

2. Full-scale trials were made on the 1000-ft-long ship in critical channels in the St. Mary's River under ice-free and ice-covered conditions.

3. Utilizing these test results, a simulation model was developed to represent the dynamic behavior of ships proceeding through the channels. Subsequently, a series of digital simulation runs were made proceeding through the critical channels in order to establish guidelines for Great Lakes ship design and operating procedures.

Results obtained from this study indicate that ice has a pronounced effect on maneuvering performance. Inherent course stability is significantly increased with greatly reduced turning performance under ice-covered conditions. Results also indicate that the effect of ice on maneuvering performance is influenced to a large extent by the stern configuration.

This paper presents results obtained from the two-phase program in the following two parts:

Part I   Identification of most significant problems

Part II   Experimental and computer-aided studies

PART I: Identification of most-significant problems

The objective of the first phase of analysis is to identify the most significant design and operating problems involving vessel maneuverability in both ice-free and ice-covered channels in

---

[1] This study has been conducted as a two-year program at Stevens Institute of Technology and Arctec under the sponsorship of U.S. Maritime Administration.

[2] Senior research engineer, Davidson Laboratory; professor of ocean engineering, Stevens Institute of Technology, Hoboken, New Jersey.

[3] Program manager, Office of Maritime Technology, U.S. Maritime Administration, Washington, D.C.

[4] Arctec, Inc.; presently, vice president, Offshore Technology Corp., Escondido, California.

[5] Numbers in brackets designate References at end of paper.

Presented at the Annual Meeting, New York, N. Y., November 17–20, 1982, of THE SOCIETY OF NAVAL ARCHITECTS AND MARINE ENGINEERS.

order to develop the subsequent Part II study plan.

Toward this objective, alternative waterways, ship types, design parameters and operating variables were ranked according to their importance to shiphandling in channels.

The data obtained and a summary of the situations identified as the most significant problem areas are presented in the following sections.

Industry assessment of waterways and vessels

Existing and potential maneuvering problems were defined by the Great Lakes industry and government personnel during a series of interviews conducted January and February 1979. Those interviewed represent nine fleet operators, one trade association, two design firms, two shipyards, one university, and three government agencies.

Participants were asked to rank the waterways based on relative maneuvering difficulties and levels of utilization. In cases where the participant did not rank all of the waterways, equal priorities have been assigned to those which were not ranked so that numerical totals could be calculated. The final rankings were determined by identifying those waterways with the highest cumulative priorities (lowest sum of priority numbers assigned by individual participants). The St. Mary's River was identified as the highest priority waterway with 16 participants ranking it No. 1 and one participant ranking it No. 2. The Detroit River and the St. Clair River were ranked second and third, respectively, and Lake St. Clair and the Straits of Mackinac received an equal ranking of fourth.

Participants were also asked to rank the alternate vessel types based on relative handling difficulties and the anticipated fleet mix in the year 2000. Final rankings were calculated in a manner identical to that used for ranking alternate waterways. Vessel types which were not ranked by a participant were assigned equal priorities and the final rankings were determined by adding the priorities assigned by all participants. The highest ranked vessel type is the 1000 × 105-ft laker, which was ranked No. 1 by 14 of the 17 participants who ranked the alternate vessel types. The 1100 × 105-ft laker and the 850 × 75-ft laker were ranked second and third, respectively.

Industry participants were also asked to identify ship and channel design and operational variables which should be included in the analysis of maneuvering in restricted channels. Channel width variations were identified as important by 15 of the 18 participants and channel depth variation was identified by 14 participants. The inclusion of bow and/or stern thrusters was identified by 10 participants and therefore ranks third, and rudder configuration and bow design received a final ranking of fourth. In the case of bow design, three of the nine participants who identified it as important said changes should be considered only for operations in ice.

Physical characteristics of connecting waterways

Preliminary analysis of the relative maneuvering difficulties experienced by vessels operating in alternate waterways can be accomplished by comparing the dimensions and configurations of the waterways. The two parameters of primary importance in a waterway with a fairly constant depth (such as dredged channels) are the number and magnitude of heading changes that must be made by the vessel, and the channel width available to accomplish the maneuvers.

Each of the interconnecting waterways in the Great Lakes/St. Lawrence Seaway system was divided into the reaches, and channel width, channel depth, and heading changes were tabulated.

A summary of the results of this analysis is presented in Table 1. The severity of maneuvers required in alternate waterways can be compared based on the average heading change per turn, the maximum heading change required in the waterway, and the number of turns (heading changes) per mile. The room

---

Nomenclature

A = reference area ($A = lH$, l^2, or BH)
a = yaw gain constant
B = ship beam
b = yaw-rate gain constant
c = sway gain constant
d = sway-rate gain constant
D_w = water depth
e = subscript e indicates value at equilibrium conditions
F_r = Froude number ($U/\sqrt{gl}$)
g = acceleration due to gravity
H = ship draft
I_z = moment of inertia referred to z-axis
l = ship length
m = mass of ship
N = hydrodynamic and aerodynamic yaw moment
$N_{\dot{r}}$ = derivative of hydrodynamic yaw moment with respect to yaw acceleration
N_v = derivative of hydrodynamic yaw moment with respect to sideslip velocity
n = propeller revolutions per second
N_δ = derivative of hydrodynamic yaw moment with respect to rudder angle
N_n = derivative of hydrodynamic yaw moment with respect to off-centerline displacement

r = yaw rate
t_r = time constant of rudder in control system
U_a = approach speed
U_t = speed in steady turning
u = component of ship speed in x-axis direction
u_e = component of equilibrium ship speed in x-axis direction
W = width of channel
v = component of ship speed in y-axis direction
v_e = component of equilibrium ship speed in y-axis direction
X = hydrodynamic and aerodynamic force component in x-axis direction
X_ρ = hydrodynamic force component in x-axis direction due to propeller
$X_{\dot{u}}$ = derivative of hydrodynamic force component in x-axis direction, with respect to surge acceleration
X_{vr} = second derivative of hydrodynamic force component in x-axis direction with respect to sideslip velocity and yaw angular velocity
X_0 = drag coefficient

Y = hydrodynamic and aerodynamic force component in y-axis direction
Y_r = derivative of hydrodynamic force component in y-axis direction with respect to yaw rate
Y_v = derivative of hydrodynamic force component in y-axis direction with respect to sideslip velocity
$Y_{\dot{v}}$ = derivative of hydrodynamic force component in y-axis direction with respect to sideslip acceleration
Y_δ = derivative of hydrodynamic force component in y-axis direction with respect to rudder angle
Y_η = derivative of hydrodynamic force component in y-axis direction with respect to off-centerline displacement
y_0 = off-centerline displacement
β = drift angle ($-\sin^{-1} v/U$)
δ = rudder angle
δ_e = equilibrium rudder angle
ψ = heading angle of ship
ψ_e = desired heading angle of ship
φ = roll angle

available to complete maneuvers can be compared based on the average channel width divided by the beam of the largest vessel transiting the waterway, and the minimum channel width divided by the beam of the largest vessel.

Based on the data summarized in Table 1, the seven waterways were ranked for each of the five criteria, shown in Table 2. The results were summed to determine a final ranking based on analysis of physical characteristics. The St. Mary's River received the highest cumulative ranking, while the St. Clair River, the Detroit River, and the Welland Canal received equal rankings of 2.

Traffic level projections

Traffic projections developed for the Army Corps of Engineers [2] were analyzed to compare alternate waterways and vessel types based on the total number of transits per year. These results were used to determine the relative levels of congestion in alternate waterways for alternate vessel types. In addition, future changes in traffic patterns were estimated.

Results of the traffic level projections are summarized in Table 3 and Table 4 for the years 1980 and 2000, respectively. The total number of vessel transits per year is shown for each waterway and vessel class, as defined in Table 5, in accordance with the Corps of Engineers' vessel classification system. Total number of vessel transits for the St. Mary's River, the Welland Canal, and the St. Lawrence Seaway were taken directly from data prepared for the Corps of Engineers. However, the total number of transits was not given for the Straits of Mackinac and the Detroit/St. Clair River. These were calculated based on total cargo tonnage projections and an assumed fleet mix for each type of cargo. The St. Mary's River fleet mix by commodity was assumed for the Straits of Mackinac and the Detroit/St. Clair Rivers since restrictions on vessel size are the same in these waterways.

Based on the total number of vessel transits in 1980 and 2000, the alternate waterways were ranked as shown in Table 6. The St. Mary's River continues to have the highest traffic levels through 2000 and thus received the highest final ranking. The Detroit/St. Clair River system and the Welland Canal both received a final ranking of 2.

Table 1   Physical characteristics of connecting waterways on the Great Lakes/St. Lawrence River

Waterway	Reach No.	Length, (miles)	No. of Turns	Average Width (ft)	Minimum Width (ft)	Average Depth (ft)	Average Change in Heading (deg)	Maximum Change in Heading (deg)	Average Width / Max. Beam	Min. Width / Max. Beam	No. of Turns / Mile
St. Mary's River		74.8	25	1267.8	200		32.4	65.0	12.1	1.90	0.33
	SMR1	11.5	6	1400.0	1200	33.0	25.5	44.3	13.3	11.43	0.52
	SMR2	9.5	4	1400.0	600	27.0	19.0	44.0	13.3	5.71	0.42
	SMR3	18.0	5	800.0	500	27.5	52.9	65.0	7.6	4.76	0.28
	SMR4	17.0	4	300.0	300	27.0	31.6	40.0	2.9	2.86	0.24
	SMR5	9.0	4	1840.0	200	28.0	32.8	39.0	17.5	1.90	0.44
	SMR6	9.8	2	1866.7	800	29.0	32.5	39.0	17.8	7.62	0.20
St. Clair River		41.2	34	1195.8	600		15.4	51.0	11.4	5.71	0.83
	SCR1	11.6	11	1287.5	600	27.0	19.1	51.0	12.3	5.71	0.95
	SCR2	13.9	12	1300.0	900	31.0	11.9	25.0	12.4	8.57	0.86
	SCR3	15.7	11	1000.0	700	26.5	15.1	23.3	9.5	6.67	0.70
Lake St. Clair	LSC1	14.2	1	700.0	700	27.0	7.0	7.0	6.7	6.67	0.07
Detroit River		47.5	24	781.5	300		20.1	40.0	7.4	2.86	0.51
	DR1	15.5	10	1672.7	900	32.0	18.0	28.0	15.9	8.57	0.65
	DR2	9.1	9	535.0	300	25.0	20.7	40.0	5.1	2.86	0.99
	DR3	7.2	1	700.0	600	28.0	21.5	21.5	6.7	5.71	0.14
	DR4	7.8	1	400.0	400	27.0	23.5	23.5	3.8	3.81	0.13
	DR5	7.9	3	600.0	600	27.5	17.0	21.0	5.7	5.71	0.38
Straits of Mackinac	SM1	8.2	2	3833.3	3000	71.0	25.5	29.0	36.5	28.57	0.24
St. Lawrence River		191.1	107	1026.5	528		16.1	70.0	13.7	7.04	0.56
	SLR1	35.3	28	637.2	528	27.5	14.6	43.0	8.5	7.04	0.79
	SLR2	28.6	15	561.0	528	40.4	12.7	34.0	7.5	7.04	0.52
	SLR3	25.1	19	554.4	528	32.0	18.8	35.0	7.4	7.04	0.76
	SLR4	25.5	15	528.0	528	42.0	16.3	34.0	7.0	7.04	0.59
	SLR5	24.5	10	1440.0	528	55.0	13.4	21.0	19.2	7.04	0.41
	SLR6	25.5	14	598.4	528	92.2	9.4	28.0	8.0	7.04	0.55
	SLR7	26.6	6	2866.3	528	87.3	27.5	70.0	38.2	7.04	0.23
Welland Canal	WC1	26.9	21	418.2	200	27.0	7.1	18.0	5.6	2.67	0.78

Table 2   Ranking of alternate waterways based on analysis of physical characteristics

Waterway	Ranking Based on Avg Channel Width/Maximum Vessel Beam	Ranking Based on Min. Channel Width/Maximum Vessel Beam	Ranking Based on Number of Heading Changes Per Mile	Ranking Based on Average Heading Change	Ranking Based on Maximum Heading Change	TOTAL POINTS	FINAL RANKING
St. Mary's River	5	1	5	1	2	14	1
St. Clair River	4	4	1	5	3	17	2
Lake St. Clair	2	5	7	7	7	28	5
Detroit River	3	3	4	3	4	17	2
Straits of Mackinac	7	7	6	2	5	27	4
St. Lawrence River	6	6	3	4	1	20	3
Welland Canal	1	2	2	6	6	17	2

Table 3 Year 1980 vessel transits by class (total number of transits per year)

Vessel Class	St. Mary's River	Straits of Mackinac	Detroit/St. Clair Rivers	Welland Canal	St. Lawrence Seaway
Class IV	362	47	168	1055	891
Classes V & VI	N.A.	N.A.	N.A.	800	371
Ocean	N.A.	N.A.	N.A.	2760	2687
Class V	3694	1311	2489	N.A.	N.A.
Class VI & Ocean	2269	546	1663	N.A.	N.A.
Class VII	2662	639	1927	2367	1162
Class VIII	763	367	534	0	0
Class IX	106	44	78	0	0
Class X	423	92	242	0	0
Class XI	0	0	0	0	0
TOTAL	10279	3046	7101	6982	5110

SOURCE: "Draft Report Great Lakes/St. Lawrence Seaway Lock Capacity Analysis," prepared by Arctec, Inc., for the U.S. Army Corps of Engineers, North Central Division.

Table 4 Year 2000 vessel transits by class (total number of transits per year)

Vessel Class	St. Mary's River	Straits of Mackinac	Detroit/St. Clair Rivers	Welland Canal	St. Lawrence Seaway
Class IV	236	31	137	1182	555
Classes V & VI	N.A.	N.A.	N.A.	687	603
Ocean	N.A.	N.A.	N.A.	4916	4844
Class V	2521	820	1702	N.A.	N.A.
Class VI & Ocean	3220	875	2692	N.A.	N.A.
Class VII	3374	757	2360	3764	1988
Class VIII	763	273	531	0	0
Class IX	106	43	89	0	0
Class X	2456	610	1626	0	0
Class XI	0	0	0	0	0
TOTAL	12678	3409	9137	10549	7990

SOURCE: "Draft Report Great Lakes/St. Lawrence Seaway Lock Capacity Analysis," prepared by Arctec, Inc., for the U.S. Army Corps of Engineers, North Central Division.

The process of ranking alternate vessel types based on project traffic levels was slightly more difficult since the type of vessel of primary importance can vary for the different waterways, and the current fleet is being replaced with larger vessels. Therefore, vessel types have been ranked for each waterway based on the increase in number of transits between 1980 and 2000, as shown in Table 7. When determined in this manner, the rankings reflect the shift in the importance of each vessel type in the future.

In the St. Mary's River, the Straits of Mackinac, and the Detroit/St. Clair River system, Class X, Class VI, and ocean vessels will be of primary importance in the future. In the Welland Canal and the St. Lawrence Seaway, ocean vessels and Class VII vessels will be of primary importance.

Analysis of damage records

The final source of information used to compare the maneuvering-related problems of alternate waterways and vessel types was historical records of vessel casualties. The data source for this analysis was a computer listing of all vessel casualties on the Great Lakes/St. Lawrence Seaway provided by the USCG Merchant Marine Safety Office for fiscal years 1969–1977. All casualties resulting from collision and groundings were tabulated by geographic area and vessel length.

Table 5 Vessel characteristics

Vessel Class	Length Range (ft) Min.	Length Range (ft) Max.	Max Beam (ft)	Maximum Carrying Capacity (s. tons)
IV	0	599	75	9500
V	600	649	75	20000
VI	650	699	75	24000
VII	700	749	75	28890
VIII	750	849	75	29960
IX	850	899	105	48150
X	900	1099	105	64200
XI	1100	1199	105	70620

Table 6 Ranking of alternate waterways based on projected traffic levels

Waterway	Ranking Based on Total 1980 Vessel Transit	Ranking Based on Total 2000 Transits	TOTAL POINTS	FINAL RANKING
St. Mary's River	1	1	2	1
Straits of Mackinac	4	5	9	3
Detroit/St. Clair Rivers	2	3	5	2
Welland Canal	3	2	5	2
St. Lawrence Seaway	5	4	9	3

Maneuvering Performance of Ships in Critical Channels

Table 7   Ranking of alternate vessel types for each waterway

Vessel Class	St. Mary's River		Straits of Mackinac		Detroit/St. Clair Rivers		Welland Canal		St. Lawrence River	
	ΔT^a	Ranking	ΔT^a	Ranking	ΔT^a	Ranking	ΔT^a	Ranking	ΔT^a	Ranking
Class IV	−126	5	−16	5	−31	6	127	3	−336	4
Class V & VI	N.A.		N.A.		N.A.		−113	4	232	3
Ocean	N.A.		N.A.		N.A.		2156	1	2157	1
Class V	−1173	6	−491	7	−787	7	N.A.		N.A.	
Class VI & Ocean	951	2	329	2	1029	2	N.A.		N.A.	
Class VII	712	3	118	3	433	3	1397	2	826	2
Class VIII	0	4	−94	6	−3	5	0	b	0	b
Class IX	0	4	−1	4	11	4	0	b	0	b
Class X	2033	1	518	1	1384	1	0	b	0	b
Class XI	0	b	0	b	0	b	0	b	0	b

^{a} ΔT = (Number of transits per year in 2000) − (number of transits per year in 1980).
^{b} Not ranked since vessel of that class will not operate in the particular waterway.

Based on the results shown in Fig. 1, the following rankings have been assigned to the various geographic areas:

GEOGRAPHIC AREA	TOTAL GROUNDINGS & COLLISIONS	RANK-ING
St. Mary's River and Straits of Mackinac	162 (= 6 + 10 + 23 + 123)	2
St. Clair River	69 (= 32 + 37)	3
Detroit River and Lake St. Clair	>285	1
St. Lawrence Seaway	35 (= 1 + 12 + 9 + 13)	4

The Detroit River and Lake St. Clair, including the Lake Erie approach to the Detroit River, experienced the greatest number of groundings and collisions of any of the connecting waterway areas. The geographic area which includes the St. Mary's River ranks second, and the area which includes the St. Clair River ranks third. One further conclusion which can be drawn from the data presented in Fig. 1 is that the geographic areas containing the interconnecting waterways experience the largest number of groundings and collisions. Geographic areas containing major ports (such as Chicago, Gary, Duluth-Superior, and Cleveland) experience the second largest number of casualties.

Final ranking of waterways, vessel types, and variables

Based on the data described in the previous section, final rankings have been developed for the waterways, vessel types, and variables under consideration. These rankings indicate the most important situations to be considered in analyses of the maneuvering performance of Great Lakes ships in the critical channels. The final rankings were obtained by combining the equally weighted ranking from each of the previously discussed information sources. As shown in Table 8, the waterway with the highest final ranking is the St. Mary's River, followed by the Detroit River and the St. Clair River.

Final rankings of vessel types were based on industry opinions, projected traffic levels, historical accident records, and a preliminary analysis of the maneuvering characteristics of the vessels. As shown in Table 9, the 1000 × 105-ft lakers were ranked No. 1, the 850 × 75-ft lakers were ranked No. 2, and the

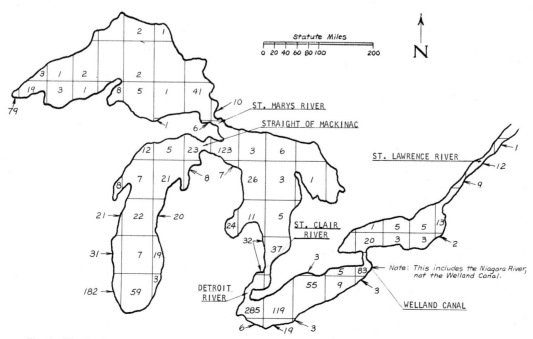

Fig. 1   Distribution of collisions and groundings on the Great Lakes and St. Lawrence Seaway (FY69-77)

Maneuvering Performance of Ships in Critical Channels

Table 8   Final ranking of waterways

	Industry Ranking	Ranking Based on Projected Traffic Levels	Ranking Based on Analysis of Physical Characteristics	Ranking Based on Historical Accident Records	TOTAL POINTS	FINAL RANKING
St. Mary's River	1	1	1	2	5	1
Straits of Mackinac	4	3	4	2	13	5
St. Clair River	3	2	2	3	10	3
Lake St. Clair	4	2	5	1	12	4
Detroit River	2	2	2	1	7	2
Welland Canal	9	2	2	2[a]	15	6
St. Lawrence Seaway	9	3	3	4	19	7

[a] Ranking assigned equal to the numerical average of the rankings for the other waterways.

Table 9   Final ranking of vessel types

	Industry Ranking	Ranking Based on Projected Traffic Levels	Ranking Based on Prelim Analysis of Maneuvering Characteristics	Ranking Based on Historical Accident Records	Total Points	Final Ranking
Tugs and barges	5	5	6	2	18	4
Oceangoing ships	5	2	5	1	13	3
Lakers less than 730 ft	6	2	4	1	13	3
730' × 75' lakers	4	3	3	3	13	3
850' × 75' lakers	3	4	2	3	12	2
1000' × 105' lakers	1	1	2	3	7	1
1100' × 105' lakers	2	6	1	4	13	3

remaining lakers and oceangoing ships were all ranked No. 3.

Table 10 shows the final rankings for ship and channel design and operational variables. The two highest-ranked variables are channel width and depth; the inclusion of thrusters was ranked third, and ship length fourth. Bow design, afterbody design, rudder configurations, and propeller type were all ranked fifth.

Finally, Table 11 shows a summary of the most important waterways, vessel types, and variables. In general, the major problems arise because vessel size has increased at a more rapid rate than channel size in critical areas such as the St. Mary's River (see Fig. 2), the Detroit River, and possibly the St. Clair River. Although the system is currently functioning, improvements are desirable especially in light of the projected increase in the number of large vessels operating in the future.

Industry personnel identified the upbound Neebish Island Channel as the critical location in the St. Mary's River. This channel requires five heading changes averaging 53 deg each and has an average width of 800 ft and a minimum width of 500 ft. It is the most difficult section of the river in terms of the severity of turns.

Part II: Experimental and computer-aided analyses

The second-phase of this program was to treat the identified problems in Part I through experimental and computer-aided analyses. Major efforts in this phase of the study include:

- captive model tests in ice-free water conditions,
- captive model tests in ice-covered water conditions,
- full-scale trajectory measurements in critical channels,
- digital simulation studies (with participation of experienced ship officers), and
- analyses and discussion of results.

Table 10   Final ranking of design and operational variables

Variable	Industry Ranking	Ranking Based on Preliminary Analysis	Total Points	Final Ranking
Channel width	1	1	2	1
Channel depth	2	2	4	2
Ship length	5	3	8	4
Ship beam	6	5	11	6
Ship bow design	4	6	10	5
Ship afterbody design	5	4	10	5
Rudder configuration	4	4	10	5
Thrusters	3	4	7	3
Steering or Kort nozzles	5	6	11	6
Machinery type	7	6	13	7
CP versus Fixed-Pitch Propellers	6	4	10	5
Icebreaker assistance	8	5	13	7
Traffic control	8	5	13	7
Nav equipment	8	5	13	7
Flanking rudders	9	4	13	7
Sail area	9	6	15	8
Pilothouse location	9	6	15	8
Automatic control	9	6	15	8

Table 11   Summary of highest-ranked waterways, vessels, and variables

WATERWAY	RANKING
St. Mary's River	1
Detroit River	2
VESSEL TYPE	**RANKING**
1000 × 105-ft laker	1
805 × 75-ft laker	2
VARIABLE	**RANKING**
Channel width	1
Channel depth	2

Captive model tests in ice-free water conditions

Rotating-arm facility and test procedure

In order to obtain hydrodynamic data for development of coefficients in the equations of ship maneuvering motion, captive model tests were performed under ice-free water conditions in the Davidson Laboratory Rotating-Arm Facility in Tank 2.[6]

Tank 2 is a square basin 75 ft on a side with a water depth (variable) of 4.5 ft for maneuvering and seakeeping model testing. The rotating-arm facility provides for the determination of hydrodynamic force and moment data (obtained from captive models) which are essential for use in the formulation of mathematical models for ship maneuvering motions.

On the basis of the results obtained in the Phase I study, two Great Lakes bulk carriers (that is, the 1000 × 105-ft and the 730 × 75-ft ships) were tested during the summer of 1979. The configurations of both ships are shown in Figs. 3 to 6. While the 1000-ft ship is equipped with twin propellers and twin rudders, the 730-ft ship is equipped with a single propeller and a single rudder. Two models (that is, $\frac{1}{163}$- and $\frac{1}{124}$-scale models of the 1000-ft and 730-ft ships, respectively) were built to the lines shown in these figures.

The two ship models were tested in open deep water, shallow water, and restricted channels. Figures 7 and 8 show these models being tested in the rotating-arm facility. The model is constrained (with freedom to pitch and heave) to the dynamometer under the rotating arm and tested at various drift-angle and turning-radius conditions. Balances mounted above the model were used to measure yaw moment, lateral force, and drag force.

The major parameter changes in the rotating-arm tests were as follows:

1. Ship speed: low speed, medium speed, and high speed (that is, 6, 8, and 10 knots in full scale)
2. Turning rate: $r' = l/R = -0.19$ to $+0.51$
3. Drift angle: $\beta' = 0$ to ± 16 deg
4. Rudder angle: $\delta = 0$ to ± 35 deg
5. Water depth: deep water, medium water depth (1.9 times ship draft), and shallow water depth (1.3 times ship draft)
6. Channel width: width/ship beam = ∞, 20, 19, 13, 12, 6

Test results

Data points were processed into nondimensional coefficients of yaw moment, lateral force, and drag based on the typical area of l^2, that is

$$\text{Yaw-moment coefficient} \quad N' = \frac{N}{\frac{\rho}{2} l^3 U^2}$$

$$\text{Lateral-force coefficient} \quad Y' = \frac{Y}{\frac{\rho}{2} l^2 U^2}$$

$$\text{Drag-force coefficient} \quad X' = \frac{X}{\frac{\rho}{2} l^2 U^2}$$

To obtain the hydrodynamic forces and moments, air tare and centrifugal forces due to the dynamometer were subtracted from the measured data. The centrifugal forces due to the rigid mass are included in the hydrodynamic data.

---

[6] Simultaneously, captive model tests were conducted under ice-covered water conditions in the Arctec Ice Model Basin during July and August 1979.

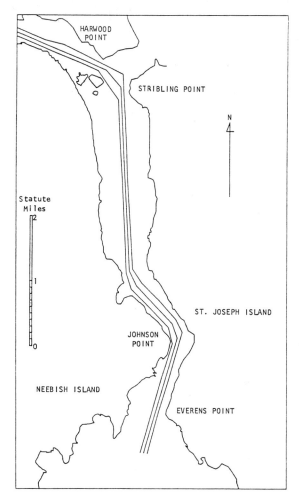

Fig. 2 Upbound Neebish Island Channel, St. Mary's River (computer-plotted for digital simulation purposes)

When a series of runs was completed, covering a range of turning radii, drift angles, rudder angles, and propeller revolutions, these hydrodynamic data were least-square-fitted to be represented in the following polynomials:

$$N' = a_1 + a_2 v' + a_3 r' + a_4 \delta + a_5 y'_0 + a_6 v'^2 r' + a_7 v' r'^2 + a_8 v'^3 + a_9 r'^3 + a_{10} \delta^3 + a_{11} y'^3_0 + a_{12} \dot{r}' + a_{13} \dot{v}'$$

$$Y' = b_1 + b_2 v' + b_3 r' + b_4 \delta + b_5 y'_0 + b_6 v'^2 r' + b_7 v' r'^2 + b_8 v'^3 + b_9 r'^3 + b_{10} \delta^3 + b_{11} y'^3_0 + b_{12} \dot{r}' + b_{13} \dot{v}'$$

$$X' = c_1 + c_2 v' r' + c_3 v'^2 + c_4 \delta^2 + c_5 \dot{u}'$$

Major examples of data points are shown together with least-square-fitted curves in Figs. 9(a) through 9(h).

Typical examples of hydrodynamic coefficients determined in the least-square analyses are listed in Tables 12(a) through 12(d).

Captive model tests in ice-covered water conditions

Model testing facility under ice-covered water conditions

The purpose of the tests was to provide sufficient data for development of coefficients in the maneuvering equations of motion for ice conditions typical of the interconnecting waterways of the Great Lakes.

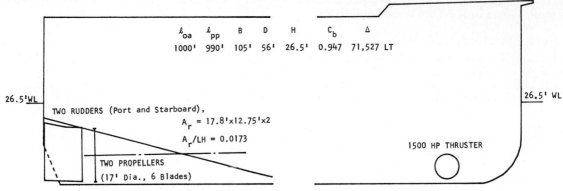

ℓ_{oa}	ℓ_{pp}	B	D	H	C_b	Δ
1000'	990'	105'	56'	26.5'	0.947	71,527 LT

26.5'WL

TWO RUDDERS (Port and Starboard),

$A_r = 17.8' \times 12.75' \times 2$

$A_r/LH = 0.0173$

TWO PROPELLERS
(17' Dia., 6 Blades)

1500 HP THRUSTER

26.5' WL

Fig. 3 A 1000-ft-long Great-Lakes bulk carrier

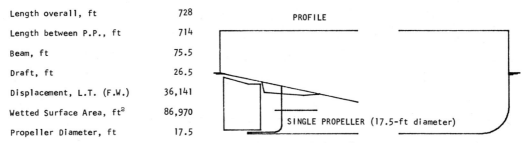

Length overall, ft	728
Length between P.P., ft	714
Beam, ft	75.5
Draft, ft	26.5
Displacement, L.T. (F.W.)	36,141
Wetted Surface Area, ft²	86,970
Propeller Diameter, ft	17.5

PROFILE

SINGLE PROPELLER (17.5-ft diameter)

Fig. 4 A 730-ft-long Great Lakes bulk carrier

The model test series was conducted in the Arctec Ice Model Basin, Columbia, Maryland, during the summer of 1979. This facility consists of a refrigerated model towing basin 100 ft long, 12 ft wide, and 5 ft deep, which is filled with a saline water solution. Ice is frozen on the surface to a thickness equal to the geometric scale of the desired full-scale ice thickness. By controlling the water salinity, freezing rates, and temperatures, model ice is produced with the correctly scaled flexural strength.

Models

The $\frac{1}{48}$ scale models were built for the 1000-ft and 730-ft ships (that is, Bay Shipbuilding Hull Nos. 718 and 715, respectively). Appendages on the model of Hull 718 included rudders, shafts with propellers, and shaft struts. Appendages on the model of Hull 715 included a centerline rudder and propeller.

Both models were equipped with propulsion systems consisting of a variable-speed electric motor, shafting, and correctly

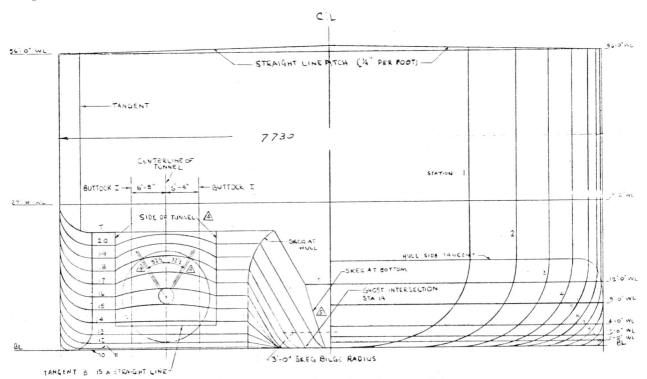

Fig. 5 Body plan (1000-ft Great Lakes bulk carrier)

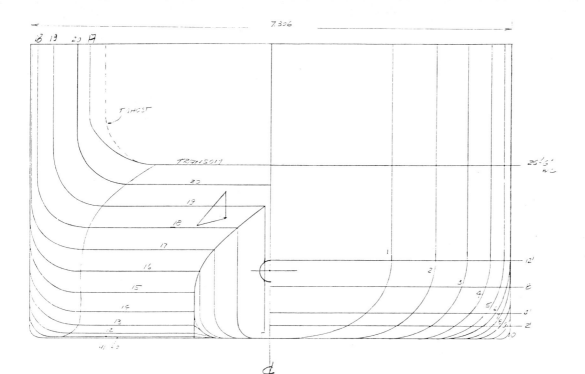

Fig. 6 Body plan (728-ft Great Lakes bulk carrier)

scaled propellers. This system was calibrated during open-water propulsion tests so that the desired thrust could be achieved by setting the motor speed. Propulsion characteristics for both models are included in the Appendix.

Ballast was added to the models to achieve the desired displacement and even trim, and the longitudinal radius of gyration was set at 0.25 *LWL* using the Bifilar Pendulum Method. The coefficient of friction between model surfaces and the ice was set at 0.25 prior to testing.

Test conditions

To satisfy the objectives of the model test program, a total of 133 different conditions were tested with Hull 718, and 129 different conditions were tested with Hull 715. Parameters were varied and included broken channel width, ship speed, propeller loading, drift angle, and rudder angle. The range of variation for each of these parameters is shown in Table 13. Specific conditions tested are listed in the Appendix along with the test data.

Fig. 7 A bulk carrier model being tested in the rotating-arm facility

Fig. 8 Two Great-Lakes bulk carrier models used in the rotating-arm tests

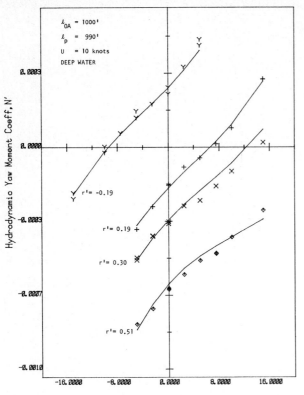

Fig. 9(a) Hydrodynamic yaw moment coefficient versus drift angle

Fig. 9(c) Hydrodynamic yaw moment coefficient versus drift angle

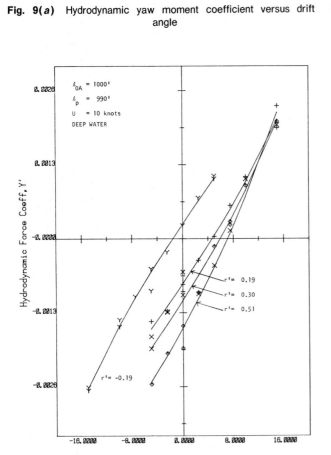

Fig. 9(b) Hydrodynamic force coefficient versus drift angle

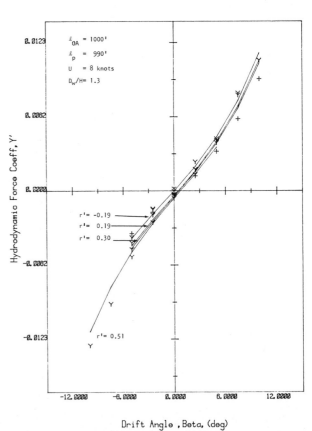

Fig. 9(d) Hydrodynamic force coefficient versus drift angle

Maneuvering Performance of Ships in Critical Channels

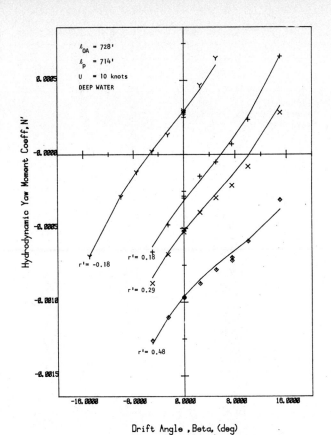

Fig. 9(e) Hydrodynamic yaw moment coefficient versus drift angle

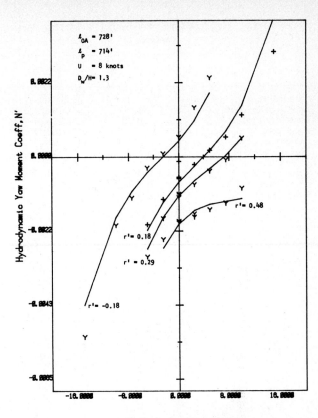

Fig. 9(g) Hydrodynamic yaw moment coefficient versus drift angle

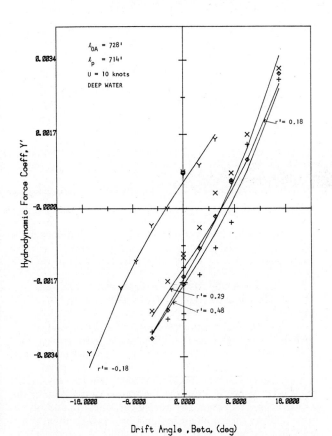

Fig. 9(f) Hydrodynamic force coefficient versus drift angle

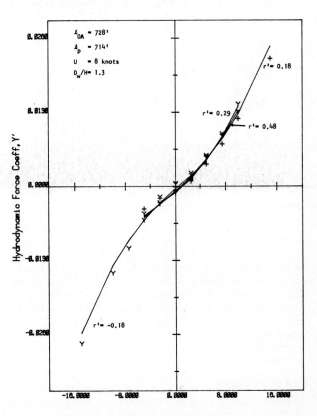

Fig. 9(h) Hydrodynamic force coefficient versus drift angle

Maneuvering Performance of Ships in Critical Channels

Table 12(a) Hydrodynamic coefficients (1000-ft ship, deep water)

		GL1HD DEEP
Ship length	L	990.000
Length beam ratio	L/B	9.420
Beam draft ratio	B/H	3.820
Block coef.	CB	0.947
Rudder area ratio	AR	0.017
Movable portion	RM/RT	0.900
Aspect ratio	ASR	1.520
Trim	TRIM	0.000
Draft/water depth	H/DW	0.000
Beam/water width	B/W	0.000
m'		0.00559
Iz'		0.00035
a 0	O	0.00000
a 1	V	−0.00172
a 2	R	−0.00121
a 3	D	−0.00125
a 4	Y	0.00000
a 5	V2R	−0.01080
a 6	VR2	−0.00070
a 7	V3	−0.01005
a 8	R3	−0.00053
a 9	D3	0.00146
a10	Y3	0.00000
$Iz' - $a11	RDOT	0.00081
a12	VDOT	0.00000
b 0	O	0.00000
b 1	V	−0.00886
$-m' + $b 2	R	−0.00275
b 3	D	0.00232
b 4	Y	0.00000
b 5	V2R	0.01540
b 6	VR2	−0.00964
b 7	V3	−0.01360
b 8	R3	0.00081
b 9	D3	−0.00230
b10	Y3	0.00000
$m' - $b11	RDOT	0.00000
b12	VDOT	0.00877
c 0	O	−0.00034
$m' + $c 1	VR	0.00789
c 2	VV	−0.00354
c 3	DD	−0.00139
$m' - $c 4	UDOT	0.00570
	SIG1	−0.401
	SIG2	−2.103
	RP/D	−2.515
	VP/D	1.042

12(b) Hydrodynamic coefficients (1000-ft ship, shallow water; $D_w/H = 1.3$)

		GL1000 DW 1.3
Ship length	L	990.000
Length beam ratio	L/B	9.420
Beam draft ratio	B/H	3.820
Block coef.	CB	0.947
Rudder area ratio	AR	0.017
Movable portion	RM/RT	0.900
Aspect ratio	ASR	1.520
Trim	TRIM	0.000
Draft/water depth	H/DW	0.000
Beam/water width	B/W	0.770
m'		0.00559
Iz'		0.00035
a 0	O	0.00000
a 1	V	−0.00974
a 2	R	−0.00326
a 3	D	−0.00192
a 4	Y	0.00000
a 5	V2R	−0.07570
a 6	VR2	0.01600
a 7	V3	−0.12450
a 8	R3	0.00173
a 9	D3	0.00201
a10	Y3	0.00000
$Iz' - $a11	RDOT	0.00173
a12	VDOT	0.00000
b 0	O	0.00000
b 1	V	−0.04640
$-m' + $b 2	R	0.00176
b 3	D	0.00525
b 4	Y	0.00000
b 5	V2R	0.07092
b 6	VR2	0.00818
b 7	V3	−0.49400
b 8	R3	0.00349
b 9	D3	−0.00666
b10	Y3	0.00000
$m' - $b11	RDOT	0.00000
b12	VDOT	0.01513
c 0	O	−0.00037
$m' + $c 1	VR	0.01362
c 2	VV	−0.01856
c 3	DD	−0.00315
$m' - $c 4	UDOT	0.00570
	SIG1	−2.476
	SIG2	0.553
	RP/D	−0.833
	VP/D	0.082

The major variation in ice conditions addressed during the test program was broken channel width, which was defined as the width of brash ice which does not have a refrozen crust on the surface (that is, areas where ship traffic keeps the ice broken). The surrounding ice consisted of similar brash with a refrozen crust. Target thicknesses were held constant throughout the test program at 1.0 in. (48-in. full scale) for brash ice and 0.15 in. (7-in. full scale) for the refrozen crust. These thicknesses represent severe ice conditions in the interconnecting waterways and the range of variation for channel width is consistent with actual conditions.

Test procedures

During the test program, models were towed at constant velocity and were rigidly attached to the towing carriage. Drift angle, rudder angle, and propeller rpm were set at the desired values prior to each test. Three different velocities corresponding to 3, 6, and 9 knots full scale were tested in each ice sheet. The test sequence for each ice sheet was as follows:

1. Collect at least 10 sec of steady-state data at the first speed.
2. Stop the model to reset carriage velocity and rpm.
3. Collect at least 10 sec of steady-state data at the second speed.
4. Repeat the foregoing procedure for the third speed.

Models were attached to the towing carriage via four strain-gaged force blocks which sensed longitudinal and transverse loads. One pair of force blocks was mounted at the midbody, and the other pair was mounted near the bow. Drift angle was varied by adjusting the transverse position of the forward force blocks on the towing carriage. In addition to surge and sway force measurements (and yaw moment calculated from forward sway force), propeller rpm and carriage velocity were measured each run. All data were recorded on

Maneuvering Performance of Ships in Critical Channels

Table 12(c)	Hydrodynamic coefficients (730-ft ship, deep water)		GL7HD DEEP
Ship length		L	714.000
Length beam ratio		L/B	9.460
Beam draft ratio		B/H	2.840
Block coef.		CB	0.905
Rudder area ratio		AR	0.017
Movable portion		RM/RT	0.900
Aspect ratio		ASR	1.520
Trim		TRIM	0.000
Draft/water depth		H/DW	0.000
Beam/water width		B/W	0.000
	m′		0.00712
	Iz′		0.00045
a 0		O	0.00000
a 1		V	−0.00325
a 2		R	−0.00165
a 3		D	−0.00174
a 4		Y	0.00000
a 5		V2R	−0.01570
a 6		VR2	0.00141
a 7		V3	−0.01890
a 8		R3	−0.00150
a 9		D3	0.00148
a10		Y3	0.00000
Iz′ − a11		RDOT	0.00102
a12		VDOT	0.00000
b 0		O	0.00000
b 1		V	−0.01211
−m′ + b 2		R	−0.00603
b 3		D	0.00305
b 4		Y	0.00000
b 5		V2R	0.01510
b 6		VR2	−0.01130
b 7		V3	−0.04580
b 8		R3	0.01490
b 9		D3	−0.00158
b10		Y3	0.00000
m′ − b11		RDOT	0.00000
b12		VDOT	0.01237
c 0		O	−0.00038
m′ + c 1		VR	0.01113
c 2		VV	−0.00484
c 3		DD	−0.00183
m′ − c 4		UDOT	0.00726
	SIG1		−0.012
	SIG2		−2.585
	RP/D		−80.687
	VP/D		40.429

Table 12(d)	Hydrodynamic coefficients (730-ft ship, shallow water; $D_w/H = 1.3$)		GL713 DW 1.3
Ship length		L	714.000
Length beam ratio		L/B	9.460
Beam draft ratio		B/H	2.840
Block coef.		CB	0.905
Rudder area ratio		AR	0.017
Movable portion		RM/RT	0.900
Aspect ratio		ASR	1.520
Trim		TRIM	0.000
Draft/water depth		H/DW	0.000
Beam/water width		B/W	0.770
	m′		0.00712
	Iz′		0.00045
a 0		O	0.00000
a 1		V	−0.01156
a 2		R	−0.00327
a 3		D	−0.00217
a 4		Y	0.00000
a 5		V2R	−0.17280
a 6		VR2	−0.00238
a 7		V3	−0.21530
a 8		R3	−0.00220
a 9		D3	0.00207
a10		Y3	0.00000
Iz′ − a11		RDOT	0.00216
a12		VDOT	0.00000
b 0		O	0.00000
b 1		V	−0.05658
−m′ + b 2		R	−0.00119
b 3		D	0.00622
b 4		Y	0.00000
b 5		V2R	0.30730
b 6		VR2	0.03337
b 7		V3	−0.39070
b 8		R3	0.00048
b 9		D3	−0.00595
b10		Y3	0.00000
m′ − b11		RDOT	0.00000
b12		VDOT	0.02287
c 0		O	−0.00042
m′ + c 1		VR	0.02058
c 2		VV	−0.02263
c 3		DD	−0.00373
m′ − c 4		UDOT	0.00726
	SIG1		−1.281
	SIG2		−2.707
	RP/D		−1.137
	VP/D		0.134

oscillograph paper and magnetic tape. Force data were averaged for each test by replaying magnetic tape force records through an integrating voltmeter.

During the course of a 13-hr test day at least three ice sheets were prepared. First, a parent ice sheet was frozen and allowed to thaw to the proper strength. This sheet was then broken and brash ice of uniform thickness was distributed over the water surface. If a refrozen crust was required, a second, shorter freeze period was conducted. After each test, brash ice was "groomed" to uniform thickness in preparation for the next test. For those cases where a broken channel bounded by refrozen ice was required, a channel of proper width was cut in the refrozen ice sheet and the ice within the channel was broken and "groomed" to a uniform thickness. Prior to each test, both brash and crust thicknesses were measured at one-meter intervals along the track of the model. These thicknesses were averaged for each data point.

Table 13   Range of variation for independent variables during ice model tests

HULL 718
Broken channel width (w)	0 to ∞
Ship speed	3 to 9 knots (full scale)
Propeller loading	1.0 to 1.5 × ship propulsion point
Drift angle (β)	0 to 15 deg
Rudder angle (δ)	−20 to 40 deg
Brash ice thickness (HB)	48 in. (full scale)
Refrozen crust thickness (HC)	7 in. (full scale)

HULL 715
Broken channel width (w)	0 to ∞
Ship speed	3 to 9 knots (full scale)
Propeller loading	1.0 to 1.5 × ship propulsion point
Drift angle (β)	−5 to 15 deg
Rudder angle (δ)	−20 to 40 deg
Brash ice thickness (HB)	48 in. (full scale)
Refrozen crust thickness (HC)	7 in. (full scale)

Fig. 10 A bulk-carrier model being tested under ice-covered water conditions

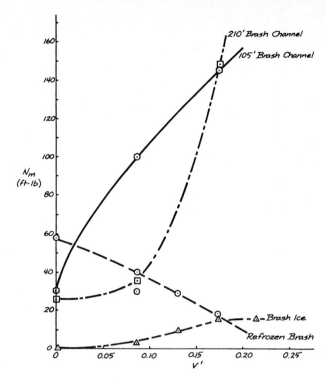

1000' BULK CARRIER MODEL @ 1.47 ft/sec

Fig. 11(a) Yaw moment measured under ice-covered water

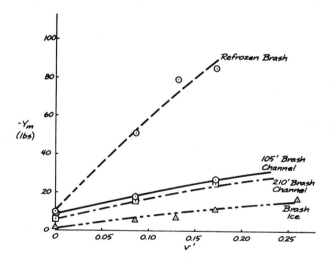

1000' BULK CARRIER MODEL @ 1.47 ft/sec

Fig. 11(b) Side force measured in ice-covered water

Full-scale trajectory measurements in critical channels

Figure 10 shows a ship model being tested under ice-covered conditions. Typical examples of data points obtained in these tests are shown in Figs. 11(a) through 11(c).

In order to make an overall check on the validity of the mathematical model, full-scale trials were made on the 1000-ft bulk carrier.[7] These trials were performed under ice-free and ice-covered conditions in November 1979 and January 1980, respectively, in the Neebish Island Channel of the St. Mary's River.

The following data were obtained during the trials:
- Heading angle (from gyro)
- Ship position (from radar display photographs)
- Rudder angle (from rudder indicator)
- Propeller rpm (from rpm indicator)
- Ship speed (from ship trajectory)
- Water depth (from charts)

Ship trials under ice-free water conditions

Figure 12 shows an example of a radar display photograph, together with a map of the West Neebish Channel. Similar photographs were taken at one-minute intervals, and were used to determine ship trajectory. Such a procedure proved to be simple and effective, particularly in harbor waterways where the shorelines could be used as ideal reference points to deter-

---

[7] The *Edwin H. Gott* of The U.S. Steel Company.

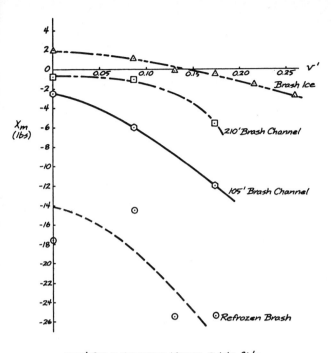

1000' BULK CARRIER MODEL @ 1.47 ft/sec

Fig. 11(c) Longitudinal force measured in ice-covered water

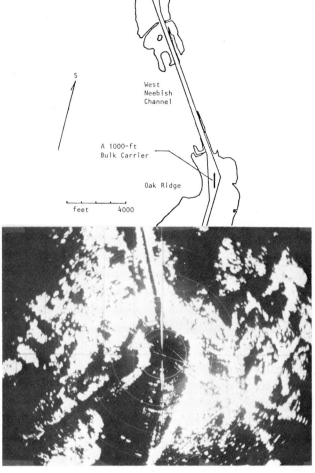

Fig. 12 West Neebish Channel

mine ship position. Figure 13 shows the ship trajectory determined through this radar picture technique. The figure also includes rudder angle, heading angle, and propeller pitch of twin controllable-pitch propellers.

In the approach area to the West Neebish Channel, a rudder angle of up to a 20-deg right rudder angle was used to negotiate the 40-deg bend at the channel entrance. When the 20-deg rudder angle is compared with a maximum rudder angle of 40 deg, it is considered that the ship has a sufficient amount of margin in turning performance for negotiating this particular bend *under ice-free water conditions.* (It should be stated here that the situation is quite different under ice-covered water conditions because the turning performance is greatly reduced due to the ice effect, as mentioned in the following section.) When the ship achieved the heading angle change and entered the channel, the rate of swing was checked by the use of only a small rudder angle of 5 deg in a steady-smooth manner without overshoot.[8] This clearly indicates that the ship has a high degree of inherent course stability characteristics due to the stabilizing effect of shallow water.

Ship trials under ice-covered water conditions

In January 1980, ship trajectory measurements were made in the East Neebish Channel (southbound) under ice conditions. The area includes Johnson Point, which was ranked the most critical channel among connecting waterways of Great Lakes in the Phase I study.

Figure 14 shows the channel from a high altitude in addition to a realistic frontal view from actual bridge height. It is seen in the figure that, for the purpose of waterway navigation, the frontal view from the bridge is fairly limited because of the relatively small height of the navigation bridge compared with the ship size and waterway dimensions.

In Fig. 15, one can see the stern views of ship trajectory on ice-covered water when the ship is proceeding on a straight

course in the waterway. An extremely high degree of inherent course stability is clearly evident from the straight-line edges of ice-breaking along the ship path. In the second picture a high degree of course stability is also shown by the straight course trajectory achieved after making a turn.

Figure 16(a) shows a front-view when the ship is approaching Johnson Point, and Fig. 16(b) a stern-view when the ship is completing a turn at the bend. When the ship is making a tight turn toward the right-hand side during a southbound transit at this location of the channel, ice buildup along the left side of the ship is shown in Fig. 17. These pictures indicate the ice buildup toward the stern along the entire ship length is due to the great sideslip velocity at the stern relative to the forward portion of ship length. This ice buildup toward the stern of the ship introduces a large reduction in turning performance as the side of the ship (in particular, the stern portion) swings into the ice.

Figure 18 presents examples of radar display photographs taken at the S-shape bends in the approach of Johnson Point. The radar pictures show a fairly clear trace of trajectories on the ice made by the transits of our own ship and also those of previous vessel transits.

Results of trajectory measurements are shown in Figs. 19 and 20.

It should be noted in Fig. 20 that *a maximum rudder angle of 40 deg was used over an extended period under the ice-covered water conditions* in the approach area of the Johnson Point in order to make a heading angle change of 60 deg. It

---

[8] Previous studies indicate that the rate of swing of a ship with inherent course stability can be checked with less rudder angle compared with the case of a less-stable ship.

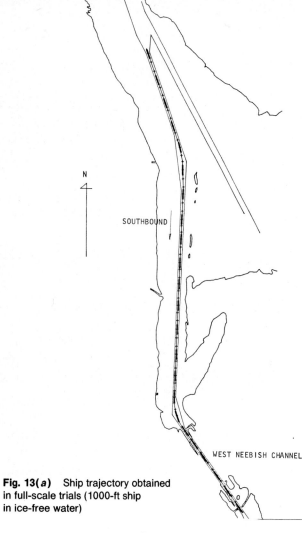

Fig. 13(a)   Ship trajectory obtained
in full-scale trials (1000-ft ship
in ice-free water)

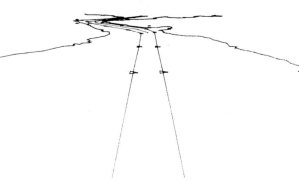

Fig. 14(a)   View of a channel from a high altitude

Fig. 14(b)   Realistic view from a navigation bridge (computer-gen-
erated for actual bridge height)

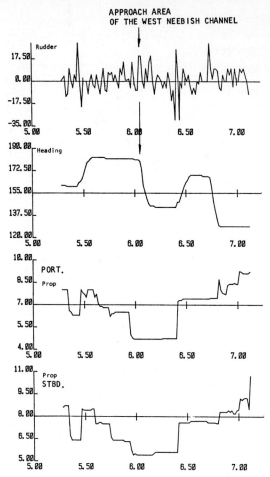

Fig. 13(b)   Time history of ship trajectory obtained in full-scale
trials

is clearly shown that this particular location of the channel is
a critical one.   The turning performance of the ship is greatly
reduced under the test conditions because of substantial stabilizing effects on inherent course stability characteristics due to
ice-breaking and shallow water.

In Figure 20, an extremely high degree of course stability
characteristics can be observed when a small rudder angle (up
to 15 deg) was used for a brief period to check the swing after
making a turn.

Digital simulation studies

Digital simulation model

Utilizing the captive model test data, a mathematical model[9]
was formulated to represent the maneuvering characteristics
of ships under various conditions [4–13] such as:
   (*a*)   in open water (that is, ice-free water)
       in deep water
       in shallow and restricted waters
   (*b*)   in ice-covered water
In addition, effects of wind and current were included in the
simulation model.

In order to evaluate ship-handling characteristics in critical
channels, the simulation model can be operated with the participation of a human pilot on the basis of a bird's-eye view of
the ship location relative to waterways of restricted channels.

---

[9] A basic mathematical model is shown in the Appendix.

Fig. 15 Straight-line edges of icebreaking along ship path

Fig. 16 Johnson Point in St. Mary's River Channel

Dynamic course stability

Dynamic stability is directly related to magnitudes of yaw and sway deviation caused by small initial disturbances. The linearized equations of motion can be applied effectively for this treatment.

The linearized equations of yaw and sway motions can be written as follows [4]

$$n'_z \dot{r}' - N'_v v' - N'_r r' = N'_\delta \delta$$

$$m'_y \dot{v}' - Y'_v v' - (Y'_r - m')r' = Y'_\delta \delta$$

Assuming the rudder is fixed amidship in the preceding equations, a set of homogeneous differential equations is obtained. The general solution can be written

$$v' = V'_1 e^{\sigma'_1 t'} + V'_2 e^{\sigma'_2 t'}$$

$$r' = R'_1 e^{\sigma'_1 t'} + R'_2 e^{\sigma'_2 t'}$$

where values are constant V'_i and R'_i depend on the initial conditions of motion. Dynamic course stability is obtained as a solution of the following characteristics equation, which is obtained by substituting the foregoing form of solution into the homogeneous differential equations (with $\delta = 0$):

$$A\sigma'^2 + B\sigma' + C = 0$$

where

$$A = n'_z m'_y$$

$$B = -n'_z Y'_v - m'_y N'_r$$

$$C = Y'_v N'_r - N'_v (Y'_r - m')$$

Thus the inherent course stability roots σ_1 and σ_2 can be readily determined from the foregoing quadratic characteristic equation.

If the real parts of σ'_1 and σ'_2 are both negative, the solution for v' and r' will vanish with time and a new straight course results. In this case, the ship is dynamically stable on course.

Fig. 17 Ice buildup during turning at Johnson Point

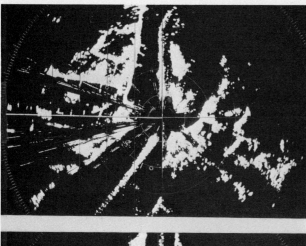

Fig. 18 Radar display photograph in the area of Johnson Point

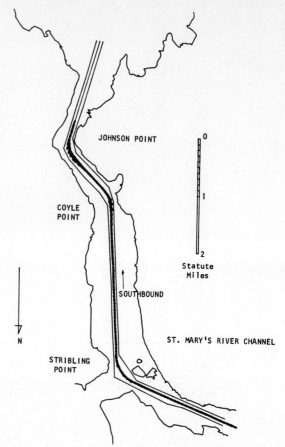

Fig. 19 Ship trajectory obtained in full-scale trials (1000-ft ship in ice-covered water)

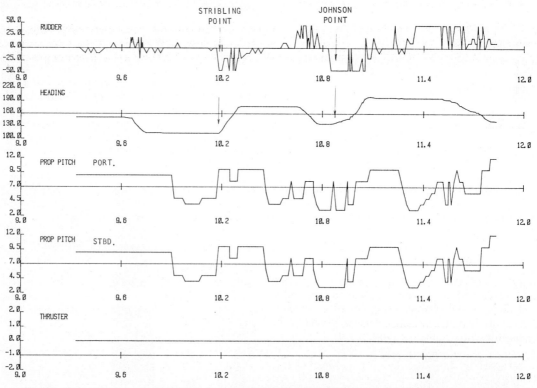

Fig. 20 Ship trajectory obtained in full-scale trials (1000-ft ship in the ice-covered St. Mary's River Channel)

Maneuvering Performance of Ships in Critical Channels

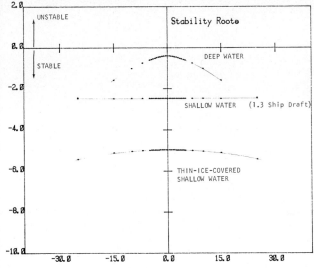

Fig. 21 Inherent course stability (1000-ft ship)

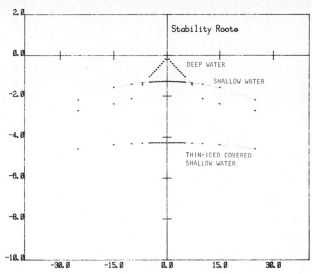

Fig. 22 Inherent course stability (730-ft ship)

On the other hand, if either σ_1' or σ_2' has a positive real part, an initial disturbance will lead to continuous increases of v' and r' (until the nonlinearity of the hydrodynamic reactions prevails) and the ship is unstable in yaw.

One of the two roots, σ_2', is always negative and algebraically less than σ_1'. Therefore, σ_1' is the critical root and is called the stability index. It is clear from the preceding forms of solutions that the motion described by the σ_1'-term persists longer than that of the σ_2'-term, after the disturbance has ended. Furthermore, the magnitudes of motion due to small disturbances are directly related to the value of σ_1'. In other words, σ_1' is more significant to the response after the disturbance than σ_2'.

The criterion that $\sigma_1' < 0$ will be satisfied if, and only if

$$Y_v'N_r' > N_v'(Y_r' - m') \quad \text{or} \quad N_r'/(Y_r' - m') > N_v'/Y_v'$$

Figure 21 shows inherent course stability characteristics of the 1000-ft ship in the form of stability index σ_1' under the following conditions:

(a) deepwater condition
(b) shallow water condition ($D_w/H = 1.3$)
(c) thin-ice-covered shallow water condition (1-ft brash ice, $D_w/H = 1.3$)

The course stability index is shown with respect to the equilibrium conditions at various rudder angles, which is shown in the abscissa of the figure. The stability index on straight course can be seen at zero rudder angle.

In Fig. 21, the stability index shows that the ship possesses the following course-keeping characteristics:

(a) fairly high degree of stability in deep water
(b) high degree of stability in shallow water
(c) extremely high degree of stability in ice-covered shallow water

Figure 22 shows the inherent course stability for the 730-ft ship. The figure illustrates that the ship is:

(a) marginally stable (that is, small degree of stability) in deep water
(b) high degree of stability in shallow water
(c) extremely high degree of stability in ice-covered shallow water

From these two figures it is clearly evident that the ice and shallow water have significant stabilizing effects on course stability characteristics. It should be noted here that a similar high degree of course stability was observed on the 1000-ft ship under thin-ice-covered water conditions during full-scale trials in January 1981 (see section on full-scale trajectory measurements).

Response to standard maneuvers

There are several kinds of standard maneuvers frequently employed to evaluate maneuvering characteristics, such as:

• Enter-a-turn maneuver
• Spiral maneuver
• Z-maneuver

These maneuvers have been widely employed in full-scale ship trials, free-running model tests, and computer simulation studies. Consequently, there exists a fairly abundant amount of data available from these maneuvers which can be used for comparison purposes.

Accordingly, in order to evaluate maneuvering characteristics of the 1000-ft and 730-ft ships under various water conditions, responses to standard maneuvers were computed utilizing a digital simulation model.

(a) *Enter-a-turn*—Figure 23 shows enter-a-turn trajectories for the 1000-ft ship in deep and shallow waters, and in thin-ice-covered shallow water. This figure illustrates that the ship possesses a fairly high turning performance in deep water. These trajectories clearly demonstrate the significant effects of ice-covered and shallow water on turning performance. A substantial reduction in turning performance with the ice and shallow water conditions is consistent with the aforementioned changes in stability index.

Enter-a-turn trajectories for the 730-ft ship are shown in Fig. 24. The ship also has a fairly high degree of turning performance in deep water. In a similar manner as with the 1000-ft ship, turning performance of this ship is also reduced to a large extent due to the ice and shallow-water conditions.

(b) *Spiral tests*—Spiral tests originally proposed by Dieudonne were to obtain steady turning equilibrium conditions for a range of rudder angles consecutively in order to evaluate the turning performance and inherent course stability of a given ship. The spiral tests consist of the following:

When the ship is steady on a straight course, the rudder is turned to an angle (for example, 15 deg) and held until the rate of heading angle change reaches a steady state. The rudder is then decreased by a small amount (for example, 5 deg) and held again until a new steady-state value of turning rate is achieved. The foregoing procedure is repeated for different

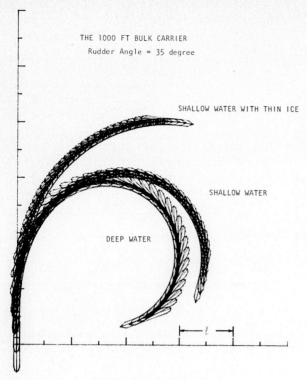

Fig. 23 Turning trajectory

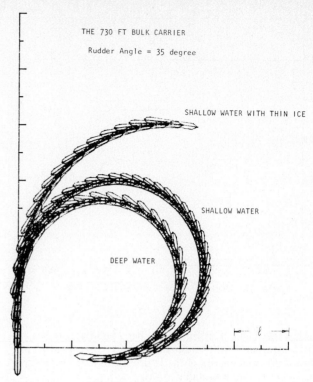

Fig. 24 Turning trajectory

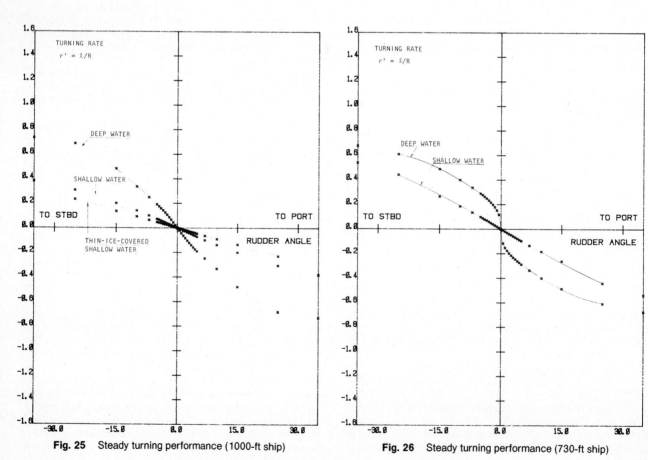

Fig. 25 Steady turning performance (1000-ft ship)

Fig. 26 Steady turning performance (730-ft ship)

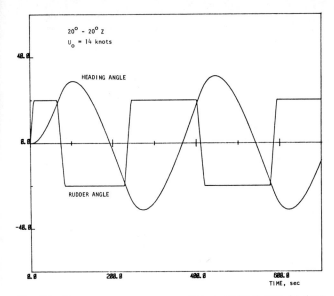

Fig. 27 Z-maneuver response prediction (1000-ft ship in deep water)

rudder angles. The rudder angle is changed by small increments starting from a large rudder angle at one side (for example, 15-deg starboard) to a rudder angle (for example, 15-deg port) at the other side. This procedure is repeated back again (for example, from the port to the starboard). In this manner, data points of steady turning rate are obtained as a function of rudder angle.

In the computer simulation runs, steady turning conditions are determined by numerically solving nonlinear equations of yaw, sway, and surge, where acceleration terms $\dot{r} = \dot{v} = \dot{u} = 0$. Under steady turning conditions, substantial speed reduction is introduced due to the increased resistance which increases the longitudinal component of centrifugal force and rudder force. As a result, a large speed reduction is introduced due to the turning of the ship. Under this circumstance, the effectiveness of rudder angle is increased due to the relatively increased propeller stream flowing into the rudder. This effect is adequately considered in order to obtain realistic steady turning solutions.

Figure 25 shows steady turning rate of the 1000-ft ship in nondimensional form ($r' = l/R$, where R is the steady turning radius) for a whole range of rudder angles under various water conditions. Reduction of turning rate is again shown in this figure due to the ice and shallow-water effects.

Figure 26 presents the steady turning rate for the case of the 730-ft ship, which indicates a similar trend in the changes in turning performance due to the ice and shallow-water conditions.

(c) *Z-maneuver response*—An ordinary Z-maneuver is accomplished as follows: With the ship on a steady-state straight course, the rudder is deflected to a certain angle (for example, 20 deg) at maximum rudder rate and maintained at this position. When the change of heading reaches the same magnitude as the rudder angle, a second rudder execution takes place shifting the rudder to the opposite direction. This procedure is continued.

The response of the 1000-ft ship to a 20-deg/20-deg Z-maneuver was computed at an approach speed of 14 knots in deep water and is shown in Fig. 27. When the change of heading angle reached 20 deg, the same magnitude as the rudder angle, the rudder was deflected to 20 deg toward the opposite direction. Before the ship started to turn toward the

opposite direction in response to the second rudder execution, the heading angle deviation reached 30 deg. At this point, the overshoot in heading angle was 10 deg. This magnitude of overshoot indicates a fairly high degree of course stability.

Figures 28 and 29 show the response of the 730-ft ship in deep and shallow waters. In these figures, higher degree of course stability is indicated by the smaller magnitude of overshoot in shallow water relative to that in deep water. A similar tendency was shown in the case of the 1000-ft ship.

Simulation runs with a human pilot

In order to evaluate shiphandling performance in critical channels in a realistic manner, simulation runs were carried out with participation of a human pilot.

The simulator used at Davidson Laboratory was a combination of digital computer model, a terminal and a plotter, and was operated in the following manner.

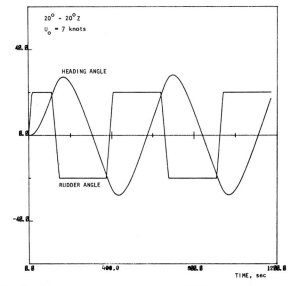

Fig. 29 Z-maneuver response prediction (730-ft ship in shallow water, $D_w/H = 1.3$)

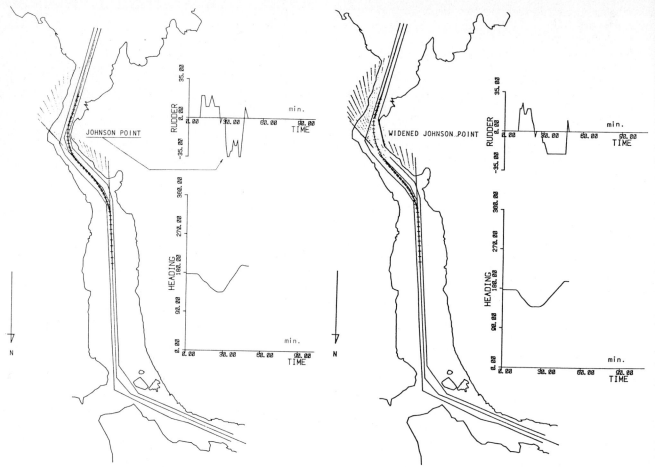

Fig. 30 Simulation run at Johnson Point (1000-ft ship in thin-ice-covered water)

Fig. 32 Simulation run at widened Johnson Point (1000-ft ship in thin-ice-covered water)

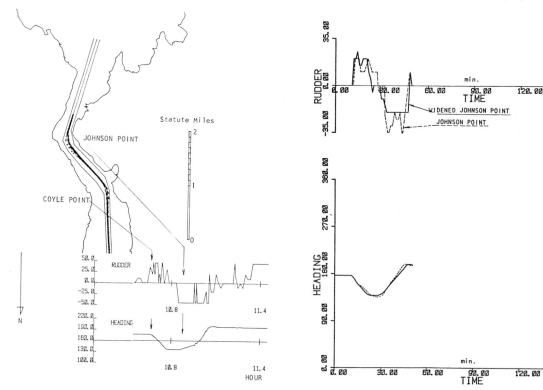

Fig. 31 Ship trajectory and rudder angle measured in full-scale trials at Johnson Point (1000-ft ship in thin-ice-covered water)

Fig. 33 Comparison of rudder angle (effect of widened Johnson Point)

Maneuvering Performance of Ships in Critical Channels

When a simulation run is initiated, the following data are drawn on the plotter:
- waterways and shorelines
- scaled ship form at initial location
- heading angle line extended forward five ship lengths from ship

Simultaneously, the ship speed in knots and yaw rate in degrees per second are typewritten on the terminal, which is located beside the plotter.

Based on the bird's-eye view location of the ship relative to the waterway, heading angle, ship speed and yaw rate, the navigator gives commands of rudder angle and ship speed on the terminal. These commands are fed into the digital computer model, which starts to compute the subsequent ship motion. One minute in real time (for example) after the new commands are given, the new ship location is plotted on the plotter together with new heading angle line extending forward five ship lengths. The bird's-eye view on the plotter is similar to the picture shown in Fig. 30. New ship speed and yaw rate are typewritten on the terminal. On the basis of new ship location and ship speed data, new commands of rudder angle and ship speed are given through the terminal to the computer model. In this manner, the navigator can steer the ship through the waterway.

During a series of simulation runs, major emphasis was placed on the two ship configurations (the 1000-ft and 730-ft ships) and the following critical channels:
- St. Mary River Channel
  1. Johnson Point (together with Coyle Point)
  2. Stribling Point
  3. West Neebish Channel
- Detroit River Channel
  1. Livingston Channel (in the area of Bois Blanc Island)

(a) *Johnson Point*—Figure 30 shows results of a simulation run on the 1000-ft ship proceeding through the approach area of Johnson Point under thin-ice-covered water conditions. The ship trajectory is shown together with time history of rudder angle and heading angle in the figure. It should be noted that a large rudder angle was used for an extended period of time in the approach area of Johnson Point.

Figure 31 shows the ship trajectory under equivalent ice-covered water conditions, which was measured in full-scale trials.

Comparing these two trajectories, encouraging correlation is evident in the following pattern of rudder activities:
1. large rudder angle executed for an extended amount of time in the approach area
2. only small rudder angle used to check the swing-rate when heading angle change was achieved

The aforementioned rudder activities clearly demonstrate that the Johnson Point area is a critical location from the viewpoint of shiphandling during winter season. Effects of the ice and shallow water are significant contributing factors to reduced turning performance of the ship as mentioned in the previous sections.

When the Johnson Point area was hypothetically widened, a similar simulation run was made. Results of ship trajectory and rudder angle are shown in Fig. 32. Rudder activity in the widened Johnson Point is compared with that in the actual Johnson Point in Fig. 33. Much reduced rudder activity is evident in the widened Johnson Point, indicating the effectiveness of dredging this particular location of the waterway.

Figure 34 shows the trajectory of a simulation run for the case where both Johnson Point and Coyle Point are widened. Reduced rudder activity is revealed in the widened approach area relative to that in the actual waterway in Fig. 35.

(b) *Stribling Point*—Figure 36 shows the trajectory of a

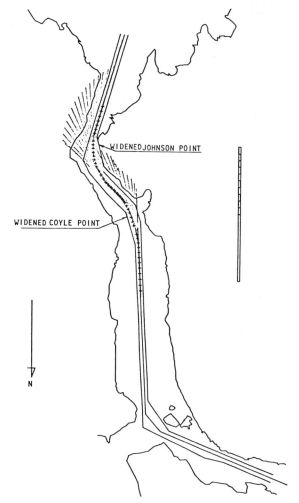

Fig. 34 Simulation run at *widened* Johnson Point and *widened* Coyle Point (1000-ft Ship in thin-ice-covered water)

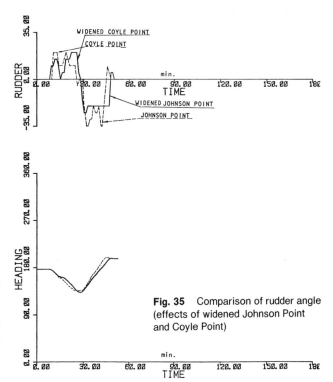

Fig. 35 Comparison of rudder angle (effects of widened Johnson Point and Coyle Point)

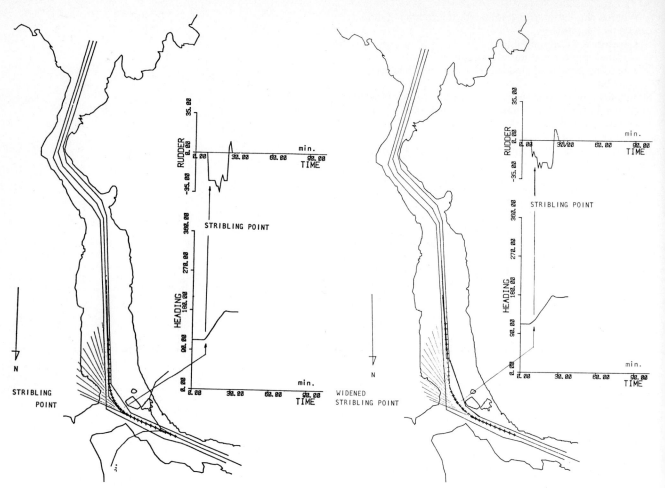

Fig. 36 Simulation run at Stribling Point (1000-ft ship in thin-ice-covered water)

Fig. 38 Simulation run at *widened* Stribling Point (1000-ft ship in thin-ice-covered water)

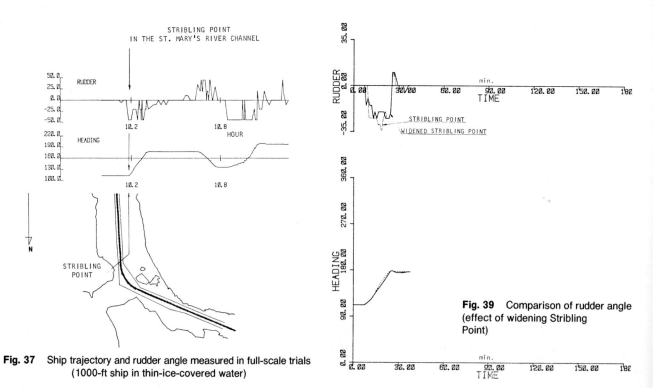

Fig. 37 Ship trajectory and rudder angle measured in full-scale trials (1000-ft ship in thin-ice-covered water)

Fig. 39 Comparison of rudder angle (effect of widening Stribling Point)

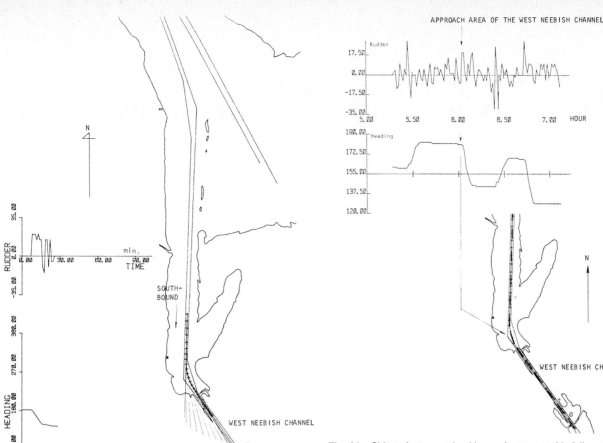

Fig. 40 Simulation run in the approach of the West Neebish Channel (1000-ft ship in ice-free water)

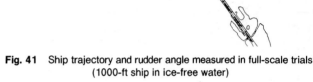

Fig. 41 Ship trajectory and rudder angle measured in full-scale trials (1000-ft ship in ice-free water)

simulation run on the 1000-ft ship in the ice-covered Stribling Point area of the St. Mary's River Channel. For comparison purposes, the trajectory measured during the 1000-ft ship trials is shown in Fig. 37, which shows similar pattern of rudder activity to that obtained in the simulation run.

Assuming that the approach area of Stribling Point was widened, a simulation run was made as shown in Fig. 38. Figure 39 shows reduced rudder activity in the widened Stribling Point relative to the actual waterway, indicating the effectiveness of dredging this approach area.

(c) *West Neebish Channel*—Under ice-free water conditions, simulation runs were made on the 1000-ft and 730-ft ships in the approach area of the West Neebish Channel in the St. Mary's River Channel.

Figure 40 shows results of a simulation run on the 1000 ft ship. The ship trajectory was measured on the actual ship in ice-free water in November 1979 and is shown in Fig. 41. It is shown in these two figures that relatively small rudder angle (up to only 20 deg) is used under ice-free water conditions in both full-scale trials and simulations.

Results of a simulation run on the 730-ft ship in this approach area are shown in Fig. 42. Rudder angle activities are compared between those on the 1000-ft and 730-ft ships in Fig. 43. It is revealed in this figure that much less rudder angle is used on the 730-ft ship relative to that on the 1000-ft ship, indicating the profound effect of ship size on shiphandling characteristics in critical channels.

(d) *Livingston Channel*—Simulation runs in ice-free water were made on the 1000-ft and 730-ft ships in the downbound Livingston Channel near Bois Blanc Island. Results for these two ships are shown in Figs. 44 and 45. Rudder activities on these two ships are compared in Fig. 46. The profound effect of ship size on ship-handling in the channel is clearly shown by the difference in the magnitude of rudder activity on these two ships.

Figure 47 shows an example of grounding during a simulation run on the 1000-ft ship in the shallow eastside of the channel, indicating a need of dredging the shallow side of the channel in this approach area.

Simulations with participation of an experienced ship officer

Captain J. B. Cooper, who commands the 1000-ft-long *Edwin H. Gott*, participated in a series of simulation runs at Davidson Laboratory during March 1980. His knowledge and expertise in ship-handling, in particular, in critical channels, were fully utilized during his participation in the simulation studies.

Detailed discussions and useful comments were given by Captain Cooper during these simulation runs. The major results obtained are summarized as follows:

1. *Critical location of connecting waterways*—In Captain's Cooper's opinion, Johnson Point is the most critical location of the connecting waterways. One effective measure that could be carried out at minimal cost would be to increase the approach area to the turn (or cutoff the corner of the Point).

2. *Ship speed*—To proceed at a proper speed is extremely important to the approach of a turn in a narrow channel. Ex-

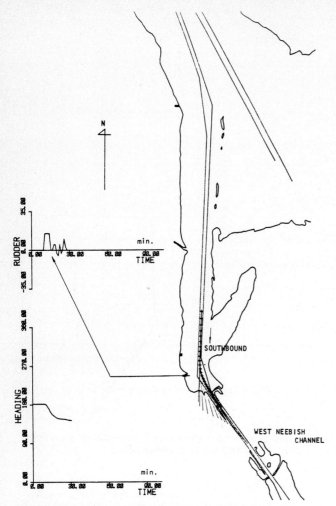

Fig. 42 Simulation run in the approach of the West Neebish Channel
(730-ft ship in ice-free water)

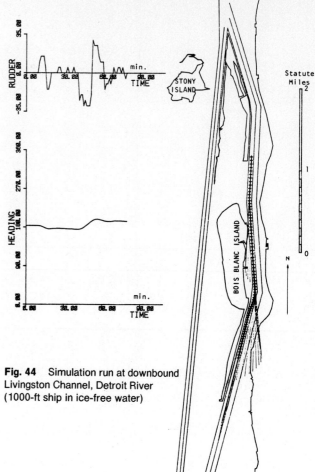

Fig. 44 Simulation run at downbound
Livingston Channel, Detroit River
(1000-ft ship in ice-free water)

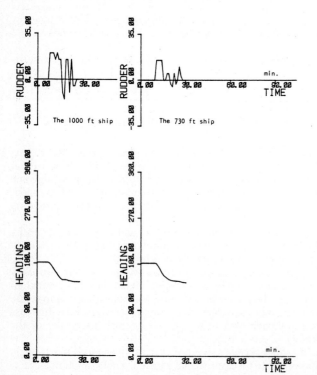

cessive speed on the approach to a turn leaves less room for
ship-handling error; on the other hand, when the ship is proceeding at a low speed, more power is readily available to make
corrections if needed. Furthermore, there exists the possibility
of vibration due to heavy propeller loading when the fully
loaded ship is proceeding at a higher speed in narrow channels.

3. *Negotiating a bend*—The basic idea when making a
turn along the bend is to proceed at a slow speed, make easy
course changes, having the ship lined up and centered as far
from the entrance as possible. In this manner, more time is
available to make any necessary corrections if the ship is off
channel centerline.

Continuous attention to the rate of swing is extremely important in actual ship handling and also in simulation runs.

4. *Maneuvering in ice*—Effects of the ice reduce the
turning performance of the ship to a great extent because of the
ice buildup at the stern when the side of the ship swings into the
ice. Accordingly, full-rudder angle is frequently used to negotiate a bend under ice conditions. The length of the ship
contributes directly to the reduction of turning performance
in this situation.

Maneuvering in ice-covered water with a round bow is more
difficult than for a ship with a sharp bow which can penetrate
into the ice.

 Fig. 43 Comparison of rudder angle during transit to the West
Neebish Channel (1000-ft and 730-ft ships, ice-free water)

Maneuvering Performance of Ships in Critical Channels

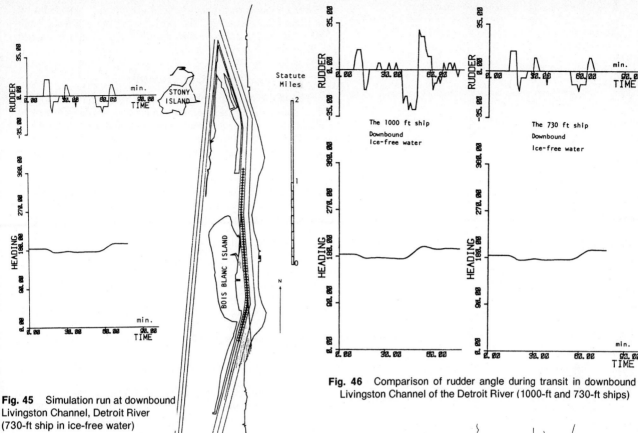

Fig. 45 Simulation run at downbound Livingston Channel, Detroit River (730-ft ship in ice-free water)

Fig. 46 Comparison of rudder angle during transit in downbound Livingston Channel of the Detroit River (1000-ft and 730-ft ships)

5. *Controllable-pitch propeller*—This eliminates a time delay in engine response during critical shiphandling.

6. *Twin-propellers and bow-thrusters*—These are effective to produce turning moment in ship handling, particularly at low speeds.

7. *Wind effects*—Wind speed and direction are critical during ship handling in narrow channels. A wind of 25 knots can be critical when entering any harbor.

8. *Lock size*—With an increase in the number of 1000-ft-long ships in the Great Lakes, a new large lock at the Soo should be a high priority.

Maneuvering performance design guidelines

Inherent course stability and turning performance

The two Great-Lakes bulk carriers examined in this study possess satisfactory course stability characteristics and turning performance in open water as indicated in the previous sections. In the meantime, results shown in the previous section also indicate that under ice-covered water conditions, the degree of dynamic course stability is greatly increased with substantial reduction in turning performance. This is due to the significant stabilizing effect of icebreaking resistance during a turn. Accordingly, an effort should be made during the preliminary design stage to improve the overall performance under ice-covered water conditions (that is, to reduce the degree of dynamic course stability with increased turning performance), although it is not an easy task.

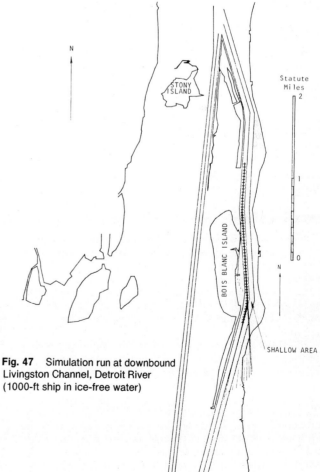

Fig. 47 Simulation run at downbound Livingston Channel, Detroit River (1000-ft ship in ice-free water)

Maneuvering Performance of Ships in Critical Channels

Table 14 Turning performance

(1) 1200-ft ship

```
                    GL12HD
                    DEEP 1200


            APPROACH SPEED KT:   14.00
            RUDDER ANGLE DEG:   -35.00

                          ADVANCE/ℓ    TRANSFER/ℓ
            90 DEGREES:  (     2.900,     1.364)
           180 DEGREES:  (     1.836,     3.060)=TACT.DIA./ℓ

            XPMAX:  (     2.935,      1.682)
            XPMIN:  (     0.000,      0.000)
            YPMAX:  (     1.532,      3.094)


            D/L:    2.81    BETA:   12.53   U/U0:    0.50
```

(2) 1000-ft ship

```
                    GL1HD
                    DEEP 1000


            APPROACH SPEED KT:   14.00
            RUDDER ANGLE DEG:   -35.00

                          ADVANCE/ℓ    TRANSFER/ℓ
            90 DEGREES:  (     2.900,     1.346),
           180 DEGREES:  (     1.890,     2.953)=TACT.DIA./ℓ

            XPMAX:  (     2.932,      1.644)
            XPMIN:  (     0.000,      0.000)
            YPMAX:  (     1.608,      2.983)


            D/L:    2.64    BETA:   12.23   U/U0:    0.48
```

The following design procedures are suggested for improvement of the maneuvering performance under ice-covered conditions.

1. Reduce the fullness of the stern waterline shape to lessen the icebreaking resistance in a turn.

2. Use additional maneuvering devices such as:
 (a) thrusters
 (b) twin-prop and twin-rudder combinations
 (c) controllable-pitch propeller

3. Increase beam at the bow relative to the mid-parallel body, such as the bow of the SS *Manhattan*, to increase sideslip angle during a turn. Overall performance of this configuration should be thoroughly examined during the preliminary design stage.

Maneuvering performance of a planned 1200-ft bulk carrier

There has been a plan of a 1200-ft bulk carrier to be constructed and operated in the Great Lakes. Accordingly, a limited study was made to examine the maneuvering characteristics of this size bulk carrier.

Preliminary evaluations of maneuvering performance of the ship (L_{pp} = 1185 ft), B = 105 ft, H = 27 ft, C_b = 0.95) indicated that the ship has satisfactory maneuvering characteristics in open water.

Table 14 is a computer printout of the estimated turning performance of the 1200-ft ship compared with that of the 1000-ft ship during an enter-a-turn maneuver. Results indicate that the 1200-ft ship possesses somewhat similar turning performance to that of the 1000-ft ship in terms of ship length. It means that the turning trajectory of the 1200-ft ship should be increased relative to that of the 1000-ft ship in proportion to the ship length. It is expected that the degree of strain in ship handling will be increased for the 1200-ft ship relative to the 1000-ft ship, when the ship is proceeding through a channel (for example, Johnson Point in St. Mary's River channel).

For efficient transportation of bulk cargo, it is essential to utilize a larger-size ship. Toward this objective, efforts should be continued to improve ship-handling performance and also connecting waterway capabilities.

Conclusions

The major objective of this study is to evaluate and to optimize ship-handling performance of Great-Lakes ships in critical channels of connecting waterways under ice-free and ice-covered water conditions.

The Phase I study was made to identify specific problem situations in terms of channels, vessel types, design parameters and operating variables.

Subsequently, in the Phase II study, maneuvering characteristics of Great-Lakes bulk carriers are evaluated in experimental and computer-aided analysis. A major emphasis was placed on two ship designs (that is, the 1000-ft and 730-ft ships) in critical channels (that is, St. Mary's River channel and the Livingston channels of the Detroit River).

Results obtained in captive model tests, full-scale trials, and simulation studies under ice-free and ice-covered water conditions indicate consistent and important findings as follows:

1. The ice and shallow water have a profound effect in increasing inherent course stability and reducing turning performance to a large extent

2. Accordingly, ship handling in ice-covered channels is a severe problem because of greatly reduced turning performance

3. To widen the approach area at a bend of waterways is a very effective procedure to reduce shiphandling difficulty in critical channels. Dredging is recommended for certain locations in critical channels, including:
 (a) Johnson Point approach area together with Coyle Point area (see Fig. 48)
 (b) Stribling Point area (see Fig. 48)
 (c) Shallow side of Downbound Livingston Channel near Bois Blanc Island (see Fig. 49)

4. Ship size has a profound effect on ship-handling performance in restricted channels. Accordingly, for a large-size ship, every effort should be made to provide satisfactory maneuvering performance during preliminary design stage. For example, consideration should be given to employing controllable-pitch propellers, twin rudders, bow thrusters, and shipboard navigational aids.

5. The 1000-ft and 730-ft ships considered in this study have satisfactory turning performance and course stability characteristics in deep water relative to most other commercial-type ships.

6. An effort was made to estimate the maneuvering performance of the proposed 1200-ft Great Lakes bulk carrier, which showed somewhat similar performance to that of the 1000-ft bulk carrier *in nondimensional terms*. For example, the turning trajectory should be increased approximately in proportion to the ship length. It is expected, therefore, that the degree of strain in ship handling will increase when this ship runs through critical channels such as Johnson Point of St. Mary's River, in particular under ice-covered water conditions.

7. Turning performance under the ice-covered water conditions can be improved by reducing the fullness of the stern waterline shape.

Acknowledgments

The authors gratefully acknowledge the cooperation and assistance provided by many members of the U.S. Maritime Administration, U.S. Steel Great Lakes Fleet Division, Arctec,

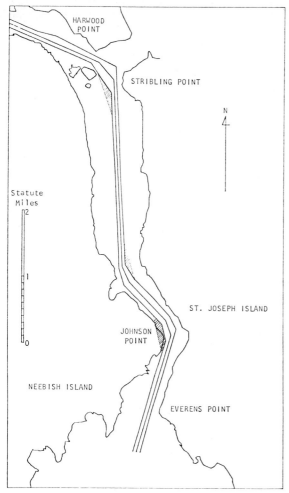

Fig. 48 Recommended dredging area in the St. Mary's River Channel (shown by shaded location)

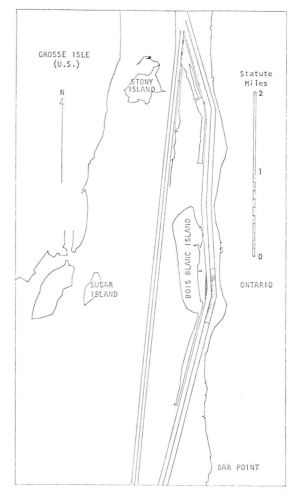

Fig. 49 Recommended dredging area in the Livingston Channels of the Detroit River (shown by shaded location)

and Davidson Laboratory during various stages of this research program.

References

1   "Final Report of Working Panels at First Review Meeting, U.S. Great Lakes-Seaway Port Development and Shipper Conference," Cleveland, Ohio, Oct. 3 and 4, 1977.

2   Kotras, T., Kim, J., and Jacobi, J., "Draft Report Great Lakes/St. Lawrence Seaway Lock Capacity Analysis," prepared by Arctec, Inc. for Department of the Army, North Central Division, U.S. Army Corps of Engineers.

3   Eda, H. and DeBord, F., "Analysis of the Maneuvering Characteristics of Great Lakes Ships in Critical Channels," Phase 1 Report, April 1979.

4   Eda, H. et al., "Ship Maneuvering Safety Studies," TRANS. SNAME, Vol. 87, 1979.

5   Crane, C. L., Jr., "Maneuvering Trials of the 278 000-DWT *Esso Osaka* in Shallow and Deep Waters," TRANS., SNAME, Vol. 87, 1979.

6   Landsburg, A., Card, J., Eda, H., von Breitenfeld, H., and Knerim, T., "Proposed Shipboard Maneuvering Data," *Proceedings*, SNAME STAR Symposium, 1980.

7   Eda, H., "Digital Simulation Analysis of Maneuvering Performance," *Proceedings*, 10th Symposium on Naval Hydrodynamics, Boston, 1974.

8   Crane C. et al, "Proposed Procedures for Determining Ship Controllability Requirements and Capabilities," SNAME STAR-α Symposium, 1975.

9   Eda, H. and Crane, C. L., Jr., "Steering Characteristics of Ships in Calm Water and Waves," TRANS. SNAME, Vol. 73, 1965.

10   Nizery, B. and Page, J. P., "Maneuverability Tests on the 213 000 Ton Tanker *Magdala*, Effect of Depth," ATMA, 1969.

11   Fujino, M., "Experimental Studies on Ship Maneuverability in Restricted Waters, Parts I and II," *International Shipbuilding Progress*, No. 168, 1968, and No. 186, 1970.

12   Eda, H., "Directional Stability and Control of Ships in Restricted Channels," TRANS. SNAME, Vol. 79, 1971.

13   Norrbin, N. H., "Theory and Observations on the Use of a Mathematical Model for Ship Maneuvering in Deep and Confined Waters," Swedish State Shipbuilding Experimental Tank Report No. 68, Göteburg, 1971.

Appendix

Basic equations of ship maneuvering motions

On the basis of captive model test results together with analytical estimations, an effort was made to formulate the equations of yaw-sway-roll-rudder motions to represent realistic maneuvering behavior of a ship.

Figure 50 shows the coordinate system used to define ship motions, with major symbols following the nomenclature used in previous papers.   Longitudinal and transverse horizontal axes of the ship are represented by the x- and y-axes with origin fixed at the center of gravity.   By reference to these body axes, the

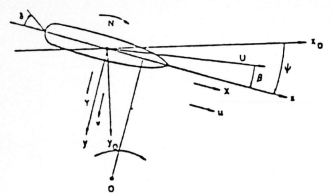

Fig. 50 Orientation of coordinate axes fixed in ship

equations of motion of a ship in the horizontal plane can be written in the form:

$$l_z \dot{r} = N \quad \text{(yaw)}$$

$$m(\dot{v} + ur) = Y \quad \text{(sway)} \qquad (1)$$

$$m(\dot{u} - vr) = X \quad \text{(surge)}$$

where N, K, Y, and X represent total hydrodynamic terms generated by ship motions, rudder and propeller.

Hydrodynamic forces are expressed in terms of dimensionless quantities, N', K', Y', and X' based on nondimensionalizing parameters ρ (water density), U (resultant ship velocity relative to the water), and A, that is

$$N' = \frac{N}{\frac{\rho}{2} U^2 A l}, \quad Y' = \frac{Y}{\frac{\rho}{2} U^2 A}, \quad \text{etc.} \qquad (2)$$

Hydrodynamic coefficients vary with position, attitude, rudder angle, propeller revolution, and velocity of the ship. For example, in the case of hydrodynamic yaw moment coefficient:

$$N' = N'(v', r', \delta, y'_0, \dot{v}', \dot{r}', n', u') \qquad (3)$$

where

$$v' = \frac{V}{U}, \quad r' = r\frac{l}{U}, \quad y'_0 = \frac{y_0}{l}, \quad n' = \frac{n}{n_e}, \quad u' = \frac{u}{u_e}, \quad \text{etc.}$$

Finally, the following polynomials were obtained for predictions of ship dynamic motions:

$$N' = a_1 + a_2 v' + a_3 r' + a_4 \delta + a_5 y'_0 + a_6 v'^2 r' + a_7 v' r'^2 \\ + a_8 v'^3 + a_9 r'^3 + a_{10} \delta^3 + a_{11} y'^3_0 + a_{12} \dot{r}' + a_{13} \dot{v}'$$

$$Y' = b_1 + b_2 v' + b_3 r' + b_4 \delta + b_5 y'_0 + b_6 v'^2 r' + b_7 v' r'^2 \\ + b_8 v'^3 + b_9 r'^3 + b_{10} \delta^3 + b_{11} y'^3_0 + b_{12} \dot{r}' + b_{13} \dot{v}'$$

$$X' = c_1 + c_2 v' r' + c_3 v'^2 + c_4 \delta^2 + c_5 \dot{u}' + X'_p \qquad (4)$$

Yaw moment, side force and longitudinal force due to the ice are superposed in the corresponding hydrodynamic coefficients such as a_2, a_4, b_2, b_4 and c_1 under each speed condition.

Under each speed and ice conditions (for example, infinite brash ice condition or a specific broken channel width), the ice effects are represented by the following expression:

$$Y' = b_{20} + b_{21} \nu' + b_{23} v'^3 + b_3 \delta + b_9 \delta^3$$

$$N' = a_{20} + a_{21} \nu' + a_{23} v'^3 + a_3 \delta + a_9 \delta^3$$

$$X' = c_{20} + c_{22} \nu'^2 + c_3 \delta^2$$

where

$$Y' = \frac{Y}{\rho/2 \, l^2 U^2} = Y^* \left(\frac{gBh^2}{l^2 U^2} \right)$$

$$X' = \frac{X}{\rho/2 \, l^2 U^2} = X^* \left(\frac{gBh^2}{l^2 U^2} \right)$$

$$N' = \frac{N}{\rho/2 \, l^3 U^2} = N^* \left(\frac{gB^2 h^2}{l^3 U^2} \right)$$

and

$$Y^* = \frac{Y \, [\text{lb}]}{\rho_w g B h^2}$$

$$X^* = \frac{X \, [\text{lb}]}{\rho_w g B h^2}$$

$$N^* = \frac{N(\text{ft-lb})}{\rho_w g B^2 h^2}$$

These ice effects are superposed in the hydrodynamic terms (for example b_{21} into b_2, a_{21} into a_2). Ylb, Xlb, and Nft-lb in the foregoing were determined from model tests.

Discussion

Ralph H. Bertz, Member

The authors are to be congratulated on a comprehensive and excellent study of ships maneuvering in the Great Lakes waterway system.

At the beginning of the decade of the 70's with the advent of the new-generation, maximum-cargo-capacity Great Lakes carriers with the full bow, full stern and pilothouse aft, there was great concern about the maneuverability of these ships in the narrow Great Lakes connecting channels. Actual operating experience has proven the design to be efficient, economical and maneuverable over a wide range of operating conditions. Since the two ships chosen for analysis in this paper are of the aforementioned design the study has certainly confirmed and quantified the adequacy of their maneuvering performance.

The authors' recommendation for hull form design modification for ice transient must be carefully evaluated, as any changes that have a negative impact on the cargo-carrying capacity must be recovered through improved maneuverability

in the relatively short period of the year when ice conditions severely impair ship passage. As an example, in the testing and evaluation of ice transiting bow forms for Great Lakes carriers by Voelker and Kim [14] (additional references follow some discussions), it was concluded that the application of an ice transiting bow form will only be marginally beneficial even in an 11-month operating season.

It is noted that in the full-scale trials of the 1000-ft ship in the ice-covered St. Mary's River the trajectory indicates that both propellers were in an ahead pitch and the bow thruster was unused during the entire 12-mile transit. If more severe ice conditions than experienced in the trials are encountered, additional maneuverability can be obtained by the use of one propeller in an ahead pitch with the other in an astern pitch coupled with the aid of the bow thruster.

It is also emphasized that adequately wide icebreaking around critical turns is very important in preventing serious maneuvering problems in an ice-covered channel.

On the basis of the computer-aided analysis quantifying the maneuvering benefits derived from channel widening at the Johnson, Coyle and Stribbling Points area in the St. Mary's River and the shallow side of the downbound Livingston Channel, it is recommended that the U. S. Army Corp of Engineers undertake the necessary dredging as indicated.

Additional reference

14 Voelker, R. P. and Kim, J. K., "Test and Evaluation of Ice Transiting Bow Forms for Great Lakes Bulk Carriers," prepared by Arctec, Inc. for the Maritime Administration, March 1978.

C. Lincoln Crane, Jr., Member

This practical paper combines modern techniques of predicting maneuvers in restricted, shallow, and ice-covered waters with practical data on waterways, traffic, casualties and opinions of users.

In Phase 1 of the work, 14 of the 18 study participants named channel depth variations as important to performance. With regard to this, in the 1977 *Esso Osaka* shallow-water maneuvering trials we found a tendency for the vessel to seek deeper water when moving in a coasting turn. This was noticed with 50 percent underkeel clearance when the vessel spontaneously reversed its path curvature against 35-deg rudder, even though the bottom gradient averaged only about 7 ft in 12 000, or about 0.06 percent. I wonder if the authors think this effect might be useful for assisting vessels to turn in channels; that is, by providing a mildly downward sloping bottom toward the center of the turn.

I have some questions regarding the actual and simulated trackings of vessels in the St. Mary's River and the Livingston Channel: First, did the authors obtain records of the off-track distance of the vessels' midship points, and were they able to calculate the "minimum bank clearance" as suggested in reference [8]? In the critical turning regions, these quantities would seem to provide the key information on risk of grounding. However, they are difficult to extract from the small charted presentations in the figures. My other question is, Was the simulator's "view from the bridge" presentation useful to shiphandlers in the critical turns? If so, were fixed navigation ranges visible on the CRT?

As master of the *Edwin H. Gott*, Captain Cooper's comments are appreciated. User's inputs are very important in studies such as this.

Regarding Figs. 9(d) and 9(h), can the authors explain why the linear segments of the Y' versus β curves vary so little with r' in shallow water? Is only the lateral center of pressure affected? Incidentally, the changes in the N' and Y' scales between the deep and shallow water figures tend to hide the very large effects of water depth on these yaw moment and side force outputs.

I also wonder why the yaw moment, N', in Fig. 11a is not close to zero at zero drift angle. Can the authors explain this?

The data on the effects of thin ice and shallow water on both turning and coursekeeping should be useful for both ship and waterway design. Regarding hull form, during the icebreaking trials of the tanker *Manhattan* in 1969, the widened bow created enough lateral clearance along the sides and after shoulders to permit reasonable turning in thick ice. On the other hand, the sloping side sponsons were more important in thin ice. Regarding the widened bow in fairly thick uniform ice, the measured turning diameter of about 7 miles agreed well with a simple calculation based on the "effective stern clearance" (most of which clearance seemed to be provided by the widened bow). In thinner ice the turning diameter was, of course, much smaller because of icebreaking accomplished by the vessel's side as it drifted laterally in a turn.

Wilbur H. Vantine,[10] Visitor

Figure 24 of this impressive paper shows the shallow water turning trajectory increasing considerably as the ship gets well into the turn, and at about 270 deg from the original heading the turning trajectory in shallow water becomes tighter than the turning trajectory in deep water. This may be so, but it seems unusual and I think that the authors might want to check this to be sure that it was not misplotted.

On page 221 Item 5 promotes controllable-pitch propellers as being desirable because they "eliminate a time delay in engine response during critical shiphandling." I think that a solid majority of pilots would argue against the overall desirability of VP props. It is true that they do offer quick increases of power when a "steering kick" is needed, but the response of a typical direct-drive diesel is about equal and that of a typical good-handling turbine is adequate and the latter two arrangements do not have the serious maneuvering difficulties inherent in the VP design.

Some troubles with the VP propeller ships are as follows: (1) When the pitch is suddenly and drastically reduced, as might become necessary when there is an unexpected delay or emergency in the channel ahead, the ship loses all steering and begins to slue about. The only way that it can be slowed in a controlled manner is to do so gradually and this luxury is not always possible. On the other hand, a conventional ship, when the propeller is stopped, will retain some steering control from the flow of water from the ship's headway to the rudder. On the VP ships the spinning propeller in zero pitch seems to block the flow of water to the rudder to such an extent that all steering control is lost. (2) It is not possible, at least with a single-screw VP ship, to hold in a stationary position as is sometimes necessary. With all headway off the ship and the propeller in zero pitch the stern will "walk" in the direction of rotation. (3) Unless the designer and builder provide a left-turning propeller, a single-screw VP ship will back the opposite direction from a conventional single-screw ship and may thereby cause difficulties. (4) It is much more likely that a mooring line will get caught in the constantly turning propellers during docking/undocking maneuvers. (5) On many VP ships, particularly after the linkage has become worn, it is very difficult to find true zero pitch. (6) When the linkage develops slack, it is always taken up so that the ship can still go full ahead at the expense of backing power. Of course these problems can be eliminated or minimized by providing the equipment to start and stop the engine as on a conventional ship. I know of one large company that agrees with this assessment. Shell Oil Company provides the facility to start and stop the engines on their VP diesel tankers. They even provide the facility to reverse the engine so that the direction in which their ships back can be influenced.

On page 221, in Item 6, twin propellers and bow thrusters are mentioned as being effective in producing turning moment in ship handling, particularly at low speeds. I agree that bow thrusters are great but the twin screws are only good if the ship also has twin rudders. Most of the commercial twin-screw ships that we get in the Panama Canal have only a central rudder which is out of the propeller race and therefore ineffective for "steering kicks." I am sure that the authors agree with my assessment of this because on page 222 twin rudders are mentioned along with the twin propellers.

Ralph E. Johnson, Member

[The views expressed herein are the opinions of the discusser and not necessarily those of the National Transportation Safety Board.]

I would like to thank the authors for their valuable paper and ask two questions. First, can the authors comment on the effect

[10] Consultant, Miami, Florida.

that increased ice thickness would have on the results presented in their paper? Second, can the results presented in this paper be applied to ship forms other than the typical Great Lakes bulk carrier hull form?

J. C. Card, Member

[The views expressed herein are the opinions of the discusser and not necessarily those of the Department of Transportation or the U. S. Coast Guard.]

The author's paper is an excellent example of applying a sound engineering approach and emerging technology to an old problem. Adequate maneuvering performance from ships has always been necessary. However, until recently, tools were not readily available to assess maneuvering capabilities during design. Most new ships were patterned after existing ones and maneuvering performance was not directly addressed. As a result, some ships have been built with inadequate or marginal maneuvering capabilities. Now that doesn't need to happen.

While this study is more involved than would be expected for most new ship or ship/waterway designs, it contains elements necessary for most assessments. As I see those elements, they are:

1. Problem definition—an important and many times overlooked step. The paper documents a well-thought-out process for choosing the types of ships and operating locations for further analysis. Since many of the decisions in this process are subjective, they are open to discussion—however important is the authors complete presentation of their process and the results.

2. Selection of the ships and their overall parameters.

3. Determining hydrodynamic or maneuvering coefficients for the particular ship. This step still requires either model testing or a professional hydrodynamicist's determination of coefficients from a similar ship. However, work currently underway in the United Kingdom, Japan, and the United States should permit estimation from basic hull parameters. At some point I believe that coefficients will be available directly from the lines drawings.

4. Digital simulation of basic vessel maneuvers and/or a particular maneuvering scenario.

5. Full-scale testing of the maneuvers to compare against digital simulation and/or verify the simulation.

6. Simulated maneuvers with experienced mariners to evaluate particular scenario.

Following these steps is the all-important one and that is deciding upon a course of action. The study, as excellent as it is, is not the end. I would like to know how the results of the study will be used? What will happen next? As my good friend and teacher in System Safety, Dr. Vernon Grose, states, "The only reason for an engineering analysis is to make a decision."

One final comment is on what I see as conflicting requirements for maneuvering characteristics in open water and ice. If open-water coursekeeping and turning are compromised in favor of better characteristics in ice, I think problems could result. This is an area where more research is needed.

Masataka Fujino,[11] Visitor

The authors should be congratulated for giving us useful information on the maneuvering characteristics of ships moving in the ice-covered water. In particular, it is very interesting that the inherent course stability of ships increases to a great extent due to the presence of the ice on the water surface. The authors succeeded in simulating the maneuvering motions of ships in the ice-covered area by making use of the digital simulation technique. Unfortunately, however, they do not indicate definitely how the hydrodynamic coefficients which are included in the maneuvering equations vary with the ice conditions, except for the experimental results of oblique towing tests carried out in the ice-covered water which are shown in Fig. 11(a)–(c). I think it would be highly appreciated if the numerical data of the hydrodynamic coefficients used during the digital simulation studies were shown.

N. E. Mikelis,[12] Visitor

In addition to congratulating the authors on their excellent report of what must have been an exciting project, the discusser wishes to make some comments and add some information that may be of use in similar studies in the future.

When a ship proceeds in a channel the hydrodynamic force and moment depend on velocity and acceleration perturbation terms, and also on displacement terms describing the asymmetry of the flow, namely, the off-centerline displacement y_0 and the orientation ψ relative to the channel's centerline. Although the first of these effects has been accounted for in the authors' mathematical model, the second one is missing. To include this effect, we add the terms $a_{14}\psi$, $b_{14}\psi$ and possibly $c_6\psi$ to the polynomial equations provided in the paper.

The absence of these quantities from the mathematical model could possibly account for the lesser amounts and fewer uses of rudder in simulation when compared with full-scale measurements (Figs. 30 and 31, 36 and 37, 40 and 41). A brief discussion on the necessary experiments to measure the orientation coefficients is given in reference [15] herewith.

The authors have discussed the rotating-arm tests used to measure the velocity and the off-centerline displacement dependent coefficients, but have not mentioned the tests or means employed to evaluate the acceleration coefficients (a_{12}, a_{13}, b_{12}, b_{13}, c_5). The discusser is interested in the method used to obtain the acceleration coefficients, as his work has shown that computations of three-dimensional potential flow around accelerating ships provide an accurate means for the theoretical prediction of such coefficients [15, 16]. Thus, until velocity and displacement dependent coefficient can also be confidently calculated, it is conceivable to use computed acceleration coefficients along with the rotating-arm tests for the evaluation of the remaining coefficients. A simpler alternative is the use of empirical formulas, obtained from existing experimental results [17]. In the latter course it must be noted, however, that very few data are published for coefficients appropriate to shallow waters or canals.

Computed acceleration coefficients have been published by the discusser [15, 18] for ships of $C_B = 0.80$ and for various other principal dimensions in shallow or deep water. It is hoped that it will prove desirable to produce similar data for ships of other block coefficients so that by successive interpolations the acceleration coefficients can be obtained, for any ship form in shallow or deep waters, from published charts.

Additional references

15 Mikelis, N. E. and Parkinson, A. G., "Acceleration Coefficients for Manoeuvring and Simulation Modelling for Ships in Deep or Shallow Waters," Conference on Behaviour of Ships in Restricted Waters, Vol. I, BSHC, Varna, Nov. 1982.

16 Mikelis, N. E. and Price, W. G., "Calculation of Acceleration Coefficients and Correction Factors Associated with Ships Maneuvering in Restricted Waters: Comparisons Between Theory and Experiments," Trans. RINA, Vol. 123, 1981, pp. 217–232.

17 Clarke, D., Gedling, P., and Hine, G., "The Application of Maneuverability Criteria in Hull Design Using Linear Theory," Paper No. 7, RINA Spring Meeting, 1982.

18 Mikelis, N. E., "Data for the Evaluation of the Acceleration Coefficients for Tankers Maneuvering in Shallow and Deep Waters," International Shipbuilding Progress, Dec. 1982.

---

[11] University of Tokyo, Japan.

[12] Lloyd's Register of Shipping, London.

Authors' Closure

The authors wish to thank all of the discussers who took the time and effort to prepare valuable contributions to the paper.

Mr. Bertz's comments are particularly relevant in that they provide a discussion of our conclusions in light of practical considerations. We agree that with current traffic levels and season extension conditions, maneuverability has proved to be adequate. This is primarily due to the foresight of the designers and skill of the operating personnel.

The subject of hull modifications to improve maneuverability of ice-worthy cargo ships is one that will no doubt receive a great deal of attention, especially for Arctic vessels. In the case of Great Lake bulk carriers, performance improvement in ice should justify increased construction cost and reduced cargo capacity. In this respect, Mr. Bertz is correct in saying that hull form modification for ice transit must be carefully evaluated in order to recover related expenses through improved performance in ice within relatively short period of the year.

We agree with Mr. Bertz that wide icebreaking around critical turns in the waterways is very important in preventing shiphandling difficulties in ice-covered channels.

We hope that the Corps of Engineers will undertake the necessary dredging in the St. Mary's River Channel and the Livingston Channel as recommended on the basis of the computer-aided analysis, model tests, and actual ship trials.

We would like to take this opportunity to acknowledge the cooperation provided by Mr. Bertz and the U.S. Steel Great Lakes Fleet Division during full-scale trials.

Mr. Crane describes an idea to provide a mild downward sloping bottom toward the centerline of the waterway for assisting a ship to turn in channels. It is an interesting idea, and could be applicable in real situations. This is similar to the case of the HMS *Nelson*, which sheered away from its course due to the sloping bottom effect. On the other hand, the slope of the bottom he refers to relative to the *Esso Osaka* trials appears to be too small to produce noticeable turning motion.

During our simulations runs in the St. Mary's River, navigation ranges were visible on the plotter, where a bird's-eye view of the ship-waterway systems was shown. Minimum bank clearance was not computed during simulation runs.

Regarding Figs. 9(d) and 9(h), hydrodynamic lateral forces shown in these figures are a fairly complicated function of r' and β. As a result, these forces plotted in the figure happened to be of approximately similar magnitude for different values of r'. Previous series of tests also have shown similar charts to Figs. 9(d) and 9(h) under certain conditions.

As Mr. Crane pointed out, nonzero moment is shown in icebreaking moment at zero angle of attack, which we cannot explain at this time.

Mr. Crane's comments on ship hull form for turning and coursekeeping are very useful, because they are based on his experience on the SS *Manhattan* during North West Passage trials and also on a USCG icebreaker during an Antarctic expedition.

We are pleased to receive Captain Vantine's comments, as he has been involved in shiphandling in the Panama Canal as a pilot for many years.

In response to his question regarding the ship turning trajectory, the computed trajectory in very shallow water shows a consistently milder turn relative to the one in deep water in Fig. 24. Although the shallow-water trajectory is intersecting the deep-water trajectory at the heading angle change of 270 deg, it is due to the greater advance made in shallow water due to smaller turning rate. The lower turning capability of the same ship in extremely shallow water relative to that in deep water is also shown in Fig. 26.

As Captain Vantine points out, it is very important for a ship with twin propellers to be equipped with twin rudders for satisfactory shiphandling characteristics. We have known a number of ships with twin propellers and a single rudder which exhibited poor shiphandling characteristics. This is due to lack of propeller stream flowing into the rudders. It should be emphasized here that the propeller stream has a major impact on rudder effectiveness, and that every effort should be made during the preliminary design stage to install twin rudders whenever a ship has a twin-propeller arrangement.

Although the effectiveness of a controllable-pitch propeller depends on specific ship conditions as Captain Vantine mentions, we believe that a controllable-pitch propeller is a promising direction to follow for superior shiphandling and increased propulsion efficiency under actual ship operating conditions.

In response to Mr. Johnson's question, the effects of increased ice thickness are in general more stabilizing; however, based on the data collected, specific aspects of behavior cannot be fully predicted for thickness outside the range of conditions tested. Results are also not entirely applicable to more conventional hull forms. The force distribution due to ice along the hull will be greatly influenced by both waterline and section shapes.

Professor Nomoto mentioned icebreaking forces and moments due to sway velocity, rudder angle, and also yaw velocity. We have obtained icebreaking forces and moments due to sway velocity and rudder angle in captive model tests. On the other hand, icebreaking force and moment due to yaw velocity were estimated and used in the simulation model to compare and verify actual ship turning trajectory.

It should be noted here that, although we have not carried out icebreaking captive model tests with yaw velocity, icebreaking force and moment were estimated and included in the simulation model, and refined by comparing with actual ship trial data in ice.

CDR Card's remark on ship-waterway design procedure is very useful by showing a step-by-step approach. We expect that his proposed procedure will be realized in an effective manner in the near future. He commented on conflicting requirements for maneuvering characteristics in open water and ice. We agree with him that to find a well-balanced compromise is important, and that more research is needed in this direction.

In response to Professor Fujino's remarks, a significant increase of inherent course stability characteristics was clearly evident in those results obtained in our studies based on actual ship trials, model tests, and computer simulations. It is needless to state here the complex nature of the icebreaking force to be represented by the mathematical model. Our effort toward the mathematical model under ice-covered water conditions is an exploratory one at this time. Accordingly, we hope that icebreaking effects can be clarified more in detail in the near future to the extent that we know hydrodynamic effects due to shallow water and restricted water.

Dr. Mikelis discussed hydrodynamic effects of the channel bank due to off-centerline displacement y_0 and the ship orientation ψ relative to the channel direction. It is believed that the hydrodynamic effect due to off-centerline displacement is a much more dominating factor than that due to the ship orientation. This is because the ship orientation ψ relative to the channel direction is only a small magnitude in actual ship operations in a channel. We hope that further study will clarify the hydrodynamic effect due to the ship orientation deviation relative to the channel direction. In this study, hydrodynamic coefficients were determined from a series of rotating-arm tests where sway and yaw velocities were kept constant. Acceleration coefficients were determined through stripwise computations in the deep-water case, and estimated restricted water effects were applied to finally determine the acceleration terms. It is our hope that further theoretical and experimental efforts will be made toward the hydrodynamic acceleration effect, in particular, in restricted water.

SNAME *Transactions*, Vol. 90, 1982, pp. 229–248

Upgrading Steering Gear Systems from Inception to Operation

Vincent W. Ridley,[1] Visitor, and **Yair Henkin,**[1] Member

Upgrading existing steering systems (higher standards for new steering system) will shortly become international law through amendments and protocols to the existing SOLAS convention. A discussion of the risk of steering failures and their characteristics shows how the "regulations" were conceived. An analysis of the casualty and failure data explains why the regulations were formulated as they were. A retrofit program for a fleet of ships operating internationally presented a management and logistics challenge to maintain a program schedule dictated by the normal ship repair periods. Computer management devices were used extensively to monitor costs and progress to ensure on-time completion. The decision to proceed with retrofitting the vessels was based on philosophy that the installations should meet the intent of IMCO to improve the availability of steering systems after a single failure occurred even if this required hardware in excess of the minimum specified by IMCO. From this criterion an emergency hydraulic rudder arresting system (EHRAS) was designed which was completely independent of the other pumps, piping, wiring, etc. The system is manually controlled from the steering gear room. The service experience of EHRAS to date has been excellent.

Introduction

THE PROPOSED and newly enacted steering gear regulations of the International Maritime Consultative Organization (IMCO) reflect the concerns of the maritime nations about the sea and coastal environments. The catalyst for the latest round of regulations was the protests following a series of steering gear-related incidents of floundering and grounding in the mid-1970's. The regulations of IMCO, the implementing rules of the maritime nations, and the response by shipowners sensitive to the public pressures influenced the regulators of the shipping industry. Fortunately, most shipowners agree on the ultimate goal of improved regulations and the upgrading of steering systems. The task is how to achieve the objective.

In February 1978, IMCO sponsored the Tanker Safety and Pollution Prevention (TSPP) Conference concerning safety and antipollution issues and the international regulations affecting steering gear controls. The results of the TSPP conference were incorporated into the U.S. Port and Tanker Safety Act (PTSA) of 1978 which mandated, unilaterally, that these TSPP provisions be met by both U.S.-flag vessels and non-U.S.-flag vessels which trade in U.S. waters. And thus began the latest process of upgrading steering gear systems, a process which continues today.

Subsequent to TSPP, the proposed IMCO regulations were strengthened by the Marine Safety Committee (MSC) of IMCO which expanded the proposed regulations into all aspects of steering gear design and operations. The latter regulations are being added to SOLAS 74 (Safety of Life at Sea) as an amendment. Therefore the regulations which evolved from the considerations of these two aspects of IMCO are found pri-

marily in the SOLAS protocols, Amendments to SOLAS 74, and flag and regulatory body rules.

Upgrading steering systems to comply with the latest regulations will affect both existing vessels and newbuildings. The regulations affect all ships in various degrees and applications, with the most stringent applying to new tankers over 100 000 dwt. Singling out tankers and chemical carriers forced tanker owners to address themselves to the problem quickly and from a different viewpoint. A tanker owner should require that the steering gear modification he installs not only meet IMCO regulations but also attain the higher reliability and availability desired. This paper deals with the implementation of the new regulation from inception to service.

Basic philosophy of the perceived problem

To understand the nature of the improvements mandated and the form of the regulations, it would be useful to understand the nature of the risk and consequences of failure as applied to steering gear systems discussed herein.

What is the risk?—The risk is a failure of the steering system, which could cause a loss of a ship through floundering, collision, grounding, etc. In the case of a tanker, a major pollution incident is possible.

Who is bearing the risk?—The risk bearers are the seamen and their families, the coastal communities, the fishermen and fishing grounds, the corporation and corporate stock holders.

What is the character of the risk?—It is a unique, insurable, low-probability, once-in-a-lifetime event that can affect a country's economy, ecology, industry, and the owning company property and reputation.

The regulations define what risk is being addressed. The regulators define solutions, the object of which is to eliminate the risk incident due to a single failure, which, unattended, could cause a complete loss of steering. The regulations then specify solutions which are acceptable. This single-failure criterion tends to favor automatic systems that take over and realign the components of the system to isolate the failed

[1] Exxon International Company, Florham Park, New Jersey.

For presentation at the Annual Meeting, New York, N. Y., November 17–20, 1982, of THE SOCIETY OF NAVAL ARCHITECTS AND MARINE ENGINEERS.

Presented at the Annual Meeting, New York, N. Y., November 17–20, 1982, of THE SOCIETY OF NAVAL ARCHITECTS AND MARINE ENGINEERS.

Table 1　Reported steering gear failures

U. S. Coast Guard: Based on 173 Steering Related Casualties	ABS: Based on 70 Steering Gear Failure Reports	Type of Steering Gear Failure
13.9%	51.4%	mechanical parts
13.9%	...	power failure
16.2%	2.9%	hydraulic system failure
15.6%	11.4%	power unit, including motor
3.4%	2.9%	cylinders, rams, rotary, vane housing
26.6%	15.7%	rudder angle indicator and control system
10.4%	15.7%	unexplained or consequential damage

component and put working components to work. The regulators assume that there will be no automation failure because that would be a second failure, which is not to be considered under the base case. Newbuilding regulations are a direct effect of this approach.

Since the major risk bearers (coastal communities) are not, by and large, directly involved with ship operation, the economics of prevention is not their primary concern. Initially, most steering gear manufacturers did not react to the momentum building up for regulations, adopting a wait-and-see attitude confident that they could conform to whatever the new rules brought. This attitude, coupled with indecision on what to do next, permitted regulators, without intimate knowledge of the systems, to propose far-reaching design requirements based upon, among other things, elimination of human error by preventing human intervention in reacting to failure. The initial regulatory proposals affecting system operation therefore were automatic systems which were to be superimposed on large tanker systems, and all newbuildings. Later, as other knowledgable people began to analyze the regulations, alternative solutions to automation were proposed for existing tankers. One such industry group that considered the problem of how best to accomplish the desired upgrading was the Oil Companies International Marine Forum (OCIMF), who made suggestions to IMCO and flag states regarding other and possibly better methods of retrofitting equipment which would ensure steering system availability after a single failure.

The character of the risk is its uniqueness and randomness. Steering gear manufacturers have provided reliable equipment. The incidents that have occurred do not follow any obvious specific patterns and, therefore, the improvement must be to isolate large portions of the system and allow for corrective action to be taken after analysis. In the retrofit cases the regulators say this can be accomplished by:

Oil tanker, chemical tanker or gas carrier of 10,000 tons gross tonnage and upwards shall comply with the following:
(1.) Two independent steering gear control systems shall be provided each of which can be operated from the navigating bridge. This does not require duplication of the steering wheel or steering lever;
(2.) If the steering gear control system in operation fails, the second system shall be capable of being brought into immediate operation from the navigating bridge; and
(3.) Each steering gear control system, if electric, shall be served by its own separate circuit supplied from the steering gear power circuit or directly from switchboard busbars supplying that steering gear power circuit at a point on the switchboard adjacent to the supply to the steering gear power circuit.

In addition, on oil tanker, chemical tanker or gas carrier of 40,000 tons gross tonnage and upwards, the steering gear shall be arranged so that in the event of a single failure of the piping or of one of the power units, steering capability can be maintained or the rudder movement can be limited so that steering capability can be speedily regained. This shall be achieved by:
(i) An independent means of restraining the rudder; or
(ii) Fast acting valves which may be manually operated to isolate the actuator or actuators from the external hydraulic piping together with a means of directly refilling the actuators by a fixed independent power operated pump and piping system; or
(iii) An arrangement so that, where hydraulic power systems are interconnected, loss of hydraulic fluid from one system shall be detected, and the defective system isolated either automatically or from the navigating bridge so that the other system remains fully operational.

The most significant and far-reaching regulation applies to every new tanker from 10 000 gross tons (grt) and up, and requires that in response to a failure the failed portion of the steering gear system be isolated and that steering capabilities be regained in no more than 45 sec.

The actual meaning of this is that some sensing device shall:
1. sense that a failure has occurred, and
2. the failed system shall be recognized and safely isolated by automatic or remote means, and that within the time limit of 45 sec, steering capability shall be regained.

In the end, it was left to the shipowner whether the IMCO regulations, which are minimum, fulfill the intent of betterment or in his specific case should be augmented.

Decision process

The decision process was focused on the retrofit requirements on tankers as these were existing systems, and were being called to task by world opinion. The newbuilding regulations were very specific and left no options to be considered. Complete statistics on failures and troubles were not and are not available; however, there are special report statistics that give strong direction to the type of problem to be expected. The tabulation of the steering gear-related casualties submitted by the U.S. Coast Guard to IMCO, and a study of American Bureau of Shipping (ABS) reports of steering gear failures, produced valuable sets of statistics. These are shown side by side Table 1. Although the statistics are not totally consistent, they give strong indication where trouble lies for failures serious enough to involve the Coast Guard or ABS. The inference of the statistics are:

• The cylinders, rams, and rotary vane housing are reliable.

• The rudder angle indicator and control system should be considered when upgrading the steering gear systems. The statistics also infer that upgrading which relies solely on automatics may also be susceptible to failure (the 1978 SOLAS Protocols and the Port and Tanker Safety Act addresses primarily the control systems and how to improve them).

• Failures of mechanical parts external to steering gear are significant; however, they do not always lead to casualty.

• Hydraulic system failure is well covered by the new IMCO regulation by the requirement of isolating the failed part of the system while maintaining control with the other part of the system.

• The unexplained or consequential damage failure deals primarily with a scenario where more than a single failure occurred, not covered by IMCO regulations. It is the authors' opinion that for those unknown and unpredictable types of failures, the Emergency Hydraulic Rudder Arresting System (EHRAS) is a unique, simple and effective solution.

These statistics add support to the direction taken by IMCO and her implementum. IMCO does not address specific failure, but stresses that the ship must be able to cope with failure which is part of the steering system, but not of the rams, vanes, or housing.

Managing the upgrading program

Once having made the decision that the ships would be retrofitted with the ERHAS, and the upgraded steering gear system brought up to the standards of TSPP, SOLAS 74, etc., during one shipyard overhaul period cycle, the task became one of managing the retrofits program for approximately 70 ships in a period of $2\frac{1}{2}$ years or about 2.5 ships/month. These 70 ships would have six separate steering gear manufacturers further divided into 26 different steering gears of both the rotary vane and the Rapson-slide types, and 11 different retrofitting shipyards in eight countries on three continents.

The program required the use of a computer management program to monitor cost and skid locations. Several items were unique and significant. Changes in the standard computer programs were made to accommodate the special needs of ships on a repair cycle. The available software is set up so that the tracking and budget monitoring was done on a "calendar basis." The modification permitted monitoring to be done on a cumulative "ship basis" and subroutines were set up to change the order of the ship's cycle. The ships' schedule changed their position in the repair cycle. A computer-based graphical reporting system was initiated to monitor the total project (Fig. 1).

It was also necessary to monitor ships on an individual basis and to forecast expenditures for shipyard cost control. Figure 2 is a typical page from the computer report. The first category is engineering and accounts for in-house manpower and subcontracted engineering sources. The second category is freight costs. Some of the units and material were air-freighted, especially in the early phase of the project when equipment deliveries prohibited ocean freight. The third category is Owner-Furnished Equipment (OFE) and other purchased services further broken down into 13 categories as follows:

0001	Arresting skid and motor controller
0002	Valves
0004	Miscellaneous piping (spool pieces; elbow rings, various flanges)
0005	Service engineer
0006	Circuit breaker
0007	Telephone headset
0008	Hydraulic oil
0009	Instruction books
0010	Spare parts
0011	Level switches
0012	Special hoses
0013	Steering failure alarm
0014	Classification fees

This also acted as a convenient checkoff list. The last category is the shipyard's costs.

Horizontally the first group of numbers is the capital budget breakdown. The second group of numbers is the actual, estimated and forecast numbers based on the currency conversion at the inception of the project. The actual column is the invoiced amount and the estimated column is the quoted or revised estimate. The forecast amount is the best estimate of the final cost of the project. In developing the forecast, the computer first looks for actual numbers; if actual amounts are absent, the computer seeks out the estimated values and if they don't exist the budget amounts are used. In this manner the forecast is built from all the latest data. The third and last group of numbers contains the same information, modified, however, by the actual currency exchange rate. The forecasted amount when compared with the budgeted amount reflects the health of the project.

Because the ships were to be retrofitted during their repair period, the time between the repair specification going to the shipyard and the time the vessel is actually in the shipyard is short. Time constraints dictated a unitized type of equipment to be owner-furnished. Bids were solicited from steering gear manufacturers as well as other qualified concerns to manufacture the rudder arresting skid. Upon analysis of the bids returned, awards were made to four companies, one in Europe, two in Japan, and one in the United States. The majority of the vessels were awarded to the U.S. Company, which was competitive in both price and delivery. The uniqueness of the main steering gear design influenced the awards to some of the companies. Also at this time, many of the steering gear manufacturers were not interested in the retrofit program.

The owner-furnished equipment was to be installed as a package and it was necessary, therefore, that the owner provide detailed sets of drawings and specifications to the shipyard to allow them to do the installation. At this time none of the ship repair yards had made such installations. The detailed sets of drawings were made dependent on a ship survey outcome, which had to be conducted on each class of ships to determine the nature of the steering gear, and any special problems that existed in running the pipe, providing electrical cables in location of the skid, and to ensure compliance with the rules. It was also necessary to determine whether the installation would interfere with the hand-steering capability of the gear.

In making these surveys, the design engineer reviewed the steering flat arrangement; the existing installation and how it related to the office copy of the contract specification; and the current piping arrangement, comparing it with the specification, and choosing the location for the EHRAS and reserve and sump tanks.

The survey program found numerous instances in the older vessels where the electrical circuitry did not allow true splitting of the electrical system. Modifications were necessary on two of the electrical installations: elimination of two separate feeders leading to a common junction and from there to each of the power motors, and the common selection switch.

A standard checkoff list has been developed to provide the design engineer with information needed to generate plans and specifications that meet the particular vessel needs. The checkoff list is given in the Appendix.

In a number of cases, it had to be determined how to get the rudder arresting skid into the steering gear room as the skid itself exceeded the access available. The total number of plans per ship varied depending on the initial installation. Usually 12 plans/ship were needed, resulting in 850 plus plans for the project. A typical plan titles list included:

—Schematic piping diagram—EHRAS
—Arrangement—EHRAS pump set
—Piping arrangement—upgraded steering system—including EHRAS
—Electric schematic diagram—EHRAS control and alarms
—New sump tank (EHRAS)
—General arrangement of steering gear modifications
—Level switches
—Modified hydraulic oil storage tank
—Three-way ball valve with adapters
—Flexible hose assembly
—Equipment list
—Two-way ball valve with adapters

The equipment list is in sufficient detail to allow the shipyard to start with preparation for the non-OFE items such as low-pressure piping and electric cables prior to ship arrival.

The schematic piping diagram was later transposed into a computer tape and copies printed in two sizes to meet regula-

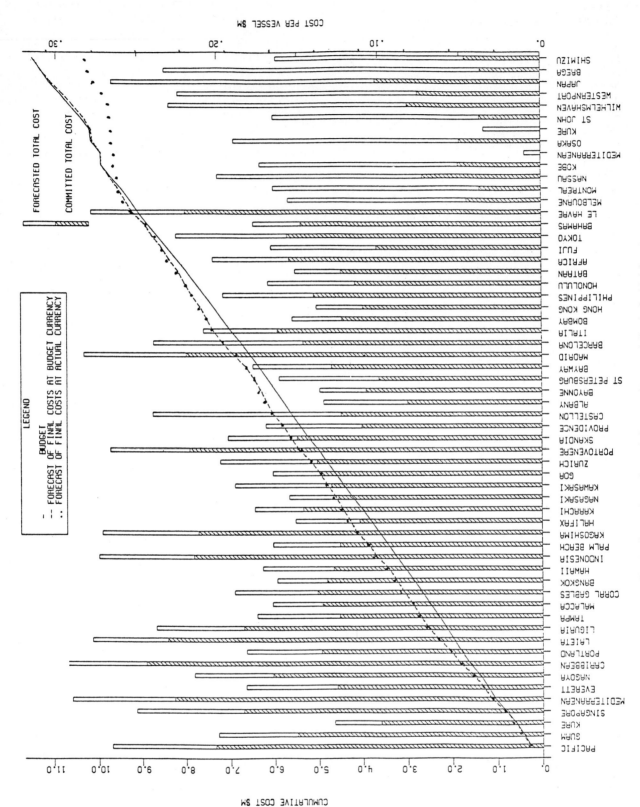

Fig. 1 Comparison of cumulative-actual to cumulative-budget total cost

tory requirements to post a mimic diagram on the bridge and steering gear compartment. The computer drawing could easily and cheaply be modified for similar installations. The final drawings were laminated and framed for mounting (see Figs. 3 and 4).

With the owner furnishing the equipment, the plans and the specifications, the complete retrofit could be accomplished easily within a normal 14-day repair period.

The delivery schedule for the OFE was monitored to meet shipyard schedule and with one exception all deliveries were made on time. Deliveries of equipment are taken and shipments consolidated and integrated with other items being prepared for the ships. The warehousing and shipment of the containers were controlled by in-house personnel and aided by the computer to monitor and control the programs.

Design basis for a retrofit of an EHRAS system

For retrofitting, the implementing philosophy is to provide a high-quality steering gear rudder arresting system that in an emergency can arrest the motion of a swinging rudder and be used to steer the ship reliably for long periods. The design addresses the permitted alternate of an external power-operated pump and piping system separate from the main hydraulic system which can be used to refill the rams (or vanes) and arrest the rudder motion in the event of failure in the main system. These implementing design criteria are not limited or delineated in the IMCO regulations, but represent the execution of the stated philosophy. The system described has greater functional capability than required by IMCO. The EHRAS is also fitted on newbuildings.

The EHRAS consists of a hydraulic power pack, associated piping, and alarms. The pumping system is a skid-mounted unit in the steering gear room and hard piped directly into the main cylinders or vanes through half-turn, quick-acting, manually operated three-way ball valves bolted directly on the steering gear housing. These valves isolate the external main steering gear hydraulic piping from the EHRAS piping.

In most cases, the main steering gear pumps have their own sumps; however, in some cases sumps common to both main pumps were fitted and in these cases the sump tanks were modified so that they are split with a separate power operation. Two modes of operation concern the main system with the main system split, where either main pump may be used to operate the steering gear independently of the other, with control on the bridge. The third mode is with the EHRAS pump, which is operated and controlled from the steering gear room. When splitting tank, care must be taken to ensure that sufficient cooling surface remains.

For a fleet operator, standardization is a normal and desirable goal. The design standard of the upgraded steering gear systems resulted in a single hydraulic system package, mounted on a skid, that can be assembled at any qualified manufacturing facility and shipped, as a unit, to an assigned destination. Standardization benefitted both the installation of the units and made it easier for the crew to operate the system.

Another advantage realized using the unit-type idea is the reduction of long-lead items to only two: (1) the rudder arresting skid and (2) the three-way fast-acting valves. It takes as much as six months to procure, manufacture, test, and deliver the long-lead items.

The skids have been designed to fit vessels of all sizes from the handy size of 20 000 dwt to the ultra large crude carriers (ULCC's) of over 500 000 dwt using identical components, with the exception of

a. electric motor—to meet pump driving power needs,

b. screw-type pump—to comply with flow/pressure requirements, and

Fig. 2 Typical page from computer output of 1980 Steers Program Budget—cost breakdown

1980 STEERS PROGRAM BUDGET COST BREAKDOWN — REPORT DATE 26MAR82, PAGE 31

SORT CODE	SHIP NAME	COMP	EQUIP	BUDGET $	CURRENCY CONV. TO BUDGET	ACTUAL BUDGET ESTIMATE	ACTUAL CURRENCY ESTIMATE	ACTUAL CURRENCY FORECAST	FUTURE CURRENCY ESTIMATE	FUTURE CURRENCY FORECAST
31000	BAYONNE	ENGR	1	19320	1.0000	22000	22000	22000	22000	22000
		ENGR		19320	1.0000	22000	22000	22000	22000	22000
		FRGT		10870	1.0000	1500	1500	1500	1500	1500
		OWNR	0001	67010	1.0000	28065	28065	28065	28065	28065
			0002		1.0000	7295	7295	7295	7295	7295
			0003		1.0000	7617	7617	7617	7617	7617
			0004		1.0000		1		1	
			0005		1.0000	430	430	430	430	430
			0006		1.0000	302	302	302	302	302
			0008		1.0000	2000	2000	2000	2000	2000
			0009		1.0000	1550	1550	1550	1550	1550
			0011		1.0000	168	168	168	168	168
			0014		1.0000	2000	2000	2000	2000	2000
31000	BAYONNE	OLAR		67010	1.0000	43877	5551	49428	5551	45428
		YARD		88900	1.0000	63480	57700	63480	57700	63480
				186100		107357	86751	136408	86751	136408

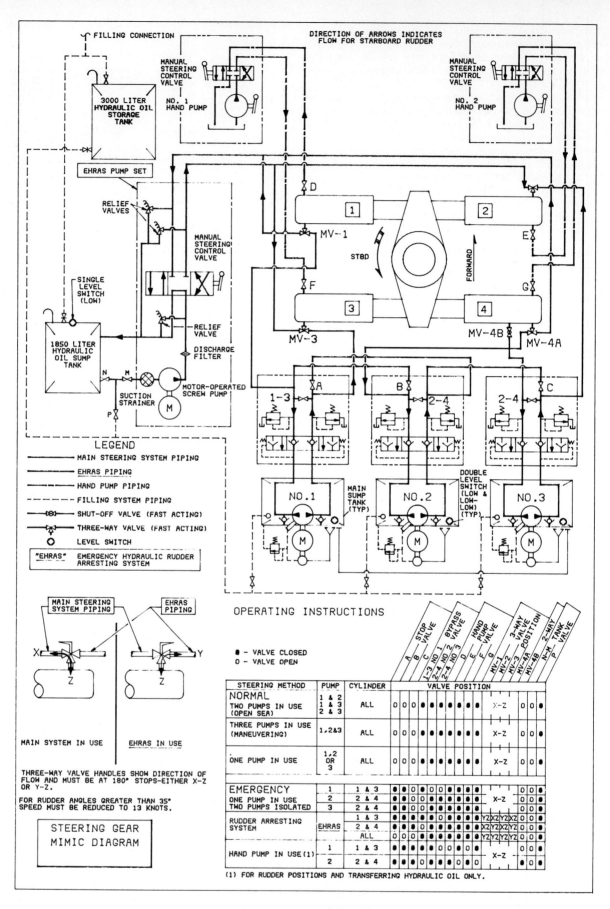

Fig. 3 Steering gear—mimic diagram

Upgrading Steering Gear Systems

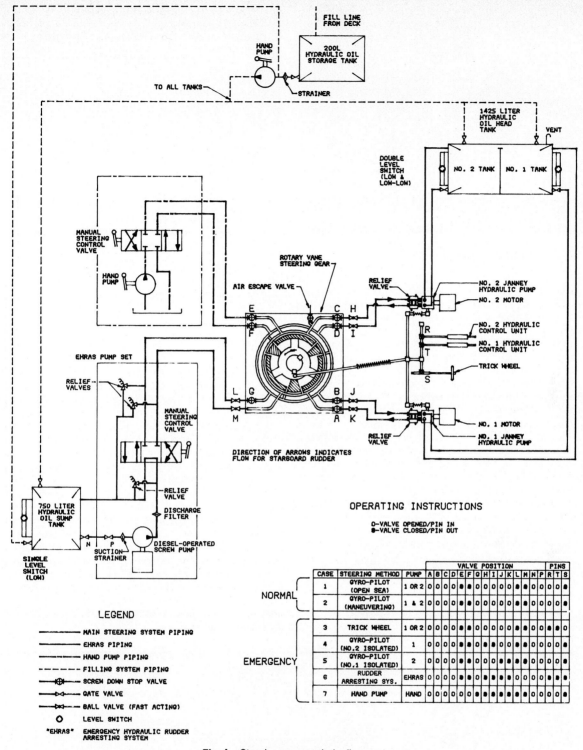

FILL LINE
FROM DECK

200L
HYDRAULIC OIL
STORAGE TANK

HAND PUMP

TO ALL TANKS — STRAINER

1425 LITER
HYDRAULIC
OIL HEAD
TANK — VENT

DOUBLE
LEVEL
SWITCH
(LOW &
LOW-LOW)

NO. 2 TANK | NO. 1 TANK

MANUAL STEERING CONTROL VALVE

HAND PUMP

ROTARY VANE STEERING GEAR

AIR ESCAPE VALVE

RELIEF VALVE

NO. 2 JANNEY HYDRAULIC PUMP
NO. 2 MOTOR
NO. 2 HYDRAULIC CONTROL UNIT
NO. 1 HYDRAULIC CONTROL UNIT
TRICK WHEEL

EHRAS PUMP SET

RELIEF VALVES

MANUAL STEERING CONTROL VALVE

DIRECTION OF ARROWS INDICATES FLOW FOR STARBOARD RUDDER

NO. 1 MOTOR
NO. 1 JANNEY HYDRAULIC PUMP
RELIEF VALVE

RELIEF VALVE

DISCHARGE FILTER

750 LITER HYDRAULIC OIL SUMP TANK

SINGLE LEVEL SWITCH (LOW)

SUCTION STRAINER

DIESEL-OPERATED SCREW PUMP

OPERATING INSTRUCTIONS

O–VALVE OPENED/PIN IN
●–VALVE CLOSED/PIN OUT

| | | | VALVE POSITION | | | | | | | | | | | | | | PINS | | | |
CASE	STEERING METHOD	PUMP	A	B	C	D	E	F	G	H	I	J	K	L	M	N	P	R	T	S
1	GYRO-PILOT (OPEN SEA)	1 OR 2	O	O	O	O	O	●	O	O	O	O	O	O	●	O	O	O	O	●
2	GYRO-PILOT (MANEUVERING)	1 & 2	O	O	O	O	O	●	O	O	O	O	O	O	●	O	O	O	O	●
3	TRICK WHEEL	1 OR 2	O	O	O	O	O	●	O	O	O	O	O	O	●	O	O	●	●	O
4	GYRO-PILOT (NO.2 ISOLATED)	1	O	O	O	O	O	●	●	O	O	●	O	O	●	O	O	O	O	●
5	GYRO-PILOT (NO.1 ISOLATED)	2	O	O	O	O	O	●	O	O	●	O	●	O	●	O	O	O	O	●
6	RUDDER ARRESTING SYS.	EHRAS	O	O	O	O	●	●	O	●	●	●	●	O	O	O	O	●	●	●
7	HAND PUMP	HAND	O	O	O	O	O	O	●	●	●	●	●	●	O	O	O	O	O	●

NORMAL — (Cases 1, 2)
EMERGENCY — (Cases 3–7)

LEGEND

——— MAIN STEERING SYSTEM PIPING
——— EHRAS PIPING
——— HAND PUMP PIPING
----- FILLING SYSTEM PIPING
—⊠— SCREW DOWN STOP VALVE
—▷◁— GATE VALVE
—▷◁— BALL VALVE (FAST ACTING)
O LEVEL SWITCH
"EHRAS" EMERGENCY HYDRAULIC RUDDER ARRESTING SYSTEM

Fig. 4 Steering gear—mimic diagram

c.   three-way valve—to interface with main line pipe size connections.

In some cases components were selected on the basis of the individual ship design and steering gear manufacturer.

The following guidelines have been followed in the design of the EHRAS.

1.   The EHRAS pump has the capability to move the rudder from +15 to −15 deg in about 60 sec with all four rams (or all vanes) in service.   The time was selected arbitrarily, and it is based on IMCO requirements for auxiliary steering gears.   The pressure developed by the pump is the same as the pressure developed by the main pump to ensure safety in extreme adverse weather conditions.   The EHRAS pump is either driven by an electric motor whose source of power is the emergency generator, or directly driven by a small diesel engine in the steering gear room.   The system with its local control is intended for emergency service, and is not intended to be another auxiliary gear (see Fig. 5).

Fig. 5 Typical EHRAS skid

Table 2   Alarm panels

Control & Alarm Requirements	Steering Gear and Cabinet	Bridge Cabinet	ECR[a] Cabinet
Power available	X	X	X
Tank No. 1 low level	X	X	X
Tank No. 1 low-low level	X	X	X
Tank No. 2 low level	X	X	X
Tank No. 2 low-low level	X	X	X
EHRAS sump tank low level	X	X	X
EHRAS feeder circuit breaker open	X	X	X
Steering Gear No. 1 power failure	...	X	X
Steering Gear No. 2 power failure	...	X	X
Steering Control System No. 1 power failure	...	X	X
Steering Control System No. 2 power failure	...	X	X
Transient alarm test	X	X	X
Lamp test	X	X	X
EHRAS motor start	X	...	...
EHRAS motor run indicator	X	...	...
EHRAS motor stop	X	...	...
EHRAS motor stop indicator	X	...	...

[a] Engine Control Room.

2.   The EHRAS pump is the constant-delivery screw type. Screw pumps are preferred for high-pressure hydraulic service although sliding-vane or gear pumps have been used for this application.

3.   The EHRAS pump has steel or ductile iron casings which are stronger than many of the other alloys used for this service. Steel is preferred for systems over 140 bars (2000 psig).

4.   The motor is totally enclosed, and fan-cooled with Class F insulation to ensure the highest reliability. It has an overload capability of 150 percent for 15 min per each hour. The motor could, therefore, run continuously in any weather.

5.   The discharge filter is steel encased and in line with the pump discharge to ensure maximum protection to the four-way control valve and the steering gear itself in the event that there should be a breaking up of the pump or the carriage of particulate matter through the pump. The EHRAS skid is made of heavy-scantlinged H-beams to provide the best foundation possible for the rotating machinery, ensuring reliability and availability of the equipment when needed.

6.   Two- and three-way high-pressure ball valves are used as isolating and transfer valves at the rams or vane housing. Ball valves meet the IMCO criterion of being fast acting. Locking devices are provided to prevent inadvertent opening or closing of these valves (see Fig. 6).

7.   The visual and audible alarms are grouped together in alarm panels. Alarm panels are located on the navigating bridge, the engine control room, and in the steering gear room itself. Also located on this panel are the EHRAS circuit-breaker alarms which are required by ABS. Test and acknowledgment buttons are provided for testing and thereby reduce the possibility of signal error (see Table 2).

8.   In many current designs sump tanks are common to both main system pumps. These sump tanks are removed and replaced with individual sump tanks or modified to be split. This permits independent operation of the main steering gear pumps. Care must be taken when modifying existing tanks to ensure that they can continue to act as heat sinks without external cooling requirements. The main sumps of many other steering gear systems are split in that each main pump has an independent sump.

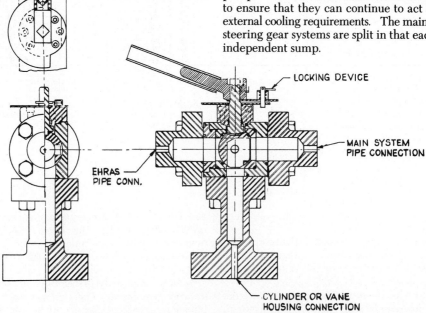

Fig. 6 Three-way ball valve assembly with spool adapters

Upgrading Steering Gear Systems

9. Reserve oil tanks and EHRAS sump tanks are provided. The reserve tank capacity is sized to meet IMCO requirements with permanent pipe connections to all sump tanks by gravity, if possible. Filling of the reserve tank is through permanent piping and strainer from the deck.

10. All new oil tanks are internally coated with two coats of 100-μm dry-film-thickness epoxy phenolic after proper surface preparation (SA-2-$\frac{1}{2}$).

11. Each of the main sump tanks is provided with two level alarm gages. The EHRAS sump tank has a single level alarm. Sight glasses are provided with automatic valves on the lower end to prevent spill in the event of glass breakage.

12. Flexible hoses and blank flanges are provided to bypass failed portions of the system. Hoses are not acceptable for long-term application. Hoses may be used only for emergency repairs to get the vessel into port, where permanent repairs must be made.

13. Rudder angle indicators in the EHRAS control stands in the steering gear room are provided for ease in determining the full scope of the rudder position.

14. American National Standards Institute (ANSI) flanges are provided as required by ABS in lieu of the more normal or older Society of Automotive Engineers (SAE) type which do not have such approval.

15. Twenty-four-volt dc electricity is supplied to the control of the EHRAS of John Hastie Ltd. design. Other steering gear systems do not have this, nor do they require it.

16. High-quality alloy steel four-way hydraulic control valves are provided for directional control of the steering gear when using the EHRAS system.

17. Antiskid surfaces and handrails are provided in the steering gear room. Antiskid paint, using copper slag, is satisfactory; however, nonskid gratings have been successfully used.

18. Safety valves on the EHRAS system ensure safe operation and protection from induced pressure due to external forces on the rudder.

Control and alarm system

A remote alarm annunciator system is provided and integrated into a complete control and alarm system. The control/alarm system is a control panel situated in the steering gear room adjacent to the EHRAS, a remote visual/audible alarm cabinet on the bridge, and another in the engine control room. All components are suitable for shipboard service and are designed to withstand shock and vibration experienced in steering gear rooms. The power for the control and alarm system is supplied from the emergency generator panel.

The annunciator system includes audible and visual alarms. Alarm activation is normally an open-field contact type. An alarm condition is brought to the operator's attention by the sounding of an audible device and flashing annunciator at each alarm cabinet. Acknowledgment and circuit testing features are included.

Table 2 itemizes the audible and visual alarms for an upgraded two-pump steering gear system and EHRAS.

Control of the EHRAS is provided in the steering gear room only. Run/Stop pushbuttons and indicator lights are provided on the panel for local control. Instructions for rudder movement are via a sound-powered telephone from the bridge.

Retrofit alternatives

Systems other than the EHRAS have been developed that fulfill the rules. Some of them can be considered as variations of the EHRAS and others are intended to fulfill the other options specified.

The available systems can be segregated into three groups:

1. Using an independent hydraulic power system connected to the ram cylinders for the Rapson-slide type steering gear and to the vane housing for the rotary vane type steering gear with isolation capability of the main power systems.

2. Capability to automatically split the main system into two subsystems and to isolate, when a single failure occurs, the failed part of the system and maintain steering capability with the other part of the system.

3. Combination of Groups 1 and 2. This system is detailed in the next section of the paper, "Steering gear—new generation," and is the author's company's choice for the newbuilding steering gear system.

These three groups can be divided into systems that meets the retrofit needs of various owners.

Group I: EHRAS and its variations—

1. Alarm annunciating system located on the bridge, engine control room (ECR) and in steering gear room. Manual changeover and steering control in the steering gear room only.

2. Alarm annunciating system located on the bridge and steering gear room. Remote switchover and control from the bridge.

3. Alarm annunciating system on bridge and steering gear room. Automatic switchover and remote control from the bridge.

4. Other variations.

Group II: Automatic isolation—

1. The Hastie Supervisory System includes a detecting/alarm system with automatic isolation, logic and control that splits the main steering gear system and isolates the failed portion, maintaining steering control.

2. The new-generation steering gear system described in this paper excluding the EHRAS portion.

Group III: Combination of automatic isolation and independent power source—

1. The new-generation steering gear system with the EHRAS as described in this paper.

2. Four-ram steering gear with redundant steering system developed for Amoco Co. See paper "Redundant Steering System" by W. P. Towner. The system includes an alarm detecting system, a remote control and isolation system, all operated from the bridge. Once a failure is detected, a pushbutton on the bridge will isolate the main power system and cut power off. It will start the emergency power system and provide instantaneous fluid pressure from accumulators to the system.

3. Cunningham method and apparatus for auxiliary control of fluid operated steering gear (U.S. Patent #4,209,986 dated July 1, 1980). Includes isolation of existing steering control system and provision of flow under pressure from external source using accumulators.

Steering gear—new generation

Influenced by the tendency of the shipping industry to automate, the first basic improvement in steering gear systems called for automatic controls to isolate the fault in the system and place the remaining working systems on line. Only later on was it realized that a fully automatic system and control may not be the best practical solution as a retrofit on many of the vessels presently in operation. It is apparent that most steering gear manufacturers are not going to improve their basic design but will comply with the regulations by adding additional control components and sensing devices.

Several solutions have been put in force which meet IMCO's criterion for a single failure and were adopted during the November 1981 meeting.

For newbuildings, automatic isolation of the steering gear system without the loss of steering capability is mandatory. The rule requirement and rationale is that no single casualty will deny a vessel steering capability. The irony is that to comply with requirements by adding components such as solenoids and actuators, each component of a system has a finite probability of failure and, therefore, increases the total probability of failure, resulting in a reduction in the total reliability of the "upgraded" system. In this case we are trading between this reduction in reliability for a presumed increase in availability.

Design requirements by owners for new constructions should contain all of the requirements approved by IMCO for newbuildings and the special needs of the owner. These requirements imposed on steering gear manufacturers will force them to upgrade their basic design to meet demand and to stay in competition. This new design can be considered as the "new generation of steering gear."

New-system description

The steering gear is of the electro-hydraulic Rapson-slide two-ram or vane type with two independent power plants, control and alarm systems, each capable of providing 100 percent of the torque necessary to meet regulatory agency requirements and arranged to provide adequate working space around assembled units.

The working space is provided with handrails and nonslip surfaces to ensure safety in the event of oil spillage. The steering gear system is designed with full regard to strength requirements, allowance for rudderstock rise, and vertical weld and rudderstock bearings.

Each main power plant has its power supply from an independent power source; that is, one power plant receives its power supply from the main switchboard whereas the other power plants receives its power supply from the emergency power source. The power supply from each switchboard is totally independent.

Each of the main power systems is provided with a relief valve and automatic shutoff valves directly mounted on the cylinder housing for ram-type steering gears or on the vane housing for vane-type steering gears. Each of the automatic shutoff valves is provided with a manual override arrangement and position-indicating device.

Where pressure-sensing-type double check valves are employed, another type of alarm signal is required to distinguish automatic shutoff during normal operation vis-à-vis one that occurred during the failure of the system. Where a steering gear system contains cross connection between two power units, the automatic shutoff or isolation valves can be located away from the cylinder or housing provided a manual shutoff valve is added at the cylinder or housing connection.

Each of the hydraulic power plants is provided with its own sump oil tank with low-level alarm indicators. Tank capacity is designed to fill the steering gear system and to be able to be used as a heat sink without external cooling.

An additional reserve tank (100 percent capacity of the main system), including the two main sump tanks, is provided with filling arrangement from the main deck. An in-line fine-mesh filter (10 to 20 μm) is provided in a bypass line receiving continuously 15 percent of the total rated flow with an alarm for a clogged condition.

All pressure piping between the hydraulic power plant and the steering gear engine is of seamless steel with wide sweeps at all bends and with flanges welded on. All servo line connections and low-pressure lines should be flanged if possible.

Otherwise, a self-sealing-type threaded connection is recommended. All refill, drain or vent lines are of the fixed-pipe type and flange connected. Threaded pipe connection is not recommended. Special considerations are required for pressure above 17.25 MPa (2500 psi).

An emergency hydraulic rudder arresting system (EHRAS) consisting of the hydraulic pump and motor with a separate pipe system, hydraulic tank, isolation valve, safety valves, and local control is provided in addition to the main steering gear system. The EHRAS is connected to the ram cylinders or the vane housing and is capable of operating the rudder from 15-deg port to 15-deg starboard in 60 sec. Power supply to this system is from the emergency generator. The pump has an adequate capacity to act as a brake to arrest and hold the rudder in the event of a steering gear failure; that is, design pressure is the same as for the main system.

The main steering gear is so arranged that the single failure in its piping or in one of the power units may be isolated automatically so that the integrity of the remaining part of the steering gear will not be impaired.

The control and alarm system is integrated as part of the ship's control and alarm system on the bridge, in the engine control room and in the steering gear compartment. A typical annunciator requirement is provided in Table 3.

An independent electrical control steering system for automatically or manually controlling the main steering gear system is provided. The control system is console-mounted in the steering section of the bridge console. Steering controls are arranged so that the helm wheel is located on the centerline of the vessel.

Two independent control systems, each of which can be operated from the navigation bridge, are provided. The electric motors can be started and stopped from the wheelhouse, the engine control room, and the steering gear room. The main steering gear power is arranged to start automatically when power is restored after failure. Audible and visual alarms are provided in the navigating bridge, engine control room, and steering gear room, so that they can be readily observed. A rudder failure alarm system is installed with a synchro-type transmitter or equivalent in the navigating bridge and rudder angle follower in the steering gear room. Overload lights for all pump motors are provided.

The two following examples illustrate the design described above. The first example illustrates an automatic isolation of the ram-type steering gear system manufactured for four 87 000-dwt crude carriers currently being built in Taiwan. The second example illustrates a vane-type fully automatic isolatable steering gear system manufactured for three special-product carriers of 43 000-dwt being built in the United States.

Figure 7 provides schematic diagrams of the two ram-type steering gear systems with fully automatic isolation capability upon loss of oil from the main sump tanks and with fully independent EHRAS system connected to the cylinder through a manually operated root-type stop valve. The failure-detecting system logic operates as follows:

A three-position oil level sensing switch is mounted on each of the main power unit sump tanks. When units operate normally the oil level switches in the sump tanks are in the "off" position. If a failure occurs somewhere in the system, such as a pipe failure when a single pump unit, No. 1 for example, is in operation, oil from the sump tank will be lost through the failed pipe. The first low-level alarm will sound at the same time that the pilot pump automatically starts. When the second low-level alarm sounds, the system isolation valve, marked "SV1," is energized to isolate the system. At this point the system operates with Nos. 3 and 4 cylinders while Nos. 1 and 2 cylinders are in a bypass mode. At this condition, two events can occur:

Table 3   Typical control and alarm system annunciator requirements

Item	Particular	Steering Gear Compartment			Wheelhouse			Engine Control Room		
		Control	Indicator Light	Alarm	Control	Indicator Light	Alarm	Control	Indicator Light	Alarm
Electric motor Main pump (each) and control system	start/stop	X			X			X		
	running		O			O			O	
	overload			⊗			⊗			⊗
	no voltage			⊗			⊗			⊗
	circuit breaker						⊗			⊗
Electric motor for steering gear pump # (each)	on/off control no voltage	X		⊗			⊗			⊗
Electric motor for servo pump (each)	start/stop (automatic start)	X	O		X	O		X X	O	
Electric motor (EHRAS)	start/stop	X								
	running		O							
	overload			⊗						
	circuit breaker			⊗			⊗			⊗
Main Sump Tank (for Each Pump)	low level			⊗			⊗			⊗
	low-low level			⊗			⊗			⊗
	low-low-low level			⊗			⊗			⊗
EHRAS sump tank	low level			⊗						
Solenoid valve (each) for Isolation	]open		O			O			O	
	]shut			⊗			⊗			⊗
Solenoid valve (bypass)	]open			⊗			⊗			⊗
	]shut		O			O			O	
Filter	clogged			⊗			⊗			⊗
Rudder failure alarm							⊗			⊗

X—control location; O—indicates lights only; ⊗—visual and audible alarms.

1.   The system will continue to operate on half its total capacity.   This will identify the failure to be at the isolated part of the steering gear system.

2.   If, on the other hand, the third low-level alarm is sounded, the isolating valve SV1 will de-energize and return to its original position and isolation valve SV2 will energize and will stop any oil leak from Cylinders 1 and 2.   When the third low-level signal sounds, personnel in control on the bridge will start No. 2 unit and shut off No. 1 unit.   When No. 2 unit is in operation, the same sequence of events will apply, except for substituting No. 2 for No. 1 wherever it appears and isolating valves SV2 for SV1 wherever they appear.

Figure 8 provides a schematic diagram of a vane-type steering gear system with fully automatic isolation capability. Upon a loss of oil pressure from the main power unit, a double-check shutoff valve sensitive to the main system line pressure will automatically shut off.   Manual shutoff valves, located between the double-check valves and the vane as part of the housing, are provided for additional security.

A fully independent EHRAS system connected to the vane housing with manual shutoff valves is provided.   The failure detection logic system in the vane-type steering gear system is even simpler than for the ram type, and functions as follows:

• The double-check valve is line pressure sensitive.   Any failure in the feed line to the vane housing will automatically reduce line pressure and will lock the rudder by automatically putting the double-check valve in the "close" position.   This will normally eliminate the possibility of losing oil and arrest the rudder to eliminate the possibility of getting air into the system.

• A loss of pressure will at the same time activate the pressure alarm gage to alert the personnel on the bridge.   A change of units from Unit 1 to Unit 2 will transfer the systems and auto-matically isolate the failed part of the system without loss of steering control.

• Any alarm in the main oil sumps will also initiate the same action, that is, change from working unit to the second unit. Once the units are changed and the system is isolated, corrective action may take place while full steering control is maintained.

Shipyard experience

The basis for imposing strict requirements demanding first-quality workmanship in the design and construction phases of the project is the result of a goal established in its inception. There was no time scheduled for error.   The time assigned for the implementation of the project was $2\frac{1}{2}$ years, equal to one shipyard overhaul period cycle; the design and implementation had to be successful at the first try.

The choice of the shipyard and its ability to undertake this type of a project was not the overriding criteria for repair yard selection.   Not all ship repair yards are familiar with the need to provide the type of service required to install high-pressure hydraulic systems with a high level of reliability.   Shipyard specifications, therefore, were written emphasizing in detail the installation requirements, especially pertaining to the high-pressure hydraulic system, such as pickling of pipes in preparation for welding, welding, flushing of the system, and hydrotesting.

During the early retrofitting program, it became evident that the world's shipyards could not procure high-pressure pipe and high-pressure ball valves in the time available between the repair specification bid and the actual installation.   It was therefore necessary for the steering gear retrofit package to get to the shipyard as a "do-it-yourself" kit which would include

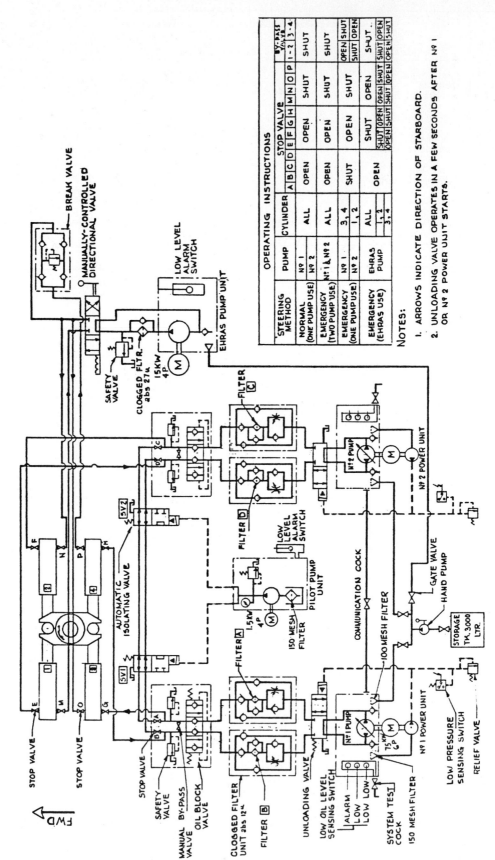

Fig. 7 Hydraulic circuit

A ROTARY VANE STEERING GEAR
VA PRESSURE CONTROL VALVE (ANALOG PROPOR)
VP PRESSURE RELIEF VALVE (BAR)
VD PILOT CONTROLLED DOUBLE CHECK VALVE
PS PUMP SET
PV AXIAL PISTON PUMP IN CASING
PC AUXILIARY PUMP
PE EMERGENCY PUMP SET
FJ FILTER
CY HYDR. ADJUSTING DEVICE
TO OIL TANK
VT SHUTTLE VALVE
VC CHECK VALVE
VU SWITCH OVER VALVE
VO OVERFLOW VALVE
SP PRESSURE SWITCH
JL OIL LEVEL
SP3 PRESSURE SWITCH
MP MEASURE POINT
V SHUT-OFF VALVE
SFT STROKE FEEDBACK TRANSMITTER (SPERRY)

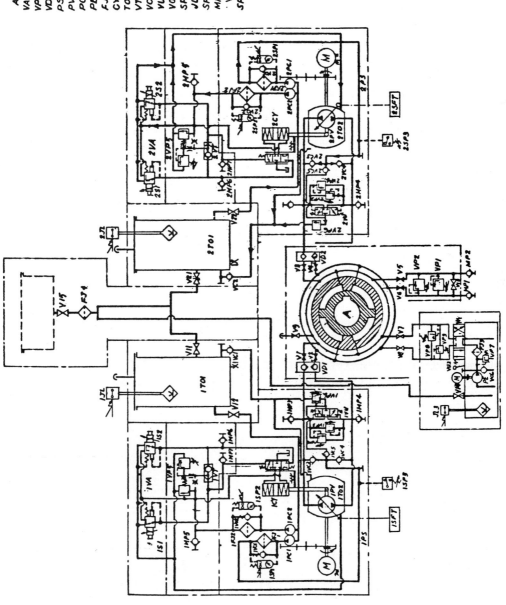

Fig. 8 Hydraulic schematic

Table 4 Sea trial for EHRAS

Vessel name		Esso Karachi		Esso Coral Gables		Esso Honolulu		Esso Laieta		Esso Mediterranean	
Vessel size		21 000 dwt		37 200 dwt		279 000 dwt		40 000 dwt (LNG carrier)		450 000 dwt	
Type of steering gear		rotary vane		Rapson slide		Rapson slide		rotary vane		Rapson slide	
EHRAS power capacity		48-hp diesel drive pump		electrical 15 hp		electrical 50 hp		electric 15 hp		electric 125 hp	
EHRAS/main system flow capacity		100%		30%		16.6%		12.5%		21%	

SEA TRIAL TESTS

Vessel Speed	Sweep Angle	Time (sec)	Pump Max. Pressure	Time (sec)	Pump Max. Pressure	Time (sec)	Pump Max. Pressure	Time (sec)	Pump Max. Pressure	Time (sec)	Pump Max. Pressure
At half speed ahead	15°P to 15°S	13.5	n/a	23		55		48		44	
	15°S to 15°P	13.5		23	550 psig	55	800 psig	56	175 psig	44	750 psig
At full speed ahead	15°P to 15°S	13	n/a	n/a		51	940 psig	52		45	
	15°S to 15°P	13		n/a		54	940 psig	67	200 psig	45	900 psig
At half speed ahead	35°P to 35°S	32	n/a	60		145		142		121	
	35°S to 35°P	32		60	750 psig	142	940 psig	152	350 psig	120	1200 psig
Time to switchover		250 sec[a]		66 sec		65 sec		80 sec		n/a	

[a] This vessel was not equipped with fast-acting valves and the changeover required manual closing of four threaded-type shutoff valves and the opening of two shutoff valves. The vessel will be equipped with fast-acting valves during her next scheduled shipyard stopover.
1 psig = 6.894 kPa.   1 dwt = 1.016 047 metric tonnes.   1 hp = 0.7457 kW.

all pipe, valves, level switches, control and alarm panels, as well as the emergency hydraulic rudder-arresting skid and the fast-acting valves.

Experience gained during the installation period of the steering gear systems in different yards identifies some typical problems that, if addressed early enough and correctly, will improve efficiency and quality of work and reduce the potential of errors during installation.

• One problem that arose often in terms of frequency and consequences was the wrong installation of the high-pressure piping system where many sections of the piping system, or all of the existing piping systems, have been replaced.

• Workmanship in the yards on occassion was less than adequate and led to problems. Most notable of these was a case where the yard reused pipe flange bolts which had been severely worn with damaged threads. Later on when the system was subjected to high-pressure fluctuation the flange could not sustain the pressure, resulting in oil leaks that could have led to a serious problem. Corrective action by the crew using the EHRAS, and later on splitting the system, maintained control of the rudder and brought the vessel safely to port.

• Equipment designated as shipyard supply (under the assumption that low-pressure fittings, valves, gages and other auxiliaries are "off the shelf" items) was found hard to get and in some cases needed special handling.

• The installation period is an excellent time to train and familiarize the crew with the new system operation and capabilities. Ample time should be allotted to train key personnel in the emergency operation.

EHRAS—sea trial procedure

A sea trial procedure has been developed to demonstrate the operation capability of the EHRAS while the vessel is underway. Maneuvering tests are performed with the vessel operating at different speeds to demonstrate rudder angle movements and to check system performance capability.

The test requirements are limited to the demonstration of time necessary to change from the main steering gear system to the EHRAS after receiving a simulated loss of main steering gear alarm. The time it takes to complete this operation and maintain control with the EHRAS is recorded. The system is tested for its capability by moving the rudder from 15° port to 15° starboard in no more than 60 sec while the ship moves at one half of its normal speed ahead.

Time data and pressure at the cylinders or vanes are recorded. The test is repeated several times to establish satisfactory data. The test is repeated with vessel speed increased to full speed ahead.

The capability of the EHRAS to move the rudder from 35 deg port to 35 deg starboard at no specified rate is conducted at one half of the normal vessel speed.

Table 4 provides some actual sea trial data taken during sea trials of some of our vessels retrofitted with EHRAS.

Steering gear inspection and testing procedures

A steering gear inspection and test procedure has been developed to protect the system and its pertinent components. This procedure is considered a guide for ship's personnel to follow as it is their responsibility to ensure system safety and availability whenever needed.

A. Within 12 hr before departure, the ship steering gear, steering control system, and EHRAS are to be checked and tested by the ship's personnel following a detailed checklist and procedure developed for that purpose by the vessel's officers and based on the following:

1. Visual inspection of steering gear room by engineering officer to ensure that steering gear equipment is completely assembled and free of any obstructions prior to operational tests.
2. Check that all fast-acting valves are in the right position and that all other valves are open and closed as shown in the mimic diagram posted in the steering gear room for the main system normal operation.
3. Check all oil tanks, sump, and reserve tanks to ensure that they are full.
4. Test all alarms related to the steering gear system by activating test patterns on the alarm panels. All communication devices in the steering gear room to other locations shall also be tested.
5. Where automatic shutoff valves and bypass valves are provided, they should be checked for adequate operation.

Upgrading Steering Gear Systems

6. Start each pump and test the main system by moving the rudder from 0 to 35 deg port and then to 35 deg starboard, then back to zero. Repeat a few times. Continue with two-pump operation running simultaneously, following the same procedure. When the system proves to be in good working condition, secure the pumps.
7. Change fast-acting valve position from the main system to the EHRAS system. Start EHRAS unit and test by moving the rudder from 0 to 35-deg port and then to 35-deg starboard, then back to zero. Repeat a few times.
8. For vessels equipped with an independent power source for the emergency steering system, such as a diesel driven hydraulic pump, the diesel engine shall be tested, started, and run in a declutched condition for a minimum of 15 min before commencing with Test No. 7 of the foregoing.

B. Within every four-week period, demonstrate emergency procedures, check equipment, and train personnel to act and take effective corrective action in the event of a steering gear failure.

1. Demonstrate the EHRAS by changing from the main system to the emergency system by repositioning the fast-acting valve. Start the EHRAS system and run it for one half hour, moving the rudder from port to starboard every so often. This operation should also be performed with a diesel-driven EHRAS.
2. Check all control and alarm systems to ensure their function by testing of the failure alarms of the following equipment:
   - remote steering control system power failure
   - steering gear main system pump unit failure
   - [2] servo pump power failure
   - main sump tank for each pump
   - low and low-low level alarm
   - EHRAS sump tank low level
   - [2] all solenoid valves for isolation of main system
   - [2] filter clog pressure difference
3. Check oil level in all sumps, reserve tanks, and grease containers.
4. Visually check all pipe and pipe connections, packing glands, valves, and gages for oil leaks.
5. Visually check Rapson-slide bearings and general condition of foundation, bolt tightness, and pipe supports.
6. Check for proper storage of flexible hoses, flanges, and blank flanges.

Conclusions

The purpose for the implementation of IMCO steering gear regulations is to minimize the *risk* of failure. The successful design and installation of upgraded systems will reduce the number of casualties with dangerous consequences.

Translation of a German local newspaper clipping is the best proof of the preceding statement, at least in one case:

DUAL STEERING GEAR SAVES TANKER

Due to a dual steering system the Liberian oil tanker, *Esso Albany*, did not became a casualty. This safety installation which became compulsory only a short time ago made it possible, after failure of one of the systems during heavy weather, to anchor safely in the Elbe Estuary. There the near-casualty waited this night for four tugs who will escort the vessel during her Elbe transit.

─────────

[2] For new vessels equipped with automatic isolation and in-line filtration systems.

The EHRAS system, due to its nature, can act as a true independent system intended by the regulation and is recommended to become an integral part of future steering gear systems. This system can be used in conjunction with automatic systems or stand by itself on retrofits, and it represents a satisfactory method of improving steering availability on existing and new tonnage.

Bibliography

Hay, P. L., "Developing Technology for Improved Steering Gear Reliability," SNAME Great Lakes and Great Rivers Section Meeting, Jan. 22, 1981.

Henkin, Y. and Ridley, V. W., "Steering Gears—Regulations and Solutions," Institute of Marine Engineers, March 27, 1981.

"Consideration and Adoption of the First Set of Amendments to the 1974 SOLAS Convention," Intergovernmental Maritime Consultative Organization, #MSCXLV/WP.3/Add. 1, Nov. 19, 1982.

"Rules and Regulations for Classification of Ships Part 5, Proposed Chapter 19, Steering Gear," Lloyd's Registry of Shipping, Print No. S.&E.1, Feb. 1, 1982.

Maxham, J. C., "Steering Gear Requirements: Changes on the International and Domestic Scene," *Marine Technology*, Vol. 18, No. 4, Oct. 1981, pp. 382–389.

"Navigation and Vessel Inspection Circular 1–81," U. S. Coast Guard, Washington, D. C., 1981.

Towner, W. P., "Redundant Steering System," presented at the API 1980 Tanker Conference, May 11–14, 1980.

Cunningham, R. F., Inventor (United States Patent #4,209,986 July 1, 1980) "Method of and Apparatus for Auxiliary Control of Fluid Operated Steering Apparatus for Ships, Boats and the Like."

Cowley, J., "Steering Gear: New Concepts and Requirements," The Institute of Marine Engineers, Jan. 18, 1982.

Appendix

Steering gear upgrading—survey data

Ship's Name_____
DWT_____
Survey Port _____

Hull No._____
SHP_____
Date_____

Class_____
Speed_____
Surveyor_____

Steering Gear Manufacturer _____
Type _____ Model No. _____
No. of Hydraulic Pumps _____ Torque per Pump _____
Max. Rudder Angle _____ Speed Limit _____
Max. Rated Torque at Rudder _____
Relief Valve Set Pressure _____ Test Pressure _____
System Oil Capacity _____
Tank (Existing) Capacity & Size _____
New Tanks Required _____
No. of Hand Pumps _____ Transfer Pump _____
Electric Motor: RPM _____ Voltage _____
    Amps _____ kW _____
Manufacturer of Control System _____
    Model _____
Rudder Angle Indicator Manufacturer _____
Remarks

_____
_____
_____

Is there room for skid? _____

Access to bring skid & tanks in? _____

Relocations necessary—Tank _____

Spares _____

Etc. _____

A. Existing Steering Gear Controls (Telemotor ____Electric _____)

    1. Are two systems completely separate

      a) Power Supply—

        Panel _____Location _____

        Panel _____Location _____

      b) Common Junction Boxes—Yes __ No __ Location _____

      c) Mode Selector Switches—

        Nav. Bridge _____

        Engine Room _____

        Steering Gear Room _____

        Selection Choices _____

    2. Can second control system be brought into immediate operation?
Yes __ No __

    3. Does control system have audible & visual alarm?
Yes __ No __
Location _____

    4. Rudder angle indicator system

      a) Location of all rudder angle repeaters _____

      b) Manufacturer & model number: Mfg. _____
Transmitter _____Repeater _____

      c) Voltage of repeater _____Scale Factor _____

      d) Number of repeaters on each transmitter circuit _____

      e) Can existing transmitter serve additional repeaters? _____
How many? _____

      f) Is space available to install additional transmitter? Yes __ No __

      g) Is system independent of steering gear remote control system? _____

    5. Manufacturer & Model of Steering Stand _____

B. Existing Steering Gear Power System

    1. Main Power Sources

      a) Motor No.

        1 Panel_____ Location_____

        2 Panel_____ Location_____

        3 Panel_____ Location_____

        4 Panel_____ Location_____

      b) Are there common junction boxes? Yes__ No__
Location_____

      c) Are there feeder transfer switches? Yes__ No__
Location_____

      d) Do motors restart automatically if power is lost

& motors not disconnected manually? Yes__ No__
Notes_____

    2. Alternative Power Source (Diesel_____ Electrical_____

      a) Motor No.

        1 Panel_____ Location_____

        2 Panel_____ Location_____

        3 Panel_____ Location_____

        4 Panel_____ Location_____

      b) How many motors can be operated?_____

      c) Are there common junction boxes? Yes__ Not__
Location_____

      d) Are there transfer switches? Yes__ No__
Location_____

      e) Emergency Generator Nameplate Data
Capacity_____ RPM_____
Volts_____ Prime Mover_____
Amps_____
Notes:_____

      f) Does emergency switchboard have room for new system circuit breaker?_____
Spare circuit breakers available (No./Size)_____

      g) Emergency Switchboard Vendor_____

      h) Circuit breaker vendor_____

    3. Steering Gear Motor Control

		Nav. Bridge	Engine Room
a)	Alarm Panel		
	Power Available	___	___
	Loss of Power	___	___
	Running	___	___
	Overload	___	___
	Circuit Breaker Tripped	___	___
	Sketch		

      b) Steering Gear Operation

        1. Can steering gear be operated from steering room? Yes__ No__

        2. Can power units be brought into operation from Nav. Bridge? Yes__ No__

      c) Communications

        1. Is there communication from Nav. Bridge and Engine Room? Yes__ No__

        2. Does sound powered phone in steering gear room have long extension headset? Yes__ No__
Manufacturer_____

      d) Are steering gear operating & changeover instructions posted in
Steering Room. Yes__ No__
Nav. Bridge. Yes__ No__

Discussion

John W. Reiter, Member

I would like to congratulate the authors on presenting a comprehensive paper on this timely topic.

There are several points in the paper which I would like to amplify and others which I would ask the authors to elaborate upon further.

First, although the authors highlight some of the key points of the new regulations of the International Maritime Organi-zation (IMO, formerly known as IMCO), the paper is not a complete listing of the regulations. The reader should refer to the *Amendments to the International Convention for the Safety of Life at Sea, 1974*, IMO Resolution MSC.1 (XLV), for a complete listing.

The IMO steering gear requirements differ for cargo vessels and tank vessels. Would the authors care to comment on this, particularly since there have been several cases where cargo ship steering problems have caused such vessels to collide with "parked" tankers?

The authors point out the irony of the new requirements in that the added components, while increasing availability, may decrease overall reliability. The authors state this rather emphatically and I would ask if they have knowledge of any studies performed which have quantitatively shown this. In this connection I question whether there is a distinction drawn between failures of these components increasing maintenance headaches and failures which can cause vessel casualties. Also regarding reliability, I would like to comment that I have found it increasingly disturbing that requirements are developed and systems designed to perform certain functions simply because "It is a good idea and technically achievable" without adequate consideration being given to the effect on overall reliability. This appears to be occurring more frequently, particularly in the case of control systems, and as a result the American Bureau of Shipping recently changed the Rules to require fault analyses for propulsion control systems. I would be interested to know if the authors' organization has had experience with similar analyses and their opinion concerning the usefulness of these studies.

In the fifth paragraph of the subsection "New-system description" it is stated that the automatic shutoff or isolation valves can be located away from the cylinder or housing when manual shutoff valves are added at the connection and there is a cross connection between two power units. While this may be true for some designs, it may not be acceptable for others. The governing criterion for automatic valve location is that they be located so that under the casualty conditions specified, steering is automatically regained or retained as required, the governing conditions being a single pipe or power unit failure in some cases and a more comprehensive requirement of failure including the actuators in other cases.

In the same subsection reference is made to Fig. 7 showing a Rapson-slide two ram-type gear and Fig. 8 showing a vane-type gear, both of which are intended to comply with the latest IMO requirements. It should be pointed out that for tankers of 10 000 grt and up, a single rotary vane actuator would be acceptable only if it met the IMO Guidelines for Acceptance of Non-Duplicated Rudder Actuators; for tankers of 100 000 grt and up, duplicate actuators are required.

I note that EHRAS is to be provided for the new systems even though it is not required. It seems that a high level of availability could be achieved at a substantial cost saving by providing for manual override of automatic values rather than installing EHRAS. I would appreciate the authors' comments concerning this alternative.

Parker L. Hay, Member

Concurrent with the program described in this paper, another independent program was undertaken, which, although very similar in objective, was also uniquely different.

The major difference was the early involvement of the steering gear manufacturer who, working closely with the shipowners, assumed total responsibility for the system design, manufacture and installation supervision.

There was a total of 14 ships ranging from 28 000 to 75 000 dwt with four different types of steering gears. The smaller numbers plus the fact that all work was to be done in the United States simplified the logistics of course, but the hydraulic system design was somewhat complicated as it was desirable that all the systems be identical. Obviously this meant that the units had to be adequate for the requirements of the larger vessels while within the electric power capability of the smaller. A search of the vessels' records was made to determine the maximum kW available on the smallest emergency switchboard. The findings so derived were confirmed by an actual ship

check, and a maximum electric motor size was established. From this point, the hydraulic pressure of the largest vessel was considered. Preliminary calculations showed that in order to attain the required pressure for rudder restraint, the volumetric displacement of the hydraulic pump was so reduced that the resultant speed was insufficient to meet the desired 15°–15° in 60 sec. This led to consideration of a dual-stage pump which could provide a high flow at lower pressures and reduced flow at high pressures. To check the validity of this possibility, tests were performed during a voyage on one of the larger vessels. The ship's speed was reduced by one half and pressures were recorded as the rudder was worked from 15° to 15° in several area states. From the information obtained it was determined that the total flow of the dual-stage pump could be used for the 15°–15° steering mode without exceeding the electric motor kW rating with a speed of just under 30 sec. The net result was that even on larger vessels, all the desired goals and requirements could be realized with minimum installed horsepower and minimum power consumption.

Once it had been determined that all the power units could be identical, logistics were even further simplified. All the systems were built and held for individual ship availability. Drawings were prepared for each vessel to reflect the physical location of the systems, required piping and electrical modifications; and any interfacing problems unique to a given vessel or class of vessels.

The value of programs of this type is best realized in terms of real experience. Several months after a system had been installed on one vessel, main steering was lost while the vessel negotiated the treacherous waters around the southern tip of South America. Using the standby system, not only was the rudder brought quickly under control, but the ship was steered with the system for $1\frac{1}{2}$ days until a convenient harbor could be reached where repairs could be accomplished.

These programs are of proven worth and will no doubt become a standard part of the "new generation" of steering gears. It is hoped, however, that they will not be viewed as the optimum in steering gear design. If manufacturers have been remiss in basic design improvements, it must be recognized that shipbuilders and owners have been equally reluctant to change, often permitting price to be the final criterion for selection as long as minimum requirements have been met. Industry-wide new and better methods must be sought. To this end, the following suggestions are offered.

1. We must severely critique current design approaches. There can be no "sacred cows" in the search for better ways to steer a ship.

2. We must find improved methods for early detection and correction of failures.

3. We must demand a higher level of training and qualification for these involved in the design, installation and operation of steering equipment.

4. We must open up specifications so that they define—not confine—design parameters, thus encouraging innovation and creativity.

Haruhiko Mishina,[3] Visitor

We at MHI have high regard for the efforts of Exxon and the authors to develop a logical approach to the problem of upgrading ship steering gear systems, not only to satisfy the IMCO requirements, but also to attain higher reliability, and, with an established philosophy regarding the future picture of the steering system, to consistently and successfully upgrade the steering gears on all the ships in their fleet. Based on our extensive technical know-how and experience gained through the steering gear upgrading jobs as ordered by Exxon and sev-

[3] Mitsubishi Heavy Industries (MHI), Ltd., Tokyo, Japan.

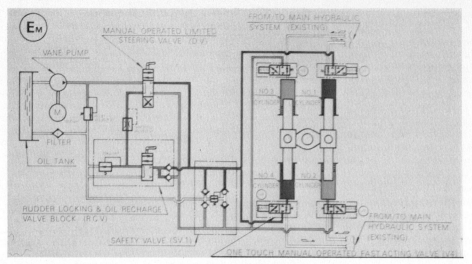

Fig. 9 EHRAS hydraulic line

Fig. 10 EHRAS simulation test equipment at shop

Fig. 11 Pump skid for EHRAS simulation test

eral other shipping companies, we have developed an emergency hydraulic rudder arresting system (EHRAS) of the kind shown in Fig. 9 accompanying this discussion, and have successfully established through shop simulation tests that it would offer very satisfactory performance. Figures 10 and 11 show the simulation testing facilities.

This MHI EHRAS, though basically the same in function as the EHRAS described in Figs. 3 and 4 of the paper, features its own characteristics in respect to hydraulic lines, performance, and the manner in which it is operated, as described in the following:

1. *Hydraulic lines*—A rudder locking and oil recharging hydraulic line consisting of nonreturn valves, oil recharge selector valve, and charging pressure setting relief valve run in parallel with that for limited steering as detailed in Fig. 9.

2. *Operation and performance*—(a) By simply switching the oil recharge selector valve to the charging position, oil is charged into the rudder actuator port and starboard steering oil chambers, simultaneously or alternately, regardless of the level and direction of external force acting on the rudder plate; consequently, the rudder is automatically and hydraulically locked at about the midway position.

(b) As the oil charge is carried out at relatively high pressures (approximately 20 to 35 kg/cm^2), the rudder can almost completely be locked regardless of the amount of air

contained in the rudder actuator and without the need of air purging. This enables the system to draw air out of the rudder actuator safely and restore the steering capability. Figure 12 shows the relevant data recorded at the simulation testing.

(c) The oil charging method mentioned poses no danger of the rudder colliding violently with the mechanical stopper from the effects of external wave force.

It is believed that the MHI EHRAS introduces commendable features in its performance and operational safety.

Because Exxon is a steering gear user with a wealth of experience as reported in the paper, the authors' comments on the MHI EHRAS would be greatly appreciated.

George Koury,[4] Visitor

In November of 1979, Modular Systems received an order for four emergency hydraulic rudder arresting systems from Exxon. During the next several months, we received the balance of the order covering 52 ship sets of these systems for the Exxon International fleet.

We worked closely with the authors of this paper.

We also worked closely on the design with J. J. Henry, the marine consultant of the project. We furnished the arresting skid and motor controller, plus the level switches, special hoses, the bridge, the control room, and the steering gear room panels

[4] Modular Systems, Rockaway, New Jersey.

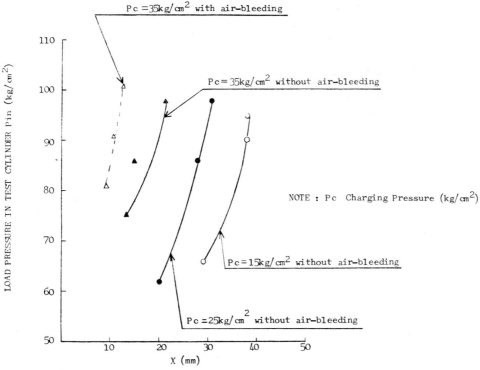

Fig. 12 EHRAS simulation test data. Piston play, *X* (mm), after charging oil into the cylinder filled with air—rudder plate (piston) locking test

related to the arresting system. One of the decisions we made on the design was to incorporate many of the functions of the system into one hydraulic block. The purpose was to lessen the amount of piping so as to make the overall system more compact and more reliable.

The units were built at our plant in Rockaway, New Jersey. They were hydrostatically tested and a rig was built so that they could be performance tested to simulate the flows and the pressures they would be required to handle in operation. All the units were witness tested in our shop by ABS.

Authors' Closure

We would like to thank all the discussers for their complimentary and constructive remarks.

In reply to Mr. Reiter's first comment: We also urge all interested persons to read the amendment to SOLAS 74, IMCO Resolution MSC.1(XLV) as well as the United States Coast Guard Navigation and Vessel Inspection Circular No. 1-81-Guidance for Enforcement of the requirements of the Port and Tanker Safety Act of 1978 (PTSA). Both these documents are listed in the Bibliography.

The authors share Mr. Reiter's apprehensions and fully agree that all classes and types of vessels should have reliance steering systems. We have implemented this philosophy in our upgrading program by applying the higher standards required for VLCC's and ULCC's to all of our international tanker fleet regardless of their size.

We also agree with Mr. Reiter that the type of incident such as the one in N.Y. Harbor where a containership struck an anchored tanker with a subsequent loss of 13 lives must be prevented by increasing steering gear reliability. Decreasing reliability of the steering system by superimposing in-line automatic valves, and controls, would not, in the authors' opinion, decrease the risk of such an incident.

The authors have no knowledge of any quantitative studies conducted to analyze a ram or vane-type steering gear with automatic isolation features other than the one conducted by the University of Hanover, Germany, at the request of AEG Telefunken, Shipbuilding Department, that analyzed the reliability of the dual vane-type steering gears proposed for tankers over 100 000 dwt. The study included calculation of the system reliability using different modes of operation.

The results showed that a single installation operating with the capability of emergency switching similar to a single rotary vane operating at all times is more reliable than a parallel installation, which is IMO's choice solution for vane-type steering gears.

We did a failure mode analysis for both the ram and vane-type steering gears and used it as guidance during the evaluation and design process, but we did not carry through to quantitative results due to the lack of statistical data or a large data base. We found the analysis, however, a very useful study. The University of Hanover in the study previously referred to uses a fault tree analysis technique to derive the result. Failure mode and effects analysis or its variants are very useful in projects concerning reliability and availability.

Logic dictates that in a case whereby a number of components with existing finite probability to failure are added "in line" to an existing system with its own finite probability of failure, the outcome is a decrease of total system reliability.

In the case of an automatic isolation-type system, the solenoid-operated isolating valve increases the number of components liable to fail. A failure in the "added" system could render the total steering inoperative or put the system in a situation equivalent to a conventional steering gear. Although the authors' company has suffered no in-service failure of automatic isolation equipment, failure of a solenoid valve caused a hydraulic lock in a dock trial test.

The vane-type steering gear system in the paper has been designed in compliance with the latest IMO requirements pertaining to tankers smaller than 100 000 dwt. We are not enamored with the duplicate-actuators design and would use it only where required by the regulations.

With reference to Mr. Reiter's suggestion that automatic valves with manual override are an alternative to EHRAS, we refer him to the paper under "New-system description" where we require manual override and position-indicating devices with alarm as the first line of defense in an automatic system. These features insure that a failure of any of the added components can be recognized immediately. However, an off-line system which can easily be put on line, and the entire main system isolated, is more "user friendly." The isolated main system can then be scrutinized in a less tense environment.

Any new component which is now part of the main system when it fails may cause a failure of the total system with unknown consequences. For example, failure of only one of the isolation valves by shutting itself off may cause a hydraulic lock of the main system with all the implications and ramifications involved. The *Esso Singapore*, as indicated earlier, experienced a hydraulic lock during the dock trial of the new automatic isolation system when one solenoid failed to function. If one of the valves sticks in an open position during a casualty, oil may be lost from both power systems, leaving the system uncontrolled for more than the 45 sec as permitted by the regulations, and with unknown results. If, for example, there had been an automatic isolation system on the *Esso Albany*, the casualty mentioned in the paper, the following situation could have occurred:

The system would not respond automatically when the casualty occurred because no loss of oil would have been registered by the low level oil indicator in the tank. The actuators having lost the oil due to rudder fluctuation allowed air to get into the system. Activating the main units would only aggravate the situation by spilling more oil on the steering gear floor. Loss of additional oil is required to activate the low level oil alarm, which will activate the automatic isolation valves to isolate the system. The actuators would be filled with air and with the rudder unrestrained flapping from side to side. With this scenario on hand it is hard to perceive that the remaining part of the main system could regain steering control. It was the EHRAS that gained steering control and allowed by manual switchover to isolate the system, bringing the ship with the remaining part of the main steering system safely to port.

Replying to Mr. Hay, we would like to thank him for sharing his experience in upgrading of steering gear systems by using an EHRAS as the basic solution. In this case the owner and the manufacturer had agreed to a "turnkey" type arrangement, which works well.

The authors fully agree with Mr. Hay's suggestions and hope that now is the time, when the regulations have been accepted, for the industry to become more active and use its technical and marketing forces to develop and provide a safer and a better steering gear system.

The conclusion of the steering gear failure episode to which he refers is "another success story" and additional proof of the viability of an EHRAS as a simple, reliable and workable solution for retrofits and for newbuildings.

Responding to Mr. Mishina's discussion, we are flattered by the confidence and credibility given to us by a well-known steering gear manufacturer. There are three points on which we would like to comment:

1. We do not see the need for an added feature to lock the rudder in position by introducing a surge of oil to all cylinders at one time when the same result can be achieved using the four-way control valves, immediately gaining control of the rudder and at the same time venting the air trapped in the system. This action was successfully proven in the case of *Esso Albany* steering gear failure.

2. We believe that the rudder will be locked at any position upon admitting hydraulic fluid to all cylinders at once, having equal pressure applied to all cylinders at the same time.

3. We recommend that the design pressure of the EHRAS system be the same as the main steering gear system to protect against any external forces acting on the rudder. We can understand that just locking the rudder does not require full pressure and that the emergency power source might be deficient and a reduction of the pressure (motor hp) could be tolerated.

Finally, in reply to Mr. Koury, one of the problems we encountered early in the upgrading program was that material specified to be shipyard furnished was not always available locally. Modular Systems provided us with an effective service in purchasing and delivering these items. Subsequently we supplied all the materials to be used and they were provided, as owner-furnished material, to the shipyards in a container.

SNAME *Transactions*, Vol. 90, 1982, pp. 249–276

Resistance and Propulsion of Ice-Worthy Ships

Jack W. Lewis,[1] Associate Member, **Frank W. DeBord,**[2] Associate Member, and **Vanya A. Bulat,**[3] Associate Member

Lewis and Edwards [1][4] presented information in their 1970 SNAME paper which established, for the first time, an engineering basis for estimating icebreaking resistance of ships. Since their paper, much work has been accomplished. Data from several full-scale ice trials and from corresponding model tests have been collected. In many instances, these trials and model tests have been performed at different times and by different organizations with the result that no consistent analysis of the data has been made. In this paper, such an analysis is made. Its purpose is to reveal information regarding propulsion factors as well as hull resistance factors. Thrust deduction, wake fraction, and relative rotative efficiency are analyzed in detail for tugboats and icebreakers in open water to show how greatly these coefficients differ during towing conditions from free-running conditions. The coefficients are then examined under icebreaking conditions using ice and open-water ship trials data as well as ice and open-water model test data. The propulsion-oriented analysis of the data leads to a method for inferring hull ice resistance from ice trials data and this method is consistently applied to all trials data. The trials resistance data are then compared with those from model ice resistance tests and it is shown that 63 percent of all trials data lie within ±20 percent of values predicted by model test data. Past model data in which hull form was purposefully varied are reviewed as well as a new analytical method for predicting hull resistance. The propulsion and hull data analyses are then combined to provide insight into new methods for selecting major propeller parameters during the design stage.

1. Introduction

AMONG the many problems which face the designer of an ice-worthy ship is the problem of selecting the power required to propel the ship through a given ice field at some desired speed. To solve this problem, the designer must have information regarding the total resistance of the hull in all types of ice, the thrust and torque characteristics of suitable propellers and the interaction between the hull, propeller and ice. The necessary information is far from complete. There is almost an infinite variety of ice types found in lakes, harbors, and northern seas and this greatly complicates the problem of determining hull resistance. Propellers for ice-worthy ships generally have large thickness and hub-diameter ratios which represent departures from standard propeller series data. There are almost no data available concerning the effects of ice on thrust deduction, wake fraction and relative rotative efficiencies.

In order to simplify the problem, it is assumed throughout this paper that the ice-worthy ship in question moves continuously (as opposed to ramming) through a homogeneous, level ice field of constant thickness and mechanical/physical properties, without any internal pressure. Real ice fields, of course, are not this simple. Instead, they are frequently interlaced with pressure ridges of varying size, and rubbled or rafted ice. The field may also be in various states of stress due to wind and water drag. Nevertheless, investigation of this idealized problem provides both meaningful design data and much insight into the problem at hand.

As a start in solving the propulsion problem, it is instructive to first consider the means available for determining the resistance and powering of an ice-worthy ship. The obvious approach is to build the ship and measure its speed in various ice fields at various power levels. If the ship does not attain the desired speed, another is built with more power and the process repeated until the desired speed is achieved. Needless to say, such an approach is quite expensive.

Another approach is to build a self-propelled model of the ship and measure its speed in various ice fields at various input power levels. While this approach is considerably less expensive, it involves a major assumption. That is, it assumes that the input power to the model can be scaled to prototype. It will be shown later that this approach could cause the designer to greatly overpower the ship due to scale effects associated with conducting self-propelled model tests in the commonly used saline/carbamide model ice.

Another approach is to build an analytical model and use it to predict powering requirements. Present knowledge of hull resistance and propeller-hull-ice interaction forces the developer of such analytical tools to rely heavily on full-scale and model-scale experimental data. Consequently, this approach brings the designer back to building ships and models in order to obtain data to build the analytic model. Obviously, there is no easy answer to the problem.

A classical approach to the problem is taken in this paper. Full-scale trials data, model-scale test data, and results of theoretical analyses are combined to provide working solutions.

[1] President, Arctec, Incorporated, Columbia, Maryland.
[2] Vice president, Offshore Technology Corporation, Escondido, California.
[3] Senior engineer, Arctec Canada Limited, Kanata, Ontario, Canada.
[4] Numbers in brackets designate References at end of paper.

Presented at the Annual Meeting, New York, N. Y., November 17–20, 1982, of THE SOCIETY OF NAVAL ARCHITECTS AND MARINE ENGINEERS.

The paper commences with a detailed analysis of the propulsion problem and establishes the framework and terminology used throughout the paper. This section, entitled "Propulsion," describes procedures for inferring "pure" hull-ice resistance from full-scale trials data and details the information required to make the necessary calculations. Data are provided from several ship trials showing pure hull ice resistance and hull-propeller-ice interaction coefficients. Open-water and ice model testing are introduced in this section as they provide necessary information to infer hull-ice resistance from trials.

The next section, entitled "Hull ice resistance," presents empirical methods for determining resistance based on full-scale trials. These methods are in turn used to demonstrate the degree of correlation with model test data obtained from towing model ships in an ice model basin. Relations between hull resistance and hull form are also discussed. This section also discusses a new analytical model for estimating hull resistance. The model was built using observations of full- and model-scale ice-worthy ships. Advantages and limitations of the model are discussed.

The last section, entitled "Propeller selection," describes procedures for selecting optimum-efficiency propellers for ice-worthy ships. This section places particular emphasis on the similarity between designing a propeller for a tugboat and designing a propeller for an ice-worthy ship.

2. Propulsion

In order to select the power required to propel a given ice-worthy hull through level ice at a given speed, it is necessary to have (i) information regarding the hull resistance in ice as a function of speed and ice characteristics; (ii) information regarding the thrust/torque characteristics of suitable propellers; and (iii) information regarding the hull-propeller-ice interaction coefficients (thrust deduction, wake fraction, and relative rotative efficiencies). An important means for determining hull resistance in ice is available through the conduct of full-scale trials. Full-scale trials, however, do not allow direct measurement of hull resistance unless the ship is actually towed or pushed through the ice. To the authors' knowledge, towed ship tests in ice have not been undertaken to date. Consequently, hull resistance must be inferred from measurements of ship speed, shaft speed, shaft thrust and shaft torque. Inferring hull resistance from such measurements requires detailed knowledge of the propeller performance in open water and of the hull-propeller-ice interaction coefficients.

The operating regime of a propeller on an ice-worthy ship is similar to that for a tugboat. For example, numerous route analysis studies of proposed icebreaking tankers have shown that the majority of shaft horsepower hours accumulated during a round-trip voyage occur at low ship speeds under nearly full-power operation. Minimum fuel consumption considerations dictate that the propeller be designed for maximum efficiency under "overload" conditions. This means that information regarding propulsive coefficients under overload conditions must be available. Thrust deduction, wake fraction, and relative rotative efficiency coefficients are considerably different under overload conditions when compared with free-running conditions. Consequently, the discussion will start with an investigation of the propulsive coefficients under open-water overload conditions and then continue with a discussion of ice effects on these parameters.

Nomenclature

C_B = block coefficient

C_p = prismatic coefficient

C_x = midship area coefficient

f = hull-ice friction factor

g = acceleration of gravity

h = ice thickness

n = propeller shaft speed

t_i = constant of proportionality or thrust deduction factor in ice (subscript i is used to denote icebreaking)

t_p = constant of proportionality or the so-called "thrust deduction factor" while towing (subscript p is used to denote pulling)

$w_i = (V - Va)/V$ = wake fraction, icebreaking

w_p = wake fraction, towing

A_0 = dimensional coefficient for ice resistance

A_1 = dimensional coefficient for ice resistance

A_x = midship area

B = maximum beam at operating waterline

C_0, C_1, C_2 = dimensionless icebreaking coefficients

D = propeller diameter

D_j = broken ice cusp depth, row j

E = ice elastic modulus

EHP = useful output power

DHP = developed horsepower

DHP_i = developed horsepower, ice-breaking

EHP_i = useful output power, ice-breaking

F = a function

G = a function

H = ship draft

$J_a = V_a/nD$, propeller advance coefficient

$J_m = V/nD$, measured advance coefficient

$K_Q = Q_0/\rho n^2 D^5$ = torque coefficient, open water

$K_{QBP} = Q_{BP}/\rho n^2 D^5$ = measured torque coefficient, towing

$K_T = T_0/\rho n^2 D^4$ = thrust coefficient, open water

$K_{TBP} = T_{BP}/\rho n^2 D^4$ = measured thrust coefficient, towing

L = ship length at operating water-line

L_j = broken ice cusp length, row j

P = tow rope pull

P/D = propeller pitch-diameter ratio

Q_{Bi} = shaft torque, icebreaking

Q_{BP} = shaft torque measured just before stern tube bearing towing

Q_0 = propeller torque measured without ship present

R_i = pure hull ice resistance

R_{iw} = ice and water hull resistance (towed)

R_{ow} = open-water hull resistance (towed)

T_{Bi} = shaft thrust (behind in ice)

T_{BP} = shaft thrust (behind pulling)

T_0 = propeller thrust measured without ship present

V = ship speed

V_a = advance speed of propeller

∇ = ship displacement

ΔR_{iw} = hull resistance augmentation due to propeller hull-ice interactions (in ice-covered water)

ΔR_{owp} = hull resistance augmentation due to propeller hull interactions (in ice-free water)

α = attack angle on propeller

β = advance angle of propeller

ϕ = pitch angle of propeller

ρ_i = mass density of ice

ρ_w = mass density of water

σ_c = ice crushing strength

σ_f = ice flexural strength

$\eta_{DP} = EHP/DHP$ = quasi-propulsive efficiency, towing

η_0 = open-water propeller efficiency

η_{HP} = hull efficiency, towing

η_{RP} = relative rotative efficiency, towing

$\eta_{Di} = EHP_i/DHP_i$ = quasi-propulsive efficiency, icebreaking

η_{Hi} = hull efficiency, icebreaking

η_{Ri} = relative rotative efficiency, ice-breaking

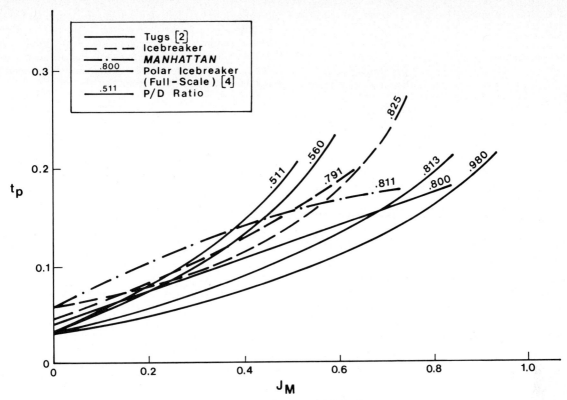

Fig. 1 Thrust deduction while towing

Interaction between hull, propeller, and ice

Thrust deduction—The force balance equation for a single screwed ship under towing conditions can be expressed as

$$T_{BP} = P + R_{ow} + \Delta R_{owp} \tag{1}$$

where

T_{BP} = shaft thrust (behind pulling)
P = towrope pull
R_{ow} = open-water hull resistance (towed)
ΔR_{owp} = hull resistance augmentation due to propeller-hull interactions

It is general practice to express ΔR_{owp} as a fraction of T_{BP}. That is

$$\Delta R_{owp} = t_p * T_{BP} \tag{2}$$

where t_p is a constant of proportionality or the so-called "thrust deduction factor" while towing (the subscript p is used to denote pulling).

Substituting (2) into (1) and rearranging gives

$$t_p = \frac{T_{BP} - (P + R_{ow})}{T_{BP}} \tag{3}$$

Usually, thrust deduction factors are plotted as a function of ship speed, V. But this is inappropriate for the towing conditions. Since R_{ow} is a function of ship speed and T_{BP} a function of ship speed and shaft speed, n, then t_p must be a function of V and n. Harvald [2] shows that the thrust deduction factor can be expressed as a function of the measurable advance coefficient

$$J_m = V/nD \tag{4}$$

where

V = ship speed

n = shaft speed
D = propeller diameter

Harvald analyzed the Parker and Dawson [3] tugboat data and showed that the thrust deduction factor varies from a low of about 0.04 at $J_m = 0$ to a high of about 0.20 at values of J_m depending upon the pitch-diameter (P/D) ratio of the propellers. Similar results can be obtained from overload model tests of ice-worthy ships. Figure 1 shows thrust deduction factors as a function of J_m for several ice-worthy ships along with the tug data analyzed by Harvald. These data clearly indicate that there is little thrust deduction at near bollard condition and that thrust deduction varies almost linearly with J_m over the range of normal towing speeds. These results were further confirmed during full-scale overpropulsion tests of a triple-screw icebreaker conducted by DeBord et al [4].

Open-water model tests are usually used to determine thrust deduction factors. Captive towed-model tests are used to measure R_{ow} and self-propelled overload model tests with varying values of towrope pull and model speed are used to measure shaft thrust. Equation (3) is then used to compute the thrust deduction factors from the measured data. These calculations are very prone to error because t_p is computed based on the difference between two very large numbers (T_{BP} and $P + R_{ow}$).

Full-scale trials can also be conducted to determine thrust deduction factors. While these tests are expensive, they are important for determining model-prototype correlation. Recently, such full-scale tests were conducted by DeBord et al [4] on a large polar icebreaker. These tests indicated that towing thrust deduction factors measured in a model agree reasonably well with those measured during ship trials. Consequently, it can be safely assumed that model-scale effects on open-water thrust deduction are negligible.

Consider now the following force balance equation for an ice-worthy ship breaking level ice:

$$T_{Bi} = R_{iw} + \Delta R_{iw} \qquad (5)$$

where

T_{Bi} = shaft thrust (behind in ice)
R_{iw} = hull resistance in ice and water (towed)
ΔR_{iw} = hull resistance augmentation due to propeller hull-ice interactions

As before, ΔR_{iw} is expressed as a fraction of T_{Bi}

$$\Delta R_{iw} = t_i \times T_{Bi} \qquad (6)$$

where t_i is a constant of proportionality or thrust deduction factor in ice (the subscript i is used to denote icebreaking).

Substituting (6) into (5) and rearranging gives

$$t_i = \frac{T_{Bi} - R_{iw}}{T_{Bi}} \qquad (7)$$

Equation (7) is quite similar to equation (3) and this similarity suggests an important means (hereafter referred to as the "shaft thrust method") to infer full-scale hull ice resistance from full-scale trials data. If the thrust deduction factor in ice (t_i) is equal to the thrust deduction factor during open-water towing (t_p) then

$$R_{iw} = P + R_{ow} \qquad (8)$$

Thus, given the function t_p versus J_m from model tests, and given a set of values V, n and T_{Bi} from full-scale trials, one could obtain R_{iw} by computing J_m, looking up t_p, and multiplying by T_{Bi} to get R_{iw}.

To investigate the validity of the assumption that $t_i = t_p$, self-propelled model data collected during ice-breaking and open-water towing are analyzed. It should be understood, before discussing the results, that a self-propelled model test in ice has only recently been attempted and hence little data are available. In order to compute t_i, a means of estimating R_{iw} must be available. For the model tests being discussed, this estimate was obtained by first conducting captive towed resistance tests in ice and then fairing the results. Unlike open-water testing, a great deal of scatter exists in ice model test data and this considerably complicates the problem of estimating t_i. The analyzed test results, shown in Fig. 2, clearly reveal the problem. In this figure, values for t_i computed using equation (7) and the ice model data are plotted along with the open-water test results. The scatter in the t_i data is so great that all one can say is that the data provide no evidence which would indicate that t_i is or is not equal to t_p. Much more work is needed in this area. In particular, more self-propelled ice model test data are needed in order to isolate data trends.

Propulsive efficiency, wake fraction and relative rotative efficiency—The input power required to sustain a given towing speed in open water depends on the propulsive efficiency. This efficiency can be expressed as the ratio of the useful output power (or EHP) to the required input power (developed horsepower or DHP). In the case of towing, EHP must include the towrope pull. Thus

$$EHP = \frac{(P + R_{ow})\, V}{550} \qquad (9)$$

The input or developed horsepower is given by

$$DHP = 2\pi n Q_{BP}/550 \qquad (10)$$

where Q_{BP} is the shaft torque measured just before the stern tube bearing. The ratio of EHP/DHP is generally referred to as the quasipropulsive efficiency, η_{DP}, and for towing is equal to

$$\eta_{DP} = \frac{EHP}{DHP} = \frac{(P + R_{ow})V}{2\pi n Q_{BP}} \qquad (11)$$

The subscript P is used as a reminder that this is for the towing condition.

The quasi-propulsive efficiency is generally subdivided into three components: open-water propeller efficiency, hull efficiency, and relative rotative efficiency. The open-water propeller efficiency, η_0, is given by

$$\eta_0 = \frac{T_0 V_a}{2\pi n Q_0} \qquad (12)$$

where

T_0 = propeller thrust measured without ship present
Q_0 = propeller torque under same conditions
n = propeller shaft speed
V_a = advance speed of propeller

The advance velocity of the propeller and the ship speed are related by the "wake factor," which is by definition

$$w_p = \frac{V - V_a}{V} \qquad (13)$$

Equations (3), (12) and (13) may be substituted into (11) to give

$$\eta_{DP} = \frac{1 - t_p}{1 - w_p} \times \frac{T_{BP}}{T_0} \frac{Q_0}{Q_{BP}} \times \eta_0 \qquad (14)$$

The first term on the right-hand side of equation (14) is called the hull efficiency while towing, η_{HP}. The second term is called the relative rotative efficiency while towing, η_{RP}. Obviously, in order to compute the power required to overcome the total resistance ($P + R_{ow}$) while towing, it is necessary to have information on the relative efficiency and the wake fraction.

The relative rotative efficiency is an artifice of data analysis procedures. That is, it exists in equation (14) because of our desire to separate out of the quasi-propulsive efficiency that part due to the open-water propeller efficiency. As such, the value of the relative rotative efficiency depends on the method (torque or thrust identity) used to obtain the open-water propeller efficiency. In the thrust identity method (used throughout this paper), the value of K_{TBP} is calculated from measured data and used as the entering argument for the open-water propeller curves. Thus, T_{BP} is assumed equal to T_0 (hence the name "thrust identity") and as a result the relative rotative efficiency is equal to Q_0/Q_{BP}. The value of J_a found from the K_T-curves is then used to find K_{Q0} and hence Q_0. The relative rotative efficiency is then easily computed. Frequently, relative rotative efficiency is reported in model test reports without reference to the method used to compute it. This misleading practice probably contributes to the mystery which seems to surround this coefficient.

The method (torque or thrust identity) used to obtain open-water propeller efficiency also affects the value obtained for wake fraction. Hence, it too is an artifice of data analysis procedures. In addition to this complication, a careful analysis of propulsion data under towing conditions reveals that values for wake fraction can be considerably different from those at the self-propulsion point. This is of great importance in tugboat design and is frequently overlooked by designers who usually work only at the self-propulsion point.

Harvald [2, 5] gives much insight into the behavior of wake fractions at extreme propeller loadings. A very useful concept was taken from his work and used in the analysis of ice-worthy ship propulsion. The wake fraction can be determined by use of propeller diagrams in which curves of the propeller coefficients behind the ship (K_{TBP} and K_{QBP}) are plotted against the advance coefficient in addition to the corresponding open-water

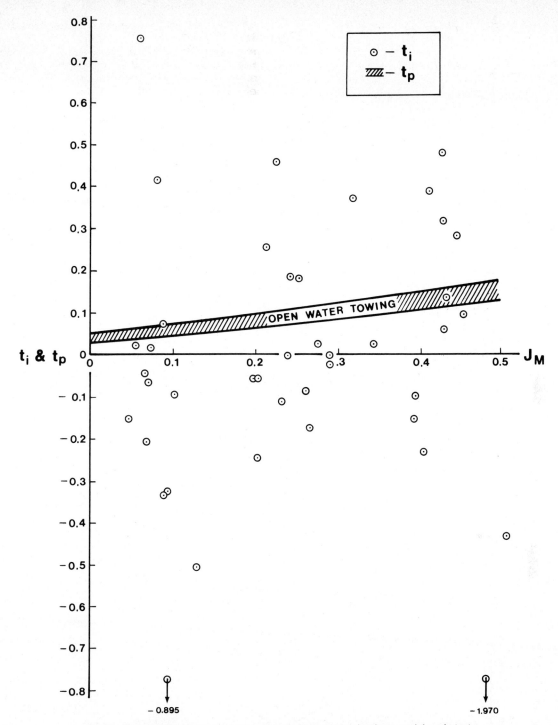

Fig. 2 Thrust deduction factors during icebreaking and towing from model scale tests

propeller curves. The following equations for V and V_a

$$V = J_m nD \qquad (15)$$

$$V_a = J_a nD \qquad (16)$$

are substituted in equation (13) to give

$$w_p = \frac{J_m - J_a}{J_m} \qquad (17)$$

Consequently, wake fraction can be obtained directly from the propeller diagrams using either the thrust or torque identity method.

Figure 3 shows the thrust identity relative rotative efficiency and wake fraction for a typical icebreaker hull form under open-water towing conditions obtained from model data. The data clearly show the large differences in wake fraction under towing and free-running conditions. The choice of J_m as the abscissa for plotting η_{Rp} and w_p is arbitrary. However, it will be seen later that this eliminates ambiguity when attempting to use relative rotative efficiency and wake fraction data during propeller design.

The input power required to sustain a given ship speed while icebreaking can be expressed in a manner similar to that used for towing. The quasi-propulsive efficiency for icebreaking becomes

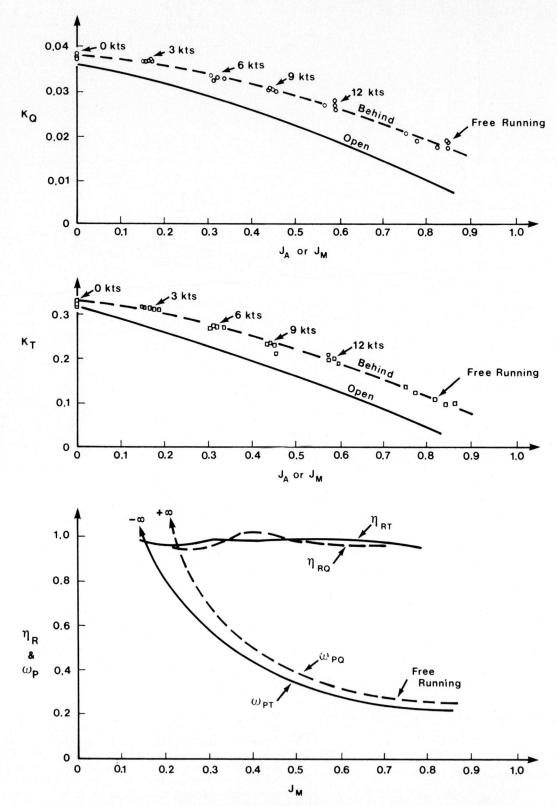

Fig. 3 Relative rotative efficiency and wake fraction in free water (free running to bollard conditions)

Resistance and Propulsion of Ice-Worthy Ships

$$\eta_{Di} = \frac{EHP_i}{DHP_i} = \frac{R_{iw}V}{2\pi n Q_{Bi}} \qquad (18)$$

where the subscript i is used as a reminder that this is for ice-breaking.

The quasi-propulsive efficiency for icebreaking can also be subdivided into the open-water propeller efficiency, hull efficiency and relative rotation efficiency. The latter two efficiency definitions are given by[5]

$$\eta_{Hi} = \frac{1 - t_i}{1 - w_i} \qquad (19)$$

and

$$\eta_{Ri} = \frac{T_{Bi}}{T_0} \frac{Q_0}{Q_{Bi}} \qquad (20)$$

where

$$w_i = \frac{V - V_a}{V} \qquad (21)$$

There is great similarity between equations (11) and (18) and this similarity suggests yet another means (hereinafter referred to as the "shaft torque method") to infer full-scale hull ice resistance from full-scale trials data. If the quasi-propulsive efficiency in ice equals the towing quasi-propulsive efficiency, then hull resistance can be obtained as follows. A plot of quasi-propulsive efficiency for towing is prepared from open-water model or full-scale data as a function of developed horsepower and ship speed. Values for developed horsepower and ship speed during icebreaking are then used as entering arguments for this plot and the quasi-propulsive efficiency obtained. Equation (18), with $\eta_{Di} = \eta_{DP}$, is then used to compute R_{iw}.

To investigate the validity of the assumption that η_{Di} equals η_{Dp}, it is necessary to determine if both the hull efficiency and relative rotative efficiency while icebreaking are the same as when towing. The hull efficiency involves both thrust deduction and wake fraction. Thrust deduction in ice has already been discussed so attention will now be given to wake fraction and relative rotative efficiency in ice.

Fortunately, both of these latter parameters can be determined from full-scale data using the previously discussed method suggested by Harvald. Plots of K_{TBi} and K_{QBi} versus J_m are prepared from the full-scale trials data and plotted along with the corresponding open-water propeller curves. Figure 4 shows full-scale thrust identity wake fraction and relative rotative efficiency data in ice for the icebreaker previously discussed in Fig. 3. The open-water towing wake fraction and relative rotative efficiency is also shown in this figure for purposes of comparison. It can be seen that the icebreaking wake fraction is considerably different from the towing wake fraction, but the relative rotative efficiencies are roughly the same.

Plots similar to those shown in Fig. 4 have been prepared for several icebreakers in which full-scale data are available. In each case, the influence of icebreaking on relative rotative efficiency and wake fraction was found to be similar to that shown in Fig. 4. Apparently the submerged ice pieces, which surround the hull and strike the propeller while icebreaking, significantly change the water flow pattern into, and the speed

of, the propeller, causing the propeller to observe a great decrease in advance velocity.

Referring back now to the discussion of the validity of the assumption that $\eta_{Di} = \eta_{DP}$, it is obvious that the wake fraction difference will render this assumption invalid unless there are compensating changes in the ice thrust deduction. Previous discussion of ice thrust deduction, however, shows that no such compensating changes are present. It is therefore concluded that η_{Di} is not equal to η_{DP} and consequently the shaft torque method of inferring full-scale hull ice resistance from icebreaking trials data should not, in general, be used.

Before leaving the subject of ice-worthy ship powering, it is of interest to investigate the input powering requirements obtained from self-propelled icebreaking model tests. Figure 5 shows plots of the K_{TBi} and K_{QBi} versus J_m for both the model and prototype. These data indicate that thrust measurements obtained during self-propelled model tests in ice are similar to those obtained during full-scale trials. The torque data from the self-propelled model tests in ice, on the other hand, are considerably higher than the full-scale trials data and the scatter is significantly greater.[6] Consequently, the powering requirements obtained from the self-propelled model test data are in excess of actual ship powering requirements. It is not clear at this time why this happens. It is believed that the problem may be due to the improper scaling of crushing strength of the model ice.

The self-propelled model ice tests were conducted in saline model ice, which is known to have too high a crushing strength (by a factor of 2 to 4) when flexural strength is properly scaled as it was in these tests. Since the propellers frequently mill ice when icebreaking, it is reasonable to assume that too high a crushing strength would result in the long-term average model shaft torque being too high while having possibly little influence on long-term average shaft thrust. This phenomenon might also explain the increased scatter in torque data as compared with thrust data since torque would be greatly influenced by the quantity of ice impacting the propellers.

Procedure for estimating pure hull ice resistance from ship trials

During the preceding discussion of propulsive coefficients, two methods of inferring hull resistance in ice were described. These methods were referred to as the "shaft thrust method" and the "shaft torque method." Uncertainties exist in each method; however, it appears that fewer uncertainties exist with the shaft thrust method and therefore this method is to be preferred.

The concept of "pure hull ice resistance" comes from the assumption that the total hull resistance can be subdivided into two additive components. One component is the open-water resistance of the hull as obtained from towed model tests in calm water, and the other is obtained from subtracting the open-water resistance from the total resistance. Thus pure ice resistance is defined as

$$R_i = R_{iw} - R_{ow} \qquad (22)$$

where R_{iw} is the total hull resistance in ice and water and R_{ow} the hull resistance in open water. This division of the total resistance into two components is arbitrary and without an analytical basis. However, it will be useful later when the full-scale trials data of several ships are analyzed and compared with model-scale test predictions.

It is assumed that a set of full-scale data consisting of measurements of shaft thrust, shaft speed and ship speed is available. For each "run" in this set of data, the measurements should be

---

[5] Juurmaa and Segercrantz [6] take a different approach. They give $\eta_{Di} = \eta_{Hi} \eta_{Ri} \eta_{0i}$ where η_{0i} is obtained from model propeller dynamometer tests in ice without the hull. This approach has not been followed in the present paper because model propeller dynamometer tests in ice are not yet known to produce meaningful results. It should also be carefully noted that Juurmaa and Segercrantz's η_{Hi} and η_{Ri} differ from those used by the present authors because the definitions of w_i differ.

[6] Similar results from self-propelled icebreaking model tests have been reported by Narita and Yamaguchi [7].

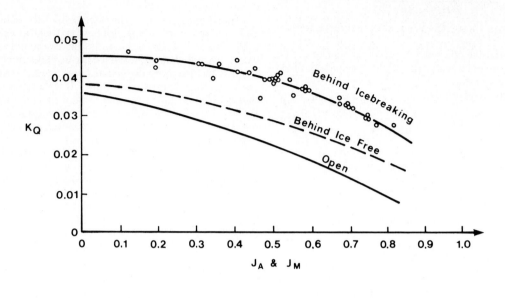

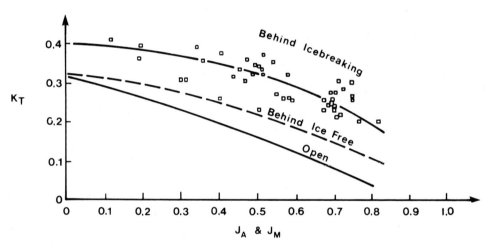

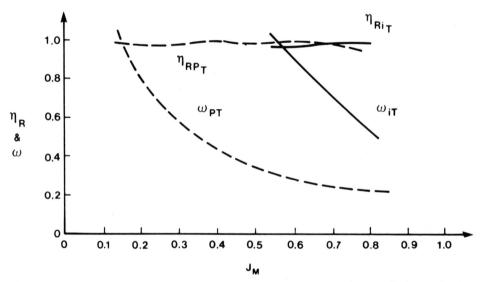

Fig. 4 Relative rotative efficiency and wake fraction during icebreaking (light to heavy ice conditions)

Resistance and Propulsion of Ice-Worthy Ships

time-averaged over several ship lengths of travel at a relatively steady speed.

To infer pure ice resistance from this set of data, it is also necessary to have available two sets of open water model test results or equivalent full-scale data. The first set consists of the open-water towed resistance test data and the second set consists of the open water, self-propelled overload or towing test data. The latter set of data is absolutely essential and great care should be given to its collection to ensure that a sufficient number of towing speeds are used to span the full-scale data and that shaft thrust is measured.

The model data are then reduced and plots of t_p versus J_m and R_{ow} versus V are prepared. The full-scale data are reduced as follows. The value of J_m is calculated for each run using the measured shaft speed and ship speed, and the diameter of the propeller. The value of t_p is obtained from the plot of the model data. The total ice and water resistance is computed using the measured shaft thrust for the run and the equation

$$R_{iw} = (1 - t_p)T_{Bi} \qquad (23)$$

The open-water resistance is found by entering the plot of model open-water resistance versus speed with the value of ship speed for the run. Equation (22) is used to obtain the pure ice resistance for the run.

The procedure is repeated for each run in the set of full-scale data. The data are then tabulated and the ship speed, ice thickness, ice flexural strength and any other pertinent data tabulated along with the pure ice resistance.

One set of full-scale data, reduced as described in the preceding, is of somewhat limited value. However, as shown in the next section of the paper, when many sets of such data are analyzed together, meaningful design data can be obtained.

3. Icebreaking hull resistance

Means for determining hull ice resistance must be available to the designer of an ice-worthy ship in order to estimate powering requirements. Full-scale data can be used for this purpose, and in this section available full-scale data will be analyzed and formulas for determining hull-ice resistance developed.

Use of full-scale data for determining hull ice resistance, however, has its limitations. It is very expensive and data are available for only a relatively few number of hull forms. Icebreaking model tests represent a much more cost-effective approach to obtaining such data, provided the results are reliable. This section will investigate the correlation between full-scale and model test data and show how model data can be used to derive effects of hull form on ice resistance.

The use of analytical theories for determining hull ice resistance is the least-expensive means available. Use of analytic methods will be discussed in this section. Particular emphasis will be placed on a recently developed theory.

Hull ice resistance based on full-scale trials data

There are so many hull, ice, water, and motion variables which could influence hull resistance that it is currently impossible to explain the effect of every one on resistance. For the time being then, one must be satisfied with methods which predict hull ice resistance only to a first-order approximation.

Past analyses of full-scale trials and model test data in level ice have shown that pure ice resistance is composed of two additive components: one speed-independent and the other speed-dependent. Analysis of near-zero speed data shows that the speed-independent term varies roughly with the square of the ice thickness. The speed-dependent term varies approximately linearly with the product of the ice thickness and the

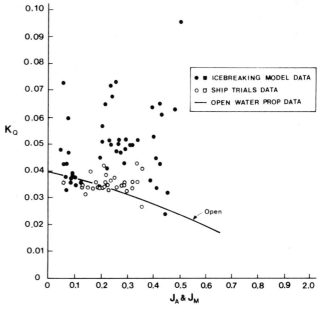

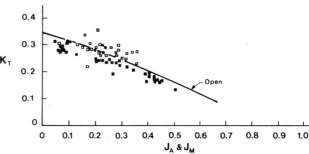

Fig. 5 Comparison of self-propelled icebreaking model and icebreaking ship trials data

ship velocity. In equation form, these past analyses show

$$R_i = A_0 h^2 + A_1 hV \qquad (24)$$

where A_0 and A_1 are constants for the particular ship in the particular ice field under study.

Through the use of dimensional analysis, it is possible to develop dimensionless variables which can greatly facilitate the analysis of data by allowing diverse sets of data to be combined, and by reducing the total number of independent variables involved. For example, consider the following functional expression for pure ice resistance:

$$R_i = F(L,B,H,\nabla,A_x,h,\sigma_f,\sigma_c,E,\rho_i,\rho_w,g,f,V) \qquad (25)$$

where

F = the function being sought
L = ship length at operating waterline
B = maximum beam at operating waterline
H = ship draft
∇ = ship displacement
A_x = midship area
h = ice thickness
σ_f = ice flexural strength
σ_c = ice crushing strength
E = ice elastic modulus
ρ_i = mass density of ice
ρ_w = mass density of water
g = acceleration of gravity
f = hull-ice friction factor
V = ship speed

Table 1 Results of regressing individual icebreaking ship trial data against equation (30)

Ship	C_0	C_2	Correlation Coefficient
A	4.354	0.194	0.956
B	7.161	0.222	0.736
C	6.065	0.230	0.705
D	1.556	0.203	0.945

The number of variables in equation (25) may be reduced through application of classical dimensional analysis. By selecting the force group $\rho_w gBh^2$ for nondimensionalizing R_i, one can obtain the following dimensionless version:

$$\frac{R_i}{\rho_w gBh^2} =$$
$$G\left(C_B, C_p, C_X, \frac{B}{h}, \frac{L}{h}, \frac{H}{h}, \frac{\rho i}{\rho_w}, \frac{E}{\sigma_f}, \frac{\sigma_c}{\sigma_f}, \frac{\sigma_f}{\rho_w gh}, \frac{V}{\sqrt{gh}}, f\right) \quad (26)$$

where G is a different function from F.

Although equation (26) is only slightly less complicated than equation (25), it does provide a basis for combining data from several different size hulls in various types of ice into one data base. Furthermore, experience has shown that many of the independent variables shown have negligible influence on the dependent variable.

Past analysis of ice resistance data indicates that much of the variation associated with the ice resistance data is removed when the ice resistance is divided by the force group $\rho_w gBh^2$. This is consistent with the findings indicated in equation (24), since dividing this equation by h^2 leaves it in the form

$$\frac{R_i}{h^2} = A_0 + A_1 \frac{V}{h} \quad (27)$$

That is, R_i/h^2 is a linear function of V/h.

It is possible to form several groups of the independent dimensionless variables given in equation (26) which will give a V/h term for a particular ship. One such group is

$$VLB = \frac{V}{\sqrt{gh}} \frac{(L/h)}{(B/h)^{1/2}} \quad (28)$$

Using this group, the dimensionless equivalent of equation (27) becomes

$$\frac{R_i}{\rho_w gBh} = C_0 + C_2 \frac{V}{\sqrt{gh}} \frac{(L/h)}{(B/h)^{1/2}} \quad (29)$$

Multiplying both sides of Equation (29) gives the dimensional equation

$$R_i = C_0 \rho_w gBh^2 + C_2 \rho_w g^{1/2} B^{1/2} LhV \quad (30)$$

It can be seen that equation (30) is equal to equation (24) if

Table 2 Full-scale ice trials information regarding hard-to-quantify independent variables

Ship	Ice Type	Bow Type	Hull Surface Condition
A	sea (284)[a]	modern	painted steel
B	fresh (920)[a]	old	painted steel
C	fresh (661)[a]	modern	low-friction coating partially worn
D	sea (376)[a]	modern	low-friction coating

[a] Mean flexural ice strength in kPa.

$$A_0 = C_0 \rho_w gB$$

and

$$A_1 = C_2 \rho_w g^{1/2} B^{1/2} L$$

The validity of equation (29) must be checked against actual data. Note that this equation indicates that the speed-independent term is proportional to the beam of the ship and that the speed-dependent term is proportional to the product of the square root of the beam and the length of the ship. In order to check this, it is therefore necessary to have data for several ships with varying beams and lengths.

Four sets of full-scale ice trials data were analyzed to determine if equation (29) reasonably fits these data. The ships varied in length from 39.6 to 295.7 m (129.8 to 969.8 ft) and their beams from 7.3 to 45.7 m (23.9 to 149.8 ft). Each set of trials data was linearly regressed with equation (29) to obtain values for coefficients C_0 and C_2, and the corresponding correlation coefficient. The results are given in Table 1.

Before discussing these results, it is important to point out that so far no consideration has been given to possible effects of ice strength, hull form or hull-ice friction factor on pure ice resistance. This was done for two reasons. First, these variables were purposely omitted at this stage of the analysis in order to determine how much of the data variation could be explained by considering only length, beam, speed of the ship, and the ice thickness as independent variables. Second, except for ice strength, it is difficult to quantify these variables. Table 2 gives a matrix of test conditions associated with each ship trial that are relevant to ice strength (Ice Type), hull form (Bow Type) and hull-ice friction (Hull Surface Condition). The mean flexural ice strength is indicated in parentheses in this table.

The results given in Table 1 clearly indicate that the speed-dependent coefficient, C_2, for each ship is essentially identical. This shows that the speed-dependent pure ice resistance component most likely varies as the product of the square root of the beam, the length, the ice thickness and the velocity ($B^{1/2}LhV$). In view of the possible variations in ice strength, bow form and friction factor indicated in Table 2, the similarity of C_2 could also indicate that this coefficient is not greatly affected by these variables.

The speed-independent coefficient, C_0, is not the same for each ship data set. It is most likely that this coefficient is influenced by the variables indicated in Table 2. It is difficult, however, to isolate this influence. An attempt was made to include the effect of ice strength by combining all of the trials data into one set and performing a multiple linear regression with the following equation:

$$\frac{R_i}{\rho_w gBh^2} = C_0 + C_1 \frac{\sigma_f}{\rho_w gh} + C_2 \frac{V}{\sqrt{gh}} \frac{(L/h)}{(B/h)^{1/2}} \quad (31)$$

The results gave $C_0 = 3.8989$, $C_1 = 0.0123$, $C_2 = 0.223$, and a correlation coefficient of 0.85.

Although equation (31) does not show any variation in resistance with hull form on hull-ice friction factor, it is of immense value to a designer in the initial stages of ice-worthy ship design. The equation first of all is derived entirely from full-scale trials data collected on ships ranging from very small to quite large. It also includes two ship variables (length and beam), two ice variables (ice thickness and ice strength), and the ship speed.

Hull ice resistance based on model-scale tests

Model/full-scale correlation—Due to the difficulties associated with attempts to isolate effects of hull form and hull-ice friction on pure ice resistance using full-scale trials data, it is natural to turn to another, less-expensive, approach. The works

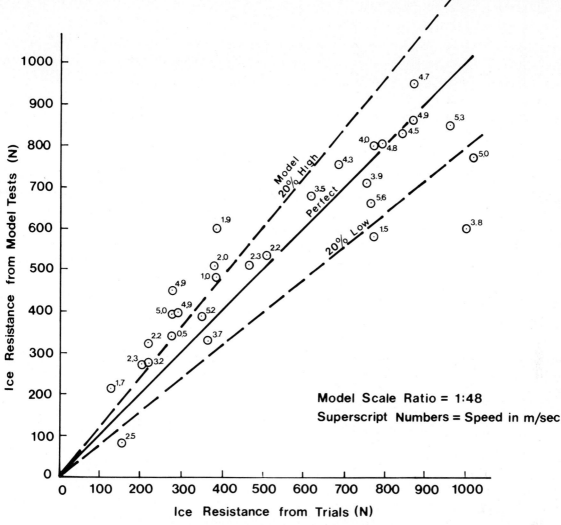

Fig. 6 Model/full-scale correlation—USCGC *Mackinaw*

of Edwards et al [8] and Lecourt et al [9] address these problems and present very useful design data. Still the validity of model test data is frequently questioned and therefore it is important to take every opportunity to address the question of model-prototype correlation when such data become available.

Within the past several years, two new sets of full-scale data have been collected for ships which were extensively tested in the model ice basin. In addition, field trials data from one old test (Edwards et al [10]) were reanalyzed using the "shaft thrust method" referred to in Section 2. The corresponding model test data are old, but still valuable.

The approach taken in this model-prototype correlation study was as follows. For each ship model test the experimenter involved presented a data-smoothing equation which best fit the model data. This equation was used to predict full-scale ice resistance by substituting values of the full-scale independent variables (that is, values for ice thickness, ice strength, ship speed, hull friction, etc.). The ice resistance predicted by the model data-smoothing equation was then plotted against the full-scale ice resistance as inferred using the shaft thrust method.

The results of this model/full-scale correlation analysis are shown in Figs. 6 through 8. On each of these plots there are three lines. The solid line represents the line for perfect match of model and full-scale data. The other two lines represent ±20

percent variation between model and full-scale data.

Figure 6 shows correlation for the USCGC *Mackinaw* ice trials and model tests. These data were previously presented and analyzed by Edwards et al [10]. The trials data used in Fig. 6, however, differ in three respects from those presented by Edwards et al. First, the trials data were reanalyzed for this paper using the "shaft thrust method" instead of the "shaft torque method" used by them. Second, the thrust deduction factor was taken into account in this reanalysis. Third, trials data in very thin ice were excluded from the analysis, because these could not be tested in the ice model basin. Of the resulting 29 data points, 16 fall within the ±20 percent limits, nine are above the upper 20 percent limit, and four are below the lower 20 percent limit. The ship speed is indicated beside each data point to show that there are no trends in the scatter associated with speed as had been previously observed by Edwards et al [10].

Figure 7 shows correlation for the USCGC *Katmai Bay* ice trials and model data. The ice trials data for this ship were presented by Vance et al [11] and the model data by Lecourt et al [9]. Vance's raw data were reanalyzed using the shaft thrust method referred to previously. Vance suggested using a hull-ice friction factor of 0.15 and this was used in Lecourt's model data-smoothing equation. The *Katmai Bay* had a low friction coating but was reported by Vance as deteriorated.

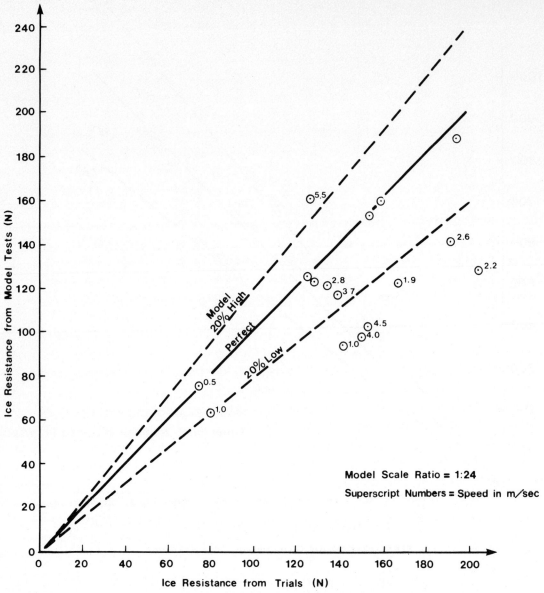

Fig. 7 Model/full-scale correlation—USCGC *Katmai Bay*

The required thrust deduction factors had to be estimated using the data presented in Fig. 1 because West [12] did not report thrust measurements taken during the open-water towing model test program. Of the 16 data points shown, nine are within the ±20 percent limit, one is above the upper 20 percent limit, and six are below the lower 20 percent limit. Notice that the range of absolute resistance values associated with these trials is only one-fifth that associated with the *Mackinaw* trials. Also note that the scale factor for the *Katmai Bay* model (1/24) is twice that of the *Mackinaw* (1/48).

Figure 8 shows correlation for the CCGS *Pierre Radisson* ice trials and model data. The ice trials data for this ship were presented by Edwards et al [13] and the model data by Bulat [14]. The Edwards et al raw data were reanalyzed using the shaft thrust method. Thrust deduction factors and open-water resistance required for application of this method were taken from the excellent work of Murdey [15].[7] The full-scale trials data for this ship are the most extensive ever collected and are

[7] This report of open-water towing and other trials can be used as an outstanding example of how such tests should be conducted, and how the data should be analyzed and reported.

a tribute to the skills and foresight of those involved with these trials. Of the 102 data points shown, 67 are within the ±20 percent limits, 20 are above the upper 20 percent limit, and 15 are below the lower 20 percent limit. For purposes of clarity, ship speed is not shown with the data; however, no speed effects were noted. Several of the data points above the upper 20 percent limit were associated within the highest ice thickness conditions, which may show a tendency for the model to overpredict resistance at high ice thicknesses. It is also of interest to point out that the model tests were conducted with a hull-ice friction factor of around 0.05.

Out of the 147 data points presented in Figs. 6 through 8, 63 percent are within the ±20 percent limits, 20 percent are above the upper 20 percent limit, and 17 percent are below the lower 20 percent limit. It would appear that the ±20 percent limits correspond to roughly one standard deviation between model and full-scale data.

Effect of hull form on pure ice resistance—The most extensive investigation to date of the effects of hull form on pure ice resistance is contained in the paper by Edwards et al [8]. The present paper can add little to this work. For the sake of

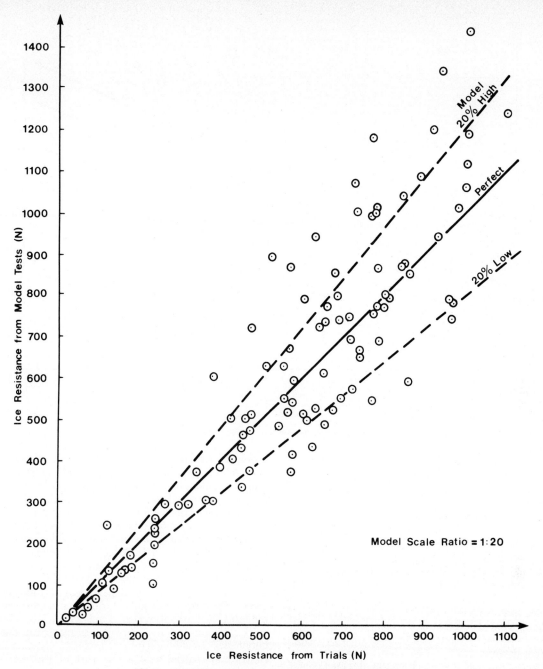

Fig. 8 Model/full-scale correlation—CGS *Pierre Radisson*

continuity, however, this section of the present paper will present a brief review of that part of the Edwards et al paper which pertains to hull form effect on pure ice resistance.

A series of seven different icebreaker models and two parallel midbodies was tested in order to determine the effect of varying length, beam, draft and block coefficient on icebreaking resistance of a typical modern icebreaker. Each of these variables was varied independently, insofar as was possible, over three discrete steps. For each model, ice flexural strength, ice thickness and ice friction factor were also varied. One hundred ninety-six data points were acquired in the test program and later subjected to a stepwise multiple regression analysis which accepted independent variables at the 95 percent confidence level.

The resulting equation, which follows, had a multiple correlation coefficient of 0.99:

$$\frac{R_i}{\rho_w gBh^2} = 5.7 + 0.147\,\frac{H}{h} - 7.83\,C_B{}^2$$

$$+ \frac{\sigma_f}{\rho_w gh}\,(-0.318 + 0.265\,f + 0.394\,C_B)$$

$$+ \frac{V}{\sqrt{gh}}\left(-68.16 + 0.048\,\frac{\sigma}{\rho_w gh}\right.$$

$$\left. + 223.73\,C_B - 181.3\,C_B{}^2 + 0.249\,\frac{H}{h}\right) \quad (32)$$

The equation was stated as valid over the following ranges of the independent variables:

$$104 > \frac{\sigma_f}{\rho_w gh} > 8$$

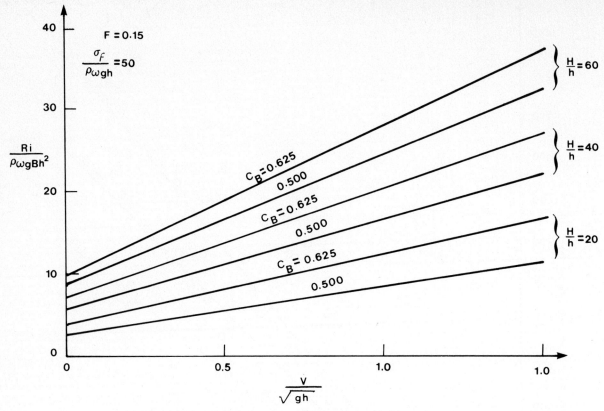

Fig. 9   Variation of ice resistance with sweep, hull size and hull form

$$2.5 > \frac{V}{\sqrt{gh}} > 0.2$$

$$0.625 > C_B > 0.500$$

$$73 > \frac{H}{h} > 10$$

No range for the friction factor f was given.

Equation (32) is rather complex and it is difficult to see how the various independent variables infuence the resistance. In order to see the effect of varying C_B and (H/h) more clearly, Fig. 9 shows plots of dimensionless resistance as a function of dimensionless speed with C_B and (H/h) as parameters and with f and $(\sigma_f/\rho_w gh)$ held constant at 0.15 and 50, respectively. These plots show that dimensionless ice resistance increases as C_B and H/h increase.

It is interesting to note that equation (32) does not contain ship length. This variable was not found to be significant in the regression analysis in spite of the fact that it was varied up to 40 percent more than the parent hull form. This is in disagreement with the full-scale data analysis reported earlier. However, the variation in length among the full-scale data is far greater than 40 percent. Equation (32) also appears to the present authors to give too much variation in resistance with ship draft.

If the designer is considering icebreaker-type ships, consideration should be given to the hull forms discussed by Noble and Bulat [16]. These forms use the CGCS *Pierre Radisson* as a parent. Since that ship obviously has outstanding icebreaking characteristics (see Ship D in Table 1), parametric form variations about this parent should be of great interest and value.

Hull ice resistance based on analytical studies

Predicting ice resistance analytically is an extremely complex problem. Ice may be treated, for example, as an elastic plate on an elastic foundation for purposes of analysis. But even simple equations for this model involve fourth-order, nonlinear partial differential equations. Further, full-scale and model-scale test data clearly show that the strength of ice has only a minor influence on the total icebreaking resistance. Even if the aforementioned differential equations could be solved, one may find that only a fraction of the problems had been solved.

This complex problem has been tackled by several investigators over the years, starting perhaps with Runeburg [17] in 1888. The most significant contributions in recent times were published by Kashteljan, Poznak and Ryvlin [18]. While their work cannot be strictly referred to as analytical, their contribution gives great insight into the problem. Another significant contribution to the field is the work of Enkvist [19]. His order-of-magnitude analysis of ice resistance components gives even greater insight into the factors contributing to icebreaking resistance.

Perhaps the first person to investigate the problem completely analytically was Milano [20, 21]. Milano's algorithm, however, shows ice resistance to be greatly influenced by ice flexural strength and only slightly influenced by hull-ice friction. This is in disagreement with full-scale trials and ice model test data.

Recently, a major contribution to the field has been made by Naegle [22]. Naegle's algorithm produces results and trends which agree reasonably well with full-scale trials and ice model test data. For this reason, Naegle's model is considered to be the best one available in the open literature today and will now be discussed in some detail.

Naegle approaches the hull ice resistance problem as a mechanics problem. All forces acting on the hull are explicitly written and Newton's law is applied. The resulting coupled differential equations are solved numerically to determine

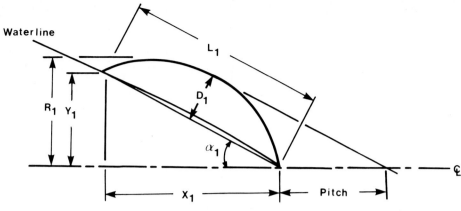

Fig. 10(a) Row 1 breaking pattern

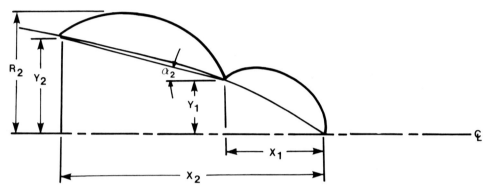

Fig. 10(b) Row 2 breaking pattern

rigid-body motions. Ice resistance is determined by setting the surge-direction velocity to a constant value and calculating average values for the surge direction forces.

Naegle considers both ice and non-ice (fluid and propulsion) forces, but only the ice-related forces will be discussed here. His treatment covers those ice forces related to breaking of the ice, turning of broken ice pieces, submersion of the broken ice pieces, and mechanical friction between the hull and the ice. Naegle starts by assuming a breaking pattern for the ice as shown in Fig. 10. He analyzed breakage patterns from full-scale ship trials and empirically derived an equation relating the ratio of cusp depth (D_j) and characteristic length of the ice to an average of the direction cosines between the hull normal and vertical axis near the forebody of the ship. He assumed values for the ratio of cusp length (L_j) and depth and used these to obtain the length of each row of cusps. The number of rows of ice broken becomes a function of the ice characteristic length, hull form and beam.

Equations for forces encountered during actual fracture of the ice were derived using primarily the work of Nevel [23]. These equations also consider mechanical friction and inertial forces and are applied up to the point where the stress in the ice sheet equals the ice flexural strength.

Once the cusps are broken, another set of equations is derived to describe the forces associated with turning the flows. These equations consider the effect of ventilation as first described by Enkvist [19]. Naegle assumes the ventilation to be linearly dependent upon speed. It is assumed absent at zero speed and present half the time at higher speeds. The turning force equations also include mechanical friction.

After the cusps are turned against the hull, Naegle derives another set of equations to describe the forces associated with

submerging the ice. The submerged floes are assumed to slide along the underwater surface of the hull and to remain in constant contact with it. Buoyancy and mechanical friction forces are considered.

Naegle's treatment of the problem essentially divides the pure ice resistance into six components: two related to ice fracture (normal and friction), two to ice floe turning (normal and friction), and two to ice floe submergence (normal and friction). The relative contribution of each of these terms to the total depends upon the ice flexural strength, ship speed, hull-ice friction, and ice thickness. In general, Naegle's algorithm produces results and trends which agree with full-scale trials and model test data. For example, a doubling of ice strength at any reasonable ship speed does not double the ice resistance since ice strength affects only two of the six ice resistance components. Doubling hull-ice friction, on the other hand, nearly doubles the total ice resistance because it affects three of the six components.

Naegle compares the results of his algorithm with several sets of full-scale and model test data and shows reasonable correlation. His resistance predictions as a function of ice thickness appear to be somewhat low, however, and he attributes this to the turning-related force equations. Naegle concludes that his algorithm could be useful in preliminary design but should not be used in place of ice model tests.

As stated previously, the present authors consider Naegle's algorithm to be the best available in the open literature. The algorithm should be useful in studying hull forms for ice-worthy ships in the feasibility design stage. In addition, the algorithm provides a fairly sound basis for future work in this area and provides great insight into the ice resistance problem associated with ice-worthy ships.

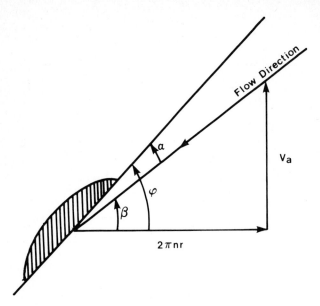

Fig. 11 Propeller blade-velocity diagram

4. Propeller design

The design of propellers for ice-worthy ships is not straightforward. As indicated in Section 2, there is not a great deal of information available concerning needed hull-propeller-ice interaction coefficients. Furthermore, there is much confusion concerning methods for applying what data are available. The design procedures discussed in this section will, it is hoped, eliminate at least some of the confusion and provide a sounder basis for propeller selection.

Classic works in this field are found in the papers by Ignatjev [24], and Enkvist and Johansson [25]. These authors give particularly practical information regarding the selection of propellers for optimum efficiency while icebreaking. The work of Enkvist and Johansson is of particular interest because they recommend departures from traditional tugboat and icebreaker design practice. The traditional approach generally involves designing propellers for maximum thrust in bollard conditions or some intermediate speed using the standard series propeller data without giving consideration to the ice. Usually this practice results in the largest practical diameter propeller consistent with cavitation criteria associated with submergence, and a rather small pitch-diameter ratio. Enkvist and Johansson claim, however, that when ice interaction with the propeller is considered, smaller diameters and larger pitch-diameter ratios result in a more efficient propeller. Their conclusions appear to be based on laboratory studies of model propellers in water-ice mixtures. Unfortunately, easy-to-use design data are not provided in their paper. Their paper also does not mention thrust deduction, wake fraction or relative rotative efficiency.

Kader [26] describes the procedures he used to design the propeller for a recent U.S. Coast Guard icebreaking tugboat (*Katmai Bay*). He employed the traditional approach. Kader mentions the work of Enkvist and Johansson but apparently could not accept the approximately 10 percent decrease in open-water thrust associated with reducing propeller diameter. While Kader's approach is referred to as traditional, it also points out some of the confusion surrounding icebreaker propeller design.

Kader sought values for propeller pitch-diameter and expanded area ratios which maximized thrust at 5 knots given the propeller diameter and delivered horsepower [2500 hp (1864 kW)]. In order to perform such calculations, it is necessary to know relative rotative efficiency, wake fraction and thrust deduction. Kader makes no mention of relative rotative efficiency. A check of his calculations shows that he assumed it to be unity.

For wake fraction, Kader used wake fraction data at the self-propulsion point for 5 knots. This is completely inappropriate, for at 5 knots the self-propulsion power requirement was only around 50 hp (37 kW), not 2500 hp. Consequently, the wake field at the self-propulsion point would be entirely different from that at a 5-knot towing condition using 2500 hp. Kader made no attempt to use wake fraction data under towing conditions which were collected by West [12], and makes only passing reference to thrust deduction in his design even though such data must have been available (although not reported) from West's work. It is interesting to note that Kader goes on in his report to present results of detailed lifting-line propeller calculations for the propeller selected with the incorrect wake fraction.

Basic concepts

The preceding discussions point out some of the interesting problems facing the ice-worthy ship propeller designer. In order to explain the design procedure recommended in this paper, it is necessary to describe in more detail the behavior of wake fraction under towing and icebreaking conditions previously discussed in Section 1. Consider the blade velocity diagram shown in Fig. 11. The advance coefficient, J_a, is directly proportional to the tangent of the angle β. The thrust and torque are directly related to the attack angle α, which is in turn a function of the difference between the pitch angle ϕ and the advance angle β. During icebreaking, ice interacting with the propeller can slow its speed as discussed in the paper by Enkvist and Johansson. If the advance speed of the propeller, V_a, were to remain constant, then the attack angle on the blade could rapidly decrease and even go negative. Thrust and torque would quickly diminish and the thrust could go negative. Such shaft speed variations, however, are nonsteady phenomena and are of concern to the propeller designer only insofar as they affect the long-term average propeller thrust and torque.[8]

In the analysis of the full-scale ice trials data previously described, such long-term averages of thrust and torque were obtained and used in the computations of relative rotative efficiency and wake fraction. Consequently, these coefficients represent average or long-term values suitable for the design of propellers.

Consider now the plot of $(1 - w_p)$ shown in Fig. 12, and the associated blade velocity diagrams and $K_T - J$ curves. Imagine an icebreaker towing a load in open water which gradually increases from nothing (self-propulsion point) to such a magnitude that it stalls (bollard point) the ship. Throughout this maneuver, the following equation applies:

$$V_a = V(1 - w_p) \qquad (33)$$

At the free-running condition, V_a will equal approximately $0.8\,V$. As the load increases, V_a slowly decreases until at *some finite ship speed*, V_a becomes zero. At this point the angle of attack on the propeller equals roughly the pitch angle. Note that this occurs when $J_a = 0$ on the $K_T - J$ curve, yet this is *not* bollard condition. Further, increase in load causes V_a to go negative. This does not mean thrust goes negative. It does mean, however, that the propeller is now operating in a regime not normally tested in open-water propeller tests. To get data for a propeller in this quadrant, the propeller must be turning ahead but towed backwards. When the load is finally increased

---

[8] Adequate blade strength assumed.

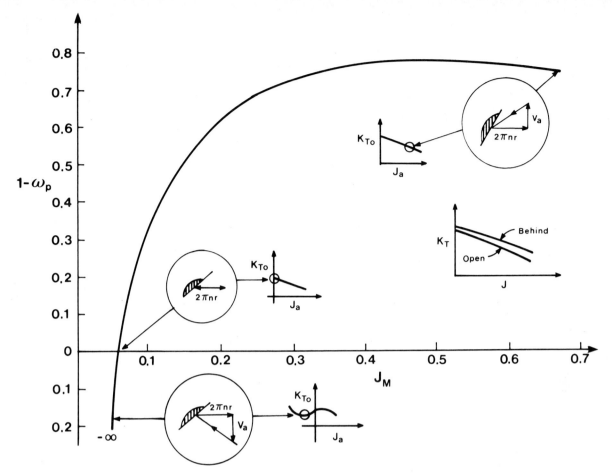

Fig. 12 Typical wake fraction under towing conditions

to the point where it stalls the ship, equation (33) can no longer be used to calculate V_{ap} because the equation is indeterminant. That is, as V approaches zero, $(1 - w_p)$ approaches negative infinity. While this behavior may at first seem hard to believe, it becomes more palatable when one understands that the $(1 - w_p)$ curve was derived from self-propelled overload model tests for the *Katmai Bay*.

The situation depicted in Fig. 12 does not necessarily occur with all icebreaker hulls. It is also possible for $1 - w_p$ to exhibit behavior as shown in Fig. 13. In this case the K_{TBp}-curve crosses over the K_T-curve at a certain value of J_a (equal to J_m) and then continues below K_T for values for J_a less than this crossover J_a. This completely different behavior of $(1 - w_p)$ shows clearly how dependent w_p is on the definition equation for w_p as well as the stern for the icebreaker. Figure 13 is derived from actual model overload test data presented in the aforementioned report by Murdey [15]. The same behavior was found during full-scale tests of a large polar icebreaker as reported by DeBord [4].

In considering wake fraction during icebreaking, there are at least two approaches that can be taken. One approach is to use an entirely new "open water" $K_T - J$ curve for referencing wake fraction computations. Juurmaa and Segercrantz [6] suggest this approach in their paper. The new open-water $K_T - J$ curves are obtained by conducting propeller dynamometer tests in an ice-water mixture, that is, without the ship being present. They show that this new "open ice-water" $K_T - J$ is similar to, but slightly below, the normal open-water $K_T - J$ curves. If sufficient data were available and could be trusted to have no model-scale effects, then thrust identity wake fractions could be obtained by referencing the wake fractions to

these new curves. The present disadvantages associated with this method are: (1) Such data are not readily available to a designer; (2) the open ice-water $K_T - J$ curves depend on the amount of ice entering the propeller; and (3) model/full-scale correlation has not been established.

Another approach is the one suggested in this paper. That is, full-scale ship trials $K_{TBi} - J_m$ data are plotted along with normal open-water $K_T - J$ data and thrust identity wake fractions for icebreaking are obtained by referencing the wake fraction calculations to the open-water $K_T - J$ curves. The present disadvantages of this method is the scarcity of data. Both of the suggested methods suffer from the fact that open-water propeller data are not normally collected in the "positive n negative V_a" quadrants and this is sometimes necessary.

Consider now an icebreaker starting at its full-power free-running speed and encountering a level ice field whose thickness gradually increases with distance of penetration. The speed of the icebreaker will decrease slowly until it reaches the ice thickness which stalls ($V = 0$) the ship. The ice-related wake coefficient ($1 - w_i$) for this situation is shown (actual computations using *Katmai Bay* ice trials data) in Fig. 14. It can be seen that the situation described for the icebreaker while towing in open water applied to the icebreaking situation also. Only in the icebreaking case, the speed (ship) at which J_a equals zero will be higher and the propeller will therefore operate in the positive-n negative-V_a quadrant over a larger range of ship speeds.

Design procedure

The procedure recommended here for designing the optimum-efficiency propeller for an icebreaker will now be de-

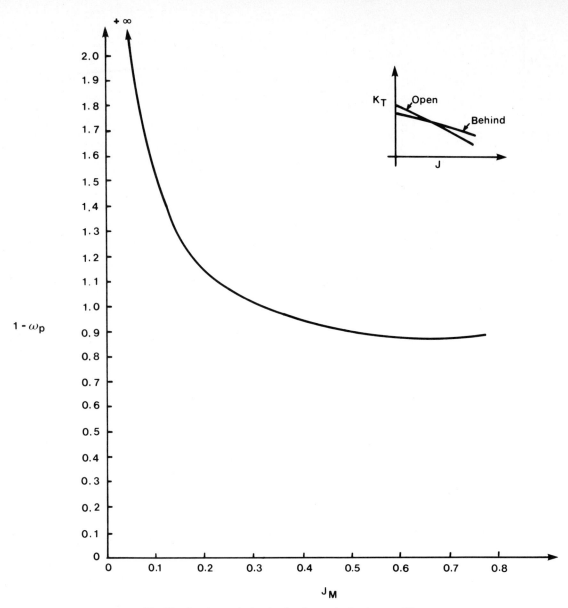

Fig. 13 Another typical wake fraction under towing conditions

scribed.   First it is presumed that thrust deduction, wake fraction and relative rotative efficiency data have been obtained from full-scale icebreaking trials and model tests for a similar ship as required.   Thrust identity coefficients should be used and plotted as a function of J_m.   The ship speed for optimization is then selected based on preliminary routing studies.   The maximum-diameter propeller should be selected consistent with adequate hull clearances for vibration and ice clearing.   It is also presumed that open-water $K_T - J$ and $K_Q - J$ propeller curves are available as a function of pitch-diameter and expanded-area ratio.

Two general cases may then be investigated.   In one case the shaft horsepower to be installed is unknown and in the other case the shaft horsepower is given.   The first case is the more general design problem and will be discussed first.

In this case, the total hull resistance is first computed given the ice thickness, ice strength, ship characteristics, etc., using the given ship speed.   Next, values for pitch-diameter and expanded-area ratio are arbitrarily selected.   A trial value of shaft speed is next selected and used to compute J_m.   Values

for $(1 - t_i)$,[9] $(1 - w_i)$ and R_i are then found from plots.   The value of J_a is calculated using $(1 - w_i)$ and J_m. K_{T0} for this value of J_a is found and used to determine T_0.   From this, the total resistance which can be overcome is found by multiplying T_0 by $(1 - t_i)$.   If the value of total resistance so found does not agree with total resistance required, shaft speed is changed and the foregoing process repeated until acceptable agreement is found.   Once convergence is achieved, the value of J_a at convergence is used to find K_{Q0}.   This can then be used in conjunction with the values of R_i and n at convergence to obtain the required shaft horsepower for the values of pitch-diameter and expanded-area ratio used.   The procedure is repeated for several values of pitch-diameter and expanded-area ratios.   The pitch-diameter ratio which gives minimum horsepower for each expanded-area ratio is then selected.   Cavitation charts such as suggested by Enkvist and Johansson are used to select the expanded-area ratio which minimizes shaft horsepower while providing sufficient safeguard against cavitation.

[9] Obtained by assuming $(1 - t_i) = (1 - t_p)$ where t_p is from overload model tests.

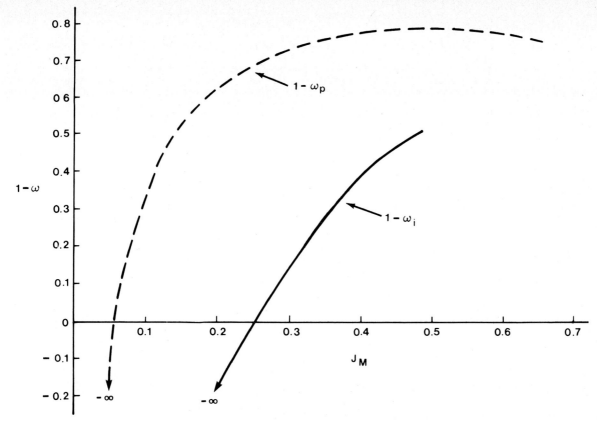

Fig. 14 Typical wake fraction under icebreaking conditions

For the case in which shaft horsepower is given, the procedure involves seeking the pitch-diameter and expanded-area ratio which maximizes thrust available for icebreaking while providing sufficient safeguard against cavitation. First, values for pitch diameter and expanded-area ratio are arbitrarily selected. Next a trial value for shaft speed is chosen and used to compute J_m. Values for $(1 - t_i)$, $(1 - w_i)$ and R_i are found. Two values for K_Q are then computed. The first is obtained using the given horsepower, the assumed shaft speed and R_i. The second value is obtained by calculating J_a using $(1 - w_i)$ and J_m, and finding K_Q from the open-water $K_Q - J$ curves. If the two values found do not match, another value for shaft speed is chosen and the process repeated until convergence of the K_Q-values is achieved. Once convergence has been achieved, the value of J_a at convergence is used to obtain K_T from the open-water $K_T - J$ curves. The values of shaft speed and $(1 - t_i)$ at convergence are then used to compute available thrust for the values of pitch-diameter and expanded-area ratios chosen. The procedure is repeated for several values of pitch-diameter and expanded-area ratios. The pitch-diameter ratios which provide maximum thrust are then selected for each expanded-area ratio considered. Finally, the expanded-area ratio which provides the required margin against cavitation and maximum available thrust is selected.

The design procedure recommended here is not considered by the authors to be the final word on this subject. Considerably more work in this area is required. More work following the approach taken by Juurmaa and Segercrantz [6] could prove very valuable. It would be extremely interesting, for example, to have the Troost propeller series tested using their dynamometer in a model ice which had crushing and shearing strength properly scaled. More self-propelled model icebreaking tests are also needed and these data should be compared with full-scale ice trials data to more adequately describe

ice-related thrust deduction, wake, and relative rotative coefficients using methods suggested in this paper.

5. Conclusions and recommendations

The following represent the major conclusions and recommendations of this paper.

(a) To understand ice-related thrust deduction, wake fraction, relative rotative efficiency, and quasi-propulsive efficiency for ice-worthy ships, it is first necessary to completely understand how these propulsion factors vary under towing or overload conditions in open water.

(b) Currently available data from model self-propulsion tests in ice do not allow one to conclude that ice does or does not affect thrust deduction. Wake fractions, however, are considerably affected by icebreaking and this has considerable effect on propulsive efficiency and propeller selection. Relative rotative efficiency does not appear to be greatly affected by icebreaking.

(c) Only the shaft thrust method should be used to infer hull resistance from trials data. Use of only the shaft torque method will lead to errors in estimating hull resistance. By carefully accounting for the thrust deduction factor, model ice resistance data will predict full-scale ship trials resistance within ±20 percent without any dependence on ship speed.

(d) Effects of hull form on icebreaking resistance may be approximated in feasibility/preliminary design using equation (31), and the works of Edwards et al [8], Noble and Bulat [16], and Naegle [22].

(e) The selection of optimum parameters for an ice-worthy ship is not a trivial task. In no case should free-running propulsion factors be used unless this is to be the point where optimum efficiency is desired. Usually route analyses will indicate a much lower design speed at full power. In this case, overloaded propulsion parameters including ice effects must be considered in the design.

References

1 Lewis, J. W. and Edwards, R. Y., Jr., "Methods for Predicting Icebreaking and Ice Resistance Characteristics of Icebreakers," TRANS. SNAME, Vol. 78, 1970.

2 Harvald, S. A., "Tug Propulsion: Wake, Thrust Deduction, and R.P.M." *European Shipbuilding*, Vol. 12, No. 3, 1963.

3 Parker, M. N. and Dawson, J., "Tug Propulsion Investigation," *Trans*. RINA, 1962.

4 DeBord, F. W., Voelker, R. P., Geisel, F. A., Coburn, J. L., and Dane, K. E., "Winter 1981 Trafficability Tests of the USCGC *Polar Sea;* Volume V—Bollard and Tow-Rope Pull Tests," Arctec, Incorporated Report No. 583C-3, Columbia, Md., 1981.

5 Harvald, S. A., "Wake and Thrust Deduction at Extreme Propeller Loadings," Swedish State Shipbuilding Experimental Tank, Publication No. 61, Goteborg, 1967.

6 Juurmaa, K. and Segercrantz, H., "On Propulsion and Its Efficiency in Ice," *Proceedings*, SNAME Sixth Ship Technology and Research (STAR) Symposium, Paper No. 17, 1981.

7 Narita, S. and Yamaguchi, M., "Some Experimental Study on Hull Forms for the New Japanese Antarctic Research Ship," *Proceedings*, SNAME Sixth Ship Technology and Research (STAR) Symposium, Paper No. 20, 1981.

8 Edwards, R. Y., Major, R. A., Kim, J. K., German, J. G., Lewis, J. W., and Miller, D. R., "Influence of Major Characteristics of Icebreaker Hulls on Their Powering Requirements and Maneuverability in Ice," TRANS. SNAME, Vol. 84, 1976.

9 Lecourt, E. J., Major, R. A., Thomas, H. L., and Naegle, J. N., "Recent United States Coast Guard Efforts to Improve Icebreaking Efficiency," *Proceedings*, SNAME Spring Meeting (STAR) Symposium, 1978.

10 Edwards, R. Y., Lewis, J. W., Wheaton, J. W., and Coburn, J. L., "Full-Scale and Model Tests of Great Lakes Icebreaker," TRANS. SNAME, Vol. 80, 1972.

11 Vance, G. P., Gracewski, A. S., and Goodwin, M. J., "Full-Scale Icebreaking Tests of the USCGC *Katmai Bay*," *Proceedings*, SNAME Sixth Ship Technology and Research (STAR) Symposium, Paper No. 25, 1981.

12 West, E. E., "Powering Predictions for the United States Coast Guard 140-Foot WYTM Represented by Model 5336," Naval Ship Research and Development Center Report No. SPD-223-16, Bethesda, Md., April 1975.

13 Edwards, R. Y., Johnson, B., Dunne, M., Comfort, G., and Bulat, V., "Results of Full Scale Trials in Ice of CCGS *Pierre Radisson*," *Proceedings*, SNAME Sixth Ship Technology and Research (STAR) Symposium, Paper No. 23, 1981.

14 Bulat, V. and Glen, I. F., "The Testing of a Ship Model in Ice for the National Research Council," Arctec Canada Limited Report No. 335C-3, Kanata, Ont., 1981.

15 Murdey, D. C., "Resistance and Propulsion Experiments with Model 327-1 and Propellers 66C and 66R," National Research Council MDSL Report LTR-SH-269, 1980.

16 Noble, P. and Bulat, V., "Final Report on Optimization of Bow Forms for a Medium Icebreaker," Arctec Canada Limited Report No. 461C, Kanata, Ont., 1979.

17 Runeburg, R., "On Steamers for Winter Navigation and Icebreaking," *Proceedings*, The Institution of Civil Engineers, Vol. 97, Part 3, London, 1888.

18 Kashteljan, V. I., Poznjak, I. I., and Ryvlin, A. J., *Ice Resistance to Motion of a Ship* (Translation), Sudostroenie, Leningrad, 1968.

19 Enkvist, E., "On the Ice Resistance Encountered by Ships Operating in the Continuous Mode of Icebreaking," The Swedish Academy of Engineering Sciences in Finland, Report No. 24, Helsinki, 1972.

20 Milano, V. R., "Ship Resistance to Continuous Motion in Ice," TRANS. SNAME, Vol. 81, 1973.

21 Milano, V. R., "Ship Resistance to Continuous Motion in Ice," Ph.D. Dissertation, Stevens Institute of Technology, Hoboken, N.J., 1972.

22 Naegle, J. N., "Ice-Resistance Prediction and Motion Simulation for Ships Operating in the Continuous Mode of Icebreaking," Ph.D. Dissertation, University of Michigan, Ann Arbor, 1980.

23 Nevel, D. E., "A Semi-Infinite Plate on an Elastic Foundation," U.S. Army Cold Regions Research and Engineering Laboratory, Research Report 136, Hanover, N.H., 1965.

24 Ignatjev, M. A., *Screw-Propellers for Ships Navigating in Ice*, Sudostroenie, Leningrad, 1966.

25 Enkvist, E. and Johansson, B. M., "On Icebreaker Screw Design," *European Shipbuilding Journal of the Ship Technical Society*, Vol. 17, No. 1, 1968.

26 Kader, R. D., "The Design of a Propeller for a U.S. Coast Guard Icebreaker Tugboat," Naval Ship Research and Development Center Report No. SPD-223-19, Bethesda, Md., Oct. 1975.

Discussion

A. Tunik, Member

Ice resistance to continuous icebreaking in smooth ice is usually divided into speed-independent and speed-dependent components. There are no principal disagreements between most authors in their definition of expressions for the speed-independent components. The speed-dependent components are the more difficult for study and model.

I'd like to touch on the problem of how ship dimensions are presented in the speed-dependent component of the ice resistance. In the 1968 Kashtelyan expression [18], the only variable in this component is $B^{1.65}$. In papers published from 1970 to 1981, by Lewis and Edwards [1], Edwards et al [10, 8], Enkvist [19], Milano [20], Lecourt et al [9], and Vance et al [11], there is a linear dependence (in the dimensional form) on the ship beam only. The dependence on $B^2 L^{-0.5}$ is used by Poznjak et al in their paper at the Ice Tech '81 Symposium. In the present work, the speed-dependent component in expressions (29), (30), and (31) is a function of the dimensional variables $LB^{0.5}$ or $(L/h)(h/B)^{0.5}$ in the dimensionless form.

This approach is very close to Kashtelyan's [18], if only icebreakers are discussed. The only difference that can be found between expression (31) in dimensional form and Kashtelyan's $(R_i = K_0 Bh^2 + K_1 Bh\sigma_f + K_2 B^{1.65} hV)$ is $LB^{0.5}$ instead of $B^{1.65}$ in the speed-dependent component. All the existing icebreakers have the L/B ratio in a very narrow range from 4 to

5. Then, the $LB^{0.5}$ to $B^{1.65}$ ratio varies also in the very narrow range from about 2.5 to 3 for the dimensions in meters (mean 2.78 with the standard deviation 0.18). Thus, for the icebreakers, it does not matter which of the ship dimensions are presented in the expression, but it does matter how it is done. That is because the icebreaker dimensions are hardly independent variables. For ice-worthy ships other than the special icebreakers, the L/B ratio can vary so significantly that the length and the beam may be assumed as the independent variables. Therefore, the structure of the speed-dependent component in the ice resistance expression is to be as physically comprehensive as possible.

Unfortunately, the authors do not explain their unusual choice of the variables specified by expression (28). It is understandable that the speed-dependent component of the ice resistance is to depend on the length or L/B ratio, but the stronger influence of L than of B is less understandable. The authors use the identity of coefficients C_2 in Table 1 as evidence in favor of the chosen expression but they specify neither the ship dimensions nor the L/B ratios. If these trials were conducted within a relatively narrow range of the L/B ratios (for the icebreakers, for instance), the Kashtelyan expression $(B^{1.65})$ or any other expression like $B^a L^b$ (where $a + b \cong 1.5$) could result in a similar identity of the speed-dependent component's coefficient (C_2). Thus, the C_2 identity provides no evidence in favor of the chosen expression if the ship parameters are not specified. It is also unclear how the authors excluded the effect of both the bow shape and the friction coefficient as stated, if all four sets of the full-scale ice trials data were obtained from different bow shapes and hull surface conditions specified in very uncertain terms in Table 2.

The model/full-scale correlation presented in Figs. 6, 7, and 8 does not prove the dependence of the speed-dependent component on $LB^{0.5}$ because the correlation relates to the total pure ice resistance. Hence, a nonassumable error of the component can result in an assumable agreement in the total resistance. In addition, when using the model tests for defining the speed-dependent component (or components) it is of course usual to use the Froud number as the similarity criterion. However, the speed-dependent components include also the forces resisting the transverse motion of ice fractures. As the ice fractures are typical bodies with turbulent flow, the Froud number models such forces with errors that increase with the increase in ship speed.

It is much easier to criticize than to create. I would not like the opinions in my discussion to be misunderstood as criticism, but rather as a wish to see convincing evidence that the approach used is physically true or at least to be aware of the range where the expressions proposed can be used. It has been my great pleasure to read this informative paper and I hope to use its data in practice. The authors are to be congratulated on their proper contribution in the methods of the ice resistance definition.

Ernst Enkvist,[10] Visitor

My comments on this extensive and important paper are intended to make the picture more complete rather than to raise objections. The authors do not clearly state that the screw-ice interaction is transient. When reference [25] was produced by the discusser and his colleague Johansson, the background was that the side screws of the *Moscow*-class of Polar icebreakers frequently stopped in ice and sometimes suffered damage because they were not able to maintain their rate of revolution. In laboratory tests the interaction could be made reasonable stationary. Afterwards, during many full-scale tests, we used to watch the rpm-meters on the bridge to learn what really happened. What we found made us drop the idea of defining stationary "ice conditions" for screw-design use. Sometimes, at high speed in brash ice the rpm-pointers reacted frequently. In Arctic conditions a huge multi-year ice floe could tilt on its edge to be milled by the screw, nearly stopping it. During many observations in heavy ice at near zero speed, however, there was no interaction whatsoever. The conclusion was that the screw-ice interaction is a frustrating and transient phenomenon which varies with ship type, draft, ice conditions, speed, hull form and stern configuration. Icebreaker evolution resulted in increasing power load on disk area and thus rpm could be maintained without any deliberately decreased diameter.

The description of interaction given in the preceding indicates that a stationary propulsion correction due to ice could be somewhat dangerous to use in connection with analyses of icebreaking full-scale tests. During breaking virgin ice with a large-draft icebreaker there is often no interaction at all, and if there is, it is occasional and requires continuous recording.

In analyzing a full-scale test to obtain ice resistance data the open-water bollard-pull full-scale test is an important reference. Such tests are normal practice for icebreakers and tugs, but not for icebreaking cargo ships. Wake measurements, free or towing, from model tests suffer from scale effects. Performing ice resistance model tests as self-propulsion tests to include in-teraction effects is certainly not to be recommended for reasons explained both by the authors and by the foregoing arguments. Such propulsion tests are useful for special qualitative interaction studies only.

Kimmo Juurmaa,[11] Visitor, and Henrik Segercrantz,[11] Visitor

In their very extensive paper concerning propeller-ice-ship interaction, the authors refer to the discussers' paper [6]. In this discussion we are going to comment on some aspects of the results obtained by the authors and to clarify our approach to propeller-ice-interaction presented in the aforementioned paper.

The authors derived equation (23) as a method for determining a ship's total resistance in ice. This method can be used without model-scale tests if the ship's propeller-ice interaction is relatively weak and the hull form is "conventional." As the accurate measurement of shaft thrust may be difficult (low strain rate compared with the strain rate of shaft torque), it can create a potential source of error. Consequently, the simplest way to derive the net thrust is to record the propeller revolutions and make t and w corrections based on open-water tow rope knowledge.

When the hull form is unconventional and the propeller-ice interaction is strong, the η_i method can be used successfully together with model tests, as presented in reference [6]. Great care must be taken to derive correct ice torque results in the model tests.

Using a model propeller dynamometer for studying the propeller-ice interaction for a propeller alone, as presented in reference [6], can be valuable when studying and comparing different propeller configurations, but this method is *not* a good approach to ship-propeller-ice interaction for determining the ice resistance. Also, the way of presenting ice thrust and torque results in the dimensionless K_T, $K_Q - J$ form is dangerous and can result in misleading conclusions as K_{Tice} and K_{Qice} are directly dependent on a specific n and D and a specific ship in a specific ice condition. As also the value of J $(= V/nD)$ is affected by the change in mean propeller revolutions due to ice, it would be of interest to know whether the curves for "Behind Ice Free" K_T and K_Q in Fig. 4 have been obtained using the same propeller revolutions as in the icebreaking condition.

Referring to Section 4 we feel that there is some major confusion concerning the wake factor close to bollard condition. The reason for this confusion relates probably to the attempt to adapt the thrust identity method for purposes where it is not suitable. It should be noted that V_a is never negative, not even when V is zero.

In practice the influence of the ice on the thrust and wake coefficients is negligible. The influence appears with complicated propulsion-hull configurations, such as tunnel sterns and ducted propellers, in heavy ice conditions. The methods presented in reference [6] are useful for explaining the overall performance of vessels in these conditions.

Yoshio Kayo,[12] Visitor

The measurements of thrust, ship velocity and ice properties are more difficult and subject to error in ice than that in open water because actual ice fields are not homogeneous and the ship speed is not steady. Even in the case of open-water full-scale trials, winds, waves, currents and other disturbances affect the data to scatter the model-ship correlations. Considering these problems, the correlation between the trial resistance data and the prediction based on model ice resistance, shown in Figs. 6, 7, and 8, can be said to be remarkable. The results clearly

[10] Helsinki University of Technology, Finland.

[11] Oy Wartsila Ab, Helsinki Shipyards, Finland.

[12] Nagasaki Experimental Tank, Mitsubishi Heavy Industries, Ltd., Nagasaki, Japan.

show a usefulness of the model resistance test in ice; on the other hand, further investigation on the self-propelled model test in ice should be made in order to provide reliable data for designers.

I have two comments on this paper:

1. For the large ice-going tankers and LNG carriers which will be realized in the future, the scale effect of resistance is considered to be of significance. Therefore, we should be more careful in correlating the model results of such large ships to full-scale.

2. The authors mention that only the shaft-thrust method should be used to estimate hull resistance from trial data. The reason is given that the wake fraction difference will render the assumption $\eta_{Di} = \eta_{DP}$. I do not agree with the authors, since the difference between the shaft-thrust method and shaft-torque method is due to the variation of η_R; that is, if we have full-scale torque data, then we can estimate the thrust in such a manner as

$$Q, n$$
$$\downarrow$$
$$K_Q = Q/\rho n^2 D^5$$
$$\downarrow$$
$$\eta_R = \text{assumed}$$
$$\downarrow$$
$$K_{Q_0} = K_Q \cdot \eta_R$$
$$\downarrow$$
$$K_T \text{ open-water characteristics}$$
$$\downarrow$$
$$T$$

or if we follow equation (18)

$$\eta_D = \frac{RV}{2\pi n Q_B} = \frac{1-t}{1-w} \frac{T_B Q_0}{T_0 Q_B} \eta_0$$

with

$$\eta_0 = \frac{V_a T}{2\pi n Q_0} \text{ and } 1 - w = \frac{V_a}{V}$$

or

$$\eta_D = (1 - t) T_B/2\pi n Q_B$$

This again shows that the problem is only the evaluation of T_B/Q_B or η_R.

Those who have challenged the full-scale thrust measurement know well how difficult it is because of the very small strain caused by thrust compared with the strain due to torque. Considering the general scarcity of full-scale ice-going performance data, I would suggest that both thrust and torque data be carefully examined.

G. P. Vance, Member

The authors are to be complimented on an extremely important and well-written paper. If there is any fault to be found with the paper, it is that it attempts to cover three very important subjects related to ships in ice—resistance prediction, propulsion efficiency, and propeller design—in one short paper.

The authors do us a slight disservice by not completely identifying Ships A, B, C, and D in Table 1. I believe Ship A is the *Polar Star* class, Ship B is the *Mackinaw*, Ship C is the *Katmai Bay* and Ship D is identified as the *Pierre Radisson*. The complete identifications make it possible for one to utilize equation (29) for ships of the same general shape and size. One should also point out that equation (31) should be used with caution, for although it includes ship beam and length (I am very glad to see the effect of length finally being recognized), it neglects the effect of the bow shape of the vessel, that is, the

Table 2   Level ice estimated thrust deduction

Run No.	T_{meas} (lb)	R_{ice} (lb)	t_i
1000.000	19 227.000	14 100.000	0.27
1020.000	41 597.000	23 900.000	0.42
1100.000	17 669.000	12 000.000	0.32
1110.000	34 626.000	23 500.000	0.32
1130.000	45 685.000	24 300.000	0.47
1200.000	32 502.000	19 500.000	0.40
1210.000	38 037.000	24 200.000	0.36
1220.000	44 096.000	25 500.000	0.42
2100.000	22 387.000	15 300.000	0.32
2110.000	35 055.000	20 500.000	0.42
2120.000	42 747.000	23 200.000	0.46
1300.000	34 004.000	25 000.000	0.26
1310.000	41 250.000	25 200.000	0.39
1320.000	47 904.000	34 400.000	0.28
1331.000	48 993.000	34 500.000	0.30
2200.000	49 248.000	35 000.000	0.29
2210.000	47 677.000	33 000.000	0.31
2221.000	41 280.000	28 900.000	0.30
2230.000	29 937.000	23 000.000	0.23
2231.000	20 724.000	15 000.000	0.28
2001.000	17 211.000	14 500.000	0.16
2300.000	44 924.000	30 000.000	0.33
2310.000	49 574.000	19 000.000	0.62

Average $t_i = 0.343$.
Standard deviation = 0.097.

Mackinaw, radically different from the *Polar Star*.

It is also of interest to note the inclusion of ship draft in equation (32) and the increase in resistance with draft as shown in Fig. 9. I have seen model test data that indicated there could be a decrease in resistance with an increase in draft. This can be partially explained by the ice not flowing along the bottom of the vessel, but being forced up to the side at the waterline as the draft was increased, thereby decreasing the ice-ship hull friction effect.

The authors' presentation of thrust deduction and wake fraction is extremely important and timely. The effect of ice on these parameters has not been given sufficient attention in the past. I have attempted to obtain a better understanding of what is happening to these parameters in ice by utilizing the data collected in the *Katmai Bay* experiments. Utilizing the data presented in Table 2 accompanying this discussion (available in an unpublished report provided to the U.S. Coast Guard in 1980), and equation (7) of the paper, and assuming that the tow rope pull provided by West [12] is equal to the icebreaking resistance, I have computed t_i and plotted it on Fig. 2 of the paper, presented with this discussion as Fig. 15. One can readily see that t_i varies from 0.25 to 0.42, which is a four- to five-fold increase in the open-water thrust deduction one would normally expect. Since the hull efficiency is so dependent on thrust deduction as shown in equation (19), it certainly deserves more attention than it has been getting in the past. Unlike the authors, I did not have sufficient information to make a similar analysis for the wake fraction.

I did have the opportunity to compare model test results with full-scale results using a method similar to the shaft thrust method, and the results are shown in Fig. 16 herewith. The comparison shows the results of Milano's technique, Kashteljan's technique, the ICEREM technique and model test results as reported by Le Court in an ARCTEC report "Icebreaking Model Tests of the 140 Foot WXTM" prepared for the U.S. Coast Guard. ICEREM is a proprietary analytical model licensed by ARCTEC. The Naegle formulation was not available at the time this comparison was made. The figure is for 12-in. level ice with no bubble system in effect. As can be seen in the figure, the Milano technique predicts high; the Kashteljan

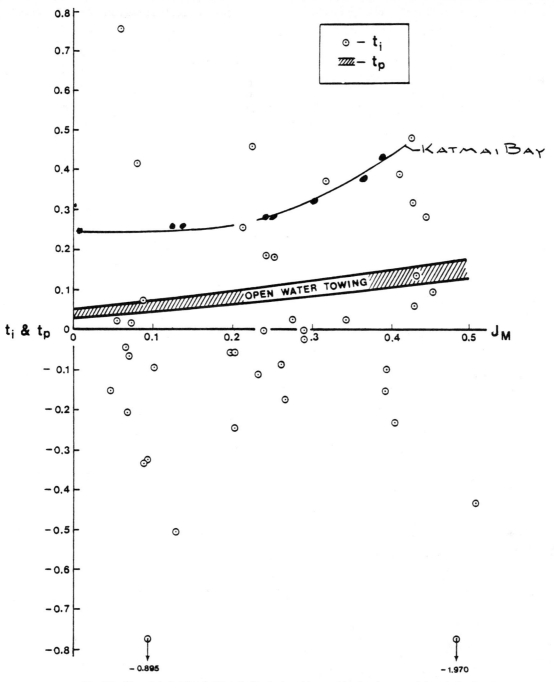

Fig. 15 Thrust deduction factors during icebreaking and towing from model scale tests

technique is high at low speeds and of the wrong slope. The model tests are the best prediction with ICEREM predicting high, but with the correct slope. It should be noted that IC-EREM is very sensitive to the friction coefficient and a slight error in this factor could cause the differences noted. A $t_i = 0.4$ was assumed for the full-scale data.

John N. Naegle, Member

[The views expressed herein are the opinions of the discusser and not necessarily those of the Department of Transportation or the U.S. Coast Guard.]

In Fig. 1 it is not clear which curves are tug data from reference [2] and which are icebreaker data from reference [4]. The towing data of reference [4] were not obtained at pitch ratios larger than approximately 0.65, yet Fig. 1 seems to show icebreaker curves at ratios higher than this.

Figure 4 indicates that the icebreaking wake fraction differs considerably from the towing wake fraction. The icebreaking curves are at higher advance ratios than one might expect during the usual low-speed icebreaking operations.

The K_T portion of Fig. 5 shows model and full-scale data points clustered about the open-water K_T curve. Presumably, the open-water K_T curve is plotted against J_A, while the trials data are plotted against J_M. If all data were plotted against J_A, then the data points would shift some amount to the left and more of these points would fall below or near the open-water curve. A similar shifting to the left in the K_T portion of Fig. 4 would bring only a few of the data points near the open-water

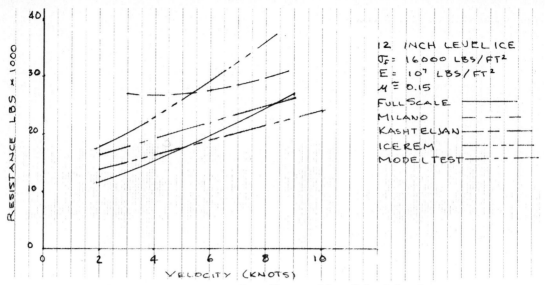

Fig. 16 Ice resistance, *Katmai Bay:* model, prediction, full scale

curve. These data seems to be contrary to those presented in Fig. 5.

Perhaps the authors would comment on the data from which these curves were derived?

Roderick Y. Edwards, Jr., Member

The authors have prepared a very interesting treatment of the hull interaction coefficients for ships which navigate in ice. The paper should serve as a catalyst for sorely needed research in the field of hull-propeller-ice interactions.

The authors present a comparison of the relationship between ice-free water thrust deduction and advance ratio with the corresponding "nonrelationship" for ice-covered waters in Fig. 2. The model used was that of CCGS *Pierre Radisson*. Those results are very discouraging. The authors suggest that the main source of dispersion is that the value of R_{iw} used to compute it must be obtained from the faired results of previous bare hull resistance trials in level ice which exhibit scatter. As long as I have simply faired or regressed model ice resistance data using *dimensional* model values for resistance, speed, ice thickness, strength, etc., I have rarely found errors of more than 10 percent in predictors for model resistance for other values of thickness, speed and strength lying within the bounds of the actual test data. Using a nominal resistance value of 20 lb force and an average thrust of say 22 lb force, a ±10 percent error in the predicted value of R_{iw} would cause thrust deduction to vary between zero and 0.1. The data shown in Fig. 2 suggest average errors in R_{iw} of as much as ±30 to 40 percent and extreme errors of over 100 percent. There must be other sources of error?

Equation (7) used by the authors to estimate it is only valid at the self-propulsion point. Were the points plotted in Fig. 2 obtained at the self-propulsion point? In ice model tests it is not a simple matter to achieve the self-propulsion point at a nice constant velocity. As I recall, for these tests we planned to bracket the self-propulsion point with discrete slightly over and under propulsion points and then fair and crossplot the results. Would the authors comment on how they finally did it?

Finally, would any trend show in Fig. 2 if the points were annotated with ice thickness values?

Shouldn't this vitally important experiment be repeated? Could the authors suggest how it can be done better next time?

Figure 4 is the crux of this paper in my view, where the behind icebreaking, behind ice free, and open KT and KQ curves are presented for real ships. The plots are thought-provoking to say the least.

In Figure 3 the behind and open plots in ice-free water are shown. Simply put, wake fraction is computed from the change in J needed to shift the "open" curve to fit on the "behind" curve. But in Fig. 4 the behind icebreaking curves cannot be made to superimpose on the open curves when behind icebreaking K_T and K_Q exceed open iT and K_Q. Is that why ω_{iT} in Fig. 4 stops at a J_m of about 0.5?

The traditional wake fraction approach only handles a lateral shift in the K_T and K_Q versus J curves. A coefficient needs to be derived which quantifies the global vertical shift of the K_T and K_Q versus J relationships apparently caused by ice flux into the screw race. This coefficient might be expected to be dependent upon hull form, ice thickness and J and should be treated as a "hull" coefficient since the hull will control the nature and density of the ice flow into the propeller.

On the subject of model/full-scale correlation, would the authors confirm that they subtracted from the full-scale resistance computed with "the shaft thrust method" the open-water resistance extrapolated from model tests and similarly subtracted the model open-water resistance from model total resistance in level ice?

In the latter part of the paper the authors encourage the careful consideration of wake at low advance ratios and high loads in the design of icebreaker screws. I think their emphasis is well directed particularly for triple-screw configurations. Design of icebreaker propulsion systems using hull interaction coefficients from lightly loaded conditions is unthinkable.

The authors offer some typical wake fraction plots for ice-free water under towing conditions. However, I don't believe that the propeller ever can really operate in the fourth quadrant (negative J–positive K_T) in steady state ahead or stalled operation. In the lowest circle in Fig. 12 for instance, I would suggest that the operating point has shifted back out along the positive J-axis to where there is an identical value of K_T.

Years ago when analyzing wake data from the *Polar Star* candidate models, I found that at bollard there was a finite apparent wake velocity; that is, observed K_T in the behind condition was always less than K_T at $J = 0$ for free-water propeller curves. Hence, we inferred that although J measured was zero, effective J was positive.

Resistance and Propulsion of Ice-Worthy Ships

Would the authors elaborate on the difference in the basic data which led to the differences in Figs. 12 and 13? How did they infer from measured K_T and open water K_T curves that J was negative?

The authors have dealt in this paper with relatively low-powered icebreakers with open screws in ice thin with respect to the propeller submergence. Hull/ice interactions might be expected to be modest.

Having model tested several high-powered tuglike icebreakers with unconventional sterns and nozzles in heavy ice, I can assure the readers of this paper that the hull/ice interaction coefficients are spectacular to the extent that effective propulsive force falls to a small fraction of that which would be measured under similar ice-free conditions in overload tests. Designers of shallow-draft, high-powered Arctic service vessels ignoring the concepts presented by the authors risk significant loss of operational efficiency in ice.

Jacques B. Hadler, Member

The authors have presented us with a synopsis of the problems associated with analyzing the propulsion performance of ships operating in ice and designing the propeller(s) to give the desired performance.

It seems to me that the clearest approach to analyzing propulsion performance in ice would be to determine the K_T, K_Q versus J characteristics of the propeller both in open water and when milling ice of the type(s) expected in service with a number of different ice concentrations in the water. When the propeller is milling ice, there will be changes in the characteristic curves, particularly the K_Q curve, due to the energy required to mill the ice. Utilizing these propeller performance curves when analyzing model self-propulsion tests in comparable ice fields should then provide much more insight into the interaction effects of the propeller and hull.

In regard to fixed-pitch propeller design, we essentially have the classical problem of designing a propeller for two widely different load conditions such as occurs in fishing vessels pulling large nets at very low speeds and then wanting to return to base as rapidly as possible. In most instances, economic analysis indicates that the propeller and engine (diesel) should be matched to achieve maximum towing power utilizing the full capacity of the engine and accepting the best speed possible on the free route operation without overtorquing the engine. This requires optimizing the propeller design for the towing condition. By analogy, the same approach would be applicable to the vessel which operates in ice most of the time. Utilizing propeller characteristic curves desired while milling ice in conjunction with wake fractions, thrust deduction and relative rotative efficiencies derived as described in the foregoing should make it possible to achieve propeller designs which provide the desired thrust with minimum expenditure of engine horsepower.

In closing, I would appreciate it if the authors could clarify the propeller blade-velocity diagram, Fig. 11, as regards angle of attack, α. Is this "angle of attack" intended to include the induced velocities? If so, how does this relate to the wake fractions in Fig. 12?

D. H. Humphreys, Member, **G. W. Morris,** Member, and **J. M. Falzarano,** Member

[The views expressed herein are the opinions of the discussers and not necessarily those of the Department of Transportation or the U.S. Coast Guard.]

We wish to thank the authors on behalf of U.S. Coast Guard Naval Engineering Design Branch for an opportunity to comment on their paper. They have done a commendable job in presenting their insights on the icebreaker resistance and pro-

pulsion problem. These comments represent the combined thoughts and personal views of several members of the design branch.

The comparisons shown in Figs. 5, 6, 7, and 8 are extremely valuable because they allow the designer to assess the value of empirically derived results. Care must be exercised, however, in extending these empirical equations in situations for which data have not been collected.

The *Katmai Bay* class of icebreaking tug has proved very successful as an icebreaker. These ships have surpassed expectations with the propeller design mentioned by the authors installed. While this design may not be optimum, it is apparently adequate for these multimission vessels at this time.

In Figs. 12, 13, and 14 the Taylor wake fraction for towing $(1 - w_P)$ and the Taylor wake fraction in ice $(1 - w_i)$ approach either positive or negative infinity as the measured advance coefficient (J_m) approaches zero. The limit of infinity is apparent in the definition of wake

$$(1 - w) = V_a/V$$

as ship's speed (V) and therefore measured advance coefficient (J_m) approach zero, wake fraction approaches infinity. The curves were determined by calculations using the thrust identity. Is there a physical significance in this extrapolation? What would these curves look like using the propeller advance coefficient (J_a) as the independent variable? Measuring the velocity of the water/ice mixture through the propeller(s) to determine propeller speed of advance (V_a) directly would be extremely valuable. Might this be possible using a laser velocity measuring system? Comparing nominal wakes (without propeller present) and effective wakes (with propeller present) in model scale with ice would also be interesting.

Ernst Radloff, Member

I concur with the authors that propellers for icebreaking ships should be based on ice interaction parameters rather than on a hydrodynamic requirement for maximum thrust at bollard condition. However, the authors neglected to mention the importance of ice milling and ice impact, which dictate the propeller strength criteria, thus influencing such design parameters as blade thickness, diameter, and hub size. Here the "pyramid strength concept" of progressively increasing strength of all shaftline components can be applied. This concept allows propellers and shafting to be designed as a unit with the weakest link in the failure hierarchy being the blade RMT. Once this primary requirement has been met the propeller hydrodynamic/ice geometry can be refined by means of an iterative procedure (see Fig. 17).

D. C. Murdey, Member

On reading this comprehensive paper, my attention was particularly drawn to the scatter in Fig. 2, and I wonder if the authors could give a little more background on the way in which the thrust deductions were derived. More details of the experiment procedure for carrying out self-propulsion tests in ice would be very useful. I should like to ask how differences in ice characteristics between the resistance and self-propulsion test were taken into account and if the test data were smoothed before calculating the thrust deduction. Do the authors consider it possible that differences in the size and trajectories of ice pieces drawn into the propeller race are related to variations in thrust deduction? It is my own feeling that it should be possible to make sufficiently accurate measurements of thrust and resistance themselves, and that the scatter is likely to arise from differences in test conditions, which may, in principle, be taken into account in the test and analysis procedures.

As a past chairman of the ITTC Performance Committee,

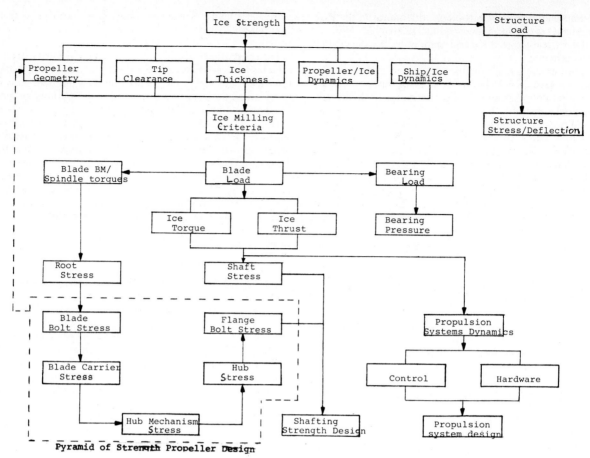

Fig. 17 Design flowchart

I am pleased to see that the so-called "rational" or "step-by-step" approach to predicting ship performance is adopted by the authors for predicting performance in ice-covered waters. However, there is one difference between the methodology described in the paper and the approach adopted for performance predictions in clear water, and that is the emphasis placed on ship resistance. The success of the prediction method is judged, in the paper, by its success in predicting ship resistance, which cannot be measured full scale, rather than ship power, which can be measured on full-scale trials. Perhaps the reasons for this are mainly historical, in that it is only recently that propulsion model tests in ice have been carried out. However, the ship designer is primarily concerned with predictions of power and rpm, and I wonder, if, in the authors' opinion, the emphasis on resistance may, in the future, be reduced?

Finally, I should like to thank the authors for their kind remarks on the tests carried out at the Arctic Vessel and Marine Research Institute at NRC in Ottawa to measure the performance of a model in clear water with an overloaded propeller. The test and analysis methods described in the reference [15] of the paper are in fact routine in the Institute and similar data have now been obtained for several models of ice-worthy ships.

Authors' Closure

We would like to thank all of the discussers for their comments. These not only provide clarification in areas where we may have been lax but also greatly add to the value of the paper by providing additional insight into several complex problems.

We appreciate Mr. Tunik's comments and would like to clarify several points made in the paper. First, the four ships for which full-scale data are considered have lengths ranging from 130 to 970 ft and beams ranging from 24 to 150 ft as stated in the paper. Although the only explanation for the choice of variables in equation (28) is experience analyzing previous data, sufficient length and beam ratios are present to test its validity. As shown through comparison of the coefficient C_2 (which varies from 0.194 to 0.222) the group does provide a very good description of the speed-dependent component. Bow form and friction factor are not included in the analysis and therefore these affects appear only in the coefficients, primarily C_0.

The model/ship correlations presented in Figs. 6 through 8 are not intended to prove or disprove correlation with the empirical equation. Actual model and full-scale data are compared, not results of the empirical equation.

Mr. Tunik's point on the validity of Froude scaling at high speeds may be relevant and in fact might explain unusual results of past tests at very high speeds in thin ice. Typically, however, model tests in ice are limited to low Froude numbers.

Dr. Enkvist's comments regarding transient propeller/ice interactions are relevant and must not be overlooked by the designer. However, in order to select propulsion parameters and propeller characteristics, a set of criteria must be chosen for which propulsive efficiency is to be optimized. We have attempted to improve our understanding of propeller/ice/hull interaction based on a quasi-static approach where effects are averaged over a sufficiently long period of time. What is first needed is sufficient interaction data to intelligently select propeller characteristics for a specified quasi-static or "stationary" set of conditions. This approach is analogous to that used for open-water propeller selection where the design is based on a steady speed even though most operations will include unsteady effects due to waves and ship motions.

We are not really in a position to comment intelligently on scale effects in open water wake and thrust deduction testing; however, we would like to briefly discuss propulsion tests in ice. Although we have demonstrated that currently self-propulsion tests in ice do not accurately predict torque and thus horsepower, a tool is required to investigate interactions quantitatively. We must develop improved techniques, modeling materials and analysis procedures if our understanding of these phenomena is to be improved. Also, additional high-quality full-scale data with sufficient measurements are required to establish correlations in propulsion parameters similar to those presented for resistance.

We apologize for not identifying the vessels in Table 1. They are: (A) SS *Manhattan*, (B) USCGC *Mackinaw*, (C) USCGC *Katmai Bay*, and (D) CCGS *Pierre Radisson*. We agree with Dr. Vance's comment that bow form is not included in equation (31); however, the correlation is still very high, indicating it explains most of the large differences in ice resistance of the various ships. As stated in the paper the equation should prove valuable in *initial* design.

Calculated thrust deduction for the *Katmai Bay* deserves further consideration before conclusions regarding ice effects can be made. The method used to calculate thrust deduction is a very straightforward approach to determining this coefficient when thrust is measured full scale; however, several cautions should be noted. First, since R_i was set equal to model tow rope pull the propeller loading due to hydrodynamic drag was not accounted for. This would tend to reduce the calculated t at high speeds but would have no effect at bollard conditions. This problem, however, can be overcome by using $P + R_w$ instead of P only. Second, determination of thrust deduction from full-scale data is analogous to resistance determination in that one cannot be determined without the other. The experimenter must know (or assume) t to determine resistance. It is for this reason that model test techniques must be improved.

We are extremely pleased to see the comparisons of resistance prediction with trials data; however, one major assumption should be noted. An average thrust deduction of 0.4 was assumed during analysis of the trials data. Even if t varied from 0.25 to 0.4 as shown in Dr. Vance's Fig. 15, resistance would be in error as much as 15 percent at the low speeds. This might explain the difference in slope between model and full-scale test results.

CDR Naegle's comments regarding Fig. 1 are the result of our failure to identify the icebreakers. The curve labeled P/D 0.8 is the USCGC *Polar Sea* from reference [4]. The 0.8 value was used since this is the design P/D value. The other two icebreaker curves are the CCGS *Pierre Radisson* ($P/D = 0.775$) and the USCGC *Mackinaw* ($P/D = 0.750$).

Data shown in Fig. 4 are from the USCGC *Katmai Bay* while those shown in Fig. 5 are from the CCGS *Pierre Radisson*. These two vessels exhibit entirely different wake fraction behavior in the behind condition. If full-scale thrust data for the *Radisson* are compared with the behind ice-free thrust data, they will be found to lie above the behind ice-free curve in a manner similar to that in Fig. 4, even though at certain advance ratios they fall on top of the open curves. For this ship, the open and behind curves intersect at a $J \approx 0.3$. Since these two vessels exhibit totally different behavior in wake fractions, icebreaking data must be compared to the behind ice-free case rather than the open case to permit valid comparisons between the two vessels.

We have purposely saved the comments of Messrs. Juurma and Segercrantz to be addressed concurrently with those from Mr. Edwards. They are in some ways similar in nature and when combined inspire several suggestions for improving our understanding.

First, we would like to answer specific questions related to our methods of analysis. Messrs. Juurma and Segercrantz asked if rpm data used in Fig. 4 are consistent. All data presented are based on actual measured rpm. Mr. Edwards tries to locate the sources of scatter in the model thrust deduction data shown in Fig. 2, and in fact a great deal of effort was expended to try to make these data converge. The method used was to enter equation (7) with faired *dimensional* model resistance data and measured thrust plus dynamometer towing force. In fact, Mr. Edwards's comment regarding the validity of this equation at points other than the self-propulsion point is correct. We did not crossplot the data to determine thrust at the exact self-propulsion point; however, results were compared with analyses which used this technique and these exhibited scatter of similar magnitude. No trends with ice thickness were observed; however, this requires further analysis.

It is felt that the principal sources of error in this experiment are: (1) determination of R_{iw} in one model ice sheet and T_{Bi} in a different sheet; (2) insufficient time-averaging of measured thrust; and (3) the inherent difficulty of calculating t from experimental results. For example, if R_i varied ±10 percent and the actual t was 0.1, the calculated t would vary from 0.01 to 0.19. Suggestions for improving experimental techniques include: (1) test two identical models side-by-side in the same ice sheet and measure resistance with one and required thrust with the other; and (2) calculate t continuously during the test period from smoothed simultaneous resistance and thrust data.

Both Messrs. Juurma and Segercrantz and Mr. Edwards comment on the derivation of the negative V_a and the result that $1 - w$ approaches negative infinity in Fig. 12. We would like to quote Harvald from reference [2] on the definition of wake fraction and advance velocity: "The effective wake coefficient is determined by the ship propeller acting as a wake measurer and wake integrater, the effective velocity of wake being defined as the difference between velocity of propulsion and that velocity which in a *homogeneous* field would enable the propeller at this definite number of revolutions to create a thrust or to absorb a torque equal to that present." In other words, advance velocity and wake fraction as used in design with open-water propeller curves exist only because of definition, and attempts to assign physical significance and relate this to velocity of flow into the propeller behind the ship are incorrect. These parameters are used to provide a means of relating propeller performance behind the ship to that in open water. They are influenced by ship velocity, hull form, rotation in the flow, spatial and temporal differences in the flow and even the presence of rudders behind the propellers.

As an example, wake fraction calculated in Fig. 12 uses open-water propeller data expanded into the fourth quadrant based on experimental results of Nordstrom.[13] This was necessary to identify an open-water advance coefficient at which K_T was equal to K_T behind the hull for J_m less than 0.05.

Mr. Edwards suggests that Fig. 4 indicates the necessity of an additional interaction coefficient to account for the shift in K_T and K_Q above those for the behind ice-free case. This is essentially the purpose of the relative ice/water efficiency approach suggested by Messrs. Juurma and Segercrantz. We agree with the need for an additional interaction coefficient; however, we feel that this coefficient must be dependent on hull form since the hull affects the quantity and distribution of ice in the flow. Even in the "simple" case of behind ice-free conditions wake behavior can vary drastically from ship to ship.

---

[13] Nordstrom, H. F., "Screw Propeller Characteristics," publication of the Swedish State Shipbuilding Experimental Tank, No. 9, 1948.

There is, therefore, no reason to suspect that ice interaction effects can be considered independent of hull form.

Both of these discussions provide opinions on the magnitude of propeller/hull/ice interaction. Mr. Edwards proposes that thick ice causes much larger interaction and Messrs. Juurma and Segercrantz suggest that there is very little interaction for open screws. We can only comment that based on our findings interactions do appear to be significant; however, additional data are required before generalizations can be made.

Professor Hadler suggests propeller tests in ice similar to those suggested by Messrs. Juurma and Segercrantz. We must reiterate that in order to determine proper interaction coefficients the concentration and distribution of ice must be accurately known and all mechanical properties of the "ice" must be scaled. Therefore, we suggest tests in ice behind the hull to relate propeller performance in this condition to that in the open condition or the behind ice-free condition using additional interaction terms. We agree completely with Professor Hadler's comments on propeller design for tugs and fishing vessels and our paper suggests a similar approach (including ice interaction terms) for icebreakers.

As discussed previously, V_a is determined by definition and therefore includes effects of all factors which affect apparent flow direction. In this sense, the angle of attack shown in Fig. 11 is an effective angle of attack and depends on the wake fractions. This definition approach is a result of using open-water propeller curves for design. If lifting-surface theory is used, on the other hand, the designer must have knowledge of the actual flow velocity into the propeller disk and thus the actual angle of attack. These are not necessarily related to V_a and apparent angle of attack as derived using the propeller curves.

The authors are in total agreement with Mr. Kayo and are pleased to have someone else point out problems in ice testing and the critical need for solution of these problems. Mr. Tanibayashi's comments on shaft thrust method point out the need to know relative rotative efficiencies in ice. The development presented assumes η_R to calculate resistance. As discussed in the paper, we know of no existing data which give η_R in ice for arbitrary ships. Also there is no evidence to support the proposition that $\eta_{Rice} = \eta_{Rbehind}$.

Mr. Radloff makes a very important point concerning propeller design. However, it is not within the scope of our paper to address this problem.

Messrs. Humphrey, Morris, and Falzarano imply that results shown in Figs. 5–8 are comparison of empirical predictions with full-scale data. We must point out that these are comparisons between model and full-scale data for specific ships. We agree that these figures in no way are applicable to other vessels. Their comments on wake fractions reiterate that they are by definition and have no physical significance. Also J_a behind the hull cannot be determined except by definition since the propeller is the measurer of J_a.

SNAME *Transactions*, Vol. 90, 1982, pp. 277–320

The Naval Auxiliary Oiler AO-177, USS *Cimarron* (U.S. Navy Photograph)

Causes and Corrections for Propeller-Excited Airborne Noise on a Naval Auxiliary Oiler

Michael B. Wilson,[1] Member, **Donald N. McCallum,**[2] Associate Member,
Robert J. Boswell,[1] Member, **David D. Bernhard,**[3] Visitor, and **Alan B. Chase,**[3] Visitor

The AO-177, first of a new class of Naval Auxiliary Oilers, experienced high levels of inboard airborne noise and initial-stage erosion damage on its skewed, seven-bladed propeller during builder's trials. This paper describes the problems, corrective design modifications considered, and procedures and rationale used to develop a successful corrective design modification consisting of a fin to improve the flow into the propeller. To evaluate the problem, extensive model experiments were conducted, including flow visualization, wake surveys, powering experiments, and a crucial series of cavitation experiments including propeller-induced hull pressure measurements in a large water tunnel. Experiments with two fin designs showed the superiority of a flow-accelerating configuration. Other experiments showed some benefits of altering the propeller blade shape. Propeller analyses were undertaken to provide design alternatives for retrofitting the ship with a new propeller. A full-scale trial with the final fin design provided evidence of a reduction of the highest levels of airborne noise, reduction in the initial-stage erosion damage, and minimal effect on ship speed. The result is that the AO-177 has been accepted by the fleet for normal service.

[1] Naval architect, David W. Taylor Naval Ship Research and Development Center, Bethesda, Maryland.
[2] Naval architect, Naval Sea Systems Command, Washington, DC.
[3] General engineer and mechanical engineer, respectively, Naval Sea Systems Command, Washington, DC.

Presented at the Annual Meeting, New York, N. Y., November 17–20, 1982, of THE SOCIETY OF NAVAL ARCHITECTS AND MARINE ENGINEERS.

The views expressed herein are the opinions of the authors and not necessarily those of DOD or the Department of the Navy.

Introduction

IN RECENT YEARS, there has been a rash of propeller-induced vibration and noise problems that have plagued certain types of commercial ships (usually of single-screw design). This has been the result of the increase of power per shaft, restrictive demands on stern geometry and propeller and shafting placements, tendencies toward high block coefficients and large beam-to-draft ratios, and trends toward single-screw designs for fuel economy. These problems normally manifest themselves in the form of unacceptable hull girder vibration in the stern region near the propeller and at the upper levels of deckhouses, structural damage from fatigue, and considerable crew nuisance, often resulting in imposed speed limitations. Although the U.S. Navy has had a minimal number of such occurrences with its single-screw auxiliary ships, there was an exception in the case of the recently completed AO-177, the first ship of a new class of Naval Auxiliary Oilers. During builder's trials, the USS *Cimarron* (AO-177) was reported to have unacceptably high levels of airborne noise and localized vibration. Close inspection revealed early-stage (incubation zone) propeller erosion damage and bent trailing edges near the tips of all seven blades of the propeller. Based on these full-scale findings, the Navy immediately embarked on a corrective program to identify the root cause of the difficulties, develop a suitable solution, and verify that the resulting modification did indeed cure the problems. In the process of satisfying these objectives, the Naval Sea Systems Command (NAVSEA) together with the David W. Taylor Naval Ship Research and Development Center (DTNSRDC) employed the services of the Swedish Maritime Research Centre (SSPA), Hydronautics, Inc. (HNI), Det norske Veritas (DnV), and several independent experts in the field of ship hydrodynamics analysis. This paper documents the problems, the experiences, the solutions proposed, the model experiments, and analytical predictions carried out for a number of alternative proposed solutions, culminating in the final choice of a wake-improving fin design and its validation with a full-scale trial.

Since 1952, when Baier [1][4] designed the first wake-modifying and anti-air-drawing fin for use in curing severe fantail vibrations of the Great Lakes ore carrier *Carl D. Bradley*, variations of this type of stern appendage have been employed—usually successfully—to help improve the flow into the propeller region of many kinds of single-screw ships. Most of the applications of such a fin have been on full-block ships such as tankers, roll-on/roll-off (RO/RO) ships, containerships, liquefied natural gas (LNG) vessels, and other bulk and product carriers [2, 3]. In most instances the effect of the fin is to divert flow into the propeller disk region, firming up slow-moving or separating boundary-layer flows in the afterbody region, generally reducing the large wake peak at the top of the disk, and thereby reducing the large flow angle excursions at the outer radii of the propeller blades. These changes apparently reduce the vibration excitation levels by reducing the fluctuating pressures induced on the hull (and resulting fluctuating hull surface forces) that arise from intermittent propeller blade cavitation, rather than by significantly reducing the bearing force excitation levels.

As will be shown in the case of the AO-177, there were possible improvements of the hull surface excitation to be achieved with alternative propeller designs as well as with the wake modification. Part of the objective of the investigation described here was to identify a corrective measure that was effective enough to do the job, yet simple enough to be deployed and verified quickly.

---

[4] Numbers in brackets designate References at end of paper.

The ship and propeller

Main particulars

The AO-177 (USS *Cimarron*) is the first of a new class of single-screw Naval Auxiliary Oilers designed by the U.S. Navy and built at Avondale Shipyards, Inc. in New Orleans, Louisiana. Its principal particulars are given in Table 1.

From the body plan lines and profile outlines given in Fig. 1, it can be seen that the ship hull has a prominent elliptical bulbous bow, rather narrow V-section shapes toward the after end, a clearwater stern, and generous propeller clearances both vertically and forward to the hull surface. The propeller clearances defined in the figure are

$$a_z/D = 0.2915$$

$$a_x/D = 0.5503 \text{ (at } 0.8R)$$

$$a_{xt}/D = 0.519 \text{ (at tip)}$$

$$b_{xt}/D = 0.192 \text{ (at tip)}$$

Some care was taken during the design stages to produce a hull design with good resistance characteristics, and this effort succeeded to a great extent because the AO-177 has a favorable power-to-weight ratio compared with similar ship types at the same speed. Purposeful slimming of the hull lines aft definitely contributed to the good resistance properties of the AO-177. Yet, these narrow aft section shapes have been determined to be largely responsible for the poor wake (rather deep, spike-like main wake shadow). It must be noted that design of the hull shape for the AO-177 was determined at a time when there was much more fragmentary understanding of the potential problems that could arise from intermittent propeller cavitation; and most of the concern then was focused on full block hull shapes.

Figure 2 shows a simplified inboard profile of the after end of the ship.

Propeller details and design

The main propeller particulars are presented in Table 2. This propeller was designed to meet the conditions outlined in Table 3. The design process is discussed in detail in reference [4], and is essentially the same as the process described in reference [5].

Upon making the required tradeoffs to meet the conditions specified in Table 3, it turned out that the geometry of the propeller was controlled largely by the requirement that the longitudinal and torsional vibration in the main propulsion system be below that specified in MIL-STD 167 [6] and that hull vibration levels meet the requirements of MIL-STD 1472 [7]. These specifications resulted in requirements which were more restrictive than those imposed by other design specifications and, therefore, controlled the selection of the number of blades, propeller diameter, magnitude and radial distribution of skew, and radial distribution of chord length.

Based on a preliminary longitudinal and torsional vibration response analysis of the main propulsion system that was available at the time of the propeller design (1975), which included only a rough estimate of the stiffness of the thrust bearing, it was concluded that a six-bladed propeller should not be used because blade frequency for a six-bladed propeller would coincide with a predicted longitudinal resonance at the full power point, that is, at approximately $100 \times 6/60 = 10$ Hz. The vibration analysis of the main propulsion system also indicated that the blade frequency thrust at full power must be less than 13.3 kN (3000 lb), that is, less than 1 percent of the time-average thrust, for either a five- or seven-bladed propeller. For this propulsion system the upper limit on blade frequency

Table 1 Main ship particulars

	SI	U.S. Customary
Length overall, L_{OA}	180.3 m	591.5 ft
Length on waterline, L_{WL}	170.9 m	560.6 ft
Length between perpendiculars, L_{PP}	167.6 m	550 ft
Beam, B	26.8 m	88 ft
Depth to main deck, D_H	14.9 m	49 ft
Draft, design full load (mean), T_m	9.9 m	32.5 ft
Draft trial (mean), T_m	9.6 m	31.5 ft
Draft ballast (mean), T_m	6.68 m	21.9 ft
Trim, design full load (down by stern)	0.46 m	1.5 ft
Trim, trial full load (down by bow)	0.31 m	1.0 ft
Trim, ballast (down by stern)	1.14 m	3.75 ft
Displacement, design full load, Δ(SW)	27 819 tonne	27 380 l.tons
Displacement, trial full load, Δ(SW)	26 810 tonne	26 390 l.tons
Displacement, ballast, Δ(SW)	17 550 tonne	17 270 l.tons
Block coefficient design, C_B	0.597	0.597
Displacement-length ratio, $\Delta/(0.01L)^3$	...	155.4 l.ton/ft^3
Full-power design	17 897 kW	24 000 hp
Design ship speed (endurance speed)	20 knots	20 knots
Maximum speed (full power)	21.5 knots	21.5 knots

thrust was much more restrictive than the upper limit on blade frequency torque; that is, any propeller for the AO-177 that has blade frequency thrust below the allowable limit will automatically have blade frequency torque below the allowable limit based on available calculation procedures. The blade frequency side forces and bending moments do not enter the vibratory requirements of the main propulsion system explicitly; however, the transverse forces could, if large in amplitude

or near a resonant frequency, excite hull vibration. Therefore, it was required that the vertical and transverse horizontal components of blade frequency bearing force at full power be less than 8.9 kN (2000 lb).

A four-bladed propeller was rejected because of possible excessive hull girder vibration at blade rate frequency, and possible longitudinal shaft resonance problems at twice blade rate frequency. The conclusion that the hull girder vibration

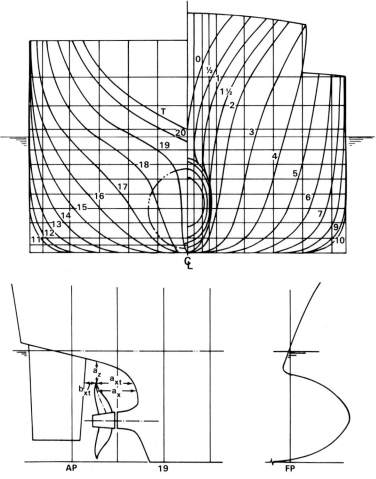

Fig. 1 Body plan and bow and stern profiles

Causes and Corrections for Propeller-Excited Airborne Noise

could be excessive with four blades was based on design stage calculations of hull vibration responses with excitation empirically derived from comparison of calculated and measured amplitudes of this type of vibration on similar U.S. Navy ships, on previous experience with this type of vibration on similar U.S. Navy ships with four-bladed propellers, and on the phenomenon that this vibratory response tends to increase as excitation frequency decreases. At the time of the propeller design, it was concluded that similar problems were possible, but less probable, with a five-bladed propeller. This alone was not justification for immediately rejecting a five-bladed propeller, but the probability of hull girder vibration would be considered in any possible design tradeoffs for selecting the number of blades.

Requirements of MIL-STD 167 are that for all operating conditions the peak periodic thrust amplitude at the thrust bearing be less than the lesser of:

1. the time-average thrust at the local operating point, or
2. one-half the time-average thrust at full-power steady ahead.

The following empirical multiplicative factors derived from

Nomenclature

A_E = expanded area of propeller, $Z \int_{r_h}^{R} c \, dr$

A_0 = disk area of propeller, πR^2

A_P = projected area of propeller

a_x = propeller clearance, horizontal distance between blade-reference line and hull at 0.8R

a_{xt} = propeller horizontal clearance forward to hull, at tip

a_z = vertical tip clearance between propeller and hull

B = beam of ship

b_{xt} = propeller horizontal clearance aft to rudder, at tip

C_B = block coefficient

C_{Th} = thrust loading coefficient

$c(x_R)$ = propeller blade section chord length

D = propeller diameter

D_H = depth of hull, keel to main deck

dB = decibel sound pressure level in octave band, $20\log(\bar{p}/20\mu Pa)$

$(F_x)_Z$ = amplitude of blade frequency harmonic of axial bearing force (thrust)

$(F_y)_Z$ = amplitude of blade frequency harmonic of transverse horizontal bearing force

$(F_z)_Z$ = amplitude of blade frequency harmonic of vertical bearing force

$(F_{Sx})_Z$ = amplitude of blade frequency harmonic of axial hull surface force

$(F_{Sy})_Z$ = amplitude of blade frequency harmonic of transverse horizontal hull surface force

$(F_{Sz})_Z$ = amplitude of blade frequency harmonic of vertical hull surface force

F_n = Froude number

$f(x_R)$ = camber of propeller blade section

g = acceleration due to gravity

H = head, distance from propeller centerline to water surface plus atmospheric pressure minus vapor pressure

$i_G(x_R)$ = rake of propeller blade section

J = advance coefficient, $J = V_A/nD$

k_1 = pressure amplitude factor (see Fig. 18)

L = length

L_{OA} = length overall

L_{PP} = length between perpendiculars

L_{WL} (or L) = length on waterline

n = propeller revolutions per unit time

$p(x_R)$ = propeller section pitch

P_D = delivered power at propeller, $2\pi nQ$

P_E = effective power

$\bar{p}$ = root-mean-square (rms) sound pressure level in specified bandwidth

R = radius of propeller

r = radial distance from propeller axis

r_h = radius of propeller hub

T = thrust

T_m = draft, mean

t = thrust deduction fraction

$t(x_R)$ = thickness of propeller blade section

V = ship speed

V_A = speed of advance, $V(1 - w_T)$

$V_R(x_R,\theta_w)/V$ = radial velocity component ratio in propeller plane

$V_T(x_R,\theta_w)/V$ = tangential velocity component ratio in propeller plane

$V_X(x_R,\theta_w)/V$ = axial velocity component ratio in propeller plane

$(V_X/V)_n$ = amplitude of nth harmonic of axial velocity component ratio in propeller plane, $\pi^{-1}\int_0^{2\pi}(V_X(\theta)/V)\cos n\theta \, d\theta$

v_r = single amplitude vibration velocity (rms)

w_T = Taylor wake fraction

x_R = nondimensional radius of propeller blade section, r/R

Z = number of propeller blades

Δ = displacement mass

Δp_Z = blade frequency amplitude of hull surface pressure

Δp_{2Z} = twice blade frequency amplitude of hull surface pressure

∇ = displacement volume

η_D = propulsive efficiency, P_E/P_D

η_H = hull efficiency, $(1 - t)/(1 - w_T)$

η_R = relative rotative efficiency

θ_S = skew angle in projected plane of propeller measured from a radial line through midchord of section at hub to radial line through midchord of section at local radius, positive in counterclockwise direction looking upstream

θ_w = wake position angle about propeller axis in propeller plane, measured counterclockwise from upward vertical looking forward, $-\varphi$

λ = linear scale ratio

ρ = mass density of water

σ = cavitation number at shaft centerline, based on speed of advance, $2gH/V_A^2$

Φ = phase angle

φ = position angle about propeller axis, measured clockwise from upward vertical looking forward, $-\theta_w$

Abbreviations

BBN   Bolt, Beranek and Newman, Inc

DL   Davidson Laboratory

DnV   Det norske Veritas

DTNSRDC   David W. Taylor Naval Ship Research and Development Center

HI   Hydromechanics, Inc

HNI   Hydronautics, Inc

ISO   International Standards Organization

MIT   Massachusetts Institute of Technology

NAVSEA   Naval Sea Systems Command

SSPA   Statens Skeppsprovninganstalt (Swedish Maritime Research Centre)

VAI   Vorus and Associates, Inc

full-scale measurements on U.S. Navy ships[5] are applied to the values that are calculated by numerical procedures based on propeller unsteady lifting-surface theory [8] including the influences of propeller geometry, propeller operating conditions, model nominal wake patterns, and calculated amplification in the shafting:

1. A factor of 3 for amplitude modulation of the periodic thrust $(F_x)_n$, where $n = Z, 2Z, 3Z$, etc. This modulation may result from a combination of large-scale turbulence in the wake, periodic time variation of the wake for steady ship conditions, periodic variation of the wake due to sea waves and ship motions, and small changes in rudder angle for course correction. It is assumed that for each n the calculated amplitude is the minimum amplitude of the modulated signal.

2. A factor of 3 for increase in $(F_x)_n/T$ at speeds from 90 to 100 percent of full speed, which may be due to the influence

[5] As described in a report of restricted distribution by A. Zaloumis and G. P. Antonides entitled "Recent Developments in Longitudinal Vibrations of Surface Ship Propulsion Systems," Sept. 1970.

of cavitation, or change in the wake pattern due to free surface (wavemaking) effects. It is assumed that the calculated amplitude corresponds to $(F_x)_n/T$ before this increase.

3. A factor of 3 for increase in $(F_x)_n$ in hard (full rudder) turns relative to the $(F_x)_n$ for the steady ahead condition at any speed. The differences between $(F_x)_n$ in hard turns and $(F_x)_n$ for steady ahead operation results from the different wake patterns, ship speeds, propeller rotational speeds, and extent of cavitation for these conditions. The manner in which these various quantities change from steady ahead to hard turns,

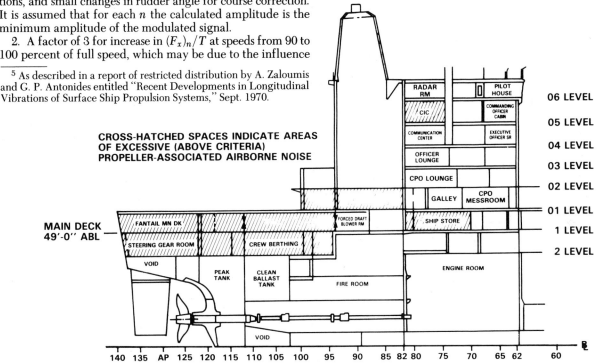

CROSS-HATCHED SPACES INDICATE AREAS OF EXCESSIVE (ABOVE CRITERIA) PROPELLER-ASSOCIATED AIRBORNE NOISE

Fig. 2 Inboard profile of stern

Table 2   AO-177 propeller characteristics

Diameter, D	6.4 m (21 ft)
Number of blades, Z	7
Expanded area ratio, A_E/A_0	0.771
Projected area ratio, A_P/A_0	0.59
Projected skew angle at tip	45 deg
Pitch-to-diameter ratio (at $0.7R$)	1.25
Section thickness form	NACA 66 (DTNSRDC modified)
Section mean line	NACA $a = 0.8$
Mean thrust (full power, full load), T	1 371 kN (308 200 lb)
Thrust loading coefficient, $C_{Th} = (8/\pi)K_T/J^2$	1.167
Rotation	right-hand
Material	Ni-Al-Bronze
Weight	31 479 kgf (69 400 lb)

Radius Ratio, r/R	Chord Ratio, c/D	Pitch Ratio, P/D	Skew, θ_s (deg)	Thickness Ratio, t/c	Camber Ratio, f/c	Rake Ratio, i_G/D
0.2	0.2070	1.125	0.0	0.2000	0.0490	0.0000
0.3	0.2456	1.223	2.2	0.1625	0.0444	−0.0017
0.4	0.2722	1.288	7.1	0.1325	0.0367	−0.0044
0.5	0.2817	1.318	13.1	0.1080	0.0314	−0.0070
0.6	0.2684	1.309	20.0	0.0880	0.0300	−0.0077
0.7	0.2320	1.250	27.7	0.0715	0.0295	−0.0049
0.8	0.1815	1.140	34.5	0.0590	0.0281	−0.0003
0.9	0.1180	0.970	40.3	0.0500	0.0263	0.0082
1.0	0.0000	0.722	45.0	0.0450	0.0240	0.0245

Table 3   Propeller design conditions

Design point: full power at full-load displacement
Diameter: 6.4 to 7.3 m (21 to 24 ft)
RPS: 1.66 at the design point
Endurance: 20 knots at 80 percent power
Cavitation criteria: 10 percent speed margin on the inception of back
 bubble at the design point. Other forms of
 cavitation to be minimized to the extent practicable
Blade skew: Use the amount practicable in order to reduce vibration
 excitation forces imparted to the propulsion machinery
 and hull in order to meet MIL-STD 167 and MIL-STD
 1472. This dictated the following limits on blade frequency bearing forces:

$$(F_x)_Z \leq 13.3 \text{ kN (3000 lb)}$$

$$(F_y)_Z \leq 8.9 \text{ kN (2000 lb)}$$

$$(F_z)_Z \leq 8.9 \text{ kN (2000 lb)}$$

especially the wake patterns and cavitation, may be sensitive to the type of hull form; for example, it may be different for an auxiliary and a surface combatant.

With these three multiplicative factors, the maximum amplitude of the periodic thrust at the thrust bearing is estimated to be 27 times the periodic thrust amplitude calculated at the thrust bearing using propeller unsteady lifting-surface theory and shafting response formulations for shaft amplification.

These factors are intended to be sufficiently conservative to ensure that the requirements of MIL-STD 167 are met for all operating conditions, including statistical variations over the lives of the ships of the class, yet not so conservative that they unnecessarily control the design of the propeller or propulsion system. Measurements on the AO-177 and AO-178 suggest that these factors are reasonable for this application; however, it is difficult to define precisely the individual factors due to variations with operating conditions, time, and between different ships of the class, and because the measurements are made on the shaft some distance from the propeller. The distance between the point of measurement on the shaft and the propeller makes it very difficult to separate amplifications in the propulsion system from increase in propeller periodic thrust. This is especially critical between 90 percent of full speed and full speed on the AO-177 Class because of the probability of longitudinal shaft resonance at approximately 10 rpm above full power.

Perhaps the most conservative part of the analysis lies in the assumption that the three factors of 3 are multiplicative to give a worst-case factor of 27. There may be some nonlinear effects between the three factors so that the maximum factor is less than 27. As stated previously, one of the criteria is to avoid thrust reversal of the main thrust bearing. Thrust reversal of the AO-177 bearing did not occur under any trial conditions; however, the thrust was not measured at the bearing. The maximum periodic thrust at the bearing, based on measurements on the main propulsion shafting and calculated amplification of the propulsion system between the measured point and the bearing, is 25 percent of the time-average thrust at full-power steady ahead operation. This represents an estimated factor of safety of four.

These amplification factors result in the requirement that the calculated blade frequency thrust amplitude at the propeller must be less than 1 percent of the time-average thrust, which is a severe requirement. It is common commercial ship practice to allow blade frequency thrust to be 8 percent of the time-average thrust, and in some cases as high as 12 percent.[6]

---

[6] Private communications with staff of DnV.

The more restrictive upper limit on the AO-177 Class is due, in part, to the requirement that it be able to execute full rudder turns at any speed, and to the higher maximum speed than is typical of commercial ship practice.

Consideration of powering, cavitation, clearances, and strength dictated the following:

Diameter, D(m): 6.4 to 7.3
Expanded area ratio, A_E/A_0: 0.77

Therefore, calculations of the six components of bearing forces and moments were made for $A_E/A_0 = 0.77$, for diameters just indicated, for five and seven blades, and a range of skew distributions. These calculations were made using the unsteady lifting-surface procedure of Tsakonas et al [8], which does not consider the influence of cavitation. These calculations were based on the pertinent harmonics of the model nominal wake at full-power steady ahead operation in a calm sea without corrections for the influence of Reynolds number, the effect of the propeller on the wake (effective wake), or possible temporal variations in the wake. The limitations concerning the lack of consideration of cavitation and the use of time-average nominal model wake are fully appreciated; however, validated procedures for quantitatively calculating the influences of these effects were not (and are not) available. Nevertheless, as mentioned previously, the influences of these effects was considered empirically in calculating the allowable limits of 13.3 kN (3000 lb) for the blade frequency thrust, and 8.9 kN (2000 lb) for blade frequency vertical and transverse horizontal force components.

These calculations indicated that in order to meet concurrently the following two requirements:

1. produce blade frequency thrust that is less than 13.3 kN (3000 lb), and
2. have a blade planform with neither a significantly concave trailing edge nor a pointed trailing edge near the tip,

it is necessary to have a seven-bladed propeller with 6.4-m-diameter (21 ft), nonlinear distribution of skew with approximately 45-deg skew near the tip, and relatively short chords at the outer radii. Concave and pointed trailing-edge planforms were judged to be undesirable from considerations of strength and damage susceptibility, especially during astern rotation. The diameter had a first-order influence on these calculations because the axial components of the fifth and seventh harmonics of the wake have a reversal of sign at radii less than 6.4 m (21 ft) as will be seen in the wake harmonics distributions. In order to reduce the blade frequency thrust to less than 13.3 kN (3000 lb) with five blades would necessitate a substantially larger maximum skew angle than with seven blades due to the combination of longer wavelength and larger amplitude of the fifth harmonic of the wake than of the seventh harmonic of the wake. The combination of higher skew and wider chords for a five-bladed propeller would result in a blade profile with unacceptably pointed trailing edge near the tip. Therefore a five-bladed propeller was unacceptable. The final skew distribution was carefully selected to obtain the most effective cancellation of periodic propeller loading over the propeller radius, so that the specified bearing force criteria were met.

These calculated values, together with values calculated in 1981 by Det norske Veritas [9] using an unsteady lifting-surface procedure based on a vortex lattice approach without cavitation, but with an approximate correction for effective wake based on the method of Huang and Groves [10] for a body of revolution, are given in Table 4. The values calculated by Det norske Veritas are greater than the specified limits.

The net inaccuracies in these predictions are judged to be 26.7 kN (6000 lb) or 200 percent of the limit on blade frequency thrust and 300 percent of the limit on blade frequency

Table 4 Bearing force components for AO-177 propeller

	Specified Upper Limit		Tsakonas et al [8]; Model Nominal Wake		Det norske Veritas [9]; Estimated Model Effective Wake	
	kN	lb	kN	lb	kN	lb
$(F_x)_Z$	13.3	3000	11.6	2600	18.7	4200
$(F_y)_Z$	8.9	2000	4.45	1000	25.4	5700
$(F_z)_Z$	8.9	2000	0.89	200	25.4	5700

Fig. 3 Seven-bladed skewed propeller on the AO-177(note installation of wake-improving fin)

transverse force components, based on the cumulative effects of inaccuracies and omissions in the analytical computational methods, and errors due to wake measurements and scaling effects. These inaccuracies are, in part, compensated for by the empirical factors incorporated in the specified limits, especially the factor of 3 for the estimated increase in $(F_x)_n/T$ between 90 percent and 100 percent of full speed, and the factor of 3 for the amplitude modulation, as discussed previously. Although these calculated results are estimated to be inaccurate relative to the small periodic propeller shaft excitation forces being calculated on the highly skewed propellers, it is believed that these calculated results give a realistic indication of the influence of propeller design parameters on the periodic propeller shaft excitation forces. Further, the methods used in the propeller design for the AO-177 Class represent the then-current state of the art for calculating these forces.

Direct measurements of the propeller shaft excitation forces were not made on the AO-177 Class; however, as discussed previously, measurements of the periodic longitudinal response were made on the shafting at some distance from the propeller. From these longitudinal shaft response measurements and a mathematical model of the shafting system, the blade rate propeller thrust is calculated to be between 0 and 26.7 kN (0 and 6000 lb); that is, $0 \le (F_x)_Z/T \le 0.02$. This agrees reasonably well with the values predicted in the propeller design process. The blade rate thrust cannot be determined more accurately from these full-scale measurements due to measured variations with operating conditions, time, and between different ships of the class, and inaccuracies in calculating amplifications in the propulsion system including possible resonances.

It was realized that propeller-induced hull forces due to transient cavitation could produce hull vibration and airborne noise. However, no reliable procedure for quantifying these effects existed. Had such a procedure existed, it would have been applied and, it is hoped, a balance would have been struck between machinery vibration and hull noise and vibration performance. In the absence of such knowledge and procedures, the machinery vibration criteria, for which design procedures did exist, drove the design. The blade tips were unloaded relative to the Lerbs optimum criterion in some attempt to reduce the periodic hull forces; however, the effectiveness of this unloading is unclear for a propeller operating in a severe wake and with transient cavitation as is the case for the AO-177. Further, it was judged that the blade skew would dramatically reduce propeller-induced hull forces relative to those induced by the corresponding propeller without skew [11, 12, 13]. Some semi-empirical criteria existed for judging the likelihood of propeller erosion and propeller-induced hull vibration; however, these are not applicable to the present design since its geometry is outside the range of the data base on which these semi-empirical methods are based. In particular, this design has narrow blades near the tip, seven blades, and high skew, which are not considered in the semi-empirical criteria.

The final pitch and camber were determined by the lifting-surface procedure of Cheng [14] with thickness corrections by the method of Kerwin and Leopold [15]. Table 2 gives the pertinent details of the final configuration. Figure 3 shows photographs of the propeller installed on the ship.

The problems

During builder's sea trials, the AO-177 exhibited several unsatisfactory symptoms at and near full-power operation:
- High inboard airborne noise levels in many spaces in the stern region of the ship, and up into some deckhouse spaces as well.
- Incubation zone erosion damage to the propeller (burnishing and dimpling) and bent trailing edge.
- Heavy localized vibrations, particularly in the areas directly over the propeller.

Airborne noise

Extensive airborne noise measurements made during the builder's trials indicated some high levels that exceeded criteria

Table 5   Criteria noise levels—permissible airborne sound pressure levels (in dB relative to 20 μPa)

| Type of Space | Octave Band Center Frequency, Hz | | | | | | | | | SIL[a] |
	32	63	125	250	500	1000	2000	4000	8000	
Large command and control	90	84	79	76	SIL	SIL	SIL	69	68	54
Small command and control, and administrative spaces	90	84	79	76	SIL	SIL	SIL	69	68	64
Living spaces	90	84	79	76	73	71	70	69	68	x
Medical	85	78	72	68	65	62	60	58	57	x
Shops, service spaces, passages and topside stations	105	100	95	90	SIL	SIL	SIL	85	85	72
Machinery	105	100	95	90	90	85	85	85	85	x

[a] Speech interference levels (SIL): In the octave bands where SIL values apply, the noise levels may exceed the SIL value in any of the three SIL octave bands provided the arithmetic average of the levels in the SIL octave bands do not exceed the specified SIL value.

given in the shipbuilding specification. Excessive noise levels in berthing, lounge, recreation, mess, and shop spaces aft of Frame 94 were identified consistently as being caused by the propeller-excitation. In all, 23 compartments were reported to have unsatisfactory noise levels associated with the propeller. Locations of the troublesome spaces within the ship are indicated by the cross-hatched areas in the aft-end inboard profile of Fig. 2. The noise level criteria for Navy ships depend on the compartment usage. The allowable sound levels applicable to the AO-177 are given in Table 5.

As an illustration of the character of the problem, Fig. 4 shows octave band sound pressure levels measured during the initial AO-177 builder's trials in four representative compartments: Crew Berthing and Dressing Nos. 4, 5, and 6, and the Gym. All these spaces have the same noise criteria. These data were measured using the approach described in Appendix 1. As indicated in Fig. 4, low-frequency noise levels in aft compartments were 5 to 15 dB above the criteria and high-frequency levels ranged from 5 dB above to 6 dB below the criteria. Similar conditions were found for most of the spaces identified as having noise problems, each with respect to the pertinent criteria levels for the space. Another space near the top of the deckhouse also experienced marginally unsatisfactory propeller-associated noise, but only at the lowest octave band, and it was discernible as a low rumbling sound.

Vibration amplitudes representative of the hull girder response were measured at several locations on main structural girders on the ship centerline in the steering gear compartment, engine room, and at the top of the stack of deckhouses. These were all found to be of satisfactory magnitude according to Navy standards and also were judged to be acceptable from the point of view of recent ISO recommendations [16]. Hence, although there was clearly excessive propeller-excitation with this ship, it was manifested principally as unsatisfactory airborne noise levels, and not as unacceptable hull girder vibration.

Propeller damage

A week after the builder's trials, the propeller was visually inspected by ballasting the ship down by bow to expose the upper third of the propeller. A blade-by-blade check revealed that damage had occurred on the suction (back) side of all blades, with most of the distress centered between the 0.8R and 0.9R radii. The damage consisted of a roughly semicircular patch of initial-stage cavitation erosion along the trailing edge of each blade about 20.3 cm (8 in.) in maximum width, and a rolled portion of the trailing edge (bent from the suction side toward the pressure side) about 30 cm (1 ft) long with a lip on the pressure side of maximum height 3 to 6 mm ($\frac{1}{8}$ to $\frac{1}{4}$ in.). A smaller, lightly dimpled patch was centered near each blade tip along the trailing edge; see Fig. 5. No distress was found on the pressure side.

Propeller cavitation

Propeller viewing and photography were performed on the AO-177 using a periscope projecting through the hull which provided a reasonably wide field of view. Photographs of the propeller were taken for a range of blade angular positions during daylight hours using ambient light.[7] Only a description of the visual observations is presented here for the full-load, full-power condition. Photographs and sketches of the cavitation are presented later.

[7] More details are presented in a report of restricted distribution by J. Kelley and S. D. Jessup entitled "Results of Propeller Vibration/Cavitation Investigation on USS *Cimarron* (AO-177) During Acceptance Trials," May 1981.

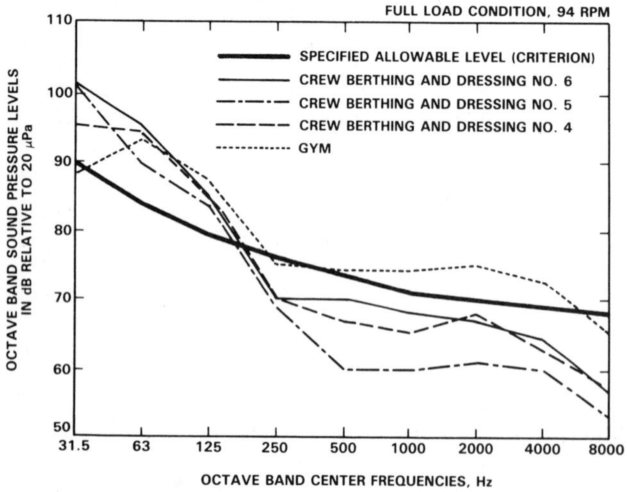

Fig. 4 Example excessive airborne noise levels measured during builder's trials

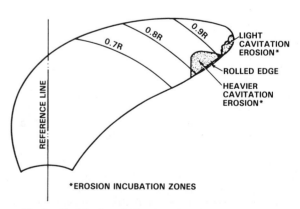

Fig. 5 Sketch of cavitation damage after builder's trials

Causes and Corrections for Propeller-Excited Airborne Noise

Clouds of cavitation were observed on the suction side of the blades from the $0.7R$ to the tip. Violent clouds of cavitation formed as each blade tip passed through the top position of rotation. Each cloud formation was then shed downstream along the starboard side of the rudder. Such formation of suction side cloud cavitation is generally associated with vigorous cavity collapse. In this case, cavitation erosion damage would be expected to occur at the suction side trailing edge near the blade tip as discussed by van Manen [17] and Lindgren and Bjärne [18]. A sharp banging sound occurred at blade passing frequency and is believed to correspond to the violent collapse of the cavitation.

Investigations and design modification

Scope

The pursuit of a successful design modification for the AO-177 was guided primarily by the results of model experiments. These were aimed at several specific objectives:

• Verify the cause of the problems.
• Formulate and develop possible solutions and obtain evaluations of them.
• Determine the most expedient correction scheme, and explore the consequence of its implementation.

At the outset, the most probable source of the problems was thought to be hydrodynamic excitation caused by intermittent cavitation on the propeller blades passing through severe velocity excursions associated with the main wake shadow. That is, airborne noise is generated by structureborne localized vibrations caused by fluctuating hull surface pressure excitation arising from the periodically collapsing blade sheet cavities. Propeller blade erosion and bent trailing edges are common symptoms of cloud cavitation that occur when blade sheet cavities collapse with sufficient violence and proximity to the blade surface [17, 19].

The mechanism producing large pressure pulse excitation and attendant propeller damage involves a complicated interaction of the cavitating flow over propeller blades with rapidly changing velocities associated with wake patterns having severe nonuniformity. Some of the important details of this interaction are described, for example, by Huse [20], and in many subsequent studies. During the past decade, there has been a tremendous growth of literature centered on surface pressure excitation and resulting ship vibration and noise problems. References [21] and [22], for instance, are representative of collections of published efforts devoted to these topics. It is generally known that steep and narrow main hull wake characteristics can give rise to excitation problems [23, 24], and that details of propeller blade planform and section geometry can also markedly influence the excitation levels. The difficult question to answer is whether some particular wake together with a given propeller configuration will cause problems at a given speed. For the evaluation of the AO-177, this question was addressed experimentally. As will be shown, there is a strong case for attributing the problems of the AO-177 to the effects of unsteady growth and collapse of sheet cavitation.

Possible solutions involve changing the wake velocity distribution, altering the propeller design, or both. The several means of modifying the wake distribution include: bulbous stern designs [2, 25] to help create more rounded wake contours (to reduce spike-like features) and produce a more uniform circumferential velocity variation; flow-improving fins [1, 2, 26–29] to guide more flow into the upper propeller disk region by increasing local axial flow speed; upstream propeller ducts [29, 30] to help induce a more stable and uniform through-flow to the propeller; and various types of wake spoilers or flow deflectors [31, 32] to induce flow changes selectively just forward of the propeller location. A bulbous stern was not pursued as a corrective measure, since the structural changes to the ship would have been much too radical and expensive. Flow deflectors such as those noted by Rutherford [25] were not pursued.

It was decided to investigate flow-improving fins, an upstream duct, and propeller design changes as the options for reducing the excitation levels on the AO-177.

Two basic fin designs were selected for model evaluation: a tunnel-type configuration modeled after a fin described by Rutherford [25] that was successful in helping to relieve excessive vibrations on a moderate-block-coefficient refrigerated pallet cargo ship, and a flow-accelerating configuration suggested by SSPA. Line drawings of these fin designs are shown in Figs. 6 and 7. Aside from the differences in shape and size, the tunnel-type fin features a tip clearance ratio of $a_z/D = 0.12$, while the flow-accelerating fin has $a_z/D = 0.10$. The detailed design of the tunnel-fin design for the AO-177 application was carried out by Hydronautics, Inc.

Experiments were conducted at both DTNSRDC and SSPA with scale models of the AO-177 hull of identical size. This made it possible to use the same model propeller (DTNSRDC Model 4677) for tests involving flow visualization, pressure pulse amplitudes, and powering. Table 6 summarizes the basic dimensions and conditions of the models.

Model flow visualization and wake studies

In order to gain preliminary understanding of the effect of a fin on the quality of wake flow near and approaching the propeller aperture, flow visualization experiments were performed in the Circulating Water Channel at DTNSRDC with the propelled AO-177 model, at the appropriate scaled propeller rpm and at the Froude-scaled speed corresponding to 20 knots full scale [33]. Both full-load and ballast conditions were simulated. Yarn tufts were attached from Station 17 aft, and to the rudder.

From observations of unstable or reversing tuft patterns it was possible to detect regions of very slow or separated flows. In the case of the AO-177 with no fin, and with the as-built propeller design, the flow along a narrow strip near the centerline of the upper aperture was found to show some variable or near-separated flow behavior in both the load and ballast conditions. It was also found that the tunnel-fin produced a noticeably less variable flow behavior in the vicinity of the propeller plane, compared with the flow with no fin. The sketch of Fig. 8 shows the superposed tuft patterns taken from photographs of the port side aft of the model in the channel, indicating the hull flows both without and with the tunnel-fin. From this comparison, the discernible effect of the installed fin seemed to be concentrated near the partial tunnel underside where several tufts (and streamlines) were deflected slightly downward from their original orientation. This corresponds to more of the buttock-aligned flow being directed into the propeller disk region.

Wake surveys were conducted at DTNSRDC with the AO-177 model operated with and without the fin configurations, in both the full-load and ballast conditions [34]. These experiments were performed with a wake rake consisting of five 5-hole, spherically headed pitot tubes rotated systematically around the complete propeller disk. For the full-load displacement condition, the measured circumferential distributions of the three velocity component ratios of the nominal wake at radius ratios $r/R = 0.359, 0.556, 0.775, 1.017,$ and 1.178 are shown in Figs. 9 through 13, respectively. The cases included are the AO-177 hull with no fin, with the tunnel-fin, and with the flow-accelerating fin. These plots are arranged to show the effect of the main wake shadow in the center of each graph. It

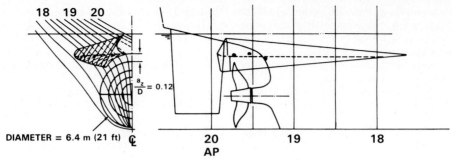

Fig. 6 Tunnel-fin configuraiton

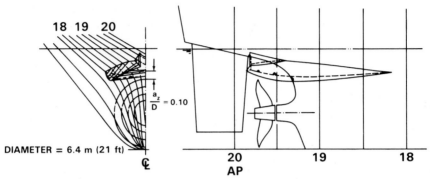

Fig. 7 Flow-accelerating fin configuration

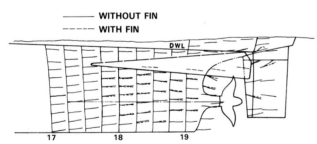

Fig. 8 Model tuft patterns with and without tunnel-fin

Table 6 Model hull and propeller geometry of AO-177 (scale ratio $\lambda = 25.682$)

Hull

length	$L_{PP} = 6.527$ m (21.42 ft)
length on waterline	$L_{WL} = 6.653$ m (21.83 ft)
beam	$B = 1.044$ m (3.43 ft)
draft (mean) full load	$T_m = 0.374$ m (1.227 ft)
material:	wood for experiments at DTNSRDC paraffin wax for water tunnel experiments at SSPA
turbulence stimulation	none on DTNSRDC model 1-mm trip wire at $0.05\,L_{WL}$ on model at SSPA

Propeller

diameter	$D = 24.92$ cm (9.812 in.)
pitch-to-diameter ratio	$(P/D)_{0.7R} = 1.25$
number of blades	$Z = 7$

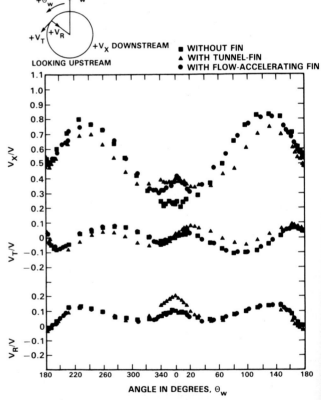

Fig. 9 Model nominal wake velocity ratios, with and without two different fins, at radius ratio $r/R = 0.359$

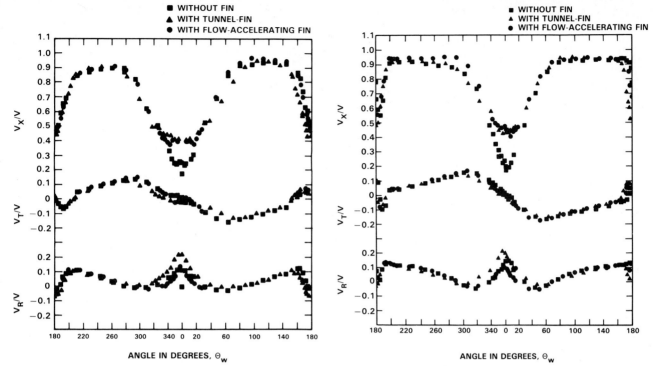

Fig. 10 Model nominal wake velocity ratios, with and without two different fins, at radius ratio $r/R = 0.556$

Fig. 11 Model nominal wake velocity ratios, with and without two different fins, at radius ratio $r/R = 0.775$

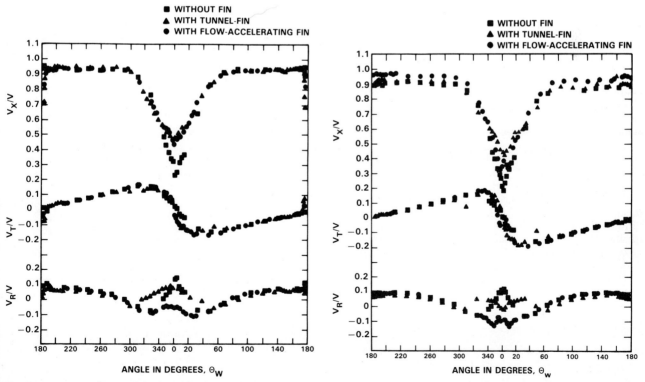

Fig. 12 Model nominal wake velocity ratios, with and without two different fins, at radius ratio $r/R = 1.017$

Fig. 13 Model nominal wake velocity ratios, with and without two different fins, at radius ratio $r/R = 1.178$

Causes and Corrections for Propeller-Excited Airborne Noise

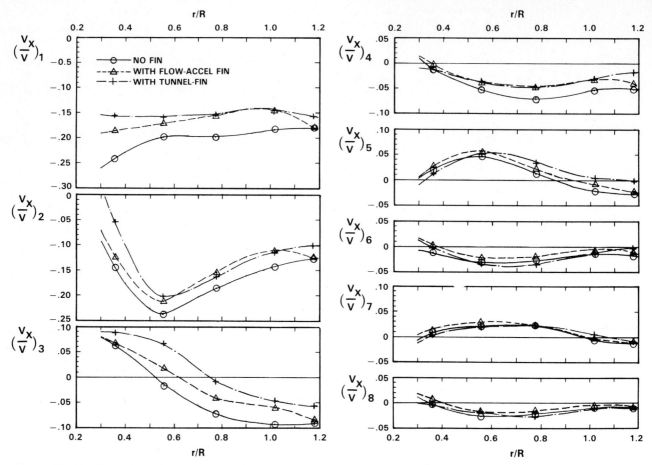

Fig. 14 Comparison of radial distributions of axial component of wake harmonics, with and without the two different fins

is noted that for each of the two with-fin velocity patterns there is an increase of the axial velocity component V_X/V (decrease of wake peak) that occurs locally within the angular interval 40 deg to either side of the 12 o'clock position. The distributions of the axial velocity components due to the two different fin configurations seem to differ little in magnitude and detail. There are, however, noticeable differences in the distributions of the tangential and radial component ratios V_T/V and V_R/V for the different fin types.

Radial distributions of the harmonic amplitudes $(V_X/V)_n$ of the longitudinal velocity component for harmonics $n = 1$ through 8 are shown in Fig. 14, comparing the full load displacement cases of the hull with no fin, with the tunnel-fin, and with the flow-accelerating fin. For the lowest harmonics, $n = 1$ and 2, the amplitudes are systematically reduced by the action of each of the two fin configurations. For the higher harmonics, the effects of the two fin systems become mixed and apparently subject to no simple or generalized trends. It is known from previous investigations and extensive comparative work (see, for example, Hylarides [3]) that the reductions of the

lowest harmonic orders of the V_X/V velocity field can produce measurable reductions in the levels of propeller-excitation due to intermittent blade cavitation. Both fin configurations under consideration were found to produce improvements in the flow to the propeller in the upper disk region (near 12 o'clock), and both fin wakes showed reduced magnitudes in the first two harmonics.

Propeller-excitation model experiments

Cavitation tunnel experiments were carried out in the Swedish Maritime Research Centre (SSPA) Tunnel No. 2 with the DTNSRDC model propeller of the AO-177 operated behind a complete wax model of the AO-177 hull. These experiments included measurement of propeller thrust and torque, systematic observations of the propeller cavitation patterns, checks on cavitation erosion tendency, and measurements of the propeller-induced pressure pulse amplitudes at several points on the hull surface. These experiments provided a crucial body of evidence that verified that propeller blade intermittent cavitation was the likely cause of the excitation and initial-stage erosion problems of the AO-177, and supplied the technical basis for choosing a design correction for the ship from among the several proposed options. The results of all these experiments are recorded in references [35–37].

Original AO-177 configuration—Initial experiments were run with the design propeller operating behind the unaltered AO-177 hull at the conditions given in Table 7. Observations of the propeller blade cavitation patterns at the simulated conditions of both full-load and ballast displacements indicated that extensive sheet cavitation appeared on the outer radii of

Table 7 Conditions for original configuration experiments

Condition	Ship Speed V (knots)	Ship Scale rpm	J	Number Cavitation σ
Full load	21.6	98.3	0.77	4.7
Ballast	23.2	100.3	0.81	3.5

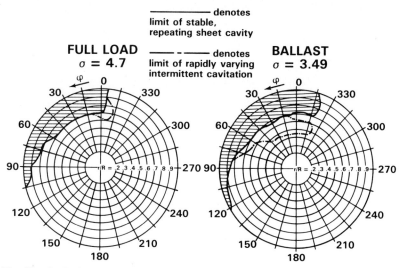

—————— denotes limit of stable, repeating sheet cavity

—— - —— denotes limit of rapidly varying intermittent cavitation

FULL LOAD
σ = 4.7

BALLAST
σ = 3.49

Fig. 15 Cavitation extent diagrams for unmodified AO-177 at full load and ballast conditions [position angle φ measured counterclockwise looking aft (downstream)]

each blade from about 0.6R to the tip as it passed through the main wake field. Figure 15 indicates the radial and circumferential extent of the blade cavitation during one revolution for the two displacement conditions. Cloud cavitation produced by the unstable breakup of the sheet cavities formed in patches downstream and overlapping the blade trailing edges around the 0.8R to 0.9R radii. SSPA's standard erosion tendency test using a coating on the blade surface predicted blade surface erosion around the 0.85R radius at the trailing edge.

The pressure pulse magnitudes at various locations around the propeller aperture were found to be rather high as shown in the longitudinal distributions of blade rate pressure double amplitudes plotted in Fig. 16. Two representations of the same pressure pulse signature are displayed: the oscilloscope-recorded value of maximum peak-to-peak at blade rate, and the mean of the highest 5 percent double amplitudes at blade rate as determined from Fourier analysis. The positive phase angle Φ here indicates the angular delay of the suction peak occurring after the blade reference line has passed the upright position. The longitudinal distribution of the phase angle is nearly constant, a typical attribute of the fluctuating pressure field from cavity volume variations.

For the point on the hull centerline directly over the propeller tip, the variations of blade rate pressure double amplitudes with ship speed are shown in Fig. 17 for both full-load and ballast conditions. The measured noncavitating pressure pulse double

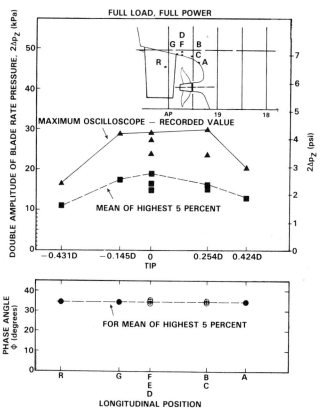

Fig. 16 Longitudinal distribution of blade rate pressure pulse double amplitude and phase angle for unmodified AO-177

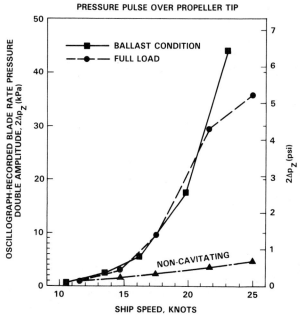

Fig. 17 Variation of blade rate peak-to-peak hull pressure over propeller tip versus ship speed

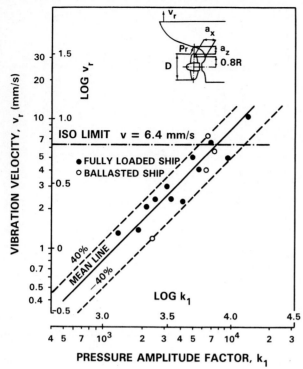

Fig. 18 SSPA pressure pulse-vibration response criterion (from reference [27])

the tip clearances a_z and a_x, as specified in the dimensional pressure factor

$$k_1 = 2(\Delta P_Z)\frac{10^3 D^2}{\nabla}\frac{a_z}{a_x}$$

where

$2(\Delta P_Z)$ = blade rate pressure pulse double amplitude (Pa)
D = propeller diameter (m)
∇ = volume of displacement (m³)
a_z = vertical tip clearance
a_x = horizontal blade clearance measured from midchord at 0.8R radius forward to hull

This criterion was developed from data on ships having propellers with fewer than seven blades. For the unaltered AO-177, using the mean-line value for the ISO limit on vibration velocity of 6.4 mm/s (252 mils/s), the allowable blade rate pressure fluctuation over the tips according to the SSPA criterion is $2(\Delta P_Z)_{\text{allowable}}$ = 9.7 kPa (1.41 psi). This is smaller than the range of values allowed by the single-point, single-value recommendations.

In any case, the propeller-excitation levels inferred from the model tests of the AO-177 are excessive, and indicate that troublesome hull vibration might be expected. As noted at the outset, the problems with the AO-177 did not appear in the form of large hull girder vibrations, either at the fantail centerline, or at the top levels of the deckhouse, but rather showed up as high-level, low-frequency inboard airborne noise, transmitted by localized structureborne vibrations. It would appear that this indicates either a model scaling-correlation difficulty with the SSPA criterion, perhaps because the AO-177 propeller has seven blades, or that there are unusual characteristics of the AO-177 structural impedance properties for girder vibrations and airborne noise. This may also be related to the excitation frequency ranges associated with the seven-bladed propeller being somewhat higher than is common practice for ships of this type.

Experiments with alternative (stock) propellers—Measurements of propeller-induced hull pressures and observations of cavitation patterns were made for three stock propellers on the AO-177 model hull without fins in the SSPA water tunnel. The objective of these experiments was to obtain data on the influence of specific propeller parameters on the cavitation patterns, tendency towards erosion, and propeller-induced hull pressures. This information was necessary for:

1. evaluating the relative potential gains to be achieved by redesigning the propeller and by modifying the hull/wake, and

2. providing guidance for a propeller redesign in the event that this option was selected.

The schedule did not permit propeller models to be designed and built specifically for these experiments; therefore, the most suitable stock propellers were selected.

The existing (stock) propeller models were chosen in an attempt to represent the following geometries:

A. A five-bladed, 21-ft-diameter (6.4 m) (full-scale) skewed propeller with wide blades near the tip, and a large skew gradient near the tip. It was speculated that a design with these general characteristics would be the most promising alternative design for reasons described in the section on propeller redesign.

B. A four-bladed, 21-ft-diameter (6.4 m) propeller, preferably with a skew distribution similar to that for the selected five-bladed propeller. This would help isolate the influence of number of blades.

C. A seven-bladed, 23-ft-diameter (7.0 m) propeller. This

amplitudes are also presented in Fig. 17. This latter comparison shows an order-of-magnitude increase in the pressure pulses due to blade cavitation in the high-speed range. This effect, the slow longitudinal diminution of the pressure amplitudes forward and aft of the propeller plane (Fig. 16), and the almost constant longitudinal distribution of pressure pulse phase angle (Fig. 16), are typical characteristics of the excitation produced by blade cavity volume variations.

Simple criteria are available for judging whether the scaled-up fluctuating pressure amplitudes are excessive from the point of view of propeller-excited hull vibrations. Typically, these prescriptions are based on correlations between hull girder vibration levels that exceed the limits recommended by the ISO or by the pertinent authority for the ship type involved. Unfortunately, there are no known elementary criteria that pertain specifically to airborne noise in this same fashion. It has been indicated, for example, by Ward and Willshare [38] that excessive airborne noise often accompanies the problem of severe aft-end vibrations, and is generally attributable to the same unsteady cavitating-propeller excitation. It is useful, for a frame of reference, to consider the present problem in terms of criteria for hull girder vibration, which deal with the lowest end of the pressure pulse excitation spectrum. The simplest criteria are the recommended single-point, single-value limits for hull pressure pulses directly over the propeller tip. The typical limiting values of blade rate double amplitude discussed in reference [39] are in the range $2(\Delta P_Z)_{\text{allowable}}$ = 15 to 20 kPa (2.25 to 3 psi). Since the corresponding model test value for the AO-177 was found to be about 29 kPa (4.35 psi), this seemed to verify the presence of an excessive excitation.

The criterion developed by SSPA [27] and embodied in Fig. 18 is based on a correlation of pressure pulse amplitude and hull vibration velocity response v_r at the fantail centerline. It provides for determining limiting values of pressure amplitudes that depend roughly upon the relative size of the ship and upon

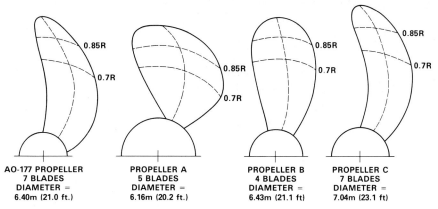

AO-177 PROPELLER	PROPELLER A	PROPELLER B	PROPELLER C
7 BLADES	5 BLADES	4 BLADES	7 BLADES
DIAMETER =	DIAMETER =	DIAMETER =	DIAMETER =
6.40m (21.0 ft.)	6.16m (20.2 ft.)	6.43m (21.1 ft)	7.04m (23.1 ft)

Fig. 19 Propellers evaluated in AO-177 experiments at SSPA

propeller was selected in an attempt to isolate the influence of diameter.

These target geometries for the alternative propeller were selected as representing the most effective candidates for providing information for improving the erosion and airborne noise on the AO-177. It was desired that all the propeller models have values of other geometric parameters which are consistent with the requirements of the AO-177, especially expanded area ratio, average pitch, and radial distributions of pitch, skew, thickness, and camber.

These requirements could be met only partially with existing model propellers; however, in most cases the geometries were sufficiently near the desired values for the objective of these experiments. The selected propeller models are compared in Fig. 19. The best available four-bladed stock propeller had neither high skew nor a suitable expanded area ratio; however, it was experimentally evaluated in an attempt to obtain some additional information on the influence of the number of blades.

Experiments were conducted at the estimated full-power, full-load point with each propeller, corresponding to the conditions given in Table 8.

The cavitation results showed that all of the propellers had cloud cavitation near the trailing edge except Propeller A. For Propeller A, the back sheet cavitation remained as a clear stable sheet that merged with the tip vortex and collapsed substantially downstream of the propeller. The resulting collapse of the sheet cavitation on this propeller appeared to be much less violent than on the other propellers. This type of behavior should be beneficial for reducing both the tendency towards erosion and periodic hull pressure amplitudes. Figure 20 compares the patterns on the model of the AO-177 propeller with Propeller A.

The hypothesized mechanism which drives the sheet cavitation on Propeller A to merge with the tip vortex is discussed in the section on the proposed redesign propeller; however, the controlling propeller parameters are thought to be the sweep angle of the leading edge near the tip, and the chord lengths near the tip. Propeller A, which is a model of a controllable-pitch propeller, has substantially wider blades near the tip than the AO-177 propeller and Propellers B and C. The leading-edge sweep angle near the tip on Propeller A is slightly larger than it is on the AO-177 propeller, and substantially larger than on Propellers B and C.

The relative magnitudes of blade rate pressure fluctuations measured on the hull centerline directly over the propellers were found to be as given in Table 9. The reduced pressure pulse amplitude with Propeller A is consistent with the observed less-violent collapse of the cavitation on this propeller. The

Table 8 Conditions for alternate propeller experiments

Propeller	Ship Speed V (knots)	rpm	J	σ
AO-177	21.6	98	0.77	4.7
A	21.3	103	0.78	4.7
B	21.6	98	0.77	4.7
C	21.5	103	0.68	4.6

higher pressures with Propeller C are due predominantly to the substantially reduced tip clearance with this propeller.

As discussed in the section on the proposed redesign propeller, the radial distribution of loading (pitch and camber) near the tip may also have an influence on the violence of the cavitation collapse, and on propeller-induced hull pressures. Propellers B and C have significantly less pitch and camber reduction near the tip than either the AO-177 propeller or Propeller A; see Fig. 21. However, the influences of radial distribution of loading near the tip on the violence of the cavitation collapse and propeller-induced hull pressures could not be isolated from these data because more than one propeller parameter was changed simultaneously.

In conclusion, these experiments suggest that if a propeller redesign is to be undertaken, desirable characteristics are wide blades near the tip with a highly swept leading edge near the tip.

Experiments with wake-improving appendages—Experiments were conducted at SSPA with three sets of stern appendages to explore the possibility of modifying and obtaining a sufficiently improved wake so that the propeller would not have to be changed. In addition to the flow-accelerating fin and the tunnel-type fin designs described earlier, a retrofit upstream duct concept modeled after a configuration discussed by Takekuma [30] was also considered. Such an upstream duct has been shown to be helpful in the reduction of propeller-excited vibrations for full ship forms, but not necessarily for slimmer hull forms like the AO-177. Figure 22 is a profile drawing of the duct fitted on the hull indicating how it was arranged ahead of the propeller. This duct features nonconstant chord lengths around its periphery.

Observations of the blade cavitation patterns and measurements of induced hull pressures were carried out for each of the cases of the modified hull at the estimated full-power condition characterized by data given in Table 10. All these tests were run with the design AO-177 propeller.

Blade cavitation patterns corresponding to operation with the two fin designs showed some slight shifts in extent both

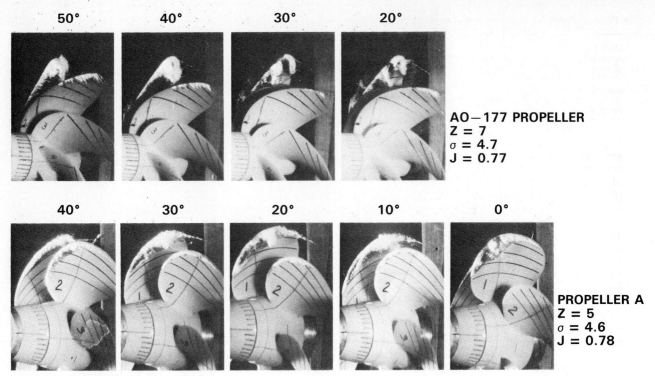

50° 40° 30° 20°

AO−177 PROPELLER
Z = 7
σ = 4.7
J = 0.77

40° 30° 20° 10° 0°

PROPELLER A
Z = 5
σ = 4.6
J = 0.78

ANGLES ARE POSITION ANGLE φ

Fig. 20 Cavitation patterns on AO-177 propeller and Stock Propeller A behind unmodified hull at simulated full-power, full-load conditions

radially and circumferentially. In these cases, the cloud cavitation associated with instability of the sheet cavities was diminished somewhat compared with the situation with the unappended AO-177 hull. With the duct, the blade cavitation extent in the upper disk was diminished somewhat but a new region of cavitation was introduced near the 5 o'clock position (looking downstream) of the disk, caused by a local wake peak at the bottom region of the duct. Also with the duct, there was observed a frequent occurrence of fine vortex core cavitation near the 12 o'clock region of the duct exit that had the appearance of lightning strokes leaping from the blade tips to the inside aft end of the duct. Pressure pulses produced by this phenomenon are known to be very large, but since no pressure

gages were located within the duct for the AO-177 experiments, the magnitudes of pressure excitation levels on the inner duct surface were not determined.

The cavitation sketches collected in Fig. 23 illustrate the changes in gross cavitation extent and cavitation appearance for the simulated full-power, full-load operation of the unmodified hull plus the three modifying appendage configurations. The slight discontinuity in cavitation extent that occurs in the blade cavitation pattern for the case of the unmodified

Table 9 Effect of propeller geometry on pressure fluctuations

Propeller	$\Delta P_Z/(\Delta P_Z)_{AO\text{-}177}$
AO-177	1.0
A	0.5
B	1.0
C	1.8

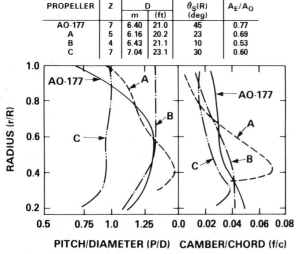

PROPELLER	Z	D (m)	D (ft)	$\theta_S(R)$ (deg)	A_E/A_O
AO-177	7	6.40	21.0	45	0.77
A	5	6.16	20.2	23	0.69
B	4	6.43	21.1	10	0.53
C	7	7.04	23.1	30	0.60

Fig. 21 Comparison of pitch and camber of propellers evaluated in AO-177 experiments at SSPA

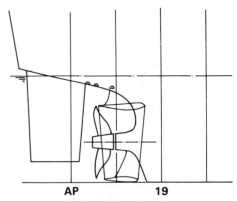

Fig. 22 Retrofit duct configuration

Table 10   Conditions for wake-improving appendage experiments

Modifying Appendage Configuration	Ship Speed V (knots)	rpm	J	σ
Flow-accelerating fin	21.5	101	0.80	4.2
Tunnel-fin	21.5	101	0.80	4.2
Retrofit duct	21.3	102	0.825	3.8

hull between position angles of 60 and 70 deg seems to have been smoothed in the sequences recorded for each of the appended hull cases. From visual observations and to some extent from photographs, it appears that for each of the appended hull cases shown, the blade sheet cavity was thinner than that for the case of the unmodified AO-177. There were also noticeable differences in the cavity termination region near the blade trailing edge. In general, for all of the appended hull cases the extent of cloud cavitation was reduced.

Erosion tendency tests were carried out with the AO-177 model propeller with the flow-accelerating fin and with the duct; in both cases, the experiment did not indicate any tendency toward erosion.

Pressure pulse measurements were made at various locations on the underside of the two fins and on the hull at positions indicated in Figs. 6, 7, and 22. For the full-power, full-load conditions appropriate to each configuration, the resulting distributions of blade rate pressure amplitudes are shown in Fig. 24. The resulting distributions of pressure pulse double am-

plitudes show that the effect of each of the two fin appendages follows a distinctive pattern. Directly over the tip, the pressure pulse levels remain large or may even increase. The tunnel-fin, with a vertical tip clearance ratio $a_z/D = 0.12$, produced a slightly greater pressure pulse level than the unmodified hull over the tip, but showed much reduced amplitudes both forward and aft of the propeller. The flow-accelerating fin, with $a_z/D = 0.10$, produced somewhat lower pressure pulse levels over the propeller, and even greater reductions of amplitude compared with the tunnel-fin forward of the propeller plane.

For both Propeller A and the duct appendage, the distributions of pressure pulse amplitudes at points along the hull showed similar reductions to about 50 percent of the levels of the original AO-177 propeller/hull combination.

There is a subtle correspondence between the appearance of cavitation patterns on the blade planform illustrated in Fig. 23 and the details of the resulting pressure pulse excitation shown in Fig. 24. Unfortunately the important properties of cavity thickness and cavity volume distribution are not indicated in Fig. 23. In fact, these properties are determined experimentally only with great research effort. Therefore the diagrams of Fig. 23 provide only a partial description of the alterations in cavity geometry that are reflected in the changes of pressure pulse levels of Fig. 24.

Figure 24 also shows the allowable pressure double amplitude obtained from the SSPA criterion (Fig. 18) for each of the configurations. The permissible level (at the point above the propeller tip) for the flow-accelerating fin is the highest because

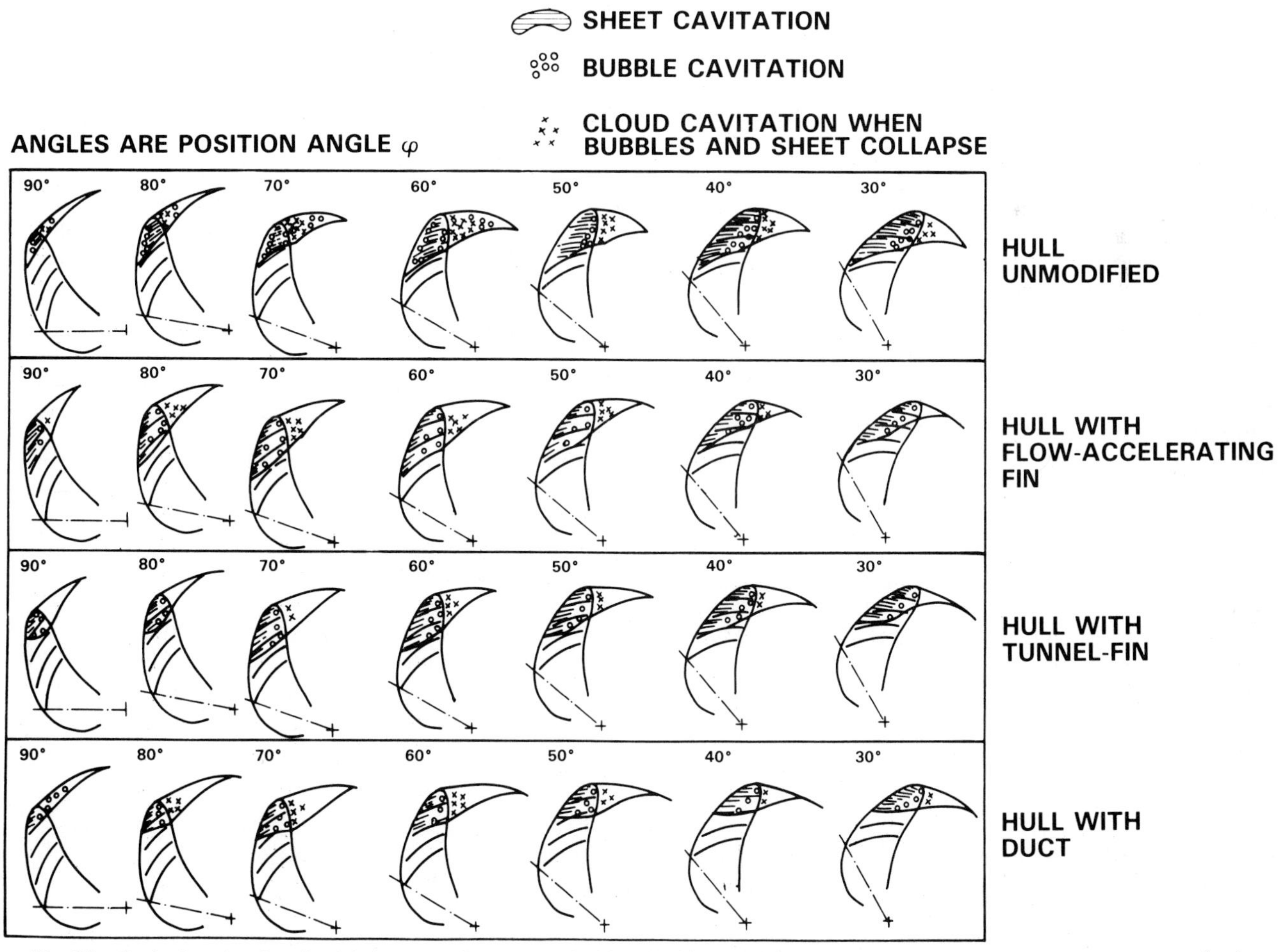

Fig. 23   Cavitation sketches for AO-177 propeller operated with and without various flow-modifying appendages (from reference [37])

Causes and Corrections for Propeller-Excited Airborne Noise

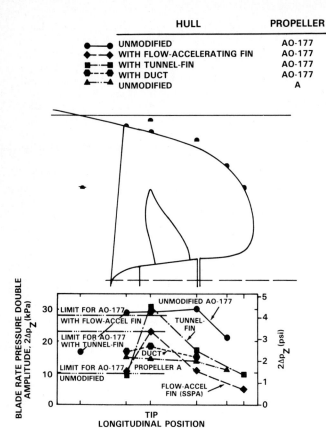

HULL	PROPELLER
UNMODIFIED	AO-177
WITH FLOW-ACCELERATING FIN	AO-177
WITH TUNNEL-FIN	AO-177
WITH DUCT	AO-177
UNMODIFIED	A

Fig. 24 Comparison of distributions of blade rate pressure double amplitudes for various corrective options for AO-177

sequent higher harmonic components, up to frequencies at least as high as 1 kHz. Therefore, over most of the hull surface near the propeller, the model experimental results indicate that both fins produce lowered overall fluctuating pressure excitation in the frequency ranges important to the production of airborne noise. There seems to be no clear-cut advantage for either fin in this regard. The better performance of the flow-accelerating fin at the blade rate harmonic was the significant factor in its choice as the final corrective design modification to be installed full scale.

In addition to the model experimental determination of the cavitating propeller excitation levels of the AO-177, analytical investigations were carried out by four independent groups under contract. Some of the results are presented in Appendix 2 for the cases of the original AO-177 and its modification with the flow-accelerating fin. In general, the results corroborate what was determined in the model tests, that compared with the unmodified AO-177, the cavitating propeller-induced surface force amplitudes and cavity thickness and volume are reduced with the improved wake and with the hull shape changes introduced by the fin.

Resistance and powering with the fin

Once the flow-accelerating fin was selected as the design modification for the AO-177, the resistance and powering penalties associated with it were determined by model experiments at DTNSRDC [40].

Figure 26 shows a comparison of the powering characteristics of the AO-177 with and without the flow-accelerating fin for the full-load displacement with trim 0.31 m (1.0 ft) down-by-the-bow. The predicted delivered power requirement was increased somewhat over the unmodified hull due to a combination of increased total resistance (P_E) and decreased propulsive coefficient η_D with the fin. At full power, these data indicate that there would be a speed loss with the fin of about 0.2 knot, which is a smaller variation than the typical accuracy of the towing tank experiments. Corresponding comparisons of pertinent propulsive factors versus speed with and without the fin are displayed in Fig. 27. It appears that the main effect of the fin in this case is to reduce the effective wake w_T (an expected result). There is also a reduction in the relative rotative efficiency η_R, and very little change in the other factors.

For the ballast condition, with trim 1.14 m (3.75 ft) down by the stern, the powering characteristics of the AO-177 with and without the fin are compared in Fig. 28. There was a measured increase in resistance with the fin, but due to changes in all the propulsive factors (see Fig. 29), the propulsive efficiency η_D is increased somewhat, so that the delivered power requirements are actually reduced compared with the case of no fin. Therefore, the speed at full power is predicted to increase slightly by 0.3 knot (again a variation that lies within the typical accuracy of the experiment).

Proposed redesign of propeller

A proposed redesign of the propeller[8] was performed for the ship as fitted with the flow-accelerating fin, as a possible solution in the event that the fin did not solve the problems with the existing propeller. The proposed redesign considered the geometric characteristics and resulting cavitation performance of the existing propeller, and of the stock propellers evaluated at SSPA. However, it is not considered to be a "final" redesign since it has not benefited from information from all the trials, nor has it been tested for propulsion or cavitation performance.

its tip clearance ratio a_z/D is the smallest of all the arrangements indicated. If it is assumed that the SSPA vibration criterion somehow has general applicability to problems associated with cavitating-propeller excitation, then the flow-accelerating fin is the only choice of the options tested that produces an acceptable level of excitation. The rapid reduction of the pressure pulse amplitudes forward and aft of the propeller location (as seen with both the tested fins for the AO-177) is an important adjunct to the SSPA criterion when it is applied to give guidance to the solution of a ship vibration problem. With the situation of the AO-177, the choice of the flow-accelerating fin for the final corrective measure was made on the basis of its performance relative to the other options. It offered a likely cure for the problems, while retaining the original propeller.

Both fin configurations were found to influence not only the blade rate component, but also the higher harmonic content of the fluctuating hull pressure characteristics. Figure 25 is a comparison of the first three harmonic components of pressure double amplitude at several points around the propeller aperture, presented in terms of the mean of the 5 percent highest amplitudes determined from Fourier analysis. The data apply to the full-load, full-power condition for the two fin arrangements and for the original AO-177. At the point on the hull directly above the propeller tip, the effect of each of the fins is to increase the second and third blade rate harmonic components, $2\Delta p_{2Z}$ and $2\Delta p_{3Z}$, relative with the no-fin case. This is apparently an isolated trend, however, because for all the other points considered, both forward and aft of the tip plane, the effect of the fins is to reduce the second and third harmonic components of pressure. From spectral analyses of typical hull pressure pulses, the reductions of the 2Z and 3Z harmonic components due to the fins tend to be repeated for all the sub-

---

[8] Described in a report of restricted distribution by S. Jessup entitled "Preliminary Redesign of the AO-177 Propeller," 1982.

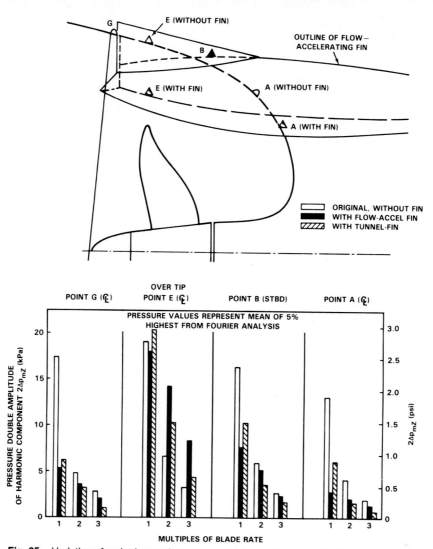

Fig. 25 Variation of major harmonic components of propeller-induced hull pressure pulses at several locations, with and without wake-improving fins

The design conditions specified for the redesign were the same as those for the original propeller (Table 3) except for modifications to minimize airborne noise and erosion. As discussed later, it was also necessary to increase the maximum allowable blade frequency bearing forces.

As discussed in a preceding section, the existing AO-177 propeller has seven blades and relatively short chords, especially near the tip; see Table 2. Although the existing propeller has 45 deg of projected skew angle at the tip, the skew angle distribution is essentially linear from the midradius to the tip. The narrow chord lengths near the tip appear to reduce the tendency of skew to reduce cavitation [41, 42] by reducing the sweepback angle of the leading edge, that is, the angle between the projected leading edge and a radial plane. The full-scale cavitation observed on the AO-177 propeller showed a two-dimensional character indicative of the narrow blades, that is, little radial motion of the cavitation or interaction with the tip vortex.

A variety of geometry changes has been suggested to reduce propeller-induced hull forces and propeller erosion problems. These suggestions are summarized as follows:

1. Increased chord length [18]: A dramatic change in this parameter could be achieved because of the abnormally short chords at the outer radii on the existing propeller. Increasing chord lengths would reduce the loading per unit area on the blades, thus reducing the volume of cavitation. Reducing the number of blades for the same expanded area ratio would produce wider blades, possibly causing a greater three-dimensional cavity structure, and reduced violence of collapse. Also, fewer blades would bring the design closer to traditional design practice.

2. Large skew variation near the tip: A large variation (gradient) in projected skew angle, θ_s, near the blade tip will produce a highly swept tip. This type of blade outline, when heavily loaded, as occurs in the wake peak, may induce turbulent separation along the leading edge extending to the blade tip. If this occurs, then cavitation forms along the leading edge and will be convected into the tip vortex and off the blade. It is believed that blade cavitation collapses gently off the blade when it merges with the tip vortex. This process has been observed by Jessup [43] and on the five-bladed stock propeller (Propeller A) evaluated on the AO-177 model hull at SSPA. This type of blade outline has been successfully adopted with controllable-pitch propellers for commercial ship applications with significant reductions in propeller-induced hull vibration [13].

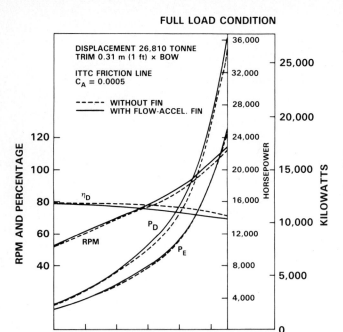

FULL LOAD CONDITION

Fig. 26 Comparison of resistance and powering properties with and without flow-accelerating fin for trial full-load displacement

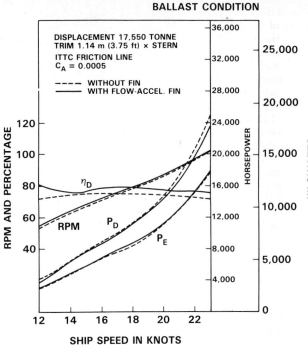

BALLAST CONDITION

Fig. 28 Comparison of resistance and powering properties with and without flow-accelerating fin for ballast condition

3. Increased loading near the tip [18]: Increased loading near the tip will increase the cavitation volume, and the blade angular extent in which cavitation occurs. This may tend to decrease erosion and the violence of the cavitation collapse, but too much loading near the tip may increase the propeller-induced hull forces.

4. Reduced loading near blade tip [18, 44]: In general, reduced loading near the blade tips will reduce the amount of cavitation. Propeller-induced hull forces may be be reduced; however, the effect of tip unloading on cavitation erosion and cavity collapse is not fully understood. In some cases, tip unloading produces undesirable unstable cavity collapse.

5. Increased angle of attack loading with decreased camber

loading [18]: Blade pitch can be increased with a corresponding decrease in camber, resulting in unchanged propulsive performance. This will alter the pressure distribution on the blade sections, providing a less severe chordwise pressure gradient near the trailing edge, which may reduce the violence of the cavity collapse.

The approach chosen for the proposed redesign of the AO-177 propeller incorporates Items 1, 2 and 3: increased chord lengths, an increased skew gradient, and slightly increased loading are incorporated near the tip region. Time-average chordwise loading corresponding to an NACA $a = 0.8$ mean line at ideal angle of attack was specified, which is the same as was specified for the existing AO-177 propeller.

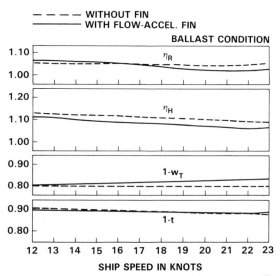

Fig. 27 Comparison of propulsive coefficients with and without flow-accelerating fin for trial full-load displacement

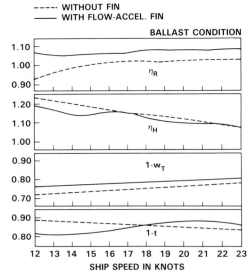

Fig. 29 Comparison of propulsive coefficients with and without flow-accelerating fin for ballast condition

Causes and Corrections for Propeller-Excited Airborne Noise

Calculations of the blade frequency bearing forces with and without the fin were made using the same methods used for the design of the existing propeller, and using model wakes with and without the fin (see Fig. 14). The limitations of these methods were discussed in the earlier subsection on propeller details and design. These calculations indicate that in order to meet concurrently the following two requirements specified for the original design:

1. produce blade frequency thrust amplitude that is less than 13.3 kN (3000 lb), and
2. have a blade planform with neither a significantly concave trailing edge nor a pointed trailing edge near the tip,

the redesign must have seven blades and essentially the same blade planform as the original design. This follows directly from the similarities of the pertinent wake harmonics with and without the fin (see Fig. 14), and the increase in required maximum skew as the number of blades decreases, for the same reasons as for the existing propeller. Therefore, for a redesign to be viable for improving airborne noise and erosion, the bearing force limits had to be increased and the subjective limitation on trailing-edge planform concavity had to be relaxed.

Full-scale measurements have indicated that the longitudinal shafting resonance for the AO-177 occurs around 13 Hz, or about 10 rpm above the full-power condition with a seven-bladed propeller, rather than at approximately 10 Hz as was predicted when the original design was carried out. Therefore, the maximum allowable blade frequency thrust to meet MIL-STD 167 increased with decreasing number of blades, with the upper limit being 13.3 kN (3000 lb) for seven blades and 35.6 kN (8000 lb) for five blades. In addition, measurements indicated no significant hull vibration due to transverse bearing forces; therefore, the restrictions on transverse bearing forces were substantially relaxed.

Four blades were unacceptable for the same reasons as for the original design, and seven blades would force the design to be almost the same as the existing design. Full-scale measurements and additional response calculations made since the original propeller design indicate that excessive hull girder vibration is no longer considered likely with a five-bladed propeller. Five blades were selected rather than six because blade frequency for a five-bladed propeller is further from the longitudinal resonance in the main propulsion system and because it allows wider chords to be used near the tip than does a six-bladed propeller.

Due to reduced clearance with the fins and other constraints as discussed for the original design, the diameter had to remain at 6.4 m (21 ft).

The design process involved choosing a blade outline to maximize sweepback of the blade leading edge near the tip with wide chords near the tip subject to the following constraints:

1. Avoid a pointed tip trailing edge from consideration of strength and damage susceptibility, especially during astern rotation.
2. Maintain periodic bearing forces to the new specified values.
3. Avoid the blade overhanging the front and back edges of the hub.

The proposed blade shape representing the best compromise of these characteristics is shown in Figure 30. The bearing forces for the redesign propeller predicted using the same procedures as for the existing AO-177 propeller are given in Table 11.

The loading near the tip was slightly greater than it was for the original design but slightly less than the Lerbs optimum. This distribution was selected in an attempt to reduce the violence of the cavity collapse without excessively increasing the loading near the tip. The radial distribution of thickness was

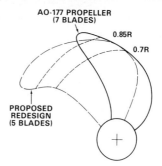

Fig. 30 Comparison of existing propeller with proposed redesign

selected in conjunction with the radial distribution of loading to ensure a 10 percent margin on inception of back-bubble cavitation at full power, ensure freedom from face cavitation at full power, and strength integrity.

Figure 30 compares the geometry of the existing propeller with the redesigned propeller. The slightly smaller tip skew for the redesigned propeller resulted from the requirements to avoid a "pointed" blade profile near the tip, and to have wide chords near the tip. The predicted propulsion performances of the two propellers are essentially equal.

Det norske Veritas, using a procedure based on unsteady lifting-surface theory, including the influence of cavitation, predicted that the proposed redesign propeller would reduce the blade rate hull pressures to approximately 70 percent of the values with the existing propeller. This reduction is predicted both with and without fin. In addition, DnV predicted that the proposed redesign would be erosion-free on the ship as fitted with the fin.

Full-scale verification

Following the installation of the flow-accelerating fin on the AO-177 at Todd Shipyards in Alameda, California the ship was instrumented for measurements of airborne noise, fluctuating pressures on the fin underside, main shaft torque, and propeller viewing.

Airborne noise

The general result of the fin installation is a reduction in compartment octave band noise levels by 10 dB or more in spaces aft of Frame 94. In some areas such as the fantail, high-frequency noise reductions in excess of 30 dB were observed. Typically, the noise levels dropped from being significantly greater than specification criteria to being within the criteria.

Example comparisons of the noise levels in four critical spaces before and after the fin installation are given in Figs. 31 through 34. Included are the applicable Navy specification criteria levels for these spaces. Figure 35 is a sketch of the ship aft end inboard profile showing a comparison of averaged low-fre-

Table 11 Calculated bearing forces on proposed redesign propeller

	SIT Procedure [8] Model Nominal Wake		DnV Procedure[a] with Estimated Model Effective Wake	
	kN	lb	kN	lb
$(F_x)_Z$	35.6	8000	26.7	6000
$(F_y)_Z$	8.9	2000	22.2	5000
$(F_z)_Z$	13.3	3000	31.1	7000

[a] Calculations by DnV.

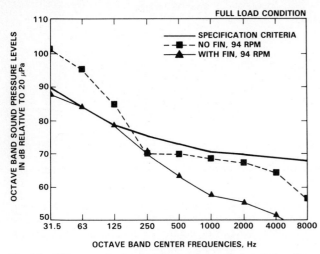

Fig. 31 Airborne noise levels before and after fin installation, Crew Berthing and Dressing No. 6

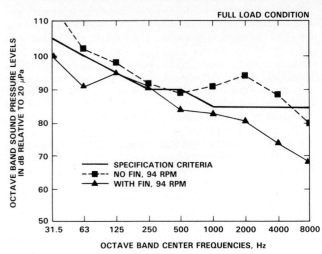

Fig. 33 Airborne noise levels before and after fin installation, Steering Gear Room

quency noise levels in several locations and how they varied with distance away from the propeller vicinity.

Dependence of airborne noise upon ship speed (or rpm) is illustrated in Fig. 36, which shows the noise levels measured in the steering gear room at 45, 75, 90, and 100 rpm for the ship in ballast condition.

In some of the living spaces, the propeller noise still remains subjectively annoying or at least noticeable and distracting, even with the significant reductions produced by the fin attachment. The annoyance factor may be related to the temporal characteristics of propeller noise being modulated at blade frequency, or possibly modulation due to ship motions in a seaway. Also, it must be pointed out that despite the satisfactory reductions of the noise to values at or below the applicable criteria levels in Table 5, the AO-177 can be judged to be a noisy ship. Quite independent of the AO-177 issue, the U.S. Navy has taken action recently to lower its acceptable noise level criteria to the values shown in Table 12, and by these new standards (not applicable retroactively) there are spaces on the AO-177 that would require further attention to produce a completely satisfactory fix.

Full-scale propeller cavitation

Propeller viewing and photography were carried out using the same periscope system that was rigged for the earlier trial.[9] The visibility and photography were not as clear, however, due to the shadow of the fin, overcast weather, and poorer water clarity.

The results discussed here are for the full-load, full-power condition. Example comparisons of the appearance of cavitation without and with the fin installed are shown in Fig. 37. The line sketches were prepared as composites from many photographs, and are provided here for both the cases without and with the fin. Corresponding sample photographs are included only for the case without the fin. At an angular position of approximately 35 deg past the upward vertical [Fig. 37(a)], the cavity without the fin appears to be thicker and extends over slightly more of the blade than the cavity with the fin. At 50 deg past vertical, the cavity without the fin forms a large thick

---

[9] More details are presented in a report of restricted distribution by I-Y. Koh and S. D. Jessup entitled "USS *Cimarron* (AO-177) Fin Survey Trial" Feb. 1982.

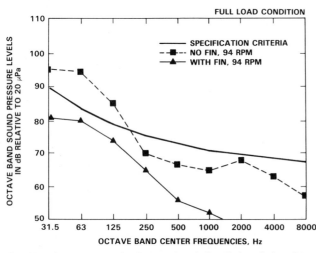

Fig. 32 Airborne noise levels before and after fin installation, Crew Berthing and Dressing No. 4

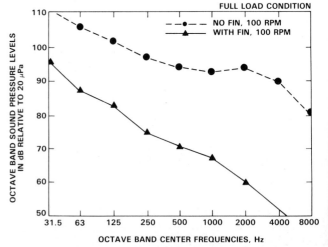

Fig. 34 Airborne noise levels before and after fin installation, Fantail-Main Deck

Causes and Corrections for Propeller-Excited Airborne Noise

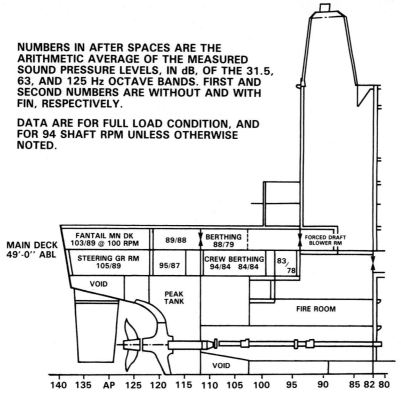

Fig. 35 Variation of averaged low-frequency noise levels in stern region, before and after fin installation

cloud behind the trailing edge which breaks into two separate tip vortices. With the fin, a thinner, more-uniform sheet extends downstream into a single vortex. At 65 deg past vertical [Fig. 37(b)], the blade is approximately 5 deg ahead of the estimated point of cavity collapse. For the case without the fin, a substantial cloud of cavitation can be seen to form behind the cavity sheet, presumably broken off from the cavity sheet at a previous instant.

The effect of the fin appears to have reduced the cavity volume, mainly by reduction of cavity thickness, because of the reduction of the maximum wake defect and the resulting decrease in the angle of attack variation on the blades, especially near the tips. This has the effect of reducing both the excursions of low-pressure fluctuations near the leading edge and the production of cavitation.

Propeller erosion tendency

The propeller was inspected in dry dock five months after the fin evaluation trial. At this time, approximately 50 hr of running at high power levels had been logged since the fin and a replacement propeller (original design) had been installed. No evidence of bending of the trailing edges was found. No erosion due to cavitation was detected, but some minor dimpling and burnishing of the suction side (back) surface near the tips could be seen after the blade tips were washed to remove deposits. It was decided, based upon this inspection, that no further action regarding the propeller was necessary, except for the periodic inspection of the propeller blades.

Propeller-induced pressure pulse amplitudes

Measurements of the blade rate pressure amplitudes were made at several points on the fin underside at locations somewhat off the centerline that have minimum radial tip clearance. Figure 38 shows the longitudinal distribution of blade rate

pressure double amplitudes, comparing model experimental results with the full-scale trial measurements at full power, full load. The model results are the maximum oscillograph-recorded values of $2\Delta p_Z$, including the cases with and without the flow-accelerating fin. The full-scale trial results represent three different runs at 100 rpm, with the rms peak-to-peak values converted to equivalent double amplitudes by multiplication by $\sqrt{2}$. Although there is scatter in the full-scale data and some differences between the average full-scale data and model data, the general trends and correlation of the results are encouraging, and seem to verify the beneficial action of the fin.

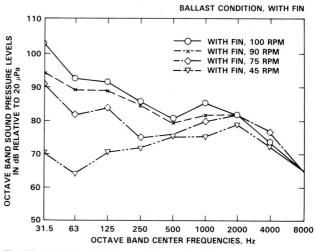

Fig. 36 Variation of airborne noise levels with speed (propeller rpm), Steering Gear Room

Table 12 New Navy noise criteria levels—permissible airborne sound pressure levels (in dB relative to 20 μPa)

Type of Space	Octave Band Center Frequency, Hz								
	32	63	125	250	500	1000	2000	4000	8000
Large command and control	72	69	66	63	60	57	54	51	48
Small command and control, and administrative spaces	81	78	75	72	69	66	63	60	57
Medical	78	75	72	69	66	63	60	57	54
Shops, service spaces, passages and top-side stations	88	85	82	79	76	73	70	67	64
Machinery	97	94	91	88	85	82	79	76	73

Operating experience

Operator feedback with the fin installed has been good. With the crew comfort improved, the ship has been run extensively with no speed restrictions, it has experienced no adverse effects on its maneuvering properties, and it has engaged in numerous underway replenishment operations. As noted earlier, the propeller erosion tendency has been noticeably reduced compared with the builder's trials performance. The ship has been shown to be acceptable for fleet duty in its intended mission.

Conclusions

The following conclusions, directly applicable to the AO-177, were drawn from the noise correction program:
• Fluctuating pressure pulses from intermittent blade cavitation caused the propeller-excitation problems of the AO-177. The situation was attributable to the combination of a poor wake due to the after hull shape, excessive unstable cavitation on the unfavorable propeller blade geometry, and the relatively high speed and power.
• The flow-accelerating fin configuration was effective in reducing blade rate hull surface pressure excitation due to reductions in propeller cavitation caused by improvement in the magnitude and steepness of the nominal wake. The fin also produced reductions in higher blade rate harmonic components (model scale) of the pressure pulse excitation, and this trend is likely responsible for reductions in structureborne noise and vibration that eventually radiate energy as diminished airborne noise inside the ship.
• The flow-accelerating fin produced a significant reduction of inboard airborne noise on the ship, to levels within the specifications.
• The propeller blade erosion tendency was measurably reduced by the flow-accelerating fin configuration.
• The flow-accelerating fin configuration produced negligible penalties on the drag and propulsion characteristics of the ship.
• Model experiments indicated that reductions of propeller-induced hull pressures could be achieved with propeller design modifications.
• It is speculated that a combination of a flow-improving fin and redesigned propeller could provide even lower surface pressure and surface force excitation than was achieved with the flow-accelerating fin alone, but with likely increases of periodic thrust and torque beyond the tight constraints.

Other conclusions and recommendations are:
• The criteria for periodic thrust that dictated important

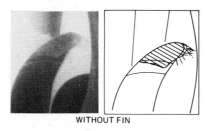 

WITHOUT FIN   WITH FIN

(a) BLADE ANGULAR POSITION φ = 35 DEG

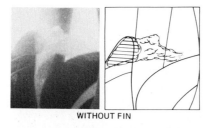

WITHOUT FIN   WITH FIN

(b) BLADE ANGULAR POSITION φ = 65 DEG

Fig. 37 Comparison of AO-177 propeller cavitation (full scale) with and without fin

details of the AO-177 propeller geometry may have to be relaxed somewhat for single-screw auxiliary ship designs.

• The excitation from propeller-induced hull surface pressures and forces should be determined routinely along with bearing force and moment excitation as part of the ship and propeller design process, especially for single-screw ships with appreciable wake.

• Great care must be exercised when the nominal wakes are predicted to exhibit large and steep peaks. Bulbous sterns or open stern arrangements should be considered seriously in early stage design.

• Crew accommodations and other occupied spaces where critical criteria must be met should be located as far from the propeller as practical, such as in the deckhouse superstructure or well forward.

Acknowledgments

The work described in the paper could not have been successfully accomplished without the contributions of many organizations and individuals, whose efforts the authors gratefully acknowledge; however, it would be impractical to name all of them. The authors would like to express their special appreciation to Stuart Jessup, Gary Hampton, Bob Perkins, Chris Noonan, Jerry Kelley, Don Drazin, and In-Young Koh from DTNSRDC for valuable contributions to model experiments and full-scale trials, to Brian Corbin of DTNSRDC for prediction and analysis of the vibratory response of the main propulsion system, and to Dan Nelson of BBN for his work on the evaluation trial. Stuart Jessup also conducted the proposed redesign of the propeller. The staff at SSPA in Göteborg, Sweden, especially Eric Bjärne, Carl-Anders Johnsson, and Gilbert Dyne, have our particular thanks for their expert guidance with model experiments and the benefit of their experience with propeller excitation problems. Considerable benefit was derived from calculations performed at Det norske Veritas (DnV) and from consultations with the staff of DnV, especially Arnst Raestad and Hans Smogli. Valuable advice and design assistance were provided by Roger Schaeffer, Otto Scherer, and Jeffrey Bohn of Hydronautics, Inc. Finally, Captain Black and the crew of the USS *Cimarron* have our gratitude for their patience and support during the various sea trials.

References

1 Baier, L. A. and Ormondroyd, J., "Vibration at the Stern of Single Screw Vessels," TRANS. SNAME, Vol. 60, 1952, pp. 10–25.

2 Vossnack, E. and Voogd, A., "Developments of Ship's Afterbodies, Propeller Excited Vibrations," Second LIPS Propeller Symposium, May 1973, pp. 103–165.

3 Hylarides, S., "Some Hydrodynamic Considerations of Propeller-Induced Ship Vibrations," Ship Vibration Symposium, SNAME Publication SY-8, 1978, pp. H-1 to H-16.

4 Valentine, D. T. and Chase, A., "Highly Skewed Propeller Design for a Naval Auxiliary Oiler (AO-177)," David W. Taylor Naval Ship Research and Development Center, Report No. DTNSRDC/SPD-544-12, Sept. 1976.

5 Boswell, R. J. and Cox, G. G., "Design and Model Evaluation of a Highly-Skewed Propeller for a Cargo Ship," *Marine Technology*, Vol. 11, No. 1, Jan. 1974, pp. 73–89.

6 Military Standard, "Mechanical Vibrations of Shipboard Equipment (Reciprocating Machinery and Propulsion System and Shafting)," MIL-STD 167-2(Ships), May 1974.

7 Military Standard, "Human Engineering Design Criteria for Military Systems, Equipment and Facilities," MIL-STD 1472A, May 1970.

8 Tsakonas, S. et al., "An Exact Linear Lifting Surface Theory for Marine Propellers in a Nonuniform Flow Field," *Journal of Ship Research*, Vol. 17, No. 4, Dec. 1974, pp. 196–207.

9 Myklebust, A. et al, "Auxiliary Oiler Tanker, AO-177, Propeller Induced Excitation Forces, Propeller Cavitation, 7-Bladed Propeller," Det norske Veritas Report 81-0120, Oslo, Feb. 1981.

10 Huang, T. T. and Groves, N. C., "Effective Wake: Theory and Experiment," Presented at the Thirteenth Symposium on Naval Hydrodynamics, Office of Naval Research, Oct. 1980; also DTNSRDC Report 81-033, April 1981.

11 Kerwin, J. E., Lewis, S. D., and Kobayashi, S., "Systematic Experiments to Determine the Influence of Skew and Rake on Hull Vibratory Excitation Due to Transient Cavitation," Ship Vibration Symposium, SNAME Publication SY-8, 1978, pp. Q-1 to Q-18.

12 Hammer, N. O. and McGinn, R. F., "Highly Skewed Propellers—Full-Scale Vibration Test Results and Economic Considerations," Ship Vibration Symposium, SNAME Publication SY-8, 1978, pp. R-1 to R-41.

13 Björheden, O., "Vibration Performance of Highly Skewed CP Propellers," *Proceedings*, Symposium on Propeller Induced Ship Vibration, The Royal Institution of Naval Architects, London, Paper No. 8, 1979, pp. 103–118.

14 Cheng, H. M., "Hydrodynamic Aspects of Propeller Design Based on Lifting Surface Theory, Part II—Arbitrary Chordwise Load Distribution," David Taylor Model Basin Report 1803, June 1965.

15 Kerwin, J. and Leopold, R., "A Design Theory for Subcavitating Propellers," TRANS. SNAME, Vol. 72, 1964, pp. 194–335.

16 Noonan, E. F. and Feldman, S., "State of the Art for Shipboard Vibration and Noise Control," Ship Vibration Symposium, SNAME Publication SY-8, 1978, pp. A-1 to A-38.

17 van Manen, J. D., "Bent Trailing Edges of Propeller Blades of High Powered Single Screw Ships," *International Shipbuilding Progress*, Vol. 10, No. 101, Jan. 1963, pp. 25–29.

18 Lindgren, H. and Bjärne, E., "Studies of Propeller Cavitation Erosion," Conference on Cavitation, Edinburg, Institute of Mechanical Engineers, Sept. 1974, pp. 241–251.

19 Tanibayashi, H. and Nakanishi, M., "On the Method of Cavitation Tests for Prediction of Tip Erosion," *Journal of the Society of Naval Architects of Japan*, Vol. 133, June 1973, pp. 57–64.

20 Huse, E., "Pressure Fluctuations on the Hull Induced by Cavitating Propellers," Norwegian Ship Model Experimental Tank Publication No. 111, March 1972.

21 *Proceedings*, Symposium on Propeller Induced Ship Vibration, The Royal Institution of Naval Architects, London, Dec. 1979.

22 Ship Vibration Symposium, SNAME Publication SY-8, 1978.

23 Takahashi, H., "Estimation of Surface Force Induced by Pro-

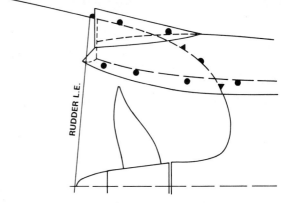

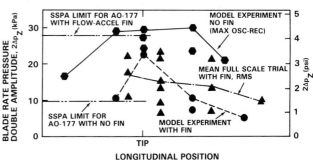

Fig. 38 Comparison of longitudinal distribution of blade rate pressure pulse double amplitudes, model experiments and full scale

peller," *Journal of the Society of Naval Architects of Japan*, Vol. 140, 1976, pp. 67–76.

24 Odabasi, A. Y. and Fitzsimmons, P. A., "Alternate Methods for Wake Quality Assessment," *International Shipbuilding Progress*, Vol. 25, No. 282, Feb. 1978, pp. 34–42.

25 Rutherford, R., "Aft End Shaping to Limit Vibration," *Trans.* North East Coast Institute of Engineers and Shipbuilders, Vol. 95, No. 4, July 1979, pp. 197–210.

26 Huse, E., "Effect of Afterbody Forms and Afterbody Fins on the Wake Distribution of Single-Screw Ships," The Ship Research Institute of Norway, Report No. R-31.74, Sept. 1974.

27 Lindgren, H. and Bjärne, E., "Ten Years of Research in the SSPA Large Cavitation Tunnel," Stone Manganese Marine/Newcastle University Conference, 1979; also SSPA Publication No. 86, 1980.

28 Reed, F. E., Bassett, N. L., and Norton, J. A., "Effects of Hull and Propeller Design Changes on the Vibration of a Lakes Freighter," TRANS. SNAME, Vol. 89, 1981, pp. 417–434.

29 Sasaki, N., Nagamatsu, S., and Ukon, Y., "Influences of Stern Fins on Wake and Propeller Cavitation," *Trans.* West-Japan Society of Naval Architects, No. 61, March 1981, pp. 99–111.

30 Takekuma, K., "Evaluation of Various Types of Nozzle Propellers and Reaction Fin as the Device for the Improvement of Propulsive Performance of High Block Coefficient Ships," *Proceedings*, Shipboard Energy Conservation Symposium, SNAME Publication SY-12, 1980, pp. 343–360.

31 Fink, P. T., Campbell, R., and Matheson, N., "A Problem in Aft End Vibrations," Lecture to The Royal Institution of Naval Architects, Australian Branch, Nov. 1974.

32 Gadd G. E., "Flow Deflectors—A Cure for Vibration," *The Naval Architect*, Nov. 1980, p. 238.

33 Hampton, G. A., "Investigations of Underwater Flow Patterns for Three Tunnel-Fin Configurations for the Naval Auxiliary Oiler (AO-177) Represented by Model 5326-1," David W. Taylor Naval Ship Research and Development Center, Report No. DTNSRDC/SPD-0544-17, Feb. 1981.

34 Hampton, G. A., "Analysis of Wake Survey for Tunnel-Fin and Accelerating-Fin Configurations for the Naval Auxiliary Oiler (AO-177) Represented by Model 5326-1," David W. Taylor Naval Ship Research and Development Center, Report No. DTNSRDC/SPD-0544-18, April 1981.

35 Bjärne, E., "U.S. Navy Oiler, AO-177 Class—Model Tests in SSPA Cavitation Tunnel No. 2—Design Propeller," SSPA Report No. 2564-1, Göteborg, Sweden, Oct. 1980.

36 Bjärne, E., "U.S. Navy Oiler, AO-177 Class—Model Tests in SSPA Cavitational Tunnel No. 2 with Alternative Propeller Models," SSPA Report No. 2564-2, Göteborg, Sweden, Dec. 1980.

37 Bjärne, E., "U.S. Navy Oiler, AO-177 Class—Model Tests in SSPA Cavitation Tunnel No. 2—Ship Model with Alternative Fins and Duct," SSPA Report No. 2564-3, Göteborg, Sweden, Dec. 1980.

38 Ward, G. and Willshare, G. T., "Propeller-Excited Vibration with Particular Reference to Full-Scale Measurements," *Trans.* The Royal Institution of Naval Architects, Vol. 118, 1976, pp. 97–112.

39 Report of Propeller Committee, *Trans.* 15th International Towing Tank Conference, The Hague, The Netherlands, Sept. 1978, pp. 231–296.

40 Hampton, G. A., "Powering Performance for a Naval Auxiliary Oiler (AO-177) Using Various Stern Fin Configurations with Model 5326-1," David W. Taylor Naval Ship Research and Development Center, DTNSRDC Departmental Report No. SPD-0544-20, June 1981.

41 Boswell, R. J., "Design, Cavitation Performance, and Open Water Performance of a Series of Research Skewed Propellers," Naval Ship Research and Development Center, Report No. 3339, March 1971.

42 Cumming, R. A., Morgan, W. B., and Boswell, R. J., "Highly Skewed Propellers," TRANS. SNAME, Vol. 80, 1972, pp. 98–135.

43 Jessup, S. D., "Reduction of Propeller Vibration and Cavitation by Cyclic Variation of Blade Pitch," M. S. Thesis, Massachusetts Institute of Technology, May 1976.

44 Glover, E. J. and Patience, G., "Aspects of the Design and Application of Off-Loaded Tip Propellers," *Proceedings*, Symposium on Propeller Induced Ship Vibration, The Royal Institution of Naval Architects, London, Paper No. 7, 1979, pp. 87–102.

45 Breslin, J. P. and Goodman, T. R., "Estimated Vibratory Pressures and Forces Induced on AO-177 Class Oiler With and Without Blade Cavitation," Davidson Laboratory Report SIT-DL-81-9-2186, Stevens Institute of Technology, Hoboken, N.J., March 1981.

46 Breslin, J. P., Goodman, T. R., and McKee, T. G., Jr., "Estimated Vibratory Pressures and Forces Induced on AO-177 Class Oiler With Stern Fin, and With and Without Blade Cavitation," Davidson Lab-oratory Report SIT-DL-82-9-2281, Stevens Institute of Technology, Hoboken, N.J., May 1982.

47 Tsakonas, S. and Valentine, D. T., "Theoretical Procedure for Calculating the Propeller-Induced Hull Forces," Davidson Laboratory Report SIT-DL-79-9-1979, Stevens Institute of Technology, Hoboken, N.J., Sept. 1980.

48 Bentson, J. and Kaplan, P., "Prediction of the Propeller Excited Fluctuating Pressures and Hull Surface Forces Acting on the AO-177 Fleet Oiler," Hydromechanics, Inc. Report No. 81-24, Jan. 1981.

49 Bentson, J. and Kaplan, P., "Prediction of the Propeller Excited Fluctuating Pressures and Hull Surface Forces Acting on the AO-177 Fleet Oiler Equipped with Flow-Improving Fins," Hydromechanics, Inc. Report No. 81-36, Oct. 1981.

50 Kaplan, P., Bentson, J., and Breslin, J., "Theoretical Analysis of Propeller Radiated Pressures and Blade Forces Due to Cavitation," *Proceedings*, Symposium on Propeller Induced Ship Vibration, The Royal Institution of Naval Architects, London, Dec. 1979, pp. 133–146.

51 Vorus, W., "Analysis of Propeller Cavitation and Propeller Induced Vibratory Forces and Pressures on the U.S. Navy AO-177," Vorus and Associates, Inc. Report, Nov. 1980.

52 Vorus, W., "Analysis of Propeller Cavitation and Propeller Induced Vibratory Forces and Pressures on a U.S. Naval Oiler" (2nd Report), Vorus and Associates, Inc. Report VAI-81-004, Nov. 1981.

53 Vorus, W. S., "Calculation of Propeller Induced Hull Forces, Force Distributions, and Pressures; Free Surface Effects," *Journal of Ship Research*, Vol. 20, No. 2, June 1976.

Appendix 1

Measurement and analysis of airborne noise

All airborne noise measurements aboard the AO-177 were made with portable instrumentation consisting of sound level meters with octave band analysis capability, and condenser microphones. The noise data were manually tabulated. Where noise levels varied with time, the meter display was visually averaged over a period typically in excess of 10 seconds for each data entry. This approach was used consistently during all the trials where airborne noise was measured, and comparison of the data with compartment noise criteria is considered valid.

Airborne noise measurements were taken at locations representative of manned positions within the various surveyed compartments. In berthing and dressing spaces, measurements typically were taken near two bunks. Measurement locations were selected on the basis of commonality with the builder's trials noise survey.

The Navy's airborne noise level criteria are assigned to shipboard spaces on the basis of compartment operational requirements. Depending on the functional nature of the space, the noise criteria are intended to minimize personnel hearing damage risk (for example, in machinery spaces), allow reliable speech communication (as in office and command and control spaces), and provide for reasonable habitability in living, mess, and recreational areas.

Table 5 shows the specific airborne noise criteria, in octave band levels, which were included in the AO-177 ship building specification. Recent changes in occupational noise control and hearing conservation requirements have established acceptable noise levels for ship spaces which are considerably lower than levels used in the AO-177 and other specifications which were written prior to 1981. To comply with public law and other operational needs, the Navy formally set maximum allowable airborne noise levels for six different categories of shipboard spaces. These criteria, first established as dBA levels and then expanded to octave band levels, are shown in Table 12.

Appendix 2

Results of analytical investigations

As part of the program of investigations for finding and verifying a cure for the problems of the AO-177, predictive calculations were commissioned from several independent sources to study the propeller blade cavitation, and estimate the propeller-excited hull pressures and surface forces. This work was undertaken to

- provide corroborative evidence on the character of the initial cavitating propeller flow and its alteration by the proposed fix,
- obtain some idea of the correspondence between levels of propeller-induced hull pressures and hull surface forces that give rise to troublesome excitation, and

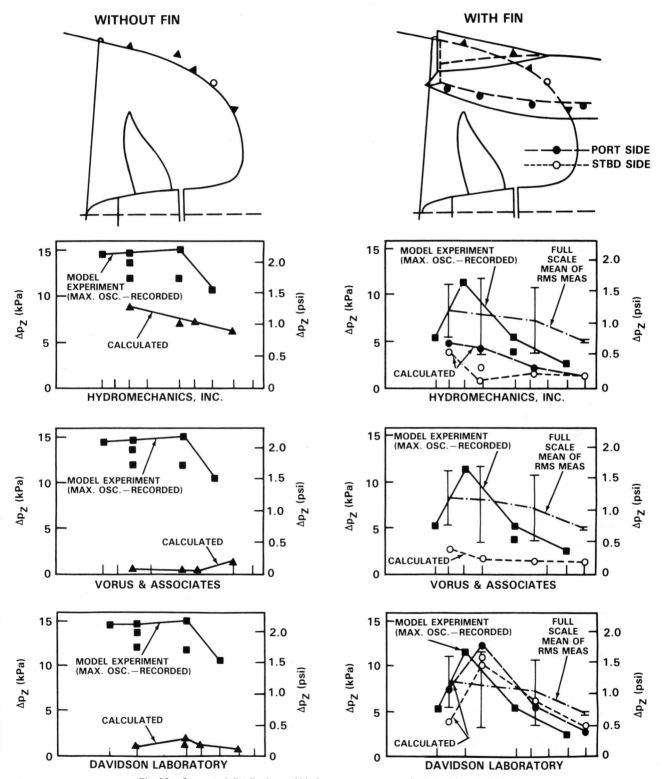

Fig. 39 Computed distributions of blade rate pressure amplitudes with and without fin

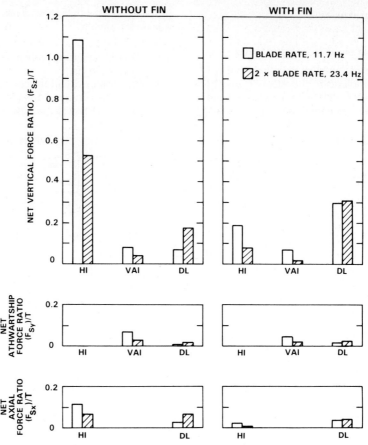

Fig. 40 Predictions of fluctuating hull force components

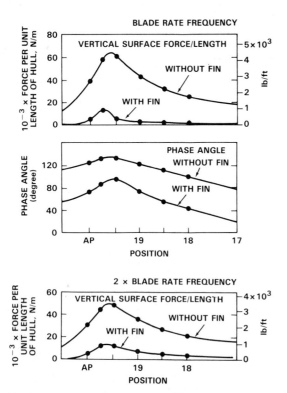

Fig. 41 Computed predictions (from DnV [9]) of vertical surface force per unit length at blade rate and twice blade rate, with and without flow-accelerating fin

- obtain correlations between measured and predicted cavitation patterns and hull pressures on a realistic example.

Ship and propeller geometry and speed-power data corresponding to the full-power, trial full-load conditions for both the original AO-177 and for the AO-177 with the flow-accelerating fin were supplied to the Davidson Laboratory (DL), Hydromechancis, Inc. (HI), Vorus and Associates, Inc. (VAI), and Det norske Veritas (DnV). These groups performed similar calculations using their existing procedures.

The Davidson Laboratory results [45, 46] were obtained using a hull-propeller analysis program [47] which accounts for the boundary reflection effects of the hull shape. The necessary velocity potential inputs appropriate for a cavitating propeller were determined using a quasi-steady, two-dimensional cavity flow theory and an approximated propagation function to model the effect of the entire propeller. The DL approach made possible the simulation of either a rigid free-surface condition or a pressure free-surface condition at the location of the zero speed waterline.

The results from Hydromechanics, Inc. [48, 49] were carried out using the approach described in reference [50] which employs a quasi-steady flow analysis to model the cavitating blade sections and a strip theory to describe the effects of the entire propeller. A lifting-line solution was used in this case to obtain the steady loading solution needed to estimate the noncavitating effective camber and angles of attack. The resulting fluctuating free-space pressure field values were multiplied by a factor of two to account approximately for the presence of the body.

The results of Vorus and Associates, Inc. [51, 52] were carried out with the theory described in reference [53]. The reciprocity theorem employed by Vorus recasts the problem into a form such that the surface forces are calculated directly rather than by means of integrating the pressures over the hull surface. Hull shape effects on the local boundary reflection properties are accounted for. Fluctuating pressures are computed independently of the basic surface force calculation scheme. The calculations also employ an unsteady cavitation dynamics analysis to solve for the effects of cavity cross-sectional area variations to be superposed on the noncavitating blade loading effects.

The DnV results [9] employ an unsteady, noncavitating vortex lattice lifting-surface theory for the blade loading effects, using an approximate accounting for effective wake. Unsteady cavitation effects are modelled with time-dependent source distributions over the panels of the lifting surface. The final free-space fluctuating pressure values were multiplied by a factor of two to account for the presence of the hull near the propeller.

These methods were (and still are) in various stages of development; therefore, some of the results are to be viewed as preliminary and in need of further refinements.

Longitudinal distributions of blade rate pressure amplitudes at points along the upper aperture are shown in Fig. 39, comparing results of three of the predictive methods. For the case with fin, the points of interest are off the centerline, where the fin undersurface is closest to the propeller disk. There is a dramatic variation in the magnitudes of the pressures predicted by the various calculation schemes. For the case without the fin, all the calculation procedures predict pressure amplitudes that are substantially smaller than those measured in the SSPA water tunnel. For the case with the fin, the predictions are somewhat closer to model and full-scale measurements. As discussed previously, the full-scale data have considerable scatter.

Figure 40 presents the predicted blade rate and twice blade rate harmonics of the net surface force component amplitudes induced by the cavitating propeller as decimal fractions of the time-average propeller thrust T. Again, there is considerable variation in the amplitudes predicted by the various methods. For the case without the fin, predictions from DL and HI indicate that vertical force is more than a factor of 10 greater than the athwartship force, whereas VAI predicts that the vertical force is only slightly larger than the athwartship force. DL and HI predict that the vertical force is substantially larger than the axial force, and VAI did not include the axial force.

For the important vertical surface component (F_{Sz}), HI predicts that the blade rate amplitude without the fin is greater

Table 13 Calculated effect of fin on vertical surface force component

Prediction Method	$\dfrac{(F_{Sz})_{Z \text{ no fin}}}{(F_{Sz})_{Z \text{ fin}}}$	$\dfrac{(F_z)_{2Z \text{ no fin}}}{(F_{Sz})_{2Z \text{ fin}}}$
DnV	10	1
HI	5.8	6.8
VAI	1.2	1.9

than the propeller thrust, and more than 10 times greater than the corresponding predictions by DL and VAI. The predictions of the blade rate harmonics of vertical force by DL and VAI are in good agreement; however, the twice blade rate amplitude predicted by DL is over four times as large as that predicted by VAI.

Det norske Veritas [9] did not calculate net surface force components, preferring instead the prediction of vertical surface force per unit length shown in Fig. 41. From this, the trends of the vertical surface force calculated by DnV can be compared with the corresponding trends predicted by the other three methods. HI, VAI, and DnV predict that the amplitude of the blade rate vertical force is greater than the twice blade rate amplitude; however, DL predicts the opposite trend. All the methods that were exercised for both wakes with and without the fin predicted that the fin would reduce the blade rate amplitude of the vertical surface force; however, the amount of reduction varied substantially between the various methods, and are summarized in Table 13. Additional information was provided from all the contracted sources on the blade cavitation patterns and cavity dynamic properties. In general, all of these predicted that by fitting the fin, the blade cavitation extent was reduced and the cavity volume velocities were diminished relative to the characteristics of the unmodified AO-177. Det norske Veritas [9] also provided the results of a calculation of the spectrum of the propeller unsteady source strength sound pressure level, with and without the flow-accelerating fin. With the fin, substantial reductions of the excitation pressure levels were predicted, relative to the original AO-177, covering a range of frequencies up to 1 kHz.

It is beyond the scope of the present paper to attempt to explain the variations in the predictions shown earlier in this Appendix. In the opinion of the authors, however, these discrepancies are representative of the present state of the art. Intensive research and development directed at improving the capability to calculate the propeller-induced periodic hull pressures, surface force distributions, and net surface forces is strongly recommended.

Discussion

E. Bjärne,[10] Visitor

I would first like to congratulate the authors on an excellent paper covering most, if not all, aspects involved in the problem. It is interesting to notice that the model-test results have given good correlation with the full-scale measurements, which apparently is not always the case with the theoretical calculations. It is also encouraging that the desired improvement with regard to the vibration and noise problems has been achieved with the recommended measures.

The paper covers most details involved, but it would have been of interest to have some information about, especially, the full-scale blade frequency vibration velocities in the extreme aft region, if those were measured.

The improvement of pressure pulses by application of accelerating fins is according to the model tests mainly concentrated on the blade frequency. The 2nd- and 3rd-order amplitudes are only slightly influenced by the fin. In spite of this the airborne noise in full scale at the 3rd harmonic was noticeably lower with fin than without, Figs. 31–34. The former values, however, refer to the 5 percent highest amplitudes. If the mean values from the model tests are compared, better correlation between the model tests and the full-scale noise measurements will be obtained. Furthermore, it could not be excluded that some of the noise is caused by rattling of construction details excited by propeller-induced pressure pulses of lower frequency.

The erosion obtained on the 7-bladed propeller was also verified by the model tests. This erosion may possibly be ex-

[10] Swedish Maritime Research Centre (SSPA), Göteborg, Sweden.

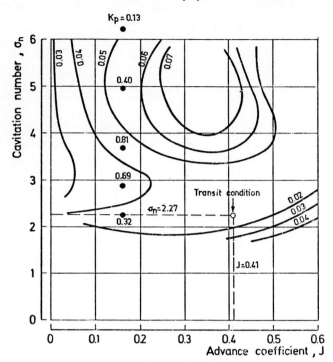

● PHV cavitation from propeller to transducer C

$K_p = 0.13$

Fig. 42 Influence of PHV cavitation on pressure pulses on the hull

plained by the relatively large camber-pitch relation for the propeller concerned. Usually when we design a propeller according to the vortex theory, corresponding relations between pitch and camber are obtained; see for instance the stock Propeller A in Fig. 21, for which the reduced blade tip pitch is reflected by a similarly reduced profile camber. This relation may, however, be influenced by the shape of blade, "skewback," and wake distribution for the design, but still the blade tip profile of AO-177 seems to be somewhat overcambered.

At tests with nozzle in front of the propeller model some vortex cavitation between the blade tips and the inside of the duct was noticed. To show the pressure pulses created by such a vortex cavitation, Fig. 42 is presented from my reference [54] (additional references follow some discussions). At the tests concerned the vortex cavitation (PHV cavitation) from the blade tip happened to hit the model hull exactly in a transducer. The pressure pulses hereby obtained are plotted in a diagram of level curves for equal pressure pulse coefficients and indicate amplifications of up to 20 times the values for surrounding areas.

Additional reference

54 Bjärne, Eric and Melitz, Dan, "Multi-Purpose Ducted CP-Propellers for a Semi-Submersible Offshore Support Vessel," Paper No. 24, International Offshore Conference, Göteborg, Sweden, Aug. 1981, p. 33.

A. Zaloumis, Member

[The views expressed herein are the opinions of the discusser and not necessarily those of the Department of Defense or the Department of the Navy.]

I wish to address my remarks to the empirical factors that are applied to the calculated propeller unsteady thrust forces.

Design stage calculations of propulsion systems include the analysis of longitudinal vibrations which describe the response of the system to propeller alternating thrust forces. Estimates

of these propeller forces in the design stage are accomplished by one or more of the following methods:

    (*a*)   Using full-scale results from similar ships.

    (*b*)   Using model wake survey data together with a propeller theory calculation scheme.

    (*c*)   Performing propeller thrust variation measurements on model ships.

The method most commonly employed is (*b*) above, because it allows a more rapid evaluation of parameter variations such as number of blades, skew, and diameter. The candidate propeller is then recommended on the basis of minimal exciting force and/or minimal response of the propulsion system (and hull—for which separate calculations are made).

When using calculated propeller forces for longitudinal vibration stud consideration must be given to certain phenomena observed on full-scale underway measurements.

    (*a*)   For free-route steady-state operation, propulsion system longitudinal vibration data consistently show various degrees of modulation such that the peak values (say the upper 10 percent) are generally several times greater than the time-average values.

    (*b*)   As shaft speeds approach full power (say above 90 percent of full power rpm), the propeller alternating thrust forces increase abruptly, perhaps several times the value that occurs throughout the operating range below 90 percent full power rpm.

    (*c*)   During turns, the alternating thrust is considerably higher than that for corresponding shaft speeds during steady-state free route operation.

In the footnoted reference, page 000, each of these three factors is given a recommended value of 3.0; that is, the free-route steady-state alternating thrust value is adjusted (increased) by factors of 3.0 to account for each of these three operational conditions. Therefore, a worst case results in an overall factor of (3 × 3 × 3) or 27 times the free route blade forces. It should be noted that none of these factors contains the effects of any resonant amplification of the propulsion shafting system. Resonant effects were accounted for in processing the measured data for the aforementioned factors.

These three factors were based on a range of values obtained on a limited number of ships wherein the upper portion of the range was used to insure some degree of conservatism in the design of a propulsion system. Using these factors, as stated, generally results in a sufficiently conservative design assumption so as to preclude the possibility of a propulsion system vibration problem. However, there are circumstances where prudent engineering judgment would suggest perhaps lower values in one or all three of these factors. Generally, the overall combination of these three factors will be between 15 and 27. For noncombatant type ships such as the AO-177, the effects of hard turns may be deemphasized since it would not be a significant operating parameter.

A. E. Raestad,[11] Visitor

This paper shows in an excellent way the thorough investigations which have been performed to identify and solve the noise problems experienced on the AO-177 auxiliary oiler. We are pleased to be one of the contributors to the reported calculations and thereby have the opportunity to compare our analysis with other analytical and experimental results.

In my opinion the reason for the problems experienced is unrealistic design criteria on propeller-induced excitation forces and cavitation which are, as I understand, empirically based upon results from quite different types of ships.

Firstly, concerning the factors accounting for amplitude modulation, cavitation and turns, the authors state that there

---
[11] Det norske Veritas, Høvik, Norway.

may be some nonlinear effects between the three factors so that the maximum factor is less than 27. However, I cannot see that there has to be any relation at all between the thrust variation of blade frequency steady ahead condition and, for example, the thrust variations in hard turns.

Secondly, even if such relations exist, it is, in my opinion, not possible to predict thrust variations within 1 percent accuracy keeping in mind the nature of the problems such as scaling of the wake and the time variations in the wake. These are always present and make it difficult even to quantify these small variations on the ship.

Regarding the choice of number of propeller blades, I miss the evaluation of the risk of exciting the natural frequency of superstructure, which is considered to be very important.

I also wish to comment on Appendix 2 where it is said that, for the case without the fins, all the calculation procedures predict pressure amplitudes which are substantially smaller than those measured in the SSPA water tunnel. If the DnV calculations had been included in Fig. 39 we would have seen that these results give somewhat larger pressure amplitudes than the model experiments.

Since the problems also were related to erosion, I miss a comparison between analytical and experimental amounts of cavitation.

The authors have demonstrated in an instructive way how analytical and experimental investigations can be applied to solve propeller cavitation related problems and I agree with the conclusions arrived at to solve the problem. However, this case also demonstrates the need for analytical methods to predict the propeller-induced noise at the design stage. In this connection it may be mentioned that by the DnV analytical method the noise reduction in the steering room was estimated at 10–15 dB(A) by mounting fins [9].

Finally, just a small comment on the title of the paper: According to common terminology this is a typical structureborne noise problem—not airborne.

K. Takekuma,[12] Visitor

The authors are to be congratulated for their interesting paper describing their extensive hydrodynamic investigations to find the cause of airborne noise phenomena experienced on a ship of relatively small block coefficient. As the authors explained in their paper, many vibration problems have been experienced in the past several years in spite of the effort to decrease the level of vibration and airborne noise during the course of ship design.

The discusser, who presented his experience in a paper for RINA in 1979 [55], would like to offer the following comments and questions on the basis of his experience in the design of hull forms and propellers:

1. On reviewing the propeller design of the AO-177, it is noticed that: (a) the diameter of the propeller was much smaller than optimum (about 7 m), or the number of revolutions should have been higher (about 120 rpm) for the selected diameter; and (b) the expanded area was smaller than by existing criteria such as those proposed by NSMB as follows:

$$AE \text{ according to NSMB } 28.5 \text{ m}^2$$
$$AE \text{ adopted } \qquad\qquad 24.8 \text{ m}^2$$

Thus, some propellers with larger expanded area could be worth investigation in addition to the three candidate propellers A, B and C.

2. The discusser considers that higher blade rate frequency components of propeller exciting force are more responsible for the airborne noise, but Fig. 25 shows that the level of blade rate frequency component is much higher than those of higher blade rate frequency components except at over tip point A. Would the author explain how they reached the understanding on the phenomena that airborne noise is much more dominant than vibration level, although high blade rate frequency components of exciting force were relatively small?

3. Regarding the results of resistance and propulsion tests, the results shown in Figs. 26 and 27 coincide with some of our experience, namely, little difference of EHPa and thrust deduction coefficient, decrease of wake fraction coefficient and little difference of power when fitted with fin. However, the results in Figs. 28 and 29 indicate that improvement of propulsive performance is obtained by a remarkable increase of relative rotative efficiency. How do the authors explain the difference in the effect of stern tunnel fin on propulsive performance of the ship?

4. Significant variation of the full-scale measurement of pressure fluctuations is shown in Fig. 38. The authors explained that those results were obtained in three runs at 100 rpm in the full-scale trial. Would the authors explain the reason for the significant variation of the pressure fluctuations when fitted with a fin?

Additional reference

55 Takekuma, K., "Vibration Problem with a Class of Cargo Liners and the Solution from Fitting a Fin," Symposium on Propeller-Induced Ship Vibration, RINA, Dec. 1979.

Paul Kaplan, Member

This paper provides an interesting saga about the consequences of unwanted propeller cavitation, as well as the procedures used to establish a successful correction of the associated problems. Although there are a number of items in the paper that can be discussed, my discussion will focus primarily on the analytical prediction of hull pressures and the comparison between theory and experiment. The comparisons are shown in Appendix 2 of the paper, with the implied result that the present theoretical methods provide results that significantly differ from experimental values. Considering only the results of theoretical calculations provided by Hydromechanics, Inc., I can make a number of comments relative to this comparison.

As a general comment I want to object to the nature of the comparison between theory and experiment for hull pressures, as shown in Fig. 39. The theoretical methods provide values of the blade rate amplitudes corresponding to a single frequency, which is obtained by a direct mathematical method that is analogous to the use of a perfect filter. Those values should not be compared with the *maximum* value of the experimental pressure signal read from an oscilloscope, which can include effects due to time variations of the actual wake that are not considered in the theory. A particular set of experimental values for comparison purposes should be perhaps the mean of the highest 5 percent of the blade rate component, as shown in Figs. 16 and 25, since that is the preferred measurement considered appropriate by the test laboratory (SSPA). If that information were used as the experimental data, the comparison in Fig. 39 of the paper would then be shown as in Fig. 43 with this discussion. In that case the degree of agreement between the Hydromechanics theoretical predictions and the experimental values of hull pressures would be quite close. The degree of correlation would then be similar to that found in other applications of this theory, as exhibited in [50], which is the basic description of our method. Thus we at Hydromechanics believe that the capabilities for theoretical prediction of pressures due to cavitating propellers are not as dismal as portrayed in this paper.

[12] Nagasaki Technical Institute, Mitsubishi Heavy Industries, Nagasaki, Japan.

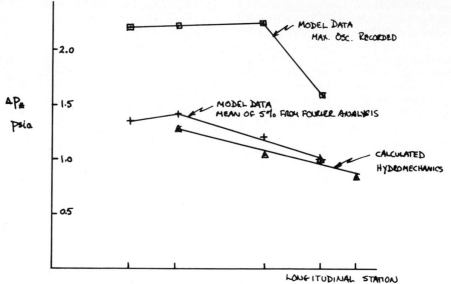

Fig. 43 Predicted versus measured hull pressures: AO-177–no fins

Also included in Appendix 2 are theoretical values of total hull force components as obtained (in the case of the Hydromechanics, Inc. analysis) by integrating the theoretical pressures over the ship hull.   Our results are quite large and we know that they are in error since they only represent the effects of the (doubled) free space pressures arising from the propeller. There is no consideration of any free-surface image effect which would result in a more rapid spatial decay longitudinally of the force, which is a more recent enhancement of our method that is described in reference [56].

We do appreciate the opportunity of participating in this program where our theoretical predictions could be compared with experimental data as well as used for basic guidance for an important practical problem.   Although the present state of the art in predicting pressures is not perfect, and more intensive studies can still be carried out to provide improvements and refinements, the method developed in [50] has demonstrated utility as a predictive tool.   It is unfortunate that theoretical work could not have been applied at an earlier stage in the AO investigation to provide design guidance.

Additional reference

56   Kaplan, P., Bentson, J., and Benatar, M., "Analytical Prediction of Pressures and Forces on a Ship Hull Due to Cavitating Propellers," presented at the Fourteenth Symposium on Naval Hydrodynamics, The University of Michigan, Ann Arbor, Aug. 1982.

Norman O. Hammer, Member

[The views expressed herein are the opinions of the discusser and not necessarily those of the Department of Commerce or the Maritime Administration.]

Shortly after the *Cimarron* (AO-177) returned from sea trials, rumors began to spread about excessive "noise and vibration" encountered on the ship.   Although not personally involved with the project, this discusser had a keen interest in the AO-177 performance since it was known well before completion of the vessel that a highly skewed propeller was planned for installation on the ship.   Since all previous highly skewed propeller installations on single-crew merchant ships had been very successful, naturally similar results were expected on this vessel. Therefore when the news was heard of unacceptable performance, many questions were raised about the highly skewed propeller which up until now have never been openly discussed.

Even after reading the excellent paper prepared by the authors, which represents the first comprehensive report on the AO-177 problems to outsiders, several questions still remain unanswered.

To start off with a provocative statement to enliven the discussion, it appears that the AO-177 design process suffered from "overengineering" at the outset.   While the authors have described the numerous design studies and considerations that influenced decisions that led to the unique propeller design, the basic ship parameters outlined in Table 1 such as speed, length, horsepower, deadweight, and block coefficient do not appear to be outside the state of the art when the AO-177 was designed. Table 14 with this discussion has been prepared comparing the AO-177 with three merchant ship designs each having highly skewed propellers.

Basically what this table shows is that these merchant ship designs have equal or greater speed, displacement, shaft horsepower than the AO-177.   The AO-177 propeller is, however, the smallest of the group and is by far the lightest in weight.

With this brief comparison, it would therefore appear, since numerous 20-knot single-screw merchant ships had been designed or were in operation well in excess of 24 000 shp with five- or six-bladed propellers prior to the AO-177 ship design, that too much reliance was given to the AO-177 predicted analytic study results without applying equal engineering judgment relative to the questionable accuracy of the propeller/ hull/machinery compatibility studies.   Emphasis must be given to the overall comprehensive meaning to the term "*propeller/hull/machinery*" studies.

Again, the rationale given in the paper to depart from proven baseline designs and select a seven-bladed propeller is not convincing.   Actually, much of the evidence presented in the paper points to an extremely irregular wake, but yet little or nothing is said about model tests or hull changes to correct this problem.   Therefore, while the original highly skewed propeller design appears to have borne the brunt of the attention, the real villain is the poor stern hull form which caused the highly irregular wake in the first place, and questionable propeller/hull/machinery analytic studies which in turn resulted in a seven-bladed propeller that provides higher blade frequency components and harmonics from a noise and vibration standpoint.

Digressing somewhat to comment on other vessels, it should

Table 14 Ship and propeller characteristics

	Class			
	Sea Bridge	San Clemente	Maine	AO-177
LBP, ft	560	855	640	550
Displacement, LT	27 580	99 210	33 765	27 380
Speed, knots	24	16.5	23	21.5
Shp	30 000	24 000	37 000	24 000
Diameter, ft	23	26	22	21
Conventional, lb	75 700	106 000	80 000	. . .
Skewed, lb	80 000	116 000	90 000	69 400
No. of blades	6	5	6	7
Rpm	110/107	92	120	100

be noted that within the past 12 months two other ship designs have suffered propeller/hull/machinery related problems. One high-powered containership design analyzed by the most knowledgeable experts was predicted to have excessive stern lateral vibration. On sea trials, however, the vessel was found to perform very well from a vibration standpoint, but instead, Murphy's Law took effect and what was not predicted happened—all propeller blades bent uniformly ten inches during the crash-astern test, resulting in a vessel operating rpm/speed restriction in piloting waters until the overall problem is resolved. A second example concerns a bulk carrier design where the propeller was found to overload the main diesel propulsion engines, necessitating cropping 18 in. from the blade tips to achieve a more proper hull/machinery match. The point to be made, again, is that the design process for propeller/hull/machinery compatibility is not an exact science and there is no substitute for good engineering judgment.

In conclusion, it is apparent that considerable effort went into the highly skewed propeller design, and analysis of propeller generated forces. Was equal attention given, however, to exploring changes to the hull form? Also, did the predicted 10 Hz longitudinal machinery resonance at full power show itself on sea trials? In other words, if the authors had a second chance to do it all over again, what changes would be made on the AO-177 propeller/hull/machinery overall vessel design if follow-on ships were to be constructed? After all is said and done, the fin installation represents the least-cost remedial choice to correct a problem generated by a poor hull form.

Edward F. Noonan, Member

The paper represents a great deal of effort by a significant number of individual investigators and an impressive array of technical talent and facilities. It provides a wealth of information but most importantly it emphasizes the need for a number of significant steps that should be undertaken as a follow-up, if we are to improve our ability to profit by our experience in the field of vibration and noise control.

In the first place, I would suggest we associate the problem with the cause, propeller-excited forces and moments, rather than with the effect, the airborne noise. Indeed no attempt to attack the problem by classical noise reduction methods was considered, but rather all efforts were properly directed at the identification and reduction of the alternating forces generated by the propeller. As a first suggestion I would have liked to have seen a complete spectral analysis of the hull and compartment vibration and hull pressure forces, with and without the fin, for correlation with the noise data. Of particular importance would be the harmonic content associated with the cavitating seven-bladed propeller and the structural response characteristics in the various compartments in which the noise was a factor. Past experience has indicated such airborne noise levels have been significantly reduced by the reduction of cavitation and hull vibration in the range of the higher har-

monics of blade rate, by the use of fins, although blade rate levels were acceptable, and little improvement of blade rate vibratioin was noted. This would appear to be the likely result of the effort carried out on the AO-177.

My second comment relates to the prediction of propeller forces in the preliminary phase of ship design. It is considered necessary to evaluate these forces against suitable criteria, to ensure satisfactory performance and/or to evaluate one proposed design against another. Propeller bearing forces are generally low and because of past work in this area can be reasonably assessed. Hull pressure forces, particularly when augmented by cavitation effects, pose a much more difficult problem. However, the work carried out by SSPA points to the possibility of developing acceptable criteria against which a proposed design may be evaluated. Work in this direction is required.

My third comment relates to the subject of the longitudinal vibration of propulsion systems, including the empirical service factors and the requirements of MIL-STD-167. It is my opinion that the combined service factor of 27 is unnecessarily restrictive and indeed may be incompatible with MIL-STD-167 reduction gear requirements. This same problem has appeared on several other designs and indicates the need for early attention to both the service factor and MIL-STD-167 requirements.

In 1975, about the same time the AO-177 design was started, the 120 000-m³ LNG carrier, a single-screw, 45 000-shp, 20-knot ship built for El Paso Gas Company by Chantiers De France-Dunkerque, was successfully tested and reported on at the Ship Structure Symposium 1975. During the development of this design SSPA model studies of propeller cavitation indicated the inception of cavitation at approximately 100 rpm. Full-scale studies, monitored by television by DnV, indicated the inception of cavitation actually occurred at 60 rpm. This is a significant variation introduced by the action of the ship's propeller on the wake and was discussed by Hylarides of NSMB at the Ship Vibration Symposium in 1978. I would like to ask the authors to comment on the current correlation of SSPA model tests with full-scale studies, such as conducted on the AO-177. How reliable are the model tests in predicting the inception of cavitation on ships in this horsepower range?

On a more general note, this study emphasizes the need for a rational design procedure for use in preliminary ship design, to minimize vibration and noise. The 1978 Ship Vibration Symposium, sponsored by the Ship Structures Committee and SNAME, paid particular attention to the subject of vibration and noise aboard ship, and the HS-7 Panel derived the Ship Vibration and Noise Guidelines published in the T&R Bulletin 2-25 in 1980. A "Proposed Five Year Ship Vibration Research Program," based on the 1979 SSC-292 Report "Report on Ship Vibration Symposium," by E. Scott Dillon, was submitted to the Ship Research Committee of the National Research Council by members of Panel HS-7 and was endorsed by the Ship

Structures Committee. From this work, the Interagency Ship Structures Committee of the National Research Council placed the "Guide for Shipboard Vibration Control" as their number two priority for the current fiscal year. The authors are to be congratulated for their efforts and we can all hope the lessons to be learned from this study will be effectively incorporated in the development of a suitable and necessary design guide.

Fred Stern, Member

The problems encountered by the AO-177 are yet another example of the need for quantifying wake peaks, propeller loadings, unsteady cavity behaviors and hull surface pressures (or forces) so that excessive levels can be avoided in future designs. In their detailed description of the AO-177 problems and the extensive corrective program, the authors have provided a considerable amount of data, mostly experimental, but also computational, which are invaluable in performing this task. The extensiveness of the corrective program is commendable. The model-scale experimental investigations were performed in such a manner that the effects of propeller geometry variations and the different wake-improving appendages could be evaluated separately, thereby demonstrating the possibility of designing propellers and hull geometries which can minimize cavitation and its often deleterious consequences. The good agreement shown between the full- and model-scale experiments indicates the usefulness of model-scale experimental data in obtaining this goal. This is in spite of the model-scale experimental difficulties: rigid wall water free-surface representation and lack of Reynolds number and cavity scaling. Accurate computational tools are also essential if this goal is to be reached. Various computational methods were implemented to predict the propeller blade cavitation and hull pressures and surface forces on the AO-177. Some of the results are given in Appendix 2. However, as will be discussed herein, it is difficult to draw many conclusions from the limited computational data presented, and in this regard, I believe the paper would have benefited if more attention had been given to the computational results.

I have also performed calculations for the AO-177 propeller blade cavitation and hull pressures and would like to present some of the results here for comparison with the other calculations shown in Appendix 2. The complete results including detailed comparisons between the predicted cavitation and the model and full-scale experiments were recently reported at the 1982 ONR Symposium on Naval Hydrodynamics [57]. The method employs a dynamical approach in which the form of the instantaneous cavity surface is modeled at each propeller cross section as a semi-ellipse. Values for the cavity length (major axis), thickness (semiminor axis) and position along the section chord are determined such that the nonlinear cavity surface boundary conditions are satisfied approximately. The pressure on the instantaneous cavity surface is obtained using a two-dimensional, thick-section unsteady potential flow computer program. Three-dimensional propeller effects are included by correcting the harmonics of the vertical component of the section inflow using the results from an unsteady propeller lifting-line computer program. The vertical component of the section inflow is obtained from the nominal wake modified to represent an effective wake using data for axisymmetric bodies.

Figures 44 and 45 herewith show the predicted cavity volume and volume velocity. The results show substantial reductions due to the addition of the flow-modifying fin. The reductions are due principally to a decrease in the cavity thickness as was also found in both the model and full-scale experiments. The cavity volume velocity (Fig. 45) has been harmonically analyzed (see Fig. 46) and the free-space pressures calculated (see Fig. 47) for comparison with the other calculations and ex-

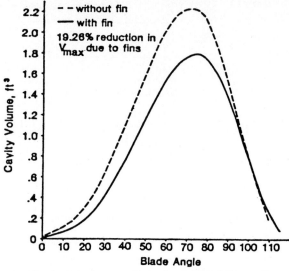

Fig. 44 Cavity volume prediction for the AO-177 propeller

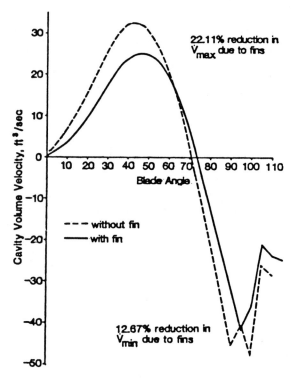

Fig. 45 Cavity volume velocity prediction for the AO-177 propeller

perimental data shown in Fig. 39 (in the paper). A value of 2 was used for the reflection coefficient in the free-space pressure calculation. This approximate procedure for calculating hull pressures due to unsteady cavitation is in common use and, in fact, was also used by HI and DnV. The results are seen from Fig. 46 to be below the model and full-scale experimental data. The results do show the same trend as the experiments with regard to the effects of the fins; that is, a reduction in the pressure magnitude except for directly over the tip where the effects of reduced tip clearance offset the reduction due to the fin in the seventh harmonic of the cavity volume velocity, $\ddot{V}_7$. The "free space/factor of two" method is correct for the limit of an infinite flat plate or an infinitely long cylinder. This

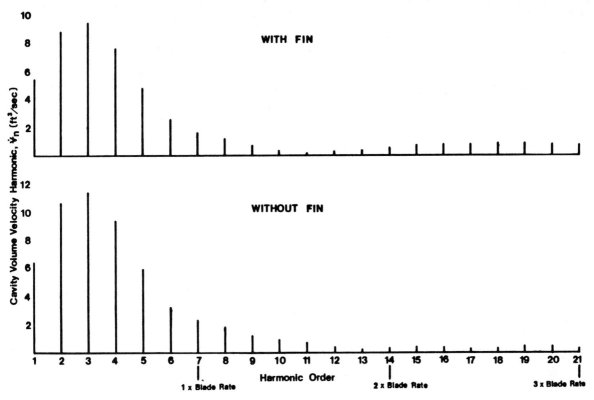

Fig. 46 Cavity volume velocity harmonics for the AO-177 propeller

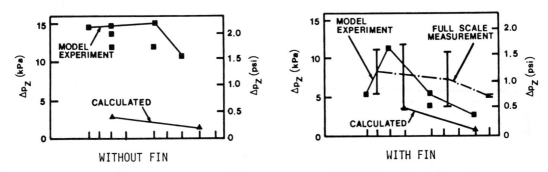

Fig. 47 Comparison of blade rate pressure amplitudes with experiments

neglects the water free-surface pressure relief effects and accurate representation of hull reflection effects. The former effect reduces the pressure magnitude. The latter effect may increase or decrease the pressure magnitude depending on the specific hull geometry. A comparison of Fig. 47 with Fig. 39 (in the paper) shows that the present results give larger magnitudes than the more sophisticated methods of VAI and SIT. This is most likely due to large water free-surface pressure relief effects. However, this is not substantiated by the experimental data. The good agreement between model-scale results obtained using a rigid wall water free-surface and the full-scale results implies small water free-surface pressure relief effects. The VAI and SIT results also show an increase in hull pressures due to the fin which seems improbable. In order to draw more conclusions it would be necessary to make a comparison between the cavity volume and volume velocity variations predicted experimentally and by the various computational methods. Such a comparison is important due to the dominating effects of cavitation on hull pressures. It is hoped, with regard to this matter, that the experimental difficulties in measuring cavity volumes and volume velocities will soon be overcome, since these data are imperative for the purpose of validating the cavity prediction tools.

I believe that the computational results are encouraging although, clearly, as stated by the authors, in need of further developments and improvements. These tools are needed particularly at the early design stage so that the relative merit of many design options can be evaluated.

Additional reference

57   Stern, F., "Comparison of Computational and Experimental Unsteady Cavitation," presented at the 14th ONR Symposium, Ann Arbor, Mich., Aug. 1982.

Jacques B. Hadler, Member

It was a pleasure to receive this paper at this time as I am involved in a number of propeller designs, one of which is for a ship that has a wake pattern with almost as severe a wake gradient and wake defect at top dead center as that of the unmodified AO-177.

In general, I agree with the authors' conclusions on the propeller-blade characteristics which seem to be most successful for reducing the likelihood of cavitation erosion, trailing edge bending and minimal higher harmonics of blade frequency with acceptable blade frequency forces. I have used the technique, whenever I have had to design a propeller for such a ship, of designing three or four propellers in which I have made small but systematic variations in either radial load distribution at the tip, variations in plan form or the amount of camber in the tip sections. A model propeller is then constructed with each blade to a different one of the designs. The propeller is then tested in the variable pressure water tunnel behind wake screens or partial hull bodies combined with wake screens which simulate the wake measured on the ship model. These tests, which can approximate both the load and ballast condition of operation, show the extent of growth and decay of the sheet and tip vortex cavitation as the blades pass through the low-velocity region. Through strobe lighting, it is easy to compare one blade with the others in directly comparable flow conditions and find the blade which produces the most stable cavity that collapses in the tip vortex of the blade. The results of this approach have always lead me to the following conclusions:

(*a*) Radial blade loading distributions which approached the Lerb's optimum were best.

(*b*) The amount of camber at the blade tips should be limited so the sections are not hollow on the pressure face.

(*c*) Plan forms which produced pointed tips even at the trailing edge were not successful.

(*d*) Wide tips are generally better than narrow although there is some evidence that there is a "best" length.

These propellers have had varying amounts of skew up to a maximum of about 30 deg. So far, all propellers developed by this approach have been successful.

I agree with the overall approach used by the authors in the new five-bladed design except for the shape of the trailing edge at the tip, which is more "pointed" than I have found successful.

I am quite surprised at the author's estimate that the periodic thrust at the thrust bearing may be 27 times that calculated by unsteady lifting-surface theory using model wake data. I agree and have witnessed on vibration trials a modulation that may approach three when there is a large amount of turbulence in the wake due to flow separation, but a factor of three is excessive in my experience for free-surface effects and for turns. The most that I have ever noted is a factor of two on twin-screw ships in a tight turn and less than 1.5 for free-surface effects. Could the authors cite their evidence for such large factors?

In closing, I cannot help but note that it almost always seems to take a design failure to precipitate a major technical investigation which can extend our fountain of knowledge. We are fortunate that the authors could share this knowledge with us.

David W. Byers, Member

[The views expressed herein are the opinions of the discusser and not necessarily those of the Department of Defense or the Department of the Navy.]

The authors have presented a comprehensive treatment of how a propeller-excited noise problem discovered during sea trials of the AO-177 was ultimately resolved. This problem arose as a result of incomplete understanding of hull-propulsor interactions on the AO-177 while under design from 1972 to 1974. I would like to briefly address the question: How are we in the U.S. Navy design community at NAVSEA ensuring that such a problem does not recur on future designs?

First of all, in the area of hull form design, we are smarter today than we were ten years ago. As suggested by the authors' references [2] and [25], the hull afterbody design in way of the propeller of an AO-177 designed today would clearly be more bulbous in character and have greater cutaway of the hull below the propeller shaft.

More importantly, the critical need to validate performance predictions of the hull-propulsor system with a sufficiently large-scale propeller model tested in the behind-the-ship condition at a facility capable of accurately modeling the wake field has been recognized. Pending refinement of the various analytic techniques for predicting hull pressure forces which are presented in Appendix 2 of the paper, such tests are now considered a standard component of model test programs for fleet auxiliaries. Subsequent to the AO-177 tests discussed in the paper, NAVSEA and the David W. Taylor Naval Ship Research and Development Center (DTNSRDC) undertook a similar cavitation test program of the Kort nozzle propulsor system on the ARS-50 salvage ship design at SSPA and are planning comparable programs for the T-AO 187 commercial oiler and AOE-6 fast combat support ship currently under design.

Testing at a foreign facility such as SSPA is necessary since no comparable facility presently exists in the United States. To rectify this deficiency, current plans call for construction at DTNSRDC beginning in Fiscal Year 1985 of a large cavitation channel with a 10-ft by 10-ft by 45-ft long test section, speed capability of 50 fps and pressurizable up to 4 atmospheres. Until this facility is operational in Fiscal Year 1989, NAVSEA will continue to rely on cavitation tanks such as SSPA for hull-propulsor system tests of auxiliaries. Coupled with the expected improvements in analytic techniques, such tests should minimize the chances of a recurrence of cavitation-related problems such as those which occurred on the AO-177.

Stephen G. Arntson, [13] Visitor, **K. Ikeda,** [13] Visitor, and **Michael Lusick,** [13] Visitor

[The views expressed herein are the opinions of the discussers and not necessarily those of the Department of Defense or the Department of the Navy.]

The authors have presented an interesting and informative paper. They have discussed "why" the flow accelerating fin was installed. It may be of some interest to describe "how" the fin was installed.

The fin installation was beset with a number of major problems, the biggest of which was the time constraint. The decision to install the fin was approved in mid-December 1980 with the proviso that the task be completed by mid-May 1981—just five months! Backing down from the completion date to allow for installation in dry dock, prefabrication, ordering materials and letting an overhaul contract, this meant the detail design had to be ready by mid-February 1981. The schedule did not allow for slippage at any point.

A second major problem involved the number of participants involved. Avondale Shipyards, Inc. (ASI), tasked through the Supervisor of Shipbuilding, New Orleans, developed the detailed drawings, including lofting, since ASI was the builder of the AO-177, and had four more AO-177 class ships under contract. However, ASI could not install the first fin as the AO-177 had already deployed to the West Coast. The AO-177 fin installation could possibly have been done by any of a number of yards from Seattle to San Diego. Subsequently, Todd Shipyard's Alameda, California, facility got the contract and worked under the direction of the Supervisor of Shipbuilding, San Francisco. The second ship of the class, the AO-178, having already been delivered, would have her fin

---

[13] Naval Sea Systems Command, Washington, D.C.

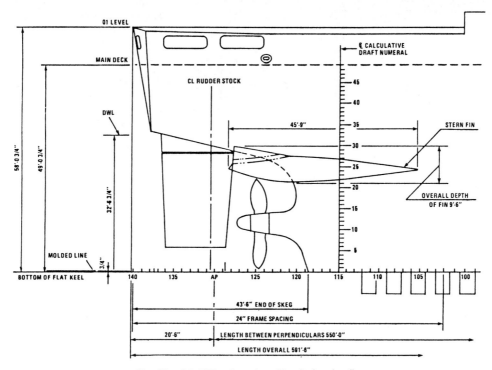

Fig. 48 AO-177 outboard profile aft showing fin

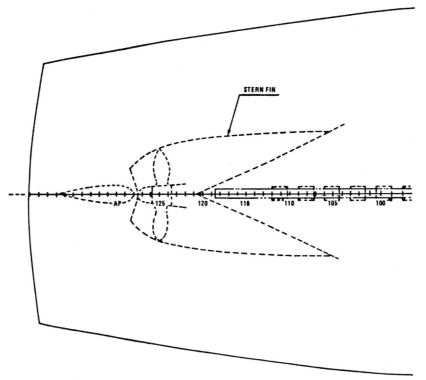

Fig. 49 AO-177 plan views aft showing fin

installed by the Naval Shipyard at Charleston, South Carolina. The fins for the remaining ships would be installed by the shipbuilder, ASI. All in all, there were two commercial yards, one naval shipyard and two SUPSHIP offices involved in addition to many codes within NAVSEA.

Considering the tight schedule and likelihood of a "too many cooks" phenomenon, it is pleasantly surprising that things went as smoothly as they did. This was due mainly to the excep-

tionally cooperative effort put forth by all concerned.

As can be seen from the figures, the fin is rather large. The overall depth of the structure was 9 ft, 6 in., with a width of about 18 ft, 6 in., and an overall length of 45 ft, 9 in. The thickness of the fin is sufficient to allow quite adequate access to the interior for welding, painting, inspection, etc. The complex shape of the fin can be seen in Figs. 48–50 herewith.

Causes and Corrections for Propeller-Excited Airborne Noise

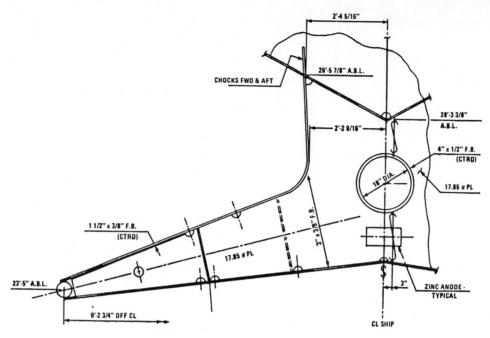

Fig. 50 Section view of fin, AO-177

The structural design of the fin was fairly straightforward, although several issues evolved to complicate it. The first cut at the scantlings maintained the general plate thicknesses and arrangement of adjacent hull structure, and was transversely framed with webs at 24-in. spacing. Analysis of the resulting structure indicated it would withstand a general slam ("beaver tail slap") to at least 12 000 psf. Since standard practice would have predicted loads of only 1000 psf, these "minimum" scantlings were maintained. Plating was commercial grade MS except for the lower face in way of the propeller, which was Navy grade HY-80 to protect against erosion. Actually, HY 100 was used for the AO-177 when sufficient amounts of HY-80 could not be acquired within the time available.

An unusual feature of the fin is that it is free flooding. In order not to have an adverse effect on the trim of the ship (down-by-the-head under certain load conditions), it was determined early on that the fin could not just be an empty void. Various concepts for locked-in liquid ballast were considered but rejected because of problems of freezing (the fin is often at or above the waterline), chemical contamination and penetrations of the hull (in case the installation was not hydrodynamically successful and was later removed). Thus it evolved that the greater part of the fin (any section over 18 in. in depth) would be free flooding. Flood holes were provided on the under surface and vent holes above (just like a submarine!). The interior was protected by coatings and zinc anodes. Access plates are provided for inspection and maintenance of the interior of the fin.

The only problem unresolved after the initial installation involved the adequacy of the propeller shipping pad eyes (flush type) installed on the underside of the fin. This was resolved by a design modification on subsequent installation by the addition of another pair of pad eyes.

In an age when it is easy to be cynical about the Navy's ability to work with industry to respond quickly and effectively, it was refreshing to be involved in a project which was as successful as this one. The authors and the major facilities involved are to be congratulated.

J. P. Breslin, Member, and T. G. McKee,[14] Visitor

Propeller-induced pressures on the afterbody of the AO-177 without fin have recently (16 November 1982) been computed as a part of the documentation of the MIT-DL propeller-hull program described in the Breslin et al paper given earlier in this volume. Comparisons of the pressures at five points as measured and reported in Fig. 16 of the present paper with those calculated are shown in Fig. 51 of this discussion. Here we compare our calculated double amplitude (for the rigid condition on the water surface) with the mean of the 5 percent highest values measured on the model at SSPA. (This is the level used by SSPA for predictive purposes as explained earlier in the Breslin et al paper.)

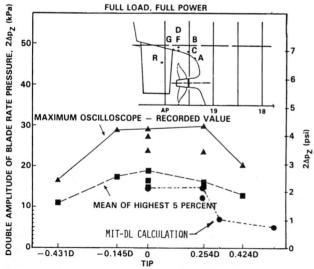

Fig. 51 Figure 16 of paper with MIT-Davidson Laboratory calculated values superposed for AO-177 without fin

[14] Davidson Laboratory, Stevens Institute of Technology, Hoboken, N.J.

It is seen that the correlation is excellent near to the propeller, but beyond 0.25D the calculated values are about half of those from measurement.

As the theory does not include temporal variations of the flow and, hence, no statistical variations in pressure amplitude (or phase), it is reasonable to question the significance of correlation with a particular part of the nonstationary model test output. The agreement might be considered as fortuitous, *but of highly practical value since the twelve-year experience at SSPA shows that their means of the 5 percent highest amplitudes correlates well with full-scale results.*

Clearly, the predictions made via an ad-hoc theory developed hurriedly at Davidson Laboratory compare poorly with the maximum amplitudes in the authors' Fig. 39 for the finless case. A decision to represent the cavity potential by only three terms (which dominate the far field) is now seen to be a poor approximation in the near field. A more effective ad-hoc model is believed to be that developed in the discussion of the Huse/Guogiang paper by Breslin, which appears earlier in this volume.

In any event, the calculation of hull pressures arising from intermittent cavitation must be regarded as still in its formative period. We must expect that theoretical conceptions, which include the physics of the phenomenon, will give far more consistent results than the ad-hoc formulations.

Schelte Hylarides,[15] Visitor

This paper contains a great amount of practical design aspects on vibration problems aboard ships as generated by the propeller. Their use—the pros and cons—the considerations as to which choice should be made between the various possibilities, are dealt with very extensively. Also is illustrated the fact that many questions are still open, so that very often the designer has to operate on intuition. I therefore think that we unanimously agree in complimenting the authors for their valuable work.

In spite of the rather extensive description, it is not clear to me why finally the flow-accelerating fin with the original propeller was selected. In my opinion we can state the problem as follows:

- the vibration level is acceptable,
- the noise level is by far too high, and
- the cause is the intermittent propeller cavitation.

Knowing this, the alterations on ship or propeller should be aimed at reducing the higher harmonics of the hull pressure fluctuations.

Looking to Fig. 25 of the paper, one directly concludes that for the higher harmonics the tunnel fin is by far more effective than the flow-accelerating fin. Although not mentioned in the text, I expect that Propeller A (the five-bladed, wide-blade propeller) is also very effective in reducing the higher harmonics. This opinion is based on the large effect of Propeller A on the pulses with blade harmonic frequency (Table 9, Fig. 24) and on the complete redesign of the propeller that has been performed. So the obvious solutions would be:

(*a*) the tunnel-fin, or
(*b*) the 5-bladed newly designed propeller.

Yet the flow-accelerating fin has been selected.

According to the paper the flow-accelerating fin was selected because, according to the SSPA vibration criterion, for this fin the pressure limit is the highest. The authors start the justification of their choice with the words: "If it is assumed that the SSPA vibration criterion has general applicability. . . ." etc. In my opinion this assumption is not correct. This criterion has been based on experiences with ships without fins and therefore

cannot be used in a case where the fin is applied.

When applying a fin the pressure field around the propeller tip will have lower amplitudes, but due to the smaller clearance the ship structure is moved into the region with high pressure amplitudes. These two aspects combined result in a different pressure distribution on the structure with respect to amplitude and phase. The integration of this pressure field can lead to lower or higher forces and moments than originally. In case, for example, that with a fin the vertical force F_z is larger than without a fin, one may expect that the vertical vibration level increases proportionally. The increase of hull stiffness due to the fin will have a negligible effect. Further, one can state that larger pressures lead to larger forces, unless the phase distribution is changed so that the pressures balance each other to a certain degree. But then a reduction of the excitation system can only be small.

Therefore at MARIN we state that pressure fluctuations have to be reduced if a fin is used. The decreased vertical clearance surely is no reason to allow a higher pressure level on the fin.

Authors' Closure

The authors sincerely thank all of the discussers. Their contributions have greatly enhanced the value of our paper.

We will reply first to points raised regarding the propeller design and propeller performance. Then we will respond to other points including those associated with hull pressures and forces, fin selection, and airborne noise.

Several discussers, including Messrs. Zaloumis, Raestad, Hammer, Noonan, and Professor Hadler commented on the severe requirements regarding maximum allowable blade rate bearing forces that were imposed on the propeller design. Essentially all of these discussers felt that these requirements were too severe. As discussed in the paper, these bearing force requirements influenced the design of the propeller on the AO-177 to a much greater degree than is usual practice. The U.S. Navy requirements and rationale that led to the maximum allowable bearing forces are summarized in the paper and amplified in the discussion by Mr. Zaloumis. We thank Mr. Zaloumis for the supplemental information in his discussion. The rationale for blade rate thrust includes:

1. MIL-STD-167 for allowable vibration level in the propulsion system.
2. Propulsion system vibratory response calculations.
3. Empirical multiplicative factors on the calculated propeller forces to consider the influence of
    (*a*) modulation,
    (*b*) nonlinear effects at high speed, and
    (*c*) turns.

Mr. Zaloumis described the derivation of the empirical multiplicative factors. His discussion answered some of the questions asked by other discussers, so those points will not be repeated here.

The empirical multiplicative factors inherently include factors of safety for the influence of phenomena that presently cannot be calculated directly, such as

1. Wake scaling effects (differences in the pertinent harmonics of the nominal wake between model and full scale).
2. Effective wake distribution (influence of the propeller on the pertinent harmonics of the wake).
3. Possible effects of cavitation on periodic propeller loads.
4. Possible effects of the free surface on periodic propeller loads.
5. Inaccuracies (including inaccuracies in model wake experiments, propeller loading calculations, shafting response calculations, bearing support stiffnesses, etc.)

[15] Maritime Research Institute (MARIN), Wageningen, The Netherlands.

The authors agree with several of the discussers who suggest that the empirical multiplicative factors are overly conservative. Conservative factors of safety are reasonable engineering tools so long as they do not lead to other problems. Unfortunately, this did not turn out to be the case on the AO-177. The authors fully endorse Mr. Noonan's suggestion that the empirical multiplicative factors should be carefully reviewed and relaxed as appropriate.

As discussed in the paper, the authors agree with Mr. Raestad that the accuracy of predicting bearing forces as low as 1 percent of the time-average thrust is poor. However, it is felt that periodic bearing force calculations do yield a reasonable indication of the relative performance (or ranking) of different candidate propellers (design options). The uncertainty in the calculated periodic bearing forces is considered in the empirical factors of safety as discussed in the preceding paragraph.

We also agree with Mr. Raestad that the bearing forces in turns and straight ahead are essentially unrelated because the wake patterns are completely different for these two cases. However, since wake data are not, in general, available in turns, the maximum bearing forces in turns are empirically estimated to be three times the maximum bearing forces in straight-ahead operations.

Mr. Hammer raised several questions regarding the propeller design. He states that the real villain in this case is the hull which produced the poor wake in which the propeller must operate, and the propeller machinery studies which dictated very small allowable blade rate bearing force components. From the propeller designer's point of view, the authors certainly agree with this assessment. However, from overall ship design viewpoint the story is more complicated.

The hull design for AO-177 was completed eight years ago. It was designed primarily for high propulsive efficiency which could be quantified through model experiments. This was a requirement imposed on the design to maximize range.

It was recognized that this hull produced a severe wake in the propeller plane. However, at the time of the hull design there was no reliable validated technique for predicting propeller-induced hull vibration and airborne noise; certainly none that was applicable to a highly skewed propeller, or to a seven-bladed propeller. However, it was judged that the combination of high skew and generous tip clearance (30 percent of diameter) on the AO-177 would minimize the likelihood of these problems. In fact, the AO-177 as built without fin was satisfactory from the vibration point of view, but suffered from

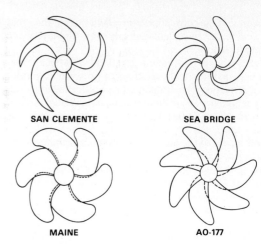

Fig. 52   Comparative skewed propellers

excessive noise. It remains the opinions of the authors that if the ship had an unskewed propeller with the same number of blades and identical other parameters then the levels of vibration and noise would be much higher than was experienced on the AO-177 with the skewed propeller. In any event, the hull designers selected a known gain in propulsive efficiency over reducing an unknown risk of problems associated with hull vibration or noise.

Mr. Hammer cited three highly successful skewed propellers applied to merchant ships. These propellers and the AO-177 propeller are shown in Fig. 52 with this closure. All of these merchant ship propellers were designed by DTNSRDC using essentially the same techniques and philosophy as was used for the AO-177 propeller design. However, the wake nonuniformity and bearing force requirements are more severe for the AO-177. These propellers exhibit a wide variety of geometries based on fine tuning of the propellers to the particular wake and design requirements. The primary departure of the AO-177 propeller from these designs was the use of seven blades and a smaller diameter. Seven blades did not directly lead to problems on the AO-177, rather the short chords near the tips which are a by-product of the high number of blades and the requirement to avoid a pointed trailing edge near the tip contributed to the airborne noise problem.

Table 15 herewith compares the blade frequency bearing

Table 15   Blade rate bearing forces on comparative skewed propellers

	AO-177 LIMITS	AO-177 EXISTING PROPELLER	AO-177 PRELIMINARY REDESIGN PROPELLER	SEA BRIDGE	MAINE	AO-177 REDESIGN PROPELLER	SAN CLEMENTE
NUMBER OF BLADES	7	7	6	6	6	5	5
SKEW AT TIP (DEGREES)	45	45	45	60	30	30	72
100X BLADE RATE THRUST / STEADY THRUST	1.0	0.9	0.9	2.4	1.2	2.9	0.5
100X BLADE RATE VERTICAL FORCE / STEADY THRUST	0.7	0.3	1.1	0.4	1.6	1.3	0.4
100X BLADE RATE TRANSVERSE FORCE / STEADY THRUST	0.7	0.1	1.3	0.7	0.6	2.6	0.8

ALL VALUES CALCULATED BY METHOD OF TSAKONAS ET AL[8] USING MODEL NOMINAL WAKE DISTRIBUTIONS WITHOUT EFFECT OF CAVITATION.

force requirements for the AO-177 with the calculated blade frequency bearing forces on the AO-177 propeller, on the three cases cited by Mr. Hammer, in their respective design wakes, and on five- and six-bladed propeller design options for the AO-177. All calculated values are based on the procedures used for the AO-177 propeller design as discussed in the paper. Table 15 shows that none of the propellers except the seven-bladed AO-177 propeller meets the bearing force requirements imposed on the AO-177 propeller design. This illustrates that the severe bearing force requirements drove the design of the AO-177 propeller.

Mr. Hammer asked what would we do differently if we were designing the AO-177 today with benefit of today's knowledge. Basically, we would do three things differently:

1. Design the hull with a bulbous stern, as discussed by Mr. Byers, to produce a more uniform wake in the propeller plane. Alternatively, use an open-stern hull design typical of many existing U.S. Navy auxiliary and combatant ships whose main hull wakes are very mild.

2. Make a different tradeoff between a hull design for maximum propulsive efficiency and one designed for reduced risks of vibration, airborne noise, and cavitation erosion.

3. Increase the maximum allowable blade rate bearing force components, and design a five-bladed skewed propeller as discussed in the paper.

Mr. Hammer asked whether the predicted resonance in the propulsion system at 10 Hz, which eliminated consideration of a six-bladed propeller, was observed in the trials. As discussed in the paper, the trials indicated that this resonance occurred near 13 Hz rather than 10 Hz. This rather poor prediction of resonance frequency is primarily due to inability to adequately predict the stiffness of the bearing support in the design stage.

Professor Hadler shared some of his design experience and model evaluation techniques with us in his discussion. The authors thank him for this. Much of his experience is similar to ours as discussed in the paper.

Professor Hadler and Mr. Bjärne cite a general guideline of low values of camber near the tip for reducing the likelihood of cavitation erosion, bent trailing edges, and minimal harmonics of blade frequency hull forces. This guideline is based primarily on experience with unskewed propellers. However, the relatively high value of camber-to-chord ratio near the tips of the AO-177 propeller is due to short chords rather than high camber. Further, these are significantly influenced by lifting surface corrections due to skew, so typical values applicable to unskewed propellers are not necessarily applicable here.

Professor Hadler recommended avoiding a pointed trailing-edge profile near the tips. Pointed trailing-edge profiles near the tips were unavoidable on both the original and redesign propellers on the AO-177 due to the severe bearing force criteria. Further, the three skewed propeller designs discussed by Mr. Hammer (see Fig. 52) had pointed trailing edge profiles near the tips without significant cavitation erosion, propeller-induced vibration, or propeller-induced airborne noise.

Mr. Takekuma correctly commented that the diameter of the AO-177 propeller is less than the diameter for optimum propulsive efficiency. The diameter for optimum propulsive efficiency, 7.0 m (23 ft), and the corresponding optimum rotational speed, 100 rpm, were selected during the preliminary design stage; however, the diameter was reduced to 6.4 m (21 ft) during the detailed design stage to meet the bearing force criteria. Calculations indicated that the smaller diameter would cause insignificant loss in propulsive efficiency and the smaller diameter resulted in a lighter propeller with larger tip clearance. The reduction gearing was fixed when the diameter was reduced, so the rpm could not be increased to its optimum value for a 6.4-m (21 ft) diameter. However, calculations

showed that propulsive efficiency is insensitive to change in design rotational speed from 100 rpm to 120 rpm.

Mr. Takekuma suggested higher values of propeller expanded area ratio than that used for the AO-177 propeller. The blade chord lengths at each radius on the AO-177 propeller were determined by analysis based upon blade section cavitation buckets. The resulting expanded area ratio A_E/A_O was checked against minimum criteria of Burrill and Emerson [58] for freedom from thrust breakdown and of Lindgren and Bjärne [18] for freedom from excessive cavitation erosion. However, Propeller A evaluated at SSPA and the proposed redesign propeller had wider blades near the tips, resulting in higher values of A_E/A_O. The values of A_E/A_O are as follows:

Propeller	A_E/A_O
AO-177	0.73
Propeller A	0.82
Proposed redesign for AO-177	0.82
Value suggested by Mr. Takekuma	0.89

Wider blades may help alleviate the problems that occurred on the AO-177; however, care must be exercised to avoid excessive blade width because increasing blade width causes increased weight, increased cost, and reduced propulsive efficiency due to increased viscous drag.

We turn now to discussion points relating to the propeller-induced excitation pressures, ship response and inboard noise, and the alternative fin designs.

Mr. Bjärne and Mr. Noonan expressed interest in information concerning the hull girder vibration and the localized vibration in the troublesome compartments of the ship. Of course we agree such data would be useful and complementary information. However, extensive local compartment vibration data do not exist, and unfortunately the hull girder vibration data for this Navy ship are restricted. Nevertheless, it may be noted that the crucial vibration components measured at the usual representative locations such as the vertical amplitudes at fantail centerline on the main deck and the horizontal amplitudes at the top of the deckhouse were found to be acceptable in terms of both the U.S. Navy standard and the ranges recommended by the International Standards Organization (see, for example, reference [16]). Therefore, the girder vibration levels are not considered to be excessive.

Mr. Bjärne's recommendation that the mean values of the third blade rate harmonic of the measured model scale pressure pulse amplitudes be used for best correlation with the observed changes in very low frequency full-scale interior noise is interesting. We believe that a reliable empirical trend for judging an interior noise correlation should be established using numerous examples, not just this one case. We may observe that there are very few published studies involving interior noise excited by the propeller. We have concentrated on judging the probable merits of our various corrective options based on the relative levels of the pressure pulse amplitudes.

In answer to Mr. Bjärne's suggestion about the possible source of interior noise, we believe that it is unlikely that there are sufficient loose bulkheads, detached stringers, etc., to explain the widespread occurrence of inboard airborne noise on the AO-177 as *rattling* response to low-frequency vibration.

We are further indebted to Mr. Bjärne for his data on the large pressure pulse amplitudes that may accompany propeller-hull vortex cavitation for a propeller in a duct.

Mr. Raestad inquired whether the characteristics of expected superstructure vibration influenced the choice of number of blades. There were numerous check calculations performed on the natural frequencies of typical panels and substructures located throughout the stern of the ship, but estimated super-

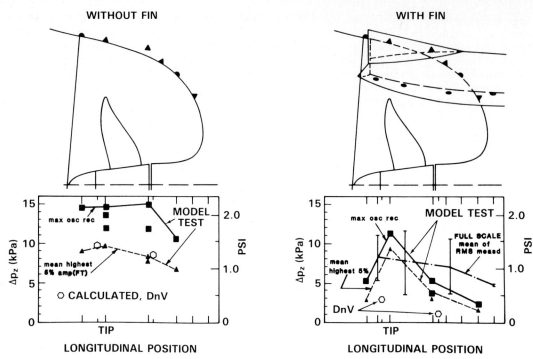

Fig. 53 Comparison of measured blade rate pressure pulse amplitudes with computed values from DnV [9]

structure resonant frequencies were not directly considered in the propeller design. Previous Navy experience has shown that fewer numbers of blades, such as four or five, are more likely to produce difficulties along these lines. Two resonant frequencies of the deckhouse were observed during vibration surveys of the unmodified ship. In each case the response was very narrowly tuned, and even after the vibration levels at the top of the deckhouse were allowed to build up to peak response, the amplitudes were not judged excessive, as explained earlier.

Mr. Raestad noted that calculations of periodic pressure amplitudes were carried out by DnV and reported in reference [9] for the AO-177 hull without and with the flow-accelerating fin. These data were not included in Fig. 39 because only two of the points fell within the longitudinal interval covered by these diagrams, so the local trend is not clearly defined. However, this omission is corrected with Fig. 53, which shows the DnV computed blade rate pressure amplitude points for each case, and comparison with the model and full-scale measurements. Included are curves for two measures of the model scale results: (1) the mean of the highest 5 percent amplitudes from Fourier analysis, and (2) the maximum oscillograph values. The calculated values fall below the maximum oscillograph recorded values for both without-fin and with-fin cases. For the case of no fin, the agreement between the DnV computed amplitudes and the highest 5 percent curve is excellent.

Mr. Raestad also pointed out that we did not include comparisons between patterns of calculated and model observations of extent of cavitation. Although interesting and potentially useful, these comparisons have not been presented because of the length of this paper.

We heartily endorse the idea stated by Mr. Raestad and Dr. Kaplan that there is a distinct need for early stage guidance on the possibility of unsteady cavitating propeller excitation problems that could be provided by analytical prediction schemes such as those described briefly in Appendix 2. At least in the U.S. Navy design community, the experience with the

AO-177 has added an impetus to activities started some years ago to upgrade capability and initiate fresh directions for research in this area.

The use of the term "airborne noise" to describe the noise levels detected with a microphone and perceived by the ear in the interior spaces of a ship conforms to U.S. Navy practice. Thus, there is simply a semantic difference between this label and the term structureborne noise mentioned by Mr. Raestad to describe the noise levels (measured in air) transmitted to the compartment by a structural path. Perhaps a better term might be interior noise.

Mr. Takekuma questioned whether it was inconsistent that airborne noise was the dominant problem on this ship while the pressure pulses measured in the model tests showed that the blade rate component of periodic pressure was larger than any of the higher harmonic components. The fact that the interior airborne noise levels instead of hull vibration was the main problem in many after spaces of this ship was simply a matter of measurement and comparison with allowable criteria. We see no reason to suppose that the absolute levels of the higher harmonic pressure pulse components (say those in the range 31 Hz to 250 Hz) need to be larger than the blade rate levels in order to cause excessive interior noise. What is involved here is a complicated transmission process that depends on the frequency-dependent impedance characteristics of the structure and the detailed noise radiation properties of the boundaries of the compartments. Without detailed (and very expensive) acoustoelastic calibration of the ship, all we can say about the particular composition of pressure pulse spectra for the AO-177 is that the higher frequency excitation levels were large enough to cause the problems described.

Mr. Takekuma pointed out that the net improvement of overall ship propulsive performance with the flow-accelerating fin installed (compared with the no fin case) seems to hinge on a noticeable increase of the relative rotative efficiency η_R. This applies only to the ballast condition with the hull trimmed 1.14 m (3.75 ft) down by the stern. Changes in the propulsive interaction coefficient η_R are often difficult to understand and motivate. In this case, there are changes in the three velocity component ratios of the nominal wake, comparing the ballast condition with the full-load condition, that may explain the improvement in η_R. Within the main wake shadow, the V_X/V values for the ballast condition are increased and wake extent is broadened, so that the tangential gradients are reduced compared with the velocity patterns of the full load condition. Similarly, the peaks of the V_T/V and V_R/V variations versus circumferential angle are reduced for the ballast condition compared with full load case. Overall then, the velocity circumferential gradients are diminished in the ballast condition wake field, and the somewhat weakened sheared flow pattern, could be responsible for the larger η_R trend in that condition.

Mr. Takekuma expressed concern with the wide band of measurements of pressure pulse amplitudes displayed in Fig. 38. This scatter reflects the character of the observed pressure signals. This may in part be attributed to temporal variations that are known to be present, especially in full scale measurements. Although the data shown here exhibit large scatter, which is rather unsettling to us as well as to Mr. Takekuma, there are other examples of measured pressure pulse data that illustrate variability, for instance, the measurements reported by Holden et al [59]. We should be advised for future measurement work to display the data in a stricter statistical manner, when an ensemble mean value is identified, along with the standard deviation, and the extent of maximum and minimum values.

Dr. Kaplan's complaint about the use of the measured maximum oscillograph amplitude of fluctuating pressure for the comparison with the analytical results is well taken. For clarity, it should be noted that it is the maximum amplitude of the blade rate *filtered* signal that has been displayed in these comparisons. Nevertheless, we agree that the mean of the highest 5 percent value determined from sequences of Fourier analysis for each revolution is a better choice, and it has been the most frequently suggested average value for correlation purposes on the basis of several investigations by SSPA. Figures 16 and 53 present the mean of the highest 5 percent of the model pressure amplitudes that may be directly compared with the analytical predictions shown in Fig. 39.

Mr. Noonan commented that the main efforts of the program outlined in this paper were directed toward the identification, verification, and reduction of the *source* of propeller-excitation, and not on classical noise reduction methods. This was certainly the case. We chose both wake and propeller modification alternatives. Anyway, it is most likely that the available noise reduction techniques would have helped little or not at all in the low-frequency range that characterizes the worst noise levels of the AO-177. There may be some additional gains that could be made by selectively stiffening certain structural elements in the after part of the ship in order to alter the susceptibility of the hull to the transmission of vibration energy to interior compartments. Mr. Noonan also argued for criteria for evaluating the surface force aspect of propeller excitation for proposed designs, and we certainly agree. In fact, because of the AO-177 experience we are trying to fill this need.

Mr. Noonan requested comment on the correlation of cavitation inception from model and full-scale observations. Inception of cavitation usually refers to the velocity conditions (rpm and ship speed) at which cavitation of a particular type first appears. Inception by itself is not an issue in the present situation. Inception of cavitation occurs at much lower speeds than the regime of excessive excitation which is a result of fully developed, sheet cavity flow experiencing periodic instability and collapse. The important cavitation scaling aspects are the scaling of the cavity volume dynamics and unsteady cavity flow patterns as they relate to the propeller excitation levels. Dr.

Stern also expressed interest in this latter issue. Correlation of model and full scale results in this area is very complicated, involving topics such as scaling model-to-full scale wake, the boundary condition simulated by the tunnel ceiling, ambient flow quality, and air content. On the basis of cavitation extent and general cavity appearance, the water tunnel results correlate fairly well with patterns observed full scale. The most current discussion of the subject of correlation with large water tunnel experiments is given by Breslin et al [60]. Regardless of the assessment of the absolute levels of pressure pulse results from SSPA, we have interpreted the results of the water tunnel tests from a point of view of relative magnitudes. That is, we defined the final choice of a design option on the basis of best relative improvement over the case of the unmodified AO-177.

Dr. Stern stated a desire for a more complete review of the computational results accumulated in the course of this project. We agree that this would be interesting and useful. Unfortunately, the length of this paper limited the attention that could be given to the analytical results. We hope to include a more complete discussion of the computational results in a future reference. In this connection, Dr. Stern offered his computed results for the AO-177 unsteady volume velocity, and estimated pressure pulse amplitudes. We thank him for this contribution.

We thank Mr. Byers for his thoughts on the steps being undertaken to avoid the recurrence of problems similar to those encountered by the AO-177.

The details of the fin structural design and the fin installation program provided by Messrs. Arntson, Ikeda, and Lusick are certainly timely and an important addition to this paper. We thank these discussers for their remarks.

Prof. Breslin and Dr. McKee presented calculations for the AO-177 without fin from the combination of computer programs from MIT and DL/SIT for the cavitating propeller and hull-propeller interaction analysis, respectively. They provided a comparison between the predicted pressure pulse amplitudes and the mean of the highest 5 percent amplitudes measured in the cavitation tunnel at SSPA. As noted previously, we agree that the average of the 5 percent highest amplitudes is probably the preferred experimental quantity for correlation. We thank the discussers for this additional information.

Dr. Hylarides raised some interesting points and challenging questions. Based on information available in the paper or inferred from his experience, he suggested a reordering of the corrective options for solving the problems of the AO-177. He reiterated the idea that for reducing the levels of interior noise, any design modification should be directed toward the reduction of the higher harmonics of the induced pressure pulses. We have previously stated this aim, but we should note that other considerations also played a role in the final choice of fin design. To shed more light on the comparison between the two fin configurations, we include in Fig. 54 the pressure amplitude spectra measured at the forwardmost point, Point A (centerline), for the unmodified hull and for each of the fins at the full-power, full-load condition. These curves represent the model scale pressure pulse levels (rms) expressed in dB versus the frequency for the model scale. These data are considered reliable up to about 1600 Hz. Here we see that both fins reduced the general levels of higher-frequency pressure pulses. In the lower frequency range, up to seven times the blade rate frequency (82 Hz full scale), the tunnel-fin produced the larger reductions, but for the higher harmonics the bigger reductions were associated with the flow-accelerating fin. From this comparison, we feel that neither fin shows clear superiority, considering the entire frequency range of interest. It appears that either fin probably would have reduced the inboard noise.

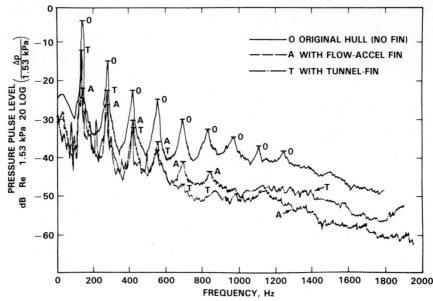

Fig. 54 Model scale pressure amplitude spectra measured at forwardmost transducer A, comparing cases without and with the two fins

With regard to the selection of a corrective option, there was a distinct need to choose a fix that could be implemented quickly and inexpensively. Since initial fin designs were ready by the time of the cavitation tunnel tests, a fin could be installed on the ship faster than any other option. If the choice had been a new propeller, it would have required approximately one year longer to have a verified design modification ready to be installed on the ship. The better performance of the flow-accelerating fin relative to the tunnel-fin in reducing blade rate periodic pressures, especially forward and aft of the tip plane, was the principal appealing feature. Secondary advantages are that the flow-accelerating fin is smaller, lighter, and cheaper to build and install. Its added drag is smaller as well. Criticism of using the SSPA criterion beyond its intended scope (hull vibration) is probably justified here, but we believe that this criterion correctly indicated that there was a greater margin of safety for avoiding possible hull girder vibration problems with the flow-accelerating fin than with the tunnel-fin. More significantly, the flow-accelerating fin produced lower blade rate pressure amplitudes over the tip, while the tunnel-fin produced slightly higher values (mean of 5 percent highest amplitudes), compared with the case of the unmodified hull. In light of Dr.

Hylarides's argument about the desirability of having reduced pressure pulse amplitudes with a fin (presumably over the tip), it seems difficult to justify a firm conviction that the tunnel-fin would have been such an obviously better choice.

All things considered, we felt that the choice between the two fins was rather close. It is perhaps an academic point since the full-scale fin evaluation trial showed that the flow-accelerating fin was a satisfactory and sufficient correction to the problems of the AO-177.

Again, the authors wish to thank all of the discussers for their significant contributions to this paper.

Additional references

58 Burrill, L. C. and Emerson, A., "Propeller Cavitation: Further Tests on 16 inch Propeller Models in the King's College Cavitation Tunnel," *Trans.* NECIES, Vol. 79, Part 6, 1962–1963, pp. 295–320.

59 Holden, K., Søntvedt, T., and Øfsti, O., "On Stability and Volume of Marine Propeller Cavitation and Corresponding Spectral Distribution in Hull Pressure Fields," Symposium on High Powered Propulsion of Large Ships, Part 1, NSMB Publication No. 490, 1974.

60 Breslin, J. P. et al, "Theoretical and Experimental Propeller-Induced Hull Pressures Arising from Intermittent Blade Cavitation, Loading, and Thickness," Trans. SNAME, Vol. 90, 1982.

SNAME *Transactions*, Vol. 90, 1982, pp. 321–338

The Naval Gas Turbine Ship Propulsion Dynamics and Control Systems Research and Development Program

C. J. Rubis,[1] Member, and **T. R. Harper,**[2] Visitor

The objective of the U.S. Navy-sponsored Gas Turbine Propulsion Dynamics and Control R&D program was to evaluate various control system approaches and tradeoffs, to develop performance guidelines and design criteria for machinery dynamics and control systems, and to determine propulsion system dynamic loads under various maneuvering and sea-state conditions. This paper discusses the problems and requirements of gas turbine ship propulsion control systems and the research approach consisting of simulations, experimental tests and trials. The work conducted under the various program phases is discussed, including the impact of this work on new ships, new propulsion systems, and the use of simulations as a diagnostic tool for solution of fleet machinery and control problems.

Introduction

WITH THE DD-963 class destroyers, FFG-7 class frigates, PHM class gunboats and other planned gas turbine ships, the U.S. Navy is committed to gas turbine propulsion for a large part of the surface fleet.

Aero-derivative marine gas turbine engines adopted by the U.S. Navy and many foreign navies worldwide for ship propulsion are lightweight, fast-responding, high-performance engines with certain mandatory automatic control requirements. The engines and propulsion control systems comprising the propulsion plants of these ships require a relatively high degree of automatic control since the number, speed and accuracy of control actions required exceed the capabilities of human operators.

The advantages of gas turbine propulsion systems have led to their adoption in naval combatant ships, but these advantages lead to increased reliance on automatic control systems and much greater attention to system dynamic performance. Gas turbine controllable-pitch (CP) propeller propulsion systems have introduced new dynamics and control problems for which there was little previous design or operating experience. Propulsion dynamics and control simulations have become an essential step in control system design necessary to assure safe loading levels throughout the drive train under all maneuvering conditions while not significantly compromising ship maneuvering performance.

Propulsion control system design is a critical part of the ship design process impacting on ship maneuvering performance and engine drive train transient loads. Controls are also the interface between men and machinery, the means by which machinery is controlled.

The Gas Turbine Ship Propulsion Control Systems Research and Development Program was initiated by the Navy and conducted by Propulsion Dynamics, Inc. with support from DTNSRDC and the fleet. Its purpose was to develop machinery dynamics and control system information. This program involved large-scale computer simulations of total propulsion systems supported by experimental hydrodynamic model tests, full-scale propulsion system tests and ships trials. While this R&D program dealt also with fixed-pitch propeller applications, the majority of the discussions contained herein are for controllable-pitch propellers. An earlier SNAME [1][3] paper reported on a portion of this total program which is now nearing completion.

Problems and requirements of gas turbine ship propulsion control systems

Gas turbine controllable-pitch propeller systems

Propulsion control systems for gas turbine ships incorporate direct throttle control from the bridge. Direct throttle control enhances the mobility and effectiveness of ships while exploiting the faster response capability of gas turbine engines. An important operational advantage of gas turbines is their extremely fast light-off and response to full-power capability. A large gas turbine can be started and ready for full power in a period of less than two minutes as compared with approximately an hour for a steam plant, while an idling gas turbine can be brought to full power in less than 10 sec. In order to take advantage of the very fast response of gas turbine engines and permit safe, correct control, the control systems must incorporate a high degree of automatic control. The use of CP propellers and multiple engines further increases system complexity and the need for automatic controls in the ship propulsion control system.

Gas turbine propulsion and CP propeller systems coupled with the increased automatic control of these plants present some new and unique problems. The Navy is using large [in excess of 40 000 hp (~30 000 kW)] controllable-pitch propellers. Because of their improved cavitation and noise characteristics, skewed CP propellers are now used. The stress problems of CP

[1] President, Propulsion Dynamics, Inc., Annapolis, Maryland.
[2] Director, Ship Systems Engineering, Propulsion Dynamics, Inc., Annapolis, Maryland.

The views expressed herein are the opinions of the authors and not necessarily those of DOD or the Department of the Navy.

Presented at the Annual Meeting, New York, N. Y., November 17–20, 1982, of THE SOCIETY OF NAVAL ARCHITECTS AND MARINE ENGINEERS.

[3] Numbers in brackets designate References at end of paper.

propellers (especially skewed propellers) particularly in maneuvering transients have been intensively studied. Emphasis on additional dynamics, control and stress analyses for gas turbine CP propeller propulsion systems was begun after the blade failure of an experimental CP propeller during ship trials in 1974.

Integrated throttle control and temperature compensation

For gas turbine plants driving controllable-pitch propellers, the propeller speed and pitch must be properly coordinated for both steady-state and transient conditions. The matching of propeller, engine and ship characteristics affects the propeller performance and ship propulsion efficiency. Since gas turbine performance is greatly subject to ambient air temperature, integrated throttle controls should be corrected for changing ambient temperature to eliminate temperature effects on engine performance.

Transient load limiting

Control of propeller pitch, pitch rate of change and engine throttle command must be integrated and designed to prevent excessively large transient loads during any type of propulsion maneuver. For example, such transients could produce very large torque loads on the shaft, engine or propeller blades (spindle torque, that is, torque required to turn the blade on its axis) or excessive propeller thrust loads.

Reversing, expecially crashback from maximum ahead, presents new problems not encountered with steam turbines. During reversing, maximum gas turbine power is potentially available. During pitch change in reversing, the propeller torque near zero pitch becomes small, hence turbine fuel and pitch must be properly coordinated to control propeller speed-up and consequent peak propeller loads. Under certain blade pitch conditions while reversing, the transient negative propeller thrust can exceed the maximum ahead thrust. In steam systems 65 to 70 percent of the drive train inertia is in the LP turbine rotor whereas in gas turbines only 15 to 20 percent is in the free turbine rotor, thus passing larger loads to the gear teeth. Crashback performance for gas turbine ships can be superior to steam turbine ships, but is limited by allowable drive train loads.

For crashahead from a maximum backing condition or for any rapid acceleration maneuver, very large engine and shaft torques as well as large peak blade spindle torques and propeller thrusts could develop. The propulsion control system should provide for automatic engine or shaft torque limiting to limit engine torques to safe levels during all maneuvering transients. Thus, for gas turbine controllable-pitch propeller ships, it is absolutely essential that the propulsion control system provide transient limiting controls. These controls must perform the following functions automatically while correcting for the effects of changes in ambient air temperature: (1) Restrict the magnitude of throttle commands for low pitch settings; (2) limit engine or shaft torque; and (3) limit pitch and pitch rate of change.

The propulsion control system should be designed to provide for safe engine operating conditions for unrestricted throttle manipulation. The operator should not be expected to exercise ultimate engine response limiting based on his method of throttle command; too much potential for machinery damage exists.

Engine overspeed

Aero-derivative gas turbines have much smaller rotating moments of inertia than steam turbines of comparable horsepower. Consequently, the overspeed hazard is potentially greater. Under a full-power load-drop condition (for example, caused by a sudden clutch opening or shaft break) a large propulsion gas turbine could reach destructive overspeed in less than a second unless fuel is immediately shut off. A fail-safe overspeed trip that shuts off fuel in response to a load-drop condition without engine damage is mandatory. Catastrophic destruction of a large propulsion gas turbine due to a malfunctioning control system on a Coast Guard Cutter occurred in 1972. The potential danger in such occurrences has led the Navy to investigate load-drop situations and the requirements of overspeed trip systems via simulations and by testing a gas turbine engine at the Navy's land-based test site. In marine application, with the high probability of greatly varying sea-imposed propeller loads, the topping governor design must protect the engine from excessive overspeeds without total engine shutdown.

Governing

The influence of the seaway causing large propeller load fluctuations has a greater effect on the engines and drive trains of gas turbine plants than steam plants due to the lower drive train inertia for gas turbine plants. Propulsion plant cycling is undesirable and is greatly affected by the propulsion control system design. Gas turbine propulsion systems are typically combinations of gas generator power governed and propeller speed governed systems. Closed-loop propeller speed governed systems, if used, should be carefully designed to provide stable operation under all conditions and provide for control gain adjustment to alleviate the cycling problem in high seas. Variable-geometry gas turbine engines operating with closed-loop propeller speed control could develop wear caused by continual cycling of the propeller in waves. In addition, the operation of these speed-governing systems should not oppose or interfere with the transient limiting systems during propulsion or turning maneuvers. The advantages and disadvantages of closed-loop propeller speed control versus power control are still under debate. Some ship propulsion control

---

Nomenclature

BTL = bridge throttle lever position
CP = controllable-pitch
$DTNSRDC$ = David Taylor Naval Ship Research and Development Center
FS = full scale
J = propeller advance coefficient
LP = low pressure
N = propeller speed
N_E = engine speed
N_{GG} = gas generator speed
$NRPMP$ = propeller speed, port
$NRPMS$ = propeller speed, starboard

N_S = scheduled shaft speed
PLA = power lever angle
$PLANS$ = propeller speed controller PLA bias, starboard
$PLAS$ = scheduled PLA
$PLATMS$ = shaft torque controller PLA bias, starboard
PR = propeller pitch ratio
PR_S = scheduled propeller pitch ratio
P_2 = compressor inlet pressure
P_{54} = power turbine inlet pressure
Q = propeller torque

Q_B = propeller blade spindle torque
Q_E = engine torque
$QTMP$ = measured shaft torque, port
$QTMS$ = measured shaft torque, starboard
S_{STOP} = reach to stop ship
T = propeller thrust
T_{AMB} = ambient temperature
$T_{AVG\ STOP}$ = average thrust to stop ship
V = ship speed
W_F = engine fuel flow rate
τ = propeller pitch stroke time
δ = rudder angle

systems are experiencing problems of stability and undesirable interactions between the closed-loop speed control and transient limiting systems. An example of a complex problem involving engine and other propulsion system controls is the lowered engine compressor stall margin during certain ship maneuvers.

Turning loads

Provision should be made to automatically limit the magnitudes of shaft torques in turning maneuvers. Recent full-scale trials on both single- and twin-screw CP propeller ships have indicated that some of the highest drive train loads occur during high-speed turns. In the DD-963 destroyer for example, during sharp high speed turns both shafts become torque limited by the propulsion control system and the propulsion system cannot maintain constant propeller speed. In addition, turning even in a calm sea causes random fluctuations in propeller torque which can be sensed by the torquemeter and can result in large, undesirable fluctuations in fuel and other engine parameters.

Automation

The requirement for automation of gas turbine engine controls arises mainly from the demands for rapid, exact, always correct control actions. To control turbine support systems and interfacing systems such as the CP propeller and to cope with multiple engine on-off sequencing requires automation of these auxiliary systems as well. Mode changing refers to actions involved in starting, stopping, paralleling or removing on-line gas turbines. For a twin-screw ship with a total of four propulsion gas turbines (for example, the DD-963) a considerable amount of logic is required for this function. These actions in turn involve controls, interlocks and safety permissives. The automatic starting of gas turbines requires that all the engine supporting auxiliaries be operational and correctly controlled. Thus, engine start-up requires sufficient stored air pressure and working pneumatic starters, an operational gas turbine control system, working lubrication and fuel oil systems, and proper conditions on doors, ducts, clutches and other interlocks assuring machinery and personnel safety. For reasons of machinery and personnel safety and consistently correct control, automation of mode changing is important. But such automation becomes essential if the fast light-off and acceleration capability of gas turbines and the ability to safely and rapidly control several engines simultaneously is to be realized. Unfortunately, this pushbutton control of engine light-off and on-line/off-line capability has the disadvantage of increasing control system complexity with increased dependence on electronic logic circuits or a propulsion systems computer. Propulsion control system hardware is complex and the design approaches differ with each ship (even with the same engine and functionally identical control requirements), adding to hardware proliferation. There is a need for control and hardware standardization based on well-developed control system specifications.

Summary

The introduction of gas turbines as naval main propulsion engines together with controllable-pitch propellers has resulted in new problems in system dynamics, loads, controls and automation. Gas turbine engines require more automation and this requirement extends to a great degree to the entire propulsion system. Some of the requirements and characteristics of gas turbine CP propeller propulsion systems are summarized as follows:

- Integrated single lever throttle/CP propeller controls.
- Light-off to full power in 2 to 3 min; automatic subsystem sequencers needed.

- Rapid response, large torques and low inertia; need transient rate/load limits in crash maneuvers.
- Require unlimited throttle manipulation capability.
- Automatic controls for overspeed protection, multiple engine mode changes (start/stop, brakes, clutches, auxiliaries . . .), ambient temperature compensation, governing, torque limiting (turns, other maneuvers).
- Seaway effects/engine cycling; potential system instability; undesirable closed-loop/transient control interactions possible.

Controls and dynamics R&D program objectives

Simulating and predicting ship propulsion plant and control system performance has become imperative for the new generation of gas turbine ships where the engines, shafting and propellers could be easily damaged by excessive torques, thrusts or overspeed conditions. The control system must provide proper and safe commands to the machinery at all times irrespective of operator commands. Control systems must be designed to avoid unnecessary restrictions on machinery response and ship maneuverability in an attempt to provide overconservative safety margins. Propulsion dynamics and control simulations can predict such important information as ship response characteristics, machinery loads and stresses, operating limits and provide a means to develop the control strategy for various conditions so that evaluations and tradeoffs involving performance, safety, complexity and reliability can be made on a quantitative basis. These simulations are used in developing the control system and propulsion plant design, thus assuring a good match between propulsion machinery and control systems. But, probably more important, such simulations provide good assurance against major design problems and machinery failures by identifying peak loads during maneuvering and sea-imposed transients and by providing for design compatibility between machinery and control systems.

The objective of the Gas Turbine Ship Propulsion Dynamics and Control Systems R&D Program has been to conduct gas turbine ship propulsion dynamics and control simulations supported by hydrodynamic model tests and ships trials; to evaluate various control system approaches and tradeoffs to develop performance guidelines, design criteria and standards for control systems; and to determine worst-case dynamic loads for the propulsion system under various maneuvering and sea state conditions.

Program phases

The Dynamics and Control Systems R&D program consisted of four phases listed in the following. For each phase, topics investigated are listed.

I *Plant dynamics/control*—Integrated throttle control, temperature compensation, system performance sensitivity, dynamic time histories, transient load limiting, dynamics/controls design effects, maneuver optimization, load-performance tradeoffs, control/dynamics criteria, controls strategy, and worst-case drive train loads during a variety of maneuvering and operating conditions.

II *Ship turning dynamics/control*—Propeller dynamics, ship turning dynamics simulations, turning-propulsion interactions, turning performance, loads, and control tradeoffs and load limiting strategies.

III *Propulsion system governing dynamics/control*—Ship simulations in seaway, engine control simulations, analyses of cycling and stability in maneuvers, controls performance, and criteria under conditions of speed and power governing.

IV *Dynamics/control machinery impacts*—Analysis of

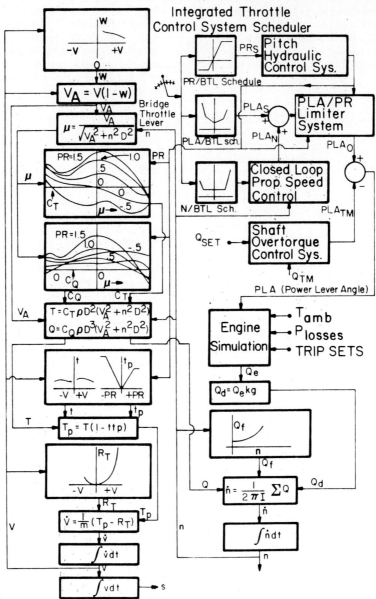

Fig. 1 Propulsion simulation computational diagram

dynamics/control design practices on propulsion machinery, including responses, loads, and safety factors for shafting, gears, clutches, brakes, bearings and propellers.

Approach

The three-pronged approach taken in conducting this program consisted of large-scale digital computer simulations supported by experimental data on engines, hull, propellers and control systems together with ship's trials verifications.

Computer simulation

Digital computer simulations representing the entire ship propulsion plant and ship maneuvers were developed using mathematical models and experimental data for control systems, engines, transmission, thrusters and the environment.

The engine dynamics and control simulation was a thermodynamic model of the gas turbine engine and its control systems (inner loop), for example, fuel control, stator vane control, torque limiting, topping governor and overspeed trip. The propulsion control system includes the outer loop controls such

as propeller pitch-speed scheduling, ambient temperature compensation, multiple engine scheduling and various maneuvering transient protection systems. It is the outer-loop portion of the propulsion control system that constitutes the unique part of each ship design while the same engine with essentially identical inner-loop controls may be used in many different ship applications. The propulsion plant dynamics and control simulation is generally concerned with one degree of freedom involving the ahead or astern motion of the ship (surge) in any steady-state or transient condition. However, all six degrees of freedom of ship motions were simulated to study, for example, the effect of pitching and heaving motions in a seaway on governing system design and turning loads with their consequences on propulsion shafting torques and control system interactions. A block diagram for a one-degree-of-freedom propulsion plant simulation is shown in Fig. 1. Additional diagrams show the engine simulation (Fig. 2) and the study ship propulsion control system (Fig. 3). These simulations numerically solve coupled nonlinear differential, algebraic and logic equations to quantitatively predict many propulsion system parameters during both steady-state and transient op-

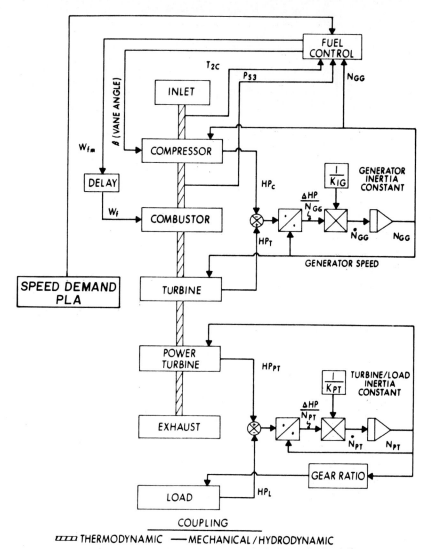

Fig. 2   LM2500 gas turbine engine thermodynamic simulation

eration.   The study ship used in most of this R&D program was the DD-963 class destroyer with twin controllable-pitch propellers driven by four gas turbine engines.   The control system was generalized to permit evaluation of various control strategies.   A block diagram of the study ship propulsion system is shown in Fig. 3.   The most complex part of the ship propulsion dynamics simulation is the engine model.   Depending on the purpose, engine simulations of varying degrees of sophistication are in use.

Figure 2 shows the block diagram for a thermodynamic

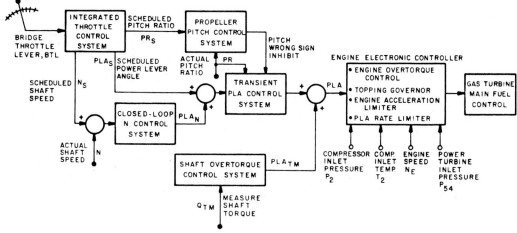

Fig. 3   Study ship propulsion control system

Table 1 Engine simulation models

Model Type	Techniques	Typical Uses
Thermodynamic	differential equations algebraic equations thermodynamic fundamentals gas tables performance data engine tests	control systems analysis and design
Quasi-dynamic	transfer functions performance maps empirical relationships transient corrections	preliminary control and system response studies trainers, simulators
Steady-state	performance maps empirical relationships	scheduling, optimization, sizing and preliminary design studies

model of the General Electric LM2500 gas turbine used for this program. This model is of the so-called functional component type wherein each major component function (for example, compressor, combustor, fuel control ...) is independently modeled. Table 1 lists three major types of gas turbine engine models from the most sophisticated (thermodynamic) to the simplest (steady state). Figure 4 shows a steady-state torque map representation of a gas turbine engine showing the engine torque-speed locus of a ship crashback transient. During Phases I and III of this program, it was mandatory to use the thermodynamic engine model. However, during Phase II (turning), an independent steady-state torque map model for each screw proved perfectly adequate. Indeed, because of the great turning simulation complexity, this was a prudent course of action.

The simulation outputs included

• about 70 gas turbine parameters, for example, temperature, pressure, flow, speed, power, enthalpy, and control actions, and

• 30 or more ship and control parameters, for example, propeller pitch, thrust, torque and speed, ship speed, and stopping distance.

Experimental data

Model basin and water tunnel tests were conducted at the David Taylor Naval Ship Research and Development Center (DTNSRDC) on scale models of ship hulls and propellers to measure performance experimentally where performance cannot readily be predicted by theory. These experimental data were used together with mathematical models in the simulations. Hydrodynamic model test data included data for fixed-pitch and controllable-pitch propellers with and without cavitation and under transient conditions such as propulsion and turning maneuvers. Propeller thrust and torque data for full maneuvering simulations must be "four-quadrant," that is, ahead, backing, crashback, and crashahead. Other hydrodynamic data included hull-propeller interactions (wake and thrust deduction factors) during crashback maneuvers and hull maneuvering coefficients to develop ship turning simulations and ship response in waves (ship motions, added resistance and propeller loading). Experimental tests were conducted on gas turbine engines to determine transient responses under acceleration, deceleration and load-drop conditions. These Navy and engine manufacturer tests were used in a continual evolution of engine simulation improvements. Additional tests conducted in laboratories or aboard ship were used to develop data on systems performance in the areas of control systems, drive trains, hydraulic systems and auxiliary machinery.

Verification

The dynamic computer simulations, based on theory and tests of machinery subsystems, were verified as a complete system by ships' trials. Highly instrumented ship propulsion systems were tested at sea with recordings of many ship, drive train, engine and control system parameters. These data after reduction and analysis were used to update, improve and verify

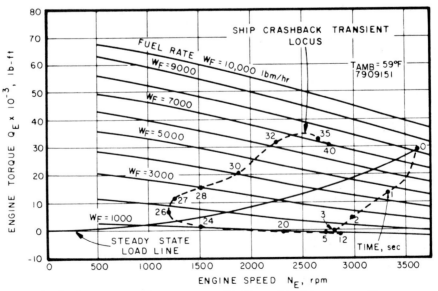

Fig. 4 Gas turbine steady-state torque with ship crashback torque-speed locus

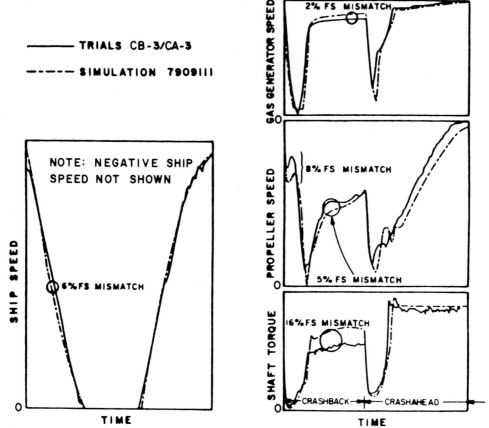

Fig. 5 Example of correlation of ship trials and simulations for crashback and crashahead maneuvers

the dynamic simulations of the total propulsion system. For numerous types of maneuvers and operating conditions, time histories of up to 160 parameters were recorded on high-density microfiche for simulation results and up to 80 parameters for ships' trials. The results, consisting of hundreds of simulations and ships' trials for various conditions and ship types, were conducted over many years and constitute a valuable data bank now in use for analysis of fleet problems and development of new ship designs.

Some sample time-history records of a destroyer crashback/crashahead maneuver from a maximum-ahead initial speed are shown in Fig. 5. The propeller data used in the simulations are based on scale-model tests. The data correlate very well in most regions of the maneuver with the exception of the shaft torque in the crashback region. Propeller model test data in the crashback quadrant results from highly turbulent conditions which do not typically correlate well with ships' trials data in crashback transients since the model tests do not adequately duplicate conditions in the region of the ship's propeller during reversing. Such difficulties have been generally reported in the literature by various investigators [2]. In our ship simulation experiences, the poorest correlation between trials and simulations is the hydrodynamic area, particularly the propeller. This is not surprising considering the scaling inaccuracies and unsteady conditions encountered during the experiments.

Reference [3] deals with the simulation techniques, limitations and results in the development of ship propulsion dynamics simulations.

Plant dynamics/control program, Phase I

Phase I consisted of three parts as follows:

1. Steady-state performance envelope

Objective—Define overall steady-state bounds for machinery and control system operation with no control compensation for a range of environmental and other conditions.

The factors considered were
- ambient temperature
- hull resistance
- propeller pitch ratio
- propeller performance degradation
- engine performance degradation

The results (for twin and single engine/shaft operation) were
- Compendium of data
- Sensitivity curves/coefficients
- Combined effects operating point predictions

Figure 6 shows an example of the sensitivity of five ship parameters to hull resistance where S_{RT} is a multiplying factor on resistance.

2. Analysis of integrated throttle control systems

Objective—Analyze performance of various integrated throttle control systems with ambient temperature compensation for the engine(s).

The conditions considered were
- ahead and astern schedules (maximum ahead to maximum astern)
- linearizing ship speed to BTL command
- ambient temperature compensation (-40 to $+140°$F) (-40 to $+60°$C)
- optimizing propeller pitch for cruising efficiency

Figure 7 shows an example of an integrated throttle control system scheduler for the study ship for a temperature range of

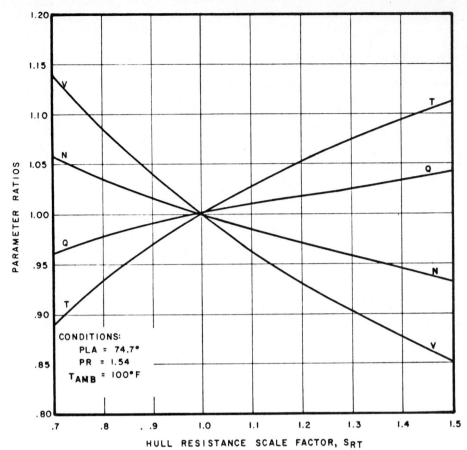

Fig. 6 Hull resistance effect on single-engine cruise operation

−40 to +140°F. Such schedulers were determined using a steady-state ship simulation at various temperatures and commanded bridge throttle lever (BTL) positions.

3. Propulsion and control system dynamics

Objective—Develop ship and propulsion control system dynamics simulations; evaluate various control system approaches to determine performance-peak transmission load tradeoffs and develop a fundamental cause-effect understanding of CP propeller propulsion systems. This part of the Phase I program was by far the most difficult to conduct and produced the most important results.

The conditions and maneuvers simulated were
- single and twin engine/shaft over −40 to 140°F ambient temperature
- acceleration, backing, crashback, crashahead at various power levels
- various control strategies for example $\dot{\tau}$, PLA/PR limiting, PLA, torque limiting, delays ...

The results were
- system dynamics and control time histories (100 variables versus time, 50 maneuvers)
- system dynamics and control cause-effect relationships
- peak loads, ship machinery and control performance in maneuvers
- evaluation of various control strategies; control to optimize maneuvering performance
- correlation of various ship propulsion simulations and trials

Two examples of important results are shown. Figure 8 shows a typical crashback time history. Many such simulations were conducted to develop tables of peak loads and maneu-

vering performance. Model tests and simulations were conducted on ship reversing dynamics and the performance of wake and thrust deduction factors during transient conditions [4]. Figure 9 shows the sensitivity of various ship load and performance parameters to the propeller pitch stroke time. This figure illustrates a typical example of an important system tradeoff area. Increasing the pitch stroke time results in decreased system loads but also poorer stopping performance.

Turning dynamics/control program, Phase II

Objective—Investigate gas turbine ship turning performance and evaluate control systems to limit shaft loads and random disturbances without significantly impairing ship performance.

The approach and conditions were
- conduct turning model tests of destroyer hull in four degrees of freedom (surge, drift, roll, yaw) to determine approximately 70 maneuvering model coefficients.
- conduct model tests of a CP propeller in turns to obtain data on propeller thrust and torque under turning conditions.
- develop ship turning simulation; compare governing methods and models and correlate with ship's trials
- compare high-speed turn performance with power and speed governing

The results were
- turning loads and control system interactions
- maneuvering performance in turns

Gas turbine ship trials have shown that some of the largest drive train loads occur during high-speed turns. These large turning loads together with crash maneuver loads must be limited automatically without a significant impact on the ship maneuverability. In addition, undesirable control system interactions and engine cycling in high-speed turns and in a seaway must be minimized. During all turns, particularly at maximum power and full rudder, random hydrodynamic loads are developed on the rudders and propellers. This buffeting with unstable flow or "hydrodynamic noise" can result in large random fluctuations of the propeller torque. For closed-loop propeller speed control systems and torque-limiting systems using measured shaft torque, this can result in undesirable engine cycling and control system interactions. Thus, every time a ship experiences a turn, random signals are introduced into the propulsion control system through the sensed shaft torque or shaft speed measuring systems. The method of controlling propeller speed also has an effect on shaft loads. Figure 10 shows the time history of a typical destroyer trials maximum-speed turn conducted with full rudder. The propulsion control system is a closed-loop propeller speed governing system that attempts to maintain a constant propeller speed. The turn is initiated to port. The starboard or outboard shaft torque exceeds the port shaft torque and the measured torque limiting signals $QTMS$ and $QTMP$ indicate highly fluctuating shaft torques during the turn. In response to a falling propeller speed $NRPMS$, the turbine power lever angle $PLANS$ increases fuel until torque limiting causes saturation of the speed controller. The signal $PLATMS$ is the output of the sensed torque-limiting control signal used to cut back PLA due to a shaft overtorque condition.

Example of turning maneuver loads

A summary of control system effects on outboard (worst-case) propeller torque for the study ship based on model tests and simulations is shown in Fig. 11. This is a time history of a turn with maximum rudder from a maximum initial speed condition. Curve 1 is a propeller speed governed case utilizing a proportional pitch control which decreases propeller pitch to limit shaft torque. Curves 2 and 3 are power and speed (with some droop) governed cases that use a torque limiter based on sensed engine parameters. Curve 4 is a power-governed condition where gas generator power (but not free turbine power) is maintained constant. This case does not use any torque limiting. Curve 5 shows a propeller speed governed case with droop because the power lever angle controlling engine fuel rate reaches a set limit. No torque limiting is used in Case 5. Curve 6 is an isochronous propeller speed governed condition with no engine fuel rate limit. This hypothetical case illustrates a worst-case condition of propeller torque presuming the engine could provide the additional power needed to maintain constant propeller speed in a turn.

Propulsion system governing dynamics/control, Phase III

Objective—Analyze performance of engine-governing systems subject to seaway disturbances and develop governing systems design guidelines and performance criteria.

The approach and conditions were

- model test ship hull and propeller in waves
- conduct spectral analysis of wave loading
- develop ship and propeller seaway disturbance models
- develop total ship propulsion simulations for various wave conditions and ship speeds

The results were

- total propulsion system simulations for operation in a seaway, power and speed governing
- cause-effect relationships
- governing criteria

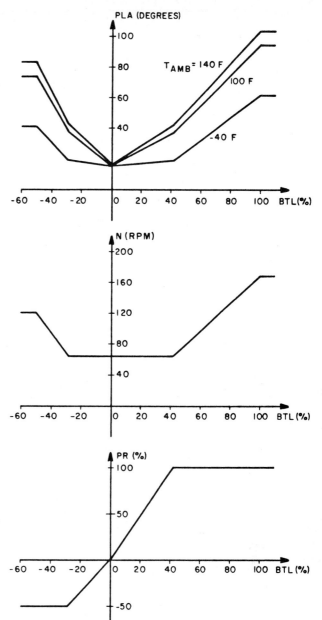

Fig. 7 Twin engine/shaft integrated throttle control with T_{AMB} compensation

Mechanism of propeller loading in waves

The wave orbital velocity is the velocity of water particles caused by the passage of waves. As a wave passes a submerged propeller, the water inflow to the propeller increases under a wave crest and decreases under a wave trough. The ship's pitching and heaving motions greatly affect the magnitude of this variational velocity as the propeller submergence changes. The varying inflow velocity manifests itself as a variation in the propeller advance coefficient J and hence a variation in propeller torque coefficient. This mechanism is the principal means by which seaway disturbances are coupled to the drive train, engine and control system.

The sequence of model tests, simulations, and analyses conducted during the propulsion system governing phase is shown in Fig. 12. This approach was taken to provide a fundamental understanding of seaway action on the propulsion system and

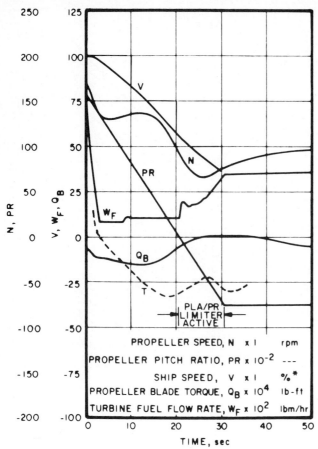

Fig. 8 Example of ship crashback from full ahead

PROPELLER SPEED, N × 1   rpm
PROPELLER PITCH RATIO, PR × 10^{-2} ---
SHIP SPEED, V × 1   %*
PROPELLER BLADE TORQUE, Q_B × 10^4 lb-ft
TURBINE FUEL FLOW RATE, W_F × 10^2 lbm/hr

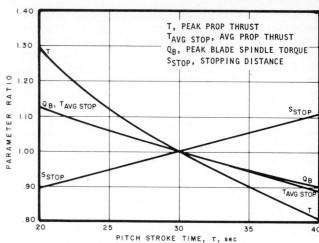

T, PEAK PROP THRUST
$T_{AVG\ STOP}$, AVG PROP THRUST
Q_B, PEAK BLADE SPINDLE TORQUE
S_{STOP}, STOPPING DISTANCE

Fig. 9 Effect of propeller pitch stroke time, τ, on crashback performance

determine general cause-effect relationships applicable to all ship propulsion systems. In particular, for gas turbine ships, the low inertia drive train, variable-geometry engines and closed-loop propeller speed control systems are susceptible to seaway-caused cycling and instability in maneuvers [5].

Figure 13 shows a simplified diagram of a ship propulsion control system using both power- and speed-governing control loops. In this case, the primary control system is a power-governed gas generator control that maintains constant gas generator speed, N_{GG}. A scheduled power lever angle (PLA_S) and scheduled propeller speed (N_S) result from the bridge throttle lever command (BTL). Similarly, BTL schedules propeller pitch ratio, PR_S.

In a gas generator power-governed control system, the free turbine and propeller speeds are scheduled by means of PLA command with no assurance that a particular shaft speed can be achieved or repeated. To eliminate the ambient temperature influence on engine power, the throttle control system should include ambient temperature compensation. A speed-governing control loop may be added as shown in Fig. 13 to provide closed-loop speed feedback to bias the scheduled PLA command. The speed controller can incorporate integral plus proportional control, sea state gain adjust and various nonlinearities to achieve a desired speed control characteristic. The closed-loop propeller speed control may achieve near iso-chronous speed control in a relatively calm sea and repeatable propeller speed response to BTL command invariant with time or system changes. Undesirable closed-loop propeller speed control characteristics include engine cycling in waves and propulsion system transients in turns.

Dynamics/control machinery impacts, Phase IV

Under this phase of the program, to be completed in 1983, the impact of the entire controls R&D program on various propulsion system design practices will be determined. This will include, for example, load levels and safety factors for gears, bearings, clutches and shafting together with ship and control system response tradeoffs under various conditions.

Solving fleet machinery and control problems

Problems unknown with steam plants are surfacing with naval gas turbine ships. These problems are a result of the application of new technologies (gas turbines, controllable-pitch propellers and increased automation) to ship propulsion. The controls R&D program has led to development of techniques and solutions for fleet problems using computer simulation of total propulsion plants. Using such simulations, a variety of machinery and control/automation problems have been rapidly resolved and hardware or operational changes identified. This capability was not initially foreseen, but developed gradually as certain types of problems became amenable to solution via simulations. These simulations have already become an important tool in providing rapid identification, assessment and solution of a multitude of control, automation and machinery problems. A partial list of problems successfully solved by this approach are given below:

• *CP propeller failure simulations*—With the failure of an experimental CP propeller on a steam frigate test ship in 1974, the U.S. Navy began an exhaustive investigation of CP propeller loads. Analyses of structures, materials, dynamic simulations of worst-case loads in maneuvers and propeller stress tests were conducted because of the importance of CP propellers to the new gas turbine ships then entering the fleet.

• *Trials performance predictions*—Performance predictions of the DD-963 class destroyers in worst-case propulsion maneuvers were conducted prior to trials. This information was used to develop trials and propeller test programs, the results of which were correlated against predictions and used to develop operational strategy and experience for control system designs. In addition, these full-scale tests provided valuable data for refining and verifying the simulations.

• *Propulsion system cycling in seaway and turns*—The controls interactions and fluctuations in turns and seaway cycling leading to premature engine wear in some parts of vari-

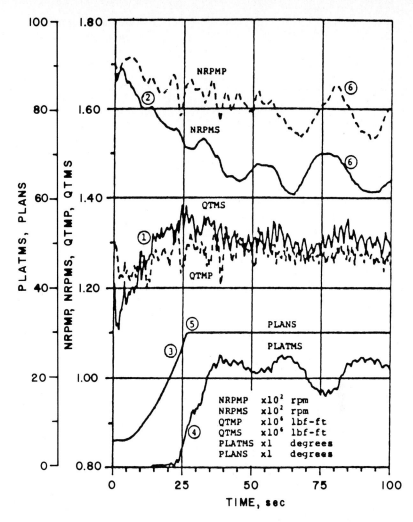

1. Turning increases Q (torque)
2. Increased Q decreases N
3. Speed controller responds to N
4. Shaft Q-controller activates
5. Speed controller saturates

NOTATIONS
NRPM = propeller speed
P = port
PLA = power lever angle
QTM = measured shaft torque
S = starboard

Fig. 10   Example of high-speed turning trials

NRPMP	x10²	rpm
NRPMS	x10²	rpm
QTMP	x10⁶	lbf-ft
QTMS	x10⁶	lbf-ft
PLATMS	x1	degrees
PLANS	x1	degrees

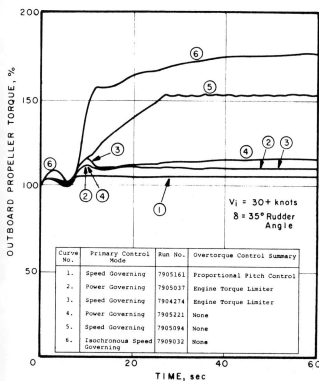

V_i = 30+ knots
δ = 35° Rudder Angle

Curve No.	Primary Control Mode	Run No.	Overtorque Control Summary
1.	Speed Governing	7905161	Proportional Pitch Control
2.	Power Governing	7905037	Engine Torque Limiter
3.	Speed Governing	7904274	Engine Torque Limiter
4.	Power Governing	7905221	None
5.	Speed Governing	7905094	None
6.	Isochronous Speed Governing	7909032	None

Fig. 11   Example of shaft overtorque control in high-speed turns

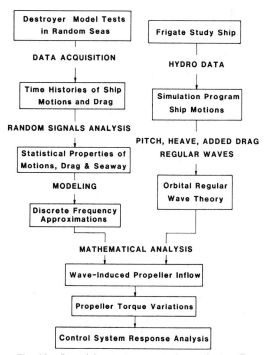

Fig. 12   Propulsion system governing project outline

Naval Gas Turbine Ship Propulsion Dynamics

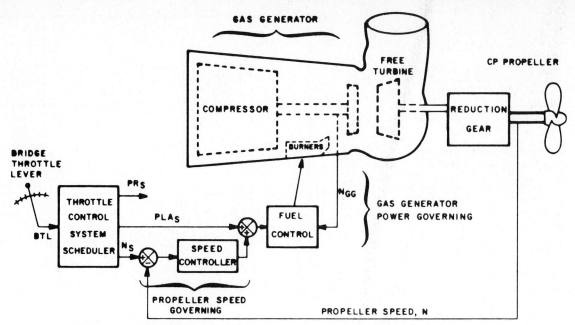

Fig. 13 Simplified ship propulsion control system showing speed- and power-governing loops

able-geometry engines are influenced by the propulsion governing system design. Simulations, model tests and trials have evaluated speed and power-governing performance. Ship trials of several governing methods are planned for 1983. These results will affect propulsion control system design on new ships and possible control system modifications to existing systems.

• *Shaft torque-limiting systems*—Ship turning, as noted earlier, can introduce very undesirable engine power fluctuations via measured torque-limiting systems in some ship types. Simulations of torque-limiting systems employing filters to remove effects of hydrodynamically induced torque variations in turns have been conducted and improved controllers have been designed and readied for trials.

• *Trials-simulation correlations*—Highly instrumented gas turbine propulsion control system ship trials have been conducted to evaluate problems related to engine and control system transients in certain maneuvers. These trials were planned and their results predicted by simulations. Analysis and interpretation of trials results have been aided immeasurably by simulations where system complexity almost precludes detailed trials interpretations without such an analytical tool. Trials results were then used to improve both simulations and control system design procedures.

• *Maneuver optimization and loads reduction*—Drive train loads reduction, ship maneuver and propeller pitch optimization, propulsion safety, and protection systems are all related to control system design. Various control methods and their tradeoffs in ship performance have been simulated with new controls being designed for ship trials and eventual fleet improvement retrofits.

• *Gas turbine ship's service electric plant overloads*—Overloads on paralleled ship's service turbogenerators can cause total electric plant shutdown if one turbine shuts down for any reason and the remaining turbogenerator is tripped out due to overload. Simulations of a ship gas turbine electric plant were conducted to study various alternatives to preserve electric plant continuity by very rapid reconfiguration of the turbine and electric load systems. This effort led to successful design of a turbine overload protection system.

Impact on new propulsion systems

Systems engineering studies utilizing dynamics, control, optimization and design simulations are being used to evaluate new propulsion, control, automation and monitoring system concepts and develop ship specifications. Completed projects which had their genesis in this dynamics and controls R&D program are listed in the following:

• *New ships*—A dynamic analysis of the propulsion control system is now a typical requirement for most Navy ships. This dynamic analysis begins with development of a simulation of the engines, ship, drive train, and thruster as well as the propulsion control system. The dynamic anlaysis is used to predict peak loads, for example propeller torques, thrusts, blade spindle torques and ship performance in acceleration, crashback, crashahead and backing maneuvers. In addition, for these maneuvers, engine and control performance is determined for various control system designs, for example pitch/rpm schedulers, *PLA* temperature compensation, control system limiters, setpoints, time constants, gains and a multitude of controllers dealing with torque limiting, shaft brakes and clutches. In effect, the propulsion control system is designed by an iterative process centered around a propulsion control system and machinery simulation. Recent examples of this approach include the DD-963 destroyers, FFG-7 frigates, PGG-511 and PCG-612 CODOG gunboats and LSD-41 auxiliary ships. The simulation process does not end with the completion of the ship; it continues with the design of propulsion plant simulators used for training operational and maintenance personnel.

• *New propulsion systems*—Dynamics and control simulations are being utilized in feasibility analyses, specifications, preliminary and/or detailed design of the following new propulsion systems: COGAS (combined gas and steam) propulsion plant [now called RACER (Rankine cycle energy recovery)] for application to Navy destroyers, superconducting electric drive, and reversing reduction gear ship transmission systems. Finally, dynamics and control results of these programs are being summarized, condensed and unified in a design guide for use by propulsion system engineers.

Reflections on approach

The ship propulsion dynamics and controls R&D program has a total history now approaching two decades encompassing well over 30 large simulation efforts. The major, most-concentrated portion of this work was accomplished over a six-year period from 1976 to 1982. The sponsoring Navy codes and staff of Propulsion Dynamics, Inc. required a long-term commitment to the program goals and persistence in the face of numerous technical and organizational problems. Their recounting is of value here for the insights that can be brought to bear on future work and guidance in similar programs.

First and foremost, this work is *systems engineering* covering a wide variety of disciplines and specialties which had to be melded and coordinated to achieve the desired results. These areas include, for example, hydrodynamics, thermodynamics, kinematics, marine engineering, control theory, computer simulation and various specialties such as propellers, hull-propeller interactions, gas turbine engine dynamics, seaway characterization, ship trials, data processing and model testing. Since the program funding would not permit fielding a large team to satisfy all these resource requirements, a limited number of systems engineers became multi-hatted in this work. Such a systems team takes time to develop and in this case the team grew with the job. However, we discovered that such broad, wide-ranging systems engineering work was not of interest to most engineers, who preferred to work in more traditional and circumscribed roles. Those who accepted the challenge became strong disciples.

A number of important lessons were learned. The model testing experiments and ships trials must be very closely coordinated and directed by the systems engineers in charge of the project and the simulation efforts. This includes preparing the test agenda and instrumentation and participating in or observing tests. Test data should be evaluated as quickly as possible before the test program terminates. Otherwise an expensive test or trials program can be jeopardized with missing or inadequate data. Particularly on ship's trials the data acquisition system should include some capability for on-the-spot data processing, analysis and playback to permit data evaluation prior to leaving the ship. Ship's trials in their entirety include planning, scheduling, data acquisition equipment installation and removal, travel, data processing and documentation. This procedure is typically very complex, frustrating and costly; hence, care must be taken to prevent the ultimate catastrophe of meaningless or nonexistent data.

As noted earlier, our experience shows that the greatest inaccuracies in ship dynamics simulations are associated with the hydrodynamic models. These models are based on experimental data subject to scaling, scatter, instrumentation and other errors. Since we are dealing with turbulent and non-steady conditions, such data can be expected to reflect scatter and inaccuracies. From our point of view, the entire simulation exists essentially to provide transient information.

Once the system modeling has been completed, the simulations should be used to investigate all conditions of interest and the results analyzed immediately, especially in the early phases of the simulations. Many iterations and fine tuning of the simulations are usually required with continual checks on conformance to reality before the simulations are ready for "production runs." Results of simulation exercises (or runs) should be analyzed and described as the work proceeds. Their complexity usually dims perception and sharp insights if the work is reported on months later. Each good simulation run should be treated as a valuable "computer experiment" with each run coded and stored (for example, on high-density microfiche) for later retrieval. Another alternative is to assume the stored simulation program will be available at a later date to generate additional runs for various new conditions or design changes. We have found that the storing of all our successful computer runs (and even a few selected unsuccessful ones) on microfiche has provided an invaluable data bank for instant access to the behavior of complete propulsion systems where the immense amount of data generated cannot be realistically reported. Often by using this approach our files contain answers to yet-unasked questions which can be handled rapidly and efficiently by a staff familiar with the history of this work.

While intuition and experience are powerful allies to the engineer, they can become a trap when dealing with very complex nonlinear systems. During the course of this program, the simulations taught us never to be overconfident in predicting or assuming system behavior. Invariably, when peculiar results were analyzed, it was found that our understanding was lacking and the simulations became a continuous learning process to extract new information. It was found that the greatest insights came from the reporting part of each phase. The discipline imposed in writing the final reports results in one of the most prolific and useful parts of the project.

Summary and conclusions

The U.S. Naval ship propulsion dynamics and control systems R&D program has proven very successful in its primary goal of developing a theoretical design basis for gas turbine propulsion systems. The orientation has been primarily dynamics, loads and performance information, but with heavy emphasis on the role of control systems. This program has resulted in a capability to conduct total ship propulsion dynamics and control simulations with good trials correlations overall. The results of this program are now used for the following:

• *New ship design*—Most Navy ship propulsion control systems are now designed and verified by computer simulations with model tests and trials as described in this paper. The results of this R&D will impact on new ship design.

• *New propulsion plant R&D*—Evaluation of new plants, control and monitoring approaches and development of system specifications, contractor guidance and monitoring are now typically conducted using simulations supported with model tests as a tool.

• *Fleet hardware analysis and improvements*—Rapid solutions for numerous systems problems related to loads, performance, environment, wear and malfunction are being developed utilizing a growing simulation and data bank capability in propulsion systems.

This paper has dealt exclusively with gas turbine propulsion systems. However, as these methods developed, they were used in all types of plants, including diesel, steam and combined propulsion systems for both naval and commercial applications.

The purpose of this paper has been to describe an important and long-running U.S. Navy R&D program begun with the advent of ship gas turbine propulsion. This paper was essentially restricted to an overview of the program, discussing problems, approaches and accomplishments. Several examples were shown to illustrate some of the results and conclusions. Future papers will deal with the detailed results of this program, which cannot be adequately covered in a single paper.

Acknowledgment

The U.S. Navy ship propulsion dynamics and control systems R&D program owes its existence to the funding support and encouragement provided by the following NAVSEA and DTNSRDC individuals who recognized the R&D needs of a rapidly changing technology: G. M. Boatwright, A. A. Wolf,

J. Abbott, R. R. Peterson, M. R. Hauschildt, C. L. Miller, R. Lisiewski, D. Tempesco and H. D. Marron. For administrative and technical direction, we valued the enthusiastic efforts of M. Resner and J. McIntire. In particular, we are indebted to the late Mr. Miller, former NAVSEA gas turbine program manager, who funded most of this program and whose untimely death in late 1981 was deeply felt by all of us in the naval gas turbine R&D community.

References

1 Rubis, C. J., "Acceleration and Steady-State Propulsion Dynamics of a Gas Turbine Ship with Controllable-Pitch Propeller," TRANS. SNAME, Vol. 80, 1972.

2 Canham, H. J. S., Mason, D., and Dorrian, A. M., "A Comparison Between Propeller Characteristics Derived From Full-Scale Trials and From Tank Results," *Proceedings*, Fourth Ship Control Systems Symposium, Den Helder, The Netherlands, 1975.

3 *Control and Dynamic Systems*, *Advances in Theory and Application*, C. T. Leondes, Ed., Academic Press, New York, Vol. 18, Chapter 7, 1982.

4 Rubis, C. J. and Harper, T. R., "Reversing Dynamics of a Gas Turbine Ship with Controllable-Pitch Propeller," *Proceedings*, Fifth Ship Control Systems Symposium, Annapolis, Md., 1978.

5 Rubis, C. J., "Gas Turbine Performance Under Varying Torque Propeller Loads," *International Shipbuilding Progress*, Jan. 1974.

Discussion

Richard S. Carleton, Member

Mr. Rubis and Mr. Harper have contributed a valuable paper to the literature covering propulsion dynamics and control systems of Navy ships. They show how a small group of farseeing engineers persisted and, at the right time, developed a new tool for analyzing complex problems. Speaking from my own experience of working for the U. S. Navy at that time, I can testify that this tool was needed. When analyzing control problems with gas turbine ships at sea, or trying to design a control system for new gas turbine ships, we automatically turned to propulsion dynamics because of the expertise they had developed in this field. Without the help provided by this analysis method, we would have been forced to rely on intuition and cut-and-try methods to solve some of the difficult problems that came up.

I would also like to add my commendations to the list of individuals in the Navy who recognized the need for this program and made sure that it was funded—in particular, Charles Miller, whose foresight not only in this program but over the past 25 years has helped the U. S. Navy introduce gas turbine engines with a minimum of problems. His death in 1981 brought much sadness to the Navy engineering community.

Referring to the paper, I would like to ask a question. On the third page, the authors speak of the complex automation required on gas turbine ships. The question is, "Have we gone too far?"

The authors speak of the need for automation of all engine supporting auxiliaries with automatic subsystem sequences, so that it may be possible to go from light-off to full power in two to three minutes. Is it really necessary to light off in two to three minutes? Perhaps a manual starting sequence that takes five to eight minutes would be satisfactory and allow less complexity of automation. Has this been studied?

I am interested in the stress that is put on ambient temperature. Studies are done with temperature ranges of −40 to 140°F. This seems rather extreme. This may be of some academic interest, but in actual practice a range of 25 to 95°F would probably cover most cases and might not result in as drastic an effect. It might also be kept in mind that the rate of change of ambient temperature is normally very slow and that any series of maneuvers would be done within a very narrow band of temperature change. Navy engines are rated so that they will have adequate margin under most ambient temperature conditions.

All of the work shown in the paper has been done for ships using controllable-pitch propellers. With renewed interest in using methods such as reversing gears or reversing clutches and fixed-pitch propellers, I wonder whether any studies have been done or will be done using these modes of reversal. I would be interested in any results the authors may have.

Gerald M. Boatwright, Member

My congratulations to the authors in the preparation of an outstanding paper covering the background, need and uses pertaining to the understanding of propulsion dynamics.

The authors are also to be commended for their multidiscipline approach and their persistence in understanding all aspects of the system from load to prime mover and controls. For example, a few years ago many analysts made the mistaken assumption that all propellers behaved the same under transient conditions. This was partly true when a great majority of propellers operated at high speed and had low pitch ratio and narrow blades. Today's propellers cover a wide spectrum of these parameters and each performs differently under transient load conditions. This was first best shown in a Russian propeller test series reported in 1958 by Minovich [6] (additional references follow some discussions). This test series was given wide distribution within the naval community after its BuShips Translation No. 697 [6] was made available. Its use was included in a paper, "Effect of Ship Maneuvers on Machinery Component Design" [7] in 1965. This paper, coauthored by this discusser J. J. Nelson, includes the following paragraph in its Introduction:

> "It is the purpose of this paper to explain in a simple manner . . . the methods used in determining propulsion plant drive system transient loadings. If the method and basic data inputs needed are better understood, more analysis will lead to more reliable propulsion systems."

The authors of the present paper have taken up this challenge and have perfected their techniques with many simulations during the past 17 years. This discusser was especially appreciative of their work on the DD 963 class destroyers during his close association with this project from 1967 to 1978.

Additional references

6 Minovich, I. Ya., "Investigation of Hydrodynamic Characteristics of Screw Propellers Under Conditions of Reversing and Calculation Methods for Backing of Ships," BuShips Translation No. 697, 1958.

7 Boatwright, G. M. and Turner, J. J., "Effect of Ship Maneuvers on Machinery Component Design," *Proceedings*, Second Annual Symposium of the Association of Senior Engineers of the Bureau of Ships, 26 March 1965.

A. Witcher,[4] Visitor

[The views expressed herein are the opinions of the discusser and not necessarily those of the Department of Defense or the Department of the Navy.]

The authors are to be commended for the preparation of an excellent paper, which provides a concise overview of the Navy's involvement in computer simulations of propulsion

---

[4] Naval Sea Systems Command, Washington, D.C.

dynamics and control and use of simulation to assist in resolution of emerging fleet machinery problems. They are modest in not highlighting the significance simulation has played in contributing to timely solution of critical fleet machinery problems. The value/usefulness that dynamics and control simulations can provide in the design and development of ships systems, other than gas turbine control systems, could have been stressed to a greater extent.

Simulation was first used to assist in solution of fleet problems in the CP propeller blade failure investigation. In this early application, simulation was not given serious consideration by the Navy engineers involved. However, as simulation became successfully applied to additional fleet problems, its use as a diagnostic tool became highly regarded. Simulation recently received its greatest recognition and accolades in the solution of the gas turbine generator overload problem. This problem occurred with the failure for any reason of any one of two paralleled gas turbine driven generating systems. The surviving generator would receive an immediate transient load and could be tripped out on an overload condition even when the connected steady-state load was within the capacity of one generator. Simulation allowed timely solution of a gas turbine control problem in this electric plant application. Corrective action was implemented in all ships of the class prior to the ships entering the fleet. Solution of this problem through the conventional method would have been a lengthy process due to the various organizations and component manufacturers involved and due to the various technical disciplines involved within these organizations. It is safe to say simulation permitted an optimum solution at least cost, in addition to providing new insights into the electrical system design. Failure to correct this problem could have placed the future use of gas turbines for ships' electrical power generation in jeopardy.

The technology and experience gained in the R&D programs show that computer simulation has application in other areas of ship system design, specifically the electrical and piping systems. Today's modern gas turbine powered combatant is almost totally dependent upon uninterrupted and sustained electrical power to carry out not only its normal functions, but also vital combat functions. Loss of electrical power during combat, due to a hit, near miss or system casualty renders the ship defenseless and essentially could be equated to loss of the ship. World War II combatants could maintain propulsion without electrical power by utilizing the steam auxiliaries, had steam-driven fire pumps, and could fire most of the ships weapons without electrical power. Surface combatants now require high-quality electrical power for all electronic and combat weapons systems to maintain propulsion and even to maintain fire-fighting and survivability capabilities operational. Because of the vital importance of the electrical generating and distribution systems to the ships' missions (in addition to its extreme vulnerability to battle damage) urgent studies should be undertaken to maximize survivability of these systems. Computer simulation is the prime candidate for such studies. Simulations can provide information for development of automated casualty detection and appropriate response equipment to keep power to the maximum number of essential ship functions after suffering battle damage. The complexity of the electrical system and its connected loads/systems no longer permits manual responses.

Fluid (piping) system design is another area in which simulation can provide a significant impact. A minimal amount of work is currently being done in this area. Excessive flow rates in the machinery seawater cooling systems are causing piping component and heat exchanger tube erosion. Simulation is being applied to determine correct orifice sizing and location so as to reduce flow rate and noise thereby enhancing ship silencing. Use of simulation in the design stage could avoid

building in and later having to correct or live with these problems throughout the life of the ship. Fire main and electronic/weapons cooling systems have annoying deficiencies that could be avoided if simulations were applied in the design phase.

The authors note organizational problems: that this area is multidisciplinary systems engineering, and that most engineers prefer not to work in this type of wide-ranging systems engineering. These problems must be addressed and resolved. The proven, successful track records demonstrate that system simulation can and should be applied to a number of other ship systems to enhance and optimize the initial design. System engineering within the Navy engineering organization must be given greater emphasis throughout the ship design phase. Recognition must be given to the fact that an engineering plant is not just a number of independent components interconnected by piping, cabling, or a mechanical drive train, but a fully integrated system that should be initially designed to function together in an optimum fashion under all operating and casualty control situations. This responsibility should be specifically assigned within the engineering organization. Program managers do not have the resources to re-engineer systems or correct problems that were inadvertently built into the system. Dynamic simulation has proven to be an extremely valuable design and diagnostic tool; therefore its use should be extended to a much wider range of applications. It must lose the connotation of an R&D investigative or design phase approach and become a full-fledged tool of the systems engineer.

Donald M. Wray, Member

The use of computer simulation for the advancement of gas turbine propulsion dynamics and control has strong merit in naval ship systems engineering. The authors are commended for providing this excellent and comprehensive paper that helps us all understand the significance of their labors.

Three areas will be discussed here: problems and requirements of gas turbine ship propulsion control, computer simulation, and solving fleet machinery and control problems.

The requirement for a relatively high degree of automation in gas turbine ships is understood. In the FFG-7 Class design every effort was made to reduce manpower. Manning level was reduced from early projections of 239 to 185 in contract design. Through the use of gas turbine engine automation and reliability centered maintenance (RCM) the reduction in manning goal was realized [8]. The paper does an excellent job of relating the importance of propulsion dynamics and simulation to attain the most effective automated control system consistent with reduced manning levels.

Regarding the integrated throttle control corrected for ambient temperature effects, I would ask how significant the ambient temperature change is to the gas turbine engine output as compared to pressure ratio and engine speed, which are major factors in the torque calculations accomplished in the free-standing electronic enclosure (FSEE). Are the temperature effects of such magnitude to warrant increasing the cost and complexity of the control system?

Engine overspeed in a load drop situation, a concern of the authors, has been evaluated at the Navy's land-based test site at the Naval Ship Systems Engineering Station in Philadelphia. It has been proved that the FSEE can adequately control the gas turbine at no load (broken shaft at full power), thereby providing required overspeed protection.

The authors are commended for achieving a viable means to conduct simulation studies to resolve machinery problems through dynamic tests with various modes and sea states. They have also developed an analytical data base to support propulsion plant control for DD-963 class ships.

A significant area of concern has been exposed by the authors, that is, an inherent limitation to accurately simulating the hydrodynamic portion of the ship's model. The previous studies of four-quadrant data do not correlate well with DD-963 class trial data. This has necessitated changing the model to better predict actual trial results. There is an immediate need for research in the hydrodynamics area which can accurately correlate with actual ship data. The realization of this will be an improved means of providing input to new construction ships to accurately predict performance prior to construction rather than reworking the computer model to reflect ship trial data. Potential inadequacies would then be highlighted instead of waiting until construction and trials are complete.

There exists a fleet machinery problem in the gas turbine area which should be a task of the R&D program. Fretting (wearing away the shroud by the trunnion of the inlet guide vane first and second stage) is a continuing and serious problem in the fleet. Replacement is required prior to 6000 hours, sometimes as early as 2500 hours. Left undetected, this would result in a catastrophic failure. Cycling of the variable-geometry gas turbine in power maneuvers, vibration and alignment have all been offered as possible culprits in this recurring maintenance problem. Perhaps computer simulation could provide the timely answer to this maintenance problem.

Additional references

8 Garzke, William A. and Kerr, George, "Major Factors in Frigate Design," TRANS. SNAME, Vol. 89, 1981.

Eugene P. Weinert, Member

[The views expressed herein are the opinions of the discusser and not necessarily those of the Department of Defense or the Department of the Navy.]

This paper includes a very comprehensive view of significant work done in design, modeling and shipboard experience with gas turbine ship propulsion control systems. The program spans about ten years and has enabled Navy ships to benefit from careful preparation and subsequent modification of several control systems.

Operational benefits of gas turbine powered ships are substantial and automation should make the most of them. I agree that propulsion control system design is a critical part of the ship design process in maneuvering performance, drive train transient loads and to provide the interface between men and machinery. But I believe steady-state performance, optimum use of people and maximum reliability of machinery are equally important contributions. Man is *the* critical closure element to the *full* control system! Early consideration of human factors is vitally important to the ultimate success of the full system. Boredom, conflicting signals and inaccurate human input to the outer loop should be minimized by early consideration in control station design.

Conflict through duplication of corrective signals in both inner and outer control loops should be resisted. For example, in most gas turbine control systems, ambient air temperature at the compressor inlet modifies the inner loop control. But to also modify the outer loop control is counterproductive duplication which can only reduce the possibility of developing full power when 100°F air enters the compressor. It should, however, protect the power turbine on a super-cold day when the bridge throttle level (BTL) calls for more torque than either the power turbine or the reduction gear can transmit. Therefore, ambient temperature override should be effective on the cold end only. Another example would be the provision of an overspeed trip for the gas generator of a split turbine engine. The power turbine needs overspeed protection; the gas generator cannot overspeed so long as it is topped by either compressor outlet pressure or turbine inlet temperature limiters.

The operator should not be expected to provide engine response in the normal operating mode. But exception should be accomplishable if the automation is so slow that manual control would be quicker in an emergency. For example, the crashback rate of current gas turbine ships could be substantially improved (more than 40 percent) by permitting the operator to move the pitch command levers with the throttle (PLA) control set for *full shaft speed*. Current doctrine in most navies calls for the throttle to be closed to IDLE setting, pitch changed slowly and steadily to reverse setting, and the engine to be brought up slowly to full astern. Fear of overspeed of propulsion machinery leads propulsion ship designers astray, however. Direct reduction of pitch causes a decrease in torque absorption by the propeller but proper timing and rotational mass aid the operator to reduce pitch through the limited region of minimum torque and changing forces on the propeller blades. Note that, with shaft speed control and *proper* timing of pitch change, torque reversal (initiator of the feared overspeed) cannot occur. Furthermore, even with intentionally incorrect timing of the pitch change, the inner loop response is far greater than the acceleration capability of the whole power train and the outer loop could be designed to automatically and correctively respond to shaft acceleration occurring with a decreasing torque. It should also be noted that the power turbine overspeed trip is designed and, for the LM2500, demonstrated to prevent overspeed with instantaneous dropping of load.

Authors' Closure

We wish to thank the discussers of this paper for their perceptive remarks and commendations, and hope our closure will answer various questions raised and provide additional elaboration in some areas.

R. S. Carleton—Mr. Carleton asks "Have we gone too far?" in the automation required for gas turbine ships. Our response to this question could require another paper. But, we will reply with brevity. This question has been and continues to be asked endlessly by almost anyone concerned with naval ship procurement, design or operation. Surely one of the major factors in this question is the explosive growth of technology upon which automation is based. It is now estimated that the fastest growing technology, namely, electronics and computers, doubles every three years. Compare this technology growth with the LM2500 gas turbine engine (a mainstay engine of the Navy). Over approximately the past 12 years since its introduction, the supporting controls/automation technology has increased by a factor of 16 assuming this change rate persisted over that time. Making these projections over the next 20 years is startling! To be more specific in answering the question: Most design engineers in this field realize that a major driving force for automation is performance. It is particularly evident with gas turbine plants where an absolute minimum of control and automation is necessary. We would rather not answer without qualifications and space well beyond the scope of these discussions whether we have gone "too far" in automation. However, it is almost certain that the trend toward increased performance and automation will greatly intensify. Once the technology is available, the pressure to use it in military systems (where performance is practically everything) is overwhelming.

Relative to subsystem sequences (as in gas turbine starting): a primary consideration is safety and always correct control of machinery. The "automation" here is almost a necessity and the speed of response is a useful byproduct. Manual backup (where feasible) is always a central consideration for damage control especially in combatant ships.

The ambient temperature range of -40 to $+140°F$ is a typical Navy specification for operating environments. Of course, these extremes are rarely encountered, but for purposes of control system design they are the extreme conditions. It is true that ship maneuvers (unlike airplane maneuvers) are executed at an essentially constant ambient temperature. Nonetheless, ambient temperature has such a large effect on engine performance that fuel control scheduling must be compensated for temperature.

As we pointed out in the paper, most of the controls R&D program centered on ship dynamics using CP propellers. However, we have done considerable work with fixed-pitch propellers, electric drive, reversing gear and hydraulic reversing systems. For example, the latter two systems are currently under investigation by our staff.

G. M. Boatwright—We are greatly indebted to Mr. Boatwright for his leadership in fostering development of ship propulsion dynamics and control simulations. As a NAVSEA program manager, his enthusiasm and funding resulted in the very first project which led to the entire controls R&D program. As the propulsion system project manager for the DD-963 class destroyers, Mr. Boatwright was to a large extent responsible for overseeing the introduction of gas turbine propulsion into the Navy. He continued in this role with distinction until his retirement after the DD-963 ships became operational.

The Miniovich series of 18 fixed-pitch propellers is a major reference work and, to our knowledge, is still one of the few complete four-quadrant propeller series available. One of our early tasks was conversion of the Miniovich propeller data from the normal K_T, K_Q versus J forms into the modified coefficient forms (see the propeller data in the left of Fig. 1 of the paper). This method of propeller representation in either of two modified forms has been used extensively by our staff over many years and is now becoming a rather standard practice in ship propulsion dynamics simulations.

A. Witcher—In commenting on Mr. Witcher's remarks, we wish to acknowledge his NAVSEA role in keeping the DD-963 class destroyers operational. He has noted with concern how the ships' electrical plant has become crucial to the operation and survival of modern combatant ships loaded with electrically dependent propulsion, auxiliary, weapons and damage control systems. Starting with the turbine overload simulation program in 1980 our staff began the development of large-scale electric plant simulations which are now continuing. The experience accumulated from the propulsion dynamics and control systems R&D program is a tremendous advantage in accelerating this electric plant dynamics and control simulation effort. These simulations and other systems engineering studies underway are part of the urgent studies he recommends to increase the survivability of vital ship systems.

We have observed for many years how badly an increased awareness and use of systems engineering are needed in this area. Unfortunately, the technological needs of systems engineering require the crossing and cooperation between various organizations, jurisdictions and disciplines. Thus, progress in systems engineering becomes a problem of many facets involving conflicting human relationships and sometimes narrowly defined interests. We wholeheartedly agree that dynamic simulation should and will be extended to a wider range of applications, including (as is now happening) its use as a diagnostic tool for fleet problems. We consider ourselves fortunate to have helped spearhead the Navy in this direction.

D. M. Wray—As noted by Mr. Wray, the LM2500 engine control system contains a torque computer which predicts engine output shaft torque based on the measured variables of ambient temperature and pressure, power turbine speed and turbine inlet pressure. The measured ambient temperature is a correction on a stored torque performance map in terms of

engine pressure ratio. Its effect on torque computation is relatively small (about 0.1 percent torque per deg F at $100°F$).

However, the effect of ambient temperature on engine power in terms of an uncompensated power lever angle is quite large, amounting to about 0.5 to 1.0 percent/deg F. It is this latter effect which requires throttle signal compensation for ambient temperature as noted in the paper.

We were involved in portions of the engine drop-load test program at NAVSSES. Based on the results of these tests the LM2500 engine simulation program was improved by the General Electric company to more accurately predict the overspeed excursions following an instantaneous drop-load condition.

We have noted in some previous publications as well as in this paper that a problem with hydrodynamic data persists. Scale-model tests are conducted on hulls and propellers. The experimental data are then used in dynamics simulations. These ship propulsion dynamics simulations essentially exist to provide transient information. Yet, the hydrodynamics part of the simulations is based on steady-state or "quasi-steady" data. The difficulties and limitations of even steady-state hydrodynamic model tests are well known, while virtually no transient hydrodynamic testing is done in this area. Reference [3] provides a discussion of the limitations of simulation involving highly complex nonlinear systems. Interesting enough, and fortunate for us, considering these limitations (not to mention cavitation, air drawing, wave effects and hull/propeller nonlinearities), the simulation results correlate remarkably well with trials except in crashback. As we note in our paper and also noted by other investigators, the propeller crashback quadrant is an area where additional research is needed to improve ship performance simulation predictions. In cooperation with DTNSRDC we conducted some work in this area including hull/propeller interactions in transients as reported in reference [4].

Mr. Wray concludes his comments with a discussion of a gas turbine wear problem influenced by engine cycling. We have been developing analytical solutions to this problem with simulations comparing power and speed governed gas turbine engines in various seaway conditions. This problem was briefly mentioned several times in the paper. Within the next year ship trials are planned to investigate the validity of these governing simulations and to test hardware modifications designed via the use of simulation to reduce engine cycling induced by turns and seaway.

Eugene P. Weinert—We welcome the remarks of Mr. Weinert, who has been a sounding board for us on numerous questions concerning performance of gas turbine engines. As part of the controls R&D program, transient testing of both the FT4 and LM2500 gas turbines together with drop-load tests were conducted at the Naval Ship Systems Engineering Station (NAVSSES) with his cooperation.

He makes an interesting control system design observation. Our investigations also indicate that engine temperature compensation should be done only once, preferably as part of the inner-loop engine controls. This should then result in engine performance essentially invariant with ambient temperature, requiring no further need of temperature compensation at various places in the outer-loop control system. Compensation of the limiting controllers (such as the FSEE overtorque controller) without compensating PLA for temperature is inadequate based on our investigations.

The operator at the handle of the propeller speed or throttle command signal should not be expected to be able to provide always proper engine response commands. This function should be scheduled or controlled so as to provide, rapid, always correctly limited machinery control irrespective of operator commands. The crashback headreach of U. S. Navy gas turbine ships is already remarkably good. Any substantial improvements would incur the penalty of greatly increased transient drive train loads during the crashback maneuver. In particular, maintaining PLA at full power and rapidly reducing propeller pitch while relying on the system topping governor and overspeed controls to prevent overspeed leads to peak thrusts and spindle torques very much greater than the maximum ahead conditions. Such increased loads indeed reduce stopping distances but are well beyond the peak values assumed for the propulsion system design. In addition, should the power turbines exceed the trip speed of 110 percent, an automatic shutdown will occur, leaving the ship with no on-line propulsion power. We studied these various tradeoffs during Phase I of the R&D program.

SNAME *Transactions*, Vol. 90, 1982, pp. 339–364

Design of a New-Generation Coal-Fired Marine Steam Propulsion Plant

Atsuo Fukugaki,[1] Visitor, **Sumio Fukuda,**[2] Visitor, **Shigemitsu Nakamura,**[3] Visitor, and **Yasuo Sakamoto,**[4] Visitor

A new-generation coal-fired marine steam propulsion plant, consisting of all-coal-fired twin-boiler installations and their associated coal bunkers, daily service hoppers, coal and ash handling systems, ash retention and disposal systems, etc., to drive a main propulsion turbine rated to develop 19 000 shp, was devised for installation in two 74 700-dwt bauxite carriers that are being built to Lloyd's Register's Rules and Guidance Note to quality as unattended machinery spaces (UMS). The boilers are equipped with a special automatic combustion control system, and coal transfer from the bunkers to daily hoppers is in the dense phase. To cope with many chemical, physical, and structural unknowns associated with using coal as a marine fuel compatible with the modern UMS principle, far-reaching research and engineering were conducted, theoretically as well as by model tests, with design emphasis on maximizing reliability and safety. As part of this project, a training simulator also was devised for training and education of the ship engine room personnel as well as for use in testing of the plant equipment.

Introduction

IN NOVEMBER 1980, a contract was awarded to the authors' company (MHI) to build two 74 700-dwt coal-fired bauxite carriers for The Australian National Line (ANL). The two ships, scheduled for delivery in September 1982 and March 1983, will be used to carry bauxite for Queensland Alumina Ltd. along the Australian coast. The first ship, named *River Boyne*, has already been installed with the main turbine, twin main boilers and most of her vital equipment, and is to be launched in April.

At the inception of the design work for these coal-fired ships, the design goal was set, primarily, at achieving the highest reliability and safety. Emphasis has therefore been on "perfection" throughout the design, construction, out-fitting and commissioning of this new generation of coal-fired steam propulsion plants.

Designing a fully automated marine coal-fired steam propulsion plant equivalent to an oil-fired plant in reliability, safety, and operational and maintenance requirements is a highly challenging task. Although a great amount of research and engineering work had been performed during the preliminary design stage to finalize the contract specifications and key plans, there still remained many unknown areas regarding

[1] Deputy general manager, Ship Engineering Department, Mitsubishi Heavy Industries, Ltd., Head Office, Tokyo, Japan.

[2] General manager, Ship Designing Department, Mitsubishi Heavy Industries, Ltd. Nagasaki Shipyard & Engine Works, Nagasaki, Japan.

[3] Manager, Machinery Equipment Designing Section, Ship Designing Department, Mitsubishi Heavy Industries, Ltd., Nagasaki Shipyard & Engine Works, Nagasaki, Japan.

[4] Project Manager, Marine Machinery Designing Department, Mitsubishi Heavy Industries, Ltd., Nagasaki Shipyard & Engine Works, Nagasaki, Japan.

Presented at the Annual Meeting, New York, N. Y., November 17–20, 1982, of THE SOCIETY OF NAVAL ARCHITECTS AND MARINE ENGINEERS.

the systems and components related to coal and ash. Neither reliable design data nor records of service results were available in these areas. Therefore, two special engineering projects were initiated prior to signing the formal contract.

The first project was a comprehensive research and development project to clarify the unknown areas so as to obtain reliable design data and establish design criteria. Intensive research work was conducted in a very limited time to facilitate the design progress, including the survey of literatures, fact-finding visits, analyses, laboratory tests and model tests. The subjects covered by the research included the chemical and physical properties and combustion characteristics of coal, vibration characteristics of the main boilers integral with the hull structure, dynamic response of boiler and automatic combustion control system, coal bunker configuration, coal transfer system, ash handling system, safety analysis against hazards associated with coal, and a simulator for personnel training and equipment check up.

The second project was a reliability enhancement program to ensure the highest reliability and safety for this entirely new plant. To this end, a close reexamination of the basic design was performed in search of any subject area where operational problems and casualties might arise. Consequently, some 160 items were picked up and thoroughly analyzed for clearance.

As of this writing, all the design work has been completed, and the authors are confident that the design goal of the highest reliability and safety has been achieved. Also, the authors believe that the successful completion of this new generation of coal-fired steamships will certainly pave the way for more and more coal-fired steamships coming on the world's sea lanes.

In preparing this paper, the authors tried to present the essentials of their research and development work in the logical order—namely, identification of problems, formulation of approaches to the problems, results of analyses and tests, eval-

Table 1 Principal particulars of ship

Class:	Lloyd's Resister of Shipping +100 Al "Ore Carrier," + LMC and UMS
Length overall:	255.0 m
Length BP:	248.00 m
Breadth (molded):	35.35 m
Depth (molded):	18.30 m
Designed draft (molded):	12.20 m
Scantling draft (molded):	12.80 m
Deadweight (designed draft, molded):	74 700 metric tons
Gross tonnage (British):	53 900 tons
Cargo holds capacity:	66 000 m³
Coal bunkers capacity:	4200 m³
Service speed:	15.8 knots
Endurance:	4500 nautical miles
Main turbine:	Mitsubishi MS-21-II × 1 set 19 000 hp × 80 rpm
Main boilers:	Mitsubishi-CE V2M-9S × 2 sets max. evaportion 35 t/hr each
Main generators:	back-pressure type turbogen. × 2 sets 1850 kW × 1800 rpm each
Emergency generator:	radiator-cooled diesel gen. × 1 set 700 kW × 1800 rpm
Coal transfer:	pneumatic dense-phase type 16 t/hr
Ash transfer:	pneumatic vacuum (by vacuum pump) type 3 t/hr
Ash discharge:	Pneumatic vacuum (by hydro-eductor) type 30 t/hr
Kind of coal:	Callide (Queensland) coal

uation of the results, and finalization of design. The first part of the paper deals with design philosophy and gives a brief description of the propulsion plant.

Design philosophy and system description

The newbuildings are intended to transport bauxite over a distance of about 1200 nautical miles between Weipa and Gladstone, along the northeast coast of Australia. Most of the route is coastwise, inside the Great Barrier Reef, characterized by very shallow waters and narrow channels. The ships are propelled by steam generated in pure coal-fired boilers. The coal used as fuel is "Callide coal" mined in Queensland, Australia, and is bunkered to ship at Gladstone, the unloading port for the bauxite. At the outset of this project, ANL asked MHI to assure the following as basic design concepts in dealing with the coal-fired propulsion plant.

(a) Maximum operational security throughout the voyage route, most of which is characterized by confined and shallow waters.

(b) Maximum utilization of coal as the energy source for all purposes, including in-port operation.

(c) Minimum downtime throughout the service life of the ships.

(d) Maximum operational flexibility.

(e) Suitability for unattended operation.

(f) Compliance with acceptable standards for environmental pollution protection.

Following the preceding guideline, design and research work was initiated toward the satisfactory completion of the first coal-fired ships of the new generation.

Hull form and propulsive power

The newbuildings are the largest permissible size for their voyage route and port facilities. The main turbine of either ship has a higher rated output than the engines of bulk carriers of comparable size to facilitate navigating, without delay in schedule, a route that is heavily dotted with shallow waters where a drop in ship speed can frequently take place. Table 1 gives the principal particulars of the ships.

General and machinery arrangements

The large machinery and bunker spaces required for a coal-fired ship greatly restrict the flexibility of overall ship design. Figure 1 and Figs. 2–4, respectively, show the general arrangement and machinery arrangement. Bunkers, one port and one starboard, are located aft of the machinery space, whereas two boilers are located at the forefront of the machinery space, all this being the result of comparative studies made of various alternative arrangements.

The particular locations of the bunkers and boilers were decided upon as a result of comprehensive engineering and operational studies with particular attention to the prevention

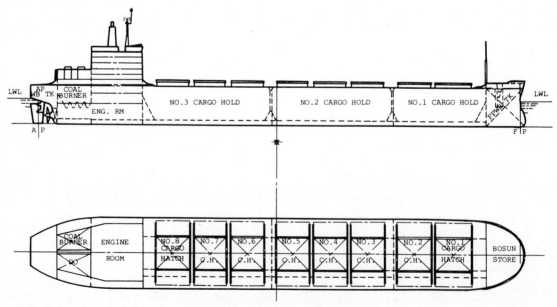

Fig. 1 General arrangement

Coal-Fired Marine Steam Propulsion Plant

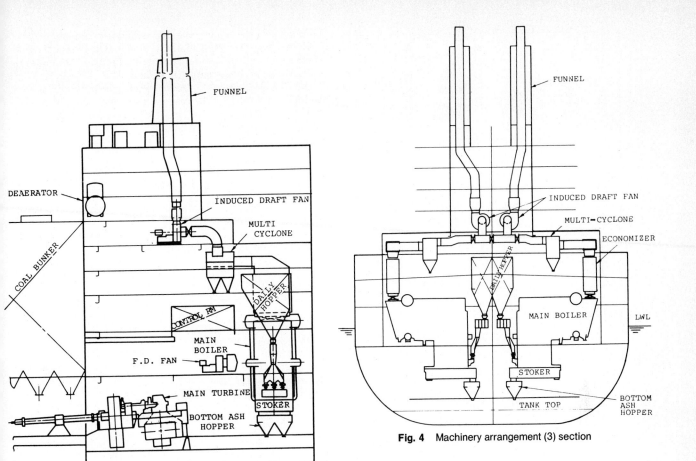

Fig. 2 Machinery arrangement (1) elevation

Fig. 4 Machinery arrangement (3) section

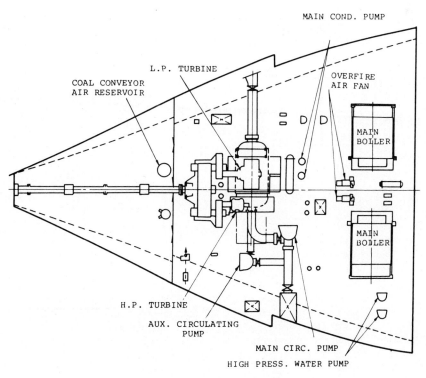

Fig. 3 Machinery arrangement (2) plan

Coal-Fired Marine Steam Propulsion Plant

341

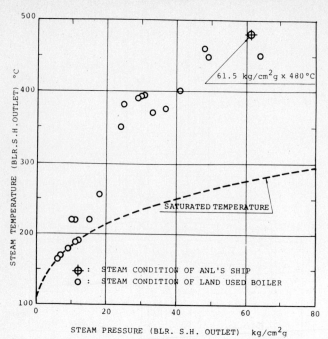

Fig. 5 Steam conditions of land-used spreader stoker coal-fired boiler (evaporation, 15 t/hr and larger unit supplied by MHI)

of boiler vibration due to the ship sailing in extremely shallow waters. The predicted vibration levels at the final stage of design are well within the acceptable limit for both accommodations and boiler support decks.

For the ship's length overall, the cargo hold space is shorter in total length than is the case with the motor ship of comparable size, for reason of the large machinery and bunker spaces required as mentioned earlier. A somewhat greater amount of steel than usual was therefore required for reinforcement against the larger sagging moment likely to be induced in the fully loaded condition, although the necessary cargo hold capacity could be maintained because of the larger specific gravity of bauxite.

The two boilers are located symmetrically, each with its firefront inboard and uptake outboard so that operation and observation of both boilers can be carried out from the same area between them. The direction of stoker grate travel is athwartships.

Steam condition

Main steam pressure at the turbine inlet is 60 kg/cm²g at a temperature of 475°C, these values being the result of studies made of past experiences with land-based stoker-fired boilers with particular attention to the ash fusion temperature of Callide coal to prevent excessive boiler fouling. Figure 5 compares steam conditions adopted for the ANL ships and land-based stoker-fired boilers.

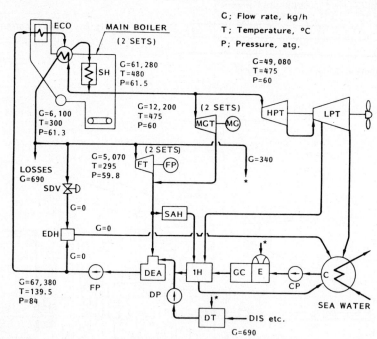

LEGEND

HPT	: HIGH PRESSURE TURBINE	SH	: SUPERHEATER
LPT	: LOW PRESSURE TURBINE	SAH	: STEAM AIR HEATER
MGT	: MAIN GENERATOR TURBINE	CP	: CONDENSATE PUMP
FT	: FEED WATER PUMP TURBINE	DP	: DRAIN PUMP
MC	: MAIN CONDENSER	FP	: FEED WATER PUMP
AE	: AIR EJECTOR	DT	: DRAIN TANK
GC	: GLAND CONDENSER	DIS	: DISTILLER
1H	: 1ST STAGE FEED WATER HEATER	SDV	: STEAM DUMP CONTROL VALVE
DEA	: DEAERATOR	EDH	: EXTERNAL DESUPERHEATER
ECO	: ECONOMIZER	MG	: MAIN GENERATOR

Fig. 6 Heat balance diagram

Coal-Fired Marine Steam Propulsion Plant

Steam cycle

A simple two-stage regenerative feedwater heating cycle is employed utilizing the steam air heater and economizer, with the following considerations in relation to stoker coal firing:

(a) maintaining suitable forced-draft air temperature for stoker grate cooling, and

(b) space saving and freedom from maintenance work for rotating parts and elements, as would be the case with gas air heater.

A specific feature of steam cycle in relation to stoker coal firing is a steam dump system designed to compensate for the slow response characteristics of coal firing as well as to cover low-load operation below the boiler minimum turn-down capacity. And due attention should be paid to the large electric power demand of the stoker coal-fired boiler plant as shown in Table 2.

Figure 6 is a schematic diagram of the steam cycle. Apart from these features, the steam cycle employed gives top priority to simplicity and low maintenance at the expense of fractional gains in fuel economy. Two back-pressure type generator turbines, exhausting into a deaerator, are employed, this arrangement making for ease of operation as well as the elimination of an auxiliary condenser. Excess steam is dumped to the main condenser, avoiding the necessity of installing an independent dump condenser. All these measures designed to provide a simple steam cycle were in accordance with ANL's desire that the conventional part of the plant should be the simplest proven system and components should be designed on the principle of "fit and forget."

Main turbine

The main turbine is of the cross-compound type of proven design with tandem articulated double-reduction gear. The arrangement of the main turbine installation is quite conventional with emphasis on simplicity.

The design features, if any, include the steam dumping connection to the main condenser and the adoption of a split-type main condenser. A special flash chamber integral with the main condenser receives dump steam. Because of the possibility of sand abrasion of condenser tubes due to the ships navigating through shallow water area for the greater part of

Table 2 Comparison of electric power demand between coal-fired and oil-fired marine steam propulsion plants

Kind of Plant		COAL-FIRED MARINE STEAM PROPULSION PLANT	OIL-FIRED MARINE STEAM PROPULSION PLANT
Kind of Vessel		74,700 dwt, bauxite carrier	74,000 dwt. oil tanker
Main Turbine Output		19,000hp x 80rpm x 1 set	19,000hp x 105rpm x 1 set
Main Boiler Capacity		35,000/32,000 kg/h x 2 sets (61.5atg x 480°C)	42,000/28,000 kg/h x 2 sets (61.5atg x 515°C)
Electlic Generating System		T/G ; 1,850kw x 2 sets E/G ; 700kw x 1 set	T/G ; 800kw x 2 sets E/G ; 250kw x 1 set
Electric Power Demand at Normal Sea Going with Air Conditioning	Main Turbine Auxiliaries	332 kw	216 kw
	Main Boiler Auxiliaries	515 kw	142 kw
	Coal Handling System	91 kw	—
	Ash Handling System	3 kw	—
	Ship Service Auxiliaries	257 kw	123 kw
	Deck Machinery	17 kw	14 kw
	Cargo Gear & Service	13 kw	—
	Lighting Etc.	41 kw	36 kw
	Total	1,269 kw	531 kw

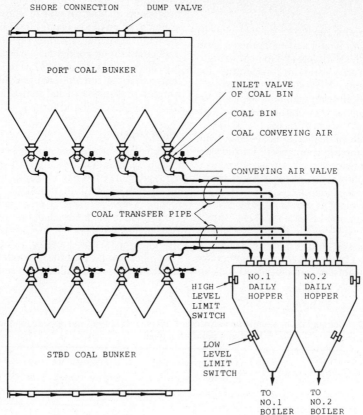

Fig. 7 Coal transfer system

the voyage, a split-type main condenser was introduced in order to permit routine inspection and cleaning to be carried out without having to shut down both main boilers.

Also, nylon inserts were fitted at the inlets of all condenser tubes to protect them from inlet attack.

Coal firing method

The first decision to be made in this project was selection of the coal firing method. The examination and evaluation narrowed down to which of two methods to use, spreader stoker firing or pulverized coal firing, both being readily available for marine application.

Finally, the spreader stoker firing method was selected in view of the following advantages:

(a) lower installation cost,
(b) smaller installation space,
(c) less maintenance,
(d) simpler control system for combustion with safety,
(e) lower dust density in boiler flue gases,
(f) less electric power required for pulverizing mill, and
(g) fewer risks of various kinds of explosions.

Number of main boilers

Twin-boiler installations, fully coal fired, are employed instead of a single boiler system with auxiliary fuel oil burner. The reasons for this arrangement are as follows:

(a) maximum utilization of coal as the energy source for all purposes, including operation in port,
(b) simplification of the automatic combustion control system without the need for oil burner control,
(c) no need for a take-home propulsion device which is required under Lloyd's rules and regulations for the single-boiler system, and

(d) greater operational flexibility compared with the single-boiler system

Coal handling system

Just as important as the firing method and ash collection and disposal system for the coal-fired ship is the coal-handling system, especially with the increasing concern for working environment and the need for a high degree of ship automation. The coal handling system employed was devised with a special emphasis on the following:

(a) safety in coal storage and transfer,
(b) smooth and uninterrupted flow of coal,
(c) ease of operation and maintenance,
(d) avoidance of segregation of lumps and fines, and
(e) elimination of coal dust in the engine room.

The dense-phase pneumatic transfer system is employed for transfer of coal from bunkers to daily hoppers because of its suitability for the pipe system of transfer, space saving, simplicity of arrangement, and dust prevention. Figure 7 is a schematic diagram of the coal handling system. Two bunkers are installed in accordance with Lloyd's "Guidance Notes for Burning of Coal in Ship's Boiler," symmetrically port and starboard and sufficient in capacity to enable the ship to run continuously 4500 nautical miles without refueling. Each bunker has four coal inlets and four coal outlets carefully arranged to prevent the formation of excessive peaks and troughs of coal inside. Each outlet from the bunker has its coal transfer line, 125 mm in diameter, which connects to the daily hopper and can transfer about 16 tons of coal per hour, almost twice the coal consumption of the two main boilers. Eight such coal transfer lines are provided in total. One daily hopper is provided for each boiler for the purpose of accumulating coal for orderly and timely supply of coal to the boiler. Their capacity

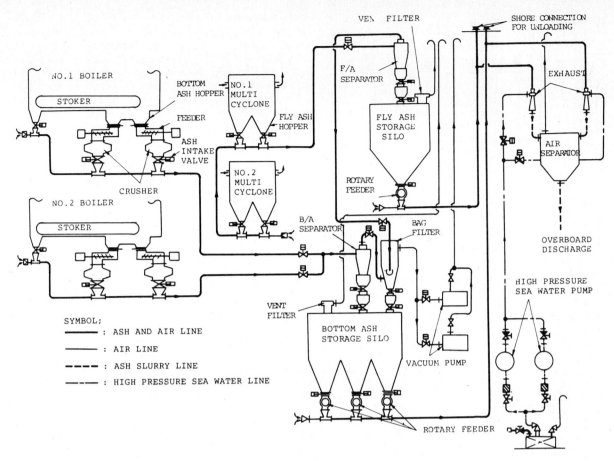

Fig. 8 Ash handling system

is sufficient to operate the main boiler for six hours of maximum boiler load without replenishment. The transfer lines are arranged above the boiler firing front between the two boilers. A coal weighing machine and a coal chute are installed between each daily hopper and boiler spreader units. The coal weighing machine serves as a mechanical means of feeding coal from the daily hopper to the coal chute as well as providing automatic batch measurement of the coal flow for checking consumption. The coal chute serves to distribute coal from one common inlet to multiple outlets connected to individual coal spreader units attached to boiler, ensuring even mass flow and uniform distribution of coal size. A nonsegregation-type conical coal chute has been adopted.

Ash handling system

The design of the on-board ash handling system, consisting principally of ash collection and transfer and storage equipment, was based on the proven system used with land-based boilers. Careful attention was paid, of course, to avoiding the leakage of dust into the machinery space and to assure uninterrupted transfer of ash. Furthermore, the ash handling system complies with relevant environmental regulations, as mentioned later.

Figure 8 is a schematic diagram of ash handling system. Two kinds of ashes with the following ratio are treated separately.

    (a) bottom ash: 70 ∼ 80 weight percent
    (b) fly ash: 20 ∼ 30 weight percent

As shown in Fig. 9, fly ash is separated from flue gases in the multicyclone-type dust collectors which are designed to

maintain the dust density within the specified limit at the funnel outlet. Bottom ash is dumped progressively into the bottom ash hoppers through the feeders and crushers. Through the crushers, ash is crushed into fines appropriate for vacuum transfer. A pneumatic-vacuum ash transfer system using a vacuum pump is employed for both fly ash and bottom ash, due to its superiority to the hydraulic transfer system in preventing environmental pollution and erosion of transfer piping. The ash transfer capacity is about twice the quantity of ash produced from boiler operation at maximum load, the former being about 3 tons/hr and the latter about 1.5 tons/hr. For shipboard ash storage, one fly ash storage silo and one bottom ash storage silo are installed in the machinery space. Each silo is designed to have a capacity sufficient to store ash produced on a round voyage between Weipa and Gladstone. Overboard disposal of ash is accomplished via a pneumatic vacuum transfer system using a hydraulic exhauster; it has the capacity to empty the silos within a half day of operation.

Combustion air and flue gas system

Figure 10 is a schematic diagram of the combustion air and flue gas system. A balanced draft system has been adopted in which the forced-draft fan and induced-draft fan are combined to keep the furnace pressure slightly negative and thus avoid the leakage of combustion products into the machinery space. The overfire air system is designed to give sufficient turbulence in the furnace for complete suspension burning of fine particles of coal. The fan capacities and number of overfire air nozzles were chosen based on the results of burning tests. In addition, a cinder reinjection system is employed to minimize the unburnt carbon loss.

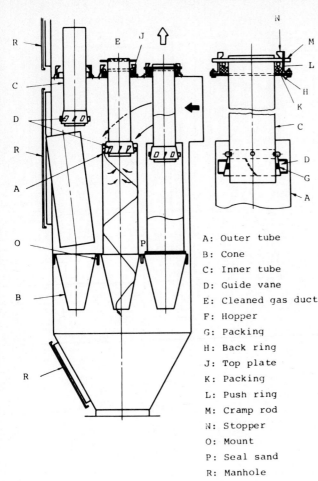

A: Outer tube
B: Cone
C: Inner tube
D: Guide vane
E: Cleaned gas duct
F: Hopper
G: Packing
H: Back ring
J: Top plate
K: Packing
L: Push ring
M: Cramp rod
N: Stopper
O: Mount
P: Seal sand
R: Manhole

Fig. 9 Mitsubishi-Lurgi standard multicyclone

Automation and remote control

The engineering control system incorporates UMS principles in accordance with Lloyd's rules and regulations. The design philosophy in this respect, therefore, remained the same as that for designing oil-fired ships except in areas where different approaches were required to use coal as a fuel.

Based on many applications of the MHI marine boiler Automatic Combustion Control System (MACCS) for oil firing, a new type of automatic boiler combustion control system, "COAL MACCS," was developed specifically to perform the control functions for the stoker coal-fired boiler. The COAL MACCS has a direct digital control system consisting of a 16-bit microcomputer, transmitters, controllers, etc. and featuring ease of adjustment. Figure 11 is a schematic diagram of the COAL MACCS system which has the following additional control functions as compared with the ordinary automatic combustion control system for oil-fired ships:

(a) steam dump control to take care of load variations below the minimum turndown capacity,
(b) smoke density control looped with combustion air control,
(c) grate traveling speed control so as to minimize the unburnt carbon content in the bottom ash,
(d) furnace pressure control to maintain a slightly negative pressure in the furnace, and
(e) overfire air pressure control.

Apart from the aforementioned automatic combustion control system, grate temperature monitoring is provided to protect the grate key from damage due to local overheating.

The coal and ash handling control systems are designed for unmanned operation, incorporating the latest in automatic and remote controls. The coal transfer from the bunkers to the daily hoppers is done by automatic detection of the coal level in the daily hoppers, and coal feed to the coal distributor by linkage with the automatic combustion control system.

Fly and bottom ash transfer from the hoppers to their respective ash storage silos is initiated and stopped automatically by detection of the ash level in each ash hopper. This operation is continued sequentially until all the hoppers are empty, and upon completing one cycle the system returns to the starting position to repeat another cycle. Starting and stopping the overboard discharge of ash from the storage silos is manually remote-controlled.

All the propulsion plant operations, including operation of the coal handling and ash handling systems, are monitored and controlled in the central control room in the machinery space.

Maintenance and repair

Pipes, valves, and other fittings used in the coal and ash handling systems are likely to suffer corrosion, abrasion, or erosion, so the materials for these items were very carefully selected, and their design carefully planned, to minimize maintenance. Materials considered most promising by current technological standards were evaluated for cost-effectiveness; however, the emphasis was placed on the fail-safe rather than safe-life principle, resulting in the selection of relatively short-life components which are to be periodically renewed, especially in critical areas.

Pollution control

The densities of dust and smoke as they leave the funnel, especially while in port, are controlled by means of a multicyclone-type dust collector of special design, in combination with the efficient boiler automatic combustion control system, to within the limits imposed by the clean-air regulation of Queensland, which specifies the following:
(a) dust density at the funnel outlet to be less than 0.45 g/Nm³, and
(b) smoke density at the funnel outlet in the steady condition to be less than Ringerman No. 2.

The ash storage silos installed in the machinery space retain the ash while navigating through restricted areas and in port. This design consideration also avoids the discharge of heated ash into the unrestricted seaway. Employment of the pipe system of coal and ash transfer and the balanced boiler draft system, as earlier mentioned, constitutes the dustproofing arrangement for the machinery space.

Chemical and physical properties of Callide coal

The characteristics of coal, although very important to the coal-fired propulsive plant, vary widely from coal to coal depending upon where it is mined and sometimes from seam to seam at the same place of origin. To achieve a successful coal-fired propulsive plant, therefore, it is absolutely necessary to know the properties of the coal to be burned and to develop thereby optimum designs for the boiler furnace, coal firing systems, and coal and ash handling system in a well-coordinated manner.

Properties of Callide coal

Table 3 lists the properties of Callide coal as determined by laboratory analysis, together with those of Taiheiyo coal, the typical Japanese coal, for reference. It was decided through this analysis that Callide coal was suitable for stoker firing in

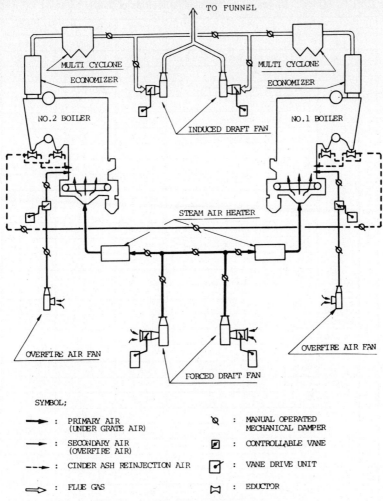

Fig. 10 Combustion air and flue gas system

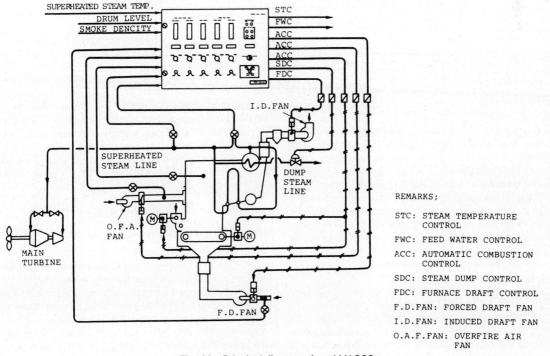

REMARKS;

STC: STEAM TEMPERATURE
CONTROL

FWC: FEED WATER CONTROL

ACC: AUTOMATIC COMBUSTION
CONTROL

SDC: STEAM DUMP CONTROL

FDC: FURNACE DRAFT CONTROL

F.D.FAN: FORCED DRAFT FAN

I.D.FAN: INDUCED DRAFT FAN

O.A.F.FAN: OVERFIRE AIR
FAN

Fig. 11 Principal diagram of coal MACCS

Coal-Fired Marine Steam Propulsion Plant

Table 3 Chemical and physical properties of Callide coal

		Production	–	Australia	Japan
		Name of Coal	–	Callide	Taiheiyo
Coal Property		High Calorific Value(Moist.Eq.)	kcal/kg	5,360	6,480
		Surface Moisture	wt.%	5.5	–
	Proximate Analysis	Inherent Moisture	wt.%	10.2	5.5
		Fixed Carbon	wt.%	50.5	38.6
		Volatile Matter	wt.%	24.3	44.2
		Ash	wt.%	15.0	11.7
		Fuel Ratio	–	2.08	0.87
	Ultimate Analysis (Moist. and Ash Free)	Carbon	wt.%	77.9	74.9
		Hydrogen	wt.%	4.2	6.2
		Oxygen	wt.%	16.6	16.9
		Nitrogen	wt.%	1.1	1.2
		Sulphur (Combustible)	wt.%	0.06	0.06
		Sulphur (Uncombustible)	wt.%	0.11	0.19
		Chlorine	mg/kg	122	72
		Fluorine	mg/kg	121	107
		Grindability	HGI	86	42
		Specific Gravity	–	1,636	1,477
		Volumetric Gravity	–	0.90	–
		Caking Factor	CSN	NA	NA
Ash Property	Fusion Temp.	Softens	°C	1,460	1,185
		Melts	°C	> 1,500	1,295
		Fluids	°C	> 1,500	1,305
	Composition	SiO_2	wt.%	43.1	45.3
		Fe_2O_3	wt.%	15.4	6.3
		CaO	wt.%	1.8	10.4
		MgO	wt.%	1.2	2.6
		Al_2O_3	wt.%	30.9	24.6
		SO_3	wt.%	2.0	4.2
		TiO_2	wt.%	1.8	1.1
		P_2O_5	wt.%	0.3	0.7
		Na_2O	wt.%	0.5	0.5
		K_2O	wt.%	0.2	0.3
		Cl	mg/kg	9	191
		Specific Gravity	–	2,878	–
		Volumetric Gravity	–	0.56	–

terms of calorific value, ash content, and ash fusion temperature.

Callide coal, however, also possesses undesirable properties, namely, a very high fixed carbon content as against relatively low percentage of volatile matter, and an extremely high Hard-grobe Grindability Index (HGI). The former suggests poor combustion characteristics in the furnace of a stoker-fired boiler, resulting in turn in an increase of unburnt carbon and slow response in accommodating boiler load change. The latter (HGI) suggests a considerable size degradation during transfer, which not only adversely affects the boiler efficiency but can even give rise to spontaneous combustion and explosion of accumulated fines and coal dust in the bunker, daily hopper, and transfer piping.

Additional analysis and tests

In view of the concerns just mentioned, three steps were taken. First, a series of combustion tests was performed to obtain sufficient data on the burning characteristics of Callide coal. Secondly, a full-scale model test of the dense-phase pneumatic coal transfer system was performed in order to ascertain the extent of degradation of Callide during transfer. Thirdly, safety analyses were performed with respect to spontaneous combustion, gas and dust explosion, and static electricity charging characteristics to determine what safety measures to take. All these tests and analyses are reviewed in detail later.

Boiler design

MHI-CE stoker coal-fired marine boiler type V2M-9S

The Mitsubishi-CE stoker coal-fired marine boiler type V2M-9S was developed for installation in the newbuildings. The design features include the following:

(a) The dropped furnace construction provides a sufficient furnace volume to give fine particles of coal adequate residence time for completion of suspension burning.

(b) The furnace outlet gas temperature can be maintained well below the fusion temperature of ash so as to be free from fouling and slagging.

Table 4   Principal particulars of boiler

Type:	MHI-CE stoker coal-fired marine boiler Type V2M-9S
Number of sets:	2 boilers per ship
Steam condition (at superheater outlet):	
steam pressure:	61.5 kg/cm^{2}g
steam temperature:	480°C (at normal rating)
Evaporation (per boiler):	32 t/hr (at normal rating)
	35 t/hr (at boiler max. rating)
Feedwater temperature:	138°C
Boiler efficiency: (air-dried, HHV basis)	83.4% (at normal rating)
Coal consumption:	4590 kg/h/boiler (at normal rating)
	4890 kg/h/boiler (at boiler max rating)
Ambient temperature:	38°C
Combustion air temperature:	120°C

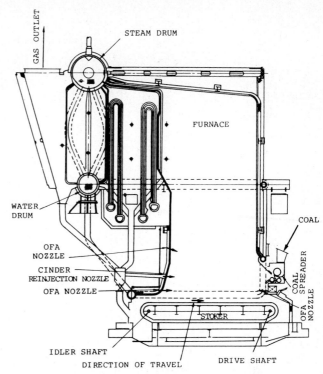

Fig. 12   Arrangement of boiler

(*c*)   The tube size and pitch selected assure freedom from fouling and erosion caused by ash.

(*d*)   Sufficient turbulence in the furnace is assured by supply of adequate overfire air.

(*e*)   Efficient cinder reinjection arrangement is provided to minimize the unburnt carbon loss.

The original V2M-9S-type design had been developed by Combustion Engineering (CE), Inc. for a stoker coal-fired boiler based on the oil-fired V2M-9-type boiler.   Twenty or more units of the latter are now in service.

Table 4 gives the principal particulars of the MHI-CE V2M-9S unit, and Fig. 12 the boiler assembly.

Study of boiler vibration

Careful studies were made on boiler vibration characteristics to avoid boiler resonance with propeller-induced hull vibration and to ensure levels of boiler and tube vibration well within acceptable limits.   In order to predict the boiler vibration characteristics, the ship hull, including the boiler installations, must be treated as a combined vibrating system so that the boiler response to external excitation as an element of the vibrating system can be determined.

Accordingly, a new system of vibration analysis, called the "modal synthesis technique," was employed, the principle of which is illustrated in Fig. 13.   In this system, a complex structure is divided into some major component structures to determine the vibration characteristics of each of the components.   Then data thus obtained are synthesized to predict how the structure will vibrate as a whole.   The aft hull structure was subdivided into a major hull part, super-structure, boiler proper, and boiler tube assemblies, and these individual component structures were analyzed.   For the boiler proper, a finite-element model of about 250 nodes was produced as shown in Fig. 14.   The final boiler structure was determined from the results of the overall evaluation by this modal synthesis technique.

Study of burning characteristics

The stoker and coal firing equipment, including the automatic combustion control system and fan capacity, must be suitably designed for the burning characteristics of the particular coal to be used.   For Callide coal especially, careful attention was required because of its inferior combustion characteristics, which had been predicted from the results of analyses of its chemical and physical properties.   In addition, the high friability of Callide coal was taken into account in designing the coal firing equipment.   In this connection, a series of combustion tests was performed to accurately determine the actual burning characteristics of Callide.

The ignition temperature and burning velocity were deter-

mined by a basic laboratory experiment.   Figure 15 shows the ignition temperature of Callide coal at which coal fines were found to catch fire spontaneously when heated to that temperature, together with data on ignition temperatures of different coals indicated in relation to percentage of volatile contents.   Figure 16 shows the burning speed of Callide as obtained by burning its smaller particles of about 3 mm in size. It can be seen from this figure that Callide coal burns very slowly, at about half of the speed of Taiheiyo coal, which was tested simultaneously for comparison.

As the next stage, actual burning tests were performed in a test furnace with a stationary grate.   A series of burning tests was performed to examine the effects of changes in parameters such as the coarse-fine ratio of coal size, surface moisture, thickness of coal layer, undergrate air flow rate, overfire air flow rate, and combustion air temperature.   Temperature and combustion gas were measured and recorded on a strip chart recorder.   Combustion characteristics derived from analysis of the test data enabled us to calculate vertical upward burning speed and burnout speed for a layer of coal spread out on the grate.   Combustion characteristics of Callide coal on the actual traveling grate of a stoker were determined quantitatively by these calculations in combination with the coal distribution rate per unit grate surface area measured separately.   Figure 17 shows the results of calculations made from these analyses.   It was predicted from this figure that when the grate speed exceeded 3 m/hr and the excess air ratio was less than 40 percent, the combustion of Callide coal would be incomplete with a resultant increase in the unburnt carbon content of bottom ash. In addition, these tests confirmed that an increase in percentage of fine coal would cause the unburnt carbon content to increase.

Based on the burning characteristics of Callide coal determined through these tests, the following improvements were incorporated into the original design of the stoker and coal firing equipment.

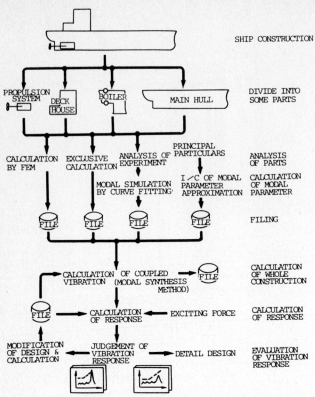

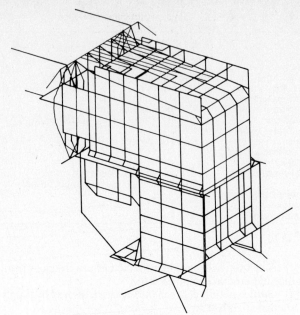

Fig. 14 Boiler model for vibration analysis

Fig. 13 Modal analysis of structural vibration of ship by modal synthesis method

(*e*) The material of the grate bar key was altered from 1 percent chromium cast iron to 4 percent silicon ductile iron in order to avoid heat damage.

(*f*) The number of overfire air nozzles under the coal spreader was increased from three to seven per spreader.

(*g*) The forced-draft fan and induced-draft fan capacities were increased to meet with the excess air requirement of 40 percent or more.

(*h*) It was agreed with ANL that the coal size distribution would be adjusted before bunkering.

It was expected that the unburnt carbon loss would be kept to a minimum by these design improvements. Figure 18 shows the stoker assembly employed for *River Boyne*, and Table 5 gives the principal particulars of the stoker.

(*a*) The lower limit of grate speed adjustable range was changed from 4 to 2 m/hr.

(*b*) The effective grate surface area was increased to make it compatible with the slow burning rate of Callide coal.

(*c*) The number of stoker undergrate air compartments was increased from three to five.

(*d*) The grate bar key shape was altered from the "flat" type to "overlapped" type in order to minimize uneven burning on the grate surface.

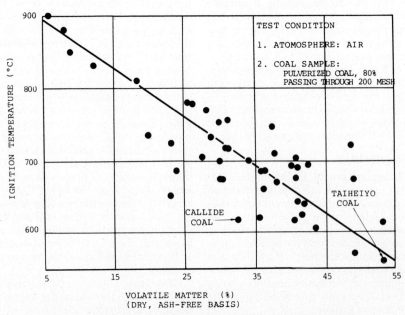

Fig. 15 Relationship between volatile matter and ignition temperature

Coal-Fired Marine Steam Propulsion Plant

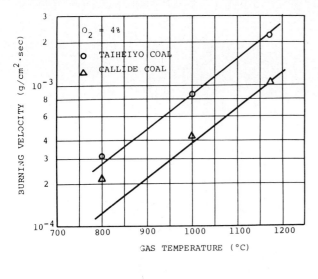

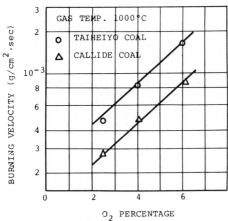

Fig. 16 Burning velocity of coarse coal sample

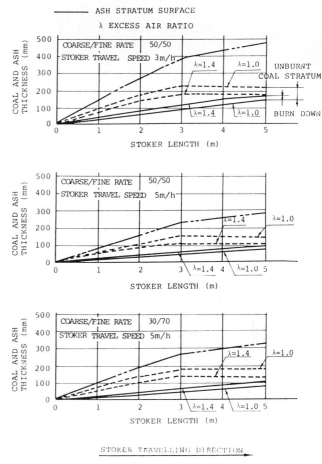

Fig. 17 Expected combusion characteristic on traveling grate

Study of dynamic response

The characteristics of boiler dynamic response also require due respect in designing the automatic combustion control system and coal firing equipment. However, available data on these were very limited and nothing was available for the marine boilers which have to respond to very quick load changes. Therefore, the following studies were performed in order to obtain basic data on boiler dynamic response.

First, studies were made of the boiler control system for the land-based spreader stoker coal-fired boilers and an initial skeleton of the boiler control system was drawn up (refer to Fig. 11), although the response characteristics varied with the kind of coal burned.

Next, computer simulation studies of boiler dynamic response characteristics were performed using mathematical models for the actual boiler furnace and stoker, coupled with the assumed combustion control system, in order to finalize the control system. A series of simulations was performed done with various combinations of parameters influencing boiler combustion, such as coal feed rate, combustion air rate, and traveling speed of stoker grate, for all the imaginable in-service boiler load changes. From these simulations, functional requirements, gains, and time constants for each control parameter could be established to maintain favorable combustion. These functions, gains, and time constants were incorporated into the final design of the boiler automatic combustion control system and dump steam control system. Figure 19 shows an

example of the simulation results in which the boiler load was increased and decreased between 100 and 30 percent, respectively, of normal load in 7 min.

Design of coal bunker and daily hopper

The reliability of the coal-fired ships depends largely on how to ensure a smooth flow of coal fuel from the bunkers to the daily hoppers and boilers through the transfer system under any seagoing condition. This problem was one of serious concern from the outset of the project and thus intensive research was carried out both analytically and empirically to arrive at a solution. The major objective was the achievement of uninterrupted discharge of coal from the daily hoppers and especially from the bunkers, which are large and very deep, having a total capacity of about 4200 m³ and depth of about 19 m. The coal discharge from hoppers is basically governed by the characteristics of bulk solid flow, but the actual performance is complicated by the combined effects of many factors, such as the following:

(a) coal characteristics (especially size distribution, surface moisture, and specific gravity),
(b) segregation into lumps and fines in the hopper,
(c) hopper configuration (especially the slope angle of the wall and coal discharge size at the outlet),
(d) depth of hopper,
(e) material for the hopper internal surface, and the

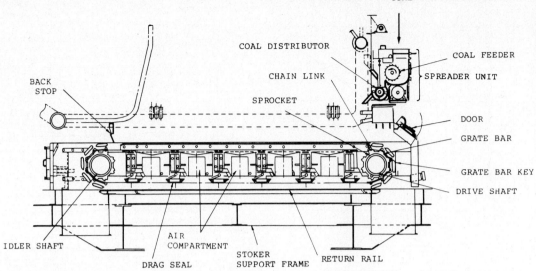

Fig. 18 Continuous ash discharge spreader stoker

(f)   effects of hull vibration and ship motions.
The coal bunkers and daily hoppers were designed in the following manner.

Design of hopper

In the field of powder technology, much valuable research has been done in both theoretical and experimental approaches to clarify the characteristics of bulk solid flow.   Development and refinement of theory as well as empirical verification are still being done on Jenike's theory, Walker's theory, and Walter's theory.   Applying the latest theory in powder technology, the configurations of the bunker and daily hopper were determined giving top priority to the achievement of good discharge performance.

The slope angle (α) of each hopper was designed to make the coal flow out by gravity without any stagnation.   Such a gravity discharge flow pattern is referred to as "mass flow."   The required slope angle of a mass-flow hopper depends on the ef-

fective angle (δ) representing internal friction of the coal and the friction angle (ϕ) between the coal and the hopper wall.   As the material for the internal surface of the coal bunker and daily hopper, stainless-clad steel was selected in view of its low friction feature and its resistance to corrosion and abrasion. Fundamental tests produced the following results:

(a)   The effective angle (δ) of internal friction was approximately 34 deg with Callide coal.

(b)   The friction angle (ϕ) between Callide coal and stainless steel was approximately 23 deg.

Figure 20 shows the relationship between ϕ and α with δ as parameter.   Accordingly, the slope angles for the coal bunker and daily hopper were made less than 24 deg for the mass flow of coal to take place most effectively.

The dimensions of each hopper outlet were chosen so as to avoid arch formation and to assure unobstructed flow at the required rate.   It is known that coal arches across the hopper outlet when the strength of the coal is greater than the stress induced in the arch.   The strength of coal as a function of consolidating pressure is expressed as the flow-function (FF) curve.   The *FF* curve for Callide coal was measured by using the direct-shear constant-rate type tester.   The stress induced in the arch as a function of consolidating pressure is referred to as the flow-factor (*ff*) curve, which is theoretically calculated from the actual hopper configuration and the friction angle (ϕ) between the coal and hopper wall.   Figure 21 shows the *FF*-curve and *ff*-curve for the coal bunker, in which the intersection of these curves represents the minimum outlet dimension necessary for discharge of coal under gravity only.

Model test

It should be noted that the foregoing procedures in which the hopper configuration was selected apply basically to the land installation.   For marine application, the influences of ship motion and vibration must naturally be taken into account. Vibration and inclination tests using a hopper model were performed.   Figure 22 shows a part of the test results.   Through these model tests it was confirmed that the influence of ship motion and vibration would be very small on the mass-flow characteristics of properly designed hoppers.

Countermeasures against arch formation

It may be very difficult in practice to entirely eliminate the possibility of arch formation or "hang-ups" in the hoppers, even

Table 5   Principal particulars of stoker and spreader unit

1. STOKER

Type:	MHI-CE continuous ash discharge spreader stoker
Number of sets:	1 stoker/boiler
Grate area (nominal):	19.4 m^2
Grate bar key type:	overlapped type
Adjust range of grate speed:	2 ~ 12 m/hr
Driving shaft:	front shaft
Driving method:	motor driven, with speed reducer and variable speed gear
Number of air compartments:	5 compartments

2. SPREADER UNIT

Type:	MHI-CE coal spreader Type 24
Number of sets:	3 units per boiler
Driving method of coal feeder:	Motor driven, with variable speed gear through one line shaft
Adjust range of coal feeder speed:	0 ~ 67 rpm
Driving method of coal distributor:	motor driven, with speed reducer
Adjust range of coal distributor:	380 ~ 700 rpm

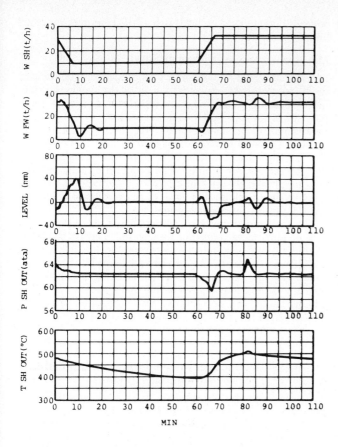

Fig. 19 Simulation of boiler dynamic response

W SH   : SUPERHEATED STEAM FLOW (t/h)
W FW   : FEED WATER FLOW (t/h)
LEVEL   : BOILER DRUM LEVEL (mm)
P SH OUT : SUPERHEATED STEAM OUTLET PRESSURE (ata)
T SH OUT : SUPERHEATED STEAM OUTLET TEMPERATURE (°C)

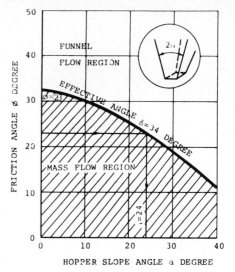

Fig. 20 Regions of mass flow and funnel flow in coal bunker

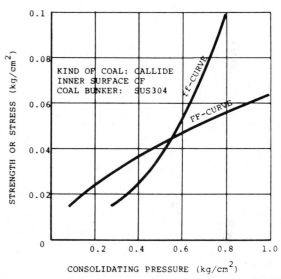

Fig. 21 Relation between flow function *FF* and flow factor *ff* for coal bunker

if they are designed with the utmost attention to an ideal configuration as described in the preceding, paying due attention to the ship vibrations and motions. Therefore, the following additional countermeasures were adopted for the coal bunker and daily hopper as a backup means of enhancing their reliability:

(*a*) Installation of slant plates at all the hopper corners.
(*b*) Installation of a deflector in the coal bunker to reduce the consolidating pressure.
(*c*) Increasing the loading points for the coal bunker to reduce the extent of coal segregation.
(*d*) Installation of arch breakers (air blaster) near the outlet.

All these design innovations for the hopper were also applied in designing the ash hopper and ash storage silo, including the countermeasures.

Design of pneumatic coal transfer system

The dense-phase pneumatic coal transfer system had successful applications in the past in many land-based applications. This, however, being the first marine application for the coal-fired newbuildings, due consideration was required of very severe operational conditions. Therefore, full-scale model tests on the transfer of Callide coal were performed to evaluate the reliability of this system for marine application as well as to obtain basic data necessary for system design.

Design of actual coal transfer system

All the coal transfer test results, plus the following considerations, were taken into account in designing the shipboard dense-phase coal transfer system:

(*a*) Coal size specifications for shore bunkering facilities were

- 30 mm maximum size,
- 95 percent through a 19-mm round-hole screen,

and

- about 30 percent through a 6.4-mm round-hole screen (this ensuring not more than 50 percent at the boiler inlet).

(*b*) Adoption of an independent coal transfer pipeline from each coal bunker outlet (eight lines total).
(*c*) Increase in transfer pipe bore to 125 mm diameter.
(*d*) Minimizing of bends and horizontal runs in piping arrangement.
(*e*) Adoption of special pipe connections and bend pieces for reduction of friction.

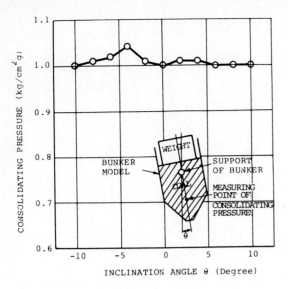

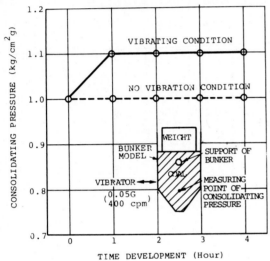

Fig. 22 Model test results of coal bunker

(*f*) Adoption of elastic supports for transfer piping to reduce noise transmission to the hull structure.

In addition, due consideration for maintenance of the transfer piping was given to specifically deal with possible coal blockage during transfer.

Design of ash handling system

The ash handling system for this marine application was developed based on the proven design employed for land-based boilers as described earlier (see Fig. 8). In addition, the following studies were performed in order to enhance the reliability of the system, with the results thereby obtained duly incorporated into the design.

Dust density control in flue gases

A greater part of fly ash carried in flue gas is caught by the multicyclone-type dust collector installed in the flue gas line before the funnel outlet. As the boiler load decreases, however, the separation efficiency falls, resulting in higher dust density in flue gases at the funnel outlet. In order to solve this problem, the split-type dust collector was developed to keep the dust density of flue gases within the specified limit even when the

boiler is operated at low load such as the case in port operation.

Ash storage and overboard disposal

Ash transferred through the pneumatic-vacuum transfer system is separated from conveying air by the cyclone and bag filter which are both fitted at the top of storage silo; the separated ash is dumped into the ash storage silo. When the temperature of the ash increases, the bag filter is automatically by-passed in order to avoid damage to the bag filter elements. Occasionally, ash separation is effected by two cyclones in series through the backup piping. The system is designed so that bottom ash and fly ash can be stored separately in their respective silos, because they have different discharge characteristics during disposal operation.

The ash disposal overboard from both ash silos is performed by a pneumatic-vacuum transfer system. The ash discharge equipment and associated transfer piping include a shore connection. In the case of overboard discharge into the seaway, a high-pressure water pump and hydro-exhauster on board are used as vacuum equipment so that ash can be thoroughly wetted and discharged in a slurry state. Also, if required, ash can be discharged in the dry state via the shore connection by using on-shore vacuum equipment.

Material selection for coal and ash handling system

Handling of bulk solid such as coal and ash is an entirely new field of technology to marine engineers. Environmental and operational needs have led to the adoption of an enclosed piped system for transfer as mentioned in the foregoing. Then the primary concern becomes wear of the piping, and evaluation of the material to be used for the system becomes necessary. Accordingly, a review of the literature and field studies on the selection of materials and rate of abrasion were carried out with particular emphasis on minimizing wear due to abrasion of the pipes and hoppers.

Summarizing the test results and analyses, the abrasion of materials subjected to the flow of bulk solids depends on the following factors:

(*a*) *Piping arrangement*—The abrasion rate increases in the order of pipe bends, horizontal piping, and then vertical piping. The bend parts especially suffer heavy abrasion.

(*b*) *Flow velocity*—The relationship between the abrasion rate (W) and flow velocity (U) can be expressed by the formula $W \propto U^3$.

(*c*) *Solid density*—The abrasion rate increases as the increase in solid density up to a certain density, where it is saturated.

(*d*) *Solid size*—The abrasion rate becomes severer with the increase in solid size.

In addition, results from the transfer piping service of the land-based boilers were closely examined.

As a consequence of the foregoing research, materials for ash transfer equipment were selected and their service lives were estimated with the results as given in Table 6. As can be seen, the bend pieces in the coal and ash transfer lines are relatively short in service life. Within the limitations of the present state of the art and with due respect to the question of cost-effectiveness, however, those listed in the table were the only materials available for use. Accordingly, the bend pieces were regarded as consumables to be periodically renewed, with emphasis on the fail-safe rather than safe-life design, and so the basic system design was arranged to permit easy replacement of those pieces at relatively short intervals.

Table 6   Materials for coal and ash handling system

Equipment	Material	Thickness (mm)	Estimated Life (year)
Straight Pipe of Coal Transfer Line	Steel Pipe (Sch40)	6.6mm	4
Bend Piece of Coal Transfer Line	Steel Pipe (Sch40)	6.6mm	2
Straight Pipe of Ash Transfer Line	Steel Pipe (Sch80)	9.5 or 8.6mm	10
Bend Piece of Ash Transfer Line	Abrasion Resistance Forged Steel	15mm	3
Coal Bunker	Stainless-clad Steel Plate	Stainless Steel: 2~3mm Steel: abt. 12mm	13 ~ 21
Daily Hopper	Stainless-clad Steel Plate	Stainless Steel: 2 3mm Steel: abt. 10mm	6 ~ 10
Bottom Ash Silo	Steel Plate	abt. 12mm	20
Fly Ash Silo	Steel Plate	abt. 10mm	20

Safety analysis against spontaneous combustion and gas and dust explosions

One of the most influential factors to be considered in the design of the coal-fired ship is the phenomenon of spontaneous combustion.   Gas and dust explosions also are just as important considerations.   As witness, many explosions have occurred in coal mines, coal-fired thermal power stations, and coal-carrying ships.   To prevent such troubles, therefore, it is absolutely necessary to know the characteristics of the coal to be used as fuel and to take adequate safety measures.   Chemical and physical analyses of Callide coal suggested the following with respect to safety.

(*a*) Callide coal is relatively high in spontaneous combustibility since it carbonizes at a low level.

(*b*) With Callide coal, dust clouds can form easily, the coal being extremely high in Hardgrobe Index.

Therefore, spontaneous-combustibility and explosibility tests were carried out with Callide coal, and precautionary measures were incorporated in the design of the coal handling system.

Spontaneous-combustibility test

A spontaneous-combustibility test was performed using Callide coal dried and pulverized to 200-mesh or smaller in size, and the rate of rise in coal temperature by oxidizing reaction was measured.   Figure 23 shows the characteristics with which the temperature of Callide coal rises, together data on the several kinds of coals for comparison.   It is evident from this figure that Callide coal has a relatively high propensity to spontaneous combustion although the time required for such spontaneous combustion to take place in the actual coal bunker is several times as long as that determined by laboratory tests.

Explosibility test

Explosion of coal dust can occur only when three factors are present simultaneously—namely, an inflammable material, air that supports combustion, and a source of ignition.   In the absence of even one of these factors, explosions can be avoided.   A series of tests was therefore carried out to evaluate the explosibility of Callide coal.

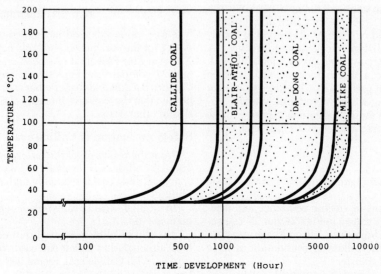

Fig. 23   Characteristics of temperature rise by oxidizing reactions from 30°C

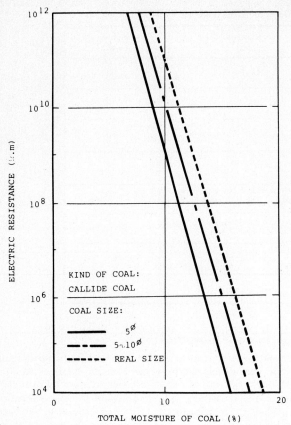

Fig. 24 Relationship betwen electric resistance and total moisture of coal

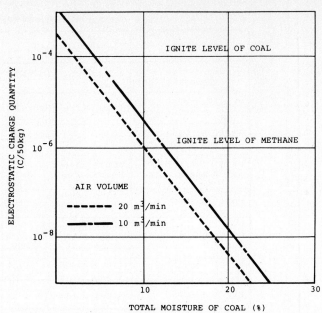

Fig. 25 Relationship between electrostatic charge quantity and total moisture of coal

• Confirmation of the presence of an inflammable material: Measurement of the quantity of gas released confirmed that the methane gas content of Callide coal was so small that it is hardly of any meaningful reading. The density of dispersed coal dust as measured by air pulse was also low, although a dust cloud could easily form.

• Evaluation of ignitability: Measurement of the minimum dust cloud ignition temperature, energy, and concentration demonstrated that the dust of Callide coal is less explosive than that of other coals.

• Verification of ignition source—frictional spark: If the energy of a frictional spark produced by a hard object hitting a steel plate is large, it could be a source of ignition in the atmosphere of methane-air mixture or coal dust-air mixture. A test on the ignitability of inflammable gas by frictional spark proved that a hard object like a piece of rock could not produce a frictional spark and that, if produced, such a spark would not develop enough energy to constitute a source of ignition.

• Verification of ignition source—electrostatic charge: The following electrostatic characteristics of Callide coal were measured:

(*a*) electric resistance,
(*b*) dielectric constant, and
(*c*) total quantity of electrostatic charge and surface voltage after transfer.

The results of measurements of electric resistance and electrostatic charge quantity are shown in Figs. 24 and 25, respectively, as a function of total moisture. From these measurements it was found that the following considerations were necessary for safety of coal transfer.

(*a*) Earthing for all coal transfer equipment.

(*b*) Restriction of total moisture content of coal to greater than 14 percent.

(*c*) Restriction of velocity of coal transfer to less than 15 m/sec.

• Explosive intensity: An explosion test with pulverized coal under 200-mesh in size was carried out with an enclosed test apparatus, and the maximum explosion pressure and maximum rate of explosion pressure rise were determined as follows:

(*a*) Maximum explosion pressure in an enclosed test vessel:

$$P_{\max} = 3.3 \text{ bar}$$

(*b*) Maximum rate of explosion pressure rise in an enclosed test vessel:

$$\left(\frac{dP}{dt}\right)_{\max} = 21.5 \text{ bar/sec}$$

(*c*) Maximum rate of explosion pressure rise in a 1-m³ enclosed vessel (European coefficient for dust explosion):

$$K_{ST} = 11.1 \text{ bar·m/sec}$$

The K_{ST}-value was used in the design of an explosion relief device for the coal bunker and daily hopper in accordance with National Fire Prevention Association guidelines. Figures 26 and 27 compare the explosive intensity, $P_{\max}$ and K_{ST}, of Callide coal dust and that of other coal dusts, from which it can be seen that the explosive intensity of Callide coal is lower than that of other coals.

Safety evaluation of Callide coal

From the results of all the foregoing tests, the safety evaluation of Callide coal reached the following conclusions:

(*a*) Callide coal is relatively high in spontaneous combustibility.

(*b*) Callide coal releases only a negligibly small amount of methane gas.

(*c*) With Callide coal, coal dust concentration is at a low level although dust clouds can easily form.

(*d*) With Callide coal, ignitability of coal dust is relatively low.

Coal-Fired Marine Steam Propulsion Plant

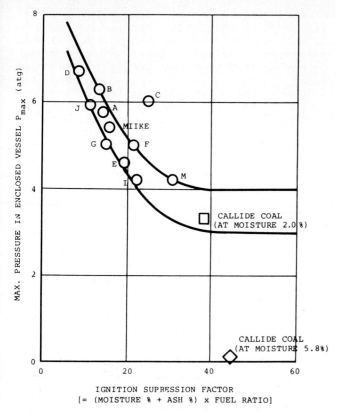

Fig. 26 Comparison of P_{max} between Callide coal dusts and other coal dusts

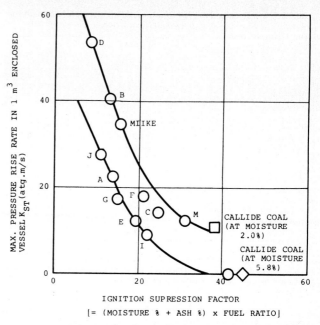

Fig. 27 Comparison of K_{ST} between Callide coal dusts and other coal dusts

(e)   A friction spark from hard objects coming into violent contact does not constitute a source of ignition.

(f)   Callide coal is moderate in electrostatic charge characteristics if its total moisture content is about 14 percent.

(g)   With Callide coal, the probability of gas-and-dust explosion is lowest.

(h)   Explosion intensity is at a relatively low level.

Countermeasures against disaster

Precautionary measures against possible problems were designed into the system as shown in Table 7, with emphasis on the prevention of spontaneous combustion of coal in the coal bunker and daily hopper based on the foregoing conclusions. For detection of spontaneous combustion, thermal sensors were employed. Table 8 outlines the temperature set points for alarms and safety devices.

Acknowledgments

The main boilers of the spreader stoker coal-fired type, the main turbine, and associated auxiliaries have already been installed in the first ship and outfitting work is underway. Var-

Table 7   Safety countermeasures against coal disaster

Countermeasures	Position	Coal Bunker	Daily Hopper
Fire Prevention	Exhaust through Bag Filter	O	O
	Natural Vent	O	
Fire Detection	Temp. Sensor	O	O
	Fire Alarm	O	O
Fire Fighting	CO_2 Flooding	O	O
	Water Drenching	O	
	Water Flooding	O	
	Drainage Pipe	O	
Explosion Prevention	Exp. Relief Device	O	O
	Portable Gas Detectors for HC and CO	O	

Mark O indicates the adoption.

Table 8 Temperature set guidance of alarm and safety device for coal bunker and daily hopper

Dangerous Grade	Temperature	Alarm	Safety Devices
First warning temp.	40 ~ 50°C	...	...
Second warning temp.	50 ~ 60°C	high temp. alarm	all ventilation to be stopped
First dangerous temp.	60 ~ 80°C	...	water drenching
Second dangerous temp.	80 ~ 100°C	high–high temp. alarm	CO_2 flooding water flooding

NOTE: Eight temperature sensors for one coal bunker and one temperature sensor for one daily hopper are fitted, respectively, and these are monitored in engine control room.

Metric Conversion Table

Original experimental data herein were measured in metric units. Following is a list of standard factors for conversion to U.S. customary values:

$$1 \text{ m} = 3.28 \text{ ft}$$
$$1 \text{ mm} = 0.04 \text{ in.}$$
$$1 \text{ nautical mile} = 1.852 \text{ km}$$
$$1 \text{ metric tonne (t)} = 0.98 \text{ long ton}$$
$$1 \text{ metric tonne (t)} = 1.1 \text{ short ton}$$
$$1 \text{ kg/cm}^2 = 14.2 \text{ psi}$$
$$1 \text{ kW} = 1.34 \text{ hp}$$

ious adjustments and on-board tests will be performed preceding the delivery and commissioning of the ship in September 1982. The authors are hopeful that all these shipboard machinery tests and subsequent sea trials will be successful and that they can touch on these test results at the Society's 90th Annual Meeting.

The authors extend their sincere thanks to The Australian National Line for their full collaboration in making this coal-fired ship project successful, and also to people at the Mitsubishi Nagasaki Technical Institute, at the Power Systems Research & Development and Ship Engineering Departments of Mitsubishi's Head Office, and at the Marine Machinery Designing Department and Ship Designing Department of the MHI Nagasaki Shipyard & Engine Works.

Bibliography

Bartknecht, W., "Gas Vapour and Dust Explosions Fundamentals, Prevention, Control."

Beggs, G. C., "Coal Burning Bulk Carriers for an Australian Coastal Trade," Trans., Institute of Marine Engineers, (TM), Paper 15, Vol. 94, 1981.

Crawley, M., "Pneumatic Transfer of Coal On Board," *Proceedings* Second International Coal-Fired Ships Conference, 1980.

Fukugaki, A., "Coal-Fired Ships—How to Make Them Really Viable," *Proceedings*, Second International Coal-Fired Ships Conference, 1980.

Horlitz, C. F. and Sabo, S. E., "Coal-Fired Boilers for the 1980's," *Proceedings*, SNAME Shipboard Energy Conservation '80, 1980.

Jenike, A. W., "Quantitative Design of Mass-Flow Bins," *Powder Technology*, Vol. 1, 1967.

Stock, A. J., "Bunker-to-Stoker and Bunker-to-Pulverizer Systems," Proceedings, Industrial Coal Conference, 1960.

Stock, A. J., "Coal Segregation, Coal Flow and Bunker Fires," *Proceedings*, Industrial Coal Conference, 1966.

Discussion

H. C. Blanding, Member

The authors are to be complimented for an interesting paper covering the reintroduction of a technology which had been all but forgotten in the marine field. I say "all but forgotten" because in the United States we have had until very recently coal-fired vessels operating on the Great Lakes.

There are a few points in the paper on which further information would be useful:

(a) Electric power demand—The total electric power demand for the coal-fired plant seems to be extraordinarily large in comparison with the oil-fired plant; the size of the turbo-generator sets and particularly the emergency generator set provided is much larger than would be normal current practice.

(b) Coal firing method—The reasons for selecting spreader stoker firing are given on page 344 and in this section pulverized coal firing is described as being "readily available for marine applications." Our research could only turn up two such installations, both experimental back in 1927. We would add to the disadvantages of pulverized coal firing the noise generated by the pulverizing mills.

(c) Light-off—No mention has been made of the method of initial light-off of boilers or relight-off if fires are extinguished for any reason. It would appear from the paper that no oil firing of any kind is intended. In this connection, I wonder if a fixed fire extinguishing system for the machinery spaces was deemed necessary since this SOLAS requirement would appear to apply only to oil-fired boilers.

(d) Condition of coal—No mention has been made of the condition of the coal as received on board or of measures taken to guard against tramp iron or other trash (wood, rags, etc., all of which are particularly troublesome).

(e) Coal handling system—The estimated lives for components of the coal and ash handling systems appear to be much less than as reported by the manufacturers of these systems.

(f) Cost—The paper has made no mention of cost, and I wonder if the authors would care to venture a cost comparison between these vessels and a diesel-powered vessel for the same service taking account of both capital and operating costs.

E. M. Palmieri, Member, and **M. T. Wahlgren,** Member

The amount of research, development and engineering effort spent by both shipyard and owner on this project is commendable, and will certainly lead to an operational success. Hence, the authors' prediction of more coal-fired steamships on the world's sea lanes will undoubtedly come to pass. In our opinion, however, such applications will be limited for some time to specialized bulk carriers on dedicated trade routes.

We have several brief questions:

1. On the second page the authors note that because of the shallow water frequently met in the trade route, the power installed is greater than on conventional bulk carriers. Was the required increase in power estimated from traditional naval architectural knowledge, or projected from actual tank model testing? In the latter case, any details of the model testing in shallow water would be appreciated, including any information of value obtained from analyzing the results of the sea trials carried out after this paper was written.

2. It appears that the use of oil has been reduced to lubricants and fuel for the emergency diesel generator. Was this

a requirement of the owner, and was it due to economic, supply, or operational considerations? It would be of interest to know how the boilers are initially lit off, and how long it takes to be ready for sea.

3. Figure 19 illustrates the prediction of boiler response under a gradual change in load. We note that the boiler level is predicted to "swell" during a decrease in power and "shrink," except for a slight upturn, during an increase in load. This is contrary to the usual short-term behavior, say, one to two minutes, of an oil-fired boiler. We would appreciate an explanation. We would also like to know if the steam dump would be actuated during this seven-minute ramp change, or if it is only used for more radical step changes that occur during maneuvering.

4. We note that the traveling grates are mounted athwartships rather than fore and aft. Was this orientation selected because the ship was not expected to roll appreciably, or is roll not a factor when installing coal-fired boilers with traveling grates?

5. We note that these vessels have the capability of either discharging ash at sea or holding it for discharge in port. Which method of disposal will be used on these vessels and why?

D. Tawse, Member

I wish to congratulate the authors on a very timely paper—the ship's acceptance trial was just on September 2 and 3, and the ship left for Australia on September 30.

It is interesting to note that while ANL/Mitsubishi decided on two boilers per ship for the reasons of maximum utilization of coal, simpler automatic combustion control, etc., Bulkships/Italcantieri for ships in identical service carrying bauxite from Weipa to Gladstone selected one boiler ship and the ships have two quite different machinery arrangements.

The ANL ships have two boilers per ship with no oil-burning capability, while the Bulkships coal-burning ships are a single boiler installation with 50 percent oil-burning capability. It is also of interest that the boilers on both ships are oriented the same way (that is, drums fore and aft); however, the stokers on ANL ships, which are of the C-E/Mitsubishi type, run athwartships while the Bulkships stoker is run fore and aft.

The comparison of electrical power demand in Table 2 shows more than double the power required for a coal-fired ship versus the oil-fired ship. I do not believe this to be the best example for comparison since it is made between a bauxite carrier and an oil tanker. It would be better to compare a bulk carrier with a bulk carrier. A portion of the increased power required is due to the coal and ash handling systems; however, I would appreciate the authors giving a more detailed breakdown of the power demands for the main turbine, main boiler and ship service auxiliaries.

It is noted that the ash handling system, Fig. 8, shows a separation between the fly ash and bottom ash; other ships have one common system for both types of ash. What led to the decision to separate fly and bottom ash? It is also noted that there is a shore connection for disposing of ash. Is it anticipated that the primary method of ash disposal will be to the shore facility?

Owing to the authors' company, MHI, being a licensee of Combustion Engineering, Inc. for oil and coal steam generating equipment for over 30 years, and there being a close working relationship between the two companies, I was priviledged to be on the acceptance trial of this ship. I have the following observations with regard to the acceptance trials:

1. The ash in the boiler resembled a coarse black and white sand, very loose. It appeared that the time intervals between soot-blowing in the superheater and boiler bank could be in-

creased. What were the original blowing time intervals, and have these times been increased?

2. It is noted that the grate temperature was monitored during the trials. How did the temperature vary with load, under a trip condition and under a banked fire condition?

3. The fuel bed on the stoker grate was very stable under trial conditions. Now that the ship has had some deep-sea running, has there been any noticeable movement of the bed?

In closing, I must say that the trials were very successful, with the Lloyd's UMS Certification being awarded after the six-hour UMS trial. Since this was originally not to be awarded for at least six months after the sea trials, it is a credit to MHI that the ship was delivered on time and with the UMS Certificate.

Gerard L. Gallinaro, Member

The authors are to be commended for allowing us an interesting and enlightening look at the design of a coal-fired marine steam propulsion plant. General Dynamics/Quincy Shipbuilding Division, presently the sole shipbuilder in the United States with a design and construction contract for a coal-fired propulsion plant vessel, can appreciate the results and conclusions obtained by the authors.

We do, however, offer the following comments and questions:

1. How long was the preliminary design phase and what did it constitute?

2. It is noted that the ship's design calls for coal to be pumped aboard through pipelines connected to a shore facility. Are there provisions for coal to be loaded at ports not equipped with compatible pumping facilities?

3. General Dynamics' ship design is to the ABS guide which recommends that provisions for emergency off-loading of bunkers be provided. With MHI building to the Lloyd's guide—which has no such requirement—does MHI provide this feature?

4. What is the concern about dumping heated ash in the unrestricted waterway?

5. It is of interest to note that the FD fans, ID fans and overfire air fans are so connected that the port units can service the starboard boiler and vice versa. What was the reason for such an elaborate scheme? Are the fans sized so that one fan can handle two boilers at full load? And, if not, what two-boiler load can they handle?

6. It is not clear why main turbine auxiliaries, deck machinery and lighting electric loads should be less for oil than for coal.

7. It appears that the authors have considerable concern about boiler vibration. Was the concern due to the method of firing being coal, or do the authors have the same concern about conventional oil-fired boilers?

8. Steam dumping and minimum turndown capacity are briefly addressed. What is the minimum turndown capacity attainable and what effect does it have on in-port operation with regards to steam dumping?

9. Please clarify the term "fail-safe rather than safe-life principle."

10. Finally, the U. S. Coast Guard has indicated to General Dynamics that the CO_2 flooding is not an effective method of extinguishing fires in coal bunkers, the rational being that the CO_2 will dissipate, leaving hot coals and thus allowing recurrence of the fire. It is noted that Lloyd's guide allows CO_2 flooding. Any comment?

Anthony C. LiCausi, Member

The marine steam propulsion plant is not an endangered species. Were this not the case, the authors would simply be congratulated on a very excellent paper, and a discussion of same would probably at some future time be the required work of a marine engineering student desiring extra credit or an advanced degree.

The coal-fired steam plant has a great potential, and it is in the pursuit of "perfection" as noted by the authors in their Introduction that these comments and queries are proposed.

• *Machinery arrangement*: 1. Why is the economizer located before the cyclone fly ash collector? Will not the fly ash laden flue gas increase the probability of economizer surface fouling and reduce heat transfer efficiency?

2. We question the use of a horizontal run of duct from the economizer to the cyclone inlet. It would seem prudent to avoid a flat horizontal surface to preclude an ash buildup. Since this arrangement does exist, are there means provided to remove any ash buildup in this area?

• *Steam conditions*: We do not understand the information contained in Fig. 5 as an aid in selecting final steam temperature. It would appear that 440°C would be more in line with past stoker experience and conservatism.

• *Steam cycle* (refer to Table 2): We are interested in knowing why the coal-fired plant requires so much more electric power than the oil-fired plant, specifically in the main turbine and ship's service auxiliaries, as well as cargo gear service.

• *Coal handling system*: 1. In Table 1, it is noted that the vessel has an endurance of 4500 nautical miles; likewise, we are advised that the route distance is about 1200 nautical miles. It would appear, therefore, that the bunker capacity is slightly insufficient for two round trips and much more than necessary for one round trip. Perhaps the authors would comment on the selection of bunker capacity.

2. There seems to be an excess of coal transfer capacity from the bunker to the day hopper, both in capacity per transfer line, as well as in number of transfer lines. The day hopper has a six-hour maximum boiler load capacity. Does this combined arrangement of multiple feed to the day hopper and day hopper capacity reflect any concern on system reliability? Are the day hoppers cross-connected at their common wall?

• *Boiler Design*: 1. Why is there no fly ash reinjection from the cyclone?

2. Was special consideration given to the choice of boiler refractory?

• *Burning characteristics*: The heart of a coal fired boiler is its burning capability, and our questions concerning the stroker are numerous:

1. Was the number of air compartments increased from three to five to improve air distribution? One would think that simplicity would dictate a large plenum, a multiplicity of air jets, and sufficient draft loss to ensure proper air distribution, rather than compartmentalization.

2. Does operational performance include variation of grate speed?

3. What is the maximum anticipated grate temperature?

4. What is the design unburned carbon loss from the grate, that is, in the bottom ash?

5. While excess air less than 40 percent will increase unburned carbon in the bottom ash, will not an increase in excess air increase carryover of fines in the flue gas and/or burning of fines in the screen or superheater tube bank?

6. What is the anticipated variation in excess air over the load range?

7. How thick is the coal layer on the grate at normal power?

8. How is coal ignition initiated?

• *Design of ash handling system*: 1. Based on the possibility of burning coals entering the bottom ash hopper, what effect will this have on the performance of the ash disposal system?

2. What is the design temperature of this system?

3. It would appear that one of the most damaging component failures would be loss of the ash removal system. Assuming this failure to occur, what is the capacity of the bottom ash hopper? Is it proportionate to the six-hour capacity of the day hopper?

We wish to emphasize that the numerous questions proposed herein in no way detract from the vast amount of knowledge offered the reader in this most informative paper. The technical expertise of the Mitsubishi Heavy Industries Marine Group is known throughout the industry.

Nonetheless, in our mutual resolve to further the use of marine coal fired steam plants, the asking of questions is the first step in the resolution of a possible problem.

William G. Bullock, Member

[The views expressed herein are the opinions of the discusser and not necessarily those of the Department of Commerce or the Maritime Administration.]

There are presently nine ships with coal-fired boilers under construction of which three are conversions. A technical paper on one of these conversions was presented at the recent SNAME Energy and Cost Symposium.

Up to the present time, the marine engineering community has only been addressing the potential of coal fired ships, their advantages and disadvantages, potential problem areas and energy/cost savings.

With this technical paper, a new era of coal-fired ships has arrived. This paper describes the two coal-fired vessels for Australian National Lines. I hope everyone noted the time frame of this project: contract signing, November 1980; delivery and sea trials, September 1982—a total of 22 months. My congratulations to the authors and their shipbuilding company for a remarkable achievement in designing, constructing and delivery of a new-old form of propulsion. There is an old saying in the marine community, "Don't be the *first* but don't be last." So I believe Australian National Lines must also be congratulated for their courage in breaking new ground and being one of the "firsts."

The test phase of coal-fired ships has now *commenced*. The real future of coal-fired ships will be determined in the *next two to three years* after the economic results of this ship and the eight others presently under construction become widely known.

The Nov. 1, 1982 issue of *Maritime Reporter* gives a short article on the first ship, *River Boyne*, so I hope the authors will give us an update of the sea trial results, particularly with respect to fuel consumption and the automated operation of the coal firing system from the hoppers to the boiler.

Because of the space limitations, the authors have been permitted to show us only the highlights of their design approach. However, the list of topics which they have discussed does serve as a valuable checklist of the significant design details which must be addressed in any coal-fired ship design.

My final comment addresses the automated, unmanned aspects of the engine room design. Since the capacity of the daily hopper is sufficient to operate the main boiler for only six hours of maximum boiler load, how was approval obtained for an unmanned engine room space of 12–16 hours???

Edwin G. Wiggins, Member

[The views expressed herein are the opinions of the discusser and not necessarily those of the Department of Commerce or the U. S. Merchant Marine Academy.]

The paper presents a well-integrated and thorough approach to the design of a coal-fired steam turbine propulsion system. I have two comments, one procedural and one substantive.

My procedural comment has to do with the use of kilograms per square centimeter as a unit of pressure. This is very common practice of course, but it is fundamentally incorrect. The standard unit of pressure in the SI system is the pascal. While the size of a pascal is a bit inconvenient for expressing commonly occurring pressures, at least it is a unit that embraces force per unit area. A kilogram is a unit of mass not force. Therefore kilograms per square centimeter is mass per unit area, which is nonsense. Most of us understand what it means, but that does not make it right. In particular, students are baffled by such a unit.

My substantive comment has to do with the use of backpressure generators. Clearly the energy extracted from one pound of steam flowing through the generator turbine is less than for a condensing turbine. This is not a true loss, however, because some of the residual energy in the exhaust steam is used for feed heating in the deaerator. Even so, there would appear to be a net fuel consumption penalty for using backpressure generators. I note that the authors state that the design "... gives top priority to simplicity and low maintenance at the expense of fractional gains in fuel economy."

It is not clear how the system will operate during maneuvering and in port. With the generator and the main feed pump turbine exhausting to the deaerator, a substantial flow of condensate would be required to maintain equilibrium. This would seem to require the steam dump control valve to remain open continuously, a very inefficient condition. Instead, the diesel generator could be used during maneuvering and in port periods. I assume this is the planned course of action, and that this is why a very large diesel generator is specified. At least part of the savings realized from omitting auxiliary condensers and pumps is expended on the larger diesel generator. In addition there must be an increment in diesel engine maintenance which exceeds the savings on maintenance of auxiliary condensers and pumps.

In the event of a loss of main condenser vacuum casualty, condensate flow would be reduced and condensate temperature would rise. Both of these effects would reduce the deaerator's ability to handle generator exhaust steam. This would effectively reduce the generator's capacity and might necessitate shifting to the diesel generator in the midst of an already hectic situation.

Clearly there are advantages to backpressure generators, but there are also significant disadvantages in capital cost, operating cost, and casualty control capability.

Richard Ciliberti, Member

I would like to amplify a comment made by a previous discusser, H. C. Blanding.

The present discusser's company, Keystone Shipping Co. of Philadelphia and our partner, New England Electric, have a U. S.-flag coal-fired, self-unloading coal carrier under construction at Quincy Shipbuilding Division of General Dynamics. Our coal-fired propulsion plant is in some ways similar to that described in the paper. We understand that the bunker coal for the vessels described in this paper is processed ashore prior to loading aboard ship. Will the authors please advise, however, what additional equipment would be installed in the Australian vessel's coal-fuel system to deal with both ferrous and nonferrous debris which might be loaded with bunker coal that is not processed ashore?

This is of concern to us because, certainly, some types of debris may well render the coal transfer system inoperative.

Authors' Closure

The authors wish to thank all of the discussers for their compliments and appreciate their comments and questions reflecting their interest in this paper. In view of the numerous questions raised by the discussers, the authors' replies constitute, for the most part, answers to questions and further explanation, with very little exchange of different views or controversial issues.

Trial results and practical experience as given in the oral presentation would be useful for a better understanding of the paper; hence the following summary:

River Boyne showed herself to be one of the most quiet ships, with peak vibration levels of 15 Gals in the aft part and noise levels in the accommodations of 41 to 54 dB (A), which proved the success of efforts made to minimize propeller-induced excitation force and the effectiveness of the aft bunker arrangement. Measured coal consumption of 488.3 g/ps.h as compared with design figure of 485 g/ps.h is a very acceptable figure in view of the fact that the coal actually burned contained quite a high percentage of fines, that is, 60 to 65 percent passing through a 6.4-mm screen against a specified 50 percent or less.

Callide coal containing much fines becomes sticky when very wet and is difficult to handle. The coal bunker and coal conveying system could discharge and transfer this out-of-specification coal with total moisture of 20 percent. Coal stagnation was experienced with very wet coal in way of the conical distributor just above the feeder and spread unit; it had to be removed by manual poking.

New systems in addition to the main boiler, such as the coal storage and transfer and feed system and the ash collection, transfer, storage and disposal system together with their sophisticated control systems, were all confirmed to satisfy their intended functions better than expected. The UMS test was perfect with no malfunction alarms in the test period of six hours' duration.

Successful completion of *River Boyne* has proved beyond doubt that modern automated coal-fired ships operated with unattended machinery spaces are no longer merely a concept but real, viable alternatives to survive through the decades of uncertainty in stable fuel oil supply. Long-term durability and reliability require some years for assessment, but the authors see no reason why they should not be highly satisfactory.

Mr. Blanding—The authors thank to Mr. Blanding for raising important points requiring further explanation.

The larger electric power demand on *River Boyne* is not necessarily attributable to coal firing. The difference in main turbine auxiliaries of 116 kW is mostly due to the larger number of ventilating fans with larger capacity and higher statical head, the latter being a necessity on bauxite carriers for additional pressure drop in the intake air filters. The difference in ship auxiliary of 134 kW is mostly due to the difference in owners' practice in accommodation. Even after correcting for the preceding, the electric power demand for the coal-fired plant is nearly twice that for an oil-fired plant.

The capacity of the emergency generator is substantially higher than the Rule requirement due to a special request of the owners to permit emergency propulsion with one boiler in operation.

The initial light-off procedure turned out to be much simpler than originally thought, after the art was mastered. We need only wooden logs and oily rags. After coal is spread on the grate to about 2 in. depth, logs and oily rags are put on the coal at front end. Then the rag is lit with a torch and in five minutes we have a good fire on the logs; the coal catches fire in another five or ten minutes. Induced-draft fans and forced-draft fans are started at this point and the flame gradually propagates to the rear end within about one hour. This method is quite primitive but it works well.

Additionally, banking as long as 24 hours is possible. There is no problem with overnight banking.

The authors agree with Mr. Blanding's comment that no fixed fire extinguishing system is necessary in machinery space. A fixed fire extinguishing system is installed only in the coal bunker and daily hopper.

A shore bunkering facility with crusher and screen is required to assure coal size as specified on page 353:

- Top size . . . 30 mm.
- 95 percent through a 19-mm round hole screen.
- About 30 percent passes through a 6.4-mm screen.

In addition, a magnetic separator to remove tramp iron is required in the shore bunkering facility.

The estimated lives listing of components in Table 6 was the best estimate we could do, based on shore experience, although Mr. Blanding's view would be generally true. We will collect data from *River Boyne* to assess practical component lifetimes.

Both capital cost and operating cost are widely spread over the world depending on the place and time. This makes economic assessment quite difficult. The *River Boyne*, with about 20 percent acquisition cost differential, could well be paid off by a fuel cost differential of about 1.5 million dollars per year.

Messrs. Palmieri and Wahlgren—The authors agree with the views of Messrs. Palmieri and Wahlgren on the immediate application of coal-fired ships most likely to dedicated trade such as *River Boyne*.

As for the shallow-water effect, speed loss rather than power increase was initially estimated by the traditional method as a function of the under-keel clearance. The power is selected to keep scheduled speed, taking account of this speed loss. Schedule keeping is very important so that the vessel can pass two extreme shallows at high tide. In addition, speed loss was confirmed by the model test. In the full-load condition, the speed loss was 0.66 knots at 32 m depth, 1.57 knots at 20 m depth, and 2.72 knots at 15 m depth. In the ballast load condition, the speed loss was 0.52 knots at 20 m depth, and 0.88 knots at 15 m depth.

Pure coal firing was the fundamental request of the owners. The reason is economy as well as simplicity of systems and operations. Another consideration was that the operating personnel would be more likely to rely on oil fuel, especially in port, with a dual-fuel installation.

The initial light-off method has already been explained in the reply to Mr. Blanding. After light-off, the time required for pressure raising is about four hours, the same as for an oil-fired unit. Regarding the simulation of boiler dynamic response, the authors believe that a correct observation of Fig. 19 agrees with the usual short-time behavior. We have initial negative response of "shrink" at power decrease and "swell" at power increase. After this initial negative response, the level upsurge at power decrease and downsurge at power increase are caused by the time delay between steam flow and water flow during ramp change.

Steam dumping will not be actuated during this mild seven-minutes ramp change, but only for more radical load changes such as a crash-stop astern reversal.

The reasons for the athwartship movement of the traveling grates, although not vital, are (1) even distribution of temperature and gas flow across boiler tube banks, (2) smaller effects of rolling such as uneven distribution of coal on the grates and meandering of strands, and (3) convenience in operation and observation of both boilers at the same area between them.

The usual method of ash disposal is overboard discharge only in the designated open-sea area between Torres Strait and Weipa, where it is recognized as being harmless to the marine environment. Finely powdered ash is an inert and nonpolluting substance in the marine environment provided that it is thoroughly cooled and wetted. Ash is not discharged over-

board within the Great Barrier Reef, where it might be liable to damage living coral. During the overboard discharging operation at the sea trial, steaming at about 17 knots, a slight grey streak was observed in the wake, but after a few seconds disappeared as the ash sank.

Mr. Tawse—The authors thank to Mr. Tawse for useful supplementary information and appreciate his supporting comments.

It is recommended for the ship's staff to do soot-blowing on the superheater and boiler bank as well as the economizer twice a day, which has not been altered yet. After checking the actual service results later, it will be decided whether the intervals of soot-blowing can be increased.

The grate temperature is about 160°C, which has almost no relation to boiler load. However, it was noted that the temperature increased by about 100°C under a banked condition.

We believe that no noticeable movement of fuel and ash bed on the grate is experienced, because it is reported by the owner that the ship remained very smooth throughout all the shallow-water passages between Weipa and Gladstone. In addition, at the first sea trial on 29–30 July 1982, we experienced big rolling of the ship in excess of 10 deg in half amplitude and no noticeable movement of the fuel bed was observed.

As for the comparison of electric power demand, we agree with the comment of Mr. Tawse that direct comparison of a tanker and a bulk carrier is misleading.

The usual method of ash disposal has already been mentioned in the reply to Mr. Palmieri and Mr. Wahlgren.

Separate storage onboard of bottom and fly ash was at the request of the owner, considering the future utilization of each ash. The bottom ash may be utilized for reclamation works and road pavement. On the other hand, the fly ash may be utilized for cement industries and fertilizer plants. In addition, operational reliability will be higher for separate systems, since bottom ash and fly ash have different density and flow characteristics.

Mr. Gallinaro—The authors thank Mr. Gallinaro for his practical comments and constructive criticism leading to wider flexibility of the coal-fired plant. It is certainly interesting to compare the design of two different coal-fired ships, namely, *River Boyne* for ANL/MHI and *Energy Independence* for Keystone/General Dynamics.

The preliminary design stage for these vessels was about ten months, from October 1979 to July 1980. All the basic design for the contract specification and technical guarantee was fixed in this period. The time required is about three times that for ordinary vessels, due mainly to evaluation of various alternatives in every respect.

The necessity of emergency loading and off-loading as pointed out by Mr. Gallinaro is one of the most important design considerations. Means for emergency coal loading are provided on *River Boyne*. Each coal bunker is provided with two emergency hatches, 2.7 by 3.6 m, through which coal can be bunkered in a traditional way, as has been demonstrated during coal bunkering for tests and trials.

River Boyne has no provision for emergency off-loading of bunkers, since the chance of off-loading is quite remote for this dedicated trade with specialized bunkering facilities ashore. The possible means of off-loading, however, would be through emergency hatches mentioned in the foregoing or by connecting rubber hoses to coal transfer lines running at main deck level.

The concern in dumping heated ash is that the ash may not be completely wetted but remains afloat and could drift to seashore and smother sea life.

In the final design of *River Boyne*, cross connections of combustion air ducts as shown on Fig. 10 were deleted for simplicity of ductwork at the owner's request. At the initial design stage these cross connections were employed in view of redundancy and operational flexibility following the good old practice in marine engineering.

The electric power demands have already been explained in the reply to Mr. Blanding.

The primary reason for the authors' concern about boiler vibration is that the voyage route of the vessel is heavily dotted with shallow waters with minimum underkeel clearance of one meter in extreme shallows. The propeller exciting force, hence stern vibration, is known to increase drastically in shallow waters. If the discusser has experience with motor tankers, he will certainly understand the authors' concern about boiler vibration. We have established a design practice to do a boiler vibration analysis in depth either for newly developed boilers or newly developed hull forms.

Boiler minimum turndown capacity is 25 percent of boiler maximum load. Hence boiler load is set to 25 percent during the in-port condition. For the maneuvering operation, however, the minimum boiler load is set at 40 percent to cover the steam demand of harbor full-ahead and astern operation. Since the boiler evaporation is fixed in the preceding operation modes, any surplus steam is automatically dumped. These minimum load settings are intergrated in the automatic boiler control system.

The fail-safe principle as adopted in the selection of material for coal and ash piping transfer means that the inspection of material shall be done at regular intervals to replace or repair the parts concerned. On the other hand, safe-life principle means that the replacement or repair work should not be done throughout the ship's life, which may result in a prohibitive cost increase.

The authors appreciate Mr. Gallinaro for picking up the point of fundamental importance—suppression of fire in the coal bunker.

The authors understand the suspicion of the U. S. Coast Guard regarding the effectiveness of CO_2 flooding. Our literature survey of the casualties with coal revealed that the cause and remedies are widely separated. Fighting a coal fire appears to be a hide-and-seek matter. We have come to the conclusion that complete water flooding will be the final means.

There is no reason, however, why CO_2 flooding should have adverse effects in fire fighting coal, as approved by Lloyd's Register of Shipping (LRS).

The authors hope that the coal-fired steamship under construction in the discusser's yard will be highly successful and are looking forward to hearing about it.

Mr. LiCausi—The authors appreciate Mr. LiCausi's compliments, but are rather puzzled at such numerous detailed questions while reflecting on his thorough reading of the paper, and his keen interest in boiler performance.

As pointed out by Mr. LiCausi, location of the multi-cyclone, whether in the upstream or downstream of the economizer, has to be carefully examined. In the case of *River Boyne*, location of the economizer at the boiler exit results in a very good machinery arrangement. No fouling of the economizer has been observed so far. We examined the horizontal run of the duct and confirmed no ash buildup. A manhole is provided to inspect the inside of the duct.

The interpretation of Fig. 5 is that we could have higher design steam temperature than that of past trends, since the ash fusion temperature of Callide coal is quite high. However, the design temperature is lower than the current temperature level of $510°C$ due to the limitation in the maximum allowable superheater area to be installed.

The electric power demand has already been explained in the reply to Mr. Blanding.

The endurance of 4500 nautical miles is based on the distance from Nagasaki, Japan, to Gladstone, Australia, via Weipa. Also, this endurance is sufficient from Australia to Singapore or Japan for annual drydocking.

The authors do not agree with the view of Mr. LiCausi that coal transfer capacity is oversized and coal transfer lines have too much redundancy. Each coal bunker is provided with four outlets so as to eliminate excessive peaks and troughs. Independent transfer lines from each outlet to day hoppers with cross connections is for the sake of simplicity and reliability. Day hopper capacity of six hours, which is half of the Rule requirement, reflects the reliability of the transfer system.

No cross-connection is provided between port and starboard day hoppers.

No fly ash re-injection is provided, since unburnt carbon content in fly ash is low. Fly ash re-injection could hardly be justified in view of the very small gains in boiler efficiency with adverse effects such as increased dust loading and complexity of the system.

No special consideration for coal-firing is given to the choice of boiler refractory. The boiler is totally water-walled and hence insulation characteristics becomes the basic requirement.

The authors believe that optimum air distribution on the grate is more important than uniform distribution. Grate speed is regulated by an automatic combustion control system so as to ensure sufficient thickness of the ash layer on the grate regardless of boiler load. The thickness of ash layer at normal load is 150 mm and the design temperature of the bottom ash is $150°C$.

Grate metal temperature and initial light-off procedure have already been explained in the replies to previous discussers.

Unburnt carbon content in the bottom ash is 5 percent.

While carryover of fines will increase with higher excess air ratio as Mr. LiCausi pointed out, furnace dust loading, however, is primarily governed by the content of fines in the coal. Anticipated variation is excess air ratio is 40 percent at full load and about 90 percent at 25 percent of boiler load with fairly wet Callide coal.

The authors' view is that a well-designed and adjusted stoker will not give rise to burning coals in bottom ash hoppers. Possible afterburning in the hopper, however, will result in clinker formation. A clinker crusher is provided to take care of this situation. The design capacity of the bottom ash hopper is six hours at full load. In the event of failure of the ash removal system of one boiler, the other boiler can propel the ship well above the safe steerable speed.

Mr. Bullock—The authors agree with Mr. Bullock that coal-fired ships now enter a demonstration period and valuable operational experience will be accumulated within a few years, which will certainly contribute to improvements in the performance of future coal-fired ships for wider application and, it is hoped, result in revitalization of the steam turbine and boiler industries.

The trial results as requested by Mr. Bullock are summarized at the beginning of the authors' closure. In short, what we have learned from the commissioning of *River Boyne* is that spreader stoker coal-fired marine boilers as well as coal and ash handling systems have much higher flexibility than initially thought, when they are carefully engineered and properly adjusted.

As for the capacity of the daily hopper for the main boiler, LRS was happy to approve the capacity of six hours to be sufficient for unattended machinery space operation in view of their thorough recognition of the reliability of the coal transfer system, that is, the prudent design of discharge hoppers for main bunkers, service-proven fully automated dense-phase pneumatic coal conveying system, and the redundant arrangement of four conveying lines to each hopper as illustrated in Fig. 7.

Prof. Wiggins—The authors agree with Prof. Wiggins that use of kilograms per square centimeter as a unit of pressure may be confusing to students, although "kilogram" is more frequently used as a unit of force representing "kilogram force" in the MKS system. The matter of units had better be included in the Society's guide to prepare technical papers, as is currently done by the Japan Society of Mechanical Engineers to use SI units. In this connection, the authors are happy to inform Prof. Wiggins that SI units are used throughout the instrumentation on *River Boyne*, such as kilopascal for the unit of pressure, including boiler draft.

As to the type of turbines for generator drive, backpressure turbines are justified if the exhaust can be effectively used for heating feed waters, combustion air and distilling plant, etc. When we have excess exhaust to be dumped to the main condenser, then we are penalized in fuel consumption. In the case of *River Boyne* marginal excess exhaust is very acceptable in view of the simplicity of the system.

Regarding the concern of Prof. Wiggins about maneuvering and in-port operation, minimum load is around 26 percent, slightly above the minimum turndown of the boilers, with generator and main feedwater pump turbines exhausting to the deaerator and steam dump control valve closed. Under this condition, an equilibrium is readily reached with about 40 percent of exhaust being used for heating deaerator and steam air heater, while the rest of the exhaust is dumped to the main condenser, giving rise to the source of condensate.

It is not planned to use the diesel generator during mini-mum-load operation in port, contrary to the guess of Prof. Wiggins. The large capacity of the diesel generator is to enable emergency propulsion as mentioned in the reply to Mr. Blanding.

The authors understand the concern of Prof. Wiggins that no heat sink is provided except for main condenser, and hence the consequence of a main condenser vacuum casualty. In order to enhance the reliability of the main condenser and to permit routine maintenance without having to shut down the plant, a split-type main condenser was introduced on *River Boyne*.

Mr. Ciliberti—The authors duly understand the concern of Mr. Ciliberti, which is also one of our concerns, since *River Boyne* relies solely on the processing facility ashore with respect to the quality of coal to be bunkered. Honestly speaking, the authors cannot help Mr. Ciliberti in this regard, because no special provision is made to deal with tramp iron and other debris. The probable consequence of such foreign matter will firstly be plugging of pipes for coal and ash transfer. Such foreign matter will most likely be carried to bottom ash hoppers and might be caught in the screw feeder and clinker crusher for the bottom ash, depending on the size. This problem was discussed in depth at the outset of design and it was decided to rely on the shore facility and not to provide countermeasures such as a last-chance screen. The rationale is that we would rather assume a remote risk due to foreign matter than to accept a more probable chance of increased maintenance due to such additional equipment.

The authors are looking forward to hearing of the successful completion of the first modern U. S.-flag coal-fired ship from Mr. Ciliberti in the coming year.

SNAME *Transactions*, Vol. 90, 1982, pp. 365–390

Residual Stresses Due to Welding: Computer-Aided Analysis of Their Formation and Consequences

Vassilios J. Papazoglou,[1] Associate Member, **Koichi Masubuchi,**[2] Member, **Edison Gonçalves,**[3] Visitor, and **Akihiko Imakita,**[4] Visitor

Results of recent investigations at M.I.T. on the subject of residual stresses due to welding are summarized. Part 1 deals with the computer-aided prediction of residual stress distributions. Both closed-form analytical and numerical solutions, the latter based on the finite-element method, to the problems of determining temperature, transient strain, and residual stress distributions are presented. Experimentally obtained data are then compared with predictions obtained by the developed computer programs to test their validity. Guidelines for the applicability of each model are also included. Part 2 discusses the computer-aided analysis of the effects of residual stresses on the service behavior of welded structures. A finite-element analysis of the fracture characteristics of high-strength steel weldments is described in some detail as a case study. The obtained results are also compared with experimental data.

Introduction

THE PROBLEM of predicting residual stresses due to welding has long been recognized by ship designers and fabricators as very important but at the same time as a very difficult one to analyze. This difficulty has its origin in the complex mechanism of residual stress formation which starts from the uneven temperature distribution caused by the intense, concentrated heat source associated with all fusion welding processes. The incompatible strains that are formed as a consequence give rise in turn to self-equilibrating stresses that remain in the welded structure after it has cooled down to ambient temperature, thus producing the so-called residual stresses.

To effectively analyze the problem and account for the nonlinear phenomena associated with it, one has to draw upon knowledge from a variety of scientific disciplines, including heat transfer, applied mechanics, numerical analysis, and materials science. On top of that, the lengthy calculations required make the solution prohibitive unless one has access to a fast electronic digital computer. It is therefore no coincidence that researchers became actively involved in the field only during the past decade or so, during which time computers and the powerful numerical techniques developed in association with them have started to be more widely used.

A logical question that could come to one's mind at this point is why should one be concerned with the prediction of residual stresses in welded structures, especially since it is such a for-midable problem. The answer is that the effect they have on the service behavior of these structures can be detrimental. Brittle fracture can occur earlier because the presence of residual stresses, combined with any external loading, can substantially decrease the critical flaw size of the weldment. Compressive residual stresses located in the regions some distance away from the weld line can substantially decrease the critical buckling stress of a structure, especially if it is composed of thin plates, causing structural instabilities. Similar effects occur in the areas of fatigue fracture, stress-corrosion cracking, hydrogen embrittlement, and others.

It thus becomes evident that the practicing engineer would like to have a design tool to account for residual stresses and their effects. More specifically, what he wishes to do is to change design and fabrication parameters, such as plate thickness, joint design, welding conditions, and welding sequence, so that the adverse effects of residual stresses (and the associated distortion) can be reduced to acceptable levels from the point of view of reliability. It is generally much better to achieve this goal during an early stage of design and fabrication rather than confronting the problem at later stages of fabrication. This is especially true when critical structures, such as submarines and other types of deep-sea submersibles, are to be built using new materials (for example, HY-130 steel, titanium alloys) or unconventional welding processes (for example, electron beam, laser beam) or both.

One of the most comprehensive sources of information regarding the problem of residual stresses and their consequences is a recently published book by Masubuchi [1].[5] This book, which can be of great value to both designers and fabricators of welded structures, represents a systematic presentation of knowledge on the subject accumulated over the past 30 or so years mainly on the basis of extensive parametric experimental investigations, which can collectively be thought of as "first generation" or "pre-computer age" methodologies. These methodologies have served and still serve their purpose in cases

---

[1] Postdoctoral associate, Department of Ocean Engineering, Massachusetts Institute of Technology, Cambridge, Massachusetts.

[2] Professor of ocean engineering and materials science, Massachusetts Institute of Technology, Cambridge, Massachusetts.

[3] Assistant professor, Department of Naval Architecture and Marine Engineering, University of Sao Paulo, Sao Paulo, Brazil.

[4] Visiting research engineer, Department of Ocean Engineering, Massachusetts Institute of Technology, Cambridge, Massachusetts; also with Mitsui Engineering and Shipbuilding Co., Tokyo, Japan.

Presented at the Annual Meeting, New York, N. Y., November 17–20, 1982, of THE SOCIETY OF NAVAL ARCHITECTS AND MARINE ENGINEERS.

[5] Numbers in brackets designate References at end of paper.

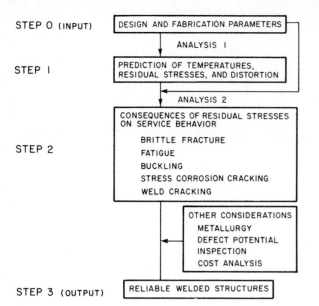

STEP 0 (INPUT)

```
┌─────────────────────────────────────────┐
│ DESIGN AND FABRICATION PARAMETERS        │
└─────────────────────────────────────────┘
              ANALYSIS 1
```

STEP 1

```
┌─────────────────────────────────────────┐
│ PREDICTION OF TEMPERATURES,              │
│ RESIDUAL STRESSES, AND DISTORTION        │
└─────────────────────────────────────────┘
              ANALYSIS 2
```

STEP 2

```
┌─────────────────────────────────────────┐
│ CONSEQUENCES OF RESIDUAL STRESSES        │
│ ON SERVICE BEHAVIOR                      │
│                                          │
│     BRITTLE FRACTURE                     │
│     FATIGUE                              │
│     BUCKLING                             │
│     STRESS CORROSION CRACKING            │
│     WELD CRACKING                        │
└─────────────────────────────────────────┘
```

```
        ┌──────────────────────────────┐
        │ OTHER CONSIDERATIONS          │
        │   METALLURGY                  │
        │   DEFECT POTENTIAL            │
        │   INSPECTION                  │
        │   COST ANALYSIS               │
        └──────────────────────────────┘
```

STEP 3 (OUTPUT)

```
┌─────────────────────────────────────────┐
│ RELIABLE WELDED STRUCTURES               │
└─────────────────────────────────────────┘
```

Fig. 1 Systematic approach for predicting residual stresses due to welding and their consequences

that have already been extensively investigated, for example, joining of mild steel structures using conventional arc welding techniques. Time and cost requirements in today's competitive world, however, do not allow them to be used when new materials and processes have to be effectively used in the construction of seagoing vessels and offshore structures. The need therefore exists for a new, more versatile and efficient computer-age methodology.

This paper discusses such a methodology based on the extensive use of computers in a very systematic way as shown in Fig. 1. Part 1 of the paper discusses state-of-the-art methods for predicting residual stresses (and distortion) due to welding; it thus corresponds to Analysis 1 between Steps 0 and 1 in Fig. 1. The methods presented range from relatively simple one-dimensional analyses to more complicated ones based on the finite-element method with nonlinearities. Comparing the obtained results with data collected through series of experiments, the predictive capabilities of the various methods are finally assessed.

In Part 2 of the paper the subject of analyzing the consequences of residual stresses on the service behavior of welded structures is addressed (Analysis 2 between Steps 1 and 2 in Fig. 1). To demonstrate how the computer can help in this respect, details of the special case of analyzing the fracture characteristics of weldments are presented. The numerical results obtained using the finite-element method are finally compared with exerimentally obtained data.

It is not the intent of the authors to present in detail all the mathematics involved in the discussed methodologies. The interested reader is referred for this purpose to other sources [2–5]. The emphasis will rather be placed on how the ship designers and fabricators can effectively use the state-of-the-art methodologies available today for solving the residual stress problem.

Part 1

Prediction of welding residual stresses

In this part of the paper the problem of predicting residual stresses due to welding is addressed. After a brief introduction on the physical aspects of residual stress formation, the various

methodologies available for calculating residual stress distributions are discussed. Particular emphasis is placed on the method based on a computer simulation of the welding process as it relates to residual stress formation. This consists of first solving the heat-transfer problem and then utilizing the obtained results to perform the stress analysis.

Throughout the discussion special reference is made to the prediction capabilities of the analyses by comparing analytical results with experimental data collected from series of experiments conducted over the past several years by Massachusetts Institute of Technology (M.I.T.) investigators.

General information on residual stresses

Residual stresses are defined as these stresses that exist in a body if all external loads are removed. Various alternative technical terms have been used and can still be found in the literature that refer to residual stresses, including internal stresses, initial stresses, inherent stresses, reaction stresses, and locked-in stresses.

Areas in which residual stresses can exist vary greatly in scale from a large portion of a metal structure down to areas measurable only on the atomic scale [1]. Regarding the former case, macroscopic residual stresses can occur in scales ranging from ships heated by solar radiation from one side to a small area on the top of a plate where grinding took place. On the other hand, microscopic residual stresses can be produced on the atomic scale during a phase transformation or near a dislocation. Furthermore, residual stresses can also be classified, according to the mechanism of formation, to those produced by structural mismatching and those produced by an uneven distribution of nonelastic strains (including plastic and thermal strains).

In the case of welding, with which this paper is concerned, residual stresses can be classified as being macroscopic in scale and as being produced by uneven distributions of nonelastic strains. Finally, it should be noted that since residual stresses exist without any external loads they should always satisfy force and moment equilibrium, that is, they should be self-equilibrating.

Welding residual stress formation

To physically understand how residual stresses are formed during welding, the simple case of a straight bead-on-plate weld will be described in some detail [1]. Figure 2 shows schematically the changes of temperature and stresses that occur during such a process. The welding arc, which is moving at a speed v, is presently located at the origin O, as shown in Fig. 2(a).

Figure 2(b) shows the temperature distribution along several cross sections. Along Section A-A, which is ahead of the welding arc, the temperature change due to welding, $\Delta\theta$, is almost zero. Along Section B-B, which crosses the welding arc, the temperature change is extremely rapid and the distribution is very uneven. Along Section C-C, which is some distance behind the welding arc, the distribution of temperature change is as shown in Fig. 2(b)–3. Along Section D-D, which is very far from the welding arc, the temperature change due to welding again diminishes.

Figure 2(c) shows the distribution of stresses along these sections in the x-direction, σ_x. Stress in the y-direction, σ_y, and shearing stress, τ_{xy}, also exist in a two-dimensional stress field.

Along Section A-A, thermal stresses due to welding are almost zero. The stress distribution along Section B-B is shown in Fig. 2(c)–2. Because molten metal will not support a load, stress underneath the welding arc is close to zero. Stresses in regions a short distance from the arc are compressive, because the expansion of these areas is restrained by the surrounding metal where the temperatures are lower. Since the temperatures of

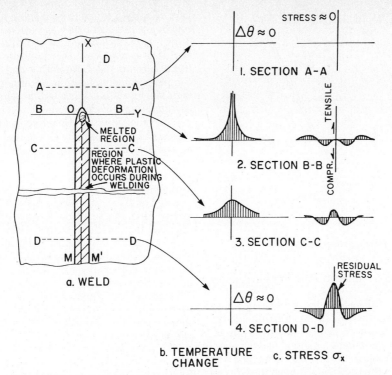

Fig. 2 Schematic representation of changes in temperature and stresses during welding

these areas are high and the yield strength of the material low, stresses in these areas are as high as the yield strength of the material at corresponding temperatures. The magnitude of compressive stress passes through a maximum with increasing distance from the weld or with decreasing temperature. However, stresses in areas away from the weld are tensile and balance with compressive stresses in areas near the weld. In other words

$$\int \sigma_x dy = 0$$

across Section B-B.[6] Thus, the stress distribution along Section B-B is as shown in Fig. 2(c)–2.

Stresses are distributed along Section C-C as shown in Fig. 2(c)–3. Since the weld metal and base metal regions near the weld have cooled, they contract and cause tensile stresses in regions close to the weld. As the distance from the weld increases, the stresses first change to compressive and then become tensile.

Figure 2(c)–4 shows the stress distribution along Section D-D. High tensile stresses are produced in regions near the weld, while compressive stresses are produced in regions away from the weld. This is the usual distribution of residual stresses that remain after welding is completed.

The cross-hatched area, M-M′, in Fig. 2(a) shows the region where plastic deformation occurs during the welding thermal cycle. The egg-shaped region near the origin O indicates the region where the metal is melted.

The region outside the cross-hatched area remains elastic during the entire welding thermal cycle.

Sources of residual stresses—In the previous section the difference in shrinkage of differently heated and cooled areas of a welded joint was identified as the primary cause of residual stress formation, resulting in high longitudinal stresses, σ_x, in the weld metal. Similar tensile stresses, σ_y, arise in the

transverse direction, too, but of smaller magnitude.

This situation is typical for the case examined. If, however, one is also interested in the through-thickness distribution of residual stresses or in materials exhibiting phase transformations, or both, two additional residual stress sources can be identified [6].

One source is the uneven cooling in the thickness direction of the weld. Surface layers of the weld and the highly heated areas close to it usually cool more rapidly than the interior, especially in the case of thick plates. Thermal stresses thus arise over a cross section which can lead to heterogeneous plastic deformation and hence to residual stresses. These "quenching" residual stresses are expected to be compressive at the surface of the highly heated areas and to self-equilibrate with the tensile ones in the inner regions.

The other source of residual stresses comes from the phase transformations that occur during cooling; in the case of steel, for example, austenite is transformed into ferrite, bainite, or martensite, or a combination of them. These transformations are accompanied by an increase in specific volume, causing the material being transformed (in the weld metal and the heat-affected zone) to tend to expand. This expansion, however, is hindered by the cooler material which is not being transformed, inducing compressive stresses in the transformed material and tensile stresses in the other regions.

The total residual stresses due to welding can thus be found by combining the effects of the aforementioned three sources.

Methods for predicting residual stresses

The incompatible nonelastic strains produced in the weldment as a result of the nonuniform temperature distribution are formed in a very complex manner as discussed in previous sections. The computational efforts required to analyze the phenomena involved, including high-temperature plasticity calculations in a multidimensional stress space, have limited investigators' efforts in the past to such simple cases as:

---

[6] This equation neglects the effect of σ_y and τ_{xy} on the equilibrium condition.

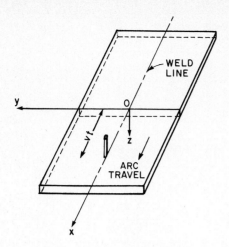

Fig. 3 Weldment configuration

1. Spot welding in which temperature and strain changes are axisymmetric.
2. Instantaneous heating along the edge of a strip in which temperature and stress changes occur in one dimension only.

In more complex cases, however, and before the advent of the era of powerful digital computers, a method had to be devised for the prediction of residual stresses. Such a method was developed by Masubuchi in the late 1950's [7,8] on the basis of Moriguchi's theory of incompatible strains [9]. This method consists of assuming an incompatible strain distribution in the weldment and calculating the residual stresses on the basis of the theory of elasticity, recognizing that this incompatibility is a form of singularity in an elastic stress field. Analyses using singular points, such as a concentrated load or a center of dilation, for solving stress problems under various boundary conditions are well established and can thus be very useful for analyzing residual stresses under similar boundary conditions.

One major drawback of this method, however, is that it is very difficult to estimate the distribution of the incompatible strains. In some representative cases the distribution has been found experimentally [10]. On that basis, estimates can then be made for other similar situations.

It is nevertheless felt that since the advent of the modern digital computer a more accurate prediction of the residual stress distribution can be made by simulating the phenomena that occur during the welding process.

Computer simulation—To accurately simulate the thermo-mechanical behavior of a weld, or for this matter any phenomenon that involves both thermal and stress analysis, one should start from first principles, which in this case is the first law of thermodynamics. This would mean that one would

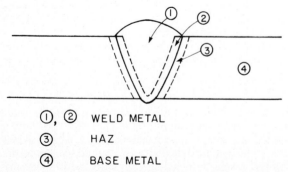

Fig. 4 The four parts of a weld subjected to different thermal histories

①, ②	WELD METAL
③	HAZ
④	BASE METAL

have to solve a problem containing mechanical and thermal coupling, a fact that makes the analysis extremely complicated, if not impossible, on the basis of the present state of knowledge, except in cases where thermoelastic modeling is sufficient. Initial attempts at formulating and investigating the more complex problem of coupled thermoplasticity have been undertaken by Mróz [11,12], but the whole subject area is still at its initial stages of development.

It becomes necessary, therefore, to uncouple the thermal and mechanical parts of the welding problem and solve each one separately. The assumptions required for this uncoupling have been examined by Hibbitt and Marcal [13]; the most critical ones are the neglect of dimensional changes and the neglect of cross-coupling between thermal and mechanical work.

Based on these assumptions the problem can be solved in two steps. First, the heat flow during welding is analyzed. The obtained temporal and spatial temperature distributions are then used as one of the inputs for the subsequent strain and stress analysis. Various analytical and numerical methods that can be used in each step are examined in the next sections of this part of the paper.

Problem characteristics—Figure 3 shows the physical phenomenon to be examined. A welding arc is traveling with a speed v between two plates, causing them to coalesce by providing filler metal.

The four parts of a weld that are subjected to different thermal histories are shown in Fig. 4. Part 1 constitutes the filler metal which is deposited molten and later solidifies as cooling begins. Part 2 is the part of the joint that melts and later resolidifies during cooling. Both these parts define the weld metal. Part 3 is the heat-affected zone (HAZ), defined for steel as that part of the joint in which the maximum temperature reached is above the A_1 but below the solidus temperature.[7] Finally, Part 4 is the base metal.

These four thermal histories and the related changes in physical properties are shown in Fig. 5 for the case of a single-pass weld [14].

Analysis of heat transfer during welding

The importance of accurately predicting the temperature distribution during welding has been recognized for many years by both scientists and engineers working with welding problems. This importance stems from the fact that most of the phenomena subsequently encountered, such as residual stresses, distortion, and metallurgical changes, have their origin in the uneven temperature distribution and the fast heating and cooling rates that occur during the welding operation.

All of the early attempts at solving the problem of heat flow during welding were analytical in nature since they were performed before the advent of the computer. As a consequence several simplifying assumptions had to be made to allow for the solution of the highly nonlinear governing partial differential equation and the accompanying boundary conditions. Starting in the mid-sixties, however, several investigators from around the world have used the computer to numerically predict the thermal history during welding with much greater accuracy.

As with any complex engineering problems, the choice of whether to use an analytical or a numerical solution has to be based on a cost versus accuracy tradeoff. Analytical solutions are much more inexpensive and, though not as accurate as the numerical ones, provide nevertheless for the establishment of the general laws and thus facilitate a good understanding of the

---

[7] A_1 temperature is defined for steel as that temperature at which the eutectoid reaction takes place. Under equilibrium conditions this temperature is equal to 723°C (1333°F). Solidus is defined as that temperature above which the liquid phase is also present.

Residual Stresses Due to Welding

phenomena involved. On the other hand, the more expensive numerical solutions are necessary whenever accuracy is of paramount importance, as for example when a metallurgical characterization of the weld metal and the HAZ is needed, or when a subsequent stress analysis to determine the transient strains and residual stresses is required.

Closed-form analytical solutions

Fundamental solutions—The first exact analytical solutions of the problem of heat flow during welding were obtained by Rosenthal [15–17] in the late 1930's and early 1940's, although a particular case was considered independently at around the same time by Boulton and Lance Martin [18]. Rosenthal solved the conventional heat conduction differential equation for constant point, line, and plane heat sources moving at a constant speed with respect to a fixed Cartesian coordinate system. To facilitate easier handling of the problem, he assumed that welding was performed over a sufficient length so that the temperature distribution around the heat source would not change if viewed from a coordinate system moving with the heat source. This phenomenon is called quasi-stationary or quasi-steady state. Additional assumptions were made as follows:

1. The physical properties of the conducting medium are constant.
2. The heat losses through the surface of the conducting medium to the surrounding atmosphere are neglected.
3. Heat created in electric welding by the Joule effect is negligible.
4. The phase changes and the accompanying absorption or release of latent heat in the conducting medium are neglected.
5. The conducting medium is infinitely large in the two-dimensional case (line heat source) and semi-infinitely large in the three-dimensional case (point source).

Based on the foregoing assumptions Rosenthal developed the following exact solutions for the two- and three-dimensional cases, respectively (see Fig. 3):

$$\theta - \theta_0 = \frac{Q}{2\pi kH} \cdot e^{-\lambda v\xi} \cdot K_0(\lambda v r) \qquad (1)$$

$$\theta - \theta_0 = \frac{Q}{2\pi k} \cdot e^{-\lambda v\xi} \cdot \frac{e^{-\lambda vR}}{R} \qquad (2)$$

where

θ_0 = initial temperature
Q = total heat input
H = plate thickness
$\xi = x - vt$
v = welding (or arc travel) speed
t = time
(x,y,z) = fixed Cartesian coordinate system
$r = (\xi^2 + y^2)^{1/2}$
$R = (\xi^2 + y^2 + z^2)^{1/2}$
k = thermal conductivity
$\frac{1}{2}\lambda = k/\rho c = \kappa$ = thermal diffusivity
ρ = density
c = specific heat
$K_0(x)$ = modified Bessel function of second kind and zero order

For the case of thin plates (two-dimensional solution) Rosenthal [16] and other investigators have suggested that heat losses through the surface to the surrounding atmosphere might have to be taken into account by replacing in the Bessel function of equation (1) the factor λv by

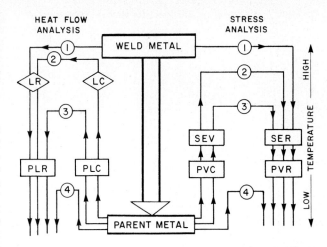

LC — ABSORPTION OF LATENT HEAT DURING MELTING
LR — RELEASE OF LATENT HEAT DURING SOLIDIFICATION
PLC — ABSORPTION OF LATENT HEAT DURING PHASE TRANSFORMATION
PLR — RELEASE OF LATENT HEAT DURING PHASE TRANSFORMATION
PVC — VOLUME SHRINKAGE DURING PHASE TRANSFORMATION
PVR — VOLUME EXPANSION DURING PHASE TRANSFORMATION
SEV — YIELD STRESS AND YOUNG'S MODULUS VANISH
SER — YIELD STRESS AND YOUNG'S MODULUS RECOVER

Fig. 5 Thermal histories and related changes of physical properties of the four weld parts

$$\left[(\lambda v)^2 + \frac{h_1 + h_2}{kH}\right]^{1/2} \qquad (3)$$

where h_1 and h_2 are the heat-transfer coefficients, assumed constant, at the top and bottom of the plate, respectively.

Furthermore, by using the so-called "method of images" or "image source method" [16], one can get solutions for the cases of large but finite thickness and/or finite breadth plates. For example, a three-dimensional solution for laying a weld bead on the top of a finite-thickness plate with adiabatic boundary conditions can be obtained by adding an infinite series to equation (2), yielding

$$\theta - \theta_0 = \frac{Q}{2\pi k} \cdot e^{-\lambda v\xi}$$
$$\cdot \left\{ \frac{e^{-\lambda vR}}{R} + \sum_{n=1}^{\infty} \left[\frac{e^{-\lambda vR_n}}{R_n} + \frac{e^{-\lambda vR_{n'}}}{R_{n'}} \right] \right\} \qquad (4)$$

where

$$R_n = [\xi^2 + y^2 + (2nH - z)^2]^{1/2}$$
$$R_{n'} = [\xi^2 + y^2 + (2nH + z)^2]^{1/2}$$

Following these initial developments many investigators tested the validity of the proposed equations experimentally. A thorough exposition of these works can be found in Myers et al [19]. Comments on this subject are reported in a later section.

Modifications to fundamental solutions—Looking at data on thermal conductivity, specific heat, and density one finds that all these parameters are highly dependent upon temperature, thus making the constant-properties assumption of the analytical solutions unrealistic, especially for the regions close to the heat source where the material exhibits very high tem-

Table 1   Values of arc efficiency for various processes

	Christensen [23]	Rykalin [25]	Tsai [26]
GMAW	...	0.65 to 0.85	...
mild steel	0.66 to 0.70	...	0.80 to 0.90
aluminum	0.70 to 0.85	...	...
SAW	0.90 to 0.99	0.90 to 0.99	0.85 to 0.98
SMAW	...	...	...
mild steel, ac	0.66 to 0.85	0.65 to 0.85	0.55 to 0.90
GTAW	...	...	...
mild steel, ac	0.22 to 0.48	0.20 to 0.50	...
mild steel, dc	0.36 to 0.46	0.45 to 0.75	...
aluminum, ac	0.21 to 0.43	0.20 to 0.50	...

GMAW = gas metal arc welding.
SAW = submerged arc welding.
SMAW = shielded metal arc welding.
GTAW = gas tungsten arc welding.

peratures. It is desirable to predict the high-temperature region as accurately as possible, however, since it is this region that is directly related to the size of the plastic zone and the accompanying residual stresses and distortion.

Researchers at M.I.T. [20–22] adopted the iteration method to take into account the temperature dependence of material properties. The fundamental heat source solution with material properties at some temperature, say $300°C$ ($572°F$), provides the first approximate solution at a particular point. This temperature is compared with the initial guess and if the two temperatures disagree by more than $0.5°C$, new properties are found for a temperature halfway in between. These new values are used to obtain a new temperature estimate. The process is repeated until convergence is reached. It should be pointed out that although this iteration method generally gives good predictions outside the fusion zone, there is no guarantee that it will converge to the correct solution since the approximation used may not satisfy the energy conservation law.

In addition, the conventional point heat source closed form solution fails to give good results in the case of multipass welding. This is due to the fact that the solution is based on the point source being located at the top surface of the plates being welded.

To accommodate the multipass welding case, a modification of the solution was made [2] enabling one to locate the heat source at any point through the plate's thickness. It thus becomes possible to simulate each welding pass by positioning the point source at the center of the pass.

The basic assumptions of the conventional solution were kept the same. Furthermore, the adiabatic boundary conditions on the top and bottom surfaces of the plate were satisfied by using the method of images. The obtained solution can then be expressed by the following equation:

$$\theta = \theta_0 + \frac{Q}{4\pi k} \cdot e^{-\lambda v \xi}$$

$$\cdot \left\{ \frac{e^{-\lambda v R}}{R} + \sum_{n=1}^{\infty} \left[\frac{e^{-\lambda v R_n}}{R_n} + \frac{e^{-\lambda v R_{n'}}}{R_{n'}} \right] \right\} \quad (5)$$

where

$$R_n = \sqrt{\xi^2 + y^2 + (OT_n + z)^2}$$

$$R_{n'} = \sqrt{\xi^2 + y^2 + (OB_n - z)^2}$$

$$OT_n = \sqrt{OB_{n-1} + 2.F}$$

$$OB_n = \sqrt{OT_{n-1} + 2.G}$$

with F and G being the distances of the point heat source from the top and bottom surfaces of the plate, respectively, and OT_n and OB_n the distances of the point heat source from the nth

imaginary ones with respect to the top and bottom surfaces, respectively. All other quantities have been previously defined.

Three-dimensional finite heat source model—Most investigators agree that perhaps the most critical input required for the welding thermal analysis is the power, Q, that enters the plate or section being welded. It is customary to express this total heat input by the formula

$$Q = \eta_a \cdot V \cdot I \quad (6)$$

where V and I are the arc voltage and current, respectively, their product giving the electric arc power. The other parameter in the equation (6), η_a, is called arc efficiency; it represents the ratio of the power introduced by the arc into the metal to the total electric arc power. In other words it provides a semi-empirical way of taking into account the various heat losses that occur through electrode tip heating, radiation to the surrounding atmosphere, metal spatter, etc.

Arc efficiency, η_a, is heavily dependent on the welding process used, the penetration achieved, the shielding gas and many other factors that make it very difficult to predict. It is therefore estimated either through experimental measurements using the calorimetry method [23–25] or through semiempirical correlations with the weld width in the case of single-pass welding [26]. Values of the arc efficiency for various welding processes as proposed by several investigators are given in Table 1.

Of equal importance to the magnitude of the total heat input is its distribution. At the solutions presented earlier a point or line heat source was assumed. As Rykalin [25] and other investigators report, however, a more realistic approach is to assume a Gaussian radial heat flux distribution of the form

$$q(r) = q_0 \cdot e^{-Cr^2} \quad (7)$$

where

q_0 = maximum heat flux at center of heat spot
   = CQ/π, [W/cm^2]
C = heat flux concentration coefficient = $3/r_h^2$, [cm^{-2}]
r = radial distance from center of heat spot, [cm]
r_h = radius of heat spot, [cm]

Equation (7) is valid for a stationary arc. High-speed cinematography reveals, however, that during welding, when the arc is moving, the arc column is not radially symmetric but rather distorted backwards. This observation led Tsai [26] to propose the following equation for the arc heat distribution instead of equation (7):

$$q(r,\xi) = q_0 \cdot e^{-Cr^2 - \lambda v \xi} \quad (8)$$

where all the symbols have been previously defined.

Based on the preceding discussion it is evident that in order to more accurately describe the temperature distribution and cooling rates in the region close to the weld, more realistic assumptions should be employed. A three-dimensional finite heat source model for solving the governing partial differential equation of heat transfer was thus developed [2] under the following assumptions:

1. Quasi-stationary state, that is, steady-state conditions with respect to a coordinate system moving with the heat source.

2. The heat input is provided by a moving three-dimensional skewed normally distributed heat source moving on the surface of the plate and given by equation (8).

3. The thermal conductivity of the material, k, is assumed to be a linear function of temperature, θ, given by

$$k(\theta) = k_0 \cdot [1 + \gamma(\theta - \theta_0)] \quad (9)$$

where k_0 is the value of the thermal conductivity at the initial plate temperature θ_0 and γ the proportionality coefficient.

4. The thermal diffusivity of the material, κ, is assumed to be constant.

5. Convective and radiation boundary heat losses from the plate's surface are taken into account through a constant average "effective" heat-transfer coefficient, h, which can be different for the top and bottom surfaces of the plate.

6. The initial temperature of the plate, θ_0, can be different from the environmental (ambient) temperature, θ_e, to allow for preheating.

7. Phase transformation and Joule heating effects can be neglected.

The final result obtained from this model is given in Appendix 1.

Numerical solutions

Since the advent of the electronic digital computer several serious efforts have been made to numerically solve field, and in particular, heat-transfer, problems. And although the finite difference method had initially the edge, the advantages of the finite-element method, especially if coupled with thermal stress analysis, are more and more recognized today.

Over the years many finite-element programs have thus been developed that are capable of performing heat-transfer analyses. Several of these codes can take various nonlinearities into account in a more or less sophisticated manner. One of the most sophisticated ones is ADINAT (Automatic Dynamic Incremental Nonlinear Analysis for Temperatures) developed by Bathe and co-workers [27,28] over a period of years. Some details of this program will be discussed later. It suffices here to mention that ADINAT can take into account temperature-dependent material properties as well as nonlinear convection and radiation boundary conditions.

The discussion so far dealt with multipurpose heat-transfer finite-element method (FEM) programs. Concurrently, however, several investigators concerned with the welding problem have developed similar programs. Hibbit and Marcal [13] developed such a program in 1973 which was later used by other investigators too. At M.I.T. a team headed by Masubuchi also developed similar programs in the early 1970's [20, 29,30]. Friedman [31-33] has also made substantial contributions in the case of GTA welding working at the Westinghouse Electric Corporation's Bettis Atomic Power Laboratory.

The way each of the aforementioned individuals approached the various aspects of the welding problem are discussed at the appropriate places in the next subsections, where some details on the finite-element formulation of the welding heat transfer problem are presented.

Governing equation—The governing incremental isoparametric finite-element equations for the nonlinear heat-transfer problem can be written in matrix form as follows [27,28]:

$$({}^t\underline{K}^k + {}^t\underline{K}^c + {}^t\underline{K}^r)\Delta\underline{\theta}^{(i)} = {}^{t+\alpha\Delta t}\underline{Q} + {}^{t+\alpha\Delta t}\underline{Q}^{c(i-1)}$$
$$+ {}^{t+\alpha\Delta t}\underline{Q}^{r(i-1)} - {}^{t+\alpha\Delta t}\underline{\hat{Q}}^{(i-1)} \quad (10)$$

or

$$ {}^t\underline{\hat{K}}\Delta\underline{\theta}^{(i)} = {}^{t+\alpha\Delta t}\underline{\hat{Q}}^{(i-1)} \quad (10a)$$

where ${}^t\underline{\hat{K}}$ is the effective conductivity matrix at time t consisting of the conductivity, nonlinear convection, and radiation matrices; ${}^{t+\alpha\Delta t}\underline{Q}$ is the heat flow vector including the effects of surface heat flow inputs, internal heat generation and temperature-dependent heat capacity; ${}^{t+\alpha\Delta t}\underline{\hat{Q}}^{(i-1)}$ is the effective heat flow vector; and $\Delta\underline{\theta}^{(i)}$ is the increment in nodal-point temperatures in iteration i:

Table 2 Temperature dependence of heat convection coefficient

	h[Btu/sec in.^{2} R]		
$\theta^s - \theta_e$[R]	Case 1	Case 2	Case 3
0	0	0	0
100	0.2×10^{-5}	0.2×10^{-5}	0.1×10^{-4}
500	0.5×10^{-5}	0.1×10^{-4}	0.6×10^{-4}
1000	0.1×10^{-4}	0.2×10^{-4}	0.1×10^{-3}
5000	0.58×10^{-3}	0.58×10^{-4}	0.6×10^{-3}
50000	0.12×10^{-2}	0.12×10^{-2}	0.12×10^{-2}

NOTE: θ^s = surface temperature.
 θ_e = environmental temperature.

$$ {}^{t+\alpha\Delta t}\underline{\theta}^{(i)} = {}^{t+\alpha\Delta t}\underline{\theta}^{(i-1)} + \Delta\underline{\theta}^{(i)} \quad (11)$$

Equation (10) represents the heat flow equilibrium at time $t+\alpha\cdot\Delta t$, where $0 \le \alpha \le 1$ and α is chosen to obtain optimum stability and accuracy in the solution. Furthermore, the solution using these equations corresponds to the modified Newton-Raphson iteration scheme.

Boundary conditions—Convection and radiation boundary conditions are taken into account by including the matrices ${}^t\underline{K}^c$ and ${}^t\underline{K}^r$ and the vectors ${}^{t+\alpha\Delta t}\underline{Q}^c$ and ${}^{t+\alpha\Delta t}\underline{Q}^r$ in equation (10). Additional external heat flow input on the boundary is specified in ${}^{t+\alpha\Delta t}\underline{Q}$ as surface heat flow input. Prescribed temperature conditions can also be specified.

With respect to the welding problem these boundary conditions can be stated in more detail as follows:

1. Convection heat losses from the plates' surfaces can be modeled according to Newton's linear law

$$ q^s = h \cdot (\theta_e - \theta^s) \quad (12)$$

where h is the temperature-dependent convection coefficient, θ_e the environmental temperature, and θ^s the surface temperature at the point under consideration. There is some difficulty in estimating the temperature dependence of h. Although most previous investigators considered h to be constant, efforts were made at M.I.T. to rationally estimate it on the basis of past semi-empirical studies. Table 2 provides the three different sets of values tested. Discussion on the obtained results are made later.

2. Radiation heat losses are very significant in the vicinity of the weld metal because of the large difference between the surface and environmental temperatures. These losses are modeled according to the quartic Stefan-Boltzman law

$$ q^s = \sigma\epsilon A(\theta_r^4 - \theta^{s4}) \quad (13)$$

where

σ = Stefan-Boltzman constant
ϵ = emissivity of surface
A = shape factor
θ_r = sink temperature
θ^s = surface temperature

In the M.I.T. studies the shape factor was taken to be unity and the emissivity coefficient 0.8.

3. Temperatures can be prescribed at any point and/or surface of a weldment. Such a case, however, seldom arises in welding analyses.

4. The heat input during welding is modeled using the concept of arc efficiency. For the space distribution of the heat input, a consistent formulation should be adopted assuming a uniform distribution over the top of each weld bead. Finally, the time distribution of the heat input is modeled in such a way that the passing of the arc over the cross section examined could be simulated (a linear increase as the arc approaches, uniform

as the arc travels over the cross section, followed by a linear decrease).

Time integration schemes—A family of one-step methods [34] is considered for the time integration using the parameter α. The scheme is found to be unconditionally stable for $\alpha \geq \frac{1}{2}$ and to generally give better solution accuracy when $\alpha = 1$ (Euler backward method). Finally the modified Newton iteration is guaranteed to converge provided the time step Δt is small enough.

Material properties—One of the significant features of the finite-element method is that it can take into account any nonlinear dependence of the material physical properties with temperature, something that is very important in the welding analysis. Furthermore, it can incorporate the latent heat of fusion or of any solid-state material transformation, which cannot be furnished by closed-form analytical solutions [13, 33].

Dimensionality of problem—At first glance even the simpler welding heat-transfer analysis looks as a three-dimensional one. If the assumptions are made, however, that the welding heat source (arc) is moving at a constant speed along a regular path (for example, a straight line in a planar weld), that the weld speed is sufficiently high relative to the material's characteristic diffusion rate, and that end effects resulting from either initiation or termination of the heat source can be neglected, the three-dimensional character of the heat-transfer problem can be simplified. This can be achieved by analyzing a cross section of the weldment of unit thickness and located in the midlength region of the weld [2,31].

Molten-pool modeling—The heat-transfer mechanism in the weld metal, when molten, is extremely complex and its physics are not well understood as of today. These complexities arise not only from the difficulty involved in modeling the welding arc heat flux correctly, but also from the behavior of the convective motion of the molten metal, the thermal properties of the molten metal (including the phase transformations that take place during melting and solidification), the electric heating due to the current flow in the base metal, the boundary conditions for heat losses, etc. Many investigators have recognized these difficulties and have tried to find ways to approximate the phenomena involved.

A look at the available literature reveals that there are generally three ways for handling the problem. The first one, still at its developing stages, tries to understand and subsequently mathematically model the physical phenomena involved, that is, the fluid flow, the convective heat transfer, etc. [35]. Since no conclusive general results are available yet, this approach cannot be generally used.

In the second way the problem is divided into two parts. First the shape of the molten pool is semi-empirically determined; then the heat flow equations are solved numerically in the solid metal only using the melting isotherm as a boundary condition [26]. This method cannot be used, however, because the temperature distribution in the weld metal has to be calculated too if a stress analysis is to follow (most plastic deformation that causes the formation of residual stresses takes place in this region).

The third and final approach tries to simulate the convective heat-transfer mechanism in the molten metal by using a value for the thermal conductivity of the molten metal an order of magnitude higher than that of the material at the solidus temperature. This approach, although strictly not physically correct, was used in the M.I.T. investigation.

Finally, since the cases analyzed involved multipass welding, it is necessary to find a way to model the laying of the various beads during the welding cycle. This was made possible by the element birth-and-death capabilities of the code used. In other words, the program ADINAT is capable of giving birth to a predetermined number of elements at predetermined time instances, thus enabling one to model the laying of a bead by specifying the appearance of the elements representing it at the time it physically appears [27].

Analysis of transient strains and residual stresses due to welding

Using the temperature distributions predicted on the basis of the techniques described in the previous section, one can calculate the transient strains, transient stresses and residual stresses due to welding since the problem is assumed to be uncoupled. The calculation of strains and stresses, however, poses a much more formidable problem than the one encountered in the heat-transfer analysis, making the use of numerical techniques a necessity. These difficulties stem from the complicated thermal-elastic-plastic state developed in and around the weld metal during welding.

Two general techniques have been developed to solve the problem. One is a simple one-dimensional analysis and the other a more sophisticated one based on the finite-element method. Both will be considered here, although emphasis will be placed on the latter.

One-dimensional analysis

The one-dimensional model for calculating stresses parallel to the weld line only was first developed in 1964 by Tall [36]. Using this model, Masubuchi, Simons, and Monroe [37] developed a computer program which was later modified and improved both at M.I.T. and elsewhere [20–22,38,39].

The basic assumption inherent in the one-dimensional stress analysis is that the only stress present is the one parallel to the weld line, σ_x, and that this stress is a function of the transverse distance from the weld centerline only. As a consequence, the equilibrium conditions are not satisfied. Despite this, however, it appears that the obtained solutions correlate reasonably well with experimental data in certain cases, as will be further explored.

The analysis lends basically the procedure originally proposed by Tall [36]; the computer code implementing the solution with the latest modifications can be found in [22].

The algorithm for solving the problem is based on the method of successive elastic solutions as proposed by Mendelson [40]. The program can take into account the temperature dependence of all material properties, any type of strain hardening and can solve bead-on-plate, edge, and butt welds of flat plates with finite width. One of the input requirements, the temperature distribution, can also be calculated if desired by the same program using the line heat source solution. The output at each time step consists of the temperature, total strain, mechanical strain, plastic strain, and stress at each of the predetermined points located at various transverse distances from the weld centerline.

Previous applications of the program have shown that it gives good results in the case of thin plates. This happens because in thin plates all stresses, except σ_x, are very small, sometimes an order of magnitude smaller than σ_x. Further discussion is delayed until the next section when experimentally obtained results are compared with analytical solutions.

Finally, it should be mentioned that the one-dimensional analysis can be used with proper minor modifications for the analysis of simple structural forms other than plates. An example is the welding analysis of built-up T-beams [20,22].

Finite-element analysis

The complex behavior of a weldment, and in particular the highly nonlinear material response and the material loading and unloading that occur in the multidimensional stress space, can be handled more accurately using numerical techniques such as the finite-element method.

One of the first applications of FEM to weld problems was presented by Hibbitt and Marcal [13], who considered a thermo-mechanical model for the welding and subsequent loading of a fabricated structure. Their model simulates GMA welding processes and accounts for temperature-dependent material properties. Friedman [31–33] also developed finite-element analysis procedures for calculating stresses and distortions in longitudinal butt welds. These procedures are applicable to planar or axisymmetric welds. Rybicki and co-workers [41] have developed similar procedures. At M.I.T. a team headed by Masubuchi has also developed two-dimensional finite-element programs capable of performing plane-strain and plane-stress analyses [1,20,29,30].

Japanese investigators have also been very active in the field. Ueda and co-workers [14], Satoh et al [42], and more recently Fujita and Nomoto [43] have all developed models to calculate transient strains and residual stresses due to welding based primarily on the initial strain method.

A recent report [44] contains an annotated bibliography of research efforts in the area that have been published since 1977.

In this subsection some details on the finite-element formulation of the welding stress problem are presented. Although the discussion pertains to the multipurpose nonlinear stress finite-element program ADINA [45,46], it is felt that what is discussed can be equally well applied to any similar code.

Finite-element formulation—Some basic considerations regarding the thermo-elastic-plastic and creep constitutive model used in conjunction with ADINA are discussed in the following.

The governing incremental finite-element equations for the problem can be written as [45]

$$^\tau\underline{K}\Delta\underline{U}^{(i)} = {}^{t+\Delta t}\underline{R} - {}^{t+\Delta t}\underline{F}^{(i-1)} \tag{14}$$

where $^\tau\underline{K}$ is the tangent stiffness matrix corresponding to time τ; $^{t+\Delta t}\underline{R}$ is the nodal-point external force vector at time $t+\Delta t$; $^{t+\Delta t}\underline{F}^{(i-1)}$ is a vector of nodal-point forces that are equivalent, in the virtual work sense, to the internal element stresses at time $t+\Delta t$ and iteration $i-1$

$$^{t+\Delta t}\underline{F}^{(i-i)} = \int_V \underline{B}_L^{T\,t+\Delta t}\underline{\sigma}^{(i-1)}dv \tag{15}$$

and $\Delta\underline{U}^{(i)}$ is the increment in nodal-point displacement in iteration i

$$^{t+\Delta t}\underline{U}^{(i)} = {}^{t+\Delta t}\underline{U}^{(i-1)} + \Delta\underline{U}^{(i)} \tag{16}$$

The solution using equation (14) corresponds to the modified Newton-Raphson iteration procedure which is helpful in improving the solution accuracy and in many cases in preventing the development of numerical instabilities. The convergence of the iteration can be accelerated using the Aitken method or, in complex material nonlinear cases (like the welding problem), improved using the BFGS (Broyden-Fletcher-Goldfarb-Shanno) matrix updating method [46].

In the thermo-elastic-plastic and creep model, and assuming infinitesimal strains, the total strain at time τ, $^\tau e_{ij}$, is assumed to be given by

$$^\tau e_{ij} = {}^\tau e_{ij}^E + {}^\tau e_{ij}^P + {}^\tau e_{ij}^C + {}^\tau e_{ij}^{TH} \tag{17}$$

where

$^\tau e_{ij}^E$ = elastic strain
$^\tau e_{ij}^P$ = plastic strain
$^\tau e_{ij}^C$ = creep strain
$^\tau e_{ij}^{TH}$ = thermal strain

so that at any time τ during the response the stress is given by the constitutive law for an isotropic thermo-elastic material

$$^\tau\sigma_{ij} = {}^\tau C_{ijrs}^E({}^\tau e_{rs} - {}^\tau e_{rs}^P - {}^\tau e_{rs}^C - {}^\tau e_{rs}^{TH}) \tag{18}$$

with $^\tau C_{ijrs}^E$ denoting a component of the elastic constitutive tensor.

The thermal strains are

$$^\tau e_{rs}^{TH} = {}^\tau\alpha_m({}^\tau\theta - \theta_R)\delta_{rs} \tag{19}$$

where $^\tau\alpha_m$ is the average thermal expansion coefficient, θ_R is the reference temperature, and δ_{rs} the Kronecker delta. This term can be modified to include, in addition to the thermal strain, the strains that are induced from the solid phase transformations occurring during the heating and cooling stages of the thermal history [2,47].

The creep strains can be determined by any of a number of different approaches proposed in the literature. Given that in the welding problem the time intervals at high temperature are short, however, creep can be neglected.

For the plastic strains, $^\tau e_{rs}^P$, the situation is more complicated. Although the classical theory of isothermal plasticity is a well-tested one, extension of the theory to nonisothermal cases is difficult to substantiate experimentally. Several investigators have proposed modifications but very few experiments have been performed. Relatively good agreement between theory and experiments has generally been reported but for temperatures up to about 538°C (1000°F) only. During welding, though, the temperatures rise to above the A_1 temperature [654°C (1210°F) for steel] inside the HAZ-base metal boundary and above the liquidus temperature in the weld metal. For lack of any alternative, however, the same nonisothermal theory of plasticity can be used throughout the temperature range encountered in welding problems.

The general form of the yield or loading function for multiaxial stress conditions is

$$^\tau F = {}^\tau F({}^\tau\sigma_{ij}, {}^\tau\alpha_{ij}, {}^\tau\sigma_y) \tag{20}$$

where $^\tau\alpha_{ij}$ and $^\tau\sigma_y$ are functions of the history of plastic deformation and temperature. For elastic behavior, $^\tau F < 0$, and for plastic behavior $^\tau F = 0$. As a consequence of Drucker's postulate for stable plastic materials, $^\tau F$ defines a convex surface in the stress-temperature space. It is also assumed that the isothermal normality condition remains valid, so that

$$^\tau\dot{e}_{rs}^P = {}^\tau\lambda\frac{\partial^\tau F}{\partial^\tau\sigma_{ij}} \tag{21}$$

where $^\tau\lambda$ is a positive scalar. The selection of a hardening rule is also required for the calculation of $^\tau\lambda$. In ADINA either isotropic or kinematic hardening can be assumed. Because cyclic plasticity is expected in the welding problem, the kinematic hardening mechanism, thought by many to better model the phenomena involved, should be chosen. The assumptions involved in this mechanism are that the size of the yield surface depends on the temperature only, whereas the translation rate of the yield surface in the stress space depends on the plastic strain rate.

Further details on the numerical aspects of the problem can be found in [46].

Geometry and boundary conditions—A cross section of the weldment in its midlength can be used to calculate the transient strains, transient stresses, and residual stresses due to welding. This is rationalized by the fact that for relatively long plates the maximum stresses are developed in this region. Furthermore, the plane-strain assumption can be used (that is, all plane sections normal to the weld line remain plane during the entire welding process).

The boundary conditions to be used in the analysis should be

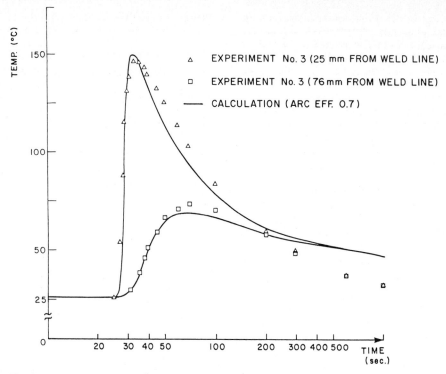

Fig. 6 Temperature distribution—analysis versus experiment (bead-on-plate weld; line heat source)

such so as to allow free expansion of the weldment in the transverse direction as well as bending. At the same time the structure should be properly restrained to eliminate all possible modes of rigid-body motion; otherwise the stiffness matrix will not be positive definite.

The foregoing holds for a relatively thick weldment. In the case of a thin plate, a plane-stress analysis can alternatively be performed over the top surface of the plate (assuming negligible through-thickness stress gradients).

Material properties—The temperature dependence of Young's modulus, E, Poisson's ratio, ν, virgin yield stress, σ_{vy}, and strain hardening modulus, E_T, are all required input for the thermo-elastic-plastic model used.

A word of caution is appropriate at this point as far as the material properties above the liquidus temperature are concerned. The material does not have any strength when molten since all its mechanical properties are zero. But due to numerical considerations, zero properties cannot generally be entered as input to the program. Hence to avoid any instabilities (or even divisions by zero) very small values for E, σ_{vy}, and E_T should be used above the liquidus temperature.

Another point is the accumulation of plastic strains in the regions that become molten during the welding cycle. When the temperature reaches the liquidus these plastic strains are physically relieved, starting to accumulate again when the metal solidifies. The presence of nonzero material properties above the liquidus, however, would cause the plastic strains not only to continue accumulating but also to reach artificially high values owing to the very low magnitude of the mechanical properties. It was therefore necessary to modify ADINA by imposing a total relief of plastic strains when the material melts.

Solution strategy—One of the most important decisions an analyst has to make when performing a nonlinear incremental stress analysis is the solution strategy to be followed, because the accuracy and the convergence characteristics of the solution depend very much on it. This is especially true for complex

situations involving highly nonlinear material behavior like the one encountered in the welding problem. It is therefore necessary to perform several numerical experiments prior to a full analysis of the problem.

Experimental verification of models

In the previous two sections various analytical and numerical methods for the prediction of temperature, transient strain, and residual stress distributions due to welding were described. It was suggested that these methods could be very useful to designers and fabricators for the prediction of residual stresses. Before the methods can be widely used, however, the level of confidence in their predictive capabilities should be well established. This can be done by comparing their predictions with results obtained from systematic series of experiments that cover different cases encountered in practice. Through these comparisons the analytical and numerical models can be tested and modified where necessary.

During the past ten or so years efforts towards this goal have been continuously made by several M.I.T. investigators. Their results have been published in a number of theses, reports, and papers [2,4,5,20–22,26,29,30,37,38,47]. In this section some of the most recent investigations will be reported. At the same time the capabilities and limitations of the several methodologies will be discussed.

Temperature distributions

Line heat source—To investigate the predictive capabilities of the line heat source solution, experiments performed on 6.35-mm thick ($\frac{1}{4}$ in.) 6061 T6 aluminum alloy plates [48] were analyzed. Bead-on-plate welds using the GMAW process were performed with an arc voltage of 19 V, arc current of 240 A, and welding speed of 13.6 mm/sec (0.54 in./sec). The plates were 76.2 cm (30 in.) long and 45.7 cm (18 in.) wide. Figure 6 shows how the experimentally obtained data compare with the analytical predictions [22] at two points located 25 and 76 mm (1 and 3 in.) away from the weld centerline and on the midsection of the plate (quasi-stationary state). It can be seen that the correlation is very favorable. Note that this would not be the case if locations closer to the weld centerline were considered because of the singularity (heat source) present on this line.

Similar good predictions have been obtained when plates up to about 12.7 mm (½ in.) in thickness and bead-on-plate or butt welded using conventional processes were analyzed. In addition, analyses of plates up to 25.4 mm (1 in.) thick and welded using high-energy-density welding processes (electron beam and laser) seem to accurately predict temperature distributions [49].

A common characteristic of all the cases for which the line heat source solution gives reasonably accurate predictions at points some distance away from the weld centerline is the presence of negligible temperature gradients in the plate's thickness direction (two-dimensional heat transfer). This characteristic can therefore be used as a criterion for when such a solution can be utilized.

Finite heat source—As previously mentioned, the line heat source solution does not give accurate results at points close to the weld centerline, even for thin plates, the reason being that the heat source introduces a singularity which does not model the phenomena in this area properly. This difficulty, however, can be overcome by the three-dimensional point heat source model discussed in an earlier section.

To test this proposition, experimental results previously obtained [26] when welding a 3.2-mm-thick (⅛ in.) low-carbon steel plate were analyzed. The welding speed was 3.80 mm/sec (0.15 in./sec) and the arc power 5000 J/sec. Figure 7 shows the comparison between experiments and analysis at two points located 10.2 and 17.8 mm (0.4 and 0.7 in.) away from the weld centerline. As postulated, the finite heat source model gives good results in this thin-plate case.

Point heat source—The point heat source solution is more appropriate when relatively thick welded plates, say more than 12.7 mm (½ in.), are to be analyzed. This is the case because in these instances the heat-transfer problem is a three-dimensional one due to the presence of temperature gradients in the thickness direction too. When joining thicker plates, however, more than one welding pass is required, necessitating the use of the modifications described at an earlier section (that is, the positioning of the point source at the center of each pass). Moreover, one should note that as in the line heat source case the temperature predictions close to the weld centerline will not be very accurate due to the singularity induced by the presence of the point source. To remedy the situation somewhat one should limit the maximum temperature calculated to a fixed value, such as the liquidus temperature; otherwise, artificially high values will be obtained.

To demonstrate the aforementioned points the first pass of a multipass welding experiment on a 25.4-mm-thick (1 in.) HY-130 plate welded using the GMAW process was analyzed. Details of the experiments can be found in [2,4,49]. Figure 8 presents some of the results obtained. Shown are the cases of constant material properties with the point heat source located on the top surface of the plate (conventional solution) and at a distance 11.1 mm (0.4375 in.) from the top (simulating the first pass of the actual welding experiment) and the case of variable properties (iterative solution).

The results show clearly the overestimation of temperatures if the conventional point heat source is applied even if the temperature variation of material properties is considered. This overestimation is even more pronounced in the high-temperature region close to the weld centerline. Finally, comparison of the modified solutions predictions with experimentally obtained data revealed good correlation [2].

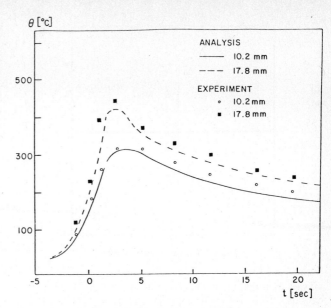

Fig. 7 Comparison of finite heat source solution with experimental data for a 3.2-mm-thick welded plate

Finite-element solution—To test the predictive capabilities of the more accurate nonlinear finite element heat-transfer program ADINAT, a series of experiments involving the multipass GMA welding of 25.4-mm-thick (1 in.) HY-130 plates was analyzed.

Figure 9 shows the test plate arrangement for these experiments. The weld joint consisted of a double-V groove with a

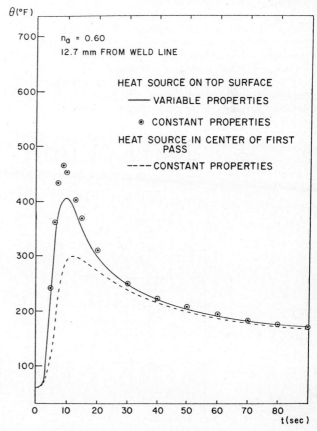

Fig. 8 Investigation of point heat source solutions (12.7 mm away from weld centerline)

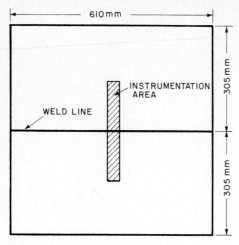

Fig. 9 Test plate arrangement

60-deg included angle in accordance with U.S. Navy specifications. The test plate support arrangement consisted of knife-edge supports located through the whole specimen length at 127 and 203 mm (5 and 8 in.) from the weld centerline on either side; this way the experiments were performed with the specimens completely unrestrained. Twelve passes were needed to complete the welding with an arc voltage of 25 V, a travel speed of 5.1 mm/sec (0.2 in./sec) and a heat input of 14.6 kJ/cm (37 kJ/in.). Temperatures and transient strains were measured throughout the welding operation using Chromel/Alumel adhesive bonded thermocouples and 90-deg Rosette electric resistance strain gages, respectively, located at preselected distances from the weld centerline (the instrumentation area is shown in Fig. 9).

A cross section of the plate at its midlength was analyzed. Figure 10 shows the finite-element mesh used for the analysis. Four- to six-node isoparametric elements were used; special care was taken not to include any triangular elements in the mesh. A total of 77 nodes and 47 elements was utilized.

Table 3 summarizes the four analyses performed. Two parameters were varied, the arc efficiency, η_a, and the temperature variation of the convection coefficient, h, given the

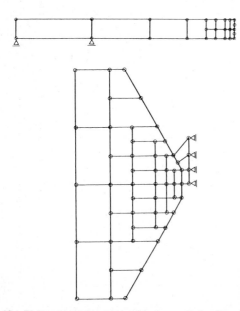

Fig. 10 Finite-element mesh used in the analysis of the welding problem

fact that some uncertainty exists regarding their true values. All other variables were kept constant in the four cases.

Cases A2, A3, and A4 are compared with experimentally obtained results in Fig. 11 for a point on the plate's top surface 12.7 mm (0.5 in.) away from the weld centerline and for the first welding pass. Considering the same heat input ($\eta_a = 0.60$), little difference is found between Cases A2 and A3. This is due to the fact that although higher values for the convection coefficient were chosen in Analysis A3, these values were not high enough to significantly alter the heat losses from the top and bottom surfaces of the plate and consequently the temperature distribution. A substantial increase in the convection coefficient was therefore chosen for Case A4; at the same time, however, an increase in the arc efficiency was made to partially compensate for the higher h and thus to obtain a good estimate of the maximum temperature reached. As seen in Fig. 11, the combination of values used in this latter analysis succeeded in bringing the cooling rate much closer to the experimental one. At the same time a 4 percent overprediction of the maximum temperature is observed. The difference, however, was very small so that any further analysis was not felt necessary.

Similar results were found at other points of the plate and for the consecutive welding passes. Case A4 always came closest at matching the experimentally obtained results.

Transient strain and residual stress distributions

One-dimensional analysis—The same experiments as the ones mentioned in the line heat source solution were analyzed to test the predictive capabilities of the one-dimensional computer program. Figure 12 shows the longitudinal strain history at a point 25.4 mm (1 in.) away from the weld centerline. Presented are experimental data and predictions based on the old [21] and new [22] versions of the program (the most important modification is a change in the numerical integration scheme). It can be seen that the analytical results have a good correlation with the experimentally obtained ones. Similar conclusions can also be drawn with regard to the residual stress distribution [22].

To investigate the limits of the predictive capabilities of the one-dimensional model, experiments on 25.4-mm-thick (1 in.) plates welded using the electron beam (EB) and the GMAW processes were analyzed. The EB specimens had the same geometric configuration as the GMA welded ones (described previously when the finite-element heat-transfer analysis was discussed), the only difference being the joint shape which was square butt in the case of EB welding.

Figure 13 shows the comparison between experiment and analysis of the longitudinal transient strain history, ϵ_x, in the EB specimen at two points 17 and 25.4 mm (0.67 and 1 in.) away from the weld centerline. Despite the thickness of the specimens [25.4 mm (1 in.)] the results show a remarkably good correlation of analysis and experiment. This can be attributed to the physics of the EB welding process which result in a relatively uniform through-thickness temperature distribution and a narrow heat-affected zone. As a consequence, stresses σ_y, σ_{xy}, and σ_z are small compared with σ_x, a fact substantiated

Table 3 Summary of analyses performed

Analysis	η_a [a]	h Case [b]
A1	0.65	1
A2	0.60	1
A3	0.60	2
A4	0.70	3

[a] η_a is the arc efficiency utilized.
[b] Refers to the cases presented in Table 2.

Residual Stresses Due to Welding

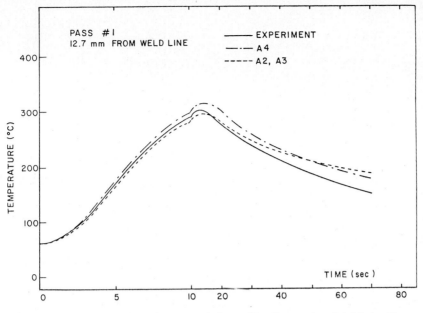

Fig. 11 Comparison of finite-element analysis results with experimental data (weld pass No. 1)

by the experimental data. The assumption of the one-dimensional theory that σ_x is the only stress present is, therefore, approximately valid. It should be emphasized once more, however, that these results apply for the midlength of a relatively long plate [longer than 457.2 mm (18 in.)], where the maximum possible stresses have been developed and where the end effects can be neglected.

The comparison between experimental data and analytical results for the longitudinal transient strain history in the GMA welded specimens at two points 25.4 and 57.2 mm (1.0 and 2.25 in.) away from the weld centerline is shown in Fig. 14. Here the story is completely different. The correlation is not good, especially for the closest point; at around 45 sec from the

commencement of welding, for example, the experimental data show a maximum positive longitudinal strain of about 0.9, whereas the analysis predicts a negative longitudinal strain 0.4 in magnitude. It is thus apparent that the assumptions involved in the one-dimensional analysis break down in the case of multipass GMA welds of thick plates. Experimental data actually confirm this by showing that the transverse strains are of the same order of magnitude as the longitudinal ones.

In conclusion, then, the one-dimensional program seems to be appropriate for analyzing thin plates welded by conventional processes or medium-thickness plates welded by one of the high-energy-density processes.

Finite-element analysis—The same experiments as the ones

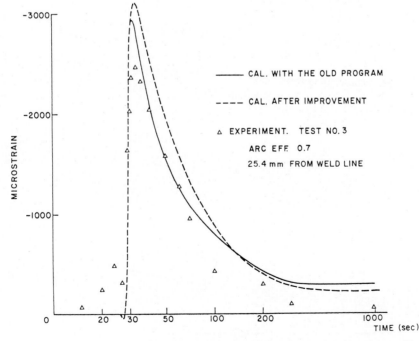

Fig. 12 Longitudinal strain history—analysis versus experiment (bead-on-plate weld; one-dimensional program)

Residual Stresses Due to Welding

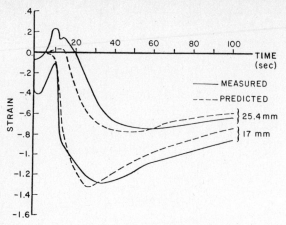

Fig. 13 Longitudinal transient strain histories for EB welded specimen (experiment and analysis)

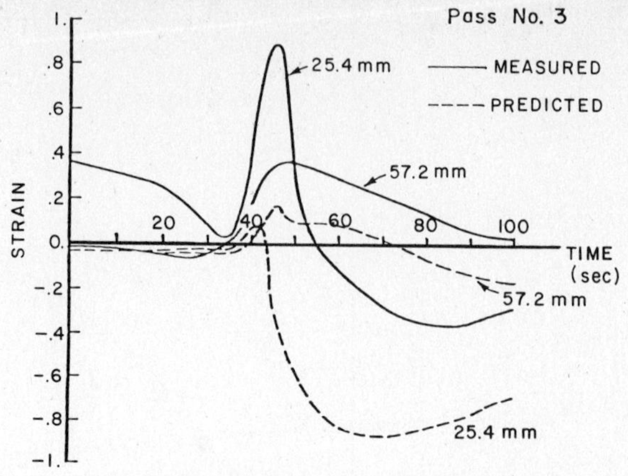

Fig. 14 Longitudinal transient strain histories for GMA welded specimens (experiment and analysis)

analyzed for the finite-element heat-transfer problem were also used in the stress analysis. The finite-element mesh used was also the same (see Fig. 10); now the appropriate nodal restraints were also imposed.

Comparison of the experimentally measured transverse transient strain history at a point located at the top surface of the plate is made with the numerically obtained results in Fig. 15. The correlation is relatively good if one takes into account the various assumptions involved in modeling the complex welding problem. A delay in the transition from tensile to compressive and again from compressive to tensile strains is observed in the analysis. The same delay as far as the occurrence of the maximum strain is also exhibited. It is believed that this phenomenon is primarily due to the relative coarseness of the finite-element mesh, and the complex loading history present in the welding problem.

Figure 16 shows calculated transient longitudinal stress distributions. Compressive stresses exist in the weld metal prior to melting. When the metal is in its molten stage, negligible compressive or tensile stresses were calculated. As cooling commences, tensile stresses start appearing in the weld metal. These stresses then build up to the residual stress pattern when ambient temperature is reached. For self-equilibrating purposes, compressive stresses exist in areas removed from the weld centerline. Note in Fig. 16 the effect of phase transformation, causing a sudden decrease in the tensile stresses.

Summarizing, it can be said that the finite-element model developed based on ADINA modified for phase transformation effects captures most of the important aspects of the welding

stress analysis. Although some discrepancies have been observed between the obtained results and experimental data, considerations of cost and the assumptions made do not allow much more sophisticated analyses at present. It is expected, however, that the dramatically decreasing computer costs, together with developments in the areas of coupled thermoplasticity, will enable investigators to perform more accurate analyses in the future.

Part 2

Analysis of consequences of residual stresses

This part of the paper addresses the problem of analyzing the consequences of residual stresses on the service behavior of welded structures. A brief introduction on the subject is first given, mostly qualitative in nature, followed by a discussion on how the various problems in the area can be analyzed. Because of the vastness of the field, however, and due to length limitations, one particular case only has been singled out and analyzed in some detail. It consists of an investigation on the fracture characteristics of weldments made of high-strength quenched-and-tempered steels.

Finally, and in accordance with the general philosophy of always testing the predictive capabilities of any analysis, the analytical results are compared with data obtained during a series of experiments.

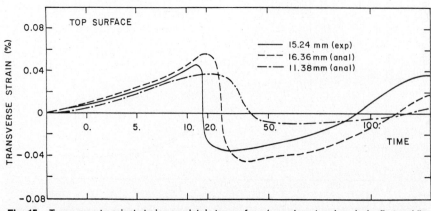

Fig. 15 Transverse transient strains on plate's top surface (experiment and analysis; first welding pass)

Effects of residual stresses

Besides the basic issues of structural and material strength, several additional factors have to be taken into account when one wishes to analyze the service behavior of a welded structure. One of the most important of these factors is the presence of residual stresses due to welding.

Unfortunately, there are no general rules that can guide the designer of a welded structure in the determination of the effects these residual stresses will have on the reliability of the structure. This is mainly due to the fact that these effects can be very complex in nature. Furthermore, and depending on the nature of the structural or material characteristic one is interested in, controversial opinions might be found in the available literature regarding the true effect the residual stresses have.

In this section an effort will be made to briefly discuss some aspects of the consequences of residual stresses on the service behavior of welded structures in a more or less qualitative manner. This discussion will thus lead to the more specific analysis of the fracture characterization of weldments.

Brittle fracture

It is widely known that to avoid brittle fracture in a welded structure, the material must have adequate notch toughness. Differently stated, and using concepts from the fracture mechanics theory [1], unstable fracture occurs when stresses are applied to a structure containing a crack longer than a given value (critical crack length). For low-carbon steel this critical crack is several inches long at the yield stress. Brittle fractures in welded structures have been observed to originate, however, from relatively short cracks and under an overall stress equal to about one-third of the material yield strength.

These catastrophic failures of welded structures from subcritical cracks, called low applied-stress fractures, are due to presence of high tensile residual stresses in areas where the cracks are located. The crack can thus grow uncontrollably even though the level of applied stress is low [1].

Fatigue fracture

Only limited studies have been made on the analysis of the effects of residual stresses on the fatigue strength of welded structures. This stems from the major difficulties that come from the change in stress distributions around a crack as it grows due to the repeated loading.

Because of these and several other reasons [1], our knowledge of the relationship between residual stress and fatigue strength is confused. An observation that has been reported by several investigators, although not conclusive, is that the fatigue strength of welded specimens seems to increase when compressive residual stresses exist in regions near the surface of a plate. It should be pointed out, however, that the fatigue strength depends greatly on the condition of the surface; the effect of residual stress is thus secondary and is overshadowed by such major factors as weld geometry and surface irregularities [1].

Stress-corrosion cracking and hydrogen embrittlement

As previously mentioned, residual stresses significantly affect those phenomena that occur under a low applied stress. Since stress-corrosion cracking and hydrogen-induced cracking of a weldment has been observed to occur without any external loading, it can be concluded that residual stresses, especially the high tensile residual stresses, do significantly affect these phenomena, leading to catastrophic failures [1].

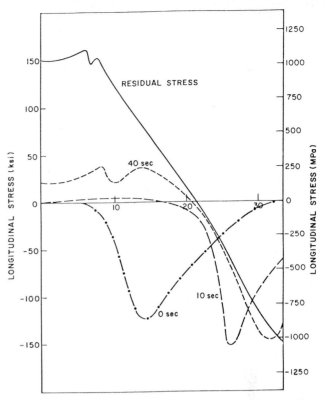

Fig. 16 Longitudinal stress distribution at several time instances (first welding pass)

Buckling strength

It is generally known that residual compressive stresses decrease the buckling strength of a welded structure, as measured for example by the externally applied critical stress. This is true for columns, plates, stiffened plate structures, spherical and cylindrical shells [1,20,38].

Methodologies for analyzing residual stress effects

In Part 1 of this paper, and in particular when discussing methods for predicting residual stresses, it was pointed out that, due to the complex nature of the problem and before the wide use of the electronic digital computer, most investigations in the area were done experimentally. This statement is even more true in the case of analyzing the effects of residual stresses on the service behavior of welded structures.

Very few analytical studies have actually been performed in the area. Moreover, these studies appear to be rather isolated attempts at addressing the various problems. A more systematic effort has been followed by M.I.T. investigators aimed at providing designers of ships and other welded structures with tools capable of aiding in the reliability assessment of these structures.

The methods used by M.I.T. investigators are both analytical and numerical. The former ones can be used whenever a rougher estimate of the residual stress effects is desirable, whereas numerical techniques, such as the finite-element method, should be used when more detailed and accurate estimates are required or when the problem is too complex to analyze otherwise.

Examples of cases that have already been studied using analytical techniques include the corrugation damage of ship bottom plating [20], the effect of residual stresses on the buck-

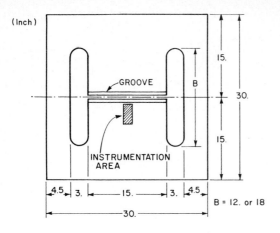

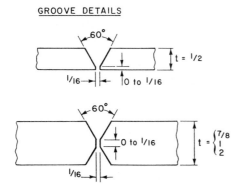

GROOVE DETAILS

Fig. 17 Configuration of simple restrained specimens

ling strength of welded plates [38], the systems analysis approach to the fatigue crack growth of surface and embedded transverse cracks in a butt weld in the pressure hull of a deep submersible [1], and others.

On the other hand, the more sophisticated numerical techniques have been used, for example, in the fracture analysis on weldments. This analysis will be the topic of the next section.

Fracture analysis of weldments: a case study

The pursuit of improved technology for designing high-performance marine vessels has led to the use of new materials having high strength-to-weight ratios, as is the case with the HY-80 steel used in present day U.S. Navy applications or the even more advanced HY-130 steel.

Unfortunately, however, these high-strength steels can be susceptible to catastrophic failures in the presence of small flaws, making the initiation and propagation of cracks in the presence of residual stress fields of the utmost concern. Presently the U.S. Navy evaluates the cracking sensitivity of the base

Table 4   Parameters of specimens for fracture experiments

Specimen Number	Type of Steel	Thickness mm (in.)	B mm (in.)	K_s (MPa/mm)
1	SAE 1020	12.7 (1/2)	305 (12)	32.5
2	SAE 1020	25.4 (1)	457 (18)	34.0
3	SAE 1020	25.4 (1)	305 (12)	65.1
4	SAE 1020	50.8 (2)	457 (18)	68.0
5	SAE 1020	50.8 (2)	305 (12)	130.2
6	HY-130	22.2 (7/8)	457 (18)	29.8
7	HY-130	22.2 (7/8)	305 (12)	56.9
8	HY-130	50.8 (2)	305 (12)	130.2

metal and welding electrodes through tests on various restrained welded specimens. The results of these tests are used on a "go" or "no go" basis, which means that when the restrained joint can be welded successfully without cracking, then the material and the welding procedures used in the test can also be used successfully during actual construction. Very little effort has been done to obtain quantitative information on the fracture potential of such weldments.

A study was thus undertaken at M.I.T. to investigate the effects of residual stresses on some of the fracture characteristics of welded structures, especially those made of high-strength quenched-and-tempered steels [3]. The methodology used and some results obtained in this study are reported next, serving as a case study of how one can analyze the effects of residual stresses on the service behavior of a welded structure.

Fracture experiments

As previously mentioned, one's confidence in the predictive capabilities of any analysis can grow only if the analytical results correlate with experimentally obtained data in a satisfactory manner. For this reason a series of experiments was performed and later analyzed as discussed in the next subsection.

Figure 17 shows the typical configuration of the simple restrained specimens used in the experimental program. A total of eight similar specimens was used as detailed in Table 4. Welding was performed using the GMAW process according to U.S. Navy specifications.

Both temperature changes and transient strains were measured during the welding operation using thermocouples and electric resistance strain gages, respectively, at preselected locations. The joint transverse shrinkage was also measured after each welding pass using a clip gage. Results of these measurements, which are not of interest in the present discussion, can be found in [3,4,49].

After the completion of welding, the crack-opening displacement (COD) was measured in all specimens. It should be noted that the COD concept can be used instead of the stress-intensity factor since both can provide similar information regarding the fracture characteristics of a weldment.

The COD was recorded while a notch, inserted in a direction parallel to the weld (x-direction) and located on the weld centerline, was continuously propagating in the specimen's thickness direction. No external stresses were applied during this process; the only stresses present were the residual stresses due to welding. Under such conditions the crack would propagate through zones of relatively constant fracture toughness (that of the weld metal) under the influence of high values of transverse residual stresses, σ_y, which can be considered to be independent of x in the central portion of the specimen.

Notches were made with 0.8-mm-thick ($\frac{1}{32}$ in.), 15.25-cm-diameter (6 in.) circular blade saws. The saw tips were ground to a 90-deg angle so that a sharp notch tip could be obtained. The COD was measured using a specially designed clip gage with four Type SP-133-20-35 semiconductor strain gages bonded on its spring steel arms. To improve accuracy and sensitivity of measurements, all four strain gages were active in the Wheatstone bridge arrangement.

Results—Curves of COD versus notch depth were obtained for all specimens tested. The relevant curves for two HY-130 specimens (Nos. 6 and 7 in Table 4) are reproduced here in Fig. 18.

It is interesting to mention that the relatively high values of COD shown were obtained with no applied external stresses. Furthermore, the nonlinear character of the curves signifies the presence of a complex through-thickness residual stress distribution.

Numerical analysis

Joint degree of constraint—As a first step towards analyzing the fracture experiments on the simple restrained specimens, the joint degree of constraint has to be calculated. This is defined by

$$K_s = \sigma_0/\delta$$

where σ_0 is a tensile stress uniformly distributed along the joint and δ is the joint transverse dispacement (for complex joints an average value is used). K_s is a kind of spring constant of the structure. Its value can thus be assigned to a number of linear springs which model the restraint imposed on the central part of the structure by the surrounding material.

The degrees of constraint for all the specimens were calculated using a simple linear elastic finite-element analysis [3]. The results are given in Table 4.

Estimation of residual stress field—The fracture experiments were performed in the absence of any externally applied stresses; the only stresses present were the residual stresses due to welding. To successfully analyze these experiments using linear elastic fracture mechanics (LEFM), therefore, it is necessary to know the residual stress field, and in particular the residual stresses perpendicular to the crack surfaces, σ_y.

One way of calculating these residual stresses is through the thermal-elastic-plastic finite-element analysis outlined in Part 1 of this paper. Such an analysis, however, of all eight specimens would be prohibitively expensive. Instead, a simplified approximate approach was used for determining the surface and through-thickness distribution of transverse residual stresses.

This approximate method is based on the fact that the COD measured during the fracture experiment was due to the elastic release of the residual stresses present around the notch. Thus by applying the superposition principle the distribution of the transverse residual stresses can be obtained by finding the stress which if applied on the notch surface would result in the same COD values as the experimental ones [3].

A finite-element code, utilizing several subroutines of the finite-element program FEABL [50], was developed to implement the method.

Figure 19 shows the finite-element mesh used, where only triangular and quadrilateral assumed displacement elements were used. From symmetry considerations only one-half of each specimen was considered; the restraint was simulated by equivalent elastic springs.

The notch depth increase was simulated by 16 incremental steps, each equal to $1/16$ of the plate's thickness. Steps 1 and 10 are shown in Fig. 19. In each step the nodal force distribution that would give the same COD as the experimentally obtained one was calculated iteratively using the method of false position.

Figure 20 shows the calculated through-thickness residual stress distribution, σ_y, for two HY-130 specimens (Nos. 6 and 7).

Calculation of stress-intensity factor—To calculate the stress-intensity factor for the specimens used in the fracture experiments a linear elastic finite-element analysis was performed. Instead of using standard finite elements, however, something that would require up to 1500 degrees of freedom to obtain reasonable accuracy, a hybrid crack element was developed enabling one to simulate the crack growth in a much more inexpensive way. The element developed is an extension of the one proposed by Tong et al [51]. It introduces stresses on the crack surface to simulate the residual stress field, whereas the original element assumed stress-free crack surfaces. Details on the development of this element are not included here. The interested reader is referred to [3,4].

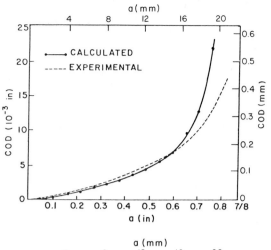

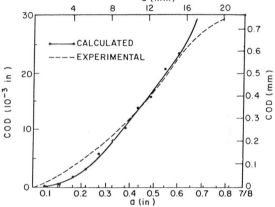

Fig. 18 FEM and experimental COD versus *a* results (Specimens 6 and 7)

The hybrid crack element was used in conjunction with FEABL to perform a linear finite-element fracture analysis of the experiments described earlier.

Figure 21 shows the finite-element mesh used in the analysis. Only the central part of a specimen is represented in the mesh; a series of springs applied on both sides of the mesh simulates the restraint the rest of the specimen exhibits on this central portion of the plate.

The crack growth was simulated by two ways: first, by increasing the size of the crack in the hybrid crack element without changing the rest of the mesh; and second, by moving the hybrid crack element deep into the mesh, something that required changes in the position of some of the other elements, increases in the number of nodes, and a renumbering of approximately half of the nodes in the mesh. The crack growth was done automatically by the program in increments of $1/16$ of the plate thickness, t, from $1/16 t$ to $14/16 t$. Figure 22 presents schematically several of these crack growth steps.

Equivalent nodal forces and distributed stresses on the crack surface were determined and prescribed automatically by the program at each step.

Numerical results of the Mode I stress-intensity factor, K_I, obtained by the finite-element analysis, are presented in Fig. 23 for Specimens 6 and 7, where K_I is plotted versus the crack depth, a.

It is interesting to note the nonlinear character of the curves, which usually show high values of K_I for cracks with depths equal to about one quarter of the plate's thickness; some of the curves even show negative values for K_I.

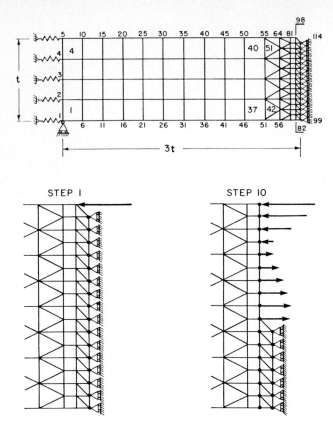

Fig. 19 Finite-element mesh used for the approximate calculation of the through-thickness residual stress distribution

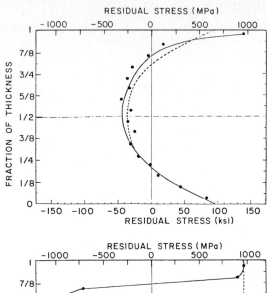

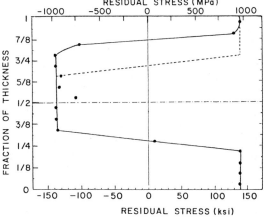

Fig. 20 Through-thickness distribution of transverse residual stress, σ_y (Specimens 6 and 7)

The calculated values of the crack-opening displacement at a distance 6.35 mm (0.25 in.) from the crack centerline are compared with the experimentally obtained ones in Fig. 18 for the same specimens. Close agreement between the two is observed for the case of small cracks. The divergence between the numerical and experimental curves observed for longer cracks is probably due to three-dimensional effects as the crack grows deeper.

Summary, conclusions and future possibilities

This paper presents computer-aided methodologies for solving the problems of predicting residual stresses due to welding and of analyzing their consequences on the service behavior of welded structures. These methodologies represent

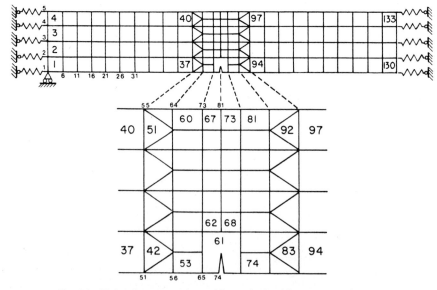

Fig. 21 Finite-element mesh used for analysis of fracture experiments

Residual Stresses Due to Welding

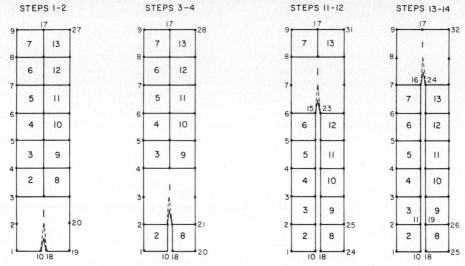

STEPS 1-2 STEPS 3-4 STEPS 11-12 STEPS 13-14

Fig. 22 Schematic representation of crack growth process

the efforts of M.I.T. investigators over a period of more than ten years in this area and can be thought of as the state of the art on a subject that is very complex but at the same time very important for the naval architectural community.

Part 1 of the paper discusses the subject of residual stress prediction. General information is first presented, including how residual stresses can be classified, how they are formed during the welding operation, and which are the physical mechanisms that should be accounted for in any accurate analysis capable of predicting them. This is followed by a historical overview of the different methodologies developed for their analysis. It is concluded that the most accurate analysis is the one based on the simulation of the whole welding operation using a computer.

The welding simulation consists of first calculating the temporal and spatial temperature distributions resulting from the application of the intense welding heat source, and subsequently of using this information as one of the inputs in a thermal-elastic-plastic stress analysis. Both analytical and numerical methods for performing each of these two steps are presented. These are then investigated with respect to their predictive capabilities and their limitations by comparing results from sample analyses with experimentally obtained data.

It is concluded that closed-form analytical solutions and simple numerical ones (that is, the one-dimensional computer program) can be used with reasonable degree of confidence in the analysis of thin plates welded by conventional processes (for example, GMAW, GTAW) and in the analysis of medium-thickness plates welded by high-energy-density processes (for example, electron beam and laser). On the other hand, if high accuracy is required (that is, when fabricating critical structures such as deep-sea submersibles) or when analysis of thick structures is desired, the only currently available technique that can be used is a numerical one based on the finite-element method.

Following completed discussion of the problem of residual stress prediction, Part 2 of the paper concentrates on the consequences residual stresses have on the service behavior of welded structures. This is a very important problem since it is well known that residual stresses adversely affect, among others, the brittle fracture, fatigue life, buckling, stress corrosion cracking, and hydrogen embrittlement characteristics of weldments.

The vastness of this subject area does not allow for a detailed

description of all the methods that can be used for analyzing the various problems encountered. For this reason, after a brief qualitative general discussion, the emphasis of Part 2 is placed on a particular subject, that of the quantitative characterization of the fracture of welded high-strength quenched-and-tempered steels. A linear elastic fracture mechanics analysis using the finite-element method is first developed. Its predictions

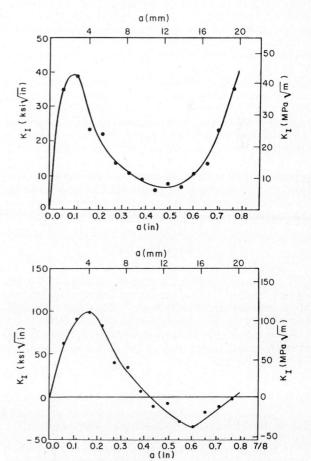

Fig. 23 Stress intensity factor versus crack depth (Specimens 6 and 7)

are then compared with experimentally obtained data.

A major conclusion can be drawn from the discussion presented in this paper. Among the various disciplines in naval architecture, including hydrodynamics, structural mechanics, and dynamics, the technology of welding fabrication has long been primarily empirical. One of the major reasons for this may be the complex, transient phenomena involved during welding. In the authors' opinion, however, computer-aided analyses like the ones presented in this paper prove that it is possible for the designers and fabricators to start incorporating manufacturing-related parameters in their analyses. It is hoped that such practice can start soon because it makes a lot of sense economically.

Future research efforts

The question that one might ask is, Where do we go from here? Although there is no single answer, it is the authors' belief that very exciting opportunities lie ahead.

For one, the fact that an analysis of such a complex phenomenon as welding has been proven to be feasible leads to the possibility of analyzing several other welding-related or more general fabrication processes. The flame heating and flame bending operations, the thermal stress relieving process, and the problem of weld metal overmatching or undermatching are just a few that come to mind. In addition, it will be well worth analyzing several of the quality acceptance tests currently used and which are mostly empirical in nature; some of them do not even provide any quantitative information but are rather performed on a "go" or "no go" basis, such as the explosion bulge test or the restrained cracking window test. There is a high probability that these analyses will aid in the rationalization of the tests or even in the development of new, more scientifically meaningful ones. We believe that the ever-increasing power and speed of the large digital computers that is spurred by such developments as parallel processing will enable analyses of this type to become more economical and hence more widespread.

On the other hand, the tremendous increase in the power of microprocessors and microcomputers, referred to by many as the second industrial revolution, will soon enable a single, inexpensive chip to perform calculations based on some of the simple models described in this paper. If one couples this with appropriate sensors, it could be possible to develop welding machines with fully adaptive automatic control that can always perform perfect welds in the presence of any external disturbances. Such machines, the dream of all fabricators, will be possible some time in the future if enough effort is applied in this direction.

Acknowledgment

This study was done as part of a $4\frac{1}{2}$-year contract with the Office of Naval Research (Contract No. N00014-75-C-0469) entitled "Study of Residual Stresses and Distortion in Structural Weldments in High-Strength Steels." The authors greatfully acknowledge the financial support provided by ONR.

We would also like to thank Mrs. Muriel B. Morey for her painstaking and highly professional efforts in drawing the figures for this paper.

References

1 Masubuchi, K., *Analysis of Welded Structures: Residual Stresses, Distortion, and their Consequences*, Pergamon Press, Oxford/New York, 1980.

2 Papazoglou, V. J., "Analytical Techniques for Determining Temperatures, Thermal Strains, and Residual Stresses During Welding," Ph.D. Thesis, Department of Ocean Engineering, M.I.T., Cambridge, Mass., May 1981.

3 Gonçalves, E., "Fracture Analysis of Welded Structures," Ph.D. Thesis, Department of Ocean Engineering, M.I.T., Cambridge, Mass., May 1981.

4 Papazoglou, V. J. and Masubuchi, K., "Study of Residual Stresses and Distortion in Structural Weldments in High-Strength Steels," 3rd Technical Progress Report to ONR under Contract N00014-75-C-0469, M.I.T., Cambridge, Mass., Nov. 1981.

5 Gonçalves, E., "Investigation of Welding Heat Flow and Thermal Strain in Restraint Steel Plates," M.S. Thesis, Department of Ocean Engineering, M.I.T., Cambridge, Mass., May 1980.

6 Macherauch, E. and Wohlfahrt, H., "Different Sources of Residual Stress as a Result of Welding," *Proceedings*, International Conference on Residual Stresses in Welded Construction and Their Effects, The Welding Institute, London, 1977, pp. 267–282.

7 Masubuchi, K., "New Approach to the Problems of Residual Stresses and Distortion Due to Welding," *Monthly Reports of Transportation Technical Research Institute*, Vol. 8, No. 12, Tokyo, Japan, March 1959 (in Japanese).

8 Masubuchi, K., "Analytical Investigation of Residual Stresses and Distortions Due to Welding," *Welding Journal*, Vol. 39, No. 12, Dec. 1960, pp. 525s–537s.

9 Moriguchi, S., "Fundamental Theory of Dislocation in an Elastic Body," *Applied Mathematics and Mechanics*, Vol. 1, 1948, pp. 29–36, 87–90 (in Japanese).

10 Kihara, H., Watanabe, M., Masubuchi, K., and Satoh, K., "Researches on Welding Stress and Shrinkage Distortion in Japan," *60th Anniversary Series of the Society of Naval Architects of Japan*," Vol. 4, 1959.

11 Mróz, Z. and Raniecki, B., "On the Uniqueness Problem in Coupled Thermoplasticity," *International Journal of Engineering Sciences*, Vol. 14, 1976, pp. 211–221.

12 Mróz, Z. and Raniecki, B., "A Derivation of the Uniqueness Condition in Coupled Thermoplasticity," *International Journal of Engineering Sciences*, Vol. 14, 1976, pp. 395–401.

13 Hibbitt, H. D. and Marcal, P. V., "A Numerical, Thermomechanical Model for the Welding and Subsequent Loading of a Fabricated Structure," *Computers and Structures*, Vol. 3, 1973, pp. 1145–1174.

14 Ueda, Y., Fukuda, K., and Nakacho, K., "Basic Procedures in Analysis and Measurement of Welding Residual Stresses by the Finite Element Method," *Proceedings*, International Conference on Residual Stresses in Welded Construction and Their Effects, The Welding Institute, London, 1977, pp. 27–37.

15 Rosenthal, D., "Étude théorique du régime thermique pendant la soudure de l'arc," *2-me Congrès National des Sciences*, Brussels, 1935, pp. 1277–1292.

16 Rosenthal, D., "Mathematical Theory of Heat Distribution During Welding and Cutting," *Welding Journal*, Vol. 20, No. 5, 1941, pp. 220s–234s.

17 Rosenthal, D., "The Theory of Moving Sources of Heat and Its Application to Metal Treatment," *Transactions*, ASME, Nov. 1946, pp. 849–866.

18 Boulton, N. S. and Lance Martin, H. E., "Residual Stresses in Arc-Welding Plates," *Proceedings*, Institute of Mechanical Engineers (London), Vol. 133, 1936, pp. 295–347.

19 Myers, P. S., Uyehara, O. A., and Borman, G. L., "Fundamentals of Heat Flow in Welding," Welding Research Council Bulletin No. 123, July 1967.

20 Masubuchi, K. et al, "Analysis of Thermal Stresses and Metal Movements of Weldments: A Basic Study Towards Computer-Aided Analysis and Control of Welded Structures," TRANS. SNAME, Vol. 83, 1975.

21 Papazoglou, V. J., "Computer Programs for the One-Dimensional Analysis of Thermal Stresses and Metal Movement During Welding," Manual No. 2 of Report to ONR under Contract No. N00014-75-C-0469, M.I.T., Cambridge, Mass., 1977.

22 Imakita, A., Papazoglou, V. J., and Masubuchi, K., "One-Dimensional Computer Programs for Analyzing Heat Flow, Transient Thermal Strains, Residual Stresses, and Distortion in Weldments," Report to ONR from M.I.T. prepared under Contract No. N00014-75-C-0469 (M.I.T. OSP No. 82558), Cambridge, Mass., Dec. 1981.

23 Christensen, N., Davies, V., and Gjermundsen, K., "The Distribution of Temperature in Arc Welding," *British Welding Journal*, Feb. 1965, pp. 161–167.

24 Rykalin, N. N., "Calculation of Heat Processes in Welding," Lecture presented before the American Welding Society, April 1961.

25 Rykalin, N. N. and Nikolaev, A. V., "Welding Arc Heat Flow," *Welding in the World*, Vol. 9, No. 3/4, 1971, pp. 112–132.

26 Tsai, C. L., "Parametric Study on Cooling Phenomena in Un-

derwater Welding," Ph.D. Thesis, Department of Ocean Engineering, M.I.T., Cambridge, Mass., Sept. 1977.

27 Bathe, K. J., "ADINAT—A Finite Element Program for Automatic Dynamic Incremental Nonlinear Analysis of Temperature," AVL Report 82448-5, Department of Mechanical Engineering, M.I.T., Cambridge, Mass., May 1977 (revised, Dec. 1978).

28 Bathe, K. J. and Khoshgoftaar, M. R., "Finite Element Formulation and Solution of Nonlinear Heat Transfer," Journal of Nuclear Engineering and Design, Vol. 51, 1979, pp. 389–401.

29 Muraki, T., Bryan, J. J., and Masubuchi, K., "Analysis of Thermal Stresses and Metal Movement During Welding, Part I: Analytical Study, and Part II: Comparison of Experimental Data and Analytical Results," Journal of Engineering Materials and Technology, ASME, Jan. 1975, pp. 81–84 and 85–91.

30 Masubuchi, K., "Applications of Numerical Analysis in Welding—Present State-of-the-Art and Future Possibilities," Colloquium on Application of Numerical Analysis in Welding, I.I.W. Annual Assembly, Dublin, Ireland, 1978.

31 Friedman, E., "Thermomechanical Analysis of the Welding Process Using the Finite Element Method," Journal of Pressure Vessel Technology, ASME, Aug. 1975, pp. 206–213.

32 Friedman, E. and Glickstein, S. S., "An Investigation of the Thermal Response of Stationary Gas Tungsten Arc Welds," Welding Journal, Vol. 55, No. 12, 1976, pp. 408s–420s.

33 Friedman, E., "Numerical Simulation of the Gas Tungsten Arc Welding Process," Proceedings, Numerical Modeling of Manufacturing Processes, ASME Winter Annual Meeting, Atlanta, Ga., 1977, pp. 35–47.

34 Hughes, T., "Unconditionally Stable Algorithms for Nonlinear Heat Conduction," Computer Methods in Applied Mechanics and Engineering, Vol. 10, 1977, pp. 135–139.

35 Dilawari, A. H., Szekely, J., and Eagar, T. W., "Electromagnetically and Thermally Driven Flow Phenomena in Electroslag Welding," Metallurgical Transactions B, Vol. 9B, 1978, pp. 371–381.

36 Tall, L., "Residual Stresses in Welded Plates—A Theoretical Study," Welding Journal, Vol. 43, No. 1, 1964, pp. 10s–23s.

37 Masubuchi, K., Simons, F. B., and Monroe, R. E., "Analysis of Thermal Stresses and Metal Movement During Welding," Battelle Memorial Institute, RSIC-820, Redstone Scientific Information Center, NAGA-TM-X-613000, N68-37857, July 1968.

38 Masubuchi, K. and Papazoglou, V. J., "Analysis and Control of Distortion in Welded Aluminum Structures," TRANS. SNAME, Vol. 86, 1978, pp. 77–100.

39 De Young, R. M. and Chiu, S. S., "Some Applications of Numerical Methods to Practical Welding Problems," Proceedings, Numerical Modeling of Manufacturing Processes, ASME Annual Winter Meeting, Atlanta, Ga., 1977, pp. 143–156.

40 Mendelson, A., Plasticity: Theory and Application, MacMillan, New York, 1968.

41 Rybicki, E. F. et al., "Residual Stresses at Girth-Butt Welds in Pipes and Pressure Vessels," Battelle Columbus Laboratory Report to U.S. Nuclear Regulatory Commission, NUREG-0376, 1977.

42. Satoh, K. et al, "Thermal Elasto-Plastic Analysis of Stress and Strain in Weld Metal During Multipass Welding," International Institute of Welding Document X-706-73, May 1973.

43 Fujita, Y., Nomoto, T., and Hagesawa, H., "Thermal Stress Analysis Based on Initial Strain Method," International Institute of Welding Document X-926-79, April 1979.

44 Imakita, A., Papazoglou, V. J., and Masubuchi, K., "Annotated Bibliography on Numerical Analysis of Stresses, Strains, and Other Effects due to Welding," International Institute of Welding Document X-996-81, July 1981.

45 Bathe, K. J., "ADINA—A Finite Element Program for Automatic Dynamic Incremental Nonlinear Analysis," AVL Report 82448-1, Department of Mechanical Engineering, M.I.T., Cambridge, Mass., Sept. 1975 (revised, Dec. 1978).

46 Snyder, M. D., "An Effective Solution Algorithm for Finite Element Thermo-Elastic-Plastic and Creep Analysis," Ph.D. Thesis, Department of Mechanical Engineering, M.I.T., Cambridge, Mass., Oct. 1980.

47 Papazoglou, V. J. and Masubuchi, K., "Numerical Analysis of Thermal Stresses During Welding Including Phase Transformation Effects," Journal of Pressure Vessel Technology, ASME, Vol. 104, No. 3, Aug. 1982, pp. 198–203.

48 Andrews, J. B., Arita, M., and Masubuchi, K., "Analysis of Thermal Stresses and Metal Movement During Welding," NASA Contract Report NASA CR-61351, prepared for the G.C. Marshall Space Flight Center, Dec. 1970.

49 Papazoglou, V. J. and Masubuchi, K., "Study of Residual Stresses and Distortion in Structural Weldments in High-Strength Steels," First and Second Technical Progress Reports to ONR under Contract No. N00014-75-C-0469 (M.I.T. OSP No. 82558), M.I.T., Cambridge, Mass., Nov. 30, 1979 and Nov. 30, 1980.

50 Orringer, O., French, S. E., and Weinreich, M., "User's Guide for the Finite Element Analysis (FEABL 2, 4 and 5) and the Element Generation Library (EGL), Aeroelastic and Structure Research Laboratory, Department of Aeronautics and Astronautics, M.I.T., Cambridge, Mass., Jan. 1978.

51 Tong, P., Pian, T. H. H., and Lasry, S. J., "A Hybrid Element Approach to Crack Problems in Plane Elasticity," International Journal of Numerical Methods in Engineering, Vol. 7, 1973, pp. 297–308.

Appendix 1

Closed-form solution of three-dimensional finite heat source model

The solution to the governing partial differential equation of heat transfer during welding under the assumptions discussed in the main text was found using the method of separation of variables, the appropriate boundary conditions, and by dividing the plate into two regions, inside and outside the heat input circle of radius r_h [2]. The obtained solution can be written as

$$\theta = \theta_0 + \frac{1}{\gamma} \cdot (\sqrt{1 + 2\gamma \cdot e^{-\lambda v \xi} \cdot \phi(r,z)} - 1)$$

where

$$\phi(r,z) = \phi^i(r,z) \cdot [u_{-1}(r) - u_{-1}(r - r_h)] + \phi^0(r,z) \cdot u_{-1}(r - r_h)$$

with $u_{-1}(r - a)$ being the unit step function and

$$\phi^0(r,z) = \sum_{n=1}^{\infty} C_n \cdot K_0(\zeta_n r) \cdot \left[\frac{h_2}{k_0 \cdot \omega_n} \cdot \sin(\omega_n z) + \cos(\omega_n z) \right]$$

$$\phi^i(r,z) = \sum_{n-1}^{\infty} \left\{ \frac{2 \cdot q_0 \cdot K_n \cdot J_0(\delta_n r) \cdot [h_2 \cdot \sinh(\chi_n z) + k_0 \cdot \chi_n \cdot \cosh(\chi_n z)]}{J_1^2(\delta_n r_h) \cdot [k_0 \chi_n (h_1 + h_2) \cdot \cosh(\chi_n H) + (k_0^2 \chi_n^2 + h_1 h_2) \cdot \sinh(\chi_n H)]} \right. $$
$$\left. + C_n \cdot K_0(\zeta_n r_h) \cdot \frac{I_0(\zeta_n r)}{I_0(\zeta_n r_h)} \cdot \left[\frac{h_2}{\omega_n \cdot k_0} \cdot \sin(\omega_n z) + \cos(\omega_n z) \right] \right\}$$

$$C_n = \frac{1}{a_n} \cdot \sum_{m=1}^{\infty}$$

$$\frac{2 \cdot q_0 \cdot K_m \cdot \delta_m \cdot [r_{mn} \cdot \tanh(\chi_m H) + s_{mn}]}{(\chi_m^2 + \omega_n^2) \cdot (J_1(\delta_m r_h)) \cdot [d_m + e_m \cdot \tanh(\chi_m H)]},$$
$$n = 1,2,3, \ldots$$

$$a_n = b_n \cdot c_n$$

$$b_n = \zeta_n \cdot \left[K_1(\zeta_n r_h) + K_0(\zeta_n r_h) \cdot \frac{I_1(\zeta_n r_h)}{I_0(\zeta_n r_h)} \right]$$

$$c_n = \frac{H}{2} \cdot \left(1 + \frac{h_2^2}{\omega_n^2 \cdot k_0^2} \right) + \frac{1}{4\omega_n} \cdot \left(1 - \frac{h_2}{\omega_n^2 \cdot k_0^2} \right) \cdot \sin(2\omega_n H)$$
$$+ \frac{h_2}{\omega_n^2 \cdot k_0} \cdot \sin^2(\omega_n H)$$

$$d_m = k_0 \cdot \chi_m \cdot (h_1 + h_2)$$

$$e_m = k_0^2 \cdot \chi_m^2 + h_1 \cdot h_2$$

$$r_{mn} = h_2 \cdot \left(\omega_n + \frac{\chi_m^2}{\omega_n}\right) \cdot \sin(\omega_n H) + \left(k_0 \chi_m^2 - \frac{h_2^2}{k_0}\right)$$
$$\cdot \cos(\omega_n H)$$

$$s_{mn} = \chi_m \cdot \left(k_0 \cdot \omega_n + \frac{h_2^2}{k_0 \cdot \omega_n}\right) \cdot \sin(\omega_n H)$$

$$\zeta_n^2 = \omega_n^2 + (\lambda v)^2$$

$$(k_0^2 \cdot \omega_n^2 - h_1 \cdot h_2) \cdot \tan(\omega_n H) = k_0 \cdot \omega_n \cdot (h_1 + h_2)$$

$$J_0(\delta_n \cdot r_h) = 0, \, n = 1,2,3, \ldots$$

$$\delta_n^2 = \chi_n^2 - (\lambda v)^2$$

$$K_n = \int_0^1 x \cdot e^{-C \cdot r_h^2 \cdot x^2} \cdot J_0(\delta_n \cdot r_h \cdot x) \cdot dx$$

h_1 and h_2 the heat-transfer coefficients at the top and bottom surfaces of the plate, respectively; H the plate thickness; $J_0(x)$ and $J_1(x)$ the Bessel functions of first kind and of zero and first order, respectively; $I_0(x)$ and $I_1(x)$ the modified Bessel functions of first kind and of zero and first order, respectively; and $K_0(x)$ and $K_1(x)$ the modified Bessel functions of second kind and of zero and first order, respectively. All other variables have been previously defined.

A computer program has been written in the FORTRAN IV language to perform the necessary calculations.

Discussion

Peter M. Palermo, Member

[The views expressed herein are the opinions of the discusser and not necessarily those of the Department of Defense or the Department of the Navy.]

The authors are to be commended for providing another valuable volume in their growing library of welding research. I have reviewed this paper and am somewhat heartened by the described relationships between predicted and experimental surface residual stresses. Unfortunately, I could not follow the method for predicting through-thickness residual stresses. But based on experimental, destructive testing methods, the general shape of the upper curve in Fig. 20 is what could be expected at a weld. However, the lower curve in Fig. 20 could use some further explanation by the authors. For example, why is the shape so different from that of the upper curve?

The authors are very correct in stating that high-strength steels can be susceptible to catastrophic failures in the presence of small flaws. Unfortunately, it can be implied that the authors are referring to HY 80 and HY 130 steels. Let me state that in the presence of a crack for thicknesses less than about three inches at temperatures above 0°F, a "pop-in" vice a catastrophic failure would be expected. For the weld metals, however, this may not be true. In those cases where the welding process gets out of control, relatively brittle conditions could be present. In the more prevalent instances where prescribed welding procedures are followed, elastic-plastic fracture response has been demonstrated for cracks up to 0.2 in. deep.

The deleterious effect of high tensile residual stress on both stress corrosion cracking and fatigue has been demonstrated. In the first instance, "out of specification" highly restrained, 2 in.-thick HY 130 welds with shallow transverse hydrogen weld cracks were subjected to cathodic potential of −1.0 V and covered with salt water. In less than two weeks, the shallow surface cracks had propagated through the thickness of the welds. Even though the tests lasted three months the cracks had not extended past the heat-affected zone (HAZ) into the base plate. Thus the less tough, more stress corrosion prone weld metal sustained flaw growth under just the action of high tensile residual stresses while the tougher base plate acted as a crack stopper.

In the second instance, under repeated compressive loadings, highly restrained welds have experienced fatigue failures [52] (additional references follow some discussions). Under high tensile residual, elastic compressive loading and unloading can be considered as tensile unloading and loading. However, the authors are correct in stating that surface conditions overshadow the effects of residual stresses. It has been demonstrated in these same tests that grinding welds smooth can increase the

Table 5   HY 80 and HY 130 acceptance requirements

Charge Wt, lb Pentolite	Standoff Dist., in.	Temp.	No. of Shots	Reduction in Area
HY 80 EB 24	17	0°F	5–6	16%
HY 130 EB 42	17	30°F	3	7½%
HY 80 CS 24	17	0	2	6%
HY 130 CS 42	17	30	2	4%

time to crack initiation by as much as a factor of three.

I must comment on the other point raised by the authors. They indicate that future directions may well lead to developing the capability to analyze "go" or "no go" type tests such as the explosion bulge test. While I concur that the explosion bulge and the crack starter tests are "go/no go" types of tests, I feel that some points should be made concerning their tremendous value as acceptance tests for base material, weldments, and for welding procedures. The explosion bulge (EB) and explosion bulge crack starter (CS) tests are only dynamic tests that evaluate base metal-HAZ-weld metal as a system, at a specific service temperature. Even though they are "go/no go" type tests, the acceptance requirements are based upon fracture mechanics principles. For example, HY 80 and HY 130 acceptance requirements are as given in Table 5 herewith.

The HY 130 requirements recognize that compared with HY 80 toughness as measured by DT energy is less because of the higher yield strength. Thus the deformation is based on the minimum amount necessary to still ensure ductile response in two-inch sections, at the expected lowest service temperature. Both tests are "brutal," but it is heartening to know that once passed, outstanding service performance can be expected.

The authors imply another exciting future possibility. The adaptive automatic controls that may someday produce the "perfect welds" of the future is an advance we would all appreciate. Adaptive controls to change welding parameters to suit joint configurations represent today's technology. The ability to include controls to minimize residual stress and distortion would be a most welcome advance to the state of the art.

Once again the authors have whetted my appetite for more. Welding once considered "blacksmithing" is becoming more and more amenable to the scrutiny of the scientific eye. Much more is needed before the designer can feel that the tools are at hand to analytically verify the adequacy of his welded design under rigorous service conditions. In fact, the designer will never be satisfied—I will always look for and expect experimental verification on a somewhat routine and regular basis.

However, the tools being developed by the authors will permit minimizing the numbers and the frequency of such testing programs.

I hope the authors take my comments in the vein in which they are offered. Critical only because it is the responsibility of the designer to question and to always want technical excellence; sympathetic because the designer has also wrestled with the problems caused by welding residual stresses; and positive because the designer recognizes that the problem is not trivial and that a simple analytic solution will only be achieved by more hard work.

Additional reference

52 Vasta, J. and Palermo, P. M., "An Engineering Approach to Low Cycle Fatigue of Ship Structures," TRANS. SNAME, Vol. 73, 1965.

B. L. Alia, Member

The American Bureau of Shipping is very concerned with the production of sound welds for ships, mobile offshore drilling units, fixed offshore installations and submersibles. In terms of welding-induced residual stresses, we are most interested in their influence upon the probability of restraint cracking during construction and fatigue fracture during service. In regard to the preceding, we inquire as to the feasibility of adapting the M.I.T. analyses for the prediction of welding residual stresses associated with large-scale production butt welding and welding of tubular T, K, and Y-joints commonly found in offshore structure design. At the current state of the art, what would be the reliability of the results and the economic feasibility of such an undertaking? The ability to reliably predict the wedling residual stresses of production joints, especially complex joints, will be of great value to the better understanding of the susceptibility to fracture of welded joints.

In addition, we recognize that thermal distortion of thin welded steel and aluminum panels used in the marine industry is of concern to many fabricators. In regard to this problem, how would the M.I.T. analyses respond to the assignment of predicting welding-induced distortion or warpage of such panels as described in the foregoing?

Joao G. De Oliveira, Member

The authors are to be congratulated for bringing to the attention of the profession such an impressive collection of methods and approaches for dealing with the important topic of residual stresses due to welding. Designers can now realize how difficult this topic is, because of the complex phenomena involved, and the variety of disciplines that must be considered in order to study the subject on a scientific basis.

In describing the finite-element approach to the analysis of transient strains and residual stresses due to welding, the authors point out several of the difficulties which are involved in such a procedure. In defining the convection heat losses, for example, we face the problem of how to estimate the temperature-dependent convection coefficient. Regarding the radiation heat losses, a shape factor and an emissivity coefficient for the surface have to be defined. In modeling the molten pool a somehow artificial value for the thermal conductivity of the molten metal has to be assumed. In evaluating plastic strains a whole theory of thermal plasticity has to be postulated. In fact, the whole computer simulation is based on the uncoupling of the thermal and mechanical components of the welding process, an assumption which must be introduced because otherwise the problem would be too difficult to solve.

The computer simulation described in the paper involves, as discussed in the foregoing, various modeling difficulties. Also, it is very costly, judging from the fact that its application to the eight simple restrained specimens described in the paper would be prohibitively expensive.

The foregoing comments bring me to the following question. In design applications, when the designer has to estimate residual stresses due to welding in a real structure, and their consequences on its performance, how can finite-element computer simulation methods be applied? This seems to require not only advances in computer technology, but also advances in pure research, in areas such as thermoplasticity and heat transfer. Could the authors please comment on the future research needed to make these methods more reliable and applicable to real structures? Also, could they comment on how they expect these methods to be translated into a practical design tool, and when could we expect this tool to be available to the engineering community?

This paper contains a wealth of information on an extremely complex subject. The methods used combine in a sound basis theory and experiment, the best way to achieve relevant results. Again, let me congratulate the authors for such a remarkable effort.

R. Latorre, Member, and A. Moshaiov,[8] Visitor

The authors are to be congratulated for this interesting paper summarizing their research in residual stress from heating/welding. Our questions deal with the details of studies the authors mentioned.

(a) In introducing equation (8), the authors speak of observations of the backward distortion of the welding arc column when moving. Have the authors conducted additional observations of the deflection of a heating torch during motion? If so, can the influence of the torch flame backward distortion be treated using a relationship such as equation (8)?

(b) The authors begin their discussion with a representation of the temperature and stresses from a welding bead on the plate and then show the FEM analysis for butt welding with notched plates. Could the authors compare these two types of welding as to the stress distribution during welding? Also, could they give the details of the FEM model results for other types of welding they studied?

(c) The authors describe the use of a finite element program to analyze the stresses during welding. Could they summarize the CPU that was needed in the analysis of the mesh described in Fig. 10? For a 3-D calculation, have the authors some idea of the CPU required?

We agree with the authors' conclusions that with the present state of the art the analysis of welding leads to the analysis of the flame bending-flame heating operation.

As part of an ongoing study on improving ship production, the discussers are examining the flame bending process. Regarding the modeling of the heat transfer from the gas torch, the work of Dr. Iwasaki and his colleagues is of interest [53, 54]. They adopted an analogous equation to equation (4) given as

$$\frac{\theta - \theta_0}{\dfrac{q}{\pi a_0}} = F(X,Y,Z,B,T) \equiv e^{-T \cdot Z} \sum_{s=0}^{\infty} A_S$$

$$(\cos X \cdot u_s + \frac{B}{u_s} \sin X \cdot u_s)$$

$$\cdot k_0(\sqrt{Y^2 + Z^2} \cdot \sqrt{T^2 + u_s^2}) \quad (22)$$

where

$$A_S = \frac{u_s^2}{u_s^2 + B^2 + 2B} \qquad \tan u_s = \frac{2B \cdot u_s}{u_s^2 - B^2}$$

$$X = (x/a_0), \quad Y = (y/a_0), \quad Z = (z/a_0),$$

$$B = a_0 h, \quad T = (a_0 \cdot v/2k)$$

[8] Graduate student, The University of Michigan, Ann Arbor, Mich.

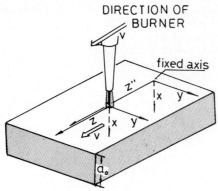

Fig. 24 Coordinate system [53]

Adopting the coordinate system shown in Fig. 24 accompanying this discussion, the temperature distribution in the point source model at point $(f[x], \eta Y, \zeta Z)$ is

$$\theta - \theta_0 = \frac{\gamma \cdot Q}{\pi a_0 \lambda} F\{f[x], \eta \cdot (Y - Y_0), \zeta(Z - Z_0), B, T\} \quad (23)$$

To develop the relationship for the temperature distribution using the measured difference between the maximum temperature and the room temperature, the following relationships were developed for equation (22). Since in the following calculations the value of Z is not required, the value of ζ was set to 1:

$$f[x] = (1 - \beta) - \beta \cdot X$$

$$\beta = \frac{a_0}{a_0 + \Delta a_0}$$

$$\eta = \beta \cdot \frac{a_0}{\Delta W}$$

$$\gamma = 1.35 \cdot \eta^{0.75} \left(\eta^{0.75} + \frac{v}{f} \right)$$

For the gas burner used in the experiments there is good agreement between the calculated and measured heat transfer when $\Delta a_0 = 17.5$ mm, $\Delta W = 27$ mm, and $f = 37$ mm/s. In the above equations the value Δa_0 is added to the top surface where the heat enters in order to have agreement with the actual temperature distribution.

The results of the actual temperature distribution are shown in Fig. 25. Figure 25 shows the results for a 19-mm-thick plate using one burner. In the figure the calculation results are indicated by solid lines while the experimental measurements are indicated by symbols. The good agreement between the experimental and calculation supports the authors assertion for the analysis of other general fabrication processes. We again congratulate the authors on their interesting study.

Additional references

53 Iwasaki, Y. et al, "Study of the Forming of Hull Plate by Line Heating Method," *Mitsubishi Juko, Giho*, Vol. 12, No. 3, 1975, pp. 51–59 (in Japanese).
54 Latorre, R., "Hull Plate Forming Process," The University of Michigan, Department of Naval Architecture and Marine Engineering, Report No. 247, Nov. 1982.

Naresh M. Maniar, Member

At the outset, I readily concede that I am not among the handful of people who are qualified to evelute the theory and details of the authors' work. I can only reflect on the overall approach and the potential of the results.

The authors have presented a paper which represents a fine example of highly theoretical and experimental research with direct link to their very practical applications. The paper succeeds in describing clearly the physical phenomena of welding and their consequences on the performance of struc-

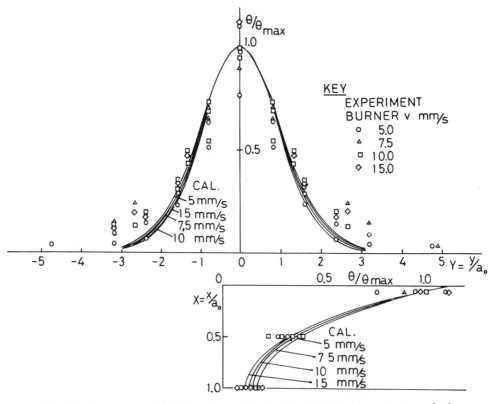

Fig. 25 Temperature distribution of $a_0 = 19$-mm steel plate heated by a gas burner [53]

ture, which is necessary in order for the designers and builders to appreciate the critical need of the analysis that is pursued.

The authors will most likely agree that the state of the art for the analysis of residual stresses due to welding is such that its application should be limited to selected critical structures of high tensile steel and/or thin plates whose characteristics meet the constraints of the proposed methods.

Considerable credit for the well-rounded work scope that was accomplished should go to the Office of Naval Research for their foresight in issuing a long-term contract of $4\frac{1}{2}$ years. Long-term contracts in the hands of capable and conscientious people permit detail planning and give time to think, which leads to good cost-effectiveness as compared to unduly short-term contracts.

I would like to take this opportunity to plead for more R&D money for the marine industry. It is popular today with politicians and policy makers to declare that U.S. industries must rely on advanced technology rather than on governmental subsidies to be competitive in the international market. Further, they have said that they would be supportive of granting R&D funds for projects with potential to enhance the necessary technology. This paper can lay claim that additional R&D money in areas such as welding of ship structure aided by American electronic computer technology holds promise for superior U.S. ships with possible reduced first cost, and certainly reduced costs for maintenance and repairs.

Authors' Closure

We would first like to express our thanks and appreciation to all the discussers for their very kind and encouraging comments. The fact that our work at M.I.T. has started to raise such interest within the naval architectural community gives us the necessary impetus and determination to continue our research efforts. Our final objective will always be to aid in the more cost-effective fabrication of reliable marine structures.

Mr. Palermo has raised a question regarding the nature of the lower curve in Fig. 20. It should be noted that the results shown are based on a rather crude method for estimating through-thickness residual stress distributions, based on the experimentally obtained COD values. Such a method became necessary when it was realized that, in order to accurately calculate these distributions for all eight specimens described in Table 4 and using the finite-element method as described in Part 1 of the paper, a prohibitively large amount of money would be needed. However, the through-thickness distributions of the transverse residual stress would be necessary for the subsequent analyses of K_I and COD. Nevertheless, we believe that the distributions shown in Fig. 20 provide the correct trends.

The authors agree with Mr. Palermo on his comments regarding brittle fracture, stress corrosion cracking and fatigue fracture of high-strength steels. Furthermore, the authors never questioned the tremendous value that "go" or "no go" tests have for ensuring adequate service performance of the whole base metal-HAZ-weld metal system. We believe, however, that an analysis of such tests using sophisticated numerical techniques, with the aid of a limited number of carefully selected experiments, would provide additional insight to these tests, probably leading to less "brutal" tests, as the discusser characterized the present ones.

Referring to the subject of adaptive automatic welding, as raised by Mr. Palermo, we would like to note the following. First of all, such systems are not presently available. What is available today are preprogrammed robotic welding systems, which at best have adaptive automatic capabilities only with respect to the seam tracking operation. What is actually needed is a welding system that can sense in real time any ex-

ternal disturbances and be able to compensate for them, by modifying the welding parameters with the aid of microprocessors, still in real time. To develop such a system, the welding process itself should be controlled. The M.I.T. research team is currently trying to develop an adaptive automatic welding system for the case of root pass welding of pipes using the GTAW process [55, 56]. Since this is, to the best of our knowledge, one of the first research efforts in this direction, the only control parameter considered is related to weld geometry. Subsequent efforts will concentrate on metallurgical and residual stress considerations, and then on the GMAW process which has the additional complexity of metal transfer.

With respect to the question Mr. Alia and Dr. Oliveira raised on the feasibility of using the methods described in the design process, and especially in more complex cases, such as in large-scale production butt welding and welding of tubular joints, the following comments are offered. The simpler models described, for example, the analytical heat transfer and the one-dimensional stress analysis models, can aid designers in the case of relatively simple geometries, by providing them with reasonable estimates of the magnitude and distribution of residual stresses. For more critical structures, where considerations of reliability override any cost factors, a two-dimensional nonlinear finite-element analysis, similar to the one presented, or even a three-dimensional analysis is warranted.

However, in all cases there is still room for improvements in accuracy. This is so because of the fact that there exist uncertainties as to the correct value of some of the parameters required as input to the computer programs (for example, heat input, surface heat loss coefficient, and temperature dependence of material properties). Three possible ways of getting around this problem can be suggested. The first is the development of more accurate models, requiring fundamental research in areas such as thermoplasticity and convective heat transfer in the molten pool. Even if it was possible to develop such models, however, the anticipated exponential increase in the costs for using them would make them impractical. The second is the incompatible strain approach discussed in the paper. Although this method can be very inexpensively implemented in a computer, its major drawback comes from the difficulty in estimating the incompatible strain distribution. The third approach involves a combination of analysis and experiments. It consists of calibrating the uncertain computer program parameters through comparisons with data taken from selected series of experiments; the programs can then be run for similar cases using as input the values so determined. On the basis of the current state of the art, this appears to be the most promising approach. At present we are at M.I.T. conducting some research along these lines.

Regarding the problem of restraint cracking, raised by Mr. Alia, the M.I.T. research team is currently engaged in a research effort to analyze (and find practical, inexpensive remedies for) the problem of hydrogen-induced cracking when fabricating low-alloy high-strength steels. It is a known fact that restraint plays a very important role in this type of cracking. We hope to be able to report before the Society results from this investigation within three years.

We share Mr. Alia's concern on the problem of thin welded steel and aluminum panels used in the marine industry. In a paper presented by the first two authors before the Society in 1978, this problem was extensively discussed [38]. All analyses and data discussed, however, were concerned with plates having thicknesses ranging from $\frac{1}{4}$ to $\frac{1}{2}$ in. Current indications show that we might want to go to even thinner structures, say $\frac{1}{8}$ in. We feel that several fabrication problems will be encountered in such a case if the procedures used today are also to be used with these thinner structures. Preliminary rough calculations made by our team tend to support this assertion. For example, the maximum allowable heat input to avoid buckling distortion due to welding seems to be proportional to the plate thickness raised to the third power ($Q \sim H^3$). This means that, if we go from $1/4$ to $1/8$-in.-thick plates, we will have to use $(1/2)^3 = 1/8$ of the heat input, that is, almost one order of magnitude lower. If we assume that the welding processes currently in use deliver a heat input equal to 40 kJ/in., we would need approximately 5 kJ/in. for welding the thinner plates. Only high power density automatic processes, such as laser welding, can provide answers to these problems.

In answer to the questions asked by Professor Latorre and Mr. Moshaiov, we would like to state the following. No additional observations on the backward distortion of the heating torch column have been made by M. I. T. investigators. However, we believe that such a behavior is very likely to be encountered in this case, too, given the fact that in both the welding and heating cases there is arc travel involved. Then, equation (8) could be used to model the phenomenon. Furthermore, the bead-on-plate welding case was discussed in a qualitative way only, in order to explain the mechanisms of residual stress formation in as simple terms as possible. No extensive finite-element stress analysis of this type of welding has been conducted (apart from simple one-dimensional calculations, see Fig. 12), though since the costs that would have incurred would not warrant the analysis of a rather impractical case. As far as other welding cases are concerned, we would like to report that the following ones have also been analyzed with the aid of the finite-element method: temperature analysis in 2D with the arc moving on the plates surface (joining of thin plates); plane stress analysis; and temperature and stress analysis of the circumferential welding of cylinders (axisymmetric geometry, instantaneous ring heat source). Finally, it is reported that the finite-element analyses presented in Part 1 of the paper were performed on an IBM 360/370 computer interactively using the Conversational Monitoring System (CMS). The stress analysis was performed in 120 time steps, with iterations and stiffness matrix reformation within each time step; 20 CPU seconds were required on the average for each time step.

The authors would also like to thank Mr. Maniar for his very kind and thoughtful remarks. We agree with his comments that shipbuilding technology has not been given up to now the appropriate attention in research funding, as other naval architecture related disciplines have. It is sensed, however, that the situation is changing. Both the industry and federal agencies have realized that better technology can ultimately lead only to higher shipyard productivity.

Additional references

55   Masubuchi, K. et al, "Improvement of Reliability of Welding by In-Process Sensing and Control," *Proceedings*, Trends in Welding Research in the United States, ASM Joining Division Conference, New Orleans, La., 1982, pp. 667–688.

56   Masubuchi, K. et al, "Improvement of Fusion Welding through Modeling, Measurement, and Real-Time Control," *Proceedings*, International Conference on Welding Technology for Energy Applications, Gatlinburg, Tenn., May 16–19, 1982, pp. 281–299.

SNAME *Transactions*, Vol. 90, 1982, pp. 391–414

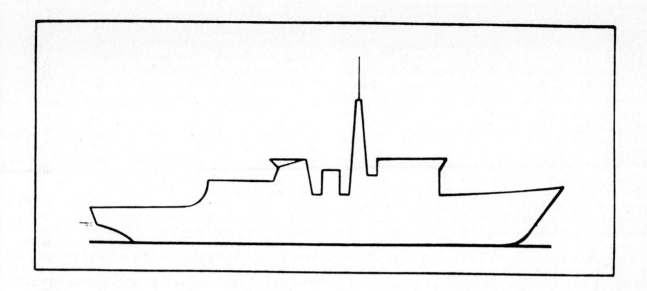

Frigate Electric Cruise Propulsion and Ship's Service Power from a Common Distribution Network

G. A. Kastner,[1] Member, **A. Davidson,**[2] Visitor, and **W. A. B. Hills,**[3] Visitor

The feasibility of providing cruise propulsion and service power from a common electrical distribution network in an ASW frigate is examined. Electric propulsion has not found acceptance in frigate-type warships due to excessive weight, volume and initial cost as compared to mechanical propulsion, in spite of such advantages as design flexibility, cross-connect capability, precise speed control, simple reversibility and low noise. Continuing improvements in electromechanical machines, the advent of high-power solid-state converters, a growing emphasis on through-life costs, the constant thrust to achieve manning reductions, pressures to conserve fossil fuel—all recommend that electric propulsion be re-considered at this conjunction of technological development and social circumstances. Having the electrical power generating plant provide both propulsion and ship's service power increases savings and fuel conservation. However, solid-state converters generate voltage waveform distortions from which some ship's service power consumers must be isolated.

Introduction

THE TYPE OF SHIP of interest in this presentation is a warship currently classed as a FRIGATE. Until recently a warship of this type would have been called a DESTROYER, a term which may be more familiar to some readers.

A frigate is a small warship having a high maximum speed. A usual feature of the operational profile of such a ship is that it will spend some 90 percent of the time underway at speeds below 60 percent of design maximum. These figures are typical, the salient point being that the ship uses under 20 percent of the installed propulsion power for 90 percent of the time at sea. Another usual and very important operational requirement is for a very low noise signature, especially for an antisubmarine (ASW) frigate.

To meet this very skewed speed-power profile requires a propulsion plant having both a high specific power ratio and the flexibility to ameliorate the fuel consumption and other economic penalties normally associated with operating heat engines significantly below rated output. As a rule of thumb, the total weight of a frigate propulsion plant should not exceed 20 percent of displacement, and of course any decrease in this permits an increase in military effectiveness in one way or another.

For several decades the propulsion plant of choice was "tailor

[1] Technical manager, German and Milne Inc., Ottawa, Ontario, Canada.

[2] Principal naval architect, German and Milne Inc., Ottawa, Ontario, Canada.

[3] Systems engineer, electrical ship propulsion, Directorate of Mechanical and Electrical Engineering, Department of National Defence, Ottawa, Ontario, Canada.

Presented at the Annual Meeting, New York, N. Y., November 17–20, 1982, of THE SOCIETY OF NAVAL ARCHITECTS AND MARINE ENGINEERS.

made" around the steam turbine. In the space of the past 15 years the gas turbine has been adapted to marine service and has become the propulsion prime mover of choice, accepting, ready made, the reduction gear technology of the precursor steam plant and relying on the controllable-reversible pitch (CRP) propeller to overcome the inability of the gas turbine to run in reverse.

The problem of matching plant rating to propulsion power demand is particularly important since the specific fuel consumption rises very sharply for an underloaded gas turbine. The conventional solution is a plant built around two gas turbines per propeller shaft, blended in size to yield acceptable performance through a range of speeds by the selection of one or other engine. This is the machinery arrangement known as the combined gas turbine or gas turbine (COGOG) propulsion plant.

In spite of this blending of two independently operable prime movers per shaft line, one to span a cruise speed range, one to span a boost speed range, the COGOG plant has poor fuel economy. The gas turbines available are marinized derivatives of aero gas turbines, hence the transition point between cruise engine and boost engine is defined by available engines rather than an optimum operational profile for the ship. Since an engine will be significantly underloaded at any speed except near the top speed in the appropriate range, the serious increase in specific fuel consumption with decreasing load mitigates significantly against the gas turbine in this application.

In addition, the necessary CRP propeller is less efficient, and when operating off design pitch is noisier, than a fixed-pitch propeller. The noise of the reduction gearing also adds to the noise signature of the ship.

There are both economic and social pressures to reduce fuel consumption and also the ever-present need to reduce the noise signature of warships. Thus alternatives to the COGOG propulsion plant must be considered. Any such alternative must be economically competitive, free of unacceptable technical risk, within established weight and space budgets, and advance the quest for a low noise signature.

It has long been acknowledged that electrical ship propulsion has several intrinsic advantages compared with the various forms of conventional mechanical propulsion. These advantages include:

(a) design flexibility
(b) inherent cross-connect capability
(c) simple and rapid reversal
(d) infinitely variable speed control
(e) low noise signature
(f) potential fuel economy

These advantages have permitted electrical ship propulsion to find application in battleships, aircraft carriers, convoy escorts, icebreakers, oceanographic research vessels, ocean liners, tankers, ferries, conventional submarines and cable layers. The technology is well developed. To date, however, electrical propulsion has not found application in frigates because of excessive weight and size. No electrical propulsion prime mover with a power output equal to the boost gas turbine in the COGOG configuration could be accommodated within the weight and space budget of a frigate without unacceptable impact on operational capability.

There is the possibility, however, that an electrical propulsion prime mover could replace the cruise gas turbine in the COGOG configuration. The potential for this to be viable would be enhanced by configuring the ship's electrical power generating plant such that it would be capable of providing electrical propulsion power over the full range of cruise speeds together with ship's service power for all operating conditions. Fuel economies might be realized to the benefit of operating costs and fuel conservation. If the electric motor is direct-connected to the propeller shaft, then its inherent quietness and the absence of reduction gearing could offer a significant reduction in noise signature at cruise speeds.

In order to examine these possibilities the Department of National Defence of Canada initiated a study to examine the feasibility of frigate cruise propulsion and ships service power from a common electrical distribution network. The study was contracted to German and Milne Inc. of Montreal with Siemens Electric Canada Ltd. as their principal subcontractor.

The Department of National Defence (DND) provided the statement of work, relevant specific technical requirements and a set of principal characteristics typical of frigates of current interest. The department also provided the speed/power and speed/time data. A table of evaluation criteria was also defined by the department including a weighted value for each criterion. The findings of the study are thus specific to a twin-shaft ASW frigate near the upper end of the displacement range for this classification of warship. The interpretation of the findings reflect the given evaluation criteria.

For such a frigate, and evaluated against the given criteria, the concept of providing cruise propulsion power and ship's service power from a common electrical distribution network is technically feasible, economically attractive and operationally advantageous. The concept has sufficient merit to warrant the development of a fully engineered design, including a solution of how to isolate some ship's service power consumers from the voltage waveform distortion generated by the high-power solid-state converters which are essential elements of the electrical propulsion system.

Design requirements

The ship shall be a twin-shaft ASW frigate having the following principal characteristics:

Length overall	131 m (429 ft)
Length between PP's	122 m (400 ft)
Molded Breadth	14.6 m (48 ft)
Draft (deep departure)	4.5 m (14.6 ft)
Displacement (full load)	4100 t (4036 tons)

The speed range 0 to 18 knots is designated the cruise speed range. The speed range from 18 knots to full speed is designated the boost speed range. The data relating to the speed/time profile and cruise range speed/power characteristic are given in Table 1.

A ship having a COGOG propulsion plant shall be taken as a baseline. Viable electric cruise propulsion variants are to be developed and compared with this baseline. The following constraints apply:

• *Mechanical propulsion plant*—Each shaft to be driven

Table 1

Speed/Power Characteristic			Speed/Time Profile	
	Power Demand- per Shaft			% of Time
Speed, knots	kW	hp	Speed Band, Knots	Under-Way in the given Speed Band
3	123	165	0 to 3	1.8
6	172	230	3 to 6	4.0
9	313	420	6 to 9	9.0
12	597	800	1 to 12	22.5
15	1156	1550	12 to 15	28.5
18	2238	3000	15 to 18	22.0
Boost speed range ———————————— 12.2				
Days per year underway ———————————— 150				
Days per year in cruise speed range ———————— 135				

by a combination of a cruise gas turbine and a boost gas turbine through a reduction gearbox.

• *Electromechanical propulsion plant*—Each shaft to be driven by a cruise power electric motor, direct-connected to the shaft and a boost power gas turbine engine through a reduction gear.

It is to be noted that the electric propulsion motors are to be direct-connected to the shafts. This means that the rotating element of the motor becomes the mechanical interconnection between the boost propulsion and cruise propulsion systems and must be capable of passively transmitting full boost power at nearly twice rated motor speed. This is a very significant constraint.

Other relevant technical requirements are summarized as follows:

• All engines shall be capable of providing full power with intake air temperatures between −32 and +43°C, and sea temperatures to +33°C (91.9°F).

• The propulsion and ship's service power machinery shall be designed for operation and maintenance by a minimum number of engineering department personnel.

• The ship will have a minimum in-service life of 25 years based on peacetime utilization.

• The machinery shall be capable of continuous operation up to full power with machinery spaces flooded to a depth of 2.5 m (8.2 ft) from the bottom of the keel with zero heel, and up to half power with a permanent heel of 20 deg.

• The machinery shall be capable of continuous operation up to full power with the ship (a) permanently heeled 20 deg to either side, or (b) rolling up to 40 deg and pitching up to 10 deg.

• The ship is required to survive a breach of the hull over 15 percent of its length, and involving complete flooding of any three adjoining machinery spaces. Under these conditions loss of propulsion is acceptable, although retention of partial propulsion capability would be very desirable. However, a minimum of approximately 750 kW of ship's service power must continue to be available.

• Machinery fitted low in the ship must withstand, without damage, high-impact shock of 120-g acceleration, while machinery fitted high in the ship need withstand only 60-g acceleration.

• Characteristics of the electrical plant shall be in accordance with STANAG 1008—Characteristics of Shipboard Electrical Power Systems in Surface Warships of the North Atlantic Treaty Navies.

• The ship's electrical propulsion system operating in any steady-state or transient condition shall not cause the electrical power plant characteristics to exceed the limits given in STANAG 1008.

• The electrical plant shall provide a total generating capacity of 3000 kW for ship's service loads, and shall also provide capacity for maximum cruise electric propulsion load.

• With sufficient generator sets on line to provide the total capacity required, there shall be two spare sets.

• The number and sizes of generator sets shall be related to providing the most economical operation possible for the following three conditions:

(a) *Peacetime cruising:* Just sufficient generator sets on line to handle ship's service and cruise propulsion loads.

(b) *Defence cruising:* As for peacetime cruising, but with one additional generator set on line.

(c) *Battle:* As for defence cruising, but all generator sets and electric propulsion motors must be independent and capable of being operated independently or in any combination.

For the purposes of equipment design and system analysis, the ship's service loads under the preceding three operational conditions may be taken as follows:

(a) Peacetime cruising	1000 kw
(b) Defence cruising	1300 kW
(c) Battle	1500 kW

It is desirable that machinery noise levels be made as low as possible.

Technical risk must be held to an acceptable level by the constraint that only equipment currently available or which will be available by the mid-1980's is to be considered.

Preliminary considerations

In spite of the optimism expressed in some research reports and technical papers published recently, it is clearly the case that the only electromechanical machines capable of being considered against the stated technical risk constraint are current state-of-the-art machines designed to the given technical requirements.

The cryogenically maintained superconducting ship's propulsion motor is not yet available. The promise of the segmented magnet machine appears unfulfilled. Increases in efficiency and reductions in size and weight by improvements in magnetic circuit materials and insulating materials continue to evolve, but no quantum improvement can be foreseen. Hydrogen or other gas-cooled machines are not economically viable in the size of interest, and the sealing problems, especially on the direct-connected propulsion motors, would be very intractable. For the direct-connected propulsion motors it is assessed that liquid cooling would not repay in reduced weight or volume the added costs and system complexity involved. The introduction of the advanced concepts would introduce design complications and risks of failure which are unacceptable until they have been fully developed and tested in the warship environment.

As noted, the ship of interest is an ASW frigate. The requirement for the lowest possible noise signature stems from the dual objectives of minimizing the probability of being heard by, and maximizing the likelihood of hearing, other vessels.

There are two principal sources of noise: the operation of machinery, and hydrodynamic noise arising from the passage of the ship through the water and the operation of the propellers.

Machinery vibration generates noise which is heard in the water because of its ability to set the hull in motion via some low-impedance transmission path. Much has been achieved to ameliorate this problem by increasing the attenuation of such transmission paths. A better solution is the employment of low-vibration-level machinery.

Just how much propulsive power should be derived from a quiet propulsion plant merits consideration. For a conventional displacement-hull form there will be a ship speed at which hydrodynamic noise becomes predominant. Both hull-generated noise and propeller-generated noise increase with speed. Thus the thrust to reduce machinery noise is fairly aimed at the low-speed regime.

The use of low-speed electric motor for cruise propulsion not only introduces a low-noise, low-vibration machine, but it also obviates the use of reduction gearing during electric propulsion. This is a feature of major significance.

It is a fact that for equivalent machines the fuel efficiency of a diesel engine is superior to that of a gas turbine at all levels and percentages of rated load. Therefore, the pressure to use diesel engine prime movers is great. However, diesel engines are heavier and excite more hull noise than gas turbines. Therefore, some guidelines for selection are required.

To exploit the fuel economy inherent in the diesel engine vis-a-vis the gas turbine, yet enjoy the inherent quietness of the gas turbine, an assessment of the top speed for quiet operation is necessary, together with an operational profile giving the percentage of time underway in the cruise speed range spent in the quiet mode. This is necessary for the rational derivation of fuel consumption and time-dependent operational and maintenance costs.

The following guidelines pertaining to the combined electric or gas turbine (COEOG) ship, were established:

• A speed of 15 knots is taken as the transition speed to hydrodynamic noise predominance, and 30 percent of the time underway in the cruise speed range will be in quiet operation mode.

• A main generator located in the machinery spaces must have a gas turbine prime mover to be available during quiet operation.

• A main generator having a diesel engine prime mover must be located high in the ship if it is to be available during quiet operation.

• Both gas turbine and diesel engine prime movers must, regardless of location, be resiliently mounted and acoustically enclosed to state-of-the-art level.

• The yoke and enclosure of the direct-connected electric propulsion motors must be hard-mounted, the rotating member being an element of the shaft.

Experience has shown that precise speed control during quiet operation provides operational advantage, and that this precise speed control is achieved more efficiently and with a lower noise signature by controlling the speed of rotation of an appropriately designed fixed-pitch propeller. It is postulated that, except for a slight decrease in efficiency resulting from the larger hub, a CRP propeller capable of being locked at the proper pitch can satisfactorily replace the fixed-pitch propeller without increasing the noise signature during quiet operation.

This postulate was supported by discussions with leading designers of warship CRP propellers. To conserve energy, the means of locking the CRP at fixed pitch should be such as to obviate an energy drain. This is achievable and assumed to be the case for this presentation.

An elementary consideration of the feasible electrical cruise propulsion motors established that only two configurations had sufficient merit to warrant detailed investigation. Briefly defined, these are:

• 1000-V, 60-Hz, 3-phase input to thyristor rectifiers feeding a dc propulsion motor, one motor per shaft.

• 1000-V, 60-Hz, 3-phase input to thyristor cyclo-converters feeding a variable-frequency, separately excited, synchronous propulsion motor, one motor per shaft.

The use of a fixed-frequency (60 Hz) synchronous motor was examined in some detail in spite of the serious inhibition that the use of such a motor would have required the active use of the CRP propeller for speed control and reverse propulsive thrust in the cruise range. Being a 60-pole motor, it must have very large transverse dimensions, making installation difficult and requiring an increase in shaft rake compared with all other propulsion methods. However, sufficient data were accumulated to suggest that if the thrust to minimize noise signature was relaxed, the 60-Hz synchronous motor would merit consideration.

The use of induction motors was rejected on the basis of achieving and maintaining an acceptable air gap, other electrical considerations and the desire for precise speed control.

The standard voltage of generation for ship's service power is 450 V. A thyristor input voltage of 1000 V was selected, however, in order to obviate a further increase in propulsion motor weight and volume beyond that imposed by the constraint of being direct-connected to the shaft. Also, at an input voltage of 1000 V the thyristor rectifier will produce an input voltage of 1200 V to the dc motor. This is the accepted maximum input voltage for satisfactory dc motor commutation.

The elementary consideration of electrical power plants capable of providing electrical propulsion power over the complete range of designated cruise speeds (0 to 18 knots) and ship's service power for all operating conditions was based on the stated technical requirements and the following comments:

• The required installed generating capacity for ship's service power is given as 3000 kW (4020 hp). This includes 100 percent redundancy since the maximum (battle) load is given as 1500 kW (2010 hp).

• The required power at the propellers for a speed of 18 knots is given as $(2240 \times 2) = 4480$ kW (6003 hp). Allowing 570 kW (764 hp) for losses and as an input to selected vital electric propulsion auxiliaries, the required installed generating capacity for electric cruise propulsion is 5050 kW (6767 hp). Propulsion power redundancy is taken as being provided by the boost power prime movers.

• To meet the electrical power demand during boost power mode and the low load in harbor, the electrical generating plant should have some main generators of appropriate capacity.

• To take advantage of the much better specific fuel consumption characteristics of the diesel engine, this engine should be the generator set prime mover selected unless ruled out by considerations of noise, weight, volume or costs.

• To assist the ship to achieve "after-damage" security of an electrical power supply, and to maximize the use of diesel engine prime movers, small generators may be located in the superstructure.

To meet the stated requirements for redundancy—"with sufficient generator sets on line to meet the total demand there shall be two spare sets"—the minimum number of main generating sets required to make up the ship's electrical power generating plant is three. However, to provide the ability to operate "split plant" under conditions of operational or navigational hazard, and to make underway corrective maintenance feasible, the realistic number of main generating sets is taken as four.

The main electrical power generating plant options may now be given preliminary consideration.

For the all-mechanical propulsion (COGOG) ship, the main electrical power generating plant will comprise four 750-kW generating sets. For reasons of fuel economy each will have a diesel engine prime mover. For reasons of logistic support the four sets will be identical. Since the intake and exhaust trunking for the four propulsion plant gas turbines demands so much space in, and above, the machinery box and contiguous superstructure, the four main generators must be located in at least two well-separated auxiliary machinery spaces situated low in the ship. The main electrical power generating plant will operate at 450 V, 60 Hz, 3 phase.

The required installed generating capacity for the ship with electric cruise (COEOG) propulsion is 8050 kW. This includes 100 percent redundancy for ship's service power as specified. The minimum number of generator sets is four. The determination of the practical maximum number of sets is not so straightforward. However, as the number of main generating sets increases, the weight, volume, cost and complexity of the switchboards and bus-ties increases, and system control becomes more complex and probably less reliable. As larger numbers of smaller sets are considered, the per-kilowatt initial cost and total plant weight/volume requirements increase more rapidly than generating capacity, although machine redundancy and both installation and operational flexibility improve. An analysis of these competing factors tends to identify the maximum practical number of main generators as eight.

Data were developed for three configurations of an electrical power generating plant capable of providing electrical cruise propulsion power over the complete range of designated cruise speeds and ship's service power for all operating conditions. The three configurations consisted of four, six and eight generating sets.

For reasons which will be defined in detail later, each variant of these three plants has two 750-kW generator sets. These sets are located in the superstructure in the space where the cruise gas turbine intake and exhaust trunks would be in the COGOG ship. They provide ship's service power during operation in the boost propulsion mode, cater for harbor service, enhance survivability and are available during quiet operation. They also meet the requirement for 100 percent ship's service power redundancy and satisfy the split-plant operating philosophy. In each variant, the remaining sets provide all electrical power during operation in the cruise propulsion mode. The two 750-kW sets may be perceived as being elements of the boost propulsion system, and as such do not contribute to fuel consumption or maintenance costs related to the electrical cruise propulsion plants.

The three electric cruise propulsion generating plants for which comparative data were developed were made up as follows:

(a)　2 × 750-kW diesel driven
　　　1 × 3500-kW diesel driven
　　　1 × 3500-kW gas turbine driven
(b)　2 × 750-kW diesel driven
　　　2 × 1750-kW diesel driven
　　　2 × 1750-kW gas turbine driven
(c)　2 × 750-kW diesel driven
　　　4 × 1100-kW diesel driven
　　　2 × 1100-kW gas turbine driven

Both the electrical and mechanical components of each generator set were selected from currently available machines. A good match between available gas turbines and generator rating was not always possible.

Hard comparative data were developed for:
• fuel consumption
• initial cost
• annual maintenance costs
• footprint area
• volume demand
• weight

These data are shown in Table 2. Configuration (a) is taken as the baseline for comparison. The comparative values for Configurations (b) and (c) are expressed as percentages of this baseline. The method used to derive these comparative data is illustrated in the following section of this paper.

A qualitative analysis was carried out to assess the impact such large electric power generating plants would have on these auxiliary ship systems:

(a)　Fuel storage, transfer and delivery system.
(b)　Lubricating oil storage and disposal system.
(c)　Oily waste storage and disposal system.
(d)　Electric power distribution system:
　　　• overall ship's service power demand
　　　• converted power demand
　　　• batteries and battery support facilities
　　　• main cabling and wiring
　　　• casualty power system
　　　• distribution hardware
(e)　Lighting services:
　　　• normal lighting
　　　• emergency lighting
(f)　Interior communications.
(g)　Data display and recording system.

Table 2　Generating plant variants—elementary comparison

Data Item	Plant Configuration		
	(a) 4 Sets	(b) 6 Sets	(c) 8 Sets
Annual fuel consumption	100	110.2	120.2
Initial cost	100	123.8	145.6
Annual maintenance costs	100	135.6	160.6
Footprint area	100	123.3	141.6
Volume demand	100	117.5	141.7
Weight	100	121.3	137.2

(h)　Climate control:
　　　• heating
　　　• air-conditioning
　　　• ventilation, including citadel air supply and NBCD filtering
(i)　Salt-water services.
(j)　Fresh-water services:
　　　• storage
　　　• distilling demand
(k)　Fire detection and suppression system.
(l)　Compressed air services.
(m)　Hydraulic services.

In keeping with the objective of the presentation, the impact of the large generating plant on the auxiliary ship systems was assessed using the COGOG ship as the basis for comparison. The overall conclusion was that the impact of Plant Configuration (a) was not significant, but the impact increases as the number of generating sets increases.

On the basis of the foregoing assessment, the four set main electrical power generating plant [Configuration (a)] was clearly the best arrangement. Detailed comparative data are developed for this plant later. Having identified major propulsion and generating plant machinery, an assessment of the effect of electric cruise propulsion on the machinery control system was undertaken. It was concluded that in terms of weight, volume, cost and manning, the machinery control system for a COEOG ship would not be measurably different from the system in the COGOG ship.

To summarize, these preliminary considerations have identified the following fundamentals:

(a)　It is necessary to select state-of-the-art machines for a current COEOG frigate.
(b)　There is a strong basis for the thrust to achieve ultraquiet propulsion at speeds of 15 knots and below.
(c)　It is necessary to establish certain fundamental guidelines relating to the selection and location of machinery.
(d)　There are two preferred motor types for electric cruise propulsion in a current ASW frigate.
(e)　The preferred configuration of the main electrical power generating plant for the COGOG ship is 4 × 750-kW, 450-V, 60-Hz, 3-phase generator sets.
(f)　The preferred configuration of the main electrical power generating plant for the COEOG variants is 2 × 750-kW and 2 × 3500-kW, 1000-V, 60-Hz, 3-phase generator sets.
(g)　It is necessary to include 4 × 1000-kVA, 60-Hz, 3-phase, 0.8 PF stepdown transformers in the COEOG variants as input power sources to the ship's service power distribution system.

Conceptual designs of the necessary propulsion and generating plants may now be developed on the given ASW frigate characteristics and technical requirements. The relevant comparative data may then be derived and the feasibility of providing cruise propulsion and ship's service power from a common network assessed.

The required comparative data should be as simple and as

stark as possible. To this end, commonality between variants will be eliminated to the maximum feasible extent. For example, in the COEOG cases, provided the magnitude of the ship's service power demand is superimposed on the cruise propulsion power demand in determining the operating point and specific fuel consumption of the generator prime mover(s), the fuel consumption and maintenance costs related to the generation of the ship's service power may be neglected, since the data would be the same for the COGOG and COEOG cases alike. Also, all ship variants will have a mechanical boost power train. If the differences in the reduction gearing as between COGOG and COEOG variants are taken into account, no other comparative data for the boost propulsion system need be developed.

Ship operation in the boost propulsion mode will be the same for all cases and no data for operating in this mode need be developed. This principle will be employed to simplify the required comparison to the maximum.

On the basis that the change from the COGOG baseline to a COEOG variant has no measurable impact on ship auxiliary support systems or the machinery control system, it is possible to examine the propulsion plant and electrical power generating plants in terms of their major system components. Only those components not common to all ship variants require the development of comparative data.

The CRP propellers and their pitch actuating and control system are taken as common. The CRP propeller will be operated as a fixed-pitch propeller during operation in the electric cruise propulsion mode.

The shafting, thrust bearings and lineshaft bearings are taken as common. The insertion of the electric motors into the shafting requires two additional journal bearing surfaces on each lineshaft in way of the motor bearings, but the cost of these will be included in the installation costs for the motors.

The 450-V main switchboards, protective switchgear, busties, bus-couplers, and related components are common. However, input power to the 450-V distribution system is derived from stepdown transformers in the COEOG variants.

Comparative data must therefore be developed for:
- mechanical cruise propulsion modules,
- electric cruise propulsion modules—two types,
- main generator set modules—two types,
- reduction gearing—two types,
- 1000-V main switchboards, protective switchgear, bus-ties, bus-couplers, etc., and
- stepdown transformers, 1000 V/450 V.

The term "module" is used to connotate a complete package capable of interfacing with the ship and the ship auxiliary support and control systems. For instance, the mechanical cruise propulsion module will consist of a gas turbine with starter, clutch, coupling and an exostructure made up of the resilient mounting base, acoustic enclosure, air supply and exhaust arrangements, generator coolers, engine mufflers and inlet filters, etc. An electric cruise propulsion module will consist of the electric propulsion motor with cooler, the associated main power converter and control cubicles, field power supply, transient suppressors, main circuit breakers and main input power cables, etc.

The 1000-V switchboard system accepts and controls the power generated by the main electrical power generating plant in the COEOG variants. Its configuration must conform to the normal warship requirements for flexibility and security of electrical power in both the cruise propulsion and ship's service power networks. The four 1000-V to 450-V stepdown transformers used to energize the ship's service power network, as replacements for the four 750-kW generating sets in the COGOG ship, may usefully be considered as components of the 1000-V switchboard system. As noted above, the 450-V

switchboard system which controls the power input to the ship's service power distribution system is common to both the COGOG ship and the COEOG variants.

The comparative data will include:
- annual fuel consumption
- area, volume and weight
- initial costs
- annual maintenance cost

In addition to the comparison based on these quantitative data, qualitative comparisons will also be made of:
- noise
- technical risk
- cross-connect capability
- speed control
- reversing capability
- installation flexibility

Equipment selection

The fundamental parameter necessary for the selection of equipment is the relevant power requirement. Once this has been established, equipment selections can proceed with appropriate reference to:
- costs
- stated design requirements
- established guidelines
- accepted principles of warship design practice

Based on the given speed/power data, Table 3 shows the required cruise speed range power demand. A cruise range speed/power characteristic based on these data is shown in Fig. 1.

Each mechanical cruise propulsion prime mover must be a gas turbine with a rated output at 43°C (109.4°F) of 2440 kW (3270 hp). A Rolls Royce RMIC engine was selected. It is the best available match to the power requirement and having a hot-end output permits a more attractive machinery arrangement than competing candidates having cold-end output.

Each electrical cruise propulsion motor must have an output of 2240 kW (3000 hp). Designs for both the dc and variable-frequency synchronous motors with this rating and capable of being direct-connected to the shaft were developed by Siemens AG. Siemens also developed the power converters, motor controllers and field power supplies for these motors.

The installed capacity required to meet the ship's service electrical power demand with adequate redundancy is 3000 kW (4020 hp). The electrical plant in the COGOG ship must have this capacity. The electrical plant in the COEOG ship must have an installed capacity of 8050 kW (10 787 hp), being the sum of:

(a) ship's service electrical power   3000 kW
(b) power to propellers at 18 knots   4480 kW
(c) motor and converter losses (worst case)   370 kW
(d) power to vital propulsion auxiliaries   200 kW

The generating plant for the COGOG ship consists of four identical 750-kW, 450-V, 60-Hz, 3-phase diesel-driven generator set modules consisting of

Table 3   Speed/power demand—cruise propulsion modes

Speed (knots)	Power Required at Propellers		Transmission Losses (kW)		Total Power Req'd (kW)	
	hp	kW	COGOG	COEOG	COGOG	COEOG
3	330	246	24	1	270	247
6	460	344	36	1	380	345
9	840	626	54	2	680	628
12	1600	1194	116	2	1310	1196
15	3100	2312	213	3	2525	2315
18	6000	4476	404	4	4880	4480

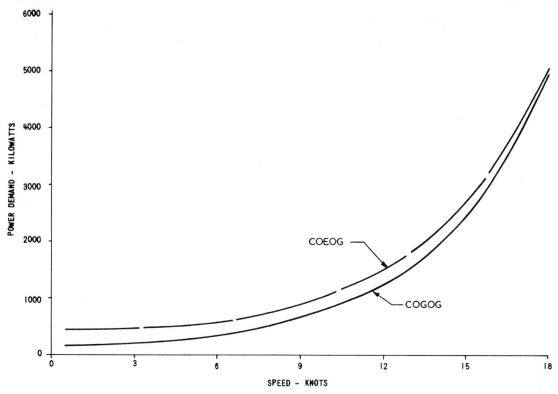

Fig. 1 Speed/power characteristics for the COGOG and COEOG ships

- GEC Paxman diesel type 8 RP 200.
- Lawrence-Scott 750-kW alternator.
- Double resilient mount, acoustic enclosure, exhaust stack and muffler, etc.

The generating plant for the COEOG variants will consist of:

(a) One 3500-kW, 1000-V, 60-Hz, 3-phase gas turbine generator set module.

(b) One 3500-kW, 1000-V, 60-Hz, 3-phase diesel generator module.

(c) Two 750-kW, 1000-V, 60-Hz, 3-phase diesel generator modules.

The major components of these modules are as follows:

- The gas turbine is a General Electric LM 500.
- The large diesel is a 1200-rpm 20-cylinder Type MTU 1163/20V.
- The small diesels are 1200-rpm 8-cylinder Type GEC Paxman 8 RP 200.
- Both sizes of alternator are Siemens AG design specific to this application.

The costs of integrating these components into appropriate modules was estimated as an element of developing the required comparative data.

In keeping with current frigate design practice, two switchboards are included in each generating plant. The switchboards are given sufficient separation to meet action damage criteria. Each switchboard is divided into sections, one section being associated with each generating set. The required comparative data for the 1000-V switchboards were developed for switchboards consisting of copper buswork, military-grade switchgear and instrumentation in a totally enclosed dead front drip-proof cubicle. Appropriate bus-tie provisions were included between the two switchboards. In both COEOG variants the 1000-V and 450-V switchboards were combined. However, only data pertinent to the addition of the 1000-V components were developed. The 450-V

switchboard components are common to all design variants.

Comparative data are developed for four 1000-V/450-V stepdown transformers. These provide the input to the 450-V switchboards in the COEOG variants. The transformers are manufactured by Jeumont-Schnieder.

BHS Werk double-input, single-output nonreversing reduction gearboxes were selected for the COGOG ship. MAAG single-input, single-output nonreversing reduction gearboxes were selected for the COEOG variants. The MAAG gearbox has an SSS clutch at the output shaft for decoupling the gearbox during operation in the electric cruise propulsion mode. Outline sketches of these gearboxes are shown in Figs. 13 and 14, respectively.

Design sketches and schematics

The design sketches and schematic diagrams listed below show pertinent details of the design variants and major system components.

Fig. 2—COGOG main propulsion plant schematic arrangement

Fig. 3—COEOG main propulsion plant schematic arrangement

Fig. 4—COEOG plant—dc module
Fig. 5—Dc cruise propulsion system, electrical schematic
Fig. 6—COEOG plant —ac module
Fig. 7—Ac cruise propulsion system, electrical schematic
Fig. 8—750-kW diesel genset, outline sketch
Fig. 9—COGOG electrical generating plant schematic
Fig. 10—3500-kW diesel genset, outline sketch
Fig. 11—3500-kW gas turbine genset, outline sketch
Fig. 12—COEOG electrical generating plant schematic
Fig. 13—Double-input, single-output gearbox
Fig. 14—Single-input, single-output gearbox

A ship's profile with the main machinery spaces identified is shown at Fig. 16.

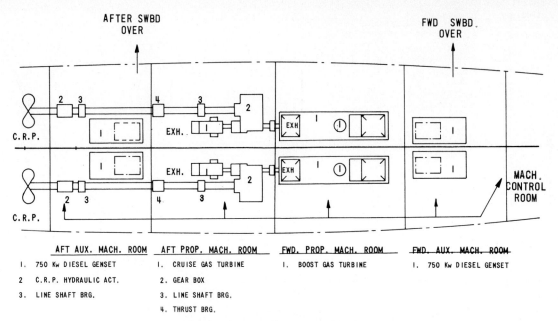

Fig. 2 COGOG main propulsion plant, schematic arrangement

AFT AUX. MACH. ROOM	AFT PROP. MACH. ROOM	FWD. PROP. MACH. ROOM	FWD. AUX. MACH. ROOM
1. 750 Kw DIESEL GENSET	1. CRUISE GAS TURBINE	1. BOOST GAS TURBINE	1. 750 Kw DIESEL GENSET
2. C.R.P. HYDRAULIC ACT.	2. GEAR BOX		
3. LINE SHAFT BRG.	3. LINE SHAFT BRG.		
	4. THRUST BRG.		

Comparative data for fuel consumption

The speed/power characteristic for both COGOG and COEOG variants is given at Fig. 1. In order to derive annual fuel consumptions, a speed/time profile is also required. It is stated in the design requirements that the ship will spend 135 days (3240 hr) per year in the cruise speed range. Based on this, an annual speed/time profile is shown in Table 4.

Specific fuel consumption (SFC) curves for the three relevant prime-movers are shown in Fig. 15.

No comparative data are derived for the fuel used for the generation of ship's service electrical power, this being common. However, in calculating the cruise propulsion fuel consumption figures for the COEOG variants, the load level on the prime mover takes cognizance of the simultaneous generation of both cruise propulsion and ship's service electrical power. As a consequence, the prime movers in the COEOG variants are never as badly underloaded as are the mechanical cruise propulsion engines. The concept of a common distribution network ameliorates the problem of badly underloaded prime movers and permits significant fuel economies.

Regarding prime mover utilization, the following must be noted:

• For the COGOG ship, no trail shaft mode is permitted in normal operation. Both cruise engines are used at all speeds in the cruise speed range.

• For the COEOG variants, generator set selection cannot be based simply on power demand. The operational profile guideline that 30 percent of the time spent in the cruise speed range is in the quiet mode must be taken into account.

(text continued on page 12)

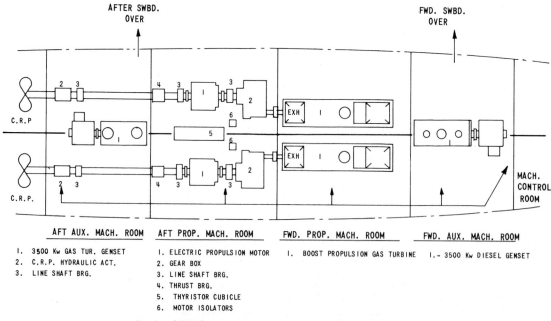

Fig. 3 COEOG main propulsion plant, schematic arrangement

AFT AUX. MACH. ROOM	AFT PROP. MACH. ROOM	FWD. PROP. MACH. ROOM	FWD. AUX. MACH. ROOM
1. 3500 Kw GAS TUR. GENSET	1. ELECTRIC PROPULSION MOTOR	1. BOOST PROPULSION GAS TURBINE	1.- 3500 Kw DIESEL GENSET
2. C.R.P. HYDRAULIC ACT.	2. GEAR BOX		
3. LINE SHAFT BRG.	3. LINE SHAFT BRG.		
	4. THRUST BRG.		
	5. THYRISTOR CUBICLE		
	6. MOTOR ISOLATORS		

Frigate Electric Cruise Propulsion

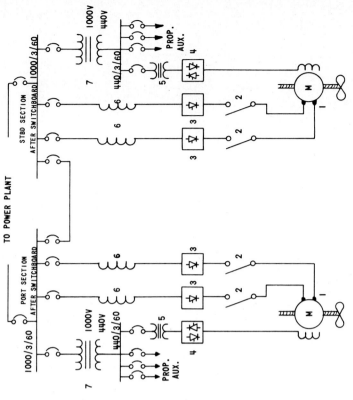

AC GENERATION – DC PROPULSION

Fig. 5 Dc cruise propulsion system, electrical schematic

1. DC PROPULSION MOTOR
2. 4 POLE ISOLATOR
3. THYRISTOR CONVERTER
4. EXCITATION AND CONTROL CONVERTER
5. EXCITATION TRANSFORMER
6. COMMUTATING REACTOR
7. SHIP'S SERVICE TRANSFORMER

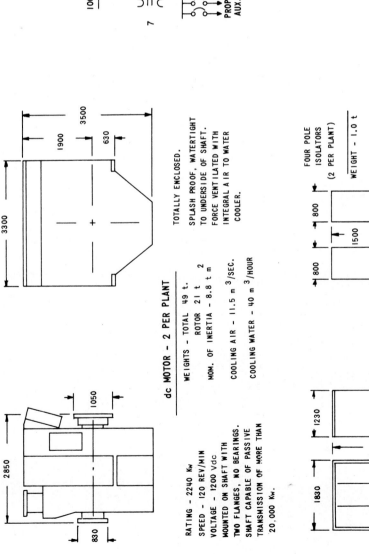

dc MOTOR – 2 PER PLANT

WEIGHTS – TOTAL   49 t.
          ROTOR   21 t
MOM. OF INERTIA – 8.8 t m²

COOLING AIR – 11.5 m³/SEC.
COOLING WATER – 40 m³/HOUR

RATING – 2240 Kw
SPEED – 120 REV/MIN
VOLTAGE – 1200 Vdc
MOUNTED ON SHAFT WITH
TWO FLANGES, NO BEARINGS.
SHAFT CAPABLE OF PASSIVE
TRANSMISSION OF MORE THAN
20,000 Kw.

TOTALLY ENCLOSED.
SPLASH PROOF, WATERTIGHT
TO UNDERSIDE OF SHAFT.
FORCE VENTILATED WITH
INTEGRAL AIR TO WATER
COOLER.

FOUR POLE
ISOLATORS
(2 PER PLANT)
WEIGHT – 1.0 t

EXCITATION
TRANSFORMER
(2 PER PLANT)
WEIGHT – 0.4 t

THYRISTOR EXCITATION AND CONTROL
CUBICLE – 2 PER PLANT
SPLASH PROOF – FRONT AND REAR ENTRY
FORCE VENTILATED – COOLING AIR – 2 m³/SEC
COMMUTATING REACTORS FITTED IN
CUBICLE.
WEIGHT – 2.0 t

Fig. 4 COEOG plant, dc propulsion module dimensions

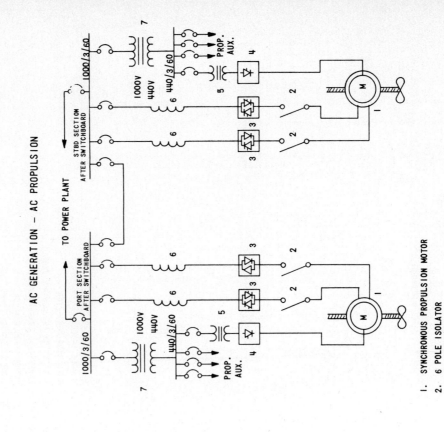

AC GENERATION – AC PROPULSION

1. SYNCHRONOUS PROPULSION MOTOR
2. 6 POLE ISOLATOR
3. CYCLOCONVERTER
4. EXCITATION AND CONTROL CONVERTER
5. EXCITATION TRANSFORMER
6. COMMUTATING REACTOR
7. SHIPS SERVICE TRANSFORMER

Fig. 7 Ac cruise propulsion system, electrical schematic

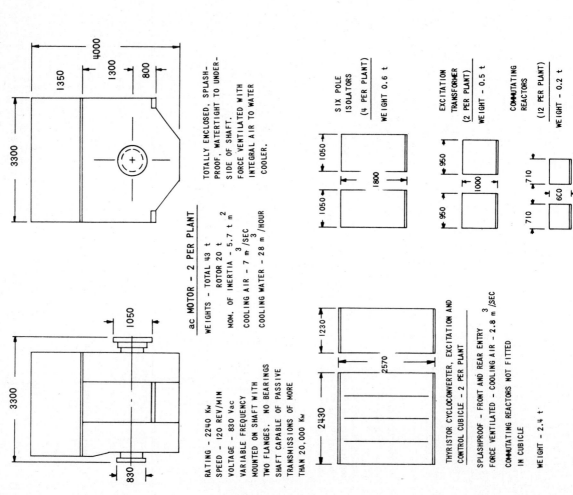

ac MOTOR – 2 PER PLANT

RATING – 2240 Kw
SPEED – 120 REV/MIN
VOLTAGE – 830 Vac
VARIABLE FREQUENCY
MOUNTED ON SHAFT WITH
TWO FLANGES. NO BEARINGS
SHAFT CAPABLE OF PASSIVE
TRANSMISSIONS OF MORE
THAN 20,000 Kw

WEIGHTS – TOTAL 43 t
ROTOR 20 t
MOM. OF INERTIA – 5.7 t m^2
COOLING AIR – 7 m^3/SEC
COOLING WATER – 28 m^3/HOUR

TOTALLY ENCLOSED, SPLASH-
PROOF, WATERTIGHT TO UNDER-
SIDE OF SHAFT.
FORCE VENTILATED WITH
INTEGRAL AIR TO WATER
COOLER.

SIX POLE
ISOLATORS
(4 PER PLANT)
WEIGHT 0.6 t

EXCITATION
TRANSFORMER
(2 PER PLANT)
WEIGHT – 0.5 t

COMMUTATING
REACTORS
(12 PER PLANT)
WEIGHT – 0.2 t

THYRISTOR CYCLOCONVERTER, EXCITATION AND
CONTROL CUBICLE – 2 PER PLANT

SPLASHPROOF – FRONT AND REAR ENTRY
FORCE VENTILATED – COOLING AIR – 2.8 m^3/SEC
COMMUTATING REACTORS NOT FITTED
IN CUBICLE

WEIGHT – 2.4 t

Fig. 6 COEOG plant, ac propulsion module dimensions

Frigate Electric Cruise Propulsion

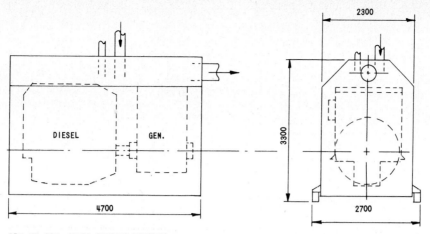

750 KW GEN. WITH PAXMAN VALENTA
8 RP 200 DIESEL — OUTLINE SKETCH

WEIGHT - 18.5 T
DIMENSIONS In mm

Fig. 8   750-kW diesel genset, outline sketch

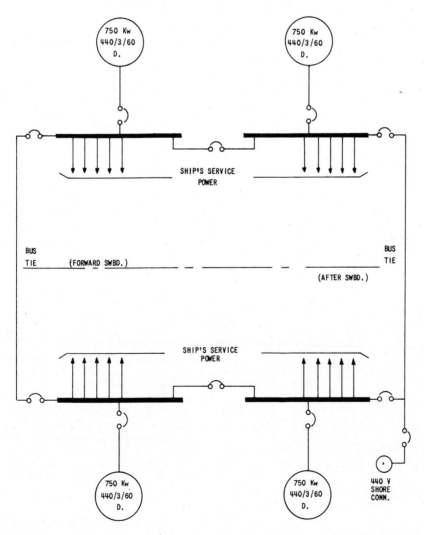

D. - DIESEL ENGINE

Fig. 9   COGOG electrical generating plant schematic

Frigate Electric Cruise Propulsion

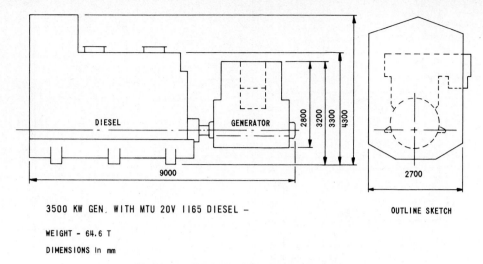

3500 KW GEN. WITH MTU 20V 1165 DIESEL —

WEIGHT — 64.6 T

DIMENSIONS In mm

Fig. 10   3500-kW diesel genset, outline sketch

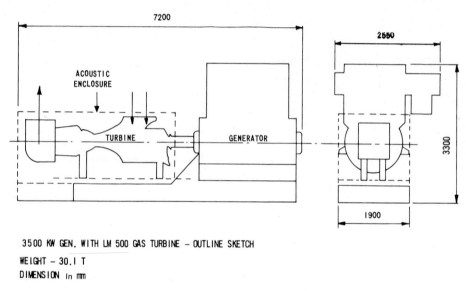

3500 KW GEN. WITH LM 500 GAS TURBINE — OUTLINE SKETCH

WEIGHT — 30.1 T

DIMENSION In mm

Fig. 11   3500-kW gas turbine, outline sketch

The annual fuel consumption estimate for cruise propulsion power for the COGOG ship is determined as follows:

• The hours per annum at speeds of 1-knot intervals is taken from Table 4.

• The propulsion power demand (kW) at corresponding 1-knot intervals is read from the COGOG speed/power characteristic, Fig. 1.

• The product of these two quantities is the annual energy demand (kWh) for speeds at 1-knot intervals through the cruise speed range.

• The necessary SFC factor at corresponding 1-knot intervals is read from the appropriate (gas turbine) curve in Fig. 15.

The complete data are given in Table 5.

The annual fuel consumption estimate for cruise propulsion power for the COEOG variants is determined by a similar procedure. In this case, however, the following steps are necessary:

• Determine the annual energy demand for cruise propulsion.

• Take cognizance of whether the energy conversion prime mover is a gas turbine or a diesel engine.

• Establish the load level on the prime mover, remembering that the total load is the demand for both cruise propulsion and ship's service power. (Note that the 1000-kW peacetime cruising ship's service power demand is used as representative.)

• Determine the SFC factor from the appropriate curves in Fig. 15 at the correct total load level.

• Recognize that 30 percent of the time is spent in the quiet mode.

The assumption is made that for generating sets operating in parallel, the load will be evenly shared between them.

The complete data are shown in Table 6. The COEOG ship permits an estimated annual fuel saving of 795 tonnes (875 tons).

Comparative data for area, volume and weight

Area, volume and weight data were developed for the ten major system components. Data were taken from manufacturers' information and design drawings where possible. Data pertaining to mountings, enclosures, ducting and other exostructure elements were estimated by making 1:100 arrange-

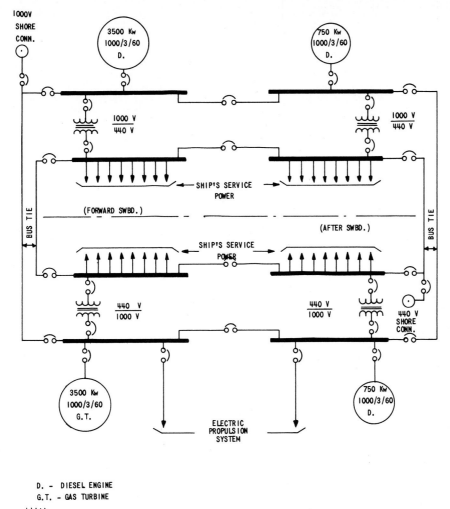

D. – DIESEL ENGINE
G.T. – GAS TURBINE
— SHIP'S SERVICE TRANSFORMERS

Fig. 12 COEOG electrical generating plant schematic

ment drawings, of which Fig. 17 and 18 are examples. The two electric motor modules are shown separately so that the major components of the electric cruise propulsion systems may be identified; see Table 7. The area, volume and weight comparative data for the ten major system components are shown in Table 8.

The comparative area, volume and weight data are shown in Table 9. The item letter designators refer to Table 8.

Comparative data for initial cost

The term "initial cost" is used to mean the sum of purchase price plus engineering and development costs (if any), acquisition costs (including procurement overheads, inspection services, transportation, storage, etc.) and installation costs.

Comparative cost data were developed for the ten major system components. The cost elements were derived as follows:

• The purchase price includes a manufacturer's price (FOB plant) plus the shipbuilder materials for the exostructure.

• Acquisition costs are an estimate related to purchase price by an experience factor for warship construction in Canadian shipyards.

• Installation costs are also an estimate related to the functional nature and weight of an equipment by an experience factor for warship construction in Canadian shipyards.

Module costs, identified by the same letter designators as used in Table 8, are shown in Table 10. The consolidated initial cost data for the three plant types are shown in Table 11.

Comparative cost data for annual maintenance

Annual maintenance costs must be estimated through the use of an experience factor which is related to purchase price and to the number of hours of operation per year. The method is to express the maintenance costs as a percentage of the purchase price of the bare machine (that is, without exostructure) per 1000 hr of operation.

The running hours per year in the cruise speed range are 3240. The major system components for which running hours are significant in terms of estimating maintenance costs are:

(a) mechanical cruise propulsion gas turbines
(b) two of the COGOG ship 750-kW generator sets
(c) double-input, single-output gearboxes
(d) COEOG dc motors
(e) COEOG ac motors
(f) 3500-KW diesel generator set
(g) 3500-KW gas turbine generator set

The single-input, single-output gearboxes are not in use during electric cruise propulsion. No maintenance costs are developed

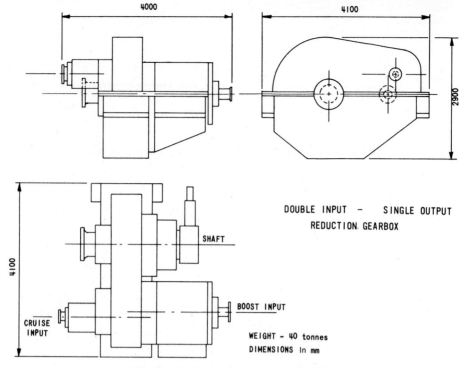

DOUBLE INPUT — SINGLE OUTPUT
REDUCTION GEARBOX

SHAFT

BOOST INPUT

CRUISE
INPUT

WEIGHT - 40 tonnes
DIMENSIONS In mm

Fig. 13   Double-input, single-output gearbox

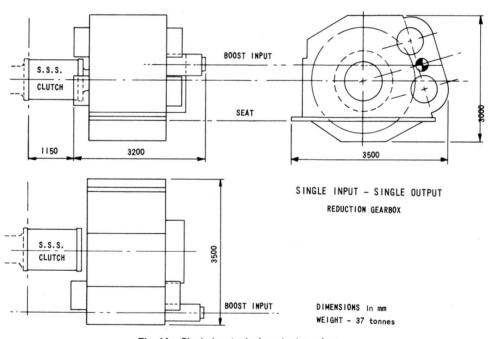

BOOST INPUT

S.S.S.
CLUTCH

SEAT

1150   3200

3500

SINGLE INPUT — SINGLE OUTPUT
REDUCTION GEARBOX

S.S.S.
CLUTCH

BOOST INPUT

DIMENSIONS In mm
WEIGHT - 37 tonnes

Fig. 14   Single-input, single-output gearbox

for the static COEOG system components.   Of the four 750-kW generator sets in the COGOG ship, two may be viewed as simply providing generating capacity redundancy.   Annual maintenance costs will be estimated for two 750-kW sets, each operating at all times when in the mechanical cruise propulsion mode in order to meet the 1000-kW peacetime cruising demand for ship's service power.   The two 750-kW generator sets in the COEOG variants will be taken as components of the boost propulsion system, and no cruise propulsion mode maintenance costs will be shown for these machines.

Of the major system components listed in the preceeding paragraph, all except the two 3500-kW generator sets are in operation whenever the ship is in the cruise propulsion mode. The annual operating hours for each of these machines is 3240.

Referring to Table 6 it is seen that for 2210 hr per year, only one 3500-kW generator need be on line.   For 30 percent of the time this must be the gas turbine generator set as per the quiet operation requirement.   Of the remaining (3240 − 2210 =) 1030 hr, both 3500-KW generator sets must be on line.   The

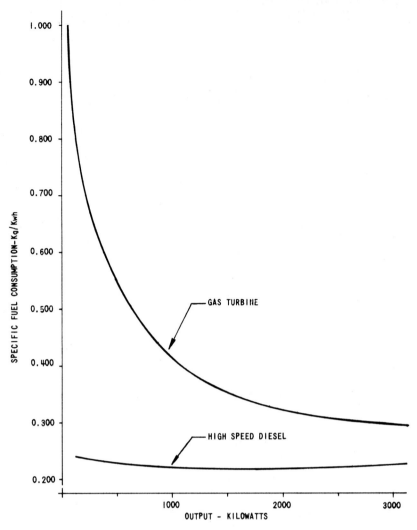

Fig. 15 Curves of specific fuel consumption

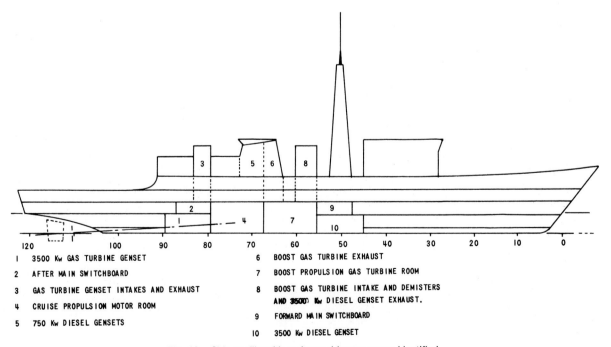

1	3500 Kw GAS TURBINE GENSET
2	AFTER MAIN SWITCHBOARD
3	GAS TURBINE GENSET INTAKES AND EXHAUST
4	CRUISE PROPULSION MOTOR ROOM
5	750 Kw DIESEL GENSETS
6	BOOST GAS TURBINE EXHAUST
7	BOOST PROPULSION GAS TURBINE ROOM
8	BOOST GAS TURBINE INTAKE AND DEMISTERS AND 3500 Kw DIESEL GENSET EXHAUST.
9	FORWARD MAIN SWITCHBOARD
10	3500 Kw DIESEL GENSET

Fig. 16 Ship profile with main machinery spaces identified

Frigate Electric Cruise Propulsion

Table 4 Annual speed/time profile—cruise range

Speed (knots)	Hours per Year Spent at This Speed	Speed, (knots)	Hours per Year Spent at This Speed
1	30	10	230
2	25	11	305
3	37	12	355
4	46	13	355
5	48	14	345
6	84	15	330
7	90	16	260
8	105	17	255
9	155	18	185

running hours per year for these machines are therefore:
• 3500-kW diesel generator set running hours per year are $0.7 \times 2210 + 1030 = 2577$.
• 3500-kW gas turbine generator set running hours per year are $0.3 \times 2210 + 1030 = 1693$.

Annual maintenance costs estimates are shown in Table 12. The same letter designators are used as in Table 8 etc. It is reiterated that the costs used are the purchase price exclusive of exostructure.

The consolidated annual maintenance cost data for the three plant types are shown in Table 13.

An assessment of the impact of the electrical cruise propulsion concepts on manning level was carried out. It was concluded that the use of electrical cruise propulsion would not affect manning levels.

The comparative data developed in the preceeding are summarized in Table 14.

Qualitative comparative criteria

In addition to the quantitative comparative data, qualitative comparisons as between mechanical cruise propulsion and electrical cruise propulsion must be made for
• noise and vibration

Table 5 Annual fuel consumption estimate—COGOG

Speed (knots)	Time per Year at This Speed (hours)	Propulsion Power Demand kW Per Engine	Propulsion Power Demand kW Total	Propulsion Energy Demand (kWh)	Specific Fuel Consumption (kg/kWh)	Annual Fuel Demand (tonnes)
1	30	85	170	5100	0.992	5.06
2	25	100	200	5000	0.974	4.87
3	37	125	250	9250	0.949	8.78
4	46	150	300	13800	0.923	12.74
5	48	170	340	16320	0.907	14.80
6	84	190	380	31920	0.872	27.83
7	90	210	420	37800	0.850	32.13
8	105	270	540	56700	0.785	44.51
9	155	335	670	103850	0.700	72.70
10	230	410	820	188600	0.626	118.06
11	305	525	1050	320250	0.559	179.02
12	355	658	1315	466825	0.498	232.48
13	355	820	1640	582200	0.456	265.48
14	345	1025	2050	707250	0.414	292.80
15	330	1272	2545	839850	0.380	319.14
16	260	1600	3200	832000	0.353	293.70
17	255	1975	3950	1007250	0.328	330.38
18	185	2460	4920	910200	0.310	282.16
Totals	3240			6134165		2536.64

Table 6 Annual propulsion fuel demand

Speed, knots	Time per Year at This Speed, h	Propulsion Power Demand, kW	Propulsion Energy Demand, kWh/y	Number of Sets on line	Load Level %	Annual Energy Conversion Diesel Prime Movers %	Annual Energy Conversion Diesel Prime Movers kWh	SFC kg/kWh	Annual Fuel Demand t	Annual Energy Conversion Gas Turbine Prime Movers %	Annual Energy Conversion Gas Turbine Prime Movers KWh	SFC kg/kWh	Annual Fuel Demand t
1	30	400	12000	1	40.0	70	8400	0.220	1.83	30	3600	0.363	1.31
2	25	450	11250	1	41.4	70	7875	0.220	1.73	30	3375	0.359	1.21
3	37	510	18870	1	43.1	70	13209	0.220	2.91	30	5661	0.355	2.01
4	46	540	24840	1	44.0	70	17388	0.220	3.83	30	7452	0.353	2.63
5	48	585	28080	1	45.3	70	19656	0.220	4.32	30	8424	0.350	2.95
6	84	620	52080	1	46.3	70	36456	0.220	8.02	30	15624	0.346	5.41
7	90	690	62100	1	48.6	70	43470	0.220	9.56	30	18630	0.341	6.35
8	105	780	81900	1	51.4	70	57330	0.220	12.61	30	24570	0.335	8.23
9	155	900	139500	1	54.3	70	97650	0.220	21.48	30	41850	0.330	13.81
10	230	1070	246100	1	59.1	70	172270	0.220	37.90	30	73830	0.321	23.70
11	305	1250	381250	1	64.3	70	266875	0.220	58.71	30	114375	0.315	36.03
12	355	1500	532500	1	71.4	70	372750	0.220	82.01	30	159750	0.306	48.88
13	355	1800	639000	1	80.0	70	447300	0.225	100.64	30	191700	0.229	57.32
14	345	2200	759000	1	91.4	70	531300	0.230	122.20	30	227700	0.293	66.72
15	330	2700	891000	2	52.9	50	445500	0.220	100.21	50	445500	0.333	148.35
16	260	3325	864500	2	61.8	50	432250	0.220	95.10	50	432250	0.318	137.46
17	255	4100	1045500	2	72.9	50	522750	0.220	115.01	50	522750	0.305	159.44
18	185	5050	934250	2	86.4	50	467125	0.225	105.10	50	467125	0.294	137.33
Totals	3240		6723720				3959554		883.19		2764166		859.14

Total Fuel Demand—1742 tonnes

- technical risk
- cross-connect capability
- infinitely variable speed control
- simple and rapid reversal
- design and installation flexibility

Noise is a topic of fundamental significance relative to the design of an ASW frigate. This topic will be discussed in some detail toward the end of this section.

The decision to select only state-of-the-art equipment, together with the maturity of electric propulsion technology, permits the assessment that there is no technical risk.

The use of electric propulsion provides full cross-connect capability through the cruise speed range. This is not the case for the COGOG ship.

Both COEOG variants employ propulsion motors which have infinitely variable speed control and any shaft speed from 0 to 120 rpm (in either direction) can be achieved and held. The COGOG ship has a minimum shaft speed (in one direction only) and all speed control then rests entirely with the CRP propeller. Propeller noise will be related to the mismatch between optimum design pitch and actual pitch setting. A reduction gear is in operation as well. The COEOG variants provide precise speed control with lower noise.

Both COEOG variants employ propulsion motors capable of simple and rapid reversal. The COGOG ship is also capable of simple and rapid reversal via CRP propellers. Indeed, an analysis of headreach and stopping times suggests that, from a speed of 18 knots, the COEOG variants would have a head reach and stopping time approximately 10 percent greater than for the COGOG ship.

Table 7   Electric cruise propulsion module—area, volume, weight

Variant	Item	No. Per Module	Area (m²)	Volume (m³)	Weight (tonnes)
dc	Motor with cooler	1	9.0	22.7	49.0
	Rectifier and control cubicle	1	2.3	5.8	2.0
	Field excitation supply	1	0.5	0.4	0.4
	Protective isolators	2	0.7	1.3	1.0
	Module Totals		12.5	30.2	52.4
ac	Motor with cooler	1	10.4	30.1	43.0
	Cycloconverter and control cubicle	1	3.0	7.7	2.4
	Field excitation supply	1	0.9	0.7	0.5
	Commutating reactors	6	3.0	1.8	1.2
	Protective isolators	2	2.2	3.8	1.2
	Module Totals		19.5	44.1	48.3

Table 8   Cruise propulsion modules—area, volume, weight data

Item Letter	Item	Area (m²)	Volume (m³)	Weight (tonnes)
A	Mechanical cruise propulsion module with exostructure	10.7	22.1	26.4
B	750-kW diesel generating set with exostructure	12.2	36.7	18.5
C	Double-input, single-output reduction gearbox	10.0	23.2	40.0
D	dc motor module	12.5	30.2	52.4
E	ac motor module	19.5	44.1	48.3
F	3500-kW diesel generating set with exostructure	21.1	64.3	64.6
G	3500-kW gas turbine generating set with exostructure	14.7	30.6	30.1
H	1000-kVA transformer for COEOG ship's service power	2.3	5.9	2.4
J	Single-input, single-output reduction gearbox	10.0	21.4	37.0
K	Increase to switchboards by addition of 1000-V components	11.4	25.1	9.7

Table 9   Cruise propulsion plants—comparative area, volume, weight

Cruise Propulsion Plant Type	Item Letter Designator × Quantity Per Plant	Area (m²)	Volume (m³)	Weight (tonnes)
COGOG	A × 2, B × 4, C × 2	90.2	237.4	206.8
COEOG—dc Variant	B × 2, D × 2, F × 1, G × 1, H × 4, J × 2, K × 1	125.6	320.2	329.8
COEOG—ac Variant	B × 2, E × 2, F × 1, G × 1, H × 4, J × 2, K × 1	139.6	348.0	321.6

Table 10   Cruise propulsion modules—initial cost data ($k)

Item Letter	Item	Purchase Price ($k)	Acquisition Costs ($k)	Installation Costs ($k)	Initial Costs ($k)
A	Mechanical cruise propulsion module with exostructure	1864	223	278	2365
B	750-kW diesel generating set with exostructure	1430	158	184	1772
C	Double-input, single-output reduction gearbox	1925	231	475	2631
D	dc motor module	3267	393	406	4066
E	ac motor module	3850	461	374	4685
F	3500-kW diesel generating set with exostructure	2471	297	682	3450
G	3500-kW gas turbine gen. set with exostructure	2375	285	464	3124
H	1000-kVA transformer for COEOG ship's service power	18.7	2.2	46.1	67
J	Single-input, single-output reduction gearbox	1773	212	446	2431
K	Increase to switchboards by addition of 1000-V components	1177	141	231	1549

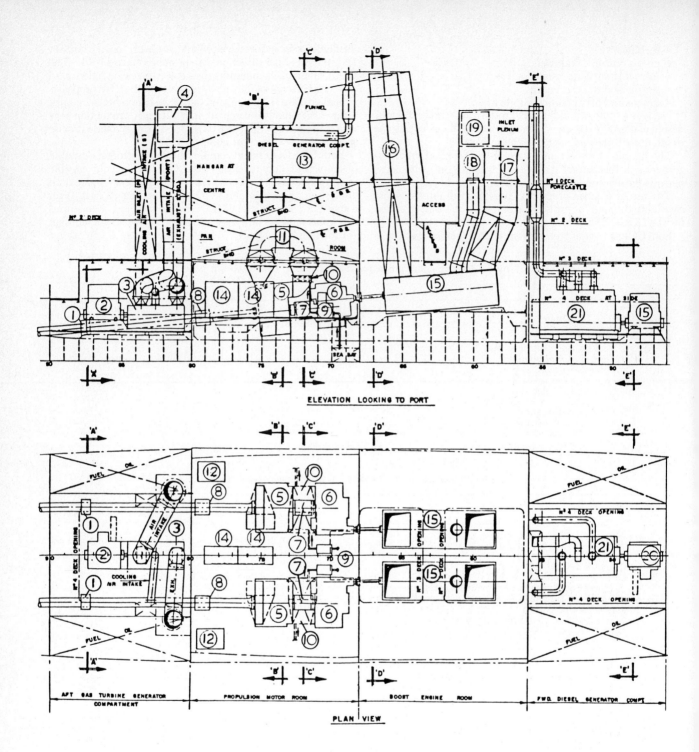

ELEVATION LOOKING TO PORT

PLAN VIEW

① LINE SHAFT B'R'G	⑧ THRUST BLOCK	⑮ BOOST GAS TURBINE
② 3500 KW GEN'R	⑨ PROP'N MOTOR COOL'G PUMPS	⑯ EXHAUST
③ GAS TURBINE	⑩ PROP'N MOTOR COOLER	⑰ AIR INTAKE
④ DEMISTERS	⑪ PROP'N MOTOR COOL'G FAN	⑱ COOLING AIR INTAKE
⑤ D.C. PROP'N MOTOR	⑫ FIN STABILIZERS	⑲ DEMISTERS
⑥ GEARBOX	⑬ 750 KW GEN'RS	⑳ 3500 KW GEN'R
⑦ CLUTCH	⑭ CONVERTER CUBICLE	㉑ DIESEL PRIME MOVER

Fig. 17 COEOG ship, machinery plant arrangement

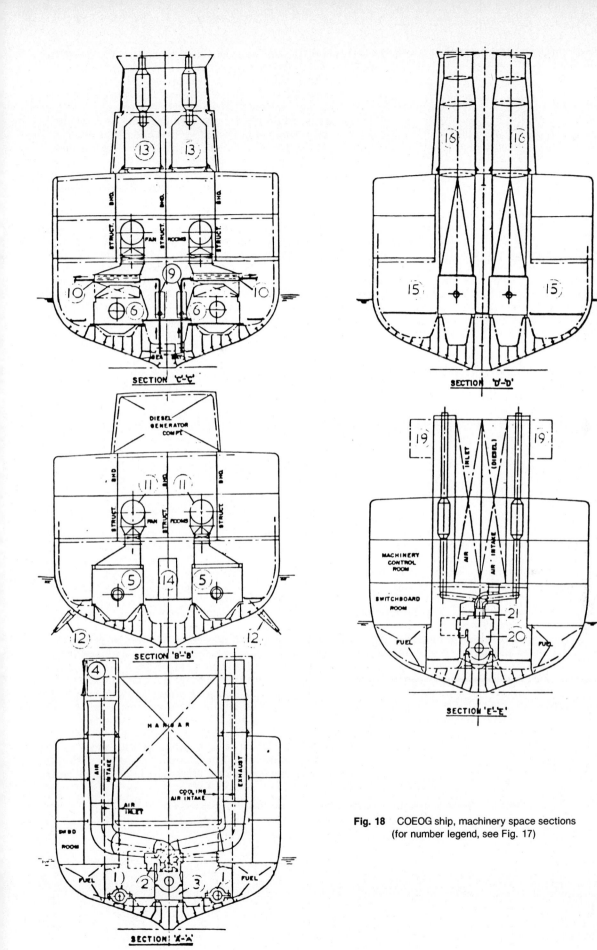

SECTION 'C'-'C'

SECTION 'D'-'D'

SECTION 'B'-'B'

SECTION 'E'-'E'

SECTION 'A'-'A'

Fig. 18 COEOG ship, machinery space sections
(for number legend, see Fig. 17)

Table 11   Cruise propulsion plants—comparative cost data ($k)

Cruise Propulsion Plant Type	Item Letter Designator × Quantity Per Plant	Initial Cost ($k)
COGOG	A × 2, B × 4, C × 2	17080
COEOG— dc Variant	B × 2, D × 2, F × 1, G × 1, H × 4, J × 2, K × 1	24929
COEOG— ac Variant	B × 2, E × 2, F × 1, G × 1, H × 4, J × 2, K × 1	26167

The necessity to have a mechanical boost propulsion power train obviates much of the design and installation flexibility which would accrue to an all electric propulsion plant. For the COEOG variants, very limited installation flexibility is available to the mechanically aligned and interactive boost propulsion prime movers/reduction gearing/electric propulsion motors. The appreciable installation flexibility in the location of electric generators, which are in effect the electric cruise propulsion prime movers, is to the advantage of the COEOG variants.

A note on noise and vibration

A major consideration in ASW frigate design is to achieve the lowest possible noise signature. The effect of machinery noise on habitability must be considered in any ship design, and the techniques for dealing with airborne noise must be invoked. However, in comparing electrical versus mechanical propulsion, it is noise in the water that is the concern. This is referred to as platform noise.

There are three principal sources of platform noise:
• hydrodynamic noise produced by the hull
• hydrodynamic noise produced by the propeller
• machinery noise produced by vibration

The discussion here is conceptually one of choices for the cruise propulsion plant in the same ship. Subject to a minor point related to cooling water, the hull-produced hydrodynamic noise is not affected by the choice of the cruise propulsion plant. Thus machinery vibration and propeller noise remain as the significant contributors to platform noise for this comparison.

It is a valid contention that a fixed-pitch propeller is less noisy than a CRP propeller operated off design pitch. The employment of electric cruise propulsion permits the CRP propeller (required for speed and thrust control during boost propulsion) to be used in a fixed-pitch mode throughout the cruise speed range. Furthermore, advantage can be taken of the precise and infinitely variable speed control to synchronize propeller speeds and reduce modulated beat propeller noise.

The principal machinery vibration sources of concern are:
• diesel engine prime movers
• gas turbine prime movers
• reduction gearing
• auxiliary machinery

In the case of the auxiliary machinery, this would be resiliently mounted in any case, for the shock protection. Hence little problem exists and the problem of auxiliary machinery is essentially the same regardless of the cruise propulsion system being considered. However, the greater volume of seawater required for electric motor cooling must be considered since this could result in larger sea bays and hull openings. These would require attention in design to prevent hull noise being generated by large openings.

The COEOG variants obviate the use of reduction gearing in the cruise speed range. The COGOG ship requires the use of reduction gearing in the cruise speed range. Gear noise is highly undesirable, and the ability to propel in the quiet mode without the use of reduction gearing is a significant advantage. Reduction gearing may be resiliently mounted in order to attenuate noise input to the water but to do so imposes the requirement for large in-shaft flexible couplings, which give rise to problems. But the salient point is that a gearless propulsion power train is superior to a geared train irrespective of how carefully the gearing is manufactured or how well the gear noise is uncoupled or attenuated from the water.

It is with consideration of prime mover engines as noise sources, and the measures that can be taken to alleviate noise, that the superiority of electric propulsion is quite significant. While gas turbines do not present difficult platform noise problems when properly mounted and enclosed, the same cannot be said for diesels. Even current technology involving double-mounted and acoustically enclosed diesels does not provide fully adequate noise isolation, particularly at the low-frequency end of the noise spectrum.

In formulating design guidelines it was taken as implicit that properly treated diesels situated high in the ship would represent a lower platform noise source than those located in machinery spaces. The option to locate diesel generators high in the ship is enhanced by the concept of electric cruise propulsion. This is due to these two factors:

• The addition of weight low in the ship (two heavy motors) allows more top weight to be carried without change to the hull form.

• The elimination of the cruise gas turbine intakes and exhausts releases deck space in a usable location without increasing the length of the ship,

There are sound economic and outfitting reasons for holding the number of generator sets to a minimum. At present there are two reasons why diesel prime-movers are preferred for the 750-kW generator sets: (1) fuel economy, and (2) lack of availability of a suitable gas turbine in the 750-kW power range.

The penalty for having diesel generator sets in the machinery spaces of the COGOG ship is reduced by the fact that both reduction gearing and CRP propellers are elements of the mechanical cruise propulsion plant. The ability to use a large gas turbine generator set as the source of quiet-mode cruise propulsion power permits enhanced exploitation of the electric cruise propulsion concept. Being able to locate additional diesel

Table 12   Cruise propulsion modules—annual maintenance cost estimate ($k)

Item Letter	Item	Purchase Price ($k)	Maintenance Cost Per 1000 Hours		Annual Running Hours	Annual Maint'ce Cost ($k)
			% of Pr.	($k)		
A	Mechanical cruise prime mover gas turbine	880	7.10	62.5	3240	202.5
B	750-kW diesel generator set	848	3.50	29.7	3240	96.2
C	Double-input, single-output gearbox	1460	0.30	4.4	3240	14.3
D	dc motor	2857	0.70	20	3240	64.8
E	ac motor	2951	0.30	8.9	3240	28.8
F	3500-kW diesel generator set	1586	3.3	52.3	2577	134.9
G	3500-kW gas turbine generator set	1387	4.3	59.6	1693	100.9

Table 13 Cruise propulsion plants—comparative maintenance cost data

Cruise Propulsion Plant Type	Item Letter Designator × Quantity Per Plant	Annual Maintenance Cost ($k)
COGOG	A × 2, B × 2, C × 2	626
COEOG— dc variant	D × 2, F × 1, G × 1,	365.4
COEOG— ac variant	E × 2, F × 1, G × 1,	293.4

Table 14 Comparative data summary

Item	COGOG	COEOG (dc Variant)	COEOG (ac Variant)
Area (m²)	90.2	125.6	139.6
Volume (m³)	237.4	320.2	348.0
Weight (tonnes)	206.8	329.8	321.6
Initial cost ($k)	17080	24929	26167
Annual Maintenance costs ($k)	626.0	365.4	293.4
Annual fuel consumption (tonnes)	2537	1742	1742

generator capacity in the superstructure adds security to the electrical power supply and provides an economical source of cruise propulsion power for very low speeds.   These machines also provide for other periods of low electrical power demand as well, such as during boost propulsion or in harbor.

In summary, the objective of realizing the lowest achievable noise signature is definitely enhanced by the concept of using electric motors as cruise propulsion prime movers.

The aspect of habitability was touched on earlier.   In general, the measures taken to protect machinery against shock and to attenuate vibration levels by proper mounting techniques adequately reduces internal structureborne noise as well.   Internal airborne noise is treated by the use of acoustic enclosures and engine mufflers.

Compliance with STANAG 1008

A stated technical requirement was that the characteristics of the electrical power generating plant must be in accordance with the specification STANAG 1008—Characteristics of Shipboard Electrical Power Systems in Surface Warships of the NATO Navies.

This specification defines the NATO standards for voltage and voltage regulation, frequency and frequency regulation, waveform and waveform total harmonic content, etc.

The stated technical requirements further state that "the electric propulsion system operating in any steady state or transient condition shall not cause the electrical plant characteristics to exceed the limits specified in STANAG 1008."

The COEOG electrical plant is not compliant with STANAG 1008 in two ways:

• The electrical plant operates at 1000 V rather than 450 V as specified.

• During cruise propulsion the thyristors used for rectification or frequency conversion generate voltage waveform distortion which exceeds the limits specified.

The lack of compliance regarding the voltage of generation is of no consequence. By the use of transformers, the voltage in the ship's service power distribution system is brought to 450 V.   This satisfactorily resolves this noncompliance.

The lack of compliance regarding voltage waveform distortion is more serious, and to make the concept of a common electrical distribution network viable this noncompliance must be eliminated or made acceptable.

The electric propulsion system user equipments are not adversely affected.   It is the presence of excessive voltage waveform distortion in the ship's service power distribution network that is the problem.   Since only a fraction of the user equipments in the ship's service power distribution system is affected by voltage waveforms distortion, steps must be taken to identify these consumers and supply them from a suitable secondary power source.   This activity must be seen as a component of fully engineering the electrical cruise propulsion concept.   This is a major task, and the problem of voltage waveform distortion must be resolved in order to make the COEOG concept fully workable.

Additional considerations

The following additional considerations merit comment:

• The main generating sets in the COEOG variants differ from the usual ship's service generators in three fundamental ways—

(1)   The voltage of generation is 1000 V.   The usual voltage is 450 V.

(2)   To cater for the reactive nature of the thyristor conversion devices as a major load, the design power factor must be 0.7.   The usual design power factor is 0.8.

(3)   To protect against the fault current capacity represented by the electric cruise propulsion system, the generator subtransient reactance must be below 15 percent, and may even require to be as low as 12 percent.

• No reference has been made to ship endurance.   However, the fuel economy which accrues to the COEOG variants may be taken to represent an increase in endurance at speeds in the cruise range.   Alternatively, endurance may be held constant and the fuel stowage reduced as an offset to the greater weight of the COEOG plants.

• A high maneuverability is a requirement for a frigate. The COEOG concept confers high maneuverability through precise speed control with rapid and simple reversal.   However, the COGOG ship with CRP propeller is slightly superior to the COEOG variants in this regard.

• The selection of electric cruise propulsion machinery can broaden the base of industrial manufacture and support of ship systems and components.

Final assessment

The final assessment is made by using the stated evaluation criteria, to each of which is assigned a weighted maximum value.   Quantitative comparative data were developed for fuel consumption, initial costs, annual maintenance costs, space and weight requirements.   Numerical ranking values are shown against these five evaluation criteria which are simple proportions of the weighted maxima.   The full weighted maximum is assigned to the top-ranked plant variant in each case. Subjective evaluations for the other seven evaluation criteria are based on the qualitative discussion in the foregoing.

The final assessment is shown in Table 15.

Conclusion

It is concluded that state-of-the-art electric cruise propulsion plants for an ASW frigate are technically feasible and are attractive on the basis of fuel conservation and through-life costs. Their low noise and vibration characteristics permit a reduction in noise signature, a feature of particular significance for an ASW frigate.   Their design and installation flexibility, infinitely variable speed control and cross-connect capability add to their

Table 15 Final assessment

Ranking Criteria	Weighted Maximum	COGOG		COEOG-dc Variant		COEOG-ac Variant	
		Quant. Data	Ranking	Quant. Data	Ranking	Quant. Data	Ranking
Initial cost ($k)	25	17080	25.00	24929	17.13	26167	16.32
Annual maintenance cost ($k)	15	626.0	7.03	365.4	12.04	293.4	15.00
Annual fuel consumption (tonnes)	10	2537	6.87	1742	10.00	1742	10.00
Volume (m³)	10	237.4	10.00	320.2	7.41	348.0	6.82
Weight (tonnes)	10	2068	10.00	329.8	6.27	321.6	6.43
Noise and vibration	10	...	2.50	...	10.00	...	10.00
Technical risk	10	...	10.00	...	10.00	...	10.00
Compliance with STANAG 1008	10	...	10.00	...	0.00	...	0.00
Cross-connect capability	5	...	0.00	...	5.00	...	5.00
Infinitely variable speed control	5	...	0.00	...	5.00	...	5.00
Simple and rapid reversing capability	5	...	5.00	...	4.00	...	4.00
Design and installation flexibility	5	...	0.00	...	3.00	...	3.00
Ranking Total			86.40		91.85		93.57

appeal. The detailed design of either variant could be undertaken now for incorporation into a near-future 4000-tonne (3920 dwt) ship.

Although larger and heavier, the ac variant has lower annual maintenance costs and this would be significant over the lifetime of the plant. he ac motor is less subject to insulation problems in the marine environment than is the dc motor. The ac variant is considered the better COEOG propulsion plant.

The major unresolved problem is how to isolate sensitive ship's service power consumers from the effects of the voltage waveform distortion consequent upon having high-power thyristors as a major load on a common electrical distribution network. It is considered that the benefits which would accrue to deriving electric cruise propulsion and ship's service power from a common network in an ASW frigate warrant a resolution of this problem. More than one viable solution exists.

Discussion

Basil R. Orr,[4] Visitor

This is an excellent paper and is so well researched and conceived that it makes a discusser's job very difficult. There is no doubt that from a fuel economy and quiet running point of view the authors have provided a very viable alternative to mechanical cruise in small warships.

It is recognized that it is necessary to establish a baseline system against which others are compared and evaluated. In this case the baseline system is a COGOG mechanical propulsion power plant with both cruise gas turbines operating at all times when the ship is operating in the cruise speed range. This means, of course, that these engines are operating in a very inefficient range from a fuel consumption point of view, even at 18 knots.

It is suggested that, in the light of the availability of cross-connected reduction gears which are now within the state of the art, the use of a non-cross-connect mechanical system for comparison purposes may be penalizing this type of propulsion system unfairly. Using the cruise gas turbine selected for the baseline system rated at 3270 hp, Fig. 1, indicates that one of these engines with a cross-connected reduction gear would be capable of providing a speed in excess of 15 knots. At these speeds the gas turbine would be operating at, or close to its design point.

With only one gas turbine operating in the speed range between 0 and 16 knots, and because, as Fig. 1 also indicates, the ship operates approximately 30 percent of the time in the 12 to 15 knot speed range, the fuel comsumption figures shown in Table 5 would be reduced by about 12 percent. The use of a second-generation gas turbine would result in further fuel savings.

It is agreed that a COGOGX system probably could not compete with the electrical system in the area of hull-transmitted noise, but one wonders if the added cost and complexity of the electrical system could be justified in order to gain a reduction of a few dB's of hull transmitted noise.

Would the authors care to comment on this?

[4] Canadian General Electric Company Ltd., Rexdale, Ontario.

Ronald d'Arcy, Member

Selecting the best propulsion plant for a naval ship application has to be one of the favorite tasks of the marine engineer. We all enjoy the creative matching of prime movers to achieve that elusively optimum propulsion plant. The problem however is not unlike trying to solve the Rubik's Cube. There are so many factors to be balanced that just establishing the design criteria is often like trying to hit a moving target.

The COEOG concept set forth in this paper is an imaginative application of today's available technology with perhaps just that proper amount of pushing the state of the art. I believe the authors have done a creditable job in comparing the COEOG to a conventional COGOG system. There are, however, several observations which I would like to offer:

One of the stated principal benefits of the COEOG concept is its lower life-cycle costs resulting from its lower fuel consumption. In developing this analysis presented in Tables 5 and 6, the authors assumed an overall transmission efficiency at 18 knots of 91 percent for the COGOG concept and 88.6 percent for the COEOG. I would expect a straight mechanical COGOG system to have an efficiency of at least 95 percent. On the other hand, I would expect the electric concept with its generator, thyristor and motor to experience an efficiency closer to 85 percent. Thus somewhat offsetting the fuel consumption advantage of the COEOG.

Another consideration which deserves more attention is the differences in the machinery control systems between the two concepts. The control system and switchgear for the integrated electric concept with thyristors are clearly more complex and costly than the COGOG concept. While I agree the authors have made a good case for electric propulsion especially for those rare opportunities in warship design when weight, volume and acquisition cost take a back seat to life-cycle cost, I do take exception to the numerical ranking system used in the final assessment. The justification for some of the criteria escapes me. For example the criterion of "infinitely variable speed control" is used to penalize the COGOG concept five points because of propeller noise, yet the COGOG plant is also penalized 7.5 points under the criterion for noise and vibration. Similarly, to rate the systems equal on technical risk seems one-sided in view of the unresolved power quality problems of the COEOG system.

I also couldn't help but come to the conclusion that, using the authors' weighted criteria, a higher ranking could be achieved by simply using a propulsion plant consisting of the two boost engines with a mechanical cross-connect. This simple system would receive the maximum rating in all categories with the exception of annual fuel consumption, noise and infinitely variable speed control. Furthermore, the fuel consumption might not be all that bad if we include the percent of time the frigate operates at speeds in the 18–22 knot range.

The authors have clearly stated strong arguments in favor of integrated electric propulsion and are to be congratulated on the thorough presentation of an innovative concept.

I. Majif, Member

The authors must be commended for the clarity with which they have considered and presented the three alternative propulsion schemes. I feel, however, that the matter of "ship endurance," of which the paper only makes brief mention, needs further examination, particularly in the light of the latest naval deployment, namely, the British Navy in the Falklands!

Endurance is defined as the total distance that a ship can travel at a specified speed without refueling. Assuming that the conditions of the bottom, the weather, the amount of helm used, the domestic load, the capacity of the fuel tanks, etc., for the alternative arrangements considered are the same, the endurance of each version will depend on the consumption rate of the propulsion plants. On cursory examination (and as stated in the paper) the COEOG propulsion seems to offer "increase in endurance at speeds in the cruise range." However, closer examination indicates that there are limitations to this statement.

Assuming a cruising speed of 16 knots, fuel consumption for the COGOG (from Table 5) is

$$3200 \text{ kW} \times 0.353 \frac{\text{kg}}{\text{kWh}} = 1.13 \text{ tonnes/hr}$$

Fuel consumption for the COEOG (from Table 6) is

$$3325 \text{ kW} \times 0.318 \frac{\text{kg}}{\text{kWh}} = 1.06 \text{ tonnes/hr}$$

The difference in fuel consumption = 0.07 tonnes/hr in favor of the COEOG variant.

The difference in machinery weight (from Table 15) is 115 tonnes in favor of the COGOG version.

So that for a given displacement the COEOG version carries 115 tonnes less fuel than the COGOG.

The break-even point for ship endurance is therefore

$$\frac{115 \text{ tonnes}}{0.07 \text{ tonnes/hr}} = 1642.83 \text{ hours of "steaming"}$$

or 26 286 nautical miles at 16 knots!!

In other words, no increase in endurance can be expected from the COEOG version unless the stated endurance requirement is in excess of 26 286 miles at 16 knots!!! However, if the economical cruising speed were to be taken as 14 knots, the break-even point becomes 7892 miles.

Authors' Closure

The authors' wish to thank the three discussers for their interest in, and valuable comments on, our paper.

Mr. Orr makes a telling point, the constraint that both cruise gas turbines must be in operation at all times when the ship is underway in the cruise speed range is recognized as being fuel inefficient. A cross-connected reduction gear is one way to ameliorate this fuel inefficiency; removing all power from one shaft and permitting it to trail is another. Both solutions add to noise signature, and this is salient. Because the answer to Mr. Orr's question as to whether the added cost and complexity is justified in order to gain a reduction of a few dB's in noise is categorically yes!

We enjoyed Mr. d'Arcy's analogy of the Rubik's Cube and propulsion plant selection. The task is almost on a par with fundamental philosophy, which has been described as imponderable answers to unanswerable questions.

Both to render the problem tractable in general terms, and to derive an optimum solution in specific terms, the important evaluation criteria must be identified and assigned appropriate weighted values. We agree that both the identification and relative weighting have a substantial subjective element. We hope we revealed and justified the judgments inherent in this aspect of our task.

With respect to transmission losses, our research and calculations tended to show that the all mechanical propulsion train had gearbox and bearing losses which were quite insensitive to the power being transmitted. Certainly a typical modern mechanical propulsion train has a power transmission efficiency greater than 95 percent at high power. The efficiency falls off as the power transmitted decreases. The figure of 91 percent represents a time and power related cruise power range average. The COEOG efficiency appears high because the propulsion prime mover is an electric motor well matched to power demand; there is no reduction gearing in the cruise propulsion train, also fewer line shaft bearings. We stand on our figure of 89 percent for the electric propulsion in the cruise speed range.

Regarding the machinery control system, our investigations drove us to the conclusion that a modern control system, based on the microprocessor, is not challenged by the additional complexity of the COEOG plant, and there would be no significant cost differential between the COGOG and COEOG machinery control systems.

The apparent double penalty arising through the use of the two ranking criteria of "infinitely variable speed control" as well as "noise and vibration" is a measure of the great importance of noise signature and the need to reduce both propeller noise and hydrodynamic hull noise in pursuit of the lowest possible noise signature.

The approach we used in assessing technical risk was to accept that if an engineering solution was available to a technical problem which was within the state of the art and could be realized without major financial or construction penalty, then technical risk was acceptable. On this basis, since the problem of the quality of power demanded by some ship's service consumers is known to be resolvable within state-of-the-art engineering without major financial or construction penalty, we assessed the technical risk for the two plants as being equal. In passing, we may note that this problem is now being examined in detail and our findings support the correctness of this earlier assessment.

We must agree with Mr. d'Arcy that a two boost engine propulsion plant with mechanical cross-connect would achieve a higher ranking in all categories except annual fuel consumption and total noise signature. We also agree that the case for such a propulsion plant improves as we extend the break point between the cruise speed range and the boost speed range. Mr. d'Arcy highlights the fact that for some other ship having some other mission profile, a study is required to determine the best propulsion plant. Rubik's Cube, here we come again!

Mr. Majif is to be congratulated upon the acuity with which he has reviewed our paper. The authors would agree that the subject of ship endurance is worthy of more than passing ref-

Table 16   Range at 16 knots (nautical miles)

	A Constant Displacement (4000 tonnes)	B Constant Fuel (430 tonnes)
Case 1		
COEOG		
(2 generators equal load)	4060	5350
Case 2		
COEOG		
(all diesel)	5300	6400
COGOG	4800	

Table 17

	Range at 10 Knots	
	COGOG	COEOG
Transit mode	6300	8000
Surveillance mode	5300	6300

erence not only in light of the recent long-range deployment of British naval forces in the Falklands, but perhaps more importantly due to the changing nature of shipborne antisubmarine surveillance operations associated with the introduction of highly sensitive towed arrays. In this latter case it is of some importance to keep the very noisy replenishment tankers well away from the area of surveillance for as long as possible. It might be further said that in conducting these surveillance operations it is imperative that the platform combine extremely low noise characteristics with superior endurance at lower speeds. In respect to these two characteristics, it is believed that the advantage lies with the COEOG propulsion system.

With reference to the comparison presented in the discussion, some clarification is required. The data presented in Table 6 show the annual propulsion fuel usage. In deriving these data, it is assumed that the COEOG ship operates on one generator which supplies both propulsion and ship service power, thereby taking full advantage of the common distribution network feature. For 30 percent of the operational time up to 14 knots, it is assumed that the COEOG ship operates in an ultra-quiet mode, that is, on one gas turbine generator only.

For the 16-knots endurance condition addressed, more than one generator is required. While the work reported assumed evenly loaded generators, it is considered to be well within the state of the art of electrical load management and machinery control systems to accommodate varied generator loads on the common distribution network. This being the case, a number of operating configurations are available to the COEOG ship. It should be noted that at this speed the baseline COGOG ship has no choice but to operate two cruise engines for propulsion. Table 16 herewith shows ranges for the COEOG ship and the COGOG ship at 16 knots for two operating configurations.

In developing the data in Table 16 a usable fuel load of 430 tonnes has been used. This is based upon 300 hours of endurance at 16 knots, a typical requirement for a frigate of this size and type. Of this, 340 tonnes is required for propulsion and some 90 tonnes for hotel load based upon 1000 kW of electrical power, which is provided by ship service diesel generators. Some 0.08 tonnes/hr, is assummed to be burnt in oil-burning auxiliaries.

In COEOG Case 1, the propulsion and ship service power requirements are met by both 3500-kW generators equally loaded. The specific fuel consumption figures given in Table 6 relate to the prime mover operating point, that is (3325 + 1000) kW. Hence, the fuel rate is $(2163 \times 0.22 + 2163 \times 0.318) + 0.08 = 1.24$ tonnes/hr. This corresponds to $(1.13 + 0.3) = 1.43$ tonnes/hr for the COGOG ship. Case 2 represents an all-diesel transit mode of operation in which the 3500-kW diesel generator and the 2×750-kW generators are operated together on the common distribution network. Investigations showed that operating the main generators together at different loadings did not appear to offer advantage to the COEOG ship.

The ranges in Column A are based upon maintaining a constant displacement, that is, compensating for the increased machinery weight by reducing fuel. While it is true that the COEOG ship does not show to advantage when operated as in Case 1, it does show some improvement when permitted to exercise its inherent operational flexibility as in Case 2. If the COEOG ship carries the machinery weight penalty and retains the full usable fuel, then a different picture emerges as the figures in Column B indicate. The additional displacement is assumed to be accommodated by sinkage of the COGOG form, resulting in a power increase at 16 knots.

When faced with a choice between a moderately heavier ship or significantly increased range, the authors have no doubt about the direction in which operators would opt.

Corresponding ranges for the COGOG and COEOG ships operating in a surveillance mode and a transit mode at 10 knots are shown in Table 17. In the surveillance mode both ships operate twin shaft, the COEOG ship utilizing the gas turbine generator to achieve an ultra-quiet noise condition. In the transit mode, the COEOG ship operates on the 3500-kW diesel generator while the COGOG ship is permitted to operate in a "trail shaft" mode.

In the surveillance mode, the range advantage of the COEOG ship is better represented as an increase in time between "on station replenishment" of 4 days—a significant operational advantage.

The authors are aware of the complexities of frigate design and the dangers of oversimplified comparisons; however, it is felt the foregoing serves to illustrate the considerations in mind when reference was made to endurance in the body of paper.

Mr. Majif is to be thanked for providing the authors the opportunity to extend the paper in the important aspect of ship performance.

SNAME *Transactions*, Vol. 90, 1982, pp. 415–453

Numerical Methods for Propeller Design and Analysis in Steady Flow

David S. Greeley,[1] Associate Member, and **Justin E. Kerwin,**[2] Associate Member

Current trends in propeller design have led to the need for extremely complex blade shapes which place great demands on the accuracy of design and analysis methods. This paper presents a new lifting-surface design procedure and a compatible lifting-surface steady analysis procedure intended to replace earlier methods developed over a number of years at the Massachusetts Institute of Technology. Numerical methods for blade surface shape generation, trailing vortex wake deformation and propeller performance analysis at off-design operating conditions are described, and comparisons are made with existing experimental and theoretical data. Viscous effects on leading-edge flow separation and cavitation inception are included using a semi-empirical model based on swept-wing data. The application of the design and analysis procedures to a specific propeller design problem is illustrated.

Introduction

DURING the past decade lifting-surface methods have become widely accepted as the most accurate way to determine the pitch and camber distribution required to generate a prescribed loading over the blades. All such methods, however, involve numerical approximations of various sorts, and involve a certain degree of simplification of the geometry of the propeller blade surface and its trailing vortex wake.

Current trends in propeller design have led to extremely complex blade shapes involving high skew and extreme changes in pitch. The successful design of such propellers requires an extremely accurate lifting-surface computational procedure. In addition, propeller designs must frequently be evaluated at off-design operating points which may be encountered due to a variety of circumstances. A compatable lifting-surface analysis procedure of comparable accuracy is therefore a major asset in the development of a propeller design.

The propeller is assumed to be operating in a prescribed axisymmetric effective wake, which may include axial, tangential and radial components. The presence of the hull, propeller hub and free surface is ignored. While the flow is largely considered as inviscid, viscous effects are addressed both in treating the problem of vortex sheet separation from the leading edge and in the problem of trailing vortex sheet deformation, as well as in the traditional manner of estimating blade frictional drag. While propeller unsteady performance is of great concern, this paper will be restricted to steady-flow aspects of the problem.

---
[1] Post-doctoral research associate, Department of Ocean Engineering, Massachusetts Institute of Technology, Cambridge, Mass.; presently, senior scientist, Bolt Beranek and Newman, Inc., Cambridge, Mass.

[2] Professor of naval architecture, Department of Ocean Engineering, Massachusetts Institute of Technology, Cambridge, Mass.

Presented at the Annual Meeting, New York, N. Y., November 17–20, 1982, of THE SOCIETY OF NAVAL ARCHITECTS AND MARINE ENGINEERS.

Determination of blade shape for a prescribed circulation distribution

The present procedure is summarized in the flow diagram shown in Fig. 1. The objective is to find the shape of the blades which will result in a prescribed radial and chordwise distribution of circulation. To accomplish this, the singularity distributions representing loading and thickness are distributed on trial surfaces representing the blades and their trailing vortex wakes, the velocities induced by these singularities are computed and the trial surfaces are then realigned with the resultant flow. Finally, the forces acting on the blade surfaces thus generated are computed. Since these forces will not necessarily be the same as those obtained from lifting-line theory, the specified circulation distribution may need to be adjusted, and the process repeated.

A measure of the success of this procedure is the extent to which the program does nothing to the trial input. In this case the component of total fluid velocity normal to the trial surface will be zero everywhere, so that the output will be identical to the input. This is not likely to happen on the first try, so a few iterations are needed to reach a desired level of accuracy.

The calculation procedure employs a vortex/source lattice representation of the continuous singularity distributions, with velocities computed at a prescribed number of control points properly located in relation to the lattice. Since accuracy and computing time are both related to the specified number of elements and control points, an efficient procedure consists of selecting a coarse lattice during the initial iterations, followed by one or two passes with a fine grid. The procedure is currently set up for an interactive time-sharing system so that the operator can make such decisions based on an immediate inspection of key information.

Once a satisfactory solution has been obtained, detailed definition of the blade shape may then be generated, either in tabular or graphical form. The method of surface definition employed in the present procedure permits the evaluation of coordinates over an arbitrary fine grid, thus facilitating interfacing with a numerically controlled machining process. This

a_l = coefficient in series representing bound circulation distribution, see equation (4)

A_{ij} = influence coefficient matrix; see equation (15)

c = blade section chord length

c_d = two-dimensional drag coefficient:
= drag$/\frac{1}{2}\,\rho c U_\infty^2$

c_1 = two-dimensional lift coefficient:
= lift$/\frac{1}{2}\,\rho c U_\infty^2$

C = leading-edge singularity parameter, defined in equation (38)

C_p = pressure coefficient:
= $(p - p_\infty)/\frac{1}{2}\,\rho U_\infty^2$

C_s = leading-edge suction force coefficient, defined in equation (20)

D = propeller diameter

f = blade camber function

f_0 = maximum blade section camber at a given radius

$\vec{F}$ = vector force on blade surface

F_s = suction force per unit length of leading edge, see equation (39)

GF = vortex weighting function, see equation (6)

J = advance coefficient:
= V/nD

J_A = advance coefficient based on speed of advance:
= V_A/nD

J_s = advance coefficient based on ship speed:
= V_s/nD

K = number of propeller blades

$K_{\vec{F}}$ = force coefficient for one blade:
= $\vec{F}/\rho n^2 D^4$

$K_{\vec{M}}$ = moment coefficient for one blade:
= $\vec{M}/\rho n^2 D^5$

K_Q = torque coefficient:
= $Q/\rho n^2 D^5$

K_T = thrust coefficient:
= $T/\rho n^2 D^4$

$\vec{l}$ = unit vector along blade chord

L = lift force

$\vec{m}$ = unit outward vector along blade:
= $\vec{n} \times \vec{l}$

M = number of chordwise panels over radius

$\vec{M}$ = vector moment on blade surface

n = propeller rotational speed, revolutions per unit time

$\vec{n}$ = unit vector normal to blade camber surface

N = number of spanwise vortices within a chordwise strip

$p = x'/x_{tw}$

p = pressure

P_∞ = ambient pressure

P = propeller pitch

$q = x'/x_{rw}$

Q = strength of concentrated line source per unit length

Q = propeller torque

r = radial coordinate

r = leading-edge radius

r_{cut} = inner radius of local tip solution, Fig. 22

r_H = hub radius

r_m = control point radii in tip solution, equation (19)

r_n = leading-edge radius of section in plane normal to leading edge; see Fig. 32

r_t = radius of trailing vortex leaving blade tip

r_w = radius of ultimate tip vortices

r_{wh} = radius of hub vortex at end of transition wake

$\tilde{r}$ = transformed radial coordinate, defined in equation (5)

R = propeller radius

R_{LE} = Reynolds number for leading-edge flow, defined in equation (21)

s = fraction of chord from leading edge

s_c = s coordinate of a control point

s_v = s coordinate of a discrete vortex or source

SF = source weighting function; see Appendix 2

$SCFACT$ = control point position factor; see Appendix 2

$\tilde{s}$ = transformed chordwise coordinate; see equation (2)

t = blade thickness function

t_0 = maximum blade section thickness at a given radius

T = propeller thrust

$\left.\begin{array}{r} u_a \\ u_t \end{array}\right\}$ = axial and tangential velocities induced by helical tip vortices

$\left.\begin{array}{r} u_a(x',r) \\ u_t(x',r) \end{array}\right\}$ = axial and tangential induced velocities due to propeller and wake singularity system

$\left.\begin{array}{r} u_{an}(r) \\ u_{tn}(r) \end{array}\right\}$ = axial and tangential induced velocities at blade trailing edge

$\left.\begin{array}{r} u_{au}(r) \\ u_{tu}(r) \end{array}\right\}$ = axial and tangential induced velocities at $x' = x_{\text{ult}}$

u_{th} = tangential velocity induced by ultimate hub vortex

U_n = component of inflow velocity normal to leading edge; see Fig. 32

U_∞ = freestream velocity

$\vec{V}$ = total velocity vector

V_A = volumetric mean inflow velocity:
= $\dfrac{2}{[1 - (r_H/R)^2]}$.

$\displaystyle\int_{r_H/R}^{1} V_A(r)\, r\, dr$

$V_A(r)$ = axial component of inflow velocity

$V_R(r)$ = radial component of inflow velocity

V_S = ship speed

$V_T(r)$ = tangential component of inflow velocity

x = distance along chord for two-dimensional foils

x' = axial distance downstream of blade trailing edge along a given streamline

x_{ult} = distance downstream of blade trailing edge at which wake pitch stops changing

$x_m(r)$ = rake, x-coordinate of midchord line, positive in direction of positive x

x_{rw} = distance from trailing edge to point where tip vortex radius is constant, defined in equation (28)

x_{tw} = axial extent of transition wake, measured from blade trailing edge

x,y,z = cartesian coordinate system fixed on propeller: x-positive downstream, y positive radially outward, and z being determined to complete the right-handed system

α = angle of attack

β = undisturbed flow angle

β_T = pitch angle of transition wake leaving blade tip

β_w = pitch angle of ultimate wake tip vortex helix

$\bar{\beta}$ = pitch angle of tip vortex separated from leading edge in global solution; see equation (10)

$\beta(x',r)$ = pitch angle in transition wake

γ = strength of vortex sheet

γ_b = strength of bound vortex sheet

Γ = strength of discrete vortex segment or horseshoe vortex

Γ_b = circulation around blade section (bound circulation)

Γ_t = strength of ultimate tip vortex

δ = incremental mean surface slope, defined in equation (9)

δ_c = contraction angle of tip vortex; see Fig. 4

Δ = maximum displacement of separated tip vortex global solution; see Fig. 12

η = open-water propeller efficiency:
= $(J_A \cdot K_T)/(2\pi K_Q)$

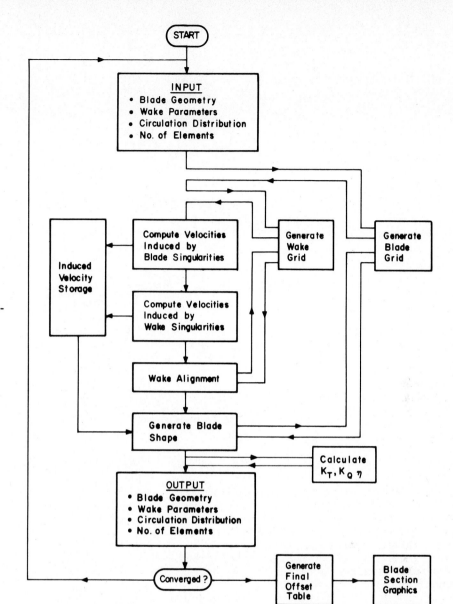

Fig. 1 Flow diagram for determination of blade shape

The flow diagram contains the following blocks:

START

INPUT
- Blade Geometry
- Wake Parameters
- Circulation Distribution
- No. of Elements

Compute Velocities Induced by Blade Singularities

Generate Wake Grid

Generate Blade Grid

Induced Velocity Storage

Compute Velocities Induced by Wake Singularities

Wake Alignment

Generate Blade Shape

Calculate K_T, K_Q η

OUTPUT
- Blade Geometry
- Wake Parameters
- Circulation Distribution
- No. of Elements

Converged ?

Generate Final Offset Table

Blade Section Graphics

blade definition includes accurate leading-edge information, but, of course, does not include hub fillets, tip rounding and special treatment of trailing edges.

In the following sections, each of the blocks of Fig. 1 will be described in more detail.

Blade geometry

The notation used in the current work is identical to that given in [1][3] and is illustrated in Fig. 2. The blade is formed starting with a midchord line, which is a space curve defined parametrically by the radial distribution of skew, $\theta_m(r)$, and rake, $x_m(r)$. By advancing a distance $\pm c(r)/2$ along a helix of pitch angle $\phi(r)$ passing through the midchord line, one obtains the blade leading and trailing edge, respectively. The blade mean surface may then be defined in terms of a camber

[3] Numbers in brackets designate References at end of paper.

θ = angular coordinate in propeller fixed coordinates:
$\quad = \tan^{-1}(z/y)$

$\theta_m(r)$ = skew angle: angular coordinate of midchord line as measured from y-axis, positive clockwise when looking toward positive x-axis

Λ = leading-edge sweep angle; from Fig. 32

ν = kinematic viscosity of fluid

$\xi = x'/x_{\text{final}}$

ρ = mass density of fluid

ρ_m = radial coordinate of endpoints of discrete vortices, defined in equations (1) and (18)

σ_n = cavitation number:
$\quad = P_\infty - P_v/\frac{1}{2}\rho n^2 D^2$

ϕ = nose-tail pitch angle of propeller blade section

ω = propeller rotational speed, radians per unit time

$\vec{\omega}$ = vorticity vector

Superscripts

I = inflow velocity

q = source

Subscripts

c = camber surface

l,t = leading and trailing edges

m = midchord

m = spanwise index

n = normal section

n = chordwise index

w = ultimate wake

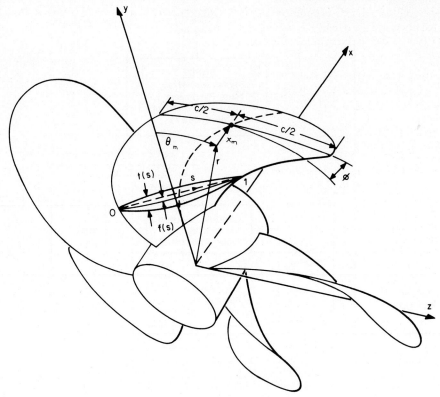

Fig. 2 Blade geometry notation

distribution, $f(r,s)$, where s is a nondimensional curvilinear coordinate along the nose-tail helix which is zero at the leading edge and one at the trailing edge. The camber, f, is measured in the plane of a cylinder of radius r at right angles to the nose-tail helix. Finally, thickness $t(r,s)$ is added symmetrically with respect to the mean line at each radius, again in a cylinder of radius r, and at right angles to f. The maximum values of f and t at a given radius are $f_0(r)$ and $t_0(r)$, and upon nondimensionalization with respect to the chord, $c(r)$ are defined as the section camber and thickness ratios.

The cartesian coordinates of any point on the mean blade surface, or on the actual blade suction and pressure surfaces, are related in a simple geometric manner to these functions, and the necessary formulas may be found in [1].

In the present work these geometrical quantities are all represented by cubic spline functions of suitably stretched coordinates, based on values specified or computed at a set of radial and chordwise stations. The number and spacing of the radial stations are arbitrary, but it is intended that these be taken at the customary even tenths of the radius, with half stations at the ends. A fixed set of 17 chordwise stations is used, following essentially the pattern of the original National Advisory Committee for Aeronautics (NACA) section data [2]. Interpolation, differentiation and integration of any blade geometrical quantity may then be carried out easily from the derived cubic spline functions. Table 1 shows a typical set of geometrical data sufficient to define a blade for the purpose of lifting-surface design or analysis.

Discretization of blade singularity distribution

The continuous distribution of sources and vortices used to represent blade thickness and loading is replaced by a lattice of concentrated straight-line elements. The elements are of constant strength, and the endpoints of each element are located on the blade mean surface.

The element arrangement used in the present work is shown in Fig. 3. The radial interval from the hub r_H to the tip R is divided into M equal intervals, with the extremities of the lattice inset one-quarter interval from the ends of the blade. The endpoints of the discrete vortices are located at radii

$$\rho_m = \frac{(R - r_H)(4m - 3)}{4M + 2} + r_H, \qquad m = 1,2,\ldots, M + 1 \tag{1}$$

Kerwin and Lee [1] discussed several chordwise distributions of singularities and concluded that a uniform chordwise distribution of singularities, with an explicit Kutta condition, was the best compromise for solving both the steady and unsteady problems with the same spacing. But since we are concerned here only with steady flow, this choice was reexamined. For the current work a "cosine" chordwise spacing of singularities is chosen in which the vortices and control points are located at equal intervals of $\tilde{s}$, where the chordwise variable s is given by

$$s = \frac{1}{2}(1 - \cos \tilde{s}), \qquad (0 \le \tilde{s} \le \pi) \tag{2}$$

If there are N vortices over the chord, the positions of the vortices, $s_v(n)$, and control points, $s_c(i)$, are given by

$$s_v(n) = \frac{1}{2}\left\{1 - \cos\left[\frac{(n - 1/2)\pi}{N}\right]\right\}, \qquad n = 1,2,\ldots, N$$

$$s_c(i) = \frac{1}{2}\left\{1 - \cos\left[\frac{i\pi}{N}\right]\right\}, \qquad i = 1,2,\ldots, N \tag{3}$$

Note that with this arrangement the last control point is at the trailing edge, and two-dimensional calculations show that this forces the distribution of vorticity over the chord to have the proper behavior near the trailing edge. This chordwise singularity distribution is also useful in that it enables the magnitude of the leading-edge suction force to be readily calculated. This is not relevant to the design problem where ideal angle of attack is specified, but is essential in the off-design analysis, treated later in this paper.

Determining the trailing vortex wake geometry

The velocity induced on the blade by the trailing vortex wake is a function of both its strength and geometry. In the design case its strength is known at the outset from the prescribed radial distribution of circulation. The geometry, however, follows in an indirect way from the requirement that to be force-free each element of trailing vorticity must be aligned with the local flow. Since this local flow depends on the trailing vortex wake geometry in a nonlinear way, an iterative procedure must be employed.

This problem is further complicated by the fact that the representation of the rotational flow region shed from the blades as a zero thickness vortex sheet is not suitable for the computation of self-induced velocities at its inner and outer extremities. It is known that much of the vorticity tends to concentrate in hub and tip vortices with finite core dimensions. While the velocity induced at a point on the blade is insensitive to the details of the formation of these vortex cores, the self-induced velocity on a particular trailing vortex element is. The self-induced velocities, in turn, affect the global geometry of the entire trailing vortex wake, which then has an influence on the induced velocities on the blade. This means that even though we have no direct interest in the local flow details of the trailing vortex wake, these details cannot be ignored due to their indirect influence on blade-induced velocities.

The fundamental problem of vortex wake deformation is common to wings, hydrofoils and propellers, and has received extensive study over the years. Particular attention has been given to the deformation of vortex sheets shed from wing leading and side edges, as discussed later in this paper. As one can imagine, extremely elaborate computational schemes have been developed requiring large computer times. Nevertheless, all such methods require artificial measures to compensate for the lack of a true viscous flow modeling of the problem.

In the past, this problem has been avoided entirely for propellers by idealizing the wake by helicoidal vortex sheets with a radial distribution of pitch obtained from lifting-line theory. More recently, Kerwin and Lee [1] developed a wake model which contained the essential features of observed wakes including slipstream contraction, concentration of vorticity into rolled-up tip and hub vortex cores and axial variation in pitch. However, the parameters defining the wake geometry had to be specified by the user on the basis of experimental observation. A sensitivity study of these parameters given in [1] indicated that wake pitch was the most critical parameter, principally because this determined the distance between one blade and the wake shed from the blade immediately ahead. While slipstream contraction was also found to affect blade-induced velocities, its sensitivity was less in relationship to the possible variation in this parameter.

This observation led to the basis for the present wake model. It is assumed here that the axial variation in radius of the trailing vortex elements can be established with sufficient accuracy on the basis of the following experimentally observed parameters:

(a) The ultimate radius of the contracted slipstream, r_w.
(b) The ultimate radius of the trailing vortices shed from the blades at the radius of the hub, r_{wh}.
(c) The axial distance, x_{tw}, from the trailing edge to the point where the vorticity can be considered to be concentrated into a single hub vortex and a set of tip vortices. The region from the trailing edge to this position is termed the transition wake.

Table 1 Input blade geometry, inflow velocities, and trailing vortex wake velocities

```
---------------------------- MIT-PBD-10 ----------------------------
  PROPELLER BLADE DESIGN FOR PRESCRIBED LOAD DISTRIBUTION
  RELEASE DATE 03/11/82   COMPUTATION DATE 3/24/82   6*29*46.00
  72 DEG SKEW-ZERO RAKE 16X8 GRID B=.8 CHORD LOAD
```

------------------------- BLADE GEOMETRY -------------------------

R/RO	P/D	XS/D	SKEW	C/D	FO/C	TO/D
0.2000	1.4387	0.0	0.0	0.1740	0.0205	0.0434
0.2500	1.5192	0.0	4.647	0.2020	0.0326	0.0396
0.3000	1.5361	0.0	9.293	0.2290	0.0387	0.0358
0.4000	1.4792	0.0	18.816	0.2750	0.0394	0.0294
0.5000	1.3772	0.0	27.991	0.3120	0.0349	0.0240
0.6000	1.2706	0.0	36.770	0.3370	0.0288	0.0191
0.7000	1.1476	0.0	45.453	0.3470	0.0231	0.0146
0.8000	1.0265	0.0	54.245	0.3340	0.0181	0.0105
0.9000	0.8999	0.0	63.102	0.2800	0.0157	0.0067
0.9500	0.8009	0.0	67.531	0.2100	0.0187	0.0048
1.0000	0.6527	0.0	72.000	0.0020	0.0263	0.0029

----- INFLOW VELOCITIES -----				TRANS WAKE INDUCED VELOCITIES			
R/RO	VX/VS	VR/VS	VT/VS	UANW	UTNW	UAUW	UTUW
0.2000	1.000	0.0	0.0	0.143	-0.093	0.275	-0.644
0.2500	1.000	0.0	0.0	0.186	-0.220	0.311	-0.581
0.3000	1.000	0.0	0.0	0.226	-0.307	0.347	-0.529
0.4000	1.000	0.0	0.0	0.295	-0.386	0.410	-0.446
0.5000	1.000	0.0	0.0	0.341	-0.373	0.446	-0.380
0.6000	1.000	0.0	0.0	0.352	-0.312	0.436	-0.312
0.7000	1.000	0.0	0.0	0.322	-0.241	0.372	-0.234
0.8000	1.000	0.0	0.0	0.256	-0.169	0.284	-0.157
0.9000	1.000	0.0	0.0	0.161	-0.103	0.215	-0.103
0.9500	1.000	0.0	0.0	0.106	-0.074	0.200	-0.091
1.0000	1.000	0.0	0.0	0.046	-0.047	0.204	-0.092

-------- MEAN LINE OFFSETS (F/C)*10**4 AT INPUT RADII --------

%C	0.20	0.25	0.30	0.40	0.50	0.60	0.70	0.80	0.90	0.95	1.00
1.0	9	17	21	21	19	15	12	10	9	12	18
2.5	22	41	50	52	46	37	30	23	22	28	43
5.0	43	77	94	97	86	70	56	44	40	52	80
10.0	80	139	169	174	154	125	100	79	71	91	136
20.0	138	230	277	282	248	202	162	127	113	140	203
30.0	178	288	345	350	308	252	201	158	139	168	240
40.0	200	320	380	387	341	280	224	176	154	184	260
50.0	205	326	387	394	349	288	231	181	157	187	263
60.0	195	309	369	378	336	278	224	174	150	177	249
70.0	169	272	326	337	301	250	201	156	133	155	214
80.0	123	206	249	260	231	192	154	119	101	118	161
90.0	60	109	134	140	123	102	81	63	55	65	91
95.0	28	54	67	70	61	50	40	31	28	34	48
97.5	13	26	33	34	30	25	20	15	14	17	25
99.0	5	10	13	14	12	10	8	6	5	7	10

(d) The contraction angle of the tip vortex as it leaves the blade tip, δ_c.

Figure 4 illustrates the axial variation of radius of a set of trailing vortex elements derived on the basis of these parameters by the relatively simple set of interpolation functions given in Appendix 1.

We now have, in effect, a set of axisymmetric surfaces which

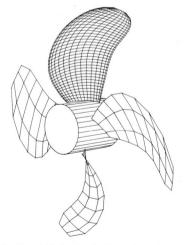

Fig. 3 Discretization of blade singularities. Note that the other blades are represented by coarser grids

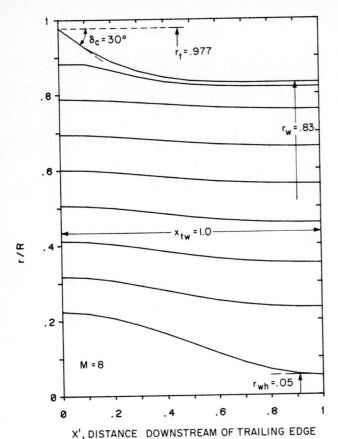

Fig. 4 Radii of trailing vortex lines in transition wake region

three-dimensional to a two-dimensional one. In addition, rather than computing the velocity directly at a large number of points along each vortex, it is assumed that induced velocities grow smoothly from the trailing edge to the beginning of the ultimate wake. An interpolation scheme described in Appendix 1 permits rapid computation of the wake convection velocities on the basis of actual velocities computed at a relatively small number of points. Finally, viscous effects on self-induced velocities are idealized by assigning a finite core radius to the hub and tip elements, determined on the basis of correlation with laser measurements of wake geometry by Min [3].

The result is a wake alignment scheme which is extremely fast, yet capable of providing the radial and axial distribution of pitch necessary for accurate determination of blade-induced velocities.

Figure 5 shows typical geometries of the trailing vortex wake, before and after alignment by the current procedure. For the initial geometry, the wake convection velocities contain no induced components so that the vorticity simply flows down the prescribed stream surfaces with the undisturbed inflow. After alignment the pitch is seen to increase as a result of the velocity induced by the blade singularities and by the wake itself.

Figure 6 shows the radial distribution of induced velocities at two axial positions obtained upon convergence of the wake alignment procedure. The first position is right at the blade trailing edge, while the second is in the ultimate wake, 1.5 radii downstream of the trailing edge. For comparison, the corresponding velocities from lifting-line theory are shown on the same graph. The latter, by assumption, are independent of axial position.

Induced velocity computation

The principal advantage of vortex/source lattice methods is the ease with which induced velocities may be calculated, regardless of the geometrical complexity of the blades and of their trailing vortex wakes. In the design case, one simply has to assign a strength to each discrete line element based on the given continuous distribution of circulation and thickness, multiply it by the velocity induced at the control point in question by a unit line element, and sum these products over all of the elements.

contain the discrete trailing vortex lines shed from the blade grid. The vorticity will now be "convected" along these surfaces by the total fluid velocity calculated on the vortex elements, thus establishing the axial variation in pitch of the trailing vortex wake.

An iterative procedure is required at this stage since the convection velocities depend on the geometry of the vortex lines. However, by prescribing the radius function for each vortex line, the problem is in some respects reduced from a

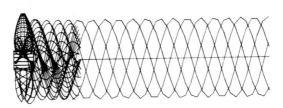

(a) WAKE FOLLOWING UNDISTURBED INFLOW

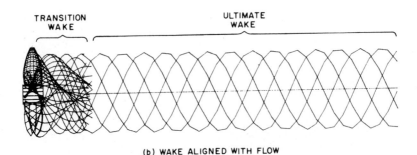

(b) WAKE ALIGNED WITH FLOW

Fig. 5 Trailing wake geometry before and after wake alignment

420   Numerical Methods for Propeller Design

The assignment of individual vortex strengths is accomplished by first solving for the total circulation at the midradius of the mth panel from the given series of coefficients, a_l, of the radial circulation distribution obtained from lifting-line theory:

$$\Gamma_b(r_m) = 2\pi R V_s \sum_{l=1}^{L} a_l \sin(\tilde{r}_m) \qquad (4)$$

where L is the number of series coefficients retained and $\tilde{r}_m$ is the transformed radial coordinate

$$\tilde{r} = \cos^{-1}\left(\frac{1 + r_H - 2r}{1 - r_H}\right) \quad (0 \le \tilde{r} \le \pi) \qquad (5)$$

The total bound circulation around this panel is then divided among the individual elements over the chord by a weighting function which depends on the type of chordwise circulation distribution and on the number of elements over the chord, N. For any chordwise circulation distribution, $\gamma(s)$, the weight assigned to the nth element is

$$GF(s_n) = \frac{\gamma(s_n)\sqrt{s_n(1 - s_n)}}{\sum\limits_{i=1}^{N}\gamma(s_i)\sqrt{s_i(1 - s_i)}} \qquad (6)$$

Equation (6) yields exact results in two-dimensional flow for flat plate and parabolic camber loading, and is extremely accurate for arbitrary distributions, as shown in [4].

We will consider here two types of chordwise circulation distributions, the NACA $a = 0.8$ distribution [2], which has become almost universally accepted for propellers, and an analytical approximation to the NACA $a = 0.8$ distribution developed by Brockett [5]. We will refer to the latter as a "$b = 0.8$" chord load. From a practical point of view both are essentially the same, but the $b = 0.8$ distribution avoids the difficulties brought about by the logarithmic singularity in section slope at the leading edge and the discontinuity in circulation slope at $s = 0.8$. Tabulated values of the weighting functions obtained from (6) for $N = 8$, 12, 16 and 20 are given in Appendix 2.

With the spanwise vortex strengths assigned, the strengths of all of the chordwise and trailing vortex elements follow from considerations of continuity of vorticity.

Blade thickness can be represented in accordance with thin-wing theory by a source distribution with density proportional to the product of chordwise derivative of the thickness form and the relative inflow velocity. The integral of the source density over a finite chordwise interval is then proportional to the difference in thickness at the ends of the interval. If each spanwise line element is considered to contain the total source strength contained in the chordwise interval between adjacent control point locations, a set of source weighting functions may then be obtained for any given thickness form and number of chordwise elements. Values of the thickness weighting function for the David W. Taylor Naval Ship Research and Development Center (DTNSRDC) modified NACA 66 thickness form [6] are given in Appendix 2.

The strength of each source element is then obtained by multiplying the appropriate weight, which is for unit thickness ratio, by the actual thickness ratio and by the relative inflow velocity

$$\sqrt{V_A(r)^2 + (\omega r)^2}$$

Since the thickness form is defined in terms of cylindrical blade sections, the source strengths obtained from thickness differences represent volumetric flow per unit radius. Since the discrete spanwise elements may be inclined with respect to the radial direction, their strength must be adjusted in inverse proportion to their length in order to preserve the same total

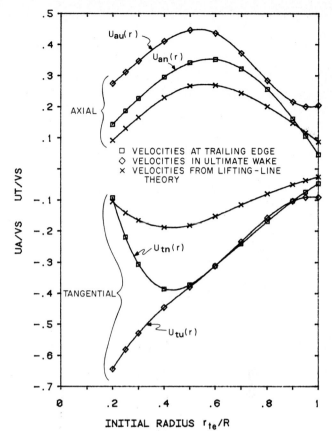

Fig. 6 Wake convection velocities versus radius

flux. This correction should not be applied to the vortex strengths, however, since the circulation around the blade at a fixed radius is independent of the angle of inclination of the concentrated line vortex elements.

Since control points must be located precisely as given by (3), Appendix 2 lists the chordwise position of each control point relative to the position of the nearest two vortices. Rather than being in the middle of each interval, they tend to be biased toward the leading and trailing edges.

The velocity induced at an arbitrary point by a line vortex or source element of unit strength may be computed from the formulas given in [1]. Since this elementary computation must be performed an enormous number of times during the course of a lifting-surface computation, it is advantageous to employ far-field approximations for distant elements, where the line elements are reduced to point singularities. It is also observed that numerical round-off errors can be incurred if the velocity is to be computed very close to a line element or its extension. This therefore requires special treatment for the case of nearby elements. Thus, the induced velocity calculation, while elementary in terms of fluid mechanics, requires careful numerical analysis for efficient and accurate execution.

Figure 7 shows a typical chordwise distribution of axial and tangential induced velocity obtained with two different numbers of chordwise elements. The appearance of the two sets of points on a common curve gives an indication of the convergence of the numerical procedure.

Table 2 shows part of a complete tabulation of induced velocities. The individual contributions of the spanwise and chordwise vortices on the blades, the trailing vortices in the wake and the blade sources are tabulated as well as the total induced velocity at each control point.

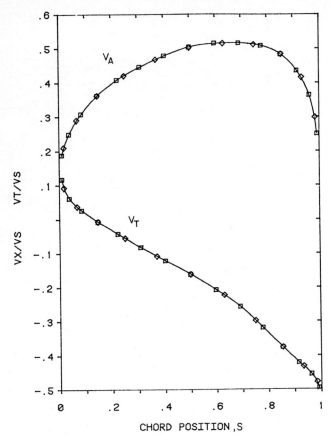

Fig. 7 Distribution of axial and tangential induced velocities over chord at $r/R = 0.426$

successful for a wide variety of geometries.

To describe the process specifically, we first look at an arbitrary control point on the blade trial surface. The cartesian components of the total fluid velocity, $\vec{v}$, are

$$V_x = v_x + V_A$$

$$V_y = v_y + \left(V_T - \frac{\pi r}{J}\right)\sin\theta + V_R\cos\theta \qquad (7)$$

$$V_z = v_z + \left(\frac{\pi r}{J} - V_T\right)\cos\theta + V_R\sin\theta$$

where (v_x, v_y, v_z) are the cartesian components of the induced velocity and (V_A, V_R, V_T) are the cylindrical coordinates of the circumferential mean inflow.

A local coordinate system on the blade surface can be defined in terms of a normal, chordwise and outward unit vector. The surface normal vector, $\vec{n}$, is constructed from the cross product of the diagonal vectors of the lattice element surrounding the control point, as shown in Fig. 8. A positive normal vector is taken to point toward the suction, or upstream side of the blade. A chordwise vector, $\vec{l}$, is formed by the intersection of a cylinder with the blade surface, and is approximated by the vector joining the midpoints of the spanwise lattice elements shown in Fig. 8. The positive direction is taken to be toward the trailing edge. Finally the outward vector, $\vec{m}$, completes the right-handed system, and is obtained from the cross product of $\vec{n}$ and $\vec{l}$.

The components of $\vec{V}$ in the local coordinate system are

$$V_n = \vec{V} \cdot \vec{n}$$

$$V_l = \vec{V} \cdot \vec{l} \qquad (8)$$

$$V_m = \vec{V} \cdot \vec{m}$$

To satisfy the boundary condition, the blade surface at this point will be rotated about the m-axis by an amount necessary to null V_n. The projection of this angle onto a cylinder yields the incremental mean surface slope δ, which can be seen from Fig. 9 to be

$$\delta = \frac{V_n\sqrt{l_z^2 + l_y^2}}{V_l(l_z m_y - l_y m_z)} \qquad (9)$$

where m_y and m_z are the components of the unit $\vec{m}$ vector in the directions indicated by the subscripts.

If the incremental slope δ is elevated at all control points at a particular radius, the corrected mean line can be obtained by integrating δ from the leading edge to the point in question, and adding it to the existing camber. This is accomplished by fitting δ over the chord by a spline cubic, which may then be integrated analytically from the leading edge to each of the 17 standard chordwise stations. The value of this integral at the trailing edge, divided by the expanded chord length, is the correction to pitch angle. The final correction to camber is then obtained by removing this "wedge" from the original function, as illustrated in Fig. 10.

This process is repeated at all radial stations containing control points. Once this is accomplished, the radial distribution of pitch, and the radial distributions of camber at the 17 standard chordwise positions, is each fitted by spline cubics, and evaluated at the originally specified input radii. Thus a new trial blade surface is formed, and is defined in a manner identical to that of the original input.

A new discretized blade grid may now be computed, which will in general have an altered set of blade vectors, $\vec{n}$, $\vec{l}$ and $\vec{m}$, and therefore an altered set of blade velocity components as given by (8). If there were no interaction between chordwise panels at different radii, V_n would now be zero as a consequence of (9). However, this will not be true in general, so that

Obtaining the shape of the blade surface

The blade mean surface must be oriented in such a way that the normal component of the total fluid velocity is zero at each point. Since we have started with an arbitrary trial surface, the computed values of the component of velocity normal to this surface will generally not be zero. The objective is therefore to move the trial surface in such a way as to satisfy this boundary condition at each control point.

If we look at a single control point, it is clear that the normal component of velocity can be nulled by rotating the surface a suitable amount around any arbitrary axis. Thus if the axis of rotation is unspecified, the solution at one particular point is not unique. However, since the displacements of all points on the surface are related, a unique solution may exist provided certain constraints are imposed.

This is not a simple matter, however, and it has been found that numerical algorithms for "growing" a blade surface frequently tend to become unstable, tying the blade surface into a complicated knot before finally crashing.

This tendency toward instability is minimized if the surface is rotated at each point about an axis which minimizes the needed angular displacement. This axis is at right angles to the resultant velocity vector, and is approximately radial in the case of a propeller.

The general scheme is therefore to perturb the mean surface along cylindrical sections, which would be all that would be necessary in linear theory. However, since the relative displacements between cylindrical sections at adjacent radii affect the surface normal vector, the process must be iterated until a specified accuracy is reached. While convergence is not guaranteed, experience to date indicates that the procedure is

Numerical Methods for Propeller Design

Table 2

```
------------------------- MIT-PBD-10 -------------------------
        PROPELLER BLADE DESIGN FOR PRESCRIBED LOAD DISTRIBUTION
        RELEASE DATE 03/11/82   COMPUTATION DATE 3/24/82  6*29*46.00
           72 DEG SKEW-ZERO RAKE 16X8 GRID B=.8 CHORD LOAD

   COMPUTATION DATE OF INDUCED VELOCITY FILE   3/24/82  6*29*46.00
   FILE IDENTIFICATION:   72 DEG SKEW-ZERO RAKE 16X8 GRID B=.8 CHORD LOAD
```

---CONTROL POINT--			-----SPANWISE----			-----CHORDWISE----			----VORTEX WAKE---			----THICKNESS----			------TOTAL------		
X	R	THETA	VX	VR	VT	VX	VR	VT	VX	VR	VT	VX	VR	VT	VX	VR	VT
-0.177	0.635	14.1	-0.169	-0.083	0.117	0.029	-0.009	-0.032	0.122	-0.071	-0.047	0.048	-0.016	0.054	0.029	-0.178	0.092
-0.169	0.635	15.7	-0.088	-0.069	0.083	0.030	-0.008	-0.033	0.124	-0.072	-0.048	0.047	-0.008	0.048	0.113	-0.157	0.050
-0.155	0.634	18.3	-0.034	-0.059	0.059	0.032	-0.005	-0.035	0.127	-0.075	-0.049	0.055	-0.015	0.049	0.180	-0.154	0.024
-0.136	0.634	21.7	0.004	-0.049	0.039	0.036	-0.002	-0.038	0.133	-0.078	-0.052	0.064	-0.026	0.053	0.237	-0.154	0.001
-0.111	0.634	25.8	0.032	-0.039	0.022	0.042	0.003	-0.043	0.139	-0.082	-0.055	0.073	-0.034	0.055	0.286	-0.152	-0.021
-0.082	0.634	30.5	0.052	-0.030	0.007	0.049	0.009	-0.049	0.147	-0.085	-0.059	0.081	-0.040	0.056	0.329	-0.146	-0.044
-0.050	0.634	35.5	0.066	-0.021	-0.005	0.059	0.016	-0.055	0.155	-0.087	-0.064	0.088	-0.046	0.058	0.368	-0.138	-0.067
-0.015	0.634	40.7	0.076	-0.010	-0.016	0.068	0.023	-0.062	0.165	-0.089	-0.070	0.093	-0.050	0.057	0.403	-0.126	-0.091
0.020	0.634	45.8	0.084	0.002	-0.027	0.077	0.031	-0.067	0.175	-0.089	-0.077	0.092	-0.050	0.051	0.429	-0.106	-0.122
0.055	0.634	50.6	0.094	0.018	-0.041	0.085	0.038	-0.072	0.187	-0.089	-0.086	0.084	-0.046	0.040	0.450	-0.079	-0.158
0.089	0.634	55.0	0.112	0.043	-0.062	0.089	0.044	-0.074	0.199	-0.087	-0.095	0.069	-0.039	0.025	0.469	-0.040	-0.206
0.119	0.634	58.8	0.124	0.066	-0.081	0.090	0.047	-0.075	0.212	-0.085	-0.104	0.045	-0.030	0.006	0.472	-0.002	-0.253
0.145	0.635	61.9	0.125	0.079	-0.090	0.088	0.049	-0.074	0.224	-0.082	-0.112	0.014	-0.018	-0.018	0.452	0.028	-0.294
0.164	0.635	64.2	0.118	0.082	-0.090	0.085	0.049	-0.073	0.234	-0.079	-0.118	-0.029	-0.001	-0.051	0.408	0.051	-0.333
0.176	0.635	65.6	0.106	0.076	-0.084	0.087	0.053	-0.076	0.236	-0.081	-0.119	-0.094	0.026	-0.103	0.335	0.074	-0.382
-0.157	0.704	21.3	-0.205	-0.078	0.107	0.019	-0.008	-0.024	0.118	-0.087	-0.045	0.038	-0.019	0.047	-0.030	-0.192	0.085
-0.150	0.704	22.8	-0.119	-0.066	0.077	0.018	-0.008	-0.024	0.119	-0.089	-0.045	0.038	-0.010	0.044	0.057	-0.173	0.052
-0.138	0.704	25.2	-0.062	-0.058	0.056	0.019	-0.006	-0.025	0.122	-0.091	-0.046	0.044	-0.018	0.045	0.123	-0.172	0.030
-0.120	0.704	28.5	-0.021	-0.049	0.039	0.022	-0.004	-0.027	0.126	-0.093	-0.048	0.052	-0.028	0.048	0.179	-0.174	0.013
-0.099	0.704	32.4	0.010	-0.039	0.024	0.027	-0.001	-0.029	0.130	-0.096	-0.050	0.060	-0.036	0.051	0.228	-0.172	-0.005
-0.073	0.704	36.8	0.033	-0.030	0.011	0.035	0.003	-0.033	0.136	-0.098	-0.052	0.067	-0.042	0.052	0.271	-0.167	-0.022
-0.045	0.704	41.5	0.049	-0.021	-0.000	0.045	0.008	-0.038	0.142	-0.099	-0.056	0.074	-0.048	0.053	0.310	-0.160	-0.040
-0.014	0.704	46.4	0.061	-0.010	-0.010	0.055	0.014	-0.042	0.149	-0.100	-0.060	0.079	-0.051	0.052	0.345	-0.147	-0.060
0.017	0.704	51.3	0.070	0.001	-0.020	0.067	0.021	-0.046	0.157	-0.100	-0.065	0.079	-0.050	0.047	0.373	-0.128	-0.086
0.049	0.704	56.0	0.081	0.016	-0.032	0.077	0.028	-0.050	0.166	-0.100	-0.071	0.073	-0.045	0.037	0.397	-0.101	-0.117
0.078	0.704	60.2	0.099	0.038	-0.050	0.084	0.035	-0.054	0.176	-0.099	-0.077	0.061	-0.037	0.023	0.420	-0.063	-0.158
0.105	0.704	63.9	0.110	0.059	-0.066	0.089	0.041	-0.057	0.186	-0.098	-0.083	0.042	-0.027	0.004	0.428	-0.026	-0.200
0.128	0.704	66.9	0.112	0.071	-0.073	0.091	0.045	-0.059	0.195	-0.098	-0.087	0.017	-0.015	-0.019	0.414	0.003	-0.239
0.145	0.704	69.1	0.105	0.073	-0.074	0.092	0.050	-0.062	0.200	-0.099	-0.089	-0.019	0.001	-0.052	0.379	0.025	-0.276
0.156	0.704	70.5	0.093	0.068	-0.068	0.103	0.061	-0.071	0.193	-0.107	-0.083	-0.072	0.026	-0.103	0.317	0.048	-0.326
-0.134	0.774	29.3	-0.235	-0.076	0.097	0.006	-0.007	-0.017	0.108	-0.101	-0.039	0.031	-0.022	0.042	-0.091	-0.206	0.084
-0.127	0.774	30.7	-0.146	-0.065	0.070	0.002	-0.007	-0.015	0.109	-0.102	-0.039	0.031	-0.015	0.041	-0.004	-0.189	0.057
-0.117	0.774	32.9	-0.088	-0.057	0.053	0.001	-0.008	-0.015	0.110	-0.103	-0.040	0.036	-0.020	0.042	0.060	-0.188	0.041
-0.103	0.773	35.9	-0.045	-0.049	0.038	0.004	-0.007	-0.016	0.112	-0.103	-0.041	0.043	-0.029	0.045	0.114	-0.189	0.027
-0.084	0.773	39.4	-0.012	-0.040	0.025	0.008	-0.006	-0.017	0.115	-0.104	-0.042	0.050	-0.037	0.047	0.161	-0.188	0.013
-0.062	0.773	43.5	0.013	-0.030	0.014	0.015	-0.005	-0.019	0.119	-0.105	-0.044	0.056	-0.043	0.048	0.203	-0.183	-0.001
-0.038	0.773	47.8	0.032	-0.021	0.004	0.024	-0.002	-0.021	0.123	-0.105	-0.046	0.062	-0.048	0.049	0.241	-0.176	-0.015
-0.012	0.773	52.3	0.045	-0.011	-0.005	0.036	0.003	-0.024	0.128	-0.105	-0.049	0.067	-0.051	0.048	0.276	-0.165	-0.031
0.015	0.773	56.8	0.054	-0.000	-0.014	0.049	0.009	-0.028	0.134	-0.105	-0.053	0.067	-0.049	0.043	0.305	-0.146	-0.051
0.041	0.773	61.1	0.065	0.013	-0.024	0.062	0.016	-0.031	0.140	-0.105	-0.056	0.063	-0.044	0.034	0.330	-0.120	-0.078
0.067	0.773	65.1	0.082	0.032	-0.038	0.073	0.024	-0.035	0.147	-0.105	-0.060	0.054	-0.035	0.020	0.356	-0.085	-0.113
0.090	0.774	68.5	0.093	0.049	-0.050	0.081	0.031	-0.040	0.155	-0.104	-0.062	0.039	-0.025	0.003	0.367	-0.050	-0.150
0.109	0.774	71.3	0.095	0.059	-0.056	0.086	0.038	-0.044	0.160	-0.105	-0.064	0.018	-0.014	-0.021	0.359	-0.022	-0.185
0.124	0.774	73.3	0.088	0.061	-0.057	0.092	0.045	-0.050	0.161	-0.108	-0.062	-0.011	0.001	-0.053	0.331	-0.001	-0.222
0.133	0.774	74.6	0.077	0.056	-0.053	0.111	0.062	-0.063	0.147	-0.121	-0.053	-0.054	0.024	-0.103	0.281	0.021	-0.272

a small residual normal velocity will be present, thus requiring another incremental correction δ.

This process is automatically repeated until the maximum correction to the blade surface is less than a specified tolerance, or until a maximum specified number of iterations has been completed. The tolerance is presently set internally as $0.0001R$ and is generally reached in well under 10 iterations. This, of course, depends on how far off the initial trial surface was, and on how complex the final blade shape turns out to be. The maximum error after each iteration is displayed at the terminal so that the operator can be warned if the procedure is not working for some reason. Finally, the success of the blade alignment procedure can be verified from a final tabulation of the blade components of velocity, as shown for example in Table 3. Here we see that a blade surface has been generated which results in zero, or nearly zero, normal velocity at all control points.

During this whole procedure the velocity field, computed from the discrete singularities placed on the trial blade surface and its wake, has not been changed. This omission is intentional since the computation of induced velocities is time-consuming, while the geometrical computations as described in this section are accomplished very quickly. However, for maximum accuracy it is advisable to repeat the entire computation, including induced velocities, with the aligned blade output serving as the input trial surface. If this is repeated until no further change

in geometry results, one will then have the "exact" solution for the geometry of a set of vortex/source surfaces of specified strength. The term "exact" requires qualification in that the singularity sheets are approximated by a vortex/source lattice whose accuracy depends on the number of elements used.

An efficient way to obtain an accurate result is to start with a relatively coarse lattice, which may then be iterated several times to obtain a very nearly correct trial blade surface. This may then be used as input to an additional calculation using a fine grid to obtain the final result.

The convergence of the blade and wake alignment procedure is illustrated in Table 4 which shows the radial distributions of pitch and camber as obtained by successive iterations starting with a trial surface having a pitch distribution corresponding to $\beta_i(r)$ from lifting-line theory, and zero camber.

Table 5 is an example of the type of amusement which one can indulge in after months of program debugging have been successfully concluded. In this example, the initial trial blade surface is set at zero pitch, and the trailing vortex wake is initially set off at the undisturbed flow angle, β. After five iterations the results are essentially identical to those obtained in four iterations starting at β_i.

Table 6 shows the effect of number of chordwise and spanwise panels on the final values of pitch and camber, together with plots of the associated blade grids. The differences in computed pitch and camber are in general quite small. The

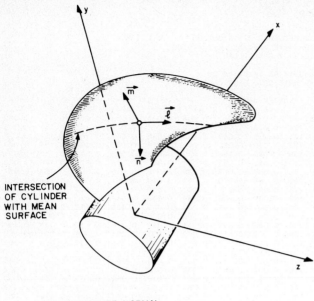

INTERSECTION
OF CYLINDER
WITH MEAN
SURFACE

CONSTRUCTION OF NORMAL

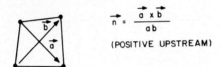

$$\vec{n} = \frac{\vec{a} \times \vec{b}}{a\,b}$$

(POSITIVE UPSTREAM)

Fig. 8 Local blade coordinate system

one exception is the result at $r/R = 0.95$ for eight spanwise panels. As is evident from the blade plot, the tip geometry of this highly skewed blade is not accurately represented by this coarse grid.

Table 7 shows the effect of chord load type and the effect of wake deformation. The $b = 0.8$ chord load requires slightly less pitch and more camber than the $a = 0.8$ load, which is confirmed by their two-dimensional characteristics. The effect of wake deformation is to produce a slightly lower pitch than for the corresponding β_i wake.

Table 8 compares the results of the present program with those obtained with its predecessor [7], and with the recent theory of Brockett [5]. Since the latter two do not have pro-

vision for wake deformation, the present results are shown for a β_i blade and wake surface.

Figure 11 is a plot of the final mean line shapes for this propeller evaluated at standard input radii, together with the shape of corresponding NACA $a = 0.8$ mean lines with the same maximum camber. It is interesting to note that the computed three-dimensional mean lines are remarkably close to their two-dimensional counterparts, even for this complex highly skewed blade.

Propeller thrust and torque

The total propeller thrust and torque as obtained by integration of local forces over the blades should be close to, but not exactly the same as, the forces obtained from lifting-line theory for the same radial distribution of circulation. These differences, while small, may nevertheless be important if the propeller is to perform as expected.

The precise calculation of forces on complex lifting surfaces is difficult, and many unresolved problems exist. Fortunately in the design case the problem is somewhat simplified since at ideal angle of attack the leading-edge suction force vanishes.

The approach used here is to derive the total fluid velocity at the midpoint of each spanwise and chordwise vortex element by interpolation based on the velocities computed at the control points. These velocities will, therefore, within the accuracy of the interpolation process, be tangent to the blade mean surface. Application of Kutta-Jowkowski's law will then yield a concentrated force on each vortex element directed normal to the blade surface. These forces, and their corresponding moment-about the axis of rotation, may then be summed to obtain the total inviscid thrust and torque. Tangential forces associated with viscous drag may be conveniently added to the existing force on each spanwise vortex, with a magnitude proportional to an assumed drag coefficient, the elementary blade area and the square of the total velocity.

The problem is complicated by the introduction of blade thickness. Stated simply, the representation of thickness in a linearized way results in perturbation velocities which increase the total flow velocity over most of the chord. This increases the local forces on the vortices according to Kutta-Jowkowski's law. This produces the paradoxical result that the total lift on a section for a fixed total amount of circulation would appear

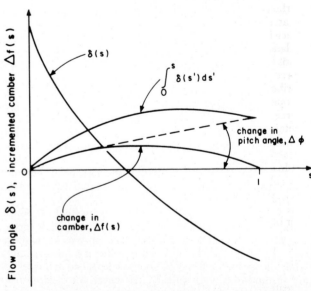

Fig. 10 Correction to mean line shape and pitch angle derived from chordwise distribution of slope function, δ

Fig. 9 Local correction to mean line slope, δ

Numerical Methods for Propeller Design

Table 3

```
------------------------------ MIT-PBD-10 ------------------------------
     PROPELLER BLADE DESIGN FOR PRESCRIBED LOAD DISTRIBUTION
   RELEASE DATE 03/11/82    COMPUTATION DATE 3/24/82   6*29*46.00
   72 DEG SKEW-ZERO RAKE  16X8 GRID B=.8 CHORD LOAD

   ----- INDUCED VELOCITIES RESOLVED INTO BLADE COMPONENTS -----

     X        R      THETA     %C     VO/VS    VN/VO    VC/VO    VM/VO
   --------------------------------------------------------------------
   -0.177   0.635    14.1    0.96     2.456   -0.000    1.039   -0.071
   -0.169   0.635    15.7    3.81     2.455   -0.000    1.038   -0.063
   -0.155   0.634    18.3    8.43     2.455   -0.000    1.040   -0.063
   -0.136   0.634    21.7   14.64     2.455   -0.000    1.044   -0.064
   -0.111   0.634    25.8   22.22     2.454    0.000    1.045   -0.064
   -0.082   0.634    30.5   30.87     2.454    0.000    1.046   -0.063
   -0.050   0.634    35.5   40.25     2.454    0.000    1.047   -0.061
   -0.015   0.634    40.7   50.00     2.454   -0.000    1.046   -0.057
    0.020   0.634    45.8   59.75     2.454    0.000    1.041   -0.049
    0.055   0.634    50.6   69.13     2.454    0.000    1.034   -0.038
    0.089   0.634    55.0   77.78     2.454    0.000    1.023   -0.021
    0.119   0.634    58.8   85.36     2.455    0.000    1.008   -0.003
    0.145   0.635    61.9   91.57     2.455    0.000    0.989    0.012
    0.164   0.635    64.2   96.19     2.456    0.000    0.966    0.023
    0.176   0.635    65.6   99.04     2.456    0.000    0.933    0.034
   --------------------------------------------------------------------
   -0.157   0.704    21.3    0.96     2.682    0.000    1.026   -0.070
   -0.150   0.704    22.8    3.81     2.682    0.000    1.026   -0.063
   -0.138   0.704    25.2    8.43     2.681    0.000    1.028   -0.064
   -0.120   0.704    28.5   14.64     2.681    0.000    1.031   -0.066
   -0.099   0.704    32.4   22.22     2.680    0.000    1.033   -0.066
   -0.073   0.704    36.8   30.87     2.680   -0.000    1.034   -0.066
   -0.045   0.704    41.5   40.25     2.680    0.000    1.035   -0.064
   -0.014   0.704    46.4   50.00     2.680    0.000    1.035   -0.061
    0.017   0.704    51.3   59.75     2.680    0.000    1.032   -0.054
    0.049   0.704    56.0   69.13     2.680   -0.000    1.026   -0.044
    0.078   0.704    60.2   77.78     2.681    0.000    1.017   -0.029
    0.105   0.704    63.9   85.36     2.681    0.000    1.006   -0.014
    0.128   0.704    66.9   91.57     2.682   -0.000    0.991   -0.001
    0.145   0.704    69.1   96.19     2.682   -0.000    0.972    0.008
    0.156   0.704    70.5   99.04     2.682   -0.000    0.944    0.018
   --------------------------------------------------------------------
   -0.134   0.774    29.3    0.96     2.911    0.000    1.017   -0.069
   -0.127   0.774    30.7    3.81     2.911    0.000    1.018   -0.064
   -0.117   0.774    32.9    8.43     2.911    0.000    1.020   -0.064
   -0.103   0.773    35.9   14.64     2.910    0.000    1.023   -0.066
   -0.084   0.773    39.4   22.22     2.910    0.000    1.025   -0.067
   -0.062   0.773    43.5   30.87     2.910    0.000    1.026   -0.066
   -0.038   0.773    47.8   40.25     2.910    0.000    1.027   -0.065
   -0.012   0.773    52.3   50.00     2.910   -0.000    1.027   -0.062
    0.015   0.773    56.8   59.75     2.910    0.000    1.024   -0.057
    0.041   0.773    61.1   69.13     2.910    0.000    1.020   -0.048
    0.067   0.773    65.1   77.78     2.910    0.000    1.014   -0.035
    0.090   0.774    68.5   85.36     2.911   -0.000    1.004   -0.022
    0.109   0.774    71.3   91.57     2.911   -0.000    0.992   -0.012
    0.124   0.774    73.3   96.19     2.912   -0.000    0.976   -0.003
    0.133   0.774    74.6   99.04     2.912   -0.000    0.953    0.006
   --------------------------------------------------------------------
```

Table 4(a) Convergence of blade and wake alignment starting with blade and wake at β_i from lifting-line theory, and zero camber. Values of P/D at three representative radii

	r/R		
Iteration	0.25	0.6	0.95
1	1.195	1.216	1.005
2	1.549	1.295	0.832
3	1.530	1.271	0.801
4	1.520	1.271	0.801

Table 4(b) Convergence of camber ratio f_0/c for conditions stated in Table 4(a)

	r/R		
Iteration	0.25	0.6	0.95
1	0	0	0
2	0.0267	0.0279	0.0158
3	0.0324	0.0289	0.0184
4	0.0326	0.0288	0.0187

Table 5(a) Convergence of blade and wake alignment starting with zero pitch and camber. Initial wake at undisturbed inflow angle β. Values of P/D compared with converged value from Table 4 starting with a β_i blade and wake surface

	r/R		
Iteration	0.025	0.6	0.95
1	0	0	0
2	1.108	1.234	0.746
3	1.540	1.284	0.793
4	1.539	1.272	0.798
5	1.520	1.271	0.799
β_i [Table 4(a)]	1.520	1.271	0.801

Table 5(b) Convergence of camber ratio f_0/c for conditions stated in Table 5(a)

	r/R		
Iteration	0.25	0.6	0.95
1	0	0	0
2	0.0151	0.0029	0.0214
3	0.0225	0.0276	0.0189
4	0.0309	0.0288	0.0187
5	0.0327	0.0288	0.0187
β_i [Table 4(b)]	0.0326	0.0288	0.0187

to increase with increasing thickness.

This was overcome in the predecessor to the present lifting-surface design program [7] by subtracting out the velocity field of an equivalent two-dimensional section at each radius. Later, Kerwin and Lee [1] showed that this apparent lift increase is balanced by the Lagally force on the sources, and this forms the basis for the force algorithm used in the PUF-2 unsteady/steady force program as well as for the steady analysis program described in the present paper. It turns out, however, that the proper balance between the Kutta-Jowkowski and Lagally forces is not achieved if the velocities on the singularities are obtained by interpolation rather than by direct calculation. This can be explained in terms of a "nose drag," as demonstrated by R. T. Jones [8].

In the present procedure the thickness paradox is eliminated by subtracting the thickness-induced velocity from the total velocity before performing the force calculation. Thus the thickness-induced velocities enter into the boundary condition for blade shape, but do not influence the force calculation.

Typical force calculation results are shown in Table 9 for two different blade grids, together with the values given by lifting-line theory. The results obtained with the two widely different grids are essentially identical, and clearly indicate greater forces than those predicted by lifting-line theory. The slight increase in efficiency over the lifting-line result may or may not be correct, and is the subject of current study.

Propeller analysis

Analysis of entire propeller

The propeller analysis problem consists of determining the load distribution on a given propeller geometry when it is operating in a specified inflow. The numerical methods used to solve the analysis problem are virtually identical to those used in the design problem, except that now the blade geometry is known and the strengths of the vortices representing the blade loading are the unknowns to be determined.

The method of discretizing the blade and wake singularity system is the same as that used for the design problem, except that a much coarser lattice is used on the key blade in the analysis problem in the interest of saving computer time. As in the design problem, the correct position of the trailing vortex

Table 6(a)   Convergence of *P/D* with chordwise elements with 34 spanwise panels

r/R	Number of Chordwise Elements, N		
	8	12	16
0.25	1.491	1.487	1.486
0.40	1.463	1.461	1.460
0.60	1.273	1.273	1.273
0.80	1.044	1.044	1.044
0.95	0.885	0.884	0.884

Table 6(b)   Convergence of f_0/c with chordwise elements with 34 spanwise panels

r/R	Number of Chordwise Elements, N		
	8	12	16
0.25	0.0320	0.0322	0.0322
0.40	0.0377	0.0378	0.0378
0.60	0.0278	0.0281	0.0282
0.80	0.0177	0.0180	0.0181
0.95	0.0173	0.0175	0.0175

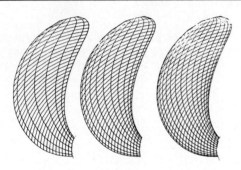

Table 6(c)   Convergence of *P/D* with spanwise panels with 12 chordwise elements

r/R	Number of Spanwise Panels, M		
	8	19	34
0.25	1.515	1.496	1.487
0.40	1.476	1.461	1.461
0.60	1.270	1.271	1.273
0.80	1.026	1.039	1.044
0.95	0.802	0.873	0.884

Table 6(d)   Convergence of f_0/c with spanwise panels with 12 chordwise elements

r/R	Number of Spanwise Panels, M		
	8	19	34
0.25	0.0327	0.0329	0.0322
0.40	0.0397	0.0381	0.0378
0.60	0.0292	0.0284	0.0281
0.80	0.0184	0.0183	0.0180
0.95	0.0186	0.0172	0.0175

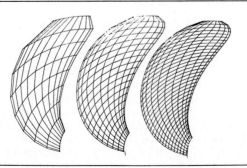

Table 7(a)   Influence of chord load and wake deformation on *P/D* using 16 chordwise and 34 spanwise elements

r/R	b = 0.8 Chord Load Deformed Wake	a = 0.8 Chord Load Deformed Wake	b = 0.8 Chord Load β_i Wake
0.25	1.487	1.493	1.507
0.40	1.461	1.468	1.487
0.60	1.273	1.278	1.293
0.80	1.044	1.047	1.062
0.95	0.884	0.886	0.894

Table 7(b)   Influence of chord load and wake deformation of f_0/c using 16 chordwise and 34 spanwise elements

r/R	b = 0.8 Chord Load Deformed Wake	a = 0.8 Chord Load Deformed Wake	b = 0.8 Chord Load β_i Wake
0.25	0.0322	0.0314	0.0323
0.40	0.0378	0.0368	0.0386
0.60	0.0281	0.0274	0.0285
0.80	0.0180	0.0175	0.0181
0.95	0.0175	0.0171	0.0169

Table 8(a)   Comparison of *P/D* values with other lifting-surface programs

	PBD-10	PBD-9[a] [7]	Brockett [5]
0.25	1.534	1.574	...
0.254	...	...	1.540
0.4	1.526	1.504	1.488
0.6	1.311	1.287	1.277
0.8	1.071	1.062	1.042
0.946	...	...	0.883
0.95	0.910	0.888	...

[a] Corrected for the difference between $a = 0.8$ and $b = 0.8$ chord loads using Table 7.

Table 8(b)   Comparison of f_0/c values with other lifting-surface programs

	PBD-10	PBD-9[a] [7]	Brockett [5]
0.25	0.0258	0.0274	...
0.254	...	...	0.0324
0.4	0.0330	0.0360	0.0369
0.6	0.0274	0.0308	0.0295
0.8	0.0174	0.0186	0.0188
0.946	...	...	0.0122
0.95	0.0142	0.0124	...

[a] Corrected for the difference between $a = 0.8$ and $b = 0.8$ chord loads using Table 7.

Table 9   Predicted thrust, torque and efficiency for 72-deg skew propeller at *J* = 0.899

		Lifting Surface		Lifting Line
		16 × 34 Grid	8 × 8 Grid	
$C_D = 0$	K_T	0.231	0.230	0.219
	K_Q	0.0419	0.0416	0.0406
	η	0.779	0.783	0.764
$C_D = 0.0085$	K_T	0.224	0.224	0.213
	K_Q	0.0461	0.0458	0.0442
	η	0.689	0.693	0.682

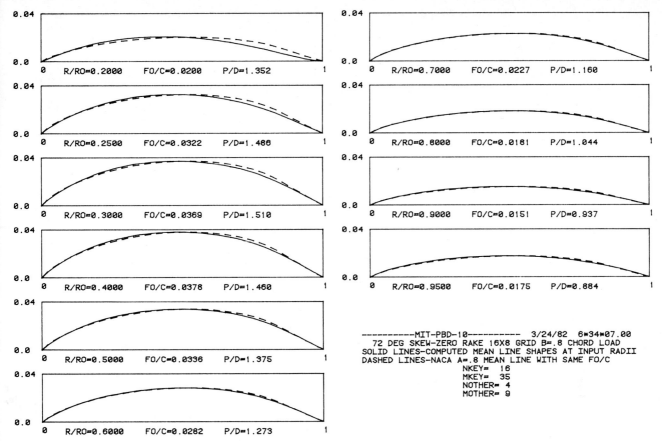

Fig. 11 Computer mean line shapes for propeller similar to DTNSRDC 4498

wake may be determined by the iterative wake alignment process described in Appendix 1.

Vortex sheet separation from tip

While it is assumed that no flow separation from leading or tip edges occurs at the design condition, these phenomena may occur when the propeller is working at off-design advance coefficients. The detailed modeling of flow separation from the tip and leading edges is discussed in the following; an appropriate representation which is adequate for calculating blade forces is shown in Fig. 12. The chordwise vortices along the tip edge of the blade are allowed to separate from the blade and coalesce at a point above the trailing edge of the blade tip. The pitch angle of the vortex leaving the leading edge of the tip panel is assumed to be

$$\bar{\beta} = \frac{1}{2}(\beta + \beta_T) \qquad (10)$$

where β is the undisturbed flow angle at the tip and β_T is the pitch angle of the transition wake tip vortex as it leaves the blade. The displacement of the trailers above the blade camber surface at the trailing edge is given by

$$\Delta = c \tan(\phi - \bar{\beta}) \qquad (11)$$

where c is the chord length of the tip panel and ϕ the pitch angle of the blade tip.

The displacement Δ is small when a propeller is operating near its design advance coefficient but increases as J is reduced, thus increasing the computed lift on the blade. This representation is sufficient to enable the thrust and torque of the propeller to be accurately calculated over a wide range of advance ratios. A more refined model of the separated tip vortex is necessary to predict the load distribution in the tip region.

Solution for vortex strengths

The solution of the propeller analysis problem consists of determining the strengths of the singularities representing the propeller blades and their trailing vortex wakes. The strengths of the sources representing the blade thickness are determined by a stripwise application of thin-wing theory at each radius, leaving only the vortex strengths to be determined.

The vortex system representing the blade and the wakes is organized into "horseshoe vortices." Each horseshoe vortex consists of a spanwise vortex and two trailing vortices extending through the blade and back along the trailing wake, as shown in Fig. 13. Note that Kelvin's conservation of vorticity theorem is automatically satisfied by this horseshoe vortex structure. The horseshoe strengths on the other blades can be expressed in terms of those on the key blade, and since there are an equal number of horseshoes and control points on the key blade, a set of simultaneous equations may be formulated to determine the key blade horseshoe strengths Γ_j.

The boundary condition to be applied is that of zero normal velocity at the control points on the key blade. Define an influence function A_{ij}, which is the normal velocity at the ith control point caused by the vortex system associated with a unit strength of the jth horseshoe vortex. Then the total normal velocity at the ith control point due to the vortex system on the blades and in the wake is given by

$$\sum_{j=1}^{(M \cdot N)} A_{ij} \Gamma_j, \qquad i = 1, 2, \ldots, (M \cdot N) \qquad (12)$$

The normal component of the velocity at the ith control point due to inflow and propeller rotation is given by

$$\vec{n}_i \cdot \vec{V}_i^I \qquad (13)$$

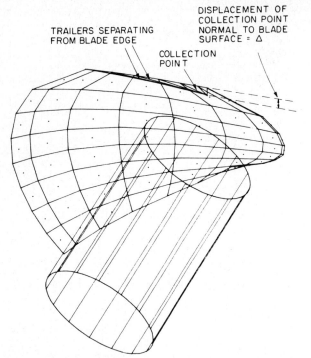

Fig. 12 Model of separation from blade tip used in global solution

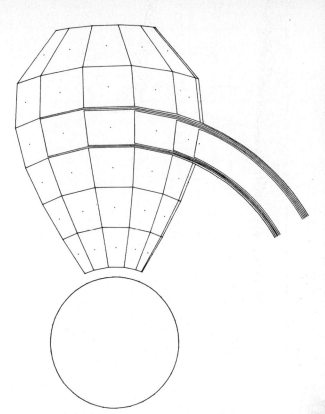

Fig. 13 Illustration of horseshoe vortices on blade and in wake

where $\vec{n}_i$ is the unit normal vector.

The normal component of the velocity due to all of the sources is denoted

$$\vec{n}_i \cdot \vec{V}_i^q \qquad (14)$$

Then the boundary condition can be written as

$$\sum_{j=1}^{(M \cdot N)} A_{ij} \Gamma_j + \vec{n}_i \cdot (\vec{V}_i^I + \vec{V}_i^q) = 0 \qquad (15)$$

or

$$\sum_{j=1}^{(M \cdot N)} A_{ij} \Gamma_j = -\vec{n}_i \cdot (\vec{V}_i^I + \vec{V}_i^q), \qquad i = 1, 2, \ldots, (M \cdot N)$$

which is sufficient to determine the unknown Γ_j values.

Since the wake alignment procedure depends on the vortex distribution over the blades, which in turn depends on the wake geometry, it is necessary to use an iterative approach to solve for the correct blade loading and trailing wake geometry. Starting with the wake following the undisturbed flow ($\beta_w = \beta$), only two or three passes through the process of solving for the vortex distribution and updating the wake geometry are usually needed to reach a converged solution. Convergence is accelerated if a reasonable estimate of the final wake geometry is used for starting the iterative process.

Determination of blade forces

Following Kerwin and Lee [1], the blade forces are computed by determining the forces acting on the line singularities representing the key blade. Assuming that the average velocity over the length of a singularity can be approximated by the velocity at its midpoint, the force on the jth key blade singularity can be expressed as

$$\vec{F}_j = \rho \Delta l_j [\vec{V}_j \times \vec{\Gamma}_j - \vec{V}_j Q_j] \qquad (16)$$

where Δl_j is the length of the line singularity, $\vec{V}_j$ the total velocity at its midpoint, and Q_j the strength per unit length of the line source. This computation is made for all of the span-

wise and chordwise singularities on the key blade except for the outermost chordwise vortices on the tip panel, which are assumed to be separated from the blade. Unlike the current design program, the analysis program obtains the velocity at the singularities by direct calculation rather than interpolating the velocities computed at the control points. This is necessary in order to calculate the leading-edge suction force at off-design advance coefficients, which appears as a chordwise force on the spanwise vortex closest to the leading edge.

The viscous drag force on the blade is represented as a force increment on each spanwise vortex, as discussed previously. The increase in viscous drag due to operation at non-shock-free entry is represented in the current program as a lack of recovery of the leading-edge suction force. As in Kerwin and Lee [1], the computed leading-edge suction force is multiplied by a "suction efficiency factor," which was set equal to $\frac{1}{3}$ for all of the performance predictions contained in this paper. This procedure appears to be sufficiently accurate for predicting the overall forces on propellers. A much more detailed analysis of the leading-edge suction is needed for predicting flow separation and cavitation, as shown later in this paper.

Viscous pitch correction

The boundary layer on the suction side of a blade section is often thicker than on the pressure side, especially near the trailing edge. This inequality of boundary-layer thickness is equivalent to a slight reduction in the pitch and camber, and hence lift, of the blade section. When solutions for propeller blade boundary layers become routinely available, this loss of lift may be rationally included in the present theory by modifying the normal velocity boundary condition [equation (15)] to account for the unequal boundary-layer displacement thicknesses.

In the present program this effect is simulated by a reduction of the pitch angle of each blade section by an amount

$$\Delta\alpha = 1.9454 \left(\frac{t_0}{c}\right) \left|\frac{f_0}{c}\right| \qquad (17)$$

where $\Delta\alpha$ is expressed in radians, as suggested by Kerwin and Lee [1]. This correction is appropriate to model propeller Reynolds numbers; presumably the correction should be smaller for full-scale propellers. This pitch correction was used for all of the propeller analysis results presented in this paper.

Influence of number of panels and wake parameters

It has been found that an 8×8 lattice on the key blade and 8×4 lattices on the other blades are sufficient for computing forces on most propellers. Increasing the number of panels on the key blade results in differences in the computed thrust and torque which are smaller than the usual errors for measurements of these quantities, and smaller than the probable errors in the current theory caused by neglecting the presence of the propeller hub. The convergence of blade forces with numbers of elements is demonstrated in [1].

Kerwin and Lee [1] showed that the most critical wake parameter is the pitch, which is now calculated rather than being provided as input data. The other wake parameters have less effect on performance predictions and may be estimated with sufficient accuracy from observations on a series of propellers [3, 9].

Correlation with experiment: DTNSRDC 5-bladed skew series

A series of six propellers with systematically varied skew and rake developed at DTNSRDC [10, 11] provides a good test of the accuracy of the present analysis program in predicting open-water performance. The series consists of four propellers with skew ranging from 0 to 108 deg, and two additional designs in which the skew-induced rake has been removed ("warped" propellers). The geometric data for these propellers were given in the 1978 paper by Kerwin and Lee [1] and are not reported here.

Figures 14–19 show the open-water characteristics as measured by DTNSRDC (solid lines) and, where available, measurements made in the Massachusetts Institute of Technology (MIT) Variable Pressure Water Tunnel (dashed lines). The differences between experiments are disturbing. Subtle viscous effects may be responsible, since the MIT experiments were made at a higher Reynolds number (1.3×10^6 versus 7.0×10^5 at DTNSRDC for $J = 0.889$) and with higher inflow turbulence. These differences could lead to different relative amounts of laminar and turbulent flow on the blades. The MIT test of Propeller No. 4381 almost certainly had fully turbulent flow over the blades, since this propeller had rough blade surfaces and badly nicked leading edges when tested at MIT (the damage due to its having spent too much time in the water tunnel!). The fact that all of MIT data presented resemble the data for this propeller (the K_T and K_Q curves tend to be flat and have similar slopes for all propellers) may indicate that the MIT tests are more representative of the "full scale" performance of these propellers.

The thrust and torque coefficients at three J-values computed using the present lifting-surface program are shown in Figs. 14–19. The lattice arrangement used for the calculations is shown in the corner of each figure. All calculations were done using an 8×8 lattice on the key blade and 8×4 lattices on the other blades. The wake alignment procedure was used for all calculations, and values of r_w and δ_c were taken from Min's [3] measurements of the wake geometry for these propellers. A section viscous drag coefficient of 0.007 was used for all computations. It should be noted that the current theory ignores the presence of the hub, both in determining the vortex

distribution on the blade and in calculating the forces on the propeller.

It is difficult to judge the adequacy of the theory, given the uncertainty in experimental results. The thrust near design $J = 0.889$ is fairly well predicted except for the 108-deg skewed propeller, No. 4384. The reason for the underprediction of torque near design J for the warped propellers is not known.

It is instructive to look at the change in thrust with skew at a given advance coefficient, as shown in Fig. 20. The unskewed propeller and the three skewed propellers were designed to have the same radial distributions of bound circulation at $J = 0.889$. The calculations indicate that these four propellers have virtually identical circulation distributions at a given advance ratio, but the computed thrust (and torque) goes up with increasing skew. The MIT data show this same trend at the three J-values shown, and the DTNSRDC data also show some of this behavior. It seems safe to say that this effect is real and not just an artifact of the current theory.

Formulation of the local problem

The propeller analysis procedure just described is adequate to determine the overall forces on propeller blades with sufficient accuracy for many purposes. Determining the load distribution on the blade with high resolution requires a much finer discretization of the blade singularity system. This leads to a tremendous increase in computer execution time because the time required to solve the system of simultaneous equations for the vortex strengths [equation (15)] is proportional to (number of panels)^3. Since the details of the load distribution near the tip are usually of primary interest because of cavitation considerations, it makes sense to use only a fine vortex/source lattice in the tip region. The computational scheme used to do this is illustrated in Fig. 21. There are four basic steps:

(a) Solve the "global" boundary-value problem for the entire propeller using a relatively coarse discretization of the blade singularity system.

(b) Choose a "local" flow domain, including the tip region of the key blade and a portion of the key blade trailing vortex wake near the tip. Set the strengths of the sources and vortices in this local flow domain equal to zero.

(c) At a series of points in the local flow domain, calculate the induced velocities caused by the remainder of the singularity system (that is, the rest of the key blade, the rest of the key blade wake, and the other blades and wakes). Since there are no singularities in this region, the induced velocity is a smooth function of position, and interpolation may be used to find the induced velocity at any point in the local flow domain.

(d) The local tip flow problem now consists of solving for the flow about the tip of the key blade only. The inflow velocity, $\vec{V}^I$, at each point on the blade tip now consists of the inflow velocity caused by the speed of advance and propeller rotation *plus* the induced velocities calculated in Step (c). Note that the influence of most of the key blade trailing vortex wake is included in the induced velocity calculation, so that only the portion of the trailing vortex wake in the local flow domain needs to be included when computing the local solution.

From this point on we need only consider the problem of determining the flow around this isolated blade tip. No further account need be taken of the rest of the key blade and its trailing vortex wake, or of the other blades and their wakes. This results in a significant saving in computer time compared with calculating the details of the tip flow as part of the global solution.

A high-resolution attached-flow tip solution, using the same assumptions used in the global solution, is discussed next. This is used to provide input data for the viscous leading-edge analysis. Finally, the tip flow solution is re-solved allowing for

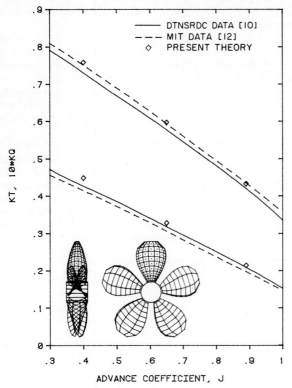

Fig. 14 Comparison of predicted performance with open-water characteristics of DTNSRDC Propeller 4381 (0-deg skew)

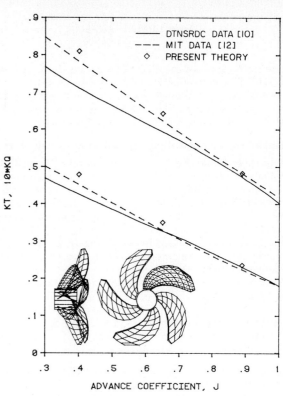

Fig. 16 Comparison of predicted performance with open-water characteristics of DTNSRDC Propeller 4383 (72-deg skew)

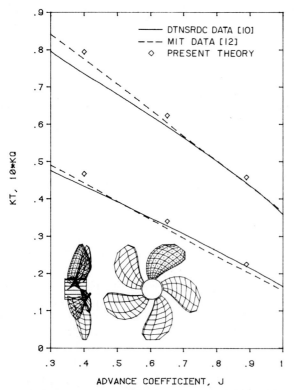

Fig. 15 Comparison of predicted performance with open-water characteristics of DTNSRDC Propeller 4382 (32-deg skew)

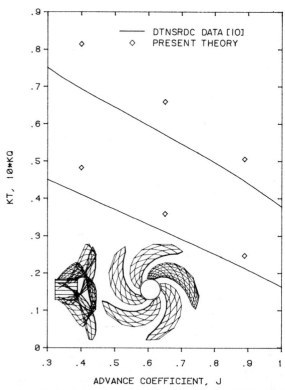

Fig. 17 Comparison of predicted performance with open-water characteristics of DTNSRDC Propeller 4384 (108-deg skew)

Numerical Methods for Propeller Design

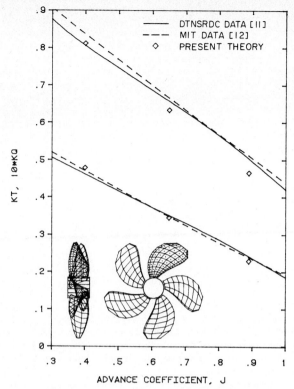

Fig. 18 Comparison of predicted performance with open-water characteristics of DTNSRDC Propeller 4497 (36-deg warp)

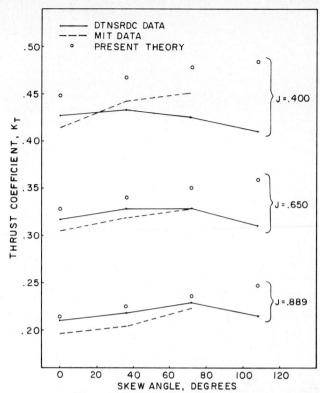

Fig. 20 Variation of thrust coefficient with skew

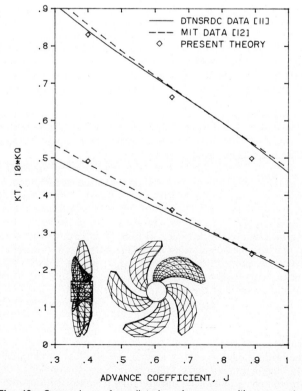

Fig. 19 Comparison of predicted performance with open-water characteristics of DTNSRDC Propeller 4498 (72-deg warp)

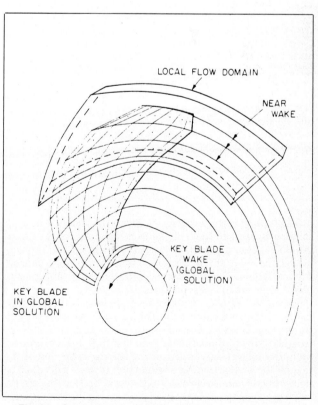

Fig. 21 Separation of problem into global and local domains

Numerical Methods for Propeller Design

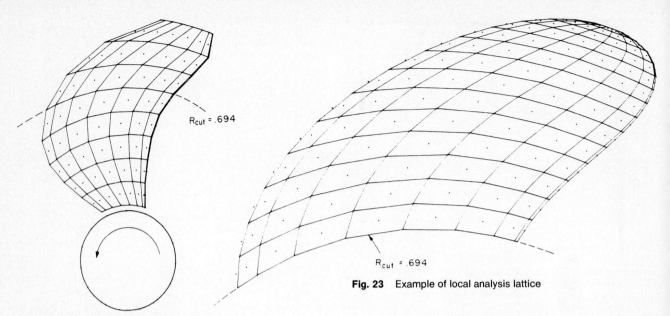

Fig. 22 Example of global analysis lattice

Fig. 23 Example of local analysis lattice

the possibility of significant flow separation from the leading edge.

Calculation of the attached-flow tip solution

The method of calculating the attached-flow tip solution is virtually identical to that used for the global solution, so that only those features peculiar to the tip solution will be discussed here.

In order to reasonably discretize a propeller blade with zero tip chord (planform having rounded tip in projected view) it was found necessary to divide the blade tip radially using "half-cosine" spacing instead of the uniform spacing used in the global solution. Dividing the tip region into M spanwise panels, the endpoints of the discrete vortices are located at radii

$$\rho_m = r_{\text{cut}} + (1 - r_{\text{cut}}) \sin\left[\frac{(m-1)\pi}{2M+1}\right],$$
$$m = 1,2,\ldots,M+1 \quad (18)$$

and the control points are located at radii

$$r_m = r_{\text{cut}} + (1 - r_{\text{cut}}) \sin\left[\frac{(m-\frac{1}{2})\pi}{2M+1}\right]$$
$$m = 1,2,\ldots,M \quad (19)$$

where r_{cut} is the separation radius between global and local solutions.

The trailing vortex wake geometry for the attached-flow tip solution is assumed to be the same as that used for the global solution. The approach developed previously for approximating the effect of flow separation from the tip is also utilized. Figures 22 and 23 illustrate the vortex lattice grids typically used for global and local analyses.

An important part of the local-tip solution is the determination of the loading near the leading edge, which is needed for the viscous leading-edge analysis. Since thin-airfoil theory (singularities on camberline instead of airfoil surface) is being used, the relevant descriptor of the leading-edge flow is the magnitude of the leading-edge suction force. This may be determined from the solution to the local tip flow boundary-value problem by placing control points along the leading edge and computing the total upwash (normalwash) there, as shown

in Appendix 3. While the leading-edge suction could be computed in the same manner as in the global solution, the method used here forms an integral part of the separated flow modeling in the tip region which is described later in this paper.

The validity of this global-local program separation has been established by extensive numerical experimentation. Some typical results are given in [4].

Viscous leading-edge flow analysis

Leading-edge separation

When propeller blades and wings having swept leading edges are operated at a high angle of attack the flow may separate from the leading edge, forming a free shear layer. This free shear layer often rolls up just behind the leading edge to form a leading-edge vortex (on highly swept leading edges) or a part-span vortex (moderately swept leading edges) which passes over the blade surface. A leading-edge or part-span vortex markedly alters the load distribution on the wing or propeller blade, usually increasing the lift and drag over that predicted by linear theory, in which vorticity is shed from the trailing edge only. In addition, the presence of a strong rolled-up vortex above the suction surface enables high angles of attack to be reached before stall occurs.

Figures 24 and 25 illustrate this leading-edge separation phenomenon on a highly skewed model propeller (DTNSRDC No. 4498) operating in the MIT water tunnel. The tip vortices have been made visible by lowering the tunnel pressure so that cavitation occurs in the low-pressure core of the tip vortex. Figure 24 shows the propeller operating near its design advance ratio where the tip vortex leaves the tip of the blade as expected. When the propeller is heavily loaded, as in Fig. 25, the "tip" vortex actually separates from the leading edge inboard of the tip and passes over the blade suction surface.

In order to model this leading-edge separation properly it is first necessary to know where the separation occurs on the blade. If propeller blades had sharp leading edges the problem would be relatively simple: separation would occur all along the leading edge except at ideal angle of attack, and a leading-edge Kutta condition could be imposed to determine the amount of vorticity shed into the flow from the leading edge. Unfortunately, propellers usually have nicely rounded leading edges to delay the occurrence of sheet cavitation, and this means

Numerical Methods for Propeller Design

Fig. 24 DTNSRDC Propeller 4498 operating near design J

Fig. 25 DTNSRDC Propeller 4498 operating at 60 percent of Design J

that a viscous analysis is necessary in order to predict the occurrence of leading-edge flow separation.

Leading-edge separation bubbles

Since the leading-edge flow behavior of airfoil sections is inextricably tied up with the behavior of laminar separation bubbles, it is worthwhile to digress for a moment and take a brief look at laminar separation bubbles on two-dimensional airfoil sections.

Separation bubbles on airfoil sections are usually classified according to their size. Short bubbles are typically less than 1 percent of the local chord in length and less than 0.01 percent of the chord in height (Fig. 26), while long separation bubbles usually extend over a significant portion of the airfoil chord (Fig. 27). At high angles of attack the flow fails to reattach to the upper surface at all and the section stalls; see Fig. 28.

The pressure distribution on the surface of an airfoil with a short bubble is shown in Fig. 29. The laminar boundary layer separates at Point S in the adverse pressure gradient following the suction peak, forming a free shear layer (vortex sheet). The separated shear layer encloses a region of quiescent fluid until Point T is reached, where the shear layer undergoes transition to turbulence. Aft of this point, turbulent mixing between the free stream and the shear layer enables the pressure rise to Point R to be negotiated, whereupon the flow reattaches to the foil surface as a turbulent boundary layer. As shown in Fig. 30, a short bubble typically affects the pressure on the foil surface only in the immediate vicinity of the bubble. For this reason the presence of short bubbles usually does not influence the lift, drag, or pitching moment.

A long separation bubble may extend over a large fraction of the airfoil chord and drastically alter the pressure distribution. Typically the suction peak (and thus the leading-edge suction force) is greatly reduced, so that the drag is increased. However, the low pressure in the bubble is extended over a large part of the chord, so that the lift does not necessarily suffer, as shown in Fig. 31. This is responsible for the gentle stall of thin airfoils, where a long bubble grows in length as the incidence is increased.

Separation bubble behavior and stall

Most two-dimensional airfoil sections will have a short laminar separation bubble present near the nose when operating slightly above ideal angle of attack. The length of this bubble decreases as the Reynolds number is increased at a fixed incidence, since the free shear layer undergoes transition sooner.

As the incidence is increased at a fixed Reynolds number, both the separation point, S, and the attachment point, R (Fig.

Fig. 26 Flow with short bubble near leading edge (height of bubble exaggerated) (from [13])

Fig. 27 Flow with long bubble (height of bubble exaggerated)

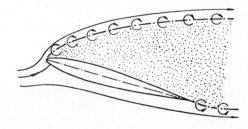

Fig. 28 Completely stalled flow with dead-air region (from [13])

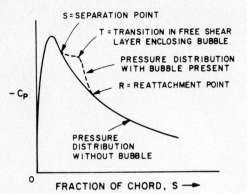

Fig. 29 Schematic of upper surface pressure distribution on foil with short bubble

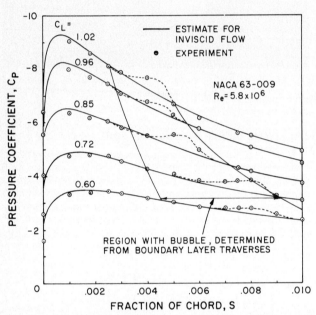

Fig. 30 Pressure distribution near nose of NACA 63.009 section

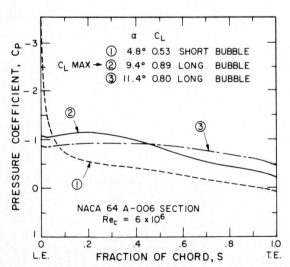

Fig. 31 Upper surface pressure distribution on foil with long separation bubble (from [13])

29), move forward, and the bubble contracts in length. At some point the short bubble "bursts," due either to the bubble being unable to negotiate the required pressure rise in so short a distance, or because the "reattached" turbulent boundary layer undergoes turbulent separation immediately downstream of R.

At this point there are two possibilities. If the shear layer fails to reattach to the foil at any point the flow breaks down completely and leading-edge stall is said to have occurred, with a loss of lift and a large increase in drag (Fig. 28). If the shear layer reattached much further downstream a long bubble forms (Fig. 27) and alters the pressure distribution over the airfoil upper surface.

Prediction of leading-edge flow behavior theory

Kuchemann [13] and Smith [14] hypothesized that part-span vortices on moderately swept wings occurred at the point along the leading edge where a short laminar separation bubble burst to form a long bubble. If we accept this hypothesis then any method we develop to predict the onset of leading-edge flow separation should predict the bursting of two-dimensional laminar separation bubbles as the leading-edge sweep approaches zero.

The viscous leading-edge flow problem for three-dimensional wings and propeller blades appears far too complicated for a direct theoretical assault at the present time. Therefore the approach used here is to identify the relevant nondimensional parameters governing the problem and collect as much data as possible upon which to regress, so that a semi-empirical model can be developed to predict the occurrence of part-span vortices.

Two major assumptions were made in developing the leading-edge flow model presented herein:

(a) It is assumed that the flow at each point on the leading edge is similar to that on an infinite sheared wing (Fig. 32) having the same leading-edge sweep and the same velocity gradients along the surface normal to the leading edge.

(b) The calculated *attached* flow inviscid load distribution is used as input to the viscous flow calculations.

If we make the further assumption that the leading-edge

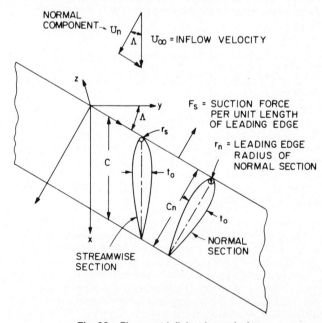

Fig. 32 Flow past infinite sheared wing

region of a wing or blade section in a plane normal to the leading edge (Fig. 32) can be satisfactorily represented by a parabola having the same leading edge radius, then the surface velocity component normal to the leading edge in inviscid flow can be calculated using the equations in Appendix 3. The only quantity remaining to be specified is the position of the stagnation point on the section normal to the leading edge (position of attachment line on infinite sheared wing). The descriptor used in the current paper is the suction force per length of leading edge, F_s. This is convenient because calculations of the attached potential flow using thin-wing theory yield the leading-edge suction force directly. A nondimensional leading-edge suction force coefficient is defined as

$$C_s = \frac{F_s}{\frac{1}{2}\rho U_n^2 r_n} \qquad (20)$$

where U_n is the component of inflow velocity normal to the leading edge and r_n is the radius of the leading edge in a plane normal to the leading edge. Note that C_s does not contain Λ.

The proper Reynolds number for describing the leading edge flow on swept wings was determined to be

$$R_{LE} = \frac{U_\infty r_n}{\nu} \qquad (21)$$

While it might be argued that U_n is the proper velocity to use, in accordance with infinite sheared wing theory, it must be remembered that the equations for the chordwise and spanwise components of the flow on a sheared wing uncouple only in the cases of inviscid flow or an attached laminar boundary layer. Once separation or turbulence appears, the chordwise and spanwise flow velocities interact. Since we are concerned about leading-edge flows involving separation and transition to turbulence, it appears that U_∞ is the proper velocity to use in forming a leading-edge Reynolds number.

Prediction of leading-edge behavior—correlation of experimental data

Wind tunnel data for swept wings [15–21] were collected and analyzed using the following procedure:

(a) For a given wing geometry, freestream Reynolds number, and angle of attack, the attached potential flow load distribution was determined using a vortex-lattice computer program very similar to the one used for the global propeller analysis.

(b) The values of R_{LE} and C_s were computed at a series of points along the span.

(c) The computed values of R_{LE} and C_s were recorded for the point along the leading edge where the part-span vortex originated (Fig. 33).

(d) The preceding process was repeated for a variety of different wings at different freestream Reynolds numbers and angles of attack. The pairs of R_{LE} and C_s-values at the observed locations of leading-edge flow breakdown were plotted together, as shown in Fig. 34.

Several other parameters describing the leading-edge flow were also investigated, but no correlation could be found between these parameters and the observed leading-edge flow behavior.

The scatter in the data in Fig. 34 is discouraging but not surprising, given the strong influence of surface roughness and turbulence shown for the 49.4-deg swept wing. There are inaccuracies in estimating C_s also, since the influence of the wing boundary layer was not considered in determining the attached flow load distirbution, the Kuchemann [21] has shown that the influence of the boundary layer increases with sweep. Nevertheless, there is a clear correlation between R_{LE} and the

computed C_s at the point where the part-span vortex separates from the wing.

Three other curves are shown in Fig. 34. The solid line is taken from Ridder [22] and represents the results of a series of tests on two-dimensional airfoil sections. The line plotted is the maximum attainable leading-edge suction force coefficient C_s (just before flow breakdown occurs) versus leading-edge Reynolds number R_{LE}. For the portion of the curve to the left of the knuckle ($R_{LE} < 8.6 \times 10^3$) the cause of the flow breakdown is bursting of a short laminar separation bubble. To the right of the knuckle ($R_{LE} > 8.6 \times 10^3$) the cause of flow breakdown is turbulent separation behind a short laminar bubble.

The line across Fig. 34 at $C_s = 6.5$ is the lower limit for the formation of laminar separation bubbles near the leading edge of a two-dimensional section. This line was calculated using the velocity distribution around a parabolic leading edge (Appendix 3) and the laminar boundary-layer separation criterion developed by Stratford [23]. This criterion is independent of Reynolds number, as expected.

The dashed line is the computed C_s at which turbulent boundary-layer separation is predicted to occur near the leading edge of two-dimensional sections. This calculation was made using the inviscid velocity distribution around a parabolic leading edge and the turbulent boundary-layer separation criterion due to Stratford [24].

The fact that both two-dimensional experimental data and the computed turbulent separation line pass through the experimental points for flow separation on swept wings is extremely encouraging. This appears to indicate that C_s and R_{LE} are proper descriptors for the state of the leading-edge flow on both swept and unswept wings. Other factors certainly influence the leading-edge flow behavior, but the limited amount of detailed swept-wing flow data available makes a correlation with these parameters difficult or impossible at present. It seems clear, however, that the suction force coefficient C_s and leading-edge Reynolds number R_{LE} are the most important parameters to consider.

Putting a line through all of the data shown in Fig. 34 results in a sort of "universal curve" for predicting the onset of leading-edge flow breakdown, which is presented in Fig. 35. If the leading-edge flow at some point on a wing has a computed C_s lying above the solid line in Fig. 35, then flow breakdown is expected. If the computed C_s lies below this limiting curve, then a short laminar separation bubble is predicted to occur. Applying this procedure to the case of propeller blades, good results are obtained in predicting the occurrence and origin of part-span vortices, as shown in the following.

The dashed curve in Fig. 35 represents the level of suction force remaining after leading-edge flow breakdown occurs. This curve is taken from Ridder [22] and represents two-dimensional airfoil data only. The importance of this curve will become clear subsequently, but for now it suffices to say that swept-wing data must be obtained to see if this curve holds for three-dimensional wings also. At present this curve must be considered as tentative only.

Comparison on predicted and observed leading-edge separation points for propellers

Very little data are available for comparing predicted leading-edge separation points with experimentally determined values. There are no full-scale data available. Obtaining model scale data is limited by two factors:

(a) Very few model propellers are available having accurately finished (and undamaged!) leading edges. The leading-edge radius near the tip of the model propeller is only several thousands of an inch.

(b) The only technique currently available for leading-edge

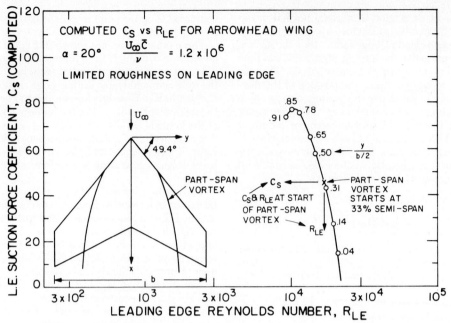

Fig. 33 Example of determination of R_{LE} and C_s at part-span vortex separation point

flow visualization is to induce cavitation in the leading-edge vortex. Unfortunately, there is only a limited range of operating conditions where other forms of cavitation (especially leading-edge sheet cavitation) do not obscure leading-edge vortex cavitation. This problem is especially severe at operation near design J, where the vorticity shed from the leading edge is weak.

The available data were taken in the MIT Variable Pressure Water Tunnel with two DTNSRDC model propellers, Nos. 4498 and 4119. Figure 36 shows the observed and calculated results. The vertical bar indicates the variability between different blades on the same propeller and the uncertainty involved in establishing the separation point from the cavitation patterns. Agreement is deemed to be satisfactory, but much more data are needed to validate the model.

Modeling of tip region separated flow

Physical description

Heavily loaded wings and propeller blades often shed vorticity into the fluid from a swept leading edge as well as the trailing edge. Since the vorticity shed from the leading edge passes very close to the wing or blade, it is essential to correctly determine the strength and location of this shed vorticity in order to determine the load distribution on the blade.

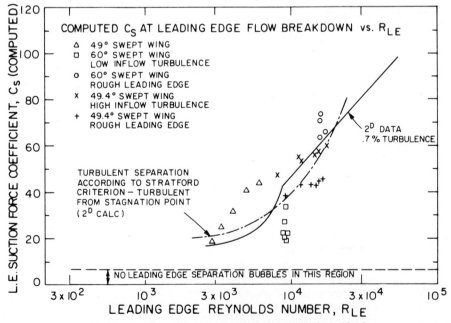

Fig. 34 C_s versus R_{LE} at leading-edge flow breakdown (data)

Numerical Methods for Propeller Design

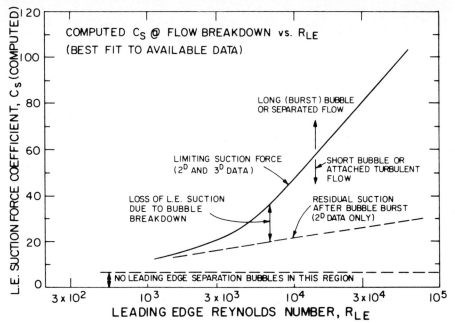

Fig. 35 C_s versus R_{LE} at leading-edge flow breakdown (best fit to data)

Figure 25 shows a heavily loaded propeller with a very strong part-span vortex being shed from the leading edge. While it may appear that vorticity is being shed from only one location on the leading edge in this case, vortex shedding is actually occurring along the entire length of the leading edge outboard of the initial separation point. The vorticity shed from the leading edge then rolls up into the part-span vortex core, so that the circulation around the core increases in the outward (downstream) direction.

At propeller loadings less severe than that shown in Fig. 25 (operation closer to design J), the initial separation point moves outward on the blade, and the strength of the vorticity shed from the leading edge is reduced. Perhaps more importantly, the tendency for the vorticity shed from the leading edge to roll up tightly is reduced. While adequate photographs of these phenomena are not available, detailed water tunnel observations of two different model propellers indicate that the tendency toward strong roll-up of the leading-edge shed vorticity is reduced as the propeller loading is reduced. Flow visualization was accomplished by noting the trajectories of minute cavitation bubbles emanating from nicks in the blade leading edges. Hence, it would appear that for many cases of interest (operation not too far away from design J) the vorticity shed from the blade leading edge tends to resemble a vortex sheet rather than a tightly rolled-up vortex core.

The amount of vorticity shed from the leading edge of a propeller blade or wing is determined by the nature of the flow at the leading edge. If the leading edge is sharp it is appropriate to impose a Kutta condition there to insure that velocities near the leading edge remain bounded. This is sufficient to determine the amount of vorticity shed from the leading edge using a variety of theoretical flow models [25, 26]. However, propeller blades typically have generous leading edge radii so that a Kutta condition at the leading edge is inappropriate. The vortex shedding rate is actually determined by the details of the viscous flow near the leading edge. A semi-empirical approach is utilized here, since the amount of vorticity shed into the flow once leading-edge flow breakdown occurs can be related to the residual leading-edge suction force. For present purposes this is taken from an empirical correlation (the dashed line in Fig. 35).

Once the amount of vorticity shed from the leading edge is determined, the major problem in completing the flow solution is to determine the proper trajectory of the shed vorticity as it passes close to the blade surface. The proper boundary condition for the shed vortex sheet is that there is no pressure jump across it. For an inviscid steady-flow model that is satisfied if

$$\vec{\omega} \times \vec{V} = 0 \qquad (22)$$

everywhere on the sheet; that is, the local vorticity vector must be parallel to the local velocity vector.

Modeling of leading-edge vortex sheet

In order to calculate the correct geometry of the vortex sheet shed from the leading edge the rolling-up process must be ac-

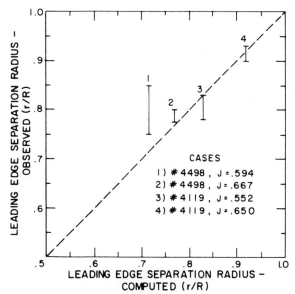

Fig. 36 Comparison of calculated and observed leading-edge separation points

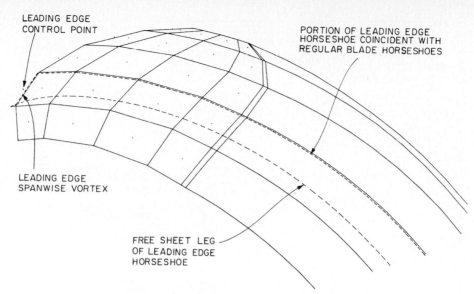

LEADING EDGE
CONTROL POINT

PORTION OF LEADING EDGE
HORSESHOE COINCIDENT WITH
REGULAR BLADE HORSESHOES

LEADING EDGE
SPANWISE VORTEX

FREE SHEET LEG
OF LEADING EDGE
HORSESHOE

Fig. 37   Schematic of leading-edge horseshoe vortex

counted for, even if the roll-up is not dramatic. This leads to severe numerical probems, since a characteristic length in the rolling-up vortex sheet is much smaller than a characteristic length of the blade tip being analyzed. Several investigators [25, 27] have developed numerical schemes for calculating the geometry of vortex sheets shed from the leading edges of delta wings at high incidence. After considerable study it was felt that their methods could not be applied directly to the propeller problem because of the more complicated geometry and the fact that the angle of attack of the propeller blade sections was usually much lower than the values typically used in delta-wing calculations. The lower incidence means that the shed vorticity remains closer to the blade surface, accentuating the numerical difficulties associated with calculating the wing/vortex interaction.

Since interest is often in propeller operation not too far from the design condition, a "first-order" model of the leading-edge vortex sheet is used here which is based on the observation that the free sheet roll-up is quite weak for operation near design J. In this first-order model the shed vorticity is convected back over the suction side of the blade along curves of constant radius. The height of the free sheet above the blade camber surface is set equal to one half of the blade thickness plus the estimated boundary-layer thickness on the suction side.

The method used for solving the analysis problem including the effect of leading-edge separation was developed by Mehrotra and Lan [27]. In addition to the usual horseshoe vortices on the blade tip a "leading-edge" horseshoe vortex is included on each radial strip for which leading-edge flow separation is predicted to occur, as shown in Fig. 37. Each leading-edge horseshoe consists of a leg coinciding with the usual horseshoes on the blade tip, a leading-edge spanwise vortex lying between the leading edge and the first spanwise vortex in the regular vortex lattice, and a leg which represents part of the vortex sheet shed from the leading edge. In delta-wing calculations [25] the position of this latter portion of each leading-edge horseshoe is obtained as part of the solution, which requires a time-consuming iterative process. In the present paper the position of this shed vortex filament is specified in accordance with the first-order model of the shed vortex sheet discussed earlier. The resulting horseshoe vortex system is shown in Fig. 38.

Appendix 3 notes that the leading-edge suction force per unit length of leading edge on a three-dimensional wing is proportional to the square of the upwash velocity computed at a leading-edge control point ahead of the first spanwise vortex. Ordinarily this calculation is done after the horseshoe strengths have been determined, but the leading-edge horseshoe strengths are additional unknowns which must be determined when solving the equation for the horseshoe strengths [equation (15)]. We introduce the correct number of additional boundary conditions by specifying the upwash velocity at the leading-edge control points for those strips having leading edge horseshoes. These upwash velocities are determined by the amount of leading-edge suction remaining after flow separation; at present these values are taken from the dashed line in Fig. 35.

Tip-flow solution procedure

The complete procedure used to solve the boundary-value problem for the flow around a propeller blade tip is outlined in the following. It is assumed that the global propeller analysis has been completed and that a local tip flow domain has already been selected.

(*a*)   A local tip-flow solution using a fine vortex lattice is done, assuming no flow separation from the leading edge of the blade.

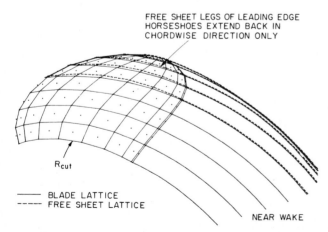

FREE SHEET LEGS OF LEADING EDGE
HORSESHOES EXTEND BACK IN
CHORDWISE DIRECTION ONLY

R_{cut}

———— BLADE LATTICE
----- FREE SHEET LATTICE

NEAR WAKE

Fig. 38   First-order model of leading-edge vortex sheet

Numerical Methods for Propeller Design

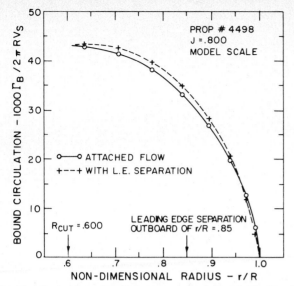

Fig. 39 Comparison of predicted bound circulation distributions for attached and separated flow

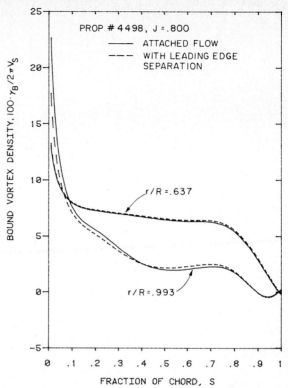

Fig. 40 Predicted chordwise loadings with and without leading-edge separation

(b) Using the singularity distribution determined in the preceding, the normal velocities at the leading-edge control points on the blade tip are calculated. As shown in Appendix 3, this allows the leading-edge suction force coefficient C_s to be determined along the leading edge.

(c) Figure 35 is consulted to determine which portions of the leading edge have suffered leading-edge flow breakdown. The assumption is made currently that vorticity is shed all along the leading edge outboard of the innermost separation point. This assumption appears to be valid for propellers having any kind of pitch distribution except for extreme unloading of the tip. For those sections of the blade predicted to have flow separation, the dashed line in Fig. 35 is used to estimate the residual leading-edge suction force coefficient.

(d) For each strip of the blade predicted to have leading-edge flow separation, the required normal induced velocity at the leading edge control point is determined from the estimated residual leading-edge suction force coefficient determined in (c).

(e) The first-order model of the leading-edge vortex sheet is set up covering all chordwise strips having leading-edge separation (Fig. 38). This first-order free sheet model comprises the shed sheet legs of the leading-edge horseshoes (Fig. 37).

(f) A set of simultaneous equations is set up and solved to determine the strengths of the blade and leading-edge horseshoes.

Calculation of blade forces

The forces on the blade tip in the separated flow solution are calculated in a manner very similar to that used in the global solution. There are additional induced velocities due to the leading-edge vortex sheet which must be included. The leading-edge suction force for those portions of the leading edge experiencing flow separation is taken from Fig. 35.

Example of tip solution with leading-edge separation

A calculation was done, using the theory outlined in the foregoing, in order to predict the flow around the tip of the blade of DTNSRDC Propeller 4498 (72-deg warp), when operating at $J = 0.800$ (Design $J = 0.899$). At model scale, leading-edge separation was predicted to occur outboard of r/R

= 0.85, and the resulting lattice arrangement used is shown in Fig. 38. Figure 39 shows the predicted bound circulation distributions, and it is seen that the presence of leading-edge separation unloads the extreme tip of the blade and increases the loading inboard of the leading-edge vortex sheet.

Figure 40 show the computed chordwise distributions of bound vorticity at two radii at which calculations were performed. As expected, the major effect of the separated flow is to reduce the loading near the leading edge in the region where leading-edge flow separation is expected to occur.

The computed values of thrust and torque on the blade tip are given in Table 10. The computed thrust is about the same for the three solutions. This is encouraging, since the global analysis does a good job predicting the propeller thrust over a wide range of J-values (Fig. 19). The change in computed torques may reflect the difficulty in computing induced drag with a swept vortex lattice, which has been noted by several researchers [28, 29].

Considerable work remains to be done in modeling the separated flow from the swept leading edges of propeller blades over a range of advance coefficients. A proper model should

Table 10 Computed thrust and torque on tip of No. 4498 blade outboard of $r/R = 0.600$, at $J = 0.800$

Solution	K_{F_x} (Thrust)	K_{M_x} (Torque)
Tip portion of global solution	−0.04019	0.007444
Attached-flow-tip solution	−0.03996	0.007249
Tip solution with leading-edge separation	−0.04098	0.007100

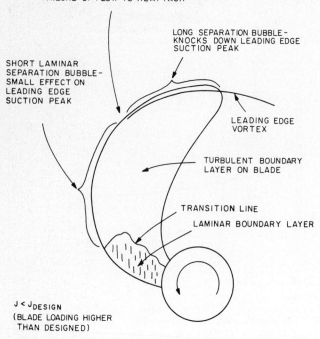

SEPARATION BUBBLE BREAKDOWN-
FAILURE OF FLOW TO REATTACH

LONG SEPARATION BUBBLE-
KNOCKS DOWN LEADING EDGE
SUCTION PEAK

SHORT LAMINAR
SEPARATION BUBBLE-
SMALL EFFECT ON
LEADING EDGE
SUCTION PEAK

LEADING EDGE
VORTEX

TURBULENT BOUNDARY
LAYER ON BLADE

TRANSITION LINE

LAMINAR BOUNDARY LAYER

$J < J_{\text{DESIGN}}$
(BLADE LOADING HIGHER
THAN DESIGNED)

Fig. 41 Schematic of suction side flow on model propeller blade

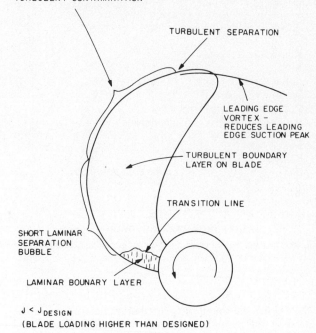

FLOW TURBULENT NEAR LEADING EDGE-
DUE TO LOCAL INSTABILITIES AND
TRANSITION OR DUE TO SPANWISE
TURBULENT CONTAMINATION

TURBULENT SEPARATION

LEADING EDGE
VORTEX –
REDUCES LEADING
EDGE SUCTION PEAK

TURBULENT BOUNDARY
LAYER ON BLADE

TRANSITION LINE

SHORT LAMINAR
SEPARATION
BUBBLE

LAMINAR BOUNARY LAYER

$J < J_{\text{DESIGN}}$
(BLADE LOADING HIGHER THAN DESIGNED)

Fig. 42 Schematic of suction side flow on full-scale propeller blade

pass smoothly from the vortex sheet model presented here to one representing a tightly rolled-up vortex core (as in Fig. 25) as the propeller loading is increased. The calculation of forces on complex lifting surfaces with free vortices in close proximity also requires considerable investigation. A more complete discussion of the problems involved is given by Greeley [4].

Implications for cavitation inception

The current viscous leading-edge flow analysis qualitatively explains the observed phenomenon that skew delays the inception of leading-edge sheet cavitation. Consider two propellers having the same chord lengths, section thicknesses, and load distribution, but let one be highly skewed and the other unskewed. The leading-edge radius of the normal section (r_n) varies inversely with leading-edge sweep angle Λ:

$$r_n \propto \frac{1}{\cos\Lambda} \qquad (23)$$

and the component of the inflow velocity normal to the leading edge (U_n) varies as the cosine of the sweep angle Λ:

$$U_n \propto \cos\Lambda \qquad (24)$$

Hence the leading-edge suction force coefficient C_s, defined by

$$C_s = \frac{F_s}{\frac{1}{2}\rho U_n^2 r_n} \qquad (20)$$

varies like

$$C_s \propto 1/\cos\Lambda \qquad (25)$$

for the two otherwise identical propellers. Similarly, the leading-edge Reynolds number [equation (21)] varies as

$$R_{\text{LE}} \propto 1/\cos\Lambda \qquad (26)$$

Referring to Fig. 35, it can be seen that the propeller with the higher leading-edge sweep Λ (the highly skewed propeller) will

operate with its sections closer to the limiting suction force line. So for a given J ($J < J_{\text{design}}$), the highly skewed propeller will have leading-edge separation extending farther inboard than on the unskewed propeller. Since the presence of leading-edge separation knocks down the minimum pressure peak at the leading edge which is responsible for leading-edge sheet cavitation, we may infer that the highly skewed propeller will be less susceptible to leading-edge sheet cavitation than its unskewed partner, for a given loading and cavitation number. This phenomenon has been observed by Boswell [10] and others.

Figure 35 also indicates that there may be significant Reynolds number ("scale") effects on leading-edge cavitation inception. Arguments similar to those given here show that leading-edge separation will occur to a greater extent on a model propeller than on its full-scale geosim, as shown in Figs. 41 and 42, when both are operating at the same advance coefficient. Leading-edge sheet cavitation will be inhibited on the model propeller because of the greater extent of the leading edge where the minimum pressure peak has been reduced due to flow separation. This means that model tests should give optimistic predictions of full-scale cavitation behavior, and indeed this often occurs.

Design example

To illustrate the use of the design and analysis procedures presented in this paper we consider here the design of a propeller for a fictitious twin-screw fisheries research vessel. Each propeller must provide a thrust of 4485 N (19 950 lb) at a free-running ship speed of 12 knots. In addition, acoustic considerations require that the propellers be free of leading-edge cavitation when the vessel is towing equipment over the side at 4 knots. The thrust per propeller required in the towing condition is 2260 N (10 050 lb).

Standard lifting-line preliminary design procedures [30, 31]

440   Numerical Methods for Propeller Design

were used to establish the values of the basic propeller parameters given in Table 11. The skew and rake distributions were chosen to minimize problems with unsteady propeller forces. The actual propeller pitch and camber distributions were calculated using the lifting-surface design program; the resulting blade geometry is given in Table 12. A perspective view of this propeller is shown in Fig. 3.

With a propeller geometry available the global analysis program was run at a series of J-values in order to generate a set of open-water curves, shown in Fig. 43. These open-water computations were done with the usual 8×8 global analysis lattice, shown in Fig. 22. The wake alignment procedure was used for all computations (even $J = 0$!) and a viscous drag coefficient of 0.007 was assumed. The reason that the computed open-water curves do not pass directly through the design point is that the viscous pitch correction was employed in the analysis calculations while no viscous effect on lift was included in the design calculations.

The thrust loading coefficient in the towing condition is $K_T/J_A^2 = 2.109$; from the open water curve we see that the towing advance coefficient is therefore $J_A = 0.374$ (113 rpm @ 4 knots).

A detailed analysis of the tip region flow was made at the towing operating condition in order to check on leading-edge flow separation and cavitation. The 12×12 tip region lattice used for these computations is shown in Fig. 23. The viscous leading-edge flow analysis indicates that the flow will remain attached at all points along the leading edge for the full-scale propeller in the towing condition. The cavitation number and computed leading-edge minimum pressure coefficient, both based on rotational speed, are shown as a function of radius in Fig. 44. The computations indicate that the full-scale propeller should have leading-edge cavitation near $r/R = 0.9$. On the other hand, if we consider a model of this propeller 0.3048 m (1.0 ft) in diameter running at 900 rpm in a cavitation tunnel at the same J_A and K_T (at roughly $1/10$ of the full-scale Reynolds number), the viscous leading-edge analysis indicates that leading-edge flow separation should occur outboard of $r/R = 0.83$, substantially reducing the leading-edge suction peak, and therefore reducing cavitation. The estimated leading-edge pressure coefficient for this case is also shown in Fig. 44, and it is seen that a model cavitation test could give very misleading results, indicating that leading-edge cavitation is no problem in the towing condition.

Since the calculations indicate that cavitation will occur in the towing condition, the design will have to be modified. One option is to increase the blade camber, so that the angle-of-attack loading will be reduced at the towing condition. This can be done by designing the propeller to have shock-free entry at some intermediate J-value between the free-running and towing conditions, with the required thrust at the J-value selected being taken from the open-water curve. In this case the free-running condition will have to be analyzed carefully to make sure that face cavitation will not occur. Another possibility is unloading the tip region, but this will entail a loss of efficiency.

The final propeller design will undoubtedly require several passes through the design and analysis procedure to arrive at a satisfactory compromise. The example given here is obviously idealized, since all unsteady effects due to operation in a circumferentially nonuniform wakefield have been ignored. Tip vortex cavitation is probably just as important as leading-edge cavitation in determining the amount of noise generated by the propeller, but its prediction and control are not considered here. However, the example does illustrate how the complementary lifting-surface design and analysis procedures presented in this paper can be used to help the propeller designer make rational design decisions when the propeller must

Table 11   Propeller design parameters

Ship speed	12 knots
Shaft speed	200 rpm
Diameter	2.54 m (8.33 ft)
No. of blades	4
Design K_T	0.187
Expanded area ratio	0.516
Volumetric mean inflow velocity $(1 - w_v)$	0.869
J_s (based on ship speed)	0.730
J_A (based on speed of advance)	0.634
Shaft immersion	2.9 m (9.5 ft)
Lerbs optimum circulation distribution $b = 0.8$ chordwise loading	

work successfully at more than one operating condition. It also highlights the fact that model cavitation tests may yield misleading information because of the low Reynolds number.

Acknowledgments

The authors wish to acknowledge the support received from the National Science Foundation, the Naval Sea Systems Command's General Hydromechanics Research Program, the David W. Taylor Naval Ship Research and Development Center, and the Office of Naval Research during the conduct of the work described in this paper.

Table 12   Blade geometry for example propeller design

```
------------------------- MIT-PBD-10 -------------------------
PROPELLER BLADE DESIGN FOR PRESCRIBED LOAD DISTRIBUTION
RELEASE DATE 03/11/82    COMPUTATION DATE 3/25/82 17*36*11.00
    SAMPLE DESIGN   LERBS OPTIMUM CIRCULATION
```

```
---------------------------BLADE GEOMETRY---------------------------
R/RO      P/D      XS/D      SKEW      C/D      FO/C      TO/D
0.2000   0.8258    0.0       0.0      0.1360   0.0453   0.0330
0.2500   0.9090    0.0026   -6.000    0.1610   0.0482   0.0313
0.3000   0.9337    0.0053   -9.300    0.1840   0.0437   0.0296
0.4000   0.9534    0.0105  -12.300    0.2300   0.0331   0.0263
0.5000   0.9640    0.0158  -12.700    0.2690   0.0253   0.0229
0.6000   0.9495    0.0210  -10.100    0.2950   0.0220   0.0195
0.7000   0.9097    0.0263   -4.400    0.3030   0.0223   0.0161
0.8000   0.8540    0.0316    3.400    0.2820   0.0250   0.0128
0.9000   0.8034    0.0368   11.600    0.2190   0.0282   0.0094
0.9500   0.7745    0.0395   15.200    0.1640   0.0316   0.0077
1.0000   0.6983    0.0421   18.300    0.0020   0.0439   0.0060
```

```
-----INFLOW VELOCITIES-----       TRANS WAKE INDUCED VELOCITIES
R/RO    VX/VS   VR/VS   VT/VS      UANW    UTNW      UAUW    UTUW
0.2000  0.820   0.0     0.0        0.061  -0.166    0.315  -0.569
0.2500  0.825   0.0     0.0        0.127  -0.278    0.335  -0.473
0.3000  0.830   0.0     0.0        0.183  -0.353    0.363  -0.402
0.4000  0.840   0.0     0.0        0.273  -0.414    0.429  -0.317
0.5000  0.850   0.0     0.0        0.338  -0.395    0.483  -0.276
0.6000  0.860   0.0     0.0        0.385  -0.341    0.495  -0.243
0.7000  0.870   0.0     0.0        0.415  -0.289    0.448  -0.192
0.8000  0.880   0.0     0.0        0.402  -0.237    0.365  -0.134
0.9000  0.890   0.0     0.0        0.312  -0.171    0.283  -0.092
0.9500  0.895   0.0     0.0        0.228  -0.129    0.254  -0.083
1.0000  0.900   0.0     0.0        0.112  -0.079    0.238  -0.087
```

```
--------MEAN LINE OFFSETS (F/C)*10**4 AT INPUT RADII--------
%C   0.20 0.25 0.30 0.40 0.50 0.60 0.70 0.80 0.90 0.95 1.00

1.0    16   22   22   18   15   13   14   15   16   18   32
2.5    39   53   53   43   35   32   33   36   38   44   74
5.0    78  101   99   81   66   60   62   68   72   82  135
10.0  151  184  178  144  116  106  108  119  128  144  224
20.0  277  311  292  232  184  165  168  187  205  228  325
30.0  372  401  370  288  226  200  203  226  252  280  384
40.0  431  458  418  321  248  218  221  247  278  309  425
50.0  453  482  437  331  253  220  223  249  282  316  439
60.0  439  473  428  322  243  209  212  237  268  302  422
70.0  386  426  387  291  217  186  188  209  236  267  375
80.0  278  325  298  224  167  141  142  158  178  204  298
90.0  129  169  157  119   88   73   74   84   95  113  181
95.0   55   81   77   58   43   36   36   41   47   58  101
97.5   24   39   37   28   21   17   18   20   23   30   53
99.0    9   15   15   11    8    7    7    8    9   12   22
```

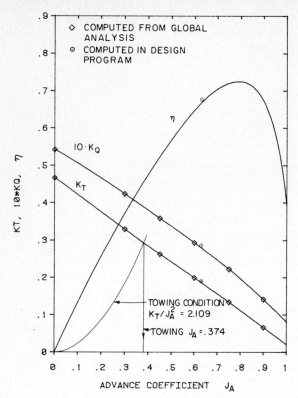

Fig. 43 Calculated open-water curves for example propeller design

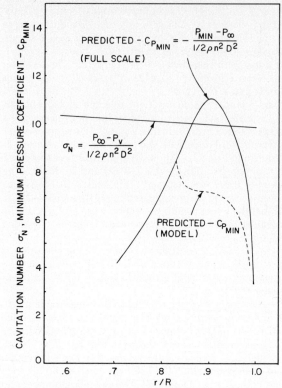

Fig. 44 Cavitation number and leading-edge minimum pressure coefficient versus radius for example propeller at towing condition

References

1 Kerwin, J. E. and Lee, C. S., "Prediction of Steady and Unsteady Marine Propeller Performance by Numerical Lifting Surface Theory," TRANS. SNAME, Vol. 86, 1978.

2 Abbot, I. H. and Von Doenhoff, A. E., *Theory of Wing Sections*, Dover Publications, New York, 1949.

3 Min, K. S., "Numerical and Experimental Methods for the Prediction of Field Point Velocities Around Propeller Blades," MIT Department of Ocean Engineering Report 78-12, Cambridge, Mass., June 1978.

4 Greeley, D. S., "Marine Propeller Blade Tip Flows," MIT Department of Ocean Engineering Report 82-3, Cambridge, Mass., Jan. 1982.

5 Brockett, T. E., "Lifting Surface Hydrodynamics for Design of Rotating Blades," SNAME Propellers '81 Symposium, Virginia Beach, Va., May 1981.

6 Brockett, T. E., "Minimum Pressure Envelopes for Modified NACA-66 Sections with NACA $a = 0.8$ Camber and Buships Type I and Type II Sections," DTNSRDC Report 1780, Bethesda, Md., Feb. 1966.

7 Kerwin, J. E., "Computer Techniques for Propeller Blade Section Design," Second Lips Propeller Symposium, Drunnen, The Netherlands, May 1973.

8 Jones, R. T., "Leading-Edge Singularities in Thin Airfoil Theory," *Journal of the Aeronautical Sciences*, May 1950.

9 Kerwin, J. E., "A Deformed Wake Model for Marine Propellers," MIT Department of Ocean Engineering Report 76-6, Cambridge, Mass., Oct. 1966.

10 Boswell, R. J., "Design, Cavitation Performance, and Open Water Performance of a Series of Research Skewed Propellers," DTNSRDC Report 3339, Bethesda, Md., March 1971.

11 Nelka, J. J., "Experimental Evaluation of a Series of Skewed Propellers with Forward Rake: Open-Water Performance, Cavitation Performance, Field-Point Pressures, and Unsteady Propeller Loading," DTNSRDC Report 4113, Bethesda, Md., July 1974.

12 Kobayashi, S., "Experimental Methods for the Prediction of the Effect of Viscosity on Propeller Performance," MIT Department of Ocean Engineering Report 81-7, Cambridge, Mass., June 1981.

13 Küchemann, D., "Types of Flow on Swept Wings," *Journal of the Royal Aeronautical Society*, Vol. 57, Nov. 1953.

14 Smith, J. H. B., "A Review of Separation in Steady, Three-Dimensional Flow" in *Flow Separation*, AGARD CP-168, 1975.

15 Black, J., "Pressure Distribution and Boundary Layer Investigations on 44 degree Swept-Back Tapered Wing," Aeronautical Research Council CP No. 137, 1953.

16 Garner, H. C., "Low Speed Theoretical and Experimental Aerodynamic Loading on Highly-Swept Curved-Tip Wings of Two Thickness," Aeronautical Research Council R&M No. 3735, Sept. 1972.

17 Garner, H. C. and Bryer, D. W., "Experimental Study of Surface Flow and Part-Span Vortex Layers on Cropped Arrowhead Wing," Aeronautical Research Council R&M No. 3107, April 1957.

18 Garner, H. C. and Cox, D. K., "Surface Oil-Flow Patterns on Wings of Different Leading Edge Radius and Sweepback," Aeronautical Research Council CP No. 583, March 1961.

19 Garner, H. C. and Walsh, D. E., "Pressure Distribution and Surface Flow on 5% and 9% Thick Wings with Curved Tip and 60 degree Sweepback," Aeronautical Research Council R&M No. 3244, Jan. 1960.

20 Woodward, D. S. and Lean, D. E., "The Lift and Stalling Characteristics of a 35 deg. Swept Back Wing Designed to Have Identical Chordwise Pressure Distributions at all Spanwise Stations when Near Maximum Lift," Aeronautical Research Council R&M No. 3721, March 1971.

21 Küchemann, D., "Boundary Layers on Swept Wings—Their Effects and Their Measurements," Royal Aircraft Establishment TN Aero No. 2370, April 1955.

22 Ridder, S. O., "Experimental Studies of the Leading Edge Suction Force," *Proceedings*, International Council of the Aeronautical Sciences, Haifa, Israel, 1974.

23 Stratford, B. S., "Flow in the Laminar Boundary Layer Near Separation," Aeronautical Research Council R&M 3002, 1954.

24 Stratford, B. S., "The Prediction of Separation of the Turbulent Boundary Layer," *Journal of Fluid Mechanics*, Vol. 5, Part I, 1959.

25 Kandil, O. A., Mook, D. T., and Nayfeh, A. H., "Nonlinear Prediction of Aerodynamic Loads on Lifting Surfaces," *Journal of Aircraft*, Vol. 13, No. 1, Jan. 1976.

26 Weber, J. A. *et al*, "A Three-Dimensional Solution of Flows Over Wings with Leading Edge Vortex Separation," *AIAA Journal*,

American Institute of Aeronautics and Astronautics, Vol. 14, No. 3, 1976.

27 Mehrotra, S. C. and Lan, C. E., "A Theoretical Investigation of the Aerodynamics of Low Aspect Ratio Wings with Partial Leading Edge Separation," NASA CR-145304, National Aeronautical and Space Administration, Jan. 1978.

28 Kalman, T. P., Giesing, J. P., and Rodden, W. P., "Spanwise Distribution of Induced Drag in Subsonic Flow by the Vortex Lattice Method," *Journal of Aircraft*, Vol. 7, No. 6, Dec. 1970.

29 Tulinius, J. et al, "Theoretical Prediction of Airplane Stability Derivatives at Subcritical Speeds," North American Rockwell Report NA-72-803, 1972.

30 Eckhardt, M. K. and Morgan, W. B., "A Propeller Design Method," TRANS. SNAME, Vol. 63, 1955.

31 Cox, G. G. and Morgan, W. B., "The Use of Theory in Propeller Design," *Marine Technology*, Vol. 9, No. 4, Oct. 1972.

32 Loukakis, T. A., "A New Theory for the Wake of Marine Propellers," MIT Department of Ocean Engineering Report 71-1, Cambridge, Mass., May 1971.

33 Sampson, R. G., "An Experimental and Theoretical Investigation of the Structure of a Trailing Vortex Wake," *The Aeronautical Quarterly*, Vol. 23, Feb. 1977.

34 Lan, C. E., "A Quasi-Vortex Lattice Method in Thin Wing Theory," *Journal of Aircraft*, Vol. 11, No. 9, Sept. 1974.

35 Lighthill, M. J., "A New Approach to Thin Airfoil Theory," *The Aeronautical Quarterly*, Vol. 3, Nov. 1951.

36 Van Dyke, M. D., "Second Order Subsonic Airfoil Theory Including Edge Effects," NACA Report 1274, National Advisory Committee on Aeronautics, 1955.

Appendix 1

Calculation of trailing vortex wake geometry

The propeller wake is divided into two parts as shown in Fig. 5:

(a) a transition wake region where the contraction and deformation of the slipstream occurs, and

(b) an ultimate wake region which is composed of K concentrated helical tip vortices and a single rolled-up hub vortex.

Although an earlier wake model (Kerwin and Lee [1]) included a strong rolling-up in the transition wake region, laser velocimeter measurements in the MIT propeller tunnel indicate that the trailing vortex wake does not roll up completely, so that the current transition wake model is probably more realistic.

Radius of trailers in transition wake

The variation of radius with axial position of the discrete vortices representing the transition wake is determined by the following set of parameters, chosen in accordance with experimental data:

- radius of rolled-up tip vortices, r_w, in ultimate wake,
- radius of hub vortex at end of transition wake, r_{wh},
- length of transition wake region, x_{tw}, and
- contraction angle of tip vortex as it leaves the blade tip, δ_c.

There will be $M + 1$ trailing vortex lines shed from each blade into the transition wake. Each will originate at the trailing edge at a point matching the corresponding trailing vortex element of the blade grid, and will extend downstream an axial distance x_{tw} measured from the trailing edge.

The first of these, which we will refer to as the hub vortex, is assumed to have a radius varying as a cubic in x, with zero slope at the trailing edge and at x_{tw}. The value of the radius at x_{tw} is specified as r_{wh}. Defining p as the fractional distance from the trailing edge to x_{tw}, the radius of the hub vortex is therefore

$$r(p) = (r(0) - r_{wh})(1 - 3p^2 + 2p^3) + r_{wh} \qquad (27)$$

The $M + 1$st trailing vortex line will be referred to as the tip vortex, which starts at a radius matching the outboard radius of the blade grid, r_t, and ends up at the specified ultimate wake radius r_w. Its initial slope with respect to x is the specified contraction angle δ_c, while its slope and curvature should be zero at the point where it reaches its ultimate radius r_w.

This can be modeled by a cubic by first defining a distance from the trailing edge to the point at which the tip vortex radius becomes constant:

$$x_{rw} = 3(r_t - r_w)/\tan\delta_c \qquad (28)$$

and defining q as the fractional distance from the trailing edge to this point. The tip vortex cubic can then be written as

$$\begin{aligned} r &= r_t + (r_t - r_w)(-3q + 3q^2 - q^3) & 0 \le q \le 1 \\ r &= r_w & q > 1 \end{aligned} \qquad (29)$$

With the radius of the hub and tip vortices defined, it then remains to fill in the intermediate values in a smooth manner. The approach which has been adopted here is to begin with the hub vortex, and to compute the position of each successive vortex line from the relation

$$r_m(p) = \sqrt{r_{m-1}^2(p) + r_m^2(0) - r_{m-1}^2(0)} \qquad (30)$$

which can be thought of as a very crude imposition of continuity, valid if the flow were axsymmetric with a velocity independent of p.

Application of (30) to the outer trailers, however, would result in radii greater than those of the tip vortex, which would not be suitable. This can be avoided by limiting the radial increment between successive trailers to

$$r_m(p) - r_{m-1}(p) \le \left[\frac{r_{m-1}(p)}{r_{m+1}(p)}\right]^2 [r_{m+1}(p) - r_{m-1}(p)] \qquad (31)$$

The introduction of (31) tends to concentrate the outermost trailers with the tip vortex, thus simulating the roll-up process which is known to occur. Figure 4 shows the resulting trailing vortex radii for $M = 8$.

Calculation of ultimate wake pitch

The ultimate wake is assumed to consist of K equally spaced helical tip vortices of strength Γ_t, pitch angle β_w, and radius r_w surrounding a single rolled-up hub vortex of strength $-K \cdot \Gamma_t$. If we examine a point in the ultimate wake sufficiently far from the propeller, it may be safely assumed that the ultimate wake extends to infinity both fore and aft, thus simplifying the geometry of the problem. In a coordinate system rotating with the propeller, the velocity seen at a point on one of the tip vortices consists of the propeller rotational velocity, the inflow velocities, the self-induced velocities due to the helical vortices, and the induced velocity due to the hub vortex. Since the tip vortices are force-free, the total velocity must be tangent to the tip vortex helix at each point. Using this fact, the pitch angle of the ultimate tip vortices may be calculated.

Loukakis [32] considered this problem in detail and noted that the local self-induced velocity of a helical vortex line is infinite. To remove this singularity it is necessary to recognize the existance of a finite core in the tip vortex, over which the vorticity is distributed. Loukakis performed extensive numerical calculations of the self-induced velocities of a set of K symmetrically located, infinitely extended, helical vortex cores, and his results are listed in Table 13. This table gives the axial and tangential self-induced velocities as a function of K and $\tan \beta_w$. The ratio (core radius/helix radius) was selected to be 0.02, as described in the following. All of the induced velocities shown are computed for $r_w = 1$ and $\Gamma_t = 1$. The actual values

Table 13 Self-induced velocities of a set of K equally spaced, infinitely extended helical vortex cores

TAN β_w	K=1 UA	UT	K=2 UA	UT	K=3 UA	UT	K=4 UA	UT	K=5 UA	UT	K=6 UA	UT	K=7 UA	UT
0.10	0.9800	0.0353	1.7169	0.1261	2.4920	0.2664	3.2513	0.2893	4.0256	0.4223	4.8161	0.5077	5.6083	0.5145
0.15	0.7416	0.0200	1.2162	0.1116	1.7158	0.2114	2.2191	0.2784	2.7277	0.3700	3.2455	0.4573	3.7647	0.5179
0.20	0.6234	0.0009	0.9668	0.0931	1.3326	0.1830	1.7059	0.2622	2.0835	0.3459	2.4663	0.4307	2.8502	0.5066
0.25	0.5503	-0.0185	0.8161	0.0748	1.1029	0.1628	1.3978	0.2457	1.6969	0.3286	1.9996	0.4121	2.3041	0.4923
0.30	0.4980	-0.0370	0.7131	0.0576	0.9479	0.1457	1.1907	0.2302	1.4377	0.3134	1.6875	0.3966	1.9391	0.4781
0.35	0.4564	-0.0539	0.6364	0.0419	0.8347	0.1305	1.0405	0.2158	1.2504	0.2996	1.4628	0.3827	1.6770	0.4647
0.40	0.4210	-0.0690	0.5757	0.0277	0.7470	0.1169	0.9254	0.2028	1.1076	0.2870	1.2923	0.3702	1.4786	0.4525
0.45	0.3896	-0.0820	0.5252	0.0153	0.6760	0.1049	0.8333	0.1912	0.9943	0.2757	1.1575	0.3591	1.3223	0.4415
0.50	0.3611	-0.0930	0.4820	0.0047	0.6166	0.0947	0.7574	0.1812	0.9015	0.2659	1.0477	0.3494	1.1954	0.4319
0.60	0.3103	-0.1092	0.4103	-0.0114	0.5215	0.0789	0.6379	0.1657	0.7571	0.2505	0.8782	0.3340	1.0005	0.4166
0.70	0.2665	-0.1189	0.3523	-0.0214	0.4474	0.0688	0.5468	0.1555	0.6487	0.2403	0.7521	0.3237	0.8566	0.4062
0.80	0.2287	-0.1234	0.3043	-0.0266	0.3877	0.0633	0.4747	0.1498	0.5637	0.2343	0.6541	0.3175	0.7454	0.3998
0.90	0.1962	-0.1141	0.2641	-0.0280	0.3386	0.0613	0.4161	0.1474	0.4954	0.2316	0.5758	0.3145	0.6569	0.3966
1.00	0.1686	-0.1221	0.2304	-0.0269	0.2978	0.0619	0.3678	0.1475	0.4394	0.2313	0.5118	0.3139	0.5850	0.3956

of the velocities can be calculated by multiplying the values in the table by Γ_t/r_w.

The velocity diagram at one of the tip vortices is shown in Fig. 45. From this we can see that the pitch angle of the ultimate wake satisfies the implicit equation

$$\tan\beta_w = \frac{V_A(r_w) + \dfrac{\Gamma_t}{r_w} \cdot UA(\tan\beta_w, K)}{\omega r_w + V_T(r_w) + \dfrac{\Gamma_t}{r_w} \cdot UT(\tan\beta_w, K) - \dfrac{K\Gamma_t}{2\pi r_w}}$$

(31)

where

ωr_w = tangential velocity due to propeller rotation
$V_A(r_w)$ = axial inflow velocity at r_w
$V_T(r_w)$ = tangential inflow velocity at r_w
$u_{th} = -K\Gamma_t/2\pi r_w$ = tangential velocity induced by hub vortex
$u_a = (\Gamma_t/r_w) \cdot UA$ = axial velocity induced by helical tip vortices
$u_t = (\Gamma_t/r_w) \cdot UT$ = tangential velocity induced by helical tip vortices

and UA, UT are taken from Table 13. Once Γ_t and r_w are specified, equation (31) may be solved to determine β_w.

It is usually assumed that the trailing vortex wake from a wing completely rolls up into two trailing tip vortices, implying that the circulation of each ultimate tip vortex is equal to the maximum bound circulation around the wing. Detailed measurements behind lifting wings by Sampson [33] show that this is not the case: the circulation of the tip vortices is only 60 to 80 percent of the maximum bound circulation. Similarly, laser velocimeter measurements behind an operating propeller show a weak vortex sheet at intermediate radii quite far downstream. It was found by extensive numerical experimentation that a (core radius/helix radius) ratio of 0.02 and an ultimate tip vortex strength Γ_t of 80 percent of the maximum circulation on the blade yielded predicted ultimate wake pitches in remarkable agreement with experimentally measured values.

Calculation of transition wake pitch

Calculation of the pitch of the transition wake is complicated by the fact that the pitch is allowed to vary in both the radial and downstream directions. The extensive laser velocimeter measurements of propeller vortex wakes by Min [3] and earlier visual measurements by Kerwin [9] indicate that the wake pitch varies smoothly with both radial and axial location. Accordingly, it was considered reasonable to calculate the pitch at a limited number of points in the transition wake and interpolate to obtain the pitch at other locations.

The velocity diagram of any point in the transition wake of the key blade is shown in Fig. 46 in a coordinate system rotating with the propeller. The pitch angle $\beta(x',r)$ in the transition wake is a function of the radius and the distance downstream of the trailing edge, x'. The pitch in the transition wake satisfies the equation

$$\beta(x',r) = \tan^{-1}\left[\frac{V_A(r) + u_a(x',r)}{\omega r + V_T(r) + u_t(x',r)}\right]$$

(32)

where $u_a(x',r)$ and $u_t(x',r)$ are the axial and tangential induced velocities due to the propeller and wake singularity system. The transition wake geometry is correct (force-free) when the induced velocities $u_a(x',r)$ and $u_t(x',r)$ calculated using an assumed pitch distribution $\tilde{\beta}(x',r)$ yield a calculated pitch distribution $\beta(x',r)$ such that $\beta(x',r) = \tilde{\beta}(x',r)$ everywhere. This requires an iterative procedure, which usually converges quite rapidly.

Although the axial extent of the transition wake region is set

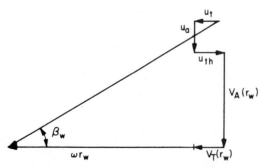

Fig. 45 Velocity diagram at ultimate tip vortex

by x_{tw}, where x_{tw} is typically one propeller radius, the pitch of the wake is allowed to change in the downstream direction until $x' = x_{\text{ult}}$, where x_{ult} is usually set to $1.5R$ based on experimental observations. In determining the transition wake geometry, the axial and tangential induced velocities are calculated at certain points and interpolated at other locations, rather than the pitch angle $\beta(x',r)$ itself. The axial and tangential induced velocities are specified in two planes: "near" wake velocities [$u_{an}(r)$ and $u_{tn}(r)$ at the blade trailing edge] and "ultimate" wake velocities [$u_{au}(r)$ and $u_{tu}(r)$ at $x' = x_{\text{ult}}$]. Note that $u_a(x' = 0,r) = u_{an}(r)$ and $u_a(x' = x_{\text{ult}},r) = u_{au}(r)$. The induced velocities are assumed to vary smoothly in the axial direction according to

$$u_a(x',r) =$$
$$\begin{cases} u_{an}(r) + (u_{au}(r) - u_{an}(r)) \cdot (3\xi - 3\xi^2 + \xi^3), & \xi \leq 1 \\ u_{au}(r) & , \quad \xi > 1 \end{cases} \quad (33)$$

where $\xi = x'/x_{\text{ult}}$. Similar expressions hold for the tangential velocities. The form of equation (33) was chosen after examining Min's [3] laser measurements of propeller vortex wakes.

The values of induced velocities at $x' = x_{\text{ult}}$ are taken from the ultimate wake pitch calculation:

$$u_{au}(r_w) = u_a$$
$$u_{tu}(r_w) = u_t + u_{tH}$$
$$u_{au}(r_{wh}) = \frac{0.75\,K\Gamma_t}{r_w \tan\beta_w} \quad (34)$$
$$u_{tu}(r_{wh}) = \frac{-0.75\,K\Gamma_t}{r_{wh}}$$

The factor of 0.75 was included after comparing computed wake velocities with experimental measurements [3].

Values of induced velocities are calculated at points just behind the trailing edge and at $p = 0.7$. Using these values and the velocities from equation (34), the wake convection velocities may be calculated at any (x',r) location by using equation (33) for axial interpolation and spline cubics for radial interpolation.

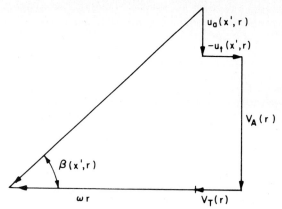

Fig. 46 Velocity diagram in transition wake

Figure 47 illustrates the variation of axial induced velocities at the key blade transition wake as a function of x' and r.

Most of the discrete trailers in the transition wake model are actually representing part of a vortex sheet, and it is reasonable to disregard the local self-induced velocity of the curved vortex line. At the tip of the blade, however, the vortex sheet rolls up considerably even before the trailing edge of the blade is reached, so that the outermost discrete trailer leaving the blade is actually representing a vortex core. In this case it is correct to assume a viscous core size and calculate the local self-induced velocity of the trailer leaving the tip. If a viscous core radius of 0.1 percent of the propeller radius is assumed, the calculated pitch of the tip vortex just behind the blade tip is in good agreement with Min's [3] measurements for several propellers over a range of advance coefficients.

It is found that the computed induced velocities in the transition wake near the hub and tip of the blade are sensitive to the number of trailers used to represent the transition wake. Any numerical scheme exhibiting this kind of behavior is usually dismissed as being unreliable. However, if the present scheme is used with eight spanwise panels on the key blade

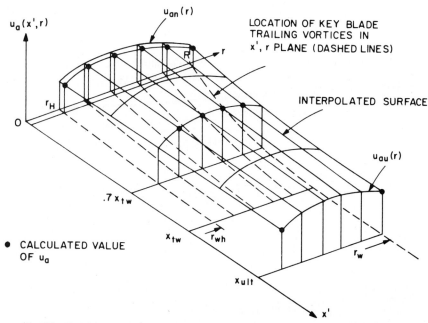

Fig. 47 Variation of axial convection velocities with radius and distance downstream

(nine trailing vortices), the computed results are reasonable and in good agreement with the experiments of Min [3] for a variety of different propellers and advance coefficients. Therefore, the current wake alignment scheme is used only with eight spanwise panels on the blade. Once the induced velocities in the wake are calculated from this analysis, they may be used to specify the wake geometry for use with any desired number of spanwise panels on the key blade.

Appendix 2

Tabulation of chord load and thickness factors

N	SV(N)	SC(N)	GF(B=.8)	GF(A=.8)	SF	SCFACT
1	0.00961	0.03806	0.03532	0.04224	0.36092	0.38111
2	0.08427	0.14645	0.11464	0.12029	0.33636	0.45075
3	0.22221	0.30866	0.18043	0.18003	0.23797	0.47960
4	0.40245	0.50000	0.21727	0.21235	0.05645	0.50000
5	0.59754	0.69134	0.21780	0.21235	-0.18424	0.52040
6	0.77778	0.85355	0.17223	0.18003	-0.34586	0.54925
7	0.91573	0.96194	0.05957	0.05068	-0.32799	0.61890
8	0.99039	1.00000	0.00273	0.00203	-0.13361	1.12869
1	0.00428	0.01704	0.01501	0.01888	0.24281	0.37769
2	0.03806	0.06699	0.05033	0.05536	0.23478	0.44324
3	0.10332	0.14645	0.08485	0.08807	0.21968	0.46723
4	0.19562	0.25000	0.11430	0.11478	0.17546	0.48108
5	0.30866	0.37059	0.13566	0.13366	0.10538	0.49122
6	0.43474	0.50000	0.14688	0.14344	0.01358	0.50000
7	0.56526	0.62941	0.14703	0.14344	-0.09814	0.50878
8	0.69134	0.75000	0.13701	0.13366	-0.19108	0.51892
9	0.80438	0.85355	0.10341	0.11226	-0.24088	0.53277
10	0.89668	0.93301	0.05148	0.04550	-0.23277	0.55677
11	0.96194	0.98296	0.01349	0.01054	-0.16788	0.62230
12	0.99572	1.00000	0.00055	0.00040	-0.06095	1.12662
1	0.00241	0.00961	0.00816	0.01068	0.18336	0.37651
2	0.02153	0.03806	0.02767	0.03164	0.17756	0.44070
3	0.05904	0.08427	0.04774	0.05139	0.17383	0.46324
4	0.11349	0.14645	0.06668	0.06916	0.16253	0.47544
5	0.18280	0.22221	0.08328	0.08427	0.13750	0.48359
6	0.26430	0.30866	0.09659	0.09614	0.10047	0.48983
7	0.35486	0.40245	0.10588	0.10432	0.05595	0.49511
8	0.45099	0.50000	0.11065	0.10849	0.00051	0.50000
9	0.54901	0.59754	0.11072	0.10849	-0.06368	0.50489
10	0.64514	0.69134	0.10647	0.10432	-0.12056	0.51017
11	0.73570	0.77778	0.09673	0.09614	-0.16267	0.51642
12	0.81720	0.85355	0.07288	0.07702	-0.18319	0.52456
13	0.88650	0.91573	0.04330	0.03924	-0.17860	0.53676
14	0.94096	0.96194	0.01861	0.01517	-0.14939	0.55930
15	0.97847	0.99039	0.00447	0.00341	-0.09901	0.62349
16	0.99759	1.00000	0.00017	0.00013	-0.03460	1.12593
1	0.00154	0.00616	0.00508	0.00685	0.14741	0.37597
2	0.01382	0.02447	0.01733	0.02038	0.14272	0.43954
3	0.03806	0.05450	0.03022	0.03340	0.14109	0.46144
4	0.07368	0.09549	0.04290	0.04561	0.13726	0.47296
5	0.11980	0.14645	0.05479	0.05669	0.12880	0.48036
6	0.17528	0.20611	0.06542	0.06638	0.11270	0.48573
7	0.23875	0.27300	0.07442	0.07443	0.08996	0.48999
8	0.30866	0.34549	0.08145	0.08065	0.06360	0.49362
9	0.38328	0.42178	0.08627	0.08488	0.03262	0.49689
10	0.46077	0.50000	0.08873	0.08702	-0.00446	0.50000
11	0.53923	0.57822	0.08876	0.08702	-0.04601	0.50311
12	0.61672	0.65451	0.08658	0.08488	-0.08397	0.50638
13	0.69134	0.72699	0.08226	0.08065	-0.11535	0.51001
14	0.76125	0.79389	0.07275	0.07443	-0.13736	0.51427
15	0.82472	0.85355	0.05600	0.05817	-0.14741	0.51965
16	0.88020	0.90451	0.03696	0.03396	-0.14447	0.52704
17	0.92632	0.94550	0.02005	0.01680	-0.12872	0.53855
18	0.96194	0.97553	0.00810	0.00636	-0.10145	0.56046
19	0.98618	0.99384	0.00187	0.00141	-0.06473	0.62405
20	0.99846	1.00000	0.00007	0.00005	-0.02224	1.12560

SV(N) = chordwise position of vortex/source elements from (3)

SC(N) = chordwise position of control points, from (3)

GF(B = 0.8) = vortex weighting factors for Brockett analytical approximation to $a = 0.8$ chord load

GF(A = 0.8) = vortex weighting factors for NACA $a = 0.8$ chord load

SF = source weighting factors for DTNSRDC modified NACA 66 thickness form

Appendix 3

Leading-edge suction

Leading-edge suction force in thin-wing theory

Thin-wing theory is used in the present work to determine the loading on the blades. This theory assumes that the effects of loading and thickness are locally separable and that the loading and thickness problems may be solved by placing singularities on the camberline instead of the airfoil surface. These assumptions work quite well everywhere over the foil except for the leading edge, where singularities occur.

Consider the two-dimensional lifting flow over a flat plate as shown in Fig. 48. The vortex distribution $\gamma(x)$ must be such that there is no normal velocity on the plate, and $\gamma(x)$ must go to zero at the trailing edge (Kutta condition). The boundary condition can be written as

$$w(x) = \frac{1}{2\pi} \oint^c \frac{\gamma(x')\,dx'}{x - x'} = U_\infty \sin\alpha, \qquad 0 < x \leq c \quad (35)$$

where $w(x)$ is the normal perturbation velocity. The solution for the vortex distribution is

$$\gamma(x) = 2U_\infty \sin\alpha \sqrt{\frac{c - x}{x}} \quad (36)$$

The pressure jump across the foil will yield a force in the z-direction only. Since lift and drag are defined relative to the undisturbed free stream, the integration of normal pressures gives

$$\begin{aligned} C_L &= 2\pi \sin\alpha \cos\alpha \\ C_D &= 2\pi \sin^2\alpha \end{aligned} \quad (37)$$

But in two-dimensional ideal flow, the drag should be zero. The discrepancy lies in the disregard of the leading-edge suction force.

From equation (36), the vortex distribution is singular at the leading edge like $(x)^{-1/2}$. Define a leading-edge singularity parameter C as

$$C \equiv \lim_{x \to 0} \left\{ \gamma(x) \left(\frac{x}{c}\right)^{1/2} \right\} = 2U_\infty \sin\alpha \quad (38)$$

Then the suction force (in the $-x$ direction) is given by

$$F_s = \pi\rho c \frac{C^2}{4} \quad (39)$$

Adding the normal pressure and suction force contributions

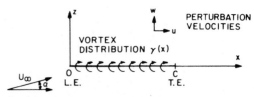

Fig. 48 Two-dimensional flat plate at angle of attack

Numerical Methods for Propeller Design

together and retaining only second-order terms, one obtains

$$C_L = 2\pi \sin\alpha \cos\alpha$$
$$C_D = 0 \qquad (40)$$

as expected.

In thin-airfoil theory this finite leading-edge suction force is the result of an infinitely low pressure at the leading edge (due to the infinitely high velocity) acting over a zero-thickness leading edge. In reality this same force arises on thin foils from very low pressures acting on small leading-edge radii. For very thick foils the suction force is actually distributed over a considerable extent of the nose region, so that the term "leading-edge suction" is somewhat misleading. However, for the thin sections near the tip of propeller blades, leading-edge suction force is a very useful concept.

Calculation of leading-edge suction

In order to determine the leading-edge suction force it is necessary to compute the parameter C:

$$C \equiv \lim_{x \to 0} \left\{ \gamma(x) \left(\frac{x}{c}\right)^{1/2} \right\} \qquad (38)$$

While this could be estimated from any numerical solution for the vortex distribution $\gamma(x)$, Lan [34] discovered that if the vortices and control points in a vortex lattice scheme were arranged using cosine chordwise spacing (as in the present paper), then the parameter C can be determined by computing the *total* upwash at a leading-edge control point for both 2D and 3D wings:

$$C = \frac{1}{N} \cdot \text{total upwash} \qquad (41)$$

where N is the number of vortices over the chord. The suction force per unit length of leading edge is then given by

$$F_s = \pi \rho c \frac{C^2}{4 \cos\Lambda} \qquad (42)$$

where Λ is the leading sweep angle. A detailed derivation may be found in Greeley [4].

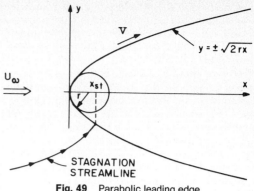

Fig. 49 Parabolic leading edge

Parabolic leading edges

The infinite velocities around leading edges predicted by thin-airfoil theory do not occur because of finite leading-edge radii. Lighthill [35] and Van Dyke [36] formulated corrections to thin-airfoil theory so that surface velocities may be accurately calculated near the nose of a foil, these corrections being equivalent to considering the flow around a parabola at an angle of attack. For the propeller case it is convenient to specify the surface velocities in terms of the position of the stagnation point rather than the angle of attack of the parabola.

As shown in [4] the surface velocity near the nose can be expressed as

$$\frac{V}{V_\infty} = \frac{\sqrt{2x/r} \pm \sqrt{2x_{st}/r}}{\sqrt{1 + 2x/r}} \qquad (43)$$

where x_{st} is the position of the stagnation point and r is the leading-edge radius, as in Fig. 49. The stagnation point location is given by

$$\frac{x_{st}}{r} = \frac{C_s}{2\pi} \qquad (44)$$

where C_s is the leading-edge suction force coefficient defined by equation (20), valid for both 2D and 3D wings.

Discussion

Gilbert Dyne,[4] Visitor

Let me first congratulate the authors on a very interesting and stimulating paper. It gives a clear description of the advanced design and analysis methods developed at M.I.T. and its treatment of the leading edge vortex separation and the local tip flow problem is certainly of great importance.

I should however like to comment on some of the assumptions made in the paper. As for the effective wake in which the propeller is working, the authors assume that it is constant in the axial direction. This implies that the axial component of inflow velocity V_A is the same in the ultimate wake as at the propeller plane, which is a considerable simplification. Due to the propeller-induced axial velocities the nominal wake is transformed into the effective wake at the propeller plane. This transformation continues, however, also behind this plane and the final wake far behind the propeller is therefore lower than the effective wake. This is especially true if the propeller is working in the stern region of a body creating both a displacement (potential) and a friction wake. The propeller and its slipstream are in this case surrounded by an accelerating flow, which has a large influence upon the contraction and thus

on the pitch of the trailing vortices. The proposal made in the paper to use parameters based on observations in uniform flow in a cavitation tunnel when determining the trailing vortex geometry seems therefore questionable.

The hypothesis that the free vortex sheets roll up in concentrated tip and hub vortices at a small distance behind the propeller was simultaneously put forward by M.I.T. in the United States and IFFM in Poland around 1970. As I told Prof. Kerwin already some years ago, I have difficulty in accepting this hypothesis, the reasons being twofold: First, in the ultimate wake, where the vortex system is assumed to have rolled up completely, the flow between the tip and hub vortices must then be vortex free and the mean induced axial velocity independent of the radius. All measurements I have seen indicate, however, that the induced axial velocity is varying in the radial direction in a similar way far behind and at the propeller. This implies that there is vorticity at almost all radii of the slipstream and not only in the tip and hub vortices. Further, the fact that the circulation is varying in the radial direction means that the mean increase in total head at the propeller disk is different for different radii. If the roll-up hypothesis is accepted, the mean total head is constant in the ultimate wake and equal to the maximum value at the propeller. There must exist then, in the

[4] Swedish Maritime Research Centre (SSPA), Göteborg, Sweden.

transit region behind the propeller, a mechanism which increases the total head for almost all radii from a lower value immediately behind the propeller to a higher value in the ultimate wake. I find it very difficult to imagine that such a mechanism exists.

It is therefore interesting to note both that recent measurements at M.I.T. "indicate that the trailing vortex wake does not roll up completely" and that measurements behind lifting wings show that "the circulation of the tip vortices is only 60 to 80 percent of the maximum bound circulation." It is certainly true that the modified roll-up assumption used by the authors simplifies and improves the calculation of the induced velocities at the propeller, but it is doubtful if it gives a correct mathematical model of the propeller slipstream, even if the viscosity is ignored.

P. Gabrielsen,[5] Visitor, and A. J. Myklebust, Member

The high quality of work carried out by Dr. Greeley and Prof. Kerwin at M.I.T. is again found in this excellent paper.

Having had the opportunity to utilize the present computer programs at M.I.T., it should be said that these programs are both clearly and logically constructed and at same time easy to use.

Our comments concern the viscous leading-edge flow analysis and the modeling of tip region separated flow. The authors have indicated that this model needs considerable improvement and that a semi-empirical approach to setting the free sheet geometry is probably the best way to proceed. We agree with the authors that free sheet geometry should be considered and feel that effort should be concentrated on a model where this sheet is rolled up just behind the leading edge to form a leading-edge vortex or a part span vortex which is allowed to pass over the blade surface. In any case an improved model may result in an increase in thrust coefficient K_T and therefore a widening of the gap between measured and calculated openwater results. It also seems reasonable to conclude that this lack of roll-up and restriction to path of constant radius will exaggerate the difference in the model and full-scale prediction of the chordwise pressure distribution in the design example presented.

Further, the authors state that the differences between experiments are disturbing. In a recent investigation by DnV [37] (additional references follow some discussions), a similar trend was found. At low J-values there was a pronounced increase in thrust and torque coefficients, K_T and K_Q, with increasing Reynold's number whereas the effect on efficiency was small. At design J, however, increasing Reynold's number resulted in only small changes in K_T and K_Q with a more significant change in efficiency. In this context it is the discussers' opinion that differences in the extent of laminar and turbulent boundary layers may be inadequate to explain the discrepancies between the differing experimental results. However, the question of boundary layer separation should also be addressed.

Several investigations with flow visualization tests show the occurrence of a so-called critical radius on the suction side. Beyond this critical radius the flow is fully turbulent from leading edge. The position of the critical radius is found to be almost independent of the blade Reynold's number, but strongly dependent on the propeller loading and geometry. The critical radius increases with increasing J-value. The authors observed a similar trend for the leading-edge separation radius. Do the authors see any link between their observation on leading-edge separation point and part span vortex, and the so-called critical radius found by flow visualization tests?

Additional reference

37 Fagerjord, O. and Andresen, K., "Are the Existing Methods to Obtain Maximum Propulsion Efficiency Appropriate?" Presented at the SNAME Ship Cost and Energy '82 Symposium, 1982.

R. E. Henderson,[6] Visitor

Dr. Greeley and Prof. Kerwin have presented a very important assessment of the use of numerical methods for the design and analysis of propellers in a steady flow. This is particularly true regarding the development of viscous flow corrections to the inviscid flow design and analysis model. The description of the physics of leading-edge viscous flows on swept propeller blades is a very useful contribution.

The use of a lifting-surface model for the design and/or analysis of a marine propeller leads to the representation of the blade surfaces by a distribution of mathematical singularities and the eventual calculation of the forces on the modeled blade surfaces. The calculation of blade forces is a logical approach since the design is specified by the requirement of producing a certain magnitude of steady thrust. This propeller thrust is the reaction to the force which acts on the fluid due to the change in momentum of the fluid as it passes through the propeller and the pressure field on it. It is therefore possible to use a different approach for the design of marine propellers by finding a solution to the momentum equations describing the fluid motion. This so-called turbomachinery or flow field approach is used extensively in the design and analysis of pumps and compressors.

My questions to the authors are concerned with the use of this flow field approach to validate the model of the trailing vortex wake used in the lifting-surface model. Figure 3 presents the calculated axial and tangential components of the wake convected velocity at the blade trailing edge and in the ultimate wake. Have calculations been done to demonstrate that the laws of conservation of mass and angular momentum are satisfied between the blade trailing edge and ultimate wake? How does the propeller torque calculated by integration of Euler's turbomachinery equation, which relates the ideal fluid torque and the change in angular momentum across the propeller, compare with the lifting-surface torque prediction?

The lifting-surface model discussed by the authors has been demonstrated to give very good agreement with experiments for a propeller operated in a uniform radial and circumferential inlet flow. It is stated that the method can also be used in an axisymmetric effective wake which includes axial, tangential and radial velocity components. Do the authors mean that there can be radial variations of these components, such as would be experienced with a propeller operated in a hull boundary layer? If so, can the authors estimate the magnitude of the radial variations which precludes the use of this irrotational lifting-surface model in a rotational inlet flow?

The viscous pitch correction presented by equation (17) is equivalent to the so-called deviation angle correction, δ, used in the design of axial-flow compressors and pumps. The general form of δ is

$$\delta = m \text{ (camber angle) [space-to-chord ratio]}^n$$

where m and n are empirically determined constants [38]. Have the authors compared their correction with the axial-flow compressor correction?

Finally, are the authors aware of experimental data which describe the thrust, torque and cavitation of skewed propellers as a function of Reynolds number (R_n) and/or the amount of leading-edge skew? The explanation of the leading-edge separation and vortex formation suggests that skewed blades are more sensitive to R_n than radial blades. Do the authors agree?

[5] Det norske Veritas (DnV), Høvik, Norway.

[6] Applied Research Laboratory, Pennsylvania State University, State College, Pa.

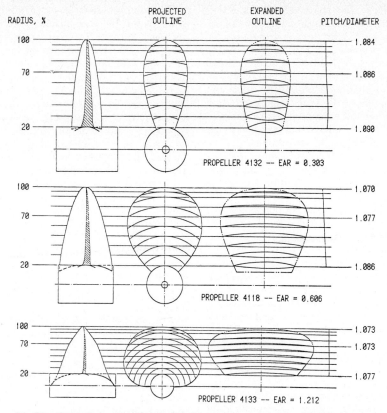

Fig. 50   Expanded area ratio propeller series (all propellers have three blades)

Additional reference

38   Horlock, J. H., *Axial Flow Compressors, Fluid Mechanics and Thermodynamics*, Robert E. Krieger Publishing Co., Huntington, N. Y., 1973.

Donald H. Fuhs, Member

[The views expressed herein are the opinions of the discusser and not necessarily those of the Department of Defense or the Department of the Navy.]

The authors have presented excellent methods for designing propellers and for predicting steady propeller performance. This discussion addresses only the steady propeller performance portion of the paper.

The propeller analysis given in this paper for predicting global forces has been independently evaluated and compared with other methods of analysis by the staff of the David Taylor Naval Ship R&D Center (DTNSRDC). The other methods of analysis evaluated at DTNSRDC are computer codes PINV1 [39], PINV2 [40], PINV4,[7] and PUF-2 [42] from the Massachusetts Institute of Technology, and PLEXVAN [43] from the Stevens Institute of Technology. Computer code GHAC-P [44], developed by Vorus & Associates, Inc. was not available at the time of the investigation. The theoretical formulation of each of these computer codes was evaluated. Predictions of steady thrust and torque were compared with measured data, for propellers having systematic variations in geometry, and operating in open water. These propellers include variations in skew (DTNSRDC Models 4381, 4382, 4383, and 4384) [45], warp (DTNSRDC Models 4497 and 4498) [46], expanded area ratio (DTNSRDC Models 4118, 4132, and 4133) [47], and thickness (DTNSRDC Model 4119) [47]. The geometry of the

expanded area ratio series propellers is given in Fig. 50 of this discussion. Some nonoptimum, wake-adapted propellers operating in open water were also used to perform the correlations at DTNSRDC. These independent calculations verify the predictions shown in Figs. 14 through 19 of the paper for the skew and warp series propellers.

Figure 51 of this discussion shows the correlations of measured and predicted open water performance for DTNSRDC Model 4118, which is the baseline for the expanded area ratio

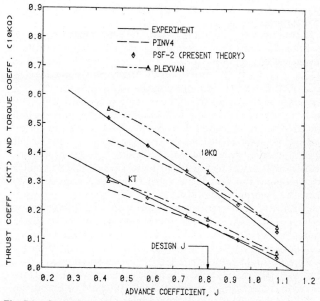

Fig. 51   Correlation of predicted and measured performance in open water for Propeller 4118

---

[7] It appears that the only documentation for PINV4 that has been formally published consists of a brief description in reference [41] of this discussion.

and thickness series propellers. The points identified as PSF-2 are predictions made using the method presented by the authors. The data shown in Fig. 51 are typical of those for the propellers in the expanded area ratio and thickness series. From this independent study at DTNSRDC, it was concluded that the theory presented by the authors is the best overall of those methods evaluated for predicting total steady thrust and torque based on considerations of the analytical formulation and correlations of calculated and measured performance.

Sensitivity studies at MIT [42] indicate that wake pitch has an important influence on predicted steady propeller performance. The method presented in this paper aligns the free vortex lines with the local flow field, including the calculated induced velocities. This should be an important advantage over other performance analysis programs that do not align the free vortex lines with the flow. The wake alignment calculations are an iterative process. For the majority of cases examined at DTNSRDC, the wake alignment calculations converged near design advance coefficient, and the final predictions of thrust and torque agreed favorably with experimental data. However, in a few cases the wake alignment calculations did not converge. When the alignment calculations did not converge, it was usually for low advance coefficient, corresponding to a high thrust loading coefficient and large induced velocities. Lack of convergence occurred more frequently for wake-adapted, nonoptimum propellers operating in open water, than for optimum propellers designed for uniform flow. Also, lack of convergence occurred more frequently when the axial extent of the transition wake, x_{tw} (input parameter TWLEN) was larger than one propeller radius. Sometimes a run that had not converged could be made to converge by using a coarser grid spacing in the spanwise direction on blades other than the key blade and the preceding blade. At the end of an iteration, the induced velocities are adjusted by a damping factor, to determine the induced velocities used to set the wake pitch for the next iteration. The purpose of this damping factor is to speed convergence. However, changing the magnitude of the damping factor does not necessarily cause unconverged runs to converge. Would the authors please comment on what they believe to be causing nonconvergence, and what can be done to correct the problem? When the alignment calculations converge, the final predictions of thrust and torque appear to be relatively insensitive to the induced velocities used to begin the iterations, for the limited number of cases examined. It is emphasized that the majority of wake alignment calculations converged.

As shown in Fig. 5 of the paper, the free vortex lines at intermediate radii are terminated at the end of the transition wake. The free vortex lines are aligned with the local flow field, so that a fluid particle, on the free vortex sheet, leaving the transition wake and entering the ultimate wake may experience a sudden change in the strength of its vorticity. This is an apparent violation of Kelvin's theorem for conservation of circulation. Granted, Kelvin's theorem is derived for an ideal fluid acted on by conservative forces, and viscous effects are generally important in the wake behind propellers. However, it should be possible to devise a wake model in which the trailing vortex lines do not roll up completely, and still satisfy Kelvin's theorem rigorously.

Sensitivity studies performed by the staff at DTNSRDC using the method presented by the authors indicate that the predicted performance depends on the radius of the ultimate wake, r_w (input parameter RULT), and the contraction angle of the tip vortex, δ_c (input parameter DCD). The recommended values for these parameters appear to be based on measurements for propellers operating in uniform flow. It would be highly desirable to experimentally determine the influence of a sheared onset flow on wake deformation.

There appears to be an error in the top line of equation (3) of the paper. This equation gives the chordwise positions of the bound vortices, $S_v(n)$, and control points, $S_c(i)$. As written, it appears that many of the bound vortices have the same chordwise position as control points, since $S_v(n)$ is equal to $S_c(i)$ whenever $(n-1)$ is equal to i. For example, $S_v(2)$ is equal to $S_c(1)$. The tabulated values of $S_c(i)$ given in the table in Appendix 2 can be computed using the equation given for $S_c(i)$ in equation (3). However, the values of $S_v(n)$ computed using equation (3) are different from the values given in the table. According to equation (3), there should be a bound vortex at the leading edge, whereas there is no vortex at the leading edge listed in the table in Appendix 2.

I would like to end this discussion by congratulating the authors for having developed a lifting-surface theory that has proven to be of considerable value in analyzing steady propeller performance.

Additional references

39 Cummings, D. E., "Numerical Prediction of Propeller Characteristics," *Journal of Ship Research*, Vol. 17, No. 1, March 1973, pp. 12–18.
40 Tsao, S.-K. S., "Documentation of Programs for the Analysis of Performance and Spindle Torque of Controllable Pitch Propellers," MIT Report 75-8, Cambridge, Mass., May 1975.
41 Frydenlund, O. and Kerwin, J. E., "The Development of Numerical Methods for the Computation of Unsteady Propeller Forces," *Norwegian Maritime Research*, Vol. 5, No. 2, 1977, pp. 17–28.
42 Kerwin, J. E., and Lee, C. S., "Predictions of Steady and Unsteady Marine Propeller Performance by Numerical Lifting-Surface Theory," TRANS. SNAME, Vol. 86, 1978, pp. 218–253.
43 Tsakonas, S. et al, "Blade Pressure Distribution for a Moderately Loaded Propeller," Davidson Laboratory, Stevens Institute of Technology Report SIT-DL-80-9-2063, Hoboken, N. J., Sept. 1980.
44 "Evaluation of an Alternative Lifting Surface Model for the Analysis of Marine Propeller Performance," Vorus & Associates, Inc., VAI-82-002, March 1982.
45 Boswell, R. J., "Design, Cavitation Performance and Open Water Performance of a Series of Research Skewed Propellers," DTNSRDC Report 3339, Bethesda, Md., March 1971.
46 Nelka, J. J., "Experimental Evaluation of a Series of Skewed Propellers with Forward Rake," DTNSRDC Report 4113, Bethesda, Md., July 1974.
47 Denny, S. B., "Cavitation and Open-Water Performance Tests of a Series of Propellers Designed by Lifting-Surface Methods," DTNSRDC Report 2878, Bethesda, Md., Sept. 1968.

Terry E. Brockett, Member

[The views expressed herein are the opinions of the discusser and not necessarily those of the Department of Defense or the Department of the Navy.]

The authors deserve our congratulations for this fine paper describing improved numerical solutions for both the design and performance prediction problems. These solutions are complex and include elements of both theoretical and empirical considerations. For the past two decades, we at the DTNSRDC have used the computer codes developed by Prof. Kerwin and his students in our design work with considerable success.

Although not stated in the paper, the method appears to be based on a mathematical identity giving a specification of a field vector in terms of singularities integrated over the bounding surface (see, for example, Phillips [48]). The surface integrals are approximated by the thin-wing assumptions and then reduced to the sum of integrals over smaller surface elements or panels. These integrals over the panel elements are approximated by a vortex/source lattice representation of the continuous distributions. The geometry of this lattice arrangement is clearly described in the text but I could not find an analytical expression of the vorticity or source strengths. The vorticity strength described in equations (4) and (6) would be in the direction tangent to the constant fraction of chord lines if continuous functions were being employed (see, for example, reference [5]). Can the authors describe the steps in going from the general expressions for the continuous source and vortex distributions to the lattice approximations, including error terms? A similar question arises relative to the approximation for the loads on the blade. The loads are defined fundamentally by an integration of a continuous pressure distribution over the blade. The authors describe several attempts at defining the lattice equivalent of these loads. Is there a direct relationship between the continuous integrals and the lattice sums to obtain loads, and can any error term be defined?

A highly desirable property of any design method is that the specified geometry be such as to produce the required thrust and torque. Table 9 indicates that the thrust predicted by the lifting-surface method increased about 5 percent relative to the thrust defined by lifting-line theory. For the Wageningen B-Screw Series (van Lammeren et al [49]), five-bladed propellers of similar area ratio would have about a 5 percent change in thrust for a 1 percent change in pitch ratio. The thrust of NSRDC Propeller 4498 at the design condition is about 15 percent greater than the design value of $K_T = 0.213$. At $r/R = 0.6$ and $r/R = 0.8$, the pitch in Table 8(a) is about 1 and 2 percent less, respectively, than that for Propeller 4498. Hence there is reason to expect the thrust prediction to be close to the experimental value if the propeller were manufactured and tested. However, as noted in the author's closure to reference [5], a highly skewed propeller was manufactured to the specifications derived from that method and the experimental loads agreed with the predictions based on both lifting-line theory and the first-order lifting-surface theory. The trends for change of load with change in pitch were considerably different than trends from the Wageningen B-Screw Series. Hence, experimental confirmation of the predicted loads is highly desirable.

The experimental/empirical data presented in the paper are of two overlapping kinds: summary/comparative with other information and that used to formulate concepts for inclusion into the mathematical model. These data lead to many questions:

1. Have powering tests in the tunnel been conducted at the same values of Reynolds number as the DTNSRDC experiments to ensure that tunnel blockage is not responsible for the minor differences in performance presented in Figs. 14 to 19?

2. Do the authors have recommendations as to how some of their empirical constants vary with Reynolds number?

3. Has the rich literature of the International Towing Tank Conference Proceedings been examined to evaluate model and full-scale performance differences in both the powering and cavitation areas?

4. Have any data for nonuniform flow been included in the specification of the separated flow geometry, including the shed vortex sheet?

5. The pitch of the shed vortex sheet is aligned with the local flow but the radial contraction is to be assigned. Can the authors describe the problems that arise when the contraction is also obtained with wake alignment?

6. Can the authors describe the reason that the point where leading-edge separation occurs is also the point of minimum pressure (and hence the first point to cavitate)?

In addition to these general questions, I have some observations about the details presented. Not all of the data presented in Tables 6 and 7 are consistent. Can more information be given about the trends in the convergence of the data in Table 8? Are the thrust and torque values in Table 9 for the contracted wake model? What are the differences in loads (both global and local values near the tip) if the wake is or is not contracted? Are run times available for the sample cases

presented? There appears to be a typographical error in equation (9) (V_l missing) and Fig. 10 (c missing). Are the lengths of the transition wakes in the hub and tip region independent? What is the basis for equation (28) defining the length of the transition region? In Figs. 37 and 38, the separated flow is modeled by vortices trailing aft from the leading edge; however my own observations, data in references [10] and [11], some of the ITTC literature, and Fig. 25 suggest that the separation vorticity is convected along the leading edge, as in the delta wing model. Can the authors describe the observations in support of the vortex trajectories they employ?

Finally, I note the importance of the leading-edge radius as defined in a cross section normal to the leading edge. To compute this quantity, it must be related to the known value of leading-edge radius for the two-dimensional blade section, r_{2D}. For the NACA 66 (Mod) thickness distribution, the leading edge radius is

$$r_{2D}/D = 0.448 \cdot (t/c)^2 \cdot \frac{c}{D}$$

To define the leading-edge radius for the section normal to the propeller outline in terms of this blade-section radius of curvature, a two-step process is required. The first step is to determine the radius of curvature at the leading edge of a section defined in a plane that contains the cross product of the radial and chordwise vectors at the leading edge and the intersection of the normal plane and plane defined by the radial and chordwise vectors at the leading edge. Let the direction along this intersection be e_i. This is equivalent to rotating the cutting plane about a directed line segment at the leading edge, and Meusnier's theory (see for example, Rutherford, [50]) states that the leading-edge radius will be increased by the inverse of the cosine of the angle between these two planes (let this angle be θ). This is similar to a chordwise shrinking (by the factor $\cos\theta$) with local offsets fixed. Next the leading-edge radius is defined for a section in a plane rotated about the intersection of the previous two planes (that is, rotated about e_i) to align it with the plane normal to the leading edge. This is equivalent to a thickness reduction with unchanged chordwise distances and hence the leading-edge radius will be decreased by the square of the cosine of the rotation angle (let this second rotation angle be δ). Thus one has

$$r_n = r_{2D} \cos^2\delta/\cos\theta$$

If the order of rotations were inverted, the general form of this equation would be preserved but the angles would be slightly different. The angles θ and δ can be computed from the components of the vector tangent to the leading edge. As described in reference [5], this is the vector $\partial s/\partial x_R$ at the leading edge. Can the authors give some details of their calculation of the leading-edge radius r_n?

Additional references

48   Phillips, H. B., *Vector Analysis*, Wiley, New York, 1933.
49   van Lammeren, W. P. A. et al, "The Wageningen B-Screw Series," Trans. SNAME, Vol. 77, 1969.
50   Rutherford, D. E., *Vector Methods*, Oliver and Boyd, Edinburgh and London, 1957.

T. van Beek,[8] Visitor

This paper describing the developments in numerical methods for propeller design and analysis is a logical step forward in the improvement of available models.

For the analysis of highly skewed propellers such as Propeller 4384 there still exists some difference between measurements and calculations, although an increase of the Reynolds number will decrease the difference as demonstrated in, for example,

---

[8] Lips Propeller Works, Drunen, The Netherlands.

Fig. 16. Two aspects of the present theory may explain these differences.

The first concerns the calculation of the forces on the discrete vortices. These forces are calculated with the aid of Kutta-Jowkowski's law for which the velocity at the vortex element must be known. The velocity can be calculated directly or can be interpolated from the velocities in the adjacent control points, as mentioned in the text. It is not clear which method yields the best results, especially for extreme propeller shapes. Also, the calculated forces may be less accurate when the four vortices adjacent to one control point (Fig. 8) are not in the same plane, which is strongly the case with extreme propeller blades.

The second aspect is the vortex sheet separation. The present model allows the chordwise bound vortex to separate from the leading edge. From the results given in Table 10 one can conclude that this has a decreasing effect on the computed torque while the computed thrust is hardly influenced. The differences, however, are not large, and therefore it is possible that the present program underestimates the effects of leading-edge vortex separation. In the case of propeller 4384, can the authors give their comment on these two aspects?

H. Tanibayashi,[9] Visitor

The discusser thanks the authors for presenting an invaluable paper establishing a milestone for progress of theoretical methods for propeller design and analysis. Of particular interest in this paper, among other things, is an approach to the local problem by the use of local analysis lattice as well as global analysis lattice. By this approach, combined with implementation of the physics of flow around the leading edge and blade tip, as shown in Figs. 40 and 44, will the present method be correlated with the cavitation inception curves of the highly skewed propeller series shown in Fig. 21 of reference [11]?

Additional reference

51 Cumming, R. A., Morgan, Wm. B., and Boswell, R. J., "Highly Skewed Propellers," TRANS. SNAME, Vol. 80, 1972.

Authors' Closure

Dr. Dyne's comments regarding the axial variation in effective wake are most welcome, and the authors agree that its presence may change the predicted geometry of the trailing vortex wake. In addition, it may directly change the prediction of blade shape due to the variation in "inflow" between the leading and trailing edge. Fortunately the numerical approach used in the present work is readily adaptable to the inclusion of this refinement. This problem is currently under study at M.I.T.

Dr. Dyne's criticism of the wake model is certainly valid. However, the intended purpose of the simplified representation of the trailing vortex wake is to yield correct induced velocities on the blade. The ultimate wake may therefore be regarded as a far-field approximation, and the abrupt change in discretization at the end of the transition wake must be accepted as locally invalid. In fact, the current wake representation yields induced velocities in the transition wake region which are in reasonable agreement with laser measurements ["Flow Field Computations for Non-Cavitating and Cavitating Propellers," 14th Symposium on Naval Hydrodynamics, Aug. 1982, Kerwin]. The representation of the ultimate wake by concentrated helical vortex lines with a properly contracted radius, while not perfect, is still far more realistic than the traditional helicoidal vortex sheet.

[9] Nagasaki Experimental Tank, Mitsubishi Heavy Industries, Ltd., Nagasaki, Japan.

We agree with *Mr. Gabrielsen* and *Mr. Myklebust* that a model for the flow separating from the leading edge should be developed which allows the vorticity shed from the leading edge to roll up just behind the edge and pass over the blade surface, as shown in Fig. 25 in the paper. This model would be appropriate for a heavily loaded propeller. However, we feel the leading-edge vortex model shown in Fig. 38 is appropriate when the propeller is operating just slightly below its design advance ratio. We agree that differences in the extent of laminar and turbulent flow are probably not sufficient to explain the observed Reynolds number effects on propellers. The critical radius mentioned by the discussers is the radius below which a laminar separation bubble will not form ($C_s <$ 6.5). This is very much a function of the propeller loading and geometry, but as shown in Fig. 35, independent of Reynolds number. There is not direct connection between the critical radius and the leading-edge separation point discussed in the paper.

Prof. Henderson raises the question of the relationship between the potential flow vortex representation of the propeller used in the present paper and the so-called turbomachinery approach. It is interesting that two such diverse approaches can be applied successfully to the same problem. It is true that the interaction of the propeller with a rotational inflow has only recently been addressed by the former, while it is inherent in the axisymmetric turbomachinery approach. On the other hand, the latter approach employs much more approximate methods of determining the nonaxisymmetric part of the problem.

It is important to recognize that the wake convection velocities shown in Fig 3 are local velocities on the vortex sheet and therefore contain, in themselves, no information regarding conservation of mass and momentum. Between the vortex sheets the flow is potential, thus automatically satisfying the relevant conservation laws. This is in contrast to the axisymmetric approach where circumferential mean velocities are derived on the basis of conservation of mass and momentum along axisymmetric stream tubes.

The difference between these two approaches is evident in considering the question of the ultimate slipstream radius. Using the vortex sheet approach, one concludes that the ultimate radius is largely governed by roll-up and is relatively insensitive to propeller loading. In the axisymmetric approach, mass conservation leads to an ultimate radius which is directly related to loading. Observations indicate that the ultimate tip vortex radius, for light and moderate propeller loadings, is insensitive to loading, and is less than that which would be predicted in axisymmetric flow.

Prof. Henderson's question as to the limit of applicability of the present theory to cases of rotational inflow is a difficult one. As indicated in our reply to Dr. Dyne, axial variations in "effective" inflow can be incorporated in our numerical approach. In the near future, it is hoped that systematic calculations can be made with varying radial gradients of inflow to determine the need for including some elements of shear-flow interaction.

We have not compared our blade pitch correction for viscous effects [equation (17)] with axial-flow compressor corrections, but we appreciate this worthwhile suggestion. Reference [10] of the paper describes the influence of skew on thrust, torque, and cavitation inception, but does not treat the question of Reynolds number. Most of the data which we have seen indicate that skewed blades are more sensitive to Reynolds number effects than radial blades.

The authors are pleased to see the results of the correlation studies carried out by *Mr. Fuhs.* The occasional lack of convergence of the wake alignment iteration procedure is probably due to a breakdown of the two-dimensional interpolation procedure used to obtain convection velocities at points on the trailing vortex sheet. This would explain why increasing the damping does not necessarily help. We have not experienced this problem, but the authors of a program always have the advantage of being able to kick the computer terminal at the opportune time. It may be worthwhile to replace the present interpolation scheme with one which will handle more irregular input.

Mr. Fuhs' question regarding the abrupt termination of the vortex lines in the transition wake has also been addressed by Dr. Dyne. We feel that Lord Kelvin would not be too upset if the model were explained from the point of view of a far-field approximation. The validity of the present wake model in a radially varying inflow field has also been questioned by Dr. Dyne and Prof. Henderson. We hope that current laser measurements in the M.I.T. water tunnel will provide some insight into this question.

We thank Mr. Fuhs for pointing out the error in equation (3), which has been corrected. The computer code did not contain this error.

Dr. Brockett has raised a large number of questions, and we thank him for his careful scrutiny of our paper. The concentrated spanwise vortex sheet is given in equation (6). This gives exact results in two-dimensional flow for flatplate and elliptical chord loads, and very satisfactory results for other loadings, including the NACA $a = 0.8$. Its suitability in three-dimensional flow has not been established formally, but as is typical in numerical lifting-surface theory, can be inferred from the convergence of the method. Since the circulation around a vortex line is not altered by its inclination, the fact that the spanwise vortex lines are not radial does not require an alteration in their strengths. This inclination will change the chordwise vortex distribution. Source strengths are obtained from thin-wing theory based on the local slope of the thickness form. Since the total flux of a concentrated source line depends on its length, the inclination of the spanwise elements must be accounted for in this case. To test the accuracy of the discrete approximation to the source distribution, a calculation was made for a propeller blade with blade outline and thickness corresponding to an ellipsoid. Comparison with the analytical solution for this special case was very satisfactory, except, of course, at the leading and trailing edge.

Dr. Brockett asks what problems arise if the radial contraction of the trailing vortex lines are to be obtained by alignment rather than by specification in advance. It is important to recognize the extreme complexity of the problem of calculating the deformation of three-dimensional vortex sheets. By constraining the motion of the vortex elements along prescribed surfaces, a much simpler algorithm can be employed, with computing times on the order of ten seconds on an IMB 370/168. Since slipstream radius appears to be relatively insensitive to propeller type and loading, it seems practical to prescribe this in advance, and to let the alignment procedure solve for the pitch. The latter is both a sensitive parameter and one which varies considerably with propeller type and loading.

The PBD-10 results given in Table 8 were obtained with the finest grid. Since the only difference here is in the undeformed wake, convergence with number of blade elements is presumed to be similar to that shown in Tables 6 and 7. Convergence of the other two methods may be found in [5]. Equation (28) sets the distance from the trailing edge to the point where the tip vortex radius becomes constant. With this value, the cubic in equation (29) has the prescribed contraction angle, and zero

slope and curvature at its downstream end. The length of the transition wake is specified independently.

Trying to validate a potential flow design method by building a model propeller and testing it completely ignores the question of viscous effects, which seem to be quite important. In response to Dr. Brockett's questions about the experimental/empirical data presented in the paper, we offer the following comments. The tunnel blockage effect could not change enough with skew to explain the difference in experimental data shown in Figs. 14–19. We have no suggestions at present for the variation of our corrections with Reynolds number, but we do recommend the coupling of blade boundary layer computation with the current programs at the earliest possible date. We have not explored the ITTC literature for data on scale effects, but would like to do so when we have the chance. Nonuniform flow effects have not been addressed in any of the work presented in this paper. It is not generally true that the leading-edge separation point is the point of minimum pressure; this just happened to be the case for the example shown. The minimum leading-edge pressures outboard of the separation point are only estimates in any event.

The observations supporting the leading edge vortex sheet model shown in Fig. 38 were made by carefully watching the trajectories of minute cavitation bubbles originating at nicks in the leading edge of a highly skewed propeller model, operating at a J just slightly lower than design. No satisfactory photographs could be made of these bubbles. As pointed out in our reply to Messrs. Gabrielsen and Myklebust, we agree that a different vortex model is required for heavier propeller loadings. We note that the design advance ratio for Propeller 4498 is 0.889, the vortex sheet model shown in Fig. 38 is claimed to be valid at $J = 0.800$, while Fig. 25 shows Propeller 4498 operating at $J = 0.533$.

We appreciate Dr. Brockett's discussion of leading-edge radii on three-dimensional propeller blades. Our current algorithm is equivalent to the equation

$$r_n = r_{2D}/\cos\theta$$

using Dr. Brockett's notation. We will add the missing $\cos^2\delta$ term (approximately equal to one for most propellers) during the next program modification.

In response to *Mr. van Beek*'s questions about Propeller 4384 (Fig. 17), we acknowledge that there are some subtle problems in calculating forces on highly distorted vortex lattices; these problems are currently under study at M.I.T. We would caution against generalizing too much from the results presented in Table 10. As already noted in our replies to previous discussers, a different model for the leading edge vortex is required at heavier propeller loadings, and different effects on thrust and torque may be predicted by such a model. Finally, we would like to mention that Propeller 4384 is no longer with us, so that it cannot be retested at differing Reynolds numbers. The possibility of geometric errors during construction and blade deflection under load must also be accounted for when dealing with such extreme blade shapes.

We agree with *Dr. Tanibayashi* that the present theory should be correlated with the cavitation inception curves of the highly skewed propeller series. We plan to do this as soon as time and money are available.

Finally, we would like to thank all of the discussers for their interest in our paper and their valuable comments and additions.

Obituary

Kenneth W. Allen
Member

Kenneth Wayne Allen, assistant vice president, ABS Technical Services, New York, died Sept. 9, 1982 after a long illness.

Mr. Allen was born in Des Moines, Iowa on May 23, 1924. After graduation from the U. S. Merchant Marine Academy in 1945, and some years of sea time, Mr. Allen joined the American Bureau of Shipping in 1956, and was a vice president of AB-STECH at the time of his death.

Mr. Allen joined the Society in 1962.

L. Stanley Baier
Member

Services were held July 30, 1982 for L. Stanley Baier at Portland, Oregon. Mr. Baier, 81, was president of L.S. Baier & Associates, Marine Designers and Engineers of Portland.

Born at Boston, Massachusetts, Mr. Baier received his elementary education in Washington, D. C. and Portland. He also attended the University of Oregon. His first employment was with the Northwest Steel Company, and he founded L.S. Baier & Associates in 1946. He joined the Society that same year.

Mr. Baier was one of the few individuals to make personal contributions to the Society's Technical and Research Program over the years.

Barry S. Brissenden
Member

Barry Samuel Brissenden died October 23, 1982.

Born October 23, 1920 in Halifax, Nova Scotia, Canada, Barry S. Brissenden received a B.S. degree in civil engineering from Queens University in 1951 and a B.S. in naval engineering from MIT in 1954. He served as a lieutenant in the Royal Canadian Navy. In 1974 Mr. Brissenden was a supervisor in the Department of Development, Marine and Port Industries, in the Province of Nova Scotia. He was an active member of the Eastern Canadian Section of SNAME and the author of several local Section papers.

Mr. Brissenden joined the Society in 1953.

Hugh J. Brown
Student Member

Hugh James Brown died of leukemia in November 1981.

Born July 28, 1957, Mr. Brown was a resident of Beaverton, Oregon. He received a degree in design engineering from Mount Hood College in 1978 and was a lecturer at the College in 1979. He began studying for his B.S.M.E. degree at the University of Portland in 1978.

His illness was first diagnosed in 1979; during that period he became very interested in naval architecture and marine engineering, and designed two sailboats for construction. In 1979 he also started his own engineering, design and drafting firm, known as "North Pacific Design."

Mr. Brown joined the Society in 1981.

John G. Calvin
Member

John Gordon Calvin was killed in the plane crash in Washington, D. C. on January 13, 1982.

Mr. Calvin was born in Northern Ireland in 1939 and began his career with Harland & Wolff, Ltd., Belfast. He came to the United States via Canada in 1970, joining the American Ship Building Company as project engineer. At the time of his death, he was Manager-Estimating & Contracts, AmShip Division, Lorain, Ohio.

He joined SNAME in 1977.

Carl D. Colonna, Jr.
Member

Carl Dunston Colonna, Jr., died December 19, 1981.

Mr. Colonna was born June 21, 1905 at Norfolk, Virginia, and graduated from the Fishburne Military School, Waynesboro, Virginia, in 1925. That same year he began his long career at Colonna Shipyards, Inc. of Norfolk, Virginia, where he held various positions over the following decades, including marine draftsman and estimator. In 1939 he became general superintendent, and by the time of his retirement he had attained the position of first vice president.

Mr. Colonna joined the Society in 1941.

James J. Convy
Affiliate

James Joseph Convy, chairman of the board, Gibbs & Cox, Inc., New York City, died on February 3, 1982 after a brief illness.

Mr. Convy was born June 29, 1919 and was a graduate of Pace College. He had been with Gibbs & Cox since 1941 with responsibilities in the areas of finance and administration.

Mr. Convy joined the Society in 1972.

Leslie Coward
Member

Leslie Coward died March 15, 1982 at North Vancouver, British Columbia, Canada.

Born July 19, 1925 at Middlesbrough, Yorkshire, England, Mr. Coward studied engineering at Salford Technical College. From 1944 to 1947 he served with the Royal Electrical and Mechanical Engineers in Europe and the Middle East. In 1948 he emigrated to Canada. He held several positions in the construction industry from 1948 to 1962, including four years with Cominco of Trail, B.C., where he was involved with purchasing and warehousing. In 1962 he was employed as a comptroller by Allied Shipbuilders, Ltd. of Vancouver, B.C., and was later promoted to the position of director and comptroller. From 1968 to 1969 he was with Newfoundland Marine Works Ltd. as director and general manager. Returning to Allied Shipbuilders Ltd. in 1969, he became director, vice president and comptroller. By 1974 Mr. Coward had formed his own consulting business, CCS Marine Associates, Ltd., and specialized in shipbuilding, ship repair and shipyard construction.

Mr. Coward was an active member of the Pacific Northwest Section, having served as chairman, secretary-treasurer, and as a member of the 1975 Spring Meeting Steering Committee. Mr. Coward joined the Society in 1964.

Carlos H. Danao

Associate Member

Carlos Higa Danao died June 2, 1982 following a motorcycle accident.

Mr. Danao was born in Okinawa on February 3, 1955 and received a B.S. degree in mechanical engineering in 1978 from Virginia Polytechnic Institute and the State University in Blacksburg, Virginia. He was a specialist in piping design with J. J. Henry Co., Inc., Arlington, Virginia.

Mr. Danao joined the Society in 1980.

Gerard J. DeCourville

Member

Gerard Joseph DeCourville died January 15, 1982.

Mr. DeCourville was born in Montreal, Quebec, Canada on May 13, 1923 and attended secondary schools there and Queens University, Kingston, Ontario. He became president of Demco, Ltd. of Canada in 1966 and subsequently was president and general manager of M.I.T. Sales Co., Ltd., Saint John, New Brunswick.

Mr. DeCourville joined the Society in 1962.

Clayton DuBosque

Permanent Member

The Society recently learned of the death of Clayton DuBosque, who passed away at the age of 80 in 1970. A graduate of Yale, Mr. DuBosque was an investment banker with F. Eberstadt & Co. and Vance Sanders Co. of Boston.

Walter B. Gallagher

Affiliate

Walter B. Gallagher, a dedicated member of the Society, died on January 7, 1982.

Born in New York City on December 15, 1928 Mr. Gallagher spent 21 years with Gibbs & Cox, Inc., New York, before joining the Society staff as Administrative Assistant in 1970. He became Manager - Administration in 1978.

In the words of his fellow workers at SNAME headquarters . . . "Walter Gallagher was totally dedicated to the objectives of our Society and (he) worked tirelessly for the benefit of each and every member." He was . . . "a loyal member, dedicated employee and true friend."

He is survived by his wife Phyllis and four children.

Tobia H. Gordon

Associate Member

Tobia Hart Gordon died July 31, 1982.

Miss Gordon was born June 9, 1910 in New York City and held B.A. and M.S. degrees in mathematics. During her early career Miss Gordon worked for the Moore Dry Dock Co. of Oakland, California, in their Scientific Section. In 1946 she joined the Bethlehem Steel Company's Shipbuilding Division at San Francisco. In later years Miss Gordon was a naval architect with the Lockheed Missiles and Space Program at Sunnyvale, California, and resided in Palo Alto.

Miss Gordon became a member of the Society in 1947.

Raymond T. Greene

Affiliate

Raymond Thomas Greene died November 5, 1982.

Born January 28, 1917 in New York City, Mr. Greene held a B.B.A. from Manhattan College, an M.B.A. from Columbia University, and a D.J. from Fordham University. He began his law career in 1940 with Kirlin, Campbell & Keating of New York City, where he became a junior partner in 1952 and a senior partner in 1954. Mr. Greene was considered one of the outstanding international admiralty lawyers in the United States.

Mr. Greene was vice president of Miami Shipyards Corporation of Miami, Florida in 1972, and he later served as president of Anchorage Ship Sales and Documentation, Inc. In 1976 he formed a new company, Anchorage Marine Brokerage and Documentation, Inc. of Miami.

Mr. Greene joined the Society in 1958.

Linda L. Grimes

Associate Member

Linda Louise Grimes died in 1982.

Born April April 14, 1960, Miss Grimes was a recent graduate (June 1982) of Florida Institute of Technology in Melbourne, Florida, where she received a B.S. degree in ocean engineering. After graduation, she relocated to Ocean Springs, Mississippi. Miss Grimes's parents reside in Windsor, Connecticut.

In July 1982, Miss Grimes became an Associate Member of the Society.

Carl E. Habermann

Life Member

Carl E. Habermann died April 13, 1982 in Vincentown, New Jersey.

Mr. Habermann was born March 24, 1915 in New York City and received his B.S. degree in chemistry from New York University in 1941. In 1935 he was employed by Socony-Vacuum Oil Co., Inc. of New York City as supervisor of the Engine Testing Lab. From 1950 to 1952, he was staff advisor to the director of the Product Development Division, Research & Development Labs. In 1952 he became research engineer for the Marine Sales Department.

Carl Habermann held a patent for an electronic detonation indicator for automotive engine equipment. His area of specialization was internal combustion engines and fuel and lubricants development.

Mr. Habermann later joined the Mobil Sales and Supply Corporation of New York City, and by 1971 was manager of Technical Services. In 1975 he retired from Mobil.

Carl Habermann joined the Society in 1952 and was a member of the Philadelphia Section. He served on Panel M-24 (Marine Fuel Systems) from 1970 to 1972. In 1971 he was honored by the Society for writing the chapter, "Petroleum Fuels," for *Marine Engineering*, and he was awarded Life Membership.

Philip Handler

Special Member

Dr. Philip Handler, former president of the National Academy of Sciences, died December 29, 1981 in Boston, Massachusetts. He was on leave from Duke University at the time of his death.

Born in 1918, Dr. Handler joined the Duke University faculty in 1939 after he received his Ph.D. at the University of Illinois. Dr. Handler also served as chairman of the Department of Biochemistry at Duke University Medical Center for 19 years. Considered one of the founding fathers of the university's Department of Biochemistry, he became chairman of the department in 1950, a position he held until his appointment to the National Academy of Sciences in 1969. He retired July 1, 1981 after serving two six-year terms with the academy.

In October 1981 Dr. Handler received from President Reagan one of the highest distinctions the federal government offers for scientific excellence, the National Medal of Science.

Dr. Handler was the recipient of numberous awards, including 28 honorary degrees. He also served on a number of government panels dealing with scientific issues.

Dr. Handler was elected to the Society as a Special Member in 1969.

Henry A. Hoffman

Member

RADM Henry A. Hoffman, USN (Ret.) died February 4, 1982.

Admiral Hoffman was born in New York City on August 24, 1923 and joined the Society when he was with the Supervisor of Shipbuilding, Newport News, Virginia in 1965. Admiral Hoffman had a distinguished career since his graduation from the U.S. Naval Academy in 1947 to his retirement in 1980. At the latter time, he commanded maintenance and resources management activities of the U.S. Pacific Fleet and the Naval Logistics Command, Pacific.

After his retirement from the Navy, Admiral Hoffman joined Engineering-Science, Inc. as head of the firm's Government Services Group, in McLean, Virginia.

He was active with the Society as chairman of the Hawaii Section in 1975 and 1976 and on the Papers Committee of the Spring Meeting/STAR Symposium in Honolulu in 1982.

Lewis C. Host, Jr.

Member

Lewis Clinton Host, Jr., a veteran of Newport News Shipbuilding and the American Bureau of Shipping, died November 11, 1982 at the age of 85.

After attending elementary and high school in Newport News, he graduated from the Webb Institute of Naval Architecture as well as the Naval Steam Engineering School at Stevens Institute of Technology.

In his early years, Mr. Host worked for the Newport News Shipbuilding Co. In 1919 he joined ABS, where 40 years later he was elected senior vice president. He retired in 1962.

Mr. Host joined the Society in 1927.

Robert H. Jones, Jr.

Associate Member

Robert Henry Jones, Jr., died in early 1982 at Kirkland, Washington.

Born June 7, 1919, Mr. Jones studied transportation at the University of Washington and the College of William and Mary before completing a marine engineering course at the U.S. Army Transportation School. From 1941 to 1961 Mr. Jones was with the U.S. Army Transportation Corps. The next ten years were spent employed as an assistant manager at Burchand and Fisken Inc. (steamship agents). In 1972 he was with the Coatings Division of Norton Corrosion Limited of Woodinville, Washington, and in 1973 he joined Northwest Ship Suppliers, Inc. of Seattle, Washington as general manager.

Mr. Jones became a member of the Society in 1973.

Sergio Jurman

Member

Sergio Jurman died in January 1982.

Mr. Jurman was born in Italy on January 11, 1932. He attended university in Italy and received his chief engineers license in 1962. After some years with Oretea Shipping Company and Gulf Oil, Mr. Jurman became chief engineer of Home Lines Cruises, Inc.

Mr. Jurman joined SNAME in 1977.

James P. Klima, Sr.

Member

James P. Klima, Sr., died June 27, 1982.

Born March 16, 1889 in Baltimore, Maryland, Mr. Klima was a graduate of the Maryland Institute, where he later taught evening classes in mechanical drafting (1926 to 1934). He began his career as a machinist's apprentice in 1905 with the Baltimore Shipbuilding & Dry Docks Co. In 1910 he became a junior draftsman at the Bethlehem Steel shipyard at Sparrows Point, Maryland, where he worked for almost a half century. In the course of his career there, Mr. Klima was chief engineer, general superintendent, assistant to the manager and, finally, chief engineer. He retired in 1956.

Mr. Klima first joined the Society in 1918, but resigned in 1926, and was reinstated as a member in 1936.

Clarence W. Levingston

Member

Clarence W. Levingston died in Orange, Texas on August 3, 1982. He was born there January 12, 1913.

A graduate of Rice Institute, Mr. Levingston joined Levingston Shipbuilding Company as a draftsman. He became assistant chief engineer and naval architect in 1951 and retired as chief engineer in 1980.

Mr. Levingston joined the Society in 1943.

Theodore J. Lund

Member

Theodore J. Lund died January 25, 1982 at Silver Spring, Maryland.

Born August 9, 1921, Mr. Lund received a B.M.E. degree from City College of New York in 1948, and a B.L.L. degree from George Washington University, Washington, D.C. in 1956. He began his career in 1948 with the Bureau of Ships as an engineer-in-training. Over the next 30 years he held various positions with the Bureau of Ships (later known as NAVSEA), including project engineer, head engineer in charge of boiler design for naval ships, and director of engineering for improvement of the 1200 psi Steam Improvement Program in Naval Sea Systems Command.

In 1977 he became founder and president of Lund Engineering Associates of Silver Spring, Maryland, and was a consultant to industry on public utilities and marine power plants.

Mr. Lund was the recipient of the U.S. Navy Superior Civilian Service Award in 1977.

Mr. Lund joined the Society in 1978.

Walter L. Martignoni
Member

Walter Lewis Martignoni died June 14, 1981, the Society recently learned. He was 91 years of age.

Mr. Martignoni joined the Society in 1935 and for many years was president of the San Francisco consulting engineering firm, Pillsbury & Martignoni, Inc. Mr. Martignoni was a salvage master and naval architect. He was born in Oakland, California.

John W. Milman
Member

John Walter Francis Milman died August 18, 1982.

Mr. Milman was born in North Wales on December 7, 1928. He held a B.S. degree in applied science from the University of Durham, England, and was with the shipbuilders J. S. White & Co., Ltd. of Cowes, Isle of Wight, England from 1945 to 1954. In 1954 he was employed as a calculations draftsman by Canadian Vickers, Ltd. of Montreal, Canada. By 1975 he was a principal consultant with Y-ARD Ltd. of Glasgow, Scotland. At the time of his death he was Manager, Merchant Ships and Auxiliary Vessels, at Vickers Stanwick Systems, Inc. in Ottawa, Canada.

Mr. Milman joined the Society in 1954, and served on Panel HS-4 (Design Procedure and Philosophy) from 1966 to 1969.

J. Davis Minster
Associate Member

J. Davis Minster died March 9, 1982.

Mr. Minster was born April 16, 1923 in Elkton, Maryland. He attended Dickinson College in Carlisle, Pennsylvania from 1946 to 1948. In 1948 Mr. Minster was employed by the Wiley Manufacturing Company of Port Deposit, Maryland, where in 1956 he was appointed chief estimator. In 1957 he became an assistant sales manager with full responsibility for the detail administration of both the sales and estimating departments. In recent years he was an independent consultant.

Mr. Minster joined the Society in 1958 and was member of the Chesapeake Section.

John C. Niedermair
Fellow and Honorary Member

John C. Niedermair died at the age of 88 on March 6, 1982 in Washington, D.C. He was one of our country's foremost naval architects and held the civilian position of Chief Naval

John C. Niedermair

Architect for the U.S. Navy from 1938 until his retirement in 1958.

Mr. Niedermair was born at Union Hill, New Jersey and grew up on Staten Island. In 1914 he was selected for a scholarship at Webb Institute of Naval Architecture and graduated at the head of his class in 1928.

In the field of basic design Mr. Niedermair occupied a preeminent position. He has been called the father of today's modern U.S. Navy. As director of the preliminary design branch of the Bureau of Ships he was primarily responsible for the basic design of all types of naval ships, some 8000 vessels, beginning with destroyers in 1932 to the nuclear submarines *Nautilus* and *SeaWolf* in the early 1950's.

Worthy of particular mention is the part he played in the design of the tank landing ship, the ubiquitous LST. This design, which was in large measure the product of Mr. Niedermair's original thinking and good engineering judgment, was sketched in a couple of hours after the requirements were given him. More than 1000 of these craft were eventually constructed, and taking part in the Pacific and Normandy landings were indispensable to bringing World War II to a victorious close.

For his outstanding services to the Navy, Mr. Niedermair was presented the Distinguished Civilian Service Award in 1945, and he was awarded the Society's David W. Taylor Medal in 1958. An Honorary Member of the Society since 1956, Mr. Niedermair was an active committee member and author, and was a regular and wise contributor to discussions of the technical papers.

Mr. Niedermair joined the Society in 1929.

Nelson Ogden

Affiliate

Nelson Ogden, 92, died February 28, 1982.

Born in Rye, New York, Mr. Ogden graduated from Stevens Institute of Technology in 1910. He joined the Kingsbury Machine Works, Frankfurt, Pennsylvania in 1922 and rose to general manager, remaining there until his retirement in 1965.

Mr. Ogden joined the Society in 1918.

D'Arcy E. Phillips

Life Member

D'Arcy Emory Phillips died October 30, 1981 in Newport News, Virginia.

Mr. Phillips was born October 18, 1919 at Hurlock, Maryland. His long career at the Newport News Shipbuilding and Dry Dock Co. spanned 45 years. He began working there as a draftsman and designer; by the end of his career, he had attained the position of project engineer in the energy building and grounds department.

Mr. Phillips was an active member of the Trinity United Methodist Church in Newport News, where he served on the administrative board, chaired the Property Committee and taught the Men's Bible Class.

Mr. Phillips joined the Society in 1956 and was made a Life Member in 1969.

Jacob Y. Pyo

Member

Jacob Y. Pyo died in early 1982.

Mr. Pyo was born in Kohala, Hawaii on February 20, 1917. After graduating from the University of Hawaii with a B.S. degree in civil engineering, he became employed in 1940 at the Pearl Harbor Shipyard.

Mr. Pyo joined the Society in 1955.

Charles P. Reddall

Affiliate Member

Charles Patrick Reddall died January 8, 1982 in Burlington, Ontario, Canada.

Mr. Reddall was born March 17, 1914 in England. He completed a three-year property management course at Knight, Frank and Rutley of London, England, and received a fellowship in the National Association of Land and Property Managers. From 1939 to 1946 he served in the British Army's Royal Artillery. He was employed by Richard Foot and Partners Ltd. from 1946 to 1948, and in 1948 joined the management at the Prince Edward Island Industrial Development Corporation of Charlottetown, P.E.I.

In 1952, Mr. Reddall began a 25-year career with the Canada Steamship Lines Ltd. of Montreal, P.Q., where he later attained the position of corporate planning officer.

Mr. Reddall joined the Society in 1972.

William C. Reynolds

Member

William Charles Reynolds died January 11, 1982 in Philadelphia, Pennsylvania.

Born October 26, 1906 at Milwaukee, Wisconsin, Mr. Reynolds received his B.S. degree in naval architecture and marine engineering from the University of Michigan in 1930. He began his career with the Bethlehem Shipbuilding Corporation in Quincy, Massachusetts, and then became manager of the Sparrows Point Shipyard in Baltimore, Maryland. In 1960 he became vice president of the Gibbs Shipyard in Jacksonville, Florida, and in 1966 was named president and chief executive officer of Philadelphia Shipyards, now the Delaware Shipyards. He was also a consultant to the Bethlehem Shipbuilding Corp. in Baltimore. Mr. Reynolds retired in the mid-1970's.

William C. Reynolds joined the Society in 1930.

Henry W. Runyon

Associate Member

The Society has learned of the death of Henry Wisner Runyon, who passed away in November 1981 at Castine, Maine.

Mr. Runyon was born in Red Bank, New Jersey on October 27, 1905. In 1926 he received an industrial mechanical engineering degree from Pratt Institute, Brooklyn, New York. From 1926 to 1941 he was employed by several companies, including Standard Motor Construction Co. of Jersey City and Worthington Pump and Machinery Corp. of Harrison, New Jersey. Among the positions he held during this time were sales and service engineer, diesel and gas engine specialist, and applications engineer. In later years he was a marine consultant. He retired in 1972.

Mr. Runyon became a member of the Society in 1941.

Theodore C. Schoening

Associate Member

Theodore Carl Schoening died August 1, 1981 at Gautier, Mississippi.

Mr. Schoening was born January 9, 1916. After graduating from Pitman High School, Pitman, New Jersey, he took courses in methods engineering and the N.Y. Ship Management Program. From 1940 to 1954 he was employed by the New York Shipbuilding Corporation, first as an estimator (for eleven years), and then as chief scheduler. In 1954 he joined Eastern Cold Storage Insulation Company; by 1975 he was construction superintendent, responsible for coordinating all the company's construction work in various shipyards, such as General Dynamics Corp. and Bethlehem Steel Corp. In 1975 Mr. Schoening was president of Seacarl Marine Industries, Inc.—Marine Consultants and Contractors, with offices in Gautier, Mississippi and Fair Lawn, New Jersey.

Mr. Schoening became a member of the Society in 1972.

Loring W. Schutz

Member

It was with sadness that the Society learned of the death of Loring William Schutz, aged 70, on September 27, 1982. Mr. Schutz, an active member of the Hawaii Section, was born in Boston and was a retired chief design engineer at the Pearl Harbor Naval Shipyard. Mr. Schutz's most recent activity with the Society was as a member of the 1982 Spring Meeting/STAR Symposium Steering Committee.

Mr. Schutz joined the Society in 1939.

Irving W. Smith

Life Member

Irving W. Smith died in the spring of 1982.

Born March 11, 1913, Mr. Smith received his B.S. degree in mechanical engineering from Lafayette College in 1934. His over 30-year career with the Maritime Administration (MarAd) in Washington, D.C. began in 1941. In 1971 he was a marine engineer in the Division of Engineering at MarAd. That same year, he was honored by the Society for his significant contribution as coauthor of the chapter, "Hull Machinery," which appears in *Marine Engineering*. During 1972–1973 he served on Panel O-37 (Air Conditioning). Upon retirement from MarAd in 1974, he relocated to Bristol, Tennessee.

Irving W. Smith became a Life Member of the Society in 1971.

Umberto Spadetti

Member

The Society has learned of the death of Umberto Spadetti in November, 1981.

Mr. Spadetti was born in Italy, March 14, 1907 and came to the United States at an early age, receiving his B.S. in electrical engineering at Rhode Island State College. He joined the Navy Bureau of Ships in 1946 and became project coordinator for the incorporation of national defense features in merchant ships. He was a registered engineer in the District of Columbia.

Mr. Spadetti joined the Society in 1966.

Theodore A. Taylor

Associate Member

The Society has learned of the death of Theodore A. Taylor in April 1980 at Pompano Beach, Florida.

Mr. Taylor was born April 12, 1920 at Brooklyn, New York, and attended New York University from 1938 to 1940. He was employed by the Todd Shipyard Corp. from 1940 to 1960, where he held various positions, including shipfitter, ship supervisor, and estimator. In 1961 he went to work for the Bailey Carpenter and Insulation Co., Inc. of Brooklyn, New York, and by 1966 had become manager, specializing in marine refrig-

eration. In later years he was vice president of Jamestown Metal Marine Sales, Inc. of Pompano Beach, Florida.

Mr. Taylor joined the Society in 1966.

Girard T. Tranchin

Affiliate

Girard T. Tranchin died in 1981, the Society has learned.

Mr. Tranchin was born in New Orleans, Louisiana on April 13, 1932. After receiving his A.B. degree from Harvard University, he joined the firm of F.F. Tranchina Co., Inc. in 1955 and rose to the position of vice president, responsible for the sales and development of various marine products, both mechanical and electrical.

Mr. Tranchin lived at Metairie, Louisiana and joined SNAME in 1970.

Leendert Van Der Tas

Member

Leendert Van Der Tas died on May 30, 1982 in Rotterdam, the Netherlands. He was born there on September 16, 1922, and after graduating from the Technical University of Delft in 1954 he worked for Werkspoor and Royal Dutch Shell in Amsterdam. Mr. Van Der Tas joined the Rotterdam Dock Yard in 1958 and rose to the position of managing director.

He joined the Society in 1963.

Nils A. Wirstrom

Associate Member

Nils A. Wirstrom of Houston, Texas died June 12, 1981.

Mr. Wirstrom was born May 19, 1918 at Norrkoping, Sweden and attended Eberstein's Institute and Goteborg's Navigation and Marine Engineering School. From 1939 to 1947 he did sea service in capacities ranging from 2nd assistant engineer to chief engineer, and was with the Swedish American Line, the Standard Oil Co. of New Jersey, Marine Transport Lines, and Lykes Bros. Steamship Co. In 1947 Mr. Wirstrom became founder and president of Bywater Sales & Service Co., Inc. (distributors of protective coatings), of Belle Chasse, Louisiana.

Mr. Wirstrom joined the Society in 1968.